Africa

Lawrence R. Sullivan

The World Today Series
2025–2026

59th Edition

BLOOMSBURY ACADEMIC
Bloomsbury Publishing Inc, 1359 Broadway, New York, NY 10018, USA
Bloomsbury Publishing Plc, 50 Bedford Square, London, WC1B 3DP, UK
Bloomsbury Publishing Ireland, 29 Earlsfort Terrace, Dublin 2, D02 AY28, Ireland

BLOOMSBURY, BLOOMSBURY ACADEMIC and the Diana logo are trademarks of Bloomsbury Publishing Plc

First published in the United States of America 2026

Copyright © Bloomsbury Academic Publishing, 2026

For legal purposes the Acknowledgments on p. vii constitute an extension of this copyright page.

Cover design: Chloe Batch
Cover images: © iStock.com/sorendls and iStock.com/Gile68

All rights reserved. No part of this publication may be: i) reproduced or transmitted in any form, electronic or mechanical, including photocopying, recording or by means of any information storage or retrieval system without prior permission in writing from the publishers; or ii) used or reproduced in any way for the training, development or operation of artificial intelligence (AI) technologies, including generative AI technologies. The rights holders expressly reserve this publication from the text and data mining exception as per Article 4(3) of the Digital Single Market Directive (EU) 2019/790.

Bloomsbury Publishing Inc does not have any control over, or responsibility for, any third-party websites referred to or in this book. All internet addresses given in this book were correct at the time of going to press. The author and publisher regret any inconvenience caused if addresses have changed or sites have ceased to exist, but can accept no responsibility for any such changes.

A catalog record for this book is available from the Library of Congress

ISBN: PB: 979-8-8818-0241-7
ePDF: 979-8-8818-5490-4
eBook: 979-8-8818-0242-4

Series: World Today

Typeset by Sue Murray
Printed and bound in the United States of America

For product safety related questions contact productsafety@bloomsbury.com.

To find out more about our authors and books visit www.bloomsbury.com and sign up for our newsletters.

CONTENTS

Africa Today vi

Historical Background (Pre-Colonial period)
Prehistoric Africa... 1
Early Civilizations of the Nile Valley and
   Mediterranean Sea 1
The Kingdom of Ethiopia 2
The Spread of Islam 3
Arabs and Traders in East Africa 3
The Empires and Peoples of West Africa 3
Peoples of Central and Southern Africa 4
European Discovery and Exploration 6
Early Ethiopian–European Contact 7
The Arabs and Ottoman Turks in North Africa 7
European Settlers in South Africa 7

The Colonial Period
The Portuguese (about 1550) 9
The British (about 1660) 10
The French (about 1830) 18
The Americans (1835, see Liberia) 25
King Leopold II and the Belgians (1885) 25
The Spanish (1885) 26
The Germans (1885) 27
The South Africans (1919) 28
The Italians (1927) 28

NORTH AFRICA
Algeria 30
Egypt 37
Libya 50
Morocco 57
Tunisia 66

WEST AFRICA
Benin 72
Burkina Faso 78
Cape Verde 84
Côte d'Ivoire 87
Gambia 95
Ghana 99
Guinea 105
Guinea-Bissau 110
Liberia 115
Mali 123
Mauritania 128
Niger 134
Nigeria 139

Senegal 149
Sierra Leone 155
Togo 161

CENTRAL AFRICA
Burundi 166
Cameroon 171
Central African Republic 177
Chad 183
Congo 190
Democratic Republic of the Congo 195
Equatorial Guinea 204
Gabon 209
Rwanda 214
São Tomé and Príncipe 222

EAST AFRICA
Djibouti 228
Eritrea 232
Ethiopia 237
Kenya 244
Somalia 253
The Republic of South Sudan 262
The Republic of the Sudan 267
Tanzania 274
Uganda 280

INDIAN OCEAN ISLAND NATIONS
Comoros 289
Madagascar 294
Mauritius 299
Seychelles 302

SOUTHERN AFRICA
Angola 305
Botswana 314
Lesotho 319
Malawi 323
Mozambique 327
Namibia 334
South Africa 340
Swaziland 365
Zambia 369
Zimbabwe 374

Web Sites and Selected Bibliography of Key
   English Language Sources 385

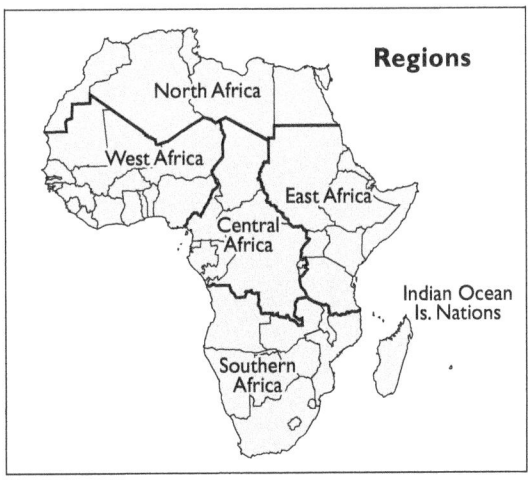

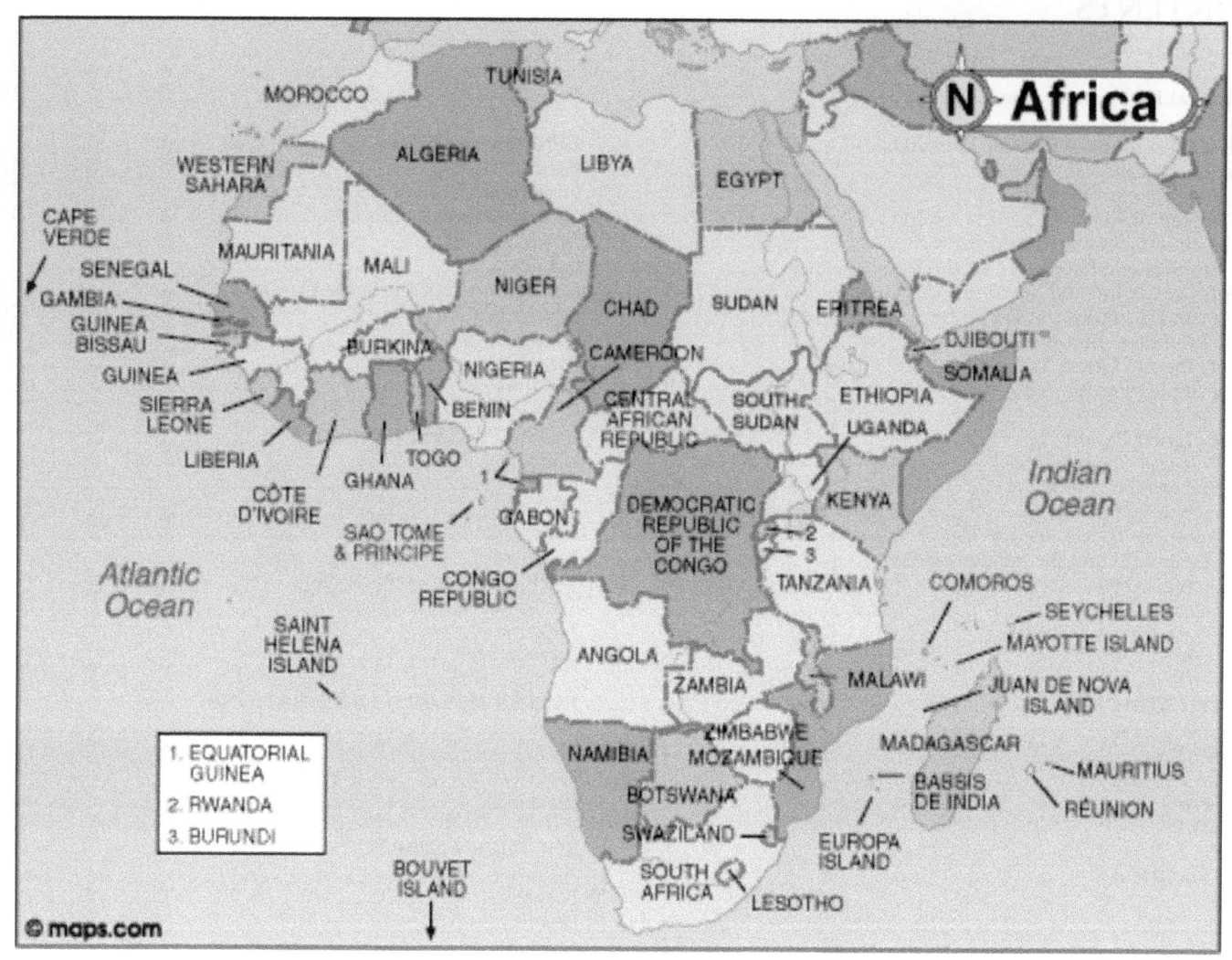

Foreword to the 59th edition

For this edition of *Africa: The World Today Series*, I have made numerous changes, but have necessarily retained much of the historical content from work in previous years. Several changes have focused on updating the empirical material. Given the size of the volume and the scope of change in so many countries over the past year, the task is necessarily ongoing. Many countries have witnessed leadership and other changes including Sudan, Liberia, DR Congo, and Zimbabwe, among others.

In this edition, I have worked to present an up-to-date statistical analysis on the continent.

The *Africa* volume is always evolving and changing, much like the continent itself. Such work benefits from suggestions, corrections, and critiques. I can be contacted at the University of Toronto, Canada.

Africa Today

THE UNITY AND DIVERSITY OF AFRICA

The continent of Africa offers a complex and sometimes contradictory picture of the human spirit, and the year 2013 to 2014 has reminded us of the breadth of African experience. From out of Africa in recent years have come some of the greatest testaments to humanity's perseverance and courage. After the death on December 5, 2013, of Nelson Mandela, much of the world paused to reflect on his remarkable and world-changing resistance to the injustice of *apartheid* rule in South Africa. As a leader of the African National Congress (ANC), Mandela refused to renounce armed struggle against South Africa's repressive "whites-only" government, yet when the *apartheid* regime finally yielded in 1990, Mandela showed neither bitterness nor vindictiveness, but rather an astonishing reserve of compassion and a profound capacity for reconciliation. Mandela's fight for equality and justice inspired millions worldwide and for a time made South Africa a beacon of hope for the continent. Yet at the other end of the spectrum, the last year has also marked the 20th anniversary of the Rwandan genocide of 1994, which has provided a striking reminder that ethnic conflict continues in Africa; as can be seen in the ongoing violent civil war in the Central African Republic, Africa encompasses a wide range of various possible futures, and many of its countries find themselves at a crossroads.

Africa has experienced a startling mix of events in the years leading up to 2014, ranging from revolutions that have toppled dictatorships to coups that have toppled democracies, and from economic booms in some countries to virtual collapses in others. In this section, I will offer some general thoughts on current trends across the continent. Specifics about each country will be the subject of the country chapters to follow. This does not substitute for those. It is instead intended as a complementary analysis for the reader who is interested in some country detail but embedded in a "big picture" view of the continent.

Understanding Africa: One Continent, Many Destinies

Africa is one continent, but it is also home to about one billion people spread across 54 quite different economies and polities. While we may speak of Africa as a single entity for some purposes (as shown by the scope of this book itself), we must also recognize that it is increasingly difficult to describe the trajectory of "Africa as a whole." We must increasingly refer to the vast differences between African countries and their experiences, and how these change over time. Africa has always been a varied and complex place. Even in the late 1800s, when the British Empire dreamed of a Cape to Cairo railroad to connect the northern and southern tips of the continent, it was clear that Egypt and South Africa differed dramatically from one another and from the tropical regions in between. In recent years, however, the trajectory of countries has perhaps become even more diverse.

Several countries in Africa are on a relatively positive trajectory, or have prospects of showing in the near future that they are on such a trajectory. This includes several relatively stable democracies, plus countries that have tentatively made progress on reducing conflict or tempering dictatorial rule. Other groups of countries are "breaking bad" or are currently subjected to considerable amounts of instability and violence. Even in the latter, there may be some "good news" in the sense that strife may slow down or stop, but these countries are Africa's basket cases and will remain so into the future until some dramatic change occurs. The dividing lines between the "good" and "bad" trajectories are not always clear, but the following sections will attempt to group similar countries together in order to illustrate that certain patterns can be found in multiple countries at the same time.

The Untold Story? Increases in Stability and Democracy

In a region where poverty is rife and economic opportunity is scarce, there are now nearly a dozen countries—including some of the poorest places in the world—that have remained stable and largely democratic for over twenty years. At first glance, this may sound unremarkable, but something of great importance can be gleaned from this statistic: democratic legacies have the ability to be self-reinforcing. Furthermore, African populations are young, with the median age under 20 years in many countries. This means that in places such as Ghana, half of the population (and an entire generation) has never known military rule, coups, or social strife. People have become accustomed to a functional democracy, even with inevitable and visible imperfections. If democratic values are given time to percolate, each passing year in a young democracy is precious. As of 2009, Ghana joined Benin as a country meeting the

Africa Today

Mitsamiouli Beach, The Comoros

"two turnover" criterion for democratic consolidation. The late political scientist Samuel Huntington argued that a democracy reaches a level of genuine consolidation when there are two democratically elected turnovers of governing power. That is, a government (or a head of state) loses an election, and then at a later date the government that defeated them loses in turn. The premise of the two-turnover logic is that it suggests all significant parties accept democracy as "the only game in town," and all recognize that losing is a reality in the realm of politics.

In recent years, Ghana has been Africa's emblem of how politics operates when democracy works as it is supposed to. The country lived up to this reputation again in 2012 when President John Atta Mills died in office in the lead-up to elections. In accordance with constitutional procedure, the vice president assumed the presidency. This interim president was then subsequently elected in a free and fair election. The leading opposition candidate—who took nearly half the vote—ultimately accepted defeat. As a result of this example, Ghana continues to serve (at least for now) as a model for other countries in Africa. At present, Ghana itself is booming economically from investment in the oil industry, and the stability in the political sphere should serve the economy well in the years to come.

Several other countries also lead the way as exemplars of democratic persistence despite the fact that poverty, social problems, and government ineffectiveness and corruption have not yet been completely eradicated. Freedom House (a non-governmental organization) ranks the southern African nations of Botswana, Namibia, and South Africa as "free," but still it should be noted that each has a dominant political party still in power since democratization, and these parties have not yet conceded power to the opposition. Several West African countries—Benin, Senegal, and now Sierra Leone—are also now considered to be fully democratic. Other democratic nations include the small islands of Cabo Verde (Cape Verde), São Tomé e Príncipe, and Mauritius. The persistence of stability and democratization make for less dramatic stories than incidents of conflict and disorder, so slow improvement does not often make the news. Regardless, these slow and steady changes are central to the improvement of the quality of life in Africa as a whole.

Other African countries have developed vibrant multi-party politics and important sets of democratic practices, though these have not yet been proven as robust as in the democracies mentioned above. Zambia fits this trend. Zambia's election in 2011 resulted in an important alternation of power away from the party that had dominated for the 20 years since the initial push for democracy. While politics in the country is still tense, there is a real chance that the country could conceivably consolidate its democratizing trend.

Even more dramatic news was the change in Kenya in the election of 2013, as contrasted with the previous electoral cycle. The major concern in 2013 was a replication of the inter-ethnic violence that killed over 1,000 people after the previous election in 2007. The Kenyan people had approved a new constitution in a 2010 referendum and prepared for open elections. Remarkably, the 2013 elections came off without major glitches and without any significant incidents of violence. Kenya thus took a meaningful step towards enhanced democracy, although the newly-elected president Uhuru Kenyatta is the subject of an ongoing proceeding at the International Criminal Court for his role in the 2007–2008 violence. If Kenya can remain stable and increasingly democratic, it will serve as an important anchor in the regions of east Africa and the Horn of Africa.

Two other countries have seen encouraging changes given the atrocities of recent decades. Sierra Leone and Liberia appear to have reemerged from their horrendous civil wars to create new and hopeful polities with improvements in civil and political rights. Liberia, led by the continent's first woman president, has once again become a major American partner on the continent (though there is still evidence of corruption), and Sierra Leone has seen a major turnaround. Both have posted solid economic growth in the range of 5% in recent years, even after completing many of the projects of post-war reconstruction. The durability of democracy in these countries is still a question, but as noted, Sierra Leone in 2013 joined the ranks of the small number of African countries that have earned the label "partly free" from the independent organization Freedom House (see chart at the end of this essay for full list of countries and their status).

Still other countries can claim a more subtle and modest achievement: the persistence of economic and social stability, combined with a creeping sense that politics is liberalizing, if not fully democratizing. Countries such as Tanzania serve as examples here. While never a fully functioning democracy, Tanzania has slowly improved civil liberties, avoided instability and coup attempts, and has managed increasingly open elections. Similar positive trends have happened in the most populous country in Africa: Nigeria. This economic powerhouse is an especially complicated case: it is simultaneously the economic motor of West Africa and the home to decades of legendary corruption, military misrule, and strife between religious and ethnic groups. Nigeria cannot be cast as a country that is thriving, especially given the active presence of substantial violence by Islamists in the north. But at the same time, it seems the economy is plowing ahead and that political and civic life is growing richer. There is even evidence that corruption is declining in some areas—most notably Lagos State (which is probably the most populous state in the country as of 2013, though the

Africa Today

numbers are disputed). Nigeria is a long way from European-caliber democracy or from China-caliber economic growth, and it is a long way from eliminating the threat of terror in the north, but it is also far from the bad old days of coups and decline.

Africa is full of these modestly improving experiences, yet they are broadly underreported and underappreciated in the west because there is little spectacular to report: as noted above, slow and moderate improvements make little news. Nonetheless, it seems clear that, in another generation, young Africans will look back to note that the Africa of the 1990s to 2010s was a very different—and many ways, much improved—place from the continent of the 1970s and 1980s: the founding fathers of independence have largely died or faded from public life, taking with them in most cases the sense that one might be ordained by divine right to be president for life. Dictatorship still exists, but is increasingly embarrassing to Africa's own leaders, who are increasingly (albeit unevenly) willing to stand up for democracy and openness. While troubles persist, the tragicomic tyrannies of decades past—epitomized by Mobutu Sese Seko of Zaire (now Democratic Republic of the Congo)—have become more the exception than the rule. Incredibly, even Somalia—a country long synonymous with state failure—may have turned a corner in 2012 and 2013 when it elected a new parliament and established what may be its first functional government in over two decades.

In many authoritarian countries, a slow shift can be seen from horrific dictatorships during the Cold War to a more subtle form of flawed semi-authoritarian regimes at present. In a range of countries, elections may not be fully free and fair and governing parties may have huge advantages, but multiple parties are at least permitted, for example. Or the press may be permitted to function more freely, even if the only media outlets with significant resources are state-owned and give favorable coverage to standing governments. Or the economy may not be booming like China's, but at least small farmers and merchants may feel more secure in their property rights and have improving access to credit. Or women may not have fully equal status to men yet, but at least fewer are subjected to official discrimination or to procedures such as genital cutting (formerly known as female circumcision). Some degree of slow change can be seen in countries across the continent, from Burkina Faso to Malawi.

Incremental changes are meaningful, and they have social origins: Africa's modest improvements can be attributed partly to several forces of modernization,

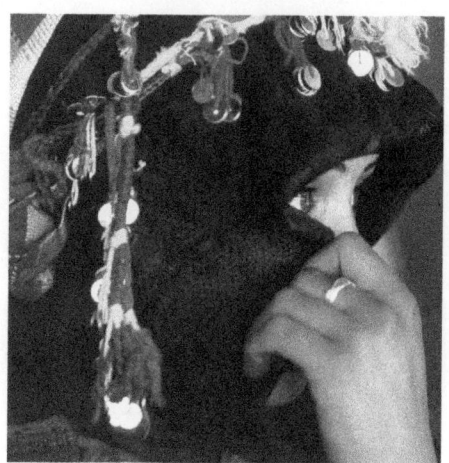

Moroccan woman

such as a rising middle class (which tends historically to be an important force that stands up for individual rights), and modern communications (which mean access to international ideas and norms). This is true especially in urban areas, but also in rural districts, where access to cell phones and improving incomes for some farmers have heightened the economic and political expectations of average citizens. On a more anecdotal level, it seems clear that access to Facebook, Twitter, and other social media have become increasingly important in facilitating the kinds of communication between citizens that governments are ill-equipped to control. This should have beneficial impacts for the growth of civil society—and potentially democracy—in the long-run, though it is certainly possible for communications technologies to be used by autocratic governments to monitor the populace as well.

The effort by the ECOWAS sub-region to bring military pressure on the 22-year rule of Yahya Jammeh of The Gambia to relinquish power to Adama Barrow is a significant way forward for example for the other regions in Africa to follow.

ECONOMIC DEVELOPMENT: GOOD NEWS AT LAST?

Instances of Economic Growth

Africa is the last region in the world where people will come out of poverty in large numbers, increasing their consumption and boosting economies as they do so. This has led to increasing interest—albeit hesitant and justifiably skeptical—in the continent's economy on the part of international investors and businesses. Africa has recently been touted as the world's final "growth frontier". Of course, the continent has long been seen as a repository of natural resources ripe for exploitation, but the economic perspective has shifted in tone somewhat over recent years, with growing attention to other areas, ranging from public infrastructure to industry to communications services to consumer goods to agricultural exports.

It would be premature to say Africa has many economic lions (beyond perhaps the long-standing economic success story in Botswana and other shorter-term successes), but a positive economic turn looks possible. The continent as a whole may grow at 5% or more in coming years, with some countries topping 7% or 8% (and yet others occasionally going into double digits for a few years when, say, oil investment really booms). Natural resources are one key to African economic development, but recent years have also seen more prosaic improvements in the agricultural production and small-scale service sectors that together employ well over half of Africa's population. Economies such as Ethiopia have grown at over 8%, not due to mineral exports alone, but rather a more balanced growth that includes increases in public and private investment, small-scale industry, services, and agricultural production.

Concerns about Dependency, Neocolonialism, and Underdevelopment

While the above trends are promising, one caveat is Africa's continued dependence on foreign investment and international markets for its exports. Given Africa's relative marginalization from the global process of economic integration, it is easy to forget how much Africa's economic outcomes are shaped by the world beyond the continent's shores. In 2008 and early 2009, Africa suffered the ripple effects of the global financial and economic crisis. This suggests that crises in Europe, the United States, or Asia can hit Africa hard. From the second half of 2009 through mid-2013, Africa has witnessed a turnaround, with growth that may average over 5%. In part, a rebound in commodity prices and investments in energy, which constitute the base of several African economies, drove the recovery. Sub-Saharan giants Nigeria (the continent's most populous nation) and Angola are two of the world's leading oil exporters, along with Algeria. Libya has largely recovered to export rates seen before the 2011 civil war. Oil also features prominently in countries as small as Equatorial Guinea, which was in several recent years the fastest growing country on earth as the destitute economy was changed virtually overnight by massive inflows of foreign investment. Ghana and Uganda, among other countries, are beginning to pump oil as well, with the former witnessing a boom that has pushed growth into double digits over the past year. Beyond oil, a range of other minerals and resources—from

Africa Today

diamonds to copper to coltan (a necessary ingredient for cell phones)—form the basis of many economies. The resources that helped Africa recover from the economic crisis could continue to spur growth for the coming years, if international demand remains intact.

It is likely that much of Africa will remain economically dependent on the rest of the world, and Africa continues to face challenges related to its post-colonial (or even neocolonial) associations with the global economy. Many of Africa's natural resource exports are unfinished products that require additional processing or manufacturing. African countries are often ill-equipped to complete these processes that add value to raw materials, and consequently much of the manufacturing is completed by developed countries. The value of the finished goods is much higher, which means the largest portion of the profits from natural resources often remains in wealthy countries, rather than being invested in African societies or coming in the form of income to African workers.

Of course, many African nations are not reaching their fullest economic potential due to problems that are more internal than external. The Democratic Republic of Congo (DRC), one of the largest nations on the continent, utilizes only a minimal proportion of its land for agriculture due to decades of conflict. Despite a UN report proclaiming that the DRC's abundant rivers have the hydroelectric potential to power the whole continent, the state suffers from weak infrastructure and planning, so the potential power goes unused. The same problem faces the Central African Republic, where natural resources are under-utilized due to economic instability. The diamond industry has the potential to be immensely profitable (as Botswana has shown) but smuggling and lack of infrastructure have reduced any positive impacts of the trade. This logic extends beyond the natural resource economy and the cause of conflict: issues such as endemic corruption also hamper investment, even in circumstances where the potential returns to capital are very high.

Social and Human Development

We must also note that Africa remains the epicenter of many of the world's greatest challenges, and home to many of the greatest human tragedies. While over recent decades the great majority of African nations have achieved considerably higher levels of social development indicators (such as literacy and life expectancy), it is still the region of the world with the lowest levels of human development. Sub-Saharan Africa is not on track to meet most of the Millennium Development Goals established to measure progress in human development by 2015. In 2011, a drought struck east Africa (especially Ethiopia, Somalia, and northern Kenya), and dangerous food shortages occurred in Niger and Chad. Even when hunger and malnutrition are less acute, Africa is still the continent with the world's lowest literacy rates, highest rates of infant mortality, and highest prevalence of poverty. Even many years of positive trends will not change the fact that the level of human development is tragically low.

Of particular note, of course, are the ongoing health crises from communicable diseases, especially HIV/AIDS, malaria, tuberculosis, and other tropical diseases. Some progress has been made in malaria treatment and prevention, and some other tropical diseases (notably Guinea worm and polio) may be on the verge of eradication. On the other hand, there is an increasingly dangerous threat that multi-drug resistant tuberculosis will spread. As for HIV/AIDS, millions of Africans continue to be infected and die of the disease every year, though estimates of prevalence and infection rates have declined in many countries. The prevalence of HIV/AIDS is especially low in some countries (such as Senegal), and this lower prevalence has been attributed to increasingly effective awareness campaigns, prevention methods, and treatment policies. In countries with the lowest rates, these programs have dated as far back as 1980, which may give hope to countries with more recently instituted prevention programs.

While there has been a perception that the worst has passed (which is no comfort to the many currently living with and contracting the virus), health officials in Zambia and other countries have warned of the emergence of strains of HIV that are resistant to current drug treatment. HIV-1 (the first strain discovered) is the more virulent, and has a higher possibility of transmission at exposure, but it is this type that anti-retroviral medicines have been produced to suppress (in large part because it became a worldwide disease). The HIV-2 strain is less virulent and has a lower rate of transmission, but it is found largely in West Africa, and anti-retrovirals have not been made to specifically counter it. This HIV-2 strain, despite its lower risk, poses a large threat to Africa. How it is addressed may be a question of how much and in what ways Africa matters to the rest of the world, a question that has been a part of the continent's history for centuries.

Even beyond HIV/AIDS, tropical Africa remains a very challenging environment for public health officials in terms of epidemiology and disease prevention. In West Africa, the year 2014 has seen an outbreak of the Ebola virus—with its deadly hemorrhagic fever –in Guinea, Sierra Leone, and Liberia. The fatal disease erupted in Guinea and later spread when the Guinean government proved unable to control the crisis; for containment, African governments have relied on assistance from international groups such as Doctors Without Borders. Though Ebola infection has a high fatality rate (of over 50%), its spread is limited by the fact that those infected can transmit the disease only when they are exhibiting rather serious symptoms. The crisis showed that countries (such as Guinea) have scant capacity at present to control such an outbreak, whereas some other neighboring countries (like Senegal) are better prepared to confront it.

POLITICAL UNCERTAINTY: THE ONLY CONSTANT IS CHANGE?

Ambiguous Trends in Formerly Troubled Countries

Earlier in this essay, I noted the slow accumulation of good news in many African countries. While that positive trend deserves more press than it gets, so too does news of the slow deterioration of governance in countries such as Rwanda and Uganda. These two countries have witnessed a slow but methodical retreat from optimism about their political prospects as recently as 10 years ago. In the late 1990s, there was hope that new leaders in these countries could turn their war-ravaged countries around. These men were thought to be a "new breed" of African leaders, representing a push towards democracy and a departure from the tyranny of older regimes. In Rwanda, it was hoped that President Paul Kagame would stabilize the country after the genocide of 1994 and bring democracy after creating political order. Yoweri Museveni had prospects for doing the same in Uganda after civil wars and horrific regimes there. Yet by 2013, it has become clear that the achievements of these leaders did not extend to crafting democracy, even if they did stabilize their countries and have brought economic growth and development. Rwanda and Uganda have become dominant-party states in which the opposition has little chance of winning the power to govern.

A similar pattern holds in Ethiopia. Even the passing of Ethiopia's longtime leader in 2012 is unlikely to alter the basic pattern of centralized domination by one party. When prime minister Meles Zenawi took charge of the country at the head of the Ethiopian People's Revolutionary Democratic Front (EPRDF) in the early 1990s, he was seen as a potential model leader for Ethiopia: he sought to give autonomy to the nation's different peoples while restoring a functioning government after taking down a brutal Marxist-Leninist dictatorship. Yet Zenawi and the

Africa Today

EPRDF came to dominate all aspects of the political system, at the national, regional, and local levels. After Meles died in August 2012, a new prime minister took his place, in accordance with the constitution. The relatively smooth transition suggests the EPRDF has settled in for the coming years, backed by over 99% of all the members of parliament and a similarly dominant position in Ethiopia's states and localities.

Rwanda, Uganda, and Ethiopia have each witnessed economic success of late, and each of the governments may well have enough genuine popularity to win even in free and fair elections, but the political style of the regimes has become depressingly familiar to observers of African politics that have seen decades of political manipulation favoring sitting governments at the expense of pluralism and civic freedoms. These countries are among those that should give pause to enthusiasts who are optimistic about African democracy, regardless of their burgeoning economic growth. At the same time, achievements on the economic front are consequential for Africa's one billion people, and they should not be obscured by a view that focuses exclusively on regime politics.

Honoring term limits have become a challenge for democratic consolidation in Africa. Two-term limits have been popular in Africa. However, Incumbent leaders have not shied away from amending constitutions to enable them to stay in power. Blaise Compaore tried to change the constitution to enable him to contest for a third term but was met with violent protest, forcing him to flee the country. Currently, Burundian President Pierre Nkurunziza is attempting a bid to enable him to run for a third term. This has already resulted in weeks of civil unrest, a refugee crisis, a coup attempt, as well as prominent politicians, such as second Vice President Gervais Rufyikiri, taking refuge in Belgium.

North Africa: Aftermath of the Arab Spring

The vast majority of Africa's population is found south of the Sahara Desert, and 49 of the 54 countries in this book are found there, but some special attention must also be paid to the region where the most well-known international news has come from in recent years: North Africa. Geographically, North Africa is situated between Sub-Saharan Africa, the Middle East, and southern Europe. Like much of the rest of Africa to its south, several North African states continue to struggle with the legacies of colonialism, the rule of long-serving dictators and autocrats, and difficult and fractious attempts at democracy. It is also home to somewhat stronger Islamist movements (as found in the Middle East) that sometimes challenge pushes toward liberal western democracy (as found in Europe to the north).

The uprisings that convulsed the Middle East in 2011 began in Tunisia, spread to the heart of the Arab world in Egypt and beyond, and then took a deadlier turn in Libya. Meanwhile the Algerian regime continues to operate as a corrupt shell "democracy", reforming at a very slow pace. In the last three years, events in Egypt and Libya and the rest of North Africa have taken remarkable twists and turns. Indeed, as this book goes to press in late June 2014, the situations in both countries remain in flux. As the events in North Africa have shown, the end of an autocratic regime is not the same as a smooth transition to democracy. The revolutions have in many ways left more questions than answers, with the varying experiences across the different cases showing that the hopes of straightforward transitions to democracy after 2011 were rather naive.

Egypt's political landscape has been in flux since early 2011, when Egyptians first began flooding into Tahrir Square in Cairo to demand the end of the regime of President Hosni Mubarak. That regime finally collapsed after weeks of protest and counterattacks, and Mubarak himself was arrested and placed on trial. In June 2012, elections resulted in a narrow victory for Mohamed Morsi, who was supported by the Freedom and Justice Party and the long-banned Muslim Brotherhood. While this progress to elections was a stated aim of the uprising, the subsequent trajectory set off a constitutional crisis, pitting the military and judiciary on one side against popularly elected Islamists on the other (with secular liberals constituting yet another front in the internal political strife). By early July 2013, the Egyptian military deposed Morsi just after he completed one year in power. Supporters of Morsi and the once-banned Muslim Brotherhood led counter-rallies, and some called for rebellion. In August 2013, hundreds of pro-Morsi protesters were killed by security forces in Cairo, and the military government declared a state of emergency and imposed curfews. In January 2014, Egyptians approved a new constitution that banned parties based on religion, and May saw the election of former army chief Abdel Fattah el-Sisi. In the last four years, Egypt has thus gone from Mubarak's autocratic regime, to the popularly elected Morsi (supported by the Muslim Brotherhood), to an interim regime backed by the military, to an elected government led by a former military leader who is not unlike Mubarak. The new government seems intent on sidelining the Islamists through police and judicial action, sometimes through startling civil rights violations like mass death sentences of hundreds of Islamists in one single day trial. The likelihood of stability and genuine western-style democracy over the coming years is rather low.

Libya has also undergone a seismic change in its political system since the fall of Muammar Qadhafi in 2011. Qadhafi was eventually defeated by a rebel movement (which was supported by NATO) after a months-long civil war. Defections within Qadhafi's inner circle and the lack of military supplies and financing finally broke the leader, who was eventually hunted down on October 20, 2011, as he tried to escape from his hometown of Sirte. Qadhafi was ultimately taunted, beaten, and killed by his rebel captors. Given the bloody nature of the Libyan conflict, it was perhaps surprising that subsequent elections went off smoothly and resulted in a victory for moderates. Yet Islamists groups and straggling supporters of the old Qadhafi regime continue to challenge the new government, leaving it subject to destabilizing violence and internal factions that may yet undermine the entire regime. Again, this evokes the complexity of revolutionary change, with a chaotic downfall of the old regime giving way to a transition that is itself the subject of much contestation.

Thus, unlike the end of the Soviet bloc in Eastern Europe in 1989, the Arab Spring looks to be followed by a long and complex period of uncertainty and efforts at state-building. Internal conflicts and remnants of old power structures remain intact, while the presence of Islamists complicates the democratic landscape in many cases. The true impact of the revolutions that swept across the region is still being written.

Turmoil South of the Sahara

The influence of the Arab Spring in Africa was mostly restricted to the northern coast of the continent, and it did not directly sweep aside regimes south of the Sahara. However, its effects were felt in other ways on other parts of the continent. The Libyan regime change indirectly brought about another collapse in a quite different country: Mali. After the fall of Qadhafi, well-armed Tuareg soldiers (a semi-nomadic group that resides in regions in and around the Sahara) migrated south across the desert. Arriving in Mali's remote northeast, they joined up with a small pre-existing Tuareg liberation movement and groups of Islamist rebels. The Tuareg groups found common cause with radical Islamist militants in their opposition to the Malian state. By March of 2012, they had advanced and taken over some regional capitals; this triggered a coup against Mali's civilian government by frustrated elements of the army that felt the civilians had not given them the power

Africa Today

and resources to stop the rebellion. These events in Mali showed that North Africa and sub-Saharan Africa share (at least partially) a common fate, notwithstanding the geographic and cultural barriers between them. The irony is that the type of regime change that occurred in Mali was the obverse of that seen in Libya: the collapse of one of Africa's most notorious dictatorships precipitated the collapse of one of Africa's most remarkable democracies. By late 2012, Mali was experiencing open war—a terrible turn for one of Africa's most peaceful and democratic countries. With the Islamist rebels (known as Ansar Dine) advancing and within striking distance of the capital, the French military suddenly intervened in its former colony; within a few weeks, the French forces turned the tide and pushed the rebels back out of the major population centers. After a national election in 2013, there are now decent prospects for the reestablishment of a full democracy in Mali, but parts of the hinterlands are still under rebel control and the regime's 2012 collapse shows more broadly the fragility of even the established democracies in Africa.

Mali was not the only country that faced an existential threat to its regime in 2012 and 2013. An old-fashioned armed overthrow took place in the Central African Republic (C.A.R.), a long-troubled country at the geographic heart of the continent. A rebel movement known as Séléka worked its way to the capital city and toppled the regime of President François Bozizé. Michel Djotodia took interim power on an interim basis, but resigned in January 2014 following claims that he was making the situation worse. Catherine Samba-Panza was appointed as interim president in January, and it is too soon to tell whether or not she will be able to make a positive impact. She faces a difficult job, with CAR suffering badly damaged infrastructure, an increased death toll, and a rising refugee count. Recently, the United Nations called the Central African Republic "a lawless country." Several other African countries—such as Guinea-Bissau and Chad—continue similarly to be plagued by the specter of atrocious civil-military relations that always leave open the possibility of coups or civil strife.

Catastrophic governance also persists in several countries that have not seen coups or overthrows. Probably the most conspicuous example at present comes from Sudan. Along the border between Sudan and South Sudan (a country that gained independence from its northern neighbor in 2011), conflict over oil-rich regions has resulted in fighting, mutual recrimination, and attempts at economic sabotage. Sudan is still governed by a president (Omar al-Bashir) who is a war criminal, while South Sudan has been unconvincing in its halting steps toward building functioning governance. Al-Bashir has repeatedly pledged to step down from his presidency in 2015, but his genocidal governance incarnates the major challenges facing Africa going forward. In South Sudan, a bitter rivalry has led to violence between the Dinka and Nuer ethnic groups. Tension between these two groups has been present in the country since the movement for independence. In mid-2013, President Salva Kiir (a Dinka) dismissed his entire cabinet, including Vice President Riek Machar (a Nuer), after accusing them of plotting a coup. Machar denied these charges and saw it as a pretext to eliminate Nuer opposition to the Dinka-ruled government. In December 2013, Machar called for rebels to fight the government and civil war broke out. Thousands of people have been killed (with the most brutal fighting occurring in Bentiu, an oil-rich town located in Unity State where hundreds of unarmed civilians were killed) and 1.5 million have been displaced from their homes. Attempted cease-fires in January and May 2014 have proved unsuccessful. The UN has threatened to impose sanctions on both sides as both are guilty of using child soldiers and killing civilians.

Another country with a worrying trajectory is Zimbabwe. Robert Mugabe has ruled the country with an iron fist since independence and has successfully fought off attempts by his main rival of late, Morgan Tsvangirai. After years of fitful attempts at power-sharing and half-steps toward democracy that Mugabe has routinely short-circuited, Zimbabwe held a constitutional referendum that was overwhelmingly approved by supporters of both men. There is still little evidence that the new regime will result in Mugabe trimming his own power, although optimists may point to this as a turning point when some modicum of procedural democracy was reinstituted. And even pessimists recognize that the time horizon for Mugabe's rule is shortening, as the leader is now 90 years old as of mid-2014. He is essentially the last of the freedom-fighting founding fathers still governing in sub-Saharan Africa, and the end of his reign in the coming years—which cannot come soon enough for many observers—will certainly mark the end of an era. However, there are speculations that Mugabe would like to extend his reign by grooming his wife Grace to be his successor. Joyce Mujuru, his vice president, has been sacked after state media and Mrs. Grace Mugabe launched a relentless campaign against her, and accused her of corruption and plotting to kill Mr. Mugabe. Joyce Mujuru was favored to succeed Mugabe when he retires from active politics.

Countries and experiences such as these—from Mali or Zimbabwe—show that the bad news out of Africa is not over. On the contrary, it is bound to continue in various forms and for some time. Messy politics can be found even in Africa's most famously successful case of democratization—South Africa—where the long-dominant African National Congress of former president Nelson Mandela has slowly morphed into a conventional African dominant party, beset by factions and internal battles, and guilty of corruption by several of its prominent members. The ANC may yet have several more years to run in its hold on power, but the quality of its work and the memories of its halcyon days are fading fast. A question that thus emerges for observers outside the continent is what this means with regard to the rest of world: what impacts do outsiders have on events in Africa? For that matter, what do the prospects for different

Africa Today

outcomes in Africa mean for those who live outside the continent?

AFRICA IN THE WORLD

How The World Affects Africa

Africa's relationship with the world is a two-way street. Before turning to the global effects of African issues (or "why Africa matters for the world"), consider how the world affects Africa, both for better and for worse. Consider first the international impacts on African public health. On one hand, the continent has benefited from increasing international support for programming to help control HIV/AIDS. On the other hand, the swine flu also reached Africa in 2009, conveyed from Mexico (almost certainly via the United States and/or Europe) by the vehicles of globalization: air travel and trade. While the pandemic did not cause large numbers of deaths in Europe or America, influenza viruses may yet spread (and will likely mutate), and such disease can be far more lethal in places where large numbers of people are immune compromised. Africa, then, benefits from many of its interactions with the world, but also is susceptible to global complications. On a continent where so many confront HIV/AIDS in precarious economic circumstances, it may be said in a literal sense that when the world coughs, Africa catches a fever.

The arrival of problems originated overseas is not new to Africa, of course. After all, this is the continent whose early economic exchanges with the world were based upon the slave trade. Moreover, during the Cold War, Africa was a central battlefield in the proxy wars for power between a First World led by the United States and the Second World of the Soviet Bloc. The corrupt and vile dictatorships that dotted the continent for 30 years were of Africa's own making but were amply aided and abetted by international powers. In short, western countries have a long history of bringing social, political, and economic disruption to Africa, alongside the genuine opportunities, new ideas, and constructive investment they also brought. Colonial history, trade, development aid, policy advice, political interventions, military engagement, and multinational enterprise have constructed a web of interactions between the west and Africa that have had ambiguous consequences for the continent.

To be clear, this history does not mean that Africa would be better off reversing its integration with the international economy. The assessment of the situation must be considerably more complex and varied, much as the continent itself is complex and varied. Rather than offering simplistic lessons, the events of the recent global economic crises suggest a dynamic interrelationship between the "globalized" world and the continent that is often seen as the least touched by globalization. Economically, Africa and the world share a mutual dependence that brings benefits and costs to each.

Chinese investment in Africa in recent years is one indicator of the importance of global integration. The investment would seem to be an unambiguous boost to African economies. China has supported mineral extraction and exploration, heavy industrial investment, construction of public venues such as sports stadiums, and even provision of artemisinin, the leading antimalarial drug. On the downside, however, Chinese investment has arguably helped to prop up dictatorships, since China (an authoritarian regime itself) stands by the principle of non-intervention in domestic affairs. Certainly, rotten governments such as those in Sudan and Zimbabwe will appreciate the Chinese investment and willingness to "look the other way" on human rights issues, but large segments of the populations are likely to suffer the consequences. Moreover, tensions have risen in many countries as Chinese firms have imported tens of thousands of Chinese laborers, many of whom have not integrated much with local society. African host countries are witnessing rising resentment over several issues with Chinese investment, including a lack of employment opportunities for Africans and a reputation for poor quality of infrastructure developments.

The world has long affected Africa in many ways, but for many years, the inverse was not true: it seemed the world could largely ignore Africa if it chose. From the 1970s through the early 1990s, the images of Africa were relatively static: famine and genocide, poverty and conflict, death and destruction and disease. But these problems were distant, almost literally of "another world," a Third World that scarcely affected the day-to-day lives of those far away. Africa had a whole set of different meanings for people living in the developed world, representing challenges and opportunities alike, but for most people these were of occasional significance at best. For some, Africa was ominous and foreboding—witness its longstanding nickname as "the Dark Continent"—while for many others it has the inexorable appeal of vivacity and resilience in the face of humanity's greatest challenges. In either case, Africa rarely "came home." In the 21st century, however, we can argue that this has changed, for reasons that seem all too familiar.

Why Africa Matters to the West, part 1: Weak States and Security

There are very concrete ways that Africa affects countries beyond the continent itself. (And it goes without saying that western nations are most likely to take interest in those African issues that affect or benefit themselves most directly.) The first reason Africa is of growing strategic importance to the rest of the world is because of its weak states. The most prominent example of this today is Somalia, where a feeble Somali government and international forces are attempting (with some modicum of success lately) to reestablish law and order. Despite these efforts, parts of the country still remain a lawless frontier. Modern day pirates have attacked ships off the coast of Somalia up to 2014, affecting vessels and merchant mariners from France, Denmark, and the United States, among other countries. This is evidence of a government's inability to perform the essential tasks of governing, such as enacting and enforcing laws. As political scientist Jeffrey Herbst has put it, African states too often fail to broadcast their power and authority over their own territory.

A recurring problem in Africa is the failure of "states" to live up to even the basic definition of statehood. While a country may have a plaque and a seat at the United Nations, it may have little internal control; or, as political scientists and sociologists would characterize the phenomenon, they may lack a monopoly on the legitimate use of force in their territory. Put more concretely, many African regimes have proven historically incapable of governing outside the confines of just a few square miles in a capital city. The most striking examples of this phenomenon came from the "warlord states" of the 1990s, when clans of roving bandits—often including child soldiers wielding machetes and automatic small arms—brought mayhem to Liberia, Sierra Leone, and Somalia. Sierra Leone and Liberia have since recovered rather admirably from this vortex, and are now relatively stable, but the basic concern with state power continues. (It should be noted here that the 1994 genocide in Rwanda was quite different in this regard. It was in fact meticulously coordinated by one of Africa's more organized state apparatuses, and was not, despite common misperceptions, a spontaneous outburst of violence by marauders avenging "ancient tribal hatreds.")

Why do Africa's weak states matter for, say, average Americans? After all, how many Americans find themselves on a ship at risk of capture by Somali pirates, or find themselves in the midst of West African civil wars? Apart from the obvious humanitarian concerns, it is tempting for some to believe that American disengagement from the continent could mean that we simply allow for "African solutions to African problems." Indeed, American disengagement from Somalia in 1993 after the

Africa Today

deaths of American troops must be understood in light of the unwillingness of the administration and American populace to stand in the middle of an African conflict. And the failure to intervene in the Rwanda genocide of 1994 must be understood with reference to the prior year's events in Somalia. So why should America involve itself in African problems? Setting aside questions of moral imperatives and those about America's historic role on the continent, there are several simple answers to such a question. A first is terrorism.

Weak states are likely breeding grounds for terrorism. Al-Qaeda, like other Islamic fundamentalist movements that advocate terrorism, thrives not in countries where they can live above ground, but rather where power itself is scarcely exercised by the government. Terrorism can flourish where the state cannot penetrate. It is for this reason that the U.S. government has, in recent years, poured money into western Africa. The aim has been to stabilize West and North African countries with large Islamic populations and prevent them from becoming safe havens for Islamic terrorists. While some of these countries (especially Senegal) are known for their relatively comfortable relations with the West and their liberal interpretations of Islam, other countries are dealing with active radical elements that are openly antagonistic towards the United States and western Europe. A dramatic change here in 2012 was the advance of the Islamic group Ansar Dine in Mali (which was partly responsible for the collapse of the former democratic regime), but the most horrific events have come in Nigeria, where the fundamentalists of Boko Haram have massacred Christians by the dozens, month after month in 2013 and 2014. Again, this problem affects Africans first and foremost, but these conflicts can and do metastasize in ways that impact the rest of the world.

A leading concern for the west is the proliferation of al-Qaeda franchises in Africa. Al-Qaeda in the Arabian Peninsula comes up to the borders and shores of Africa, while the militant group al-Shabaab ("The Youth") in Somalia developed an on-again-off-again affiliation with the leadership of Al-Qaeda. An especially dangerous unit has been al-Qaeda in the Islamic Maghreb (AQIM). Originally formed in Algeria under another name, it began bombings and kidnappings, and later took became an al-Qaeda franchise by 2006. In recent years, the organization has reached further south from the Mediterranean into the Saharan states of Mali, Niger, and Mauritania. And here, state weakness matters, as resource-poor governments in these countries have considerable difficulty establishing a rule of law in their vast Saharan hinterlands.

Further, extreme poverty within many of these countries allows Al-Qaeda to recruit new members who desperately need the income the terrorist group is able to provide. In those conditions, AQIM can more freely expand and extend its reach. Without much exaggeration, it can be said that America's response places it in a low-intensity war with Al Qaeda on yet another front in western Africa.

Beyond terrorism, weak states also present challenges to the ability of global actors to prevent other social problems. The "war on drugs" is an example. Here, Africa plays a key role, even if it does not make the front pages. Much of the world's illicit drug supply is processed or transshipped through West African countries with weak or corrupt states, like Guinea-Bissau. Where corruption is rampant and governmental control is woefully inadequate, the black market can thrive as much as terror cells. Corruption in Nigeria or the deterioration of civil-military relations in Guinea-Bissau (with the assassination of its president by the military in 2009 and continued indications of state failure up to 2014) scarcely register in the United States, but the consequences of these events come home to Americans every day in the form of heroin on the streets of Atlanta, or even email phishing scams that coax gullible readers into divulging valuable personal information.

Even for beneficial pharmaceuticals (i.e., "good drugs"), weak states present a difficulty: a government that cannot govern cannot control dangerous processes of counterfeiting and piracy. Improper or dangerous products may find their way into the world commercial market. (Even if safe, unlicensed generics often infringe patents and copyrights; the effect may well be affordable drugs for Africans, and morally defensible in the case of national health emergencies but is certainly a question that gives western governments and pharmaceutical corporations pause.) Finally, another possible threat to public health comes from the inability of inept state management of the possible pandemics that threaten to become the new "plagues" of the 21st century, whether viruses directly affecting human health or crop diseases that may destroy yields. Of course, the direct impacts of these are felt most often in Africa itself, but it serves to illustrate that strengthening Africa's states is also a matter of self-interest for the world's wealthiest nations. One of the more dire prophecies of the 21st century is that the world, now accustomed to global travel and interaction, will be struck by a particularly virulent form of influenza or infections (such as tuberculosis or other bacillary diseases) that are resistant to drug treatments. Already, there is worry that the massive international push to eradicate polio may founder just short of the finish line, and Nigeria or another African country may well be the last on earth where the virus holds out and lives to infect another generation.

Why Africa Matters to the West, part 2: Energy

Beyond concerns with state weakness, Africa is back on the world map as an arena of great power contestation for the coming century for one principal reason: energy supplies. Not since the Cold War have the world's leading powers *needed* Africa in the way the United States, China, and Europe need Africa today. Already, Africa supplies almost as much oil to the United States as the Persian Gulf provides, and Africa's share of the American market is growing. Libya, Nigeria, Algeria, and Angola are leading suppliers to the world, with Gabon, Cameroon, and Congo historically providing major supplies. The gross domestic product of the tiny nation of Equatorial Guinea has skyrocketed in the last decade as oil investment and production have taken off, though little of the wealth has trickled down to the population. The new nation of South Sudan has abundant oil but has an ongoing conflict that has ruined the capacity and conditions needed for profitable extraction and transportation to market. Ghana and Uganda, meanwhile, are up-and-coming producers. (This economic future may well be one unstated reason—among many other compelling reasons—why President Barack Obama chose Ghana as his first African country to visit, over his father's homeland of Kenya.)

The struggle between the United States and China for access to energy supplies in Africa fits the mold of great power contestation over access to resources, and African governments are enthusiastic about the attention they are receiving—a sort of new scramble for Africa. In the days of the Cold War, the competing interests of the U.S. and the Soviet Union meant that African client states could count on financial support for their willingness to take sides. While the current great power rivalry is more economic (and thus has a somewhat lesser feel of a zero-sum game), it looks like African governments gain from being argued over. Countries with natural resources are targeted for investment and lavished with diplomatic attention. In short, the bargaining power of African governments increases when the world wants the resources over which they preside. Much Chinese investment in Africa is linked to oil and other natural resources, though China has also invested in infrastructure and prestige projects across the continent. The rivalry between the U.S. and China takes on

Africa Today

difficult overtones as the former tries to push (perhaps selectively) for a recognition of universal human rights, while the latter expresses support for the principle of "non-intervention" in Africa's domestic affairs. The result is a willingness on the part of China to be cozy with some of the continent's worst dictators (such as those in Sudan and Zimbabwe), though the United States also has a checkered history that blends accommodation and indignation in regard to African governance.

To bring together these threads, we may say that Africa matters beyond Africa for several reasons. Viewed from an American perspective, for instance, we can say that nowhere else in the world do several of today's most prominent foreign policy issues intersect: concerns about radical Islam and terrorism, drugs and piracy, access to natural resources, and the economic rise of China. The continent may well matter more for America—and the rest of the world—in the coming decades than it has for centuries.

Desperate and Dangerous: Report on the human rights situation of migrants and refugees in Libya (20 December 2018)

For full report see: https://www.ohchr.org/Documents/Countries/LY/LibyaMigrationReport.pdf

Migrants and refugees suffer unimaginable horrors during their transit through and stay in Libya. From the moment they step onto Libyan soil, they become vulnerable to unlawful killings, torture and other ill-treatment, arbitrary detention and unlawful deprivation of liberty, rape and other forms of sexual and gender-based violence, slavery and forced labor, extortion and exploitation by both State and non-State actors. Despite the overwhelming evidence of human rights violations and abuses, Libyan authorities have thus far appeared largely unable or unwilling to put an end to violations and abuses committed against migrants and refugees. UNSMIL and OHCHR regret that the Libyan authorities have failed to implement the recommendations included in their joint report "Detained and Dehumanized": Report on Human Rights Abuses Against Migrants in Libya. issued on 13 December 2016.

Given the lack of progress in addressing the rampant human rights violations and abuses against migrants and refugees in Libya, their situation has not improved in the past two years, despite overwhelming evidence of horrific abuses and increased attention given to the issue at global and regional levels. Years of armed conflict and political divisions have weakened Libyan institutions, including the judiciary, which have been unable, if not unwilling, to address the plethora of abuses and violations committed against migrants and refugees by smugglers, traffickers, members of armed groups and State officials, with near total impunity. The vacuum left by the State following the 2011 uprising and armed conflict has been filled by a multitude of armed groups in control of large swaths of Libya's territory, borders, and key installations. These armed groups were increasingly integrated into State institutions without any vetting processes to remove those with problematic human rights records, although the Government of National Accord, following the outbreak of violence in Tripoli in September 2018, has promised to take steps to diminish the influence of armed groups on state institutions. This climate of lawlessness provides fertile ground for thriving illicit activities, such as trafficking in human beings and criminal smuggling, and leaves migrant and refugee men, women, and children at the mercy of countless predators who view them as commodities to be exploited and extorted for maximum financial gain. Abuses against sub-Saharan migrants and refugees, in particular, are compounded by the failure of the Libyan authorities to address racism, racial discrimination and xenophobia. Libyan law criminalizes irregular entry into, stay in or exit from the country with a penalty of imprisonment pending deportation, without any consideration of individual circumstances or protection needs. Foreign nationals in vulnerable situations, including survivors of trafficking and refugees, are among those subjected to mandatory and indefinite arbitrary detention. Libya has no asylum system, has not ratified the 1951 Convention relating to the Status of Refugees, and does not formally recognize the United Nations High Commissioner for Refugees (UNHCR), while defacto entities allow the agency to register some asylum seekers and refugees from a limited number of countries.

In practice, the overwhelming majority of migrants and refugees are arbitrarily detained as they have never been charged or tried under Libya's migration legislation. They languish indefinitely in detention until they are returned though the International Organization for Migration's (IOM) Voluntary Humanitarian Returns program, evacuated by UNHCR or forcible deported by the Libyan authorities. While conditions vary across detention centers, they are generally inhuman, fall far short of international standards and, in some cases, may amount to torture. During visits to the Directorate for Combatting Illegal Migration (DCIM) detention centers in 2017–2018, UNSMIL staff have consistently observed severe overcrowding, lack of proper ventilation and lighting, inadequate access to washing facilities and latrines, constant confinement, denial of contact with the outside world, and malnutrition. Conditions lead to the spread of skin infections, acute diarrhea, respiratory tract-infections and other ailments, and medical treatment is inadequate. Children, including those separated or unaccompanied, are held together with adults in similarly squalid conditions. UNSMIL has also documented torture and other ill-treatment, forced labor, rape and other forms of sexual violence perpetrated by DCIM guards with impunity. The fact that women are held in facilities without female guards further facilitates sexual abuse and exploitation. UNSMIL staff found that female detainees are routinely subjected to strip searches by or under the gaze of male guards. Many of those detained at DCIM centers are survivors of horrific abuses by smugglers or traffickers and are in need of tailored medical and psychological support and rehabilitation. They are systematically held captive in abusive conditions, including starvation, severe beatings, burning with hot metals, electrocution, and sexual abuses of women and girls, with the aim of extorting money from their families through a complex system of money transfers, extending to a number of countries. They are frequently sold from one criminal gang to another and required to pay ransoms multiple times before being set free or taken to coastal areas to await the Mediterranean Sea crossing. The overwhelming majority of women and older teenage girls interviewed by UNSMIL reported being gang raped by smugglers or traffickers or witnessing others being taken out of collective accommodations to be abused. Younger women travelling without male relatives are also particularly vulnerable to being forced into prostitution. Countless migrants and refugees lost their lives during captivity by smugglers or traffickers after being shot, tortured to death, or simply left to die from starvation or medical neglect. Across Libya, unidentified bodies of migrants and refugees bearing gunshot wounds, torture marks and burns are frequently uncovered in rubbish bins, dry riverbeds, farms, and the desert.

UNSMIL continues to receive credible information on the complicity of some State actors, including local officials, members of armed groups formally integrated into State institutions, and representatives of the Ministry of Interior and Ministry of Defense, in the smuggling or trafficking of migrants and refugees. These State actors enrich themselves through exploitation of and extortion from vulnerable migrants and refugees. In addition to detention on the grounds of breaking immigration legislation, migrants and refugees are vulnerable to being arbitrarily arrested and detained, including by armed groups nominally under the control of the Ministry of Interior, in relation to accusations of theft, drug-related offences, sex work, alcohol consumption, and terrorism. Hundreds are thus held, most without charge or trial for prolonged periods or following grossly unfair trials. UNSMIL documented that migrants and refugees held at facilities under the Ministry of Interior, in particular at the Mitiga detention facility controlled by the Special Deterrence Force armed group in Tripoli, are subjected to torture and other ill-treatment, forced labor, prolonged solitary confinement, and inhuman detention conditions. Security forces in Libya, including armed groups integrated into the Ministry of Interior, have used excessive or unwarranted lethal force against migrants and refugees in the course of law enforcement operations, leading to loss of life and injury. Even at liberty, migrants and refugees in Libya are not safe and live under a constant risk of deprivation of liberty and arbitrary arrest, assault, theft, and exploitation by State and non-State actors, who are well aware of their vulnerability and inability to access justice or redress. Migrants and refugees are at risk of arbitrary arrest or capture at checkpoints or on the streets by security forces, members of armed groups and private citizens, even if they have proper documentation. Migrants and refugees are frequently exploited by unscrupulous employers who refuse to pay their wages, knowing that in practice they have no recourse to justice. The lack of liquidity in Libyan banks has left migrants and refugees employed in the public sector such as teaching, nursing, and engineering struggling to withdraw their salaries for the past two years. UNSMIL gathered information that sick and injured migrants and refugees, as well as pregnant women in labor, have been turned away from public hospitals. Migrants and refugees whose rights have been abused, including survivors of trafficking and rape, refrain from lodging complaints with the police or prosecution, fearing arrest and re-victimization. While recognizing the significant security and political challenges faced by the Libyan authorities, OHCHR and UNSMIL call on them to respect, protect and fulfil the human rights of migrants and refugees and to place respect for human rights at the center of their approach to managing migration. This includes releasing all migrants and refugees detained arbitrarily, closing all detention centers that fail to uphold minimum standards, guaranteeing unannounced and unimpeded access for human rights monitors, introducing alternatives to detention, and improving detention conditions. The authorities should also clearly signal that atrocities against migrants and refugees will no longer be tolerated, regardless of whether perpetrators are smugglers, traffickers, members of armed groups or State officials. Judicial investigations into violations and abuses committed against migrants and refugees should be undertaken and completed, with a view to holding perpetrators accountable in proceedings meeting international standards for fair trial. Tackling impunity would not only end the suffering of tens of thousands of migrant and refugee women, men, and children seeking a better life, but also undercut the parallel illicit economy built on the abuse and exploitation of migrants and refugees. Eradicating this predation on migrants and refugees would reduce a key source of income for criminal gangs and armed groups and help establish the rule of law and national institutions.

OHCHR and UNSMIL recommend that the European Union and its Member States step up their search and rescue operations in the Mediterranean Sea and facilitate the life-saving work of rescue vessels operated by humanitarian organizations. They are also urged to put in place measures to ensure that any cooperation with Libyan institutions in the management of migration includes safeguards to ensure respect for international humanitarian, human rights, and refugee law, and does not contribute to or facilitate, directly or indirectly, the commission of human rights violations. Any future support should be contingent upon the Libyan authorities showing progress in upholding human rights law and standards. This should include working towards an end to the mandatory, automatic, and arbitrary detention of migrants and refugees in irregular situations, stamping out of torture and ill-treatment, sexual violence, and forced labor in detention, and ending all return practices that would violate the strict prohibitions on collective expulsion and refoulement.

The World Bank in Africa: The World Bank's overview of Africa for the year 2019
http://www.worldbank.org/en/region/afr/overview
This portion is solely a report from the World Bank in the assessment of the African continent. It is wholly obtained from the above weblink.

Context:
Growth in Sub-Saharan Africa is estimated at 2.3 percent for 2018, down from 2.5 percent in 2017. Economic growth remains below population growth for the fourth consecutive year, and although regional growth is expected to rebound to 2.8 percent in 2019, it will have remained below three percent since 2015.

The slower-than-expected overall growth in 2018 reflects ongoing global uncertainty, but increasingly comes from domestic macroeconomic instability including poorly managed debt, inflation, and deficits; political and regulatory uncertainty; and fragility that are having visible negative impacts on some African economies. It also belies stronger performance in several smaller economies that continue to grow steadily.

In Nigeria, growth reached 1.9 percent in 2018, up from 0.8 percent in 2017, reflecting a modest pick-up in the non-oil economy. South Africa came out of recession in the third quarter of 2018, but growth was subdued at 0.8 percent over the year, as policy uncertainty held back investment. Angola, the region's third largest economy, remained in recession, with growth falling sharply as oil production stayed weak.

Growth picked up in some resource-intensive-countries like the Democratic

Quick Reference Table (2023 Estimates)

Country	GDP per Capital Nominal IMF 2023 EST.	PPP IMF 2023 EST.	Projected Real GDP growth (Annual % change) (2023 IMF)	Freedom House (2023)
Algeria	4481	13,507	2.6	Not Free
Angola	3204	7225	3.5	Not Free
Benin	1390	4300	6	Partly Free
Botswana	7270	19,398	3.7	Free
Burkina Faso	900	2726	4.9	Not Free
Burundi	249	891	3.3	Not Free
Cameroon	1699	4665	4.3	Not Free
Cape Verde	4278	9661	4.4	Free
Cent. African Rep.	534	1127	2.5	Not Free
Chad	667	1787	3.5	Not Free
Comoros	1360	3463	3	Partly Free
Congo Rep.	2584	5155	4.1	Not Free
Côte d'Ivoire	2646	7011	6.2	Partly Free
Dem. Rep. Congo	695	1447	6.3	Not Free
Djibouti	3802	6894	4	Not Free
Egypt	3644	16,979	3.7	Not Free
Equatorial Guinea	9777	18,510	-1.8	Not Free
Eritrea	715	2188	2.8	Not Free
Ethiopia	1475	3724	6.1	Not Free
Gabon	9294	19,197	3	Not Free
The Gambia	861	2804	5.6	Partly Free
Ghana	2024	6974	1.6	Free
Guinea	1549	3218	5.6	Not Free
Guinea-Bissau	974	3072	4.5	Partly Free
Kenya	2269	6569	5.3	Partly Free
Lesotho	1208	3251	2.2	Partly Free
Liberia	805	1788	4.3	Partly Free
Libya	6763	24,599	17.5	Not Free
Madagascar	536	1916	4.2	Partly Free
Malawi	496	1682	2.4	Partly Free
Mali	889	2656	5.0	Not Free
Mauritania	2475	7437	4.4	Partly Free
Mauritius	11,548	29,164	4.6	Free
Morocco	3748	10,460	3.0	Partly Free
Mozambique	587	1556	5.0	Partly Free
Namibia	5100	11,440	2.8	Free
Niger	613	1600	6.1	Partly Free
Nigeria	2280	6178	3.2	Partly Free
Rwanda	970	3090	6.2	Not Free
São Tomé & Príncipe	2695	4874	2.0	Free
Senegal	1719	4515	8.3	Partly Free
Seychelles	19,536	39,662	3.9	Free
Sierra Leone	415	2082	3.1	Partly Free
Somalia	544	1374	2.8	Not Free
South Africa	6485	16,091	0.1	Free
South Sudan	467	516	5.6	Not Free
Sudan	975	4471	1.2	Not Free
Swaziland (Eswatini)	4146	11,492	2.8	Not Free
Tanzania	1348	3600	5.2	Partly Free
Togo	990	2754	5.5	Partly Free
Tunisia	4671	13,2700	1.3	Partly Free
Uganda	1105	3224	5.7	Not Free
Zambia	1423	4041	4.0	Partly Free
Zimbabwe	1851	2627	2.5	Not Free

Note: GDP is gross domestic product, a measure of income (in this case per capita, or per person). PPP refers to purchasing power parity, a measure used to adjust incomes for the purchasing power of what a dollar can buy in a given country; it is, roughly speaking, an adjustment for the cost of living. Freedom House category refers to the level of political rights and civil liberties in a country, or roughly the level of democracy. The World Bank data of annual percentage growth in real GDP growth is an indication of the direction of the country's economic growth for the coming years.

Africa Today

Elmina Castle; Also called the door of no return. Used as a slave hold up for onward shipment to North America and the Caribbean.

Republic of Congo and Niger, as stronger mining production and commodity prices boosted activity alongside a rebound in agricultural production and public investment in infrastructure. In others, like Liberia and Zambia, growth was subdued, as high inflation and elevated debt levels continued to weigh on investor sentiment. In the Central African Economic and Monetary Community, a fragile recovery continued as reform efforts to reduce fiscal and external imbalances slowed in some countries.

Non-resource-intensive economies such as Kenya, Rwanda, Uganda, and several in the West African Economic and Monetary Union, including Benin and Côte d'Ivoire recorded solid economic growth in 2018.

However, many challenges remain. Public debt levels and debt risk are rising, which might jeopardize debt sustainability in some countries; the availability of good jobs has not kept pace with the number of entrants in the labor force; fragility is costing the subcontinent a half of a percentage point of growth per year; and poverty is widespread. While growth is expected to increase in 2019, it will remain insufficient to reduce poverty significantly. Total poverty headcount at the international poverty line ($1.90/day in 2011 PPP) is projected to decline only marginally.

Strategy:
The World Bank Group strategy for Africa builds on opportunities for growth and poverty reduction to support structural transformation, economic diversification, resilience, and inclusion. The region is made up of a combination of low, lower-middle, upper-middle, and high-income countries. 18 countries are fragile and conflict-affected states. Africa also has 13 small states, characterized by a small population, limited human capital, and a confined land area. The Bank is responding to this diversity by providing a wide range of instruments—both traditional and innovative—tailored to the needs of the countries.

Achieving higher inclusive growth and reaping the benefits of a demographic dividend will require going beyond a business-as-usual approach to development for Africa. Going forward, it is imperative that the region undertakes the following four actions, concurrently: invest more and better in its people; leapfrog into the 21st century digital and high-tech economy; harness private finance and know-how to fill the infrastructure gap; and build resilience to fragility and conflict and climate change.

The strategy focuses on the following priority areas:

Empowering women to change fertility dynamics and accelerate human capital gains: The World Bank, via its new Human Capital Project (HCP) is at the forefront of helping countries strengthen their human capital. 44 countries, including 15 from Africa, have joined a first cohort of HCP countries committed to invest more and better in their people. While every country faces unique obstacles and opportunities, three widespread challenges put at risk young Africans' survival, education, and health: (i) high fertility; (ii) fragility, conflict, and violence; and (iii) suboptimal financing. Boosting women's empowerment is at the crux of these three challenges and our work will continue to support efforts that ensure that women are educated, healthy and able to decide when and how many children to have, helping reduce fertility and investing in the next generation. A population that is healthy, educated, and well-equipped for the future is the best way to eradicate poverty in Africa and contribute to the world's stability and prosperity.

Accelerating Africa's digital economy: Africa has the opportunity to harness the digital economy as a driver of growth and innovation, but if it fails to bridge the digital divide its economies risk isolation and stagnation. With digital economy investments and reforms, Africa may be able to accelerate, possibly even leapfrog the traditional growth model, and transition from an agriculture-based economy to a digital economy, leaping over intermediate steps, while building core infrastructure, systems, and competencies. The World Bank Group, through the Digital Economy for Africa (DE4A) Moonshot initiative, is helping the region catalyze digital transformation and massively scale-up efforts and resources to build the foundations of a thriving digital economy.

Climate change: Africa's poor are likely to be hit hardest by climate change, particularly changes in temperature and rainfall patterns. In the face of increasing climate-related risks, investing in climate change adaptation and resilience mechanisms and disaster risk management will remain a top priority. The Africa Climate Business Plan, launched in 2016, has delivered significant results ahead of schedule, particularly in the areas of climate-smart agriculture, integrated watershed management, climate-smart ocean economies, climate resilience in coastal zones, social development, and renewable energy. Since its launch, the World Bank has approved a total of 176 projects for a total commitment of $17 billion of Bank financing. This is twice the Bank's 2020 resource mobilization target of $8.5 billion set out under the ACBP when it launched.

Regional integration: Regional integration in Africa remains a critical emphasis of our strategy to improve connectivity, leverage economies of scale, and get collective action by countries to address shared challenges. There will be a greater focus on fewer and bigger operations in areas like the digital economy, promoting power trade, human capital, and sub-regional fragility hotspots. The World Bank Group will continue to scale up successful regional and country level approaches.

Maximizing finance for development: At a time when public resources are

Africa Today

increasingly scarce, and the aspirations of African populations are rising, the World Bank Group has embraced the Maximizing Finance for Development approach to systematically leverage all sources of finance, expertise, and solutions that will help create an enabling environment for investors, particularly those in the private sector. While private participation in Africa is on the rise, with total investment in infrastructure increasing by 151% from $2.5 billion in 2014 to 6.3 billion in 2015, there is still much more scope for all actors to work together. Thanks to the concerted efforts of the WBG, most of the energy generation conducted in Africa is handled by the private sector, and in a clean way. Through the maximizing finance for development (MFD) approach, we have mobilized over $2 billion in private investment in Kenya and nearly a billion in Cameroon so far.

Boosting resilience to conflict and violence: Sub-Saharan Africa faces serious challenges related to fragility, conflict, and violence (FCV) that threaten to undermine development gains. With violent conflict surging, the fight to end extreme poverty in Africa will require a stronger focus on addressing the underlying drivers of fragility in order to create opportunities for peace and shared prosperity. Through the IDA 18 Risk Mitigation Regime, we are providing more resources for countries such as Niger and Guinea to mitigate the drivers of FCV. Together with the United Nations, the International Committee of the Red Cross, and global technology firms, the World Bank is developing the Famine Action Mechanism, a new initiative that harnesses technologies such as Artificial Intelligence and Machine Learning to strengthen our ability to forecast famine risks and ensure funds are released before a crisis emerges. In countries like Somalia or the Central African Republic, we are focusing our efforts on building state capacity and legitimacy, strengthening accountability and inclusive institutions, and ultimately building the trust needed between citizens and the state for long-term peace and stability to take root.

Knowledge: Knowledge is essential to our effort to improve development outcomes and make aid more effective. Country Economic Updates, produced in consultation with member countries and other stakeholders, help promote substantive discussions around key policy issues. Analytical work on structural transformation, on macroeconomic vulnerabilities, on fragility and poverty, on improving governance, but also on more specific areas such as private investment opportunities in Africa, women's entrepreneurship, stunting, learning and access to education, and urbanization have also been recently completed.

Results:

As of January 2019, the Bank had an active portfolio in Africa of 618 projects totaling $73 billion. Key focus areas include boosting human capital and empowering women, promoting regional integration particularly in the Horn of Africa and the Great Lakes regions, increasing access to affordable renewable energy, building resilience to climate change, and maximizing finance for development.

A few highlights of our development results include:

Fostering women's and youth's economic empowerment

The Great Lakes Emergency Sexual and Gender Based Violence and Women's Health Project has benefitted more than half a million women, including more than 21,000 poor and vulnerable women benefitted from economic empowerment activities and 18,000 youth benefitted from reproductive health services.

The Girls' Education and Women's Empowerment and Livelihood Program (GEWEL) in Zambia targets girls and women at two critical phases, supporting 14,000 adolescent girls to attend secondary school and 75,000 working-aged women to gain access to grants, trainings and mentoring to increase livelihood productivity. The program adopts a "cash-plus", productive inclusion model of social protection with linkages across government and private sector to achieve multi-dimensional outcomes promoting increased earnings, gains in education and health, women's rights, birth and national registration, and financial inclusion. This coordinated approach supports the client's goal to build a national flagship empowerment program to help combat poverty.

Investing in the early years to build resilient human capital

Of the 250 million children under the age of five in Africa, one-third are stunted and less than one-quarter are enrolled in preschool. Early years investments are key to unlocking a country's human capital potential and driving economic growth and social development. Children who are well nourished, nurtured and protected from stress carry advantages with them that last a lifetime. The World Bank is employing a multisectoral approach to reduce stunting, expand access to early learning and harness social protection opportunities to reach the most vulnerable. In Rwanda, the Bank is supporting a multifaceted approach to address chronic malnutrition through health and nutrition interventions, high quality child feeding and hygiene practices, enhanced access to food through cash transfers and support for improvements in household food security and dietary diversity through biofortification, labor saving technologies, and promotion of micro-nutrient enriched foods.

Adapting to climate change and building climate resilience

Africa is the lowest carbon emitter and yet is more vulnerable to climate change than other regions. The World Bank's Africa Climate Business Plan (ACBP) has proven to be a galvanizing platform for climate action in the region and is supporting African governments in their urgent response to climate change. The ACBP has financed 176 projects and $17 billion in IDA and IBRD financing for climate-resilient development throughout Sub-Saharan Africa, exceeding the Bank resource mobilization target set out for 2020.

In Zambia, Mali, Côte d'Ivoire, Lesotho, and Zimbabwe, ACBP support has led to the development of dedicated Climate-Smart Agriculture Investment Plans, which are contributing to efforts to increase food security for the rural poor through crop diversification, solar-powered irrigation, boreholes, rehabilitated canals, and mainstreaming climate knowledge via national development plans. In Mozambique, integrated landscape management is maximizing finance for development through the mobilization of commercial resources for agriculture and forest value chains. It is also leveraging private equity for protected area management. By promoting partnerships between the private sector and communities, the ACBP is making headway in creating more sustainable models that strike a balance between economic and conservation goals.

Harnessing technological developments to improve access to clean and reliable energy

At only 37%, energy access in Africa lags behind other regions, placing an unsustainable drag on growth. The Bank is supporting operations in Africa to increase access through grid extension and expansion of the transmission network, innovative off-grid electrification solutions, expansions of renewable generation capacity, development of regional power pools and improvement of service efficiency. For example, the Nachtigal Hydropower Project in Cameroon is crowding in private capital and reducing public debt as well as lowering the overall costs of service for electricity as the country starts meeting its energy demand through renewable sources. In addition, the Bank is supporting the development and adoption of new technologies such as solar storage solutions, smart meters, mobile

Africa Today

utility payments, satellite mapping and imaging, high-voltage DC transmission, and solar home systems and mini-grids.

Deepening regional integration

Regional projects create synergies, reduce costs, and make the provision of public services more efficient through economies of scale. For example, more than 40 million people are meeting their basic energy needs through products provided with the support of the joint World Bank-IFC Lighting Africa Program. This innovative effort was created for low-income families, with the aim of providing off-grid solar lighting to 250 million people in the next decade. 1,792,090 metric tons of greenhouse gas emissions were avoided in Africa in the past year.

AFRICAN UNION (AU) CORNER

Note: All materials and discussions sourced from www.au.int.

With Africa's population estimated around 1.2 billion sustained by improved health conditions and increase and life expectancy, the need to refocus the continent's attention to important regional and global agenda has inevitably become necessary. It is for this reason that the continent's leadership discussion on the way forward to achieve stronger regional integration and compete globally is the step in the right direction.

AGENDA 2063 was adopted at the 24th Ordinary Assembly of African Heads of State in Addis Ababa on January 31, 2015. This is one of the major initiatives yet by African leaders to integrate and enhance security and development on the continent. This volume will henceforth feature some of the discussions and raise relevant questions to assist in this direction. For this volume, we shall concentrate on AGENDA 2063 initiative document itself and present the objectives and expectations.

Agenda 2063: The Africa We Want (Overview)

AGENDA 2063 is Africa's blueprint and master plan for transforming Africa into the global powerhouse of the future. It is the continent's strategic framework that aims to deliver on its goal for inclusive and sustainable development and is a concrete manifestation of the pan-African drive for unity, self-determination, freedom, progress and collective prosperity pursued under Pan-Africanism and African Renaissance The genesis of Agenda 2063 was the realization by African leaders that there was a need to refocus and reprioritize Africa's agenda from the struggle against apartheid and the attainment of political independence for the continent which had been the focus of The Organization of African Unity (OAU), the precursor of the African Union; and instead to prioritize inclusive social and economic development, continental and regional integration, democratic governance and peace and security amongst other issues aimed at repositioning Africa to becoming a dominant player in the global arena.

As an affirmation of their commitment to support Africa's new path for attaining inclusive and sustainable economic growth and development African heads of state and government signed the 50th Anniversary Solemn Declaration during the Golden Jubilee celebrations of the formation of the OAU/AU in May 2013. The declaration marked the re-dedication of Africa towards the attainment of the Pan African Vision of an integrated, prosperous and peaceful Africa, driven by its own citizens, representing a dynamic force in the international arena and Agenda 2063 is the concrete manifestation of how the continent intends to achieve this vision within a 50-year period from 2013 to 2063. The Africa of the future was captured in a letter presented by a former chairperson of the African Union Commission, Dr. Nkosazana Dlaminin Zuma.

The need to envision a long-term 50-year development trajectory for Africa is important as Africa needs to revise and adapt its development agenda due to ongoing structural transformations; increased peace and reduction in the number of conflicts; renewed economic growth and social progress; the need for people centered development, gender equality and youth empowerment; changing global contexts such as increased globalization and the ICT revolution; the increased unity of Africa which makes it a global power to be reckoned with and capable of rallying support around its own common agenda; and emerging development and investment opportunities in areas such as agri-business,

Term Limit Regimes in Africa

Country	Head of state/government		Other	
	Title	Maximum number of terms	Office	Maximum number of terms
Algeria	President	Two 5-year terms		
Angola	President	Two 5-year terms		
Benin	President	Two 5-year terms		
Botswana	President	Two 5-year terms		
Burkina Faso	President	Two 5-year terms		
Burundi	President	Two 7-year terms, since 2018 Constitutional Reform.		
Chad	President	Two 6-year terms, since 2018 Constitution.		
Cameroon	President	Unlimited 7-year terms, from 2008 Constitutional Reform.		
Cape Verde	President	Two 5-year terms, third term only after 5 years.	Prime Minister	No term limits

Africa Today

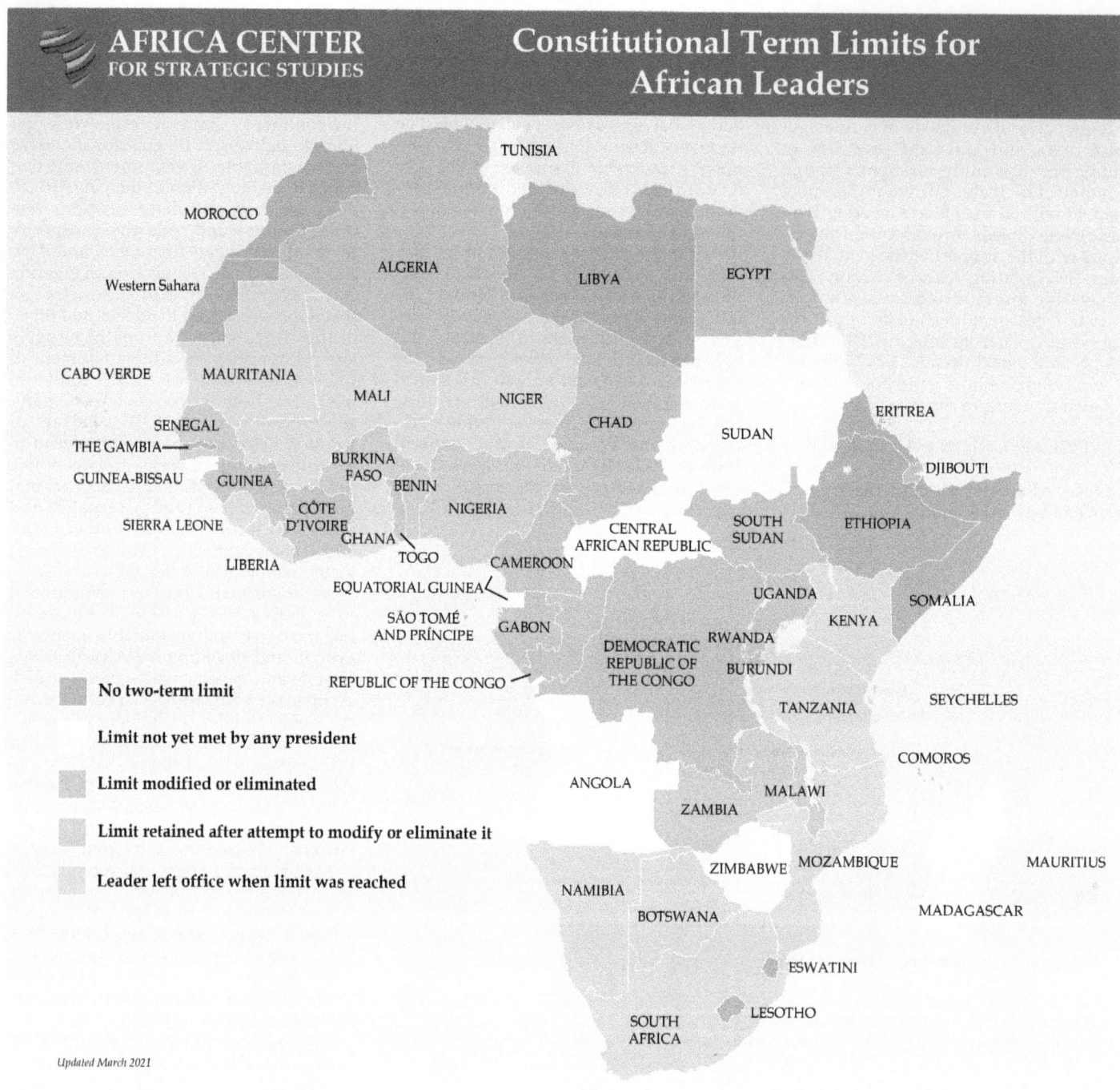

infrastructure development, health and education as well as the value addition in African commodities

Agenda 2063 encapsulates not only Africa's Aspirations for the Future but also identifies key Flagship Programmes which can boost Africa's economic growth and development and lead to the rapid transformation of the continent.

Agenda 2063 also identifies key activities to be undertaken in its 10-year Implementation Plans, which will ensure that Agenda 2063 delivers both quantitative and qualitative Transformational Outcomes for Africa's people.

Flagship Projects of Agenda 2063

The flagship projects of Agenda 2063 refers to key programs and initiatives which have been identified as key to accelerating Africa's economic growth and development as well as promoting our common identity by celebrating our history and our vibrant culture.

The Flagship projects encompass amongst others infrastructure, education, science, technology, arts and culture as well as initiatives to secure peace on the continent.

1. INTEGRATED HIGH-SPEED TRAIN NETWORK

The project aims to connect all African capitals and commercial centres through an African High-Speed Train Network thereby facilitating the movement of goods, factor services and people. The increased connectivity by rail also aims to reduce transport costs and relieve congestion of current and future systems.

Africa Today

AFRICA CENTER FOR STRATEGIC STUDIES
Constitutional Term Limits for African Leaders

No Constitutional Two-Term Limit	Countries with Two-Term Limit in Constitution			
	Limit Not Yet Met by Any President (Year Limit to Be Reached)	Two-Term Limit Reached		
		Attempted Modification or Elimination of Limit		Left Office (First Leader to Adhere to Limit)
		Limit Modified or Eliminated	Limit Retained	
Eritrea	Sudan (2022)[4]	Guinea (Conté, 2001)(Condé, 2020)[6]	Zambia (Chiluba, 2001)	Tanzania (Mwinyi, 1995)
Ethiopia[1]	Madagascar (2023)	Togo (Eyadéma, 2002, 2019)[7]	Malawi (Muluzi, 2003)	Ghana (Rawlings, 2001)
The Gambia	Central African Republic (2025)	Gabon (Bongo, 2003)	Nigeria (Obasanjo, 2006)	São Tomé and Príncipe[19] (Trovoada, 2001)
Lesotho[1]	Angola (2027)	Uganda (Museveni, 2005, 2017)[8]	Senegal (Wade, 2012)	Cabo Verde[19] (Monteiro, 2001)
Libya[2]	Zimbabwe (2028)[5]	Chad (Deby, 2005, 2018)[9]	Burkina Faso (Compaoré, 2014)	Mali (Konaré, 2002)
Morocco[3]	Guinea-Bissau (2029)	Cameroon (Biya, 2008)	Benin (Talon, 2017)	Mauritius[19] (Uteem, 2002)
Somalia	Tunisia (2029)	Algeria (Bouteflika, 2008, 2016)[10]		Kenya (Moi, 2002)
Eswatini[3]	Equatorial Guinea (2030)	Djibouti (Guelleh, 2010)		Mozambique (Chissano, 2005)
	Seychelles (2030)	Burundi (Nkurunziza, 2015, 2018)[11]		Sierra Leone (Kabbah, 2007)
		Rwanda (Kagame, 2015)[12]		Botswana (Mogae, 2008)
		Republic of the Congo (Nguesso, 2015)[13]		South Africa (Mbeki, 2008)
		South Sudan (Kiir, 2015, 2018)[14]		Namibia (Pohamba, 2015)
		DRC (Kabila, 2016)[15]		Liberia (Sirleaf, 2018)
		Comoros (Azali, 2018)[16]		Mauritania (Abdel Aziz, 2019)
		Egypt (Sisi, 2019)[17]		Niger (Issoufou, 2021)
		Côte d'Ivoire (Ouattara, 2020)[18]		

Updated March 2021

2. FORMULATION OF AN AFRICAN COMMODITIES STRATEGY

The development of a continental commodities strategy is seen as key to enabling African countries to add value, extract higher rents from their commodities, integrate into the Global Value chains, and promote vertical and horizontal diversification anchored in value addition and local content development. The strategy aims to transform Africa from simply being a raw materials supplier for the rest of the world to a continent that actively uses its own resources to ensure the economic development of Africans

3. ESTABLISHMENT OF THE AFRICAN CONTINENTAL FREE TRADE AREA (AfCFTA)

Accelerate intra-African trade and boost Africa's trading position in the global marketplace. The AfCFTA aims to significantly accelerate growth of Intra-Africa trade and use trade more effectively as an engine of growth and sustainable development by doubling intra-Africa trade, strengthening Africa's common voice and policy space in global trade negotiations

4. THE AFRICAN PASSPORT AND FREE MOVEMENT OF PEOPLE

Remove restrictions on Africans ability to travel, work and live within their own continent. The initiative aims at transforming Africa's laws, which remain generally restrictive on movement of people despite political commitments to bring down borders with the view to promoting the issuance of visas by Member States to enhance free movement of all African citizens in all African countries.

5. SILENCING THE GUNS BY 2020

To achieve the goals of Agenda 2063, Africa needs to work towards ending all wars, civil conflicts, gender-based violence, violent conflicts and preventing

Migrant remittance inflows (US$ million)	2021	Remittances as a share of GDP in 2021 (%)
Algeria	1791	1.1
Angola	12	0.0
Benin	230	1.3
Botswana	57	0.3
Burkina Faso	560	2.8
Burundi	48	1.7
Cabo Verde	302	15.6
Cameroon	430	0.9
Central African Republic		
Chad		
Comoros	287	22.2
Congo, Dem. Rep.	1347	2.4
Congo, Rep.	12	0.1
Cote d'Ivoire	440	0.6
Djibouti	79	2.3
Egypt, Arab Rep.	31,487	7.8
Equatorial Guinea		
Eritrea		
Swaziland (Eswatini)	132	2.8
Ethiopia	447	0.4
Gabon	14	0.4
Gambia, The	547	26.8
Ghana	4167	5.4
Guinea	34	2.1
Guinea-Bissau	178	10.9
Kenya	3770	3.4
Lesotho	499	20
Liberia	338	9.6
Libya		
Madagascar	439	3.0
Malawi	258	2.1
Mali	1131	5.9
Mauritania	13	0.1
Mauritius	272	2.4
Morocco	10	7.5
Mozambique	453	2.9
Namibia	46	0.4
Niger	353	2.4
Nigeria	19,483	4.4
Rwanda	391	3.5
Sao Tome and Principe	10	2.0
Senegal	2657	9.6
Seychelles	9	0.7
Sierra Leone	232	5.7
Somalia	1735	22.7
South Africa	926	0.2
South Sudan	135	9.5
Sudan	1119	3.3
Tanzania	569	0.8
Togo	674	8.0
Tunisia	3083	6.6
Uganda	1082	2.7
Zambia	241	1.1

genocide. In addition, progress in the areas are to be monitored through the establishment and operationalization of an African Human Security Index (AHSI).

6. IMPLEMENTATION OF THE GRAND INGA DAM PROJECT

The development of the Inga Dam is expected to generate 43,200 MW of power, to support current regional power pools and their combined service to transform Africa from traditional to modern sources of energy and ensure access of all Africans to clean and affordable electricity.

7. ESTABLISHMENT OF A SINGLE AFRICAN AIR-TRANSPORT MARKET (SAATM)

The SAATM aims to ensure intra-regional connectivity between the capital cities of Africa and create a single unified air transport market in Africa, as an impetus to the continent's economic integration and growth agenda. SAATM provides for the full liberalization of intra-African air transport services in terms of market access, traffic rights for scheduled and freight air services by eligible airlines thereby improving air services connectivity and air carrier efficiencies. It removes restrictions on ownership and provides for the full liberalization of frequencies, tariffs, and capacity. It also provides eligibility criteria for African community carriers, safety and security standards, mechanisms for fair competition and dispute settlement as well as consumer protection.

8. ESTABLISHMENT OF AN ANNUAL AFRICAN ECONOMIC FORUM

The annual African Economic Forum is a multi-stakeholder meeting that brings together the African political leadership, the private sector, academia and civil society to reflect on how to accelerate Africa's economic transformation harnessing its vast resources to enhance the development of the African people. The forum discusses key opportunities as well as the constraints that hamper economic development and proposes measures to be taken to realize the Aspirations and goals of Agenda 2063.

9. ESTABLISHMENT OF THE AFRICAN FINANCIAL INSTITUTIONS

The creation of African Continental Financial Institutions aims at accelerating integration and socio-economic development of the continent through the establishment of organizations which will play a pivotal role in the mobilization of resources and management of the African financial sector. The financial institutions envisaged to promote economic integration are the African Investment Bank and Pan African Stock Exchange; the African Monetary Fund and the African Central Bank.

10. THE PAN-AFRICAN E-NETWORK

This aims to put in place policies and strategies that will lead to transformative e-applications and services in Africa; especially the intra-African broad band terrestrial infrastructure; and cyber security, making the information revolution the basis for service delivery in the bio and nanotechnology industries and ultimately transform Africa into an e-Society.

11. AFRICA OUTER SPACE STRATEGY

The Africa outer space strategy aims to strengthen Africa's use of outer space to bolster its development. Outer space is of critical importance to the development of Africa in all fields: agriculture, disaster management, remote sensing, climate forecast, banking and finance, as well as defense and security. Africa's access to space technology products is no longer a matter of luxury and there is a need to speed up access to these technologies and products. New developments in satellite technologies make these accessible to African countries and appropriate policies and strategies are required to develop a regional market for space products in Africa.

12. AN AFRICAN VIRTUAL AND E-UNIVERSITY

This project aims to use ICT based programs to increase access to tertiary and continuing education in Africa by reaching large numbers of students and professionals in multiple sites simultaneously. It aims to develop relevant and high quality Open, Distance and eLearning (ODeL) resources to offer students guaranteed access to the University from anywhere in the world and anytime (24 hours a day, 7 days a week.

13. CYBER SECURITY

The decision to adopt Cyber Security as a flagship program of Agenda 2063 is a clear indication that Africa needs to not only incorporate in its development plans the rapid changes brought about by emerging technologies, but also to ensure that these technologies are used for the benefit of African individuals, institutions, or nation states by ensuring data protection and safety online. The Cyber Security project is guided by the African Union Convention on Cyber Security and Personal Data Protection

14. GREAT AFRICAN MUSEUM

The African Charter for African Cultural Renaissance recognizes the important role that culture pays in mobilizing and unifying people around common ideals and promoting African culture to build the ideals of Pan-Africanism. The Great African Museum project aims to create awareness about Africa's vast, dynamic and diverse cultural artefacts and the influence Africa has had and continues to have on the various cultures of the world in areas such as art, music, language, science, and so on. The Great African Museum will be a focal center for preserving and promoting the African cultural heritage.

15. ENCYCLOPAEDIA AFRICANA

The Encyclopedia Africana aims to provide an authoritative resource on the authentic history of Africa and African life. The Encyclopedia provides Africans a body of truth to guide and unite them in their development with foundations in all aspect of the African life including history, legal, economic, religion, architecture and education as well as the systems and practices of African societies. The Encyclopedia Africana provides an African worldview of the people, culture, literature, and history of Africa and is a key tool to be used to educate, inform and set the records straight regarding the history, culture and contributions of African people throughout the world.

Key Transformational Outcomes of Agenda 2063

Agenda 2063 identifies several key benefits to Africans if the programs identified in the strategic development framework are initiated and implemented in the FTYIP.

Africa is expected to show improved standards of living; transformed, inclusive and sustained economies; increased levels of regional and continental integration; a population of empowered women and youth and a society in which children are cared for and protected; societies that are peaceful, demonstrate good democratic values and practice good governance principles and which preserve and enhance Africa's cultural identity.

Improvements in Living Standards

· Real per-capita incomes would be a third more than 2013 levels.

· Incidence of hunger, especially amongst Women and Youth will only be 20% of 2023 levels.

· Job opportunities will be available to at least one in four persons looking for work.

· At least one out of every three children will be having access to kindergarten education with every child of secondary school age in school and seven out of ten of its graduates without access to tertiary education enrolled in TVET programmes.

· Malnutrition, maternal, child and neonatal deaths as at 2013 would be reduced by half; access to anti-retroviral will be automatic and proportion of deaths attributable to HIV/AIDs and malaria would have been halved.

· Nine out of ten persons will have access to safe drinking water and sanitation; electricity supply and internet connectivity will be up by 50% and cities will be recycling at least 50% of the waste they generate.

Africa Today

Linking Agenda 2063 and the SDGs

	Agenda 2063 Goals	Agenda 2063 Priority Areas	UN Sustainable Development Goals
1.	A high standard of living, quality of life and well-being for all citizens.	Incomes, jobs and decent work Poverty, inequality and hunger Social security and protection, including persons with disabilities Modern, affordable and liveable habitats and quality basic services	1. End poverty in all its forms everywhere in the world 2. End hunger, achieve food security and improved nutrition and promote sustainable agriculture. 8. Promote sustained, inclusive and sustainable Economic growth, full and productive employment and decent work for all. 11. Make cities and human settlements inclusive, safe, resilient and sustainable.
2.	Well educated citizens and skills revolution underpinned by science, technology and innovation.	Education and science, technology and innovation (STI) driven skills revolution	4. Ensure inclusive and equitable quality education and promote lifelong learning opportunities for all.
3.	Healthy and well-nourished citizens.	Health and nutrition	3. Ensure healthy lives and promote well-being for all at all ages.
4.	Transformed economies.	Sustainable and inclusive economic growth STI driven manufacturing, industrialization and value addition Economic diversification and resilience.	8. Promote sustained, inclusive and sustainable economic growth, full and productive employment and decent work for all. 9. Build resilient infrastructure, promote inclusive and sustainable industrialization and foster innovation.
5.	Modern agriculture for increased productivity and production.	Agricultural productivity and production	2. End hunger, achieve food security and improved nutrition and promote sustainable agriculture.
6.	Blue/ocean economy for accelerated economic growth.	Marine resources and energy Port operations and marine transport	14. Conserve and sustainably use the oceans, seas and marine resources for sustainable development.
7.	Environmentally sustainable and climate resilient economies and communities.	Bio-diversity, conservation and Sustainable natural resource management. Water security Climate resilience and natural disasters preparedness	6. Ensure availability and sustainable management of water and sanitation for all. 7. Ensure access to affordable, reliable, sustainable and modern energy for all. 13. Take urgent action to combat climate change and its impacts. 15. Protect, restore and promote sustainable use of terrestrial ecosystems, sustainably manage forests, combat desertification, and halt and reverse land degradation and halt biodiversity loss.
8.	A United Africa (Federal or Confederate).	Frameworks and institutions for a United Africa	
9.	Continental financial and monetary institutions established and functional.	Financial and monetary institutions	
10.	World class infrastructure crisscrosses Africa.	Communications and infrastructure connectivity.	9. Build resilient infrastructure, promote inclusive and sustainable industrialization and foster innovation.
11.	Democratic values, practices, universal principles of human rights, justice and the rule of law entrenched.	Democracy and good governance Human rights, justice and the rule of law	16. Promote peaceful and inclusive societies for sustainable development, provide access to justice for all and build effective, accountable and inclusive institutions at all levels.
12.	Capable institutions and transformative leadership in place.	Institutions and leadership Participatory development and local governance.	16. Promote peaceful and inclusive societies for sustainable development, provide access to justice for all and build effective, accountable and inclusive institutions at all levels.

Africa Today

13. Peace, security and stability is preserved.	Maintenance and preservation of peace and security	16. Promote peaceful and inclusive societies for sustainable development, provide access to justice for all and build effective, accountable and inclusive institutions at all levels.
14. A stable and peaceful Africa.	Institutional structure for AU instruments on peace and security Defence, security and peace	
15. A fully functional and operational APSA	Fully operational and functional APSA all pillars	
16. African cultural renaissance is pre-eminent.	Values and ideals of Pan Africanism Cultural values and African Renaissance Cultural heritage, creative arts and businesses	
17. Full gender equality in all spheres of life.	Women and girls' empowerment Violence and discrimination against women and girls	5. Achieve gender equality and empower all women and girls.
18. Engaged and empowered youth and children.	Youth empowerment and children's rights	4. Ensure inclusive and equitable quality education and promote lifelong learning opportunities for all. 5. Achieve gender equality and empower all women and girls.
19. Africa as a major partner in global affairs and peaceful co-existence.	Africa's place in global affairs Partnerships	17. Strengthen the means of implementation and revitalize the global partnership for sustainable development.
20. Africa takes full responsibility for financing her development Goals.	African capital markets Fiscal systems and public sector revenue Development assistance	10. Reduce inequality within and among countries. 17. Strengthen the means of implementation and revitalize the global partnership for sustainable development.

Goals & Priority Areas of Agenda 2063

Aspiration	Goals	Priority Areas
1) A Prosperous Africa, based on Inclusive Growth and Sustainable Development	(1) A High Standard of Living, Quality of Life and Well Being for All Citizens	Incomes, Jobs and decent work
		Poverty, Inequality and Hunger
		Social security and protection Including Persons with Disabilities
		Modern and Livable Habitats and Basic Quality Services
	(2) Well Educated Citizens and Skills revolution underpinned by Science, Technology and Innovation	Education and STI skills driven revolution
	(3) Healthy and well-nourished citizens	Health and Nutrition
	(4) Transformed Economies	Sustainable and inclusive economic growth
		STI driven Manufacturing / Industrialization and Value Addition
		Economic diversification and resilience
		Hospitality/Tourism
	(5) Modern Agriculture for increased productivity and production	Agricultural Productivity and Production
	(6) Blue ocean economy for accelerated economic growth	Marine resources and Energy
		Ports Operations and Marine Transport

Africa Today

	(7) Environmentally sustainable and climate resilient economies and communities	Sustainable natural resource management and Biodiversity conservation
		Sustainable consumption and production patterns
		Water security
		Climate resilience and natural disasters preparedness and prevention
		Renewable energy
2) An Integrated Continent Politically united and based on the ideals of Pan Africanism and the vision of African Renaissance	(8) United Africa (Federal or Confederate)	Framework and Institutions for a United Africa
	(9) Continental Financial and Monetary Institutions are established and functional	Financial and Monetary Institutions
	(10) World Class Infrastructure crisscrosses Africa	Communications and Infrastructure Connectivity
3) An Africa of Good Governance, Democracy, Respect for Human Rights, Justice, and the Rule of Law	(11) Democratic values, practices, universal principles of human rights, justice and the rule of law entrenched	Democracy and Good Governance
		Human Rights, Justice, and The Rule of Law
	(12) Capable institutions and transformative leadership in place	Institutions and Leadership
		Participatory Development and Local Governance
4) A Peaceful and Secure Africa	(13) Peace Security and Stability is preserved	Maintenance and Preservation of Peace and Security
	(14) A Stable and Peaceful Africa	Institutional structure for AU Instruments on Peace and Security
	(15) A Fully functional and operational APSA	Fully operational and functional APSA Pillars
5) Africa with a Strong Cultural Identity Common Heritage, Values and Ethics	16) African Cultural Renaissance is pre-eminent	Values and Ideals of Pan Africanism
		Cultural Values and African Renaissance
		Cultural Heritage, Creative Arts and Businesses
6) An Africa Whose Development is people driven, relying on the potential offered by African People, especially its Women and Youth, and caring for Children	(17) Full Gender Equality in All Spheres of Life	Women and Girls Empowerment
		Violence & Discrimination against Women and Girls
	(18) Engaged and Empowered Youth and Children	Youth Empowerment and Children
7) An Africa as A Strong, United, Resilient and Influential Global Player and Partner	(19) Africa as a major partner in global affairs and peaceful co-existence	Africa's place in global affairs.
		Partnership
	(20) Africa takes full responsibility for financing her development	African Capital market
		Fiscal system and Public Sector Revenues
		Development Assistance

Transformed, Inclusive and Sustainable Economies

· GDP will be growing at 7% and at least a third of the outputs will be generated by national firms.

· Labour intensive manufacturing, underpinned by value addition to commodities and doubling of the total agricultural factor productivity will be attained by 2023

· The beginnings of value addition blue economy—fisheries, eco-friendly coastal tourism, marine bio-technology products and port operations—will emerge.

· Creative arts businesses will be contributing twice as much in real terms their 2013 contribution to GDP.

· ICT penetration and contribution to real GDP in absolute terms would be double of 2013 levels.

· Regional industrialization hubs linked to the global value chains and commodity exchanges will be in place by 2023.

· At least 17% of terrestrial and inland water and 10% of coastal and marine areas would have been preserved and 30% of farmers, fisher folks and pastoralist will be practicing climate resilient production systems.

Integrated Africa

· There will free movement of goods, services and capital; and persons travelling to any member state could get the visa at the point of entry.

· The volume of intra-African trade especially in agricultural value added products would increase threefold by 2023.

· The African Customs Union, an African Common Market and an African

Africa Today

Monetary Union will be operational by 2023.
· The African Speed Train Network will have passed the inception stage and will be taking its first passengers between two connected cities.
· African Skies will be open to all African Airlines.
· Regional power pools boosted by at least 50% increase in power generation and the INGA dam will be operational and will contribute to the powering of the industrial transformation of the continent and comfort of the citizenry.
· African Education Accreditation Agency and a common educational system are in place and the African Youth will have the choice to study at any university and work anywhere on the continent.

Empowered Women, Youth and Children
· All obstacles related to Women owing/inheriting property or business, signing a contract, owning or managing a bank account would be removed by 2023.
· At least one in five women would have access to and control of productive assets.
· Gender parity in control, representation, advancement will be the norm in all AU Organs and the RECs.
· All forms of violence against women would have been reduced by a third in 2023.
· All harmful social norms and customary practices would have ended by 2023.
· The African Youth will be mobile and 15% of all new businesses will emanate from their ingenuity and talent and the proportion of 2013 youth unemployed will be reduced by at least a quarter.
· Child labour exploitation, marriages, trafficking, and soldiering would have ended by 2023

Well-governed, peaceful and cultural centric Africa in a Global Context
· Democratic values and culture as enshrined in the African Governance Architecture would have been entrenched by 2023.
· At least seven out of ten persons in every member state of the union will perceive elections to be free, fair, and credible; democratic institutions, processes, and leaders accountable; the judiciary impartial and independent; and the legislature independent and key component of the national governance process.
· African Peer Review Mechanism will have been ascribed to by all Member States and its positive impact on governance metrics felt.
· All guns would have been silenced by 2023.

· All Member States of the Union will have in place local and national mechanisms for conflict prevention and resolution.
· All Member States of the Union will have in place a dual citizen's program for the diaspora.
· The Encyclopedia Africana will be launched by the 2023 Assembly of the Union.
· One in five polytechniques will be offering programs in the creative arts and management of micro cultural enterprises to support the growth of the creative arts businesses.
· Local content in all print and electronic media would have increased by 60%.
· At least 30% of all cultural patrimonies would have been retrieved by 2023.
· An African Space Agency would have been established by 2023.
· An African Global Platform will be in place by 2017 and will contribute to an increase in the share of Africa's exports in global exports in 2023 by at least 20%.
· The African Investment Bank, the African Guarantee Facility, the African Remittances Institute and at least 2 Regional Stock Exchanges would have been established and functioning.

Our Aspirations for the Africa We Want
Agenda 2063 seeks to deliver on a set of Seven Aspirations each with its own set of goals which if achieved will move Africa closer to achieving its vision for the year 2063. These 7 Aspirations reflect our desire for shared prosperity and well-being, for unity and integration, for a continent of free citizens and expanded horizons, where the full potential of women and youth are realized, and with freedom from fear, disease and want.

Aspiration 1: A prosperous Africa based on inclusive growth and sustainable development
We are determined to eradicate poverty in one generation and build shared prosperity through social and economic transformation of the continent.
Goals:
1. A high standard of living, quality of life and well-being for all
· ending poverty, inequalities of income and opportunity; job creation, especially addressing youth unemployment; facing up to the challenges of rapid population growth and urbanization, improvement of habitats and access to basic necessities of life – water, sanitation, electricity; providing social security and protection;
2. Well educated citizens and skills revolutions underpinned by science, technology, and innovation

· developing Africa's human and social capital (through an education and skills revolution emphasizing science and technology)
3. Healthy and well-nourished citizens
· expanding access to quality health care services, particularly for women and girls;
4. Transformed economies and jobs
· transforming Africa's economies through beneficiation from Africa's natural resources, manufacturing, industrialization and value addition, as well as raising productivity and competitiveness
5. Modern agriculture for increased proactivity and production
· radically transforming African agriculture to enable the continent to feed itself and be a major player as a net food exporter;
6. Blue/Ocean Economy for accelerated economic growth
· exploiting the vast potential of Africa's blue/ocean economy;
7. Environmentally sustainable climate and resilient economies and communities
· putting in place measures to sustainably manage the continent's rich biodiversity, forests, land and waters and using mainly adaptive measures to address climate change risks

Aspiration 2: An integrated continent, politically united and based on the ideals of Pan-Africanism and the vision of Africa's Renaissance
Since 1963, the quest for African Unity has been inspired by the spirit of Pan Africanism, focusing on liberation, and political and economic independence. It is motivated by development based on self-reliance and self-determination of African people, with democratic and people-centered governance.
Goals:
1. United Africa (Federal/Confederate)
· accelerating progress towards continental unity and integration for sustained growth, trade, exchanges of goods, services, free movement of people and capital through establishing a United Africa and fast-tracking economic integration through the of the CFTA
2. World class infrastructure crisscrosses Africa
· improving connectivity through newer and bolder initiatives to link the continent by rail, road, sea and air; and developing regional and continental power pools, as well as ICT
3. Decolonization
· All remnants of colonialism will have ended and all African territories under occupation fully liberated. We shall take measures to expeditiously end the unlawful occupation of the Chagos Archipelago, the Comorian Island of Mayotte and

Africa Today

affirming the right to self-determination of the people of Western Sahara.

Aspiration 3: An Africa of good governance, democracy, respect for human rights, justice and the rule of law

An Africa of good governance, democracy, respect for human rights, justice and the rule of law. Africa shall have a universal culture of good governance, democratic values, gender equality, and respect for human rights, justice and the rule of law.

Goals:

1. Democratic values, practices, universal principles for human rights, justice and rule of law entrenched
· consolidating democratic gains and improving the quality of governance, respect for human rights and the rule of law;
2. Capable institutions and transformed leadership in place at all levels
· building strong institutions for a development state; and facilitating the emergence of development-oriented and visionary leadership in all spheres and at all levels.

Aspiration 4: A peaceful and secure Africa

Mechanisms for peaceful prevention and resolution of conflicts will be functional at all levels. As a first step, dialogue-centered conflict prevention and resolution will be actively promoted in such a way that by 2020 all guns will be silent. A culture of peace and tolerance shall be nurtured in Africa's children and youth through peace education.

Goals:

1. Peace security and stability is preserved
· strengthening governance, accountability and transparency as a foundation for a peaceful Africa;
2. A stable and peaceful Africa
· strengthening mechanisms for securing peace and reconciliation at all levels, as well as addressing emerging threats to Africa's peace and security
3. A fully functional and operational APSA
· putting in place strategies for the continent to finance her security needs.

Aspiration 5: An Africa with a strong cultural identity, common heritage, shared values, and ethics

Pan-Africanism and the common history, destiny, identity, heritage, respect for religious diversity and consciousness of African people's and her diaspora's will be entrenched.

Goal:

1. Africa cultural renaissance is pre-eminent
· inculcating the spirit of Pan Africanism; tapping Africa's rich heritage and culture to ensure that the creative arts are major contributors to Africa's growth and transformation; and restoring and preserving Africa's cultural heritage, including its languages.

Aspiration 6: An Africa, whose development is people-driven, relying on the potential of African people, especially its women and youth, and caring for children

All the citizens of Africa will be actively involved in decision making in all aspects. Africa shall be an inclusive continent where no child, woman or man will be left behind or excluded, on the basis of gender, political affiliation, religion, ethnic affiliation, locality, age or other factors.

Goals:

1. Full gender equality in all spheres of life
· strengthening the role of Africa's women through ensuring gender equality and parity in all spheres of life (political, economic, and social); eliminating all forms of discrimination and violence against women and girls;
2. Engaged and empowered youth and children
· creating opportunities for Africa's youth for self-realization, access to health, education, and jobs; ensuring safety and security for Africa's children, and providing for early childhood development.

Aspiration 7: Africa as a strong, united, resilient, and influential global player and partner

Africa shall be a strong, united, resilient, peaceful, and influential global player and partner with a significant role in world affairs. We affirm the importance of African unity and solidarity in the face of continued external interference including, attempts to divide the continent and undue pressures and sanctions on some countries.

Goals:

1. Africa as a major partner in global affairs and peaceful co-existence
· improving Africa's place in the global governance system (UN Security Council, financial institutions, global commons such as outer space);
2. Africa takes full responsibility for financing her development
· improving Africa's partnerships and refocusing them more strategically to respond to African priorities for growth and transformation; and ensuring that the continent has the right strategies to finance its own development and reducing aid dependency.

Continental Frameworks

Several continental frameworks have been developed to address the development of key sectors such as Agriculture, trade, transport, energy and mining. These sectors are seen as key in enabling Member States of the Union to achieve their development goals. To ensure coherence and convergence, these frameworks have been captured in the priority areas of the First Ten Year Implementation Plan.

The continental frameworks include the Comprehensive African Agricultural Development Programme (CAADP), The Programme for Infrastructure Development in Africa (PIDA), The African Mining Vision (AMV, Science Technology Innovation Strategy for Africa (STISA), Boosting Intra African Trade (BIAT), and Accelerated Industrial Development for Africa (AIDA).

Comprehensive African Agricultural Development Programme (CAADP)

CAADP is a continental initiative to help African countries eliminate hunger and reduce poverty by raising economic growth through agriculture-led development. Through CAADP, African governments agreed to allocate at least 10% of national budgets to agriculture and rural development, and to achieve agricultural growth rates of at least 6% per annum. Underlying these main targets are targets for reducing poverty and malnutrition, for increasing productivity and farm incomes, and for improvements in the sustainability of agricultural production and use of natural resources. CAADP also supports member states to enhance resilience to climate variability through development of disaster preparedness policies and strategies and early warning response systems and social safety nets. CAADP has 4 priority areas, namely:

1. Extending the area under sustainable land management and reliable water-control systems
2. Improving rural infrastructure and trade-related capacities for market access
3. Increasing food supply, reducing hunger, and improving responses to food emergency crises
4. Improving agriculture research, technology dissemination, and adoption

In addition, CAADP places emphasis on African ownership and African leadership to set the agricultural agenda and the stage for agricultural change. This change emphasizes Africans truly being the drivers of CAADP, rather than the more typical case of leadership and direction coming from donors or other international partners. CAADP is thus an inward-looking policy framework where African leaders who have championed CAADP in their countries can influence their counterparts towards agricultural transformation.

Africa Today

The Programme for Infrastructural Development in Africa (PIDA)

The Programme for Infrastructure Development in Africa, PIDA, provides a common framework for African stakeholders to build the infrastructure necessary for more integrated transport, energy, ICT and trans-boundary water networks to boost trade, spark growth and create jobs. As a multi-sector program PIDA) is dedicated to facilitating continental integration through improved regional infrastructure and implementing it will help address the infrastructure deficit that severely hampers Africa's competitiveness in the world market, transform the way business is done and help deliver a well-connected and prosperous Africa.

PIDA's long-term strategic planning for Africa's regional infrastructure has been conducted under the coordination of the African Union Commission, the African Union NEPAD Planning and Coordinating Agency, the United Nations Economic Commission for Africa and the African Development Bank in cooperation with all African stakeholders.

The African Mining Vision (AMV)

The African Mining Vision calls for the "Transparent, equitable and optimal exploitation of mineral resources to underpin broad-based sustainable growth and socio-economic development." The AMV envisages an African mining sector that is:

1. Knowledge-driven and contributes to growth & development which is fully integrated into a single African market;
2. Sustainable and well-governed and effectively garners and deploys resource rents, is safe, healthy, gender & ethnically inclusive, environmentally friendly, socially responsible and appreciated by surrounding communities;
3. A key component of a diversified, vibrant and globally competitive industrializing African economy
4. Helping to establish a competitive African infrastructure platform, through the maximization of its propulsive local & regional economic linkages;
5. Optimizing Africa's finite mineral resource endowments and that is diversified, incorporating both high value metals and lower value industrial minerals at both commercial and small-scale levels;
6. Harnessing the potential of artisanal and small-scale mining to stimulate local/national entrepreneurship, improve livelihoods and advance integrated rural social and economic development;
7. A major player in a vibrant and competitive national, continental, and international capital and commodity markets

Science Technology Innovation Strategy for Africa (STISA)

The AU Science, Technology and Innovation Strategy for Africa places science, technology, and innovation at the epicenter of Africa's socio-economic development and growth and the impact the sciences can have across critical sectors such as agriculture, energy, environment, health, infrastructure development, mining, security and water among others. The strategy envisions an Africa whose transformation is led by innovation and which will create a Knowledge-based Economy. STISA is anchored on six (6) priority areas, namely:

1. Eradication of Hunger and Achieving Food Security
2. Prevention and Control of Diseases
3. Communication (Physical and Intellectual Mobility)
4. Protection of our Space
5. Living together in peace & harmony to build the society
6. Wealth Creation.

The strategy further defines four mutually reinforcing pillars which are prerequisite conditions for its success namely: building and/or upgrading research infrastructures; enhancing professional and technical competencies; promoting entrepreneurship and innovation; and providing an enabling environment for Science Technology and Innovation (STI) development in the African continent.

Boosting Intra African Trade (BIAT)

The objective of BIAT to deepen Africa's market integration and significantly increasing the volume of trade that African countries undertake amongst themselves from the current levels of about 10-13% to 25% or more within the next decade. The BIAT Action Plan provides for the assessment of Africa's overall trade flows and the potential for boosting intra-African trade by addressing key priority areas (both supply-side and demand-side) and identifying which areas are important to make trade an important driver of regional integration, structural transformation, and development in Africa.

The BIAT Action Plan identifies seven (7) critical pillars (Clusters) to address challenges facing intra-African trade such as infrastructural bottlenecks, improving trade facilitation, enhancing opportunities for intra-African trade through trade information networks, addressing financial needs of traders and economic operators through improved finance, addressing adjustment costs associated with FTAs and trade liberalization to ensure equitable outcomes for Member States. Specifically, the Clusters are:

1. Trade Policy
2. Trade Facilitation
3. Productive Capacity
4. Trade Related Infrastructure
5. Trade Finance
6. Trade Information and Factor Market integration

Accelerated Industrial Development for Africa (AIDA)

The Action Plan for the Accelerated Industrial Development of Africa (AIDA),

	Summary of STISA-2024 Priority Areas	
	Priorities	Research and/or innovation areas
1	Eradicate Hunger and ensure Food and Nutrition Security	• Agriculture/Agronomy in terms of cultivation technique, seeds, soil and climate • Industrial chain in terms of conservation and/or transformation and distribution • infrastructure and techniques
2	Prevent and Control Diseases and ensure Well-being	• Better understanding of endemic diseases: HIV/AIDS, • Malaria Hemoglobinopathie • Maternal and Child Health • Traditional Medicine
3	Communication (Physical and Intellectual Mobility)	• Physical communication in terms of land, air, river and • maritime routes equipment • and infrastructure and energy • Promoting local materials • Intellectual communications in terms of ICT

Africa Today

4	Protect our Space	• Environmental Protection including climate change studies • Biodiversity and Atmospheric Physics • Space technologies, maritime and sub-maritime exploration • Knowledge of the water cycle and river systems as well as • river basin management
5	Live Together—Build the Society	• Citizenship, History and Shared values • Pan Africanism and Regional integration • Governance and Democracy, City Management, Mobility • Urban Hydrology and Hydraulics • Urban waste management
6	Create Wealth	• Education and Human Resource Development • Exploitation and management of mineral resources, forests, aquatics, marines etc. • Management of water resources

is a pan-African program developed by the United Nations Industrial Development Organization (UNIDO) in 2008 at the request of the African Union, together with African governments and the private sector. The strategy aims to mobilize both financial and nonfinancial resources and enhance Africa's industrial performance.

The AIDA focuses on driving the integration of industrialization in national development policies especially in poverty alleviation strategies, development and implementation of an industrial policy with priority accorded to maximizing the use of local productive capacities and inputs, through value addition and local processing of the abundant natural resources of the country. AIDA also seeks to support the development of small-scale and rural industries, including the informal sectors as well as intermediate and capital goods industries with high linkages to other sectors of the economy as potential sources of employment creation.

The AIDA strategy further seeks to improve Investment and Mining Codes to support local processing of mineral resources whilst at the same time encouraging mineral resources-rich countries to set aside portions of commodity price-surge related premiums for investment in programs/projects of economic diversification. The program also expects the continent to leverage Africa's Partnerships, especially with the Newly Industrializing and Emerging Powers of the South, for the development and transfer of technology, for the establishment of joint industrial enterprises in Africa, and for greater market access for African manufactured products.

Climate Change Is an Increasing Threat to Africa

Retrieved from/Courtesy UNCC: https://unfccc.int/news/climate-change-is-an-increasing-threat-to-africa

UN Climate Change News, 27 October 2020 – Increasing temperatures and sea levels, changing precipitation patterns and more extreme weather are threatening human health and safety, food and water security and socio-economic development in Africa, according to a new report devoted exclusively to the continent.

The State of the Climate in Africa 2019 report, a multi-agency publication coordinated by the World Meteorological Organization (WMO), provides a snapshot of current and future climate trends and associated impacts on the economy and sensitive sectors like agriculture. It highlights lessons for climate action in Africa and identifies pathways for addressing critical gaps and challenges.

"This report shows increasing climate change threats for human health, food and water security and socio-economic development in Africa. Because of this, we need accurate and current data for adaptation planning," said Ovais Sarmad, Deputy Executive Secretary, UN Climate Change.

The UN Climate Change secretariat is supporting countries in identifying and managing climate risks through the formulation and implementation of National Adaptation Plans (NAPs).

Advancements in systematic observations and research that WMO is undertaking plays a key role in providing critical input to these efforts.

The report was released on 26 October at a ministerial-level launch to highlight the urgency of climate action in Africa and the current state of capacity. The risks are becoming more severe.

"Climate change is having a growing impact on the African continent, hitting the most vulnerable hardest, and contributing to food insecurity, population displacement and stress on water resources. In recent months we have seen devastating floods, an invasion of desert locusts and now face the looming spectre of drought because of a La Niña event. The human and economic toll has been aggravated by the COVID-19 pandemic," said WMO Secretary-General Petteri Taalas.

"Science-based climate information is the foundation of resilience building, a cornerstone of climate change adaptation, as well as an oasis for sustainable livelihoods and development. The State of Climate Report for Africa has, therefore, a critical role to play in this respect, including in informing our actions for achieving the goals of the Africa Agenda 2063," said H. E. Josefa Leonel Correia Sacko, Commissioner for Rural Economy and Agriculture of the African Union Commission.

"The limited uptake and use of climate information services in development planning and practice in Africa is due in part to the paucity of reliable and timely climate information. This report, focusing on Africa, will go a long way towards addressing this gap. The contribution of the Economic Commission for Africa to the production of this report, through the African Climate Policy Centre, seeks to highlight the nexus between climate change and development, and to emphasise that building forward better from the Covid-19 pandemic requires a development approach that is green, sustainable and climate resilient, informed by the best available science. The participation of multiple institutions and agencies in producing the report reinforces our principles and approaches of working as one," said H.E. Vera Songwe, Under-Secretary-General and Executive Secretary of the United Nations Economic Commission for Africa.

Rising Temperatures

The year 2019 was among the three warmest years on record for the continent. That trend is expected to continue. African temperatures in recent decades have been warming at a rate comparable to that of most other continents, and thus somewhat faster than global mean surface temperature.

The latest decadal predictions, covering the five-year period from 2020 to 2024,

Africa Today

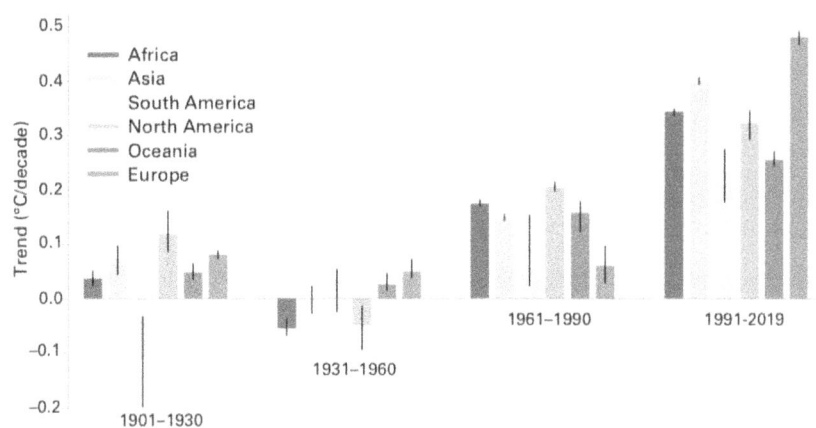

shows continued warming and decreasing rainfall especially over North and Southern Africa, and increased rainfall over the Sahel.

Extensive areas of Africa will exceed 2 °C of warming above pre-industrial levels by the last two decades of this century under medium scenarios as reported in the Intergovernmental Panel on Climate Change Fifth Assessment Report. Much of Africa has already warmed by more than 1 °C since 1901, with an increase in heatwaves and hot days. A reduction in precipitation is likely over North Africa and the south-western parts of South Africa by the end of the century, according to the Intergovernmental Panel on Climate Change (IPCC).

Rising Sea Levels and Coastal Erosion

There is significant regional variability in sea-level trends around Africa. Sea-level increase reached 5 mm per year in several oceanic areas surrounding the continent and exceeded 5 mm per year in the south-western Indian Ocean from Madagascar eastward towards and beyond Mauritius. This is more than the average global sea-level rise of 3–4 mm per year. Coastal degradation and erosion is also a major challenge, especially in West Africa. About 56% of the coastlines in Benin, Côte d'Ivoire, Senegal, and Togo are eroding and this is expected to worsen in the future. Sea level rise is currently not the dominant contributor but is expected to combine with other factors in future to exacerbate the negative consequences of environmental changes.

Extreme Events

The report documents high-impact events in 2019. Tropical Cyclone Idai was among the most destructive tropical cyclones ever recorded in the southern hemisphere, resulting in hundreds of casualties and hundreds of thousands of displaced.

Southern Africa suffered extensive drought in 2019. In contrast, the Greater Horn of Africa shifted from very dry conditions in 2018 and most of 2019 to floods and landslides associated with heavy rainfall in late 2019. Flooding also affected the Sahel and surrounding areas from May to October 2019.

Food Security Impacts

In the drought-prone sub-Saharan African countries, the number of undernourished people has increased by 45.6% since 2012 according to the Food and Agriculture Organization of the United Nations (FAO).

Agriculture is the backbone of Africa's economy and accounts for the majority of livelihoods across the continent. Africa is therefore an exposure and vulnerability "hot spot" for climate variability and change impacts.

IPCC projections suggest that warming scenarios risk having devastating effects on crop production and food security.

Key risks to agriculture include reduced crop productivity associated with heat and drought stress and increased pest damage, disease damage, and flood impacts on food system infrastructure, resulting in serious adverse effects on food security and on livelihoods at the regional, national, and individual household levels.

By the middle of this century, major cereal crops grown across Africa will be adversely impacted, albeit with regional variability and differences between crops.

Under the worst-case climate change scenario, a reduction in mean yield of 13% is projected in West and Central Africa, 11% in North Africa, and 8% in East and Southern Africa. Millet and sorghum have been found to be the most promising crops, with a yield loss by 2050 of just 5% and 8%, respectively, due to their greater resilience to heat-stress conditions, while rice and wheat are expected to be the most affected crops with a yield loss by 2050 of 12% and 21%, respectively.

Health Impacts

Increases in temperature and changes in rainfall patterns also significantly affect population health across Africa. Warmer temperatures and higher rainfall increase habitat suitability for biting insects and the transmission of vector-borne diseases such as dengue fever, malaria and yellow fever.

In addition, new diseases are emerging in regions where they were previously not present. In 2017, an estimated 93% of global malaria deaths occurred in Africa. Malaria epidemics often occur after periods of unusually heavy rainfall. In addition, warming in the East African highlands is allowing malaria-carrying mosquitoes to survive at higher altitudes.

Economic Impacts

According to the International Monetary Fund, adverse consequences of climate change are concentrated in regions with relatively hot climates, where a disproportionately large number of low-income countries are located. The African Climate Policy Centre projects that the Gross Domestic Product in the five African subregions would suffer significant decrease as a result of a global temperature increase. For scenarios ranging from a 1 °C to a 4 °C increase in global temperatures relative to pre-industrial levels, the continent's overall GDP is expected to decrease by 2.25% to 12.12%. West, Central

Subregions	GDP (% Change/Year)			
	1° C	2° C	3° C	4° C
North (n = 7)	−0.76 ± 0.16	−1.63 ± 0.36	−2.72 ± 0.61	−4.11 ± 0.97
West (n = 15)	−4.46 ± 0.63	−9.79 ± 1.35	−15.62 ± 2.08	−22.09 ± 2.78
Central (n = 9)	−1.17 ± 0.45	−2.82 ± 1.10	−5.53 ± 1.56	−9.13 ± 2.16
East (n = 14)	−2.01 ± 0.20	−4.51 ± 0.34	−7.55 ± 0.63	−11.16 ± 0.85
Southern (n = 10)	−1.18 ± 0.64	−2.68 ± 1.54	−4.40 ± 2.56	−6.49 ± 3.75
Whole of Africa (n = 55)	−2.25 ± 1.52	−5.01 ± 3.30	−8.28 ± 5.12	−12.12 ± 7.04

Africa Today

and East Africa exhibit a higher adverse impact than Southern and North Africa.

Climate Action

Africa's Agenda 2063, Ih was concluded in 2013, recognizes climate change as a major challenge for the continent's development.

Since 2015, the Nationally Determined Contributions (NDCs) to the Paris Agreement have become the main instrument for guiding policy responses to climate change. Fifty-two (52) African countries have submitted their first NDCs and are now in the process of submitting revised NDCs in 2020.

Africa and the small island developing States are the regions facing the largest capacity gaps regarding climate services. Africa also has the leIloped land-based observation network of all continents. Africa has made great efforts in driving the global climate agenda. This is demonstrated by the very high levels of ratification of the Paris Agreement—over 90%. Many African nIave committed to transitioning to green energy within a relatively short time frame. Clean energy and agriculture are, for example, prioritized in over 70% of African NDCs. This ambition needs to be an integral part of setting the economic development priorities of the continent.

One promising approach throughout the continent to reducing climate related risks and extreme event impacts has been to reduce poverty by promoting socioeconomic growth, in particular in the agricultural sectIIn this sector, which employs 60% of Africa's population, value-addition techniques using efficient and clean energy sources are reported to be capable of reducing poverty two to four times faster than growth in any other sector.

Solar-powered, efficient micro-irrigation, for example, is increasing farm-level incomes by five to 10 times, improving yields by up to 300% and reducing water usage by up to 90% while at the same time offsetting carbon emissions by generating up to 250 kW of clean energy.

Women constitute a large percentage of the world's poor, and about half of the women in the world are active in agriculture—in developing countries, this figure is 60%, and in low-income, food-deficit countries, 70%. Reducing poverty by means of growth in Africa's agricultural sector is therefore of particular benefit to women. It also may be the case that in some instances, women do not have access to weather and climate services; it is important that all individuals be provided with access to these services in order to enhance their individual resilience and adaptive capacity.

Africa's Strategic Efforts at Addressing Climate Change

Climate change impacts every facet of Africa's life, most significantly its economy. Africa's economy, like most developing countries, is predominantly agriculture and rural. The rIas are the less developed on the continent. Thus, as Africa combats climate change and its impact, strategic resources need to be invested in the rural areas to stem the economic impact of climate change. The African Union Commission Department of Rural Economy and Agriculture (DREA) is assisting the continent in this area. The Department's mandate is to boost AU Member States' rural economy development and agricultural productivity by supporting the adoption of measures, strategies, policies, and programs on agriculture. It works closely with the Regional Economic Communities (RECsIother partners. Key tasks include developing programs to ensure food security; promoting rural communities' initiatives and transfer of technologies; coordinating efforts to eradicate poverty and combat desertification and drought; promoting agricultural products by small-scale producers; supporting the harmonization of policies and strategies between the RECs; and initiating research on climate change, water, and sanitation management. The Department has three divisions: Agriculture and Food Security; Environment, Climate Change, Water, Land and Natural Resources; and Rural Economy (https://au.int/en/rea/department).

DREA's work on sustainable environment and natural resources focuses on:(https://au.int/en/directorates/sustainable-environment)

1. AdvaIAfrica's Climate Change Agenda, including supporting Africa's negotiations on climate change at global level, through facilitation of effective coordination around African Common Position on Climate Change, and formulation of an African Climate Change Strategy.
2. Enhancing capacities of Member States and RECs to access near-real time environmental, natural resources, and climate information for policy and decision-making, and development planning by improving Africa's exploitation of earth observation technologies through the implementation of the Monitoring for Environment and Security in Africa (MESA) program formerly called the African Monitoring of the Environment for Sustainable Development (AMESD) Program; and operationalizing, in partnership with UN-ECA and AfDB, the program on Climate for Development in Africa (ClimDEV Africa).
3. Building Member States' capacities for improved performance in terms of discharging their responsibilities and derive benefits from Multilateral Environmental Agreements (MEAs);
4. Implementation of the Great Green Wall for the Sahara and Sahel Initiative (GGWSSI)—as part of the efforts to combating land degradation and desertification. The Initiative serves as an important platform and instrument towards bringing together key actors and partners at various levels for a concerted action.
5. Advancing the African Water and Sanitation agenda, in terms of implementation of the Sharm El-Sheikh Commitments on Water and Sanitation and supporting the Water Basin initiatives.
6. Facilitating the formulation and implementation of Integrated African Strategy on Meteorology (Weather and Climate Services) to enhance weather and climate service delivery for sustainable development through cooperation among AU Member States in collaboration with the African Ministerial Conference on Meteorology (AMCOMET), and its Secretariat, the World Meteorological Organization.
7. Facilitating and coordination of the implementation of the Africa Regional Strategy on Disaster Risk Reduction (DRR) and its Programme of Action (PoA) in line with the Hyogo Framework for Action.

Achievements on Implementation of Programs on Environment Climate Change, Water and Land Management Division

i. Addressing Africa's Vulnerability to Disaster Risk

Efforts have been exerted to put in place systems, mechanisms and capacities that will enableIica to transition from managing crises, which has dominated the scene, to managing risks of disasters. These efforts have led to three interrelated achievements.

The first concerns development and adoption of a Programme of Action for the implementation of the Africa Regional Strategy for DisaI Risk Reduction (for the period 2006–2015), which provides strategic guidance for disaster risk reduction intervention of MemIStates, RECs, and development partners—based on which institutional mechanisms and legislative frameworks are now in place in most of the Member States and RECs.

The second relates to theIrationalization of the African Risk Capacity (ARCIhich was established as a Specialised Agency of the AU, which has now held twice its Conference of Parties since February 2013. ARC is envisaged as African owned, standalone financial entity that will provide African governments with timely, reliable, and cost-effective contingency funding in the event of a severe drought by pooling risk across the continent.

The third is concerned with refocusing of the thrust of one of DREA's technical agencies such as (SAFGRAD) to explicitly address the challenges of resilience. EIve implementation of these and other related initiatives, including the Climate for Development in Africa (ClimDEV Africa), the African Monitoring for Environment and Security (MESA) the Multilateral Environmental Agreements (MEAs), the Great Green Wall for the Sahara and Sahel Initiative (GGWSSI), is expected to contribute towards improved capacity of Member States and RECs to access and utilize climate information for policy making purposes and therefore better preparedness, improved response, and enhanced resilience of African economies to risks of natural disasters.

ii. Harnessing Africa's Collective Strength: Climate Change, Desertification, and Sustainable Development

Since 2007 the AU Commission, through DREA has become an important interlocutor and regional and global player in matters of climate change, desertification, and biodiversity. This was largely due to the histoIAU Assembly Decisions adopted from February and July 2009 onwards which essentially charted the way for Africa to do 'business unusually' in matters of climate change, desertification, and biodiversity negotiations, with Africa to have articulated its Common Position on Climate Change and to negotiate it with a single voice.

Subsequent Assembly Decisions estabInd further refined coordinating mechanisms, notably mandating the Committee of African Heads of State and Government on Climate Change (CAHOSCC) to provide political guidance to the negotiation process. CAHOSCC has since been providing the much-needed guidance and direction on strategic issues.

Africa had a prominence on climate change on the margins of the UN General Assembly in New York in September 2013 as CAHOSCC met to exchange views on Africa's preparations for the Nineteenth Conference of the Parties to the United Nations Framework Convention on Climate Change (UNFCCC) (COP 19) and endorsed the updated key messages of the African Common Position on Climate Change for basis of Africa's negotiations at the global climate change negotiations (COP 19 /CMP 9). The African Union Commission supported the African Group of Negotiators on Climate Change (AGN) at the March 2013 session of the Ad-hoc Working Group of the Durban Platform for Enhanced Action held in Bonn, Germany; the African preparatory held in May 2013 in Libreville, Gabon for the Bonn (Germany) June 2013 Climate Conference that prepared for the Warsaw Climate Conference ; the African Preparatory for the development of the key messages on the AfriIan Common PosiIion on Climate Change held in Mbabane, Swaziland in May 2013; and in October 2013 in Gaborone, Botswana for Africa to defend and uphold Africa's interest under the political guidance of the African Ministerial Conference on Environment (AMCEN) and leadership of CAHOSCC during the World Conference on Climate Change (COP 19) held in Warsaw, Poland in November 2013, where Africa once again demonstrated leadership in setting pace in the global climate change arena.

Subsequently, CAHOSCC also prepared its position on climate change in December 2013 in Paris for the Elysée Summit on Peace and Security in Africa in the engagement between Africa and France on the issues of climate change; and a major part of Africa's position was the excerpt in the Elysée Summit Declaration on Peace and Security in Africa.

Similarly, a substantive show of African solidarity on environmental affairs was for example demonstrated during the Rio+20 conference since Africa submitted the 'Africa Consensus Statement'. It is through the unity drive of this collective belief that the issues concerning the evolution of a Green Economy in the context of sustainable development are intimately linked.

The AU Commission, through DREA, has been actively engaged in providing the much-needed facilitation of coordination of these endeavors, and in due course has created crucial caIor use by African stakeholders. An African Climate Change Strategy has been developed and is soon to be submitted to the African Ministerial Conference on Environment (AMCEN) for validation and endorsement. A Climate Change and Desertification Unit has been established within the Commission, and work towards operationalizing it is currently in progress, as an integral component of the Climate for Development in Africa (ClimDEV Africa) initiative, one of the programs that the Commission joined hands with the AfDB and the UNECA to champion and further enhance Africa's capacity to access and utilize climate information for policy making purposes.

iii. Combating Desertification

CCDU participated in the Second Ministerial Council and Heads of State Summit for the Great Green Wall for the Sahara and Sahel Initiative (GGWSSI) in Ndjamena, Chad from 5 to 19 April 2013: During this Summit the implementation of the United Nations Convention to Combat Desertification (UNCCD) within the framework of the Great Green Wall Initiative was discussed and CCDU provided technical guidance to the Expert Session on the ten-Year Strategy of the UNCCD. The Ministerial conference acknowledged the GGWSSI as an important platform for implementing UNCCD in Africa.

iv. Development of the African Climate Change Strategy

The Commission is in the final stages in the development of the African Climate Change Strategy. During 2013, meetings were held with the RECs and consultants to review and validate the draft strategy. The strategy, once finalized, will provide the RECs and Member States with a single source of strategic direction that would enable them to mitigate and adapt to the challenges and opportunities of climate change.

v. Mainstreaming Water Resources into Climate Change

On Water, CCDU has been working to train national experts on integrating water resources management issues as adaptive measures into climate change and desertification policies. Also to create awareness of the important linkages between water, energy, and climate change for the sustainable development of Africa given the serious developmental challenges facing Africa.

vi. Development of a Continental Natural Resource Accounting Framework Document and Guidelines

In 2013, CCDU has embarked on a process of developing a continental Natural Resource Accounting Framework to valorise natural resources (impacted by climate change) on their contributions to (i) climate change adaptation (ii) mitigation and (iii) sustainable development. Under this a regional workshop was organized at the AUC HQ and a Conference in collaboration with partners.

vii. The Monitoring for Environment and Security in Africa (MESA) Programme, (formerly, the African Monitoring of Environment for Sustainable Development (AMESD) Programme)

Under the African Monitoring of the Environment for Sustainable Development (AMESD) program (now the Monitoring for Environment and Security in Africa (MESA) programme, the AUC, through DREA has been supporting African decision-makers and planners in designing and implementing national, regional and continental policies and development plans towards sustainable development thereby advancing the socio-economic progress and well-being of Africans towards achievement of the MDGs. In close collaboration with the RECs, the AUC completed facilitation of installation of 107 sets of infrastructure for accessing and analyzing satellite Earth Observation (EO) and meteorological data and information in Member States. This ensures continued access to near-real time environmental, natural resources, and climate data and information for timely intervention, development planning, and policy and decision making in Africa.

In 2013, the AU Commission, in collaboration with RECs and regional specialized institutions, i.e., the Regional Implementation Centres (RICs), concluded the facilitation of production and dissemination of 12 region-specific environmental and climate information services (i.e., monitoring of droughts, floods, vegetation, bush/wildfire, agriculture, water levels and flow rates,, monitoring of water balance and flooded forests, land degradation mitigation, natural habitat conservation, fisheries management, ocean biological and physical indicators, oceanographic climatology, marine currents forecasting, and providing early warning systems). The program, further, facilitated the development of three continental information packs which provided environmental outlooks and were distributed to Member States. Production and dissemination of services and information packs have been successfully taken up by the MESA program, which succeeded AMESD and kicked-off early 2013.

In order to ensure sustainability in the use of EO-based environmental and meteorological data and information, four African training centres i.e. Ecole Africaine de la Météorolgie et de l'Aviation Civile (EAMAC) in Niamey, Institute for Meteorological Training and Research (IMTR) in Nairobi, South African Weather Service (SAWS) in Pretoria, and the National Meteorological and Hydrological Services (NMHS) of Mauritius were equipped with computers and training software licenses to allow for continued continental training on EO including satellite meteorology. Furthermore, about 1000 African experts were trained, creating a critical mass of technicians with basic skills in EO data, satellite meteorology, e-Station software suite, system administration, EO data processing, production of environmental monitoring bulletins, and maintenance and operation of infrastructure. The program trained 60 African Experts as Regional Trainers, who are presently conducting trainings at national level in an effort to ensure that capacity development continues.

The AU Commission, through MESA, continues with capacity development of African institutions and experts, upgrade and provision of infrastructure and facilitation of the production of products and services produced under AMESD and newly introduced services on climate monitoring, forest management, and coastal and marine resources management. As an environmental monitoring program, it provides development planners and policy and decision makers with near-real time information that informs sustainable development planning, and policy and decision-making processes. The MESA programme runs from 2013 to 2018.

viii. The Great Green Wall for the Sahara and Sahel Initiative: GGWSSI

Implementation of the GGWSSI in thirteen (13) participating Member States commenced with elaboration of a Harmonised Regional Strategy for the implementation of the Initiative. Thirteen countries have developed National strategies and Action Plans (NAP) through technical and financial support made available through collaboration with the EU, FAO and Global Mechanism. Of the thirteen countries engaged in the project, 11 have completed and launched their National Action Plans (NAP) with Egypt and Sudan still to launch to complete and undertake their launching ceremonies. The Initiative, with support from the Department obtained funding from the World Bank and GEF to support the implementation of plans in 14 countries with 12 of the countries being part of the focal countries in the GGWSSI. The funds will be implemented through the BRICKS (Building Resilience through Innovation, Communication and Knowledge Services) and SAWAP (Sahel and West Africa Program in support of the GGWSSI), The AUC was nominated the head of the steering committee of the above programs. DREA also work with Partners (FAO & Global Mechanism) in resource mobilization initiatives that have resulted in the raising of over EU 54 million to undertake two projects in the next five years to support the implementation of the NAP in selected countries through two projects, Action Against Desertification and FLEUVE.

ix. Trans-boundary Forest Management and REDD+ Regional Strategy

Within the framework of revitalizing the contribution of forest and other biological resources to sustainable development and poverty eradication in Africa, the Commission has been working with RECs and regional forest Commissions toward enhancing regional collaboration in forest resources management through policy harmonization and capacity building through developing trans-boundary forest management systems and mechanisms. An Africa Regional Strategy on REDD+ is being development in collaboration with Centre for International Forestry and FAO to serve as guideline for AU Member States and the RECs when developing their plans and strategies.

x. Water Resources Management

Following the 2008 Sharm-El Sheikh Declaration on Water and Sanitation [Assembly/AU/Decl.1 (XI)], DREA's efforts, through technical and financial support provided by Germany (GIZ), has been directed towards collaborating with the African Ministerial Council on Water (AMCOW) with a view to putting in place a monitoring and evaluation (M&E) mechanism for tracking progress on achievement of Sharm El-Sheikh Commitments by Member States, and to promote sound water resources management on the continent.

DREA has successfully been engaged for the last two years, in mobilizing the key stakeholders and development partners to strengthen the partnership with AMCOW, the Member States and the Regional Economic Communities (RECs) for establishing the M&E mechanism with a view to preparing a regular progress report on implementing the commitments on water and sanitation, to the African Union Assembly on an annual basis. Moreover, in consultation with MS, RECs and African Institutions, the African Water Common Position and its targets and indicators for implementation were finally considered and included in the Global Post-2015 Development Agenda. DREA has furthermore been involved in guiding the African Common Position for a Water goal in the framework of the SDGs processes.

Two continental taskforces, namely the African Water and Sanitation M&E Task Force and the African Water and Sanitation M&E Steering Committee, have been formed as part of the M&E mechanism to provide political and technical guidance to regularly guaranty the quality of the annual report to the AU Policy Organs. DREA has also prepared a program for the Establishment of an African Water and Sanitation Information and Reporting System that has received a commitment, from the African Water Facility, of two million Euro for a two-year project to implement Phase 1 of the program hosted at AMCOW-Secretariat. The estimated program cost for operationalizing this system is eight million Euro; mobilization efforts for which are currently under way.

DREA is continuing with the on-going efforts to foster the implementation of the Africa Water Vision 2025, in the Phase II of the GIZ Support Programme for implementing the 2008 Sharm El-Sheikh Declaration, which was commissioned in June 2013 with a two million Euros contribution from the Government of the Republic of Germany.

xi. Capacity Building Project on Multilateral Environmental Agreements (MEAs)

Since its launch in 2009, the Project has been implementing activities in the areas of enhancing negotiation skills of African negotiators on climate change, desertification, and Mercury, among others, through facilitating training as well as interaction between political leaders and the technical experts. Following the strategy developed by the MEAs Project to promote ratification of the Maputo Convention and endorsed by the AMCEN of 2012, 3 additional ratifications were obtained in 2013 (Guinea, Ivory Coast and South Africa). The Project supported the organisation of the 1st Conference of Parties to the Bamako Convention in Bamako, Mali in June 2013. In the same year, Comoros, Congo, Ethiopia, Mali, and Lesotho held workshops to validate their multi-stakeholder collaboration strategies. In 2013, Uganda, with support of the Project had in place its Regulations on Persistent Organic Pollutants (POPs).

xii. Improved Meteorology (Weather and Climate Services) in Africa

The African Union Commission in collaboration with the World Meteorological Organization (WMO) and Partner Institutions facilitated the establishment of the African Ministerial Conference on Meteorology (AMCOMET) by Member States in 2010. Subsequently, AMCOMET developed the Integrated African Strategy on Meteorology (Weather and Climate Services) that was endorsed by the January 2013 AU Summit. The Strategy sets out priority actions that can be undertaken at national, regional, and continental levels. These priority actions are supported by a set of institutional partnerships that bring together AMCOMET and Development Partners to support meteorological (weather and climate) services in the African continent. Currently, the Implementation Plan and Resource Mobilization Strategy for the Integrated African Strategy on Meteorology (Weather and Climate Services) have been developed.

HISTORICAL BACKGROUND

PREHISTORIC AFRICA

As advances in archeology, population genetics and linguistics continue to flesh out our understanding of human evolution, it is clear that the ancestral home of humankind is Africa. Recent DNA research suggests the Vasikela Kung of the northwestern Kalahari Desert of southern Africa are a population that lies close to the root of modern humans' origins. Similarly, the Turkana people of Kenya show the greatest genetic diversity of any known human group, and high diversity is usually indicative of a species' place of origin. Regardless of the specific place of origin, it is clear that Homo sapiens, modern humans, evolved in sub-Saharan Africa and, in a later split, migrated out of Africa some 50,000 years ago to populate the rest of the world. And this wasn't the first migration of hominids out of Africa, as recent findings date such occurrences back well over one million years ago. Archeologists, like population geneticists, continue to add to our store of knowledge of human development. In the Republic of Georgia, scientists have discovered a 1.7-million-year-old hominid skull that shows clear linkages with African fossils. Tools found with the Georgian skulls resembled tools found in the Olduvai Gorge of Tanzania and dated at about 1.8 million years. Discoveries of the migration routes of early hominids now allow scientists to trace the incredible journeys out of Africa.

Early African peoples also adopted signature human customs earlier than once thought. A cave site in Zambia has revealed pigment and paint-grinding equipment that dates back 400,000 years, suggesting the ancestors of *Homo sapiens* were decorating themselves much earlier than ever thought. A recently discovered site along the Red Sea coast of Eritrea appears to be 125,000 years old and documents the utilization of marine resources—clams, crabs, and oysters. These are some of the tantalizing discoveries that will form the basis of a fuller understanding of human development in Africa, just as archeological remains testify to the richness of African civilization. Such richness could be seen in its full splendor long before the arrival of European explorers on the continent, as the rest of this brief historical survey will demonstrate.

EARLY CIVILIZATIONS OF THE NILE VALLEY AND MEDITERRANEAN SEA

The Nile Valley was settled, and agricultural skills developed by 5000 B.C. This population was able to form one of the first centrally organized societies of the western world by about 3000 B.C., the beginning of the Egyptians. Under the control of the succession of kings (Pharaohs), the social organization of the people permitted rapid evolution and development of writing, architecture, religion and the beginning of scientific thought.

The Egyptians' early religious efforts were varied; they conceived of a god represented by a variety of animal forms. Under the rule of the dynasties, these individual symbols were gradually discarded in favor of the obelisk (a tall, usually pointed four-sided structure with ornate carvings and frescoes which was used as a symbol of *Re*. It is probable that *Re* was associated with local gods which the people were accustomed to worship, but this concept of God led to the development of the first-known beliefs in life after death. The development of writing, first in hieroglyphics (illustrations portraying a variety of thoughts and concepts) and later in abstract symbols (an early "alphabet") in turn enabled the development of a highly stylized literature. A calendar of 365 days was adopted. The religious concept of life after death led in turn to invention of embalming methods to preserve the human body after death. This further resulted in the combination of early geometry with architecture, which permitted the construction of obelisks and elaborate and immense pyramids, the burial tombs of the pharaohs.

The Egyptians under the pharaohs reached their period of greatest power in the 2nd millennium before the Christian era, and gradually declined in strength and organization until they were invaded by a succession of other Mediterranean powers—the Assyrians in the 7th century B.C., the Persians and finally the Greeks under Alexander in the 4th century B.C.

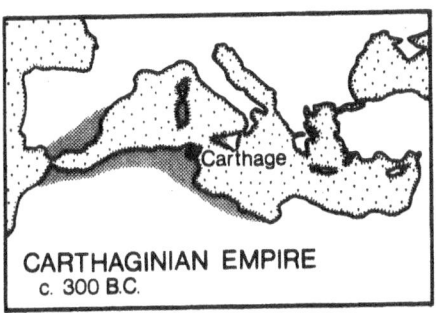

Phoenician traders on the northern coastline of the African continent combined over many centuries with the small number of other people of Middle East origin, emerging into the unified society of Carthage in the 9th century B.C. in what is now Tunisia and part of Algeria. The Carthaginians fought with the inhabitants of Sicily and Sardinia for about four hundred years, eventually winning control of the two islands after many changes in the fortunes of war in the 2nd century B.C. Carthaginian control was brief—the

1

Historical Background

powerful Roman Empire was able to completely conquer Carthage by 122 B.C.

As early as 1000 B.C., the Phoenicians established themselves along the coastline of present-day Libya, founding what later became the city of Cyrene. Three coastal cities to the west were given the name *Tripolitania*, or *three cities*, by the Romans—Sabratha, Leptis Magna and Oea. The first two are now ruins. Oea became Tripoli. Ruins of imperial structures throughout Libya are intermixed with those of earlier temples and buildings dating back to 1000 B.C. In Tripoli, Marcus Aurelius constructed a great arch as a monument to Roman power. After the fall of the Roman Empire, Libya was successively invaded and ruled by Vandals, Byzantines, and Greeks. A massive Arab invasion from the east subdued the people in the 8th century, bringing Islam to the native Berber people.

So too in Morocco, many centuries before the birth of Christ, the Phoenicians established trading posts and settled numerous people in the land. From the 1st century B.C. until the 5th century A.D., Morocco was a Roman province, providing foodstuffs for the people of the empire. After the fall of the Roman Empire, there was a quick succession of Vandals, Visigoths, and Byzantine Greeks who conquered Morocco. In the 9th century, Arab forces arrived, bringing Islam to the people whom they subdued. The Berbers of inland Morocco were readily converted to this religion. The first rulers of the country claimed to be direct descendants of the Prophet Mohammed. The next centuries were a period of strife between the Muslim-Berbers and the Arab invaders.

After achieving some degree of unity in the 12th century, Morocco began to expand. Its borders ultimately reached from the Atlantic to Egypt and as far as Timbuktu to the south. After consolidating this immense territory, the Moors (the name given to mixed Arab-Berber peoples) conquered almost all of Spain, Ih became a Moroccan province, and advanced into present-day France. The slow decline of this vast empire culminated in the first part of the 16th century.

South along the upper Nile, the ancient history of Sudan, one of the oldest civilizations in the world, revolves around the pharaohs of Egypt and the Nubian people. Gigantic formations of stone in the Nile area to the north furnished the material from Ih many of the picturesque temples and burial grounds of ancient Egypt were carved and built. In the 8th century B.C., Kushite kings from Nubia, now northern Sudan, conquered Egypt and created the 25th Dynasty. At the beginning of the Christian era, Sudan split into a collection of small, independent states. There were some conversions of people to Christianity in the 6th century, but much of the country remained pagan until there was widespread adoption of Islam, primarily in the north, at the end of the 13th century.

THE KINGDOM OF ETHIOPIA

By tradition, the Ethiopian kingdom dated back to a visit by the Queen of Sheba (a city in Yemen also known as Saba or Sabah) at the court of Solomon. Menelik I, son of Solomon and the Queen, founded the Ethiopian monarchy. There are other indications that the Ethiopians had progressed at a relatively early date in African history. Herodotus, a Greek writer of the 5th century B.C. described Ethiopia; Homer refers to the Ethiopians as a "blameless race" in his writing of about 800 B.C., but for the ancient Greeks, "Ethiopian" referred generally to "the most remote of men," most likely Nubians whose descendents live in modern Sudan, not present-day Ethiopia. There are forty-five references to Ethiopia in the Bible, but again, they point to the lands south of Egypt, Nubia, rather than the area of modern Ethiopia.

Little else is known of the history of Ethiopia at the beginning of the Christian era. The Coptic Christian Church established outposts in Ethiopia and Eritrea in the 4th century, and Islam arrived most probably as a result of continued contact with Arabs by the first part of the 8th century. The capital was moved from the ancient city of Axum to Addis Ababa and the distinctive Amharic language of the Ethiopians slowly evolved. The Christian Church in Ethiopia was established as a branch of the Coptic Christian Church headed by the Patriarch of Alexandria in Egypt. Contact with other Christians was later severed by the Islamic-Arab conquest of North Africa in the mid-10th century.

Although tradition holds that the ancestors of the Somali people, of Cushitic origins, lived in present-day Somalia more than 2,000 years ago, the earliest traces of people date to the 7th century A.D. The Koreishite Kingdom was established at that time by a group of people from nearby Yemen.

Roman Imperial Ruins, Sabratha, Libya

Photo by Pat Crowell

Historical Background

THE SPREAD OF ISLAM

The teachings of Mohammed, a religious prophet of the neighboring Arabian peninsula, were the basis for the religion known to billions today as Islam. The writings of Mohammed, together with his teachings, are gathered together in the Koran. He envisioned his prophecy to be supplemental, adding to and completing previous revelatiIncluding those of Judaism and Christianity, of a single God. Preaching a belief in *Allah*, a single, all-powerful God, Mohammed was supposed to be the last prophet of God. He preached the Last Judgment, a duty to donate to the poor, and an obligation to engage in a daily system of prayer. A line of Islamic rulers established Ihemselves In Damascus in Syria, and from that base other Muslim leaders conquered most of North Africa within a century, even going further to seize most of Spain.

Islam spread southward from the 8th century AD, converting most of the semi-arid regions south of the sands ofIahara. Because of this contact with Islamic Arabs whose faith was based on a written text and who employed writing in their commercial transactions, we have much more exteIe materials on which to build a history of this area. Al Umari, Ibn Khaldun and especially Ibn Battuta who visited the Mansa of Mali in the 14th century, have all left important materials to supplement local oral traditions.

Islam reached the western end of the Sahara as well as the eastern end. The first inhabitants of Mauritania were West African peoples, dating back to the Neolithic period. In historical times, both sub-Saharan peoples and Berbers have inhabited the area. It was the Berbers who founded the austere Almoravid movement and spread its version of Islam throughout the area in the 11th century A.D. An influx of Arabs, following commercial caravan routes, produced the mixed Arab-Berber culture known as Moorish. Federations of Moorish nomadic tribesmen came to dominate sedentary African farmers, many of whom adopted the Islamic faith of their conquerors.

ARABS AND TRADERS IN EAST AFRICA

From the 8th to the 10th centuries A.D., the Arabs penetrated the shoreline of East Africa in increasing numbers, establishing trading posts at Mogadishu (Somali Republic) and Mombasa (Kenya) and in what is now Mozambique. Ivory and African slaves were the basis of a brisk trade, as well as gold, shipped primarily to India. This coId in one form or another until control of the area was seized by European colonial powers in the last part of the 19th century. Persian, Arabic,

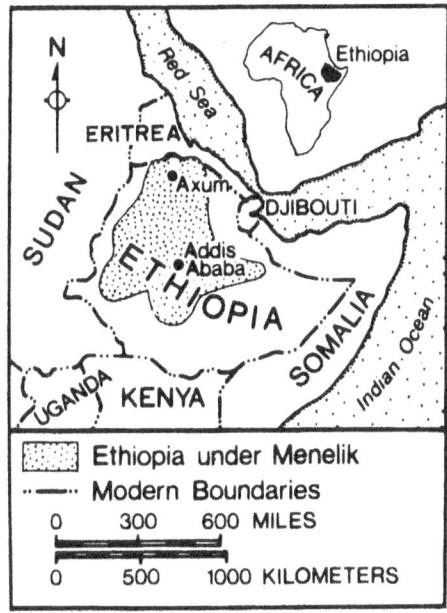

Indian and Portuguese traders engaged in lively trade with various coastal peoples in and around Ipresent-day Tanzania, including the island of Zanzibar, a region that had been settled long before by large numbers of Bantus and smaller groups of Nilotic Ieople. Portuguese mariners landed in Kenya as early as 1498, seeking a sea route to the Far East. In the 19th century, Arab and Swahili caravans in search of ivory and slaves penetrated the interior. Colonial activity in the area was first initiated by GermanI, followed by the British.

Islands in the Indian Ocean were also accessed first by maritime traders. Probably during the first millennium of the Christian era, people known as the Hovas settled in the highlands of the island of Madagascar and possibly reached the east coast of Africa. The Comoros were first settled by Arab seafarers about 1,000 years ago. The Arabs brought in slaves from Africa and established a series of small sultanates on the different islands. It was not until 1527 that the Portuguese cartographer Diego Ribero depicted the Comoros islands on a European map. The Dutch arrived at Mauritius, uninhabited by man prior to the time, in 1598, naming it after a prince of Holland. They remained for a century and started sugar production at the time the last clumsy dodo birds walked upon the island. (Concluding that the island offered no profit, they withdrew, and the French arrived in 1715.) The small group of settlers on Mauritius was augmented by African slaves, who worked the sugar plantations that came to dominate the island. The firsI recorded landfall on the Seychelles islands was madI by an expedItion of the British East India company in 1609.

THE EMPIRES AND PEOPLES OF WEST AFRICA

A segment of people living in the area south of the Sahara gathered together in the first "empire" of West Africa in the 4th century A.D., eventually controlling a large area that is now part of Burkina Faso, southern Mali and eastern Senegal. The basis of this early group of people was a lively trade in gold and slaves with the nomadic people to the north. *Ghana*, as this empire is historically known, should not be confused with the modern state bearing that name. Its existence continued until it was conquered by the Islamic Berbers from the north in 1076, who converted the local people to their faith.

West Africa's history after Islam arrived in the sub-Sahara dry regions is one of conflict between various tribes and kingdoms, all located within the same general area. ThInghai Empire based in western Niger, which had controlled the region since the 7th centurIdopted Islam, as did the Mandingo Empire which arose in Mali. Initially, most of West Africa from about 1000 to 1200 A.D. was divided between the Songhai and Mandingo rulers, with the exception of areas closer to the coast in what are now parts of Guinea, Côte d'Ivoire, Ghana, and Burkina Faso.

Trade with the Arabs to the north and east was lively for several centuries, with caravans linking Timbuktu, Gao (Mali), Kano (Nigeria) and the Lake Chad region with the Middle East by way of the Sudan and Egypt. The more affluent Islamic people journeyed on traditional pilgrimages to Mecca from this area of West Africa. Other trading was conducted with the Arab-Berber people of the North where Morocco, Algeria, Tunisia, and Libya are now located.

Historical Background

The Mande rulers gradually acquired more territory at the expense of the neighboring ethnic groups after 1200 A.D. A brief domination by the Sosso people of Guinea, led by Sumanguru Kanté, was ended when the kingdoms of the savannah were rallied to overthrow Sosso's oppression in the early 13th century. The leader of this liberation struggle, Sundiata Keita, became the first of the Mansas or Emperors of Mali. Timbuktu, located in a remote part of what is now Mali, became a center of culture and progress fabled throughout West Africa, and was visited by many Arab merchants and travelers. The Empire of Mali disintegrated in the 15th century when Timbuktu was invaded and sacked by desert Tuaregs. A generation later, in 1468, the Songhai rulers were able in turn to expel the Tuaregs. The Songhai reached their greatest power in the following six decades, at a time when the first Portuguese explorers began to penetrate the area.

Several initially non-Muslim kingdoms arose along the southern coast of West Africa at about the same time the Islamic empires of the upper Niger River were powerful. The Fulani, also known as Peulh, established several states from what is now Senegal to Nigeria, occupying an area between the Muslim empires and the coastal lands, and gradually were converted to Islam. Closer to the coastline, the Mossi created two distinct states within what is now southern Burkina Faso and Ghana, also adopting Islam.

The Ashanti became established in what is now central Ghana, as did the Soso in Guinea, the Yorubas in Dahomey and south-western Nigeria and the Ibos in southeastern Nigeria. Togolese oral history indicate that in the 15th to 17th centuries Ewe clans from Nigeria and the Ane fIGhana and Ivory Coast settled in the region, which was already occupied by Kwa and Voltaic peoples. Coastal Sierra Leone was thinly populated by the Sherbro, Temne, and Limba peoples who had probably lived in the area for thousands of years by the time the Portuguese explorer, Pedro de Cintra, visited the coastal area in 1460. Impressed by the beauty of the mountains of the southeast, he named the territory Sierra Leone—"Lion Mountains." Already established by this time were Iande-speaking peoples who settled inland. Islam was introduced by Muslim traders and took root initially in the north, but later spread throughout the area.

Early migrations of peoples from the east were long-established in and around Senegal and Gambia rivers by the time of the first European explorations in the 15th century. Paleolithic and Neolithic artifacts have been found near Dakar (Senegal), and early copper and iron objects have been found elsewhere. Berbers from the north established a Muslim monastery in the Senegal River region in the 11th century, converted local populations to Islam, and began a military expansion that ultimately resulted in the conquest of both Ghana and Morocco and the invasion of Spain. The region was strongly influenced by Islamic revival movements from the later 17th century well into the 19th century.

Some of the most important archeological work in Africa has been done in Nigeria, producing evidence of human habitation that goes back thousands of years. The oldest evidence of a widespread organized society is associated with the Nok culture (c. 500 BC–200 AD). Yoruba peoples were established in the southern coastal region by the 11th century, and by the 14th and 15th centuries the Yoruba empire was a regional power. Hausa kingdoms were gradually formed after the 12th century in the north and began to undergo conversion to Islam by the 14th century. Fulani (Peulh) nomadic herdsmen became rulers in the Hausa regions of the North as a consequence of an Islamic reformist jihad in the late 19th century. In the densely forested southeast region Ibo peoples organized themselves in small-scale political units centuries before the arrival of the first Europeans.

Farther south, archeological evidence suggests that Cameroon has been occupied for at least 50,000 years. Originally populated by pygmies, who are now found only in small numbers along the southern border, Cameroon was successively invaded by other groups. There is evidence of Iy state-building societies, the most important of which is Sao, centered in the Lake Chad area. In 1472, a Portuguese explorer, Fernão do Pó (Fernando Po in Spanish) arrived on the coast of what is now Cameroon.

PEOPLES OF CENTRAL AND SOUTHERN AFRICA

Humans have inhabited the area of the present-day Central African Republic for at least 8,000 years, as polished flint and quartz tools testify. Huge stone megaliths near Bouar date back 2,500 years and suggest a relatively large-scale society with specialized labor. A wide variety of Niger-Congo and Nilo-Saharan languages suggest widespread migrations into the area, dating back to the 10th century. Oral tradition also conveys the story of the mighty Kingdom of the Kongo, probably founded in the 14th century. It was not until 1482 that the first European, the Portuguese navigator Diogo Cao, explored the coastal areas of present-day Congo-Brazzaville. Little is known of the pre-colonial period of present-day Equatorial Guinea; the Fang and other Bantu people settled thinly in Rio Muni and the Bubis settled on Bioko Island.

In Rwanda and Burundi, the original inhabitants were the Twa, a pygmy hunting and gathering people. The Twa were followed by the Hutu who established themselves as farmers. In the 14th century, the pastoral Tutsi appeared and imposed their dominance over the mass of Hutu agriculturalists by military power. The Hutu were reduced to serfdom, each choosing a Tutsi lord protector who gave them the use (but not ownership) of

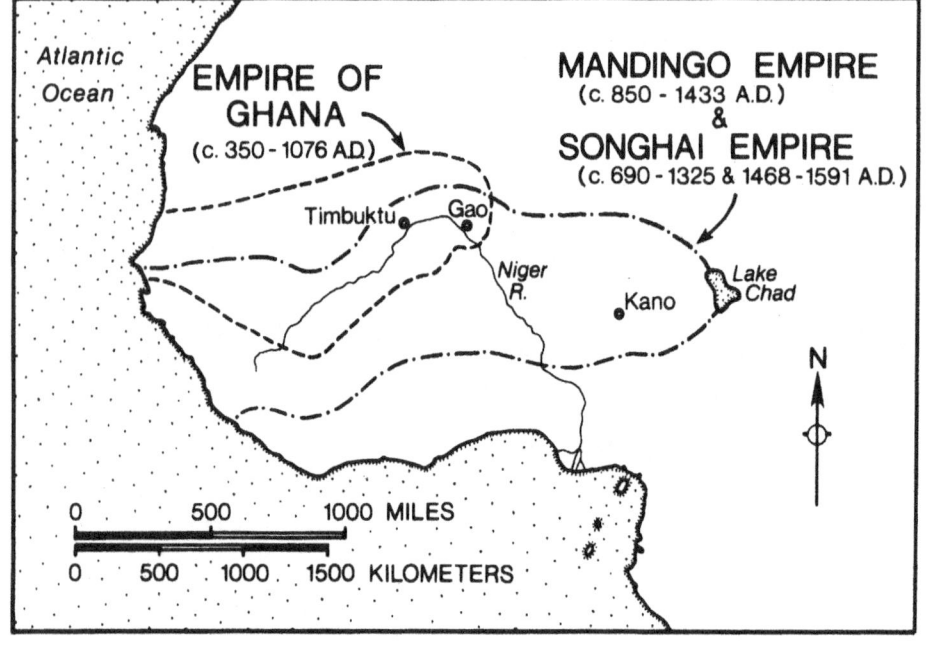

Historical Background

Royal Enclosure, 17th-Century, Gondar, Ethiopia — Photo by Judi Iranyi

cattle, the most important status symbol and source of wealth among the Tutsi. In the 15th century a Tutsi kingdom was founded near Kigali, which by the late 19th century had rounded out its borders to become a unified state whose Mwami (king) ruled through a centralized military bureaucracy. Local chiefs and military captains received tribute from Hutu communities.

Moving toward southern Africa, it becomes more difficult to trace with any precision the migrations of the Bantu people whose descendants live in countries such as Uganda, Malawi, and Zambia today. It is not possible to determine the exact time when the Nilotic groups came to northern Uganda. It seems that before the waves of Bantu migration arrived many centuries ago, the region around Malawi and Zambia was probably scantily settled. Restive Bantu peoples from the north expanded slowly southward from about the 10th century onward, sending successive waves of transients through this country on their journey to the south. Some stayed as permanent settlers, forming into distinct tribes based on common ancestry. As far south as Swaziland, it seems lands were thinly inhabited by a variety of Bantu groups who migrated to the area from what is now MozamIilue about 1750.

Regardless of the timing of the migrations, it iI clear the Bantu people emerged into rather powerful societies in what is now Uganda and the Congo River basin. The Kabaka, king of a Bantu state in Uganda, who was deposed in 1966, claimed to be the 37th monarch in an uninterrupted rule of a single family. Since there was a lack of the written word during the early centuries, our knowledge of the area's history is dependent on oral sources. In many societies specialists, like the *griots* of West Africa, memorized the history and traditions of their peoples and passed them on to their sons. Spoken and sung, very much lIke the epics of Homer, these histories provided inspiration and identity for families and communities. Today, they remain an important source for historians attempting to reconstruct an African past.

The Bantu and Sudanic groups expanded at a relatively rapid rate during the first millennium of the Christian era, perhaps as early as the 4th century A.D. There was an initial expansion of Bantu peoples into the eastern regions of Africa, into what is now Tanzania, Zambia and Zimbabwe. The imposing stone constructions at Great Zimbabwe, located in the southwestern part of the nation now bearing that name, suggest a wealthy and privileged elite in control of a powerful state. The site was the capital of a Bantu kingdom that stretched from eastern Zimbabwe over parts of Botswana, Mozambique, and South Africa. The first known permanent settlemeIt was established around the 11th century and building continued into the early 15th century. The large quantities of stone used to build on the site suggest control over considerable labor. The state's prosperity was based on trade in gold with Swahili speakers on the eastern African coasts. The Zimbabwe ruins, the only pre-European remnant of architecture found below the Sahara in Africa, are attributed to people known as the Monoma and are dated sometime between the 9th and 13th centuries, A.D. The Shona settled at an unknown time in the region; the Zulu and Barotse passed through during their migration to the south, and the Ndebele, a brancI of the Zulu that split off from Chaka Zulu, migrated to the area in the 19th century.

Zimbabwe is the Anglicized version of the Shona word *Dzimbahwe*, meaning stone houses—later understood as graves, or dwellings, of chiefs. The significance must run far deeper. Built in a gentle valley, it is believed to be a sacred place where a person could communicate with his ancestors. Stone huts attached to portions of the ruins indicate that it later became a home for the living. Zimbabwe was abandoned in the early 19th century when fierce Zulu warriors destroyed the Shona confederation.

The Bantu expansion farther southward continued at a slower rate. As it pushed more deeply into the south, it encountered Khoisan speaking pastoralists. When European sailing ships, mainly Dutch and English, began to make regular voyages around the Cape in the 16th century, they too encountered Khoisan pastoralists, eager to sell their surplus animals in exchange for iron, copper, tobacco, and beads. The original inhabitants of Botswana were the San people (Bushmen). Bantu peoples of central and east Africa migrated into the area in the 16th century; during the following centuries, intermarriage and population

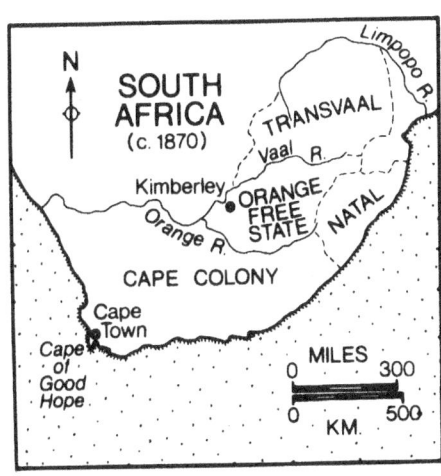

Historical Background

growth of the Bantus reduced the number of pure Bushmen to a handful. The Tswana remained split into hundreds of tribes and clans until they gathered together under Khama III, If of the powerful Bamangwato tribe; this was a loose federation which emerged in the last half of the 19th century. Bushmen groups also settled in what is now Namibia, followed by several Bantu tribes. Ovambos and Damara—Hereros became the most numerous groups.

EUROPEAN DISCOVERY AND EXPLORATION

The first exploration of the African coastline started early in the 15th century when Portuguese navigators reached Senegal, Guinea and the islands lying adjacent to the West African coast. By 1492, Fernão do Pó reached the island off the coast of Cameroon, which ultimately came to bear his name, translated into Spanish—Fernando Po (now Bioko Island of Equatorial Guinea). Fifteen years later, Bartolomeu Dias, usually referred to in English as Bartholomew Diaz, was blown by a storm in a southerly direction to the bottom of the continent. Turning eastward, he became the first European to navigate around the Cape of Good Hope.

In 1497, shortly after Columbus' second voyage to America, Vasco da Gama sailed around the African cape in search of a way to India, using the primitive navigation information supplied by Diaz. He stopped at Mozambique, Mombasa, and Malinda on the east coast of Africa, and was able to obtain the information necessary to proceed onward to India from the Arabs who were already established along the African coast.

With the arrival of increasing numbers of Portuguese vessels, quarrels with the Arab traders intensified. Francisco de Almeida was sent with a squadron to control Arab interference with Portuguese shipping; he took Mombasa in 1505 and ultimately demolished the Arab fleet in 1509, establishing Portuguese supremacy in the eastern coastal area of the continent.

In spite of this rather rapid navigational discovery, there was to be almost no penetration inland by the Europeans for more than three hundred years. With the exception of a Dutch settlement at the Cape of Good Hope, the sub-Sahara inland African regions remained the same dark, forbidding land that was first seen by the Portuguese. Following the precedent of the Arabs of East Africa, the Europeans started a lively West African trade in human cargo—slaves to perform the tasks of labor needed to colonize other parts of the world.

It was an easy task, with little exception, to acquire slaves along the so-called Gold and Ivory Coasts of West Africa. Anchoring their slave ships in natural harbors, the Europeans negotiated with the chiefs of the more powerful ethnic groups that lived inland. When a suitable price (in terms of value, almost nothing) was agreed upon, the men and sometimes the women of a weaker neighboring tribe would be brought to the coast in bondage after a brief skirmish. They were delivered as promised to the slave traders. It was in this manner that black Africans, tempted by their desires for the wealth offered by the white slave traders, sold the bodies of other black Africans into slavery. Africans were split in their views on trade; along with obvious resistance to plunder, some viewed themselves as disposing of undesirable social elements that they believed represented a threat to them, their families, and their tribe.

Packed shoulder to shoulder in quarters on the slave ships that were so cramped no one could stand, the cargo of humans, regarded as animals, was transported across the sea, usually to the Western Hemisphere. Those unable to survive were dumped overboard at suitable intervals following their death. The remaining survivors were sold at a handsome profit compared to the sum paid for them along

The Imperial Family of Ethiopia, 1930

Historical Background

the African coastline—a profit possible even if more than one-half of the ship's cargo died during the trip to the "new world." The fact that an individual slave had survived this journey was testimony to his hardiness and stamina as compared to his less-fortunate brethren who had perished. Arriving at a particular destination in the Western Hemisphere where he was sold, the slave was to begin a new and incredibly difficult life in a totally strange surrounding, where he would be judged by his physical ability to perform long, long hours of hard manual labor.

EARLY ETHIOPIAN–EUROPEAN CONTACT

In the late dark ages of Europe, a letter from a supposed Christian king of Africa received widespread acclaim as possibly being from an unknown people dating from Biblical times. Inspired by this, a Roman Catholic Pope dispatched several Dominican brothers in the 14th century to locate this Christian kingdom. The results of these efforts are not clear, but an Ethiopian emissary did reach Venice in 1402, arriving later at Lisbon and Rome. In turn, European kings and the Pope sent emissaries to Ethiopia, hoping to enlist help in the continuing "crusades" against the Islamic people of the Middle East and North Africa. This diplomatic effort continued unevenly for four centuries, and there was no other significant contact between this region of Africa and Europe during the passage of those years.

Increased penetration of Ethiopia by Europeans occurred in the 19th century. Although Ethiopia was not formally colonized by any European power, it became subject to a variety of "spheres of influence" of the British, French, and Italians in the latter part of the century. The succession to the Ethiopian throne was irregular—every time a king died there was usually a two- or three-way contest for the throne. The somewhat weak character of the nation was further complicated by periodic skirmishes and quarrels over territory with the neighboring Sudanese who were led by religious-political figures with the title *Mahdi*. The Somalis to the east, who were Islamic, also claimed Ethiopian territory, sometimes with the assistance of the French or the Italians. The borders of the kingdom changed countless times during this period.

The modern history of the country begins with the reign of Emperor Menelik II, the first monarch to choose that name since the reign of the son of Solomon and Sheba. It was under the second Menelik that Ethiopia began to have regular contact with the outside world. Although he was at first forced to acknowledge an Italian protectorate over Ethiopia, by 1896 he had consolidated his power sufficiently to send a military force that decisively defeated the Italians. Lidj Yassu, the grandson of Menelik II succeeded to the throne in 1913, but was deposed in 1916. Zauditu, Menelik's daughter, was installed as empress. Her cousin, Ras Tafari Makonnen ascended the throne in 1930, taking the name *Haile Selassie*, which means "the power of the Trinity" in Amharic.

THE ARABS AND OTTOMAN TURKS IN NORTH AFRICA

The Arab-Berber rulers of North Africa who came to power with the spread of Islam were known first as the Almavorid and subsequently the Almohad dynasty. Initially these Muslim kingdoms were characterized by a centralized power, but in the 13th to the 16th centuries there was gradual division into countless numbers of local rulers. Just as Christianity had split into numberless sects, so also had Islam been divided. Although the internal unity of the Arabs diminished, they were usually able to unite against non-Arabs on the infrequent occasions when outsiders threatened their territory.

The Muslim rulers of the Turkish Ottoman Empire gained control of most of Egypt and Libya at the beginning of the 16th century; their power in this area was not absolute since both regions quickly became no more than tribute-paying vassal states of the empire. The Ottoman rulers were almost continuously occupied in wars with Europe and had insufficient resources to bring North Africa directly within the Empire as was done in Syria and Iraq. It was not long before most of North Africa was within the Ottoman sphere.

With the exception of Egypt, the remainder of North Africa continued under the loose control of the Ottoman Empire until World War I. Egypt remained under the Ottomans until the invasion by Napoleon in 1798. The Turks sent Mohammed Ali from an Ottoman military family (probably of Albanian origin) as commander of forces opposing the French; together with the British under Lord Nelson, they were finally able to expel the invaders in the summer of 1799.

Mohammed Ali quickly established his personal rule in Egypt as an Ottoman *Pasha*. Although he and his successors were able to avoid absolute domination by the Ottoman rulers, in reality Egypt continued to be a tributary vassal of the Empire for about 75 years until the British influence became paramount. Khedive Ismail, grandson of Mohammed Ali, ruled as king but under the authority of the sultan and caliphs of the empire; he had received a European education for several years. The Suez Canal was under construction principally in order to provide the British with a shorter route to their possessions in India and the Far East, although the construction effort was in the name of a cooperative effort of most of the European nations and Egypt. In anticipation of the revenues expected from the canal which opened in 1869, Ismail borrowed large sums of money at extremely high interest rates from European banks. When he was unable to repay the loans on schedule, the British used this as a pretext to assert their authority in Egypt, initially with Egyptian cooperation, in order to bring areas bordering the Red Sea waterway and in the Sudan under control. By 1876 Khedive Ismail had been forced to sell all Egyptian shares in the Suez Canal, and Egypt was placed under the supervision of British and French financial controllers. That is considered the start of the colonial period in Egypt; although the Khedives continued to be the nominal power, they were little more than the instrumentality through which the British ruled.

EUROPEAN SETTLERS IN SOUTH AFRICA

Holland, seeking a food and fuel station for its ships sailing to the Dutch East Indies, established a small station on the Cape of Good Hope (near Africa's southernmost tip) in 1652. A fort was constructed to guard against the Hottentots and Bushmen found in small numbers in the area. This outpost developed rapidly, with the outlying farms worked by slaves brought from the East.

There was a slow expansion of this Dutch community into the interior, though such was not actively pursued by the Dutch East India Company. A substantial number of Huguenot religious refugees from France arrived in 1688, adopting the Dutch social patterns. Further settlement of the interior by the Dutch *Burghers* continued for the next hundred years, since there was little opposition to their desire for additional farmland. It was not until the Dutch had penetrated 200 miles to the northeast that they first encountered the Bantu people who were then in a process of migration from the southeast lake region of Africa. Bitter frontier warfare between the two groups of migratory people continued for the next 75 years, with large numbers of casualties on both sides.

The British took possession of Cape Town in 1795 in the name of the Prince of Orange, who then reigned in Holland and in England when his nation was overrun by the French. The British handed the area over to the Batavian Republic, a puppet state of France, in 1803 (all of this was a product of shifting alliances in Europe involving Napoleon's activities). But in 1806 the British returned; the Cape Colony was

7

Historical Background

officially ceded to it in 1814 and it became a Crown Colony. A substantial migration of British settlers arrived in the succeeding 30 years, which by 1834 caused widespread unrest among the Dutch farmers of the Eastern Cape, who resented British rule.

Led by hardy souls like Andries Pretorius, for whom Pretoria is named, the Voortrekkers, or pioneers, journeyed in covered wagons to the northeast, overcoming severe hardships and fighting fierce Bantu peoples. In 1839, they founded a new republic calledNatal but were later pushed even farther into the interior by the arrival of British military forces. Crossing the Drakensburg (Dragon Mountains), they went into the Orange Free State and Transvaal. In each area, a Boer republic was proclaimed. Thus, toward the end of the 19th century, there were two Boer republics and two British colonies in what is now the Republic of South Africa. Discovery of a huge 84-carat diamond on the banks of the Orange River by an African shepherd boy in 1869 set off the South African diamond rush. Fortune hunters from all over the world flocked to South Africa. In 1886 the world's largest goldfields were discovered on the Witwatersrand, adding to the influx of non-Boers. With these discoveries, South Africa was transformed. From an economic backwater, it became a major supplier of precious minerals to the world economy.

THE COLONIAL PERIOD

Queen Elizabeth inspects the Second Battalion of the King's African Riffles in British Gold Coast

This chapter details Africa during the colonial period, from settlement to the waves of decolonization in the 1960s and thereafter. The organization is according to the European country that colonized and ruled in each territory, reflecting the shared colonial Ies of many countries.

THE PORTUGUESE
Coastal West Africa: Portuguese Guinea

Inching their way down the African coast under the inspiration of Prince Henry—known as "The Navigator"—Portuguese mariners reached the Senegal coast around 1444; they established trading posts at the mouth of the Senegal River, on the island of Gorée, and at Rufisque, all in the region of present-day Senegal that would later come under French control. The Portuguese explored the coastline of Guinea as early as 1446, and this area remained a slave trading coastal region for about the next 450 years. Portuguese control of the area occurIly because it was permitted by the other, more aggressive colonial powers; Portuguese Guinea was deemed somewhat poor territory—what was left after the French and British had colonized West Africa.

The final boundaries of Portugal's African dominions were delineated only in 1905, after both Britain and France had appropriated parts of Portuguese Guinea. Penetration by the Portuguese into the continent's interior was negligible until about 1912; in the years prior the Portuguese had only sporadic control Ihe region, which was still theoretically a part of European Portugal. It was declared independent on September 10, 1974, with the mainland territory coming to be known as Guinea-Bissau and the islands off the Atlantic coast of Senegal becoming Cape Verde (Cabo Verde).

Equatorial West Africa: Angola and Cabinda, São Tomé e Príncipe

Portuguese navigators discovered the uninhabited islands of São Tomé and Príncipe in the late 15th century. By the mid-16th century, the colonial power had imported slaves and converted the islands into a major exporter of sugar. A slave-based plantation economy characterized the islands well into the 20th century, whereupon coffee and finally cocoa emerged with the decline of sugar exports. The rich volcanic soils of São Tomé proved especially well-suited to cocoa trees, and by 1908 the island had become the world's largest producer of cocoa. The crop was grown on extensive plantations called *roças*—owned by Portuguese companies or absentee landlords—that occupied all productive farmland. The *roças* system inevitably led to abusive treatment of African farm workers, and the history of the islands is filled with slave revolts and resistance to labor demands. Local dissatisfaction with working conditions on the plantations led to an outbreak of riots in 1953. In what became known as the "Batepa Massacre," over 1,000 *Forros* (the descendants of freed slaves) were shot by Portuguese troops for refusing to work the *roças*. The massacre is seen as the beginning of the nationalist movement in those islands. Príncipe is a small and poor island barely supporting the handful of descendants of freed slaves. These islands became independent on July 5, 1975, as The Democratic Republic of São Tomé and Príncipe.

Angola was first explored in 1482 by Diego Cao, who found this region of Africa controlled by the Bacongo people, led by a mighty King of the Congo. A scattering of Portuguese immigrants arrived during the following decades, but

The Colonial Period

they were restricted to the coastal areas by the native Africans as a result of a series of bloody clashes. The King was overthrown, but later reestablished by the Portuguese in 1570.

During the 17th and 18th centuries, Angola was the prime source for slaves deported to Brazil to work the huge coffee plantations in that Portuguese Latin American colony. The Portuguese also established an infamous penal colony there. During the late 19th and early 20th centuries, a multitude of treaties between Portugal and the British, French, Belgians, and Germans gradually fixed the boundaries of Angola and Cabinda (an enclave separated from Angola by the Congo River delta). The colony was given a form of internal autonomy in 1914, but this was strictly under White minority rule. Economic development under the Portuguese consisted of agriculture in the form of coffee and cotton production and mineral extraction based on diamonds in northeast Angola.

Periodic uprisings in Portuguese Africa occurred in tIth century. In its Africa policy, Portugal had almost exclusively favored the Portuguese immigrants and their descendants. After a protracted battle for independence that occasioned the fall of the dictator António de Oliveira Salazar in Lisbon, Angola too gained its independence in 1975. Having received Cuban assistance for a Soviet-backed rebel group, Angola became a Marxist state upon decolonization.

Southern Africa: Mozambique (Moçambique)

The Portuguese presence along the coast of Mozambique dates back to the voyage of Vasco da Gama in 1498. He found a number of trading posts that had been established by the Arabs, who offered little resistance to Portuguese construction of settlements and forts during the next century. These stations were intended more as an aid to Portuguese efforts in India and the Far East and were little more than stopping places for commercial vessels bound to and coming from those areas.

Shortly after Africa was partitioned at the Berlin Conference of 1885, both the French and Germans recognized Portuguese supremacy in Mozambique; Britain, preoccupied with its own colonial ambitions, largely ignored the Portuguese. Five years later, after expanding into neighboring Nyasaland (now Malawi), the British reached an agreement recognizing Portuguese claims. At the same time, the Mozambique Company was chartered to manage and invest in the colony, backed by substantial amounts of British capital. A massive uprising of Africans at the close of the 19th century hampered economic development in the territory. An early attempt was made in 1907 to establish a legislative council with membership restricted to White settlers in the colony.

As a result of the German defeat in World War II, the Portuguese added a small piece of German East Africa to Mozambique. The colonial period was relatively eventless between the two world wars, apart from the establishment of railroad lines from the port of Beira to Nyasaland (Malawi), Southern Rhodesia (Zimbabwe), Northern Rhodesia (Zambia) and as far as the southeastern province of Katanga (Shaba) in the Belgian Congo, now DR Congo. Though Portugal resisted attempts on the part of the native African majority to obtain independence during the postwar period, the revolution in Portugal itself brought independence (as with elsewhere in Portuguese Africa) in mid-1975.

THE BRITISH

Coastal West Africa: (The) Gambia

The claimant to the throne of Portugal granted English merchants, in exchange for an undisclosed sum of money, the exclusive right to trade with the people along the GambiI River. Queen Elizabeth I confirmed this sale by granting letters patent to English businIssmen, and in 1618 James I granted a charter to the Royal Adventurers of England, giving the company trade franchises in Gambia and in the Gold Coast.

At the same time the British merchants were developing trade in the river area, French interests were expanding in Senegal, and the Gambia River was the best route to the interior of Senegal. Hence, an intense rivalry arose between the two nations in this area of colonial Africa. Their disputes were partially resolved by the TrI of Versailles in 1783 which granted Gambia to the British but reserved for the French a small enclave across the water from Bathurst. There had been little exploration or penetration up the river to the interior until after 1860 when British explorers went inland and negotiated treaties with the local chief to obtain additional territory. The city of Bathurst remained a separate entity for the next two decades, sometimes administered from Sierra Leone, otherwise governed as a separate colony.

The present boundaries of The Gambia were delineated by a British-French

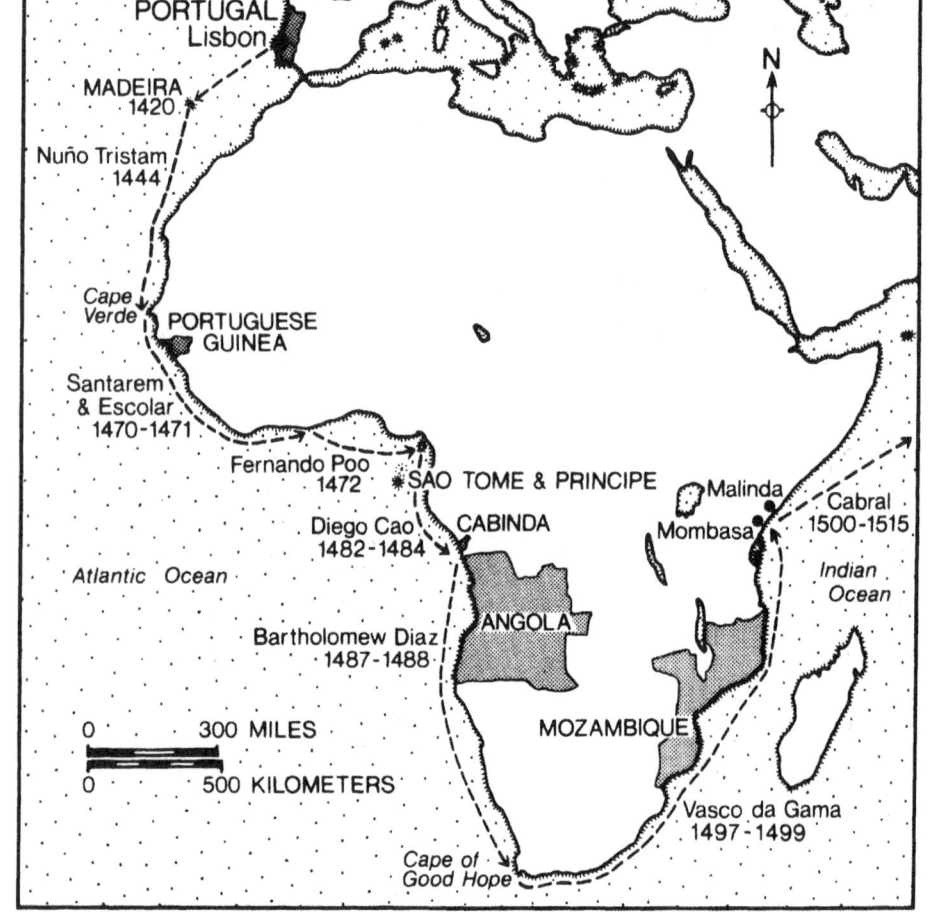

The Colonial Period

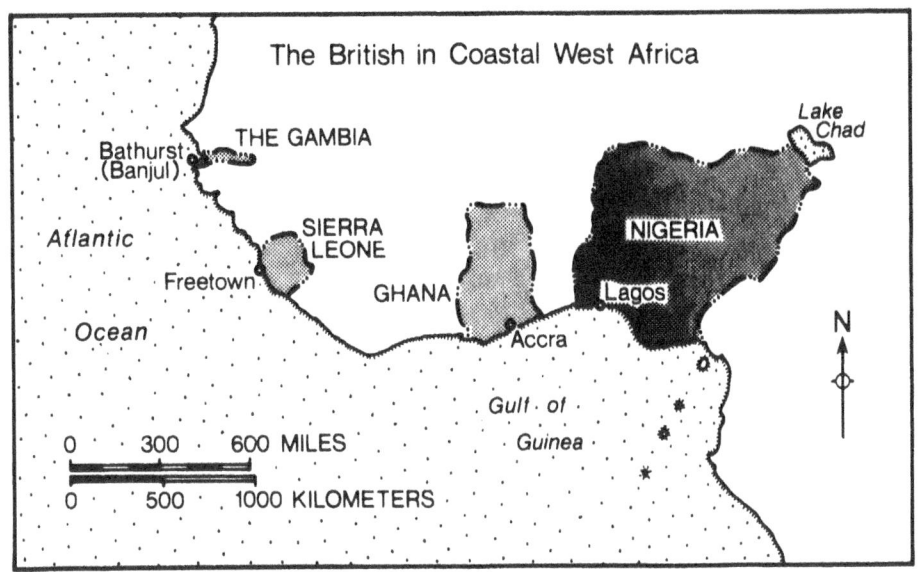

agreement in 1889. Although the exportation of slaves had been prohibited, it was not until 1906 that the local practice of slavery within Gambia was abolished by British decree. From the turn of the century until after World War II, there were few significant historical events in Gambia. Periodic efforts of the French to acquire control of the area were unsuccessful. With the exception of Bathurst, no Europeans here.

During World War II, Gambia not only served as an important naval base for military convoys but contributed soldiers who fought valiantly in the Burma campaign of General Stilwell against the Japanese. The postwar period saw the birth of nationalist sentiment in Gambia. The governor-general granted increasing powers of self-government to the Africans of the country and established an advisory council.

In the late 1950s, Gambian leadership gathered into four political parties: the Progressive Peoples Party; the United Party; the Democratic Congress Alliance; and the Gambian Congress Party. The leaders of these groups actually had few differences, except with regard to possible association or federation with Senegal. Ultimately, internal self-government was granted to The Gambia in 1963, followed by explorations of the possibility of union with Senegal. A UN recommendation for unity between the two was turned down.

Coastal West Africa: Sierra Leone

The people of the European mercantile powers, particularly in England, had felt increasing antipathy toward the principle of slavery by the end of the 18th century after the American Revolution. A Society for the Abolition of Slavery was formed under the Iership of Granville Sharp, which planned to establish a colony in Sierra Leone for the slaves that were to be set free. In 1788, the Temne King, Naimbana, and his subordinate chiefs, sold a portion of the coastal area of Sierra Leone to the Society, which was then settled initially by a group of 300 Africans freed as a reward for their service in the British armed forces in the battles of the American Revolution, joined by some former Jamaican slaves. The diminutive settlement was administered by the Sierra Leone Company and was immediately burdened by the task of fending off attacks from neighboring groups and French warships.

The area of Freetown, the capital, was originally sold to the British by the Temne ruler, King Tom, as a trading post. Controversial from the start, the sale provoked local skirmishes, which were not subdued until 1808 when Britain began using the harbor as a naval base in its operations against the slave trade, outlawed in 1807. British ships patrolling the Atlantic would capture slaving ships and return them to the Freetown base where the captives would be liberated. Between 1807 and 1864 more than 50,000 captives were resettled. Much like Americo-Liberians, these resettled former slaves formed a culture separate from hinterland peoples. They were a heterogeneous lot, coming from all over western Africa, but had in common the English language and Christianity. With British encouragement they were turned into a more homogenous Christian community, known as Creoles (or Krios), by the efforts of Protestant missionaries and the black pastors of Freetown churches.

There was little growth—the burden of defense, development and settlement proved to be severe for the Company—and in 1808 Sierra Leone was taken over by the British as a Crown Colony. The English Parliament had abolished slave trade in 1807. Freetown, the name of the Company settlement, became a base for a squadron of ships which sailed the shores of West Africa searching for and intercepting the privateer slave ships. The first slave ship found was quickly condemned in 1808; its human cargo, so recently abducted from other African areas, was released at Freetown. As further slave ships were captured in the succeeding years, thousands of Africans of great diversity in origin were released, most of whom elected to remain in Sierra Leone, settling largely in the areas closest to the coast.

Coastal Creoles had privileged access to European education in the Sierra Leone colony. Fourah Bay College was founded in 1846 by the Church Missionary Society to train teachers and missionaries. Given full degree-granting status by affiliation with Durham University in England only ten years later, Fourah Bay is sub-Saharan Africa's oldest university, proudly earning Freetown the title of "the Athens of Africa." Through access to university education, Creoles prospered, entered the professions, and qualified as doctors and lawyers, becoming an educated elite.

British influence gradually extended inland from the coastline, and in 1895 a protectorate was proclaimed over the colony's hinterland. In the protectorate, the British preference for indirect rule prevailed. Local chiefs ruled under the direction of district commissioners. It was not a system that encouraged the transformation of tradition. In general, the protectorate lagged behind the colony in social and economic development.

The period of the 19th century was one of gradual development by the British in Sierra Leone, with the establishment of a flourishing trade, schools, a college and Christian church missions. The former slaves, called Creoles, isolated from their native peoples and traditions, adopted many English customs which prevail today among their descendants, now numbering more than 125,000. In 1896, a British protectorate was established over the territory, Ih by then had definite boundaries with the adjacent French territories as a result of treaties signed in 1861.

The roads to democracy Ind independence were ones of relatively peaceful development of responsibility and unity among the Creoles and the inland groups, with the first elections for local office being held in 1924. Sir Milton Margai, a Creole leader, was appointed to successive offices in 1954 and the following years, becoming the first prime minister in 1960.

The Colonial Period

Kwame Nkrumah

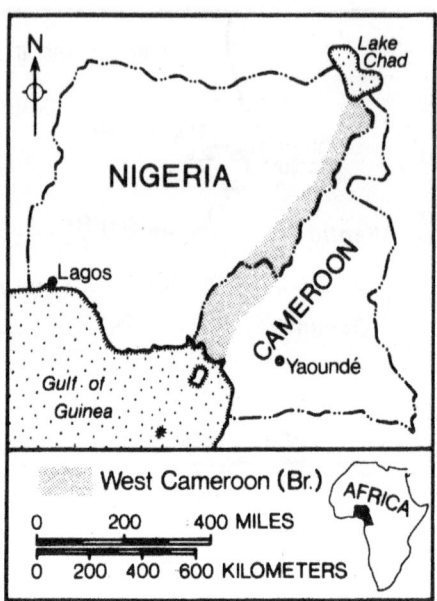

Coastal West Africa: Ghana (Gold Coast)

The Portuguese initially landed in Ghana as early as 1470; they were followed in 1553 by an English arrival on the shores of what was then known as the Gold Coast. English, Danish, Dutch, German, and Portuguese commercial interests controlled ports on the Gulf of Guinea during the next 250 years. By 1750, only the English, Dutch, and Danes remained.

Great Britain assumed control of English commercial settlements in 1821, negotiating treaties with the local chiefs in the southern areas in 1844. Shortly thereafter, the Danes and Dutch ceded their interests to the British. English forces fought a long series of battles against the Asante of the interior; there were four major campaigns in which the British subdued them: 1824–27, 1873–74, 1893–94 and 1895–96. It was only in 1901 that colonial authority spread through the entire country. After seizing Togoland (Togo) from the Germans during World War I, the British administered it from Accra. With the exception of the commercial activity in the south coastal area, there was little economic development during the colonial period.

Following World War II, there was a sharp rise of nationalism among the Africans of higher education in Gold Coast, as the colony was called. The United Gold Coast Convention, led by J. B. Danquah, exerted continuous pressure for autonomy and independence. Political developments quickly came to revolve around one person: Kwame Nkrumah. After receiving college educations in the United States and Great Britain, obtaining several degrees in advanced courses of study, he returned to the Gold Coast from England in 1947. As Secretary of the UGCC, he assisted in promoting riots and strikes in early 1948. Both he and Danquah were exiled to a remote northern village by the British Governor; the British accused Nkrumah of being a communist.

Under continuing pressure, the British in 1949 promulgated a new constitution and released the exiled leaders. Nkrumah, restless under the leadership of Danquah, formed his own political party, the Convention Peoples Party (CPP). Further civil disobedience under Nkrumah's leadership resulted in his arrest, conviction, and sentence to a two-year jail term. Constitutional reforms in 1951 provided for election of a greater number of Africans to a legislative council and Nkrumah was freed from prison to head the new government.

A new constitution of 1954 established a cabinet composed entirely of African representatives. The subsequent elections again resulted in a majority for the *CPP*. Two years later, Nkrumah, as prime minister, demanded independence. The British held new elections in 1956, which perpetuated the majority of the *CPP* (71 out of 104 seats). Independence was declared in 1957.

Central West Africa: Nigeria

The Portuguese were also the first explorers to land at Nigeria in 1472. For the next 300 years, traders from all nations called briefly in Nigeria, but there was no settlement. The principal purpose of their visits was to obtain human cargo to work in the colonies of the Western Hemisphere. The hundreds of Nigerian tribes periodically attacked each other, and the victor carried off the defeated to be sold into slavery for never more than the equivalent of $10.00 each. Transported across the ocean, they brought prices of up to $300.00. Slavery was not outlawed internally in Nigeria until 1901.

British penetration into the interior of Nigeria following the Napoleonic wars was slow. The British annexed coastal Lagos in 1861 as part of its continuing efforts to suppress the slave trade, but they were unwilling to incur the costs of maintaining an administration in Nigeria. To keep costs down, Lagos was first administered from Sierra Leone. Only in 1886 did Lagos become a separate colony. Later, two other protectorates were declared, one over the Oil Rivers and the other over the Lagos hinterland. In 1894 both entities were merged into the Niger Coast Protectorate. Twenty-three years later, the Niger River Delta was established as a British Protectorate and British influence in Nigeria was formally recognized at the conference of European powers at Berlin in 1885. The British continued to expand in Nigeria through the Royal Niger Company, but in 1900 the territory came under the control of the British Colonial Office.

The people of northern Nigeria were believers in Islam; the Hausa and Fulani, as they are known, were feudally governed by a variety of rulers known as emirs (also spelled *amirs*). In the north the first British High Commissioner, Frederick Lugard, set about controlling the emirs. Some were deposed, some defeated in battle, and others collaborated. By 1903, Lugard's conquest of the emirates was complete. Though defeated, the emirates were not dismantled. To spare the British treasury administrative costs, Lugard developed a policy of "indirect rule," relying on existing administrative structures of the emirates. Much of the north's traditional feudal structure was thus maintained. In 1914, northern and southern administrative areas were consolidated into Nigeria, and the difficult tasks of balancing regional interests and identities would dominate Nigerian colonial history.

Even after penetrating into areas of Nigeria, the British had difficulty in

The Colonial Period

controlling the people; there were widespread disturbances and revolts in southern Nigeria in 1904 and an uprising in the Sokoto region of northern Nigeria in 1906. It was not until 1914 that northern Nigeria was fully brought under control, at which time the Colony and Protectorate of Nigeria was formally established. Shortly after World War I, African legislators were included in the Council governing Lagos and southern Nigeria. The British enlarged tin mines on the Jos Plateau and improved the roads, schools and port facilities of Nigeria during the succeeding decades. Following World War II, the Colonial Office adopted successive constitutions which expanded African participation in Nigerian administration on a representative, federal basis. Three political parties evolved on a regional basis: the Nigerian Peoples Congress (North), the National Convention of Nigerian Citizens (Southeast) and the Nigerian National Democratic Party (Southwest). The latter two of these parties pressed energetically for full independence, but the Nigerian Peoples Congress advocated a lesser nationalistic outlook because it feared domination by a combination of the other two parties.

Discussions were held in London in 1957, at which time there were demands by 15 ethnic groups that they become individual and independent nations within the territory of Nigeria. The British resisted these demands and established a central parliamentary government with many powers reserved to the individual provinces; independence was granted in 1960.

Central West Africa: Cameroons

The British had early colonial ambitions in Cameroon and dispatched an emissary to negotiate treaties with the local chieftain in 1884. He arrived on the coast five days too late—the German representative had already concluded agreements with the coastal people, and Cameroon was to remain a German colony until 1916.

The British and French waged a protracted campaign against the German forces in Cameroon during the First World War. The fighting ended with the surrender of the Germans in 1916 (in Cameroon) and under the Treaty of Versailles Britain was awarded the smaller West Cameroon territory and France obtained East Cameroon. The fact that there were two colonies where there had been one gave rise to the plural name *Cameroons* for the area, creating confusion, which persisted after they were again joined together in 1961.

The British held a mandate over its part from the League of Nations and subsequently under a trusteeship from the United Nations. Because of the language difference between the colonial powers of the two countries, there was wide divergence of opinion among the people of West Cameroon as to the political future of the territory in the late 1950s. The British conducted a plebiscite under UN supervision in 1961 to determine whether the people of West Cameroon desired to become a part of the English-speaking Nigeria to the northwest, or to join the French-speaking East Cameroon in a federation. Rather than conduct the plebiscite on the basis of all votes cast in the entire territory, it was decided to count the votes of the northern and southern portions separately. The North voted to become part of Nigeria and the South opted for federation with the former French Cameroon. The voting procedure was strongly opposed by East Cameroon, with considerable numbers of Cameroonians believing that the vote should have been counted as a whole. Had this been done, it seems certain no part of West Cameroon would have merged into Nigeria.

South Africa

The complex history of South Africa's colonial period is addressed in detail in the chapter on that country. In addition, however, the British maintained continuous control over three territories in the South African orbit: Botswana (or Bechuanaland, pronounced Beh-*kwa*-na-land), Lesotho (called Basutoland, pronounced Ba-*soo*-toe-land) and Swaziland (*Swah*-zee-land). During the colonial period, which ended in 1967–68, all three were economically dependent upon what is now the Republic of South Africa, though they were colonies of Great Britain.

Southern Africa: Botswana (formerly Bechuanaland)

The Tswana, as the majority of the people of Botswana are called, remained split into hundreds of tribes and communities until Khama I, Chief of the powerful Bamangwato tribe, consolidated them into a loosely constituted group in the last half of the 19th century. As the *Boers* of South Africa were pushed northward from the Cape by the British, they attempted to penetrate into what is now Botswana, and battles erupted between the two peoples. Khama I, a Christianized native, appealed to the British for assistance, and the country was proclaimed to be under British protection. Khama I reigned over the loosely united country until his death at the age of 93 in 1923, and was succeeded by his son, Sekgoma, who died three years later in 1926.

The British did little more than maintain peace in Bechuanaland during the period of the protectorate, although in later years they provided an annual grant to assist the colony's economy. In 1920 they set up two advisory councils—one for the native African people and one for the European settlers and their descendants who had come in small number to the area. Later, in 1934, they established a constitution which granted authority to the local chieftains and native courts.

The native rule of the Bamangwato passed to Seretse Khama, then the four-year-old son of Sekgoma, under the regency of Tshekedi Khama, brother of the dead ruler. The British had difficulty in controlling Tshekedi—at one time he was deposed as regent for a short time after having had a Briton flogged. Seretse Khama left for England in 1945 to pursue higher education; while studying law he met a young English woman, Ruth Williams, and married her. This interracial marriage of 1949 infuriated the white population of South Africa, and the embarrassed British Government removed Seretse Khama from office and forced him to remain in England until 1956.

After obtaining a renunciation of his chieftainship, the British permitted him to return to Bechuanaland in 1956 as "Mr. Khama." Many of the lesser chiefs opposed his return, as did his uncle, Tshekedi. The British established a Legislative Council in 1958 composed of 35 members equally divided between the races to advise and consent to the acts of the British High Commissioner, who was also executive authority in Swaziland, Basutoland and Ambassador of Great Britain to South Africa. Tshekedi was removed as regent-chief in 1959; the avowed purpose of establishing the council was to prepare Bechuanaland for independence.

Political parties emerged rapidly after the first council meetings—K. T. Motsete formed the Bechuanaland People's Party in 1960, demanding immediate independence and removal of political power from the white settlers. The British tacitly permitted Seretse Khama to enter politics because of his popularity, which had grown since his return from exile. He formed the Bechuanaland Democratic Party, with membership from both races, and advocated a policy of non-racism in government, a move toward internal self-government by 1965 and independence as soon thereafter as possible.

The British reviewed the status of Bechuanaland in 1963 and established a new constitution in consultation with the representatives of the political parties. The first elections in 1965 under the new system were won by Khama's Democratic Party and he was named prime minister. Further negotiations led to an agreement for full independence which became effective on September 20, 1966; Bechuanaland took the name Botswana—land of the Tswana.

The Colonial Period

Seretse Khama and his wife shortly before Botswana's independence

Southern Africa: Lesotho (formerly Basutoland)

The people of what is now Lesotho, although composed almost entirely of what are now referred to as South Sotho people, were organized in a multitude of subgroups and tribes in the early 19th century. Raids from neighboring Zulus and Matabeles had depleted their number, and the remainder were gathered together in a loosely united kingdom by Moshoeshoe I, a chieftain from the northern region of Lesotho. The land was mountainous, hilly, and generally regarded as unsuited for farming by *Boer* descendants of the original settlers of South Africa who had been driven from the Cape region into the interior of South Africa by British pressures.

But pressures for more land led to a 12-year war between the whites of the Orange Free State and the Sothos between 1856 and 1868, which weakened the latter; they lost a substantial portion of their territory, still referred to as the "Conquered Territory." Facing total defeat, the Sothos appealed to the British for protection in 1868. The land area of the protectorate was poorly defined; the British resisted further *Boer* expansion but had difficulty establishing control in what was considered a remote (from the Cape) land.

Basutoland was annexed to the British Cape Colony in 1871, an act which was resented by the Basutos at the time because the English were just as eager for expansion in southern Africa as were the *Boers*. The unstable union was plagued by disturbances within Basutoland; the British, faced with a state of near anarchy among the people, placed the colony directly under the control of Her Majesty's Government in 1884. The British High Commissioners spent most of their time in Basutoland settling tribal differences and settling the ever-contentious question of who was Paramount Chief; since the reign of Moshoeshoe I the land had been governed by about 22 lesser chiefs, who were in turn superior to approximately 2,000 minor chieftains. Little was done to improve and modernize the lives of the people living in the remote wilderness of the highlands.

The Basutoland Council was informally constituted in 1903 to provide direction in internal matters, and it was recognized officially by the British in 1910 as a legislative body to be consulted on internal affairs of the colony. The Council requested further reform in 1955 in order that its decisions might be conclusive on all internal questions. After a period of negotiation, a revised constitution was adopted in 1959, to take effect the following year, which granted the wishes of the Legislative Council.

Pressures for total independence slowly gathered momentum, and Britain decided on a course of action in early 1965. Elections were held in April of that year to determine the popular will with respect to leadership of the colony. The Basutoland National Party of then-moderate Chief Leabua Jonathan gained 31 of the 60 parliamentary seats. The opposition party, the Panafricanist Congress Party, led by Ntsu Mokhele, a leftist, received 25 seats, and the right-wing Maramatlou Freedom Party, which supported the aspirations for power of Moshoeshoe II, hereditary Paramount Chieftain, won 4 seats. One delegate from the Maramatlou party defected to the National Party shortly after the election. Although Chief Leabua Jonathan, who conducted his campaign from a helicopter provided by the Republic of South Africa, had received a minority of 44% of the popular vote, he negotiated for independence with the British in London.

An independence agreement was reached on June 18, 1966, whereby Basutoland was to become independent and was to be called *Lesotho*, indicating the lowlands of the Sotho—the area they traditionally occupied.

Southern Africa: Swaziland (Eswatini)

The Swazis came to their present territory during one of the many Bantu migrations southward through Africa. In the 18th century, Zulu raids into their country forced the tribal chieftain of Mawati to seek British assistance through the Agent General in Natal, who mediated a peaceful relationship between the two groups. For a time, the Transvaal Republic (now a province of South Africa) protected and administered Swaziland. After the *Boer War* (see the Republic of South Africa), control of the territory passed to the British. In 1907, administration of Swaziland was charged to the British High Commissioner for South Africa. A proclamation was issued in 1944 by the Commissioner which recognized the Paramount Chief and Council as native authority for internal matters.

The British agreed in 1967 that Swaziland was to be independent after September 6, 1968. Internal self-government was established in April 1967 and elections were held shortly thereafter. The Imbokodvo National Movement (also known as The Grindstone Movement), led by Prince Makhosini Dlamini, won all 24 seats in the National Assembly. King Sobhuza II ascended the throne at the time of independence. Dr. Ambrose Zwane, leader of the opposition Ngwane

The Colonial Period

Nyasaland (Malawi) into the Federation of Rhodesia and Nyasaland in 1953, but this crumbled because of the overwhelming opposition of the African majorities in what are now Zambia and Malawi. Although there were earlier visits by traders and missionaries, the first significant penetration of Malawi was by the intrepid Scotch missionary, Dr. David Livingstone, on September 15, 1859. For almost 15 years, he explored southeastern Africa to proselytize and bring Christianity to the native people. Formal annexation of the area occurred in 1883 when a representative of the British government accredited to the kings and chief of central Africa appeared and negotiated treaties with them. In reality, this was no more than an effort to exclude Portugal and Germany from the area. The British energetically andIly ended slave trade of Arab raiders.

During the colonial period, particularly after the discovery of gold and diamonds in South Africa and copper in Rhodesia (Northern), the men usually spent several years working in the mines of those territories, bringing their limited wages back home toIland. Because of this, and the prevalence of the Christian faith among the people, there was no rapid surge of nationalism. This changed in 1953 when Nyasaland was joined into the Federation of Rhodesia and Nyasaland—the Nyasas greatly feared the white supremacy movements that were strong in the other two members of the federation. In an eIo suppress opposition, the British tried to arrest the chief of the Angoni tribe who advocated a passive resistance to the federation. The attempted arrest was unsuccessful but was the source of an even higher level of mistrust of the British and other white people by the Nyasas. There was a gradual transition to internal autonomy from 1961 to 1963Ied upon elections in which the Malawi Congress Party of Dr. Hastings Kamuzu Banda won an overwhelming victory. The despiIed federatIon was dissolved in 1963 and independence was granted the following year.

East Africa: Kenya, Uganda, Tanzania (Tanganyika & Zanzibar), and the Indian Ocean

The first British efforts in East Africa occurred in 1823 when Admiral William Owen entered the coastal area, supposedly in an attempt to end the Arab slave trade that had been going on for centuries along the coast. In theory, the Sultan of Muscat on the Arabian coast was the ruler of the region, and his authority was exercised by a viceroy (Sayyid) on the island of Zanzibar. The British, using a combination of threats and treaties, gradually established their control about the turn of the century.

National Liberation Council, pressed charges that the elections were rigged before the Organization of African Unity and in the UN. Both organizations listened but did nothing.

Southern Africa: Rhodesia, Zambia, Malawi

A steady, but small procession of traders and missionaries of many European nations established themselves in Mozambique after the Portuguese in the 16th century, yet there was no real colonial effort until almost 400 years later, when diamonds and gold were discovered in the former *Boer* states of South Africa, Transvaal, and Orange Free State. Transvaal had been successful in maintaining its independence. In an effort to surround the people of Dutch ancestry, the British commissioned the British South Africa Company in 1889, giving it all rights to an area north of Transvaal without limit.

Under the leadership of Cecil Rhodes, the town of Salisbury was founded in 1890 in what was then known as Mashonaland, inhabited by Matabele (Bantu) people; the city would later come to be known as Harare. Leander Jameson, a close friend of Rhodes, was appointed administrator of the thinly settled area which included what is now Zambia and the name Rhodesia was adopted in 1895. Since the most valuable of the natural resources of this part of Africa were then believed to be only in South Africa, the settlement of Rhodesia was slow. For decades, Salisbury was a rural town with wooden sidewalks and was the only urban settlement in what was a vast agricultural area. In the early 20th century, Zambia was recognized as a distinct state called Northern Rhodesia; both areas were granted full internal autonomy in 1923, when Rhodesia was declared to be a Crown Colony instead of the property of the British South Africa Company.

The white Rhodesians were few in number, but steadily grew into an industrious, conservative society. The African people, with the exception of a few missionary efforts, were largely ignored, and restricted to the poorer lands in the ensuing decades. Salisbury emerged as a cosmopolitan and large city by the end of World War II, which was the beginning of a period of migration of more thousands of white Europeans—principally British—to Rhodesia.

The African people of Rhodesia became increasingly restless after 1960 as many colonies of Africa were granted independence under African leadership, but the resulting limited political effort was unsuccessful because of the power of the white minority which was firmly established. Southern Rhodesia was joined with Northern Rhodesia (Zambia) and

The Colonial Period

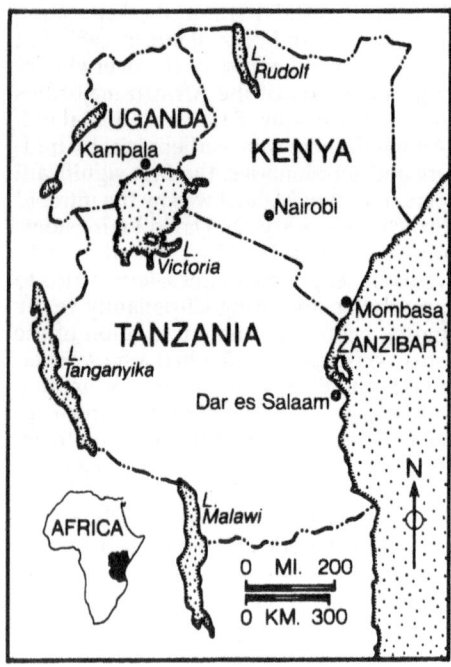

Jomo Kenyatta

German exploration and annexation of Tanganyika and part of southern Uganda from 1878 to 1885, in turn, aroused the interest of the British in Kenya and Uganda. The Sultan of Zanzibar granted the British East Africa Company a 50-year lease of what is now Kenya in 1887; this in turn was changed to the East Africa Protectorate, governed by a commissioner, by the British government in 1895.

The last quarter of the 19th century in the eastern region of Africa was turbulent. There were efforts by both the Britisld Germans to enter Uganda, which was divided into four semi-autonomous kingdoms—Buganda, Busoga, Butoro, and Bunyoro, of which Buganda was the most powerful. King Mwanga of Buganda, who reigned from 1884 until he was captured and exiled in 1899, tried to play the British off against the Germans by alternating his allegiance. In addition to this swirl of activity on behalf of Germany and Great Britain, there were roving remnants of Arab slave traders and religious conflicts involving and between Catholic and Protestant missionaries and believers, as well as those of Islamic faith.

The borders of this region were adjusted countless times, and not generally along the lines of actual colonial power. By a process of bargaining and trading, accompanied by line-drawing, particularly in Berlin in 1885, the eventual boundaries of the German, British, and Portuguese territories, as well as those of King Leopold of Belgium were fixed. The almost straight line that now separates Kenya and Tanzania cuts almost through the center of the territory inhabited historically by the Masai people.

The British encouraged immigration of white settlers to Kenya after the turn of the century, and they established immense plantations in the most select parts of the colony. The tribes people of Kenya, particularly large numbers of the Kikuyu (referred to as "kooks" by the British) were relegated to the poorer, tsetse-fly-infested farmlands. White immigrants entered Uganda only in very small numbers.

At the start of World War I, 300,000 British, South African, and colonial Indian troops invaded German East Africa, renamed Tanganyika following the establishment of British control after the war. A force of slightly more than 200 German officers, commanding native troops numbering between 2,500 and 4,000 fended off the massive force for four years under the brilliant leadership of General Paul Von Lettow-Vorbeck. After the war, the British sent the German settlers from Tanganyika, confiscating their lands; a small number were permitted to return within a few years. Kenya was completely dominated by the white farmers and a substantial number of Indians who were descendants of workers brought in to complete a railroad between Nairobi and Mombasa, which had opened in 1895. Uganda was governed through the local kings, and the cultivation of cotton and coffee quickly rose to be the source of the leading exports, permitting Uganda to become the richest British colony in Africa.

Government in Kenya was through a variety of commissioners sent from Britain; it was at a relatively late date that local councils were permitted, and initially even these consisted of people appointed by the commissioners. The white farmers of Kenya requested a regional council for Kenya, Uganda and Tanganyika as early as 1926, but were turned down since it was felt that this was merely an effort of theirs to preserve and extend their power, which excluded the African majority from sharing in government.

Following World War II, the ability of the British to rule effectively in Kenya and Uganda sharply decreased. The population of Kenya was stratified into three groups: the rich, landowning white (a small minority), the Indian and Arab merchant class, and (at the bottom) the huge majority of Africans. The African population had doubled in 25 years, creating tremendous pressure for expansion into the lands exclusively held by white farmers. The white population, instead of recognizing the needs of the Africans, instituted progressively more strict and severe laws directed against the majority.

From the mid-19th century, British interest in the region grew and in 1895 Kenya was declared a protectorate. Railroad construction from the port of Mombassa to Lake Victoria encouraged development of trade and settlement, and in 1920 Kenya became a crown colony administered by a British governor.

Africans were not permitted representation on the colony's legislative council, so developed their own pressure groups. Most active in these developments were members of the Kikuyu tribe, who supplied the bulk of labor used on European farms. By the 1930s, there were several organizations to represent the tribe's grievances, among which were low wages and exclusion from profitable coffee growing.

Anti-British Africans formed a terrorist organization, the *Mau Mau*, to achieve their goals. Dreadful brutality became commonplace. The *Mau Mau* attacked whites and mercilessly slaughtered those of their own people who were servile to and worked for the whites. White retaliation was equally brutal. Jomo Kenyatta, the political leader of the majority of African people, educated in Europe, was arrested, tried and convicted for participating in the *Mau Mau* conspiracy and was sentenced to seven years in jail. In 1957, Kenya erupted in a total state of civil anarchy, as *Mau Mau* terrorism had spread into almost every area of the country. Africans suspected of participating in this secret society were shot on the spot by Whites. Even long-trusted house servants had by this time joined the secret organization. It became increasingly apparent that in order to bring stability to Kenya, the British would have to accede to the demands of the *Mau Mau*. Most of the British farmers departed, and in 1960 an agreement was reached in London that gave the Africans a majority in the Legislative Council.

The Colonial Period

Dissension and political quarrels among the Africans in Kenya retarded the goal of full independence. Kenyatta, released from jail, headed the Kenya-African National Union (KANU), which represented the larger tribes of the country. The Kenya African Democratic Union drew its support from the many smaller tribes. After prolonged discussion in London, a complicated constitution was adopted providing for a loose, federal system of government.

The election conducted in May 1963 resulted in an overwhelming victory for KANU. Under pressure from the majority, the constitution was amended to strengthen the authority of the central government. The British recognized the independence of Kenya in December 1963.

Uganda was not without disturbance during the postwar period, although not as bloody as that in Kenya. In 1953, with the intent of establishing a central government, the British commissioner informed the kabaka (king) of Buganda that there were to be reforms in administration which would undermine his authority. Edward Mutesa II, the kabaka, adamantly refused to accept these regulations and he forthwith was dismissed as king and put on a plane for London. The Buganda people regarded this as nothing short of an outrage. The British had to constitute a form of martial law to control the people throughout Uganda, and the economy suffered a steep decline.

The British attempted to solve this state of affairs by proposing that the *Lukiko*, the Ugandan tribal assembly, be permitted to vote on whether a new king should be chosen; the Assembly would not listen to the proposal. Kabaka Edward Mutesa was subsequently returned and the British set up a ministerial system of government, increasing African membership in the Legislative Council. The United Kingdom of Uganda was granted full independence in October 1962.

The movement toward independence was relatively tranquil in Tanzania (Tanganyika). The British had received a mandate from the League of Nations to administer the former German colony. This continued under a UN trusteeship. A gradual development of internal self-government was undertaken by the British, starting with a Legislative Council appointed by the government in 1926. Subsequent elections were held in 1958 and again in 1960, the latter of which was won by the Tanganyikan African National Union of Julius Nyerere, who was president of Tanzania until 1985. He retired that year, but is still a figure of power in the country. Full independence was granted in December 1961.

Britain also seized several French possessions in the Indian Ocean and was the colonial power for Mauritius and the Seychelles for most of the 19th and 20th centuries. On the Seychelles, the abolition of slavery and the shift to small-scale agricultural production in the 19th century triggered an influx of Asians—Chinese, Indians, and Malays. Over the years the populations intermarried, producing the islands' present mixed population, in which descendants of former slaves have remained an underclass.

Northeast Africa: Egypt and the Sudan

During the first half of the 19th century, interest in European technology and education grew rapidly in Egypt, ruled by the khedives (kings) nominally subject to the control of the Turkish Ottoman Empire's sultan. The basis for the construction of the Suez Canal lay in this interest, coupled with British and French desires for a shorter route to India and the Far East.

After negotiation with Khedive Ismail, European powers, working through their financial institutions, began construction of the canal, which was completed and opened amid great fanfare in 1869 with a multitude of European royalty present; they later heard the first performance of the opera *Aida*, by Giuseppe Verdi, erroneously said to have been written for the occasion. Egypt had been enriched by the demand for cotton created by the United States Civil War but had also heavily borrowed at high interest rates to help finance the construction of the canal. From 1870 to 1883, the British succeeded in conquering most of the Sudan, penetrating as far as Uganda, supposedly in partnership with Egypt. The prime interest initially in this area was to end the oppressive slave trade that was firmly entrenched.

A financial crisis compelled the khedive to sell all of the Egyptian shares in the Suez Canal to Great Britain in 1876, giving the British a majority interest. Further financial deficits and inability to repay European loans were the basis of increasing British control of Egypt. The khedives rapidly became figurehead kings, totally subject to British control, which led to an early rise of Egyptian nationalist desires. An army revolt, coupled with a popular nationalist uprising was the excuse used to invade Egypt, and absolute British control of the region resulted.

Although the khedives were retained as the nominal rulers, their power quickly became almost nonexistent in the face of growing pressures of the nationalist leaders. Eventually, a scheme of rule was devised under the so-called Organic Law which included a legislative council and cabinet with advisory powers. The khedive was controlled by a "Resident and Consul-General" of the British; all high Egyptian ministers had a British "advisor."

In the Sudan, Mohammed Ahmed, a leader known as Mahdi, quickly achieved wide popularity following 1880—in addition to his political military support, he was regarded by his followers, the dervishes, as a modern-day prophet of Islam. By 1884, he had all but completely demolished British and Egyptian forces within the territory. An expedition sent by the British offered the Mahdi some concessions, which were flatly rejected; the Mahdi immediately laid siege to Khartoum, where General Charles Gordon and his forces were located.

After several months, the Mahdi entered the city and the British were slaughtered; General Gordon was impaled by a dervish spear. A relief force sent to help arrived in Khartoum three days later but was greeted only by smoking rubble and the stench of death. Fearful of also being wiped out by the fanatical Sudanese, the rescue force beat a hasty retreat. The control of the Sudan remained with the Mahdi and his successor for ten years. The British, faced with the growing French expansion on the western side of the Nile River in the Sudan, sent a large force under General Sir Horatio Hubert Kitchener to reconquer the territory in 1896–98. The Mahdi had died, and the dervishes were disorganized; in the ensuing battle almost 10,000 Sudanese lost their lives and were only able to claim that of 50 British and Egyptians in return. One of the young

The Colonial Period

King Farouk at 16 in 1936

Gemal Abdel Nasser

lieutenants in the British force was none other than Winston Churchill, destined to lead Britain through World War II.

Kitchener was later entitled Lord Kitchener of Khartoum in recognition of his leadership. Entering Khartoum, he emptied the revered tomb of the original Mahdi and dumped the corpse into the river, and then quickly captured and killed the *Khalifa*, successor of the Mahdi. Kitchener marched rapidly southward, meeting the French at Fashoda (now Kodak) in an effort to reassert British power. The result was the Fashoda Crisis (discussed under *The French*) that was finally ended by agreement on areas of control which roughly defined the boundaries between what is now the Sudan, Central African Republic, and Chad.

Great Britain and Egypt set up a joint administration of the Sudan; although they were nominally equal partners, the British were in fact the dominant power. After World War I, the British had to institute increasingly harsh measures to maintain their control in Egypt and the so-called Anglo-Egyptian Sudan. At the start of World War I, the Ottomans in Turkey demonstrated sympathy for the German cause, and as a result, the British declared war against them. Although the Ottoman control in Egypt was little more than imaginary, the British used the war as a pretext to proclaim a protectorate status over Egypt, which aroused a great deal of local opposition. The Nationalist, or Wafd Party, quickly became dominant, opposing both the British and the khedives.

A multitude of successive administrations under a semidemocratic constitution ruled following World War I. Ahmed Fuad, the khedive, repeatedly dissolved nationalist governments and announced new elections, in all of which the nationalists scored tremendous victories and returned to power. The nationalist movement was not genuinely popular, however; its primary support came from the wealthy, land-owning *pashas* who had become established during the Ottoman era. The protectorate status was withdrawn in 1922 and Egypt achieved internal autonomy as a result of Wafd efforts.

There were some efforts at economic development during the period between the two world wars based upon the opening of dams along the Nile to partially control the age-old flood and drought cycle of the river. Constitutional reforms gave increasing power to the Egyptian *pashas*. The worldwide depression of the 1930s further lessened British control, and upon the death of King Fuad I in 1936, his handsome 16-year-old son, Farouk, came to power. Colorful and pleasure seeking, he was at first very popular. With the consent of the British and other European powers, Egypt became nominally independent in 1936 and was admitted to the League of Nations a year later. British military control was limited to the Suez Canal area.

The king dissolved the *Wafd* government in 1938, and the election that followed was a complete victory for the new pro-king party. Initially arming itself for World War II, Egypt maintained a passive neutrality during the conflict, although it was the scene of battles between the Allied and Axis powers.

Following World War II, the Egyptians sought to end the last vestiges of British domination. Weakened by the war, England was in no position to offer opposition to this demand. The picture was further complicated by the presence of the new state of Israel, carved out of a portion of Palestine, opposed by the Arabs, which led to a brief Egyptian–Israeli battle in 1948, won by the Israelis.

The Wafd Party again returned to power in 1950 after several changes of government reflecting the desires of the nationalists and unrest among the army leadership. Egypt demanded withdrawal of British troops from the Canal Zone and from the Sudan. Great Britain immediately retaliated with a plan for Sudanese independence; this appeared realistic in view of the traditional hatred for and distrust of Egyptians by the Sudanese. Events moved swiftly—the UN requested that Egypt lift its embargo forbidding use of the Suez Canal by ships bound for or coming from Israel. Egypt replied by abrogating its treaties with the British of 1899 and 1936 and the British navy attacked Port Said and landed forces in the area. Riots erupted in Cairo and there were two rapid changes of government. King Farouk, having grown fat and dissipated at the age of 32, was overthrown and exiled by the military in July 1952; a new era began in Egypt that is now generally thought of as the beginning of true independence in the modern age.

Prior to the defeat of Farouk, the British offered the Sudan a plan of internal self-government which was condemned by Egypt. The colonial government was able to work out a compromise arrangement with the military junta that succeeded Farouk, which provided that the Sudanese should decide whether they were to be independent or part of a federation with Egypt. In 1953 an overwhelming number of the Sudanese voted for independence, which was granted in 1956.

THE FRENCH
North Africa: Algeria, Morocco and Tunisia

With the exception of Morocco, all of Arabic-speaking North Africa was, at the turn of the 18th century, part of the vast Ottoman Empire; the area consisted of a number of small principalities ruled by Turkish military men who had titles of Bey or Dey, depending upon the location. Commerce consisted of trade with regions to the south, and piracy of European shipping in the Mediterranean Sea. The booty seized from the vessels consisted not only of cargo, but the crew as well, which was sold into slavery.

After other nations had sent expeditionary forces against the Arab raiders, France sent a force into Algiers in 1830,

The Colonial Period

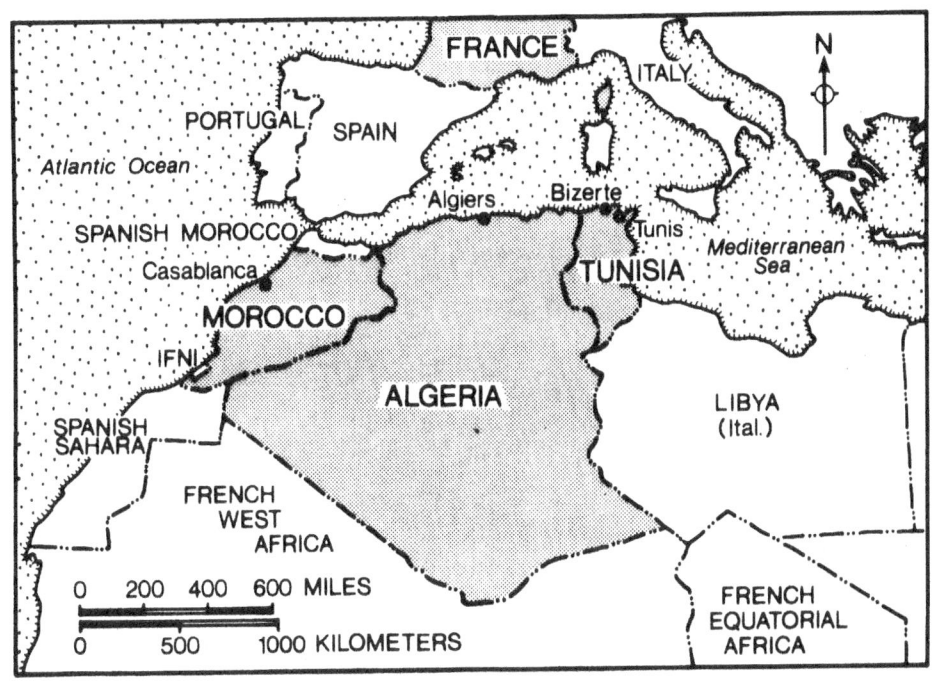

of all stripes gathered and challenges to French rule mounted. French attempts to divide Berbers and Arabs backfired and nationalists initiated a new national day, the *Fête du Trône* or Throne Day in 1933. It accentuated the monarch's role as symbol of national unity.

Popular enthusiasm for the young king was often accompanied by anti-French demonstrations. Political parties soon emerged seeking greater Moroccan self-rule. The explicit demand for independence logically followed the country's experiences in World War II. Muhammad V urged cooperation with France when war broke out in 1939, and Moroccan troops fought valiantly to defend the colonial ruler. A defeated France shone less brightly, and Vichy's racial laws were offensive to a monarchy that had a large Jewish population. The Allies, meeting in Casablanca in 1943, expressed little enthusiasm for continued French presence in Morocco, and by 1944 an Independence Party, *Hizb alIstiqlal*, was formed.

The monarch's willingness to permit existence of the independence movement annoyed the French administrators. He roused further hostility by refusing to countersign decrees of the French resident general, denying them legal validity. Seeking to divide Arabs and Berbers, French administrators began to cultivate Berber leadership as a counter foil to a nationalist monarch. One of the most formidable,

deposing the dey and seizing a few of the coastal towns. Another dey was selected by the local people, who promptly marshaled attacks upon the French. Eventually the occupying forces had to recognize the new dey, Abd el-Kader. He engaged in sporadic warfare for 15 years against the French, who relinquished to him their claim to interior lands initially, but later drove him into Morocco where other French forces invaded and captured him in 1847.

After the conquest of Algeria, France slowly subdued Morocco, which had initially escaped domination by colonial powers, although the major powers had forced a treaty in 1880 that protected the rights of foreigners within the country. After a 13-year-old boy succeeded as sultan in 1894, the internal conditions deteriorated, reducing Morocco to virtual anarchy by the turn of the century. In exchange for concessions in Libya, Italy relinquished any claim it might have had in Morocco and the British later also acknowledged French supremacy in 1904. A nominal French–Spanish control was established in 1906 after a visit to Morocco by German Kaiser Wilhelm II as evidence of a German interest; negotiations led to an acknowledgment of French domination of the country in 1909. This was given by Germany in exchange for some economic guarantees and a section of the French Congo, which became part of Germany's colony of Kameroun (now Cameroon).

The French–Spanish administration quickly gave way to a French Protectorate under the terms of the treaty of Fez in 1912. When Sultan Moulay Yusuf died in 1927 the French chose his younger son, Sidi Muhammad, as sultan. Known for his retiring disposition, the prince turned into a skilled and forceful king as Muhammad V. Around him Moroccan nationalists

Habib Bourguiba celebrates Tunisian independence

The Colonial Period

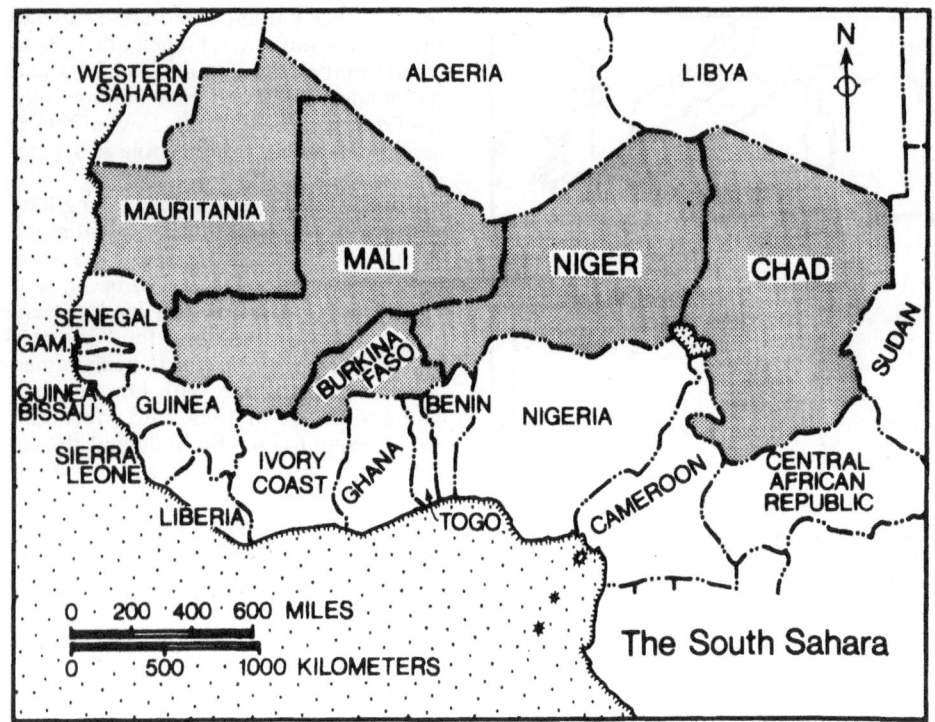

The South Sahara

Thami al-Glaoui, the feudal overlord of Marrakesh, condemned Muhammad V as not being the sultan of Moroccans as much as he was the sultan of *Istiqlal*.

Together al-Glaoui and France worked to depose the sultan, but when the French removed him from office in 1953, it made Muhammad a nationalist hero. The Algerian uprising in 1954 diverted French attentions from Morocco and under the overwhelming influence of a popular monarch and a strong nationalist party, Morocco became independent in 1956.

Although the French presence in the area now known as Algeria was initially military, efforts were made to settle colonists from France in the 1860s and 1870s when most of what is now Algeria was gradually brought under colonial control. In Tunisia, the French had economic competition from England and Italy. In return for control of Cyprus, the British acknowledged France's authority in Tunisia. Because of an outbreak of violence, a naval force seized Bizerte in 1881 and forced the Bey of Tunis to accept the status of a French protectorate over the area. The British, Italians, and Turks all protested, but France had the support of Germany in the move, given in exchange for French support of German colonial ambitions elsewhere in Africa.

Though France had juridical control of North Africa by 1910, *de facto* control was much less complete. During the entire colonial period from the 19th century until about 1960, the Arabs were almost in constant rebellion. Riff tribesmen of the Moroccan mountains and the Berber and Tuareg horsemen of southern Algeria never accepted French dominance. Arab unrest also came from the Muslim *Senussi* sect in neighboring Libya that spilled over into Tunisia, which was populated by Italians as well as French immigrants.

Further complicating the peaceful colonization of North Africa, the immigrants to the area from France were principally military personnel and their families—they quickly developed a militant and conservative attitude as evidenced by their armed opposition to French efforts in the 1870s to placate the restless Arabs. Substantial numbers of Arabs went to France during the colonial period, but both in Africa and in France the two ethnic groups—French and Arab—resisted integration with vigor.

The French colonists assumed the dominant position in North Africa, both economically and in terms of status derived from education. Lower schools were provided for those of French ancestry, but with little exception, no comparable effort was made on behalf of the Arabs. The local rulers were allowed to retain nominal powers, since it was actually easier to rule through them rather than try to depose them.

The earliest signs of Arab nationalism in the region—in Morocco in the 1930s—were partly a response to the world economic depression. Based almost entirely on the agricultural production on farms of European immigrants and their descendants, the whole North African economy was severely impacted by the worldwide economic slowdown. Initial nationalist efforts were the basis of continuing anti-French sentiment among the Arabs, to which was added growing worldwide liberal-nationalistic ideals—only temporarily interrupted by World War II.

Upon installation of a pro-German government under Marshal Henri-Phillipe Pétain in France following the German invasion of that country in World War II, Algeria, Morocco, and Tunisia were brought under the nominal authority of the Vichy government which he headed, named after a town in central France from which part of France was administered by his regime in 1940–1944. Although only a relatively insignificant number of French troops loyal to the Axis powers were stationed in the area, the Allies felt that it was necessary to establish Free French control in the area prior to invading Italy.

A combined American–British force invaded Morocco and Algeria on November 8, 1942, and three days later a cease-fire arranged with Admiral Jean François Darlan, the Vichy commander, led to Allied control of French North Africa within a short time, with Admiral Darlan achieving the post of Chief of State with Allied approval. Following his assassination shortly afterward, the Anglo-American command tried to install the aging General Henri Giraud as commander of French forces outside France in spite of the more energetic anti-Axis, anti-Vichy activities of the Free French led by the younger General Charles de Gaulle. His forces had conducted assaults in and from Brazzaville, French Congo. A brief German offensive in North Africa was repulsed by the Allies in May 1943.

The French were restored to continued colonial control of North Africa following World War II. Their rule was no more effective than the unstable and numerous governments of mainland France. In Algeria, the conservative colonists (*colons*) of French ancestry completely dominated all phases of government, although Algeria was legally supposed to be an integral part of France. The Communist Party had been outlawed in Morocco, a colony, but this could not be done in Algeria since the communists were not outlawed within France. The *National Liberation Front* quickly rose in power and spearheaded a revolt that started in late 1954 and lasted for seven years. This group was a leftist-socialist-communist Arab party, united in opposition to French colonial rule.

A last-ditch effort of the Secret Army Organization (OAS), composed for the

The Colonial Period

most part of French-descended Europeans, failed to stem the overwhelming tide of revolution in spite of cruel and terroristic anti-Arab measures in 1961. A ceasefire was finally negotiated in March 1962 and President Charles de Gaulle, who had promised the French to end the bloody conflict, recognized Algerian independence on July 3 of that year.

In Tunisia, there was also a postwar surge of nationalism. A large middle class of well-educated people had emerged and backed this movement, led by an Arab lawyer educated in France, Habib Bourguiba. His New Constitution Party succeeded the older Constitution Party. Bourguiba's life during the French colonial period alternated between periods of exile and/or imprisonment and periods of nationalistic leadership. Exiled in 1934, he returned in 1936, was rearrested in 1938 and later was freed by the Germans in 1942. He again was arrested when the French returned, but escaped and went into exile. When he returned in 1952, he was arrested, and in 1954 was banished into exile.

By this time, Tunisia was in a full state of insurrection requiring the presence of 70,000 French troops to attempt to control the colony. France granted internal autonomy to Tunisia in 1955, which also provided amnesty for all freedom fighters. Bourguiba was permitted to return, and full independence was achieved on July 20, 1956.

The South Sahara: Mauritania, Mali, Upper Volta (Burkina Faso), Niger, Chad

Colonization of the southern Sahara region was much slower process than in other areas of the continent because the almost uniformly arid land held little importance to the French. The only reasons for colonization were in order to connect other more valuable colonies and to exclude other foreign colonial effort in the region.

At the Berlin Conference, arranged by Otto von Bismarck of Germany and the French foreign minister in 1884–85, the major world and colonial powers officially decreed that African slavery was to be abolished and that there was to be free navigation of the major rivers of the continent. It was further decreed that colonial power in the area was to be based on presence and actual control. Unofficially, and more important, the representatives took a map of the continent and drew lines indicating areas of interest of the respective powers.

The maps of the continent at that time were uncertain—boundaries differed sometimes more than a thousand miles, depending on the map and the nationality

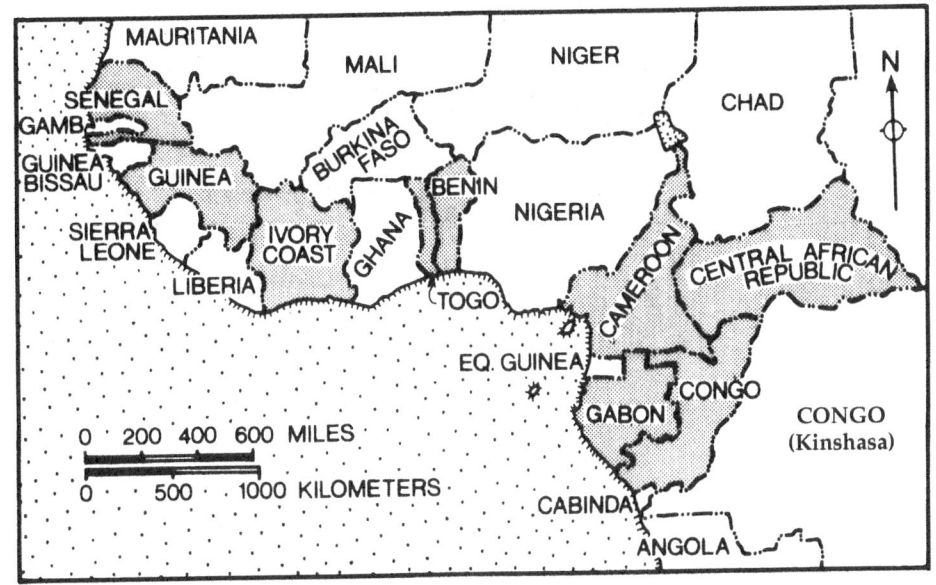

of the cartographer. In their effort to connect the West African and Equatorial African colonies, the French, in 1896–98 sent an expedition under Jean Baptiste Marchand that pushed rapidly northeastward as far as Fashoda (later named Kodak) on the Nile River. At the same time, having defeated the Sudanese, supposedly on behalf of Egypt, British Lord Horatio Herbert Kitchener was leading his forces southward along the Nile from Omdurman, and a second British expedition was pushing north on the river from Uganda. Further complicating the picture was the imminent arrival of an Ethiopian army on the right bank of the Nile at Fashoda, accompanied by another group of French forces.

The result was the Fashoda Crisis in which the British and French were eyeball-to-eyeball on the brink of total war. However, France was preoccupied with a complicated political scandal involving top military figures in Paris (the Dreyfuss Affair), Ih had political and religious overtones. The French blinked first, ending the crisis with an agreement on the lines of French and British authority in the arI- which approximately fixed the present eastern borders of Chad and the Central African Republic with the Sudan.

Although the major powers of the world recognized French authority in this barren land by the end of the 19th century, the nomadic people who lived in the south Sahara region refused fully to submit to foreign rule for several years afterwards. In the final analysis, France was compelled to rule this part of Africa through local tribal leaders who possessed a large measure of autonomy. This permitted nominal French control without large-scale military Ies, which would have been necessary for direct rule.

The region was administered as a whole as part of French West Africa. Mali, Niger, Chad, and southern Algeria were also known as French Sudan, the French Iling of which was Soudan.

The lives of the people were hardly disturbed by colonial rule. There was virtually no immigration of Europeans such as occurred in North Africa; the only French presence was essentially military. Occasional reIs occurred, which were contained, rather than defeated by the French.

Although there was some sporadic German penetration in World War II during the North African campaigns of 1942–43 in the Mali, Niger and Chad regions, the local people were not involved in the battles. Free French forces under General Jean LeClerc fought several engagements with the Germans in the northern Chad area. With little exception, there was no political movement toward independence from France following World War II in the south Sahara. Niger shared in the development of the Democratic African Rally Party, but in this respect was dominated by the members from the Ivory Coast under Félix Houphouët-Boigny. As a result of unrest of the Muslim Mossi people in what was then called Upper Coast, the area now constituting Upper Volta (Burkina Faso) was separated after World War II from Ivory Coast, taking the French name Haute Volta.

Following the election of Charles de Gaulle as President of France, the French Community was established in 1958—a plan whereby France's colonies in Africa were granted internal autonomy. This was an effort to satisfy independence

The Colonial Period

Duchess of Kent dancing with the Ghanaian Prime Minister, Kwame Nkrumah, at the Ghana Independence Ceremonies in Accia, Ghana, March 1957   Photo by Judi Iranyi

movements in areas of French Africa outside the south Sahara. It proved to be unsatisfactory in many respectIot the leastIch was continued opposition to French authority over foreign relations by a multitude of African natiIts within the Community. Because of this, France granted independence to the remaining south Sahara and West African colonies, numbering 13, in 1960. Thus, without any substantial internal effort to promote independence, the south Sahara rIn was freed of French authority (which in reality had never been firmly established).

Coastal West and Equatorial Africa: Senegal, Guinea, Ivory Coast, Togo, Dahomey, East Cameroon, Central African Republic, Gabon, Congo

France initially had no colonial ambitions along coastal Africa—scattered missionary stations were established in the 17th and 18th centuries and slave trade was also prevalent at the time. Following the abolition of slave trade in 1815, France maintained very small "factories" (trading posts) along the various parts of the coast.

Colonial interest quickened during the mid-19th century when the IEuropean powers feared that one or another of them would obtain some valuable territory available to all nations, with a potential discovery of valuable metal ores and gems. In reality, with the exception of widely scattered and exaggerated tales brought to Europe by occasional explorers, almost nothing was known of the interior coastal lands of West and Equatorial Africa.

Senegal was the first area of increased French activity—General Is Faidherbe headed an armed force in 1854, which was immediately resisted by the natives and their Tukuler ruler, El Hajj Omar Tall, but it was gradually able to subdue most of the area. The most commercially important region of Senegal—the Gambia River Basin—had been seized by the British decades prior to the arrival of the French. Under French rule, the trading sites of St. Louis, Gorée, Dakar, and Rufisque were granted special political rights. Regardless of race, inhabitants of the "Four Communes," as they were called, were French citizens with the right to elect a representative to parliament in Paris. Initially these representatives were French or mulattos, but in 1914 electors chose the first African, Blaise Diagne, as the Communes' Deputy to the National Assembly. Diagne was given the rank of governor-general to assist in recruiting African soldiers to aid France in World War I. Some 200,000 were eventually recruited from all of French West Africa.

At about the same time, a military mission was sent to Guinea, but because of the fierce resistance of the people of the region, penetration into the interior was slow. A local chieftain, Samory Toure, initially signed a treaty that permitted him to claim additional territory to the northwest. This peace was short-lived; further French military efforts were necessary in 1885–86, and a dire threat to the French was mounted when Toure united with the Tukuler people previously driven from Senegal into Mali.

The French offensive was on two fronts—north and east in Guinea and north and west in Ivory Coast, which finally resulted in the defeat of Toure in 1898. He was exiled to Gabon after his capture, where he died two years later. Penetration from southern Ivory Coast had also been slow. Although treaties were signed with the coastal chieftains of the Grand-Bassam and Assime regions, the Agnis and Baoules, two groups closely related to the warlike Ashanti people of Ghana to the west, offered fierce resistance to drives into the interior. Farther north, the Mandingo people of Samory Toure and the Tukuler Africans prevented progress; Ivory Coast was not fully conquered by the French until about 1915.

As a result of a treaty signed with the French in 1851 by Ghezo, ruler of Abomey (Dahomey) a small commercial effort was initiated in that country. Coutonou was ceded as a trading post in 1868. The colonization of Dahomey was not uncontested—the Portuguese and British attempted to encourage intertribal rivalries in order to unseat the French from the coastal area, but without success.

Dahomey, with the exception of its narrow coastal strip, was left virtually untouched until 1890 when Benhazin, the last powerful king of Abomey, refused

The Colonial Period

Tirailleurs sénégalais (Senegalese riflemen) training. France employed significant numbers of African troops in both World Wars I and II.

to sign additional treaties with France. Military occupation of Coutonou was ordered, swiftly followed by a violent uprising, which continued with periodic interruptions until 1894, when Benhazin surrendered. The interior of Dahomey was slowly subdued during the following decades.

Togo was not gained by the French until World War I. The larger part of this former German colony was occupied by French troops in 1916; this control was converted into a mandate by the League of Nations, which divided the colony between France (East) and Britain (West). The British area was joined with the Gold Coast (Ghana). The East Cameroon region was also acquired from Germany in a similar fashion in 1916, also resulting in a League of Nations mandate.

Count Pierre Savorgnan De Brazza of France entered the northern side of the Congo River region of coastal Africa at about the same time that the British-American explorer Henry Stanley was claiming the southern side of the river region on behalf of King Leopold of Belgium in the first part of the 1880s. An Italian count and later French citizen and naval officer, de Brazza signed treaties of protection with a number of African chiefs of the once mighty Kingdom of the Congo, a Bantu empire that at its peak had extended from Gabon to Angola including an area several hundred miles inland from the coast. After exploring most of Congo (Brazzaville), De Brazza went into Gabon and established a small coastal outpost, founded the city of Brazzaville, and governed the area from 1886 to 1897. When horrific reports of abuse of African workers by companies holding concessions in the colony became insistent enough to require action, de Brazza was sent to investigate in 1905. Two years later, France restricted the use of forced labor by concessionaires. In 1910, the French joined Moyen-Congo (Middle Congo), as the colony was known, with three others to form French Equatorial Africa (AEF). Brazzaville served as the capital of AEF.

The area that is now the Central African Republic was not penetrated by the French until about 1889, when an outpost was established at Bangui, the present capital. The French named this territory Ubangi-Shari after its two principal rivers. It was not until after the turn of the century that effective French control was imposed on Congo, Gabon, and the Central African Republic, all of Ih were combined in 1910 to form French Equatorial Africa, a distinctive administrative area. Upon receiving a mandate from the League of Nations over East Cameroon, a section of the former German colony (Kameroun) was made a part of French Equatorial Africa.

Mauritania, Senegal, Guinea, Ivory Coast, Dahomey, Mali, Upper Volta, and Niger had been joined together as French West Africa in 1904; the entire territory was administered from Dakar, Senegal. The part of former German Togoland acquired after World War I was joined into this vast colony.

A variety of local councils were permitted by the French, giving the Africans a limited voice in their local affairs during the colonial period. European-style education was introduced, but never achieved widespread enrollment due to a shortage of trained teachers willing to live in Africa. Small numbers who did obtain secondary education usually went to France if they desired higher level studies.

Roads and railroads were constructed to the extent necessary to commercially develop this area of the continent, such as in Ivory Coast, to permit export of agricultural products and in Gabon to support wood production.

After obtaining the necessary medical education, Dr. Albert Schweitzer, world-renowned German philosopher and musician, received permission to establish a Protestant Christian medical mission and hospital at Lamborene in the interior of Gabon. He labored among the people from 1913 until his death in 1965. He adapted medical methods to harmonize with the customs of the Africans.

Other than medical facilities provided principally for Europeans living in West and Equatorial Africa, almost none were established for the benefit of the African

Leopold II of Belgium

The Colonial Period

people during the colonial years, but there was some improvement in the post-World War II period. Boundaries were stabilized over a number of years by agreements with the British, Belgians, and Liberians; the map of colonial Africa underwent no substantial change in West Africa after 1920.

The World Depression of 1929 and the following years had great impact in the coastal colonies of French West and Equatorial Africa, where agricultural products usually were the sole exports. The sharp drop in prices paid for foodstuffs meant a corresponding decrease of income, and accompanying lower living standards, which had not really been much more than marginal.

When France fell to the overwhelming might of the German Nazi military machine, a puppet, pro-German administration was established in France—the *Vichy* government (1940), named for its location in central France. It quickly dispatched administrators and personnel to take control of French Africa; they were generally disliked by the French living in the colonies. Their policies tended in many cases to be openly racist and repressive. French General Charles de Gaulle led a force, aided by British vessels, which attempted to seize Dakar, Senegal in 1940, but it was repulsed. A month later, he was able to capture Douala, Cameroon; Brazzaville was also occupied, and a powerful transmitter was erected in order to make daily Free French broadcasts heard in distant areas.

Following World War II, colonial rule continued, but there was a rapid upsurge of nationalism among native Africans. France itself had been economically devastated by the war and only slowly recovered with great amounts of foreign assistance provided by the United States. Political extremism, both rightist and leftist (communist) was rampant, making orderly French government all but impossible. Félix Houphouët-Boigny, a nationalist leader in Ivory Coast, organized the Democratic African Rally (RDA) with associated parties in most of France's West African colonies; the allied party succeeded in electing almost all of the area's deputies to the Assembly in Paris between 1947 and 1950. The relatively small number of African delegates allowed by the constitution allied themselves with the communist deputies during this period in an effort to gain support for their nationalist viewpoint, but that allegiance was discontinued in 1950.

France was severely drained by the communist rebellion within its Indochinese colonies, including Vietnam, during the postwar period which ended in a military disaster for the French in 1954. Immediately, a second total rebellion was mounted by the Algerian National Liberation Front which resulted in devastating warfare within that colony for seven more years, with accompanying additional strain upon the French economy. Principally for those reasons, the French were in no position effectively to oppose nationalist demands of their African colonies.

The Overseas Reform Act (*Loi Cadre*) of 1956 gave the African colonies internal autonomy, leaving matters of defense and foreign policy to France in an effort to quiet the demands for total independence. After Charles de Gaulle assumed almost absolute powers in France in 1958, he announced the creation of the French Community, the first step toward granting total independence to the colonies. Guinea, led by Sékou Touré, rejected the plan and that colony gained immediate independence.

Senegal and Mali were joined into the Federation of Mali in 1959 and France made some other minor changes but granted full independence to all its remaining colonies in West and Equatorial Africa in 1960.

East Africa and the Indian Ocean: Madagascar, French Somaliland, and Indian Ocean Islands

The immense island of Madagascar was known to navigators since the 15th century, but there was no attempt at colonization. The Hindu Merina (Hova) people of Indonesian and Malaysian descent lived in the central highlands; persons of Arab and African heritage inhabited the coastal areas. There was only a brief period when the island was under single control during the 16th century, established by Sakalava (Arab) rulers.

The Merina Kingdom became dominant in the 18th century under King Andrianampoinamerina (1787–1810); he and his successors alternately encouraged the French and British in their tentative efforts at colonization so that neither would gain the upper hand. Between 1775 and 1824, the island was a stronghold of marauding pirates, including John Avery, Captain Mission, and William Kidd. The pirates even formed a republic called Libertalia, which was of brief duration.

Other nations of the world later established commercial relations with the Malagasy people; a treaty of peace, friendship and commerce between the United States and Madagascar was signed in 1881. During this period, British influence in the interior became strong. In 1869, Merina Queen Ranavolona I and her Court were converted to Protestantism. French interests continued to dominate the coastline.

At the Berlin Conference of 1885, as a result of concession by the French to the British in other parts of Africa, Great Britain supported the establishment of a French Protectorate over Madagascar. This status led to the end of the Merina Kingdom. General Joseph Simon Galliene, the first French governor, with the aid of French troops, unified the entire island.

The people—particularly the Merinas—had little use for French rule. In 1916 they rose unsuccessfully in bloody rebellion. The differences between the pro-French coastal inhabitants and those of the interior was expressed in this movement for independence, which was limited to the people of the highlands. After the fall of France in World War II, Madagascar, first administered by the Vichy (pro-Nazi) government of France, was occupied in 1942 by the British to prevent possible Japanese seizure of the strategic island. The Free French gained control in 1943. By 1947, an independence movement had become overwhelming and there was a national uprising suppressed only after months of bitter fighting, which resulted in the deaths of more than 10,000 people on the island. Subsequent constitutional reform in France lessened the tensions in Madagascar, and led to the establishment of the Malagasy Republic within the French Community in 1958. The Republic became fully independent in 1960.

France also colonized smaller islands chains in the Indian Ocean, including the Comoros and the Seychelles, as well as the island of Mauritius. Elsewhere, France colonized Mayotte in the Comoros islands in 1843 and extended its influence to the whole archipelago. In 1912, the four Comoros islands formally became a French colony administered from Madagascar. At French settlements in Mauritius, some intermarriage between French and Africans resulted in the evolution of a stable group of people now known as Creoles. France colonized the Seychelles in the 18th century but lost them to Britain as a consequence of the Napoleonic Wars.

The tiny, sun-blistered colony of French Somaliland came into existence when treaties were signed with local chieftains in 1862. This colonization, as well as that of the British and Italians in the area, was to secure the regions south of the Suez Canal, then under construction, in order to prevent any disruption of shipping. The only asset of the territory was a deep, natural harbor facing the Gulf of Aden. At the turn of the century, a railroad from Addis Ababa, Ethiopia, to Djibouti was completed and was thereafter the prime source of revenue. This colony achieved independence from France in June 1977 and is now known as the Republic of Djibouti.

The Colonial Period

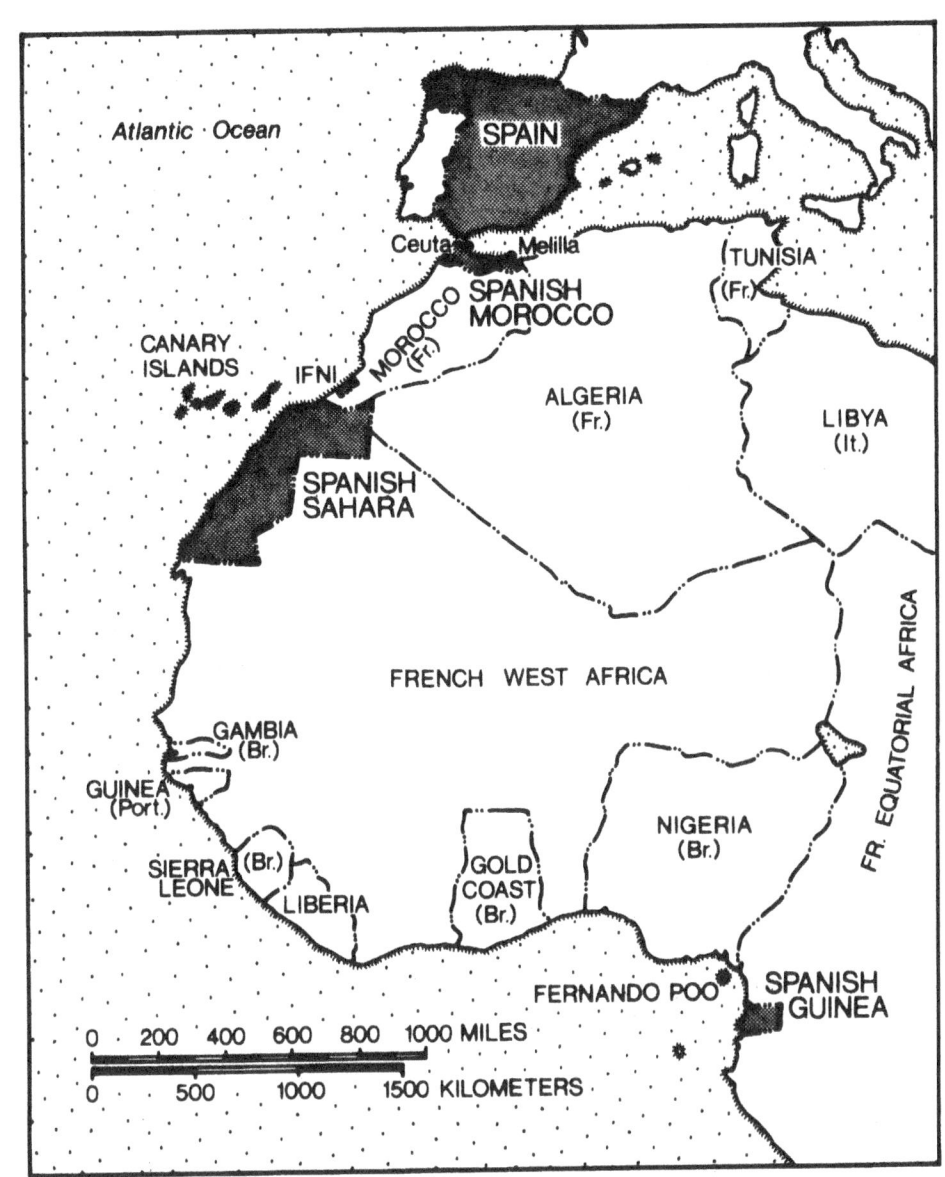

between the European colonial powers, King Leopold had personally been awarded the area south of the Congo River as far as Portuguese possessions in the Angola region. Although the area was referred to as "The Congo Free State," the yearsthat followed were harsh. King Leopold used forced labor and torture were to wring production and wealth from the colony; it is estimated that up to 8 million Africans lost their lives during the 23 years of Leopold's exploitation. By 1904, knowledge of these repressive conditions had become known in Europe and the United States; in response to pressure from Britain, Germany, and the U.S., King Leopold sent a commission to investigate conditions. The report of the commission, issued in late 1905, indicated that the actions of Leopold's administrators were scandalously cruel and improper. Bowing to continued international pressure, the Belgian parliament passed an act in 1908 annexing the Congo State of Belgium.

During the period at the turn of the century, there was friction between the British, French and King Leopold over control of the upper (southern) Nile area in the region near Lake Albert. As a result of a compromise, the Congo Free State received a small portion of territory known as the Lado enclave, which reverted to the Sudan (Anglo-Egyptian Sudan) at the death of Leopold in 1910. There were a variety of treaties between the several colonial powers that gradually and firmly demarcated the borders of the Congo region.

Under Leopold, the copper-rich Katanga (now Shaba) area had been opened up, and economic development based on

Kaiser Wilhelm II of Germany

THE AMERICANS

For detail on the role of the United States in Africa's colonial period, see Liberia, under *The Past: Political and Economic History*.

KING LEOPOLD II AND THE BELGIANS

The Belgian Congo, Ruanda-Urundi

The Belgian efforts at colonization in the Congo region of West Africa call to mind the name of one man: Henry Stanley. Following his birth in Wales, he migrated to the United States, where he became an author, soldier, and adventurer, fighting on both sides in the American Civil War. Seeking new adventure, he turned to Africa and went to locate the Scottish missionary, Dr. David Livingstone, who had disappeared while exploring central Africa. After locating Dr. Livingstone on the shores of Lake Tanganyika in 1871, he explored the lake regions of the continent and then proceeded westward to the Congo River region. It took him three years to traverse the length of the river; he arrived on the Atlantic coast in 1877 and departed for Europe.

Stanley was immediately summoned by King Leopold II of Belgium, who saw in this explorer a means to compete in the scramble for colonial territory in Africa. Stanley accepted the offer of employment and returned to the Congo, entering into treaties on behalf of King Leopold with the native chieftains. The curious thing about this colonization is that it was not on behalf of the Belgian nation—this was Leopold's personal project.

At the Berlin Conference of 1885, when great portions of Africa were divided

The Colonial Period

Benito Mussolini

that region's wealth proceeded forward under Belgian administrators. The general approach was that the native Africans should not be given too many privileges lest they become restless. Due to efficient administration, however, the per capita income rose to be one of the highest in colonial Africa.

Belgian forces moved to occupy the northwestern part of German East Africa at the start of World War I. This region, consisting of what is now Rwanda and Burundi, was then called Ruanda-Urundi and became a mandated territory assigned to Belgium in 1923; it was joined administratively with the Congo, which was given a wide degree of autonomy at the same time. Between the two world wars, Belgium made substantial capital investments in the Congo, including construction of railways connecting Kinshasa (then called Leopoldville) to the mineral wealth of Shaba (then called Katanga).

Nationalist pressures on the part of the native Africans mushroomed after World War II. Belgium, prostrated by the battles and German occupation of the war, was actually in no position to resist this movement. In a completely unexpected change, Belgium announced in January 1960 that it would grant independence to the Congo as of June 30th of the same year. It is highly probable that the Belgians hoped that a quick grant of independence would result in chaos to a degree that would justify continued colonial control. This hope, motivated by the desire for further wealth, was almost realized.

THE SPANISH

Spanish Sahara, Spanish Guinea, Ifni, Ceuta, Melilla

The colonization and division of Africa between the major powers in the 19th century was during a period when Spain, having formerly been a powerful colonial nation, was in a state of decline. The result was that Spain succeeded in claiming Spanish Sahara (also called Spanish Morocco, Rio de Oro), a barren desert area, and Spanish Guinea, a small section of oppressive jungle on the west coast at the Equator, which included the island of Fernando Poo. The enclaves of Ifni, Ceuta, and Melilla along the coast of Morocco were holdovers from the time when both Morocco and Spain were controlled by Moorish Arabs. The areas in which Spain was able to lay claim were available largely because of lack of interest in them on the part of other stronger colonial nations.

Although Spain was technically supposed to be in partnership with the French in Morocco during the colonial period, the actual control was by the French. Spain ceded its theoretical protectorate right to Morocco in 1956 when the French granted it independence; a small part of southern Morocco was relinquished in 1958. The enclave of Ifni was returned to Morocco in 1968; Ceuta and Melilla, coastal cities along the coast where Spain and Morocco are closest, remain under Spanish control with the tacit consent of the king of Morocco.

Wind-swept and arid, Spanish Sahara is inhabited by a handful of nomadic Berber-Bedouin tribesmen who had been left to themselves by the Spanish. There had been almost no interest in this area on the part of the rest of the world prior to 1966 when extensive and rich deposits of phosphate were located. After withstanding pressures from the UN, Morocco and Mauritania for a decade, Spain vacated the territory in 1976 (see Western Sahara).

In 1778, Portugal ceded the island of Fernando Pó to Spain. (The Treaty of Tordesillas of 1494, by which the Pope settled territorial claims between Spain and Portugal stemming from the discovery of the New World, had given gave the Portuguese exclusive rights in Africa.) In the 19th century, however, Fernando Pó was used by the British navy in its efforts to suppress the slave trade. Many of the freed slaves were settled on the island and the British assumed responsibility for its administration. The island was abandoned for this purpose when the British shifted their operations to Sierra Leone in 1843. Spain reoccupied the island in 1844 and by 1879 was using it as a penal settlement for Cubans considered too dangerous to be kept on that island. Economic development only began after the Spanish-American war of 1898, when Fernando Pó and its neighboring coastal enclave became Spain's last significant tropical colony. The two provinces were collectively known as Spanish Guinea. There was no significant nationalist movement reported during the postwar period and no effort was made to prepare the colony for independence. The mainland portion of present-day Equatorial

Haile Selassie enters Addis Ababa in 1941

The Colonial Period

French troops invaded Togo from their respective neighboring colonies, Gold Coast and Dahomey. German forces surrendered unconditionally, and Britain and France occupied separate areas of the territory. Germany renounced its colonial territories in the Treaty of Versailles,Ich concluded the war. In 1922, the newly created League of Nations charged France and Britain with the administration of their respective spheres of occupation as part of the League Mandate system. The territory was jointly administered for five years but was then split into two areas with the British in a smaller, western portion and the remainder controlled by the French. The British area became part of what is now Ghana, formerly known as Gold Coast.

The Portuguese navigator, Fernão do Pó (Fernando Pó in Spanish) had explored the coast of Cameroon in 1472; the prolific shrimp in the River Wouri inspired the sailors to christen the river *Rio dos Camarões*, meaning "River of Shrimp" in Portuguese. There was a variety of commercial activity during the 19th century precolonial period, a time when no single European nation dominated Cameroon. The British decided in 1884 to annex Cameroon and sent an emissary to sign treaties with the local inhabitants. He arrived just days too late—spurred by the rush for colonies, a German consul had already visited Douala, the seaport, and obtained the signatures of the chieftains on treaties annexing Cameroon to Germany; the area was named Kameroun, a Germanization of the original Portuguese name.

The colonial rule of the Germans was similar to that in Togo—exploitative and often cruel. There was some penetration into the interior but control was not established in the northern regions by the Germans. Throughout the colony it became difficult to locate the tribal chieftains, who went into hiding to avoid possible punishment or being held hostage by the colonial administrators. In exchange for support of French claims in Morocco, Germany was granted about 100,000 square miles of Congo (Brazzaville).

Cameroon was the scene of an extensive campaign early in World War I. British and French forces wrested control from Germany, and by the terms of the Treaty of Versailles, Cameroon was split between the two powers. Kamerun, as it was then called, was stripped from Germany, and made a mandate of the League of Nations in 1922; administrative responsibilities for the mandate were shared by Britain and France. Modern Cameroon results from the merger of the French and a portion of the English areas.

The Italians in Africa

Guinea consisted of an undesirable, oppressively hot and humid area acquired at the Berlin Conference in 1885, which was joined administratively to form a single colony with Fernando Pó.

In the mid-1960s, Spain began to bring increasing pressure on the British to cede the Gibraltar peninsula on the ground that it, lying at the entrance to the Mediterranean Sea, belonged to Spain by virtue of natural geography. In order to reinforce its arguments, Spain granted Spanish Guinea independence in 1968, giving little prior indication of its intention to do so.

THE GERMANS

West Africa: Togo, Cameroon

Although there was some German missionary and trading activity on the coasts of Togo and Cameroon from 1845 onward, these areas also were open to religious and commercial efforts of the remaining European nations. German missionaries arrived as early as 1847, followed soon by German traders. In the rush to acquire colonies during the 1880s, Gustav Nachtigal negotiated treaties with the Ewe chiefs of the region at Togoville, located on the banks of Lake Togo. The most powerful of them was King Mlapa III.

During the thirty years that followed, the announcement of a German protectorate in Togo, there was slow penetration into the interior. The borders with the surrounding colonies were adjusted several times by treaty. The rule of the German administrators was harsh and exploitive; there was no effort to provide any benefit to the people of the region, since the only interest was commercial. Large numbers of Togolese were jailed and forced to labor for the Germans. At the outbreak of World War I, British and

The Colonial Period

South Africa: South West Africa

The Germans first entered the region of South-West Africa in the 1840s in a strictly missionary effort, similar to British efforts in South Africa among the native Africans. This outpost, called the Bethany Mission, slowly expanded during the following decades, and numbers of Germans went into the interior from Walfish (Walvis, Walvisch) Bay. The German missionaries twice asked for the British to assume protection of the Bay area, and in 1877 this request was granted.

There was substantial German migration into South-West Africa during the last quarter of the 19th century. After quarreling with the British for several months, the Germans proclaimed a protectorate over the area in 1884; administration initially was by the German Colonial Company, but in 1892 South-West Africa came under the control of the German government. The migrants to the area were principally farmers and herdsmen who occupied the scarce and choice lands suitable for cultivation and grazing. Discovery of mineral wealth led to further measures designed to exploit the wealth of the land for the benefit of the Germans. The Bantu Hereros, also known as Damaras, rose in bloody revolt from 1904 to 1908, requiring 20,000 German troops to finally defeat them. Several thousand of these people fled to neighboring Botswana (then Bechuanaland) during the revolt.

Within a year of the start of World War I, a combined British and South African *Boer* army was able to defeat the German force of about 3,500 stationed in South-West Africa. The territory was assigned to the British-*Boer* Union of South Africa as a mandate by the Allied Council and later by the League of Nations.

East Africa: Tanzania (German EastAfrica)

Initial exploration of the East African coast area occurred in 1860–1865 when Karl von der Decken entered the region, but it was not until 1884, when Karl Peters signed a series of treaties with native kings that the colonial effort actually started. The agreements provided for a sale of land to the Germans for a very small fraction of its probable value. The German status in the area was recognized at the Berlin Conference of 1885, and the German East Africa Company was created to administer the colony.

In the early colonial period, the Germans also acquired lands in adjacent Uganda and coastal Kenya by signing treaties in the former, and coercing the Arab viceroy in Zanzibar to surrender lands in the latter. These were given up by treaties to the British in exchange for a somewhat worthless island in the North Sea and other minor concessions; treaties were also entered into with King Leopold of Belgium and the Portuguese which fixed the border of German East Africa. Penetration into the interior was slow and difficult. The native Africans resisted the German movement; there was a violent uprising of the Muslim Arabs along the coast (1888–90), a revolt of the Wahehe (Wahaya) people (1891–93) and a combined Muslim-Angoni rebellion (1903–05). The Angonis, a Bantu group related to the warlike Zulus of South Africa, were all but exterminated during this conflict, known as the Maji-Maji Rebellion, in which the Germans ruthlessly destroyed crops and villages, rendering a large area completely desolate.

In 1914, 300,000 British, South African *Boer* and Indian troops invaded German East Africa. A force of slightly more than 200 German officers, commanding native troops numbering between 2,500 and 4,000 fended off the massive attack for four years under the spirited and brilliant leadership of General Paul Von Lettow-Vorbeck.

With great effort, the allies slowly pushed Lettow-Vorbeck from German East Africa into Mozambique and Rhodesia. The Germans refused to stop fighting, and the battles ceased only when their commander was informed that the Armistice of November 11, 1918 had been signed, ending World War I, and providing for the evacuation of Germans from German East Africa.

The British received a mandate from the League of Nations to administer the former German colony, which was renamed Tanganyika. Substantial numbers of German immigrants who had established large, prosperous farms and plantations, were deported to Germany; a few were later permitted to return to the British colony.

In 1890, the Tutsi kingdoms of Ruanda and neighboring Urundi were incorporated into German East Africa. During World War I Belgians occupied the area, and in 1923 Belgium was granted a League of Nations mandate to administer Ruanda-Urundi. It administered the mandate through existing Tutsi political structures. As a consequence, the Tutsi remained a privileged and dominant minority in Ruanda after World War II. These colonies would later become present-day Rwanda and Burundi.

THE SOUTH AFRICANS
Namibia (German South West Africa, South-West Africa)

The Union of South Africa received a mandate from the League of Nations in 1919 over what had been German South-West Africa. After The UN came into existence, it exerted pressures to grant the people of Namibia their independence, a goal that was finally achieved only on March 21, 1990.

THE ITALIANS

The Eastern Horn: Somalia, Ethiopia, and Eritrea

In comparison to other European nations, Italian colonial efforts were relatively weak and delayed, largely because Italy itself was a weakly defined nation through much of the 19th century. Following agreement among the stronger powers in 1885, the Italians signed treaties during the next four years with the three Muslim sultans in the "horn" region of East Africa. Although Italian Somaliland was acquired as a colony, full control was not established in the area until as late as 1927. The bleak, uniformly hot and dry region was considered to be valueless as a colony and the nomadic Cushites and Somalis who lived in the region, including part of Kenya and Ethiopia, were difficult to control.

Eritreans continued to live a life of localized independence until swept into the maelstrom of events set off by two contending forces in the late 19th century: Italian efforts to colonize the area and efforts of Menelik II, king of Ethiopia, to assemble, by conquest, modern Ethiopia. British and French Somaliland, both areas somewhat more desirable, separated Somaliland from Eritrea, a semiarid expanse given to the Italians by a lack of interest on the part of more powerful colonial nations. Benito Mussolini, the fascist dictator, came to power in Italy in 1922. He began to flex colonial muscles, eyeing with envy the vast territories taken without resistance by the rest of Europe in Africa and elsewhere.

From bases in Eritrea, Italian forces invaded ancient Ethiopia in 1936; Emperor Haile Selassie begged for assistance at the League of Nations, but his plea fell on deaf ears. The fate of Ethiopia had been decided earlier in Paris, when the British and French gave the Italians wide authority over Ethiopia in an effort to appease Mussolini. The figurehead King of Italy proclaimed himself Emperor of Ethiopia, a title recognized at once by Austria and Germany and in 1938 by Great Britain and France.

Ethiopia was joined with Somaliland and Eritrea to form Italian East Africa; initially there was some effort at economic development and road building. However, an attempt was made to assassinate the Italian governor at Addis Ababa in 1937. A reign of terror followed, with widespread arrests and summary executions in an

The Colonial Period

attempt to terrorize the population. Further unrest became intense, and by 1940 the Italians were besieged from within by Ethiopian terrorists and from without by British forces. Exactly five years after the first entry of Italian troops, Haile Selassie entered Addis Ababa at the head of a British–Ethiopian force and Italian rule was ended.

During the postwar period, a plan whereby Eritrea was to become a part of Ethiopia was promulgated at the UN; following its acceptance, the two were joined. The UN granted a trusteeship over Somalia to Italy in 1949; this area had been occupied by the British since the early years of World War II. The trusteeship provided for complete independence within ten years, which was achieved in 1960.

North Africa: Libya

Although many Italian immigrants had settled in North Africa, particularly in Libya and Tunisia, there was no effort to colonize the area until the 20th century. The ambition had then been present for decades—when the British and French settled the Fashoda Crisis (see *The French*), the Italians protested since they did not share in the division of the Sahara region of the African continent. Using a short-term ultimatum to provoke a conflict, Italian forces invaded Libya in 1911 in an attempt to seize control from the Ottoman Turks. After taking a few coastal towns, a protectorate status was proclaimed by the Italians.

The Muslim *Sanusi* sect immediately organized a revolt that continued until about 1931 at various places within Libya. Because the Arab-Berber people were given only the poorest parts of the land in which to live, the people of Libya, though eventually subdued, continued to have a smoldering hatred for the Italians.

Italian rule was ended in the two years following 1940. Extensive campaigns were waged by the Allies throughout the land against the Nazis, who had gained control of North Africa when it became apparent that Italy could not act with military authority in the area. The country, historically divided into three provinces of Cyrenaica, Tripolitania, and Fezzan, was split between Allied powers at the end of World War II. Fezzan was occupied by the French, and the remaining two provinces were under British administration. Libya's status was submitted to the United Nations, which adopted a resolution providing for independence by the end of 1951.

Ethiopia's Emperor Haile Selassie aboard a U.S. warship with President Franklin D. Roosevelt, then on his way home from the 1945 conference in the Crimea.

NORTH AFRICA

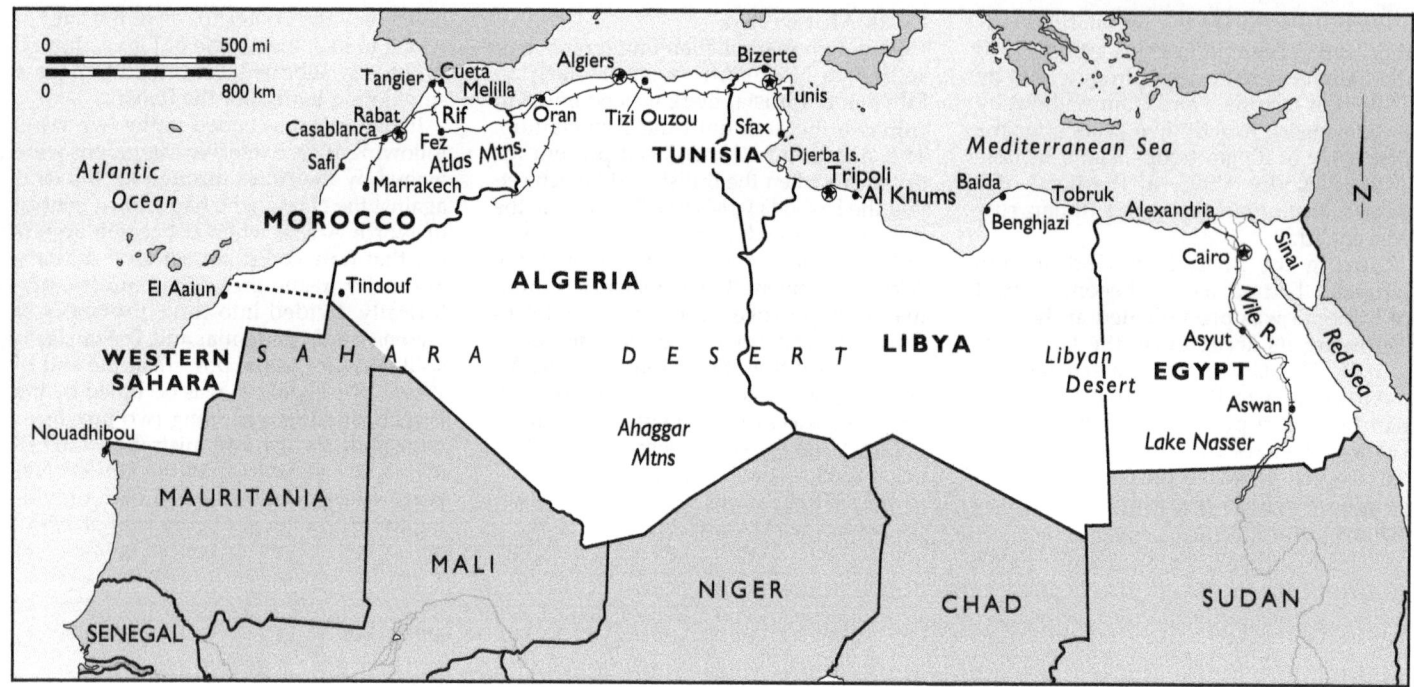

The Democratic and Popular Republic of Algeria

BASIC FACTS

Area: 2,381,740 sq. km. = 919,595 sq. mi. (almost as large as the U.S. east of the Mississippi River) World Bank 2014 est.
Population: 44,758,398 (July 2023 est.)
Capital City: Algiers
Government Type: Presidential republic
Neighboring Countries: Morocco (north-west); Tunisia and Libya (east); Niger (southeast); Mali, Mauritania (south-west)
Official Language: Arabic
Other Principal Languages: Berber languages, including Kabyle, Tamazight, Taznatit, Tumzabt; Tamahaq, spoken by Tuaregs, and French
Ethnic Groups: Arab-Berber 99%, European less than 1%
Principal Religions: Sunni Islam (state religion) 99%, Christianity and Judaism 1%.
Former Colonial Status: French Colony (1831–1870); part of France (1870–1962)
Independence Date: July 5, 1962
National Day: Revolution Day, November 1
GDP Per Capita (IMF 2023 est.): $4,481 (nominal), $13,507 (PPP)
Gini Index: 27.6 (2011 est.)
Currency: Algerian dinar, 1 USD = 135.23 dinar (2023)
Inflation Rate: 7.23% (2023 est.)
Chief Commercial Products: Petroleum and natural gas 97%

Foreign Direct Investments (FDI) net inflows: 1,200,000,000
Literacy Rate: 81.4% (2022 est.)
Life Expectancy at Birth: 78.7 years (2023 est.)
Head of State: Abdelmadjid Tebboune, President (since December 12, 2019)
Head of Government: Prime Minister Ayman Benabderrahmane (since July 7, 2021)

LAND AND PEOPLE

Algeria was a seat of civilization long before recorded history. Its ports and commerce were the lifeblood of early times. The city of Algiers, founded about 1,000 years ago, is a cosmopolitan crossroads of the East and West, climbing the Atlas Mountains from the blue Mediterranean. South of the fertile coastal regions and the mountainous areas stretches the vast Sahara Desert, where caravans still cross the arid wastelands. Gleaming modern highways, the densest on the continent, now lead to green oases and oil fields.

Algeria has a 620-mile coastline on the Mediterranean. Two Atlas Mountain chains cross the country horizontally, dividing Algeria into three geographic zones: the northern Mediterranean zone, the high arid plateau between the ranges, and the Sahara. The northern zone, known as the Tell, is a sun-bathed coastal area where vineyards, and orange, fig, and olive trees flourish in valleys and on hillsides. The high plateau is primarily the home of grazing herds of goats, sheep, and camels. South of the Sahara, the immense Ahaggar Mountains are the territory of the Tuaregs, a Berber group known for fiercely defending their autonomy.

Algeria's Berber-speaking minority, representing 20% to 30% of the population, struggles to maintain its own language and identity. The original inhabitants of North Africa, the Berbers fled to the mountains

Algeria

A workman with wire for new railway signal lines

to resist successive waves of invaders—Romans, Arabs, Turks, and French—and preserved both language (*tamazight*) and customs despite conversion to Islam. The singer Lounès Matoub, who was assassinated in an ambush in 1998, gave musical voice to Berber nationalism.

HISTORY TO PRESENT DAY

For early history, see *Historical Background* and *The Colonial Period: The French*.

Independence (1962) and the FLN to 1979

France granted independence to Algeria after a bitter eight-year struggle against Arab nationalists from 1954 to 1962, during which time more than one million French citizens and other European residents had fled the country. Ahmed Ben Bella, a prominent member of the National Liberation Front (FLN), which had led the fight for independence, headed the new government and undertook a wide range of reforms, including the redistribution of land. Ben Bella established closer ties with the European communist-bloc nations but internal tensions within the FLN led to the quiet removal of Ben Bella in 1965.

Colonel Houari Boumedienne was installed as chief of state in 1965 with widespread support of the FLN party leadership. Boumedienne, the former defense minister, established a 26-man Revolutionary Council to govern the nation, and weathered a 1967 attempt to oust him and a 1968 assassination plot.

In 1967, the FLN government began creating new political institutions to consolidate the party's control of the state. The FLN began with communal and provincial assemblies and adopted a new Marxist-oriented constitution in late 1976. Under the new charter, President Boumedienne was reelected with a 99% majority. A new National Assembly was elected in 1977, the 261 members selected from a list of 783 candidates chosen by the FLN.

Following President Boumedienne's death in late December 1978, elections were called for early 1979. Again, there was but one candidate: Colonel Chadli Bendjedid, a former commander and informal coordinator of defense during Boumedienne's illness. He also became secretary-general of the FLN, the two positions being closely interwoven in the single-party structure.

The Military and the Fundamentalist Challenge

In early 1980, Algeria was shaken by riots led by Muslim fundamentalists who sacked hotels, cafes, and restaurants where alcohol was served, a violation of Islamic law. Algeria had always been one of the most secular nations of the Arab world, keeping religion strictly out of government, but the successful Islamic revolution in Iran in 1979 had sparked a wave of back-to-Koranic-basics movements across Islamic countries. The rioters also attacked several "pleasure houses" provided for Algerian troops stationed near the border with Tunisia. Islamic fundamentalism, while initially unpopular in the early 1980s, began to emerge as a viable alternative to the FLN.

President Bendjedid was elected to a second and third five-year term in 1984 and 1989, but in the first decade of his rule, Algeria's public finances and development prospects had deteriorated sharply as a result of nonproductive spending by the FLN. The external debt of $28 billion required 80% of export earnings for debt service to pay principal and interest. There was little hard currency left for social services and productive investment. The FLN leadership had squandered oil revenues in populist projects that sustained its popularity (at least on the surface) but failed to produce development. By the 1990s, widespread corruption in the government existed alongside an unemployment rate of skilled people of over 30%.

In this deteriorating economy, Algeria's Islamic fundamentalists came into increasingly direct conflict with the secular and westernizing elements of the FLN regime. When President Bendjedid legalized political parties in 1989 in response to external and internal pressures, the first to register was the Islamic Salvation Front (FIS). It had already been clandestinely exploiting discontent among young people. As the movement gathered steam, FIS candidates won clear majorities in municipal and provincial elections in 1990 and set the stage for an energetic campaign in the forthcoming parliamentary elections.

The government declared a state of siege in an attempt to undermine the FIS. It arrested and jailed two FIS leaders—Abassi Madani and Ali Belhadj—and postponed the elections. When the elections were finally held in December 1991, the first round produced a striking victory for the FIS, which won 188 seats outright and seemed virtually certain to obtain an absolute majority in the second round.

Before the runoffs could take place in January 1992, however, President Bendjedid resigned and the army intervened to cancel the elections. A five-member Higher State Council, chaired

Algeria

by Mohamed Boudiaf, imposed military rule. The military regime declared a state of emergency, disbanded the FIS and dissolved all 411 FIS-controlled local authorities. On June 29, Boudiaf was assassinated by a member of his own bodyguard with alleged links with Islamists. Violence spiraled out of control and Algeria descended into civil war. The Armed Islamic Group (GIA: *Groupe Islamique Armé*) became the main group behind the violence.

Brig. Gen. Liamine Zéroual, subsequently chosen as interim president, faced armed fundamentalist forces, principally the GIA and the Islamic Salvation Army (AIS: *Armée Islamique du Salut*), who were well equipped with modern weaponry supplied by Iraq and Iran via Sudan. The military embarked on a campaign against the Islamists in 1994–5, interning rebels in camps in the remote desert and arming informal militias as self-defense forces in rural areas. To legitimize military rule, General Zéroual held presidential elections in 1995, and won a comfortable majority of 64.5%. According to official figures (usually inflated), 75% of the electorate turned out for the election.

The victorious military proposed a new constitution in November 1996. Even though it proclaimed Islam as the state religion, it provided that no party or candidate could have a religious affiliation as a basis for candidacy. Infuriated Islamists opposed it, and the GIA vowed to slit the throat of any person who left home to vote. The government mustered some 300,000 military and police to safeguard the election, and 85% of the electorate approved the proposed changes.

The first parliamentary elections under the new constitution were held in 1997 and resulted in Algeria's first multiparty legislature. For the election, the state made a major show of civic force. It deployed 300,000 security forces around the country to guard voters against attacks by Islamist militants and became more directly involved in the electoral politics by creating a new party to support President Zéroual, known as the National Democratic Rally (RND: *Rassemblement National et Démocratique*). The RND won a plurality of votes and seats, but not a majority, taking 156 seats (out of 380) with 38% of the vote. Coming in a distant second was the moderate Islamic party, Movement of Society for Peace (MSP), which won 69 seats. The FLN, once Algeria's only party, came in third, taking 64 seats. Two rival secular Berber-based parties, the Socialist Forces Front (FFS) of Hocine Aït-Ahmed and the Rally for Culture and Democracy (RCD) of anti-Islamist Saïd Sadi, each won 19 seats.

Despite building a governing coalition, President Zéroual surprised his countrymen by resigning his office in September 1998, effective with the selection of a successor in April 1999 elections. In politics behind the scenes, Zéroual had lost the confidence of Algeria's real rulers: the army. With the president's resignation, hopes that new elections could help national reconciliation and move Algeria beyond its current impasse abounded. Zéroual himself had promised free and fair elections, but they were not to be.

Abdelaziz Bouteflika (1999–present)

By January 1999, it was clear the army had rallied to a consensus candidate, the former foreign minister, Abdelaziz Bouteflika. In March, seven candidates were in the running, but when Zéroual refused to meet with them to discuss charges of electoral fraud, the other six withdrew, leaving Bouteflika as the sole candidate. The election was held; Bouteflika was "elected," and once again Algerian hopes were dashed.

Given the dubious nature of his election, President Bouteflika needed to prove his autonomy from the military powers. In July, Bouteflika proposed a "civil concord" initiative that offered amnesty to all but the worst offenders in Algeria's eight-year civil war. The initiative required that the rebels lay down their arms by mid-January 2000 or be wiped out. The government formalized a deal with the Islamic Salvation Army (AIS), the largest rebel group and military wing of the banned Islamic Salvation Front (FIS). However, the two most notorious armed movements—the Armed Islamic Group (GIA) and the Salafist Group for Preaching and Combat (GSPC)—rejected the amnesty and stepped up their attacks, killing 9,000 Algerians in 2000 Organized into small cells, the militants proved difficult to eradicate and violence remained as intractable as ever, though somewhat diminished.

Early in 2001, the governing coalition—which included the FLN, RND, RCD, MSP, and other parties—criticized Bouteflika for failing to deal with the nation's social and economic crisis. Almost 40% of Algeria's 30 million people lived below the poverty line and official figures put unemployment at 40%. The housing stock was inadequate, and there had been riots over the government's allocation of apartments. Even more dramatically, anti-regime violence exploded in the spring with riots by youths in Kabylia, the Berber heartland. One of their main rallying slogans laid bare Algeria's social and economic crisis: "You cannot kill us/We are already dead." The targets of their destructive rage were the symbols of government presence and occupation.

Violence in Kabylia persisted through the legislative elections of 2002. By then, security forces had killed more than 100 young people and the regime seemed incapable of resolving the crisis. In March 2002 President Bouteflika announced that Tamazight, the Berber language, would be recognized as a national language. In April the National Assembly amended the constitution to this effect, but the symbolic gesture did not placate. Instead, Berber leaders noted the language was only "national," not "official" and thus not the equivalent of Arabic; they rejected the government's offer and called on Berbers to boycott the May elections. Both Kabylia-based parties, Saïd Sadi's RCD and Hocine Aït-Ahmed's FFS, boycotted the elections in deference to local opinion. Activists closed virtually every polling place in Kabylia, and where that was impossible, physically prevented the few people who wanted to vote from getting to the polls. In the administrative region of Tizi Ouzou, the Berber capital, voter turnout was 1.8%.

The FLN was again the top party in the 2002 elections, winning 199 seats—an absolute majority—in the National Assembly, albeit with only 35% of voters turning out. Much of the credit for bringing the party back from the wilderness went to Prime Minister Ali Benflis, the party's new secretary-general. He had campaigned vigorously and suggested both the party's capacity to reform itself and his own desire to do so. During the campaign he openly denounced the party's old guard and antiquated policies, declaring they barred younger people from participating and believed in keeping women at home.

The election revealed Algeria's fundamental political pattern of three main ideological blocs. About a third of the electorate could be described as nationalist, supporting the FLN or other government-endorsed party like the RND. An Islamist bloc attracts the loyalty of 15% to

President Abdelaziz Bouteflika

Algeria

Berber cultural claims sometimes erupt in violence

20%, while a Berber bloc (FFS, RCD) can secure the support of 10% to 15%. Given this distribution of sentiment, coalition governments will remain a constant feature of the political system.

Prime Minister Benflis grew in popularity with his commitment to reform in office, which may have prompted his firing by Bouteflika in early May 2003 (well in advance of the April 2004 general election). The sacking splintered the FLN and when Benflis supporters moved to make the dynamic young leader the party's presidential nominee, Bouteflika loyalists immobilized them in the courts with the acquiescence of compliant jurists. In the April 2004 election, President Bouteflika ran for a second term against five opponents, one of whom was Ali Benflis. Defying expectations, Bouteflika won by a landslide, taking 84.99% of the votes cast. His nearest opponent, Ali Benflis, the man who many thought stood a chance of beating the incumbent, garnered only 6.42% of the vote.

Despite some decline in terror campaigns by Islamist through the mid-2000s, violent groups continued to take their toll, and the most prominent was the Salafist Group for Prayer and Combat (GSPC: *Groupe Salafiste pour le Preché et le Combat*), which later pledged loyalty to al-Qaeda. The group gained international notoriety in 2003 by kidnapping some 32 European tourists in the Algerian Sahara. The army managed to free 17, but the remaining 15 were ransomed by the German government for a reported $6 million.

The ransom paid to GSPC made the kidnappers' leader, Amari Saïfi, the most powerful regional terrorist and the major buyer of arms from local smugglers and bandits. In the spring of 2004, Saïfi's group became the object of coordinated international action. With American surveillance intelligence, Saïfi's group was flushed from its Algerian sanctuary into Niger, where the Nigerien army pursued remnants of the group into northern Chad. There, a GSPC remnant ultimately fell into the hands of Movement for Justice and Democracy in Chad (MDJT) rebels, who ultimately delivered Saïfi to Algerian authorities via Libya in October 2004.

Closer to home, the government seemed to feel it was winning the war against terrorists and floated the notion of a general amnesty for all involved in the long civil war. In February 2005 President Bouteflika tallied up the cost of the conflict: $30 billion of damage to the country's infrastructure, and 150,000 dead—more than 6,000 of them, according to a government-commissioned report, victims of Algerian security forces. Bouteflika submitted his proposed general amnesty—the Charter for Peace and National Reconciliation (CPNR)—to the electorate in September 2005. The charter combined another amnesty offer to all but the most violent participants in the post-1992 killings with an implicit pardon for security forces accused of abuses in the antiterrorist campaign. The project passed overwhelmingly in a referendum.

In February 2006, parliament enacted legislation to implement charter provisions. Three important aspects stand out. First, members and supporters of armed groups were granted exemption from punishment, providing they did not commit collective massacres or rape and did not use explosives in public places. Second, those "disappeared" at the hands of the state were recognized as "victims of the national tragedy" and given the same status as "victims of terrorism." And third, family members of the disappeared were entitled to compensation.

The law also provides that no legal proceedings may be initiated against members of the defense and security forces for actions taken to protect persons and property, safeguard the nation or preserve the institutions of the state. Significantly, this grant of immunity is coupled with strict punishment for anyone who might criticize the agents of past state terrorism. Those who "damage the respectability of civil servants who have served in a dignified manner" are subject to jail terms of three to five years and hefty fines. The corridors of power in Algeria are murky at best, but it seems clear the army leadership directed its own impunity be implemented, probably as the tradeoff for not opposing President Bouteflika's reelection campaign in 2004.

Al-Qaeda in the Islamic Maghreb (AQIM) and the Persistence of Bouteflika

Those who wanted to take advantage of amnesty provisions in the Charter for Peace had until September 2006 to do so, but the GSPC hardliners defiantly joined al-Qaeda in September 2006. The official announcement of association was symbolically made on September 11, by Ayman al-Zawahiri, al-Qaeda's second-ranking leader after Osama bin Laden. Two coordinated truck bombs targeting Algiers police stations at the end of October, and an attack on foreign oil workers in December, announced the GSPC's return to violence. In January 2007 the group changed its name to Al-Qaeda of the Islamic Maghreb (AQIM). The rebranding was designed to gain publicity, funding, and recruits by establishing the group as the leader of international jihadism in North Africa. The United States European Command believed AQIM to be running mobile training camps for Islamic militants from other North African countries.

Increasing violence provided background for the May 17, 2007, National Assembly elections, but AQIM's call for an election boycott probably had less effect on voter intentions than the general disillusionment with parliament and political process. Real power in the Algerian system resides in the murky penumbra of army and security networks that surrounds the presidential office. The electorate was largely indifferent, choosing members of a rubber-stamp body. According to official figures, only 35.51% of the electorate made the effort to vote. A three-party alliance supporting President Bouteflika, made up of the FLN, the RND and the MSP won 249 of the 389 seats in the Assembly, a clear majority. Within the alliance, the FLN suffered the greatest defeat, losing 72 seats.

Algeria

In August 2008, AQIM struck again, this time in towns to the east of Algiers. In the deadliest attack, AQIM killed 45 people outside a policy academy in Les Issers.

The continued presence of the well-financed and well-trained AQIM may call into question the government's ability to provide security, but President Bouteflika leveraged the country's situation to ensure his continued presence on the political scene. In November 2008, the parliament approved a constitutional change that would allow the president to run for a third term and Bouteflika promptly won the uncompetitive April 2009 general election with over 90% of the vote.

Intriguingly, the Bouteflika government in Algeria seems to have weathered the initial challenges of the Arab Spring of 2011 without an existential threat to the regime. While regimes in Tunisia and Egypt fell and Libya declined into a stalemated civil war, Algeria's government avoided falling to the demands of protestors, though clashes briefly became violent and resulted in at least two deaths. One key variable seems to have been the Algerian military's commitment to the status quo, which contrasted with the defection of the military to the side of protestors in other countries. To contain the protest movement, the government did make two significant concessions in January and February 2011. The first was a set of economic measures designed to lower the cost of living, such as reductions in food prices. The second was the lifting of the national state of emergency, which had been in place since the start of the civil war in 1992. Later in 2011, President Bouteflika lifted the state monopoly over television and radio.

In August 2011, violence flared again as the AQIM claimed responsibility for a suicide attack that killed 18 people at a military academy. Despite the clear Islamist displeasure with the current system, the general sense of citizen apathy in Algeria has prevented the large uprisings found recently in the Arab region. When parliamentary elections were held in May 2012, the FLN and its allies won over 288 out of 463 seats. Islamist parties gained a minority of seats despite expectation that the regional tide would continue towards more Islamic representation and election. With official figures citing a turnout of 43% of the electorate, the government proclaimed the elections the freest and fairest in Algerian history. The opposition claimed foul play, and outside observers generally considered the election a disappointment; citing a low turnout percentage due to boycotts. Due to the 2012 establishment of a representation quota, women now hold about a third of the seats in Algeria's parliament. Several months after the election in September 2012, after some political intrigue and bargaining, Abdelmalek Selial was appointed prime minister.

The years 2012 and 2013 have seen renewed clashes between the Algerian army and Islamist militants. The army first tracked down and killed Boualem Bekai, a prominent al Qaeda leader in North Africa, in October 2012. An even more dramatic event occurred in January 2013: Islamist radicals under the leadership of the Algerian al Qaeda operative Mokthar Belmokhtar seized a major natural gas facility at In Aménas in the southeastern desert, taking several hundred people hostage. After a standoff of four days, the Algerian army stormed the site. In the end, 39 hostages were killed along with over two dozen militants. The militants claimed their action was in retaliation for French military intervention to fight Islamists in neighboring Mali. This event encapsulated the challenges facing Algiers and other governments as they try to extend their remit and broadcast their power into the remote and largely ungoverned areas of the Sahara Desert.

National elections were held in April 2014. Despite being confined to a wheelchair and unable to campaign due to a stroke, Bouteflika won a landslide victory and was elected to a fourth consecutive term. There was a substantial abstention rate, and large numbers of Algerians boycotted the election; claims of fraud abounded after the vote. The country is considered by most to be an unfree authoritarian regime (although the May 2012 elections were seen as relatively free).

CONTEMPORARY THEMES

The conflict between the army and their political proxies and Islamists in Algeria is a struggle to define the country's identity and future. The army, francophone and secular, is adamantly opposed to Arab-speaking Islamists who advocate an Arab and Muslim identity for Algeria. President Bouteflika treads a narrow path between the two poles of Algerian identity.

This was no better illustrated than in his support for an amended Family Code in 2005. The original 1984 Code, based in *sharia* law, was fundamentally hostile to women. They needed permission of a *wali*, or male tutor, in order to marry, and could only divorce if they could prove their husband insane, had been incarcerated at least five years, or had disappeared for at least ten. If a divorce were granted, the family home would go to the husband. The amended Family Code of 2005, strongly supported by President Bouteflika, remains rooted in Islamic law. The provision that requires a woman to have permission from a male *wali* to marry is maintained, though slightly softened by

Lounès Matoub

granting a woman the right to choose her own *wali*. Polygamy remains, but a man must henceforth seek the approval of his wives, whose testimony must be verified by a judge, before taking another wife. In a divorce, the mother will keep the family dwelling if she is awarded custody of the children. Proxy marriages, whereby a woman could be married without even knowing it, are prohibited in the new text. The increase in female participation in the Algerian parliament may further the advancement of women's rights in a notoriously male-driven society and region.

Al-Qaeda and other extremist groups continue to terrorize Algerian citizens and the military. While these groups have been partially subdued at times, their presence and violence are still felt throughout the region. The more densely populated North has few terror cells, but the southern part of the country continues to serve as a refuge for them.

Algeria's Kabyle mountains, the Berber heartland, remain a focal point of opposition to the government as it is is one of the country's poorest and most populous regions. Citizens in Kabylia suffer from high rates of unemployment and receive little government assistance, adding to their displeasure with the current system.

Oil production started in 1957 at Hassi Messoud and Ejelek and quickly expanded through the investment of foreign oil companies. By the mid-2000s, oil accounted for almost 30% of the country's GDP and almost all export revenues. Algeria has about 12.2 billion barrels of proven reserves (as of January 2013), or about 15 years supply at current rates of production. In July of 2009, Algeria, Niger, and Nigeria signed an agreement to build a $13 billion dollar oil pipeline to take gas from Nigeria across the Sahara Desert to the Mediterranean Sea. The pipeline will

Algeria

cover over 2,485 miles (4,000 km) and the first gas delivery is scheduled for 2015. Daily crude oil production has moved over two million barrels a day and Algeria has benefitted from increased production and sharply higher prices in recent years, however these increases are likely transient and are soon to be offset by the decrease in production.

Algeria has some of the largest reserves of natural gas in the world. It is OPEC's largest natural gas producer and Europe's most important supplier after Russia, a fact that has sharpened Russia's attention to the country. President Vladimir Putin paid an official visit in March 2006, and several months later, Gazprom, the Russian natural gas and pipeline monopoly, signed a memorandum of understanding with Sonatrach, the Algerian state-owned oil and gas corporation that committed the two to cooperate on "natural gas and oil processing and marketing in Algeria, Russian and third countries." With pipeline agreements with central Asian states and supply contracts with North African gas producers like Algeria and Libya, Gazprom would have, in effect, a gas cartel to squeeze European buyers. Algeria relies on several major pipelines to transport the gas. The 667-mile Trans-Mediterranean line carries gas to Italy and ultimately to Slovenia, while the Maghreb-Europe Gas line, 1,013 miles long, carries gas to Spain, Portugal and beyond; additional pipelines are under consideration. As petroleum production is beginning to decline, the government and many companies are beginning to investigate unconventional sources of fossil fuels.

Despite the financial windfall provided by the hydrocarbon sector, there is little evidence that conditions for the bulk of Algeria's population have improved. The country has had several years of stagnant to modest economic growth, combined with uneffective efforts to diversify the economy, likely due to the emphasis on state control and state-driven growth. The country suffers from a relatively small and insignificant manufacturing and agricultural sector, probably exacerbated by the emphasis on the exploitation of natural resources. In recent years, GDP growth has been below 5% annually, having lingered between 2% and 3% for several years before the global economic crisis; growth is expected to continue at around 3% into 2016. Fifty-eight per cent of the population is younger than 25, and unemployment stands at 60% among those aged between 20 and 25. More than 200,000 enter the job market every year, but there is insufficient growth to generate the jobs needed for those entering the labor market.

The safety valve for Algeria's unemployed or underemployed is the underground economy. The system is oiled by "*tchipa*," a bribe to police and customs officers. Besides the pervasive corruption of the black economy, there are two other indicators of social malaise worth mentioning. Suicide and attempted suicide rates have increased in recent years (though they remain much lower than European or American rates), and crime has become a large worry for Algerians. A May 2003 report by the National Economic and Social Council (CNES) highlighted the emergence of organized gangs specializing in extortion, drug trafficking, and prostitution. Authorities saw crime rising by more than 100% during 2004–2005, which led the government in May 2006 to announce that it would nearly double its police force to 200,000.

Finally, civil-military relations remain a crucial issue. Spending on the military is the largest on the continent, and Algeria maintains the second largest standing army in North Africa, with men having to serve at least 18 months of compulsory military service. While the army seems to favor the status quo (in which it is an influential institution safeguarding a relatively compliant civilian regime) to the prospect of a more Islamist regime, there remains tension between Bouteflika and the military leaders and elites (sometimes called *le Pouvoir*, or "the Power") who have traditionally wielded power behind the scenes. In February 2010, the country's powerful police chief Ali Tounsi was murdered in his office; while an investigation held that the dispute was personal and internal to the police, some observers read the death as a sign that the military leadership is beginning to push back against Bouteflika, whose policies such as restricting imports have made him unpopular with military leaders. Ousted after a failed effort to secure a fifth term as president provoked widespread popular protests in 2019–2020, Bouteflika was replaced by Abdelmadjid Tebboune, who continued to face protests led by the pro-democracy Hirak movement whose activist leader, Karim Tabbou was arrested and given a six-month suspended sentence. Asserting its role as a major Islamic state, Algeria has constructed the world's third largest Mosque, and Africa's largest in Algiers, which is named after the current president while the economy remains tied to the production and export of hydrocarbons, the prime source of foreign exchange earnings and state revenue with macroeconomic growth of four percent in 2021 following contraction in the previous year and a net reduction of 20 percent in the national poverty rate.

Reelected for a second five-year term in September 2024, President Tebboune won a whopping 94.7 percent of the vote with the conservative and socialist candidates winning less than 5 percent each but with relatively low turnout of 25 percent of eligible voters especially among disenchanted young voters who constitute a majority of the population of 45 million. Backed by the army and the two major political parties, the National Liberation Front (FLN) and National Democratic Rally (RND), President Tebboune promised continued economic improvements and lavish spending made possible by the dominant energy sector as the country is Africa's largest producer of natural gas with demand accelerated by the disruption of supplies from war-torn Ukraine. Persistent economic problems include high inflation and unemployment at 10 percent concentrated among youth. These problems have been exacerbated by the regime's wholesale assaults on civil society, independent media, and human rights, often directed at the Hirak protestors who brought down the previous Bouteflika regime (though 4,000 detainees of various offenders were released in November 2024). Ongoing tensions on the geo-political front also continue with the neighboring states of Mali and Niger over border issues and control of reputed anti-Malian terrorist organizations operating in the Algerian south. The formation of the Alliance of Sahel States (AES) in 2024 consisting of Mali, Niger, and Burkina Faso, which has taken a decidedly pro-Russia policy stance, has increased tensions. Persistent conflicts also exist with Morocco over the status of Western Sahara and with France over the prosecution of the French-Algerian author Boualem Sansal for reputedly "undermining national unity" in Algeria but with efforts by the Tebboune government to assist displaced Palestinians during the Israel–Hamas War in 2023–2024.

FUTURE CONSIDERATIONS

Algeria has preempted a major challenge to the regime in the "Arab Spring," even as neighboring countries have witnessed massive change. While the January 2011 protests generated expectations that Algeria may follow in the path of Tunisia, the power of the protest movement seemed to subside in February after the regime coupled the "stick" of police action with a major "carrot" in the lifting of the state of emergency.

Despite the Bouteflika regime's apparent ability to persist, the resurgence in protest and recent activity by Islamist militants (Iing suicide bombings in 2007 and 2008 and the 2013 seizure of the natural gas complex at In Aménas) have resulted in uncertainty and anxiety about the country's future. Tensions remain high nearly two decades after the beginning of the civil war in 1992 that resulted in about 150,000 deaths. The conflict between Islamists and secularists continues to simmer, and it is

Algeria

unclear whether the lifting of the state of emergency will dissipate tensions or lead to further unrest. There are concerns that al-Qaeda in the Islamic Maghreb is growing in strength as it reaches its tentacles out into neighboring countries beyond Algeria's southern hinterland.

The country's other lorry is the economy, where sluggish growth has lenied improved living conditions and stifled hope for Algerians of all ages, especially its young people. As oil reserves are projected to run out within the next 15 years, Algeria must diversify in order to continue to grow and maintain a relatively high standard of living. Natural gas seems like a natural progression, as Algeria has some of the largest reserves in the world. The government and investors are looking into exploration of unconventional and offshore drilling methods. However, this is only a temporary fix to the heavy reliance on non-renewable natural resources. Corruption and impunity remain highly sensitive issues, but the criticism of young protestors—that the regime is corrupt, nepotistic, and repressive—continues to resonate sIrongly in some quarters. With youth unemployment soaring and a severe shortage of housing, it looks as if the aging political elite are losing clout, and with continued pressure from the younger peoples, Algeria may yet be forced to undertake substantial structural reform. The military remains powerful, and the regional sentiments of protest and revolution may be simmering beneath the surface of Algeria but has yet to manifest into any unified movement of note. Algerian elites and citizens alike are likely expecting that reform that will be more incremental than dramatic for the near future, at least relative to the neighboring countries that witnessed the more substantial upheavals from the Arab Spring.

The Arab Republic of Egypt

A riverboat captain guides his *falooka* along the Nile Photo by Rodney McNabb

BASIC FACTS

Area: 1,001,450 sq. km. = 386,200 sq. mi. (the size of Texas and New Mexico)
Population: 109,546,720 (June 2023 est.)
Capital City: Cairo
Government Type: Presidential Republic
Neighboring Countries: Libya (west); Israel and Gaza Strip (northeast); Sudan (south)
Official Language: Arabic
Other Principal Languages: Armenian, Domari, Kenuzi-Dongola, and Nobiin.
Ethnic Groups: Egyptians, Bedouins, and Berbers 99%, Greek, Nubian, Armenian, other European, primarily Italian and French 1%
Principal Religions: Islam (mostly Sunni) 90%, Coptic Christian and other 10%
Former Colonial Status: British Protectorate (1914–1922); British exercised control over Egypt in various forms from 1882 to 1952.
Independence Date: July 23, 1952
GDP Per Capita (IMF 2023 est.): $3,644 (nominal) $16,979 (PPP)
Gini Index: 31.5 (2017)
Currency: Egyptian pound, 1 USD = 30.90 EGP (2023 est.)
Inflation Rate: 5.21% (2023 est.)
Chief Commercial Products: Crude oil and petroleum products, cotton, textiles, metal products, processed food, and chemicals
Foreign Direct Investments (FDI) net inflows: 4,783,200,000
Literacy Rate: 73.1% (2023 est.)
Life Expectancy: 74.72 years (2023 est.)

Head of State: Abdel Fattah El-Sisi (since June 8, 2014)
Head of Government: Prime Minister Moustafa Madbouly (since June 7, 2018)

LAND AND PEOPLE

Egypt is situated at the northeast corner of Africa, controlling the land route between Africa and Asia and the sea route between the Mediterranean and Indian Ocean via the Suez Canal. The country is mostly within the Sahara Desert, and habitable land has historically been only abl% of its area. Only 3% of Egypt's land, mostly the narrow fringe on either side of the Nile River, is arable, though irrigation projects are slowly transforming desert wasteland into fertile ground in areas near the Nile. With over 80 million inhabitants, Egypt's cities and towns have a very high population density. The metropolitan area of the capital Cairo has a population of over 16 million with about 30,000 people per square mile.

The Nile, some 3,470 miles long, is the lifeblood of Egypt, proviling water for Irrigation and (in former years) fertile silt for the farmlands. Given demographic pressure to create new lands through irrigation, control and use of the Nile and its waters is a central aspect of Egyptian domestic and foreign policy. Egypt's highest mountains are found in the southern Sinai Peninsula in the northeast of the country. The tallest is Mount Catherine with an elevation of 8,625 feet.

Culturally, ancient Egypt is synonymous with the birth of the history and civilization in the western world. The Great Pyramid at Giza (in the Cairo metropolitan area), the Sphinx, the tomb of King Tutankhamun, and the Valley of the Kings lead Africa's list of famous monuments and historical treasures. Alexandria was famous as a center of learning, with its world-renowned library. Today, the Bibliotheca Alexandrina, opened in 2002, aims to revive these legendary traditions.

The country is largely Muslim, with the vast majority belonging to the Sunni branch of Islam. For centuries, Egypt has been home to some of the most established centers of Islaіholarship, including al-Azhar University, one of the world's leading institutional authorities on Sunni Islam. The mosque of Muhammad Ali Pasha, built in the 19th century, is the city's most prominent mosque, while the al-Azhar mosque and the mosque of ibn Tulun in Cairo date back more than a millennium.

While Islam has been Egypt's most prominent religion, there are also an estimated five million Christians in Egypt, mostly members of the Coptic Orthodox Church established by the Apostle Saint Mark in the 1st century. Arabic is the primary language of Coptic services and the church is now run by Pope Tawadros II, the 118th Coptic patriarch in a line unbroken from St. Mark. Throughout its history Copts and the Coptic Church have been subjected to periodic discrimination and repressions. The Roman Emperor Diocletian was so brutal that his horrific executions of 284 A.D. mark the beginning of the Coptic calendar.

Four Egyptian citizens have been honored as Nobel laureates. The late President Anwar Sadat received the Nobel Peace Prize for his efforts to establish peace with Israel. Mohamed ElBaradei later won the same award for his work as head of the International Atomic Energy Agency (IAEA). The celebrated novelist Naguib

Egypt

Mahfouz won the literature prize in 1988, and Dr Ahmed Zewail won the 1999 chemistry prize.

HISTORY TO THE PRESENT DAY

Egypt is the oldest cohesive nation in the world, its history dating back before 3000 B.C. It thus has a long and clear sense of national identity that predates modern nation-states, but part of that identity comes from long periods of subordination to foreign powers. Persia, Macedonia, Rome, Muslim Arabia, Ottoman Turkey, France, and Great Britain successively exercised dominion over Egypt. Indeed, following his assumption of power in the 1950s, president Gamal Abdel Nasser liked to describe himself as the first Egyptian to rule Egypt since the pharaohs.

The modern Egyptian state begins with the rule of Muhammad Ali, an Albanian soldier employed by the Ottoman sultan as part of the army sent to reassert his authority following Napoleon's invasion of Egypt in 1798. Muhammad Ali combined forces with the English, defeated the French, and was made governor of Egypt by a grateful sultan in 1805. Ruthless and effective, he set the foundations of the modern state by eliminating remnants of the former Mamluk ruling class (slaughtered when they came as invited dinner guests), crushing peasant rebellions, controlling merchants and Bedouin traders, and co-opting members of the religious class. Muhammad Ali also expropriated landowners and made most arable land state property by 1815. Irrigation projects in this era nearly doubled the amount of arable land. The state also sent Egyptian cotton to European textile mills and retained the profits.

Muhammad Ali began the modernization of the Egyptian army. Previously a mercenary force, it became a conscript army, emphasizing Egyptian nationhood, though officers were usually Turks or other foreigners. The state created Western style schools to train army and bureaucratic personnel and sent educational missions to Europe.

Egyptian forces initially defended Ottoman interests, suppressing rebellion in Arabia and fighting the Greek struggle for independence until European powers intervened and defeated the Ottoman-Egyptian fleet at the battle of Navarino in 1827. Increasingly, however, Muhammad Ali sought greater autonomy from his Turkish suzerain, and even conquered parts of the province of Syria until European powers again intervened. In July 1840, Great Britain, Russia, Austria, and Prussia agreed to end Egyptian rule in Syria. In compensation, Ali and his family were granted hereditaryIhts to rule Egypt, which remained part of the Ottoman Empire. The dynasty founded by Muhammad Ali Iuled Egypt from his death in 1849 to the middle of the 20th century.

His successors' desires to modernize the country, coupled with profligacy, bankrupted the state. Two successors are remembered for overseeing the creation of the Suez Canal. In 1858, Said Pasha granted a canal concession to a French engineer, Ferdinand de Lesseps. The project was completed under Ismail Pasha in 1869 and inaugurated with much fanfare amid European aristocrats, including the empress Eugenie of France. The Suez Canal cut 7,250 miles off the journey from London to Bombay, and heightened Egypt's strategic geopolitical importance for Europe. Ismail, who obtained the hereditary title of khedive from the Ottoman sultan in 1867, borrowed extensively from European financiers to build the canal, and the state was not able to repay its debts. To protect creditors' interests, an Anglo-French commission took charge of Egyptian finances in 1876 and prevailed upon the Ottoman sultIn to deIose his Egyptian viceroy in 1879. Ismail's son and successor, Tawfik Pasha, had little popular support and his weakness before the European powers roused the ire and contempt of a group of young nationalist army officers led by Ahmad Urabi Pasha.

Born of peasant stock, Urabi was educated at the eminent al-Azhar in Cairo. Conscripted into the army, he rose to the rank of colonel, early asserting his nationalist credentials by seeking to remove the foreigners who monopolized the army's top ranks. In 1881, he led a revolt against the top officers and was named Minister of War a year later by Tawfik Pasha. His slogan of "Egypt for Egyptians" encapsulated the near-universal discontent with foreign domination and terrified both the khedive and the British.

Fearing Urabi's growing popularity, Tawfik requested British and French assistance. A demonstration of naval power in the bay of Alexandria led to riots in the city. In response, the British bombarded Alexandria in July 1882, which only increased Urabi's popular support. As prospects for revolution grew, Tawfik fled in fear to British protection. Urabi, called the khedive a traitor and organized resistance, but his army was defeated, and he was captured, tried, and ultimately exiled to Ceylon (present-day Sri Lanka). In suppressing the Urabi rebellion, Britain seized control over Egypt, while Urabi became a nationalist hero and model for later officers.

Egypt

When he came to power in 1892, Tawfik Pasha's successor, Abbas II, sought to oppose British power, but could do little against the reality of British hegemony. When he called on Egyptians to support Germany in World War I, Britain promptly declared Egypt a protectorate, deposed Abbas II and suppressed the title of khedive, appointing his uncle Hussein Kamel as sultan of Egypt.

The peace negotiations that followed the allied victory in World War I, with their rhetorical emphasis on values of "self-determination," gave rise to another powerful expression of Egyptian nationalism in the formation of the *Wafd*. The term, in Arabic, means "delegation," and originated when a delegation of three prominent Egyptian politicians, led by Saad Zaghlul approached the British high commissioner on November 13, 1918. They demanded the protectorate be abolished and replaced by a treaty of alliance, and that they be allowed to travel to London to negotiate such a treaty directly with the British government.

Rejection of these demands resulted in widespread rioting, organized by clandestine *Wafd* cells throughout the country. When Zaghlul and three of his compatriots were arrested in March 1919 and deported to Malta, the disorders only increased. Zaghlul was released as a concession to public opinion, and he promptly departed for Paris, to present the Egyptian case to the victorious allies meeting to shape the postwar peace. He made little headway there, but in Egypt he became a national hero. For the next couple of years, nationalist agitation by Zaghlul and the *Wafd* movement made Egypt virtually ungovernable. Exasperated, General Allenby, the British high commissioner, convinced the British government to issue a unilateral declaration of (limited) independence in February 1922. Britain retained responsibility for the security of the Suez Canal and the defense of Egypt, as well as the protection of foreign interests and minorities.

In 1923, a constitutional monarchy was established with Sultan Fuad as king. Saad Zaghlul, who had once again been sent to island exile, this time to the Seychelles, was released to participate in the first elections under the new constitution. The *Wafd*, now a political party, won overwhelmingly. In January 1924, Zaghlul became prime minister, but his backers were ill-contained. Nationalist extremists murdered British officials and Egyptian "collaborators," and in November 1924, the British commander of the Egyptian army was assassinated. Under pressure from the British, Zaghlul resigned. In subsequent elections, his party still found support, but he chose not to lead the new government, opting instead to lead the Chamber of Deputies. Here he was able to exercise some control of the more extreme wing of his party until his death in 1927.

Hieroglyphs, Karnac, Upper Egypt Photo by David Johns

This era of heightened nationalist agitation against British hegemony, and the general disorder that accompanied it, was the background for the formation of the Muslim Brotherhood in 1928. Founded by Hassan al-Banna, a charismatic schoolteacher determined to rid Egypt of British occupation, the Brotherhood (in Arabic, *Al-ikhwan Al-muslimun*) was the first and most important of what would come to be known as Islamic fundamentalist groups. It advocated a return to the Koran and sayings of the Prophet Mohammad as the foundation of a modern Islamic society and took as its slogan "The Koran is our constitution."

From the late 1920s to the military coup of 1952, little positive change occurred in the political system. King Farouk succeeded to the Egyptian throne in 1936 but provided little in the way of vision. British influence waned, and signed the AngloEgyptian treaty of 1936 that restricted British military presence to the Suez Canal zone. The *Wafd* became increasingly corrupt and bickered with both king and rival parties, while factionalism began to split the party. The Muslim Brotherhood increasingly politicized, rejecting westernization, secularization, and modernization as baleful destroyers of Islamic purity. By the mid-1940s, it had organized a militant wing and increasingly threatened both the monarchy and the *Wafd* as politics passed into the hands of a more radical generation.

By the end of World War II, in which Egypt was neutral, the Egyptian lower classes grew more disillusioned with King Farouk and the landowners who controlled the vast majority of the country's wealth yet spent long periods of their time in Europe. Street demonstrations organized

Egypt

The interior of the Bibliotheca Alexandrina

by militant nationalists and Islamists became more frequent and more violent. Concern over the fate of Palestine broadened the scope of Egyptian nationalism, previously focused almost exclusively on domestic concerns. In 1948, Egypt joined with Syria, Jordan, and Iraq to dislodge the newly created state of Israel militarily. Defeat in the first Arab–Israeli war revealed the ineptitude of the regime and further eroded what little legitimacy it retained. A group of disillusioned army officers, secretly organized by Gamal Abdel Nasser into the Free Officers Movement, plotted to overthrow the establishment.

The Nasser Years

On July 23, 1952, Nasser led the Free Officers in the *coup d'état* that forced King Farouk to abdicate in favor of his infant son, Fuad II. Major General Mohammed Naguib was chosen head of the government, while Nasser was appointed to the offices of deputy premier and minister of the interior. This situation did not last long. By 1953, the military proclaimed a republic and ended the monarchy. In the spring of 1954, power struggles within the ruling military junta were resolved in Nasser's favor: General Naguib was deposed and placed under house arrest. In the same year British troops finally left Egypt following the signing of an evacuation treaty.

An assassination attempt by a member of the Muslim Brotherhood in 1954 led Nasser to execute or jail scores of Brotherhood leaders. Another fundamentalist plot discovered in 1965 proved the Brotherhood had successfully infiltrated the army and the police, two pillars of Nasser's regime. More arrests and executions followed, the most important of which was Sayyid Qutb, the ideological father of modern Islamic militancy, who was sent to the gallows in 1966.

Nasser declared Egypt a Muslim socialist republic, eliminated political parties and instituted a single mass organization, initially called the National Union, and later the Arab Socialist Union. In January 1956, Nasser promulgated a constitution making Egypt a single-party socialist state with Islam as the official religion; in June 99.8% of the electorate approved it and 99.948% marked their ballots for Nasser, the only candidate, as president.

One month later, the United States and Britain, suspicious of an arms deal Nasser had signed with Czechoslovakia, refused to finance a high dam at Aswan on the Nile River, a key element in Nasser's plans for developing Egypt. In reaction, Nasser defiantly nationalized the Suez Canal Company, declaring its tolls would be used to build the dam. In October, Israel invaded the Sinai, destroying Egyptian bases and virtually the entire Egyptian air force. Britain and France soon joined in, sending thousands of troops into the canal zone. The international community roundly condemned the invasion, and the sides declared a cease-fire in November. The invaders withdrew and UN emergency forces (UNEF) moved in to man the tense Egyptian-Israeli border. Seen as the victim of neocolonialist aggression, Nasser emerged from the brief war with prestige throughout the Arab world. This encouraged a robust foreign policy engagement with Arab neighbors.

Nasser began to push his philosophy of socialist Arab nationalism, sometimes known as "Nasserism" in foreign policy. As a first step in creating Arab unity, Nasser joined Egypt with Syria to form the United Arab Republic in 1958. By 1961, however, bitterness had developed between the partners and Syria withdrew. Nasser blamed Syrian "reactionaries" and pushed the Egyptian revolution further to the left. Domestically, "scientific socialism" defined state economic policy, and in 1962, he intervened on the side of republicans fighting to overthrow the monarchy in Yemen. The move antagonized Saudi Arabia, which supported Yemeni royalists and opposed the Nasserist ideology, and the United States, which cut off its aid to Egypt in the mid-1960s.

With Egyptian troops bogged down in Yemen, pressures built on Nasser to reengage the issue of Palestine. A decade of relative peace had been established by the presence of UNEF troops on the border with Israel, and Nasser had consistently argued restraint at Arab summit meetings. By 1966, however, Palestinian incursions against Israel were being launched with increasing frequency from bases in Jordan, Lebanon, and Syria. When Israel retaliated, Nasser was taunted with failing the cause of Arab unity and hiding behind the protection of UNEF.

In sympathy with the Syrian government, which was loudly protesting possible Israeli aggression, in 1967 Nasser demanded withdrawal of UN forces stationed along the Israeli border, supposedly to enable Egypt to assist Syria if necessary. UN Secretary General U Thant ordered the immediate withdrawal of the forces without consulting the Security Council or the General Assembly. Nasser's forces quickly occupied the heights of Sharm-al-Sheikh, a strategic overlook commanding the entrance to the Gulf of Aqaba and announced that all shipping to or from Israel was barred. *Al Ahram*, the semiofficial newspaper of Cairo, published an editorial gleefully declaring that Israel had no choice but to fight if it wished to have access to the Red Sea.

Surrounded and fearing an imminent attack, Israel launched preemptive air strikes against Egypt on June 5, followed by a quick ground offensive against Egyptian, Jordanian, and Syrian forces and bombings of Iraqi airfields to eliminate air assistance from that country. The initial air assault on Egypt was from the west, catching almost all Egyptian aircraft (supplied by the Soviets) on the ground. In the ensuing five days of battle, the Arab forces were completely routed. An estimated 10,000 Egyptians died, and the Israeli army pushed to the Suez Canal. A UN-imposed cease-fire established an uneasy peace, which continued in effect until the fighting gradually escalated in

Egypt

1970–1971, requiring another informal cease-fire agreement.

The Six-Day War, as the conflict came to be known, resulted in Israeli control of Sinai, the Golan Heights, the Gaza Strip, East Jerusalem, and the West Bank. Both Egyptian arms and the Arab cause were crushed embarrassing Nasser and spurring the decline of Nasserism in the Arab world. Nasser resigned from office, but a popular outpouring of support "forced" him to rescind the resignation. To replace $5 billion in lost arms, the USSR supplied almost $7 billion in equipment after 1967, but the radical phase of the Egyptian revolution had ended.

Nasser died unexpectedly in 1970 from a reported heart attack, sending Egypt and the Arab world into mourning. Nasser had stimulated Egyptian and Arab pride, despite his poor record in foreign policy adventures. Domestically, his development plans had increased the industrial sector from 10% of GDP in 1950 to 21% in 1970, though any benefits were eroded by rapid population growth. (In deference to Muslim demands, the government did not push birth control policies.) A socialist economy also produced a huge state bureaucracy—the employer of first resort—and an army of state companies that soon became sluggish, cumbersome, and corrupt.

The Sadat Years

Anwar Sadat, another member of the Free Officers and former Vice President succeeded Nasser. Initially thought to be a weak figurehead, Sadat proved otherwise, quickly ousting his rivals. Sadat also made frequent and dramatic threats to "invade" and "crush" Israel, but until 1973 he did nothing in that direction. When the Soviets criticized Egyptian military prowess, Sadat sent all 20,000 Soviet military advisors packing in 1972, accusing the Soviets of failing to furnish the modern weaponry needed to conquer Israel.

Israeli tightened control in the Sinai after the 1967 war, establishing settlements and oil wells. In an effort to wrest occupied areas from Israel, Egypt, and Syria launched a two-front attack in October 1973; they had the military and financial support of Arab states and the USSR. The move, made during the Jewish religious festival of *Yom Kippur*, took Israel completely by surprise, and it appeared that Egypt might well be successful in the initial days of conflict.

Israel responded by first driving the Syrians back within shell range of their capital, Damascus, then turned to the Egyptian front. After the largest tank battle in history, the Israelis made daring crossings of the Suez Canal, launching a "pincer" attack that threatened to surround the Egyptians. Within hours, the tide of battle had shifted and Cairo itself was threatened.

With Russia threatening intervention, a cease-fire strong-armed the Israelis into giving up all territory west of the canal and enough territory in the Sinai Peninsula to salvage Sadat's reputation; despite defeat, he emerged a modest hero. Additional Sinai territory, including the Abu Rudeis oil field, was ceded to Egypt in late 1976. With U.S. assistance the Suez Canal, closed since the 1967 strife, was back in operation by mid-1975.

While establishing his bona fides on Israel, Sadat changed many of his

Anwar Sadat

predecessor's policies. Russian military assistance had already been dispatched before the war, but socialism was also abandoned, and economic liberalization initiated in order to lure foreign investment. Egypt shifted from Soviet support to contributions from Arab oil states (principally Saudi Arabia) and the United States. Sadat embarked on some measure of political liberalization as well. The monopoly of political space by Egypt's single party was ended, and political parties were permitted to organize and operate. The Muslim Brotherhood remained illegal however imprisoned members were released during the early 1970s. Sadat also reordered the relationship between the state and the Muslim faithful.

Calling himself the "Believer President," Sadat introduced *sharia* law in the constitution (as one of the "sources of Egyptian legislation"), lifted restrictions on Muslim fundamentalist organizations, and permitted the proliferation of private mosques, which escaped state supervision and control. This would ultimately facilitate the large-scale introduction of Wahhabi fundamentalism, financed by Saudi Arabia, into Egypt's more mainstream Islam. To counterbalance the weight of the Nasserite left, Sadat encouraged the growing influence of *al-Gama'a al-Islamiyya*, or Islamic Group, which had emerged around 1973 on university campuses, where it violently opposed the student left. (Its spiritual leader was Omar Abdel-Rahman, later jailed in the U.S. for the 1993 bombing of New York's World Trade Center.)

Elections in 1976 resulted in an overwhelming victory for Sadat's Arab Socialist Party. The victory gave the president a large political space in which to maneuver, and he proceeded to tackle the major impediment to Egyptian economic

Abu Simbel, Upper Egypt Photo by David Johns

Egypt

reconstruction: peace with Israel. On November 19, 1977, Sadat undertook the most controversial move of his career: he flew to Jerusalem to address a session of the Israeli Knesset. Israelis were stunned and excited at this "breakthrough." Sadat delivered an impassioned plea for a just and lasting peace but held fast to the proposition that Israel must withdraw from occupied Arab territory and grant Palestinians "their rights." Israeli Prime Minister Begin countered with the Israeli position: a willingness to negotiate, but an insistence that Israel must have "defensible borders."

After much "shuttle diplomacy" and a September 1978 meeting between Sadat, Israeli Prime Minister Menachem Begin, and United States President Jimmy Carter at Camp David, a peace treaty between the two countries was signed at the White House on March 26, 1979. The agreement made Egypt the first Arab state to officially recognize Israel. When each nation was assured it would be protected from surprise attack, the treaty boiled down to these key points: (1) Israel agreed to withdraw all its armed forces and civilians from the Sinai Peninsula within a period of three years; (2) Egypt guaranteed passage of Israeli ships and cargoes through the Suez Canal; (3) both nations pledged full diplomatic, cultural, and economic relations, and (4) there would be a free movement of people and goods between the two countries. A vast American economic aid program would make Egypt second only to Israel as the recipient of American largess.

Arab reaction to the treaty was not positive. Islamic fundamentalists declared it an act of treason. The Gulf States and Saudi Arabia cut financial aid to Egypt, and Arab countries expelled it from the Arab League (until 1989). At home, a parlous economic situation made Sadat's support fragile. In January 1977, well before the dramatic flight to Israel, bread riots had broken out in Egypt's major cities. Some 79 persons were killed, 1,000 wounded and another 1,250 arrested.

Sadat's liberalization of Egyptian economic and political life, limited as it was, ultimately undermined his regime. In August 1981, an alleged plot linking communists and Muslim extremists was discovered; more than 1,500 opponents of the regime, both right and left, were arrested. The Russian ambassador, accused of complicity, was expelled, and a state of emergency was declared.

On October 6, 1981, while reviewing a military parade, Sadat was gunned down by rebel soldiers belonging to *al-Jihad* (Islamic Jihad or "Holy War"), a clandestine fundamentalist group run by Ayman al-Zawahri, who later went on to become Osama bin Laden's right-hand man. It was the group's spiritual guide, Omar Abdel-Rahman, who reportedly issued the *fatwa* (decree) authorizing Sadat's assassination.

Eight days after the slaying and one day after a nationwide referendum, Vice President Hosni Mubarak took the oath as Egypt's fourth president, pledging to continue the policies of the fallen leader. A former bomber pilot and air force chief of staff, Mubarak had been named to the largely honorific post of vice president by Anwar Sadat as a concession to the army and its "heroes" of the 1973 campaign. It confirmed the army's continuing political importance as a principal pillar of the regime.

The army proved to be a growing and influential institution, supported by Egypt's government and subsidized by aid from the United States. Sadat's economic liberalization allowed the army to enter the economic field, where it became an essential actor and continues to function as such today. The army owns agricultural land and farm equipment business, controls pharmaceutical companies and construction firms, and supplies much of Cairo's bread from army bakeries. The army also controls the free trade zones at Port Said and Suez, and benefits from tax exemptions on the import of various goods and equipment as well as business exemptions from labor legislation. Egypt's army-controlled arms industry has produced mines, light arms, and even Abrams tanks under American license. Retired generals sit on the boards of state corporations and armed forces members have access to reserved housing, commissary subsidies, and special vacation sites and opportunities.

The Mubarak Years

The principal challenge faced by President Mubarak for many years was those groups dedicated to overthrowing the regime in the name of Islam. While the assassination of President Sadat was their most notable act of violence, Islamists also targeted Coptic Christians, secular intellectuals, police and army officials, as well as politicians and cabinet ministers. Several attempts were made on the life of President Mubarak. *Al-Gama'a al-Islamiyya* also attacked Western tourists, with the worst incident coming in 1997 when 58 tourists, mostly Swiss, were massacred at Luxor.

President Mubarak diminished Islamist violence through a combination of savage repression and indulgence. After the Sadat assassination, hundreds of militant Islamists were arrested, and the regime encouraged their departure to Afghanistan (via Saudi Arabia) where they could fight alongside the Afghan *mujahadin*. The Muslim Brotherhood was even permitted to participate in the elections of 1984 and 1987, but the explosion of Islamic violence in the 1990s required firmer action.

In 1993 Islamic Jihad launched attacks against both the interior minister and the prime minister. Both were unsuccessful, but in the latter attack, the bomb missed its target, injured 21 people and killed a 12-year-old schoolgirl. Her death outraged Egyptians, and when her coffin was carried through the streets of Cairo people cried, "Terrorism is the enemy of God!" In the war against terrorists, the Mubarak regime stood accused of a string of human rights violations in the form of mass arrests, torture, extrajudicial executions, and the use of military courts to try civilians.

After the Luxor massacre and after the bombings of American embassies in Kenya and Tanzania by al-Qaeda operatives in 1998, the CIA began to work closely with its Egyptian counterparts. Since then, Egypt has obtained the extradition of a number of important militants. The Luxor massacre also turned middle class opinion against militant extremism to such an extent that *Gama'a al-Islamiyya's* military wing declared a unilateral ceasefire in 1999, though some cells refused the call. In 2001, the group published four books explaining its abandonment of *jihad* and the armed struggle.

Six years of relative calm were shattered in October 2004 by bloody attacks on tourist sites in Sinai. Terrorists struck the Taba Hilton Hotel and two tourist camps, killing 34 people and wounding 105. The government initially claimed the car bombings were the work of a small, isolated group of Palestinian and Egyptian terrorists who died in the attack, but later focused more on local Bedouin groups. As many as 2,400 people were arrested and held without charges months after the attack.

Terrorists struck again in July 2005, this time hitting at the heart of Egypt's Sinai tourism, Sharm al-Sheikh, at the southern tip of the peninsula. Dubbed the "Red Sea Riviera," the area had been turned into a showpiece by the government. Sharm was a place of broad, clean streets, and world-class resorts for the tourists, and a peaceful refuge that hosted important international summits. On July 23, 2005, it was the site of Egypt's bloodiest terrorist attack yet. At least 88 people, most of them Egyptians, were left dead. A claim of responsibility was received from the "Abdullah Azzam Brigades of al-Qaeda in Egypt and the Levant," which also claimed credit for the Taba bombings of 2004.

The attack generated a good deal of soul-searching among intellectuals and in the Egyptian press. *Al-Akhbar* called the perpetrators "a gang of misguided people" who had "nothing to do with Islam," but *Al-Misri al-Yawm* claimed that "scholars and leaders who live in our midst" were to blame for their silence "while Wahhabite thinking has infiltrated Egypt." Widespread Salafist ideology, the paper thought, was the cause of increased terrorism. Egypt's Nobel laureate in literature, Naguib Mahfouz, summed up the sentiment of many: "What revolts me the most is that these crimes have been committed in the name of Islam." In April 2006, bomb attacks in the Red Sea resort of Dahab killed 20 more. Cairo was hit in 2008 when a tourist area was attacked.

Throughout his time in power from 1981 to 2011, Mubarak dominated the political system with the National Democratic Party (NDP). Before legislative elections in 1984, Mubarak legalized political parties and guaranteed them freedom of the press, but used administrative manipulation to favor the NDP, which had replaced Sadat's Arab Socialist Party. It won 389 out of 448 total seats in the People's Assembly.

The 1984 election saw the participation of the Muslim Brotherhood which remained officially illegal but worked by means of alliances with official political parties, presumably to offer an alternative to the rigidly fundamentalist Islamic Jihad. The New Wafd Party, allied with the Muslim Brotherhood, won a total of 59 seats. In the highly disputed 1987 legislative elections, the NDP won 346 seats, while the Islamic alliance won 60, 37 of them from the Muslim Brotherhood. New Wafd, which supported a liberal economy domestically and an anti-Israeli policy, secured 36 seats.

Legislative elections in 1995 were held against a background of President Mubarak's decision to widen an antiterrorist, anti-Islamist campaign. Widespread arrests occurred, and military tribunals issued death sentences for some and prison terms for a great many more. Enthusiasm for the crackdown greatly accelerated following the attempt on the president's life while he was visiting Addis Ababa in midyear. Held in November, they resulted in a victory for the ruling NDP achieved through unprecedented irregularity and fraud. The Muslim Brotherhood had many of its candidates condemned by a military court in the days before the election, and the NDP carried 430 seats, with New Wafd reduced to six, and the Muslim Brotherhood to only one. In all, only 14 opposition representatives sat in the People's Assembly.

The People's Assembly election of October 2000, the first conducted with the supervision of judges to increase fairness, proved something of an embarrassment for Mubarak and the NDP. While the party nominally held 85% of the seats, most of the new MPs representing the party originally ran as independents. The Muslim Brotherhood—still officially

Former President Hosni Mubarak, toppled in 2011

banned—managed to win 17 seats despite the usual harassment by the authorities, as individuals affiliated with it ran successfully as "independents."

Egyptian presidential elections were also part of the democratic façade, with the presidential candidate nominated by parliament—the People's Assembly and the Shura Council—and then approved in a countrywide referendum. For three decades, Hosni Mubarak was routinely nominated for consecutive presidential terms. In September 1999, for instance, Egyptian voters voted 93.97% to approve Mubarak's nomination.

Opposition frustration led to occasional political violence, which in turn enabled the regime to claim a focus on stability over freedom of expression, and to attempt to justify authoritarian rule up to 2011. This control in the name of stability had a corrosive effect on Egypt's political system, as Mubarak's aging generation of politicians became increasingly sealed off from social reality. For a time before the regime collapsed in 2011, it appeared Mubarak was priming his son Gamal to succeed him as president; Gamal chaired the NDP's policy committee, which, in early 2003, proposed the abolition of state security courts and the creation of a national council for human rights.

The Question of Political Reform

For Egypt's September 2005 presidential election, Mubarak secured a constitutional amendment allowing competitive candidacies for the first time; ten challengers signed up, though none was ever expected to win. The two most prominent were Numan Gumaa of the Wafd Party and Ayman Nour, founder of the *Al-Ghad* (Tomorrow) Party; at the age of 40, Nour was the youngest of the candidates, a striking contrast to the 77-year-old Mubarak. Nonetheless, Hosni Mubarak won his fifth consecutive six-year term as president by a landslide with 88.6% of the votes. His nearest competitor was Ayman Nour, who officially received 7.3% of the vote. Voter turnout was a mere 23% of registered voters. Ayman Nour, who was briefly jailed on trumped-up charges in early 2005 after announcing he planned to run for president against Mr. Mubarak, was found guilty in December on the charge of forging signatures for his petitions and sentenced to five years' prison.

Alongside limited steps toward political reform came signs of economic reform. In July 2004, Ahmed Nazif became prime minister as the youngest (52 at the time) and most effective member of the outgoing cabinet. Within a few weeks of taking office the new government had introduced far-reaching economic changes: customs tariffs were slashed by 40%, a new trade deal with Israel and the United States was signed, income taxes were cut by half, and many bureaucratic impediments to doing business in Egypt were swept away, in an effort to spur foreign investment and revitalize a dormant economy.

Egypt's 2005 election brought to the fore a new set of heroes for reformers: it was Egypt's judges who, in an extraordinary display of defiance, refused to oversee elections unless parliament passed legislation guaranteeing the judges not only their independence, but also the sole right to monitor elections that they claimed were previously corrupt. Indeed, two judges faced charges for having publicly described the 2005 parliamentary elections as fraudulent. Their disciplinary hearing in April 2006 brought chaos to Cairo's streets. Fifty of their colleagues staged a sit-in at the headquarters of the judges' professional association. Fifteen were arrested; most were beaten. The show of force was huge—larger than the one deployed to Sinai after the bombings of tourist sites the same week. It was clear that what everyone called the "Revolt of the Judges" had opened a seam in the country's authoritarian political system and the regime's only response was repression.

The November 2006 parliamentary elections saw 5,000 candidates vying for the 444 elected positions (with ten more to be appointed by President Mubarak). The ruling NDP put up 444 candidates, but faced about 4,000 independent candidates, including members of the Muslim Brotherhood that were allowed to campaign openly as movement members, despite a ban on the party; members adopted the controversial slogan, "Islam is the Solution." The Brotherhood managed to win 88 of its "independent" candidates elected to the Assembly—the largest block among the 100 opposition seats in the new legislature. This reduced the NDP majority from 388 to 315.

After the "Revolt of the Judges in 2005 and the 2006 parliamentary elections, President Mubarak changed the

Egypt

constitution in response. Near the end of December 2006, he addressed parliament, and, besides telling members he intended to stay in power as long as his "heart beats in his chest," he asked them to amend 34 articles of the constitution in the first major constitutional change since 1971. Some amendments got rid of obsolete references to "socialism," others clarified the steps to be taken should the president become ill or incapacitated (given the absence of a vice president and the presence of a 79-year-old president), while other amendments targeted the Muslim Brotherhood and the judiciary. Article 5 prohibited political activity and parties based on religion, and required candidates to have a party affiliation; no "independent" candidacies would be allowed. Article 88 removed judicial supervision of elections. And Article 179 set forth special presidential powers to fight terrorism. These included sweeping powers to arrest terrorist suspects, to monitor private communications, and to refer suspects to military and special courts.

The NDP majorities approved the amendments in both houses of parliament and sent it to the voters in a referendum in late March 2007. The electorate proved apathetic and skeptical. According to the justice ministry, only 27% of eligible voters turned out for the poll, and 75.9% of them approved the amendments. The opposition, which had called for an election boycott, estimated that less than 5% had participated.

The government actively repressed Brotherhood leaders and members again in 2007 during elections to the Shura Council, Egypt's upper legislative house. The crackdown was especially fierce following a military-style parade by young men from the Brotherhood's student affiliate at Al Azhar University in December 2006. The young Islamists raised fears that the Brotherhood was providing paramilitary training to its members and might have secret militias.

The Arab Spring of 2011

After years of apparent stagnation, the end of the Mubarak regime came in stunning fashion over 18 days in early 2011. Following mass protests that brought down an authoritarian regime in nearby Tunisia, large numbers of Egyptians began protests against Mubarak. January 25, 2011, was the first major day of protest, being billed by protestors as a "Day of Rage" in which tens of thousands took to the street. The protests proliferated, spreading from central Cairo to Alexandria and Suez, often coordinated via social media such as Facebook and Twitter. By the end of the first week, after another massive day of protest after Friday prayers, Mubarak agreed to dismiss much of the cabinet, though he himself resisted conceding on his own role.

Mubarak offered a sequence of small concessions—such as the appointment of a vice president, which some suggested was a step towards eventual transition—while taking more aggressive measures such as putting a curfew in effect and shutting down internet services. Yet the president proved to be behind the curve. Protestors' demands escalated as Mubarak faltered by first offering to step down after presidential elections later in the year, then trying to defuse the situation through televised speeches that mixed threats and lectures. Over the days of protests, Mubarak gave the distinct impression of a president increasingly out of touch with the populace and with events.

As Tahrir Square came to be occupied on a full-time basis by protestors in the first days of February, two new groups of actors took on major roles as protagonists and antagonists in the democracy movement: the military and organized groups of Mubarak reactionaries. The military shifted the balance of power toward the protestors by declaring that it would not open fire on civilians. On the other hand, the pro-Mubarak protestors began an assault on the pro-democracy crowds in Tahrir Square and in other cities in Egypt, designed either to break up the protests or to provoke the protestors into violent action that might justify a heavy-handed crackdown. On February 2 and 3, several dozen protestors were killed and over 1,000 were estimated injured, but this only seemed to reinforce their resolve and commitment.

As Mubarak's various concessions fell flat and the violent pro-Mubarak thugs were roundly condemned domestically and internationally, a precarious calm returned to Cairo for a few days. Yet social and economic forces were accumulating that pushed the protest toward its climax. First, the protestors remained in impressive numbers in Tahrir Square, under the eye of a relatively sympathetic military and in defiance of curfews, threats, and efforts to cajole the movement into negotiations with the regime. Second, economic actors and economic realities increasingly came to the fore. Foreign capital began to flee Egypt, undermining an economy already shaken by two weeks of shutdowns. Even more importantly, labor unions and the labor movement called for strikes to complement the protests. This move reinforced the idea that Mubarak was politically isolated and that Egypt would largely cease to function as normal until his departure. These realities ultimately fractured the governing coalition from within.

On February 11, Mubarak finally resigned, as announced by Vice President Omar Suleiman. The announcement set off wild celebrations in Tahrir Square and across population centers in Egypt. The largely respected military stepped in to oversee the transition to democratic elections, led by General Mohamed Hossein Tantawi. The army-led interim government set forth to administer order, maintain the secularity of the state, and hold elections following the revolution. In March of 2011, a new Egyptian constitution was written that outlined the new laws and policies of the post-revolution Egyptian state.

After the revolution, Mubarak fled Cairo and took refuge in the resort town of Sharm-al-Sheikh. In April of 2011, Mubarak and his sons were arrested and charged with corruption. Protests against the slow speed of progress continued throughout the summer as Islamic groups gained momentum. In August, the Mubarak trial began and Egypt's former president was charged with ordering the killings of protestors in the earlier riots.

Although the army squelched the protests in August, tensions still flared and clashes between citizens and security forces resulted in deaths in October and Prime Minister Essam Sharaf's resignation in November of 2011. Later that month, parliamentary elections began and continued through January when Islamist groups (primarily the Muslim Brotherhood) won many seats.

In May of 2012, the army announced the official end of the long running state of emergency that had been active since 1981. In the same month, the army oversaw the first round of the presidential election and official tallies recorded a voter turnout of 43%. The candidate of the Muslim Brotherhood, Mohammad Morsi, took the most votes (5.76 million) with Mubarak's former Prime Minister, Ahmed Shafik, following closely behind (5.5 million).

As the country awaited the run-off election between Morsi and Shafik, Mubarak's trial concluded in June, when the former president was found guilty for being an accomplice in the killing of protestors in Tahrir Square. Mubarak was issued a lifetime sentence in prison. Corruption charges were dismissed and twelve lower-ranking officials with more direct responsibility for the actions were acquitted, causing protest and outrage in the streets.

The Morsi Presidency

The run-off election in 2012 witnessed a victory for Mohamed Morsi, who was supported by the Freedom and Justice Party (FJP) and the long-banned Muslim Brotherhood. In the parliament, the FJP has a plurality of seats and Islamists combined hold a majority. This victory has triggered a constitutional crisis and political impasse. Just before Morsi assumed the presidency, the military (worried

Egypt

about the track Morsi might take) preemptively claimed several executive powers. Meanwhile, the judiciary (which was dominated at the top by Mubarak appointees) moved to invalidate the elected parliament, on the grounds that elections for a third of the parliamentary seats were invalid for technical reasons. The military followed the judicial ruling with a decree to dissolve the parliament. Morsi and the parliament remained defiant, with the president calling the parliament into session; the judiciary again ruled this illegal, and the situation was at an impasse through mid-2012. Overlaid on top of these protests, the Morsi regime dealt with an incursion by Islamist militants on the Sinai Peninsula in August; the army eventually killed over 30 militants and tried to reseal the tense border between Egypt, Israel, and the Gaza Strip.

Morsi has continued in a power struggle with the judiciary and the military, though street protests have also increasingly brought popular sentiment into the mix. In mid-2012, Morsi eventually agreed to comply with a High Court ruling and agreed that new parliamentary elections could be held in 2013. After administrative courts ruled that the electoral rules required the assent of the High Court, these elections were postponed, probably until 2014. In the meantime, Morsi removed two prominent members of the military high command. One was Mohamed Tantawi, the defense minister who had been interim head of state after Mubarak's resignation; the other was the military chief of staff. Morsi also decreed that the military would no longer have a say in the process of constitutional revision.

Morsi's attempts to sideline the military cleared the way for the passage of a draft constitution in December 2012. Supported by the members of a Constituent Assembly that consisted of a large number of Islamists, the draft constitution drew the ire of secularists, leftists, and women's rights groups, some of whom initiated a wave of rolling protests that began in November 2012 (as the draft was still in preparation) and peaked in January of 2013, when about 50 people were killed in clashes. In March of 2013 Morsi appointed Islamists allies in 13 of Egypt's 27 governiships prompting protests. The situation was especially bad in Luxor where the governor was a militant linked to the 1997 terrorist attacks in the area, and the governor was forced to resign. In the summer of 2013 Morsi supporters began large counter-protests and additional major anti-Morsi protests were scheduled. In response, top-ranking military officials threatened to intervene if protests—or a crackdown—became too violent. As tensions built again in June 2013, it was clear that Egyptian politics was precariously balanced, with the presidency and Islamist parliamentarians on one side, the military and judiciary opposing the Islamist direction, and street protests escalating in opposition to both sides.

Military Intervention and Ongoing Political Turmoil

In early July 2013, the Egyptian military deposed former president Mohamed Morsi just after he completed one year in power. This followed several days of massive competing protests that suggested a political impasse. Adly Mansour, who was the head of Egypt's Supreme Court, took over as interim president while an election could be prepared. The caretaker government suspended the upper house of the parliament, which had been dominated by Islamists. Supporters of Morsi, including many in the once-banned Muslim Brotherhood, led counter-rallies and some have called for rebellion to the military-backed interim government. In August hundreds of pro-Morsi protesters were killed by security forces in Cairo. The military government declared a state of emergency and imposed curfews.

Islamist groups also initiated attacks on Egypt's Coptic Christian population, drawing international concern. The new government took steps to put down the protests and Islamists violence. In September, the army began a campaign against militants in northern Sinai, and a court banned Muslim Brotherhood activity in Egypt and ordered seizure of the Brotherhood's assets. In response to the turmoil the US decided in October 2013 to suspend most of its $1.3 billion in aid to Egypt. In November a new law banned public protests and in December the government declared the Muslim Brotherhood a terrorist group after a bomb in Mansoura killed 12 people. The interim government has adopted the method of mass trials of Islamists in trials that have been questioned by the international community.

In January of 2014, Egyptians approved a new constitution drafted after the July 2013 overthrow of Morsi. The new basic law bans parties based on religion. In February, the government of Prime Minister Hazem el-Beblawi resigned with no explanation. In March 2014, Army chief Abdul Fattah el-Sisi resigned his military position to stand in a presidential election set for May 26 and 27. He faced only one opponent, left-wing candidate Hamdeen Sabahi, who came in third in the 2012 poll.

The May 2014 election offered little suspense and resulted in a major victory for el-Sisi. El-Sisi was supported by the military and most of the mainstream political parties and took 97% of the vote. The major threat to the legitimacy of the new government came not from the result of the poll itself, but from the fact that the Muslim Brotherhood (whose candidate had won the last presidential election) had called for a boycott. The election of el-Sisi, however decisive in percentage terms,

Egyptian judges protest disciplinary action against colleagues who spoke out against electoral violations
©Serene Assir/IRIN

Egypt

Former Pope Shenuda III, of the Egyptian Coptic Church, who died in 2012

thus does not project any sense of political consensus in the country. Rather, the expectation is that the army, secular liberals, leftists, and socialists, and Islamists will continue to represent quite different poles in a divided political system.

CONTEMPORARY THEMES

Economic and Political

Continued political unrest threatens the economic and social structure of the Egyptian state. With the ousting of the Mohamed Morsi, Egypt's first democratically elected president, by the military serious questions about the future of Egyptian democracy remain. As Islamists, the military, and various other factions continue to face-off civil liberties are threatened, the nation faces a rising tide of government debt, a stagnating economy, rising unemployment, and continued violence among other issues. Upcoming elections, in which the former chief of the military is likely to stand for election also raise concerns about civilian control of the nation and could spark a new wave of unrest.

Economic growth in Egypt was in the 7% range for the period from 2006 to 2008 but declined to under 5% with the global recession of 2009. Political instability since the 2011 Arab Spring has led to further decline. In 2011, the growth rate dipped to -4.3%. In early 2012, the country rebounded with a 5.2% rate, however since then it has steadily declined reaching around 1.5% by the end of 2013. Previously, a host of international events had placed Egypt's economy under pressure. The recent political turmoil has driven away both tourism and investment. Tourism accounted for 13% of GDP in 2010 with 14 million visitors. In 2011, that number dropped to 9.5 million. In 2013 tourism receipts were down to less than half of the 2010 level. Other sources of hard currency for Egypt—oil, fees from the Suez Canal, and workers' remittances—were also affected by the terrorist attacks of 2001. The Iraq war after 2003 was another shock to the Egyptian economy, as Iraq was Egypt's number one trading partner, with exports exceeding $1.7 billion in 2002. As a consequence of these external events, the economy slowed for a time: real GDP grew at under 5% in 2004 and 2005, and even less per capita, since population growth continued at about 2%.

Unofficial estimates place Egypt's unemployment in the 15% to 25% range, with the rate is highest among young job seekers, and each year 800,000 more of them enter the job market. Given the government's policy of admitting all high school graduates into the university system (12 government universities, with eight affiliated branches and 20 campuses), the annual number of university graduates is around 195,200. Unfortunately, the market has proved unable to absorb the many university students graduating each year.

In recent years, oil revenues have represented about 40% of Egypt's foreign exchange, but oil production from the Gulf of Suez and Sinai has been declining. Egypt's crude oil production peaked at near a million barrels a day in 1996 but is now down to about two-thirds of that level. Offshore exploration in the Mediterranean is under way, but to date, most discoveries off the Nile Delta have been natural gas. Foreign oil companies began active exploration for natural gas in the early 1990s, and found significant deposits in the Nile Delta, offshore from the Nile Delta, and in the Western Desert. Over the last five years exploration has resulted in the discovery of at least 33 major fields—those whose output exceeds 100 million barrels of oil equivalent. Egypt's natural gas production nearly doubled between 1999 and 2003, and in 2004 it had reached 3.6 billion cubic feet per day (Bcf/d); daily production was expected to rise to around five billion cubic feet by 2007. The government estimates Egyptian natural gas reserves at 58.5 trillion cubic feet (Tcf). Given these resources, natural gas is likely to be the primary engine of growth for the Egyptian economy in the coming years. In a rare example of economic cooperation between Arab states, Egypt and Jordan inaugurated a gas pipeline in July 2003, marking Egypt's first exports of natural gas. The pipeline moves natural gas from Egypt to Jordan and is part of a longer line planned to eventually reach Turkey and Europe.

For its own electricity needs, which are growing at 7% a year, Egypt has opted for an alternative source: nuclear energy. At a NDP meeting in September 2006, Gamal Mubarak announced that the country was ready to resume its nuclear research program, suspended twenty years earlier after the Chernobyl disaster. Hosni Mubarak later confirmed his son's statement, and the NDP energy minister announced construction of a nuclear power plant on the Mediterranean coast, ostensibly to help water desalinization efforts. It would cost $1.5 billion, produce 1,000 MW of electricity, and could be completed by 2015.

Prior to 1967 the economy was largely dependent on a single crop: cotton. Egyptian long staple and extra-long staple cotton is probably the best in the world. It is stronger and can be spun more finely than nearly any other variety in the world. In America it is associated with the most luxurious bed sheets; in Europe, with the finest shirts, and in India, with the thinnest saris. Despite its reputation, however, the Egyptian cotton industry is dying and the area devoted to cotton cultivation has gradually fallen from 1.3 million acres in 1980–1981 to 780,000 acres. Almost all of this acreage is devoted to extra-long and long staple cotton, but only about a third of total production is exported. Roughly 200,000 tons goes to the domestic market, which cannot adequately process high-end cotton. When Gamal Abdel Nasser nationalized the industry in the 1950s, emphasis was placed on creating jobs and import substitution to clothe the country's poor population. Eastern European-supplied machinery could only process much coarser grades of cotton. Ready-to-wear textile manufacturers today prefer to import cheaper short-fiber cotton than use home-grown material.

Only about 3% of Egypt's total land mass is arable, basically the narrow strip of land that borders the Nile and its delta. Agriculture, which is dominated by small landholders, contributed 13.9% to GDP in 2005 and employed about 35% of Egyptian workers. Despite this, Egypt still imports more than half of its food. To sustain the agricultural sector the Mubarak government sought to open new farming lands through two vast irrigation projects. Both involve Nile waters, both are designed to create hundreds of thousands of acres of arable soil for land-starved Egyptian farmers, and both costing billions of dollars. In the south, the Toshka Project, at an estimated cost of $2 billion, is to pump 5 billion cubic meters of water a year from Lake Nasser into the Western Desert to

Egypt

put 1.04 million acres of land under cultivation. The project, known as "Mubarak's pyramid" in reference to its large scale and slow building pace, has yet to come to fruition. The initial completion date was pushed back to 2022 and no public data is available on the current state budget for the project. In the north a similar irrigation project has started to bring water to the Sinai desert through four 42-meter-deep ducts that carry Nile waters under the Suez Canal. The project, which is designed to add over half a million acres of arable land, also has cost estimates in the range of $2 billion. Financing has come mainly from the emir of Kuwait.

Cairo, with all its suburbs, contains more than 16 million people (and about two million cars) and is the largest city in Africa and the Middle East. The city is also home to heavy industry—cement, iron, chemical and metal factories and smelters—that leaves the city veiled in a yellow-gray haze. Cairo's governor has plans for the chaotic city: extending water, sewage, and telephone systems, as well as garbage collection; reclaiming the banks of the Nile for public parks. Taxis, minivans, and city buses are switching to compressed natural gas—a fuel system in which Cairo is now a world leader.

Foreign Policy Issues

Like Libya, Egypt has turned its attention to sub-Saharan Africa. The interest is both economic and political. Egypt joined the Common Market for Eastern and Southern Africa (COMESA) in 1998 and shortly afterwards, acceded to COMESA's free trade area. Tariffs on imports from COMESA countries have been reduced by 90%, but trade with these countries accounts for only 1.1% of exports and 1.3% of imports (2000). Far more important are strategic necessities. African states represent potential threats for Egypt on the issue of sharing and using the Nile waters. The existing Nile Water Agreement was signed in 1929, ratified in 1952, and barred states from using the waters of Lake Victoria without Egypt's permission. (Sudan and Egypt renegotiated the agreement in 1959 to permit construction of Aswan High Dam.)

The agreement, which benefited only Egypt and Sudan, became outdated as other states on the river and its tributaries made plans to use the waters for their own development. Not being independent in 1929, and thus not themselves signatories to the original agreement, the other riverine states pressed for renegotiation.

Ethiopian proposals to construct a series of dams on the Blue Nile galvanized action, and in June 2001 the Nile Basin Initiative (NBI) was created. It linked ten Nile Basin states: Burundi, the Democratic Republic

Former president Mohamed Morsi, deposed by military coup on July 3, 2013

of Congo, Egypt, Eritrea, Ethiopia, Kenya, Rwanda, Sudan, Tanzania, and Uganda. In 2003 Kenya announced its intention to disregard the treaty's provisions and Tanzania began diverting water from Lake Victoria in early 2004. NBI crisis meetings were convened in Uganda the very next month. Under the 1929 treaty, Egypt received 55 billion cubic meters (bcm) of the Nile's estimated annual allotment of 83 bcm, or two-thirds of the flow. Virtually its entire agricultural sector, especially irrigated developments in the south, depends on the Nile, and the country has repeatedly said it would reject any proposal to lower its quota. It has searched for water alternatives for its neighbors, including financing the digging of wells in Kenya, but it is unlikely these will provide adequate replacement waters.

Egypt is in negotiations with other nations regarding water from the Nile. However, Uganda, Tanzania, Kenya, and Rwanda signed an agreement in May that allows them to use river water for developing infrastructure, such as dams and irrigation channels. Egypt has insisted it has the power to block the construction of dams and the government has declared that the agreement "lacks legitimacy."

Egypt has frequently served as a key Arab player in the fragile balance of power in the Middle East that has prevented major assaults on Israel. Negotiations were necessitated in October of 2011 when Egypt and Israel exchanged prisoners after Egypt accused an American Israeli citizen of spying. A potential flare up was avoided in the region in April of 2012 when a dispute between Egypt and Saudi Arabia over a detained Egyptian was settled, preserving the relationship between the two countries and allowing Saudi Arabia to continue serving as a large financial benefactor of Egypt.

The government's crackdown on the Muslim Brotherhood in Egypt has created tension with Hamas, especially in the Gaza border region. Hamas was closely allied with the Brotherhood and the new military authorities have banned all Hamas activities and a court-ordered seizure of all its offices and assets. As a result of the crackdowns commerce between the Palestinian territory and Egypt have plummeted. Political unrest has also jeopardized Egyptian foreign relations more broadly. The United States suspended a significant portion of Iid to Egypt in 2013, and by April of 2014 the future of aid hung in the balance as the US Senate moved to withhold funding.

Social Issues

Egyptian women are slowly gaining legal protection and rights in a male-dominated society. In December of 1997, the country's highest judicial authority, the Council of State, banned the practice of excision (female circumcision), even when the consent of child or parent is given. The court ruled that excision—surgical removal of the clitoris—was physical mutilation as defined in the Penal Code and was therefore punishable by the law. Although there is no Koranic sanction for the practice, female circumcision had long been practiced in Egypt. Indeed, the operation has traditionally been seen as a mark of virtue and guarantor of modesty. In 1997, a detailed demographic survey indicated that more than 97% of women and girls had been through the ordeal.

In early 1999, the government introduced a modification of law codes to give women greater divorce rights. Islamic law allows a man divorce by simple repetition of a ritual formula three times—and divorce is immediate. A woman, on the other hand, might have to go through years of

President Abdel Fattah al-Sisi

Egypt

litigation if her husband were unwilling to grant divorce. Every year, 20,000 women went before the courts requesting a divorce and if it was not given immediately, the woman remained under the legal tutelage of her husband who could, for example, prevent her from getting a passport.

The new code was finally approved in January 2000 after heated controversy (though it is unclear what will result with the new more Islamist constitution). The reforms of Egyptian family law were far-reaching. A woman can now divorce her husband without his assent, though she is required to return any dowry or its equivalent in cash or property. According to the 2000 code, women also can call on the Egyptian government to garnish her husband's wages if he refuses to provide for her and can draw from a special state bank if men fail to pay a court-ordered living allowance. Lost in the compromise was a provision that would have allowed Egyptian women to travel abroad without the permission of their husbands.

Despite some improvements in women's rights, women continue to experience high rates of sexual assault and sexual harassment, and women protesting in Tahrir Square have been victim to high especially high assault rates. CBS correspondent Lara Logan was verbally, physically, and sexually assaulted by a gang of Egyptian men during the initial February 2011 riots, just one of the numerous reported instances of violence against females in the region.

Homosexuals are also subject to severe repression in Egypt. For years the media and government have pretended homosexuality was a Western "disease" that hardly existed in Egypt. In May 2001, however, the police raided the so-called "Queen Boat"—a three-deck floating discotheque moored on the Nile that attracted a sizable gay clientele—and arrested dozens of attendees. After releasing foreigners, the Egyptians were jailed. Then, using the detainees' address books and confiscated mobile phones, the police tracked down and arrested dozens more. Prosecutors argued that their actions defiled Islam and constituted a risk to the state, justifying the trial of 52 gay men in the State Security Court—an institution created by emergency laws passed after Anwar Sadat's assassination in 1981. Human Rights Watch reported they were subjected to humiliating "forensic" examinations, tortured, and given long jail terms for "debauchery." Twenty-three were convicted and jailed for one to five years. There is no appeal from the State Security Court, and there was no intervention on the defendants' behalf by human rights organizations.

Recent events include the reelection of President el-Sisi to a third six-year term in December 2024 made possible by an amendment to the national constitution with the president winning 87 percent of the vote against candidates from several small parties. Pledging to a policy of stability and security, el-Sisi has been accused of jailing thousands of political prisoners while promoting major infrastructure projects, most notably construction of a new administrative capital outside Cairo at an expected cost of $58 billion. Financed by a surge in public debt, results include dramatic increases in the cost of living and downward pressure on the national currency with increasing reliance on loans from the International Monetary Fund (IMF). Reform proposals emphasize reducing the influence of the army and scaling back government regulation of the economy. On the foreign policy front, Egypt has played a major role in attempting to broker a peace deal between Israel and the forces of Hamas in the Gaza Strip in 2024, with Egypt issuing a plan for reconstruction of the territory without displacing the local Palestinian population at a regional meeting of Arab leaders held in Cairo in March 2025. Persistent problems in the Egyptian domestic economy, the second largest in Africa, include high inflation rates, particularly for food and other staples, lack of critical foreign currency, and continued dependency on financial assistance from the IMF as approximately 30 percent of the population lives below the official poverty line. While new parliamentary elections are preliminarily scheduled for August 2025, President el-Sisi remains firmly in control but with the country plagued by corruption and poor governance. Engaged in an ongoing territorial dispute with neighboring Sudan over the Halai'ib Triangle, Egypt confronted the disastrous sinking of a tourist submarine off the country's coast resulting in multiple fatalities in March 2025.

FUTURE CONSIDERATIONS

The end of the Mubarak regime in the revolution of 2011 gave rise to significant hopes for political change in Egypt and across the Arab world, but the revolution in Egypt (like many revolutions) has resulted in considerable uncertainty. Mohamed Morsi's presidency pitted the Muslim Brotherhood's vision against the secularism of traditional power players in the army and other governing institutions, including the judiciary. This conflict continued under the interim government with the repression of the Islamists and was not resolved by the victory of former Army chief el-Sisi in the 2014 presidential election. The president, the courts, the military, and mobilized masses on the streets all have some power to shape events, but none can do so as they please. As this book goes to press in 2014, Egypt is at a point where its future is very uncertain; it may have turned toward consolidating a transition that began with the Arab Spring (albeit not with highly democratic features), or it may be setting up for many more years of turmoil and internal strife between political groups with irreconcilable differences.

Egypt's economic growth is slowing in response to the political atmosphere and the massive challenges of overcoming extensive poverty and inequality remain. Cairo continues to grow as a city, but this also gives rise to classic urban problems such as overcrowding, congestion and pollution; these and other social problems are among the factors that shaped

Camel market in Cairo

Egypt

the events of early 2011. Additionally, the Cairo bombing in February 2009 confirms that Egypt still wrestles with the existence of a radical form of Islam, and westerners are periodically reminded that it is this political environment that gave rise to movements such as Islamic Jihad and individuals such as al-Qaeda's Ayman al-Zawahiri.

Even as Egypt faces the challenge of establishing a stable, democratic regime over the long-term, it continues to face international dilemmas. One of these is tension with Israel over the question of the Palestinian authorities, especially with Morsi's ouster. Another is the water supply. Egypt relies almost exclusively on the Nile, which originates to the south and flows through Ethiopia and Sudan before reaching Egypt; with water widely predicted to be the resource over which the major wars of the 21st century will be fought, Egypt must constantly keep an eye on this precious resource.

Libya

Modern Tripoli Photo by Pat Crowell

BASIC FACTS

Area: 1,759,540 sq. km. = 679,362 sq. mi. (slightly larger than Alaska)
Population: 7,252,573 (June 2023 est.)
Capital Cities: Tripoli
Government Type: In transition
Neighboring Countries: Algeria and Tunisia (west); Egypt (east); Sudan (south-east); Chad and Niger (south)
Official Language: Arabic
Other Principal Languages: Italian, English, and Berber languages
Ethnic Groups: Berber and Arab 97%, other 3% (includes Greeks, Maltese, Italians, Egyptians, Pakistanis, Turks, Indians, and Tunisians)
Principal Religion: Sunni Muslim 97%, other 3%
Former Colonial Status: Turkish Colony (1553–1911); Italian Colony (1911–1943) British-French jurisdiction (1943–1951)
Independence Date: December 24, 1951
GDP Per Capita (IMF 2023 est.): $6,763 (nominal), $24,599 (PPP)
Gini index: N/A
Currency: Libyan dinar, $1US = 4.74 Dinars (2023 est.)
Inflation Rate: 3.7% (2022 est.)
Liberation Day: October 23 (2011) CIA Factbook
Chief Commercial Products: Crude oil, refined petroleum products, natural gas, and chemicals
Foreign Direct Investments (FDI) net inflows: 50,000,000
Literacy Rate: 91% (CIA 2015)
Life Expectancy: 77.12 years (CIA 2023 est.)
Chief of State: Chairman, Presidential Council, Mohammed Al Menfi (since February 5, 2021)
Head of Government: Prime Minister Abdul Hamid Dubaybah (since February 2021)

LAND AND PEOPLE

Libya covers a vast area of central North Africa, most of which lies within the blistering Sahara Desert. The coastal area is fertile and populous in an otherwise dry countryside. Farther inland, mountains rise in plateaus to heights of up to 3,000 feet. There is irregular rainfall in the region due to the perpetual struggle between the moist winds of the Mediterranean and the dry, hot air of the desert. A short distance inland, rainfall becomes increasingly light. Sudden showers, when they occur, overflow the typically dry riverbeds and sweeping valuable topsoil to the sea. Temperatures in winter often go below freezing, but they may rise quickly because of the *ghibli*, a hot, arid wind from the desert.

The low mountains, with scattered scrub vegetation, provide forage for Barbary sheep, which need little water to survive. The sands of the Sahara take charge about 50 miles from the sea, where temperatures may soar as high as 137°F in the shade. In the extreme south, the land rises to heights of 10,000 feet or more in the remote Tibesti Mountains.

Compulsory, free education greatly reduced a pre-1951 illiteracy rate of 90% to less than 50%. High schools and technical colleges emphasize the development of practical skills calculated to contribute to the growth of the economy.

Libya contains a remarkable collection of sites that bear witness to the life that flourished there during prehistoric, Punic, Greek, Roman and Byzantine eras. One rock art site alone—Tadrart Acacus on the southwest border, east of the city of Ghat—contains thousands of cave paintings in different styles, dating from 12,000 B.C. to 100 A.D. They catalogue the changing fauna, flora and lifestyles of the populations that succeeded one another in this Saharan region.

Three sites, Cyrene, Leptis Magna and Sabratha all have tourism potential. Cyrene, founded in the 7th century B.C., is one of the most complex archaeological sites in the Mediterranean region. Cyrenians built the biggest Greek Doric temple in Africa in the 6th century B.C.—the Sanctuary of Zeus, comparable to the Temple of Zeus at Olympia. Leptis Magna was enlarged and embellished by

Libya

Septimius Severus, who was born there and later became emperor. It was one of the most impressive cities of the Roman Empire, with its imposing public monuments, marketplace, storehouses, shops and residential districts. Sabratha, once a Phoenician trading post that served as an outlet for the products of the African hinterland, was later Romanized and rebuilt in the 2nd and 3rd centuries A.D. with an impressive theater, victory arch, and arena.

HISTORY TO PRESENT DAY

For early history, see *Historical Background* and *The Colonial Period: The Italians.*

By the turn of the 20th century, Libya had been historically divided into three provinces—Cyrenaica, Tripolitania, and Fezzan. At the close of World War II, the four main allied powers—the United States, France, Great Britain, and the Soviet Union—could not agree on the future of Libya. Italy had renounced all rights to the colony under the terms of the peace treaty it signed in 1947. The provinces of Cyrenaica and Tripolitania were under British control and the French administered Fezzan.

At about the same time that the so-called "Big Four" submitted the question of Libya to the UN, the British recognized Emir El Sayyid Muhammad al-Mahdi el-Senussi as head of state in Cyrenaica; he took the name King Idris. A grandson of the founder of the Senussi sect of Islam, Idris set up a government and proclaimed independence of all Libya. The UN debated for many months but ultimately passed a resolution providing for Libyan independence by 1951. The National Constituent Assembly met and proclaimed Idris to be King of Libya; a constitution was prepared which came into effect with formal independence in 1951.

Initially a loose federation under the monarch, Libya adopted a new constitution in 1963, which provided for a central government and merged the provinces. The kingdom had a two-chamber legislature and there were no political parties. The king appointed the Senate and the people elected the Chamber of Deputies.

Because Idris failed to ally Libya firmly enough with the Arab cause against Israel, a group of army officers, headed by 1st Lt. Muammar al-Qadhafi deposed the king in September 1969. Ironically, the king, because of illness, was prepared to announce his abdication the next day. He died in Cairo in 1983.

The Beginning of the Qadhafi Era

Under Qadhafi, the government was placed in the hands of a revolutionary council that implemented radical changes. Qadhafi's early moves made him popular with the international revolutionary left. Libya closed U.S. military bases and 25,000 Italians either left or were expelled, many of them leaving their property behind.

Qadhafi spent the subsequent years financing various revolutionary movements throughout the world, using Libya's immense oil wealth as his resource, while attempting to secure Arab unity under his

King Idris I on his 75th birthday, 1965

leadership. He failed to persuade the leaders and people of Arab nations (even the tiny nation of Malta) to enter into a union with Libya and a frustrated Qadhafi denounced and increasingly distanced himself from other Arab leaders.

Qadhafi attempted a range of administrative and structural reforms in the 1970s and began buying up large amounts of military equipment. In 1976, he annexed a 60-mile-wide strip of northern Chad and involved Libya in the country's civil war, supporting rebel troops against the central government. In 1987, Chadian troops, with French assistance, removed the Libyans and captured about $1 billion of Soviet-manufactured military materiel.

In 1979, Libyan mobs sacked the U.S. Embassy and relations between the two countries came to a standstill while the U.S. insisted Libya take full responsibility for the attack. Qadhafi called it a "spontaneous demonstration by students," and offered neither apology nor admitted responsibility. He heightened the verbal offensive against the United States in 1981 after the U.S. shot down two Libyan jets over the Gulf of Sidra. The U.S. said the incident resulted from an unprovoked attack on U.S. jets, but Qadhafi accused the U.S. of aggression.

Qadhafi's style of leadership rhetorically denied the top-down nature of his rule. He preferred the title "Eternal Guide" or "Leader of the Revolution" to the term president. He decreed that Libya has no central government, but a series of "People's Congresses" whose decisions are carried out by layers of committees and a general secretariat. He made military training mandatory for both girls and boys in secondary schools and formed a "People's Army" of students. These changes made conservative elements of the military very apprehensive, but the military remained loyal due to its secure command over a substantial flow of resources.

International terrorism was an integral part of Col. Qadhafi's foreign and domestic policy in the 1980s. In 1984–1986, terrorism was primarily directed at Libyan dissidents living in exile. By late 1985, Qadhafi's anti-Americanism had become virulent enough for President Ronald Reagan to urge all Americans living in the country to leave and travel visas to Libya were forbidden. The U.S. sent a naval task force into the Gulf of Sidra, past what Qadhafi had labeled "the line of death," sank two Libyan patrol boats, and conducted air raids against Libyan radar and missile installations on the mainland. Shortly thereafter a bomb ripped a discotheque in West Berlin, killing two U.S. servicemen; irrefutable evidence indicated Libya was responsible. When the trial of those responsible finally took place in November 2001, a German court blamed Libya's intelligence service, and four people, including a former Libyan diplomat, were sentenced to prison terms of 12–14 years.

In April 1986, Reagan ordered an air strike against Libya from bases in England, hitting Qadhafi's residence. The colonel was home at the time although an American spokesman denied that the U.S. military denied having that knowledge. Qadhafi was shaken up by the attack and when he finally appeared on television about five weeks later, he seemed to be heavily sedated. For the next 18 months, Qadhafi remained on the move, sleeping in different locations for fear of being targeted. His popularity plummeted as basic commodities disappeared from markets.

The Lockerbie Bombing and its Aftermath

Things got worse in 1989, when the international community fully turned on Libya following the bombing of a Pan American flight that exploded over Lockerbie, Scotland in December of 1998. 270 people were killed, a majority of them American (35 students on a Syracuse University program) and the attack was

Libya

Muammar al-Qadhafi

linked to Libyan citizens. When Qadhafi refused to hand over the alleged Lockerbie perpetrators, the UN Security Council ordered air and military embargoes in 1992. The lifting of the sanctions was contingent upon the Libyan government turning the Lockerbie suspects over to the courts.

The UN sanctions were tightened in 1993 to include the freezing of Libyan funds and financial resources in other countries, and a ban on the sale of equipment for oil and gas operations. Taking it a step further, the United States imposed its own unilateral sanctions in 1996, banning investments in Libya's oil or gas sectors.

By 1998, the UN and US sanctions were taking a serious toll on Libya's economy and Qadhafi was desperate for foreign investment in the oil industry. Being shunned by the leaders of the international community and largely marginalized by other Arab states, Qadhafi turned increasingly to his sub-Saharan African neighbors. In June 1998, the Organization of African Unity (OAU) voted to ignore the UN air embargo on Libya, and several African presidents flew into Tripoli to visit the colonel. Libya downgraded its "permanent" status at the Arab League, scrapped its Arab Ministry, and changed the name of its radio from the "Voice of the Arab Nation" to "Voice of Africa." The ever-mercurial Qadhafi told an Arab delegation that "for good or worse, nothing will ever link me to Arabs," and that he wanted "Libya's interests to be in Africa and remain there."

Libya's African supporters encouraged Qadhafi to take responsibility for the Lockerbie case and allow the country to move forward. The suspects were transferred for trial in the Netherlands under Scottish law. UN sanctions were automatically suspended and diplomatic relations with the UK moved towards restoration. The Lockerbie trial began in April 2000, and the panel of three Scottish judges found on of the suspects, Abdel Basset al-Megrahi, a Libyan intelligence agent, guilty of murdering 270 people. Al-Megrahi was sentenced to twenty-years to life imprisonment in a Scottish jail and his appeal was denied in March 2002. In August 2009, however, al-Megrahi was released and returned to Libya despite protests from both the United States and the UK and died in Libya in 2012.

In 2003, Libya formally took responsibility for the Lockerbie bombing in a letter to the UN Security Council and signed a compensation deal for the families of Lockerbie victims worth $2.7 billion. In September the UN Security Council permanently lifted its sanctions against the regime and Libya began to restore its international image.

Another plane bombing in 1989—of a UTA flight from Brazzaville to Paris—was linked to Libyan citizens and caused international outrage. Over 170 passengers died on the flight that exploded over Niger, the majority of whom were French citizens. Qadhafi refused to give up any suspects of information for five years but allowed the French to investigate in 1996 in an attempt to restore Libya's image and regain investment. Abdallah Senussi-Qadhafi's brother-in-law and second-in-command of the Libyan intelligence services was charged with having given the order to bomb the UTA flight. Five others were also named in the indictment, and their trial *in absentia* took place in Paris in March 1999. All were found guilty and sentenced to life in prison and Libya later paid some $31 million as compensation to the victims' families.

Changing Libya's Image

Following the resolution of the two bombings, Qadhafi presented himself as a reformed leader in the 2000s and devoted himself to the African cause. The high point of Libya's Africa-first policy came in March 2001, when an extraordinary OAU summit met in Sirte and agreed to the creation of an African Union (AU). The AU was inaugurated in July 2002, with South Africa's Thabo Mbeki the new formation's first president. In March and April 2007 Col. Qadhafi became actively involved in the most pressing of the continental crises at the time: the Sudanese genocide in Darfur.

As relations with Africa warmed, relations with the Arab League chilled to the point of rupture. At an early March 2003 League summit called to discuss the situation in Iraq, Qadhafi and the Saudi Crown Prince, Abdullah bin Abdul Aziz, traded public insults while embarrassed Egyptian TV operators sought to pull the plug on live transmission. The Saudi paper *Okaz* called for Qadhafi's overthrow, whereupon the colonel withdrew his ambassador to the kingdom and demanded to withdraw from the League. He told reporters that Libya was "above all an African country . . . the African Union is sufficient enough." The decision to leave the League definitively was announced as "irrevocable" in April 2003, but was never implemented.

Internally, the government faced continuing opposition that intensified as economic conditions deteriorated. Violent clashes with militant Islamist opposition groups occurred in the eastern region in 1997. The government tightened security measures, made hundreds of arrests and conducted military operations in the affected areas. Members and sympathizers of banned Islamic groups were closely monitored and activities at mosques were put under surveillance. In March 1997, the People's Congress approved a collective guilt and punishment law. By this law, any group, large or small, including towns, villages, local assemblies, tribes, or families can be punished in their entirety if accused by the People's Congress or a People's Committee of sympathizing, financing, or in any way helping, protecting or failing to identify perpetrators of crimes against the state. The crimes included "obstructing the people's power, instigating and practicing tribal fanaticism, possessing, trading in or smuggling unlicensed weapons, and damaging public and private institutions and property."

During the heyday of socialist economics, members of so-called "Popular Committees" terrorized the bazaars of Tripoli and other cities. Formed in 1996 and made up of volunteers, often students and army officers, the committees were charged by Colonel Qadhafi with purifying cities of the "satanic filthiness of the West." The committee's targeted street peddlers, confiscating imported items and fining sellers. One Palestinian merchant was accused of "inundating the Libyan market with Israeli aphrodisiac chewing gum." Punishment for deviance was severe: under laws passed in 1996 any Libyan could be punished by death for speculations in food, currency, clothes, or housing during a state of war or blockade—which included the UN sanctions. Over time, however, the multilateral sanctions worked to push Qadhafi toward free markets and investments. After 2000, Qadhafi marginalized the revolutionary committees and articulated his vision of the new Libya: "Now

Libya

is the era of economy, consumption, markets, and investments. This is what unites people irrespective of language, religion, and nationalities."

Libya's development of a missile program, with Chinese and North Korean assistance, remained a principal U.S. security concern after the Lockerbie file had been closed. Libya was accused of trying to acquire weapons of mass destruction (WMD), and the George W. Bush administration chose not to lift American sanctions when the UN Security Council did so. Tensions persisted into early 2010, when Libya reached a nearly $2 billion deal with Russia to acquire fighter jets, tanks, and air-defense systems.

The invasion of Iraq in 2003 again altered Qadhafi's incentives as he sought to keep Libya off of the list of candidates for American-led regime change. In December 2003, Qadhafi announced that Libya would abandon its programs to develop weapons of mass destruction. The country's nuclear projects were opened to international inspection and the UN's International Atomic Energy Agency (IAEA) indicated there was evidence that Libya had produced a small amount of plutonium. Though it was insufficient to make a bomb, it was clear Libya was close to obtaining nuclear weapons capability. In terms of nuclear intelligence, Libyan cooperation provided information on the vast nuclear black market operated by the Pakistani physicist, Dr. Abdul Qadeer Khan, revered as the "father" of Pakistan's nuclear bomb. To enrich uranium obtained from North Korea, Libya had purchased some $100 million worth of materials (primarily centrifuge technology) from the Khan network.

Following the dismantling of its nuclear program, the international community reopened their arms to Libya and the country began its return to the family of nations. By the end of 2004, British Prime Minister Tony Blair, Gerhard Schroeder of Germany, Italian Prime Minister Silvio Berlusconi, and French President Jacques Chirac had all had meetings with Qadhafi. In Washington, President George W. Bush had removed virtually all American unilateral sanctions, helping Libya attract badly needed foreign investment. Allegations that Col. Qadhafi had approved a plan to kill Crown Prince Abdullah, Saudi Arabia's ruler, did, however, keep Libya's name on America's list of state sponsors of terrorism. Col. Qadhafi's regime officially renounced terrorism in May 2006, turning over a new leaf and gaining further international diplomatic recognition.

In 2008, U.S. Secretary of State Condolezza Rice visited Libya and proclaimed that US-Libya relations had entered a new phase (Libya was one of the few Middle Eastern countries to denounce the September 11 attacks). In 2009, Qadhafi was elected chairman of the African Union and Libya seemed poised to stay in global good standing. The slow reintegration of Libya into the international community made the events of 2011 all the more surprising.

The Arab Spring of 2011

Following the uprisings in Tunisia and Egypt that brought down long-standing regimes in those countries, Libyans took to the streets beginning in mid-February 2011. The first major news came in the days after February 15th, as the city of Benghazi—the second largest in the country—progressively fell under the sway of anti-Qadhafi groups, even as the regime employed snipers in the city to shoot the protestors. By February 21, Qadhafi's authority had collapsed in Benghazi and the uprising had spread to several Libyan cities, including the capital Tripoli. Defections from the Qadhafi regime began, most notably with air force pilots who flew to the island of Malta rather than follow orders to bomb civilians. As expectations grew that Libya may be following in Tunisia's and Egypt's footsteps by sweeping away a long-time dictator, the leader made a bizarre appearance on state television, holding an umbrella and sitting in a van in front of a house in Tripoli to confirm his presence and authority.

Roman Imperial theater at Sabratha Photo by Pat Crowell

Libya

Libya opens to the world. Thousands view the total eclipse of the sun, March 29, 2006

Photo by Beverly Ingram

Eastern Libya rapidly fell under the control of anti-Qadhafi forces, while Qadhafi loyalists (including mercenaries and paramilitaries) reasserted control in Tripoli in the west. While the partition generally split between east and west, the western city of Misrata took up the banner of the "Libyan Republic" while Qadhafi's hometown of Sirte farther east remained firmly under the regime's control. East of Sirte on the road to Benghazi, Qadhafi's forces began pitched battles in late February and early March with poorly organized and ill-equipped rebels, contesting the cities of Ras Lanuf, Brega, and Adjabiya.

By March 17, Qadhafi's forces had pushed the rebels back and had advanced to the outskirts of Benghazi, where they looked set to crush the rebellion until the UN Security Council passed an eleventh-hour resolution authorizing member states to defend Libyan civilians. Qadhafi immediately responded by accepting a cease-fire, but days later NATO forces (initially led by French, British, and American fighter jets) began bombing Qadhafi's military assets. This intervention tipped the scales back to the rebels for a time.

In April, battles raged in Misrata and around the town of Brega in the east, while NATO continued to fire on Qadhafi's forces and several countries opened a diplomatic front by recognizing the rebels as the legitimate government of Libya or encouraging the rebels' political leaders to begin dialogue toward such recognition.

By May, the war had turned into a stalemate, with Qadhafi unable to advance forces on the rebels, and the rebels unable to claim Tripoli. NATO targeted Qadhafi's residences, which led the regime to claim hundreds of civilian deaths, but otherwise proved unable to dislodge the loyalists from their positions in Tripoli. Attempts by South African president Jacob Zuma to negotiate a ceasefire failed and the rebels looked to the west for arms.

In July, the National Transitional Council (NTC), the leading opposition force, was internationally recognized as the legitimate governing body in Libya. August saw the opposition making strides after months of stalemate, and the NTC took Qadhafi's compound in Tripoli. Col. Qadhafi went into hiding and his family fled to Algeria as the opposition solidifies its hold over the country. Later in the summer of 2011, the African Union officially recognized the NTC.

The End of Qadhafi

The end of Qadhafi's 42 years in power officially came in October of 2011, when his last holdout was taken and he was captured by rebels in a drainage ditch as he tried to flee his hometown of Sirte. After being beaten and bloodied (in incidents captured on cell phone video), Qadhafi was killed by his captors. After Qadhafi's death, the NTC declared Libya to be officially liberated and began plans to restructure the government and the nation. The NTC set in motion plans to establish an interim government with elections for June 2012; these were eventually pushed back into July. Qadhafi's eldest son, Saif al-Islam was captured in November, marking the last member of the Colonel's family to be seized or killed. The NTC stated that he would be put on trial for crimes against humanity during the war. As this book goes to print in July 2012, al-Islam is awaiting trial, and four representatives from the International Criminal Court delegation to Libya have just been detained and jailed. Reasons for their detention are still unclear, but one, an Australian woman, is accused of having attempted to pass information to al-Islam. Libya has requested that the ICC allow al-Islam to be tried in Tripoli but The Hague has insisted upon an international trial.

Civilian unrest boiled over in January 2012 as clashes erupted in Benghazi over the slow pace and the nature of the new government. The small militias created during the war continued to challenge the NTC, and the continued violence caused the NTC's initial Deputy Head, Abdel Hafiz Ghoga, to resign. More clashes occurred in the southeast in February, this time between Arabs and Africans, resulting in numerous deaths and highlighting the ethnic tensions within Libya.

The NTC faced many challenges in its interim period: imposing order, mollifying the remaining rebel militias, establishing compromises between the Islamists and secularists, rebuilding the economy

Libya

and protecting the oil industry, and setting the foundation for a smooth and timely transition of power. In May of 2012, truckloads of armed men attacked the government headquarters in Tripoli.

National elections were held on July 7, 2012, for a parliament known as the General National Congress (GNC). These were the first reasonably free and fair elections in six decades. The election was for a 200-seat parliament. Seculars and liberals outpolled the Justice and Construction Party, a conservative Islamist party affiliated with the Muslim Brotherhood. The GNC elected Mohamed al-Magarief as interim head of state until a constitution could be drafted, and new elections held. However, Magarief stepped down from the post in May 2013 after angry gunmen surrounded the parliament and demanded that any politician who had previously worked with Muammar Qadhafi be disqualified. Magarief was replaced by an acting chair of the GNC (Nouri Ali Abu Sahmain), but his ouster left Ali Zidan—another liberal—as the country's leading political figure. Zidan was elected prime minister by the parliament in 2012 and assumed office in November of that year.

The largest international news to come out of Libya in 2012 happened on September 11, when militants attacked the U.S. consulate in Benghazi. The attack resulted in the death of four Americans, including the ambassador, and resulted in investigations and political blowback in Washington. On the ground in Benghazi, groups of locals counterattacked and drove groups of militants from the city. In response to the incident, several other countries reevaluated the security of their diplomatic personnel in Libya.

Libya's crisis has continued through 2013 and 2014. The GNC, intended to be a transitional assembly, extended its own mandate, and eventually pushed legislative elections back to June 2014. (These elections are just getting underway as this book goes to press.) At the same time, the public security situation has deteriorated markedly, with Libya suffering suicide bombing attacks in 2013 and a growing rebel insurgency that has primarily taken the form of attacking and occupying parts of the country's oil infrastructure. Prime minister Ali Zidan was briefly kidnapped in 2013, and a deputy minister was assassinated in early 2014. As rebels increasingly exhibited their capacity to threaten the government, the GNC dismissed Ali Zidan and replaced him with a new prime minister, Ahmed Maiteg. The likelihood of stability for the incoming government is relatively low against this backdrop of violence and decaying public order.

CONTEMPORARY THEMES

Libya's economy is dependent on its petroleum industry. Production was seriously disrupted during the war of 2011, but has since largely recovered. Qadhafi devoted himself to the cultivation of the oil industry during his time in power and the NTC made it a priority to protect the industry while acting as the interim government. According to the World Bank, in the mid-2000s, oil accounted for 95% of foreign earnings, 93% of government revenues, and 72.6% of GDP. UN sanctions hurt the economy and hydrocarbon sector badly, and Libya reported estimated losses amounting to nearly $27 billion. Economic growth was tepid at best in the late 1990s, and moderate (at 3.5% to 4.6%) in the mid-2000s.

Prior to the war, the Qadhafi government had announced ambitious plans to increase production to 2 million barrels/day by 2008–2010, and 3 million by 2015, which would be comparable to Libya's peak production from the 1970s. The war brought production to a halt, but it had recovered to over 1 million bpd by the end of 2011 and is estimated once again at over 1.5 million bpd in mid-2012.

Libya's reserves are estimated at about 75 billion barrels of oil as of 2010, the largest in Africa and the fifth-highest in the world. In addition, Libyan oil is extremely high-quality, low-sulfur content crude. Low production costs in Libya further incentivize production. Onshore costs can be as little as $5 a barrel, and given the shallowness of the Mediterranean, and even offshore costs are low by world standards. About 80% of Libya's known reserves are located in the Sirte basin, but huge areas of the country are unexplored and untested. Oil industry analysts see excellent potential for additional oil discoveries.

Since the NTC has taken over, the oil-rich Benghazi region has taken steps to demand more autonomy, especially in regard to oil production. This regionalism has been at odds with the NTC's more unitarist view, and has made the transition to a permanent government more difficult. Around the July 2012 elections, the

African Unity billboard

Photo by Pat Crowell

Libya

main pockets of unrest were found around Benghazi, where locals (who deemed themselves to have been the inspiration and cradle of the revolution) object to the underrepresentation of the region in the upcoming parliament.

Libya's proven reserves of natural gas also have enormous potential for the economy. By shifting to the domestic use of gas rather than oil, more oil would be freed up for export, thereby increasing petroleum profits and benefiting the economy. Libya is looking to Russia to tap into the gas export market. Gazprom, the Russian natural gas and pipeline giant won a 10% stake in a Libyan offshore exploration block in January 2007, and planned to invest some $200 million on the project. With pipeline agreements with central Asian states and supply contracts with North African gas producers Algeria and Libya, Gazprom would have, in effect, a gas cartel to squeeze European buyers.

With 1,340 miles of undeveloped coastline and remarkable architectural ruins, Libya offers enormous opportunities in tourism if stability can be reestablished under a functioning regime. In addition to seaside locations along the coast a short distance from southern Europe, the country has five UNESCO World Heritages sites (Leptis Magna, Sabratha, Cyrene, Ghadames, and the southwestern rock art sites of Tadrart Acacus)

Current Situation in Libya

The instability in Libya has resulted in the country becoming a destination and transit of people from sub-Saharan Africa to forced prostitution and labor. Most of these foreign migrants are on their way to Europe and see Libya as a place they could work and raise money for the final leg of their adventure to cross the Mediterranean to Europe. Employers recruit migrants from detention centers as forced laborers on construction sites, farms, and so on. The women, on the other hand, find themselves in forced prostitution in Libyan brothels. The Libyan government does not have the appropriate resources to handle human trafficking problems in order to separate victims from perpetrators. As a result, all illegal migrants are detained and punished at detention centers.

Lacking a single unified government since the overthrow of Qadhafi in 2011, the country, including the capital city of Tripoli, has been plagued by the presence of independently operating militias that terrorize neighborhoods leading to major losses of life and constant disruptions from armed checkpoints and blockaded streets. Foreign parties have also become involved including the notorious Wagner Group from Russia while the stream of migrants from Syria and other centers of conflict hoping to reach Europe continues unabated with persistent cases of overloaded vessels lost at sea. The internationally recognized National Unity Government based in Tripoli exists in the west with the contending regime of the Government of National Stability in Benghazi in the east. Persistent problems involving migrants and refugees from Sub-Saharan Africa transitioning Libya for Europe include the discovery of mass graves at several remote sites in the country along with criticisms by human rights groups of continued systematic abuse at detention centers often run by state-supported militias. While European countries led by Italy concerned with migrant inflows have gone easy on Libyan officials at the center of the network of detention camps, including the chief of the Judicial Police of the government in Tripoli, accusations have been directed against the United Nations for nefarious attempts to alter the demographic makeup of Libya, a view denounced as an example of anti-black racism. An attempted assassination of a state minister in Tripoli in February in 2025 indicates ongoing concerns over political stability in a deeply divided country.

FUTURE CONSIDERATIONS

Change in Libya has been dramatic in recent years and the removal of Col. Qadhafi from power (and his subsequent death) ushered in a new era. One irony of Qadhafi's fall is that Libya had looked increasingly likely to move toward improved relations with the international community before 2011. It was no longer universally reviled as a pariah state until the Qadhafi regime began its violent crackdown on the uprisings in the east of the country. Qadhafi had erratically brought Libya back toward the international community, with renunciations of terror and compensation for the 1980s bombings. These had led to a lifting of sanctions and inflows of investment in the energy sector in the 2000s. Libya was a middle-income country that looked on a path to more constructive economic integration with Europe, while remaining culturally and geographically Arab and African. The uprising of 2011 changed all this, however, as the Qadhafi regime calculated that it could not endure an existential threat to its rule. The crackdown sent Libya back into the category of rogue and pariah regimes and was once again condemned by the international community.

The Arab Spring brought hope and the civil war brought despair. The transitional government has balanced precariously between these two. The establishment of a functioning (albeit interim) government in 2012 was a positive step, but the continued presence of militants—as seen with the 2012 attack on the American consulate, and the 2013 and 2014 attacks on infrastructure and civilian leaders—raises doubts about whether a functional Libyan Republic may emerge. There is little certainty about whether the new leadership will be able to create law and order or sustain a liberal democracy. Continued unrest among rebel militias and internal divisions within Libya will be two of the challenges facing the central government.

Exodus from Libya during the civil war of 2011

The Kingdom of Morocco

The World Heritage site of Ait Benhaddou — Photo by Jinny Lambert

BASIC FACTS

Area: 446,550 sq. km. (larger than California; the disputed territory of Western Sahara is another 266,000 sq. km. = 102,703 sq. mi.)
Population: 37,067,420 (June 2023 est.)
Capital City: Rabat
Government Type: Parliamentary Constitutional monarchy
Neighboring Countries: Algeria (east, southeast); Mauritania (south); Morocco claims the territory of Western Sahara, and occupies most of the territory
Official Language: Arabic
Other Principal Languages: Amazigh (Berber; official), French, Spanish (largely in the enclaves of Melilla and Ceuta)
Ethnic Groups: Arab-Berber 99%, other 1%
Principal Religions: Muslim 99%, Christian 1%, Jewish about 6,000
Former Colonial Status: French Protectorate (1912–1956)
Independence Date: March 2, 1956
GDP Per Capita (IMF 2023 est.): $3,748 (nominal), $10,460 (PPP)
Gini index: 39.5 (2013)
Currency: Dirham, $US1 = 9.98 Dirhams (2023)
Inflation rate: 1.4% (2023 est.)
Chief Commercial Products: Clothing and textiles, electrical components, inorganic chemicals, transistors, crude minerals, fertilizers, petroleum products, citrus fruits, vegetables, fish
Literacy Rate: 73.8% (CIA 2018)
Personal Remittances: 7,418,557,947
Foreign Direct Investments (FDI) net inflows: 3,582,296,216 (US$)
Life Expectancy: 73.95 years (CIA 2023 est.)
Head of State: King Mohamed VI (since July 1999)
Head of Government: Prime Minister Aziz Akhannouch (since October 7, 2022)

LAND AND PEOPLE

Situated in the northwest corner of Africa, Morocco is separated from Spain by the narrow Strait of Gibraltar. Three ranges of the high, rugged Atlas Mountains extend through the central and eastern portions of the country for more than 500 miles. In the hinterland of Fez, the Middle Atlas meets the Rif Range, which forms a crescent of land 6,000 feet high flanking the Mediterranean. To the south, the Middle Atlas is succeeded by the High Atlas, some of whose peaks reach a height of 13,000 feet. The Atlas, stretching almost the entire length of Morocco, form a natural barrier between the fertile coast and the dry Sahara Desert and give the country three major environmental zones: relatively well-watered coastal lowlands, the mountain highlands, and the eastern deserts. Temperatures are cool in the highlands and bitterly cold in the winter. They are often snowcapped in the summer. Rainfall is concentrated in the cooler months from October to May, while summers are dry.

57

Morocco

The coastal region is fertile, with a gentle climate. When ample rainfall arrives intense cultivation of the land is possible, but precipitation is irregular, and droughts are not uncommon. White beaches along the coast stretch for almost 1,700 miles along the Atlantic Ocean and the Mediterranean Sea, providing ample opportunity for the development of tourism.

Many of Morocco's cities are rich in history and are cultural and tourist attractions: Casablanca, Marrakesh, Fez, and Tangier are among them. The Alawite dynasty has provided the country's sultans since the mid-17th century. Moroccan princes are referred to with the title Moulay, or "master," unless their name is Mohamed, since the only "Master Mohamed" is the Prophet. Princes named Mohamed are addressed as *Sidi*, or "my lord" and Princesses are given the title *Lalla*. Like his predecessors, King Mohamed bears several titles—Commander of the Faithful, Savior, and Shadow of the Prophet on Earth—that reflect the dynasty's claim to be directly descended from the Prophet Mohammed. The claim has been the traditional means by which Moroccan kings have legitimized their rule and, more recently, checked the claims of Islamists.

HISTORY TO PRESENT DAY

For early history, see *Historical Background* and *The Colonial Period: The French.*

Independence to King Hassan (1961-1999) and Party Politics

Upon attaining independence from France in 1956, power in independent Morocco was concentrated in the hands of the monarch. Sultan Muhammad V (who officially adopted the title of king in August 1957) chose his ministers personally and maintained control of the all-important army and the police forces. He was assisted by a Consultative Assembly of 60, which he himself named, and his eldest son, Moulay Hassan, who became chief of staff. Royal absolutism was slightly modified by a royal charter issued in May 1958 creating a constitutional monarchy.

When the leading *Istiqlal* party split along generational and ideological lines in 1959, the king positioned himself as neutral arbiter above the political fray. *Istiqlal*'s main faction, containing older and more traditional elements, was headed by Muhammad 'Allal al-Fasi. A smaller section headed by Mehdi Ben Barka was formed of younger men, intellectuals who favored socialism and had republican leanings. To pursue these goals, they formed the National Union of Popular Forces (UNFP).

Upon the unexpected death of his father in 1961, Moulay Hassan was elevated to the throne as King Hassan. He promptly drafted a new constitution providing a parliamentary government and elections for the National Assembly were held in 1963. Both *Istiqlal* factions were in opposition, while a miscellany of royal supporters coalesced in the Front for the Defense of Constitutional Institutions. After one year without consequential policy change, the king dissolved parliament and returned to personal rule.

The king's most formidable opponent, Mehdi Ben Barka, was forced into exile. Once the king's mathematics instructor, Ben Barka later turned radical, touting a Nasserist "Arab revolution" against Morocco's "reactionary" monarch. His support of revolutionary Algeria led to subsequent charges of high treason, including allegations of plotting against the life of Hassan II and he was sentenced *in absentia* to death. From his home in Paris Ben Barka became leader of the opposition to Hassan—until his kidnapping and disappearance in October 1965. Numerous observers have suggested that the Ben Barka plot was managed by General Muhammad Oufkir, the king's minister of the interior.

A period of constitutions and coups followed, none of which were successful. Army rebels opened fire at the king's birthday party in 1971, killing 98 guests, one of which was the Belgian ambassador. A year later General Oufkir apparently led a second coup, which almost downed the royal plane. Hassan survived, as he did some eight other attempts on his life. (For his devotees, such luck meant he must be a good ruler, gifted with *baraka*—a kind of divine grace.) His opponents were less fortunate; General Oufkir died at the royal palace, supposedly by his own hand, and hundreds of suspects, including family members, were imprisoned. While Crown Prince and army chief in 1958, Hassan had suppressed a rebellion in the Rif Mountains for which rumors stated that rebel ringleaders were flown out to sea in helicopters and shoved overboard. True or not, it certainly contributed to the prince's fearsome image. Hassan II faced down plots, periodic riots, strikes, and other manifestations of discontent. He tightened his grip on power through constitutional changes that reinforced the monarchy: royal decrees could not be debated, and it was a crime to question the royal finances.

Hassan's forceful policies to absorb Spanish Sahara increased his popularity in the mid-1970s, as he turned Western Sahara into a nationalist cause. Good relations with Israel and Washington provided the weaponry to defeat the Polisario Front, a guerrilla insurrection seeking independence for the area. Ultimately the war evolved to a stalemate. (See the section below on Western Sahara.)

By the early 1980s, bad harvests, a sluggish economy, and the continuing financial drain of the Sahara war increased domestic strains. Islamic fundamentalism was finessed by the king's claim of descent from the Prophet, but its growing influence among both the educated and the impoverished suggested fundamental weaknesses in the system. The king responded with selected reforms, granting amnesties to some opponents long imprisoned in remote places and announcing curbs on the powers of security and police forces.

Rissani Suq, Tafilat Photo by Ross Dunn

Another constitutional referendum was held in 1992, but its provisions were superseded by yet another constitutional change submitted to referendum in 1996. The new arrangement included a bicameral parliament with an indirectly elected upper house and, for the first time since independence, a directly elected popular assembly. While this was reform, it remained royally directed change from above.

The 1997 elections were Morocco's first direct elections for the lower house of parliament and an effort to spread democracy to rural areas. Three main political groups took almost equal numbers of seats in the Chamber of Deputies. The *Koutla* left-wing opposition block took 102 seats. Its dominant partner, the Socialist Union of Popular Forces (USFP) won 57 seats to become the largest party in parliament. The right-wing *Wifak* block won 100 and a center-right grouping received 97. The relatively equal distribution of seats among the principal forces resulted in more stalemate than action. For the first time a fundamentalist religious party, the Islamist Popular Constitutional Democratic Movement (MPCD), also won seats in parliament, taking nine with the remaining seats in the 325-seat chamber went to a scattering of minor parties. The big loser in the elections was *Istiqlal* which won only 32 seats, down from 43 in 1993 elections, and blamed its loss on fraud and electoral manipulation by the Interior Ministry.

Though nominally a parliamentary system, government derived largely from the king and Hassan II reserved the right to appoint and fire ministers. The king asked Aberrahmane Youssoufi, the 73-year-old leader of the USFP, to form a government, but retained more direct control over two of the most important ministries. The Interior Ministry assignment went to the king's right-hand man, Driss Basri and Defense remained in the hands of the king as supreme commander of the Royal Armed Forces. As minister of the interior for over 20 years, Basri controlled a web of security agents and spies who informed him of the slightest hint of dissent or opposition and oversaw appointments of governors and other regional and local officials. The police were under his control and his jails were places of detention and torture. Even critical foreign-policy questions were under his purview. In many ways the Interior Ministry was a parallel government that operated above the law and responded only to the king.

King Mohamed VI (1999-present) and Political Liberalization

After 38 years of rule, King Hassan died in July 1999. He was succeeded by his unmarried elder son, Crown Prince Sidi Mohamed. In his first speech as King

King Mohamed VI

Mohamed VI, the new monarch ignited optimism by evoking the poverty of his people, the fate of women, and the need for change. Action followed words and the king fired corrupt governors and released 10,000 political prisoners. He also recognized the victims of human rights abuses and offered state compensation to relatives of several thousand Moroccans who had been "disappeared" under Hassan II. In November 1999, King Mohamed confirmed his commitment to change by dismissing Driss Basri.

Mohamed also began the process of bringing his father's political opponents home from exile or freeing them from house arrest. The most notable of the exiles was the 73-year-old Abraham Serfaty. Head of the Marxist-Leninist *Ila al-Amam* group, Serfaty had been sentenced to life in prison for making statements in favor of self-determination for the Western Sahara. After a 17-year incarceration and an 8-year exile, the young king invited him back to Morocco. The family of Mehdi Ben Barka, who "disappeared" under mysterious circumstances in 1965 while living in France, had their passports restored and were allowed to return to Morocco.

Also restored was the 72-year-old Islamist leader Sheikh Abdessalam Yassine, the most radical of King Hassan's challengers. Yassine was head of *al-Adl walIhsane* (Justice and Charity), the country's biggest Muslim fundamentalist organization, Ih was active mainly on university campuses and in the poor districts of large cities. Sheikh Yassine had long been a thorn in the side of King Hassan and in the 1970s he had been detained without trial for more than three years for criticizing the king for copying Western values and demanding the application of *sharia* law. Government ministers had long called for his release, but palace officials argued he should first acknowledge the religious authority of King Mohamed VI, who bears the title *Amir al-Mu'minin* or "Commander of the Faithful." Sheikh Yassine addressed a 35-page letter to the king in February 2000, raising one of the most taboo subjects: the royal family's wealth. It called on the king to return billions of dollars that Islamists allege his father had stashed abroad. Despite the directness of the challenge, King Mohamed VI released Yassine ten years of house arrest in May 2000.

Despite the vigor of the new king, political reform was limited as Mohamed VI possessed extraordinary sources of constitutional power and legitimacy. Still, some progress was made on human development initiatives as Mohamed VI took practical action to deal with the abiding problems of illiteracy and unemployment. In August 2000 he announced that Morocco's mosques would be used to dispense literacy courses, as well as religious, civic and health education. Women—whose literacy in the rural areas was estimated as low as 10%—were to be primary beneficiaries.

The 2002 legislative elections were the fairest elections yet to be held in Morocco and featured several innovations. Proportional representation was employed, with electors voting for a party list rather than individual candidates. To assure female representation in parliament, voters also selected ten percent of their future MPs from a national list of exclusively female candidates. This set-aside assured Morocco of having the largest contingent of women in its legislature among all Arab states. For the first time also, ballots featured party logos to facilitate recognition by illiterate voters. To dissuade fraud and fixing, more than 50,000 bottles of indelible ink were imported to dab the hands of voters, and prison sentences were introduced for vote-buying by candidates—a great tradition of Moroccan politics.

The election produced no seismic change, but the changes did mean a greater number of political parties participating (with 26 nominating 5,873 candidates in 91 electoral districts) and a more fragmented parliament in which 22 parties took seats in the new legislature, up from 15. Retiring Prime Minister Youssoufi's USFP claimed the largest number of seats, with 50 in the 325-member House of Representatives. *Istiqlal* took second place with 48 seats, while the moderate Islamist Party of Justice and Development (PJD) made the biggest gain, winning 42 seats up from its previous 14. Sheikh Yassine's fundamentalist Justice and Charity party called for an election boycott and ran no candidates.

Paradoxically, the new government that emerged from Morocco's cleanest, most

Morocco

An olive seller Photo by Jinny Lambert

transparent, and most democratic election was not party based. Following the election the king appointed the businessman Driss Jettou as prime minister. Unaffiliated with any political party, Jettou—a former shoe manufacturer—headed a team in which four other major ministers—including defense, foreign affairs, and Islamic affairs—were appointed by the monarch. The king presided over meetings of this select cabinet, which operated in parallel with the Prime Minister's own cabinet and made most important policy decisions.

In 2002, security forces dismantled an al-Qaeda sleeper cell, directed by three Saudis, with plans to blow up American and British war ships passing through the Strait of Gibraltar. Then on March 16, 2003, al-Qaeda–linked terrorists set off five bombs near Western and Jewish targets in Casablanca, killing 43 people (including 12 terrorists) and wounding more than 100.

Parliament reacted to the Casablanca bombings by passing a strict antiterrorism law, but the king, the embodiment of official Islam, remained silent. An investigation showed the May 16 perpetrators were mostly Moroccan and indigenous fundamentalism proved a major threat to Morocco's developing democracy. Symptomatically, municipal elections were postponed from June to September, giving the government more time to campaign against the possibility of a fundamentalist takeover of the country's biggest cities: Casablanca, Rabat, Fez, and Tangiers.

The September 2003 local elections were dominated by the two leading traditional parties: Istiqlal and the socialist USFP together won more than 30% of the vote for 23,000 local seats. The one legal Islamist party, the PJD, won less than 3% of the vote, but only because it discreetly chose to run candidates in only 20% of the constituencies. In Casablanca, Morocco's largest city, the PJD won in all eight districts where it presented candidates; had it chosen to run in the city's other eight districts, Casablanca would likely have had an Islamist government.

The Growing Threat of Islamic Fundamentalism

All across North Africa and across the Mediterranean in Europe, governments are in a fight against international terrorism spear-headed by AQIM (Al-Qaeda in the Islamic Maghreb). Arrest announcements detailing terrorist plots come often in Morocco, and this has dominated the international news out of the country in recent years. In early September 2006, police reported that 56 terror suspects had been swept up in an antiterrorist investigation. The suspects were, police officials said, members of a group calling itself *Ansar al-Mahdi* (Supporters of the *Mahdi*, a figure whose arrival is said to herald the end of the world in Islamic tradition) and had amassed material to make far more explosives than had been used by the Casablanca bombers in 2003. Among those arrested were four women, including the wives of two pilots for the national airline, Royal Air Maroc, and at least five former soldiers with training in the use of explosives. The interior minister tried to put the best possible spin on the obvious: militant Islamists had penetrated the military and security services in their recruitment. The number of those recruited, said minister Benmoussa, was "very limited and involved isolated and marginal cases."

Nevertheless, reaction was swift and airports throughout the kingdom were placed on high alert. Security control of passengers was tightened and security patrols at airport perimeters intensified. At Mohamed V airport outside Casablanca security cameras were modernized to record all movement at the airport and all female workers were prohibited from wearing the veil. The king also acted promptly to deal with the infiltration of his armed forces, firing both the head of military intelligence and the director of national security, reorganizing the royal security apparatus reorganized, and military conscription.

More Casablanca suicide bombings in March and April 2007 turned out to be more sophisticated, better funded, and better armed than originally thought. Though government officials played down possible international connections, others were quick to point out the upsurge of similar recent incidents in Algeria and Tunisia, for which AQIM had claimed credit.

A string of arrests followed in 2008 and 2009, including 36 people in February 2008 and 35 more in July of that year. An additional 15 arrests were made in August, of alleged members of Fath al-Anadalous (an al-Qaeda-affiliated group). At the same time, the Moroccan justice system was completing convictions against several terror masterminds, including Abdelkader Belliraj, the alleged leader of al-Qaeda in Morocco, who was extradited to Belgium. In February 2009, Saad Housseini was convicted and sentenced to 15 years for his role in the 2003 Casablanca bombings. Also in 2008, two Moroccan men were convicted of participation in the Madrid train bombings.

While combating fundamentalist Islam, the Youssoufi government sought to boost the social and economic status of women, who are typically disadvantaged in the male-dominated society. In March 1999 the government introduced a series of proposals that aimed alter the country's traditional Islamic marriage statutes; banning polygamy and raising the minimum age for marriage from 15 to 18. A system of legal divorce was proposed that would have replaced the norm of simple verbal dissolution through repudiation by the husband. Under the new proposals divorce would be in the hands of a judge and a couple's assets must be shared after divorce.

After the government announced its reforms, fundamentalists and modernists staged dueling marches in Casablanca and Rabat. An estimated 500,000 traditionalists demonstrated in Casablanca against the project, dwarfing a 40,000-person

Morocco

demonstration by supporters of the plan in Rabat. The government buckled under pressure from the fundamentalists and the reform of the family code languished.

When Islamists kept a low profile following the bloody Casablanca bombings, the king revisited the issue and proposed a new family code in October 2003. It was passed unanimously by both chambers of parliament, even winning the support of the Islamic PJD party. The new code, which became effective in February 2004, recognized the equality of the sexes, suppressed the husband's right of repudiation, raised the age of consent to 18 and rendered polygamy virtually impossible to practice.

Elections in 2007 saw Istiqlal take the most seats in parliament, with 52 of 325. The King appointed Abbas al-Fassi as Prime Minister at the head of a coalition comprised of Istiqlal and four other parties, including the USFP. The opposition Islamist PJD gained four seats to a total of 46, suggesting a sort of regularization and normalization of Morocco's political process, in which democracy remained incomplete but operated on increasingly standardized rules.

The Arab Spring of 2011 and Limited Reform

The events of the Arab Spring in 2011 looked like they might bring fundamental change to Morocco as they did in the nearby countries of Tunisia, Egypt, and Libya, but the King (generally held to be more popular than leaders in the other North African countries) held on to power. In February 2011, several thousand people took to the streets in some of Morocco's larger cities, including Rabat, demanding constitutional revisions that would reduce the power of the king, more jobs, and an end to corruption. Some incidents of looting followed and a handful of protestors were killed, though it was unclear whether the forces of order were responsible for the deaths. King Mohamed VI announced he would create a commission to propose reforms, and that the proposal would be put to a referendum; he also reduced the sentences of nearly 200 Islamists that had been imprisoned for several years. While some smaller protests took place into April and May and generated occasional clashes between riot police and demonstrators, it seemed the King had weathered any threat to his rule.

As the wave of protests across the Arab world subsided in April 2011, Morocco faced another destabilizing event in the form of a bomb attack that killed 16 people on April 28 at a café popular with tourists in the city of Marrakesh. This was the deadliest attack in the country since the Casablanca bombing of 2003 and served as a reminder of the persistence of a terrorist strain of political Islam.

King Mohamed's proposed constitutional referendum was passed in July of 2011. The reform lessened the King's powers and gave the Prime Minister's seat to the parliamentary majority party. It also enshrined a greater degree of gender equity before the law, building on more progressive reforms to the family code (known as *Mudawana*) in 2004, although there are still elements of Morocco's penal code that discriminate against women. Two days after the passage of the 2011 constitutional reform, protests began again demanding further reductions in royal power, though the majority of the population seemed pleased with the changes.

In November of 2011, the PJD won the majority in the parliamentary elections, ushering in a new era of Islamist influence in the legislature. With new powers to appoint ministers and dissolve parliament, Prime Minister Abdelilah Benkirane faced protests when trade unionists felt he and his new government had not delivered on reforms in May of 2012. By ceding more of his power to the legislature, King Mohamed proved able to deflect protest and citizen displeasure. Some upheaval in late 2013 led to a reshuffling of the government, though Benkirane remained as prime minister.

Overall, King Mohamed VI is one of the few regional leaders that have had the sense to cede some authority when his people have demanded more say. Making a huge effort to distance himself from the authoritative and violent practices of his father, King Mohamed VI has made strides to help the poor and disenfranchised Moroccans while working slowly towards increased liberties and citizen participation in government. When the people call for change in government, it is generally directed at various ministers and not at the King himself. This respect towards the monarch has helped to reduce the likelihood of an uprisings or revolution of the sort that has prevailed in several of Morocco's neighbors recently.

Western Sahara

Western Sahara, formerly known by the names of its two former subdivisions, Saguia el-Hamra and Rio de Oro, lies within one of the most oppressive parts of the immense Sahara Desert. A narrow band along the coast receives torrential thunderstorms wafted inland by the steady trade winds. These rains result in rapid land erosion: most of the water that is not swallowed up by the scorched land spills into short rivers that empty silt into the Atlantic Ocean. This thinly populated desert region became a Spanish colony during the scramble for colonies at the close of the 19th century. For details of earlier and colonial history, see *Historical Background* and *The Colonial Period: The Spanish.*

The territory, then known as Spanish Sahara, came under Moroccan-Mauritanian rule as a result of a series of diplomatic and military actions after the Spanish left in 1975 following pressure from Morocco, Algeria and Mauritania. Spain dragged its feet while mining the phosphate deposits, which were the colony's only resource, until guerrilla activity commenced in 1974 and sabotaged phosphate extraction, after which Spain surrendered the territory. Morocco, Mauritania, and Algeria each forwarded rival claims and positions. Morocco, then backed by Mauritania, insisted that Spain should "return" the Western Sahara as part of greater Morocco. The Algerians supported the Polisario Front (Popular Front for the Liberation of Saguia el-Hamra and Rio de Oro)—an organization that claimed to represent the national ambitions of the people of the former Spanish Sahara.

To press Morocco's claim, King Hassan announced a "green march" into Spanish Sahara in 1975, during which 200,000 Moroccan civilians crossed the border and penetrated six miles into the territory. Spain transferred administrative responsibility to Morocco and Mauritania, and the Polisario proclaimed the existence of the Sahrawi Arab Democratic Republic (SADR), which was immediately recognized by Algeria as the former colony's only legitimate government. Armed conflict soon broke out between the various actors.

Moroccan and Mauritanian troops quickly solidified their position in Western Sahara, while Algeria supported Polisario's campaign of sabotage and violence. Initially, Morocco and Mauritania seemed in firm control, but Polisario guerrilla activities succeeded in securing Mauritania's withdrawal in 1978 through incursions into Mauritania that threatened the capital Nouakchott.

King Hassan proclaimed Western Sahara the 37th province of Morocco, and Morocco now controls all but the easternmost portion of Western Sahara, which is walled by a ten-foot-high "berm" intended to keep Sahrawi "rebels" out. Since that time, rebel activity has been irregular. Most Sahrawi not under Moroccan dominion, as more than 150,000 of them are sheltered in camps near Tindouf, Algeria.

The UN has been trying to hold a referendum that would allow the Sahrawi to determine their own future, but the parties have been unable to agree on who is a Sahrawi and who should be eligible to vote in the referendum. Former U.S. Secretary of State James Baker launched a UN-backed drive to resolve the dispute in May 2000. In 2002, Baker submitted four possible resolutions to the UN Security Council. The first

Morocco

three were: working toward a referendum without the agreement of both parties on specifics; significant autonomy for Western Sahara as a region of Morocco, followed by a Sahrawi referendum after five years; a partition of the territory between contending parties. The fourth proposal indicated the degree of frustration the issue has provoked: it was simply to stop diplomatic efforts and admit that the UN was unable to solve the problem.

The Security Council met in April 2002 to choose a course of action and could not agree. After several years with little success, Baker resigned as mediator in June 2004. In September that year, Morocco received its most significant diplomatic rebuke in years when South African President Thabo Mbeki extended diplomatic recognition to the self-proclaimed Sahrawi Republic. Morocco responded by promptly withdrawing its ambassador from South Africa.

Meanwhile, Polisario had lost its nearly mythical military commander and cofounder, Lahbib Sid'Ahmed Lahbib Aouba, better known by his *nom de guerre*, Commandant Ayoub. Commandant Ayoub defected to Morocco, pledging his personal allegiance to King Mohamed in September 2002. Perhaps more significantly, international oil firms began seeking concessions for offshore exploration. TotalFinaElf, France's largest oil firm, and the Oklahoma City-based Kerr-McGee Corporation, both signed exploration contracts with Morocco to explore for oil deposits off the coast. When the SADR began offering overlapping and competitive blocks in its own licensing round, Kerr-McGee allowed its Moroccan-granted rights to lapse.

Morocco and Polisario remain without agreement after 35 years. In March 2006, King Mohammad VI made his third visit to the territory. He consulted with local notables and appointed a royal advisory council of 140 members and signaled a willingness to discuss a broad grant of autonomy within a framework of Moroccan sovereignty.

In 2009, Western Saharan activist Aminatou Haidar had her passport confiscated by Moroccan officials after she refused to state her citizenship as Moroccan and was denied entrance to the Elayoun region of the Western Sahara. Following her expulsion to the Spanish Canary Islands, she undertook a 32-day hunger-strike. Facing international pressure, Morocco allowed Haidar back into the Western Sahara. Although this event brought public awareness to the complexities facing Western Sahara, the discussion of autonomy has remained stagnant. By 2010, tensions had risen again as Moroccan security forces took over a protest camp in November, which resulted in demonstrations in Elayoun, the largest town in Western Sahara. Clashes followed in December as the BBC reported that Western Sahara delegates in South Africa attempted to replace a Moroccan flag with an anti-Moroccan banner. As of 2014, little advancement has been made and resolution of Western Sahara's status thus seems less unlikely in the near future. In fact, tensions have arisen between the United States and Morocco, given US support for UN monitoring of the human rights situation in Western Sahara.

CONTEMPORARY THEMES

The Economy

Morocco's economic growth has been volatile in recent years, alternating between about 3% and up to 7%, depending on a variety of conditions. Agriculture contributes about one-eighth of Morocco's GDP and accounts for about half of the labor force, but the conditions of rural farmers are difficult at best. Morocco is considered to have the best agricultural land in North Africa and produces wheat, barley, beans sugar beets and citrus fruits, but production is highly dependent on rainfall patterns and much of the arable land remains unused due to underdeveloped irrigation systems. Recently, the cactus plant has become a valued and profitable crop in southern Morocco. Used to create various skin-care products and in demand from European countries, the cactus has started to provide a source of revenue and employment to local Moroccans, particularly women.

There are no official statistics on Morocco's cannabis crop (known locally as *kif*), but Morocco is among the crop's largest producers, though production declined in the mid-2000s. Its cultivation and sale is the economic basis for much of the Rif Mountains of northern Morocco, where over 200,000 acres are devoted to its production that is later exported as hashish to Algeria, Tunisia, and Europe. About two-thirds of the 800,000 people of the Rif, most of them Berbers, depend on cannabis for their income. For most Rif inhabitants, cannabis cultivation is a matter of survival, as the region is isolated, underdeveloped, impoverished, and alienated, with minimal infrastructure.

Attempts to diversify the economy have produced mixed results. The mining sector remains crucially important and there are about 90 mining companies producing about 20 different mineral products. Phosphates account for 92% of mineral production as Morocco has the largest phosphate reserves in the world—110 billion tons. Morocco is the world's number one phosphoric acid exporter, averaging 1.7 million tons of exports annually. Phosphates and their by-products account for 18% of Morocco's total exports. Heightened demand, largely spurred by China's natural resource needs, have increased phosphate exports and revenues; the Chinese group Sino-chem signed an agreement with Morocco's *Office Chérifien des Phosphates* (OCP) to increase phosphate

A local vegetable retailer

Photo by Taylor O'Connor

Morocco

exports to China in 2005, and also signed a joint venture agreement to produce phosphoric acid and fertilizer in Morocco.

A fishing industry is developing, but over-fishing by aggressive industrial fishing fleets has severely reduced the stock of available fish, and Morocco has had to declare an occasional "biological repose" in response. Much of the over-fishing was done by European fishing fleets, and Morocco refused to renew its fishing agreement with the EU until recently when the EU paid Morocco $187 million dollars for four years of fishing rights in Moroccan waters beginning in 2007.

Another minor source of potential wealth for the Moroccan economy lies with the discovery of oil at several locations across the country, though production and proven reserves remain very modest to date. For years, Morocco has had to import virtually all of its oil and gas. To encourage exploration and development, it drastically overhauled its investment code: required participation by the state was reduced from 50% to 25%, and companies were offered ten-year tax abatement.

The World Bank argues that the country's bloated and heavily unionized administration is hindering economic dynamism. The state employs some 750,000 people, including security forces and para-military forces, under the direct control of the Interior Ministry. The wages of this army of civil servants take a full 12% of Morocco's GDP. The effects are clear: Morocco budgets more for education than its neighbors but achieves less because of excessive administrative costs. One out of two children of school age do not go to school in Morocco, and one in two Moroccans can neither read nor write. More than 60% of Moroccan women are illiterate, for example, with the rate rising to 90% in poor rural areas. The rates are worse in many isolated Berber communities, which contribute to the sense of abandonment in those communities.

Unemployment is at least 16% and more in the urban centers—up to 25%. Among young people, unemployment figures rise to at least 30%. The economy needs to create approximately 250,000 jobs a year to accommodate the young who enter the job market annually. Given limited opportunity, an estimated 100,000 or more Moroccans head abroad each year as illegal immigrants seeking work in Europe.

Plans to build a high-speed train running between Casablanca, Rabat and Tangier are underway. The project is expected to cost $4 billion dollars and will be funded by France, Kuwait, the United Arab Emirates, and Saudi Arabia. However, given the infrastructure needs of a growing and relatively poor country, many critics are arguing that investment in a high-speed train should be put on the backburner and funds should be used towards roads, schools, and hospitals. Campaigns against constructing cited that the projected costs of the train would build 25,000 schools in rural areas, 25 fully equipped major university hospitals and 16,000 community centers.

Foreign Relations: Immigration to Spain and Related Issues

Morocco's proximity to Spain has led to a unique relationship between the two nations that has been, at times, tension-filled. In October 2001, King Mohamed VI withdrew Morocco's ambassador to Spain, signaling the depth of tensions that had developed between the two countries. Relations had soured over Spain's continued support of the Algerian-backed Polisario Front and its claims for self-determination in Western Sahara. This was, however, only one of several issues that made Spanish relations so tricky.

While other sources of tension have been economically fueled, like disputes over access to fishing waters, the biggest issue continues to be immigration. Every year, thousands of young Moroccans (often uneducated young men), enter Spain in search of employment. Only a 90-minute boat ride away, Spain is a natural first stop, and in 2006 some 47,000 illegal immigrants from West Africa arrived in Spain. In many ways North Africa is to southern Europe as Mexico is to the U.S., with the threat of Islamic fundamentalism thrown in.

The jumping-off spots for many of those seeking clandestine entry into Spain are the two Spanish enclaves of Ceuta (Sebta to Moroccans) and Melilla—microscopic residuals from an earlier era. Ceuta, barely seven square miles in size, is a peninsula across from Gibraltar that is, like Melilla, an autonomous Spanish region. Moroccans have lived, worked, and bought duty-free goods in both of the enclaves for years. With increased illegal migration (a profitable activity of organized crime groups), Spanish authorities heightened security measures, ringing both enclaves with doubled razor-wire fences that were constantly observed by 37 infrared cameras, 230 searchlights and 21 watchtowers. When the fences proved insufficient to arrest the floodtide of immigrants, the Spanish government increased coastal patrols and installed a $120 million radar system to monitor the strait. As a consequence of these heightened security measures, most illegal immigrants now attempt to enter Spain through the Canary Islands.

Relatively large immigrant populations are a continuing source of tension between the two countries. Moroccans are the largest immigrant group in Spain, numbering well over 300,000. To service their spiritual needs, there are an estimated 1,000 mosques, functioning out of sight from outsiders in apartments, garages, or workshops with often radical preachers. From this milieu came the al-Qaeda-linked terrorists responsible for the March 11, 2004, train bombings in Madrid. They killed 191 people, wounded more than 1,500, toppled an incumbent government, and transformed relations between Morocco and Spain.

Spanish authorities identified most of the 18 Madrid bombers as Moroccans. One of the ringleaders, a Tangiers native named Jamal Zougam, had connections to two banned Moroccan groups: Salafist Jihad (SJ: *Salafiya Jihadiya*) implicated in the 2003 Casablanca bombings, and the Moroccan Islamic Combat Group (GICM: *Groupe islamiste combattant marocain*), which claims to struggle for an Islamic state in the kingdom. Facing a common threat from Islamist militancy, Morocco and Spain now cooperate closely in both legal and security issues concerning illegal immigration, international terror and, increasingly, its ties to drug trafficking and organized criminal networks. An agreement dating to 2004 provides for a Spanish judge to be based in Rabat and a Moroccan judge in Madrid to speed up judicial procedures involving both countries. That cooperation has become increasingly important as militant Islamists have regionalized their organization of jihadist terror.

A nesting stork   Photo by Taylor O'Connor

Morocco

Tourism is of growing importance, but subject to sharp fluctuations reflecting world events. The industry saw a decline following the terrorist attacks on New York in September 2001. In 2002, the invasion of Iraq and terrorist attacks in Casablanca made the situation worse; prompting Prime Minister Youssoufi to announce a tourism development scheme. Dubbed *Plan Azur*, the program aimed to add 40,000–50,000 hotel rooms as part of a plan to attract ten million tourists to the country. Five coastal sites, including the walled city of Essaouira—known for its close-knit community of Sephardic Jews and particularly its Jewish musicians—were selected for development. The coastal site of Saïdia was slated for 29 hotels providing 17,000 rooms, three 18-hole golf courses, a marina to accommodate 700 boats, and a three-mile seaside promenade. The *Ansar el-Mahdi* arrests in September 2006 highlighted just how vulnerable the infrastructure of tourism in Morocco is—and how expensive it is to provide security.

Morocco is considered a non-NATO ally of the United States and continues to serve as a supporter of the United States in the Middle East The U.S. and Morocco signed a Free Trade Agreement (FTA) in June 2004 after 13 months of tough negotiations. Morocco's largest exports to the U.S. are semiconductors, minerals, and clothing, while the largest U.S. sales to Morocco are grains and civilian aircraft. Ratified in 2006, the FTA has lifted the total trade between the two countries from around $850 million in 2003 to around $1 billion in 2006. Before trade volume can increase much more, Moroccan ports will have to be brought in line with international security standards. Both the ports of Casablanca and Tangiers, nerve centers of the kingdom's economy, are considered vulnerable. In contrast, Morocco's largest and most modern port, the Tangiers Med, opened in July 2007 with a full range of modern high-tech security devices: thermal image cameras, explosive detectors, biometric ID controls and security badges.

Recent events include the devastating earthquake on September 8, 2023, in the mountain regions outside the heavily touristed city of Marakesh with 3,000 fatalities and 60,000 dwellings damaged or destroyed. While recovery has been slow in some regions with survivors still living in tents, tourism into the popular site has rebounded as the country vies for contracts with major international aircraft manufacturers for local production of components and parts supplies, most notably Safran Aircraft of France, backed by government subsidies to the $2 billion industry. On the foreign policy front, Morrocco has maintained military and security ties with Israel even as popular pro-Palestinian protests have broken out but with no apparent loss of popularity by the king while the country continues its claim to Western Sahara.

Reacting to continued violence in the Gaza Strip, thousands of Moroccans took to the streets in the capital of Rabat in April 2025 protesting against both Israel and the United States for the prolonged 18-month war with banners portraying assassinated Hamas leaders and displaced Palestinians. Cancelling trade deals that had allowed Morocco to export fish and agricultural products from the disputed Western Sahara region to the European Union (EU), the European Court of Justice (ECJ) confirmed an earlier ruling that declared the exports breached the region's population right to self-determination, a decision criticized by the Moroccan government as "blatant political bias." On the domestic front, the country continued to confront ongoing water supply problems as individual villages have set out to integrate ancient and modern water management techniques to combat water scarcity while the central government pursues more large-scale interventions to achieve water sustainability.

FUTURE CONSIDERATIONS

The Arab Spring of 2011 tested Morocco's political system, and while King Mohamed VI has held onto power with relative ease thus far, it is clear that the system has certain fragilities. Constitutional changes in 2012 increased powers of the legislature and separated the judiciary from the executive, but the majority of power still rests in the Monarch's hands. While the 2007 elections were one more small step towards political openness, the forces that are likelier to bring change (for better or worse) are those outside the narrow confines of regime politics: the street protestors or the Islamic fundamentalist groups that necessitate responses by the government.

The biggest challenges in the political arena include the continued threat of terrorism that Morocco witnessed most tragically in 2003. The wheels continue to turn in the criminal justice system as Morocco seeks to prosecute alleged terrorists, and

Ruins of the Roman city of Volubilis. Many of the city's buildings were destroyed to provide building materials to construct the palaces of Moulay Ismail in nearby Meknès.

Morocco

a steady stream of arrests and verdicts seems likely over the coming years. The most recent example occurred in February 2009, when Moroccan Islamist militant Saad Housseini, who had learned bomb-making techniques in Afghanistan, was charged for his involvement in the 2003 Casablanca bombings and sentenced to 15 years in prison. Nonetheless, bombings in 2007, 2008, and again in 2011 showed that Morocco remains a locus of terrorist ideology and a target of extremists.

Economically, the country remains on a fair trajectory, albeit one that does not presage dramatic economic growth or poverty reduction. Unemployment remains a problem, but inflation is low and the economy is stable and growing at a moderate pace. While the economic base is vulnerable, the economy can anticipate growth going forward.

Tunisia

The Roman colosseum at El Djem

Photo by Beverly Ingram

BASIC FACTS

Area: 163,610 sq. km. = 63,170 sq. mi. (slightly larger than Florida)
Population: 11,976,182 (June 2023 est.)
Capital City: Tunis
Government Type: Parliamentary Republic
Neighboring Countries: Algeria (west); Libya (east, southeast)
Official Language: Arabic
Other Principal Languages: French
Ethnic Groups: Arab 98%, European 1%, Jewish and other 1%
Principal Religions: Muslim 98%, Christian 1%, Jewish and other 1%
Former Colonial Status: French protectorate (1881–1956)
Independence Date: July 20, 1956
GDP per capita (IMF 2023 est.): $4,071 (nominal), $13,270 (PPP)
Gini index: 32.8 (World Bank 2015)
Currency: Tunisian Dinar, $US1 = 3.04 Dinars (Apr. 2023)
Inflation Rate: 7.7% (2022 est.)
Chief Commercial Products: Clothing, hydrocarbons, textiles, phosphate and chemicals, mechanical goods, electrical equipment, agricultural products (olives, olive oil, grain, dairy products, tomatoes, citrus fruit, beef, sugar beets, dates, almonds)
Foreign Direct Investments (FDI) net inflows: 1,004,668,149
Literacy Rate: 81.8% (CIA 2015)
Life Expectancy: 77.07 years (CIA 2023 est.)
Head of State: President Kais Saied (since October 23, 2019)
Head of Government: Prime Minister Najla Bouden Romdhane (since October 11, 2021)

LAND AND PEOPLE

Tunisia, the smallest country of North Africa, lies near the center of the Mediterranean Sea coastline, with a seashore almost 1,000 miles long. The coastal belt, with an average of 50 miles in width, is the site of farmland. The coastline extends horizontally for 140 miles in the North and then proceeds irregularly southward for a lineal distance of 300 miles; there are also three large gulf areas. The coastal strip is succeeded by a gently rolling tableland with an average altitude of 1,600 feet—an area of grass and forestland. This, in turn, is followed by the semi-desert to the south-southwest where there is little rainfall, and shallow salt lakes. Though this sparsely settled territory is within the desert, it is not quite as dry and hot as the central Sahara.

A variety of well-maintained museums offer testimony to the diverse cultural heritage of Tunisia. The National Museum of the Bardo, located in the old palace of the bey (the Ottoman governor) in a Tunis suburb, is the finest archeological museum in the Mahgreb. Its attractions include mosaic floors from the Roman cities of northern Tunisia, rich evidence of the extraordinary wealth and luxury of Rome's breadbasket province. Further evidence of Tunisia's importance to Rome is the grand amphitheater of El Jem. After the coliseums of Rome and Capua, the one at El Jem was the third largest ever built by the Romans; it accommodated 30,000 spectators. Dougga, 70 miles southwest of Tunis is another spectacular Roman site where a temple dedicated to Jupiter, Juno, and Minerva

Tunisia

dominates the ruins. Near Kairouan, the sacred city of Islamic Tunisia, one can visit the national Museum of Islamic Art with its collection of ceramics and calligraphy. In Mahdia, in the heart of the east coast tourist areas and still an important weaving center, the Textile Museum of the Dar el-Himma features a fine collection of traditional Tunisian costumes.

HISTORY TO PRESENT DAY

Historical Background The Colonial Period: The French.

France recognized Tunisian independence on July 20, 1956, and the old monarchy was abolished in 1957 when the Constituent Assembly established a republic, naming Habib Bourguiba president. Following adoption of a constitution, the first elections were held in 1959 in which there was only small opposition to the New Constitution Party of President Bourguiba. After being elected to a third term in October 1969, Bourguiba was proclaimed president for life in 1975.

The Bourguiba Presidency (1957–1987)

During his time as president, Bourguiba protected the religious freedom of the state and angered many Islamic fundamentalists by doing so. Although Islam is recognized by the Tunisian constitution as the state religion, Bourguiba made many changes to preserve a sentiment of secularism between mosque and state. Bourguiba abolished most of the powers of the Muslim religious courts and rabbinical tribunals and turning their functions over to the civil courts. Women were given the right to institute divorce proceedings against their husbands and were also encouraged to enter the workplace in a variety of trades and professions that had not previously been open to them. In 1984, Bourguiba even appointed two women to his cabinet. Islamic fundamentalists did not respond lightly to the challenges to their religious views and in 1981, a group of fundamentalists raided and largely destroyed a beach resort frequented by Europeans. This attack was a terrible blow to Tunisia's profitable tourist industry and marked the beginning of the state's crackdown on the Islamic fundamentalists.

Besides the creation of a secular state, Habib Bouguiba's other lasting contribution to the development of modern Tunisia came in the emphasis he gave to education. Access to primary, secondary, and higher education was made free and the curriculum was modernized. Until universities were established, large numbers of Tunisian students benefited from scholarships that allowed them to attend universities in France or elsewhere. The development of higher education has been particularly remarkable. At independence there were only two universities in Tunisia; today there are over a dozen. In 1955, there were 2,374 students enrolled for university education and in 2005, Tunisian universities enrolled 346,000 students. The government's focus on education facilitated economic growth and the creation of a significant middle class.

In 1987, after 30 years in power, Habib Bourguiba became visibly senile after suffering from Parkinson's disease. His persecution of Islamic fundamentalists, whose numbers had been swollen by migration to the cities from rural areas, had become more aggressive in recent years and the growing fundamentalist population was pushing for a change of power.

The Ben Ali Years (1987–2011)

On November 7, 1987, former Prime Minister Zine Abidine Ben Ali declared Bourguiba incapable of carrying out his office and removed him, thus becoming president, a move that had widespread support from all elements and factions within Tunisian society. Among his first acts as president, Ben Ali reduced the sentences of several hundred Islamic fundamentalists and suggested he would dissolve the parliament and hold elections in November 1989 rather than the scheduled date in 1991. When it appeared that he and his party were well ahead of any competitor, President Ben Ali advanced the contest to April 1989. His judgment was correct—the Democratic Constitutional Rally (RCD), the new name of Bourguiba's party, won more than 80% of the vote and all of the seats in the National Assembly.

By late 1991, the Islamic fundamentalists had again bloomed and their actions were seriously threatening a booming tourist industry. Ben Ali led his own crackdown, and the government, acting through the military, brought 171 members and leaders of the outlawed Ennahda group before the Tunis military court in 1992. Of those tried, 35 received life sentences, 142 received sentences of three to 20 years, and four were acquitted.

Ben Ali increasingly repressed other political groups besides fundamentalists, as hundreds of political prisoners were taken from opposition parties. The government also closely controlled the press, which came to be more lapdog than watchdog. The Tunisian constitution required potential presidential candidates to secure the nominating signatures of 30 members of parliament, but with the president's RCD holding a monopoly in parliament, no opposition party was able to secure the necessary signatures to put forth a candidate in the 1994 presidential elections. Unopposed, Zine Abidine Ben Ali won 99.9% of the vote. In the legislative balloting of the same year, four opposition parties were only able to win 19 seats in parliament, while Ben Ali's RCD won 144 seats.

During Ben Ali's presidency, the apparatus of surveillance and control grew to dominate Tunisian life. The International Federation for the Rights of Man called Tunisia a "police state" as the number of police quadrupled and new surveillance agencies were established. Membership in the RCD became a political necessity as a membership card was often the first thing shown to police when stopped for questioning.

A local artisan embosses souvenir plates Photo by Beverly Ingram

Tunisia

Habib Bourguiba

Former President Ben Ali, deposed in 2011

New election laws in 1999 permitted the possibility of multiparty elections for the first time in Tunisian history. The 30-signature requirement was abolished and all leaders of political parties who had been in that role for five years, and whose parties were represented in parliament, were eligible to run for president. Only two candidates besides the president met these requirements: Mohamed Belhaj Amor, secretary-general of the *Parti de l'unité populaire* (PUP), and Abderrahmane Tlili of the *Union démocratique unioniste* (UDU). Official election results were not credible and Ben Ali was "reelected" by 99.4% of the voters.

Despite a network of 132,000 policemen and a reported 5,000 wiretaps on the telephone lines of its citizens, the regime did not anticipate the social unrest that rocked both Tunis and several southern cities in early 2000. Taxi drivers disabled the capital for three days in February, protesting a new driving code with increased fines. In the same month several Tunisian cities witnessed protests against stiff increases in the price of gasoline, transport, and food products, especially bread. In some places the protest began in secondary schools and colleges, where the students were supported by locals, mainly youth and mostly unemployed.

These events were not reported in the local press, as the Tunisian Press Code allowed the government to review and censor publications. Politically sensitive articles were sent to the Interior Ministry for review, and each edition had to be registered with the ministry before publication. Information critical of the government was not considered fit to print, and legitimate and unbiased news sources were hard to come by.

In November 2000, Ben Ali attempted to appease his citizens by making cosmetic efforts to put forth a new face of the regime. He announced future amendments to the Press Code to eliminate physical punishment of journalists, and specifically suggested reducing punishments for "libel of public order," a crime that the president recognized as "rather murky" and open to "various interpretations." Ben Ali also announced that the state would compensate any individual unlawfully arrested and detained. These presidential announcements followed just days after a Paris news conference where four Tunisian students gave graphic accounts of beatings, rape, and torture endured at the hands of Tunisian security agents; at the same press conference, the Committee for the Respect of Freedom and Human Rights in Tunisia announced publication of a 200-page report entitled "Torture in Tunisia." Despite international attention, Ben Ali remained firmly in power and worked on plans to extend his tenure.

President Ben Ali was scheduled to end his constitutionally permitted third term in 2004, but a series of constitutional amendments proposed in 2002 allowed him to run for an unlimited number of terms. Government propaganda promoted the creation of a second legislative house (the Chamber of Councilors) and the requirement that there be runoff elections to assure a majority vote for the presidency. Less mentioned were the provisions that increased presidential powers and gave immunity from prosecution, during and after his presidency, for any official acts. The constitutional amendments easily passed the RCD-dominated legislature and were then submitted to a popular referendum—a first in Tunisian history. When the interior minister announced the "results" of the May 26, 2002, voting, he claimed 99.56% approved with 95% percent voter participation

Presidential and parliamentary elections in October 2004 saw Ben Ali win convincingly over three opponents, taking over 94% of the vote; his nearest competitor, Mohamed Bouchiha of the

A stone carver

Party of Popular Unity took a mere 3.8%. For parliament, the RCD took 152 of 189 seats in the Chamber of Deputies and five parties shared the remaining seats. The Movement of Socialist Democrats became the largest parliamentary opposition with 14 deputies. Perhaps the most interesting result of the election was the significant representation of women in parliament. President Ben Ali made the decision to allocate 25% of positions on the RCD party's district slates to female candidates, and as a consequence, 43 newly elected members of parliament were women.

Under Ben Ali, Tunisia became an important ally of the United States in the war on Islamic fundamentalism. The most lethal incidents since the attack on the island of Djerba in 2002 occurred in late 2006 and early 2007 and were claimed by Al-Qaeda of the Islamic Maghreb (AQIM). In January 2007, Tunisian authorities announced they had killed 12 Islamic extremists and captured 15 more, six of whom had crossed into the country from Algeria. Their leader, Lassad Sassi, was a former Tunisian policeman who had run a terrorist cell in Milan until May 2001, when he fled to Algeria before dying in the clash with the Tunisian policemen, According to the Interior Minister, explosives and satellite images of the American and British embassies were found in the group's hideouts.

Ben Ali won a fifth term in office in the multi-party elections of October 2009 with roughly 90% of the vote. Officially, the RCD won 161 of the 214 seats in the Chamber of Deputies, on turnout of 84% of registered voters. Despite criticisms from human rights groups and the opposition that the elections were less than free and fair, Ben Ali settled in for another term.

Despite minimal efforts at reform, the regime continued political repression. In November 2009, journalist Taoufik Ben Brik, a noted critic of Ben Ali, was jailed for assault in a politically motivated case. His imprisonment was condemned by various

Tunisia

human rights organizations, including Amnesty International, who called Ben Brik a "prisoner of conscience." Six months later, Ben Brik was released, but the situation only further solidified Tunisia's political reputation as closed to dissent.

The Arab Spring in Tunisia (2011)

The end of the Ben Ali regime came suddenly in early 2011, and it came in a form that sent shock waves around the world. Mohamed Bouazizi, a 26-year-old fruit vendor from Sidi Bouzid quite literally lit the spark that started the revolution. On December 17, 2010, Bouazizi was confronted by a local policewoman for using an unlicensed cart; she confiscated his cart, and allegedly insulted him and his family, slapped him, and spat on him. After getting no hearing at the local municipal office, Bouazizi doused himself with flammable liquid and lit himself on fire to protest the police and the lack of opportunity in the Tunisian state. His story quickly spread and by the time he died of his burns on January 4, 2011, anger had grown throughout Tunisia into an uprising that threatened the Ben Ali regime. Ben Ali had attempted to put out the proverbial fire by visiting Bouazizi's bedside in a show of official empathy, but he was unable to defuse the situation. Bouazizi's funeral became a major rallying point for opposition.

The protests in December 2010 and January 2011 rapidly went beyond the control of Ben Ali, as growing numbers of Tunisians protested against high unemployment and the rising cost of living, as well as corruption and lack of democratic rights. Some protests turned violent and Tunisian forces fired on protestors on some occasions, killing at least two people. The protests spread to Tunis and crossed class lines as professional groups—most notably lawyers—joined labor unions, students, and informal workers in the protest movement.

The police response to the protests became more violent by January 12, 2011, when protests in the towns of Kasserine and Thala were met with violent crackdowns, and snipers in the towns shot and killed several dozen protestors. The infuriated Tunisians heightened the protests and by January 13, the movement had generalized into a direct challenge to the regime. Around the world, the events came to be known as the Jasmine Revolution.

Ben Ali made a last-ditch attempt to end the crisis on January 13 when he announced economic and political reforms, investments, and job programs. The president vowed to investigate the deaths of protestors and even promised not to seek a future presidential term in 2014, but these concessions came as too little, too late. By January 14, Ben Ali declared a state of emergency and looked increasingly set to return to a more repressive approach, but the president ultimately fled the country at night. After being refused the right to land in France, Ben Ali took refuge in Saudi Arabia.

The Bardo Museum, Tunis, has one of the world's best collections of Roman mosaics.
Photo by Beverly Ingram

In the aftermath of Ben Ali's flight, Tunisia attempted the difficult transition from the toppling of a regime to the reconstruction of public authority. An estimated 78 protesters had died and another 94 injured during the demonstrations. Prime Minister Mohammed Ghannouchi of Ben Ali's RCD party took the reigns as the interim head of the transitional government. However, Ghannouchi was quickly forced to reisgn by citizens who called for a clean break with the past. Fouad Mebazaa, the former parliamentary speaker, took over and prepared for elections. After Ghannouchi, Mebazza and various other former-ministers disaffiliated from the RCD, Ben Ali's former part was officially dissolved by court order, signaling a new era of party-politics in Tunisia.

Protests continued throughout the interim government's rule, as citizens demanded quicker and more efficient change. A curfew was imposed in May 2011 following street protests that challenged the status quo. In June of 2011, Ben Ali and his wife were tried *in absentia* and convicted of theft and unlawful possession of cash and jewelry. Ben Ali was sentenced to 35 years in prison with an additional $65 million fine. The verdict pleased the many who had fought for his removal from power and had been victims of his crimes. In June of the following year, Ben Ali was tried again and received another 20 years for incitement to murder during the Jasmine Revolution, although his exile in Saudi Arabia indefinitely delayed his punishment.

In October 2011, the interim government held elections for the constitutional assembly. The Ennahda Islamist party gained many seats, but failed to win a majority, ensuring diverse party representation and a secular government for the time being. Work began on a new constitution in November of 2011 and one month later the National Assembly elected Moncef Marzouki, a human rights activist, as president. Ennahda leader Hamadi Jebali was sworn in as Prime Minister. (In the current Tunisian government, the president is secondary to the prime minister in power and presidential action often requires consultation with or approval from the prime minister.)

The year 2012 saw new waves of violence and presaged a future in which fights will persist over the role and interpretation of Islam in society. First, hundreds of Islamic extremists attacked a police station in Jendouba in May 2012 following disputes over the sale of alcohol. Protests by Islamists continued into June as riots erupted in several cities, causing the government to establish an overnight curfew in eight regions. The government had tried to stop protests by banning them on Avenue Bourguiba in Tunis (a rallying location much like Tahrir Square in Cairo), but groups protested the ban and continued to voice their opinions and state their demands to the government. Then counter-protests in August 2012 were led by moderates and liberals that were angered by a draft constitution that suggested women were subordinate to men.

Most recently, Tunisia has witnessed escalating protests by the militant group Ansar al-Sharia. This included an attack on the U.S. Embassy in September 2012 that resulted in several Tunisian deaths (This occurred at about the same time as attacks on the American Consulate in Benghazi, Libya left several Americans dead, including the US Ambassador to Libya.) The group has also protested art

Tunisia

exhibits and movies it deems blasphemous, and its clashes with police in May 2013 left at least one person dead.

Tumult spilled over into representative politics as well. On February 6, 2013, the prominent politician Chokri Belaid of the Democratic Patriots' Movement (a secular and left-leaning group) was assassinated outside his home. Prime minister Hamadi Jebali of the Ennahda party resigned over a conflict with his party over what to do in the aftermath; Jebali preferred a technocratic government of national unity, which displeased the Ennahda rank-and-file. Ali Laarayedh of Ennahda replaced Jebali as prime minister on March 14, but the Belaid assassination was followed by that of another politician: Mohamed Brahmi was killed outside his home (allegedly by the same gunman) on July 25, 2013. This led to further outcry against the Ennahda government, and ultimately a political stalemate. The Ennahda party and the opposition ultimately agreed in late 2013 to form a caretaker government until a new constitutional assembly could be formed. Mehdi Jomaa, a political independent and technocrat, took the role of prime minister. At present, it is clear that Tunisia does not have a settled political environment, but rather remains in the midst of a long transitional phase in the wake of its national revolution.

CONTEMPORARY THEMES

Tunisia was historically a granary of the Mediterranean, and for years petroleum production became its biggest moneymaker. Oil production is now declining from peak output in the 1980s. Proven reserves are modest, as are proven natural gas reserves, most of which is located offshore; the state-owned *Société Tunisienne de l'Électricité et du Gaz* (STEG) has successfully encouraged a shift to gas as an energy source for domestic use. According to STEG figures, natural gas consumption accounted for 44% of Tunisia's energy usage in 2005, up from only 14% in 2003.

Agriculture employs about 30% of the workforce and accounts for less than 10% of GDP. Relatively rich and productive, around 30% of the land is arable, though desertification has destroyed a growing proportion of fertile land. Olive oil is Tunisia's most important agricultural export and it is the world's fourth-ranked producer, after Spain, Italy, and Greece. Tunisia also produces table grapes and over 60 types of wine from its vineyards in the north.

Tourism replaced oil as Tunisia's biggest foreign exchange earner in 1999 but dropped after the 9/11 attacks and the April 2002 attack on the Ghriba synagogue on Djerba Island. Twenty people were killed, including 13 German tourists, and the attack was linked to al-Qaeda. Built in the 1920s, Ghriba sits on the site of Africa's oldest synagogue, believed to have been built about 2,500 years ago. According to tradition, the first Jews came to Djerba in biblical times, bringing a stone from the First Temple, destroyed by the Babylonians in 586 BC. The stone is kept in a grotto at Djerba's synagogue. The thousands who make an annual *Lag Ba'omer* pilgrimage to the synagogue were down to hundreds in 2002. A turnaround in worldwide tourism by 2005 saw Tunisia receive 6.4 million international visitors, up from five million in 2002, and in 2005 the tourism sector earned over $2 billion, around 7% of GDP. The sector was vulnerable to the downturn in 2008 and 2009, and the recent political upheaval has no doubt tarnished Tunisia's image as a tourist destination for the time-being.

With tourism, the textile industry is the most important sector of the Tunisian economy, accounting for 6% or more of the country's GDP. The industry has generated some 280,000 jobs and 2,000 companies, but the expiration of multilateral textile agreements in 2005 and the opening of markets to a flood of Chinese products has forced some restructuring in the industry. The unemployment rate remains high, and were a key factor in the protests that brought down the Ben Ali regime. For years, official estimates held that unemployment was in the range of 10%–14%, but it was widely assumed that these understated the magnitude of the problem.

A secular state, Tunisia allows greater freedom to its women than most other Muslim countries. The foundation of that emancipation was the 1956 personal status code that abolished polygamy, divorce by a husband's simple repudiation, and male tutelage of women. In the cities younger women dress in Western attire, but increasingly one sees women wearing the Islamic scarf to cover their heads. In comparison to other Arab countries, Tunisia provides greater gender equality and more professional opportunity to women than anywhere else and women make up large percentages of Tunisia's lawyers, teachers, judges, and journalists. However, the constitution of the new government will not likely remove the existing section that entitles women to only half as much inheritance as men.

The presence of Islam in society has grown more public in recent years. In addition to the increased usage of the headscarf, sociologists also note an increased attendance at Friday prayers. Both were seen—in part—as a form of resistance against the few opportunities for political expression under Ben Ali.

The Ben Ali government pursued a policy of Arabization. While tolerating bilingualism, the government reduced the use of French by forcing shopkeepers to remove signs employing the Latin alphabet and ordering civil servants to use the country's official language in all documents since 2001. In education, the question of which Arabic to use is a challenge, however. Tunisians speak a dialect of Arabic, but the language of instruction in schools is introduced written classical Arabic. An Intermediate Arabic between the two has been developing, but dialectical differences in Arabic complicate the issues as ensuring the availability of textbooks with standardized terminology in the sciences.

Elected In 2019, President Kais Saied has pursued Increasingly authoritarian policies dissolving the parliament and suspending the constitution In July 2021 while charging the speaker of the parliament and main opposition leader, 82-year-old Rached Ghannouchi and head of the Ennahdha Party, with illicit receipt of foreign funds. Domestically, the major Issue Involves treatment of black refugees from sub-Saharan Africa attempting to make their way to Europe, who face Increasingly arbitrary detention and a generally hostile environment in the country are vulnerable to kidnapping and ransom. While a strong supporter of Palestinian rights against the state of Israel, at least rhetorically, President Saied has been widely criticized for lack of any concrete actions of support, a common feature of many strongman leaders in the Arab world. Struggling to stabilize the economy while dramatically increasing domestic political repression, President Saied dismissed his second prime minister since his 2024 reelection and appointed Sara Zaafarani in March 2025, the country's second female prime minister in history. Criticizing the performance of state ministers, including the recently deposed finance minister, the president called on Zaafarani to "coordinate government action and overcome obstacles" as the population becomes increasingly concern over deteriorating public services including health care, transportation, and public utilities. With economic growth stagnating at a tepid 1.4 percent in 2024, the country public finances are in peril as key commodities such as rice, sugar, and coffee remain in short supply which the president blames on "conspiracies" by criminal gangs while jailed opposition leaders numbering 40 individuals, including the once largest party in parliament, the Muslim Democrats, face state conspiracy charges as the president continues a policy of weakening the judiciary against domestic and international criticism including by the United Nations. Confronting widespread criticism over an unprecedented migrant crisis with thousands of people heading from sub-Saharan Africa in an attempt to reach Europe, thousands of migrants and refugees are living in tents located in forests near southern towns prevented by state authorities from travelling to the Mediterranean while fending off conflicts with local residents.

FUTURE CONSIDERATIONS

Tunisia's future will depend upon the resolution of the uprisings of 2011 and the efficiency of its new government that began work in 2012. The protest movement—or Jasmine Revolution—successfully purged most of the important representatives of the Ben Ali regime, especially those from the now-banned RCD, but this does not mean government is settled for the future. The current caretaker government has to navigate an increasingly fractious debate between the moderate Islamists of the Ennahda party, more liberal secularists, and hardliners.

Tunisia has major economic challenges, but also promise: it is a largely middle-class country (with over 60% of the population being in this category), yet the uprisings of 2011 must be understood as having their origins in the lack of economic opportunity and political openness. Tunisia has also thus far better resisted the advance of al-Qaeda in the Islamic Maghreb than its neighbor Algeria although Islamists continue to make themselves seen and heard through violence and protest. Tunisia is a relatively tolerant and open society has allowed for continued relations with the west and has become a model for democratic aspirations across North Africa and the Middle East, but with recent arbitrary state actions against political opponents of the sitting government undermining this long-standing pro-democracy image.

WEST AFRICA

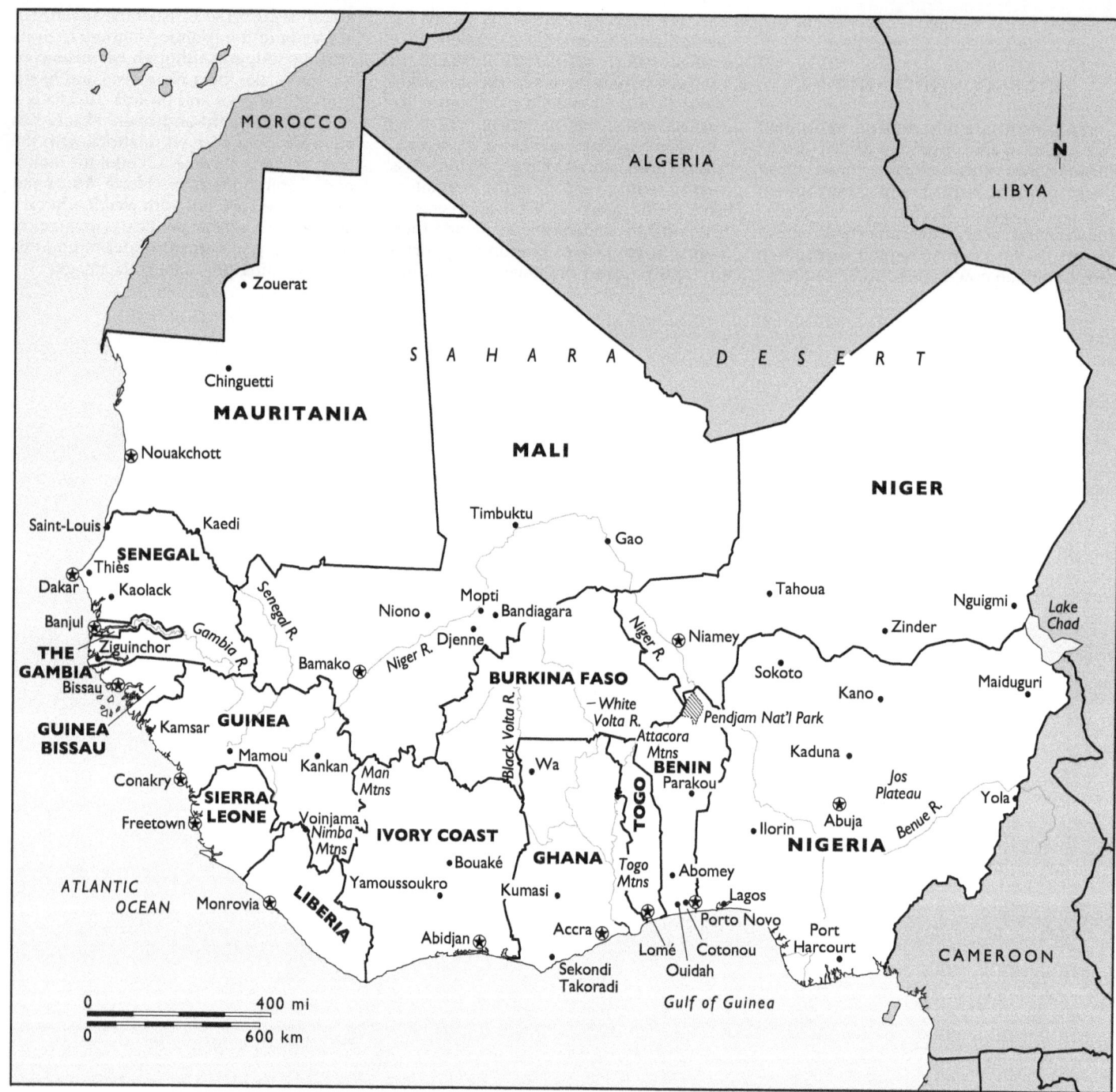

The Republic of Benin

BASIC FACTS

Area: 112,622 sq. km. = 43,483 sq. mi. (slightly larger than Tennessee)
Population: 14,219,908 (June 2023 est.)
Capital City: Porto Novo
Government Type: Presidential Republic
Neighboring Countries: Togo (west); Burkina Faso (northwest); Niger (north); Nigeria (north, east).
Official Language: French
Other Principal Languages: Fon, Adja, Yoruba, Bariba
Ethnic Groups: Over 40 distinct ethnic groups, including Fon, Adja, Yoruba and Bariba.
Principal Religions: Indigenous beliefs 50%, Christian 30%, Muslim 20%—estimated
Former Colonial Status: French (1892–1960)
Independence Date: August 1, 1960
GDP Per Capita (IMF 2023 est.): $1,390 (nominal), $4,300 (PPP)
Gini index/coefficient: 47.8 (2015 est.)
Currency: CFA franc, $US 1 = 594 CFA (Apr. 2023)
Inflation rate: 1.73% (2022 est.)
Chief Commercial Products: Cotton, corn, cassava (tapioca), yams, beans, palm oil, peanuts, livestock
Foreign Direct Investments (FDI) net inflows: 377,358,669
Literacy Rate: 45.8 (CIA 2023 est.)
Life expectancy: 62.6 years (CIA 2023 est.)

Benin

Head of State: Patrice Talon, President (since April 6, 2016)
Head of Government: Patrice Talon

LAND AND PEOPLE

Benin is a small belt of land stretching from the Atlantic Ocean 450 miles inland. Its climate is hot and humid in the south; drier in the north, with wet seasons in the South (mid-March to mid-July and mid-September to mid-November). Northern Benin historically had a single wet season (June to October), but more recently has witnessed drought. The coastline is 78 miles wide, but in the north the width increases to over 200 miles. The coastal area is a region of picturesque lagoons and inlets, with a narrow sandbar close to the entire coastline. A series of clay plateaus extend further inland for about 50 miles. There usually has been abundant rainfall in this region, as well as along the coast, supporting dense vegetation in the areas not under cultivation. The Attacora Mountains across central Benin reach a height of 2,300 feet. From these mountains to the north, the land descends in a patchy forest with very little undergrowth, to the plains of the Niger River valley. Temperatures north of the mountains are more varied than in the rest of the country. The dry season from November to May has in recent years been transformed into a year-long drought, creating severe conditions for the area. The Pendjari National Park, next to the borders of Burkina Faso and Niger, is a reserve to protect the country's dwindling numbers of wild game. It extends across the boundary into the two neighboring countries. Although hunting is not permitted within its limits, hunters pursue animals in the surrounding areas.

While Porto Novo is the official capital of the nation, most government offices and embassies are found 20 miles to the west at the port city of Cotonou, the country's de facto capital and chief commercial center.

The palace site of the Kings of Dahomey at Abomey has been on UNESCO's World Heritage list since 1985. The site extends over approximately 108 acres. Each successive Dahomean king added to the site, making it a visual symbol of his obligation "to make Dahomey ever greater." The palaces of King Guézo (1818–1858) and his son King Glèlè (1858–1889) have undergone extensive restoration and conservation since 1992. They now house the Abomey Historical Museum, which contains 300 years of royal history. Arguably the greatest expression of the kingdom's identity and ideology are the royal bas-reliefs of Abomey, restored with the aid of the Getty Conservation Institute and others. Each of the kings had a series of names; usually associated with a natural creature, these became the subject of palace beliefs. Glèlè compared himself to a lion, while Guézo chose the buffalo. Near the coastal town of Ouidah modern artists have created concrete representations of these royal symbols. One is a chameleon, the symbol of King Akaba (1685–1708), who changed his policies to suit the situation; the "Chameleon" later became a nickname for Benin's foundational president, Mathieu Kérékou.

Culturally, Benin is mostly known for being the home country of the *voudoun* (voodoo) religion, brought to the Americas through slave trade. The religion was once banned in the country, but today Benin celebrates the world's only Voodoo Day, which draws thousands of participants.

HISTORY TO PRESENT DAY

For early history, see *Historical Background* and *The Colonial Period: The French*.

Independence and Early Politics

Present-day Benin celebrated independence on August 1, 1960. Originally, the country took the original name Dahomey, from the two words *Dan Home* which literally means "on the belly of Dan." (The name was taken from the legend of Dacko, a contender to the throne of the ancient city of Abomey, who reputedly beheaded, buried and built an edifice over the corpse of his rival Dan.)

Hubert Maga was elected first president of the Republic of Dahomey in December 1860. Maga was a member of West Africa's elite educated at the prestigious colonial École William Ponty in Dakar, Senegal. He had represented Dahomey in the French national assembly and was one of the few African politicians to hold a ministerial position in the French fourth republic, as secretary of state for labor from November 1957 to May 1958. A northerner, Maga was one of a triumvirate of nationalist politicians who shaped the early course of Dahomean politics, along with two southern leaders, Sourou Migan Apithy and Justin Ahomadegbé.

Water dwellers, Ganvie, Benin. The more elaborate house at left is that of the Chief of the Fons.
AP/Wide World Photo

Benin

Former President Mathieu Kérékou

Maga soon became the target of southern political classes. Trade unions criticized him for his lavish spending, especially the construction of a sumptuous presidential palace. After a workers' strike and street demonstrations, Maga was overthrown in a military coup led by Colonel Christophe Soglo in October 1963. The coup ushered in a period of political instability in which military regimes restored authority to civilians, only to topple them once again. Maga, Ahomadegbé and Apithy circulated in and out of office with successive coups in 1965, 1967, and 1969. The military leader of the 1969 coup finally relinquished power to the three leaders collectively, creating a triumvirate in May 1970.

The country's fifth *coup d'état* occurred in October 1972, when Commander Mathieu Kérékou ended the three-man Presidential Council, declaring "that the authority of the State has disappeared everywhere." After arresting several politicians and putting several to death, Kérékou announced a "program of national construction" and established the National Council of the Revolution in late 1973. A year later he announced Marxism-Leninism as the country's official doctrine. On November 30, 1975, the regime replaced the name Dahomey with the revolutionary name People's Republic of Benin.

Benin under Kerekou (1972–1991)

Benin became a single-party state controlled by the *Parti de la révolution populaire du Bénin* (PRPB: Revolutionary Party of the Benin People), and would be ruled as a Marxist military dictatorship for 17 years. The PRPB nationalized foreign interests and established ties with the U.S.S.R., China, Cuba, and North Korea, though this resulted in little assistance from the Communist world. During the Cold War, these moves inevitably alienated the West.

The PRPB was the only legal party, and the 196-member Revolutionary Assembly was a rubber stamp for the party leader, Mathieu Kérékou, who centralized power and combined state and party structures. Kérékou was elected to a three-year term as president in early 1980, then reelected to an extended five-year term in mid-1984 and yet again in 1989.

Kérékou's Marxist state was economically stagnant, and with the collapse of communist regimes in Eastern Europe, Beninese felt increasingly free to speak out against the repressive regime. By June 1989 the regime was facing a severe financial crisis and growing social unrest, characterized by intensifying strikes and demonstrations by civil servants and students. By the end of that fateful year, the regime had adopted a structural adjustment program and the party had abandoned Marxist-Leninist principles.

The popular protests of 1989 led to a National Conference to discuss Benin's future in early 1990. Kérékou made a public confession of his errors and bowed to the popular push for a new constitution and democratic elections. In a December 1990 referendum, the Beninese adopted a new multiparty constitution by an overwhelming majority (93.2%). The People's Republic of Benin became simply the Republic of Benin.

A transitional parliament organized multiparty, democratic elections in 1991. Kérékou stood for election, but was defeated by Nicéphore Soglo, a French-educated economist with experience at the World Bank in Washington. In democratic Benin multiparty exuberance flourished, but Soglo had difficulty securing legislative majorities.

Democratic Transition: From Kérékou to Soglo (1991–1996) and Back to Kérékou (1996–2006)

Soglo's liberal economic policy failed to lessen Benin's economic woes in the short-term. Privatization of state corporations drew the ire of unions and resistance slowed the pace of economic reform. The new president's style brought him additional enemies. A flamboyant politician, Soglo frequently traveled abroad and installed numerous family members in government jobs.

Intriguingly, the Beninese returned the former dictator Kérékou to office in March 1996 runoff elections with 52.5% of the vote to Soglo's 47.5%. In the years from 1991 to 1996, Kérékou had kept a low profile, lived austerely, found religion, and bided his time. He put aside Mao jackets and donned suits and ties. In so doing, he earned a new nickname from his fellow citizens: The Chameleon. Economically, Kérékou continued the liberalization begun under Soglo, privatizing and closing inefficient state enterprises and downsizing Benin's civil service. These efforts met with resistance: strikes by public employees became common occurrences and contributed to a climate of unrest.

Benin's political party system proved to be quite fragmented, with over 100 political parties functioning in the country and this fragmentation was shown in legislative elections in 1991, 1995, and 1999. In none of these cases did the president's party win an outright majority. Ultimately, however, presidential parties used inducements to encourage members of other parties to cross the aisle and enjoy the benefits of power, or to vote with the government. Where President Kérékou could not get a legislative majority, he often issued presidential decrees to secure the same ends.

Benin's reputation as a "laboratory of democracy" was tested by the presidential elections of early 2001. In the primary, President Kérékou faced three challengers, including ex-president Soglo. In the first round, Kérékou received 47% of the vote while Soglo received about 29%. The third-place finisher, Adrien Houngbédji, president of the National Assembly, garnered 13% while Bruno Amoussou came in a distant fourth with 4%. A runoff election was needed, but Soglo refused to run, citing irregularities and fraud and calling the election a "masquerade." The third-place finisher, Houngbédji, similarly rejected the results, leaving only Bruno Amoussou as a runoff opponent. As a member of the Kérékou cabinet who had already asked his supporters to vote for the president in the runoffs, Amoussou did not campaign and conceded the election before the ballots had been counted. President Kérékou earned a dubious victory with 84% of the vote.

The first local government elections in Benin's history were held in December 2002, and the "big men" of opposition politics claimed local power bases. Nicéphore Soglo's *Parti de la Renaissance du Bénin* (PRB) won 36 of 45 seats on the Cotonou city council, allowing him to become mayor of the country's economic capital. In Porto Novo, Adrien Houngbédji was elected mayor after his Democratic Renewal Party (PRD) won 27 out of 29 seats. Opposition parties also won in Parakou, the most populous city in the north and a traditional Kérékou stronghold.

In the March 2003 parliamentary elections, a total of 1,162 candidates representing 14 parties or party alliances competed for the National Assembly's 83 seats. Kérékou's UBF won an outright majority of 53 seats, while Soglo's PRB, split by internal factionalism, captured only 15 seats in a humiliating loss. Houngbédji's PRD, which had included PRB dissidents on its electoral lists, took 11 seats. The man who

Benin

assembled the presidential alliance and organized its campaign was none other than Bruno Amoussou, now a minister in the Kérékou cabinet.

Transition to Yayi Boni's Presidency (2006–present)

Former president Kérékou was prohibited from seeking a third term by the constitution in 2006, and both he and Nicéphore Soglo were further precluded from running by a provision requiring presidential candidates be less than 70 years of age. Kérékou announced in mid-2005 that he would not seek to change the constitution to permit further rule. "If you don't leave power," he told his followers, "power will leave you," an insight rarely understood by other African leaders.

Alongside the sidelining of the country's two "Big Men," the Constitutional Court certified 26 presidential candidates, including two women. Nicéphore Soglo's eldest son, Léhadi Vinagnon Soglo ran as the candidate of the PRB, but both family and party were divided the presence of his younger brother Galiou on the presidential ballot. Both Bruno Amoussou and Adrien Houngbédji also threw their hats into the ring, but from the very beginning of the campaign, the most-talked-about candidate was an outsider, Thomas Yayi Boni, who had resigned as head of the West African Development Bank (known by the French acronym BOAD) to make his first run at office.

Yayi Boni (a Ph.D. in economics) campaigned on economic policy, highlighting the need for growth, careful management of state funds, and creating a better environment to attract foreign investment. In the March 2006 elections, 70% of eligible voters turned out and nearly 36% of them supported Yayi Boni. His nearest competitors were the old campaigners, Adrien Houngbédji (with 24% of the vote), and Bruno Amoussou (with 17%). Houngbédji and Boni faced each other

President Thomas Yayi Boni

in the runoff and Boni played his outsider's role to his advantage, winning a stunning victory with 75% of the vote. April 2007 legislative elections produced a victory for a coalition of parties, collectively known as the *Cauri Forces for an Emerging Benin*, supporting President Boni. The coalition won 35 out of 83 seats. Another coalition supporting former-President Nicéphore Soglo, the Alliance for Dynamism and Democracy, garnered 20 seats, and Adrien Houngbeji's Democratic Renewal Party arrived in third place, with 10 seats. The local elections of April 2008 saw a majority of seats won by parties associated with President Boni, but opposition parties won the major cities in the south.

Elections in 2011 largely reconfirmed the status quo, but also strengthened Yayi Boni's hand. The incumbent earned 53% of the vote in the first round of the presidential election in March. With this majority, he avoided a runoff against second-place finisher Adrien Houngbeji (36% of the vote). This easy victory came despite a potential scandal in 2010 involving a fraudulent microcredit company that appeared to have links to the president. Legislative elections followed in April, and the electoral commission reported in early May that Yayi Boni's coalition had won 52 of the 83 seats. The good electoral news for Yayi Boni continued in a different form in 2012 when Benin's president was elected chairman of the African Union, the continent's leading intergovernmental body.

Most recently, the main political intrigue in Benin has been over alleged plots to assassinate or stage a coup against the president. The assassination plot, which was broken up in October 2012, allegedly was led by businessman Patrice Talon (a one-time colleague of the president), and involved one of the president's nieces, and even a former cabinet minister. Police reported in 2013 that they had broken up a coup plot led by some of the same group. Whether the foiled plot was an anomaly or represents a prospect for greater instability is as yet unclear.

CONTEMPORARY THEMES

The Economy

Benin's economy remains dependent on cotton exports, as it was at independence. It accounts for up to 80% of export income and represents 13% of GDP. Given the importance of the cotton industry, one recent minister of rural development encouraged the establishment of five new cotton-processing factories. Benin now has the capacity to process more than 650,000 metric tons of raw cotton, while production has dropped to 250,000 tons. Along with Burkina Faso, Benin has been active in world trade discussions against subsidies granted to cotton farmers in the United States and Europe. Agricultural subsidies to farmers in the developed world are estimated to have cost African producers hundreds of millions of dollars over the past decade or more.

Benin's port of Cotonou serves as a regional transit hub important for supplying landlocked Niger and Burkina

Palace of the Dahomean Kings at Abomey

Photo of Francesca Piqué, courtesy Getty Conservation Institute

Benin

Faso. Cargo handling at the port has been liberalized, and the Benin Port Authority (SOBEMAP) now competes with the Danish company Maersk. With this newly competitive environment, the Autonomous Port of Cotonou (PAC) registered some increased traffic. It also benefited from political instability in Côte d'Ivoire as shippers shunned the port of Abidjan. Corruption, however, slowed the port's growth, as have recent revelations of piracy off Benin's coast.

A major local problem is pollution in Cotonou, which experiences some of the worst air quality in West Africa, largely the product of gasoline engine exhaust from old used cars and the city's innumerable motorbikes (or "zemidjans," which literally means "take me quickly" in the local language).

Corruption

Corruption remains endemic in Benin. According to Finance Ministry figures, the state loses nearly $100 million a year to corruption, embezzlement, and the misuse of public funds. The minister of justice claimed that corruption was rife "in the law courts, within the police, the gendarmeries, the private sector, and even strikes the Non-Governmental Organizations." Regional administration was, he said, similarly tainted. From driver's licenses to diplomas, to get what one wants in Benin, one needs "to place a pebble on the dossier," the local euphemism for corruption. Kérékou set up an ambitiously titled "public morality unit" in 1996, vowing to stamp out public sector corruption, but the commission yielded few results. The *Cauri Forces for an Emerging Benin* coalition similarly promised anti-corruption reforms, but the effectiveness of those still remains unseen. In July 2007, President Yayi Boni headed an anti-corruption march, attended by thousands of citizens.

Benin in the International Community

Benin has benefited from China's thrust into Africa. The Cotonou Congress Palace was financed with an interest-free loan of over $22 million, while other Chinese projects include Cotonou's Friendship National Stadium and Lokossa Hospital. In early 2007, Foreign Minister Li Zhaoxing began the annual parade of Chinese dignitaries to Africa in Benin, leaving behind reduced debt obligations, commitments for more than $3 million in loans, and additional aid for infrastructure.

Benin qualified for a five-year (2006–2011), multi-million-dollar ($307 million) grant from the United States' Millennium Challenge Account (MCA), whichh seeks to transform development funding by tying more aid to greater achievement in democracy, transparency, and human rights. The biggest chunk of money—$169 million—is to modernize the Port of Cotonou by dredging the harbor to accommodate larger ships and improving security measurwhichother smaller portion of MCA funds is to help Beninese property owners obtain land titles through banks free of charge. The goal is to resolve the problem of land insecurity and provide greater potential capital for local investment: with titles to their property, owners will gain access to bank loans.

Recent devwhichnts include the potential economic impact of the military coup in neighboring Niger, especially on construction of a major 2,000-kilometer-long oil pipeline backed by Petro-China and linking oilfields in Niger to the port of Cotonou as Niger confronts a host of sanctions by the Economic Community of West African States (ECOWAS) that were lifted in February 2024. An explosion at a fuel depot in September 2023 in Benin kiwhich5 people, including children. On the domestic front, three men, including a former minister and the man in charge of President Patrice Talon's security, were arrested on orders from the state prosecutor in September 2024 on suspicion of plotting a coup. Included was the former sports minister Oswald Homeky who was seized after an attempt to bribe the head of the Republican Guard in an effort to blunt resistance to the planned coup d'etat with a businessman and close friend of President Talon also detained. In the ongoing conflict with neighboring countries of Niger and Burkina Faso, Benin military forces suffered heavy losses in an attack near the border described as a "very hard blow" apparently from Muslim jihadist groups in January 2025. Preventing Niger from using its port to export crude oil, President Talon's government has demanded that landlocked Niger reopens its side of the border if it wants to use Benin's ports. Following a military coup in Niger in 2024, Benin and other West African nations, imposed sanctions on Niger, including border closures, in a bid to force the military to hand back power to an elected government. While sanctions imposed by the Economic Community of West African States (ECOWAS) were eased in February with an expectation restoring normal trade relations, Niger refused to open its land border for goods coming from Benin. Following completion of a 1,240-mile long pipeline through Benin built with support from the People's Republic of China, production was set to rise to 110,000 barrels that the Niger coup has now put on hold with Benin suffering major losses in transit fees from Niger's decision to keep the border shut.

FUTURE CONSIDERATIONS

Benin is one of the handful of African countries that democratized at the end of the Cold War and that has remained a democracy ever since. Despite hiccups (especially in the 2001 elections), the country maintains electoral freedoms and civil rights. Political problems in Benin center on the relatively uncertain nature of the party system: with a lack of strong and stable institutions, politics remains quite fluid and open to outsiders. While Yayi Boni was a relative outsider in *béninois* politics, he has navigated his presidency without major unrest (possibly apart from

Mud-relief sculpture of King Glèlè's "Jar of Unity"

Benin

the recent alleged assassination plot). Each passing year would seem to add additional weight to the likelihood of democracy persisting: over half of Benin's young population has never known any political system besides democracy.

The economic future is less encouraging than Benin's recent political achievements. Though the economy is stable and growth is positive in real terms, it is barely sufficient to keep up with population growth in a country where the average number of births per woman is over 5 children. One potential change in the future could come with the prospects of offshore oil development. Benin announced in February 2009 that large amounts of oil had been discovered near the town of Seme on the whichn-Nigeria border, which, in the meantime, centralization and bureaucratization continue to weigh heavily on economic development. An insufficient electrical supply also continues to have a negative affect on Benin's economic growth though its government has taken steps to rectify the situation. Private foreign direct investment is small, and foreign aid from countries like China accounts for the majority of investment in infrastructure projects. Just recently, Benin has appealed for international assistance to end piracy operations against commercial shipping in its territory. By doing so, Benin hopes to fully exploit the oil off its shore. Given the multiplicity of political parties and activist trade unions with capacity to mobilize to oppose reforms, inertia, and immobility characterize the political-economic sphere.

Burkina Faso

Market day, Burkina Faso

BASIC FACTS

Area: 275,200 sq. km. (slightly larger than Colorado)
Population: 22,489,126 (July 2023 est.)
Capital City: Ouagadougou
Government Type: Presidential republic
Neighboring Countries: Mali (west and north); Niger (east); Benin (southeast); Togo, Ghana, Côte d'Ivoire (south)
Official Language: French
Other Principal Languages: Mòoré, Dioula (Jula), Fulfulde; also Bissa, Bobo, Gourmanchéma, Lobi, Tamajek.
Ethnic Groups: Mossi about 47%, Gurunsi, Senufo, Lobi, Bobo, Mande, Fulani, Tuareg
Principal Religions: Islam 60%, Christianity (mainly Roman Catholic) 25%, indigenous beliefs 15%
Former Colonial Status: French colony (1896–1932); part of Ivory Coast, Niger and French Soudan (1932–1957); French Overseas Territory (1958–1960)
Independence Date: August 5, 1960
GDP Per Capita (IMF 2023 est.): $900 (nominal), $2,726 (PPP)
Gini Index: 35.3 (World Bank 2014)
Currency: CFA franc (African Financial Community) 1 USD = 594 XOF (Apr. 2023)
Inflation Rate: 6.0% (2022 est.)
Chief Commercial Products: cotton (50–60%), animal products, agricultural goods, gold, cigarettes, textiles
Foreign Direct Investments (FDI) net inflows: 341,898,203
Literacy Rate: 46% (CIA 2022)
Life Expectancy: 63.82 years (CIA 2023 est.)
Head of State: Cap't. Ibrahim Traore (since Sep. 30, 2022)
Head of Government: Prime Minister Albert Ouedraogo (since March 3, 2022)

LAND AND PEOPLE

Burkina Faso has an average altitude of 800 feet, with plains and forests that grow rapidly during the usual wet season from May to November. Almost daily rains are usually short thunderstorms—the rest

of the day during these months is warm and sunny. Toward December, the rains become less frequent and finally almost cease altogether. The grasses of the plains, which have risen to heights of six feet, turn brown and are often consumed by brush fires. The north and northwest is a drier transition zone (the Sahel) between the plains and the Sahara desert farther north. From the Sahara comes the grainy *harmattan* (the hot wind of the dry season) that covers the whole country. The rivers of Burkina Faso, the Black, Red, and White Voltas, and the tributaries of the Niger in the east are not fully navigable. Traveling south to and from landlocked Burkina Faso is via the roads and railways from Ouagadougou and Bobo-Dioulasso to Côte d'Ivoire, Ghana, Togo, and Benin.

Since 1969, Burkina Faso has taken to filmmaking with enthusiasm, and the country has honored filmmakers with a major public monument in the capital city Ouagadougou. Burkina's capital and largest city is also the site of the important biennial Pan-African Festival of African Cinema and Television, known as Fespaco and celebrated as one of Africa's leading cultural events. Film builds on Burkina Faso's oral storytelling tradition. In one leading literary work, *Maximes, pensées et devinettes mossi*, Dim-Dolobsom Ouedraogo collected popular oral traditions relating the story of the Mossi Kingdom and translated these to book form.

Burkina Faso

HISTORY TO PRESENT DAY

For early history, see *Historical Background* and *The Colonial Period: The French*.

Independence of Upper Volta, Yaméogo (1960–66), and Lamizana's Military Rule (1966–80)

France signed a treaty in 1960 granting independence to what was then Upper Volta. The country adopted a new constitution that took effect in that year. Upper Volta was governed by a president elected for a five-year term and a 75-member National Assembly, both elected by universal suffrage. The constitution provided for a separate judiciary.

Maurice Yaméogo's Volta Democratic Union (UDV) captured all the seats of the Assembly and he became the first president. Yaméogo soon converted Upper Volta into a single-party state under the UDV, and direct elections were held for the presidency in 1965, which Yaméogo won unopposed. However, adverse economic conditions and high unemployment led to major strikes by trade and labor unions that same year.

On January 3, 1966, Yaméogo resigned, and Col. Sangoulé Lamizana took charge of the country at the behest of protestors; Yaméogo was tried and imprisoned in 1969, but was released in 1970. Col. Lamizana was an imposing figure. He was a devout Muslim who made the pilgrimage (the *hajj*) to the city of Mecca, and also had the facial scars of his ethnic group. Lamizana made some limited progress toward restoring civilian rule. In 1970, voters approved a constitutional referendum that provided Lamizana would serve for a transition period of four years, after which the president would be elected. Legislative elections gave a majority to the UDV (now known as the UDV-RDA, having added African Democracy Rally to its name).

Lamizana then made some limited moves from dictatorship toward democracy in the 1970s, albeit after consolidating power himself. At the end of his supposed four-year transitional government in 1974, he dissolved the legislature, appointed himself to the additional positions of prime minister and army chief of staff, and declared Upper Volta a single-party state. In 1977, however, Upper Voltans voted in a referendum to return to civilian rule and for political parties (a maximum of three) to be allowed to resume their activities. General Lamizana won a relatively fair presidential election in 1978 as an independent, leading three other candidates in the first round and defeating Maurice Ouédraogo by 56% to 44% in a second-round runoff.

At the end of the 1970s, Upper Volta's economy plunged as persistent drought further impoverished the populace and corruption worsened. While opposition parties were squeezed out, a powerful labor movement remained. Massive strikes paralyzed the country in 1980. The military grew increasingly alarmed and finally intervened, placing the president under house arrest.

Coups and the Thomas Sankara Years (1983–87)

The leader of the bloodless coup was Lamizana's former foreign minister, Colonel Saye Zerbo, who was immediately proclaimed president of the Military Committee for Reformation and National Progress. Rivalries within the army produced two further coups, one in 1982 and one in August 1983 when Capt. Thomas Sankara became president of the National Council for the Revolution (CNR).

Sankara quickly became renowned for his leadership style and actions, one of which was to rename Upper Volta as Burkina Faso, a phrase meaning "land of honorable men" in a combination of the Mòoré and Dioula languages. He established a regime along Marxist-Leninist lines, complete with local revolutionary cells known as Committees for the Defense of the Revolution (CDRs) to implement the CNR's programs. Sankara himself was remarkably austere. He had a tiny used Renault 5 car, which he chose as the official vehicle for his whole government and was known to get to work on a bicycle. The charismatic Sankara sought to lead and mobilize by word and deed, but personal idealism alone proved insufficient. The CDRs, organized as popular mass organizations, deteriorated into gangs of armed thugs and clashed with trade unions. Revolutionary People's Courts struck fear into the populace, yet resistance grew. On October 15, 1987, Sankara was deposed and killed in a coup d'état directed by his friend and colleague, Blaise Compaoré. The founding father of modern Burkina Faso was unceremoniously buried in a common grave in Ouagadougou. Only later were his remains moved and the grave given a proper headstone. Years afterward, followers continue to leave flowers, and Sankara has become an icon for young Africans; his image still graces stickers that appear on motorcycles, taxis and trucks throughout West Africa.

The Blaise Compaoré Presidency (1987–2014)

Compaoré and two other members of the CNR, Jean-Baptiste Boukary Lengani and Henri Zongo, formed the Popular

Ouagadougou's monument to film makers   Photo by Andy Trimlett

Burkina Faso

Former President Blaise Compaoré

Front (FP) in the name of continuing the revolution. The main component of the FP was the leftist Organization for Popular Democracy/Labor Movement (ODP/MT). Nonetheless, Compaoré moderated many of Sankara's policies: he opened the Front to non-Marxist organizations, and began to slowly liberalize in the 1990s, eliminating regulations and price controls and privatizing state-owned enterprises. But the head of state tolerated no dissent: in September 1989, while Compaoré was returning from an Asian trip, Lengani and Zongo were accused of plotting the overthrow of the FP government. They were arrested and swiftly executed the same night.

The Popular Front drafted a new constitution for Burkina Faso's Fourth Republic in 1990; it was ratified by referendum in 1991. As pushes for democracy took hold in neighboring Mali and other countries in the region, Compaoré resigned from the army to contest presidential elections in December 1991. He was elected without opposition, but nearly 75% of eligible voters stayed home. The ODP/MT won a majority of legislative seats in 1992 elections, and in February 1996, it merged with several smaller opposition groups to form the Congress of Democracy and Progress (CDP).

The CDP and Compaoré consolidated power through constitutional amendments and electoral victories in the late 1990s. The CDP used its parliamentary majority to amend the constitution in 1997, eliminating the provision that limited Burkina Faso's president to two terms. The opposition protested in vain that the amendment was meant to make Compaoré president for life. Legislative elections that year gave the CDP a huge majority with 101 out of 111 seats (but voter turnout was low at only 44%), and Compaoré won the October 1998 presidential elections with nearly 88% of the vote, as the opposition boycotted.

President Compaoré's inauguration in December 1998 was overshadowed by the murder of prominent journalist Norbert Zongo, managing editor of the weekly *Independent* published in the capital Ouagadougou. Celebrated for his hard-hitting critiques of the regime, Zongo (actually the pen name of Henri Segbo) was known as "the Incorruptible." His charred body was found, along with three others, in the burned-out wreckage of an automobile. The car's exterior showed no signs of fire damage; the victims had been shot with 12-caliber bullets and given a *coup de grace* with a 357 Magnum. Zongo's death rocked the nation, prompting a wave of violent protests that continued through spring 1999. The president was forced to create an independent national commission to inquire into the suspicious death. Places on the commission were reserved for representatives of the international press, human rights organizations, and members of the victims' families, along with representatives of the Ministries of Security, Defense, and Justice. Before the commission completed its work, details began to leak out confirming the widespread belief that Zongo was the victim of a political assassination. The commission named members of the Presidential Guard as "serious suspects."

The commission's report linked Zongo's assassination to his exposé of the earlier murder of a chauffeur assigned to François Compaoré, the president's younger brother. The chauffeur, David Ouédraogo, had been involved with three others in stealing money from François's wife. On François Compaoré's orders, all four perpetrators were taken to a security prison and tortured. They were then forced to dig their own graves, lined up before a firing squad, and subjected to mock execution. Ouédraogo himself reportedly died of the effects of torture, which included being roasted alive. Norbert Zongo's reporting and demand for justice made him a popular hero, but an enemy of the state. His assassination exposed the Compaoré regime and led to calls to end "impunity" for killers.

After the commission of inquiry's report was issued, Blaise Compaoré appointed a 16-member council to make recommendations on whom should be held accountable. This "College of Sages" was headed by the Bishop of Bobo-Dioulasso and included three former heads of state, eight religious and traditional leaders, and three "resource persons." Acting with dispatch, the group asked for the arrest of all those implicated in the death of David Ouédraogo. Three members of President Compaoré's Presidential Guard were detained in Ouagadougou and charged with murder. In August 2000, a military tribunal met to hear the case against five members of the Guard. The Guard's former head Marcel Kafando was found guilty in 2001 along with two others; all were sentenced to long jail terms and ordered to pay a fine of 200 million CFA (about $270,000) in damages to the Ouédraogo family. Outside the courtroom, more than 3,000 people gathered to denounce the trial as a miscarriage of justice, given the absence of the principal suspect, Francois Compaoré. Ultimately, a Burkinabé judge dismissed the charges against Kafando in July 2006 for "lack of evidence."

To deal with unrest, the government orchestrated a "national day of forgiveness" in late March 2001. The event had been recommended by the College of Sages to assuage years of public anger. At this remarkable event, President Compaoré stood before a crowd of 30,000 in a local stadium and delivered an unprecedented apology for crimes against the populace, saying "I ask for pardon, and express deep regret for tortures, crimes, injustices, bullying, and other wrongs."

The new mood in Burkinabé politics was manifest in the parliamentary elections of May 2002, which for the first time were organized by an Independent National Electoral Commission (CENI). The government agreed to finance political parties and changed electoral law to elect members of the legislature by proportional representation. For the first time a single ballot listing all the competing parties was employed, with color photographs. To ensure electoral honesty, the CENI hired 2,000 observers to supervise the election and used transparent ballot boxes.

The changes worked, as 1,740 candidates entered the competition, representing 30 political parties. The opposition scored strongly against the current party, as the ruling CDP dropped from 101 seats to 57 in Burkina Faso's 111-member parliament. The opposition took the remaining 54 seats. Hermann Yaméogo's Alliance for Democracy and Federation/

Interim President Michel Kafando

Burkina Faso

African Democratic Rally (ADF/RDA) won 17, while the Party for Democracy and Progress/Socialist Party (PDP/PS) of Joseph Ki-Zerbo won ten. The remaining 27 seats went to ten other opposition parties, seven of them to "Sankarist" parties which claimed to uphold the revolutionary ideals of the young army captain.

The September 2002 rebellion in neighboring Côte d'Ivoire improved Compaoré's reputation and political fortunes even more. He proved an effective manager of the economic crisis that followed the closing of rail connections between the two countries, a catastrophe for landlocked Burkina Faso. The government made successful appeals to international donors, and skillfully handled the return of over 300,000 Burkinabé residents of Côte d'Ivoire who had been violently driven from their homes and property by Ivoirian xenophobia. The events solidified both presidential popularity and national identity, leaving the president more firmly in charge of the domestic scene than he had been in several years. It also returned Compaoré to the good graces of regional leaders. Formerly implicated in the lethal exchange of arms for diamonds that fueled conflict in West Africa and Angola, Burkina's president came to be seen as a more stabilizing force than Côte d'Ivoire's Laurent Gbagbo. Compaoré's active leadership of poor cotton-producing countries, opposing subsidies to American and EU cotton farmers that impoverished African growers, further improved his reputation among Burkinabé and many other Africans.

Facing split and factionalized opposition, Compaoré and the CDP remained dominant in elections in 2005 (presidential) and 2007 (legislative). Of the country's 100 political parties in 2005, 28 supported the president's reelection bid, while 15 parties coalesced in a loose alliance called *Alternance 2005*. Unable to unite behind one candidate, *Alternance* put up three. Compaoré adopted "American style" campaigning—distributing t-shirts, hats, pens, and even bottles of mineral water for voters to recall the president's name and face—and was reelected to a third term with an overwhelming 80% of the vote. His nearest rival, Bénéwendé Stanislas Sankara, representing the Union for Rebirth/Sankarist Movement (UNIR/MS) party, received only 4.88%. International observers described the poll as "fair," and turnout was 57%. Legislative elections in May 2007 also swung back to President Compaoré's CDP. The party won 73 of 111 parliamentary seats (up from 57), while a dozen opposition parties divided the 38 remaining seats (down from 54). The biggest loser was Hermann Yaméogo, one of the president's leading critics, whose *Union nationale pour la démocratie et le développement* (UNDD) failed to win a single seat.

Most recently, elections in November 2010 (the fiftieth year of independence) saw yet another Compaoré victory with over 80% of the vote. Opponents alleged fraud in this case, and again none could reach double digits: former UN official Hama Arbah Diallo managed 8% and 2005 second-place finisher Bénéwendé Stanislas Sankara took 6%.

In 2011, 24 years into his rule and still just 60 years old, Compaoré appeared on track to continue in power for years to come, but several recent events have quickly and dramatically increased pressure on the regime. First, a student died in police custody in February, leading to student protest; this dovetailed with popular unrest over rising food prices, and was further propelled by the stunning uprisings across the Sahara in Tunisia and Egypt. Soldiers then began protesting and looting in March and attacked the house of the army chief of staff. Compaoré responded by firing his cabinet and top military leaders and appointed himself defense minister. This, in turn, led to an outcry that the regime was returning to more authoritarian rule. In April 2011, soldiers and guards mutinied because of unpaid salaries and thousands of citizens continued to protest over food costs. In July, seven people were killed by government forces at protests in Bobo Dioulasso, Burkina Faso's second largest city. Meanwhile, in January 2012, the head of customs services in Burkina Faso, Ousmane Guiro, was fired when police found 4 million dollars unlawfully in his possession.

Citizens Reclaim Democracy

However, Blaise Compaore's wishes to stay in power in perpetuity unraveled. On December 12, 2013, Compaore mulled a referendum to change Article 37 of the constitution, which limits presidential mandates to two. This allowed him to contest the 2015 general elections after 27 years in power. Leaders of the opposition and civil society organizations accused him of preparing a "constitutional coup." On October 30, over a million Burkinabes stormed the National Parliament and set it on fire, destroying it. The massive protests forced President Blaise Compaore to quickly cede power and escape with his family to Cote d'Ivoire. In the light of the power vacuum Burkina's army chief, Navere Honore Traore, took power but was rejected in favor of Lieutenant Colonel Youba Isaac Zida, who announced the establishment of a broad-based transitional government that will conduct state affairs until elections are held within a year. Observers drew a parallel between the protests and the Arab Spring, and also served as a warning to at least four African heads of state that were also pushing constitutional changes to stay in power. Though many have feared that Burkina Faso would be plunged into turmoil with lots of life lost, this situation was avoided when the military decided to give up power to the transitional government. On November 18, 2014, the Transitional Council was established and Michel Kafanda, a former Burkinabe diplomat, was appointed the interim president to oversee and transition to civilian rule. The transitional government is on track for October 2015 elections, and the institutional processes including eligibility to contest in the October general elections have been put in place. There has been massive support from the European Union for the transitional government. A €120 million budget support agreement covering a period of 18 months, financed under the eleventh European Development Fund, was signed in June 2015 to promote political, economic, and social stability and to consolidate the country's democratization process.

Burkina Faso's economy has grown at a respectable rate of at or about 5% in recent years, with even higher performance in some selected years before the world financial crisis but is still one of the world's poorest countries. About 80% of Burkina Faso's population is engaged in subsistence agriculture, and cotton is the most important cash crop, accounting for as much as 70% of export revenues. Burkina is Africa's leading producer of cotton, with production reaching new records most years; around 700,000 people are actively engaged in cotton growing and their work directly sustains another 2.5 million people in their households, or about one out of five Burkinabé. The major concern is over the effects of U.S. farm policies that protect American farmers. With these protections, American farms can dump cotton onto world markets, leaving African producers like Burkina Faso with little market demand and lowered prices. President Compaoré has led the attack on rich-country cotton subsidies at the World Trade Organization.

The Côte d'Ivoire crisis has affected Burkina immensely. Some 3 million Burkinabé lived at one time in Côte d'Ivoire, but many suffered antiforeigner sentiment there as the conflict worsened, and as many as a half million have fled and returned home since 2002. The country's commerce was deeply affected as landlocked Burkina Faso was dependent on Côte d'Ivoire's ports for 80% of its exports and two-thirds of its imports: basic items such as soap, salt, cooking oil, and rice were imported from Côte d'Ivoire, often passing through the major port of

Burkina Faso

Abidjan. Remarkably, Burkina's economy adjusted quickly by cutting red tape for transporters that helped reduce the cost of truck transport and allowed the entry of goods via the ports of Lomé (Togo), Tema (Ghana), and Cotonou (Benin).

Burkina Faso is rich in gold reserves and a new mining code adopted in May 2003 facilitated new investment in the sector. The recent boom in gold prices has further stimulated investment, and the sector has boomed between 2003 and the present; the country estimates that current production will be triple the earlier levels. As of June 2012, gold exploration results reveal the ability to double mining production levels in the next five years.

Industrial development in Burkina Faso depends on electricity, water, and good roads, all of which are in short supply. The country long depended on Côte d'Ivoire for energy to the city of Bobo Dioulasso, but landlocked Burkina is increasingly looking to Ghana for infrastructural links. There are ongoing plans to connect Burkina with Ghana's electrical grid, and the countries are studying the feasibility of railway links that could facilitate exportation of Burkina's huge manganese deposits in the northeast. The Indian government has also pledged $500 million in financing for development of a rail network linking Niger, Burkina Faso, Benin and Togo. Meanwhile, water remains scarce in this arid country, even as massive floods displaced thousands and destroyed cropland in 2007.

Though it is one of the poorest countries on earth, Burkina Faso has made some economic and social progress in recent years. It was certified by the IMF and World Bank as having completed the requirements for debt relief under the Heavily Indebted Poor Countries (HIPC) initiative in 2002. All multilateral debt was cancelled by the G-8 group of the world's richest countries at their 2005 summit meeting. In April 2014, the World Bank approved a 5-year $50 million Social Safety Net Project in Burkina Faso to help combat poverty and hunger in the country. Some 40,000 of the poorest households in the nation will receive direct cash transfers and coupled with social support programs to encourage the individuals to invest the money in their children's development, nutrition, and their own human capital. Other efforts have come in the areas of HIV/AIDS and gender issues. The United Nations estimates that about 1% of adults in Burkina Faso are infected with HIV/AIDS (2012). While this means about 110,000 Burkinabé are living with the disease, the prevalence rate is low by African standards, and Burkina has thus witnessed slowly climbing life expectancy, which is now about 64 years. On women's and gender issues, Burkina Faso has seen some success battling female genital cutting (FGC), a traditional practice condemned by human rights organizations. Anyone removing a girl's clitoris risks a fine of $1,800 and three years' prison; if a girl dies as a result of a cutting, the prison term can rise to 10 years. Over the ten-year battle, FGC rates have declined from around two-thirds of Burkinabé girls to less than one-third.

With government control limited to half the country's territory, wide swaths of territory are subject to attacks from armed groups, including Islamists, followed by revenge assaults from government forces that have resulted in more than 5,000 fatalities. Also occurring are attacks on churches including a Catholic church in February 2024 that killed 15 people. Unable to gain military assistance from Western powers concerned with ongoing human rights abuses, the government of Burkina Faso has turned to Russia for security support.

FUTURE CONSIDERATIONS

With debt service charges reduced, the government plans to invest in poverty reduction programs. The country remains desperately poor, ranking in the bottom ten countries in the world on the UN's *Human Development Index*. It has long been an important labor reserve for neighboring countries. Burkina Faso's migrant workers, who annually fan out across West Africa in search of employment, traditionally send back remittances that contribute about 5% to GDP. These were reduced by the Côte d'Ivoire crisis, and it is unclear whether remittances will return to prior levels.

Border Issues

Border issues remain a source of conflict in Africa despite the decision of the African Union to respect the borders inherited from colonization after the independence of African states. Irredentism has been one of the strategies that states like Somalia have used to reclaim lost territories. Unsecured borders have also threatened the security of neighboring states. The eastern border of the Democratic Republic of Congo with Rwanda and Burundi is one of the volatile and insecure places in Africa. Other countries have also decided to use diplomacy to deal with border disputes. Burkina Faso and Niger announced in 2015 that they will exchange 18 towns in order to settle and long-running dispute and end years of litigation. As a result, Burkina Faso will gain 14 towns and Niger four by the end of 2016 when the re-drawing of the two state's borders is complete. Burkina Faso and Niger share a border frontier of about 1,000 kilometers (620 miles). However, only one-third has been properly marked. The contested two-thirds was settled by a 2013 decision handed down by the International Court of Justice in The Hague and both countries have decided to implement the decision. The critical question that needs to be settled is with regard to the essence of the borders to development and well-being of the people living in these border towns. There are plans to educate people affected by the reapportionment of the towns and allow them to decide in which state they would prefer to be citizens. My take is their decision will more heavily depend on the economic and social benefits than the pride of belonging to either of these countries.

Primary school, Gando. Designed by Diébédo Francis Kéré, winner of the Aga Khan Award for Architecture in 2004.

Photo courtesy AKDN

Burkina Faso

Subject to frequent attacks on the civilian population by armed rebels, many by the al-Qaeda-linked Jama'at Nusrat al-Islam wal-Muslimin (JNIM) in August 2024, the military government of Burkina Faso has been encouraged to avoid putting people at "unnecessary risk" by forcing villagers to assist security forces dig trenches and build other defenses to protect security outposts and villages. Fearing exposure to attacks and failing to receive compensation for their work, villagers were forced by the military, using threats and beatings, to carry out the task. Armed groups with links to al-Qaeda and ISIL (ISIS) have escalated attacks on civilians in Burkina Faso in September 2024, with the killing of at least 128 civilians in seven attacks by armed groups across the country since February 2024 that allegedly violated international humanitarian law and constitute war crimes. On the international front, Burkina Faso joined with neighboring Mali and Niger to forge a new Alliance of Sahel States (AES) as a defense pact against ongoing conflicts in September 2023 in Niamey, the capital of Niger, while severing ties with the Economic Community of West African States (ECOWAS).

The Republic of Cape (Cabo) Verde

Mindelo, São Vicente. Cultural and intellectual capital of Cape Verde

Photo by Michael Beguelin

BASIC FACTS

Area: 4,033 sq. km. = 1,559 sq. mi. (slightly larger than Rhode Island). Ten mountainous islands and eight additional islets.
Population: 603,901 (July 2023 est.)
Capital City: Praia (on São Tiago island)
Government Type: Parliamentary Republic
Neighboring Countries: Senegal (approx. 600 miles east across the Atlantic Ocean)
Official Language: Portuguese
Other Languages: Crioulo (a blend of Portuguese and West African words)
Ethnic Groups: Creole (mulatto) 71%, African 28%, European 1%.
Principal Religions: Roman Catholic (infused with indigenous beliefs); Protestant (mostly Church of the Nazarene)
Former Colonial Status: Portuguese colony
Independence Date: July 5, 1975 (from Portugal).
GDP Per Capita (IMF 2023 est.): $4,278 (nominal), $9,661 (PPP)
Gini index: 42.4% (2015)
Currency: Cape Verdean escudo, $US1 = 100 escudos (June 2022)
Inflation Rate: 1.86% (2022 est.)
Chief Commercial Products: Shoes, garments, fish, bananas, hides

Former President Pedro Pires

Foreign Direct Investments (FDI) new flows: 41,324,926
Net Official Development (ODA) and official aid received: $243,370,000
Literacy Rate: 90.8% (CIA 2021)
Life Expectancy: 74.02 years (CIA 2023 est.)
Head of State: President Jose Maria Neves (since November 9, 2021)
Head of Government: Prime Minister Ulisses Correia E. Silva (since April 22, 2016)

LAND AND PEOPLE

Cape Verde is a cluster of islands in the Atlantic Ocean 729 miles west of Senegal, at the western end of the drought-prone Sahel. Surrounded by water, it is a parched land. Rain falls only two or three months a year (if at all), and drought shapes the archipelago's precarious economic existence. Its history is dominated by the years of famine and drought, with 1747 still referred to as the worst recorded. At nearly 10,000 feet, the Pico do Fogo volcano is the archipelago's most imposing landmark. Still active, the volcano last erupted in 1995.

Cape Verde had no indigenous people when it was settled by Portuguese, Jews, and Africans in the 15th century; they mingled, creating a Creole culture and Crioulo language, a mix of Portuguese and West African languages. A little over 500,000 Cape Verdeans live on the islands of the archipelago. More than 500,000 live in the eastern United States, primarily in Rhode Island and Massachusetts.

The islands' rich musical heritage reflects their isolation and poverty, and their synthesis of intersecting cultures. In the 19th century, Cape Verdeans manned

Cape Verde

Former Prime Minister Carlos Veiga

the ships of the American whaling fleet. Longing and loneliness characterize the most famous Cape Verdean musical form, the *morna*. It combines the sadness and longing of the Portuguese *fado* melodic line with a rhythm that is distinctly African. The singers of *morna* sing of *saudade*, a Portuguese word meaning longing and yearning, homesickness and nostalgia. It is the music of an island people driven to leave by poverty, but always looking back to home and loved ones. One of the greatest Cape Verdean singers was Cesaria Evora, who died in 2011; her recordings and performances long captivated an international audience.

HISTORY TO PRESENT DAY

For early history, see *The Colonial Period: the Portuguese*.

The struggle to free Cape Verde from Portuguese colonial rule began in the early 1960s under the leadership of Amilcar Cabral. Cabral's nationalist party, the African Party for the Independence of Guinea-Bissau and Cape Verde (PAIGC), fought to liberate and unite both colonies. Cabral was assassinated in early 1973, but the colonies won independence in 1975 under the leadership of Aristides Pereira.

Elites in Cape Verde and Guinea-Bissau continued sporadic efforts in the 1970s to unite the countries, but the prospects for union ended with the 1980 *coup d'état* in Guinea-Bissau in which Nino Vieira overthrew Luis Cabral. In Cape Verde, the governing PAIGC renamed itself the *Partido Africano da Independência de Cabo Verde* (African Party for the Independence of Cape Verde), or PAICV.

Pereira maintained a left-leaning authoritarian regime until 1991, when multi-party elections were held in Cape Verde (alongside much of West Africa) after the end of the Cold War. The elections were won by the *Movimento para a Democracia* (MPD). The MPD's Antonio Mascarenhas became president and Carlos Veiga became Prime Minister. President Mascarenhas was reelected in 1996 without much opposition or participation; only about 40% of the electorate turned out.

The MPD government reversed many of Pereira's socialist policies and liberalized the economy, privatizing state enterprises and liberalizing prices and exchange rates. Over time, the openness encouraged donors, lenders, and even some foreign investors who sought to make use of Cape Verde's abundant low-wage employment.

The 2001 elections came down to thin margins between the PAICV and the MPD. In legislative elections in January, the PAICV won just under half of the vote (49.5%), which translated into 40 of 72 seats, while the MPD took 30 seats with 41% of the vote. José Maria Neves of the PAICV became Prime Minister (and remains so to the present). The next month saw an even closer election for the presidency, and indeed one of the closest presidential elections in world history. Pedro Pires of the PAICV led after the first round, with 46.5% to just under 46% for Carlos Veiga of MPD. Since neither won a majority outright, a second-round runoff was held, which Pires won by an incredible 12 votes: 75,827 to 75,815. In a credit to Cape Verdean democracy, Veiga and the MPD continued in loyal opposition.

The same rivals faced off again five years later. Based largely on diaspora support, the PAICV retained power in the January 2006 elections by winning 41 out of 72 parliamentary seats. The MPD won 29 seats, and Independent and Democratic Christian Union (UCID) captured the remaining two seats. MPD leader Agostinho Lopes, claimed the election was the "greatest electoral fraud" in the country's history, and even President Pires admitted "small irregularities," but international observers generally credited it with being free and fair. Pires of the PAICV then once again beat the MPD's Veiga in the presidential election, this time by a 51%–49% margin.

The PAICV controls the executive and legislative branches, but the MPD retains an important role in governing because some financial legislation requires a two-thirds majority. When the constitutional court declared parts of the 2002–03 budget unconstitutional because it had not received the two-thirds majority, the PAICV government began to talk about amending the constitution, but that too requires a two-thirds majority. As a result, some consensus between the country's two major parties remains a necessity.

The electoral rivalries of the PAICV and MPD continue to the present, and divide Cape Verdeans, both on the islands and in the (more numerous) diaspora community of migrants in America. The community is also divided over conceptions of race and color. Lighter-skinned Cape Verdeans frequently refer to themselves as Portuguese, while others identify themselves as black Africans. Cape Verde grants voting rights to anyone born in the islands, so many Cape Verdean emigrants participate in the parliamentary and presidential elections. Absentee ballots are not employed. Instead, polling places are set up in community centers wherever a concentration of islanders lives. There were nine official polling places in Massachusetts, Rhode Island, and Connecticut for the 2006 cycle.

The year 2011 brought another election cycle, with the legislative election held in February and the presidential election in August. In the legislative election, the PAICV repeated its performance from 2001 and 2006 with a victory over the rival MPD. The governing party took 53% to 42% for the opposition. The seat totals worked out to 38 for the PAICV, 32 for the MPD; a third party, the Independent and Democratic Cape Verdean Union (*União Caboverdeana Independente e Democrática*, or UCID) took the last two seats, as it did in 2006. Jorge Carlos Fonseca of the MPD won the presidential election in August. Coming out of the first round of voting as the front runner with 38% of the vote, he ultimately beat his competitor Manuel Inocencio Sousa of the PAICV in the second-round runoff. Fonseca was the Minister of Foreign Affairs from 1991–1993 and had unsuccessfully run for president in 2001.

CONTEMPORARY THEMES

Cape Verde has extremely limited natural resources. An archipelago of ten larger islands, only nine of which are habitable, and eight smaller islets, Cape Verde has little land to cultivate. Only 20% of the land is arable, and the country is subject to persistent periods of drought, interrupted by torrential rains and floods that erode what

Cape Verde

useful land is available. Some 73% of GDP is from the service sector and less than 10% from agriculture. The country regularly must import 80% or more of its food, which results in a large trade deficit. During years of drought and failed crops, the country is dependent on the international community for food. Cape Verde must also import all petroleum products, and the government's budget has been hard hit by recent oil price increases because it has set aside subsidies for energy and fuel.

Cape Verde suffers some of Africa's common problems but is relatively removed from others. On the positive side, development indicators are much better than most of the continent: incomes are higher, life expectancy is comparable to rich countries at over 70 years, and HIV/AIDS prevalence rates are very low (at under 0.5%). On the other hand, Cape Verde has become a major transit point for the shipment of cocaine from South America to Europe. With more than 1,200 miles of ill-patrolled shorelines and an endless supply of "mules" in nearby West Africa, the country is a top target for international drug syndicates and criminal networks. The government has recently committed to a new law enforcement program that will upgrade air and sea security for the islands. The investment has yielded some results: in 2006 a Guinea-Bissau-registered ship carrying three tons of cocaine was intercepted in Cape Verde waters.

By some accounts, Cape Verde is on the verge of exiting the Least Developed Countries category and becoming a "middle income" state. GDP growth has been strong in recent years, with several years at or above 8% between 2005 and 2010. Tourism development has helped: the government has encouraged foreign investment in the industry, which now brings some 170,000 visitors to the islands and contributes over 10% of GDP. However, tourism-led growth is asymmetrical: it mostly benefits the capital Praia, the port city of Mindelo (on São Vicente), and the island of Sal, where the international airport is located. The rural areas of Fogo, Brava, and Santo Antão have benefitted much less, and this has led to an exodus of the young from rural areas to tourist centers.

Linkages to the international economy are extremely important to the Cape Verdean economy. An estimated 20% of the GDP—about $100 million annually—is derived from remittances sent home by expatriates, and no visit of a Cape Verdean president to the United States is complete without a stop in Massachusetts and Rhode Island, where the wealthiest of the Cape Verdean diaspora reside. Chinese investment has also been important, with development projects financed by China, including the construction of a National Stadium, a second hydroelectric dam at Figueira Gorda on the island of São Tiago, and a cement factory, as well as investments in the ceramic and fishing industries. Finally, the government is also firming its ties to the European Union. The Cape Verdean escudo was once tied to the Portuguese escudo, and is now linked to the Euro. One of the most stable democracies in all of Africa, Cape Verde relies heavily on a tourist-driven economy while also dealing with periodic episodes of refugees and migrants requiring rescue offshore from fishing boats and other unstable craft plying the Atlantic Ocean along with a build-up of trash on its pristine beaches carried to its shores by ocean currents. Notable developments in the island nation include a declaration of achieving malaria-free status by the World Health Organization (WHO) in January 2024 based on the absence of a single case of local transmission over the last three years. A huge killer on the continent, malaria was responsible for 580,000 fatalities in 2022, 95 percent of the global total. Effective measures adopted by Cape Verde over the course of several years include strengthened health care systems and an increase in public access to diagnosis and treatment of all known cases. In a trip to Africa in December 2024, United States President Joe Biden stopped off in Cape Verde on his way to Angola.

FUTURE CONSIDERATIONS

Cape Verde's outlook, while very limited by climate and geography, remains solid, if unspectacular. The 2011 elections were smooth, providing the sense of stability and continuity that attract investment. The country has also invested in government transparency through an Internet-based government financial management system. The aim is to attract more investors by providing easy access to information about open bids for goods and services. The system also improves communications with Cape Verdean citizens that live outside the islands, and this is particularly important given the importance for the country of the diaspora and its remittances.

Cape Verde maintains open ties with the international economy, and the country's stability and unique location provide opportunities for the expansion of investment. Tourism and fishing appear to be among the most promising areas of development. While seeking to maintain close and favorable relations with China, the country has also sought tighter association with the United States.

Cape Verde is an African case apart, both literally and figuratively. The small and remote country faces few of the conflicts and menaces that plague other parts of West Africa. This makes for a more peaceful society, but also for greater difficulty in maintaining linkages to the rest of Africa. There is no reason to expect the country to regress or backslide, but with a small and geographically fragmented domestic market, there are questions about the natural limits to its economic growth.

A gracious town square in Mindelo

Photo by Michael Beguelin

The Republic of Côte d'Ivoire

The government established the French form of *Ivory Coast* as the country's official designation.

Our Lady of Peace, Yamoussoukro—the world's largest Christian church

BASIC FACTS

Area: 322,463 sq. km. (somewhat larger than New Mexico)
Population: 29,344,847 (June 2023 est.)
Capital City: Yamoussoukro
Government Type: Presidential republic
Neighboring Countries: Liberia, Guinea (west); Mali, Burkina Faso (Upper Volta-north); Ghana (east)
Official Language: French
Other Principal Languages: 60 native dialects of which Dioula is the most commonly spoken
Ethnic Groups: Akan 42.1%, Voltaiques or Gur 17.6%, Northern Mandes 16.5%, Krous 11%, Southern Mandes 10%, other 2.8% (includes Lebanese and French)
Principal Religions: Islam 38.6%, Christianity 32.8%, indigenous 11.9%, none 16.7% (2008 est.) The majority of migrant workers practice Islam (70%) and Christianity (20%).
Former Colonial Status: French Colony (1839–1960)
Independence Date: August 7, 1960
GDP Per Capita (IMF 2023 est.): $2,646 (nominal), $7,011 (PPP)
Gini Index: 41.5 (World Bank 2015)
Currency: CFA franc (African Financial Community), 1 US dollar = 594 (Apr. 2023)
Inflation Rate: 4.09% (2022 est.)

Chief Commercial Products: Cocoa, coffee, tropical woods, petroleum, cotton, bananas, pineapples, palm oil, and fish
Foreign Direct Investments (FDI) net inflows: 462,038,433
Literacy Rate: 89.9% (CIA 2023)
Life Expectancy: 62.71 years (CIA 2022 est.)
Head of State: President Alassane Dramane Ouattara (since December 4, 2010)
Head of Government: Prime Minister Patrick Achi (since April 19, 2022)

LAND AND PEOPLE

The Republic of Côte d'Ivoire is located in the center of the south coast of West Africa. The coast along the Gulf of Guinea is 340 miles long; from the border of Ghana for a distance of 185 miles to the west, it is flat and sandy, with many inland lagoons. The remainder of the coast towards Liberia has numerous sharp rocks and is higher. Dense forests and green jungles spread farther inland, covering almost 40% of the country. Tall niagou, samba and mahogany trees make for impressive forests. Midway to the north, the trees gradually become thinner and are succeeded by low scrub trees, grasses, and brush vegetation. In the northernmost region, the foliage gives way to a semiarid climate, which has in the past supported grasslands, occasionally interrupted by taller growth. The country is mostly level except for the Man Mountains in the area closest to Liberia and Guinea. The southern and central portions of the country have traditionally received ample rainfall and have high humidity. Temperatures are warm in the North, with less rainfall; with the African droughts of recent years, this northern region has become increasingly desolate.

Côte d'Ivoire's population is an ethnic mosaic consisting of some 60 groups, roughly divided into four linguistic families—Akan, Kru, Mandé and Voltaic—having distinct characteristics and regional identifications. Akan speakers dominate the southeast, and the most prominent subgroup, the Baulé, have also settled in savanna regions of central Côte d'Ivoire. Catholic missionaries were first active in the southeast, bringing mission education and literacy, which provided access to employment in the colonial civil service. From that position of privilege, Akan speakers came to dominate Ivoirian politics. Both presidents Houphouët-Boigny and Bédié were Baulé.

The southwestern region is dominated by Kru-speaking peoples. Though Protestant missionaries were active in the southwest, most people there practice indigenous religions. Ethnic differences map onto politics. Former president Laurent Gbagbo comes from one of the Kru subgroups, the Bété. Southern Mandé speakers predominate in the western regions, and coup leader General Gueï belonged to the Yacouba subgroup. "Northerners" are almost equally split between Northern Mandé speakers and Voltaic speakers like the Sénoufo. The Northern Mandé include Malinké and Jula (or Dyula), traditionally long-distance traders; Alassane Ouattara, Côte d'Ivoire's current president, hails from this group.

Côte d'Ivoire

While Southern Mandé practice a variety of indigenous religions and Christianity, Northern Mandé are almost all Muslims and members of their merchant class have settled in most of the major cities of the south where they have become influential enough to dominate the local politics of several southern cities.

HISTORY TO PRESENT DAY

For early history, see *Historical Background* and *The Colonial Period: The French*.

The Félix Houphouët-Boigny Years (1960–93)

When full independence was gained by Côte d'Ivoire on August 7, 1960, Félix Houphouët-Boigny became its first president. A Baulé with a line of chiefs as ancestors, Houphouët-Boigny had attended the prestigious École William Ponty in Dakar, Senegal where he was trained as a *médecin africain*. The school brought together the very best students from each of the French West African colonies and prepared them for positions in the colonial civil service or French commercial enterprises. Perhaps even more important for future political developments, Ponty created the educated elite that would ultimately bring the various colonies of the French West Africa to independence.

Prior to Côte d'Ivoire's independence, Houphouët-Boigny traveled the colony extensively as a rural doctor and in 1940 inherited large coffee-producing tracts of land from his father, a wealthy planter and chief. Using modern techniques, he was able to expand their output, becoming a very wealthy man in a relatively short time. By the 1940s, he was acknowledged as leader of disgruntled African planters and in 1944 he founded the African Agricultural Union, which fought colonial policies that favored French planters and worked to end forced labor of Africans on white-owned plantations.

In 1945, Houphouët-Boigny formed the *Parti démocratique de la Côte d'Ivoire* (PDCI), mobilized African planters, and was elected a deputy to the French National Assembly in 1945 and again in 1946. In the Assembly, Houphouët-Boigny initially affiliated with the French Communist Party, but after long and persistent harassment by colonial officials he broke with the communists in 1950 and began to cooperate with the French. In West Africa, the PDCI was part of the *Rassemblement démocratique africain* (RDA: Democratic African Rally), a Federation-wide party.

In 1958, when General de Gaulle offered the possibility of immediate independence to France's colonies, Houphouët-Boigny campaigned vigorously for self-government within the Franco-African

Former President Laurent Gbagbo, arrested in 2011

Community. He was an equally vigorous opponent of any large federation of independent states, refusing to see Côte d'Ivoire's wealth used to subsidize French West Africa's poorer states. Houphouët-Boigny became prime minister of the Côte d'Ivoire in 1959 and in 1960 was elected the first president of the independent state. He was the architect of Côte d'Ivoire's rise to become a relatively wealthy republic through policies of fiscal orthodoxy and a focus on development of exports.

His political base was with the African planting class, and economic development reflected their interests. Commercial export of coffee and cocoa was encouraged and facilitated by development of roads. The port of San Pedro in the southwest was built to facilitate exports of the two crops. To work the plantations, migrant workers from Côte d'Ivoire's overpopulated and underdeveloped north were encouraged to travel south. Similarly, migrant labor from Mali, and what is now Burkina Faso, was encouraged to travel to the plantations. Land ownership and even citizenship were made possible for the newcomers.

For 30 years, the PDCI remained the country's sole political party, and Houphouët-Boigny governed by crafting an alliance between Akan-speaking southerners and largely Muslim northerners. When young northerners complained of unemployment and uneven regional development in the 1970s, a flurry of projects was started in the north, but by the early 1990s northern resentments and frustrations could no longer be so easily bought off.

As elsewhere in Africa, waves of sentiment for multiparty democracy were felt in Côte d'Ivoire in the late 1980s. In response to popular demand, and a bit of pressure from the World Bank, free formation of political parties was permitted for the first time during the 1990 elections. One of the most critical voices was that of Laurent Gbagbo, a member of the minority Bété community. A former history professor, Gbagbo founded the *Front Populaire Ivoirien* (FPI) and ran for president in 1990, losing to Houphouët-Boigny. However, Gbagbo's FPI gave expression to the frustrations felt by those who had long suffered under a government dominated by Akans and gained support despite the electoral loss. Ominously for the future, Gbagbo charged that Houphouët's power was based on the vote of "foreigners."

Decline under Henry Konan Bédié (1993–99)

Côte d'Ivoire's founding father died in December 1993 and was succeeded by his protégé—another Baulé speaker—Henri Konan Bédié. Less confident and less politically skilled than Houphouët-Boigny, Bédié seemed not to understand the basic pragmatism by which Houphouët had ruled, winning over opponents through cooptation and cooperation, consensus, and compromise. As tough economic restructuring began to be implemented, Bédié began to scapegoat Côte d'Ivoire's "foreigners," and more specifically, northerners.

Northern resentments built up over the years as Northerners felt they were not receiving a fair return for their political support and economic contributions. They received fewer political appointments, and economic development of the region was stinted. They were too frequently hassled when trying to obtain national identity cards and complained of being treated not like citizens, but as foreigners. Their answer was to split from the PDCI.

The *Rassemblement des républicains* (RDR: Republican Rally), based mainly in the north, was founded in September 1994 only a few months after Houphouët-Boigny's death. Its leader was Houphouët's prime minister and rival with Konan Bédié as his successor, Alassane Ouattara.

Faced with an increasingly desperate economic situation and deprived of the PDCI's traditional northern support, Konan Bédié resorted to the baser instincts of his countrymen. "Foreigners" were stigmatized; a populist Ivorian ethno-nationalism was generated. It was not the first time the regime had diverted attention from its problems by arguing that foreigners exploited the colony's wealth. Dahomeans (from present-day Benin) had been the object of attack in 1958, but now it was the turn of Burkinabé and Malian migrant laborers. It was easy, by extension, to include Bédié's lapsed allies—northern Muslims.

First articulated by Bédié in an August 1995 speech to the PDCI faithful, the concept of Ivorian identity—*Ivoirité* in French—became central to political discourse in the country and was used to justify what developed into violent xenophobia. "Ivoirization" was instituted in

Côte d'Ivoire

1996, a direct reversal of the open borders policy of the country when plantation labor was needed. Now, to officially be a citizen, one had to prove his or her parents and grandparents were born in Côte d'Ivoire. Strict nationality rules for presidential candidates were introduced into the Ivorian electoral code.

Alassane Ouattara, once a prime minister under Houphouët-Boigny, was effectively prevented from running in 1995 because of these rules. He later accepted an appointment as IMF deputy director. When, in April 1998, he announced that he would not seek reappointment and would be available to serve his country, the controversy reemerged with a vengeance. One PDCI leader accused him of being a foreigner. Increasingly virulent of attacks on Ouattara suggested the nervousness and even paranoia of the political class. He was both a northerner and Muslim, the "other" for the Akan-speaking Christian core of PDCI support. Like his predecessor Houphouët-Boigny, President Bédié was a Christian politician in a country increasingly turning to Islam.

Raw statistics describe a situation ripe for xenophobic reaction: At the time, Côte d'Ivoire had an estimated three million people officially described as "residents of foreign nationality." Another two million were residents of foreign origin—migrant workers and their descendants, largely Muslim. In short, 30% of the population could be demagogically defined as "foreign."

Bédié's campaign to promote Ivorian nationalism produced increasing hostility directed at foreigners and ethnic minorities. Smoldering resentment against "foreigners," particularly in the south, erupted in ethnic pogroms in several communities. Anti-ethnic riots and continuing political demonstrations took place against a background of deteriorating economic conditions. (The cocoa industry was particularly affected after the European Union agreed to allow chocolate manufacturers to use less cocoa butter in their confections.)

Economic problems fueled political tension throughout 1999 as the country approached its presidential election. The government vigorously repressed its critics, imprisoned opposition leaders, and prohibited street demonstrations as the campaign against Ouattara grew increasingly personal. When one judge ruled that Ouattara qualified as a presidential candidate, the Justice Ministry forced that judge to resign and replaced him with a jurist who ruled that Ouattara's identity papers were forged. In early December 1999 the government issued a warrant for Ouattara's arrest.

The Coup of 1999 and its Aftermath

The country's cumulative crises culminated in a coup d'état on December 24, 1999, when General Robert Gueï, a former army chief of staff, assumed leadership of disgruntled soldiers demanding back wages and overthrew the Bédié government. France, with significant commercial interests at stake—20,000 citizens actually resident in the country, and 550 soldiers stationed there—did not act to restore the *ancien régime.* The country at large seemed initially to greet the coup with a sense of relief.

However, the military intervention did not cool political temperatures, and after the coup Côte d'Ivoire was plagued by violence and instability. General Gueï moved quickly to draft a new constitution that was submitted to voters and massively approved in July 2000. Yet, the new constitution carried into the Second Republic the seeds of division cultivated in the First Republic: presidential candidates were required to have two Ivorian parents. Bédié's *Ivoirité* was given formal constitutional recognition.

Presidential elections were organized for October 2000, and nineteen people submitted candidacy papers, of which fourteen were declared ineligible by the Supreme Court. Included among the disqualified were representatives of the largest opposition parties—Émile Constant Bombet of the long-governing PDCI and Ouattara of the RDR.

The campaign came down to a battle between Gueï and Laurent Gbagbo, the former history professor who, as the leader of the socialist *Front Populaire Ivoirien* (FPI), had opposed the governing PDCI since 1990. When the electoral commission proclaimed Gueï the winner in October elections, Gbagbo called out his supporters to protest. As Ivoirians took to the streets in massive demonstrations, the general fled and Laurent Gbagbo proclaimed himself winner and president.

Attacks against "foreigners" did not end with Gbagbo. Instead, the Gbagbo regime found the ethno-nationalism of "*Ivoirité*" as politically useful as did its predecessors, and the regime's security forces repressed minorities and engaged in outright murder. The worst incident occurred at the Abidjan suburb of Yopougon, where gendarmes slaughtered 57 individuals and dumped them in a mass grave because they were Muslim or had "northern" names.

Once installed as president, Laurent Gbagbo refused all suggestions that the election be rerun despite its dubious legitimacy (with major candidates excluded and low turnout as a result). For legislative elections in December 2000, a Gbagbo court excluded Alassane Ouattara (Gbagbo's one time ally) from running for the National Assembly. Demonstrations followed and the RDR boycotted the election with such success that in some northern areas absolutely no one turned up at the polling stations. The FPI obtained 96 seats in the 225-seat Assembly—not enough to govern alone—with the former governing Ivory Coast Democratic Party (PDCI) garnering 94 seats. Twenty-two independents would act as swing votes between the contending factions.

However, municipal elections in March 2001 showed the political capacity of Ouattara's RDR, which now participated on a nationwide basis and dominated by selecting candidates who were representative of local constituencies. The RDR gained control of all towns in the northern region and some of the largest southern cities, including Gagnoa, Laurent Gbagbo's birthplace. With these elections the RDR proved itself a national party that could be successful in a fair election.

Laurent Gbagbo (2000–11) and a Divided Country

Desperate to end the turbulence that threatened its internal power and external support, the Gbagbo regime convened a National Reconciliation Forum in late 2001, but ultimately regime behavior was little changed. Persecution and discrimination persisted, and the regime's impunity for perpetrators of violence emboldened xenophobes.

Tensions exploded on September 19, 2002, when dissident divisions of the Ivoirian army mutinied, allegedly over issues of pay and demobilization. In coordinated attacks, the mutineers took control of the northern city of Korhogo and the central city of Bouaké. There was fighting in Abidjan, the commercial capital, though loyalist troops retained control of the city. During the fighting the interior minister was killed and the minister of defense attacked. The government claimed it was an attempted *coup d'état* and used the occasion to eliminate its enemies.

President Alassane Ouattara

Côte d'Ivoire

Troops in army fatigues murdered General Gueï—who had just withdrawn his party from the governing coalition and was suspected of planning a coup—along with his wife, aides, and other family members. A similar death squad arrived at Alassane Ouattara's home, but he had been forewarned and had escaped over a wall into the neighboring German Embassy and was later given sanctuary in the French Embassy.

The army mutineers soon incorporated civilian elements, named themselves the *Mouvement patriotique de Côte d'Ivoire* (MPCI), and announced their complaints and policy demands: They were fighting a "dictatorship" that treated them like "slaves," as one spokesman put it. They demanded Laurent Gbagbo's resignation and a transitional government that would organize new presidential elections open to all. Despite defense agreements with the country, France chose not to interfere in the politics, but limited its action to protecting French citizens and evacuating them from the rebel-controlled cities of Korhogo and Bouaké.

With no outsider willing to fight the rebels, Gbagbo was forced to rely on his own ill-trained, under-equipped, demoralized, and disorganized army, making the effort to retake Bouaké a failure. To prevent further deterioration, France secured a cease-fire and established a buffer zone between government and rebel forces. The country was effectively divided in half and rabid anti-French sentiment became the order of the day.

The Gbagbo regime accused hostile neighbors (Burkina Faso and Liberia) of arming and aiding the rebels and began to acquire arms and men from Eastern Europe and Angola. The government whipped up ethno-nationalist fervor in the streets and on the airwaves. Muslims, "foreigners," and political opponents became the object of virulent attack, and none more so than Alassane Ouattara (who to his detractors fit all three of these categories). The low point was reached when one daily, *La National*, proposed a simple word game: by using the letters in the name Alassane Dramane Ouattara, wrote the author, one could spell out the words "Satan," "demon," "*meurtre* (murder)," and "torture."

Mobs demanding Ouattara's head plagued the French Embassy and nearly broke in. In early October 2002, MPCI rebels retaliated with a massacre of dozens of gendarmes at Bouaké. Death squads that the UN linked to the government began to roam through Abidjan, selectively assassinating regime opponents and intimidating others into silence by kidnapping and torture.

The government began passing even more worrisome laws. In Bonoua, only 30 miles from Abidjan, "foreigners" could not be allocated any stall at the local market, or land on which to build. They were also forbidden to work as transporters or to enter into a mixed marriage, and, in the language of the legislation, every family was "strictly forbidden to have recourse to any procedure to integrate a foreigner into our ranks."

As violence and fear intensified in the cities, the war in the countryside took on larger regional dimensions, and came to involve rebel groups, mercenaries, and France. Two new rebel groups located in Western Côte d'Ivoire announced themselves in November 2002—the *Mouvement populaire ivoirien du Grand Ouest* (MPIGO: Ivorian Popular Movement of the Greater West) and the *Mouvement pour la Justice et la Paix* (MJP). Both claimed to be fighting to avenge the murder of General Gueï and to remove Laurent Gbagbo. Both drew support from President Charles Taylor of Liberia and recruited from his reserve of mercenaries without borders. France gathered representatives of the various forces together in a Paris suburb and hammered out an agreement in January 2003 on a government of national unity, in what came to be known as the Marcoussis peace accords. A joint operation by rebels, the Ivory Coast army, and 900 French troops cleared western areas of the Liberian mercenaries. The accords, imposed on a reluctant Laurent Gbagbo, created a government of national unity that included ministers from the rebel groups (now collectively called the *Forces Nouvelles de Côte d'Ivoire*, or "New Forces"). The government was headed by a consensus premier, the northerner Seydou Diarra.

The Diarra government found itself regularly impeded. Fearing assassination, rebel ministers were hesitant to attend initial cabinet meetings in Yamoussoukro. In Abidjan, the hardliners around Laurent Gbagbo organized public demonstrations of opposition and private acts of terror against those thought to support the New Forces. Foremost among these thuggish forces was the Alliance of Young Patriots headed by Charles Blé Goudé. Goudé was a former leader of the powerful student union—*Fédération étudiante et scolaire de Côte d'Ivoire* (Fesci)—and was known for his steady stream of anti-French invective. Blé Goudé's followers became the regime's storm troopers, and he was known as "the general of the young" (and to his friends as "the machete"). Blé Goudé patrolled Abidjan surrounded by his Kalashnikov-bearing bodyguards, considering himself the incarnation of what he called opposition to "the dictates of Paris."

Though he periodically swore to uphold the Marcoussis agreement, President Gbagbo consistently delayed, circumvented, and obstructed progress towards peaceful resolution. He was received by French President Chirac with all the dignity of a head of state in February 2004, and seemingly emboldened by the recognition, he became even more intransigent. When the opposition proposed to demonstrate against the president's actions, Gbagbo decreed a prohibition on demonstrations.

Despite prohibitions by Gbagbo, opposition parties organized a peaceful march in Abidjan to support Marcoussis, to which the president responded with brute force: Gbagbo cut off the city, monitored the participants from helicopters, and sent defense and security forces to crush the demonstration. A UN report said that the government security forces and the militia killed at least 120 people. When they had completed their work, President Gbagbo congratulated his forces. The UN report called the deaths "indiscriminate killing of innocent civilians," and noted that individuals from northern Côte d'Ivoire and immigrants from Burkina Faso had been "specially targeted" even though these communities had "little or nothing to do with the march." Following the massacre, New Forces rebels and the four main opposition parties in parliament withdrew their 26 ministers from the government of "national reconciliation" and broke off dialogue with President Gbagbo.

The government also continued to buy arms and hire mercenaries and by November 2004 it launched aerial raids against five rebel strongholds in the north and west. During the last, on November 6, a government plane bombed a French military installation in Bouaké, killing nine French soldiers and one American civilian. France retaliated by destroying virtually the entire Ivoirian air force. Anti-French mobs rioted in Abidjan, largely targeting their mayhem and violence at French property and personnel; the rioters burned and pillaged shops, raped women, and beat men.

Angry voices throughout the city fanned ultranationalist and anti-French

Charles Blé Goudé

©IRIN

Côte d'Ivoire

sentiments. Young Patriots, a target audience for disinformation, were told the French intended to remove President Gbagbo from office. They responded by surrounding the principal sources of regime power: the Presidential Palace and the national radio and television station. In the chaos, at least 20 and perhaps as many as 60 Ivoirians were killed.

The UN Security Council issued an immediate arms embargo and gave leaders one month to get the peace process back on track or face a travel ban and a freeze on their personal assets. The African Union enlisted President Mbeki of South Africa to lead an African mediation effort, which resulted in the April 2005 Pretoria Agreement. It declared the war to be ended, reiterated previous accords, and reaffirmed a determination to organize presidential elections in October 2005. President Mbeki dealt deftly with the central issue of those elections: the candidacy of Alassane Ouattara. The intransigent Laurent Gbagbo was pressured to abandon his demand for a constitutional referendum on the topic, and in late April he announced that he was invoking "exceptional measures" to suspend the normal rules for the next election to allow Alassane Ouattara to participate in the presidential election.

The Decline and Fall of Gbagbo

In 2006, Ouattara and Henri Konan Bédié ended their long political feud to join forces against a common enemy, Laurent Gbagbo. The RDR and PDCI (plus two smaller opposition parties) created a new opposition coalition: *le Rassemblement des Houphouëtistes pour la démocratie et la paix* (RHDP: Rally of Houphouëtists for Democracy and Peace).

At the end of June, after two days of talks in the South African capital, Pretoria, the government and rebel movement agreed to a calendar for disarmament and a revision of several laws, including the important text on nationality. Deadlines came and went however, and each side accused the other of undermining the agreement. The government refused to act until rebels had begun disarming, and rebels refused to disarm because political reforms had not been implemented. Given the political paralysis that overtook the country, the international community turned up its rhetoric to shame foot-dragging politicians. UN Secretary General Kofi Annan took the lead. A presidential election in October 2005 wasn't possible, he said in early September, "because political leaders and parties have not cooperated." He went on to accuse them of trying to "destroy" their country and threatened sanctions to bring them to their senses.

The AU was spurred to action by President Obasanjo of Nigeria and recognized an extension of President Gbagbo's terms for "not more than 12 months." It offered a new peace plan that included an appointed prime minister with "full authority over his cabinet" to lead the country toward elections in October 2006. The UN Security Council quickly endorsed the proposal as Resolution 1633.

The resolution created an important new body to make sure disarmament and elections took place by the October 31, 2006, deadline: the International Working Group (IWG). Broadly constituted, the IWG was designed to bring the full weight of the international community to bear on the country's fragile peace process. It consists of representatives of the UN, the AU, the European Union, IMF, and World Bank, and *Francophonie* (the international grouping of French-speaking countries), as well as representatives from South Africa, Benin, Ghana, Guinea, Niger, Nigeria, France, the United Kingdom, and the United States.

In November, the IWG set forth a road map for translating the Pretoria Accord and UN Resolution 1633 into reality. Three of Africa's most prominent leaders, Obasanjo of Nigeria, Mbeki of South Africa, and Mamadou Tandja of Niger (then head of the West African regional grouping ECOWAS), shuttled between the various parties and finally designated Charles Konan Banny, the governor of West Africa's central bank, as Côte d'Ivoire's interim prime minister. His mandate from the UN Security Council was to organize elections by October 2006 and disarm contending forces: northern rebels and southern pro-Gbagbo militias.

Prime Minister Banny was sworn into office in early December and presented his cabinet by the end of the month. As usual, the most difficult negotiator was Laurent Gbagbo, who wanted his own men controlling the ministries associated with revenue and force—Economy and Finances; Defense and Security. Banny's cabinet managed the difficult task of bringing on board representatives of the rebels, government, and major opposition parties, but the new prime minister was almost immediately tested.

On January 2, 2006, a minor military mutiny took place in the capital. At the same time, Gbagbo supporters mobilized to fight the IWG's recommendation not to extend the mandate of the National Assembly, which had expired in December. Protesters took to the streets and condemned UN interference in the country's affairs, paralyzing the city and terrorizing UN personnel. As usual, Charles Blé Goudé was in the thick of the street theater. Some 2,000 of his Young Patriots blockaded the main UN bases in Abidjan and other cities until he told them to go home. (With the installation of the Banny government, some of the traditional funding sources to support groups like the Young Patriots had been squeezed off; with nothing to be paid out, the demonstrators quickly lost interest.) On February 7, 2006, the UN Security Council imposed a 12-month travel ban and assets freeze on Blé Goudé and two others for hampering peace efforts. He was cited for "public statements advocating violence against United Nations installations and personnel . . . direction of and participation in acts of violence by street militias, including beatings, rapes and extra-judicial killings . . ." (In an Orwellian turn, Laurent Gbagbo named Blé Goudé an "Ambassador of Peace" in May 2007.)

Prime Minister Banny was charged with preparing elections and with disarming rebels in the north and loyalist militias in the south but was confronted by irreconcilable demands posited by the Gbagbo regime and the New Forces. For the government, disarmament was the *sine qua non* of all else; for the New Forces, issuance of identity papers and a resolution of the question of one's Ivoirian identity was paramount. Gbagbo wanted elections without an increased electorate, many of whom would be northerners systematically excluded and abused by his and previous administrations. For northern rebels, the arms they possessed represent the sole trump they hold. Recognizing both processes—identification and disarmament—were intimately linked, the Banny government committed itself to pursuing each simultaneously. Gbagbo and company resisted.

A pilot scheme registering immigrants to obtain certificates of national and voter

Ex-Prime Minister Charles Konan Banny
©IRIN

Côte d'Ivoire

cards was denounced by the president for opening the way to "massive fraud" in the areas under the control of the New Forces. Young Patriots took to the streets to protest, while the pro-Gbagbo press mounted vicious attacks on Alassane Ouattara. Prime Minister Banny himself came under attack for being a puppet of France and the UN. Once the registration scheme expanded, obstructionists reacted even more violently. In July, the president of Gbagbo's FPI, Pascal Affi N'Guessan, demanded the Young Patriots halt registration by all means possible, and Gbagbo himself scathingly denounced the UN as pro-rebel, which only intensified the depredations of loyalist militias. Given this environment, there was no way elections could be held in October.

With peacekeeping costs mounting and results becoming more uncertain, the UN Security Council unanimously voted Resolution 1721 in early November 2006, extending the terms of both Gbagbo and Banny for another year and calling for elections to be organized by the end of October 2007. Prime Minister Banny was to have "all necessary powers" needed to carry out his mandate, including the power to issue laws by decree within governmental and cabinet meetings. The resolution also gave the prime minister authority over the country's army and defense forces. Resolution 1721 sent Laurent Gbagbo's survival skills into overdrive. With umbrage and vehemence, he denounced the grant of enhanced authority to the prime minister as unconstitutional—but said nothing about the equally unconstitutional extension of his own term of office.

In August 2006, Prime Minister Banny had suspended the chief of Abidjan's port authority after it was revealed that European toxic wastes had been allowed to enter the port and had been distributed in 15 sites around the city; at least ten people had died after being contaminated. A November investigation fingered the port chief, Marcel Gossio, as "an accomplice" of the polluters, but he and two others suspended by the prime minister in the wake of the scandal—Gbagbo men all—were reinstated in early December by the president. Street manifestations multiplied; burning tires, broken windows and thrown rocks—urban guerilla warfare—devastated Abidjan. The confrontations lasted eight days and at least three Ivoirians were killed.

Gbagbo offered a multidirectional defense. To his political base he presented himself as a populist nationalist, defending his country against French neocolonialism. To his fellow West African leaders, he argued the dangerous precedent set by Resolution 1721, which in effect superseded national constitutions and national sovereignty. But his cleverest ploy was to divide the *Houphouëtistes* by directly sounding out the young Catholic leader of the New Forces, Guillaume Soro. It was an end run around imposed prime ministers and the whole apparatus of conflict resolution created by the international community. Best of all, it could be marketed as an African solution to African problems. Timing favored the great manipulator: his two nemeses, the UN's Kofi Annan and French president Jacques Chirac were both leaving office.

The Gbagbo-Soro discussions were mediated by Burkina Faso's president, Blaise Campaoré, and resulted in a peace accord signed on March 4, 2007. The agreement envisioned restarting the citizen identification process, presidential and legislative elections by October, disarmament and integration of a limited number of northern rebels and loyalist militiamen into the national army, and suppression of the "zone of confidence" separating north and south by gradual withdrawal of both UN and French forces.

Having no alternative, the international community cautiously accepted the accord. Guillaume Soro, one-time leader of the country's militant student union, was similarly hesitant, but accepted Gbagbo's proposal to become prime minister. Soro conceded much more than he got in negotiations with Gbagbo. The President's supporters occupied the two most important ministries in the new cabinet—interior and defense—and constituted the largest voting bloc—11 of 33 members. The FN held seven portfolios, while the PDCI and Alassane Ouattara's RDR were given five each, with the remainder going to smaller parties and civil society.

Elections for the presidency were finally held after multiple delays in 2010. Initially scheduled for October 2008, they were postponed several times over issues of identity cards and the nationality of candidates. In the first round, Gbagbo took 38% of the vote and Ouattara 32%, which necessitated a second-round runoff between the two. The tense runoff was held in November, and the results were announced in December. The national electoral commission declared Ouattara the winner (with 54% to 46% for Gbagbo), but the incumbent was (not surprisingly) unwilling to go quietly.

Gbagbo rejected the results of the electoral commission as fraudulent and asked the Constitutional Council (presided over by a close ally) to rule on the election. The Council duly called Gbagbo the winner. This ruling was rejected in turn by Ouattara, election observers, and the international community (including the United Nations, the African Union, and ECOWAS), which were all persuaded that Ouattara was the rightful winner.

As had been the case in Côte d'Ivoire for a decade, the regime politics spilled over into the street, but this time Ouattara came out on top and claimed the presidency at last. In December 2010, after the competing claims of electoral victory by the two camps, forces loyal to Gbagbo clashed with pro-Ouattara forces in Abidjan and other towns. About two dozen people died at the end of 2010 and violence worsened into 2011; hundreds of thousands of Ivoirians fled their homes to avoid the fighting. Eventually, in March, forces loyal to Ouattara swept down from the north and occupied most of the country, descending upon Gbagbo's last refuge in the presidential palace in Abidjan. After several days of deadly fighting in the streets of the once-cosmopolitan city that took the death toll to over 1,000 Ivoirians, Ouattara's forces surrounded Gbagbo's compound and eventually stormed in, capturing Gbagbo alive in April.

The Alassane Ouattara Presidency (2011–present)

Alassane Ouattara was officially sworn in as president in May of 2011. He established the Truth, Reconciliation and Dialogue Commission in September of 2011 with the purpose of providing unity in the wake of post-electoral violence. Following internal investigations, Laurent Gbagbo was turned over to the International Criminal Court in The Hague to be tried for crimes against humanity during his time as President. As of April 2014, Gbagbo has been charged with four counts of crimes against humanity including murder, sexual violence, and persecution. His trial has been postponed twice to accommodate for the defense's request for more time and Gbagbo's poor health. As of 2014, Gbagbo is still awaiting trial. Also awaiting trial by the ICC is Charles Blé Goudé, who was arrested in Ghana in January 2013 and extradited

Former Prime Minister Guillaume Soro

Côte d'Ivoire

to Côte d'Ivoire. His trial is scheduled to begin with a confirmation of charges hearing in August of 2014. Meanwhile, the UN arms embargo was renewed in April of 2012 and for an additional year in April 2013, as the international community continues sanctions on the Ivory Coast in an effort to maintain a modicum of stability in the volatile country.

Côte d'Ivoire under Ouattara has seen some degree of stabilization. The government presided over parliamentary elections in December of 2011 that went smoothly despite a boycott by Gbagbo supporters; the same was true for local elections in 2013. The government has reformed the cocoa industry and begun road repair. Meanwhile, foreign investment and foreign aid have both begun again, and the economy has grown an estimated 8% in the year since Ouattara's inauguration.

Nonetheless, there is still a considerable degree of uncertainty in the country, as epitomized by the destabilizing influence of Gbagbo adherents and the Ouattara government's hair-trigger reactions to unrest. In June 2012, the government alleged that Gbagbo supporters were behind an attack that killed UN peacekeepers. It further maintained that this group—comprised of Gbagbo's malcontents and Liberian mercenaries—had prepared to stage a coup against Ouattara. This was followed by another small-scale attack at an army post along the Ghanaian border, for which the government forwarded the same explanation. This suggests that the embers of the conflict between Gbagbo and Ouattara are still glowing, even after Gbagbo's arrest. Also in 2012, President Ouattara wrestled with politics internal to the government, as he shuffled his cabinet to try to keep his restive coalition intact. From these events, it seems evident that Ouattara has yet to consolidate authority.

CONTEMPORARY THEMES

After two decades of economic success in the 1960s and 1970s, Côte d'Ivoire's economy performed poorly in the 1980s and has suffered since 1999 as a result of the persistent conflict. The wars and unrest destabilized transportation and disrupted production by forcing many people of Burkinabé ancestry to flee the country. The economy was basically stagnant through the 2000s but has shown growth since Ouattara took the helm.

The economy is heavily dependent on agriculture, with cocoa, coffee, timber, and palm oil as principal exports. Together, they produce about 70% of total export earnings and contribute 40% of GDP. Côte d'Ivoire is the world's largest cocoa producer, representing about one-third of the world's cocoa output. There are some 620,000 cocoa and coffee farmers out of a population of 16 million, and another three million people depend directly on the commodities for their livelihoods.

One consequence of the reliance on earnings from cocoa, coffee, and palm oil is that vast areas of tropical rainforest have been destroyed to create commodity plantations. Dependent on migrant labor, cocoa plantations, particularly in the western region, were the scene of many of the vicious anti-foreign pogroms under Gbagbo. Many of the migrants, often from Burkina Faso and Mali, lived in the region for years and had even bought property. Hyped up by the government's xenophobic rhetoric, locals chased thousands of northerners from their homes, lands, and livelihoods. Control of the cocoa-producing areas was the major source of the Gbagbo regime's revenues. There was virtually no transparency, but donor-nation diplomats estimate that as much as 20% of those revenues were siphoned off to buy arms for the regime and to support the thuggish activities of loyalist militias like the Young Patriots.

The principal economic resource in the north is cotton. A number of factors have compromised the industry's productivity. Planters and cooperatives have not been paid by processors, which has dissuaded many from replanting their fields. The absence of banks in the north impedes the transfer of funds, and cotton processors find it difficult to finance cotton shipments. With the division of the country, transportation costs also rose 40%. As a consequence, stocks accumulate at the factories and run the risk of deteriorating. The sector—like elsewhere in Africa—suffers from farm policy in the United States and elsewhere that subsidizes farmers in wealthy countries to produce cotton that undercuts African producers.

Like the agricultural sector, the city of Abidjan has suffered in recent years. The former capital city was once considered the most modern and sophisticated city in francophone Africa, but years of impunity for crime and violence have dampened its luster. The city, located on lagoons inland from the coast, now has a population of more than 3.5 million—the equivalent of the population of the entire country at independence in 1960. Despite years of hostility and attack, Abidjan is home to most of the French citizens who still remain in the country, a population well off from an estimated 60,000 in 1978.

Côte d'Ivoire also has a nascent oil sector, possessing proven oil reserves of some 100 million barrels, most of it located offshore. In 2008, some 55,000 barrels per day were being produced. Though the books are hardly transparent, it may be that oil income has replaced cocoa as the principal source of revenue for the state. Significant declines in cocoa bean production, also afflicting Ghana, stem from a multiplicity of problems, including widespread illegal gold mining, spreading plant disease, climate change, and general mismanagement resulting in major global price increases of chocolate. The country also continues to recover from armed conflicts in 2011 resulting from land disputes and corruption while prosecuting individuals involved in Islamic terrorist actions in 2017.

Joining a growing list of African countries cutting military ties with the once greatly influential former French colonial power, the government of Côte d'Ivoire announced that French military forces that have been in the country for decades would be expelled in January 2025. Claiming the country's military forces were "now effective," the announcement by President Alassane Ouattara puts Côte d'Ivoire on the same path as Chad and Senegal of expelling French troops, joining several Sahel countries that had earlier done the same beginning in 2021, indicating a general loss of influence by France on the continent. French soldiers have been assisting the Ivorian army in the fight against armed groups operating in the Sahel and expanding into countries along the Gulf of Guinea, including Ghana, while France also operated as part of a United Nations peacekeeping mission during Côte d'Ivoire's long civil war from 2002 to 2011. In a country where anger against France is growing, Ouattara's close relationship with French President Emmanuel Macron has bred deep resentment against the government. On the economic front, one of the top producers of cacao in the world, the country's growers continue to suffer from poor harvests, largely from the severe effects of the El Niño weather pattern which, by raising average sea surface temperatures in the equatorial Pacific Ocean, has brought drier conditions to the West Africa region with similar deleterious effects in other major producers, including Ghana.

FUTURE CONSIDERATIONS

The situation in Côte d'Ivoire remains fragile despite the dramatic turns of events in 2010 and 2011. The successful prosecution of Alassane Ouattara's claim to the presidency likely came as a relief to the international community and to most Ivoirians, though it came at the cost of over a thousand lives. (It should be noted that most of these deaths are on the conscience of former president Gbagbo, but that there are serious accusations of atrocities committed by pro-Ouattara forces during the brief war in 2010 and 2011.) The political situation remains delicate

Côte d'Ivoire

after Ouattara assumed the presidency, but there are hopes that Gbagbo's forces are slowly dissolving and disbanding (or are being reincorporated into a more constitutional national army) after their defeat. The outcome of the Gbagbo trial is still pending. Whether or not the trial will dissuade Gbagbo supporters or merely agitate them is yet to be determined.

Côte d'Ivoire was West Africa's economic star for much of the first three decades after independence; which provides the country with an industrial base and an economic memory that is the envy of many neighbors. While uncertainty over the economy will continue until the Ouattara administration can demonstrate that the country has stabilized, Côte d'Ivoire shows some economic promise with foreign investors designating it "one of the best environments for investors in Africa". Prime Minister Daniel Kablan Duncan claims his country is on track to reach double digit economic growth in the year 2014 and become an emerging economic market by 2020. The discovery of oil offshore by French company Total is also an influential economic opportunity for the country. Despite this encouraging outlook, economic challenges will remain as Côte d'Ivoire works towards patching the wounds of its past. Côte d'Ivoire has greater prospects for stable peace and forward-looking governance than any time in the past decade, but this outcome is not a guarantee and will depend heavily on whether the decisions taken can reestablish a stable rule of law in the coming years.

The Republic of The Gambia

Mothers lined up for food   Photo by Ken Brown

BASIC FACTS

Area: 11,295 sq km = 4,361 sq miles (smaller than Connecticut)
Population: 2,468,569 (2023 est.)
Capital City: Banjul
Government Type: Presidential republic
Neighboring Countries: Senegal (enclosed on three sides).
Official Language: English
Other Principal Languages: Fulfulde, Jola, Mandinka, Soninke, and Wolof
Ethnic Groups: Mandinka 42%, Fula 18%, Wolof 16%, Jola 10%, Serahuli 9%, other 4%, non-African 1%
Principal Religions: Muslim 90%, Christian 8%, indigenous beliefs (Voodoo/Animism) 2%
Former Colonial Status: British Colony (1816–1965)
Independence Date: February 18, 1965
GDP Per Capita (IMF 2023 est.): $861 (nominal), $2,804 (PPP)
Gini Index: 35.9 (2015 est.)
Currency: Dalasi, 1 USD = 60.1 dalasi (Apr. 2023)
Inflation Rate: 7.37% (2022 est.)
Chief Commercial Products: Groundnuts and peanut products, fish, re-exportation of textiles
Foreign Direct Investments (FDI) net inflows: 28,404,021
Literacy Rate: 58.1% (CIA 2021)
Life Expectancy: 67.9 years (CIA 2023 est.)
Head of State: President Adama Barrow (since January 19, 2017)
Head of Government: President Adama Barrow (since January 19, 2017)

LAND AND PEOPLE

The Gambia has the smallest area of any independent nation on the African mainland and is seldom more than 20 miles in width. It is a fingerlike projection in the territory of southern Senegal, by which it is surrounded with the exception of The Gambia's small stretch of coastline along the Atlantic Ocean. The country largely follows the Gambia River, which is navigable by oceangoing vessels for 150 miles inland; smaller ships can traverse its entire length. The estuary contains one of the finest natural harbors in Africa. The country lies within an area smaller than Jamaica. It was named *The* Gambia by the government to avoid confusion with Zambia.

The entire territory is low-lying, never exceeding a height of 120 feet. On each side of the broad river, thick swamps contain mangrove trees which can reach heights of up to 100 feet. Farther inland from the river is a region of swamps and river flats. This swampy belt is succeeded by round hills and rolling plateaus with thick growths of grass and periodic clumps of trees. There is ample rainfall for cultivation.

The Gambia's population is 90% Muslim, but this is mixed with many indigenous beliefs such as voodoo and animism. As in much of West Africa, Islam in Gambia has traditionally tolerated indigenous practices. While this flexibility has allowed for more religious freedom, it also allowed such traditional practices as female genital cutting (FGC) to persist for some time; most adult Gambian women have had their clitoris removed, but local mobilization from women's groups and others have now worked to scale back FGC dramatically.

HISTORY TO PRESENT DAY

For early history, see *Historical Background* and *The Colonial Period: The British*.

The PPP Government (1965–1994)

The Gambia was previously a British protectorate in 1894 until conferences between the British colonial rulers and The Gambia in 1964 led to full independence on February 18, 1965, when David K. Jawara was installed as the first prime minister. The Gambia voted by referendum to become a republic within the British Commonwealth in 1970, whereupon Prime Minister Jawara nominally became president.

Though the country was relatively democratic for three decades, elections from the outset were dominated by the People's Progressive Party (PPP) and by President Jawara. In the inaugural elections in 1960, and again in 1962 and 1966, the PPP won a majority over the second-place United Party. The PPP's dominance in legislative elections was consolidated in successive elections in 1972, 1977, 1982, 1987, and 1992. In each case, the PPP won a clear majority with 25 or more seats (out of a total that ranged between 32 and 36). Direct presidential elections were first held in 1982, 1987, and 1992. Jawara was elected and reelected by comfortable majorities, each time beating out Sheriff Mustapha Dibba of the National Convention Party (NCP), who could never surpass 30% of

Gambia

the vote. The only hiccup for the regime was an unsuccessful coup attempted in mid-1981 when Jawara was at the royal wedding in London.

The Yahya Jammeh Coup and Authoritarian Rule (1994–Jan. 2017)

Despite the patina of stability, unrest bubbled just below the surface from at least the mid-1980s onward, especially among army personnel who had not been paid while government corruption grew increasingly rampant and obvious. Lieutenant Yahya Jammeh finally staged a military coup in mid-1994. Jammeh established a five-man ruling council and held a referendum on a new constitution. He resigned his commission and was elected president with 56% of the vote in September 1996, with Ousainou Darboe of the United Democratic Party (UDP) taking 36%.

Legislative elections in January 1997 were contested by Jammeh's Alliance for Patriotic Reorientation and Construction (APRC) and Darboe's UDP, along with the People's Democratic Organization for Independence and Socialism (PDOIS), the National Reconciliation Party (NRP), and five independents. The APRC won more than a two-thirds majority with 33 seats, while the UDP won seven, the NRP two and the PDOIS one. The elections were controversial and most observers thought them neither fair nor free, and The Gambia's once-proud democracy showed clear signs of decline.

Jammeh's regime proved authoritarian and oppressive, with the president dominating the country and controlling the instruments of force and fear. He held direct authority over the Ministry of Defense and the National Intelligence Agency. The regime followed opposition activity closely, especially the UDP; Darboe's party was frequently denied permission to hold public rallies, and its members were arrested and regularly accused the police of torture. The regime prohibited members of parliament from criticizing the president and outlawed discussion of any matter involving the courts.

The government increasingly used brute force against the citizenry, with the governing APRC using its youth wings as storm troopers for breaking up opposition rallies and beating opposition candidates and their supporters. After an APRC supporter was killed at a UDP meeting in 2000, Ousainou Darboe and 20 of his followers were promptly arrested and charged with murder. Most were acquitted, but Darboe and his four close associates were not acquitted until June 2005. Jammeh called the acquittal decision "a disaster to the maintenance of the rule of law," and the state appealed the court's ruling.

Jammeh won another five-year term in October 2001 elections with a margin of 53%, just enough to avoid a runoff with Darboe. Against expectations, the election itself was described as "relatively free and fair" by observers. The election used simple technology to minimize fraud: voters indicated their preference by dropping a marble into the drum of their chosen candidate (nominally in an enclosed and secret space), and the marble struck a bell inside the drum to ensure that multiple voting could be detected; bicycles were banned from the vicinity of polling stations to avoid confusion with their bells.

After his victory, Jammeh fired several top civil servants for alleged disloyalty. The dismissals came after an explicit campaign threat: "You are supposed to be loyal to the ruling party as civil servants and not opposition forces," Jammeh had warned. "Anybody who does not cherish my party will not be working with us. I am ready to sack all opposition sympathizers in my government." After heavy lobbying, many top officials were reinstated, but Jammeh had made clear that he intended to politicize the civil service.

Legislative elections in January 2002 resulted in triumph for Jammeh's ruling APRC after the UDP withdrew, claiming manipulation of the voter lists. Non-APRC candidates won only three seats in the legislature, now totaling 53 seats. With its overwhelming majority, the APRC made it even more difficult for future presidential candidates to compete against Jammeh. It amended Section 48 of the constitution to eliminate the need for runoff elections; henceforth a candidate could be elected by a mere plurality of votes.

The 2002 election split the UDP; the party's former propaganda secretary, Lamin Waa Juwara, openly called for Darboe's resignation, and was promptly expelled, whereupon he formed his own party—the National Democratic Action Movement (NDAM). Juwara and the NDAM became the regime's most vigorous opponents. Juwara was regularly arrested and detained by security forces, being sentenced to six months in jail in 2004 for "uttering seditious words" by calling for demonstrations to protest the continuing decline of the currency, worsening economic conditions, and endemic regime corruption.

The regime increasingly cracked down on independent media after 2002. In 2003, *The Independent* newspaper came under particular attack: the paper's staffers received death threats, its editor-in-chief was detained by the National Intelligence Agency following publication of an article critical of the president, and unidentified men set its premises ablaze. In May 2004, Jammeh took to the airwaves to excoriate journalists who failed to register with the National Media Commission (NMC). "We believe in giving each fool a long rope to hang themselves [sic]," he said. If they failed to register in the remaining three month grace period, he warned, "[t]hey will either register or stop writing or go to hell."

In December 2004, Deyda Hydara, the editor of *The Point* newspaper and one of the country's leading journalists, was murdered, shot three times in the head after he had sharply criticized newly passed press laws that made all press offenses, including libel, punishable by imprisonment. Media owners were required to purchase expensive new operating licenses and to put up their homes as collateral to pay the hefty new libel penalties in case they published such material. The investigation of Hydara's murder was quietly put to rest, with a 23-page intelligence report from the government calling Hydara was "an instigator who stirred up the anger of a number of people." In August 2009 six journalists were jailed for criticizing Jammeh, though they were later pardoned.

Opposition leaders sought to transcend their differences in January 2005. Juwara of the NDAM and Darboe of the UDP joined with leaders of the other small parties—the NRP, PDOIS, and the remnants of the old PPP—to sign a memorandum of understanding establishing an opposition alliance: the National Alliance for Democracy and Development (NADD). The agreement called for a common candidate to challenge Jammeh in the 2006 presidential election.

Despite this attempt at unity, the opposition remained divided and weak before the September 2006 presidential elections and 2007 legislative elections. State harassment of opposition exacerbated the weakness. President Jammeh was reelected for a third term in 2006 with 67% of the vote, while Ousainou Darboe secured 27% and Halifa Sallah finished third with 6%. The president's APRC won a similar landslide victory in the January 2007 legislative

President Adama Barrow

Gambia

elections: 47 seats to the UDP's four. One additional seat went to NADD, and a single independent took the final seat. Only 38% of voters participated.

While opposition parties are historically weak in the Gambia, the Jammeh regime has been shaken by several attempted coups. The latest was in March 2006 and was led by the armed forces chief of staff, Col. Ndure Kham. The coup attempt proved embarrassing for the regime, coming just months before Banjul would host the African Union summit. Jammeh promised that any attempt to overthrow his government would be "crushed without mercy," and even threatened to kill human rights workers in late 2009 because he suspected they were saboteurs. The 2006 coup attempt resulted in a death sentence in 2010 for several officials and army officers, including former Chief of Defence Lang Tombong Tamba. Those sentenced are currently having their appeal heard in court. The regime executed several prisoners in 2012, though the president subsequently announced a suspension of capital punishment after an international outcry. Jammeh continued to demonstrate his "iron-fist" style of rule when in January 2012 he sentenced former information minister Amadou Janneh to life in prison for distributing shirts with the slogan "An End to Dictatorship".

The presidential elections of 2011 held little prospect of an alternation in power. Jammeh won with a reported 72% of the vote, with Ousainou Darboe taking 17%. The results were widely criticized by international observers, including the West African regional body ECOWAS, as being neither free nor fair. The lead-up to the elections was marred by intimidation of voters and state control of the media. In the wake of the presidential election, leading opposition parties decided to boycott the March 2012 parliamentary elections. The result was a near sweep for Jammeh's APRC, which took 43 of 48 elected seats; four independent candidates and a single member of the NRP took the remainder.

In October 2013, Jammeh announced Gambia's withdrawal from the British Commonwealth and described it as a "neo-colonial institution".

CONTEMPORARY THEMES

The Gambia's economy is based on agriculture and largely dependent on groundnut export earnings, despite hopes for diversification. About 75% of the country's workforce is engaged in farming, though this contributes only about one-third of GDP. About 60% of all cultivated land is planted in groundnuts (peanuts) and their export provides nearly 85% of all export earnings. A once promising tourism industry has declined. More recently, Jammeh has expressed a desire to turn The Gambia into the "Silicon Valley" of West Africa by inviting information technology firms to establish a presence. President Jammeh has sounded similarly optimistic in announcing that oil reserves exist in offshore waters, but these are unproven after decades of fruitless exploration by multiple companies.

Corruption remains a serious problem, despite the government's anticorruption commission that examined the assets of active and retired ministers and senior military officials. The commission submitted a four-volume report detailing tax evasion and fraud among several senior government officials. Several cabinet ministers (and others) lost their jobs and forfeited assets to the state, but some of these were reappointed later after paying a fine, undermining any sense that the regime had cleaned house. There are also questions about the role of government officials in the transshipment of drugs through the country to international markets. President Jammeh, whose salary was about $100 per month when he overthrew the government in 1994, now owns a zoo (for which he imports expensive exotic animals from around the world), an expensive mansion in his home village, and reportedly a personal airline.

While the economy has grown at about 5% and 6% in recent years and inflation has been under control, public finances are messy. In part this reflects public investment: the Jammeh regime has created a national university, increased access to education (especially for girls), built new hospitals, paved hundreds of kilometers of roads and introduced national television. Still, the country's accumulated debt is substantial and debt servicing consumes about substantial portion of the national budget. To make up for revenue shortfalls, the government imposed massive tax increases in 2004, comparable to a year's salary for many Gambians, on the small business owners that people the urban economy.

Adama Barrow became the new president of The Gambia when he was sworn into office in Dakar, Senegal on January 19, 2017. Born in Mankamang Kunda, a village near Basse Santa Su-a major town located in the Fulladu East District, on the far eastern section of the River Gambia-he became the treasurer of the United Democratic Party (UDP), an opposition party. He became its leader in September 2016 after the previous leader was jailed, and subsequently the UDP candidate in the 2016 presidential election. Barrow won the 2016 presidential election with 43.34% of the vote, defeating long-time incumbent Yahya Jammeh. Barrow was forced to flee to neighboring Senegal when the incumbent President Yahya Jammeh reneged on his initial acceptance of the election results after being in office for more than two decades. Barrow was inaugurated into the office of the presidency at the Gambian embassy in Senegal on 19 January 2017. Thereafter, on January 21, West African troops led by Senegal forced Jammeh into exile in Equatorial Guinea.

Barrow returned to the Gambia on January 26, 2017. For security reasons he asked ECOWAS troops when had helped forced out Jammeh to stay on and stabilize the fragile security in the country after Jammeh's departure. The troops totaling about 2,500 were asked to stay for six months. On February 18, 2017, Barrow again took the oath of office a second time, this time within his own Sovereign state of The Gambia during an inaugural ceremony held at Independence Stadium in Bakau outside the capital Banjul.

Some reforms that have been introduced by Barrow include the following:

- The official long-form name of the Gambia would be reverted from 'The Islamic Republic of the Gambia' to 'The Republic of the Gambia'
- Ensure freedom of the press in the country
- The return to Commonwealth of Nations membership
- Release of all persons detained without trial under the repressive regime of Jammeh. A total of 171 prisoners held in Gambia's infamous 2 Mile Prison were set free
- End human rights violations and join the International Criminal Court
- Set up a truth and reconciliation commission to investigate possible crimes committed by his predecessor Yahya Jammeh who is currently exiled in Equatorial Guinea.
- Rebuild Gambia's institutions including the Supreme Court and the Judicial system

The road ahead for the Gambia and the Barrow Administration is a rough one. With Gambia's economy around one of the lowest in the world, the new administration needs effective planning in its strategy to deliver growth, security, and stability that is very much anticipated by the Gambian people. Major contemporary issues include proposals to overturn the anti-female circumcision law inaugurated in 2015 with opposition centered among women's rights groups as prosecution of Ousman Sonko, a former interior minister accused of major human rights abuses, proceed in Geneva, Switzerland. Harvesting and sale of rare rosewood timber in the country also continues despite an official ban. After months of heated debate

Gambia

and responding to domestic and international pressure, Gambian lawmakers voted in July 2024 to uphold a 2015 ban on female genital mutilation (FGM), rejecting a controversial bill seeking to overturn the law. The Women's (Amendment) Bill 2024, which had sought to decriminalize the practice of female circumcision, had passed a second reading in March with only five out of 53 lawmakers voting against it, raising concerns among rights groups that The Gambia would become the first country to reverse a ban on the practice. On the international front, the trial of Ousman Sonko, a former interior minister of The Gambia began in January 2024 in a federal court in Switzerland. One of a few cases to be prosecuted involving individuals accused of crimes against humanity committed under the leadership of the former Gambian dictator, Yahya Jammeh, Sonko could face life imprisonment.

The Republic of Ghana

Street scene in Ghana   Photo by Nay Lin

BASIC FACTS

Area: 238,533 sq. km. = approx. 92,098 sq. mi. (slightly smaller than Oregon)
Population: 33,846,114 (June 2023 est.)
Capital City: Accra
Government Type: Presidential Republic
Neighboring Countries: Côte D'Ivoire (west); Burkina Faso (northwest); Togo (east)
Official Language: English
Other Principal Languages: Twi, Akan, Ewe, Fante, Ga, Moshi-Dagomba
Ethnic Groups: Akan/Asante 45%, Moshi-Dagomba 15%, Ewe 12%, Ga 8%, other 10%
Principal Religions: Christian 71.2%, Islam 17.6%, Traditional 5.2%, none 6.1%, other 0.7%
Former Colonial Status: British Colony (1821–1957)
Independence Date: March 6, 1957
GDP Per Capita (IMF 2022 est.): $2,024 (nominal), $6,974 (PPP)
Gini Index: 43.5 (World Bank 2016)
Currency: Cedi; 1 USD = 11.77 cedis (Apr. 2022)
Inflation Rate: 9.97% (2022 est.)
Chief Commercial Products: Gold, cocoa, timber, tuna, bauxite, aluminum, manganese ore, and diamonds

Foreign Direct Investments (FDI) net inflows: 3,363,389,444
Literacy Rate: 79% (CIA 2022)
Life Expectancy: 69.7 years (CIA 2022 est.)
Head of State: President Nana Addo Dankwa Akufo-Addo (since January 7, 2017)
Head of Government: President Nana Addo Dankwa Akufo-Addo (since January 7, 2017)

LAND AND PEOPLE

Ghana is situated in the center of Africa's Gulf of Guinea coast, with a 334-mile-long coastline that includes many lagoons and some mangrove growth. In the eastern inland coastal area, the terrain consists of scrub and grassland and in the inland western coast there is an area of rainforest supporting dense growths of tall. Some 175 miles north from the ocean, dense vegetation gives way to grassland areas with less rainfall and shorter, more sparsely distributed trees. The harmattan,

Ghana

a dry wind from the Sahara, blows from November to April. Temperatures in the grassland region are high and in the extreme North, rainfall is very scarce and there has been significant desertification in recent years. There are no true mountains in Ghana—the highest elevation is 2,900 feet at a point in the southeast.

Traditional kingdoms continue to flourish in Ghana, and their rulers exercise influence inside and outside the country. The Asantahene, paramount chief of the Asante Federation, occupies the Golden Stool of the Asante. Nana Kwaku Duah, a London-trained accountant and business executive, assumed the throne in 1999 at the age of 48, and took the name Osei Tutu II, after the first Asante king. His coronation, an "enstoolment" among the Asante, took place on the Golden Stool, which is believed to have descended from Heaven in a cloud of white dust, landing on the lap of Osei Tutu I. Asantes believe the stool contains the soul of the Asante nation.

Ghana is home to proud artistic traditions and Highlife music. In literature, the country gave birth to prominent writers such as Ayi Kwei Armah, whose novel *The Beautyful Ones Are Not Yet Born* captured the pathologies and disillusionment of the Ghana's post-independence decline. Ghanaians have also developed unique forms of fabric, including famous *kente* cloth and imprinted fabrics using symbols known as *adinkra*; these art forms were traditionally used in clothing for royalty, and are still prominent in Ghanaian clothing today. In more eclectic folk art, the Accra suburb of Teshi has become an attraction point for its specialization in creative coffins. The "Black Stars," the national football (soccer) team, had resounding success at the World Cup finals in 2006 and advanced even farther in 2010, reaching the quarterfinals and coming one missed penalty kick away from being the first African team ever to reach the semifinals.

The country is rich in historical sites of interest. As Ghana was the origin of much of the transatlantic slave trade, the country is a leading destination for tourists from the Americas who seek to explore their African heritage. The castles at Elmina and Cape Coast are solemn reminders of the historical injustices during the slave trade.

HISTORY TO PRESENT DAY

For early history, see *Historical Background* and *The Colonial Period: The British*.

Independence and the Kwame Nkrumah Years (1957–1966)

The independence of Ghana in 1957 was an inspirational event that led many of the continent's other colonies to clamor for independence. The plea for independence was led by Kwame Nkrumah, a nationalist and pan-Africanist leader who went on to be Ghana's first head of state.

Nkrumah modeled his government on the communist world and his Convention People's Party (CPP) became the instrument of all political thought. Nkrumah acquired the power to jail people for ten years without trial, and the press was rigidly censored. Establishing close ties with China and the Soviet Union, Nkrumah regularly accused the Western nations of "neo-colonialism" and followed a socialist development model, attempting to use the state to direct and fund rapid industrialization.

The country's economic prospects were excellent in 1957: it was rich by African standards, had a relatively full treasury, a good education system, an efficient civil service, and was the world's leading cocoa exporter. Yet it declined catastrophically after independence while Asian countries (and even neighboring Côte d'Ivoire for a time) plowed ahead, and Ghana became one of Africa's greatest economic disappointments for many years. To fund investment, the state depleted the accumulated surpluses of the Cocoa Marketing Board, a government institution that took most of the profits from the trade in cocoa beans. Most state enterprises were poorly managed and lost money and the state's budget went into deficit to such a degree that cocoa surpluses could not cover the budgets, especially after cocoa prices slipped precipitously on world markets. Nkrumah's government borrowed large sums of money from abroad, and squandered the funds on lavish prestige projects of little productive value. Agricultural development was largely ignored, and by 1966, Ghana was in economic meltdown. Nkrumah left a large debt burden to subsequent governments and a legacy of mismanagement and corruption.

Army officers seized power early in 1966, deposing Nkrumah and forming the National Liberation Council. The new regime released almost 1,200 prisoners of the CPP from jail, but conversely arrested Nkrumah's sympathizers and expelled Communist technical and political personnel. Nkrumah went into exile in Guinea, where his friend, Sékou Touré, bestowed on him the honor of titular head of state, and where he died in 1972.

Years of Instability (1966–1979)

Following the Nkrumah regime, Ghana endured a string of military coups punctuated by sporadic attempts at civilian rule. The first military regime was the National Liberation Council, first headed by Gen. Joseph Ankrah, which sought to remove Nkrumah's leftist policies and personnel from Ghana's political scene. The military leadership tried to return the country to civilian rule three years later, and a brief civilian interlude known as the Second Republic occurred between 1969 and 1972. Kofi Busia and his Progress Party won the 1969 election and Busia became the head of government as Prime Minister, with independence leader Edward Akufo-Addo as ceremonial president.

The Busia government put its stamp on the economy with two highly controversial decisions. In 1969, it deported several hundred thousand Nigerian immigrants, most of whom were traders and important actors in Ghana's economy, on the pretext of helping Ghanaians. Later, Busia devalued the currency dramatically. This devaluation was intended promote domestic production and make exports such as cocoa more competitive, but it also rendered imports more expensive. This raised the cost of living for many Ghanaians, including army soldiers, whose discontent contributed to another coup in 1972.

Colonel Ignatius Acheampong ruled from 1972 to 1978 at the head of a military body known as the National Redemption Council. In these years, the regime undertook a number of efforts at promoting economic "self-reliance," but these too floundered and the regime became known primarily for an encrustation of corruption in the political system. Acheampong was then deposed by another military leader, Lt. Gen. Fred Akuffo, in 1978. Each of the post-Nkrumah regimes failed to solve the problems left by their respective predecessors and inflation, corruption, unemployment, and debt prevented economic recovery through most of the 1970s.

The Rawlings Regimes (1979–2000)

In 1979, Flight Lt. Jerry Rawlings, with a group of young officers, took over the government in yet another military coup. Rawlings established the Armed Forces Revolutionary Council (AFRC) and engaged in what he termed a "housecleaning." Most startling was the rapid decision to execute the two previous heads of state—Acheampong and Akuffo—among other prominent leaders found guilty of corruption. The AFRC also seized assets from corrupt officials and returned them to state coffers.

Given the bloody start to his rule, Rawlings and the AFRC surprised many when they promptly oversaw elections for a new civilian government as promised, just months after seizing power. Dr. Hilla Limann was elected president (of Ghana's Third Republic) in September 1979 as the head of the People's National Party, but the newly elected government lasted only until New Year's Eve, 1981, when Lt. Rawlings once again deposed the

Ghana

Former President John Agyekum Kufuor

elected chief executive, citing economic mismanagement. Rawlings suspended the constitution, abolished Ghana's political parties, and created a new governing body known as the Provisional National Defence Council (PNDC).

The new Rawlings PNDC government adopted radical rhetoric and called upon the citizens to become actively involved in "the decision-making process." Rawlings was himself an admirer of Libya's Col. Qadhafi at the time, and the regime installed Libyan-style "People's Defense Committees" and "Committees for the Defense of the Revolution" in city neighborhoods, rural villages, and industrial plants. The stated purpose of these committees was to act as watchdogs against corruption.

As the economic decline continued, Rawlings adopted conservative policies to try and cause a change; he rejected leftist approaches and established an Economic Recovery Program with the guidance of the IMF and the World Bank in 1983. The government abolished subsidies and price controls, devalued the currency, restored fiscal discipline, improved tax collection, and generated a budget surplus by 1986. In 1986, Rawlings began a second phase of the recovery program with deeper structural adjustments: he trimmed the bloated and costly bureaucracy by firing tens of thousands of civil servants, liberalized foreign exchange policy, overhauled the investment code to encourage foreign investment, privatized state enterprises, and adopted a less radical rhetorical style.

Rawlings also liberalized in the political arena, allowing a multiparty system to develop in the early 1990s. Before elections scheduled for November 1992, he resigned from the air force (as required by new election laws) and ran for president as a civilian. Rawlings won with a bit under 60% of the vote, with the second-place finisher, Adu Boahen of the New Patriotic Party (NPP), gaining 30%. Rawlings thus became the first African head of state to make the conversion from military ruler to democratic civilian leader and the new regime that took effect at the beginning of 1993 came to be known as the Fourth Republic. While the return to democracy was an achievement, the economic consequences of the transition were troubling: Rawlings had granted large raises to public employees to gain their electoral support, and the strategy depleted five years' worth of surpluses, increased inflation and debt, and weakened the currency still more.

Ethnic tension in the north was heightened in 1994 when 1,000 were killed and over 150,000 displaced during clashes over land rights between the Kokomba and the Nanumba. Although a peace agreement is signed, a government curfew was imposed in 1995 following renewed ethnic violence and 100 more deaths.

Despite ethnic tensions and economic difficulties, Rawlings and his National Democratic Council (NDC) won another mandate in 1996. Rawlings retained the presidency with 57.4 % of the vote. His nearest rival was John Kufuor of the NPP, who won a respectable 39.6%. In legislative elections the NDC won an absolute parliamentary majority with 133 of 200 seats, while the NPP consolidated its role as the lead opposition party with 60 seats. Yet by 2000, the country's economic woes had worsened. Prices of major exports, such as gold and cocoa, declined and petroleum prices soared; the declining value of exports and increasing costs of imports put more pressure on public accounts. Inflation soared to 60% and interest rates to nearly 50%. Unemployment hovered around 50% while the value of Ghana's currency, the cedi, had collapsed from 2.75/dollar In 1981 to 6,800/dollar in 2000. Per capita income of $410 in 1981 had dropped to $360 by 2000. As a consequence, the 2000 democratic election led to a victory for the NPP over the NDC.

The NPP: The John Kufuor Administrations (2000–2008)

The 2000 elections were a momentous achievement for democracy in Ghana. Constitutionally prohibited from seeking a third term, Rawlings handpicked his vice president, John Evans Atta-Mills, to be his successor as NDC candidate. The NPP again nominated John Kufuor, an Oxford-trained lawyer, businessman and prominent member of the influential Asante tribe. Though marred by some violence, the vote count was generally fair and the NPP won 100 of the 200 parliamentary seats. Its presidential candidate, Kufuor, nearly won a first ballot victory, taking a lead of 48.44% to John Atta-Mills' 44.8%. In the runoff, all five minor candidates threw their support to Kufuor, who won with an impressive 57%. When Atta-Mills telephoned his concession speech, Ghanaians could boast that their country hadIly achievId a rarity in Africa: the democratic transfer of power.

The trInsition had its problems and tensions, as Kufuor had to deal with the legacy of former President Rawlings. A public holiday celebrating Rawling's military coup was cancelled in an attempt to rally support around the Kufuor administration. Rawlings called for "positive defiance" and even refused to participate in Ghana's celebration of its 50 years of independence in 2007, instead issuing a message to Ghanaians, criticizing the government for, among other things, "pervasive corruption at all levels, missed opportunities for genuine progress, nepotism, tribalism and known cases of political torture and killings."

Ghana's National Reconciliation Council (NRC) submitted a 2004 report on human rights abuses during "periods of unconstitutional rule." Much like its South African model, the commission's mandate was to allow citizens (especially victims) hear and discover the truth about past abuses; it also sought to help abusers come to tI the experience and obtain forgiveness. The Rawlings years of "unauthorized" rule (1979; 1981–1993) featured prominently in the hearings and former President Rawlings testified at the commission during the investigation.

President Kufuor's style was more mild-mannered than that of Rawlings. He marked the end of his first year in office by holding an unprecedented public question-and-answer session. Dubbed the "people's assembly," the event featured Kufuor and his entire cabinet hearing complaints and answering questions posed bIcapacity audience, which filled Accra's international conference center. Such assemblies proved commonplace throughout Kufuor's leadership as the government focusedIrepairing the economy, which neceIed some political risks, including doubling fuel prices.

The December 2004 eleItions were a reprise of the matchup in 2000 of the NPP's Kufuor and John Atta-Mills of the NDC. With strong world prices for cocoa and gold pushing Ghana's economic growth to over 5% a year and with substantial debt reduction from the World Bank and major Western donors, the economy basics favored the incumbent. President Kufuor won a solid 52.75% against John Atta-Mills, who won a respectable 44.32% of the vote; an impressive 83.2% of eligible voters turned out. Observers agreed the election was free and fair, an important consolidation of democracy for the country. Indeed, Imentary elections saw many MPs, including ministers, lose

Ghana

their seats. Kufuor's NPP garnered 129 seats in the 230-member house, while Atta Mills' NDC took 88; the remaining seIre distributed among smaller parties, including the once dominant CPP, which won just four seats.

The NDC: The Atta-Mills and Mahama Administrations (2008–2016)

In 2008, Ghanaians witnessed the secoleful democratic transition of power to the opposition, as John Evans Atta-Mills of the NDC won the presidential election in his third attempt. Kufuor, prevented by term limits from running after two terms as president, passed on the NPP candidacy to Nana Akufo-Addo. Akufo-Addo actually took the lead in the first round and nearly won, with just over 49% of the vote to 48% for Atta-Mills. In the second-round runoff between the two men, however, most of the remaining votes broke for Atta-Mills, who ended with 50.23% to 49.77% for Akufo-Addo. Initial tensions after the cliffhanger vote quickly dissipated as Akufo-Addo accepted the result and graciously agreed to attend Atta-Mills' inauguration. The election was deemed open and fair, reinforcing Ghana's reputation as one of the freest countries on the continent.

In 2011, Atta-Mills was chosen as the NDC's candidate to run as the incumbent in the December 2012 presidential election, but the president passed away of natural causes in July 2012. There had been some tension in the months prior to Mills' death—with Akufo-Addo engaging in more overt I rhetoric and other less prominent public figures (including one member of parliament) calling for violence—but Ghana's reputation for free, fair, and peaceful transitions of power was retained as Vice President John Mahama became interim president until electiIns were held on schedule in December.

The December 2012 elections saw interim president John MIof the NDC face the NPP's Nana Akufo-Addo. The result was another relatively close outcome: Mahama was elected with just under 51% of the vote, and Akufo-Addo took about 48%. The NDC also took a majority of the electoral districts for the legislature and ended up with 148 out of 275 seats. This happened despite the NDC failing to win a majority of the overall vote. The NPP actually outpolled the NDC by a small amount (reaching 47.5% of legislative votes to 46.4% for the NDC), but its votes came overwhelmingly from very strong tallies its heartland in central Ghana (where it took well over 80% or more of the vote in many constituencies), and it thus won only 123 seats total. Nana Akufo-Addo, two-time presidential candidate of the NPP, has vowed to run for president again in the 2016 elections.

Akufo-Addo first ran for President in 2008 and again in 2012, both times as the candidate of the New Patriotic Party (NPP) but was defeated on both occasions by NDC candidates: John Atta Mills in 2008 and John Dramani Mahama in 2012. In 2016 Nana Akufo-Addo, being three time lucky, defeated the incumbent President John Mahama in the first round of the elections by receiving 53.85% of the votes cast.

Nana Akufo-Addo is not a stranger to Ghanaian politics. His father, Edward Akufo-Addo, became the President of Ghana from August 1970 to January of 1972 with Dr. Kofi Abrefa Busia as Prime Minister. Nana Akufo-Addo became the first Attorney General and Minister for Justice in the Kufuor era administration. He was later moved to the Ministry of Foreign Affairs and New Partnership for Africa's Development (NEPAD). Since the end of the Kufuor Administration, Nana assumed leading role in the New Patriotic Party (NPP) Culminating in his election as the Party's flagbearer and president.

During the 2016 election campaign, Nana Akufo-Addo highlighted ten (10Icy priorities that he will pursue when elected president. These include managing the economy competently to stimulate growth, energy sufficiency and affordability, industrial production- by developing the entire agrobusiness value chain to create jobs and increase income, quality and well-funded health and education for all, reducing and/or eliminating corruption, create real job opportunities with good pay for the youth, rapid development of infrastructure at value for money, deepening financial and banking sectors to ensure inclusiveness, and the completion of the long-delayed national ID system. Nana Addo has started making good on his campaign promises with legislations targeting the roll-out of his promises. Currently, Ghanaians are confident about this early stage of his administration. It is just a matter of time that we would be able to assess the actual impact of his policy priorities on the economic and social life of the Ghanaian people.

Nana Addo Dankwa Akufo-Addo was inaugurated into office as the 5th President of the Fourth Republic of Ghana on 7 January 2017.

CONTEMPORARY THEMES

Ghana's dramatically economic position is much improved, with increased growth, reduced inflation, lower interest rates and government borrowing, and a stabilized currency. The achievements came through tough political choices that imposed austerity and caused hardship, such as increased utility rates and school fees and the elimination of gasoline subsidies. Growth has been at or above 5%

Akufo-Addo

since the mid-2000s, while the number of Ghanaians in poverty has declined to under one-third from 40% in 2000. Along with an improved investment climate, better policy, and high international prices for gold, Ghana has benefited from debt relief; its windfall under the Heavily Indebted Poor Countries (HIPC) initiative and decisions by the G-8 in the 2000s, was estimated at $4.1 billion, about 80% of the country's external debt. In 2006, Chinese Premier Wen Jiabao committed $66 million to fund development projects in Ghana, securing China's role in the growing and resource-rich economy. The IMF provided a $600 million loan to Ghana in 2009. In May 2013, Ghana scrapped costly fuel subsides to help restore fiscal stability after overshooting its 2012 budget by nearly 100 percent. Recently, there has been much discussion of enabling the IMF to bail out Ghana. Keeping this in mind, President Mahama has been taking the steps to improve the economy by endorsing a National Economic Forum.

Cocoa remains one of Ghana's largest industries, along with gold mining and timber. Nearly three million acres are planted in cocoa, worked by 700,000 farmers. Most of the holdings are small, which contributes to Ghanaian cocoa's reputation for high quality, as the smallholder takes the time to sort bad nuts from the cocoa and more carefully tends the fermentation and drying process than do large-scale farmers.

Gold is probably the country's biggest foreign exchange earner, thanks in part to a liberalized mining code designed to encourage foreign investment. Ghana is Africa's second largest gold producer after South Africa, and the income represents about 45% of the country's foreign exchange revenues. The first six companies receiving mining licenses (for gold

Ghana

and bauxite) committed themselves to invest a total of over $2 billion, though some are controversial. A coalition of local and international NGOs vigorously opposed some developments, especially Newmont Mining's Ahafo project; the company claimed the $470 million project would generate $300 million to $700 million in revenues for Ghana, while opponents argued it would displace more than 9,000 people subsistence farmers, and employ "significantly less stringent human health or environmental standards" than used in the United States. Of particular concern is contamination of drinking water from arsenic used in the mining process; the government recently fined Newmont, the world's second largest gold mining firm, $4.9 million over a cyanide spill.

In 2007, oil reserves, an estimated 3 billion barrels, were discovered offshore of Ghana, sparking international interest and significant investment. Offshore oil production began in 2010 and has contributed to Ghana's very rapid growth of an estimated 14% in 2012. The UK-based Tullow Oil plans to spend at least $4 billion to develop the underwater oil fields. If reserves are as estimated, exploration will bring billions to the country in investment, setting it up to be an "African Tiger" according to former President Kufuor.

The Ghanaian economy is linked to the international economy through the Ghana diaspora although emigration of professionals is a mixed blessing. On the one hand, remittances and money transfers from Ghanaians abroad have skyrocketed, having reached several billion dollars per year. On the other hand, the Ghanaian government is seeking new arrangements with wealthy countries regarding migrants; from Ghana's perspective, emigration of professionals (nurses, e.g.) has meant that Ghana is providing expert training only to see its people contribute to primarily to economies elsewhere once they have finished their education. This brain drain phenomenon will continue until Ghana is able to provide adequate jobs within its own borders for highly qualified professionals.

While credited with many achievements, Ghana continues to suffer many of the afflictions common in Africa. The prevalence rate of HIV/AIDS is only about 2% of the adult population, which is low by African standards, but still amounts to about a quarter of a million Ghanaians living with the virus. Estimated life expectancy saw a minor decline from over 59 years in the 1990s to just under 57 years in 2009, but there has been a major increase, to roughly 64 years as of 2011. Controversial actions by the government include passage by the parliament of an anti-LGBTQ law punishing advocates of rights for gays and lesbians with prison time. Also occurring are increased attacks against independent journalists prior to the 2024 general elections despite government efforts at enhanced protection. Suffering from significant declines in cocoa bean production along with neighboring Cote d'voire, Ghana is also being urged to take on more asylum seekers by the European Union while conflicts continue over the impact of excessive fishing off its shores by local artisanal craft and large foreign trawlers—especially from China.

Two Ghanaian Children

Photo by Nay Lin

Ghana

Sworn in for a second term as president in January 2025, John Mahama won 56 percent of the vote in the nation's presidential election on December 9, defeating ruling party candidate and Vice President Mahamudu Bawumia, who secured 41 percent. Taking over from outgoing President Nana Akufo-Addo, who served two terms in power, the new president from the National Democratic Congress (NDC) party rode to power on concerns about how to tackle a worsening economic crisis spurred on by major problems in the cacao industry. Voters also cast ballots to elect the country's next parliament, with about 18.8 million people registered to vote in a nation of 34 million. Other problems include the lucrative gold mining industry, which suffers from insufficient water supplies stemming from extreme contamination of main rivers from small-scale mining activities with protests in the capital city of Accra warning against a "looming environmental catastrophe" with some leaders arrested and imprisoned for weeks on charges of illegal assembly. While the former ruling New Patriotic Party (NPP) was voted out, environmental activists have little faith in the new president, John Mahama, to keep the mounting pollution of Ghana's rivers and soil in check.

FUTURE CONSIDERATIONS

Today, far from being a basket case, Ghana is one of Africa's success stories. Ghana's political stability is the envy of many neighboring countries, and with the transitions from the NDC to NPP and back again, Ghanaians take pride in the fact that democracy has slowly consolidated over the past decade. Ghanaians enjoy an increasingly robust democracy, with an improving rule of law and rather secure civil liberties.

Ghana remains a relatively low-income country, like most in the region, but the direction of change is positive and rapid growth has resulted in the country being counted among the ranks of middle-income nations by some measures. The discovery of oil off Ghanaian shores is promising, though caution and prudence is needed. Ghana has begun pumping oil and is planning on over a billion dollars in state profits annually for the next twenty years, in addition to further proceeds from natural gas. In an effort to avoid the tragic fate of Nigeria, which has seen its oil revenues squandered with corruption, Ghana's government is seeking expertise on extraction and savings from countries such as Norway (which has established a best practice in managing resource wealth by carefully setting aside its own oil proceeds in a "rainy day" fund totaling several hundred billion dollars. A proposed bill will split the revenue between Ghana's national budget (for current use) and two funds that are to be used only when the oil price drops or the oil dries up. Further development opportunities exist in mining and minerals, timber, fishing, and tourism.

Due to its relatively strong recent record in governance, the country is regularly included in lists of "model" African countries that perform well on economic and political criteria. *The Economist* magazine called the 2008 election "a fine example for the rest of Africa," and the 2012 election followed suit. While there were some small concerns about heated rhetoric in 2012, these seemed to subside as the election approached, and Nana Akufo-Addo again conceded a narrow defeat. Any efforts to foment social divisiveness have generally been condemned by the press and members of civil society. After conducting another successful and peaceful democratic election in 2012, and with oil exports taking off and investment booming, Ghana's trajectory is likely to continue to be far preferable to many of its African neighbors.

The Republic of Guinea

Guinean family outside traditional thatch-roofed home

BASIC FACTS

Area: 245,857 sq. km. = 95,000 sq. mi. (about the size of Oregon)
Population: 13,607,249 (June 2023 est.)
Capital city: Conakry
Government Type: Presidential Republic
Neighboring Countries: Guinea-Bissau (west); Senegal, Mali (north); Ivory Coast (east); Liberia, Sierra Leone (southeast)
Official Language: French
Other Principal Languages: Baga, Dan, Fuuta Jalon, Kissi, Malinké, Maninka, Mano, and Susu
Ethnic Groups: Peuhl 40%, Malinké 30%, Soussou 20%, smaller tribes 10%
Principal Religions: Muslim 85%, Christian 8%, indigenous beliefs 7%
Former Colonial Status: French Colony (1894–1958)
Independence Date: October 2, 1958
GDP Per Capita (IMF 2023 est.): $1,549 (nominal) $3,218 (PPP)
Currency: Guinea franc, $US1 = 8,639 Guinian francs (June 2023)
Gini Index: 33.7 (World Bank 2012)
Inflation Rate: 12.7% (2022 est.)
Chief Commercial Products: Bauxite, alumina, diamonds, gold, coffee, fish, and agricultural products
Foreign Direct Investments (FDI) net inflows: 566,000,000
Literacy Rate: 45.3% (CIA 2021)
Life Expectancy: 64.27 years (CIA 2023 est.)
Head of State: Col. Mamady Doumbouya (since October 1, 2021)
Head of Government: Prime Minister Bernard Gomou (since August 20, 2022)

LAND AND PEOPLE

Guinea has an irregular, but level, coastline on the North Atlantic Ocean. Grassy plains, interspersed with trees, are found in the north coastal region and plains and plateaus are found farther inland. The Fouta Djallon Mountains rise to heights of 6,000 feet in central Guinea and are the source of three large West African rivers: the Niger, the Gambia and the Senegal. In the northeast, the land slowly descends to flat grassland, which has greater variation in temperatures than the more humid coastal area. Vegetation grows rapidly in the northeast beginning in March and continuing through the rainy season, which lasts until November. Southeastern Guinea contains somewhat higher dense forests with a pattern of rain similar to that of the plains.

There are more than a dozen distinct ethnic groups within the country, the great majority of which profess Islam as religion. Despite the efforts of the former ruling party, traditional values have survived. Female genital cutting (FGC) is still practiced in Guinea, although it was officially banned in 1984 and is on the decline. Prior to about 2000, the vast majority of Guinean women were circumcised, but the practice has since declined to under 20% of young girls.

HISTORY TO PRESENT DAY

For early history, see *Historical Background* and *The Colonial Period: The French*.

In the 1958 constitution of the French Fifth Republic, General Charles De Gaulle gave France's colonies the choice of full independence or autonomy within the French Community. Under the leadership of the young trade unionist, Ahmed Sékou Touré, Guinea became the only French colony to opt for full independence, with a referendum resulting in an overwhelming 95% of Guineans voting "No" to continued French power. Guinea was proclaimed a nation on October 2, 1958, and Ahmed Sékou Touré became the country's first president.

Sékou Touré (1958–1984)

Sékou Touré created a single-party dictatorship modeled on Marxism-Leninism, declaring the Democratic Party of Guinea (PDG) the official political force in the country. Sékou Touré was the DPG's Secretary-General and membership in the party may have reached as many as 2 million people, organized into thousands of local committees. Presidential elections in 1968, 1974, and 1982 were mere formalities, with Touré running unopposed. The DPG was the only eligible party in legislative elections, asserting that the party expressed the will of the people. Opposition was considered tantamount to treason, and critics suffered grievously. Touré especially singled out the Peul (or Fulani) ethnic group for persecution, and the brutality of Touré's repression increased,

Guinea

reaching a peak in October 1971 when thousands were killed.

The economic legacy of the Touré regime was one of decline and failure. State enterprises created bloated bureaucracies whose salaries devoured profits from bauxite (the raw material for aluminum). With little money invested productively, growth and development languished, while smuggling and the clandestine economy flourished. As the government lost tax revenues, Guinea's infrastructure deteriorated.

The Touré regime became emblematic of Africa's tragedies of the 1970s and 1980s: dictatorial excess, economic mismanagement and corruption, and growing overtones of ethnic and social division. The case of Guinea was especially upsetting to many observers because of the early hope and optimism after its 1958 declaration of independence. After Touré's death in 1984, Prime Minister Louis Lansana Beavogui, immediately took control of the government, but a group of young military officers, disgusted with what they called a "bloody and ruthless dictatorship," took over the country on April 3, 1984. A Military Committee for National Recovery (CMRN) was established and immediately began to release some political prisoners from Conakry's notorious Camp Boiro, where as many as 50,000 people were assassinated or "disappeared."

Lansana Conté (1984–2008)

The new military government was initially led by Col. Lansana Conté as President and Col. Diarra Traoré as prime minister, but rivalry soon split the two leaders. Conté demoted Traoré in December 1984, and Traoré led an attempted coup in July 1985 while Conté was at a conference out of the country. The president returned to Guinea, restored control with relative ease, and ordered the execution of dozens of people involved, including Traoré. The coup attempt and crackdown smacked of worsening ethnic tension, as Traoré and most of those killed were of the Malinké ethnic group while Conté was of the Soussou minority.

Guinea embarked on a more liberal economic course under Conté, and while the economy never thrived, it stopped its decline, managing modest growth averaging a couple of percent a year, just about enough to keep pace with population growth, and even saw some sporadic foreign investment. France, which had given Touré the cold shoulder after Guinea opted for independence and socialism, agreed to lend development money, and the International Monetary Fund granted a line of credit to rebuild the economy. Under the new economic scheme, the government cut the bloated bureaucracy and privatized government-owned enterprises that were products of Touré's socialism.

The CMRN regime altered the economic model but continued the human rights abuses of the earlier government. Amnesty International described "arbitrary arrests, torture, [and] deaths in detention" as common in Guinea under Conté. Military trials in 1986–87 of about 200 officials of the former Touré regime resulted in 60 death sentences, 21 of them *in absentia*. The purpose of the trials was to instill fear, particularly in urban areas, where CMRN government popularity had plunged due to desperate economic conditions.

The CMRN bowed to the winds of change following the collapse of communism and presided over a referendum that approved a new multiparty constitution in late 1990, but political changes were mostly superficial. President Conté formed the Party of Unity and Progress (PUP) and won a presidential election in December 1993 that was seen as neither free nor fair. The opposition, which was split among several candidates, called it an "electoral masquerade."

The army proved a challenge for Conté, who barely survived a military mutiny in 1996 when army units rebelled, demanding higher pay. The mutineers burned down the presidential palace, looted shops and led the president off to an army base. Fifty people were killed in the incident and President Conté was forced to sign a five-point accord with the mutineers before being returned to power. The president held trials in early 1998 against soldiers from outside the president's Soussou ethnic group. The government handed down sentences of 20 years hard labor to many of the convicted, and it was later revealed that some of the confessions were extracted by torture. President Conté's then conducted an ethnic purge

Capt. Moussa Dadis Camara

of the army, removing many Malinké officers and soldiers. Conté's Soussou ethnic group made up only 15% to 20% of the population but dominated the PUP and the machinery of repression: the Ministry of the Interior, police, and security forces.

Presidential elections in December 1998 demonstrated the sharpness of ethnic division as Conté faced four opponents, three of whom concluded an electoral alliance aimed at stopping the president from winning on the first ballot. The Coordination of Democratic Opposition (CODEM) was led by Mamadou Ba (a Peul), Alpha Condé (a Malinké), and Jean-Marie Doré of a smaller ethnic group. If the alliance could force the president into a second ballot, all agreed to support his opponent in the runoff. However, in dubious balloting, the Ministry of Interior awarded Conté a first-round victory with 56.12% while Ba won a quarter of the vote and Alpha Condé slightly less than 17%.

Two days after his victory, President Conté had Alpha Condé arrested—despite his status as a member of parliament—and charged with state security offenses. Riots broke out in the principal Malinké communities and several people were killed. In Conakry, women bared their breasts—a traditional sign of mourning—in protest and were arrested for assaulting public modesty. Fourteen leading members of the Malinké opposition, including members of parliament, were arrested, charged with threatening public order, found guilty and jailed. Similar treatment of Malinké leadership within the army soon followed, with a major purge occurring in March 1999 in which armed forces Chief of Staff Col. Oumar Soumah and 30 other officers were fired for association with the 1996 army mutiny. Guinea's internal conflict began to spread to neighboring Sierra Leone, where RUF (Revolutionary United Front) fighters trained by some 1996 mutineers launched deadly border raids on several northern Guinean towns.

Amid the rising tension and violence, the regime concluded its trial of Alpha Condé in September 2000, in which the State Security Court convicted Condé of sedition and sentenced him to five years in prison. Kept in virtual isolation and denied audience with his lawyers and family members, Condé was given little opportunity to defend himself. The Condé trial became a focal point of regime criticism nationally and internationally, as President Wade of Senegal offered asylum and encouraged his release. Under pressure, Conté ultimately granted Condé a presidential pardon in May 2001.

President Conté and the PUP furthered their dominance in the early 2000s and in November 2001 the government organized a referendum to amend the constitution

Guinea

The Guinean coastline ©Photographie Michel Hasson

to permit President Conté a third term. Official results indicated 87% of registered voters voted, with 98% in favor, but the opposition, which had boycotted the referendum, claimed that less than 20% of registered voters actually took part. President Conté, reportedly extremely ill from diabetes and heart problems, ran for a third term in December 2003. All major opposition parties boycotted the elections and Conté claimed 95% of the total vote. In the meantime, long-postponed parliamentary elections were held in June 2002, and a boycott among leading opposition forces resulted in a massive victory for Conté's PUP, which won 90 of 114 seats.

Even before the 2003 elections, signs of restiveness emerged within the army, as dozens of junior army officers and soldiers had been arrested in a series of swoops on army barracks and private homes throughout the country. In November 2005, Conté furthered his purge of the army by dismissing more than 1,800 officers over the age of 60, many of them ethnic Peuls, leaving the security apparatus firmly in the hands of the president's Soussou confreres.

Popular anger increased with spiraling inflation, the Conté government's failures in providing basic public services such as electricity and running water, and endemic corruption. By 2006, Guinea was ranked the second-most corrupt country in the world by Transparency International. Militant action by students and workers continued throughout 2006. In December, when President Conté personally visited the local jail to free two friends and collaborators facing trial for embezzlement of public funds, Guinea's two most powerful labor federations took to the streets to protest corruption and judicial interference. In early January 2007 Guinea's unions pushed their demands further, successfully calling for an unlimited general strike and civil disobedience. Fourteen of the country's political parties supported the call, including the two leading opposition parties: Alpha Condé's Rally of the Guinean People (RPG) and Mamadou Ba's Union for Progress and Renewal (UPR). Shops, offices and markets closed, and public transport shut down starting January 10th.

Eight days into the 2007 strike, protesters upped the ante, demanding the National Assembly declare the presidency vacant because Conté was "physically weakened," "visibly forgetful," and in a "degraded state of health" and therefore unable to carry out the duties of his office. Still, the government repressed the protests violently and arrested their leadership. On January 22, security forces killed 20 protesters and wounded 150 more. Two days later, a weakened president agreed to cede some powers to a consensus prime minister; unions agreed the concessions were sufficient to end the strike, which had resulted in the deaths 59 Guineans over 18 days.

However, respite was brief, and when Conté appointed Eugène Camara (one of his strongest loyalists) as prime minister in February 2007, unionists relaunched the general strike, and demanded Conté's resignation. The government responded by declaring a state of emergency, with the president noting that "Orders have been given to the heads of the armed forces to take all necessary measures to re-establish public order." In the first day of the emergency, at least 11 more Guineans were killed, including a soldier lynched by protesters. On February 26, President Conté announced the appointment of Lansana Kouyaté as Prime Minister. Kouyaté, a former diplomat and UN under-secretary general, was one of five names supplied by unions and opposition parties as acceptable. With Kouyaté's appointment, Guinea's second major general strike in less than two months ended with a casualty total of 137 deaths and another 1,700 wounded. Lansana Conté survived the unrest, barely, by maintaining the loyalty of the army. In May 2008, President Conté sacked Kouyaté and appointed Ahmed Tidiane Souaré to the post, but by that time the opposition had grown disenchanted with Kouyaté for his failure to include opposition members in the cabinet or in dialogue and his firing caused little unrest.

Transition and Elections

Lansana Conté died on December 22, 2008, having battled illness for years. Following his death, the military organized a new coup d'état, toppling the provisional government and establishing a junta known as the National Council for Democracy and Development (CNDD), led by Capt. Moussa Dadis Camara. The ousted civilian government initially rejected the CNDD, but after seeing the reaction of the populace many former ministers aimed to be incorporated into the junta.

Dadis Camara, a civilian, was appointed as Prime Minister and insisted that he would hold elections in 2010. However, a dramatic turn of events shifted the political climate when soldiers opened fire on a crowd at a major opposition rally against Dadis Camara at a Conakry stadium in September 2009. Although the government said only 57 died, the Guinean Human Rights Organization put the numbers at 157 killed and 1,200 or more injured. The European Union, the African Union, and the United States instituted sanctions and the UN established a tribunal to look into the incident; in February 2010, the International Criminal Court determined that the event constituted a crime against humanity. The government subsequently banned all activities that could be considered "subversive", but the opposition continued their fight.

Another shocking development followed in December 2009, when Dadis Camara was shot in the head by a former aide. After receiving treatment in Morocco, Camara went to Burkina Faso to recuperate, handing over power to his deputy General Sekouba Konaté. In Camara's absence, Konaté appointed civilian and pro-democracy opposition leader Jean-Marie Doré as the interim prime minister, and charged Doré with leading a power-sharing government and bringing the country back to stability and civilian rule.

Guinea

These turns culminated in the dramatic 2010 presidential election, in which no incumbent ran and no single candidate had the clear backing of the state. The result was almost certainly the most free and fair voting process in the country's history. In the first round, Cellou Dallein Diallo (a Peul leading the Union of Democratic Forces of Guinea, UFDG) took a commanding lead with almost 44% of the vote, while Alpha Condé came in a distant second with 18%, with the remaining voters divided up over many other candidates. Despite Diallo's large initial lead, Condé gained the vast majority of support for other candidates in the second-round runoff; the end result was 52.5% for Condé and 47.5% for Diallo. The voting showed a clear regional split, with Condé dominating in the eastern regions and Diallo in the central regions, with the western coastal regions (including Conakry) almost evenly divided.

Some unrest followed immediately after the results were announced, particularly between the security forces and Diallo supporters. After a brief respite, new hints of unrest followed in April and May 2011. First, crowds of Peuls gathered to welcome their candidate Cellou Diallo back from a trip, and Malinké soldiers cracked down on them, reportedly shouting anti-Peul slurs. Then in early May clashes erupted in the southeast of the country region between Malinkés and members of the Kpele ethnic group, killing over two dozen people. In July 2011, armed men attacked President Conde's residence, although he escaped harm. Former army chief General Nouhou Thiam was arrested just hours after the incident. Protests and clashes continued throughout the year, causing parliamentary elections to be delayed in September and then again in April. President Condé announced elections would be held in 2013, and though these were repeatedly delayed, parliamentary elections were finally held in September. The president's party, the Rally of the Guinean People (RPG) won the most seats (53 out of 114) and formed a coalition with allied parties to secure a legislative majority of 60 seats. The opposition, led by Cellou Dalein Diallo and the UFDG, claimed the election was unfair.

Recent Bad News

Other bad news has come out of Guinea in recent years, and in various forms. First was the deaths of two would-be reformers. First, the head of the treasury, an anti-corruption advocate, was assassinated in 2012. Then in 2013, Kelefa Diallo, the chief of staff of the armed forces who was also reputed to be reform-minded, died in a plane crash in neighboring Liberia. There has not been an indication of foul play in the crash. Given the centrality of corruption and civil-military relations in Guinea's political life, this was a double whammy that set back the reform agenda.

More recently, an outbreak of the deadly Ebola virus (a deadly hemorrhagic fever) in 2014 took place mostly in Guinea. though cases were also found in neighboring Liberia and Sierra Leone. As of June 2014, the outbreak was not fully contained, and has already resulted in nearly 400 cases in Guinea, and at least 270 deaths. While the outbreak is centered in the countryside, there have been cases in the capital Conakry, which has raised concerns that the contagion could become even more difficult to stop due to the greater mobility of infected persons. Ebola is contagious only when individuals are manifesting the deadly symptoms, so the likelihood of a global pandemic is low, but the prospects for continued transmission within Guinea and West Africa is a real worry.

CONTEMPORARY THEMES

Guinea has considerable economic potential for such a poor country. It is rich in natural resources—bauxite, iron, gold, and diamonds—and the water to produce the energy needed to process and convert those raw materials. Similarly, agricultural potential is considerable, as Guinea is in many ways a vast garden: with abundant rains and many foodstuffs that can be grown year-round, including rice, coffee, cocoa, bananas, and melons. However, despite these conditions, agricultural productivity remains low.

The main economic constraints seem to come from those areas where government provision of services is needed: infrastructure, especially ports and roads; basic provision of the rule of law and a functional climate for enterprise; and the development of human capital. Educational attainment is very poor in Guinea, with the United Nations estimating that only 30% of the population literate; while illiteracy is clearly most prevalent among older Guineans, two-thirds of young men and only half of young women are literate. Health indicators are also generally poor, but there is cause for optimism: life expectancy is about 58 years and the country's HIV/AIDS rate is low compared to other regions of Africa, at under 1.5%.

Guinea's export economy is dominated by its mining sector. Bauxite, alumina, gold, and diamonds produce about 90% of export revenues. Bauxite alone accounts for nearly 80% of foreign exchange earnings, and the country produces 14.5 million tons of bauxite annually, making it the world's second largest producer after Australia. In the 2000s the government signed major deals with mining interests (from Russia to Canada to Brazil) to develop, finance, construct and operate massive new refineries. The projects and all their economic linkages called for the refinery, mines, a power plant, a dam for water supply, upgrades of railroad lines to the coast, and an expansion of port facilities. In June of 2012, Guinea launched operations at its first iron mine, built as a joint venture between African Bellzone and the China International Fund (CIF). Total investment in the project is estimated at over $300 million, with an expectation of over 4 million metric tons of production a year.

There has been much friction in the past between the Guinean governments and mining companies. Tensions ran high when Capt. Dadis Camara accused foreign mining companies of not providing enough compensation for their operations in Guinea, and Alpha Condé has continued the trend of taking on major corporations. Dadis Camara threatened to close companies and investigated several agreements and contracts signed by the Lansana Conté government. Mining companies claimed they were being targeted and worried about the uncertain investment climate. Condé has more recently sought to increase the state share in many concessions, has threatened to revise or rewrite contracts with companies including the giant corporation Rio Tinto, and has cancelled contracts with other major mining firms. The Bellzone-CIF project guarantees the government of Guinea at 15% stake in the venture, as part of a resource-for-infrastructure deal.

The stakes are high as gold and diamond mining both present major potential growth industries alongside the more traditional bauxite. Gold has a long history here, as the region of Guinea even gave its name to Britain's first gold coin. Commercial production of both precious commodities expanded through the 2000s; an estimated 90% of Guinea's mined diamonds are gem quality. Overall, Guinea is estimated to have 25 to 30 millions of carats yet to be mined. The extent of investment and the terms of contracts will be major issues going forward.

Major political developments include the announcement of a general strike in reaction to the dissolution of a transitional government by military leaders who seized power in 2021 and established a transitional administration in 2022. Investigations of the previous president Alpha Conde also continue while the country experiences major acts of sabotage such as an oil depot explosion in December 2023. On the political front, with continuing repression by the country's military leaders who dissolved the ruling government in February 2024, lawyers throughout the country went on strike in August 2024, which effectively paralyzed the court system in protest to "arbitrary arrests" and "secret

Guinea

detentions," the latest sign of growing outrage over the arrest of two prominent activists campaigning for a return to democratic rule. While many Guineans initially welcomed the coup, the military is now accused of cracking down on dissent and reneging on a promise to hand back power to a democratic government. In the trial of former military ruler Dadis Camara on charges of crimes against humanity for the killing of more than 150 people during a protest against military rule in 2009 including the rape of scores of women, he was initially jailed but received a pardon in May 2025. The announced strike by lawyers followed the arrest on 9 July 2024 of Oumar Sylla and Mamadou Bah, leaders of a citizens' movement that has been critical of the junta-led government. The junta has also been criticized for suspending media outlets, restricting Internet access, and brutally suppressing demonstrations when a mass stampede at a football match in December 2024 resulted in 135 fatalities.

FUTURE CONSIDERATIONS

There is high degree of mistrust in Guinea on several fronts: between ethnic groups; between many civilians and the ever-restive security apparatus; and between the government and major international investors. The intermittent clashes since the election—which have twice pitted Malinkés against other groups—are worrying. If reasonably fair legislative elections are eventually held and can come off without inter-ethnic violence and without clashes between crowds and security forces, that will be an indicator Guinea's politics has some prospects for longer-term improvement.

The economy is likely to continue to benefit from high global demand for raw materials, including precious metals, with the caveat that mining investment is subject to the perilous state of relations between business and the government. At the same time, sustained economic growth will likely require more robust diversification. Despite a wealth of natural resources, Guinea's economic growth has

Daily life in a household *Das Parlament*

been consistently sluggish. Even as GDP shows modest rises of about 4%, this has barely been sufficient to keep up with population growth, meaning there is little gain in GDP per capita. Although Guinea is rich in mineral wealth, its people remain some of the poorest in the region.

As elsewhere in Africa, political stability and economic performance mutually inform one another. For Guinea to leverage its natural resources into growth, development, and poverty reduction, the country must invest its mining proceeds in infrastructure and building human capital as well exploit its comparative advantage in labor-intensive agriculture. Yet the legacy of a corrupt state bureaucracy hinders the country and political uncertainty makes productive investment all the more challenging. All of these challenges even have fed into the country's poor response to the Ebola outbreak in 2014; Guinea's government has shown that its capacity to manage crises is very low. The relatively democratic election in 2010 brought one reason for greater optimism than at many points in the past, but prospects are still quite shaky for Guinea—a country that was an early leader at independence but has declined since as continuing repression by the military junta dim hopes of any return to democratic rule.

The Republic of Guinea-Bissau

A quiet area near Bissau

BASIC FACTS

Area: 36,125 sq. km. = 13,984 sq. mi. (the size of Connecticut and Massachusetts)
Population: 2,078,820 (2023 est.)
Capital City: Bissau
Government Type: Semi-Presidential Republic
Neighboring Countries: Senegal (north); Guinea (southeast)
Official Language: Portuguese
Other Principal Languages: Crioulo (the lingua franca in much of Guinea-Bissau), Balanta Fulfulde, Mandinka, Mandyak, Papel
Ethnic Groups: Balanta 30%, Fula 20%, Manjaca 14%, Mandinga 13%, Papel 7%, European and mulatto less than 1%
Principal Religions: Muslim 50%, Indigenous beliefs 40%, and Christian 10%
Former Colonial Status: Portuguese Colony (1885–1974).
Independence Date: September 10, 1974 (The date on which Portugal recognized independence; unilateral declaration of independence was September 24, 1973.)
GDP Per Capita (IMF 2023 est.): $974 (nominal), $3,072 (PPP)
Gini Index: 50.7 (World Bank 2010)
Currency: CFA (Communauté Financière Africaine) franc, $US1 = 594 francs (Apr. 2022)
Inflation Rate: 2.24% (2022 est.)
Chief Commercial Products: Cashews, fish, shrimp, peanuts, palm kernels, lumber
Foreign Direct Investments (FDI) new flows: 21,459,644
Literacy Rate: 52.9% (CIA 2021)
Life Expectancy: 64.1 years (CIA 2023 est.)
Head of State: President Umaro Cissoko Embalo (since February 27, 2020)
Head of Government: Prime Minister Nuno Nabiam (since February 27, 2020)

LAND AND PEOPLE

Bordering the Atlantic Ocean, most of Guinea-Bissau is swampy coastal lowland with ample rainfall and abundant vegetation. The Fouta Djallon mountain range of Guinea run along its eastern and southern borders and about sixty small islands lay close to the shoreline.

The Balanta people of the coastal lowlands live mainly by subsistence agriculture while the Mandingas and Fulani of the interior place greater emphasis on the ownership of livestock. A tiny handful of Africans lived as *assimilados*, speaking Portuguese and adopting European customs during colonial rule. Cape Verde Creoles long dominated the business scene in Bissau and assumed a higher social status than darker-skinned mainlanders, causing ethnic divisions.

Guinea-Bissau's most famous cultural export is probably "gumbe" music, which fuses folk and several West African styles. Manecas Costa is one of the best-known proponents of the style.

HISTORY TO PRESENT DAY

For early history, see *Historical Background* and *The Colonial Period: The Portuguese.*

Independence: Amilcar Cabral and the PAIGC

The armed struggle against Portuguese colonial rule in Africa began in 1961 under the leadership of Amilcar Cabral and the *Partido Africano da Independência da Guiné e Cabo Verde* (PAIGC: African Independence Party of Guinea and Cape Verde). The rebellion forced Portugal to maintain some 35,000 troops in the territory—half of whom were African—to oppose 10,000 rebels who operated as guerrillas in the dense rain forests. Portuguese forces controlled only the coastal urban enclaves while rebels dominated the interior and established basic schools and services to govern the area. International support came from Soviet and Chinese arms and Cuban trainers in neighboring Guinea, where the PAIGC established its headquarters.

Cabral was assassinated in early 1973 in Conakry, reportedly by agents of the Portuguese dictatorship and was succeeded as head of PAIGC by his Cape Verdean half brother, Luís de Almeida Cabral. By 1974, the liberation struggle reached military stalemate, draining men, material, and morale from colonial Portugal. Disgruntled Portuguese army officers finally overthrew the Lisbon dictatorship and quickly negotiated independence with the country's colonies.

Guinea-Bissau's independence was recognized on September 10, 1974, and the Portuguese left the country within a month. Luís de Almeida Cabral became independent Guinea-Bissau's first president and the PAIGC proclaimed itself the country's only party and organized politics and the economy along Marxist-Leninist lines. The Cabral regime ruthlessly suppressed

Guinea-Bissau

political dissent; members of the PAIGC ultimately admitted to politically motivated killing of opponents. The regime also presided over a food crisis in the late 1970s that further contributed to discontent. The issues of the Cabral administration were exacerbated by the dominance of a *mestizo* intellectual minority representing a mere 2% of the population, and the Cabral regime ultimately collapsed.

Nino Vieira (1980–1999) and State Dysfunction

In 1980, João Bernardo Vieira, known as "Nino," seized power from Cabral in a military coup. The Vieira coup in Bissau definitively split the PAIGC movement, which had long witnessed tension between the Creole leadership from Cape Verde and the less educated mainlanders from Guinea-Bissau. In Cape Verde, the governing party renamed itself the *Partido Africano da Independência de Cabo Verde*, or PAICV, severing the party links between mainland and islands.

General Vieira was elected to five-year terms as president in 1984 and again in 1989. The Marxist approach of the Cabral years vanished as Vieira sought to re-establish ties with Portugal and the West. By 1992, however, Guinea-Bissau was still a single-party state, and only grudgingly did the government open political space to multiparty competition. After several delays, the government organized elections in July 1994 in which President Vieira and his PAIGC triumphed. Although the losing parties accused the government of election fraud, international observers termed the contest a fair one.

By 1997, the PAIGC was paralyzed by conflicts between two major party factions—one led by Vieira, and another led by former prime minister Manuel Saturnino da Costa, the party's national secretary. Vieira's removal of da Costa as prime minister set him at odds with major PAIGC factions. Latent hostilities within the political class broke into open conflict with President Vieira's sacking of Army Chief of Staff Ansumané Mané in June 1998. Mané was charged with insufficient control of cross-border arms trafficking and the army rose in revolt to support its popular leader and soon controlled most of the capital city. President Vieira called upon Senegal and Guinea for assistance against the rebels, but foreign troops were not enough to crush a popular rebellion as the army and its civilian supporters controlled the countryside and a good portion of the capital. The rebellion came to an end in May 1999 when the army once again rebelled as Senegalese and Guinean troops withdrew. President Vieira fled the burning executive palace to seek sanctuary in exile in Portugal.

Kumba Ialá (2000–2004) and Deteriorating Civil–Military Relations

Malam Bacai Sanhá, the parliamentary speaker and leader of one of the anti-Vieira factions in parliament, had been made interim president when Vieira fled to Portugal Parliament drafted a new constitution and set multiparty elections for both parliament and president, to be held in November 1999 and January 2000, respectively. The leading contenders for the presidency were Sanhá and Kumba Ialá, a former PAIGC militant who ultimately became disaffected and left the party, going into opposition and heading up the Party for Social Renewal (PRS).

Kumba Ialá won with 72% of the ballots; thereby ending a quarter-century of PAIGC domination. Ialá was a Balanta, the country's largest ethnic group, and never appeared in public without the bright red bonnet of a senior Balanta initiate. For many the bonnet symbolized his ethnic identity and his rejection of imported colonial religions like Islam and Christianity. Ialá made clear his beliefs that the Balanta had provided the bulk of fighting men who brought the country to independence and that they had been treated unjustly by the previous regime. This sense of ethnic identity and grievance led to accusations that he favored Balanta over others in civil and military appointments and ethnic tensions heightened.

In the legislative elections that followed, Ialá's PRS and the Guinea-Bissau Resistance party (RGB) were the principal victors, but neither achieved a parliamentary majority. The once-dominant PAIGC did poorly, coming in third place. In February 2000, the PRS and RGB formed a coalition government, with the PAIGC the principal opposition. The coalition left unresolved the most sensitive issue facing the country: the relationship of army and junta to the new civilian government.

Long-simmering tensions between state and army culminated in November 2000 when General Mané canceled army promotions made by the president and declared himself army chief of staff. The PAIGC and other opposition parties welcomed Mané's declaration, but the general was tracked down and killed in a shootout with loyalist troops. Ialá exacerbated the growing political tensions with erratic leadership. At odds with a fractious parliament and having no majority party, Ialá exacerbated the growing political tensions with erratic leadership. He ran through five prime ministers and changed ministers so rapidly some embassies gave up on maintaining a current cabinet list. Ialá also dismissed judges and appointed their successors without consulting the National Assembly—thus undermining judicial independence—and threatened to fire the bulk of the civil service.

Ialá's presidency began to unravel at the end of 2002 as he dissolved parliament (which had voted on a new constitution curtailing presidential powers) and began to rule by decree. He harassed and jailed opponents, and shuttered newspapers and radio stations causing the opposition to take to the streets, accusing Ialá of trying to turn the country into a dictatorship. Virtually bankrupt, the government had no money to pay its employees and soldiers were given bags of rice instead of paychecks and unpaid civil servants began public sector strikes. In an attempt to end the political paralysis, Ialá succumbed to pressure to hold new parliamentary elections, which were ultimately set for October 2004.

Army leaders, who had already warned the president their restless troops needed to be paid, deposed Ialá on September 14, 2004, and installed in power a 32-member Military Committee of the Restoration of Constitutional Order and Democracy (CMROCD). Army chief of staff General Verissimo Seabra Correia announced he would act as interim president until new elections could be held but under pressure from presidents Obasanjo of Nigeria and Wade of Senegal, he agreed to the appointment of a civilian president. A 17-member ad hoc commission headed by Bissau's highly respected Roman Catholic Bishop chose a politically unaffiliated Creole businessman close to the church, Henrique Pereira Rosa, as interim president, while the army insisted upon Antonio Arthur Sanhá, general secretary of the PRS, as prime minister. The ad hoc commission also recommended creation of a Transitional National Council (TNC)—a broad-based council of civilian and military representatives that would

**Former President
Joaõ Bernando "Nino" Vieira**

Guinea-Bissau

act as a nominated legislature until parliamentary elections could be held.

By the end of September, the new government was sworn in, and the TNC, consisting of 56 members headed by General Seabra Correia, was put in place. Elections for a new National Assembly were held in March 2005 and about 75% of the voting population cast their ballots in what observers described as a free and fair election. The PAIGC won 45 seats in the 102-member legislature, while the Kumba Ialá's PRS came in second with 35 seats, followed by the United Social Democratic Party (PUSD) with 17.

In May 2005, parliament appointed the PAIGC's Carlos Gomes Júnior, a businessman who was reportedly the richest man in Guinea-Bissau, as prime minister. His selection represented the political ascendancy of Creoles, culturally more westernized and better educated than other groups within the PAIGC, and his cabinet appointments emphasized the selection of men with advanced technical expertise and skill, something considered a handicap during the days of Kumba Ialá.

However, civilian technical expertise proved incapable of controlling the military when a contingent of soldiers who had served as UN peacekeepers in Liberia mutinied in October, demanding back wages and benefits and improved living conditions. The mutiny resulted in the brutal murder of head of the armed forces, Gen. Seabra Correia, and several others. To observers, their deaths had ethnic overtones: those killed were Papels while their killers were Balanta. Having decapitated military leadership, the mutineers forced the government to offer amnesty for actions extending back to the coup of 1980 and imposed their choice of new military commanders. General Tagme Na Wai, a Balanta and a former guerilla fighter who fought in the liberation war, was appointed armed forces chief of staff.

The Return and Death of Nino Vieira (2005–2009), Malam Bacai Sanhá (2009–2012), and Continuing State Failure

Presidential elections in mid-June 2005 were meant to end Guinea-Bissau's transitional period but seemed to further divide the country. Three heavyweight contenders entered the electoral ring. Kumba Ialá represented the PRS again, while the PAIGC nominated Malam Bacai Sanhá and former President Vieira chose to run as an independent. An exceptionally high turnout—87% of registered voters—cast their ballots but gave none of the three candidates a majority. Ialá threw his support to Vieira, who took 55% of the runoff vote, compared to Sanhá's 45%. Sanhá claimed fraud and said he would not recognize the result.

Former President Kumba Ialá campaigns again in the presidential election of June 2005. ©IRIN

As prime minister, the PAIGC's Carlos Gomes Júnior provoked an institutional confrontation between parliament and President Vieira. After 14 pro-Vieira dissidents defected from the PAIGC to sit as independents in September, Gomes lost his parliamentary majority and was dismissed by Vieira. Five days later, Vieira appointed his close ally and former campaign manager, Aristides Gomes, as the new prime minister. The PAIGC challenged the dismissal of Carlos Gomes Júnior but lost its appeal to the Supreme Court in January 2006.

On January 4, 2007, Commander Lamine Sanhá, a former navy chief of staff was shot by unidentified gunmen outside his home in the capital; he died two days later, and his death set off riots in Bissau. Two people were killed in clashes between security forces and demonstrators, and a good deal of property was destroyed, including a house reportedly belonging to President Vieira. Carlos Gomes Júnior—Vieira's onetime ally and now archenemy—misguidedly sought political advantage from the tragedy. In interviews, Gomes recklessly claimed that Vieira was systematically ordering the killing the members of the military junta that overthrew him in 1999. The government issued an arrest warrant for Gomes, who promptly fled to a UN office for protection. The crisis lasted for 17 days, during which time the UN fully secured withdrawal of the warrant. Gomes was allowed to return home with promises from the government that both he and his family would be protected.

The government's arrest warrant provided a moment of unity for the normally dysfunctional National Assembly. (Gomes had, in theory, immunity from arrest as a member of parliament.) By mid-March 2007, PAIGC loyalists cobbled together enough votes to censure Prime Minister Aristides Gomes and call for a new government of national unity. President Vieira initially refused but ultimately agreed in April to a government of national unity (including the PAIGC, the PRS, and the PUSD) for one year. Vieira appointed Martinho N'dafá Cabi of the PAIGC, a former defense minister, to replace Aristides Gomes at the head of government. By February 2008, the PAIGC withdrew support from N'dafá Cabi. The government postponed the March 2008 legislative elections, however, and Vieira extended the mandate of the legislature. This arrangement lasted until July 2008, when the PAIGC left the government. In August, Vieira dissolved parliament and appointed Carlos Correia as interim head of government.

Tensions between state and army grew as political instability continued. In November 2008, Nino Vieira narrowly escaped an attack by soldiers at his home, part of an apparent coup attempt. The PAIGC won an outright majority in legislative elections that month, but the focus on the political sphere was redirected to the relationship between state and army. In early 2009, General Tagme Na Wai accused Vieira's presidential guard of attempting to assassinate him by shooting at his car, and on March 1, he was killed in a bomb attack at the military headquarters in Bissau.

On March 2, 2009, the day after the killing of Tagme Na Wai, elements of the army retaliated by attacking the presidential residence; they killed President Vieira as he attempted to flee. The military leadership assumed control of the country, called for elections within months, and named Raimundo Pereira, the speaker of Parliament, as interim head of state.

Sanhá won the July 2009 runoff election over Ialá and took office as president on September 8, 2009. The election was deemed rather free and fair by international observers. On April 1, 2010, several soldiers removed the Army Chief of Staff and temporarily arrested Prime Minister Carlos Gomes. The leader of the military action, General Antonio Indjai was later rewarded for his decisive action against civilian rule by being made army chief in June. The year 2011 saw thousands take to the streets in protest against Prime Minister Gomes and rising food prices; in 2011 as well, the EU suspended development aid, citing concerns over governance and the rule of law in Guinea-Bissau.

Guinea-Bissau

President Sanha died in office in January of 2012 and was temporarily succeeded by National Assembly head Raimundo Pereira. In the lead up to the new presidential elections, the military saw the opportunity to take control and began its assault on the interim government in April of 2012. After some skirmishes, the army detained Pereira along with Prime Minister Carlos Gomes. It then established its own transitional government, led by Manuel Serifo Nhamadjo. The transitional military government had claimed that elections would be held within the year, per a deal brokered by the Economic Community of West African States (ECOWAS), but elections were not scheduled until 2014. Peacekeeping troops from across the ECOWAS region were stationed in Guinea-Bissau following the events of April 2012, and the UN Security Council imposed a travel ban on leaders of the military coup.

A New Start? The 2014 Election

In 2014, Guinea-Bissau finally held a viable presidential election. Importantly, the election took place without any of the three men who had long dominated the country's personalized politics: Kumba Ialá died weeks before the election (and Vieira and Sanhá had previously been killed or died in office). The winner was of a new generation: José Mario Vaz of the PAIGC took the most votes in the first round against a dozen other candidates and won in the runoff on May 18 against Nuno Gomes Nabiam with 62% of the vote. He assumed the presidency on June 23, 2014. Vaz is a former finance minister who previously stood accused of diverting aid money for private gain, though the case against him was never proved. The PAIGC also won a narrow majority in the legislature, taking 57 of 102 total seats. This election has generated some hope for a normalization of civilian politics (and an end to military rule), but it should not be assumed that one election will immediately transform the poisonous civil–military relations in Guinea-Bissau.

CONTEMPORARY THEMES

Guinea-Bissau is one of the poorest and least developed countries in Africa and in the world. Its social statistics make depressing reading: life expectancy is only 48 years, one of the lowest in West Africa. More than two-thirds of the population lives below the poverty line of one dollar a day. HIV/AIDS prevalence is estimated at 2.5% of adults, which is low compared to countries in southern Africa, but higher than many other better-governed countries in West Africa.

An economy already in crisis was devastated by the civil conflict earlier this decade that destroyed roads and bridges. The government remains the country's largest employer and 80% of government revenue goes to the public sector payroll, of which a substantial portion must be used to keep soldiers happy. Cash-strapped, however, it has regularly fallen behind in its salary obligations, and striking public workers, demanding months of back pay, are a regular feature of Guinea-Bissau's public life. The country now depends heavily on foreign assistance for its revenues, creating a huge foreign debt.

Under normal circumstances Guinea-Bissau's economy is heavily dependent on exports of cashews and timber and the sale of fishing licenses. Agriculture provides jobs for 80% of the population and generates about 55% of GDP and 90% of exports. The main food crop is paddy rice, which is grown on nearly 20% of all cultivated land. With Chinese assistance, Guinea-Bissau has attempted to expand out-of-season rice production through irrigation most notably at Contuboel, about 100 miles east of Bissau. Unfortunately, the standing water in the rice paddies has increased the incidence of malaria in the region. Cashew nuts account for 90% of Guinea-Bissau's exports, most of which are shipped to India for processing. Guinea-Bissau is currently ranked as the world's fifth-largest producer of cashews. Imaginatively, the government has announced plans to build a series of small thermal plants around the country that would use the dried waste of the cashew fruit to produce electricity.

Guinea-Bissau's unpatrolled islands and inlets have become West Africa's major transit point for drugs moving from South America to Europe. Local police seized millions of dollars of Latin American cocaine in 2005, but the capacity of West African criminal gangs to elude far outpaces the capacity of local authorities to surveil and capture. Experts fear government stability is threatened as drug traffickers extend their influence into ministries, the army, and the police. Rear Admiral José Américo Bubo Na Tchuto has emerged as the mastermind behind the Guinea-Bissau drug trade, gaining large amounts of power, money, and influence. Relations with the international community have frayed over the issues of the military in politics and Guinea-Bissau's growing role as a point in the drug trade. As much as $1 billion or more of cocaine is estimated to move through Guinea-Bissau annually, leading to huge unofficial drug-based income (Ih is not broadly distributed) in an otherwise destitute country. While relatively free elections were conducted in June 2023 with the PAIGC party emerging as the winner, the country still suffers from political instability brought on by factional groups in the national guard who attempted a cIup in December 2023.

A notorious drug trafficking hub serving as a key conduit for the transport of cocaine from Latin America destined for Europe, Guinea-Bisau has been officially designated by the United Nations as a "narco-state" with drug traffickers and networks highly influential and well-entrenched in the country's government. Often funding election campaigns for politicians willing to protect the illegal trade, Malam Bacai Sanha, Jr., son of a former president, planned to use the proceeds to fund his ambitions to become Guinea-Bissau's president through a coup that failed in in February 2022 leading to his extradition to the United States where he pled guilty to conspiring to illegally import drugs. The 52-year-old, known as "Bacaizinho" in Guinea-Bissau, has held several roles in the government, including as his father's economic adviser. On the international front, a delegation from ECOWAS to help resolve an election dispute left the country in March 2025 after President Umaro Sissolu Embalo threatened to expel it. Sent to help reach a "political consensus" on how to hold elections scheduled for November 2024 (which Embalo postponed), 30 November 2025 has been announced as the new date, a delay hotly opposed by the political opposition, with the Supreme Court ruling to extend Embalo's term in office to September. The delegation plans to present its report to the Ecowas president, including a proposal for an agreement leading to "inclusive and peaceful elections." Two attempts to overthrow Embalo have occurred, the latest in December 2023, which led him to dissolve the opposition-dominated parliament with the government deploying security forces across the capital and Embalo visiting Moscow for talks with Russian President Vladimir Putin.

FUTURE CONSIDERATIONS

Guinea-Bissau is one of West Africa's most fragile and unstable countries, as demonstrated by the assassination of President Vieira in 2009 and the coup after his successor Malam Bacai Sanhá's death in 2012. The aI which insists that it was not staging a coup when Vieira was killed, maintains a veto over government

Guinea-Bissau

policy even when civilians are in power. The relative impunity of the current heads of the army and navy show how civilian leaders can be beholden to military men in Guinea-Bissau. Factional division within and between the country's main political parties is a further challenge to stability and the recent takeover by the army signifies the decreasing strength of civil society and government in general. In brief, no leader in Guinea-Bissau's forty years of independence has finished his allotted term of office and the country's political prospects are among the worst in West Africa. The election of José Mario Vaz in 2014 has generated some hope that a corner has been turned, but the verdict is still out on his new presidency.

Guinea-Bissau's economy is also fragile, especially considering the natural resource potential of the land. The country continues to rely on select cash crops, most notably cashews, for foreign exports. Guinea-Bissau's economy remained relatively stable throughout the financial crisis of 2008–9 with only a small decline due to falling export prices. Yet the performance has been modest at best: growth rates have not surpassed 5% in the last decade, when much of Africa has boomed. Moreover, the emergence of the drug trade as a major economic activity has promised some quick cash for enterprising outlaws, it also suggests the decay of social order in a society where institutions are already weak. The most recent coup, like many before it, has generated assertions that it will bring stability and progress to Guinea-Bissau, but there is little auspicious in the country's history that suggests robust development and democracy are around the corner.

The Republic of Liberia

Voinjama in the far northeast ©IRIN

BASIC FACTS

Area: 111,370 sq. km. = 43,000 sq. mi. (Slightly smaller than Pennsylvania)
Population: 5,506,280 (July 2023 est.)
Capital City: Monrovia
Government Type: Presidential Republic
Neighboring Countries: Sierra Leone (west); Guinea (north); Côte d'Ivoire (northeast, east)
Official Language: English
Other Principal Languages: Various ethnic group lles including Bassa, Dan, Gola, Grebo, Kisi, Kpelle, Krahn, Loma, Mano, Manya, Vai
Ethnic groups: Kpelle 20%, Bassa 13%, Grebo 10%, Gio 8%, Mano 8%, Kru 6%, Lorma 5%, Kissi 5%, Gola Iher 20% (including Americo-Liberians, descendants of immigrants from the U.S.)
Principal Religions: Christian 86%, Muslim 12%, Traditional and other less than 1%, none 1.4%
Former Colonial Status: N/A; settled by Americans
Independence Date: July 26, 1847
GDP Per Capita (IMF 2023 est.): $805 (nominal), $1,788 (PPP)
Gini Index: 35.3 (2016 est.)
Currency: Liberian dollar; 1 USD = 165.96 LRD (Apr. 2023)
Inflation rate: 8.2% (2022 est.)
Chief Commercial Products: Diamonds, iron ore, rubber, timber, and coffee
Foreign Direct Investments (FDI) net inflows: 362,967,566
Literacy rate: 48.3% (CIA 2017)
Life expectancy: 65.8 years (CIA 2023 est.)
Head of State: President George WEAH (since January 22, 2018)
Head of Government: President George WEAH (since January 22, 2018)

LAND AND PEOPLE

Liberia is located on the southern part of the west coast of Africa, facing the warm equatorial waters of the Gulf of Guinea. It is within the tropical region of Africa and has a hot, humid climate. There is a wet season from April to November and a drier season from December to May. From the floor of the jungle, shrubs and small trees entangled with vines rise from 40 to more than 100 feet. Interspersed with this thick growth are the solled crown trees, which bear foliage only at immense heights and have trunks up to 12 feet in width. The coastal area of Liberia, receiving the most rainfall, is dotted with lagoons, tidal creeks, and marshes. During the eight-month rainy season, most days see an inch or more of rainfall. Six rivers flow from the interior southwest to the Gulf of Guinea but they are generally not navigable for more than a few miles inland and are bounded by level land suitable for cultivation. Further inland the terrain rises slowly to a level of 1,000 feet in a series of plateaus obscured by the dense undergrowth. Low mountains rise occasionally in the northeast of the country, seldom reaching a height of more than 3,000 feet, with the exception of the Nimba

Liberia

and Wale mountains, which are 4,500 feet high. Liberia is incredibly rich in natural resources, such as iron ore, timber, diamonds, and gold. Established as a haven for freed slaves, Liberia came to be home to a variety of ethnic groups; indigenous, European, and American.

HISTORY TO PRESENT DAY

Portuguese mariners were the first to describe the Liberian coast and identify its commercially valuable products in the 15th century although Kru, Gola and other ethnic groups had lived for countless centuries in Liberia before the arrival of Europeans. The area came to be called the Grain Coast because of the grains of the Melegueta pepper, as valuable as gold to a Europe cut off from the Asian spice trade—a consequence of Ottoman conquests. The market for field labor on the plantations of the southern colonies of America and in the West Indies was immense and some local chiefs along the Grain Coast willingly sold conquered peoples to slave traders. Traders often took only the men for heavy work, leaving the women and children to fend for themselves.

The American Colonization Society

The origins of Liberia took vague shape as early as 1691 when the Virginia legislature passed a law requiring that any slave owner granting freedom arrange passage out of the colony for the freedman within half a year. Where they went was not spelled out, but there was a growing feeling among early American elites that it was dangerous to allow slaves and freed Africans to mingle.

More than a century passed before Virginia lawmakers once again considered the problems caused by slavery after the 1789 slave revolt in Haiti had sent a chill through plantation owners. Thomas Jefferson expressed the view that there should be a plan for colonizing blacks, and the Virginia legislature requested President James Monroe to obtain land outside the United States, preferably in Africa, for this purpose.

The American Colonization Society was founded in 1816 with the objective of transporting freeborn blacks and emancipated slaves back to Africa. In Henry Clay's words, such colonization would "draw off" free blacks, lest they incite a slave rebellion. In 1818 representatives of the American Colonization Society visited the Grain Coast of West Africa and after several failed attempts to secure land for the colonization project, the Society finally signed an agreement with local chiefs granting it possession of Cape Mesurado in 1821. The first American freed slaves landed in 1822.

By 1830, the tiny colonization effort had grown to a thousand people and this new "land of liberty" was named Liberia, from the Latin root for "free." Its capital came to be named Monrovia, after President James Monroe. The colony continued to expand, and its trade increased as the settler's preferred American food and goods, which had to be brought in by ship. The settlers united in 1839 to form the Commonwealth of Liberia under a governor appointed by the American Colonization Society. In 1847, Governor Joseph Roberts, a freeborn black man who hailed from Virginia, proclaimed the Free and Independent Republic of Liberia. The new nation was recognized within a short time by the European powers, but not by the United States until 1862.

Life for the descendants of the freed slaves was harsh and Liberia was a difficult place to survive becausee settlers had little Africa-specific agricultural knowledge and little interaction with the indigenous tribes. Liberia's economic and political elite of Americo-Liberians remained largely in the urban coastal communities. They were Christian people who spoke English and preferred American styles in dress, particularly valuing formal attire (including tuxedos and top hats, notwithstanding the tropical climate). The government could not exert effective authority for more than 20 miles inland. As a consequence, it was not until the 1930s that there was any real penetration of the interior by the Americo-Liberians.

The early Liberian state ran up a huge debt, and in 1909 President Theodore Roosevelt appointed a commission to investigate Liberia's finances. The commission proposed a bailout plan that involved a loan raised by international bankers, guaranteed by the Liberia's customs revenues. The customs receivership, administered by British, French, German, and American officials, brought some stability to Liberia's finances, but the country's financial

Liberia-Counties

Liberia

reorganization was scuttled by World War I. When the Firestone Tire and Rubber Company secured a concession of one million acres to establish a rubber plantation in 1926, the Liberian government arranged a loan through the company to consolidate its debts. The loan helped to stabilize the country's finances, but the administration of its customs and internal revenue was placed in the hands of an American advisor. The government was not able to liquidate its external debt until 1952—the first time since it took its first loan in 1871.

Liberia's special relationship with the United States intensified with the coming of World War II. With most Asian sources of rubber cut off by the Japanese, Liberia was virtually the only source of natural rubber available to the allies. A defense agreement signed in 1942 brought vast infrastructure developments to Liberia as strategic roads, an international airport, and a deepwater harbor were constructed. The American dollar was declared legal tender in 1943.

The Tubman and Tolbert Years (1944–1980)

William V. S. Tubman was elected to a four-year term of office as president in 1944 and he would ultimately be elected to seven successive terms. Although a descendent of American immigrants, Tubman grew up in poverty, peripheral to the core of the Americo-Liberian elite. A self-made man, he studied the law after work and passed his bar examination at age 23. He joined the True Whig Party, the Americo-Liberian political machine that controlled Liberia economically and politically and held a variety of public offices. At 35, he was elected to the Liberian Senate, where he became a bit of a gadfly opposing the Americo-Liberian establishment.

To remove the pesky critic, the True Whig leadership booted him "upstairs" with an appointment as an associate justice of the Liberian Supreme Court. From here Tubman unexpectedly announced his candidacy for President in 1943, Iy campaigned and won easily. He dominated Liberian politics for the next 28 years, dying in office in 1971.

Tubman realized the True Whig Party's continued hold on power depended on extending its reIeyond its Americo-Liberian constituency. He was the first president to appoint "country people"—that is, indigenous Africans—to high positions. Tubman made efforts to establish linkages between Americo-Liberians and traditional authorities in the hinterland. Despite limited efforts at outreach to indigenous Liberians, foreign investment under Tubman led to uneven development, with the hinterlands receiving very little in the way of economic opportunity, only exacerbated tensions between the Americo-Liberian elite and indigenous Liberians.

When President Tubman died in 1971, he was succeeded by his vice president William Tolbert. Tolbert was the first Liberian president to speak an interior tribal language, and he attempted to follow through on Tubman's efforts to incorporate indigenous Liberians. For his efforts to expand educational opportunities and bring interior peoples into the elitist government, President Tolbert was criticized by Americo-Liberians for having "let peasants into the kitchen."

By 1979, long-term inequalities, rural poverty, and economic mismanagement had brought the country to a crisis point. When rice sIs dropped because farmers found it more profitable to work as laborers on the large rubber plantations, the government proposed a price increase from $22 to $26 per hundred pounds to encourage greater production. Since rice is the staple food, the plan touched off populist rioIn Monrovia during which there was widespread looting; about 5Ile were killed, and another 500 injured. Ninety percent of the businesses in the capital were either partially or totally destroyed, with damage said to be about $50 million. President Tolbert imposed a curfew on the city, and Congress granted him emergency powers, but these proved too late to stem the tide of rebellion.

Samuel Doe (1980–1990) and the Collapse into Warlordism (the 1990s)

Enemies of the establishment surfaced, and on April 12, 1980, a group of noncommissioned officers led by Master Sergeant Samuel K. Doe stormed the Executive Mansion, assassinated President Tolbert (and disemboweled him), seized power and set up a People's Redemption Council (PRC). Doe and his fellow noncommissioned officers represented a variety of back-country peoples who had traditionally been excluded from power by Americo-Liberians. Members of indigenous ethnic groups could achieve NCO status in the army, but Americo-Liberians, dominated most of the upper ranks. Doe was a member of the Krahn people, while his two principal partners, Thomas Quiwonkpa and Weh Syen, were Gio and Kru, respectively. Ten days after the coup, the PRC organized the public execution of 13 high officials of the deposed government.

In 1983, Charles Taylor, a deputy minister of commerce in the Doe government, was charged with corruption. Among other things, he had ordered $1 million worth of bulldozers, which never arrived. The money was stashed in American bank accounts, and when he fled Liberia for his life, Taylor headed straight to the U.S. Arrested and jailed, he managed to escape and made his way back to Africa. In 1988, Taylor, still a fugitive, was reportedly supported and trained by Muammar al-Qadhafi at a Libyan terrorist base.

Doe set about transforming himself into a civilian ruler to pacify potential international donors. A new constitution was approved in July 1984, and in October 1985, general elections were held to implement its provisions. Doe, now head of the National Democratic Party of Liberia (NDPL) was elected president. The NDPL claimed victory by a slender margin—50.9%, but the election was seen as utterly fraudulent by most observers. Under President Doe, Krahns were given most of the authority in the military and the most significant posts in government and ethnic rivalry intensified as a consequence.

During the 1980s, the Reagan administration poured over $400 million into President Doe's eager hands while Liberia became an important listening post and staging base for CIA operations in central and southern Africa. But by 1987 most of the money couldn't be accounted for, and when the U.S. sent in the auditors, Doe simply refused to cooperate.

Shortly after the 1985 presidential elections, Thomas Quiwonkpa, the former army commander, returned to Liberia via Sierra Leone and attempted a coup against President Doe. The coup failed and Quiwonkpa was apprehended, killed, and dismembered. According to some reports (and a recurring theme in the Liberian tragedy), his executioners consumed parts of his body. A nationwide pogrom ensued against Quiwonkpa's Gio people and the closely related Mano people. Execution, flogging, castration, dismemberment, and rape became commonplace as Liberia sank into bloody civil strife.

Liberia's civil war broke out in earnest in December 1989 when former Deputy Minister Charles Taylor led an invasion of

Samuel K. Doe

Liberia

insurgents from Côte d'Ivoire. They called themselves the National Patriotic Front of Liberia (NPFL) and received support from Libya, Burkina Faso, Côte d'Ivoire and Liberians living abroad. Mano and Gio youth flocked to Taylor's NPFL to avenge the sufferings of their people. General disgust with Doe rallied others, and soon Taylor's forces had overrun most of the country with the control of rich diamond-producing areas supporting the rebellion's efforts. The violence was grim and both sides earned reputations for brutality and stood accused of atrocities.

By August 1990, anarchy prevailed and other West African states decided to intervene militarily to spare the nation. The military force they created was called ECOMOG, standing for the ECOWAS (Economic Community of West African States) Monitoring Group. The intervention contributed to a fragmentation of the NPFL and localization of warlord activities. One of Taylor's principal aides, Prince (a relatively common Liberian first name, having nothing to do with royal affiliation) Yormie Johnson, formed his own rebel force, called the Independent National Patriotic Front of Liberia (INPFL), and in September 1990 captured President Doe when he left the besieged Executive Mansion to meet with the head of ECOMOG. Doe was tortured, mutilated, and executed—and the violence preserved on videotape that was released to the international media.

During the period from 1990 to 1994, the well-respected Amos Sawyer nominally served as interim president (and was followed by several other short-term interim presidents), but the interim government exercised little practical authority on the ground. By mid-1995, Monrovia was a wasteland in which teenage rebels cruised the streets with loaded automatic weapons and medium artillery. The extent of the destruction that took place in Liberia's civil war was staggering. More than 5% of the population was killed, more than half a million Liberians fled the country, and 50% of those who remained were displaced from their home villages. When rebel factions began ambushing ECOWAS forces, Nigeria's military ruler Sani Abacha intervened. Abacha summoned faction leaders to Abuja, ordered disarmament, set an election date, and appointed the last of the interim presidents of the period—Ruth Sando Perry, who had been a senator during the Doe period.

Charles Taylor: Warlord President (1997–2003)

Multiparty elections were finally held in July 1997 and Charles Taylor emerged victorious. Seventy-five percent of the Liberian electorate placed their desire for peace in

Charles Taylor

the hands of the man most responsible for the devastating civil war. His National Patriotic Party (NPP) won an absolute majority in both houses of the legislature; security agencies loyal to Taylor took control and began appalling abuses of human rights. The army (AFL), once dominated by the Krahn people for former president Doe, was marginalized and its members reduced to begging for money on street corners or pleading at the Defense Ministry for their unpaid salaries. In effect, the AFL was replaced by militiamen, often little more than bodyguards for Taylor, kept loyal by regular payments in rice and dollars.

Taylor also sought to destabilize his neighbors and became the principal patron of the vicious Revolutionary United Front (RUF) in Sierra Leone, offering training, weapons, staging grounds for attacks and safe haven for retreat. The effort was paid for by Sierra Leone diamonds mined by the rebels, from which President Taylor exacted a share. As a result, the UN Security Council voted unanimously to impose sanctions on all diamond exports in March 2001; it also renewed its arms embargo, but these sanctions proved ineffective. To pay for its arms shipments, the Taylor government diverted money from the Liberian International Ship and Corporate Registry (LISCR).

The Taylor government justified its illegal arms purchases by citing the insurgency it faced at home. Meanwhile, the rebels seeking the overthrow of his regime came together in a loose coalition calling itself Liberians United for Reconciliation and Democracy (LURD), which was united only by a common antipathy for Charles Taylor. For his part, Taylor (correctly) accused Guinea of aiding and abetting his enemies and as the rebel forces grew in strength, President Taylor increased his arms purchases, little impeded by UN sanctions.

President Taylor's support of two rebel groups in western Côte d'Ivoire (MPIGO: *Mouvement populaire ivoirien du grand ouest*, and MJP: *Mouvement pour la Justice et la Paix*) also boomeranged. In April 2003, a new rebel group, the Movement for Democracy in Liberia (MODEL)—financed by Côte d'Ivoire's president, Laurent Gbagbo—began to harass Liberian government forces from the southeast.

By June 2003, the Taylor regime was rapidly unraveling. While MODEL forces attacked from the south, fighters from the main rebel group (LURD) swept south in an attempt to capture the capital. Peace talks aimed at ending the two-pronged rebellion were organized in Ghana but were overshadowed by President Taylor's indictment by the Sierra Leone Special War Crimes Court in March 2003. A ceasefire agreement was reached, but proved short-lived as rebels pressed their advantage, demanding President Taylor's resignation and departure as the price of peace.

As fighting intensified and fatalities mounted, ECOWAS agreed to supply peacekeepers. Taylor then resigned and flew away to exile in Nigeria on August 11; U.S. forces, which had remained at sea, finally entered Liberia. In Ghana, rebels and representatives of the former Taylor regime signed an agreement formally declaring a ceasefire and end to Liberia's civil war on August 18, 2003. With guns quieted, the UN began what would become one of its largest peacekeeping missions, 15,000 troops. The Accra conferees chose a politically neutral figure: Gyude Bryant, a little-known businessman without ties to either the former government or the rebels, as interim president. The interim transitional government's principal task was to organize elections for a new government in October 2005.

The United Nations Mission in Liberia (UNMIL) was assigned the arduous task of disarming combatants and organizing opportunities for reintegration into civil society. By March 2007, some 75,000 out of 100,000 demobilized former combatants had either completed or were participating in reintegration programs, including formal education and vocational skills classes. While these figures do not cover the thousands of child soldiers enlisted in the various militias that ravaged Liberia during the Taylor years, 11,000 former child soldiers were identified as beneficiaries of reintegration programs. Administered by the UN's Children's Fund, the program had provided opportunities to 9,704 former child combatants by early 2007.

The international community pledged $520 million for Liberia's reconstruction, and the United States pledged $200 million

Liberia

for reforming the security sector. The cause of such costly national reconstruction, Charles Taylor, was initially given gracious exile in a government guest house by President Obasanjo of Nigeria in 2003. Pressures to extradite Taylor were resisted as Obasanjo indicated he would only respond to a specific request from a democratically elected government in Liberia.

Election and Presidency of Ellen Johnson-Sirleaf (2006–present)

The elections that produced such a democratic government were held in October 2005. Thirty parties entered the fray, fielding over seven hundred candidates for the Senate (30 members) and lower house (64 members); twenty-two candidates vied for the presidency. In the first round, the leading candidate was George Weah, a hugely popular professional soccer player representing the Congress for Democratic Change (CDC), who won 28.3% of the vote. He was followed by Ellen Johnson-Sirleaf, a Harvard-educated economist who had once worked for the World Bank and the United Nations, the nominee of the United Party (UP) with 19.8%. Weah and his supporters asserted massive fraud and claimed an astounding 62% of the vote, a position supported by neither international observers nor the NEC (National Elections Commission). With no candidate garnering the required 50%, a runoff election was needed. The final results in the second round of the presidential election showed Liberian voters valued political and economic experience over soccer fame: Ellen Johnson-Sirleaf obtained 59.4% of the votes, becoming Liberia's—and Africa's—first elected female president.

One of Johnson-Sirleaf's first challenges was the fate of Charles Taylor in exile. With pockets of supporters scattered throughout the country, and a phone to keep in touch, Taylor had already been accused of plotting against his archenemy, Guinea's President Lansana Conté. Johnson-Sirleaf preferred to focus on rebuilding war-battered Liberia (where running water and regular electricity were nonexistent), which she announced as her first priority in her inaugural address. Yet demands built up regarding Taylor's fate, as victims, international human rights organizations, and even foreign officials pressured her to request his repatriation. On the eve of her first official state visit to the United States in March 2006, she formally requested his return from Nigeria.

Amply forewarned, Charles Taylor fled his villa, but was apprehended by Nigerian authorities. He was immediately whisked off to the prison compound of the International War Crimes Tribunal in Sierra Leone, but nervous authorities there were unwilling to have him present in the country. Appeals were made to have him express delivered to The Hague, where it was expected the Dutch could provide escape-proof detention, allowing Liberia's new government at last to get down to the daunting tasks of reconciliation and rebuilding. Taylor's trial began in June 2007 and was scheduled to last for 18 months.

The Charles Taylor trial ended in April of 2011 and a year later in April 2012, Charles Taylor was convicted of aiding and abetting war crimes during the Sierra Leone civil war. In May of 2012, Taylor was sentenced to 50 years in prison for his role in the atrocities of the war, become the first head of state convicted by an international tribunal since the Nuremburg trials after World War II. His sentencing set a new precedent that heads of state who commit crimes against humanity can (at least sometimes) be held accountable for their actions. During the lengthy trial, an American court in Miami sentenced Taylor's son, a US citizen, for his role in perpetrating terror under his father's regime.

By January 2007, one year after her election, President Johnson-Sirleaf could present her countrymen a relatively positive balance sheet; peace had prevailed, there was progress on economic recovery and growth in public revenues, and electricity and pipe-borne water were being provided to some parts of Monrovia. There was even hesitant movement on the crippling problem of endemic corruption after President Johnson-Sirleaf declared a "zero tolerance" policy. Charles Gyude Bryant and several former ministers of the National Transitional Government were implicated in a report on economic crimes prepared by ECOWAS auditors and charged with financial malfeasance. Edwin Snowe, an ally of Charles Taylor who served as Speaker of the House of Representatives until forced to resign in early 2007, was also being investigated—for misappropriation of one million dollars from the Liberian Petroleum Refinery Company; Snowe had been the company's managing director during the transitional regime. Despite its rhetoric on the subject, Johnson-Sirleaf's administration has also had its problems with corruption; in 2010, she had to remove her information minister and force her brother, the internal affairs minister, to step down because of corruption allegations.

The year 2011 saw the reelection of Ellen Johnson-Sirleaf in an election tarnished by low voter turnout. Johnson-Sirleaf has been accused of not providing the progress that had been hoped for during her first term but earns praise for the level of stability and the efforts toward reconciliation that she has overseen. In 2011, Johnson-Sirleaf was recognized by the international community when she was awarded the Nobel Peace Prize for her efforts to secure peace, promote economic and social development, and strengthen the position of women in society.

CONTEMPORARY THEMES

Monrovia, the capital city, still suffers the effects of destructive civil conflict. Its

A child soldier, once the terror of Liberia Photo by AFP/George Gobet

Liberia

power system was knocked out in 1990 and the reintroduction of electricity has been a slow process, with the sound of thousands of private generators filling up the evening air. The war also stopped the flow of water from the city's taps, and residents have been dependent on polluted wells, expensive truck-delivered purified water, or jerry cans of water sold from handcarts on the city streets. President Johnson-Sirleaf has worked towards rebuilding the water lines but as the water distribution pipes are so old, rusted, and broken, they will have to be ripped up and replaced in order to supply drinking water to residents and the costs tremendous.

Apart from destroying Liberia's infrastructure, the 14-year civil war destroyed the country's economy, and its recent growth has largely been driven by reconstruction. GDP dropped to about half of its prewar levels during the war, and per capita income sank to $140—the country was at the very bottom of the UN's *Human Development Index* for 2002. Since 2003, however, there has been economic improvement; after a calamitous decline of 31% in 2003, the country's GDP rose from all-time lows by a modest 2.6% in 2004 and 5.3% in 2005. Results continued to improve to 8% in 2006 and a growth rate of over 9% in 2007. In 2008, the country mustered another 7.5%, before growth returned to a more modest 4.6% in 2009; the global financial crisis took a toll, but Liberia's economy is growing again. In 2011, growth rates shot up again to 8.2% and have stayed relatively constant since. The 2013 estimate of economic growth rate was 8.1%. This gives an income per capita that is much improved from just five or ten years ago, though it is still incredibly low and leaves 80% under the poverty line.

The economy is predominantly based on agriculture, which accounts for over 70% of Liberia's GDP, while industry only accounts for 7%. Prior to 1990 the economy was primarily based on iron ore, rubber, timber, diamond, and gold exports. With substantial investments in rich iron ore deposits, Liberia was once the world's fifth largest exporter, but war completely disrupted the industry. In 2005, Mittal Steel, one of the world's largest steel companies, signed a deal with transitional government authorities to develop some billion tons of iron ore reserves in Nimba County, close to the Guinea border. Over 25 years, the company committed to spending $900 million to develop not only the mines, but also rail and port infrastructure to evacuate the ore. The contract was controversial from the beginning, with charges of a $100,000 bribe having been handed under the table to Transitional Chairman Gyude Bryant. Global Witness, the British NOG committed to exposing the corrupt

President Ellen Johnson-Sirleaf
Photo courtesy White House/Shealah Craighead

exploitation of natural resources, also weighed in: Mittal, it noted, was allowed to opt out of human rights and environmental laws in the contract. When Ellen Johnson-Sirleaf took office, one of her most popular engagements was a promise to review all contracts signed by the interim government. By December 2006, the Mittal contract had been investigated and renegotiated. Mittal's investment was increased to $1 billion and the Liberian government was to retain ownership of rail and port infrastructure.

Before the war the rubber industry generated over $100 million annually in export earnings. Some 50,000 people earned their living through the industry. The Firestone rubber plantation, roughly 188 square miles containing 8 million rubber trees and 670 miles of roads, was the largest rubber plantation in the world. It has yet to recover fully from war damages. Many of its trees were over-tapped by looters and will have to be cut down and replanted. It takes seven years for a rubber tree to mature and be ready for tapping. After new logging legislation intended to prevent corruption and mismanagement in the timber industry was passed, the UN Security Council lifted its three-year ban on logging in June 2006. Sanctions on the notorious "blood diamonds" were maintained until April 2007. Diamond exports have resumed legally under the Kimberley Process.

In February 2005, the transitional government extended Firestone's land concession for 36 years as part of its efforts to revitalize the economy. For its part, Firestone indicated it planned to invest more than $100 million in the rubber industry. Among other things, the company planned to give 600,000 rubber stumps to small-scale farmers to help them replant their plantations. But Liberia's rubber plantations face a grimmer reality. In May 2006 a UNMIL report indicated at five out of seven of the country's rubber plantations were plagued by gangs of mostly young men—former fighters from the civil war—who were illegally tapping trees and profitably selling it to local merchants. They could earn anywhere from $60 to $150 a week, a powerful inducement to illegal tapping in a country where 80% of the population is unemployed, and the World Bank estimates that most people live on less than one dollar a day. In August 2006, the government, backed by UN peacekeepers, repossessed the Guthrie plantation in northwestern Liberia from 500 ex-rebels who had controlled it since the end of the war. The Liberian Rubber Planters Association now oversees the enterprise, with UN soldiers standing guard. Some of the former rebel squatters who once controlled Guthrie are now employed tapping trees.

In 2000, Liberia recorded exports of $61.6 million, led by rubber and timber. The figures represented a 23% increase over 1999 and illustrated the feverish logging activity in Liberia's forests. The post–civil war rebuilding of the Liberian economy has put estimates on exports at $929.8 million. Like much of Liberia's economic activity, the timber industry was dominated by Charles Taylor. Global Witness examined the importance of timber for President Taylor and concluded it was more financially valuable to him and his security forces than was the diamond trade: revenues from timber constituted 50% of the country's export earnings before the UN Security Council imposed sanctions in July 2003 in an effort to restrict Taylor's regional threat. The timber industry in Liberia is cause of great controversy as the government's Private Use Permits have ended up selling a quarter of Liberia's land to foreign logging companies. Over half of the country's rainforest has now been surrendered to these timber companies. Additionally, Global Witness identified illegal logging as a major problem infecting half of the Liberia's forests despite government initiatives to stop such activity.

Liberia's "flag of convenience" ship registry was long a honey pot for the Taylor regime. The registry is second only to Panama's, and includes more than 2,000 vessels. (The Liberian flag covers thirty-five percent of the world's tanker fleet and a large number of cruise ships.) Fees brought in about $18 million annually and helped to pay for President Taylor's arms purchases. Under President Johnson-Sirleaf, the Liberian government plans to renegotiate the management contract for the ship registry to secure more revenues.

Liberia

As part of its antiterrorism campaign, the U.S. government signed an accord with Liberia in February 2004, which allows the U.S. Navy to board Liberian flagged vessels in international waters to inspect for unconventional weapons. The agreement was the first of its kind and resulted from fears that terrorist networks would use ships to attack the American economy. American and Liberian authorities have also been in cooperation to stop cocaine smuggling between the countries and several arrests were made and several smugglers were extradited and are on trial now in the United States.

In February 2012, energy companies reported the discovery of oil off the coasts of Liberia and Sierra Leone. Reserve estimates could be in the range of millions of barrels. The offshore waters were divided into 30 blocks by the government established National Oil Company of Liberia, and the blocks have begun being auctioned off to oil companies, such as Chevron and Exxon. This potential new resource could prove highly beneficial if managed correctly to the Liberian economy by prompting large amounts of foreign investment that could help rebuild the infrastructure.

President Johnson-Sirleaf has increased the national budget to over $400 million; while still tiny by international standards, this is up from just $80 million in 2006. Their total expenditures are around $520 million. However, the president convinced the IMF to remove its $4.9 billion in external debt. This was followed in September 2010 by an additional debt forgiveness of $1.2 billion by the Paris Club of donor countries. With sanctions removed from Liberia's diamonds and timber, a newly negotiated contract with the steel company ArcelorMittal, and the potential of a new source of revenue in oil, Liberia is poised for greater stability and economic growth from its low base.

In terms of health, Liberia has one of the world's highest infant mortality rates, and there is still malnutrition, often arising from unsafe water sources. In 2014, West Africa experienced a frightening outbreak of the Ebola virus. It initiated in Guinea and spread across the borders into Liberia; over 140 people died from the disease in those two countries before Liberia was able to quell the outbreak and was declared Ebola free.

Over 50,000 Ivorians have taken refugee in Liberia as the civil conflict in Ivory Coast escalated in past years. A country like Liberia with over 80% of its people below the poverty line has limited capacity to support 100,000 refugees. There was fear the Ivory Coast conflict would spill over into Liberia reigniting its devastating civil conflict, however that fear seems not to have materialized.

George Oppong Weah: President of Liberia

George Weah is the current president of Liberia and a former football player who played as a striker for many European clubs. Born and raised in Monrovia, Liberia, George played football for local Liberian leagues and in 1988 he embarked into the French football scene with a place in the club Monaco. His football (soccer) career took him to clubs such as Paris-Saint German and Milan. In 1995, he was honored with the FIFA World Player of the Year award and a Ballon D'Or and became the first African player to receive the honors. George Weah entered politics after retiring from football.

Weah is a devoted humanitarian for his war-torn country. During his playing career he became a UN Goodwill Ambassador.

In 2014, he ran for election to the Senate as a Congress for Democratic Change candidate in Montserrado County. He was overwhelmingly elected to the Liberian Senate on 20 December 2014. Weah defeated Robert Sirleaf, the son of President Sirleaf, becoming the first Liberian international athlete elected to represent a county in the Legislature. He won a landslide victory, receiving 78% of votes.

In April 2016, Weah announced his intention to run for President of Liberia in the 2017 elections as a candidate for the Coalition for Democratic Change. After winning the first round of the 2017 election with 38.4% of the vote, he and Joseph Boakai of the Unity Party went into the second round of the election. In the second round, Weah was elected President of Liberia, winning a run-off against Vice President Joseph Boakai with more than 60% of the vote. Weah was sworn in as president on 22 January 2018, making him the 4th youngest serving president in Africa. His main policy goals include fighting corruption, reforming the economy,

George Oppong Weah

combating illiteracy and improving life conditions. After evidently failing to enact promised reforms, Weah was defeated by Joseph Boakai in November 2023 who will serve a six-year term and has made tackling poverty and corruption a top priority while also setting up a war crimes court to deal with previous human rights abuses during the years of civil war.

Unable to get government officials onboard the much-touted anti-corruption campaign, the president announced suspensions of more than 450 top government officials for failing to declare their assets to the anti-corruption agency. Having contravened the code of conduct calling for full transparency of state employees, the officials were suspended without pay in February 2025 for an entire month until submission of the required declarations to ensure government accountability because all public officers were under obligation to declare their wealth before taking up their posts. When leaving positions in government, a list of affected officials was published by the Liberia Anti-Corruption Commission (LACC) as prescribed by law. Reducing his own salary by 40 percent, Boakai hoped to set a precedent for "responsible governance" and demonstrate "solidarity" with average Liberians. This is in contrast with his predecessor George Weah, who faced accusations of corruption and lavish spending, sparking mass protests amid a rise in the cost of living, though some civil society groups described the move as insufficient and largely symbolic. Also affecting the domestic political scene was a huge fire of the country's capitol building in December 2024, which occurred the day after plans were announced to the reigning speaker of the House of Representatives had sparked a tense protest with the country's Supreme Court unable to solve the internal dispute.

FUTURE CONSIDERATIONS

Civil conflict killed more than 200,000 people and displaced at least half the prewar population of 2.5 million. The legacy of war is appalling. Child soldiers, who were routinely given drugs to fortify their fighting resolve, pose difficult social problems. Medical experts estimate that up to 70% of all ex-combatants continue to use drugs, and many have become addicts. Unless a place in society (care, support, and education) is found for these former combatants, violence could re-ignite. Moreover, the flow of drugs into Liberia is largely unimpeded. Law enforcement agencies seem unable or unwilling to stop the smuggling of illegal substances. Weak security and judicial systems have resulted in major human rights problems on such issues as police conduct and

Liberia

human trafficking. Liberia is believed to have become a transit point for drug trafficking throughout the region. Liberia has the economic potential with oil and other resources (including agriculture) to continue to improve the standard of living in country and decrease the poverty rates. With these growing economic sectors, Liberia will have to remain attentive to the potential detrimental environmental impacts of deforestation and oil pollution.

That said, the future looks brighter for Liberia than it has at most any point in recent memory, in some cases literally: since the arrival of Ellen Johnson-Sirleaf, Monrovia has seen some electricity flow for the first time in 15 years. To say that Liberia is better off today than several years ago may be faint praise, but nonetheless it is clear the country is moving in the right direction. The country is a staunch American ally in the region and President Johnson-Sirleaf even visited the U.S. to meet with President Obama in 2010. In its post-conflict reconstruction phase, it has become a favorite of development agencies, winning a $15 million grant from the Millennium Challenge Corporation (MCC) in June of 2010. In November of the same year, she dismissed her cabinet, seeking a "clean slate," as the BBC reported. There is a long way for the country to go, and there is undoubtedly high-level corruption that persists in Liberia, but major social strife may be in the country's rear-view mirror.

The Republic of Mali

A traditional Dogon granary   Photo by Dan Silver

Literacy Rate: 35.5 (CIA 2018)
Life Expectancy: 62.8 years (CIA 2023 est.)
Head of State: Assimi Goita, Transition President (since June 27, 2021)
Head of Government: Prime Minister Choguel Maiga (since June 7, 2021)

LAND AND PEOPLE

Some 60% of Mali is covered by the Sahara Desert. This region receives virtually no rain and is only sparsely inhabited, mostly by semi-nomadic descendents of Berber tribes. The otherwise flat terrain is broken occasionally by rocky hills. The country becomes more hospitable to the south of fabled Timbuktu, which was once an important emporium on an ancient caravan route of Arab merchants. The Niger River flows across the country from west to east, past the capital Bamako and the ancient cities of Djenné and Mopti, making a great bend to the south near Timbuktu and then continuing to its delta in Nigeria. With its tributary, the Bani River, the Niger forms a large inland delta, which creates a rich farming heartland. The country becomes more temperate south of the Niger, receiving greater rainfall in average years. This section is part of the so-called Guinea Savannah, a brush and low tree belt stretching from the Atlantic coast 3,000 miles inland to the east.

Mali has a number of rich sites of archaeological and historical interest, several of which are UNESCO World Heritage sites. Timbutktu itself remains a tourist destination, with part of its allure being its remoteness even today. Djenné is one perhaps the finest examples of the monumental mud-building traditions of the West African Sahel, most notably at its Great Mosque. Similarly, the Tomb of the Askia in Gao is a 55-foot-high pyramidal structure built in mud in 1495 by the first of the emperors of Songhai, the Askia Mohamed.

BASIC FACTS

Area: 1,204,350 sq. km. = 545,190 sq. mi. (more than four times the size of Nevada)
Population: 21,597,722 (July 2023 est.)
Capital City: Bamako
Government Type: Semi-Presidential Republic
Neighboring Countries: Senegal (southwest); Mauritania (north, northwest); Algeria (northeast); Niger (east, southeast); Burkina Faso, Côte d'Ivoire, Guinea (south)
Official Language: French
Other Principal Languages: Bambara (or Bamana), spoken by 80% of the population. Bomu, Boso, Dogon, Fulfuldé, Kassonké, Malinké, Senoufo, Songai, Soninké, Tamashek
Ethnic Groups: Mandé 50% (Bambara, Malinké, Sarakolé), Peul 17%, Voltaic 12%, Songhai 6%, Tuareg and Moor 10%, other 5%
Principal Religions: Muslim 90%, indigenous beliefs 9%, Christian 1%
Former Colonial Status: Part of French West Africa (1890–1960)
Independence Date: September 22, 1960
GDP Per Capita (IMF 2023 est.): $889 (nominal), $2,656 (PPP)
Gini Index: 32.3 (World Bank 2018)
Currency: CFA franc, $US 1 = 594 CFA (Apr. 2022)
Inflation Rate: 8.0% (2022 est.)
Chief Commercial Products: Gold, cotton, and livestock
Foreign Direct Investments (FDI) net inflows: 198,927,339

Mali

The villages of the Dogon country also astound visitors, being built into and upon rock escarpments and cliffs near the towns of Bandiagara and Douentza.

Mali's musical traditions are among the most distinguished in West Africa. Traditionally the preserve of socially influential bards called *griots*, music has breached the boundaries of caste in the modern era. One of Mali's greatest musical stars is Salif Keita, who was born an albino in a culture where albinos are believed cursed; ostracized by his father, Keita and his mother were only allowed to return to his village when the local imam predicted great things for him. Equally impressive are the husband-and-wife duo Amadou Bagayoko and Mariam Doumbia, known as Amadou & Mariam, who met at Mali's Institute for the Young Blind, and have since become musical sensations. Other examples of Mali's musical greats as Issa Bagayogo, Toumani Diabaté, Habib Koité, the late Ali Farka Touré, and Boubacar Traoré. Many of these mix modern electronic influences with traditional Sahelian instruments such as the kora, a 21-stringed harp with a large drum-like body that is held by two handles and picked with the thumbs.

While Mali is a country with low levels of education on average, it has given rise to several prominent intellectuals, including scientists and writers. Mali's most distinguished scientist is the astrophysicist Cheikh Modibo Diarra, who masterminded NASA's Pathfinder mission to Mars. Many of the country's leading writers have worked to document the ancient traditions of Mali's medieval empires; perhaps the leading writer was Amadou Hampaté Bâ, who died in 1991.

HISTORY TO PRESENT DAY

For early history, see *Historical Background* and *The Colonial Period: The French*.

Independence, Modibo Keita (1960–1968), and Moussa Traoré (1968–1991)

Present-day Mali was known in the colonial period as French Soudan. It became part of the French Community in 1958, with almost complete internal autonomy. With French permission, Soudan and Senegal joined in 1959 to form the Mali Federation, but this was dissolved in 1960 when Senegal dropped out. After achieving independence in 1960, the government headed by Modibo Keita withdrew from the French Community, which had evolved into an economic union of former French colonies in association with France. Mali issued its own currency, the Malian franc, which lasted from 1962 until 1984.

Keita announced that Mali was a socialist nation and sought assistance from the

Former President Alpha Oumar Konaré

Soviet Union and later from communist China. Mali received Russian aircraft and weapons, and the Chinese sent technical assistance and some financial aid. The ruling Soudanese Union-African Democratic Rally (US-RDA) controlled the press, labor unions, and state youth organizations, but gradually splintered into two groups. One group favored a total socialist commitment, while the other saw advantages in economic cooperation with France and its former colonies.

Under Keita, Mali's fragile economy gradually declined and by 1967 the economy was in disarray and the government bankrupt. In 1967, Mali devalued the Malian franc to reset its value vis-à-vis the French franc. This had the effect of reducing the buying power of the small segment of Malians who were engaged in the wage economy. Unrest resulted, and Keita dissolved the Political Bureau of the state party because "it ceased to enjoy the confidence of the people."

In 1968, a group of young army officers seized control, establishing a Military Committee for National Liberation (CMLN). The military placed Keita in a distant prison in Kidal, deep in the Sahara. Lt. Moussa Traoré became Mali's president and dominant political figure from 1968 until the 1990s. The new military leaders attempted economic reform but were debilitated by internal political struggles and a disastrous drought. Ultimately corrupt and repressive, the Traoré regime sustained itself in power for years. A new constitution created a single-party state in 1974, and in 1976 Traoré created a new party, the Democratic Union of the Malian People (UDPM). He led the party in sham elections in 1979, winning 99% of the vote.

The economy declined under the inefficient state through the 1980s; students and actors from within the military occasionally challenged Traoré but were brutally suppressed. By 1990, unrest hit the north in the form of a Tuareg rebellion. Tuareg nomads were generally pastoralists, and they had been pushed to the brink of starvation under the Traoré regime: their flocks had been decimated and their water holes had dried up. They called themselves the Azawad Popular Movement (*Movement populaire de l'Azawad*, MPA), and took up arms after thousands of tons of food destined for starving nomads was stolen by the army. When the army proved ineffective in limiting Tuareg raids on farmers along the Niger River, the farmers themselves organized a militia, which they called *Ghanda Koy*—Masters of the Land—to strike back at nomads.

Desperate to improve the economy, the government approved plans for economic liberalization and signed an agreement with the IMF. By 1990, the austerity demanded of such plans had begun to pinch all but the ruling clique. The Soviet Union's collapse encouraged demands for multiparty democracy, something Traoré was unwilling to concede. In early 1991, student-led antigovernment demonstrations broke out, and these were met with repression. The protests turned into street rioting by March 22, when an estimated 200 people were killed by government forces. On March 26 a military coup d'état overthrew the president, suspended the constitution, and set in motion the process by which Mali would return to civilian rule. Lt. Col. Amadou Toumani Touré headed up the National Reconciliation Council. Touré promised democratic reforms and kept his word; he came to be known by his initials as ATT.

The National Conference and Democracy (1991–2012)

A cross-section of Mali's political leaders held a momentous National Conference in July and August 1991, which established the processes for multiparty democracy.

Former President Amadou Toumani Touré

Mali

ATT stepped down and transferred power to the elected civilian government after Malians enthusiastically participated in presidential, legislative, and local elections from January to April 1992. In all, 21 political parties participated and 11 won seats in parliament. Alpha Oumar Konaré, an archeologist, defeated nine other candidates for the presidency, and his Association for Democracy in Mali (ADEMA) secured a parliamentary majority.

During his first five-year term, Konaré won plaudits for helping consolidate democracy. In one major step, he devolved more governing powers to local authorities, which created some legitimacy among neglected and restive groups such as the Tuareg in Mali's remote areas. Political expression flourished as 40 independent newspapers and journals appeared (in French, Arabic, and local languages) and often criticized the government. Radio stations proliferated and were the most important source of news, given low levels of literacy. For Western states, Mali became a showcase for democracy.

In 1995, Konaré put a temporary end to the long-running Tuareg rebellion, as the rebels and the farmers who fought them rallied to Konaré's peace and reconciliation program. The program disarmed the armies, paid 9,000 fighters $210 each, and made efforts to integrate some of the former combatants into the army, a task rendered more difficult by the preference of Tuaregs for Arabic language over French. In March 1996, President Konaré symbolically set fire to several thousand weapons to seal the peace.

A committed democrat and by all accounts a humane leader, Konaré commuted death sentences meted out to Moussa Traoré and several of his cronies to life imprisonment; he closed the notorious and terrifying prison at Kidal. President Konaré looked set to cruise to a second five-year term in 1997, but the presidential and legislative elections that year proved a logistical disaster. They were so poorly administered and produced such dubious results that a court threw them out, requiring that they be repeated. The opposition—and there were now 62 parties in Mali, many organized around a single personality—screamed foul and took to the streets. Security forces used tear gas to control mobs. Nearly all of the opposition boycotted the second round of elections and thousands stayed away from the polls, fearful for their personal safety. Konaré and ADEMA won handily, but with a much-weakened mandate and with less legitimacy.

After the 1997 electoral fiasco heightened political tension and led to further complications (with municipal elections being postponed repeatedly, for example), Konaré sought constitutional revisions. He established regional forums in December 1998 to discuss electoral changes, and delegates made final recommendations in 1999. At Konaré's suggestion, a two-term limit was established for the presidency. The state agreed to provide funding for political parties and agreed that journalists should no longer be imprisoned for offending press laws.

The presidential election of 2002 was held against a backdrop of worsening economic conditions and a fragmenting political scene. The vital cotton sector was in crisis, and export income had fallen nearly 50%. Family incomes shrank while gas and electricity prices soared. Women took to the streets with their pots and pans to complain about the high cost of living. ADEMA splintered, divided by disputes between reformist youth and political veterans. The younger elements rejected the presidential ambitions of former Prime Minister Ibrahim Boubacar Keïta (known as IBK) and drove him from the party, whereupon he formed the Rally for Mali (*Rassemblement Pour Mali*: RPM), which became Mali's 74th party. The incumbent ADEMA prime minister, Mandé Sidibé, resigned to run as an independent. ADEMA formally endorsed Soumaila Cissé, a former finance minister. Having split among three candidacies, ADEMA stood little chance of winning the election in the first round.

The favorite was Amadou Toumani Touré (ATT), who ran without party affiliation, but was backed by a coalition of some 28 parties. The man who overthrew the dictatorship of Moussa Traoré had developed an enormous popular following after he returned power to civilian authorities in 1992. With 24 candidates in the first round, ATT led the vote with 28.7%, followed by the ADEMA's Soumaila Cissé with nearly 21.3%. IBK, who had received the backing of Bamako's imams during their pre-electoral Friday sermons, arrived in third place, a mere 4,000 votes behind Cissé, with 21.03%. He protested and claimed fraud, but ultimately accepted the Constitutional Court's results, urging his followers to vote for ATT.

In the runoff, ATT won a crushing victory, defeating his rival 65% to 35%. Having run without his own party, and having declared he would not create one, ATT promised to work closely with whatever parliamentary majority emerged from Mali's 2002 legislative elections. The elections gave RPM and ADEMA substantial positions in the National Assembly, but neither achieved a clear majority. IBK was overwhelmingly chosen as the parliamentary speaker. ATT chose a Tuareg, Ahmed Mohamed Ag Hamani, as prime minister and head of government. A trained statistician and former ambassador, Ag Hamani had no party affiliation and formed a cabinet of national unity, including representatives from a broad range of Malian parties. With two non-party leaders at the helm, Mali entered a period of politics by consensus.

Mali's northern region became a new front in international terrorism during the period of ATT's first term. Algerian Islamists, known in French as the *Groupe Salafiste pour la Prédication et le Combat* (GSPC: Salafist Group for Preaching and Combat) kidnapped 32 European tourists near the Libyan-Algerian border in 2003 and transported some of them to Northern Mali. To free its citizens, Germany paid a ransom of nearly $6 million, making the GSPC leader, Ammari Saifi, the most powerful Islamic militant in the region. Saifi used his hostage booty to buy arms

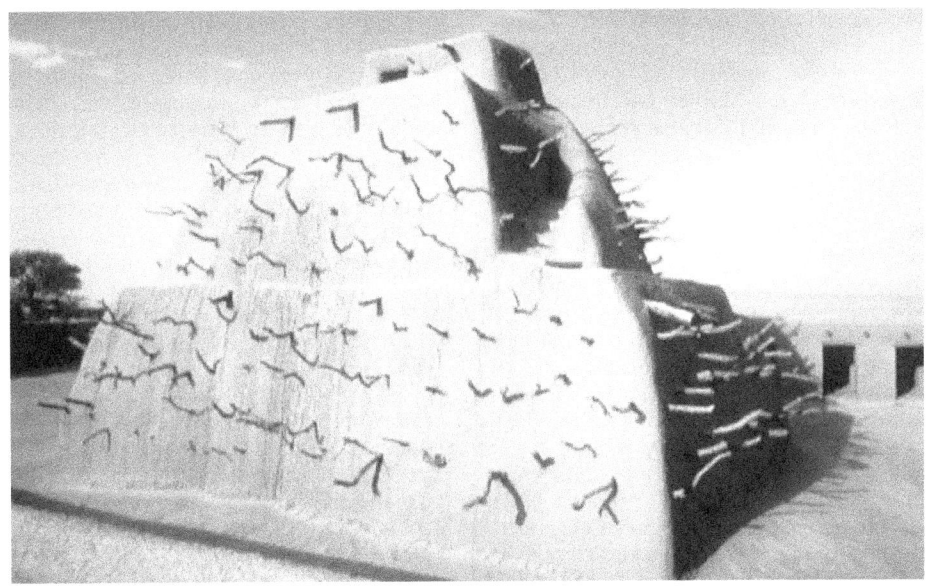

The tomb of the Askia in Gao. Named a UNESCO World Heritage site in 2004.

Mali

and recruits in Northern Mali. His movements were monitored by American and Algerian intelligence, and when notified of his whereabouts, Malian troops forced him into Niger, from whence he was chased into Chad, where 43 of his men were killed or captured. The GSPC eventually took the al-Qaeda name and became Al-Qaeda in the Islamic Maghreb (AQIM). Its zone of action in northern and eastern Mali has been plagued by banditry, smuggling and kidnapping.

Despite the 1992 peace agreement with the government, Tuareg factions in the north and east also remained resentful, feelings exacerbated by the activities of the Malian army and American-led counterterrorism forces in the region. In May 2006, Tuareg dissidents attacked two military sites in Kidal and another in Menaka, near the Niger border, and held them long enough to abscond with a large supply of weapons. The leader of the raid was Lieutenant-Colonel Hassan Fagaga, one of the highest ranking Tuaregs to have been integrated into the national army following the Tuareg rebellion of the 1990s. Col. Fagaga had deserted the army in February 2006, demanding better work and living conditions for former rebels in the army and the creation of a new political district in the Kidal region for better representation of Tuareg interests.

The government and Tuareg rebels agreed to a ceasefire and peace settlement over the months of 2006. The rebels gave up demands for regional autonomy, and the government agreed to speed up development of the three northern provinces. Details were finalized in February 2007: deserters were permitted to return to the army, and rebels agreed to return stolen arms and munitions. The settlement was festively celebrated in early March. A convoy of 200 cars brought about 2,000 former rebels to Kidal; thousands lined the streets in welcome and watched them hand back the stolen weapons.

Peace in the north helped ATT's reelection campaign for 2007. The redoubtable Ibrahim Boubacar Keita opposed the incumbent, along with seven other candidates. Forty-four separate parties supported ATT's reelection bid, and he garnered nearly 70% of the vote, shocking his opponents with a first ballot victory. Low turnout—less than 40% participated—suggested voters might be skeptical of politics and politicians.

Unrest in the north and east reemerged in 2008 and 2009. Tuareg rebels attacked a military base in December of 2008, taking hostages and killing about two dozen people. By February 2009, Malian forces had retaliated by assaulting several Tuareg rebel bases and inducing the surrender of several hundred militants. In May 2009, Algeria sent military equipment to Mali, as part of the shared operation against al-Qaeda. By July, ex-rebels from Mali had decided to work with the army in an arrangement orchestrated by the Algerian ambassador.

The Coup and Rebellions (2012–present)

Mali's government proved unable to deal with the Tuareg rebellion, and the country was dramatically destabilized in 2011. One contributing factor was the collapse of Muammar Qaddafi's regime in Libya, which triggered migrations southward (into Mali, Niger, and Chad) by Tuareg nomads. These warriors—well-armed from their time in Libya—swelled the ranks of restive Tuaregs in Mali's Saharan hinterland, forming a group known as the Azawad National Liberation Movement (*Mouvement National pour la Libération de l'Azawad*, MNLA). These forces besieged the northern city of Kidal. Army officers demanded that ATT's government do more to put down the rebellion, but the cash-strapped administration was unable or unwilling to take additional action; this drove a serious wedge between the former army leader and elements of the military, with the latter claiming that civilians inadequately supported the army's fight against separatists and extremists.

On March 22, 2012, army Captain Amadou Sanogo staged a coup that toppled ATT's government. International observers, surprised by the turn of events in a long-standing democracy, condemned the coup. Protests began to demand a prompt return to democracy, though these were met with counter-protests in support of the army junta. Amadou Toumani Touré eventually went into exile with his family in neighboring Senegal, after a period of time in which his whereabouts were unknown. After some days of uncertainty, the military leaders called on civilians to form a caretaker government. Dioncounda Traoré was placed in the presidency on April 12, followed by Cheick Modibo Diarra as prime minister on April 17. Diarra appointed several military figures to important ministerial posts.

In the meantime, violence and unrest continued. The MNLA forces advanced south and west until they controlled the major northern cities of Kidal, Gao, and Timbuktu. On April 6, they declared independence from Mali under the banner of the nation of Azawad; the declaration was not recognized by the African Union, nor other international actors. In May, the MNLA (which had mainly secular aims) allied with the Islamist group Ansar Dine in a marriage of convenience and strategy: the combination of forces increased the chance that Azawad would be able to resist any government counteroffensive, and the Islamists secured the opportunity to institute sharia law in some of the areas under their joint control.

Violence also reared its head in the capital Bamako in May, where acting president Dioncounda Traoré was attacked and beaten unconscious by a mob at the presidential palace after reports that the regional body ECOWAS and the coup leaders (led by Capt. Sanogo) had agreed on a one-year extension of Traoré's interim presidency. While Traoré survived, he required evacuation overseas for treatment. This chain of events highlighted how Mali's political life suddenly deteriorated in the space of a single year. Meanwhile, Prime Minister Cheick Modibo Diarra attempted to contain the intrigue in Bamako by padding the cabinet with supporters of Capt. Sanogo and shuffling ministers. This did little to halt the rebellion and Diarra resigned in December 2012

The combined forces of the MNLA and Ansar Dine pushed southwest through the country, rapidly seizing control of the important population centers and symbolic towns of Kidal, Gao, Douentza, and Timbuktu by late 2012. In the areas they controlled, the Ansar Dine rebels instituted draconian and reactionary forms of Islamic sharia law. Apart from eliminating many women's rights and meting out harsh punishments for blasphemy, they began the systematic destruction of invaluable cultural artifacts from Mali's centuries-old Islamic tradition. This attempt at cultural "cleansing" included the smashing of temples and shrines in Timbuktu, along with the destruction of ancient manuscripts.

As Ansar Dine grew in strength, the West African group ECOWAS (Economic Community of West African States), the African Union, and the United Nations began diplomatic preparations for a peacekeeping force. However, the pace of events soon outstripped these efforts. With the last major towns on the road to the capital Bamako falling to the rebels, the former colonial power France quickly assembled its own military response in January 2013. It deployed well-armed and well-trained French troops to strategic points along the Niger River and routed the rebels, reclaiming the population centers and pushing the rebels back up to the most remote northeastern stretches of the desert. In the midst of the fighting, it became clear that a key split had emerged between the relatively secular Tuareg liberation movement (the MNLA) and the Islamists of Ansar Dine. This division of the rebellion facilitated the pacification of many localities. By April 2013, France began its withdrawal in favor of a multinational African peacekeeping force, and in June the Malian government has signed an accord with the MNLA that will allow

Mali

for elections to proceed at the end of July 2013, in exchange for the Tuaregs having a degree of autonomy in their regions of the Sahara in northeast Mali.

After the upheaval, Mali held an election on July 28, 2013, that nominally restored democratic practice. Ibrahim Boubacar Keita took the largest portion of the vote in the first round of the election (against about two dozen other candidates), and then won convincingly in the runoff against Soumaila Cissé. Keita (known to many Malians as IBK) took nearly 78% of the vote, with Cissé taking the remaining 22%. This was followed by a parliamentary election in December 2014 that gave IBK's party a clear majority with 115 of 147 seats. After prime minister Oumar Tatam Ly resigned in early 2014 (for reasons that remain unclear), IBK appointed Moussa Mara as the new prime minister. Mara's appointment was seen as an attempt to create a unity government that would help control the situation in the north.

The 2013 elections took place under relatively calm conditions, but the ability of the new president to contain the nation's civil conflicts is yet undetermined. In early 2014, there has been a back and forth between the Malian government forces and the enduring separatist and extremist movements in the northern hinterland around the town of Kidal. In May, prime minister Moussa Mara visited Kidal and the result was clashes that led to the deaths of 50 government soldiers. These clashes have been followed by preliminary attempts at a ceasefire between the Tuaregs and the government.

CONTEMPORARY THEMES

Mali's economy is agriculture-based and cotton is the principal cash crop; it supports nearly a quarter of the population directly or indirectly and has traditionally accounted for half of Malian export earnings. Yet, the industry is withering for several reasons. One main difficulty is that China and the United States privilege their own cotton farmers. American farm policy protects American farmers from international market prices, allowing otherwise uneconomic farms to dump cotton onto world markets at prices that undercut those of Malian farmers. Mali has joined Burkina Faso, Benin, and Chad in highlighting the devastating effects of rich-country subsidies on African cotton farmers in various world trade meetings. Domestic factors also make the Malian cotton farmer less productive: poor quality seeds, expensive fertilizers and insecticides, small growing plots, declining fertility and limited irrigation, deteriorated roads, and large administrative costs of the state marketing body all reduce production and returns. Malian farmers produce on average a ton of cotton per hectare, while farmers in China and Brazil produce three tons per acre. Finally, conflict in Côte d'Ivoire shut down Ivoirian ports and increased transportation costs for cotton shippers as good had to be reoriented to ports in Ghana or Togo. This seriously burdened road infrastructure; between 70% and 90% of all vehicles using the route were found to surpass weight limits, accelerating road deterioration and raising maintenance costs.

Gold replaced cotton as Mali's biggest income producer in 2000. In 2004, Mali became the fourth-largest producer in Africa (after South Africa, Ghana, and Tanzania). South African interests jointly own the country's two major mining operations, Morila and Loulo, with the Malian government.

In early 2003, the IMF announced that Mali was to benefit from debt relief amounting to approximately $675 million under the enhanced Heavily Indebted Poor Countries (HIPC) initiative. Additional relief came in 2005, when the leaders of the G-8, the world's richest countries, agreed to cancel the multilateral debt (owed to agencies like the World Bank and IMF) of 19 of the world's poorest countries, Mali led. Mali's accumulated debt, almost all of it owed to multilateral lenders, amounted to $3.129 billion. Debt repayment and service charges can now, in principle, be used to fund anti-poverty programs.

Fundamental social challenges remain. Health and education indicators are among the lowest in the world. For every 1,000 births, an estimated 50 newborns will die, and a total of 100 will die by their first birthday and nearly 200 by the age of five (2009 estimates). Despite a steady rise, life expectancy is still under 49 years. Even among the young, where indicators are improving, literacy and education are limited. Only about half of adult men are literate and about half of young men attend secondary school. The statistics are worse for women, with about a third of adults being literate and a third of girls today reaching secondary school. There have been some improvements in women's rights, however, as some of the statistical gaps are closing. In addition, women are gaining more social rights: female genital cutting was common as of the early 1990s but has declined as an informal coalition of urban residents, devout Muslims, and the state has combined to condemn and limit the practice. With large swaths of the country ungovernable, armed groups of Islamists and various ethnicities continue to plague these regions with major loss of life in January 2023. After fostering a military alliance with Burkina-Faso and Niger in 2021, United Nations peacekeeping forces were ejected from Mali as the country deals with major heatwaves. Economically, Mali has proposed with other Western African states dropping the French-based currency, the central African Franc (CFA), which is considered a major hedge against inflation.

FUTURE CONSIDERATIONS

As of early 2012, Mali had spent 20 years of its half-century of independence in relative freedom, even after decades of misrule from the 1960s to the 1980s. This was all the more impressive given the country's crushing poverty. The collapse of the government in 2012 showed that even in Africa's more robust democracies, institutions remain fragile and political situations precarious. There is hope that Mali has made the first steps in a return to full democracy with the presidential election of 2013, but tension will continue while the Tuareg situation remains unresolved and while Islamist movements flourish in the desert hinterland. Mali's enduring difficulty is the rule of law in remote areas. The question became especially salient with the resurgence of Tuareg demands for autonomy that precipitated the 2012 coup. The current government of Mali—led by Ibrahim Boubacar Keita—is aware of the problems posed by the vast and largely ungoverned regions of the north and east. Beyond the Tuareg rebellion, the central government has wrestled with Ansar Dine and the southerly movement of the AQIM (al-Qaeda in the Islamic Maghreb) terrorist organization, which thrives in the weakly-governed regions of the Sahara and north-central Africa.

In social and economic terms, addressing poverty is the principal task for Mali's government (once it stabilizes). Mali remains one of the poorest countries in the world, though the years leading up to 2012 saw steady growth rates in the range of 4% to 5% per year. Economic opportunities are limited, though recent debt relief allowed the government to channel investment into social services and stimulate productive investment. The recent boom in gold prices should begin to show up in Mali's economic figures, assuming exploration and investment continue to increase. For a country that was long seen as politically stable and economically under-resourced, the main question for the future is whether the political situation is re-stabilizing enough to allow the country to advance on economic and social indicators.

The Islamic Republic of Mauritania

Crane operator at a mining site near Nouadhibou

BASIC FACTS

Area: 1,085,210 sq. km. = 419,000 sq. mi. (one and one-half times the size of Texas)
Population: 4,244,878 (June 2023 est.)
Capital City: Nouakchott
Government Type: Presidential Republic
Neighboring Countries: Senegal (southwest); Western Sahara (northwest); Algeria (northeast); Mali (east and southeast).
Official Languages: Hasaniya Arabic, Wolof
Other Principal Languages: Fulfulde, Soninke, Zenaga; French
Ethnic Groups: mixed Moor/black 40%, Moor 30%, black 30%
Principal Religion: Islam
Former Colonial Status: French Colony (1920–1960)
Independence Date: November 28, 1960
GDP Per Capita (IMF 2023 est.): $2,475 (nominal), $7,437 (PPP)
Gini Index: 32.16 (World Bank 2014)
Currency: Ouguiya; 1 USD = 34.39 MRO (Apr. 2023)
Inflation Rate: 4.9% (2022 est.)
Chief Commercial Products: Fish and fish products, iron ore, and gold
Foreign Direct Investments (FDI) net inflows: 501,852,411
Literacy Rate: 67% (CIA 2021)
Life Expectancy: 65.54 years (CIA 2023 est.)
Head of State: Mohamed Ould Cheikh El Ghazouani, President (since August 1, 2019)
Head of Government: Prime Minister Mohamed Ould Bilal (since August 6, 2020)

LAND AND PEOPLE

Mauritania lies on the upper west coast of Africa, almost wholly within the immense Sahara Desert. The northern two-thirds of the country is totally flat and stony, with virtually no rain. Its *ergs* (huge areas of dunes) are constantly transformed by hot, dry winds, which make the implementation of road infrastructure virtually impossible. Thunderstorms occasionally intrude and brief but heavy rainfall collects into streams and rivers within a few minutes. Shortly after the end of storms, there is no sign of moisture. In some places, the water descends to great depths, supporting a few green oases, which stand out in the otherwise empty landscape. Southern regions are subject to sporadic torrential rain showers, which can wreak much damage.

A narrow band of semiarid land stretches from west to east in the southern region of the country. Its rainfall of about four inches per year supports low, sparse scrub vegetation. The most heavily populated area of the country lies along the Senegal River. The rich soil is periodically flooded during normal years by the river, which, when added to the rainfall of 10 to 25 inches, permits cultivation and cattle raising.

At independence in 1960, some 83% of the population was nomadic. Today that figure is less than 5%, the consequence of devastating droughts in the 1970s and their periodic reoccurrence. Animal herds were decimated, and traditional family life and the rural economy were virtually destroyed. The result was a massive migration to the principal urban centers. Nouakchott and the port Nouadhibou were among the fastest-growing cities in the world. In the space of 40 years, the capital's population grew from 40,000 to 1.4 million. Eighty percent of the country's urban population lives in the two cities of Nouadhibou and Nouakchott. Surrounding both Nouakchott and Nouadhibou today are encampments of the impoverished, mud-built shanty towns. Forty percent of the country's entire population lives in and around the capital. Most live from odd jobs, and their homes have neither electricity nor running water. Traditionally, agriculture and fishing have

Mauritania

formed the foundation of the Mauritanian economy, though these industries are vulnerable to drought and over-exploitation, respectively. More recently, Mauritania has begun to exploit its offshore oil reserves, which are expected to produce millions of barrels.

Desert oases, once thriving commercial and cultural centers, are now prey to an advancing Sahara. Chinguetti, the legendary seventh holiest city in Islam, once boasted a population of 3,000; 30,000 camels annually drank its waters. Today it is almost a ghost town. UNESCO has named it part of the world's patrimony in recognition of its spiritual and cultural importance. In Chinguetti eight families guard its greatest treasures: thousands of manuscripts—verses of the *Koran*, treatises on religion, astronomy and traditional medicine, works of poetry. The oldest go back to the 12th century. None have been translated and almost all are in advanced stages of deterioration.

Mauritania's other great treasure is the *Parc National du Banc d'Arguin* (PNBA), which UNESCO made a World Heritage site in 1989. Located on the Atlantic coast, the park provides a unique example of the transition zone between the Sahara Desert and the Atlantic Ocean. It covers an area as large as Lebanon, equally distributed between land and sea and was founded in 1976 for its bird life. More than two million wading birds rest there on their annual migrations, and during breeding season 45,000 pairs of aquatic birds—pelicans, flamingos, spoonbills, herons, cormorants, and others—nest in the park.

The government has declared that Mauritania is an Islamic republic. Non-Muslims are not considered to be citizens and must be granted permission by the government to worship in private.

HISTORY TO PRESENT DAY

For early history, see *Historical Background* and *The Colonial Period: The French*.

Independence and the Ould Daddah Presidency (1961–1978)

Mauritania achieved full independence in 1960; the government adopted the presidential system, with a president elected for a five-year term by all citizens. The first presidential elections were held in 1961 and resulted in victory for the Republic's founder, Moktar Ould Daddah. President Ould Daddah was reelected in 1966, 1971 and 1976. The unicameral National Assembly of 40 members was also elected by universal suffrage. The People's Party was dominant after 1959, holding all seats in the National Assembly.

Mauritania's relations with Morocco and Algeria were quite close. In the heady days of African liberation from colonial rule, they each had an interest in Spain's holdings in Spanish Sahara—rich with a billion tons of phosphate. Wearied of guerrilla activity in its African territories, Spain decided to surrender Spanish Sahara. Mauritania joined with Morocco to exclude Algeria from the desert wasteland. The end result was a de facto partition of the former Spanish colony, with Mauritania receiving a portion in the south and Morocco receiving a larger northern area. Algeria supported the Polisario Front, Spanish Sahara's independence movement, and Mauritania soon found itself at war.

France pledged to help Mauritania against attacking Polisario guerrillas, and after the guerrillas established the Saharan Arab Democratic Republic in Spanish Sahara and made forays into Mauritania, the French launched air strikes from bases near Dakar, Senegal. Badly drained by a staggering military budget, which had increased army strength in two years from 1,500 to 15,000 men, the economy sagged noticeably. Things worsened when the Polisario attacked the railroad moving iron ore, the country's principal moneymaker, to the port of Nouadhibou.

In these circumstances the army intervened to topple the Ould Daddah government in mid-1978. In 1979, Mauritania officially ended its role in the desert war over the Western Sahara. Drained by its costly struggle with Polisario guerrillas, it renounced all claims to the territory. In 1983, it officially recognized the Saharan Arab Democratic Republic.

Mauritanian politics have traditionally been dominated by the cultural and ethnic divide that divides the population. An artificial creation of the colonizer, Mauritania joins Moors, northern nomadic peoples of Arab-Berber culture, with southern black Africans, agriculturalists concentrated in the Senegal River valley. The Moor segment of the population itself is divided into two groupings: so-called "White Moors," descended from the region's Arab-Berber conquerors, and "Black Moors," black Africans of Arab-Berber culture, traditional servants and slaves of the conquerors. Moors speak Arabic, while the Afro-Mauritanians of the south tend to speak French in addition to their indigenous languages. Virtually all are Muslim, but Moors tend to take a single wife, while Afro-Mauritanians tend to be polygamous. This has resulted in a more rapid population increase among Afro-Mauritanians, now about one-third the population. These racial identities are the historical basis of social tensions.

At independence, White Moors held political power, while Afro-Mauritanians were more numerous within the civil administration. Founding President Moktar Ould Daddah was able to keep the tensions in check, but with the beginning of the Saharan conflict in 1978 power became increasingly concentrated, especially after Ould Daddah's overthrow in 1978, in the hands of White Moors. "Arabization" policies were pursued in schools and workplaces, to the protests of Afro-Mauritanians. Several military regimes followed until Colonel Maouya Ould Sidi Ahmed Taya (or simply Ould Taya) took power in 1984.

Cultural Divides and the Ould Taya Administration (1984–2005)

Afro-Mauritanians became fearful when Moors began to invest in southern agricultural lands as early as 1983. Municipal elections of 1986 seemed to increase the power of Moors even further, just as the economic consequences of economic liberalization began to impact Afro-Mauritanians most heavily. The clandestine Front for the Liberation of Africans in Mauritania (FLAM) staged a failed *coup d'état* in 1987; racial conflicts followed in the Senegal River valley in 1989, resulting in massacres of African farmers and retaliatory racial onslaughts against Moors in Senegal. From 1989 to 1991, about 95,000 Afro-Mauritanians were expelled or fled, mostly to Mali and Senegal.

The discovery of another plot against the regime in 1991—the details of which remain obscure to this day—resulted in hundreds of Afro-Mauritanian soldiers being arrested, tortured, maimed, and executed. Parliament passed an amnesty bill in 1993 to preclude any legal pursuit of those involved but has not acknowledged responsibility or wrongdoing. It has, however, given pensions to the widows of some of those killed.

The appearance of what seemed to be racial purges, coupled with the regime's support of Iraq during the Gulf War, led

Ex-President Sidi Ould Sheikh Abdellahi

Mauritania

to international isolation and diminished foreign aid, but Col. Ould Taya managed a turnabout by beginning the process of controlled democratization in 1991. After 14 years as head of the military junta, he announced a referendum on a new constitution and general elections. The new constitution was approved and legislation legalizing political parties passed shortly thereafter.

Ould Taya's opponents coalesced to form the *Union des Forces Démocratiques* (UFD) and the outgoing regime responded by creating the *Parti Républicain et Démocratique et Social* (PRDS), which brought together Ould Taya's supporters—prominently local notables, tribal chiefs and businessmen. In the presidential elections of 1992, the UFD nominated Ahmed Ould Daddah, half brother of Mauritania's first president, but Ould Taya won with 63% of the votes. Still, Ould Daddah's 33% was more than respectable, given the "irregularities" of the election. Refusing to accept the results of a fraudulent election, the UFD boycotted parliamentary elections later that year, allowing the PRDS to dominate the legislature. Losses led to defections from the UFD as the pragmatic and opportunistic migrated to the PRDS. As a result of this influx of new supporters, the PRDS became the sole vehicle of meaningful political expression in Mauritania; internal clashes between factions became more important than contests between rival parties in Mauritanian politics.

President Ould Taya showed himself to be a keen political pragmatist by reversing alliances. In October 1995, the Iraqi ambassador was thrown out and Iraqi citizens loyal to the Arab nationalist *Ba'athist* movement of Saddam Hussein were accused of creating secret missions throughout Mauritania. In November, Ould Taya's government recognized the state of Israel, definitively reorienting Mauritania's political direction.

The opposition, given a new issue with the recognition of Israel, regrouped in 1995. One part of it formed Action for Change (AC). The party was led by Messaoud Ould Boulkheir, a "Harratin," or Black Moor descended from slaves, and presented itself as the champion of the oppressed, articulating both the grievances of Black Moors and Afro-Mauritanians. Multiparty legislative elections in 1996 reinforced PRDS power; the party won 70 out of 79 seats in parliament. The AC won only a single seat, the remaining going to independents. Massive fraud on both sides was reported, with the opposition charging the government with running voters from polling station to polling station in minibuses. Still, only 30% of those registered to do so actually voted.

Colonel Ely Ould Mohamed Vall

In advance of the presidential elections of December 1997, UFD and AC joined to create a United Opposition Front but were no more successful than before. President Ould Taya was reelected to a second six-year term, winning more than 90% of the vote against four opposition candidates. His main challenger, economist Ch'Bih Ould Cheikh Malainine, did pull some support in Mauritania's two major urban centers. After his victory, President Ould Taya announced that he would "wage war without mercy" on poverty, but no mention was made of the growing concentration of wealth in the hands of an emerging, but extremely narrow, middle class. During the campaign, Malainine revealed that 39 Mauritanians held 70% of the country's wealth, and 27 of them were members of a single tribe, President Ould Taya's own Smassids.

Throughout the period, the Afro-Mauritanian political movement calling itself FLAM continued to call for the autonomy of southern Mauritania and a resolution of the issue of 70,000 deported black Mauritanians who have been living in Senegal and Mali since 1989. FLAM accused the regime of "Mauritanian apartheid," characterized by exclusion of Afro-Mauritanians from public affairs, generalization of Arabizing policies, and affirmation of the exclusively Arab character of the country.

Mauritania took its 1995 recognition of Israel to its logical conclusion and agreed to establish full diplomatic relations with the country in October 1999. It became the third Arab state to do so, after Jordan and Egypt. However, the policy ignited a firestorm of controversy within and outside the country, and the opposition organized regular and ongoing protest demonstrations.

As usual, the government's response was repression. Ahmed Ould Daddah's rechristened *Union des forces démocratiques-Ere Nouvelle* (UFD-EN) was banned in October 2000 because, said the government, it was waging a "smear campaign against the country" and calling for violence.

In December 2000, President Ould Taya announced a series of political reforms to give his image a more liberal sheen. Proportional representation, enhancing the opposition's chances to gain representation in parliament, was introduced for multimember districts in the country's three largest cities—Nouakchott, Nouadhibou, and Selibaby. To strengthen political parties, the state agreed to fund them on the basis of their showing in forthcoming municipal elections and give them access to state-controlled media; the new law prohibited independent candidacies.

The first elections to take advantage of the new provisions were the parliamentary and municipal polls of October 2001. Eighty-one National Assembly seats were up for grabs. Only President Ould Taya's PRDS presented candidates in each of the 45 electoral districts. The Rally of Democratic Forces (RFD: *Rassemblement des forces démocratiques*), which had emerged from the remains of Ahmed Ould Daddah's UFD-EN after it was banned in October 2000, competed in only 20; Messaoud Ould Boulkheir's Action for Change (AC) presented candidates in just 15. As additional confidence-building measures, the government issued new tamper-proof identity cards, published voter lists on the Internet, and employed transparent ballot boxes. Participation was up considerably—50% of those registered—from 30% in the 1996 legislative elections.

When the results were tallied, Ould Taya's PRDS won 64 out of 81 seats; six additional seats went to small parties backing the presidential majority. The opposition garnered 11 seats, with four of them going to Action for Change and three to the Rally of Democratic Forces; Cheikh Malainine's FPM won a single seat. The EU praised the conduct of the elections and called upon Mauritanian parties to maintain a constructive dialogue "so as to strengthen confidence in democratic institutions and create an environment in which all shades of opinion can be freely expressed." President Ould Taya was not, however, willing to tolerate criticism when presidential elections approached.

In January 2002, the government banned Action for Change, accusing it of inciting violence and racial tension. The decision followed a debate on government policy in 2002, during which opposition members repeatedly questioned officials on what would be done to improve race relations and end slavery. AC's leader, Messaoud Ould Boulkheir—himself a descendant of slaves—reacted by succinctly describing the Ould Taya regime: "It is a military

Mauritania

government, an undemocratic government that cannot accept a dissenting view, a government that is ready to trample on all rights in order to achieve its objectives."

Despite numerous political parties, Mauritania under President Ould Taya remained more authoritarian than democratic. Ould Taya ruled with an iron fist banning any opposition parties that pushed too hard, subjecting their leaders to imprisonment; he systematically censured the press and prohibited unions from holding public demonstrations. The PRDS operated as a political machine for winning elections and distributing patronage—access to political positions and the resources they control. Factional disputes within the party were largely tribal, ethnic, and regional. White Moors from Adrar (President Ould Taya's native region) and Brakna were highly influential; the majority of the Black Moor elite was to be found within the party, along with leading Afro-Mauritanian figures. Frequent ministerial reshufflings allowed an efficient redistribution of spoils to reflect any necessary change or tweaking of influence within the party.

Of all the tribal factions within the PRDS it was President Ould Taya's Smassids who took a lion's share of the spoils. They constituted a virtual financial cartel with significant interests in every economic sector. Thus, Ch'Bih Ould Cheikh Malainine's comment that 39 Mauritanians held 70% of the country's wealth, and 27 of them were members of a single tribe. Thus, too, the finding of the UN's Development Program that wealth in Mauritania is very unequally distributed: the richest 20% control 44% of the nation's wealth; the poorest 20% control a mere 6.4%.

Collapse of the Ould Taya Regime

The combustible political situation—fueled by inequality, repression, and the debate over Israel—provided fuel for Arab nationalists and Islamic fundamentalists, as well as violent action by elements of the armed forces, who attempted to overthrow the Ould Taya government in June 2003. Rebels overran the presidential compound, but Ould Taya rallied his personal guard, shot his way out to nearby police headquarters and sustained a 36-hour siege. Loyalist army forces, directed by President Ould Taya himself, suppressed the attempted coup, but it was a close call.

With his vulnerability obvious (and opposition politicians lamenting the coup's failure) Ould Taya decided not to postpone presidential elections scheduled for November. Instead, he boldly appointed a Black Moor, Justice Minister Sghaïer Ould Mbareck as his new prime minister; he became the first Harratin to occupy the office. The appointment had clear political implications. Ould Mbareck hailed from Mauritania's far eastern province of Hodh el-Chargui, where many of the rebels had their family roots.

In the November 2003 presidential elections, five opposition candidates challenged Ould Taya's bid for a fresh six-year term. His most formidable opponent was Mohamad Khouna Ould Haidalla, the former military ruler who had been overthrown by Ould Taya in 1984. Haidalla attracted a heterogeneous group of opportunists to his campaign: liberal reformers, Arab nationalists, and Islamic fundamentalists—all united by a common distaste for the incumbent. Still, President Ould Taya won 67% of the ballots; Ould Haidalla placed second with about 19% of the vote. The opposition complained of fraud, but hard-to-fake voter cards and transparent ballot boxes undermined the credibility of such charges.

After the 9/11 terror attacks in New York, President Ould Taya committed himself to the war on terror, and Mauritania, with its little-patrolled desert crossings, alleged al-Qaeda cells, and large segments of its Muslim population sympathetic to Osama bin Laden and Saddam Hussein, has received special attention from U.S. planners as part of the Pan-Sahel Initiative and later the Trans-Saharan Counter Terrorism Initiative, designed to train and prepare local armed forces to combat terrorist groups in the Sahara.

Suspected extremist Islamist activity had been on the rise in Mauritania for some time. As part of the government's ongoing struggle with Islamist opposition, police conducted extensive raids against suspected terror cells, including mosques, in April and May 2005. They accused al-Qaeda of pouring vast sums into mosques and Islamic schools to recruit insurgents and send them to the front lines of holy wars in Iraq and Afghanistan. Seventeen alleged members of the Algerian-based GSPC (Salafist Group for Preaching Combat) were charged with plotting acts of terror. In June, an army base in the Sahara was attacked by elements of the GSPC; 15 Mauritanian soldiers were killed, some with their throats slit. On its website, the group claimed the attack "was in revenge for the violence perpetrated against our brothers in prison," referring to the 17 fundamentalists arrested in April raids.

The pressures, internal and external, were building up on President Ould Taya. After three successive coup attempts, his own security forces set in motion the fourth and final coup against him during his absence from the country in August on the occasion of the Saudi monarch's funeral. On August 3, 2005, troops seized state radio and television buildings, closed the capital's airport, and announced Ould Taya's overthrow.

Transition from Military to (Semi-) Civilian Rule?

Army officers calling themselves the *Conseil militaire pour la justice et la démocratie* (CMJD) declared the armed forces had unanimously decided to "end the totalitarian practices of the deposed regime." With Colonel Ely Ould Mohamed Vall—the head of national security—as its leader, the CMJD announced it would exercise power for two years to allow time to put "open and transparent" democratic institutions in place. True to its word, the CMJD organized a referendum on a new constitution in June 2006. The new text, which limited a serving president to two terms in office and cut the presidential terms from six to five years, was approved by 96.9% of Mauritanian voters; a remarkable 76.5% of all eligible voters participated in the foundation of a new state. The constitution provided for a bicameral legislature: a 56-member Senate, elected for six-year terms by municipal leaders, and a 95-member National Assembly, chosen by popular vote to serve five-year terms.

Some 25 political parties submitted lists of candidates for the first round of Assembly elections in November; to these were added numerous independent candidates. Electoral rules set aside 20% of the seats for female candidates, a first for Mauritania. When the runoff elections were completed in December, Mauritanian voters had produced a varied and potentially contentious lower house. Twelve political parties were represented, including Arab nationalists, Afro-Mauritanians, liberals, and Islamists.

Ostensibly the Assembly's largest cohesive bloc was represented by former opponents of the Ould Taya regime. Eleven opposition parties joined together as the Coalition of Forces for Democratic Change (CFDC) and won 41 seats; the largest element within the CFDC is represented by the 15 seats of the Ahmed Ould Daddah's Rally of Democratic Forces (RFD). Parties associated with the former presidential majority, most importantly, the Republican Party for Democracy and Renewal (PRDR)—a renamed PRDS—secured 13 seats, but the real power brokers were the 41 members elected as "independents." Several of them were Islamists since sectarian parties and movements were banned from electoral participation.

Presidential Election of 2007 and Beyond

The presidential election, which concluded the 19-month transitional process, took place in March 2007. A record 20 candidates joined the fray, making a first-round victory impossible. Constituent members of CFCD presented four candidates, the most prominent of whom was the RFD's Ahmed Ould Daddah. For the first time a

Mauritania

Harratin, Messoud Ould Boulhkeir of the *Alliance populaire progressiste* (APP), was a candidate for the country's highest office. Eighteen parties, generally supportive of the former regime and calling themselves "The Charter," united behind the candidacy of Sidi Ould Cheikh Abdallahi. His credentials were mixed: he had been a minister under ex-President Ould Taya but had also been put under house arrest by Ould Taya. "Sidi," as his backers called him, presented himself as a man of consensus and stability. Abdallahi received 25% of the votes in the first round of balloting; Ahmed Ould Daddah arrived in second place with slightly more than 20% of the vote.

In the runoff election, Abdallahi received crucial backing from the third-place finisher, Zeine Ould Zeidane, a former governor of the Bank of Mauritania, and, much to the surprise of the traditional opposition, from the fourth-place finisher, Messoud Ould Boulhkeir, the "Harratin" descendent of slaves. Abdallahi's campaign stressed reconciliation to heal the wounds that still lingered from racial conflicts going back to 1989, and his message prevailed. He won 52.85% to Ould Daddah's 47.15%. Boulhkeir received his political reward when the National Assembly convened in April and elected him its president. Zeine Ould Zeidane was named prime minister, though he later resigned in May 2008. High in Sidi's priorities was reinforcing the national unity of a country riven by ethnic and socio-economic divisions. He promised special legislation criminalizing slavery (officially abolished in 1981) and rehabilitating the rights of Afro-Mauritanians subject to abuse and expulsion between 1989 and 1991.

The Sidi government did not last long, however. On August 6, 2008, Gen. Mohamed Ould Abdel Aziz and the military overthrew the president in a bloodless coup. They did so in apparent retaliation for Sidi's attempts to dismiss top military brass, most notably the coup perpetrators themselves. Gen. Abdel Aziz himself resigned from the head of the junta in April 2009, in order to be eligible to run in forthcoming elections called by the military. The acting head of state was Ba Mamadou Mbaré, former president of the Senate.

Elections were held on July 18, 2009, and Ould Abdel Aziz won with 52% of the vote; parliament speaker Messaoud Ould Boulkheir won 16%. Voter turnout was reported at 61%. Opposition groups and challengers called the results "prefabricated," but the international community accepted the election.

More recently, politics in Mauritania have taken to the streets. In 2011, as the Arab Spring movements spread across North Africa, protestors held a "day of rage." However, the regime held firm,

President Mohamed Ould Abdel Aziz

using tear gas to disperse the crowds. Further clashes continued into September 2011 and thousands protested in May 2012. President Abdel Aziz was also shot in the arm in late 2012; while the government claimed this was accidental, it raised suspicion about the stability of the regime and the popularity of the president. While the regime remains intact, it has made some concessions, including a national dialogue on reforms and some liberalization of the media. Mauritania is scheduled to hold its next presidential election on June 21, 2014, just after this book goes to press. Abdel Aziz, the current president, has declared that he will run for re-election; it is unclear who else will run, as several opposition figures are proposing a boycott, citing the unlikelihood of a free and fair process.

CONTEMPORARY THEMES

Mauritania emerged from the terrible drought conditions of the 1970s and 1980s with a few years of decent rain. Animal flocks that had been devastated were gradually reconstituted. Cattle, which had fallen to 7.6 million head in 1973, rose to 11 million head by 1999, but three consecutive years of drought devastated both food and cattle production. More than 100,000 head of cattle died, and herders had to lead their herds farther south in search of greener pastures. Only in August 2003 did the rains return, temporarily removing the looming specter of drought and famine.

The agricultural sector traditionally employs 60% of the population and contributes 23.7% of the GDP (2005), but these figures are always subject to the absence of water. In 2002, rainfall was so inadequate peasant farmers were unable to sow sorghum and millet, the principal cereal grains grown. The farmer's life is one of constant struggle: "The land teaches us much," runs the Mauritanian proverb, "because it resists us." Mauritania has experienced approximately a 6% economic growth rate since 2010, which is attributed to relatively abundant rainfall, a growing fishing industry, and public works projects, among other factors.

For years, Mauritania's principal source of income was iron. The iron ore industry is centered on the open-pit mines of Zouérat in the north. Ores are processed and then transported by train to the coastal port of Nouadhibou, 400 miles away. Convoys of up to 250 ore-bearing cars, pulled by four engines and extending a mile and a half in length, evacuate the desert's wealth. On their return trip, the trains bring food, water and supplies to Zouérat, a town of 40,000 built to sustain the mines. The industry is operated by SNIM (*Société Nationale Industrielle et Minière de Mauritanie*), which is mostly state-owned. To accommodate growing iron exports, major work on the port at Nouadhibou was undertaken in the years leading up to 2005 and again up to 2012. Mauritanian officials expect the nation to increase its production of iron ore significantly throughout the next decade by spending billions of dollars on the construction of new processing plants. In October 2013, individuals discovered a new deposit in the northern portion of Mauritania that is extremely rich in iron ore.

Waters off the Mauritanian coast are rich fishing areas, such that the area was overfished through the use of industrial-scale fishing in the late 1990s. The depletion of fishing stock resulted from a fishing agreement with the European Union that brought Mauritania $600 million in cash over six years in exchange for unrestricted fishing rights for EU ships. In 1998, the government began the process of declaring a two-month "biological rest" to help fishing stocks renew themselves, but even this proved ineffective. It has occasionally banned all fishing, except traditional non-motorized fishing by local communities. Fishing currently accounts for about half of Mauritania's export income and contributes 10% of GDP. Japan is the biggest buyer of Mauritanian fish, and Mauritania maintains a sizable trade surplus with the Asian country. Given its dependence on iron and fish, Mauritania desperately needs to diversify its economy, but diversification requires investment and there is little capital available. International financial aid accounts for a large portion of the country's investment budget.

While Mauritania faithfully followed structural adjustment programs, balanced its budget (with foreign assistance), restrained inflation, and experienced reasonable growth, the country remains impoverished and highly unequal. The staggering inequalities of Mauritanian life are suggested by a simple fact: 80% of Mauritania's value added tax was once paid by a mere 12 individuals. Slavery is still prevalent within Mauritania, though

Mauritania

the government has tried to abolish the practice on numerous occasions. There exists a great disparity with respect to the standard of living of slave owners and slaves; typically, access to medical care and sanitary drinking water are reserved for light-skinned Arab slave owners, whereas the black slaves are denied these necessities. The United Nations ranks Mauritania at 155 out of 187 countries in the 2013 version of its Inequality-adjusted Human Development Index. About half the population lives in poverty, and nearly a third of all children under the age of five suffered from malnutrition in 2000; almost half the adult population is illiterate, and life expectancy is 62 years (as of 2014). These figures are dire, but Mauritania benefited from debt relief under provisions of the Highly Indebted Poor countries (HIPC) initiative and from decisions in 2005 and 2006 to cancel the multilateral debt of 19 of the world's poorest states.

Mauritania is now an oil-producing nation, though production has been modest. The Australian company Woodside began production at the Chinguetti offshore field in February 2006. Located in the Atlantic some 43 miles from Nouakchott, the field was initially predicted to produce 75,000 bbl/d (barrels a day) for ten years, but actual production proved disappointing—around 33,000 bbl/d. Woodside cut its estimates of total reserves in the field by 57% in November 2006 and estimates of current production are lower than those in the late 2000s At least two other major fields, await development but the expectation is that oil revenues will double the country's GDP are looking overly optimistic.

Nonetheless, oil prospecting has brought some rapid investments, which can explain sudden surges in growth rates like 19% in 2006, according to the World Bank (followed by –6% the following year). Chinese state petroleum companies have moved with alacrity to stake a claim in Mauritania's oil bonanza. China National Petroleum Corp. (CNPC) bought a 65% stake in offshore Block 20: for $8.6 million, it received the rights to a promising area covering nearly 4,000 square miles in Mauritania's Coastal Basin; CNPC operates the adjacent Block 12, providing ample opportunity for logistical and operational efficiencies.

Sensitive to the abject failure of oil revenues to improve the lives of people living in oil-producing countries, the government of President Vall (2005–2007) endorsed the Extractive Industries Transparency Initiative (EITI), which is designed to improve transparency and accountability in the use of natural resources. As part of its EITI commitment, the government has appointed a committee to oversee the use of oil and mineral revenues and ensure they are used to benefit all Mauritanians. The committee consists of representatives of government, oil industry, and civil society, including the press, unions and NGOs.

Major political developments nclude trial of former president Mohammed Ould Abdel Aziz for amassing an illicit fortune while serving eleven years in office as corruption remains a major problem in the country. A prime conduit for migrants attempting to reach Europe, primarily the Canary Islands off the coast of Spain, Mauritania sealed a deal with the EU aimed at enhancing border security and providing more local employment. Protests and riots against harsh government have also occurred with police crackdowns resulting in the killing of a local human rights advocate.

Winning a first term as president in 2019, Mohamed Ould Cheikh El Ghazouani secured a second term in July 2014 with 56.12 percent of the votes in the first round of the presidential poll well ahead of his main rival, anti-slavery activist Biram Dah Abeid, who won 22 percent, and Hamadi Ould Sid' El Moctar, who heads the Tewassoul party, who came in third with 12 percent. Total election turnout was 55 percent, lower than in 2019, while opponent Abeid said he would not recognize the results, which he accused of being manipulated by the government. The election victory gives former army chief Ghazouani, 67, a second term as head of the vast desert country, which has been relatively stable in the volatile Sahel region. Set to become a gas producer, the country and has been free from any reported attack on its soil in recent years unlike neighboring Mali. Ghazouani has also made helping the young a key priority in a country with a population of 4.9 million, where almost three-quarters of people are under age 35 with plans to boost the economy from major investments in renewable energy and expanded gold, uranium, and iron-ore mining. As with many countries in the region, Mauritania has dealt with disasters involving migrants fleeing sub-Saharan Africa including the capsizing of a boat carrying 300 passengers capsized near Mauritania's capital Nouakchott that originated from The Gambia; the United Nations migration agency said 120 people had been rescued by the Mauritanian Coast Guard. The Atlantic migration route from the coast of West Africa to the Canary Islands is typically used by African people seeking asylum or better work opportunities in Europe. The European Union promised Mauritania financial support worth $210 million to deal with the ongoing crisis.

The SNIM train carries iron ore from the desert to the port of Nouadhibou

The Republic of Niger

Former President Mamadou Tandja

BASIC FACTS

Area: 1,266,700 sq. km., slightly less than twice the size of Texas (CIA World Factbook 2014)
Population: 25,396,840 (June 2023 est.)
Capital City: Niamey
Government Type: Semi-Presidential Republic
Neighboring Countries: Burkina Faso (southwest); Mali (west); Algeria (northwest); Libya (north); Chad (east); Nigeria and Benin (south).
Official Language: French
Other Principal Languages: Arabic, Fulfuldé, Hausa, Kanuri, Songai, Tamajek, and Zarma
Ethnic Groups: Haoussa 55.4%, Djerma Sonrai 21%, Tuareg 9.3%, Peuhl 8.5%, Kanouri Manga 4.7%, other 1.2% (2001 census)
Principal Religions: Islam 80%, remainder indigenous beliefs and Christianity.
Former Colonial Status: French Colony (1921–1960)
Independence Date: August 3, 1960
GDP Per Capita (IMF 2023 est.): $613 (nominal), $1,600 (PPP)
GINI Index: 34.3 (World Bank 2014)
Currency: CFA franc, 1 USD = 594 CFA (Apr. 2022)
Inflation Rate: 5.0% (2022 est.)
Chief Commercial Products: Uranium ore, livestock products, cowpeas, onions
Foreign Direct Investments (FDI) net inflows: 768,985,316
Literacy Rate: 37.3% (CIA 2018)
Life Expectancy: 60.5 years (CIA 2023 est.)
Head of State: President Mahamadou Bazoum (since April 2, 2021)
Head of Government: Prime Minister Ouhoumoudou Mahamadou (since April 3, 2021)

LAND AND PEOPLE

The Republic of Niger covers an immense area in north-central West Africa. It is one of the most thinly populated nations of the continent. A huge plateau, the country is desolate but diversified, sometimes rocky and sometimes sandy, furrowed in many places by fossilized beds of ancient Saharan rivers. Hot and dry, it is pockmarked with small basins in the southern area which briefly turn into ponds during the "winter."

The only fertile region is a narrow belt of territory in the south that stretches the entire width of the country. Little more than 2% of the land area is under cultivation, most of which is gathered around the 185-mile-long portion of the Niger River within the country's boundaries. The river floods from June to September, helping to provide moisture for the surrounding vegetation. The climate is exceedingly hot and dry during eight months of the year. This area of trees and shrubs, interspersed with cultivated land supported by irrigation or wells, gives way quickly to a transition zone where the trees become smaller, and the lack of moisture supports only sporadic grazing by nomads' animals. In the northern two-thirds of the territory, the shifting sands of the hot desert render human life virtually impossible (except in the region of uranium mines).

An expedition into the Tenere desert (part of the Sahara) at a site known as Dabous discovered extraordinary rock carvings on the slopes of Aïr Mountains—huge giraffes carved into desert sandstone 9,000 years ago. The largest is over 20 feet tall and its proportions are meticulously accurate. After years of concealing the site for preservation purposes, archaeologists and foundations have worked to produce casts of the carvings and have begun to ponder how to provide tourist access while preserving them.

HISTORY TO PRESENT DAY

For early history, see *Historical Background* and *The Colonial Period: The French.*

Niger became an autonomous member of the French Community in 1958 but opted for independence in 1960 with Hamani Diori as the country's first president. Under the first post-independence constitution, Diori's Niger Progressive Party was the official and only legal party. It held all seats of the National Assembly and dominated the government. Like many of the other single-party states in Africa in the 1960s and 1970s, the NPP came under fire for a string of abuses: elitism and ethnic favoritism, corruption and fraud, economic malpractice, and intolerance of criticism coupled with repression. The regime did an especially poor job in responding to the droughts that afflicted the country in the late 1960s and early 1970s; the 1970s and 1980s were characterized by economic volatility (with little sustained growth) and continued poverty.

Trends of Violence and Instability

In 1974, the single-party regime was overthrown in a military coup led by Lt. Col. Seyni Kountché. Through the early and mid-1980s, Kountché ruled as a military dictator. His regime too was marked by tragedy, conflict, and mismanagement. Horrific droughts received a poor response and increasingly serious conflict between the regime and the Tuareg peoples, culminating in the expulsion of many Tuaregs from the country.

Kountché died in Paris of AIDS in 1987 and was succeeded by his cousin Col. Ali Saibou. Initially the leader of the Supreme Military Council, Saibou attempted to manage a controlled transition to single-party civilian rule with himself as president, but was ultimately unsuccessful. By 1990, a growing Tuareg rebellion and increasing protests had put pressure on the regime. At a moment when much of West Africa was going through rapid political change at the end of the Cold War, Saibou grudgingly agreed to a sovereign constituent assembly (known as the National Conference) and the drafting of a new constitution, which was approved in 1992. The new constitution greatly curtailed the power of the military and mandated

multiparty elections, which were held in 1993. A 43-year-old economist, Mahamane Ousmane, of the Social Democratic Convention (Convention Démocratique et Sociale, CDS) won a majority.

Ousmane quickly alienated most of the political class; Brig. Gen. Ibrahim Maïnassara and elements of the military then staged a coup in January 1996, arresting the president and prime minister. The military regime adopted a new constitution and held new elections in July. Maïnassara won, running essentially as an independent (though he formed his own loose political party). The opposition contested the results, and the crisis deepened four months later when the eight main opposition parties boycotted legislative elections. Pro-government parties and sympathizers claimed all 80 seats in the National Assembly.

On a more positive note, the government signed a peace agreement in April 1995, with two main rebel movements, the Organization of Armed Resistance (ORA) and the Coordination of Armed Resistance (CRA). The rebellions sought to give greater voice to the Tuareg and Toubou peoples and the peace agreement called for reintegration of former rebels into Nigerien society; some were even integrated into the army. Parliament voted to approve amnesty for all desert guerrilla groups in March 1998. Shortly afterward, the two main rebel fronts handed over their arsenals of heavy machine guns, rocket-launchers, antitank mines, and ammunition. Thereafter, Tuaregs were regularly appointed by the prime minister as members of the Cabinet.

General Maïnassara's difficulties increased after the 1995 peace agreement (though not necessarily because of it). After years of economic stagnation, salaries to soldiers and civil servants went unpaid for months, as did scholarships for students. This resulted in a series of strikes, protests, mutinies, and rebellions. Political instability reached a climax in early 1999 when local elections were held for the first time; after results early in the day showed the opposition winning handily, armed men appeared in pro-opposition polling areas and began destroying ballots and electoral results. The outraged opposition called supporters to the streets and widespread unrest ensued; they then called upon the president to resign.

On April 9, 1999, President Maïnassara was murdered by his security command as he was preparing to depart from Niamey airport. Eyewitnesses reported that Presidential Guard members repeatedly shot the president with a truck-mounted large-caliber machine gun, nearly severing his body in two. The commander of the Presidential Guard, Major Daouda Mallam

Ex-President Ibrahim Mainassara Barre

Wanké, emphasized to reporters that Maïnassara's death was not premeditated, but merely an "unfortunate accident."

The military junta quickly established Major Wanké as president of the National Council for Reconciliation (CRN), dissolved the National Assembly and Supreme Court, and suspended the constitution and political parties. France (on whom the Niger economy was largely dependent for investment and exports) suspended all military aid and economic assistance and the international community condemned the assassination. In need of a response, Wanké announced that the junta would return the country to civilian rule by the end of the year, with a referendum on a new constitution to be followed by elections in which members of the military and security forces were specifically banned from standing for election. The junta scrupulously followed its established timetable.

The constitution of the Fifth Republic was approved by a nearly 90% majority in a June referendum, though only about 30% of the electorate participated. The new constitution created a unicameral legislature with executive power shared between the president and the prime minister. Under the new constitution, the president is required to name the prime minister from a list of three candidates proposed by the parliamentary majority. Article 141 of the new constitution provided amnesty to those responsible for "the *coups d'état* of January 27, 1996, and April 9, 1999." After the referendum, multiparty presidential and parliamentary elections followed in October and November.

Niger Under Tandja Mamadou (1999–2010)

In the 1999 elections Tandja Mamadou of the National Movement for a Developing Society (MNSD) won the presidency. He beat Mahamadou Issoufou of the Niger Party for Democracy and Socialism (PNDS) by a margin of nearly 60% to 40% in the second round of balloting. Tandja, a retired military officer, had helped oust Niger's first president Diori Hamani in 1974, then served as interior minister for

Niger

military presidents Kountché and Ali Saibou. Under the latter, he was responsible for the bloody repression of Tuaregs in 1990. An ethnic Kanouri, Tandja profited from a runoff alliance with Mahamane Ousmane, a member of Niger's influential Hausa majority, leader of the Convention Démocratique et Sociale (CDS) and the country's last democratically elected president. His younger Hausa opponent, Mahamadou Issoufou, spent lavishly and campaigned vigorously in what Nigerien commentators called "an American style."

In elections for the National Assembly, Tandja's MNSD and CDS alliance won an absolute majority of 55 out of 83 seats. The electoral system virtually eliminated minor parties and only three other parties were represented in the new parliament: Issoufou's PNDS won 16 seats, and the Rally for Democracy and Progress (RDP) of former President Maïnassara won eight.

Tandja faced military mutinies in 2002 from enlisted soldiers upset about low pay, but by the time his first term of office ended in 2004, he had brought some stability to Niger, having maintained peace, promoted rural development, and normalized payments to urban civil servants. Tandja faced five opponents in the October 2004 presidential elections. His principal rivals from 1999, Mahamadou Issoufou of the PNDS, and Mahamane Ousmane of the CDS headed the opposition. President Tandja took the lead in the first round of balloting won the November runoffs convincingly over Issoufou with 65.5% of the vote. Tandja became the first elected leader of Niger to have completed a term of office without being assassinated or ousted by coup. In parliamentary elections, Tandja's National Movement for a Developing Society (MNSD) elected 47 deputies, while five other parties supporting the president brought the presidential majority to a comfortable 88 seats. Mahamadou Issoufou's PNDS affirmed its role as the principal opposition party with 25 seats. Niger's fragile democracy seemed to be maturing, which would make the chaotic change of 2009 all the more disappointing.

During Tandja's second term, Niger faced major problems once again far from the politics in the capital Niamey. First, another food crisis emerged in 2004 and 2005; the extent of the drought and its human toll were never clarified as the Nigerien government and international agencies differed in their assessments of the situation. Second, a restive force of dissident Tuaregs began launching attacks on military outposts and mining camps in the north in early 2007. The group, calling itself the *Mouvement des Nigériens pour la Justice* (MNJ), called for redistribution of the benefits of the region's natural resources and

Niger

greater political inclusion of marginalized Tuareg peoples into Niger's political life. The government deemed them bandits bent on destabilizing the country. (In 2009, the MNJ and the government agreed to cease hostilities, though it is not clear the situation has been resolved entirely.)

The north was also the scene of banditry and tourist kidnappings that forced trans-Saharan traffic to travel in convoys protected by heavily armed soldiers. The presence of Al-Qaeda in the Islamic Maghreb (AQIM) in the same geographical area further complicated the security situation. In March 2004, one band of Salafist radicals, involved in kidnapping over 30 European tourists in Algeria, engaged Nigerien forces and was chased into neighboring Chad (where it was annihilated by Chadian troops).

The instability attracted international attention. Niger became part of American-led efforts to track Islamic fundamentalists operating in the region. The Trans-Saharan Counter-Terrorism Initiative program furnished training and equipment (especially communications materials) to enable surveillance; this provided the intelligence to pinpoint members of the Salafist group GSPC (which later allied itself with al-Qaeda and rebranded itself AQIM), where it had been working with armed bandits, using hideouts and caches left over from the 1990s Tuareg rebellion.

As Tandja Mamadou's second (and ostensibly final) term as president was drawing to a close in 2009, the president plunged the country into a constitutional crisis. He proposed a referendum on the possibility of a third term in office, though the Nigerien constitution explicitly forbade any such referendum or any constitutional amendment to extend presidential term limits. Tandja then disbanded the legislature and proposed new legislative elections, a referendum on a new constitution, and subsequent presidential elections in which he wished to run (all within a matter of a few months). When the Constitutional Court ruled against Tandja's scheme, the president began to rule by decree. In August, Tandja won a referendum designed to keep him in power for three more years: it granted his extension to term limits and expanded his powers. Tandja dissolved the parliament and called for October elections. The opposition boycotted, and Tandja's supporters won a large majority. For refusing to delay the elections (to give the opposition more time to organize), Niger was suspended from the Economic Community of West African States.

Reinstatement of Democracy

In February 2010, a military coup ousted Tandja. Col. Salou Djibo, a senior military officer, was named head of the junta, known as the Supreme Council for the Restoration of Democracy. The junta claimed it would bring competitive politics back; the African Union suspended Niger as a result of the coup, but further condemnation was slow, with the international community waiting to see when and how elections would be held. By March 2010, the military had created a transitional government with a civilian, Mahamadou Danda, as a prime minister, and stated that the junta itself and its transitional government would be barred from participating in the forthcoming elections.

Early 2011 saw both lawlessness in the hinterlands and an improving rule of law in the capital. The bad news was the kidnapping and killing of two French nationals held hostage by what was presumed to be the al-Qaeda branch AQIM. Their death came during an attempted rescue. While many more Nigeriens than French have suffered the depredations of bandits, kidnappers, and terrorists in Niger, the fact that French citizens were killed made the incident into international news and called global attention back to Niger's enduring problem.

In better news, Niger held a reasonably free and fair presidential election in 2011. Mahamadou Issoufou of the PNDS led after the first round on January 31 and took 58% in the runoff against Seyni Oumarou of the MNSD in March. Legislative elections were held on the same date as the first round of the presidential election; the results gave a plurality of 34 seats out of 113 to Issoufou's PNDS, with the MNSD winning 25, and the Movement of a Democratic Niger for an African Federation (MODEN-FA) winning 23 and backing the PNDS. The remaining 31 seats are divided among several other smaller parties, such that if democracy holds, the government will need to compromise to maintain a coalition or to pass legislation.

Since the 2011 election, the Issoufou government has been menaced by attempted coups in the capital Niamey and insurgent Islamists in the hinterland. Five soldiers were arrested in July 2011, just a few months after the new government took the reins, for allegedly plotting a coup. Members of al-Qaeda in the Islamic Maghreb (AQIM) kidnapped a provincial governor in Niger in January 2012, and further kidnappings of European citizens have persisted.

The most significant attack by Islamists to date came on May 23, 2013, when suicide bombers conducted simultaneous attacks on an army barracks in Agadez (where eighteen soldiers and one civilian were killed) and on a French-run uranium mine at Arlit (where one person was killed and more than a dozen were injured). There are indications that Islamic fundamentalism is on the rise in Niger, among both black Africans and peoples of Arab lineage.

CONTEMPORARY THEMES

Niger is challenged by a host of social and economic dilemmas and a devastating poverty that are overwhelming even by African standards. By 2010 estimates, over half of the population survives on less than $1 per day, and only about 28.7% of all adults are literate. Niger's economy has seen limited growth and development since independence; the UN Development Program's Human Development Index ranked Niger in 2012 as the least developed country in the world, tied with the conflict-ridden Democratic Republic of the Congo. Niger even witnesses some traditional slavery among its nomadic peoples, though slavery is banned by law and now subject to increased prison terms of 10 to 30 years and fines.

Niger's women and their young children bear particular burdens. Women here have the highest fertility rate in the world, averaging 6.89 children per woman, and suffer one of the world's highest infant mortality rates. Out of every 1,000 live births, an estimated 63 died on average in 2012, and 114 of every 1,000 children died before they tuned five. More than 15% of children suffer from severe malnutrition according to a May 2006 UNICEF report; 43.9% of them suffer stunted growth. Malnutrition often leads to an early death for the children. Their deaths result from long-term starvation diets that weaken the immune system and can lead to death by malaria, meningitis, and diarrhea. All of these figures are even worse for girls, on average.

Social and religious traditions, coupled with high levels of poverty, produce an extremely high number of early marriages. According to the UN Children's Fund, 36%of Niger's young women are married by age 15 and 75% are married by age 18. Half of all Nigerien women have their first pregnancy while still teenagers. Female genital cutting (FGC) is practiced more here than in most any country in the world, with 2.2% of women aged 15–49 victims of genital mutilation according to a 2006 UNICEF estimate; traditional observers of the practice justify the practice by claiming that the removal of the clitoris reduces a woman's sex drive and guarantees marital fidelity. The practice was outlawed in 2001, but it remains widespread and there are reports no one has ever been prosecuted for performing the operation.

Economically, Niger's future seems to depend upon mining and exploration. The country is the world's fourth largest uranium producer (after Kazakhstan, Canada

Niger

and Australia); most of the product is sold to nuclear powers France and Japan. The French holding company Areva, which has a controlling interest in two major two mining concerns, was the object of protests in the remote mining town of Arlit (over 600 miles north of Niamey) in 2006 and 2007. In addition to charges of exploitation and profiteering, the protesters, backed by the French anti-nuclear lobby and environmental groups, demanded an investigation of radioactive contamination in mining communities; Greenpeace echoed these accusations in 2010. In April 2007, Tuareg rebels from the Movement of Nigeriens for Justice (*Mouvement des Nigériens pour la Justice*, MNJ) attacked a French uranium-prospecting camp in the area. On December 31, 2013, Niger's ten-year contract with Areva lapsed after the government of Niger and the company were unable to come to a new agreement. In an effort to boost the struggling economy, the government of Niger has pushed for increased revenue from uranium, while Areva claims that increasing royalties would make its operations in Niger unprofitable. As of April 2014, negotiations between the government and the company had turned for the better and a new contract seemed imminent.

Uranium is the main source of export revenues and accounted for as much as 80% of the national budget in the 1980s, so the future of the industry is watched closely. For a long while after the 1980s diminished demand and reduced prices seriously affected government revenues, but expanding Asian economies have recently driven commodity prices higher and made mineral exploration more attractive. Niger's uranium production thus increased significantly and this has supported the national budget. The deposits were long dominated by French interests, but Niger's government has granted more exploration licenses. British, Canadian, and Chinese firms are now active in the area.

Gold and oil are hopes for a diversification away from dependence on uranium. Canadian and Moroccan interests are developing two neighboring gold mines known as Samira Hill and Libiri. Gold production began in 2004 and Koma Bangou, located slightly more than 100 miles southwest of Niamey, witnessed a gold rush after 2001. Niger has explored for oil since before independence, spurred by the massive discoveries in nearby oil-producing states: Algeria, Libya, Chad, and Nigeria. Major multinationals such as Exxon Mobil, Malaysia's Petronas, and Algeria's Sonatrach have concessions and exploration permits, as does the China National Petroleum Company. Given Niger's landlocked geography, transportation of any product is costly, and large reserves and infrastructural development are necessary for production to be profitable. As of 2008, the Chinese firm was planning increased investment to bring production online. In 2014, geophysical samples revealed signs of oil in the previously uncultivated region of Tahoua and uranium in Tillaberi, presenting new economic options for Niger to pursue in the future.

One of the relatively good pieces of economic news for the country in the 2000s was that Niger qualified for participation in debt relief programs under the Highly Indebted Poor Countries (HIPC) program and the Multilateral Debt Relief Initiative. Niger is one of the countries that benefited most from the cancellation of multilateral debts: external debt stood at over $2 billion in 2003, but this was reduced by about $1.3 billion, taking Niger's debt burden from 76% of GDP to under 15%.

Reflecting growing ant-colonial sentiments in the country, Niger has called for the withdrawal of troops from France and the United States that have engaged in anti-terrorism operations in the area while the country has pivoted toward Russia with its forces occupying a former U.S. base. Along with neighboring Burkina-Faso and Mali, Niger is also in favor of dropping the Central African Franc (CFA) while also quitting the Economic Community of West African States (ECOWAS), which has lifted sanctions aimed at encouraging the country to return to civilian rule.

Reflecting continuing instability and subjugation by armed militias, at least 44 people were killed in an attack on a mosque in the country's southwest in March 2025. Assaulted in the Fambita quarter of the rural border town of Kokorou, the victims were targeted by armed fighters linked to the al-Qaeda and ISIL (ISIS) groups that took over territory in neighboring north Mali after the 2012 Tuareg rebellion. The Nigerian defense ministry blamed the attack on the Islamic State in the Great Sahara (EIGS) an affiliate of ISIL. The military-run government of Niger frequently fights armed groups in the region. Civilians are often the victims of the violence, and 2,400 people have been killed in Niger since July 2023.

On the economic front, France's majority state-owned nuclear conglomerate Orano revealed that the military government of Niger has assumed "operational control" of its Nigerien uranium mining subsidiary, Somair, in December 2024. Orano says it first began to encounter difficulties in running Somair in July 2023, soon after a group of high-ranking army officers, led by General Abdourahamane Tchiani, ousted Niger President Mohamed Bazoum. As a response to the coup, regional bloc ECOWAS suspended Niger's membership and imposed sanctions on the country, including trade sanctions that brought all exports via Benin to a halt. The military government dealt a further blow to Orano's interests in Niger by revoking the permit its other subsidiary, Imouraren SA, held for mining the Imouraren uranium deposit, believed to be one of the world's largest, on the grounds that the French company's plans for development did not meet expectations. Since assuming power, Niger's military rulers have been voicing their discontent with the process by which foreign companies are able to secure lucrative mining licenses, claiming the land-locked African nation's 27 million citizens ought to derive greater profit from its rich uranium deposits. Despite all its natural resources, Niger is one of the world's poorest countries; almost half of its population lives in extreme poverty, 13.1 percent face severe food insecurity, and only one in seven Nigeriens has access to modern electricity services. The West African country has ranked 189th out of 193 countries on the United Nations Development Program (UNDP) Human Development Index for 2023–24.

FUTURE CONSIDERATIONS

While there have been some improvements in the economy in the last five years with a modicum of stability, the backlog in providing education and health services is crushing, with little prospect for rapid improvement. The country remains very near the bottom of most statistical tables depicting the standard of living in countries around the world. Even substantial improvements year-on-year will not bring development in short order. The social benefits of Niger's natural resources seem a long way off.

Niger's twin problems of food insecurity and banditry in the desert have resurfaced once again. The years 2010 and 2012 brought more concerns about food crises, though once again (as in 2004–2005) there were varying reports on the severity of the situation. Meanwhile, violent conflict between the government and Tuareg peoples in Niger seemed to subside in 2009, but the international attention paid to the Islamist insurgents in the Sahara (and the coup precipitated by the Tuareg rebellion in neighboring Mali) has reminded international observers about the precarious state of the rule of law, especially in the more remote regions of the country.

The growing presence of refugees fleeing conflict in Nigeria presents a new challenge for Niger. The UN estimates that 50,000 people have now crossed into Niger, and the mass exodus shows no signs of stopping with 500 Nigerians

Niger

arriving every week. The Niger government has thus far been reluctant to build camps for the refugees for fear that they will become recruitment centers for the terrorist organization Boko Haram. Already Boko Haram has begun to cross the border into Niger in an attempt to recruit new members to the organization, targeting established gangs and criminal groups which can be bribed to perform violent acts for cash. Niger's ability to handle the growing refugee crisis and minimize Boko Haram's influence will prove crucial to preventing further instability in the country. It is also worth mentioning that Niger has been very instrumental in the four-nation African Union coalition to dismantle the atrocious operation of Boko Haram in northeast Nigeria. The other nations are Nigeria, Chad, and Cameroon. Nigerien army and security forces have either captured or killed numerous Boko Haram fighters that cross the border into Niger. In some cases, the army has pursued the fighters into Nigerian territories..

The Federal Republic of Nigeria

National Mosque—Abuja

BASIC FACTS

Area: 924,630 sq. km. = 357,000 sq. mi. (A little larger than Texas and Oklahoma together)
Population: 230,842,7483 (June 2023 est.)
Capital City: Abuja
Government Type: Federal Presidential republic
Neighboring Countries: Benin (west); Niger, Chad (north); Cameroon (east).
Official Language: English
Other Principal Languages: Morre than 450 languages are spoken. Prominent are Edo, Fulani, Hausa, Ibibio, Igbo, Ijo, Kanuri, Nupe, Tiv, and Yoruba.
Ethnic Groups: Several hundred, of which the most prominent are the Hausa, Fulani, Yoruba, Ibo, and Ijaw.
Principal Religions: Islam 50%, Christian 40%, indigenous beliefs 10%
Former Colonial Status: British Colony (1914–1960).
Independence Date: October 1, 1960
GDP Per Capita (IMF 2023 est.): $2,280 (nominal), $6,178 (PPP)
Gini Index: 35.1 (World Bank 2018 est.)
Currency: Nigerian Naira, 1 USD = 461.33 NGN (Apr. 2023)
Inflation rate: 11.3% (2019 est.)
Chief Commercial Products: Petroleum and petroleum products 95%, cocoa, rubber
Foreign Direct Investments (FDI) net inflows: 4,655,849,170
Literacy Rate: 62% (CIA 2018 est.)
Life Expectancy: 61.79 years (CIA 2023 est.)
Head of State: Maj. Gen. (ret.) Muham-madu Buhari, President (since May 29, 2015)
Head of Government: Maj. Gen. (ret.) Muham-madu Buhari, President (since May 29, 2015)

LAND AND PEOPLE

Nigeria has the largest population of any African nation, with about 177 million

Nigeria

of the estimated one billion people living on the continent. The country faces the Gulf of Guinea on the southern coast of West Africa. From the ocean the land has a flat appearance; there is a belt of dense swamp ten to 15 miles wide. This marshy coastal area resembles a bayou or mangrove forest, particularly in area around the delta of the Niger River.

Farther inland, there is a region 50 to 100 miles wide where the vegetation is thick green tropical forest rising from more stable ground, where the trees can grow up to 200 feet. This warm and humid forest area and the coast receive up to 150 inches of rainfall per year. The land then rises slowly in a series of foothills to the Jos Plateau, reaching altitudes up to 1,000 feet. Tall grasses grow rapidly between widely spaced trees. The dry season, from October to April, evaporates moisture from the ground, hardening the earth so that when the spring rains come, the soil erodes into the rivers.

There is a semiarid to arid region in the extreme north, close to Lake Chad and Niger. It is the transition zone lying between the Sahara Desert and the green forests and jungles of the south, receiving 25 inches or less of rain per year. In recent years, the area has been threatened by the expansion southward of the great desert. During the dry season, particularly in December and January, the *harmattan*, the hot wind blowing from the desert, reaches all the way southward to the Gulf of Guinea, lowering the humidity and raising dust storms in the interior.

Nigeria has given birth to some of the most important African writers, most notably Chinua Achebe (author of the world-famous *Things Fall Apart*, among other award-winning novels) and Nobel Prize winner Wole Soyinka. Chimamanda Ngozi Adichie, author of *Half of a Yellow Sun* and *Purple Hibiscus*, is perhaps the most prominent young female author on the continent today. Many of the soap operas and films shown on television in English speaking Africa are produced in Nigeria, in what has been dubbed "Nollywood." Also famous for its music (with the likes of Fela Kuti, Femi Kuti, and King Sunny Adé), Nigeria stands out as one of Africa's cultural powerhouses.

HISTORY TO PRESENT DAY

For early history, see *Historical Background* and *The Colonial Period: The British*.

Independence and the 1960s to the Biafra War

In Nigeria's 1947 constitution, the British introduced a federal system of government that entrenched the dominant interests of the colony's three major regions: the mainly Muslim Hausa and Fulanis in the north, the predominantly Catholic Ibo in the east, and the mostly Anglican Yoruba in the west. When Nigeria became an independent dominion of the British Commonwealth in October 1960, led the distinguished nationalist, Nnamdi Azikiwe, Even at this time, regional differences were inevitable as much of the nationalist agitation that culminated in independence came from southerners, who were better educated after longer contact with European missionaries and traders.

Balancing regional tensions quickly became a recurring issue in Nigerian history and politics. When Nigeria became a federal republic in 1963, Nnamdi Azikiwe (from the Ibo ethnic group prominent in the southeast) became president, while the federal prime minister was a northerner, Abubakar Tafewa Balewa; elections in 1965 revealed tensions between the regions as the Northern People's Congress swept the north with enough seats to create a parliamentary majority without winning a single seat in the south (then divided into Eastern, Western, and Mid-Western regions plus the Lagos Federal Territory).

Resentment against northern domination of the federal system resulted in a bloody *coup d'état* in January 1966, the first military intervention that would come to characterize Nigerian political life. Led by Major-General Johnson Aguiyi-Ironsi, an Ibo, the coup resulted in the brutal murder of the most prominent northern politicians, including Prime Minister Balewa and Ahmadu Bello, the powerful Sarduana of Sokoto who was the premier of the north. Southerners, especially Ibos, who, because of their educational achievements had been employed and posted throughout Nigeria, became the object of bloody reprisals in the north. Ibo families fearing for their lives began a mass exodus to the eastern region.

General Ironsi was killed in a counter-coup in July 1966 and was replaced by neither a northerner nor a southerner, but a man of the Middle Belt seen as a compromise president, Lieutenant-Colonel Yakubu Gowon. The new president attempted to manage ethno-regional politics through the transformation of the regions into 12 states. But conferences to settle the regional conflict were unproductive and with the leadership of Colonel Odumeg-wu Ojukwu, an Ibo, three eastern states seceded from the federation in 1967 to form the independent Republic of Biafra.

From 1967 to 1970, Nigeria was consumed by the civil war sometimes known as the Biafra War. The world took note when images of famished Biafran children, their bellies swollen in starvation and their hair turned orange by Kwashiorkor (protein deficiency) became features on

President Shehu Shagari (from 1979 through 1983)

nightly television news. The war abruptly ended in 1970 when Ojukwu fled and the Biafrans surrendered: it was estimated that between one and two million people had died during the war.

Economic and Political Crises: 1970s–1990s

The early 1970s were dominated by efforts to rebuild the nation's economy, severely damaged by the war, and to reintegrate the eastern region into the federal system. Some of this work was facilitated by the oil boom of the period. As a consequence of its oil production, Nigeria became one of Africa's wealthiest states, but in many ways, oil has been as much a curse as a boom.

As the country increased its dependence on petroleum, it suffered from price fluctuations—boom in the 1970s, bust in the early 1980s when the price of oil plummeted. Investments in the energy sector diverted money from the development of the agricultural sector, just as petroleum-related jobs drew thousands from their fields, resulting, in part, in the current food crisis in the countries surrounding Nigeria (See chapters on Benin, Niger, Cameroon). As Nigeria has grown, the country has increasingly imported food from neighboring countries, rather than relying on its own agricultural sector. In addition, the vast income derived from oil only intensified regional discontent. Producing areas suffered environmental degradation and felt as though "their" resources were siphoned off to the central government, from which they received few benefits. Oil income also encouraged lavish, often superfluous, construction projects and provided endless possibilities for corruption. The construction of the new federal capital city at Abuja was inspired by orderly planned capitals such as Washington, Canberra, and Brasilia, but became a classic example of Nigerian corruption. By the mid-1980s, half-completed government buildings and luxury hotels

Nigeria

Northern Nigeria's ancient Muslim city of Kano at the edge of the Sahara   AP/Wide World Photo

were everywhere, replete with poor quality design, workmanship, and materials.

In 1975, General Gowon was overthrown and replaced by Brigadier Gen. Murtala Mohammed who began the process of moving the federal capital to Abuja. However, Murtala was assassinated in a 1976 coup while caught in a Lagos traffic jam. His replacement, Lieutenant-General Olusegun Obasanjo, led the effort to introduce a new, American-style presidential constitution. Elections under the new constitution brought a northerner, Alhaji Shehu Shagari, to power in 1979.

Oil revenues, which peaked in 1980, provided prosperity that drew attention away from regional and ethnic tensions. By 1983, an election year, income from oil had dropped by half. The government responded to popular pressures and expelled more than one million foreigners, mostly Ghanaians, saying they had overstayed their visas and were taking jobs from Nigerians. The act proved popular in Nigeria, and Shagari was reelected in an election deeply flawed by irregularities.

Fraud, corruption, and waste under the Shagari government were massive and economically debilitating, which led the military to take power under the leadership of Major-General Muhammadu Buhari and later General Ibrahim Babangida. After 25 years of turbulence and corruption, a wide variety of Nigerians—intellectuals, the press, businessmen and even former politicians—supported Babangida. The new government instituted military tribunals for officials suspected of corruption and executed violent criminals in public. General Babangida's government was under heavy external and internal pressure to return power to civilians by the beginning of the 1990s. Suspicious of the proliferation of parties, Babangida decreed that there be only two: a Social Democratic Party on the center-left and a National Republican Convention on the center-right.

Elections were held in June 1993, but were annulled when preliminary results showed victory by Chief Moshood Abiola, a super-rich Yoruba businessman who also happened to have good connections with some northern politicians. Soon thereafter President Babangida resigned from office. Chief Ernest Shonekan was appointed head of the Interim National Government, but the interim was brief: on November 17, Defense Minister Sani Abacha staged yet another coup. With Abacha, Nigeria entered one of its darkest periods.

Corrupt and brutal, Abacha flouted both civil and human rights, and violently suppressed opposition. The regime outlawed political parties, abolished labor strikes, and seized state, local and federal government offices. When Abiola proclaimed himself president in 1994, Abacha had him arrested and imprisoned. The military government worked through local, traditional rulers to maintain control of Nigeria, particularly in the oil-producing regions.

In 1990, ethnic groups in the Niger Delta mobilized to call for a redistribution of wealth and opportunity in the country, particularly for the oil-rich delta region that had seen little of the benefits of

Nigeria

A Nok Sculpture from Nigeria's earliest great civilization
Photo Courtesy Galerie al Farahnick, Brussels

Nigeria's oil boom. The mobilization was led by the Ogoni playwright Ken Saro-Wiwa. His Movement for the Survival of the Ogoni People (MOSOP) issued an Ogoni Bill of Rights that described local misery and posited a vision of Ogoni autonomy and self-determination—"political control of Ogoni affairs by Ogoni people"—and their right to control and use a fair proportion of Ogoni economic resources. It was, in short, a claim for Ogoni statehood made symbolically concrete in 1993 with an Ogoni national day—January 4—complete with Ogoni flag and anthem. In 1994 four traditional Ogoni leaders were gunned down, and the government charged Saro-Wiwa and eight cohorts on trumped-up charges of incitement to the murders. Abacha appointed a special court and had the proceedings conducted in private; the foretold result was the death sentence for all nine men, and these were carried out (by hanging) despite massive international protest.

General Abacha planned to run in an election for the Nigerian presidency later in 1998, but the Abacha era came to an abrupt end on June 8 when the dictator suddenly died. General Abdusalam Abubakar, chief of the defense staff, succeeded him as head of state and effected a transition to civilian rule. Abubakar released political detainees, including General Olosegun Obasanjo, who had been detained since 1995 as a suspect in an anti-Abacha coup. Chief Abiola, in detention since 1994, suddenly collapsed on July 7 and died as he was about to be released. The sudden deaths of both men gave rise to speculation and conspiracy theories about possible poisoning or other foul play.

The transition under Abubakar gave rise to elections for a civilian government. Northern power brokers—known as the Kaduna mafia—agreed to a shift in power that would bring a southerner to the presidential office for the first time. For the presidency, two Yoruba opposed each other. Olu Falae, a former finance minister, was the standard bearer of the progressive Alliance for Democracy and the more conservative All People's Party (APP). Olusegun Obasanjo, the only military man actually to hand back the reins of government to civilians, represented the centrist People's Democratic Party (PDP). Obasanjo, who clearly had the backing of northern politicians and the army, won 62.8% of the vote to Falae's 37.2%. The PDP also won a clear majority in both houses of parliament.

President Obasanjo's first term consisted of four years of crisis management. The return to democracy placed extraordinary demands on the government. After 15 years of iron-fisted military rule, Nigerians had a bevy of grievances, complaints and demands, and these often descended into ethnic, regional or sectarian conflicts—most of which went back to the very origin and creation of the state. At the heart of the current controversies are the nature and definition, if not the existence, of the Nigerian state: What should be the balance of resources and power between the central government and individual states?

The Niger Delta Conflicts

Regional tensions persist in north and south. In the south, crisis is centered in the Niger Delta area, source of Nigeria's wealth, but an area in which the processes of extracting that wealth have created an ecological nightmare. Since 1986, millions of barrels of oil have been spilled on the land and creeks of the Delta region, decreasing crop yield and land productivity, while also polluting the waters, depriving local inhabitants of their traditional means of livelihood. After a large oil spill in 2012, locals now say they have to walk over two hours to find a suitable fishing area, which exacerbates hunger. The inability to fish also further limits the already poor economic success of the local people. In order

Former President Olusegun Obasanjo

Nigeria

Natural gas storage sphere, Escravos Project Photo courtesy Chevron

to contain spills, environmentalists have speculated that local contractors are hiring locals to burn the contaminated area. While this practice may effectively contain the oil, it results in numerous other ecological degradations. Additionally, for years, eight million cubic feet of natural gas has flared daily, adding harmful carbon dioxide and methane emissions and providing deadly illumination to the ugly process of extraction.

Despite its generation of fabulous wealth, the Niger Delta area remains one of Nigeria's poorest and least developed regions. For residents, which are from a number of small ethnic communities, there is an undersupply of schools, drinking water, electricity, and medical care. Regional complaints grew in scale over time as residents demanded a greater share of petroleum profits. The most intractable of demands came from young members of the Ijaw community, probably the fourth largest ethnic group in Nigeria.

On December 11, 1998, some 5,000 members of the Ijaw Youth Council (IJC) from the delta region met in Kaiama, Bayelsa State, and passed what has become known as the Kaiama Declaration. The IJC declared that it ceased to recognize all decrees "enacted without our participation and consent," which was tantamount to a declaration of secession from Nigeria. The declaration went on to claim ownership of all natural resources found in Ijaw territory and demanded that the oil companies stop exploration and exploitation activities. Oil workers were given an ultimatum to vacate Ijaw land or face the consequences. The deadline for cessation of activities and withdrawal of personnel was set for December 30. Then, the declaration said, "Ijaw youths in all communities in all Ijaw clans in the Niger Delta will take steps to implement these resolutions."

To ease tensions, the government agreed to implement a constitutional provision that allocated 13% of oil revenue to each oil-producing region. But the legislation creating a Niger Delta Development Commission (NDDC)—caught in a dispute between legislature and executive—was long delayed, and the basic question of whether the provision covered both offshore and onshore oil production proved difficult to resolve.

Funding of the NDDC remained controversial. By law, the federal government was to contribute 15% of its oil revenues, the state governments 10% of theirs, and oil-producing companies 3% of their budgets to the commission. Oil-producing states refused to contribute, saying the federal legislature could not statutorily allocate monies constitutionally granted to the states, while both the federal government and companies have been slow to fulfill their allotments.

Ethnic violence, amounting to a virtual rebellion by militant Ijaw youth, surged, forcing oil companies like ChevronTexaco and Royal Dutch Shell to evacuate the region and the federal government to establish a heavy security presence in the regional center of Warri. Given the exclusivity of Ijaw demands, interethnic conflicts have increased as other communities have sought establish subnational identities and assert their claims on Delta resources. The entire area increasingly became ungovernable, a fact underlined by the emergence of yet another claimant in early 2006—the Movement for the Emancipation of the Niger Delta (MEND).

Unlike previous incarnations of ethnic grievance, MEND rejected secession from Nigeria; it claimed to fight for greater regional autonomy and resource control. MEND brought a new level of sophistication to the guerilla struggle in the Delta. Speedboats quickly attacked targets in rapid succession; radically improved firepower and combat training made the attacks lethally and destructively successful. MEND's highly mobile units kept both Shell's western-trained private security forces and elite Nigerian units off balance and unable to protect the company's production network. On April 19, 2006, MEND took its guerilla war directly to that security complex, detonating a car bomb at a military barracks in Port Harcourt. The group's statement claiming responsibility for the attack said it was, "symbolic rather than strategic" and meant to warn "the Nigerian military, oil companies and those who are attempting to sell the birthright of the Niger Delta peoples for a bowl of porridge." Guerrilla attacks on Delta oil production had already cut output by 550,000

Nigeria

barrels a day and MEND promised no let up, saying its aim was "to totally destroy the capacity of the Nigerian government to export oil."

Faced with this assault on Nigeria's economy, President Obasanjo offered concessions. Greater employment opportunities for Delta youths in the oil sector, navy, and police were promised, as was a major development plan that involved a $1.8 billion highway through the region generating 20,000 new jobs. The Ijaw National Council reiterated its claim that denial of Ijaw rights had forced their youths into armed action. Among other things, it demanded immediate demilitarization of the region. When elected IYC president in 2001, Asari, a founding member of the Ijaw Youth Council, changed the group's slogan to "Resource Control and Self Determination By Every Means Necessary." The strategy resulted in the creation of the NDPDF and a damaging guerrilla campaign against the government and oil companies. For its part, MEND was even more categorical in its rejection of President Obasanjo's Delta plan. One MEND negotiator told Reuters that the struggle had gone "beyond just development." The inevitable MEND e-mail warned oil companies and workers to "leave while they can," promising to "resume attacks with greater devastation and no compassion on those who choose to disregard our warnings."

Sectarian Tensions and Boko Haram

The Obasanjo government faced sectarian crisis after the governor of a small northern state decided to implement *sharia* law for the state's Muslim population. Sharia imposes a variety of harsh and punishments. At independence, Nigeria's legal system incorporated aspects of Islamic, Western, and customary law. Customary law applied to land and marriage matters in parts of the Christian and animist south, for example, while Islamic law applied strictly to personal matters (not criminal matters) in the north. Under *sharia* law some states have banned gambling and alcohol consumption, while others have introduced single-sex schools and taxis. Sentences include death by stoning for adultery or sodomy, amputation of limbs for stealing, and public flogging for premarital sex or drinking alcohol in public. The introduction of sharia as applied to criminal matters by the northern states— now some 12 of a total 36 states in number—has resulted in destructive sectarian and communal riots in some areas and sharia law is an ongoing source of tension. Nigeria's minister of justice, meanwhile, described sharia penalties as unconstitutional. "A Muslim," he wrote, "should not be subjected to a punishment more severe than would be imposed on other Nigerians for the same offense. Equality before the law means that Muslims should not be discriminated against."

President Obasanjo ran for reelection in April 2003, facing nominees from 20 political parties. In practical terms, his principal opponent was another retired general and former president, Muhammadu Buhari, nominated by the All Nigeria People's Party (ANPP), the renamed APP. As the governing party, the People's Democratic Party (PDP) had significant advantages, and it won majorities in both houses of parliament, the bulk of state governorships (27 out of 36). Obasanjo soundly defeated Buhari for the presidency, 62% to 32%. Constitutionally limited to two terms, Obasanjo initially worked to amend the constitution to permit a third term. The issue divided administration, party, and country; there was also considerable international pressure on the president to desist in his efforts. The third-term push ended in mid-May 2006 when the Nigerian Senate, amid swirling accusations of hugely expensive vote-buying, voted down the proposed amendment.

The ruling PDP nominated Umaru Musa Yar'Adua, the little-known governor of the impoverished northern state of Katsina, who was personally chosen by Obasanjo to be his successor. Yar'Adua was seen as pious and reclusive, but his governorship was characterized by financial prudence and accountability, and he was one of the few Nigerian governors absolved of corruption by the country's anti-graft agency. As his running mate, Yar'Adua chose Goodluck Jonathan, an Ijaw who had only recently become governor of the Delta's oil-rich (and very corrupt) Bayelsa state. Of the two dozen other candidates, the only other nominee with a meaningful chance was again Muhammadu Buhari of the ANPP; to his credit, Buhari was known for his relatively successful fight against corruption when in office. Obasanjo's vice president, Atiku Abubakar, who had opposed the third-term amendment, bolted the PDP and secured the nomination of the Action Congress, largely composed of disgruntled former PDP members.

Backed by a well-funded electoral machine superior to any other in Nigeria, the PDP won another victory in the April 2007 elections. Umaru Yar'Adua collected 70% of the votes, and his nearest rival received only about one-fourth of that amount. Former vice president Atiku came in third with less than 10% of the vote. By objective standards, the election was hopelessly flawed, and local election monitors called the voting a "charade."

Plateau State election billboard, 2007, illustrating the careful balance between Christian and Muslim candidates for governor and deputy governor ©David Hecht/IRIN

Nigeria

Presidential weakness under Yar'Adua produced strains in Nigeria's delicate balance of power. Sporadic fighting broke out between ethnic groups and the government over the mismanagement of oil, while religious tensions heightened between Christian and Muslim groups. This was exacerbated by Yar'Adua's poor health, as his scarce appearances in public and frequent and sudden travels abroad for treatment limited crucial communication with the public. After several years of declining health, Umaru Yar'Adua traveled to Saudi Arabia in November 2009 for treatment of his chronic heart condition. Soon thereafter, a constitutional crisis erupted in which many political leaders (including Members of Parliament) called for Yar'Adua to step down. Finally, in February 2010, Parliament voted to empower Vice President Goodluck Jonathan as acting president, until Yar'Adua was able to resume his duties. Jonathan quickly reshuffled the cabinet to assert his executive authority.

This transfer of power raised the prospect of upsetting an unwritten agreement among Nigerian politicians. By convention, northern Muslims and southern Christians in the governing PDP have carefully balanced power within the party, alternating presidential nominations between the two regions and ensuring that the vice presidency goes to the opposite region from the president.

Clashes between Muslims and Christians erupted again in March 2010 in the city of Jos in Plateau State, in central Nigeria along the fault line between the regions. The fighting, mainly between Hausa-Fulani northerners and Yoruba southerners, resulted in hundreds dead. This followed smaller similar clashes over several days in January 2010 that killed an estimated 200 people. Conflicts in and around Jos over the years have included the burning of numerous churches (including a deadly burning that followed in July 2010), mosques, and homes. On December 24, 2010, a series of bombs went off in villages around Jos, killing 32 people and wounding 74 more. Violence continued in Bauchi State and Plateau State in January 2011, when several dozen more were killed.

In the midst of the upsurge in sectarian violence, President Yar'Adua died on May 5, 2010, apparently of heart and kidney disease. Goodluck Jonathan was sworn in as the official head of state until the next presidential election. Jonathan nominated Namadi Sambo (governor of Kaduna State) as vice president, and this was confirmed by the National Assembly on May 18, 2010. Nonetheless, the death of the northern Muslim Umaru Yar'Adua during his term of office further upset the delicate north-south balance, as Goodluck Jonathan decided to run for election the presidency to complete what was originally Yar'adua's term; this was objected to by many northerners and Muslims who asserted that a southern Christian was upsetting the balance of power.

Goodluck Jonathan successfully retained the presidency for himself and for the PDP in elections in April 2011, winning 59% of the vote, but only at the expense of a controversy that may further destabilize the country on regional and sectarian lines. The electoral map was stark: Jonathan swept the south (with the exception of a single state that voted for the third-place candidate, the anti-corruption reformer Nuhu Ribadu) and lost every state in the north to runner-up Muhammad Buhari, a Muslim former general who was head of state in the 1980s. Moreover, while election results are not yet fully available as this book goes to press, the PDP appeared to suffer major setbacks in the legislature and at the state level; it seems likely to retain a majority in the legislature, but its dominance is under serious threat for the first time.

Further outbursts of violence have followed in the last four years in Nigeria, and the pattern appears to be worsening. Sectarian strife and atrocities are increasingly a part of the backdrop of Nigerian political life, with the leading terror group being the Islamic fundamentalists known as Boko Haram, which means "Western education is sacrilege." The first major set of sectarian clashes claimed the lives of several hundred people in Kaduna state and across the country in April 2011. In late May 2011, a series of bomb blasts shook the towns of Bauchi (capital of Bauchi State) and the city of Zaria in Kaduna State. Even as the government considered negotiating with Boko Haram, these were followed by a suicide bomb attack on the UN headquarters in the capital Abuja in August that claimed 23 lives. Another set of attacks in the northeast killed several dozen more people in November 2011. The security forces engaged Boko Haram in December, and over 60 more were killed. On Christmas Day, Boko Haram claimed responsibility for attacks that killed 37 more people.

Boko Haram followed its 2011 atrocities with a spate of killings in 2012 to 2014. One of the deadliest days came on January 22, 2012, when the group terrorized the population of Kano, the north's largest city, killing over 180 people with grenade and gun attacks. Near a church in Kaduna on Easter Sunday, another explosion killed at least 38. Attacks continued through the remainder of the year across northern Nigeria, with suicide attacks and church bombings claiming the lives of more than 200 people in mid-2012. The Nigerian army took the initiative to attack Boko Haram's stronghold in the city of Maiduguri (capital of Borno State), starting in August 2012. In the subsequent months, they managed to kill over two-dozen militants and arrested a Boko Haram commander (and Boko Haram has also come under attack from vigilante groups at the same time), but attacks have continued sporadically up to the present. Boko Haram attacked a military base in May 2013, killing over 55 soldiers. They also have clashed with vigilantes (killing over a dozen in a fight in June 2013) and proceeded with terror against civilians, attacking two schools in Maiduguri and Damaturi (Yobe State) in June and killing at least 22 children.

Boko Haram's attacks on civilians have become increasingly deadlier, killing roughly 120 civilians from July to September 2013 by means of gunning down sleeping students, teachers, and individuals in a mosque, and bombing of motorists. In the first months of 2014, this violence only grew. Incidents included the burning of residents' houses (killing about 70 villagers) in two separate attacks; the gunning down of over 110 villagers; and the killing of students in February. Overall, Boko Haram's attacks have claimed over 1,500 lives in the first several months of 2014 in three of Nigeria's north-eastern states. Although the Nigerian government claims Boko Haram's attacks are limited to the north-east, a major bombing on April 14, 2014, claimed more than 200 lives in the capital, Abuja. This attack suggests that Boko Haram is determined to extend their area of violence and is capable of doing so.

In addition to the rampant killings, Boko Haram has committed numerous mass kidnappings in recent years, the most recent being the mysterious abduction of over 200 schoolgirls on the same night as the April 14 Abuja bombing. While the army's counteroffensive seemed briefly to shake Boko Haram, such counter-terrorism mechanisms have gained recent critique as excessive military force may have unintended consequences. After roughly four years of insurgency, limited understanding of Boko Haram keeps counter-intelligence units from piecing together a definitive strategy for responding to the group.

CONTEMPORARY THEMES

Economic and Political Development

The petroleum industry, centered on the Delta region of the Niger River, dominates Nigeria's economy. In recent years, it has accounted for nearly 95% of foreign exchange earnings, 80% of federal government revenues, and a whopping 50% to 55% of GDP. Nigeria still possesses massive oil reserves—most of them along

Nigeria

the Niger River Delta. Royal Dutch Shell is the biggest company in the oil patch, accounting for nearly half of Nigeria's total oil production; other major players are the American firms Exxon-Mobil and Chevron-Texaco, the Italian company ENI/Agip, and France's TotalFinaElf.

Oil production has been regularly interrupted by local protest and ethnic violence in the Delta region. Sabotage, occupation of oil facilities, hostage taking and kidnapping are all employed by local activists, whose legitimate claims are increasingly drowned out by the violence with which they express their claims. Major oil firms like Chevron and Shell have been compelled to shut down their operations in the area. At the height of the troubles in 2003, Nigeria's oil exports were cut by 40% of normal production. Nigeria has lost billions in oil and gas revenues because of the continuing crisis in the Delta region.

Shell and other oil producers have also incurred losses from organized thievery, or "bunkering," by lethally armed criminal networks. Estimates of daily losses from bunkering vary widely, but the governor of Delta state said that thieves were at one time stealing 300,000 barrels of Nigerian crude every day; Shell alone reported losing 100,000 barrels a day. This is hugely profitable for thieves, even if the black-market oil is sold at a discount to international prices. Working with the tacit support of local and foreign business mafias and abetted by powerful local military or political "godfathers," these criminal networks are important sources of funding for local militias and fueling the Delta's destabilizing arms race.

There are also huge environmental impacts from bunkering, chiefly as a result of several hundred pipeline vandalizations per year in the 2000s. Most of these were puncturing to steal oil, but after puncturing the pipelines, the thieves leave them leaking. The resultant spills have damaged wetlands, forests, and farmlands; they are also linked to the deadly fires that occur when local villagers attempt to scoop up the leaked oil. Pipeline fires have claimed more than 2,000 lives. The destroyed land increases food prices in the whole region, causing hunger in neighboring countries as well. Under-equipped and overwhelmed by the magnitude of bunkering, the government stepped up patrols of the Niger Delta, aided by seven ships donated by the United States.

The unrelenting and intensifying bunkering in the Niger Delta has caused some oil companies (such as ENI) to halt all activities in the area, claiming that the thief had "recently reached unsustainable levels regarding both personal safety and damage to the environment." The rampant nature of the oil theft in Nigeria has caused officials to suspect the involvement of at least multiple interest groups, such as oil workers, security forces, and the community; this complicates investigations and prosecution, despite the high crime rate.

China has begun to invest in Nigeria's oil wealth. Shortly before President Hu Jintao's April 2006 visit, China National Offshore Oil Corp (CNOOC), confirmed it had signed a deal to buy a 45% share of a Nigerian offshore oil field in the company's biggest overseas purchase to that date. China agreed to invest an additional $4 billion in oil and infrastructure projects, making it a major player in Nigeria. American companies remain active as well, of course, with Vulcan Petroleum inking the most recent major deal in July 2012 for about $4.5 billion to build six refineries to produce fuel for domestic consumption.

Nigeria is moving to diversify and decrease its dependence on oil in part through expanding into natural gas, which is closely associated with oil. The move to gas production originally came from the government's desire to curb flaring, burning off gas associated with oil drilling and pumping. It was estimated that at one time three-fourths of all gas found at oil sites was flared, making Nigeria one of the world's worst heat polluters; fortunately, most flaring has now been eliminated. Still, gas production faces the same problems of order and stability as the oil industry. Only 30% of Nigeria's gas reserves are offshore. Another 30% are in swamplands, and the rest are on dry land where production is vulnerable to violence and sabotage.

Pervasive corruption, colossal economic mismanagement, and excessive dependence on oil are largely responsible for the country's poor economic performance over the decades (though the economy has boomed with high oil prices from 2009 to the present). An estimated two-thirds of the population lived below the poverty line of a dollar a day in the mid-2000s, compared to only 43% in 1985. The education system is also under pressure, even though Nigeria has the most universities in Africa. According to USAID, only 60% of those eligible are enrolled in primary school and nearly half of them eventually drop out before completing primary education; of those who complete sixth grade, only 40% are functionally literate.

Social Development

The country's health statistics are worsened by poverty and by events in northern Nigeria. Along with generally lower access to health services, obscurantist religion and politics collided in 2003 when Muslim clerics in four states—Bauchi, Kano, Kaduna, and Zamfara—claimed that polio vaccines were contaminated and may be responsible for the spread of AIDS; they forced a halt in the World Health Organization's program to eliminate the crippling disease in Nigeria. Along with remote regions of Pakistan, Nigeria is proving to be the last frontier for the complete eradication of polio worldwide; a recent massive push has brought polio down to just a few dozen cases per year; the rate in 2013 dropping 58% from that in 2012. However, the risk is that the eradication attempt will fall just short, and that the disease will again begin to spread.

Legislation signed into effect in January 2014 takes a dramatic stance against same-sex couples. Although homosexuality was already outlawed in the country, new laws state that same-sex couples may face 14 years in prison, and 10 years for participating in homosexual behaviors such as attending gay clubs or showing public displays of affection for the same sex. Furthermore, these laws prevent others from providing services to those viewed as homosexual. The international community views this as a large issue, since this convention means that HIV services provided for homosexuals are now outlawed.

The recent violence of terrorist groups like Boko Haram in the country has brought much criticism of Goodluck Jonathan's counter-terrorism strategies. Governor Murtala Nyako of Adamawa State (part of north-eastern Nigeria) has accused Jonathan and the Federal Government of committing genocide against the people of northern Nigeria. More specifically, Nyako claims that the government is using military force to kill and kidnap civilians, while quickly blaming these acts on the Boko Haram. Although these claims are likely false, the rhetoric has furthered the politicization of the war on terror in Nigeria.

Finally, Nigeria remains an important hub of international criminality. It has the dubious distinction of being the country most associated with a range of email and "phishing" scams designed to lure gullible westerners into revealing bank account numbers and other personal data. Nigeria is also a major hub in the international illicit drug trade and in the growth of elaborate money-laundering schemes. These are so extensive that the American Secret Service maintains a separate Nigerian fraud squad in metropolitan Washington.

Despite its many problems, Nigeria is one of Africa's top industrial economies, with conglomerates dominating West African markets in areas from food processing to concrete. The country is also a telecommunications leader, with Nigerian satellites offering broadcasting, telecommunications, and broadband Internet services for Africa.

Nigeria

Major problems confronting the country in the early 2020s is the recurrence and proliferation of kidnappings especially of young school-age girls held for ransom by armed groups operating most prominently in the restive north and northeast but with cases also occurring in other regions including the capital city of Abuja. With the army and internal security forces unable to put a halt to the practice, vulnerable families have often responded by pulling their daughters from school, lowering the overall education level of the general school-age population. Persistence of the phenomenon is attributed to continued economic insecurity resulting from high inflation especially of food, rising youth unemployment, and a drop in the value of the national currency causing price spikes in imports along with flagging global prices for oil.

Ongoing conflicts in the northern region of the country include the killing of 20 Nigerian soldiers by in January 2025 in a suspected attack by fighters from the ISIL affiliate in West Africa Province (ISWAP). Targeting an army base in the remote town of Malam-Fatori in the northeastern Borno state, ISWAP members arrived on gun trucks and attacked the Nigerian Army's 149th Battalion in Malam-Fatori, gateway to the border with Niger while Nigerian air raids against so-called "bandit" forces mistakenly killed civilians. Boko Haram and ISWAP fighters mainly operate in Borno attacking both security forces and civilians, killing and displacing tens of thousands of people. ISWAP split from the mainstream Boko Haram in 2016 to become the dominant armed faction in northeastern Nigeria which, although weakened by military assaults and internal fighting over the years, Boko Haram and ISWAP have stepped up attacks in Borno in 2025, killing dozens of farmers and fishermen in a series of raids. The 5-year-old conflict has killed nearly 40,000 people and displaced around two million from their homes in the northeast with the violence spilling over into neighboring Niger, Chad, and Cameroon.

Africa's largest oil producer is currently grappling with the worst cost-of-living crisis in a generation. The price of petrol in Nigeria has soared more than 400 percent since President Bola Tinubu scrapped a decades-old subsidy when he came into office in May 2023. This has led many to risk their lives to recover fuel during tanker truck accidents. A fuel tanker explosion in Niger State in northern Nigeria killed 86 people and injured dozens, after individuals attempted to transfer gasoline from one tanker into another truck using a generator. A similar accident left 150 people dead in Jigawa State also in the north in October 2024 when people tried to scrape up the spilled fuel for sale in the black market.

FUTURE CONSIDERATIONS

Nigeria is on a knife's edge. On the one hand, the country has managed an improbable run of relatively democratic elections and is growing economically at an impressive clip. Politically, it appears that the fractious opposition is merging and coalescing around a party coalition known as the All Progressive Congress (APC); if this holds together, it may represent a formidable challenge to the dominant PDP and could place Nigeria on the path toward a more stable political party system. At the same time, Nigeria seems to be making modest progress on the long-time national challenge of corruption. Economic growth is steady, and governance has improved dramatically at the state and local level in recent years in some areas, most notably the commercial capital and largest city, Lagos.

President Muhammadu Buhari

Nigeria

On the other hand, regional and sectarian tensions—between north and south, Christian and Muslim—have stretched the national fabric dangerously. The dramatic upsurge in violence from 2010 to the present has both epitomized and heightened the tensions. The Islamist group Boko Haram is a major threat, having grown in strength in the past year after taking a setback from a military crackdown. It has demonstrated continued capacity to execute the deadly attacks they began in 2010. It states that it will continue its jihad until all Christians leave northern Nigeria so that Islamic *sharia* law can be put in place.

Apart from conflicts over *sharia* law, the country still witnesses titanic corruption (because even steady improvements will take a long time to put a major dent in Nigeria's political culture) and a longstanding reputation for poor governance. While Goodluck Jonathan has a majority mandate, he faces gargantuan challenges and his mere presence in office is an irritant to many Nigerians.

In recent years, conflicting views of Boko Haram as a terrorist organization on one hand and as the opposition party to the PDP on the other, along with the perception of Goodluck Jonathan's counter-terrorist methods as attacks against northern Muslims, has created a growing opposition to the PDP. It seems like the larger this opposition grows, and the more divided the country becomes, the more opportunity for terrorist attacks there are. Boko Haram has previously exploited this divide during the previous election, and this is of increasing concern as the 2015 election approaches.

Even the robust economy gives reason for worry. While recent oil price recoveries have benefitted Nigeria and growth is at around 7%, the country is infamous for failing to parlay its windfalls into productive investment. The oil-producing regions of Nigeria have not reversed their long decline, and conflicts around production of the commodity are perpetuated with each passing year. Nigeria's economic potential will not be fully realized in the coming years unless the country develops much improved systems of governance and invests in ways that distribute the proceeds of natural resources broadly. Industrial and agricultural development will need to stabilize to complement the boon from extractive resources. More generally, social stability and governmental predictability are needed to accelerate the country's precarious turnaround. The election of Muhammadu Buhari, the candidate of the opposition All Progressives Congress (APC), as president seems to bring hope that good governance and stability could be entrenched in Nigeria. President Buhari, a Muslim from northern Nigeria, is seen as one of the incorruptible and disciplinarian leaders Nigeria has ever had. He promised after his March 28, 2015, election to fight corruption and stop the brutality of Boko Haram in the northern part of the country. There are signs that he is up to the task of bringing stability to Nigeria, and also help consolidate the country's democracy.

The Republic of Senegal

Presidential palace

BASIC FACTS

Area: 196,722 sq. km (slightly smaller than South Dakota)
Population: 18,384,660 (June 2023 est.)
Capital City: Dakar
Government Type: Presidential Republic
Neighboring Countries: The Gambia is a finger-like projection extending eastward from the Atlantic coast to the interior; Mauritania (north); Mali (east); Guinea-Bissau, Guinea (south).
Official Language: French
Other Principal Languages: Over 30. Prominently: Bambara, Pulaar (Peul), Diola (Jola), Malinké, Serere, Soninké, and Wolof, spoken by about 75% of the population.
Ethnic Groups: Wolof 43%, Peul 24%, Serer 15%, Jola 4%, Mandinka 3%, Soninké 1%, European and Lebanese 1%, other 9%
Principal Religions: Muslim 94%, Christian 5% (mostly Roman Catholic), indigenous beliefs 1%
Former Colonial Status: French Colony, a part of French West Africa (1895–1960).
Independence Date: 4 April 1960
GDP Per Capita (IMF 2023 est.): $1,719 (nominal), $4,515 (PPP)
Gini Index: 40.3 (World Bank 2011)
Currency: CFA franc, 1 USD = 594 CFA francs (Apr. 2023)
Inflation rate: 3.0% (2022 est.)
Chief Commercial Products: Fish, ground nuts (peanuts), petroleum products, phosphates, cotton, iron, and other metals
Foreign Direct Investments (FDI) net inflows: 342,650,072
Literacy Rate: 56.3 (CIA 2021)
Life Expectancy: 70.25 years (CIA 2022 est.)
Head of State: Bassirou Diomaye Faye, President (since 2 April 2024)
Head of Government: Ousmane Sonko, Prime Minister (since 3 April 2024)

LAND AND PEOPLE

The Republic of Senegal is located at the westernmost tip of Africa and lies in a transitional zone between jungles to the south and the Sahara Desert to the north. Its unique position has made it a true "crossroads" of the world between Africa and the European and the Americas.

It is a mostly flat country of almost no mountains, with rolling plains of grasslands and low tree vegetation. In the southwest, there is a small area of jungle and the coastline is often marsh or swampland. Several large rivers—most notably the Senegal River that forms the border with Mauritania and the Gambia and Casamance Rivers in the wetter south—flow in largely parallel courses from east to west. These rivers are navigable to a substantial distance inland from the Atlantic, particularly during the wet season.

The strong winds from the Sahara usher in the traditional dry season each November. This wind of dry months, called the *harmattan*, occasionally rises to almost torrential velocity, producing severe dust and sandstorms. Frequently, the high wind lasts year-round, creating severe droughts and causing intrusion of the Sahara at the rate of about four miles per year.

Not far from Dakar is Lake Retba, also known as the Pink Lake (*lac Rose*). This naturally pink lake contains very high amounts of salt. With such great amounts of salt, Lake Retba isn't home to much aquatic life, but many local people collect the salt that lies at the bottom of the lake. Lake Retba attracts tourists from all around the world.

Dakar, the busiest seaport and capital, has long been a center for tIincluding the slave trade in the colonial era) and for visitors to Africa. The city has grown rapidly

Senegal

to more than three million inhabitants and has been marred by urban congestion. Massive investments in infrastructure and sanitation are underway to improve traffic flow, phase out polluting older vehicles, and improve garbage collection.

Wielding great influence in this Muslim nation are the Sufi orders or "brotherhoods." The orders—two major ones and several smaller—are hierarchically organized around religious lineages. Disciples are organized into associations and owe both loyalty and labor to their *marabouts* or spiritual guides. The most numerous of these is the *Tijaniyya* order, divided into several branches. Smaller but more cohesive is the *Mouride* order, founded in 1883 by Cheikh Amadou Bamba and headquartered in the holy city of Touba. The Mouride order owns the largest peanut plantations and is generally considered the most influential of the brotherhoods. Each has its own spiritual leader, or *Caliph Général*, whose authority is transmitted through family dynasties that formed after the deaths of the orders' founders. Even Senegalese president Abdoulaye Wade nominally swore spiritual allegiance to the new leader of the Mourides—Serigne Cheikh Maty Leye Mbake—in 2010, after his predecessor passed away.

With a rich and vital cultural life, Senegal is famed for its writers, filmmakers, and musicians. Senegal's founding president, the poet and philosopher Léopold Senghor, died in December 2001 at the age of 95. Senghor was one of the originators in the 1930s and 1940s of the concept of *Négritude*, a notion celebrating the authenticity of African values and their contribution to what he called the "civilization of the universal." In 1984 Senghor became the first black elected to membership in the *Académie Française*, France's most prestigious cultural society whose membership is limited to 40 members at a time, known as the "Forty Immortals." Famous Senegalese writers have included Ousmane Sembène with God's Bits of Wood (*Les Bouts de Bois de Dieu*), Mariama Bâ with So Long a Letter (*Une Si Longue Lettre*), Aminata Sow Fall with The Beggars' Strike (*La Grève des Bàttu*) and many more writers. The country is also home to renowned musicians such as Youssou N'Dour, Baaba Maal, and Cheikh Lo.

HISTORY TO PRESENT DAY

For early history, see *Historical Background* and *The Colonial Period: The French*.

Presidency of Léopold Sédar Senghor (1960–1980)

With the creation of France's Fourth Republic after World War II, Senegal's two socialist deputies, Lamine Guèye and Léopold Sédar Senghor, worked to restore and extend the rights of full French citizenship that had been offered to residents of selected Senegalese cities (Dakar, Gorée, Rufisque, and Saint-Louis) the in latter years of colonial rule. Senghor later led Senegal to complete independence in 1960.

Senghor dominated Senegalese politics for the first two decades of the country's independent existence. Renowned as a brilliant thinker and poet (and indeed even responsible for much of the language of the Fourth Republic's constitution), he also had political skills. He was a Roman Catholic president in an overwhelmingly Muslim country and a member of the Serer ethnic group in a predominantly Wolof nation, but he was popular across religious and ethnic lines. He collaborated with the grand *marabouts*, leaders of Senegal's major Islamic brotherhoods, and maintained close ties with the former colonial ruler, France.

In and after 1960, Senghor's Progressive Senegalese Union (UPS) ruled as a single dominant party. While many West African states went this route of one-party socialism, Senegal developed a more tolerant and pluralist state than most of its neighbors. An early political rivalry developed between the relatively moderate President Senghor (who could be characterized as center-left) and the somewhat more radical Prime Minister Mamadou Dia (who espoused more orthodox socialist views). In 1962, Dia was accused of plotting a coup; he was forced to resign and was later imprisoned.

The early years were a true one-party state: Senghor won presidential elections unopposed in 1963, 1968, and 1973, while his party (renamed the *Parti Socialiste* or PS) won all the seats in the National Assembly. But in 1976 Senghor authorized opposition parties, beginning the slow liberalization of Senegalese politics. Despite greater political openness, the new parties had little electoral success, and Senghor was overwhelmingly reelected in 1978 to another five-year term. The elections that year to the National Assembly were marginally more significant, as the opposition Senegalese Democratic Party (PDS: *Parti Démocratique Sénégalais*) took 17 of the 100 seats from the PS. The economy had turned from a poor performance through most of the 1960s to much more impressive growth in the 1970s.

In perhaps the most orderly transfer of power seen to that point in post-independence Africa, the aging president resigned his office on December 31, 1980, and turned it over to his able prime minister, Abdou Diouf. The economic record of the Senghor administration was modest overall, but the country had grown in the 1970s and had retained a commitment to education exemplified in its humanist president. The transfer of power further heightened Senghor's reputation internationally.

Abdou Diouf Presidency and Alternation of Power (1981–2000)

After completing Senghor's term of office, Diouf won an impressive victory in relatively democratic elections in February 1983; he and the PS received more than 80% of the vote, while seven other parties competed in the contest. Opposition to the Diouf administration centered around Abdoulaye Wade's PDS, the principal opposition party in the elections in 1983, 1988, and 1993. Diouf won in each case, and Wade and three other opposition leaders even joined the PS in a coalition government from 1988 to 1992. Wade and the other opposition members resigned in 1992, complaining they had been consulted on only trivial issues, but remained divided, allowing Diouf and the PS to roll to victory again in 1993. Yet PS dominance was clearly waning, as the vote for Diouf declined from 83% (1983) to 74% (1988) to 58% (1993), while Wade's support grew

Former President Abdoulaye Wade

Senegal's first president, Hon. Léopold Sédar Senghor

Senegal

over the same elections from 15% to 26% to 32%.

Presidential elections in February 2000 went much differently. The two principal candidates were familiar—Diouf for the long-dominant PS and Wade for PDS—but after 40 years in power, the PS had become increasingly dysfunctional as a political family. Two PS defectors were strong candidates and hurt the party with their ability to criticize Diouf and the PS from the inside: Djibo Leity Kâ represented the Union for Democratic Renewal (URD) and Moustapha Niasse, a former foreign minister, enjoyed an international reputation and access to considerable campaign financing. At 73 years of age, Abdoulaye Wade was the grand old man of Senegalese opposition, but the darling of the young. His campaign stops drew enthusiastic crowds. Change was in the air and "*Sopi*," the Wolof word for change, was the chant of the crowds. If elected, he promised he would organize a referendum to dissolve the national assembly and change the constitution.

Change, indeed, was what the Senegalese voters delivered. With a host of international observers watching, the PS set aside the usual mechanisms of electoral manipulation, and President Diouf dramatically failed to obtain a majority in the first round of voting, heightening

A former Khalif of the Mourides

The Khalif of the Tijanis

the expectation. In the runoff, Wade won 58.5% of the vote. Diouf graciously admitted defeat and announced his retirement from politics. (He then became the secretary-general of La Francophonie, the international organization of former French colonies and protectorates, basically equivalent to the Commonwealth.)

Abdoulaye Wade Presidency (2000–2012)

President Wade quickly drafted a new constitution. Among a number of important changes, presidential terms were reduced to five years from seven. The Senate, an ineffective retirement home for faded PS politicians, was abolished (though it was reinstated years later) and the National Assembly reduced from 140 members to 120. The president was granted the right to dissolve the Assembly (dominated by the PS) after two years. The right to form opposition parties was entrenched; the prime minister's duties were enhanced and the judiciary given more independence. For the first time women were given equal property rights with men. In early January 2001, 94% of Senegalese approved the new constitution.

Elections to choose the members of the new National Assembly were held at the end of April 2001, and a coalition of 40 pro-Wade parties calling itself "Sopi" swept the field, winning 90 of 120 seats. The landslide victory gave President Wade a free hand to effect the changes his constituents demanded, but also highlighted the fragile nature of Wade's coalition. Relations between President Wade and Moustapha Niasse, his first premier, had already deteriorated. In the April 2001 legislative elections, Niasse's Alliance of Progressive Forces (APF) campaigned independently, won 11 seats—just ahead of the former ruling PS—and became the leading opposition.

On September 26, 2002, Senegal experienced national tragedy when the Joola, a ferryboat run by the Senegalese military and carrying three times as many passengers as allowed, capsized in the Atlantic while making its way from Zinguinchor to Dakar. The tragedy came at the end of school holidays, and many of those who drowned were among the best and brightest of Casamance's students returning to their academic work in the capital. In the final assessment, 1,863 died—more than the *Titanic*. Only 64 were rescued. The vast majority of them were from Zinguinchor, the regional capital—a terrible toll for a sleepy county seat of only 200,000 people: In Casamance, they speak of a "lost generation." The Joola sinking also took a political toll. Both the transportation and armed forces ministers resigned, and the country's navy chief was fired. After her initial dismissal of government responsibility for the accident, Prime Minister Mame Madior Boye was also replaced by President Wade and her cabinet was dissolved.

Wade struggled to reach accommodations another prime minister after Moustapha Niasse. Idrissa Seck was a close aide of the president who and had been instrumental in Wade's electoral success, but ran into difficulties with the chief executive, reportedly over the inclusion of Djibo Leity Kâ, a key opposition figure, in the cabinet. Wade fired the man he called his "son" in April 2004. Initially accused and questioned about excess spending in a local construction scandal, Seck was later charged with endangering state security. Supporters took to the streets shouting "Idy for President" and had to be dispersed with tear gas. By August, political repression began in earnest: Seck was expelled from the PDS and arrested; parliament voted to try him before a special court. Jurists resisted, however, and an investigating panel of the Senegalese high court ordered his release and the dropping of the most serious charges in 2006. President Wade next appointed Macky Sall as prime minister—his fourth since 2000—to replace Seck. Sall had earlier served as both minister of mines and interior minister and, being apparently less threatening to the president at the time, managed to serve longer than any of his predecessors in the office of prime minister.

At eighty years of age, but still vital and charismatic to his followers, Abdoulaye Wade ran for a second term of office in February 2007. Opponents included former prime ministers Moustapha Niasse and Idrissa Seck, as well as Ousmane Tanor Dieng, who had succeeded Abdou Diouf as the leader of the Socialist Party (PS), and his arch-rival within the PS, Robert Sagna. Significantly, Sagna was mayor of Ziguinchor and had severely criticized Wade's efforts to resolve the Casamance rebellion as "amateurish." While the economy grew at a few percent per year for most of Wade's first term, the government had sowed some discontent with a predilection for promising *grands travaux*—large-scale public works projects such as new highways, tunnels, and a new international airport—that only began to materialize slowly.

Wade consolidated executive and legislative authority with victories in 2007. In the first round of the presidential election, he won 55.9% of the votes against a badly divided opposition, meaning no runoff election was needed. The opposition had counted on the election going two rounds to unify behind a single candidate. It resorted to claiming electoral fraud, but election observers disagreed, calling the polling "free and fair." Some 70% of all

Senegal

Waiting for the evening catch

registered voters participated, a new record for Senegalese elections. Following the defeat, the principal opposition parties announced they would not participate in legislative elections scheduled for June 2007. The result was a huge victory for the PDS/Sopi coalition in the enlarged National Assembly: the government won 131 of 150 seats, 60 of which were elected proportionally from national lists and 90 of which were chosen in single-member districts. Also in 2007, Wade reestablished the Senate as a second chamber. It had somewhat less democratic legitimacy as a legislative branch; of 100 seats, 65 would be appointed by the president and 35 elected by local and municipal councilors. The Sopi coalition and PDS took 34 of the 35 elected seats. Wade appointed as head of the Senate a close ally, Pape Diop.

Local elections in 2009 told a different story, and represented the first major electoral setback for Wade's government. A new opposition coalition called *Benno Siggil Senegaal* (United to Boost Senegal, in the national *lingua franca* Wolof) claimed several large cities, including the big prize, Dakar. Widely interpreted as a referendum on the government's popularity several years out from the 2012 presidential elections, the local elections give a preliminary sign the electorate is seeking further *alternance* after a decade of Sopi and the PDS. While the local elections are not as consequential as national results, the government's relatively statesmanlike acceptance of the defeat bodes well for continued democratic practice.

In the south of the country, the Movement of Democratic Forces of Casamance (MFDC) has been intermittently fighting 20 years for the region's independence. Located south of The Gambia, the Casamance province has long thought of itself as exploited, virtually colonized by northerners. Unlike most north/south conflicts in Africa, the struggle in Casamance does not pit an Islamic north against an animist south because most of the region's people are Muslims, including a slight majority of the dominant ethnic group, the Diola. Instead, the conflict is economic. Casamance has more natural wealth than other parts of the country: it produces peanuts, but also has rich fishing grounds, and enough fresh water to produce rice (Senegal's staple, which is increasingly imported from Asia). It produces cotton and has dense and rich forests but lags economically. Its residents demand more distribution of wealth from Dakar and deplore the degradation of the region's forests and fish stocks. Ironically, while Dakar is blamed for harming the region's economic prospects, demand in Dakar for marijuana served as the financial basis for the rebel movement.

One factor complicating settlement over the years has been the factional division of the MFDC. The movement's historic leader, Abbé Augustin Diamacoune, got as far as signing a peace accord with the government in 2004, but a hardline dissident faction led by Salif Sadio continued to disrupt the area from villages and bases it controlled in neighboring Guinea-Bissau. In mid-March 2006, the Sadio faction engaged in firefights with a rival faction, disrupted the area's cashew harvest, and displaced thousands. The Guinea-Bissau army intervened, destroying the rebels' base of operations, and driving them north to the Gambian border. There Sadio managed to find a new patron in Gambian president Yahya Jammeh, who in turn reportedly introduced Sadio to Libya's Muammar Qadhafi, a sort of venture capitalist for such rebel movements. The death of Abbé Diamacoune in January 2007 removed from the scene an important tempering and unifying element and increased the likelihood of conflict among MFDC factions and continuing disruption of Casamance. Indeed, during the months of September and October 2009, rebels and Senegalese troops clashed in the region. And again in December 2011, the situation escalated when several people were killed on a military base in the Casamance region.

Macky Sall (2012–2024)

The early part of 2012 witnessed upheaval and violence leading up to the presidential election. President Wade sought a third term, though the constitution has a two-term limit; Wade argued that his first term, during which the rule was established, should not count toward the limit. The tumult climaxed with major political protests against Wade taking place in January and February. A violent crackdown left several people dead and called into serious doubt Senegal's long-standing democratic credentials.

Despite the violence surrounding the protests, the first round of the presidential election came off peacefully in February. Wade took the highest total with 35% of the vote and entered into a second-round runoff with his former prime minister (and former PDS member) Macky Sall of the *Alliance pour la Republique* (APR), who took second place with 27%. For the runoff of March 25, other opposition leaders united around Sall's candidacy, and the challenger defeated Wade with 65.8% of the vote. Macky Sall then appointed Abdoul Mbaye, a banker and political independent, as prime minister.

Since his inauguration, President Sall has followed a tendency of other Senegalese presidents: centralizing power after a democratic election. Sall's supporters voted to abolish the Senate (much as Wade had done years before), saying it was a wasteful institution that entrenched the old order, and that public money could better be spent on such issues as flood control. The abolition had the ambiguous effect of eliminating a potentially ineffective institution while also deliberately strengthening the grip of the president and his party on the political system.

Upon assuming office, Macky Sall took judicial action on a couple of fronts. The first related to the presence of Hissene Habré, the ex-president of Chad who had lived in exile in Senegal from 1990 to 2013. On June 20, 2013, Habré was arrested in Dakar and was accused of crimes and killings of thousands of political opponents during his presidency in Chad. This followed several years of uncertainty. In April 2008, Senegal had amended its constitution to allow Habré to be put on trial, the International Court of Justice (ICJ) at

Senegal

The Hague and the ECOWAS Court of Justice had aimed in 2009–10 to convince Senegal to put Habré on trial or extradite him. The Wade administration contemplated sending Habré back to Chad, but later suspended the extradition process, defying multiple requests from Belgium in the process. Senegal later established a special purpose court (known as the Extraordinary African Chambers) to proceed with a trial against Habré, but the investigation and preparations for trial have occurred under the Sall presidency and have marked the major turning point in the Habré matter. Sall's administration also arrested one of the most influential religious leaders, Cheikh Béthio Thioune, who was accused of murder. Mr. Thioune was previously seen as an emblematic figure by the Wade regime but was put in jail in 2012 after Macky Sall took office.

Other recent political news has centered around Abdoulaye Wade's son, Karim Wade, who was a minister of state in his father's administration (and unsuccessful candidate for the position of mayor of Dakar). Karim Wade accumulated considerable wealth during his time in office and has been arrested and charged with corruption. Two years after departing to live in France, Abdoulaye Wade announced his return on April 25, 2014 (just after a court ruled that his son must stand trial for corruption). Abdoulaye Wade was met by crowds of PDS supporters upon his return, and expressed a belief that his son will run for the presidency in 2017.

CONTEMPORARY THEMES

Economy and Social Issues

Senegal's economy has been dependent upon the production of peanuts for employment for decades. Though surpassed by other exports in terms revenue, groundnuts remain the most important source of employment in Senegal. Forty percent of cultivated land is used for peanut production and agriculture employs 70% of the country's work force.

After years of reforms and adjustments, including the CFA franc devaluation of 1994 that raised import prices but boosted domestic production, Senegal has managed relatively steady (albeit modest) economic growth since the mid-1990s. Growth has been between 2% and 6% most every year since 2000.

Since the CFA devaluation in 1994, several export industries have grown to complement the traditional exporting of groundnuts. Growth industries have included fishing, phosphates, and tourism. Fishing has become Senegal's principal revenue earner, as the nutrient-rich cold waters off the Senegalese coast are extremely rich fishing area; however, the arrival of foreign trawlers badly overfished the area and increased competition from Asian producers has displaced some Senegalese exports to Europe. The government has thus worked to create a more robust industry in aquaculture (fish farming). The tourism sector has developed strongly and has become another important earner of foreign exchange, given Senegal's beautiful beaches, rich culture, and important historical sites like "the door of no return" through which many Africans passed onto waiting ships to be sold into slavery in the Americas. The government's strategy is to reorient the tourist industry to higher-end traffic instead of the adventurous backpacking tourist. The country has also invited investment to extract iron reserves and phosphates (which are used for fertilizer). A number of independent oil companies have shown interest in Senegal's offshore prospects, especially in an area known as the Casamance blocks, but until commercially viable discoveries are made, Senegal will remain without major natural resources.

The government's biggest economic concern is unemployment. A 2007 estimate placed unemployment at 48%, making Senegal one of the ten worst economies in the world on that measure. Every year an additional 100,000 young people leave school and enter the job market, but value-added jobs are scarce. Many look to join the growing exodus of Africans and Asians seeking to reach Europe. In addition to legal emigrants, Senegal has gained some notoriety as a springboard for illegal migration. A common attempt is to board small, canoe-like fishing boats and head for the nearest European footfall—the Spanish-owned Canary Islands, 900 miles away. The International Organization for Migration estimated that 27,000 migrants journeyed by boat to the Canaries in 2006 alone. Spanish authorities estimated that another 500 died at sea.

Basic social statistics reveal the magnitude of the challenges facing the government. Per capita income is roughly $1,000 and life expectancy at birth is about 63 years. Over 60% of adult men are literate, and for women, the figure is about 40%. The fertility rate is 4.5 births per woman on average, but estimated infant mortality is 52 per 1,000 births and 93 out of 1,000 children die by the age of five, according to CIA estimates in 2014. This is despite relatively steady improvement over time on many indicators.

Foreign Affairs

Senegal has sought to balance close relations with the west and growing relations with China. Barack Obama visited Senegal in June 2013, and praised the enduring democracy in Senegal. Recent years have also witnessed Chinese investment. In October 2005, Senegal reestablished diplomatic relations with China, which in return offered development support. Sino-Senegalese cooperative projects have included road building and the renovation of 11 regional sports stadia. Somewhat more grandiose was the construction of the biggest theater

A young Mouride prays before a photo of his Khalif at Touba, Senegal ©IRIN

Senegal

in West Africa, seating 18,000 and providing parking for 3,000 cars at a price tag of $35 million.

Winning the presidency in April 2024, Bissirou Diomaye Faye with 54 percent of the vote is a left-wing pan-Africanist who at the age of 44 is the youngest president in the history of the Republic of Senegal. Released from prison a mere two weeks before the vote, the new president has vowed to reinvigorate the artisanal fishing industry of the country afflicted for years by the intrusion of foreign boats, especially from China, and illegal trawlers that have undermined sustainable fisheries crucial to the protein intake of the local population. Also promised are efforts to rein in local corruption and better manage the country's vital natural resources.

Setting terms for a withdrawal of all French soldiers stationed in Senegal by the end of 2025, France and Senegal agreed to establish a joint commission to oversee the "departure of French elements" from the country and "a restitution of [military] bases with the foreign ministries of both countries committed to "a new defense and security partnership." As Senegalese President Bassirou Diomaye Faye has announced that French army bases were "incompatible" with the country's sovereignty, 350 soldiers are slated to leave as the country marked the 80th anniversary of mass killings of West African soldiers by French colonial forces in 1944. Soldiers of the Tirailleurs Senegalais unit, despite fighting in France's war against Nazi Germany, had protested delays in salaries and poor living conditions when colonial soldiers fired on them an event now known as the Thiaroye massacre recently officially acknowledged by French President Emmanuel Macron in 2024. Senegal's rejection of its colonial past continues a trend across West and Central Africa, where nations are downgrading ties with France. Senegal has also embarked on a campaign to renegotiate contracts in the mining, oil, and gas sectors, where French companies and conglomerates predominate.

On the domestic political front, the ruling Pastef party won a resounding victory in legislative elections, securing 130 of 165 seats in parliament, November 2024 which granted newly elected President Bassirou Diomaye Faye a clear mandate to carry out ambitious reforms promised

during the campaign, including include fighting corruption, revamping the fishing industry, and maximizing natural resources benefits. The main opposition coalition, led by former President Macky Sall, won 16 seats as two other major opposition leaders also conceded defeat with Ousmane Sonko, Pastef's highly charismatic prime minister, considered the mastermind behind the legislative landslide. Faye and Sonko have promised to diversify political and economic partnerships, review hydrocarbon and fishing contracts, and re-establish Senegal's sovereignty, which they said has been sold abroad.

FUTURE CONSIDERATIONS

The Senegalese economy has grown in recent years, but only at a measured pace of about 3% on average over the last decade, and with some degree of consumer inflation. With debt relief having helped the country immensely, there is little risk of economic collapse; by the same token, there is little expectation of dramatic achievements. The economy will continue to be helped by foreign assistance, which flows into Senegal by virtue of its stability (at least outside the Casamance) and relatively positive track record in governance.

Senegal remains one of Africa's most democratic states, a reputation it has earned slowly over several decades. The country witnessed some "backsliding" in recent years as Abdoulaye Wade moved to centralize power; he reestablished a Senate dominated by the executive branch (and by his PDS) and repeatedly delayed local elections. On the other hand, electoral results in local elections in 2009 and at the national level in 2012 helped to reconfirm Senegal's democratic credentials. The spasms of violence prior to the 2012 election provided a real test of Senegal's institutions, and the sense of relief was palpable among Senegalese and international observers at the alternation of power with Macky Sall's victory over Wade. While Sall's presidency and personal leadership are yet be evaluated, Senegal as a country remains a leader among African states with its free and fair elections.

The Republic of Sierra Leone

Panoramic View of Freetown

BASIC FACTS

Area: 71,740 sq. km. = 27,900 sq. mi. (slightly smaller than South Carolina)
Population: 8,908,040 (June 2023 est.)
Capital City: Freetown
Government Type: Presidential Republic
Neighboring Countries: Guinea (north and northwest); Liberia (southeast)
Official Language: English
Other Principal Languages: Mende (principal vernacular in the south), Temne (principal vernacular in the north), Krio (English-based Creole, a lingua franca and a first language for 10% of the population but understood by 95%).
Ethnic groups: Temne 35%, Mende 31%, Limba 8%, Kono 5%, Creole 2% (descendants of freed Jamaican slaves who were settled in the Freetown area in the late 18th century), Mandingo 2%, Loko 2%, other 15% (refugees from Liberia's recent civil war, small numbers of Europeans, Lebanese, Pakistanis, and Indians).
Principal Religions: Muslim 60%, indigenous beliefs 30%, Christian 10%
Former Colonial Status: British Colony (1808–1961)
Independence Date: April 19, 1961
GDP Per Capita (IMF 2023 est.): $415 (nominal), $2,082 (PP)
Gini Index: 35.7 (World Bank 2018)
Currency: Leone; $US1 = 22,575 leones (Apr. 2023)
Inflation Rate: 17.3% (2022 est.)
Chief Commercial Products: Diamonds, rutile, cocoa, coffee, and fish
Foreign Direct Investments (FDI) net inflows: 690,349,249
Literacy Rate: 47.7% (CIA 2021)
Life Expectancy: 59 years (CIA 2023 est.)
Head of State: President Julius Maada Bio (since April 4, 2018)
Head of Government: President Julius Maada Bio (since April 4, 2018)

LAND AND PEOPLE

Sierra Leone lies on the west coast of Africa that extends westward into the Atlantic above the equator. Its climate is hot, rainy and humid. The Freetown area along the seacoast receives 150 inches of rain each year, and the relative humidity seldom drops below 80%. The coastal belt, averaging 60 miles in width, is a region of dense mangrove swamps quite similar to the Florida Everglades.

Stretches of wooded hill country rise from the coastal belt to rolling plateaus in the north and mountains rise to heights of 6,000 feet in the southeast area near the Moa River. Although there is a nominally dry season from November to April, heavy rains, especially in July, August, and September, contribute to the dense, jungle growth characteristic of portions of Sierra Leone.

Sierra Leone

The population is made up of some 18 different ethnic groups, each exhibiting similar cultural features, including governmental systems based on chieftaincies and patrilineal descent, secret societies, and subsistence agriculture. The Mende, found in the east and south, and the Temne, in the north, are the two largest groups and constitute over 60% of the population. Creoles, descendants of freed blacks who arrived in the 19th century, live mainly in Freetown and the western region. There has been much intermarriage between groups and 11 years of civil war displaced massive numbers of people from their traditional home areas.

Paramount chiefs are the traditional rulers of Sierra Leone, especially in the provincial areas. There are 149 paramount chieftaincies in the country and 63 of the incumbents died during the 11-year civil war. Elections to replace them were held in early 2003. In 13 of the districts, there were strong protests and threats of violence where the elections had been politicized. In each, the governing SLPP was accused of selecting candidates who were party supporters rather than representatives of the traditional ruling houses.

HISTORY TO PRESENT DAY

For early history, see *Historical Background* and *The Colonial Period: The British*.

World War II gave rise to much nationalist ferment in West Africa, and following the war Britain began the process that would lead to independence. The privileged status of Sierra Leone's Creole elite was not entrenched. In the constitution of 1951, the notion of majority rule, which privileged hinterland peoples, prevailed. The Sierra Leone People's Party (SLPP), a Mende-dominated party led by Milton Margai, headed the first government elected under the new constitution.

Siaka Stevens and the APC (1968–1985)

Following independence in 1961, the parliamentary government was controlled by the SLPP, led initially by Sir Milton Margai and then by his brother Sir Albert Margai after his death in 1964. The All People's Congress (APC), led by Siaka Steves, hotly contested the elections held in 1967. Favored by coastal Creoles, the APC was initially a coalition party of Temnes, Creoles, and Limbas brought together by Stevens to counter the strength of the Mende-dominated SLPP. A preelection attempt by Margai to outlaw the APC failed and early returns indicated that the APC had captured 32 seats in the parliament to 28 for the SLPP. Governor General Sir Henry Josiah Lightfoot Boston (a Creole) quickly gave the oath of office to Siaka Stevens, making him prime minister. The military arrested both Stevens and Boston ten minutes later.

A National Reformation Council, established by military officers, continued in power until April 1968, when privates and noncommissioned officers mutinied, imprisoned their officers, and restored parliamentary rule under Stevens and the APC. Stevens ruled with increasing repression, using the army to subdue hinterland supporters of the SLPP. In 1971, he declared Sierra Leone a republic, distanced the government from Britain, and set about to consolidate his authority even further. In 1978, he proposed a constitutional referendum to create a single-party state, something he claimed was more authentically African, and generated a huge majority—97.1%—in its favor. When sworn in for a seven-year term under the new constitution he rejoiced in the voters' rejection of "the worn-out, multiparty (system) . . . inherited from our colonial master, Britain."

Much of Sierra Leone's current civil strife began during Siaka Stevens' repressive single-party rule. The notorious Internal Security Unit—groups of unemployed urban youth, fed with drugs and promises of employment—was used to terrorize and intimidate regime opponents. Stevens and his cronies looted state resources and institutionalized corruption. The economy declined, the tax base virtually disappeared, and what remained of the economy went underground. The state's ability to supply services collapsed. Rural Sierra Leone was increasingly isolated from the capital (the railroad linking Freetown to the hinterland was dismantled in the 1970s and no roads replaced it) and spiraled into abject poverty.

As his term of office was drawing to an end in 1985, the elderly Stevens designated Army Chief Maj. General Joseph Momoh his successor. Weak and easily manipulated by Stevens, Momoh was expected to protect his predecessor's extensive business interests. Faced with the economic chaos that was Stevens' legacy, President Momoh turned to international lenders. Austerity measures insisted on by the IMF raised the cost of living and social tensions. Subsidies of rice and fuel were gradually reduced, while anger increased. Government corruption became pathological. When workers were forced to appear personally to pick up their pay in cash it turned out that 75% of those listed as employees didn't exist.

Military Leaders, Ahmad Tejan Kabbah (1996–97, 1998–2007), and the Rise of the RUF

A rebel insurgency led by Foday Sankoh, aided by Muammar al-Qadhafi of Libya and Charles Taylor of Liberia, broke out in 1991. It found willing recruits in the

Captain Valentine Strasser

communities of southeastern Sierra Leone that had suffered much from the corruption of the APC regime and Momoh increasingly lost control of the government and of the country. His poor prosecution of the war against Sankoh's Revolutionary United Front (RUF) and failure to support his troops in that effort led junior officers to take power in April 1992 under Captain Valentine Strasser.

Strasser, then 26 years old, and the National Provisional Ruling Council (NPRC) had some initial successes. The educational system worked for the first time in years, and teachers were paid on time. Clinics were stocked with medicines and there was a national cleaning day every Saturday to scrub up local communities. Youth took to the streets and picked litter, cleaned out gutters and drains and beautified walls with painted murals. However, Strasser's own profligate spending roused resentment among the military, and senior officers again lost control of their troops.

A palace coup led by Strasser's army colleague, Brigadier Julius Bio, on January 16, 1996, removed Strasser out of power. Bio agreed to hold elections to restore civilian rule. In the 1996 elections, 13 parties competed and six managed to elect members to the House of Representatives. The largest number of seats, 27, went to the SLPP, followed by 17 seats for the United National People's Party (UNPP).

The SLPP's Ahmad Tejan Kabbah and the UNPP's John Karefa-Smart topped the field of ten presidential contenders, and in the runoff election Kabbah was declared the victor with 59.5% of the vote. A former UN official, he slowly built confidence in his leadership and in late 1996 the RUF agreed to discontinue its rebellion and surrender all arms. A promising beginning ended abruptly in May 1997 when army enlisted men revolted over unpaid wages, possible cutbacks in their rice rations, and possible reductions in force. Kabbah fled his capital and the rebellious

Sierra Leone

troops installed Johnny Paul Koroma, a major who had been jailed for treason, as head of an Armed Forces Revolutionary Council (AFRC) to govern Sierra Leone.

The AFRC did not restore order, but instead the country descended into anarchy. Soldiers began looting indiscriminately and within days were joined in the robbery and mayhem by fighters of the rebel front eager to share the spoils. Foreign ministers from across the Economic Community of West African States (ECOWAS) met in neighboring Guinea in late June 1997 to negotiate a return to civilian rule, but diplomacy with the AFRC failed. The West African states then decided to intervene militarily.

War raged on, involving three major components: ECOWAS forces (known as ECOMOG), the AFRC and their RUF allies, and a variety of traditional hunter societies, generally referred to by the Mende term, "Kamajors," loyal to the deposed Kabbah. Armed and trained by private security companies guarding Sierra Leone's diamond mines, the Kamajors became a major element in the ensuing struggles and were eventually recognized by the government as the Civil Defense Force (CDF). The conflict became notorious, bloody, and horrific, with estimates of over 100,000 killed and hundreds of thousands more mutilated, raped, or permanently injured. Besides these atrocities, the war was known for the widespread brainwashing and use of child soldiers.

In February 1998, ECOMOG forces (largely Nigerian troops) drove the military junta from Freetown, and Ahmad Tejan Kabbah triumphantly returned to his war-ravaged capital in March. Mutineers and rebels had stolen anything of value: schools and Fourah Bay University were stripped; foreign embassies were sacked before the mutineers withdrew to the countryside. Opponents of the AFRC, local supporters of President Kabbah, and members of the Kamajor hunting groups were singled out for particularly vicious reprisals.

Kabbah's ECOWAS-supported government exercised only a tenuous control over the country and in early January 1999 the rebels launched a brutal attack on the capital. After nine days of intense fighting, the rebels, who had come close to capturing the city, withdrew, but not before a fifth of all the capital's buildings were destroyed. Under intense pressure from the international community, the government and the rebels gathered in Lomé, Togo, and signed a peace accord in July 1999. Remarkably, RUF leader Foday Sankoh was put in charge of Sierra Leone's diamond production, and Major Johnny Koroma, head of the Armed Forces Revolutionary Council (AFRC) that overthrew President Kabbah, was named Chairman of the Commission for the Consolidation of Peace.

President Ernest Bai Koroma

Despite offers of amnesty even for those who elaborated, directed, and implemented the war, UN peacekeepers received little cooperation from RUF leaders. Few rebels surrendered their arms, and peacekeepers were kept out of RUF-controlled areas. Rebel diamond production continued and was easily filtered out through The Gambia, Burkina Faso, or Liberia to pay for weaponry.

In May 2000, when the Nigerian-led ECOWAS peacekeeping force announced its departure, the rebels attacked, held several hundred UN peacekeepers captive, and advanced on Freetown. In August a renegade army faction renowned for its brutality, calling itself the West Side Boys, kidnapped 11 British soldiers. Britain's Tony Blair intervened militarily, sending in British Special Forces that secured the kidnapped soldiers, and killed or imprisoned their captors.

Faced with the British response, the RUF returned to the conference table. They were hastened to negotiations by the capture and imprisonment of RUF leader Foday Sankoh in May 2000 and by intensified international pressure on Liberian president Charles Taylor to end his support of the rebels. RUF representatives signed a ceasefire in November 2000 and slowly began to disarm. By January 2002, 45,000 combatants had handed over their weapons, and UN peacekeepers declared the war over.

President Kabbah's term of office expired in March 2001, but was prorogued by parliament. With stability restored, long-postponed presidential elections were held in May 2002. Given an opportunity to choose their leader freely and safely, a remarkable 80% of registered voters turned out to choose among nine candidates. Given the credit for bringing in the British and restoring peace by his fellow citizens, Ahmad Tejan Kabbah won a stunning 70.6% of the popular vote, eliminating the need for a runoff with his nearest rival. Alimany Paolo Bangura, the candidate of the RUF, was supported by only 1.7% of Sierra Leone's voters.

By early 2007, one could be guardedly optimistic about Sierra Leone. The security situation remained stable, but fragile. The United Nations Mission in Sierra Leone (UNAMSIL) demobilized more than 70,000 former combatants, and after five years on the job, UNAMSIL withdrew its last troops in December 2005. To focus on the country's postwar needs, the Security Council unanimously approved creation of the UN Integrated Office in Sierra Leone (UNIOSL) in January 2006 to help the government reinforce human rights, fulfill development goals, enhance transparency, and conduct free and fair elections in 2007.

Sierra Leone's Truth and Reconciliation Commission (TRC), appointed in May 2002, submitted its final report in October 2004. The main report weighed in at 1,500 pages, with a 3,500-page annex, bearing the testimonies of more than 8,000 who had been brutalized by the country's 11-year civil war. The commissioners assessed the causes of the conflict and concluded that the country's political conflicts were all about power and the benefits it conferred. "Tragically," said the commissioners, "these characteristics persist today in Sierra Leone." Corruption, which had been one of the elements initially prompting Foday Sankoh's rebellion, remained pervasive in their eyes, and if not curtailed, it would provide grounds for further conflict.

Egregious examples of corruption were easy to find. Teachers routinely went without their salaries because school authorities had stolen the funds. Clinics were built, but no drugs were supplied because of what was graciously called "seepage." Schools were constructed, but there was no money for blackboards or desks because so much had been siphoned off in kickbacks and bribes. Huge quantities of desperately needed supplies and materials simply disappeared, presumably stolen and sold for personal gain. One government report found that the Health Ministry had failed to distribute 95% of the medicine and equipment intended for public hospitals.

Under considerable outside pressure, an Anti-Corruption Commission (ACC) was set up, and internal investigations and trials began for those indicted on charges of crimes against humanity during the civil war. Former militia leaders and commanders were arrested and tried in Sierra Leonean courts. Sam Hinga Norman, once Sierra Leone's minister of internal affairs and the former leader of the pro-government militia known

Sierra Leone

as Kamajors, faced prosecutors in early 2006. The 66-year-old Norman, a high chief in southern Sierra Leone, was charged with war crimes, including unlawful killings, the use of child soldiers, looting and burning, and terrorizing civilians. To many Sierra Leoneans he was a national hero for leading the Kamajor hunters against the RUF. The competing narratives were made moot by Norman's death in February 2007. The trials of Norman and others have helped to develop Sierra Leone's court system and provide the people with a sense that their country is serving justice and working towards reconciliation.

Civilian Transition: Ernest Bai Koroma (2007–2018)

In 2007, Sierra Leone prepared to effect the first transition from one civilian government to another since civil war ravaged the country in the 1990s. The SLPP selected Vice President Solomon Berewa as its leader, automatically making him its candidate for the presidential election. For its part, the All People's Congress (APC) chose as its standard bearer Ernest Bai Koroma, a Fourah Bay graduate and businessman. Defeated in his campaign to become SLPP leader, Charles Francis Margai, son of a former president and nephew of another, testily resigned from the party and announced the formation of yet another opposition group: the People's Movement for Democratic change (PMDC).

Much depended on a successful organization and conduct of this election. The country has few viable political institutions, a population grown cynical with war and corruption, and disillusionment with a self-serving political class. To ensure transparency and effectiveness, UNIOSL worked to develop operational capacities of the National Electoral Commission and a voter registration taskforce. Election costs were subsidized by a variety of international actors, but a budgetary deficit of several million dollars is still expected. The leaders of eight political parties signed an electoral code of conduct in November 2006, but the greatest responsibility in this area rests with the SLPP government. The temptation is strong to exploit the advantages of incumbency and control of state resources to the benefit of electoral victory.

Ernest Bai Koroma emerged victorious in the 2007 elections, and the APC took the majority of seats in the parliament, with the SLPP in second place. The government set to the task of restoring the functioning of failed institutions and ending the semi-lawless environment have contributed to Sierra Leone's culture of corruption. After his election, President Ernest Bai Koroma pursued free-market policies and has encouraged foreign investment although many countries have been slow to enter (with the notable exception of China).

In 2010, the UN Security Council lifted all remaining sanctions against Sierra Leone, applauding the government for its reconstruction efforts and declaring a sustained end to the violence that had ravaged the country in years past. In the years following the end of the civil war, the UN Security Council established a War Crimes Court for Sierra Leone at The Hague in order to try those who bore the greatest responsibility for human rights abuses. Combining both international and local jurists, the court culminated its work in 2012 when it sentenced Liberia's Charles Taylor to 50 years in jail for aiding and abetting crimes against humanity during the civil war; Taylor became the first head of state to be convicted by an international court since the Nuremburg Trials in 1945. Apart from Taylor, eight other individuals were sentenced by the court for various crimes linked to the atrocities of the 11-year war. These included three former high-ranking officials of the RUF in April 2009; Issa Sesay (52-year prison sentence), Morris Kallon (40-year sentence), and Augustine Gbao (25-year sentence).

General elections in 2012 largely replicated the result from 2007. Ernest Bai Koroma of the APC again won the presidency with 59% of the vote, easily beating the SLPP's Julius Maada Bio, who took 37%. For seats in parliament, the APC took 67 seats to 42 for the SLPP (with another dozen reserved for traditional chiefs). The SLPP alleged electoral fraud, but the international community found the elections were free and fair. (Unlike 2007, this election was the first undertaken without UN supervision.) The result seemed to confirm the status quo and represented a vote of confidence that the country had turned a corner in terms of political and social stability.

CONTEMPORARY THEMES

Despite steady economic growth and reconstruction since the end of the war in 2002, Sierra Leone is still one of the poorest countries in the world. Over half of its population lives in abject poverty, earning less than a dollar a day; three-quarters of those between the ages of 18 and 35 are unemployed, and life expectancy in 2010 is under 48 years. A major issue that the government must face moving forward is effective reconstruction, as the infrastructure in Sierra Leone requires serious investment.

One issue that needs attention is the healthcare system. In the chronically poor country, healthcare access and quality are not up to par. In 2010, Sierra Leone had the highest child mortality rate in the world, and there continues to be an enormous shortage of qualified medical professionals and supplies to administer proper care. European governments and international organizations have stepped in to provide funding for increased prenatal care as well as overall improvements in the medical infrastructure of the country. Huge improvements have already been seen (a 214% increase in the number of children under 5 getting care at health facilities), but it will take many more years before Sierra Leone is able to run a successful universal healthcare program.

Following the civil war, the Kabbah government struggled to regain control over the country's territory and economy, based on agriculture and mining. The bulk of the population is engaged in subsistence farming, with plantation agriculture significant only in certain parts of the country. Agriculture was seriously disrupted during the civil war. Overall,

Working with a Chinese tractor   Photo by Catherine Bolten

Sierra Leone

agriculture traditionally contributed 50% of GDP and employed between 65% and 80% of the population. The most important commercial crops are cocoa and coffee, and the government's goal is to revitalize both commodities and assure food security by boosting domestic production of rice. (Sierra Leone exported rice until the 1980s, but since then has been an importer of the grain.)

Mining has long been the major bulwark of Sierra Leone's economy, with rutile (an important source of titanium) and diamonds the principal source of government revenues. Sierra Rutile Ltd. (SRL), the world's largest producer of natural rutile until it was closed for security reasons in 1995, was the country's largest taxpayer, private sector employer and foreign export earner. The company shipped its first consignment of the mineral since 1995 in March 2006. Lebanese merchants control the majority of Sierra Leone's diamond trade (both legal and illegal). In 2004, one Lebanese company, owned by a Sierra Leonean-born Lebanese trader, exported almost half of all officially certified diamonds.

Sierra Leone's alluvial diamond fields lie in areas once controlled by the rebels, and in recent years the government has worked to clean up the reputation of Sierra Leone diamonds after the horrific stories out of the mines during the war. The bulk of RUF diamond production was smuggled to Liberia where it was converted to cash with which to buy arms. Arms were sourced in eastern European states and supplied to the rebels through Liberian or Burkinabé connivance, with Liberia's former president profiting handsomely as middleman in these operations. The international community branded these war diamonds as "blood" or "conflict" diamonds, and ultimately banned their sale. Under a system of the international controls aimed at ending the illicit trade in "conflict diamonds," the value of Sierra Leone's official diamond exports has increased significantly, from $76 million in 2003 to $127 million in 2004 and $150 million in 2005. The total value of the country's annual diamond production, however, is estimated at between $250 million and $300 million. The difference is smuggled out of the country to finance a variety of (usually) illicit activities.

Because of the capital investment required, deep mining of diamonds buried in kimberlite pipes is insignificant compared to alluvial (surface) mining. The first industrial mining company to undertake the task, however, saw its operations and revenues dramatically expand from and the operation produced 78,500 carats worth $13.86 million in 2004, increasing to 116,700 ct, worth $22.5 million in 2005; it is likely more deep mining operations will be undertaken as peace and stability become the norm.

Corruption will continue to be an ingrained societal issue and so widespread is it that a rich vocabulary of terms; "Kavei," for example, means cheating, while "guyu-guyu" refers to shady practices. An opinion survey taken in 2000 showed that 94% of Sierra Leoneans thought corruption was rampant and widespread in most institutions. . The dismissal of the UN Mission Chief for Sierra Leone at the behest of then President Ernest Bai Koroma was an attempt to bolster the president's re-election chances. Elected in 2018 and reelected in 2023, President Julius Maada Bio has overseen charges brought against former president Koroma for a failed coup orchestrated by Koroma's personal bodyguards with the former president allowed to seek medical care abroad. Persistent domestic problems include high youth unemployment estimated at 60 percent and human trafficking of vulnerable people to promised employment in Middle Eastern countries, such as Lebanon and Oman.

On the medical front, Sierra Leone declared a public health emergency after two cases of Mpox were reported in January 2025. This disease is caused by a virus from the same family as smallpox known as monkeypox. The disease manifests in a high fever and skin lesions, called vesicles with most human cases were seen in people in Central and West Africa who had close contact with infected animals. This is the first confirmed case in the country since the health watchdog of the African Union declared a public health emergency over the growing mpox outbreak on the continent in 2024. Neither case had known recent contact with infected animals or other sick individuals according to the Ministry of Health and Sanitation. The first case involved recent travel to the airport town of Lungi in the northern Port Loko District. Sierra Leone's medical system was ready to respond to cases based on experience gained during the Ebola and COVID-19 outbreaks in previous years. The virus was confirmed for the first time to spread via sex when outbreaks were triggered in more than 70 countries across the world in 2022. Sierra Leone was the epicenter of the Ebola outbreak that ravaged West Africa in an epidemic killing 4,000 people, including nearly 7 percent of the country's health workers, between 2014 and 2016.

A country with dwindling wilderness and forests, Sierra Leone relies on teams of rangers from the National Protected Area Authority (NPAA) who are tasked with guarding the rainforest from encroaching illegal mining and logging though with only 62 wardens it is an arduous game of cat and mouse in the Kambui Hills Forest Reserve in Sierra Leone's Eastern Province, which borders Guinea and Liberia. This province has large reserves of gold, rutile, and diamonds. The trade of so-called blood diamonds largely financed the country's brutal 11-year civil war. While mineral-rich, Sierra Leone is one of the poorest countries in the world, with the rangers blaming economic hardship for the escalating exploitation of the natural landscape. Sierra Leone has one of the highest deforestation rates in the world, losing more than 35 percent of total

A slightly rundown dormitory, Fourah Bay College   Photo by Catherine Bolten

Sierra Leone

tree cover and 14 percent of humid primary forests since 2000. Home to a diverse range of mammal species, Kambui Hill sports the western chimpanzee, the black and white colobus monkey, the brush-tailed porcupine, and Maxwell's duiker. The lush forest also provides a habitat for threatened birds such as the white-necked rockfowl. Over the past decade and a half, the government has stepped up conservation efforts, with the creation of the NPAA in 2012 and the Ministry of Environment and Climate Change in 2018.

FUTURE CONSIDERATIONS

There is room for cautious optimism about Sierra Leone, though corruption and popular disillusionment with the pace of progress will temper that optimism and challenge the government. In terms of risks, the country's external debt was about $1.5 billion in 2005, but the IMF and World Bank have provided significant debt relief under the Heavily Indebted Poor Country (HIPC) initiative. In recent years, 50% of the government's budget has been funded by grants and loans from international financial institutions. Such dependence will likely continue for the near future. Investment in infrastructure will continue to be a necessary priority as Sierra Leone works towards reconstruction and development; healthcare, roads, and government transparency will merit special consideration.

The recent rulings from international tribunals have provided some reconciliation and justice for the millions affected by the tragedies and loss of the civil war. The sentencing of Charles Taylor and others involved in the bloodshed gives hope that Sierra Leone can move forward and that future perpetrators of similar crimes will be held accountable for their actions.

Politics in Sierra Leone (like those in neighboring Liberia) seem to have taken a turn toward stability and a degree of promise. The relatively peaceful elections of President Ernest Bai Koroma in 2007 and 2012 (and the presence of both the APC and SLPP parties in the legislature) have been a good sign. The APC has focused on infrastructure development, health, and education while reacting to socio-economic challenges. While crime and social problems remain rampant, the likelihood of civil strife and open warfare has subsided. There was some violence in recent local elections, but the violence never generalized. The country is not yet a full-blown democracy, but its trajectory gives reason to hope that its greatest challenges going forward will not be war and conflict, but the reconciliation and reconstruction needed in its aftermath.

The Republic of Togo

A balanced conversation in Lomé   AP/Wide World Photo

BASIC FACTS

Area: 56,785 sq. km
Population: 8,703,961 (June 2022 est.)
Capital City: Lomé
Government Type: Presidential Republic
Neighboring Countries: Ghana (west); Burkina Faso (Upper Volta, north); Benin (east)
Official Language: French
Other Principal Languages: Ewe and Mina in the south, Kabye (or Kabiye) and Dagomba in the north.
Ethnic Groups: Ewe and Kabye, and over 30 others; European and Syrian-Lebanese less than 1%
Principal Religions: Indigenous beliefs 51%, Christianity 29%, and Islam 20%
Former Colonial Status: German Colony (1885–1916), French Colony (1916–1960)
Independence Date: April 27, 1960
GDP Per Capita (IMF 2023 est.): $990 (nominal), $2,754 (PPP)
Gini Index: 43.1 (World Bank 2015)
Currency: CFA Franc 1 USD=594 CFA (Apr. 2022)
Inflation Rate: 4.6% (2022 est.)
Chief Commercial Products: Phosphates, cotton, coffee, and cocoa.
Foreign Direct Investments (FDI) net inflows: 292,085,515
Literacy Rate: 66.5 (CIA 2022)
Life Expectancy: 71.71 years (CIA 2023 est.)
Head of State: Faure Essozima Gnassingbé, President (since April 24, 2005)
Head of Government: Prime Minister Victorie Tomegah Dogbe (since September 28, 2020)

LAND AND PEOPLE

Togo is a long, narrow country stretching 360 miles from the Atlantic north into the Sahel. This small nation is only 31 miles wide at the coast and 100 miles wide at its broadest point. As is common to this region of Africa, the climate of Togo is predominantly hot and humid on the coast with a drier region in the north. Picturesque Lake Togo, with quiet, fresh water, is along the central coast. The central section is traversed by the Togo Mountains and the north-central region of the country includes several escarpments.

The people of the populous southern coast area have better development indicators than those of the sparsely settled north. The largest ethnic group is the Ewe, who predominates in the capital Lomé and in the south, while a number of other ethnicities are most numerous in different villages and regions farther north. Some tension continues to exist between the Ewe and the Kabyé ethnic group, which includes long-time president Gnassingbé Eyadema and his son, current president Faure Gnassingbé.

The Koutammakou landscape in northeastern Togo, which extends into neighboring Benin, was made a UNESCO World Heritage site in 2004. Home to the Batammariba people, the landscape is characterized by distinctive architecture: many two-story tower houses and granaries that are almost spherical above a cylindrical base. UNESCO called Koutammakou "an outstanding example of a system of traditional settlement that is still living and dynamic."

HISTORY TO THE PRESENT DAY

For early history, see *Historical Background* and *The Colonial Period: The Germans* and *The Colonial Period: The French*.

Independence

French Togoland became an autonomous republic within the French Union in 1956 and achieved its independence in 1960. Also in 1956, as the Gold Coast (present-day Ghana) neared independence, a UN-sponsored plebiscite allowed the people of British Togoland to vote on joining the Gold Coast. The residents of British Togoland opted to unite with the Gold Coast and in 1957 became independent as Ghana. Pre-independence elections in French Togoland, held in 1956, installed Nicholas Grunitzky of the Togolese Progress Party (*Parti togolais du progrès*, PTP) as premier. His brother-in-law Sylvanus Olympio advocated for independence at the head of the Committee for the Unity of Togo (CUT: *Comité de l'unité togolaise*), later renamed the Party for the Unity of Togo (PUT, *Parti*

Togo

de l'unité togolaise). In elections in 1958, Olympio defeated Grunitsky's PTP and became premier.

The Coups of the 1960s

Sylvanus Olympio went on to become Togo's first head of state when the country became independent in 1960. He excluded other parties from political contestation and moved Togo in the direction of a one-party state under the PUT, a trend occurring in many other neighboring countries. Olympio developed a thorny relationship with Ghana's Kwame Nkrumah, partly over ideological differences (with Olympio more pro-western) and partly over ethnic differences (as Olympio was an Ewe, which represented a prominent minority in Ghana). More consequentially, perhaps, Olympio refused to expand the size of the army and refused to bring in many Togolese veterans who had fought overseas for France. This led to increasing friction with the members of the 250-man force, as well as with those who wished to join.

On January 13, 1963, soldiers burst into Olympio's home in Lomé and assassinated him at the gates of the U.S. Embassy next door, where he had fled seeking refuge. This was the first outright coup d'état in Africa after the wave of independence in the late 1950s and into 1960 and has often been considered a watershed moment that ushered in an era of military takeovers. After two days of political uncertainty under the so-called Insurrection Committee, Grunitzky returned and was named prime minister by Sgt. Gnassingbé Eyadéma, a prominent member of the group that killed Olympio. (Eyadema indeed claimed to have personally shot Olympio himself.) In May 1963, voters approved a new constitution in a referendum and elected Grunitzky to the presidency unopposed along with a slate of unopposed candidates to the National Assembly.

Eyadema's Rise to Power and Long Rule (1967–2005)

Over the subsequent four years, Gnassingbé Eyadéma (now a Lt. Colonel), seized power in a 1967 bloodless coup that toppled Grunitzky and abolished all parties. Eyadéma later formed the Rally of the Togolese People (*Rassemblement du Peuple Togolais*, RPT) and ran in 1972 as the sole candidate for president, supposedly receiving 99% in favor of his continuing his rule in a "yes"-or-"no" contest.

President Eyadéma and the military governed Togo for some 38 years, and for three decades assassination, torture, and routine abuse of civil liberties and human rights characterized the regime. Gilchrist Olympio, the son of assassinated President Sylvanus Olympio, was almost killed in a 1993 assassination attempt after he emerged as a potential rival to President Eyadéma. He retreated to exile in France, fearing he would not survive in Togo. The Togolese army, on which Eyadéma's repression relied, was largely recruited from members of the president's northern Kabyé ethnic group. Eyadéma systematically appointed northerners as generals and placed the elite Presidential Guard under the command of his son, Colonel Ernest Gnassingbé; another son, Commandant Rock Gnassingbé, led a motorized division.

Presidential elections under Eyadéma were held in 1972, 1979, 1986, 1993, and 1998, but were shams in each case. Eyadéma ran unopposed in 1979 and 1986, and virtually unopposed in 1993. For 1998, the manipulations took a different form as Eyadéma staffed several electoral institutions with supporters, including a

Former President Gnassingbé Eyadéma

new constitutional court created to hear any election disputes, a new communications authority to oversee the media, and a new electoral code that gave responsibility for organizing and supervising the elections to Eyadéma's Ministry of the Interior. The government also controlled the calendar, and announced in March that the elections originally scheduled for August were advanced to June; this tactic gave the opposition little time to organize.

Eyadéma was reelected by a modest 52.13% of the votes cast, just enough to avoid a runoff election. Immediately prior to the announcement of election results, the head of the electoral commission resigned, saying she had received telephone calls threatening her life, and four other members of the commission also resigned. Eyadéma's principal rival, Gilchrist Olympio, still living in exile, was allotted 34.1% of the ballots by the interior ministry, which ran the election. Opposition protests were met with tear gas grenades. Olympio said his own calculations showed he won 59% of the vote and vowed to use all peaceful, legitimate, and constitutional means to have the results annulled, all of which were of no avail. The spring 1999 legislative elections were equally farcical, as the opposition boycotted and candidates of Eyadéma's RPT won 79 of 81 parliamentary seats.

In May 1999, Amnesty International described Togo as a "state of terror," characterized by executions and extra-judicial executions perpetrated by authorities throughout the political crisis from 1993 to 1998. Hundreds had been killed in the days leading up to the 1998 elections alone. Evidence gathered from fishermen in Togo and neighboring Benin indicated that manacled opponents had been thrown into the sea from Togolese air force planes.

Eyadéma's brutal repression left Togo in a state of permanent political crisis and economic stagnation. Only in 1999, after years of economic sanctions had taken their toll, were there signs of willingness to compromise with his opponents. "National reconciliation" discussions took place in July under the authority of the EU and La Francophonie, the French equivalent of the Commonwealth. On a visit to West Africa President Jacques Chirac of France forcefully announced that only national reconciliation would enable the EU to resume Iid. After conversations with Eyadéma, Chirac announced that Togo's president would step down at the end of his presidential term in 2003, respecting the constitution by not presenting himself for a third term. Eyadéma would also dissolve the contested National Assembly and call new parliamentary electIons in March 2000. He also agreed to the creation If an independent electoral commission. All parties present affixed their signatures to what was called the Lomé Framework AgreIOpposition intransigence, however, scuttled the effort. Gilchrist Olympio, fearing for his life, refused to participate in the Lomé reconciliation talks for security reasons. Internal opponents of the regime objected to details. In exasperation, the international advisers sent their recommendations directly to the NatioIAssembly, which approved a new election code in March. When the legislature amended the pI code, the opposition again objected and withdrew from reconciliation discussions. The elections of 2000 never took place.

Also in 1999, Togo stood accused of massacres and summary executions. The Benin League for the Defense of Human Rights reported that more than 100 bodies were found in coastal villages, having been dumped into the sea prior to the presidential elections in 1998. Some were headless, handcuffed, or riddled with bullets. The

Togo

League said they were "pushed from low-flying planes and helicopters coming during the night from Togo." By June 2000, a joint commission between the United Nations and the OAU began investigating the massacres just as Eyadéma had begun serving a term as OAU chairman. The inquiry team made clear that individuals linked to Togolese security forces, working in cooperation with the Togolese police and allied militias, had indeed carried out summary executions of the government's political opponents. The Fowler Report to the UN Security Council of March 2000 also identified Eyadéma as one of those facilitating the continuing arms supply of Jonas Savimbi's UNITA forces in Angola. A follow-up report accused Togolese authorities of accepting "blood diamonds" from Savimbi in exchange for illegal arms and fuel shipments.

Eyadéma's RPT government returned to its suppression of civil liberties up to the 2002 elections. Yaovi Agboyibo, the former head of Togo's Bar Association, was jailed in August 2001 for having accused Prime Minister Agbéyomé Kodjo of "complicity with criminals" while heading the Lomé Port Authority. Two call-in radio talk shows were suspended for broadcasting "defamatory" programs. The RPT also passed a series of self-serving amendments to the elections code, most notably a provision (targeted at Gilchrist Olympio, who was in exile in Ghana) that required presidential candidates to have lived in Togo continuously for 12 months immediately preceding an election. Street demonstrations against the new code ensued, even in the face of contingents of riot police. When Togolese voters went to the polls in late October 2002, most opposition parties boycotted the election once again. Eyadéma's RPT won 72 of 81 seats, and the renewed RPT majority amended Togo's constitution again in December to allow Eyadéma to seek reelection yet again. The state then proceeded to intimidate, arrest and torture opposition leaders, and banned marches and public meetings.

As the 2003 presidential elections approached, the opposition fell into disarray. Gilchrist Olympio's *Union des Forces du Changement* (UFC), Togo's main opposition party, withdrew from the umbrella group known as the *Coalition des Forces Démocratiques* (CFD) to nominate Olympio as their candidate for the presidency, only to have his candidacy banned for technical irregularities in his nomination papers. Unable to agree on a single nominee, the eight remaining CFD parties decided to present individual candidates. The UFC nominated its deputy leader, the 75-year-old Emmanuel Bob-Akitani, a retired mining engineer who essentially ran as a proxy for Gilchrist Olympio. After the

President Faure Gnassingbé

June 2003 ballot, the electoral commission announced that Eyadéma won 57.22% of the votes cast and the UFC's Bob-Akitani came second with 34.14%, with the remaining votes shared by four other opposition candidates.

Eyadéma died suddenly in early February 2005, ending 38 years of dictatorial rule. The army quickly closed the borders, keeping the president's constitutional successor, the speaker of the Assembly, out of the country and installing as president Eyadéma's son, Faure Gnassingbé. The National Assembly, filled with ruling-party placement, gave political cover by amending the constitution to permit the succession. Togo's streets filled with protesters and the international community waxed indignant. The AU denounced the action and ECOWAS imposed sanctions; Faure Gnassingbé resigned after three weeks, promising elections in 60 days, but prepared to run in the subsequent election.

The opposition actually managed some semblance of unity, nominating the UFC's elderly Emmanuel Bob Akitani, who everyone understood to be the stand-in for Gilchrist Olympio. With its skills at electoral fraud homed in past elections, and enormous financial resources, the Togolese People's Rally (RPT) generated a victory for Faure Gnassingbé with 60.15% of the vote against 38.25% for the opposition. Mass protests ensued; in Lomé, gangs of opposition supporters erected burning barricades and pelted vehicles, but the army stepped in and crushed the insurrection. Between 400 and 500 people were killed, and thousands—at least 30,000—fled to Ghana or Benin.

After two years of intense negotiation, an agreement between government and opposition emerged in August 2006 (brokered by president Blaise Compaoré of Burkina Faso) that established an Independent National Electoral Commission (CENI) to organize legislative elections for 2007. The CENI consisted of 19 members—five from the presidential movement, two each from five opposition parties, and a further two representing civil society and two more representing the cabinet. To coordinate and implement the various agreements, dialogue participants also agreed to form a national unity cabinet.

Faure Gnassingbé (2005–present)

By September 2006, President Gnassingbé had appointed a new prime minister to head the transitional government—Yawovi Agboyibo, a 63-year-old lawyer who had spent much of his life trying to end the Eyadéma dictatorship. His hopes of becoming prime minister dashed, Gilchrist Olympio rejected the new government. The UFC refused to join the unity cabinet, though its second vice president, Amah Gnassingbé, was permitted to enter the government as a minister of state on an individual basis.

In 2007, Togo held what may have been the freest elections in its history, though the ruling RPT clearly had a number of advantages in the run-up to voting. Unsurprisingly, Togo's dominant party won the legislative elections; more surprisingly, the elections were hailed internationally as relatively free and fair. The European Union soon afterwards reestablished international cooperation with Togo, a state that had been one of Africa's pariahs for many years.

In 2008, Gnassingbé appointed a new prime minister, Gilbert Houngbo. But perhaps more dramatic news came in April 2009 when Faure Gnassingbé's ambitious half-brother and erstwhile ally, Kpatcha Gnassingbé, was detained by Togolese security forces as he attempted to flee into the U.S. Embassy for sanctuary (in a scene somewhat reminiscent of the Sylvanus Olympio assassination in 1963). Kpatcha Gnassingbé claimed he was the victim of assassination attempts, while Faure Gnassingbé suspects Kpatcha's participation in coup plotting. Later that same month, Togolese news sources reported that another half-brother Essolizam Edem Gnassingbé, had also been detained along with others allegedly involved in a coup plot. While details are sketchy, the conflict within the Gnassingbé clan may suggest some wider rift among powerbrokers in a country where power has seemed indivisible for decades.

Gnassingbé was re-elected in March 2010, with 61% of the vote. Jean-Pierre Fabre, leader of the opposition, won 35%. Once again, the opposition alleged fraud and led protests. In May 2010, UFC leader Gilchrist Olympio approved a deal which would bring his party into the government

Togo

in a power-sharing agreement, but following public protests the UFC rejected the deal and suspended Olympio from his position.

The RPT put in place changes to parliamentary election rules in 2012 that reconsolidated their power. These included gerrymandered districts that heavily favored the president's party and a ten seat increase to the legislature. Demonstrations stalled the October 2012 election date until July of 2013. The UFC lost 24 of their 27 seats, losing its position as the largest opposition party. Opponents denounced the results for evidence of fraud and irregularities; they had hoped to gain control of Parliament in hopes of reinstating a presidential term limit to prevent Gnassingbé from running again in 2015, but outside officials from the EU and ECOWAS accepted the results, calling the election fair and transparent.

CONTEMPORARY THEMES

The Togolese economy is mainly dependent on subsistence agriculture, which accounts for nearly 75% of jobs. Combined exports of commercial crops like cotton, cocoa, and coffee, account for nearly 40% of total export earnings. Cotton is Togo's most important commercial crop. About a quarter million Togolese earn their living from cotton, but their livelihoods are always subject to fluctuating weather and world prices.

The mining sector accounts for more than one-third of export earnings; phosphate mining is the most significant element of the sector, contributing 26% to 28% of export earnings—vying with cotton for primacy of place. Togo is the world's fifth largest exporter of calcium phosphate and possesses large reserves, estimated at over 150 million tons of high-grade ore. Togo generates only 30% of its own electricity needs. For much of the rest, it depends on electricity supplied by Ghana's Akosombo Dam or on natural gas from Nigeria.

Togo continues to suffer economic malaise, largely caused by its long-term political crisis. Togo has seen only limited international investment since 1991. As the economy shrank, an informal—and increasingly criminalized—economy developed. Illegal weapons and drugs, money laundering, human trafficking, and smuggling of all types came to dominate the country's trade. Togo is now considered one of the world's drug trafficking hubs. The government has turned some of its efforts towards targeting illegal ivory trade; in 2013 and 2014, officials made arrests and seized several tons of ivory at shipping ports in Lomé.

Lomé has the deepest water of West Africa's ports and for a time picked up business with shippers frustrated by delays at container ports in Lagos and by conflict in Côte d'Ivoire that dissuaded shippers from Abidjan. Yet it also competes with the modern port at Tema in Ghana and Cotonou, Benin. As a consequence, Togo has sought to upgrade and expand its container-handling facilities.

In terms of social challenges, Togo is confronting an HIV/AIDS epidemic that affects about 3% of the adult population. While lower than rates in southern Africa, this is worse than in many other countries in West Africa. Despite this, Togo's life expectancy continues to climb slowly, and now has reached an estimated 63 years (2009 World Bank estimate), which is relatively high by African standards. Literacy remains a challenge as well; it is estimated at only about 60%, but over 80% for younger Togolese (though there are differences between young men and young women, with the former having more schooling).

Current controversies include efforts by the parliament to alter the process of presidential elections from direct popular election to selection by the parliament which opposition leaders see as a blatant attempt to extend the presidency of Gnassingba until 2033 as changes would include a two-term limit but with no consideration of previous time in office.

In a legislative vote in April 2024, lawmakers approved changes to the constitution linked to presidential terms along with creation of a parliamentary system replacing the presidential one, which some opposition politicians and civil society groups denounced as a constitutional coup. With all 87 lawmakers present agreeing to the new parliamentary system and the few opposition lawmakers boycotting the proceedings, the president will no longer be elected by universal suffrage, but by the parliament for a single presidential term of six years along with creation of a prime minister. By not taking into account time already spent in office, this enables President Gnassingbe to remain in power for several more years. Those opposed to the changes, including church authorities, fear further extension of the president's 19-year rule and his family's grip on power as his father and predecessor Gnassingbe Eyadema seized

power in a coup in 1967. Opposition coalition Dynamique Pour la Majorité du Peuple (DMP) declared the constitutional changes a political maneuver to allow Gnassingbe to extend his tenure for life and termed the action a virtual coup d'etat as future elections were postponed.

FUTURE CONSIDERATIONS

Faure Gnassingbé seems to have settled into power with the confidence of the RPT and the military after a tumultuous beginning of his presidency, and both his detention of his half-brothers in 2009 and his 2010 re-election are likely to further cement his control. Both party and army seem likely to retain their power and privilege. Now holding 62 out of 91 seats in Parliament, President Gnassingbé's party can fend off any opposition attempt to reinstate a presidential term limit, thereby ensuring his ability to run (and probably win) for a third term in 2015. The country remains a long way from full democracy, a fact made more striking by the relative consolidation of democratic practice over the last two decades in neighboring Ghana and Benin. Sporadic outbursts of opposition in Lomé are routinely contained. The RPT regime remains in control, and the ever-fractious opposition shows few signs of being able to overcome the dominance of the party and the military-state apparatus.

Economically, Togo seems likely to continue underperforming the continental average; with economic growth expecting to fall below 5% in upcoming years, Togo's economic expansion is barely sufficient to keep pace with the population growth of nearly 2.5%. With few natural resources and a still-lagging reputation among international donors, the prospects for major investment are scant. With domestic resource mobilization too limited to accelerate growth, Togo will likely find itself envying its West African neighbors for years to come.

CENTRAL AFRICA

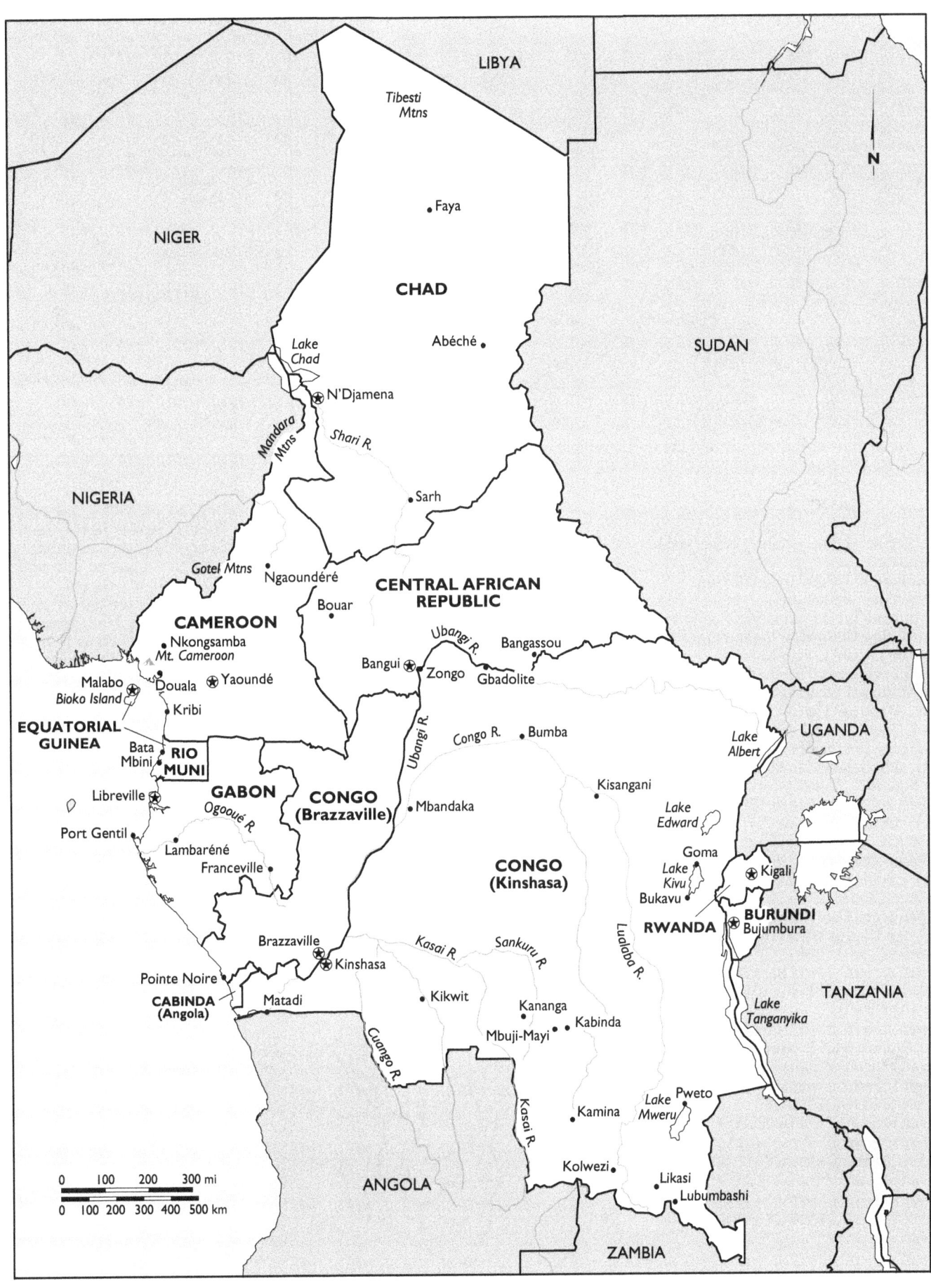

The Republic of Burundi

Aerial view of Bujumbura and the northernmost extent of Lake Tanganyika

BASIC FACTS

Area: 27,830 sq. km. (slightly larger than Maryland)
Population: 13,162,952 (July 2023 est.)
Capital City: Bujumbura
Government Type: Presidential Republic
Neighboring Countries: Rwanda (north); Tanzania (east): Congo-Kinshasa (west).
Official Languages: French, Kirundi
Other Principal Language: Swahili
Ethnic Groups: Hutu 85%, Tutsi 14%, Twa (Pygmy) 1%, small numbers of Europeans and South Asians
Principal Religions: Christian 67% (Roman Catholic 62%, Protestant 5%), indigenous beliefs 23%, and Muslim 10%.
Former Colonial Status: Part of German East Africa (1899–1917); occupied by Belgian troops (1916), Belgian trust territory under League of Nations and United Nations (1923–1962).
Independence Date: July 1, 1962
GDP Per Capita (IMF 2023 est.): $249 (nominal), $891 (PPP)
Gini Index: 38.6 (World Bank 2013)
Currency: Burundi Franc, 1 USD = 2,083 BIF (Apr. 2023)
Inflation Rate: 9.2% (2022 est.)
Chief Commercial Products: Coffee, tea, sugar, cotton and hides
Foreign Direct Investments (FDI) net inflows: 6,884,807 (2013)
Literacy Rate: 74.7% (CIA 2021)
Life Expectancy: 67.77 years (CIA 2023 est.)
Head of State: Evariste Ndayishimiye, President (since June 18, 2020)
Head of Government: Evariste Ndayishimiye, President (since June 18, 2020)

LAND AND PEOPLE

A cool, pleasant land of mountains and plateaus, the Republic of Burundi was known as Urundi before its independence; it was the southern portion of Ruanda-Urundi. Burundi is situated in the highlands of central Africa, and though only two degrees below the Equator, the climate is tempered by altitude. The legendary Lake Tanganyika, the longest freshwater lake in the world, separates Burundi and the Democratic Republic of the Congo. This amazing body of water is more than 2,500 feet above sea level on the surface, yet its floor reaches a depth of about 2,000 feet below sea level. The lake is rich in fish, hippopotamuses, crocodiles, and other native species.

The country is also crossed by the unique land feature known as the Great Rift Valley, an area of grassy, upland plains. The wet season has characteristic daily downpours with intermittent clear, sunny weather. Almost no rain falls during the five-month dry season.

Burundi is characterized by an ethnic division between the Hutu majority and the Tutsi minority, much as in neighboring Rwanda. Hutu-Tutsi tensions have underpinned much of the political and social conflict in Burundi over the decades, with representatives of both ethnic groups committing atrocities in efforts to maintain or claim power. Burundi is currently in a rebuilding and recovery phase following years of tribal warfare between the Hutus and Tutsis, which has produced approximately 250,000 deaths and 500,000 refugees. The Twa people are less than 1% of the population and are politically marginalized.

Like many other African nations, Burundi has a long and deeply rooted musical heritage. Music is played at family gatherings and other special social events. The men sing kwishongora songs, with shouts and thrills, while women often sign bilito music. "Whispered singing" is a type of Burundian music that is performed at a low pitch, so that the music instruments can be heard properly.

The Republic of Burundi faces many challenges. It is one of the poorest countries in the world, which can be attributed to its landlocked geography, its disorganized and ineffective legal system, the HIV/AIDS epidemic, and other factors. The people of Burundi face famine and food shortages; approximately 57% of children under the age of 5 suffer from malnutrition. Burundi features an extremely weak education system; more than half

The Republic of Burundi

Former President Pierre Buyoya

of the population is illiterate and only half of Burundian children attend school. Burundi relies heavily upon foreign aid to combat these issues.

HISTORY TO PRESENT DAY

For early history, see *Historical Background, The Colonial Period: The Germans* and *King Leopold and the Belgians.*

Independence and Ethnic Violence in the 1960s–1970s

In the great wave of decolonization that began in the 1960s, Urundi was separated from Ruanda-Urundi and became a constitutional monarchy in 1962. The Kingdom of Burundi was given independence as a monarchy under Mwami (King) Mwambutsa IV, but even at birth, the country was characterized by instability. In the lead-up to independence, legislative elections had resulted in a victory for the Union for National Progress (UPRONA), whose leader was Prince Rwagasore, the eldest son of Mwami Mwambutsa. UPRONA was a Tutsi-Hutu coalition party, but was dominated by Tutsi nobles of the *Ganwa* clan. Prince Rwagasore's assassination in October 1961 ushered in a period of political instability that characterizes Burundi to this day.

In 1963, ethnic violence forced thousands of Hutus to flee into Tanzania. Political violence erupted again in January 1965 when a Tutsi gunman killed the Hutu prime minister, Pierre Ngendandumwe. Following legislative elections in May of that year, in which Hutus had won 23 out of 33 seats in the National Assembly, Mwami Mwambutsa refused to appoint a Hutu prime minister, preferring to appoint his private secretary, Léopold Biha, and keep power centered in the crown. This prompted a coup attempt by Hutu policemen in which Prime Minister Biha was seriously wounded by gunfire and Mwambutsa departed for Switzerland. After the incident, Hutu leaders were executed and defense minister Michel Micombero was given power. Mwambutsa made a halfhearted effort to return to his kingdom but was ousted by his son Ntare in July 1966.

A few months later when the youthful king was out of the country, Micombero proclaimed himself president of the first Republic of Burundi in November. He had the support of the Bahima clan of the Tutsi, traditionally jealous of Ganwa power.

Restless Hutus living in exile in Tanzania plotted revolution in mid-1972. Emboldened by drugs and assurances of invincibility from local folk priests, they mounted a swift campaign. The plot involved Mwami Ntare, but he was later put under house arrest and ultimately killed "while escaping." About 2,000 Tutsis were mercilessly slaughtered; they responded with a genocidal blood bath that took the lives of more than 200,000 Hutus (especially educated Hutus) within six weeks—about 5% of the population. A second wave of Hutus poured over the Tanzanian border in May 1973.

The 1972 events generated the distrust and hatred in both Tutsi and Hutu communities, which lie at the heart of Burundi's problems today. They also became a source of tension within the Tutsi minority. Ultimately this led to the 1976 overthrow of Micombero in a military coup led by Col. Jean-Baptiste Bagaza, who initiated the Second Republic.

In 1980, Bagaza commenced a series of anti-Catholic Church measures; by 1987 more than 450 foreign priests had been expelled as he sought to bring the Church more thoroughly under the control of the state. He viewed the Church as an instrument of potential Hutu rebellion. Belgian Catholic priests were frequently Flemish, with their own sense of ethnic and linguistic identity. Flemish priests had a strong sense of identity with and sympathy for oppressed Hutu because they themselves had suffered oppression by French speaking Walloons in Belgium.

The crisis in Church-state relations provoked yet again another military coup. Bagaza was ousted by a fellow clansman, Pierre Buyoya, in September 1987, and the Third Republic was declared. The new leader quickly welcomed back the expelled Catholics despite the suspicions of right-wing Tutsis. Buyoya introduced several progressive measures to deal with ethnic resentment. Efforts were made to achieve ethnic parity within the government, and a national commission was created to seek ways of strengthening national unity. Ideas developed in the capital, however, did not always translate well in the provinces. There, Tutsi civil servants continued to discriminate against Hutu citizens.

Another outburst of ethnic hatred followed in 1988. Provoked by local officials and encouraged by Rwanda-based exiles, Hutus in the northern provinces killed 500 Tutsis in August 1988. In the backlash, 20,000 people were killed, most of them Hutu. Thousands more fled to Rwanda.

The Violence of the 1990s

President Buyoya secured ratification of a new multiparty constitution in March 1992, and the country's first free, democratic elections followed in June 1993. The new constitution explicitly prohibited political organizations that advocated "tribalism, divisionism, or violence" and stipulated that all political parties must include both Hutu and Tutsi representatives. In the June 1993 elections, Melchiore Ndadye, a Hutu, defeated Pierre Buyoya to be elected president. He ruled only until October, however, when paratroopers loyal to former president Bagaza assassinated Ndadye.

Ndadye's assassination set off another round of recriminatory ethnic slaughter. An estimated 50,000 Burundians were killed in the following months alone, as Hutus first staged genocidal attacks on Tutsis, and the Tutsi-led army retaliated against rebels and civilians into 1994. For more than a decade afterward, Burundi was gripped by a cycle of terror and counter-terror referred to as *la crise*—the crisis.

Amid the violence, Burundi's parliament finally chose Cyprien Ntaryamira, a moderate Hutu, as president. Ntaryamira took office in February 1994, but was killed just a few months later in the same plane crash that killed Rwanda's president and signaled the beginning of the Rwandan genocide that year. Amid general agreement that the security situation in Burundi did not permit another round of elections, parliament eventually appointed another moderate Hutu, Sylvestre Ntibantunganya to the presidency.

Tensions persisted as rogue elements of the army, controlled by Tutsis, and extremist Hutu militias engaged in ongoing atrocities against civilians. In November 1995, Burundi and its neighbors agreed to a regional peace initiative, designating former Tanzanian President Julius Nyerere as mediator between the various factions. Yet mediation only seemed to intensify hostilities.

The Burundian army intervened in July 1996, as Major Pierre Buyoya seized power for a second time and Ntibantunganya went into hiding. In order to force a restoration of democracy, Burundi's neighbors united to impose economic sanctions; the goal was not achieved, and the consequences were disastrous. The economy further

The Republic of Burundi

deteriorated, malnutrition rates soared, and atrocities continued; sanctions could not stop the flow of arms into Burundi.

Efforts at Reconciliation (1998–2003)

In June 1998, the government signed a Transitional Constitutional Act (TCA) designed to pave the way for the Tutsi-led government to share power with the mainly Hutu opposition. The TCA enlarged parliament by 57 new seats to make it more representative. The government appointed 27 members from Burundi's civil society; small parties not heretofore represented appointed nine of the new members, and the Hutu opposition party, *Front pour la démocratie au Burundi* (FRODEBU), designated the remaining 21 seats. With these power-sharing reforms as background, 17 delegations began peace discussions in Arusha, Tanzania, again with Nyerere as mediator. The most militant of the Hutu rebel groups, the Forces for the Defense of Democracy (FDD) and the hardline *Party for the Liberation of the Hutu People-National Liberation Forces* (PALIPEHUTU-FNL) were excluded from the talks. Progress, which was sluggish at best, was brought to a halt by Nyerere's death in October 1999.

Africa's most distinguished ex-president, Nelson Mandela, was prevailed upon to take on the role of mediator and assumed the duties in February 2000. His presence brought great publicity to previously obscure discussions, while his moral stature allowed him publicly to chastise all parties and his international prestige and contacts allowed him to proffer the carrot of aid to reconstruct a devastated country.

Nineteen parties signed the Arusha Peace and Reconciliation Agreement in August 2000, but key issues—including the leadership of the transitional period and agreement for a cease-fire—remained unresolved until July 2001. It was agreed then that President Buyoya would lead the first half of the three-year transition, with Domitien Ndayizeye of the main Hutu opposition party, FRODEBU, as vice president. In the second half of the transition, Burundi would have a Hutu president and a Tutsi vice president. Both Hutu militant groups—the FDD and the FNL—were excluded from the discussions and increased military activity against Buyoya's government.

Negotiation with the rebel movements was complicated by their splitting into separate factions and wings (more by personality than policy), but by late 2002 it began to look as though the long negotiations were at last fruitful: two smaller FLN and FDD factions signed a cease-fire in October. In December, President Buyoya and Pierre Nkurunziza, head of the principal FDD faction, signed a historic

Former President Domitien Ndayizeye
Photo by AFP/Peter Busomoke

cease-fire (the first since 1993) in Arusha. Only the hardline PALIPEHUTU-FNL rebels refused any cease-fire discussions.

Buyoya relinquished office as scheduled in April 2003, and was succeeded by his Hutu vice president, the FRODEBU leader Domitien Ndayizeye. Yet the whole structure of the transitional government remained fragile. Agathon Rwasa's PALIPEHUTU-FNL refused to join the peace process, rejected the transitional government, and showed its strength by periodically assaulting the outskirts of Bujumbura. Mistrust and low-level intermittent fighting between government and rebels continued, leaving the country in shambles.

Regional leaders kept the pressure up for Burundians to work out their differences through the new power-sharing institutions. The most sensitive issue was the reconstruction of the army. The old army was to be dismantled and a new army was to be created, made up of 50% government forces and 50% Hutu rebels. For Tutsis, the army had been the bulwark of security for the minority, while for Hutus it had been the instrument of their oppression. Reconciling the two was a task fraught with hazards and stumbling blocks, but the army's senior officer corps ultimately opened to members of the Hutu majority for the first time in Burundi's history.

President Ndayizeye scheduled a referendum on a new constitution for the country in late February 2005. The text affirmed power sharing by ethnic quota: In the National Assembly 60% of the seats went to Hutus and 40% to Tutsi, with three seats reserved for Twa representation. Allocation of government positions followed with same distribution pattern: 60% for Hutu and 40% for Tutsi, while Senate membership was equally distributed between the two ethnicities with three seats reserved for Twa. Some 91.2% of the country's three million registered voters approved the charter.

The Nkurunziza Presidency (2005–present)

Legislative elections held in July 2005 demonstrated the political dominance of the FDD in open voting; the party won nearly 70% of the vote, while President Ndayizeye's FRODEBU came second, followed by UPRONA. Pierre Nkurunziza, the FDD leader, was nominated to be president and was overwhelmingly elected to office in August, during a joint meeting of the two houses of parliament. Nkurunziza sought stability once in the presidency, but also belonged to the younger generation of Hutu leaders radicalized by the assassination of President Melchior Ndadaye. He was born in 1963, the son of a former governor killed during anti-Hutu massacres in 1972.

The FNL rebel group initially refused to recognize the legitimacy of the power-sharing government and the election of President Nkurunziza, but by October 2005 it had split into rival factions. One of the factions, headed by Agathon Rwasa's former top lieutenant, Jean Bosco Sindayigaya, favored peace talks with Bujumbura. Rwasa and his faction, on the other hand, remained hostile. His faction was the only one of Burundi's seven Hutu groups outside the peace process until March 2006, when he agreed to unconditional negotiations held in Tanzania (long supportive of the FNL) and mediated by South Africa.

Discussions between the government and Rwasa's FNL concluded in early September 2006, when Rwasa and President Nkurunziza signed a ceasefire agreement. The peace talks had gone on for more than a decade following the assassination of Melchior Ndadaye, the country's first Hutu president, in 1993. During the time from 1993 to 2006, around 1.2 million people had been internally displaced, more than 300,000 people had been killed and about 15% of Burundi's children had been orphaned. When the civil war subsided at long last, the ceasefire was followed by integration of FNL troops into the armed forces and transformation of the FNL into a political party.

The government received a rebuke in September 2006 when one of President Nkurunziza's two vice presidents, Alice Nzomukunda, resigned. A Hutu and member of the ruling CNDD-FDD party, Nzomukunda summarized her frustrations with the government and party: the country was on the path to overcome its problems, she said, "but corruption and economic embezzlement are undermining it." She specifically laid out an attack on party chairman Hussein Radjabu, accusing him of constant interference in the government's work, not respecting the country's institutions, obstructing efforts to create a functional peacetime government, and misleading the population: "The government's

The Republic of Burundi

hands," she told a press conference, "are tied by Hussein Radjabu." Nzomukunda also questioned the existence of a coup plot the government had allegedly uncovered. The events surrounding the alleged coup went back to March 2006 when President Nkurunziza himself accused unnamed politicians of conspiring with officers of the national defense and police forces to overthrow his government. In August, the government arrested former President Domitien Ndayizeye, head of the principal opposition party, as part of the conspiracy. Observers began to fear the Nkurunziza regime was increasingly intolerant of dissent and opposition.

In January 2007, Burundi's Supreme Court agreed with Nzomokunda. At the end of a trial that had begun in November, and in which the prosecutor had asked for death sentences, former President Ndayizeye and four of his co-accused were cleared of all charges. The one man who was toppled in this affair was CNDD-FDD's chairman, Hussein Radjabu, who had been linked to the now-failed prosecution of former-President Ndayizeye and blamed for the deteriorating human rights situation in Burundi. At a party meeting in February 2007, members vote to oust Radjabu from his chairmanship.

In early 2008, sporadic clashes in the capital Bujumbura briefly suggested that the FNL had not succeeded in convincing all its factions to end the struggle, but in June 2009 the FNL laid down its weapons and established itself as a political party. In January 2010, 13 Hutu and Tutsi soldiers were arrested after they were found collaborating in a plot to attempt a coup against President Nkurunziza. Although this incident sparked concern, the trepidation was less focused on the event itself, and more on what it implied for the 2010 elections.

The stability of Burundi was tested throughout 2010 when presidential elections were held in June and legislative elections in July. After early local poll results suggested victories for Nkurunziza and the CNDD-FDD party, the five leading opposition candidates claimed fraud and withdrew from the presidential race opposition. This included FNL ex-rebel leader Agathon Rwasa, who went into hiding claiming he feared for his life. The boycotting candidates called for the resignation of the nation's electoral commission and declared the election a "joke" and a "masquerade" when the electoral commission announced on June 29, 2010, that President Nkurunziza won a second five-year term. Parliamentary elections held in July followed a similar logic: most of the opposition boycotted and the ruling CNDD-FDD dominated, taking 81 of 106 seats.

The election results led to subsequent tensions and renewed fears of civil strife,

President Pierre Nkurunziza
©IRIN

as numerous opponents were arrested into fall 2010. According to a Human Rights Watch report, the regime tortured several prominent political prisoners in 2010 and harassed and intimidated journalists for *Radio Publique Africaine* (RPA), an independent radio station. This seemed to result in small-scale cross-retaliation among the various political entities, as several FNL members were found killed in September and an attack on Agathon Rwasa's home in May 2011 (though he remains in hiding) resulted in the deaths of several people; this was attributed to FNL militants. The ability of the government to reduce postelection tensions will determine Burundi's stability for the near future.

Political violence worsened in 2011 and instability has been on the horizon since. In May of 2011, a gunman opened fire on a restaurant in the capital city and in September dozens of gunmen attacked a bar, killing 36 people. In November of that year, an advocacy group estimated that over 300 people had been killed in the past five months because of their political affiliation. Meanwhile, Burundi peacekeeping troops were sent to Somalia where between six and 70 troops were killed by Somali rebels in October—the number does not seem to be clearly known. At present, there is a growing number of political rebel movements, and these are garnering resources from allies and from finding sanctuary in neighboring countries. As many as a half-dozen named insurgencies have arisen in Burundi in the last several years. While none has yet posed a significant threat to the regime, their presence is indicative of underlying instability.

CONTEMPORARY THEMES

Economic growth was modest in Burundi over the second half of the 2000s, at around 4% most years. Agriculture is the mainstay of the economy, representing about 50% of GDP. Most cultivated land is devoted to subsistence crops—mainly cassava, bananas, and sweet potatoes, but widespread violence has driven many farmers from their fields. Cattle rearing is also an important source of food, as fishing on Lake Tanganyika until it was banned by the government as a security measure to prevent rebel infiltration. The main cash crop is coffee, more than 90% of which is high-quality *arabica*. Coffee exports have accounted at times for over 95% of Burundi's foreign exchange revenues. With such heavy reliance on a single crop, the economy is seesawed by fluctuations in world coffee prices and periodically ravaged by natural calamity. Currently, Burundian leaders are working to strengthen the nation's business climate with the hopes of increasing employment and income among the population. The Doing Business Survey, an annual statement issued by the IFC that ranks countries according to the environment they provide for businesses to grow and flourish, places Burundi at 140 in its 2014 edition. This ranking is regarded as a significant improvement from its position of 169 in 2011.

Burundi's government did receive good economics in the form of eventual debt forgiveness. The IMF long refused to give money to Burundi, claiming that it was only used to purchase arms, but a national teachers strike led some Western governments (primarily France and Belgium) to urge support during the transitional period, lest the peace process be jeopardized. Presently, Burundi is striving toward new levels of development with the support of external funds. In January 2004, the IMF approved a $104 million arrangement to support the country's economic reform program over the next three years. Five years later, in January 2009, Burundi completed the HIPC initiative, which means that its debt cancelation will total approximately 1.6 billion dollars. This saves Burundi about 75 million dollars a year in debt service, some of which has already been used in eliminating primary school fees and building over 1,100 new schools. Additionally, in March 2009, the Paris Club creditors officially cancelled the $134.3 million dollars of debt that Burundi owed, freeing these resources toward general poverty reduction. In April 2014, the World Bank approved a $100 million grant to Burundi to finance the construction of two new hydro stations. This project is celebrated as a critical step in alleviating the nation's energy crisis and improving the standard of living for many Burundians, as presently only 4% of Burundians have access to electricity.

With less than half its population literate, the government has made primary-school education free, creating new demands on

The Republic of Burundi

infrastructure (classrooms) and supplies (books and desks). Belgium, which for historical reasons has a significant commitment to Burundi, granted it $12.5 million for education, road construction and rural water supply. Of that total, $5.6 million is dedicated to book purchases for students and teachers and manufacture of 50,000 desks for primary schools.

The scourge of AIDS has probably infected over 250,000 HIV-positive people in the country, and 25,000 Burundians died of AIDS annually at the peak of the epidemic. Yet estimates of HIV prevalence rates have been revised downwards in recent years, to the range of about 1.3% of the population between the ages of 15 and 49 (2012). Partly as a consequence of the war and AIDS, life expectancy declined in the 1990s, but has now climbed back to about 51 years. Beginning in 2012, Burundi launched its National Strategic Plan, an initiative to raise $349 million for programs geared toward HIV/AIDS prevention and care.

The government has announced plans to move the capital from Bujumbura, at the western edge of the country, to Gitega, its most central city. The move promises to set off a building boom there, helping economic growth and providing much needed employment. In June 2009 the World Bank approved a 45 million grant to support sustained reconstruction in Burundi; some of this money, which is to be reimbursed over a 5-year period, will be spent to provide better infrastructure and services that contribute to the government's goal of decentralization.

Burundi continues to be one of the poorest and most corrupt countries in the world. The country's problems are greatly exacerbated by the corruption and conflicts in neighboring Congo and Rwanda. Human rights violations are rampant and political turmoil and related violent killings are on the rise in 2012 (as insurgencies increased), according to Human Rights Watch. The presidential election of 2015 is one primary source of ethnic tension and violence between the Hutus and Tutsis. Though the United Nations has intervened in Burundi by encouraging dialogue and peacemaking between the Hutus and Tutsis, history indicates that elements of these two groups will continue to conflict.

Accusing neighboring Rwanda of backing intrusions by the rebel group Red Tabara since 2015 including the killing of 20 people in December 2023, Burundi closed its border in January 2024. Domestic developments include the arrest of former prime minister Alain Guillaume Bunyani in April 2023.

Continuing to grapple with humanitarian challenges, including poverty, inequality, and access to healthcare, the country has also been impacted by the war in Ukraine and the COVID-19 pandemic while also hit by major flooding requiring international assistance from the United States. The country also faces a refugee crisis as thousands of people flee fighting in neighboring Democratic Republic of Congo (DRC) seeking refuge in Burundi.

FUTURE CONSIDERATIONS

The greatest challenges facing Burundi are ethnic reconciliation, stabilization, and reconstruction. Success in these tasks will depend, in considerable measure, on the country's ability to step back from the brink of renewed conflict. The development of Burundi is highly dependent on the dynamic between the Hutu and Tutsi ethnic groups. If current efforts to maintain peace and establish a constructive relationship between these two groups prove successful, then Burundi may be able to recover from years of internal warfare and direct its resources toward other pressing issues. It will also depend in part on the international community, which is the basis for many of the specific reconstruction plans forwarded by the Nkurunziza government. In recent years, international organizations and foreign nations have aided Burundi more actively by funding expenditures on educational programs, HIV/AIDS awareness and prevention initiatives, and modern technologies to improve the standard of living for millions of Burundians. This external assistance is certainly a reason for Burundians to feel optimistic about the future. Conflict has devastated the economy and Burundi is now one of the poorest countries in the world, and its economy is estimated to have contracted by 25% during the war years. By some measures, GDP per capita fell to as low as $90 in 2004, though it has recovered somewhat since then. About 68% of the population survives on less than one dollar a day, with many relying on subsistence agriculture. Even years of positive performance will not fully reverse the tragedies of recent decades.

The country seemed to have stabilized a bit after 2005, albeit with continued cause for concern. The presidential elections in 2010 were a double-edged sword: an opportunity to move beyond the civil war that raged in the 1990s and 2000s, but also a focal point for political and ethnic tensions. The announcement of Nkurunziza's victory raised tensions once again, and there are increasing reports of repression of the opposition. Tensions have crystallized in the form of the multiple small-scale insurgencies and rebel movements that simmer in the countryside. Enthusiasm that the 2010 elections might lead to release of political tensions and movement toward more democratic and open politics have proved to be overly optimistic.

In the worst crisis since the Burundian civil war ended in 2005, Pierre Nkurunziza's bid to contest for a third term in office has made the country vulnerable to grave insecurities. Burundi's opposition has announced that they will boycott the June 29, 2015, parliamentary elections, and the postponement of the presidential elections from June 26 to mid-July does not seem to allay the fear and violence that has gripped the country. A series of events that started with an announcement of a military coup d'état on May 13, 2015, by Maj. Gen. Godefroid Niyombare claimed to dismiss President Pierre Nkurunziza and his government while the president was away in Tanzania attending an emergency conference about the situation in the country. Since then, there have been repression, arrests, grenade attacks, killings, and the assassination of opposition leader Zedi Feruzi on May 23 resulting in many Burundians fleeing the country.

However, civil society organizations are still leading protests as violence intensified. The international community including the European Union, United States, and the African Union are concerned that portions of the Cotonou and Arusha Agreements are being violated. The U.S. has threatened to pull out electoral assistance and other aids in the light of the continued insistence of the president to go ahead with the disputed upcoming elections and is prepared to hold certain individuals responsible for undermining democracy and the rule of law in the country.

Term limits have been a concern to African leaders prompting a May 19, 2015, meeting in Accra, Ghana, of leaders of ECOWAS states to discuss the issue. At the end of the one-day meeting, the general consensus was to put the "hot potato" issue aside for now since the Togolese and the Gambian leaders who are already serving their terms pushed back very hard on the issue. The argument was that each state's political context is unique, and therefore it will not be prudent to have a mandatory two-term rule.

The Burundian situation is likely to have a serious ramification on the rest of Central Africa. If President Pierre Nkurunziza succeeds to win a third term and stay in office, other leaders such as Paul Kagame of Rwanda, Joseph Kabila of the Democratic Republic of Congo, and Dennis Sassou-Nguesso of Congo-Brazzaville will be emboldened to seek third terms and beyond. In the meantime, Burundian nationals are caught up in the Mediterranean migrant crisis, as hundreds of them try to cross the Mediterranean to enter Europe despite the enormous risk to avoid violence and poverty in the country.

The Republic of Cameroon

BASIC FACTS

Area: 475,440 sq. km. (slightly larger than California)
Population: 30,135,732 (June 2023 est.)
Capital City: Yaoundé
Government Type: Presidential Republic
Neighboring Countries: Nigeria (northwest); Chad (northeast); Central African Republic (east); Congo, Gabon, Equatorial Guinea (south)
Official Languages: French (East Cameroon) and English (West Cameroon)
Other Principal Languages: There are 24 major African language groups, involving more than 275 separate languages. Prominent are Bamiléké, Bamoun, Bulu, Duala, Ewondo, Fufulde, Kom, Lamnso', and Medumba. Cameroon Pidgin, an English-based Creole language, has become a lingua franca.
Ethnic Groups: Cameroon Highlanders (Bamiléké, Bamoun) 31%, Equatorial Bantu (Beti) 19%, Kirdi 11%, Fulani 10%, Northwestern Bantu 8%, Eastern Nigritic 7%, other African 13%, non-African less than 1%
Principal Religions: Christianity (40%), traditional beliefs (40%), Islam (20%
Former Colonial Status: German Colony (1884–1916), British Colony in West Cameroon (1916–1961); French Colony is East Cameroon (1916–1960)
Independence Date: January 1, 1960 (Independence of French Cameroon); October 1, 1961 (British Cameroon joins the Republic of Cameroon to form Federal Republic of Cameroon)
National Day: May 20, 1972
GDP Per Capita (IMF 2023 est.): $1,699 (nominal), $4,66 (PPP)
Gini index: 46.5 (2014)
Currency: CFA franc, 1 USD = 594 CFA francs (Apr. 2023)
Inflation rate: 2.9% (2022 est.)
Chief Commercial Products: Crude oil and petroleum products, lumber, cocoa beans, aluminum, coffee, and cotton.
Personal Remittances: 334,097,289 (2020)
Foreign Direct Investments (FDI) net inflows: 501,200,000
Literacy Rate: 77.1% (CIA 2018)
Life Expectancy: 63.24 years (CIA 2022 est.)
Head of State: Paul Biya, President (since November 6, 1982)
Head of Government: Prime Minister Joseph Dion Ngute (since January 4, 2019)

LAND AND PEOPLE

Cameroon is a land of contrasts, containing almost every species of flora and fauna of tropical Africa and numerous varieties of wild game. The country stretches north from the Atlantic at the hinge position between West and Central Africa. The country boasts beaches along the Bight of Biafra, and mountains that proceed directly north into West Cameroon. Mount Cameroon, the tallest peak in western Africa at almost 14,000 feet high, is an active volcano. The Southern and the Eastern regions of Cameroon are characterized by a low coastal basin with equatorial forests. In the Adamaoua region of the country, there is a series of grassy plateaus whose heights reach 4,500 feet, but in the Far North region near Lake Chad, there is

Cameroon

only marshland, and the dry climate supports only seasonal grazing and nomadic herding. Cameroon's flag symbolizes the country: the vertical green stripe represents the hope and forests of the south, red center with a yellow star represents unity, and yellow represents the sun, happiness, and the savannah of the north.

Cameroonians have a long history of dances and craft. Many tribal groups produce pottery, textiles, and sculptures that are very elaborate and are used in everyday practices. The Bamiléké and Bamoun, in the Western region of the country, are particularly notable for their displays of blue and white clothing called Ndop, and beaded calabashes. The Bamoun are also known for their bronze sculptures made using a special process known as lost-wax and their intricate wood carvings.

Cameroonian arts feature prominent literary figures who documented the failings of colonialism. Ferdinand Oyono was author of the renowned novel *Houseboy* (*Une vie de boy*) and Mongo Beti wrote the much-acclaimed *The Poor Christ of Bomba* (*Le Pauvre Christ de Bomba*). Among musicians, Manu Dibango is a major international promoter of the popular Cameroonian dance music known as *makossa*.

Cameroonians are also known for their soccer team, the Indomitable Lions, Ih has won the African Cup of nations four times. Major Cameroonian players that have one the African Golden Ball are Samuel Eto'o (four times) and Roger Milla and Thomas Nkono (twice). The Cameroonian soccer team was the first African team to get to the quarterfinals of the World Cup in 1990. The Cameroonian team will participate in the World Cup in Brazil 2014.

HISTORY TO PRESENT DAY

For early history, see *Historical Background and Colonial Period: the Germans* and *Colonial Period: The French*.

Independence and Ahmadou Ahidjo (1960–1982)

Cameroon resulted from a merger of French Cameroon and British Cameroon (South West and North West regioIwhich gained independence respectively on January 1, 1960, and on October 1, 1961. Under the leadership of Ahmadou Ahidjo, the *Union nationale camerounaise* (UNC), the country adopted a federal constitution that enshrined a single-party system. President Ahidjo (a Muslim from Garoua, North Cameroon) and Vice President John Foncha (from Bamenda, North West Cameroon) received 97.5% of the vote in 1970 elections. Constitutional reforms in 1972 eliminated the state government of the two regions, but guaranteed continuation of the French language and English

President Paul Biya

in the South West and North West region of the country.

The legislative and presidential elections, held in 1978 and 1980, respectively, confirmed the dominance of Ahidjo and the UNC. Ahidjo was elected to a fifth five-year term, and all candidates for parliament were from the UNC. During his 23-year rule, power was centralized in the capital, and in Ahidjo's hands. The authoritarian regime was repressive and justified its suppression of civil and human rights by a need to contain ethnic division.

Paul Biya (1982–present)

President Ahidjo suddenly resigned on November 6, 1982, handing over power to his prime minister, Paul Biya a Christian from the Southern region, who completed Ahidjo's term of office. The former president was said to be exhausted, but he retained his leadership of the UNC, the country's sole political party until the next year, April 1983. Biya soon ousted Ahidjo from party leadership and sent him into exile. In January 1984 elections, President Biya, was the only candidate in the 1984 presidential elections to a five-year term in office. He was elected by a margin of 99.98%. With this mandate, Biya set about consolidating his own power.

To eliminate potential competition, Biya convinced the parliament to amend the constitution to remove the office of prime minister. To emphasize the unitary nature of the state, most of whose powers he held personally, Biya had the country's name changed from the "United Republic of Cameroon" to simply the "Republic of Cameroon."

In early April 1984, Biya's Republican Guard mutinied. Fierce fighting erupted in Yaoundé—members of the Republican Guard, composed mostly of Islamic northerners, waged a pitched battle with regular army units. After the rebellion was contained, Biya announced that Ahidjo had organized it. The official number of deaths was "about 70," but the actual number was probably close to 1,500. Within weeks, 35 insurrectionists were tried and summarily executed. Ahidjo was tried in absentia and condemned to death for complicity in the plot.

A year later, to demonstrate his "New Deal" policies, President Biya renamed the country's sole legal party, the UNC to the Cameroon People's Democratic Movement (RDPC). To add democratic content to the newly renamed party, 324 candidates were approved to contest 180 seats in the legislative elections of April 1988. Given a choice, voters sent a number of aging political lions into retirement. The result was a National Assembly with younger members. The president was reelected with a 98.75% majority. With his renewed mandate, Biya announced wide-ranging programs to deal with Cameroon's economic crisis.

Biya needed to implement structural adjustments and budget cuts in order to receive international aid. He agreed to downsize the bureaucracy and cut government expenditures. Belt-tightening hurt and resentments rose. To accommodate demands for greater democracy, product of political changes in Eastern Europe and stronger western emphasis on democracy as a precondition for aid, Biya approved a multiparty system in 1990.

Opposition parties proliferated. Some 48 contested the legislative elections in March 1992, but fractured, the opposition stood little chance against the RDCP. The ruling party won 88 of 180 seats in the National Assembly. The principal opposition party was the National Union for Democracy and Progress (UNDP), which elected 68 members to parliament. Sixteen opposition parties boycotted the election; the two main leaders of the boycott were John Fru Ndi—the Social Democratic Front (SDF) and Adamou Ndam Njoya's Cameroonian Democratic Union (UDC).

The presidential election was advanced from the spring of 1993 to October 1992 to catch the divided opposition unprepared, and when finally conducted it was marred by massive fraud, irregularities, and unfairness. The state-owned television, the Cameroonian Radio and Television (CRTV) for example, gave two-and-a-half hours of time to Biya, but only 16 minutes to the opposition.

The same pattern prevailed in the 1997 legislative elections, with the RDCP increasing its legislative majority to 109 of 180 seats. John Fru Ndi's Social Democratic Front captured 43 seats to become the principal opposition party. As usual, widespread intimidation and fraud were reported.

October 1997 presidential elections were virtually meaningless. President

Cameroon

Biya refused to allow an independent electoral commission to organize them, and the main opposition parties refused to participate. Most citizens treated it as a non-event, but the government reported that 60% of registered voters participated and gave 80% of their votes to Biya.

Political power in Cameroon is concentrated in the office of president. The president appoints the cabinet, which serves at his pleasure. He names judges, generals and governors, district administrators and the heads of state corporations. Parliament, dominated by President Biya's Cameroon People's Democratic Movement (RDPC), consistently defers to the legislative program chosen by the executive.

Biya's Consolidation of Power (1990s–present)

Unsurprisingly, Biya's control has been used to increase presidential powers. Constitutional amendments in 1996, for example, increased the presidential term to seven years. In general, presidential power is maintained through active repression of the political opposition, especially in election years.

The government closely controls the electoral process, which is organized through the Ministry of Territorial Administration. Members of oppositional ethnic groups and those living in areas dominated by the opposition are effectively prevented from registering to vote. The government operates almost all broadcast media (a small private Catholic station rebroadcasts programs from Vatican Radio), and coverage of opposition activity is underwhelming. Print media, of small circulation and limited to urban distribution, are subject to considerable government restrictions and libel laws.

Tensions continue in the Anglophone areas of Cameroon, which feel marginalized by the Francophone majority. Separatist demonstrations in the western regions are a regular occurrence. So is their repression by state security forces. Northern resentments, going back to the events of 1984, persist. Many feel discriminated against and excluded from a fair share of national riches.

Legislative elections were held in June 2002, and in advance President Biya effected a major revitalization of the RDPC. Biya banned tribal chiefs from standing for party posts and urged party activists not to be swayed by candidates willing to buy themselves into power. In a March 2002 party voting, 70% of grassroots RDPC leaders were replaced. Party barons lost to young men and women, suggesting the party was reinvigorating itself with a bit of new blood.

The June elections resulted in a crushing victory for the RDPC, which took 149 of the 180 seats. John Fru Ndi's Social Democratic Front (SDF), driven by internal conflicts, won only 22, but remained the principal opposition party. The loss, in percentage terms, was even greater for the *Union nationale pour la Démocratie et le Progrès* (UNDP), which went from four seats to one. The Cameroonian Democratic Union kept its five seats since the 1997 election.

The RDPC victory, worthy of a single-party state, may have been achieved by means typically associated with those regimes. A Roman Catholic NGO monitoring the election reported numerous irregularities, including phony polling places, and Douala's Cardinal, Christian Tumi, called them "obviously and intentionally" mismanaged.

In assembling his cabinet, President Biya seemed to have an eye on the 2004 presidential elections, enlarging it to nearly 50 to include every relevant region and ethnicity. In this cabinet of national union, even the UNDP, which had been reduced to a single parliamentary seat, was given two cabinet portfolios.

In order to balance Cameroon's delicate ethnic and regional differences, prime ministers are traditionally English-speakers, and Biya reappointed his Anglophone premier, Mafany Musonge, who holds an engineering degree from Stanford University. (Cameroon's third most important office, the speakership of the National Assembly, is traditionally held by a northerner.)

Premier Musonge acted as Biya's campaign manager in the October 2004 presidential elections. After 22 years in power, President Biya had little opposition and the voters had little enthusiasm. The opposition leaders, prior to the 2004 elections created a coalition and decided to elect one major opposition leader that would challenge Paul Biya. Adamou Ndam Njoya of the UDC was chosen as the opponent; embittered by the choice, John Fru Ndi of the SDF withdrew from the deal and ran separately. Because of the defection of the SDF and the dismantling of the coalition, the election provided minimum challenge to Paul Biya. The Interior Ministry announced a landslide for Biya—75% of the vote with 80% of those eligible voting. The government figures were scarcely believable. Symptomatically, only 4.6 million of an estimated eight million people over the age of 20 who were qualified to vote actually got their names on electoral registers. Cardinal Tumi expressed the sentiment that people had lost confidence in the government's ability to hold a fair and impartial election. All of them since independence, he forcefully declared, had been "surrounded by fraud." A Commonwealth observer group said many young people had failed to vote because they felt alienated from the political process. To give a veneer of change, President Biya appointed a new prime minister, Ephraïm Inoni. Like his predecessor, the new prime minister was an English speaker from the southwest, with degrees from the National School of Administration and an American MBA.

Legislative and municipal elections took place July 2007, and followed the standard Cameroonian experience: continued manipulation and domination by the RDPC.

Traditional fishing

Photo by E. Dounais
Courtesy of APFT-ULB

Cameroon

The opposition, particularly John Fru Ndi's SDF, was more divided than usual. The RDPC took 153 of 180 seats, and the SDF only 16, Adamou Ndam Njoya dropped from five seats to four after having given another seat to an oppositionist party. In April 2008, Biya arranged to change the constitution to extend his term of office in what was termed a "constitutional coup". Biya announced on December 31, 2008, an intention to amend the 6th Article of the constitution as an effort to "democratize" the system. The major proposed contribution to Cameroonian democracy was to remove the pesky two-term limit for president such as himself. An alleged coup plot by some government officials was uncovered in fall 2010, but it is unclear whether this was a real challenge to Biya or a top-down preemptive strike to eliminate political threats on trumped-up charges.

President Biya won yet another term of office in the 2011 presidential election. Biya took a reported 78% of the vote. Biya's opponents, led by John Fru Ndi (who came in second with only 11% of the vote) rejected the result, alleging fraud. International observers, including the US ambassador, concurred that the election was not free or fair.

The Cameroonian Constitution had provided for the establishment of a senate since 1996, but only on April 2013 did the government organize senatorial elections. Municipal advisors were to elect 70 senators in their respective departments. Paul Biya nominated 30 of the 100 senators. Of these 30, Biya gave 14 to the SDF and several seats to another supposedly oppositionist party. For most, this represents the cooptation of the opposition. In the Western region (particularly in the Noun department) the SDF allied with the RDPC against the UDC party, the only remaining opposition party not linked to the RDPC. The UDC was unable to attain any seats in the first senatorial elections.

In the 2013 legislative and municipal elections, the RDPC dropped by five seats in the parliament, now having 148 seats out of 180. The SDF increased by two seats and now have 18 seats, the UNDP lost one seat and has 5 seats and the UDC remains with four seats.

CONTEMPORARY THEMES

Social Issues

As of 2012, about 600,000 people were estimated to be HIV-positive in Cameroon. Of these, an estimated 59,000 are children, while 330,000 children have been orphaned due to AIDS. Among adults the prevalence rate is 4.5% (though much higher is some regions), and the rate of mother-to-child transmission is 5.7% (with proper testing and treatment this number has become virtually zero in other parts of the world). The rate of new infections has plateaued, but has not decreased yet. Tuberculosis is associated with 40% of Cameroon's HIV cases. As of 2012, 35,000 people had died from AIDS and less than 40% of people who need anti-retrovirals were receiving treatment. Recently, Cameroon has made a huge push to increase HIV testing. The country has cases of HIV Type O, a relatively rare form that is not detected by normal testing procedures; it means that those who have lived in Cameroon are not eligible to donate blood in the United States. Like much of Africa, HIV/AIDS is an immense problem for public health, the economy, development, society, and culture.

Political Issues

For two years in a row in the late 1990s, Cameroon had the dubious distinction of topping Transparency International's list of countries perceived as being the most corrupt. Stung by this classification and with its consequent investor mistrust and diplomatic chastening, President Biya's government lumbered into an anticorruption campaign. Progress was slow; by 2006, Cameroon was still only five steps above the most corrupt country in the world—bottom-ranked Haiti.

In July 2006, President Biya declared a zero-tolerance policy on corruption and this time around appeared to give meaning to words. By October, Cameroonians were treated to the relatively rare experience of seeing former ministers (Finance, Energy, and Water) and high-level civil servants indicted for a variety of financial scams and embezzlement. The government initiated Opération Épervier (or Operation Sparrowhawk) to crack down on absence at ministries. Corruption was once again brought to light in April 2010, when the editor Germain Ngota died in prison. Ngota was officially detained on charges of fraud, but the Ie to Protect Journalists (CPJ) says NgIta was investigating allegations of coIruption involving government figures; his death was attributed to a lack of medical attention. Since then, a number of ministers and high-ranking elites have been imIed, including the ex-Prime Minister Ephraïm Inoni, who had initially created the anticorruption operation. He was arrested on April 16, 2012. Other influential personIs in jail include Marafa Hamidou Yaya an ex-minister and Yves Michel Fotso, who were charged with embezzlement. On March 31, 2014, the Secondary Education Minister Louis Bapès Bapès was arrested while he was sitting in his office without "previously being deprived of function."* This was a general surprise, for before being arrested ministers were deprived of their functions, Bapès Bapès was released from jail the next day.

Cameroon faces border tension with several neighbors. With Nigeria, there have been disputes over the Lake Chad basin area and tensions over the Bakassi peninsula, a 400-square mile swampy region along Cameroon's southwest border that is thought to hold significant oil reserves. Both countries submitted their Bakassi claims to the International Court of Justice (ICJ) and in October 2002, the court decided in favor of Cameroon. In mid-June 2006, Presidents Biya and Obasanjo signed an agreement ending nearly a half-century of dispute. In November 2007, a suspected

Rainforest logs reach the sea

Photo by G. Philippart de Foy
Courtesy APFT-ULB

Cameroon

Nigerian killed 21 Cameroon soldiers in Bakassi, but by August 2008, Nigeria withdrew its troops and formally handed over the peninsula to Cameroon. Full administrative control of the area by Cameroon occurred in 2011. Border demarcation of Bakassi began in late 2005 and is the largest—1700 kilometers—and most expensive demarcation process currently being undertaken by the UN. It is still in process but is moving toward conclusion.

The poorly regulated border between Nigeria and Cameroon has caused in the past three years the kidnappings of French tourists and religious figures in northern Cameroon by the Nigerian Islamist group Boko Haram. On February 19, 2013, a French family on a safari in the Far Northern region of Cameroon was kidnapped by Boko Haram and was taken to Nigeria. They were released two months later but this didn't stop the Islamist group to kidnap a French priest in November 2013 who was released the following month. In April 2014, an Italian priest and two nuns were kidnapped, it is still unclear who the kidnappers were but there are many clues that it could be Boko Haram.

On the eastern side of the country Cameroon is hosting over 100,000 refugees from the Central African Republic.

Economic and Environmental Issues

In the parched northern region, Cameroon's plans for irrigated agriculture brought it into conflict with both Nigeria and Chad. Nigeria has threatened to bring the country back to the ICJ over disputes involving development projects on the Benue River. Chad has threatened similar action over irrigation and rice production projects on the Logone River, and the border with the Central African Republic has seen several conflicts.

Cameroon's economy was based on agriculture until the discovery of oil in the 1970s, but oil production peaked in 1985 at 158,000 barrels a day (bbl/d) and has been in decline ever since and is now at less than half its peak. Current major oil fields are nearly depleted, and total reserves of 200 million barrels as of 2010 will last only about six or seven more years at current rates of production. In 2002, the government revised its petroleum laws to provide greater investment incentives and subsequently there has been new exploration in all three of its major petroleum basins, but findings have been minor.

Cameroon briefly benefited from the construction of the oil export pipeline from neighboring Chad. The World Bank, despite stiff opposition from environmentalists, supplied 3% of the financing for the $3.5 billion pipeline project, and a consortium of major oil companies—Exxon Mobil, Petronas (the Malaysian National Oil Company) and Chevron undertook the project. The pipeline was the largest single investment project in sub-Saharan Africa and was completed in July 2003, one year ahead of schedule. Pipeline construction supported GDP growth in Cameroon, but once ended, economic growth slowed to a mere 2.6% in 2005. Other projects related to mining and energy are underway: in March 2007 Cameroon announced that the United States planned to invest nearly $3 billion in the country's eastern province to mine cobalt, and in 2011 the country announced it had secured a loan from China to build a deep-water port at the end of the Chad–Cameroon pipeline.

Aside from oil, the country's main revenue earners are cocoa, timber, cotton, and aluminum (mostly produced from bauxite imported from Guinea). Together, they account for about three-fourths of export receipts. Cameroon is the world's fifth largest cocoa producer, and cocoa provides about 40% of its exports though declining world market prices resulted in reduced production for a time. In several areas, parts of cocoa plantations have been destroyed to pave the way for food crops such as tomato, vegetables, and plantain. About 40% of Cameroon's land is forested, but the forests are disappearing rapidly because of irresponsible logging activity. Logging concessions are awarded by a bidding system. The winner is traditionally not the highest bidder, but the company prepared to offer the highest financial inducements to officials. Concession holders are often unrestrained by law or morality. Environmental groups have documented abuses. In 2003, Greenpeace exposed the work of three Dutch companies logging Cameroon's forest, saying they all operated illegally, causing severe ecological and economic damage. Logging operations destroyed local villagers' subsistence and cash crops, while depriving the government of vital taxes, since none were paid on the illegal cuttings. Friends of the Earth-Cameroon estimated that half the timber logged in the country is illegally cut, costing the state around $2.7 million a year in lost revenues. Some suggestion of the illegal trade comes from comparing declared exports to European countries with declared imports. In 1998, for example, Cameroon declared 57,038 cubic meters of timber destined for Portugal, while Portuguese figures for the same year indicated imports from Cameroon of 91,111 cubic meters. The poor roads in the area complicate access to the refugee camps. In early 2012, poachers from Chad entered Cameroon and killed about 300 elephants in a national park for their ivory tusks.

Cameroon qualified for debt relief under the Highly Indebted Poor Countries (HIPC) program in late 2000 but was cut off from program benefits in August 2003 after an IMF mission found "considerable deterioration in Cameroonian public finances in 2003–2004." After his reelection in 2004 President Biya became more cognizant of his country's disastrous economic condition and more actively pursued policies to complete the HIPC program, including the anti-corruption program. Despite some skepticism, the IMF and World Bank indicated Cameroon had completed its obligations under the HIPC initiative in May 2006. It has

Cameroon

received more than $1 billion in bilateral relief and multilateral aid. External debt will be reduced by 50%.

There is a significant and growing Chinese presence in Cameroon. From as early as 1983, with the Lagdo hydroelectric dam on the Benue River, China has made major infrastructure contributions. Following President Biya's 2003 trip to China, the China International Water & Electrical Corporation offered to build several dams to supply the National Electricity Company. Most recently a Chinese consortium, China Road and Bridge Corporation, won the contract to repair the dilapidated roads in and around Douala, the business capital. Chinese President Hu Jintao began his 2007 eight-nation tour of Africa—his third since taking office—with a stop in Cameroon. He left after approving more than $54 million in grants and preferential loans and signing a series of health and education accords. China's most recent major projects are the construction of two 20,000 seated stadiums in Bafoussam and Limbé by the China Machinery Engineering Corporation (CMEC) and the aforementioned port at Kribi, terminus of the Chad Cameroon pipeline. With Paul Biya as the world's oldest leader and the recent death of a major opposition leader, political change is unlikely in the foreseeable future.

At the age of 91 years, President Paul Biya makes rare public appearances as the government banned any discussion in the media of his health in October 2024 while ordering that "monitoring cells" charged with tracking online content be set up. Labeling the physical condition of the nonagenarian president as "a matter of national security," violations of the order would "face the full force of the law." Biya was last seen in public at the China–Africa summit in Beijing in September while he failed to attend gatherings at which he had been expected, including the United Nations General Assembly in New York and a summit of French-speaking countries in Paris. These absences sparked "rumors of all kinds . . . through the conventional media and social networks about the president's condition," which the government denounced as "pure fantasy" declaring the president is in "good health." "Trying to hide behind national security on such a major issue of national importance is outrageous," said Angela Quintal, head of the Africa Program of the Committee to Protect Journalists. In the absence of a clear succession plan, Biya's death would likely bring political turmoil to West and Central Africa, which has seen eight coups since 2020 and several other military attempts to overthrow governments. President of Cameroon for more than 41 years, his lengthy rule in Africa is second only to 82-year-old Teodoro Obiang Nguema Mbasogo, who has held power in Equatorial Guinea for 45 years.

FUTURE CONSIDERATIONS

Slow economic growth and the repressive nature of the political system leave Cameroon as one of Africa's great disappointments. The immense potential benefits of oil wealth have been squandered in one of the world's most corrupt countries, and investment in human capital has lagged (though the country maintains a relatively high literacy rate). Recent riots in major cities over the rising prices of staple commodities are an indicator of the public's dissatisfaction with the government. In 2011, there were even some protests in the wake of the Arab Spring, as Cameroonians seized on the momentum in North Africa against long-time authoritarians presiding over sclerotic regimes; however, these seem to have posed little threat to the well-entrenched Biya government.

Politically, the regime's electoral manipulations have increasingly alienated voters, especially the young. While some other countries have slowly developed somewhat improved democratic credentials, Cameroon seems to be stuck in time under Paul Biya's regime. Elections up through 2013 have been dominated by the governing party.

With this said, there are some positive notes as well. In March 2009, Pope Benedict XVI visited Cameroon and congratulated the country for the relatively peaceful coexistence between Muslims and Christians. This was especially noteworthy, given the worsening sectarian conflict in neighboring Nigeria and other countries in central Africa. The aforementioned recent kidnapping by Islamist militants of French nationals has raised some fears that sectarian tensions will spill across the porous borders of central Africa into Cameroon, but the verdict is still out. Echoing this uncertainty, Cameroon's economic and political future looks mixed: the country has prospects for further economic investment from China and the western world, but the likelihood of improved governance under Biya is extremely low.

The Central African Republic

The important, but costly, transportation of timber products

BASIC FACTS

Area: 622,984 sq. km. (slightly smaller than Texas)
Population: 5,552,228 (June 2023 est.)
Capital City: Bangui
Government Type: Presidential Republic
Neighboring Countries: Republic of Congo and Democratic Republic of Congo (south); Cameroon (west); Chad (northwest); Sudan (northeast); South Sudan (east)
Official Language: French
Other Principal Languages: Sangho (lingua franca and national language), Arabic, Hausa, Swahili
Ethnic Groups: Baya 33%, Banda 27%, Mandjia 13%, Sara 10%, Mboum 7%, M'Baka 4%, Yakoma 4%, other 2%.
Principal Religions: Indigenous beliefs 35%, Protestant 25%, Roman Catholic 25%, Islam 15%, Note: animistic beliefs and practices strongly influence the Christian majority.
Former Colonial Status: French Colony (1894–1960)
Independence Date: August 11, 1960
GDP per Capita (IMF 2022 est.): $534 (nominal), $1,127 (PPP)
Gini Index/Coefficient: 56.3 (World Bank 2013)
Currency: CFA franc, $US 1 = 594 CFA francs BEAC (Apr. 2022)
Inflation Rate: 4.0% (2022 est.)
Chief Commercial Products: Diamonds, timber, cotton, coffee, tobacco
Foreign Direct Investments (FDI) net inflows: 3,475,008
Literacy Rate: 37.4% (CIA 2018)
Life Expectancy: 55.96 years (CIA 2023 est.)

Head of State: President Faustin-Archange Touadera (since March 30, 2016)
Head of Government: Prime Minister Felix Moloua (since February 4, 2022)

LAND AND PEOPLE

The Central African Republic is located in almost the exact center of Africa. It is a vast, rolling plateau rising 2,000 to 2,500 feet above sea level. This sun-drenched land of agricultural and forest products found its original wealth in ivory from its once large herds of elephants. Wild animals still roam the countryside today, making it one of the most zoologically interesting areas of Africa.

There is a small area of forest in the southwest, followed by the rolling plateaus of the plains, rising to the mountains of the northeast. Heavy rainstorms occur almost daily during the wet season from June to October. November is the start of the dry season when the leaves of the trees turn into brilliant foliage because of lack of moisture. In the following weeks, leaves fall and grasses dry (having grown to the height of more than five feet); wildfire is a major danger in this season. The Ubangi River flows along a good portion of the southern border, and past the capital Bangui, then turns south to join the waters of the Congo River.

The conga drum is the primary instrument used in the CAR. It is made out of wet leather, stretched over a hollowed-out drum. They come in every size and shape and can be over a yard tall and can be heard several miles away, these drums were often used as speaking drums transmitting messages from one village to another. Xylophones are also very popular musical instruments, made with wood and gourds.

HISTORY TO PRESENT DAY

For early history, see *Historical Background* and *The Colonial Period: the French*.

French Colonialism and Independence

Central African Republic's independence is intimately associated with the work of a Catholic priest, Barthélémy Boganda. The first African Catholic priest in Ubangui-Chari, as the colony was then known, Boganda represented the territory in the French National Assembly in 1946. His nationalist sentiments developed rapidly, and he left the priesthood and formed his own political party, the *Mouvement pour l'Évolution Sociale de l'Afrique Noire* (MESAN) in 1949. Boganda was responsible for the country's name (*la République Centrafricaine*), its flag, national anthem, and motto. Immensely popular, he was reelected deputy in 1951 and 1956.

Boganda was among those African nationalists who opposed the balkanization of the former French Federations into independent states, but when his federal notions received little support, he returned to Ubangui-Chari to work for its eventual independence. Boganda did not see the fruit of his labors. He died the year before independence, in a plane crash in March 1959.

Independence came on August 11, 1960, and the territory took the name Central African Republic, with David Dacko as the first president. Dacko soon created a single-party state and established close relations with the communist Chinese. Dacko was reelect unopposed in 1964, but the influx of Chinese technical and diplomatic personnel aroused the resentment of the military, which ousted Dacko on the night of December 31–January 1, 1966. General Jean-Bédel Bokassa assumed power, abolished the constitution, dissolved the legislature and centralized the administration in his appointed cabinet.

Dictatorship: Jean-Bédel Bokassa (1966–79) to André Kolingba (1981–93)

Bokassa quickly became one of the most notorious dictator's in Africa's history. In late 1976 a new constitution created the Central African Empire. In late 1977, in sweltering Bangui, a crowd of more than 3,000 guests witnessed Jean-Bédel Bokassa place a crown on his head—encrusted with 2,000 diamonds—and proclaim himself Emperor Bokassa I. The spectacle was said to have cost over $22 million in a country where the average per capita annual income was $120.

Opposition to Bokassa developed quickly at home and abroad. While

Central African Republic

visiting Libya in September 1979, he was overthrown by his cousin and advisor, former president David Dacko. With the support of French armed forces, Dacko reestablished the Republic, but the CAR continued to be plagued by corrupt, inept government. Elections held in 1981 and Dacko emerged victorious over Ange-Félix Patassé, but the polls were clouded by charges of fraud. Four months later, Army Chief of Staff General André Kolingba demanded President Dacko's resignation and Dacko quickly complied.

General Kolingba operated a virtual military dictatorship for the next decade. A new constitution of 1986 provided him a single-party state and a six-year term as president. He organized a new political party, the *Rassemblement démocratique centrafricain* (RDC), and in parliamentary elections in 1987 all candidates for the National Assembly had to belong to the party. With command over party and state in a country with few other competing institutions at the national level, Kolingba exercised virtually uninhibited power.

The constitutional referendum in 1986 occurred shortly after the unexpected return of the former emperor Jean-Bédel Bokassa, who had fled virtual house arrest in France. Bokassa was put on trial, charged with murder and a variety of other crimes. After several months of intermittent action, the trial concluded in 1988 with Bokassa's guilt and death sentence. President Kolingba commuted the sentence to life in prison and later shortened the prison term; the so-called emperor died of natural causes in 1996.

Kolingba's authoritarian rule lasted a decade, during which time the regime restricted civil liberties and systematically abused human rights. Over the same time, the economy deteriorated, and the treasury emptied. By the early 1990s, strikes and work stoppages by government employees—who had gone unpaid for months—culminated in riots. In April 1991, Kolingba, under heavy pressure, promised to allow political opposition. The newly responsive National Assembly revised the constitution to transform the country into a multiparty democracy. Kolingba proposed a "Grand National Debate" (GND) to discuss democratic transformation.

In August 1992, members of the United Democratic Forces—a coalition of 14 opposition parties—decried Kolingba's planned GND, demanding a genuine national conference to bring democracy to the country. In response, Kolingba sent in the troops. Soldiers attacked the marchers with tear gas, and then plowed into the crowd swinging their rifle butts. One Iion leader was savagely beaten to death.

CAR's political situation continued to deteriorate through 1992. The government scheduled elections, then postponed them; causiIopposition to split. In May 1993, Kolingba's presidential guard mutinied, demanding its back wages, marking the first time the armed forces had rebelled against the regime.

The Ange-Félix Patassé Regime (1993–2002)

In the 1993 elections, Ange-Félix Patassé of the Movement for the Liberation of the Centrafrican People (MLPC) beat out Abel Goumba in a runoff to become president; Dacko and Kolingba came in third and fourth place, respectively. This election ended twelve years of military rule, but President Patassé faced an empty treasury, a disgruntled civil service, an unpaid army, and a deeply divided country. The trickiest of these issues was the army: years of military dictatorship had elevated army power and prestige, and soldiers were little prepared to see these cut back, as President Patassé had to do. In April 1996, when the government could not find sufficient funds to pay them, the troops mutinied again. French troops crushed the mutiny and Patassé came up with money and promised amnesty, but soldiers mutinied a second time in May, after accusing Patassé of violating the amnesty by arresting some of the April mutineers. In November, troops mutinied yet again, escalating their demands to include the President's resignation.

In addition to the parlous state of national finances, the army's demands highlighted the regional and ethnic conflicts in the country. The mutineers were southerners, mostly members of the Yakoma tribe of ex-President Kolingba, while Patassé was a northerner and member of the competing Baya tribe.

Mali's respected former military ruler, Amadou Toumani Touré, was invited to mediate the impasse between government and army. The Bangui Accords he brokered involved amnesties for mutineers, a government of national unity, and the deployment of African peacekeepers to replace French troops. Both parties signed the Accords in January 1997, but this did not restore peace.

The Inter-African Surveillance Mission for the Bangui Accords (MISAB) was barely in place before it faced another mutiny in June. French and Chadian troops responded with a "muscular offensive" against the mutineers, forcing them into another cease-fire in early July 1997. French troops withdrew in mid-April 1998 and were replaced by the UN Mission in the Central African Republic (MINURCA).

Legislative elections in November and December 1998 did little to build a climate of trust. The initial results were inconclusive, as the MLPC and its allies held 51 seats, while the opposition together held 53 and seven independents constituted the swing votes. "Discussions" with the independents went on, and suddenly resulted in defections to Patassé's coalition, prompting calls from the opposition that the defectors were "bought."

The political climate that preceded the September 1999 presidential elections was fractured. The opposition could not agree on a single candidate to confront President Patassé, so ten names appeared on the presidential ballot. The most prominent candidates were former presidents David Dacko and André Kolingba. The fractured opposition rejected the results even before the election was held and hopes that Patassé would be forced into a runoff election were dashed: the president won reelection by a slim majority of 51.6%. Kolingba received 19.3% of the votes and Dacko came in third with 11.1%. Observers declared the election free and fair. Any irregularities, they said, would not affect the overall result.

General André Kolingba

Central African Republic

"Rebels" in north-central Central African Republic ©Nicholas Reader/IRIN

The election brought no stability, and CAR teetered on the brink of implosion. Unable to pay civil servants their salaries, students their stipends, or retirees their pensions, the government faced an ongoing series of protests and demonstrations. A near-permanent strike of government workers began in November 2000 when demonstrators set up barricades and burned tires in the capital before being dispersed by security forces. They demanded nearly 30 months of back wages.

CAR represented an awful scenario for an abjectly poor state: economic crisis exacerbating political tensions and leading to social disintegration. Crime in the capital and banditry in the countryside increased in the early 2000s and has only escalated since then. The state had little capacity to project its authority beyond the Bangui city limits, and armed banditry reached insurrectional proportions, threatening the state's authority in the provinces. Bandits raped, robbed, and murdered, disrupting trade between nearby Chad and the Cameroonian port of Douala, the CAR's main outlet to the sea.

In May 2001, General Kolingba instigated a *coup d'état* against the Patassé government, but the attempt was repressed by outside forces, notably Libyan troops and several hundred *Mouvement de Libération du Congo* (MLC) troops of the Congolese rebel Jean-Pierre Bemba, who crossed the Ubangui River from their northern Congolese bases. Bemba and the MLC were accused of committing war crimes and crimes against humanity during their time in CAR. The International Criminal Court (ICC) investigated and ultimately issued a warrant for Bemba's arrest in May 2008 for crimes committed in the CAR between October 25, 2002, and March 15, 2003. He was charged with five counts of war crimes and three counts of crimes against humanity, including murder, rape, and torture. Arrested on May 24 and turned over to The Hague on July 3, Bemba became the first person arrested for the atrocities committed in the CAR. Bemba's trial commenced on November 22, 2010, and is ongoing. Forty witnesses and five victims have been called to testify.

The Patassé regime turned increasingly paranoid. The president fired his defense, interior, security, and disarmament ministers in August, and army chief of staff General François Bozizé in October. Bozizé fled to neighboring Chad in November after an attempt to arrest him led to five days of fighting between his supporters and troops loyal to the government.

The Coup of 2002 and the François Bozizé Years (2002–2013)

As the country deteriorated socially and economically, only foreign arms kept President Patassé in power. Forces loyal to General Bozizé invaded Bangui's northern suburbs in October 2002. After ten days of destructive fighting, they were driven out with the help of Libyan and Congolese forces. For Bangui's suffering citizenry, salvation was nearly as bad as rebel assault: undisciplined, Bemba's MLC troops raped and robbed residents of the capital. This further alienated CAR's citizens from President Patassé.

Soldiers loyal to General Bozizé, aided by Chadian mercenaries, left their sanctuary in Chad in March 2003 and completed the work they had begun the previous October. Bangui fell to the rebels in a day, as there was almost no one left willing to defend the Patassé regime. General Bozizé returned from Paris and was greeted as a liberator by Bangui crowds. Reportedly a deeply religious man, the general showed himself tough in his initial pronouncements, saying "thieves and other looters will henceforth be considered military targets." The violence and looting in Bangui, particularly against figures of the former regime, ended quickly. Beginning the process of national reconciliation, Bozizé amnestied all those who had plotted the overthrow of President Patassé in May 2001.

To head a transitional government of national unity, Bozizé called upon the man with the cleanest reputation among CAR's top politicians, Abel Goumba. Nearly 77 years old, Goumba was a companion from the early days of Barthélémy Boganda, the republic's founder. A man of principle, Goumba had opposed each of the republic's four presidents (Dacko, Bokassa, Kolingba, and Patassé). At the time of his appointment, he was the leader of the Patriotic Front for Progress (FPP) party and head of a 12-member coalition of opposition parties.

The new regime's most pressing problem was the restoration of security. Achieving this in the capital was the easier task. Once done, Bangui's citizens felt free to "walk anywhere, even late at night, without worrying about getting shot or robbed," as one local put it. Outside the capital, however, the government still works to reassert its authority. In January 2004, after receiving vehicles and equipment from China, France, Morocco, and Sudan, the army sent 1,000 troops into the southwestern region—where most of the country's mines are located—to restore order. It also dispatched specially trained forces to fight banditry in the northern provinces.

In many cases, it was difficult to determine who the "bandits" were. Some were Chadian mercenaries, hired to support Bozizé's invasion, who had not yet been sufficiently paid for their services. Others were unemployed soldiers loyal to former president Patassé or his defense minister Jean-Jacques Demafouth, while still others were simply opportunistic highway robbers who set up roadblocks, plundered

Central African Republic

Former president François Bozizé

travelers, and held the more prosperous for ransom. In late April 2004, President Bozizé agreed to pay the Chadian fighters the local equivalent of $1,000 to encourage their return home.

Some of the money may have come from a $2 million interest-free loan given by China to help chronically cash-short Bangui deal with unpaid civil servants. The IMF and World Bank also offered emergency post-conflict aid, the first time the institutions had provided funding since October 2002. The financing helped the regime push forward with its other central task, the restoration of democracy.

Voters overwhelmingly approved a new constitution in December. The transitional constitutional court approved only five of fifteen individuals who submitted their candidacy papers to run for president. Among the approved were François Bozizé (who declared himself an independent candidate), his vice president Abel Goumba, former president André Kolingba, and two others. The court disqualified all candidates from the MLPC, the country's former ruling party. After considerable public outcry, Bozizé allowed three of them—Jean-Paul Ngoupandé, Martin Ziguélé, and Charles Massi—to seek the presidency.

Bozizé won the election, polling 43% of the vote in the first round and 64.23% in the runoff election against the leading MLPC candidate, former prime minister Martin Ziguélé. Yet the election assured neither security nor stability. Initially aided by Chadian "irregulars" in his efforts to topple the Patassé regime, Bozizé saw the country increasingly threatened by the spillover effects of civil conflict in Darfur and Chad. In early April 2006, Bozizé closed the border with Sudan after a column of 20 pickup trucks loaded with Chadian rebels took a shortcut through CAR on their way to overthrow President Déby of Chad.

Birao, situated in the three-frontier-zone where the borders of CAR, Chad and Sudan meet, became a high priority target for Sudan-supported troublemakers. On October 30, 2006, rebels identifying themselves as men of the *Union des forces démocratiques pour le rassemblement* (UFDR: Union of Democratic Forces Coalition) captured the town; they were a mixture of Central Africans and remnants of the Chadian mercenaries who once had fought for General Bozizé. Their arms and logistical support were Sudanese.

The CAR government invoked defense agreements with France and French firepower quickly destroyed rebel mortars and heavy machine guns. Their threatened advance on Bangui stopped, rebels fled back to their Sudanese sanctuary. This scenario was virtually replayed in March 2007, this time with support from French paratroopers and Mirage fighter jets, as France acted robustly to contain the spillover effects of conflict in Darfur.

The March attack on Birao came less than a month after President Bozizé had signed a peace deal, brokered by Muammar al-Qadhafi of Libya, with one major rebel group, Abdoulaye Miskine's *Front démocratique de libération du peuple centrafricain* (FDPC). By mid-April, even the UFDR military commander was saying that "the time has come to make peace and work together for the reconstruction of our country" as he too signed a peace accord with Bozizé.

The rebels agreed to sequester their men in an army cantonment from where they would eventually be integrated into the national army. In return, the government accepted the UFDR as a political party and committed itself to introducing a law extending amnesty to former UFDR fighters. In March, following the French bombardment to oust the rebels, the UN reported that 90% of the population of the city of Birao had fled. Out of a population of 14,000, only 600 people remained; 70% of the city's houses had been burned or partially destroyed, and neither schools nor hospital remained.

The parliament passed legislation in 2008 granting amnesty to the UFDR and another major rebel group. In December 2008, it also pledged to establish a new form of unity government. In January the new structure of the government was unveiled, including François Naouyama of the APRD and Djomo Didou of the UFDR, but the opposition said the changes to the cabinet were insufficient. April 2009 saw violence continue, and the UN established a new peacekeeping office for the CAR, and in August 2009 the UN estimated that over a million people have been affected by CAR's instability.

Tension between the government and the opposition was heightened after the death of Charles Massi, a former minister who joined the UFDR in 2008. Massi was reputedly arrested by the government, most likely in 2009. Reports then leaked in early 2010 that he had been tortured and killed. According to various human rights groups, the opposition, and the French government, Massi was tortured to death while in custody of the Bozizé government. The government denied the allegations of torture, but eventually confirmed Massi's death.

Despite the continued violence, presidential and legislative elections were held again in January 2011. President Bozizé led a regime that was under scrutiny for rights abuses but could plausibly claim some success in reducing conflict and restabilizing the country. He ran against former president Ange-Félix Patassé in the election. Now at the head of the "Kwa Na Kwa" (National Convergence) coalition, Bozizé swept to victory in the first round with nearly two-thirds of the vote. Patassé, hampered by age and ill health, took 21%. Just a couple of months later, on April 5, 2011, Patassé died of natural causes in Cameroon, reportedly of complications from diabetes.

The Séléka Rebels, Civil Conflict, and State Collapse (2012–present)

President Bozizé's term that began in 2011 lasted barely two years. By 2012, a number of rebel movements (many of which had fought alongside Bozizé in CAR's various bush conflicts over the years) united in opposition to the government. This coalition (known as Séléka in the local Sangho language) progressively moved across the country, capturing successively larger towns and moving to within shelling distance of the capital Bangui. Bozizé made several last-ditch efforts to salvage his regime: he shuffled his cabinet, offered a ceasefire in January 2013, and called upon South African and Angolan soldiers to support it. Nonetheless, the Séléka rebels moved on the capital in March, killing over a dozen South African troops in addition to about 50 regulars from the CAR army. The rebels seized the presidential palace on March 24 as Bozizé fled across the Ubangi River into the neighboring D.R. Congo.

Upon taking power, the Séléka movement identified Michel Djotodia as interim president. Djotodia dissolved the government, but reappointed the prime minister Nicolas Tiangaye. The government claimed it would be transitional.

In September of 2013 Djotodia nominally dissolved the Séléka, the Muslim rebel group that had put him into power. The Séléka thereupon began committing atrocities against Christians. In response,

Central African Republic

militant Christians formed the paramilitary Anti-balaka, which have allegedly committed atrocities against Muslims in western CAR. Clashes between the two groups escalated, with former Séléka rebels murdering two priests on Easter Sunday. In April of 2014, two churches were burned down in the capital city of Bangui. Meanwhile, the Anti-balaka have been recorded saying that they would like to rid CAR of Muslims. In February of 2014, the Human Rights Watch learned from witnesses that the Anti-balaka are responsible for the deaths of 72 Muslim men and boys. With both groups responsible for countless acts of violence – including the murder of children – it is difficult to anticipate a positive resolution.

French peacekeepers deployed in CAR have not been able to stop the violence. In October of 2013 the United Nationals Security Council approved a resolution to stabilize the Central African Republic, but UN peacekeepers will be deployed only in September of 2014. The UN and other human rights bodies have expressed concerns that the situation could become a genocide, calling the Central African Republic a "lawless country." Clashes throughout the year have left numerous civilians dead.

Michel Djotodia resigned in January of 2014, which brought on celebrations in the country. A sovereign body known as the National Transitional Council elected Catherine Samba-Panza (formerly the mayor of Bangui) as interim president until elections in 2015. She was sworn in January 23, 2014, and became Africa's third female president. She is a Christian but has defied the Anti-balaka's insistence that they should be given positions in the government. Samba-Panza has called for both the Séléka and Anti-Balaka to lay down their arms and end the violence. She also asked the international community to fund the reconstitution of the CAR's security force. In response, France has agreed to increase its troop presence and US President Obama has issued an executive order authorizing the use of sanctions in response to the state of emergency in CAR.

Unfortunately, the change in leadership does not appear to have stabilized the government. Tensions between the Muslims and Christians are so intense that separate refugee camps for each group are required. Most recently, the United Nations are seeking $247 million in emergency donations to help the refugees from the conflict, many of whom have fled Democratic Republic of Congo, the Republic of the Congo, Chad, and Cameroon. Contrary to expectations, a largely peaceful election to the presidency was held in 2016 and won by Faustin-Archange Touaderra.

CONTEMPORARY THEMES

CAR's economic situation remains precarious. The coup of 2013 and the growing tensions between Christians and Muslims have further heightened uncertainty, discouraged investment, and set back the prospects for development. Mismanagement for decades (since Bokassa in the 1960s) and continuing civil strife have led to general economic deterioration and deepening poverty for most citizens. Average annual incomes are still at levels of about 20 years ago. Symptomatic of the country's abject poverty, life expectancy is estimated at just 47 years (2009). According to one UN report, more than two-thirds of the population lives on less than a dollar a day.

Civil conflict has devastated the country, and regional banditry continues to disrupt the economy and displace people. The UN Secretary General Ban Ki-Moon called the Central African Republic one of the most unstable countries in Africa. Doctors Without Borders estimated that the number of refugees from CAR tops 220,000 and that the violence within the country is keeping the organization from delivering aid.

Agriculture and forestry are the mainstays of the economy. These account for over half of GNP and employ two-thirds of the workforce. Subsistence farming dominates, with farmers growing cassavas, yams, bananas, sorghum, millet, and rice. Cotton and coffee are cash crops, grown for export, but prices for both commodities have declined on world markets.

The country has significant forestry potential, with over 60 commercially viable varieties of trees. Development of the sector is hampered by high transportation costs and delivery problems that can add 60% to production costs. CAR must send its logs down-river via Brazzaville to Pointe-Noire, or by road to Douala in Cameroon—a costly proposition given the dilapidated conditions of roads across the region. Neighboring countries that are not land-locked also appear to have an advantage in industrialization.

Diamonds have traditionally contributed half of CAR's foreign earnings, but production has been affected by political instability. An estimated 80,000 small-scale miners recover about 500,000 carats each year, however smuggling remains a problem. Estimates found that those numbers only represent half of the diamonds sold abroad.

China is keenly interested in CAR's resources. When President Bozizé met with Chinese President Hu Jintao in August 2004, the Chinese leader said China was interested in exploring cooperation in the oil, diamond, iron ore, and timber sectors. With its plans to build new nuclear power plants, China is also interested in CAR's uranium deposits in the Bakouma basin. In 2006, President Bozizé opened the country's first major uranium mining operation in the Bakouma, run by the South African firm UraMin.

HIV/AIDS is prevalent in the Central African Republic. In July 2006, President Bozizé named it the "principal cause of death". UN figures estimate 5% of the working-age population is affected by HIV/AIDS.

With proposals to eliminate presidential term limits, it appears evident that President Touaderra is seeking a life-time presidency while former strongman and ex-rebel leader Abdoulaye Hissene has been charged with war crimes as Russia's Wagner Group becomes more active In the country.

Activities by the Wagner Group in the CAR include eviction and outright violence against local small-scale miners, many of them women and children, panning for gold and diamonds perpetrated in the 2020s. After President Faustin-Archange Touadera asked for help to deal with rebel groups in the CAR in 2017, Russia's Wagner Group arrived and has since amassed significant security and economic power by creating a "complex network of operations to plunder diamonds, gold, and other natural resources" in the country taking control of gold mines in the central and eastern regions and extending northward. Attempts to seize gold mines involved summary executions of local miners by the Russian paramilitaries committed to serving Russian geopolitical interests as the CAR government has rescinded the exploration permits and mining license for Ndassima gold mine from Axmin, a Canadian company, and then granted them in 2020 to Midas Resources, a company affiliated to the Wagner Group. The Russian private military company paid rebels from Union for Peace (UPC), a local group which controlled the mine at the time, to ensure that staff and properties owned by Midas Resources were secure. When its relationship with the UPC went sour, Wagner mercenaries began a

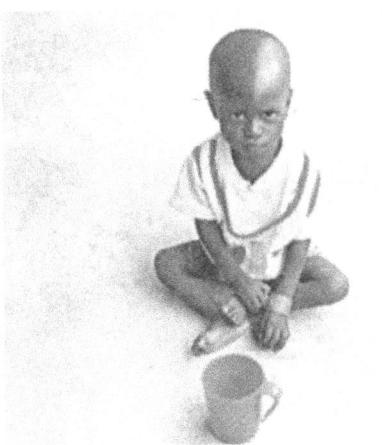

Central African Republic

counteroffensive in 2021 against the rebels but they also targeted civilians, especially artisanal miners who lived near the mine. Following the incident, Midas Resources gained complete control of the Ndassima gold mine, which has a gold deposit valued by the CAR government at an estimated $2.8 billion. Other such killings occurring in the towns of Aigbado and Yanga and the Andaha region.

FUTURE CONSIDERATIONS

The Central African Republic has long been one of Africa's weakest states: poor administration and weak governance have characterized CAR since independence. President Bozizé reasserted control with his victory in the January 2011 general election, only to see his writ collapse. The Séléka rebels and President Djotodia saw their own collapse soon thereafter. Despite the joy and hope associated with Catherine Samba-Panza's interim rule, the country has failed to stabilize. Since January of 2014, the situation has deteriorated rapidly.

Even the prospects of increased mineral wealth do not suggest a brighter future; in the presence of instability, corruption, and political strife, subsoil resources often go unexplored due to lack of investment or exacerbate social tensions more than they resolve them. The past year has demonstrated ever-worsening conditions, regardless of efforts by the international community. Economic stagnation, political conflict, and social distrust, all worsened by recent instability, suggest strongly that the Central African Republic will continue on one of the most difficult trajectories in all of Africa.

The Republic of Chad

Tibesti Region, Northern Chad

BASIC FACTS

Area: 1,284,640 sq. km. = 496,000 sq. mi. (the size of Texas, New Mexico, and Arizona)
Population: 18,523,165 (June 2023 est.)
Capital City: N'Djaména
Government Type: Presidential Republic
Neighboring Countries: Cameroon (southwest); Niger and Nigeria (west); Libya (north); The Sudan (east); Central African Republic (southeast and south)
Official Languages: French and Arabic
Other Principal Languages: Sara in the south, and over 120 different languages and dialects Iing Gulay, Kanuri, Karanda, Maba, Marba, Marfa, Masana, Mundang, Musey, Ngambay, and Sango (a Creole trade language)
Ethnic Groups: Muslims: (Arabs, Toubou, Hadjerai, Fulbe, Kotoko, Kanembou, Baguirmi, Boulala, Zaghawa, and Maba). Non-Muslims: (Sara, Ngambaye, Mbaye, Goulaye, Moundang, Moussei, Massa). Nonindigenous: 150,000
Principal Religions: Muslim 51%, Christian 35%, animist 7%, other 7%
Former Colonial Status: French colony (1910-1960)
Independence Date: August 11, 1960
GDP per Capita (IMF 2023 est.): $667 (nominal), $1,787 (PPP)
Gini Index: 39.8 (2013)
Currency: CFA Franc; 1 USD = 594 CFA francs BEAC (Apr. 2022)
Inflation Rate: 4.1% (2022 est.)
Chief Commercial Products: Oil, cotton, cattle, and gum arabic
Foreign Direct Investments (FDI) net inflows: 760,500,000
Literacy Rate: 26.8% (CIA 2021)
Life Expectancy: 59.57 years (CIA 2023 est.)
Head of State: Albert Pahimi Padacke, prime minister (since February 20, 2021)
Head of Government: Mahamat Idriss Déby (since February 20, 2021)

LAND AND PEOPLE

Landlocked Chad, more than 1,500 miles from any seaport, lies almost in the center of Africa and is one of the transitional nations between the desert to the north and the fertile southern area of the continent. For centuries it has been the crossroads of traders going back and forth between the Sahara-Mediterranean Sea region and the tropical areas of West Africa. Contact with Muslim traders may explain the conversion of some populations living in the Sahel region to Islam as early as the 9th century before the arrival of nomadic Arab tribes.

Chad resembles a shallow basin and has three distinct topographical regions. The Chadian Sahara in the North is a land of dry desert sand dunes that rise up to a height of 12,000 feet above sea level in the Tibesti Mountains. The vast expanse of desert, scorching by day, sinks to below freezing levels at night and is home to only 1.2% of the population of Chad, mostly tribal nomads.

The central portion is a semiarid land of treeless plains;Is which traditionally has received just enough rainfall to support caI experiences periodic and devastating droughts. The green southern area, with more ample rainfall, supports 45% of the country's population, who mainly engage in cotton cultivation.

Five countries share thIke Chad Basin, which is fed by the Shari and Logone Rivers in the southwest corner of the nation. Lake Chad, a former inland sea, was once one of Africa's largest lakes but has been drying up and is now a mere fraction of its former size.

In July 2002, the French paleoanthropologist Michel Brunet presented a skull, unearthed in the Chadian north, which could be as old as seven million years old. Named "Toumai," the skull reveals both ape and human features. The skull could be the oldest example of a pre-human ancestor that walked upright; the species is *Sahelanthropus tchadensis*. Some scientists suspect Toumai is the closet specimen yet to the evolutionary split between humans and apes. Excited by the discovery, which was older than any fossil found in the Rift Valley, Brunet told a Chadian audience that "the cradle of humanity is in Chad. Toumai is your ancestor."

HISTORY TO PRESENT DAY

For early history, see *Historical Background* and *The Colonial Period: The French*.

Independence and Tombalbaye Presidency (1960–1975)

Under provisions of the constitution of the French Fifth Republic, Chad became an autonomous republic within the French Community in November 1958. At independence in August 1960, Chad had a deep geographical and cultural divide between the Christian south and Muslim north. In the south, the population had traditionally been more receptive to colonial rule, adopting the French language and culture, converting to Christianity, and reaping the benefits of increased educational opportunities and improved healthcare. Conversely, the north restricted education to Arabic and Koranic

Chad

teachings. There is also a climactic difference between the regions, and as a result of these various factors, the north's economy experienced relative stagnation while the south witnessed some modest prosperity as a result of cotton cultivation.

At independence, the southerner François (later Ngarta) Tombalbaye, a teacher and trade union leader, became the country's first president. In 1963, Tombalbaye dissolved all political parties except his own *Parti progressiste tchadien* (PPT) and increasingly repressed both his fellow southerners and northerners. Northern Muslims coalesced behind the Chadian National Liberation Front (Frolinat) and rebelled against the central government. What started as reaction against the banning of political parties in 1963 turned into civil war by 1966.

Frolinat operated primarily in the north with the support of Libya, where it maintained bases, and advocated for closer ties with the Arab states of North Africa and a reduction of French influence in Chad. French military forces were brought in to suppress the revolt in 1973, but Frolinat continued its guerrilla operations with the help of Libyan weapons.

Tombalbaye saw this French intervention as an attempt to unseat him, and, in reaction, pursued an "Africanization" program. He abolished the use of Christian forenames, dropping François and renaming himself Ngarta, as well as the use of French names for streets and places. The only exception was made for Avenue Charles de Gaulle in the capital Fort Lamy (renamed N'Djaména). The PPT was also renamed and became the National Movement for Cultural and Social Revolution.

Power Struggles and the Emergence of Hissane Habré (1970s–1980s)

Economic conditions worsened and dissatisfaction increased, especially among the military, and in 1975 southern officers killed President Tombalbaye and replaced him with another southerner, Colonel Félix Malloum. By this time Frolinat had split (a continuing tendency among northern groups) into two factions, one willing to accept support from Libya under Goukouni Oueddeï, and an anti-Libyan faction headed by Hissène Habré. To unify a divided country, Col. Malloum agreed to share power with Habré, but the coalition was short-lived.

Malloum and Habré soon split, and, after losing a violent power struggle, Malloum was forced to flee N'Djaména in 1979. Northern faction leaders formed a coalition government headed by Goukouni Oueddeï, with Hissène Habré as prime minister. At this point Chad's civil conflict became less a struggle between north and south and more a struggle among northern warlords.

French forces were asked to leave the country in May 1980 and most Europeans followed. The U.S. Embassy was closed and the streets of N'Djaména became a no-man's land as the armies of Oueddeï and Habré struggled for supremacy. Libya offered military help to Oueddeï's beleaguered forces, and from December 1980 to November 1981 Libya occupied most of the country. Habré's rebels, unable to compete with well-equipped Libyans, faded into eastern Chad to await a better opportunity to seize power.

This chance arose in late 1981, when Oueddeï asked Libyan forces to leave in late 1981. Within days, Habré's troops had seized a large part of the country and he seemed to be on his way to an easy victory over Oueddeï. However, peacekeeping forces from the Organization of African Unity (OAU) quickly moved in, checking the rebel advance and driving Habré back to eastern Chad.

Life in N'Djaména temporarily returned to a semblance of order, but in mid-1982 Habré swept out of eastern Chad and, amid bitter fighting, seized the capital. The OAU troops remained neutral, Oueddeï escaped to Cameroon, and Hissène Habré declared himself president. The OAU recognized Habré's government, and its troops withdrew by the end of June, marking the beginning of Habré's violent rule.

With Libyan help, Oueddeï continued to resist the N'Djaména government, while France and Zaïre supported Habré. With destructive forces evenly balanced, fighting became sporadic after early 1984. However, diplomatic mediation remained fruitless given Chad's endemic factionalism.

When Libyan forces began building an airfield at Ouadi (Wadi) Doum in the northern desert, the French responded. The airfield was hit, and a Libyan plane bombed N'Djaména the next day. Then came the surprise: Oueddeï announced his resignation as head of the rebels (who deserted the cause) and declared his solidarity with Hissène Habré. Libya promptly placed him under arrest in Tripoli, leaving Libya's Col. Qadhafi the sponsor of a revolution without a leader. With French assistance, the Chadian army struck Libyan units in northern Chad with devastating effect and by 1987 Libya had been forced out of the entire northern region, apart from the Aouzou strip and parts of Tibesti which were later awarded to Chad by the International Court of Justice. Habré regained control of N'Djaména in November 1988, but proved unable to master the country's divisive factionalism.

The Rise of Idriss Déby (1990–present)

In April 1989, Idriss Déby, one of Habré's leading generals, defected and fled to Sudan, from where he invaded Chad in November 1990. On December 2, his troops entered war-exhausted N'Djaména without battle, President Habré and the forces loyal to him having fled. Déby's Patriotic Salvation Movement (MPS) approved a national charter in February 1991, and he became the new Chadian president.

The country's first free, multiparty presidential elections were held in June 1996

Cattle herding ©Photographie Michel Hasson

Chad

and Idriss Déby won nearly 70% of the vote in a runoff election in July, though the election was vigorously protested by the 14 other candidates who had run against him. In the 1997 legislative elections, Déby's MPS fell short of an outright majority, winning only 55 of 125 seats, while the Union for Renewal and Democracy (URD)—the party of his southern presidential rival General Wadal Abdelkader Kamougué—won 31. Kamougué rallied to the government and was elected speaker of the National Assembly, and as part of the calculus of coalition, Déby also appointed a southerner as prime minister.

The south remained restless, and by 1997 there was a resurgence of factional resistance. The revolt was triggered by discussions over the development of a major oil field, and, once again, the question of who controls resources and how they will be used. To highlight demands for greater participation in making those decisions, groups resorted to kidnapping Europeans.

Once President Déby had resolved the issues in the south, there was an upsurge of kidnappings in the north, and by October 1998 it was apparent that the government had to deal with yet another northern rebel movement. Led by a former defense minister, Youssouf Togoïmi, the *Mouvement pour la démocratie et la justice au Tchad* (MDJT) was centered in the sparsely populated Tibesti region—a mountainous, semi-desert area ideal for guerrilla warfare and heavily populated with landmines.

The war continued through 2001 at considerable cost to the government. Libya offered mediation and ultimately got the two sides to sign a peace deal that ended three years of conflict. The accord provided for an immediate ceasefire, release of prisoners, rebel integration into the national army, and "government jobs" for MDJT leaders.

Tactically, the accord gave the MDJT, reportedly suffering from major resupply difficulties, badly needed breathing space. The government, in need of political stability to assure financing of the Doba oil project and smooth spring parliamentary elections, fulfilled its obligations. After the parliament voted an amnesty bill for the rebels in February and political prisoners were released, it seemed the country was heading for its spring parliamentary elections in an atmosphere of uncharacteristic calm.

However, discussions broke down over the specifics of those "government jobs," and Youssouf Togoïmi demanded nothing less than the premiership, a position discarded by the government as "unconstitutional." The rebels themselves were divided; the intransigents supported Togoïmi in rejecting the agreement, but his deputy, Adoum Togoi, a former ambassador to Libya and reputedly close to the Libyans, argued for it. Togoi was briefly jailed and in September 2002, Togoïmi died in a Libyan hospital after having been badly wounded in a landmine explosion. With its leader dead, the MDJT split between a military high command hostile to President Déby and a political branch in exile more willing to negotiate.

The MDJT military wing reaffirmed its awkward presence in the spring of 2004 when it announced it had captured fleeing members of an Algerian terrorist group. Known in French as *Groupe salafiste pour la prédication et le combat* (GSPC, or Salafist Group for Preaching and Combat), the terrorists were part of an Algerian Islamist organization wanted in connection with the kidnapping of several European tourists the year before. The U.S. military was working with local security forces in Algeria, Chad, Mali, Niger, and Mauritania to capture or kill members of the Salafist group. GSPC members were detected at the Niger-Chad border; the Chadian army attacked and killed several while those who survived fled to rugged mountains of Tibesti where they were captured by MDJT soldiers.

The capture posed delicate diplomatic and logistical problems for the governments wanting the Salafists: to deal directly with the MDJT would insult Chadian authorities, who had identified them as terrorists; to accept them from the MDJT, without government approval, would violate international law. Diplomats did not want to enter the area anyway, given safety concerns. When asked to bring their captives to the Niger border, the MDJT admitted the territory was so dangerous even they could not provide security. A resolution came when Libya successfully negotiated with the MDJT to hand over Ammari Saifi (aka Abderezak El Para) the Salafist leader. He was extradited to Algeria in October 2004.

The MDJT conflict is one example of Chad's highly fragmented political culture and the inability of N'Djaména to project its authority throughout the country. These problems were background to two important elections. In May 2001 presidential balloting, Déby won a controversial first round victory over six opponents. Chad's Constitutional Council verified the final results: Déby, 67.17% of the votes while his nearest competitor, longtime critic and opponent Ngarlejy Yorongar, only polled 16.35%.

European Union observers regretted the "numerous defects and irregularities" that were observed. The government had restricted campaigning, used force to prevent demonstrations, and violently (but briefly) arrested opposition candidates. Threat,

President Idriss Déby Itno

intimidation, and violence also characterized the April 2002 legislative elections, with similar success. President Déby's ruling Patriotic Salvation Movement (MPS) took 112 of the 155 seats, assuring him of a solid legislative majority, which allowed him to amend Chad's constitution.

The elections suggested President Déby was a man firmly in power, but power is often an illusion in Chad. When civil conflict broke out in the Darfur region of neighboring Sudan, it destabilized all of eastern Chad and nearly ended the Déby regime. Sudanese efforts to suppress a rebellion by ethnic cleansing produced a large exodus of refugees into eastern Chad, among those most affected were numerous Zaghawa people, ethnic kin of President Déby and his inner circle.

Déby sought to mediate the crisis, but Zaghawa people in his army and security forces thought direct support for persecuted ethnic kin a more appropriate response. Déby's opponents supplied arms clandestinely to Sudanese Zaghawa and organized a mutiny against the president. The attempted coup began the evening of May 16, 2004, led by officers of some of Chad's elite forces: the Republican Guard, the Nomadic National Guard, and the Presidential Security Guard. Loyalist forces stopped the mutineers and rapidly reasserted order in the capital with no loss of life on either side, but the incident showed the fragility of Déby's power.

The Decline of Idriss Déby's Power and Chad as Failed State (2000s–present)

President Déby's efforts to extend his presidential tenure further eroded his support among those closest to him (and most desirous of succeeding him). In parliament, Déby's MPS pushed through a controversial constitutional amendment

Chad

Darfur children in a Chadian refugee camp ©IRIN

removing a two-term limit on Chadian presidents. Approved by voters in June 2005, it allowed Déby to run for a third term in 2006, but solidified opposition against him.

The president became increasingly isolated as friends, family, and members of the presidential guard—the last line of defense—deserted him. By October 2005 the guard defections were so serious that Déby simply dissolved it. Several hundred military deserters fled to hideouts in Eastern Chad and announced creation of the *Socle* (Platform) *pour le changement, l'unité nationale et la démocracie* (SCUD). As defections from N'Djaména grew, new rebel groupings proliferated, and new dissenters met the old opposition in Eastern Chad.

One such group was the *Rassemblement pour la démocratie et la liberté* (RDL), composed primarily of Chadian "Arabs" and led by a former officer in the Chadian army, Mahamat Nour Abdelkerim. Nour had defected in 1994 and remained an intransigent resistant, dedicated to overthrowing the "tyrant" Déby. He and his men reportedly found support and employment from the regime in Khartoum as it battled to repress rebellion in Darfur. They rode, it is alleged, with the *janjaweed* in their terror raids against Darfur villagers.

By December 2005 at least eight rebel formations existed in eastern Chad. Mahamat Nour Abdelkerim created the United Front for Change (*Front uni pour le changement*: FUC), but it was unclear how if differed, if at all, from the RDL. With the RDL as its core, FUC was probably the largest and best organized of the rebel formations, and, with its Sudanese-supplied equipment, the best armed. To demonstrate its aptitude, FUC launched a major attack against the Chadian border city of Adré on December 18, easily crossing the border in a convoy of lightly armed, brand-new Toyota trucks. Chadian troops loyal to President Déby, some of them recently trained in counterterrorism by American forces, beat them and chased them back into Sudan and at least 300 died in the incident.

The attack on Adré was the most serious threat to the regime thus far. The president declared a "state of belligerence" and accused Sudan of being "the common enemy of the nation" as he sought to mobilize regional and international opinion to the support of his government.

In early January 2006, the government's relations with the World Bank turned hostile when Déby backed a law to reduce the amount of oil money to be set aside for development—the money was needed, said the government, to defend the country. The World Bank had initially placed restrictions on Chad in 1999, fearing oil income would be siphoned off by corruption or diverted from poverty alleviation projects. The revenue law, passed in January 1999, mandated that 85% of the oil earnings be dedicated to national health, education, agricultural and infrastructure projects; 5% was to go to the producing region of Doba, and another 10% was reserved for "future generations," deposited directly in a blocked account at Citibank in London, under control of the World Bank. Déby demanded the World Bank release funds deposited in the London account after parliament changed the basic oil revenue distribution law. The bank suspended loans and ordered the account that collected oil revenues to be frozen; the president responded by threatening to cut off oil deliveries before a compromise was reached with the Bank in April 2006 agreeing to allow some loans to Chad.

At this time after the attack on Adré (and while Déby was seeking access to funds offshore), the president's opponents continued their efforts to overthrow the regime. The government announced it had thwarted an attempted military coup in March, and less than a month later, FUC re-launched military action from the east, this time aiming directly at N'Djaména. Another column of Sudanese-supported rebels, driving the inevitable Toyotas, entered Chad in the south, after having passed through the Central African Republic.

With the danger of regime collapse apparent, France, with some 1,200 soldiers stationed in Chad, acted to prevent the inevitable chaos that would occur if the capital fell. French intelligence and logistical assistance helped the government fight off the attacking rebels and protect the city of N'Djaména. Following its military defeat, FUC's coalition fragmented along ethnic lines.

A triumphal Déby proceeded to carry out presidential elections in May of 2006, but the main opposition refused to put up a candidate and was unanimous in calling on citizens to boycott the election. Déby faced four relatively unknown opponents, and none gathered more than 10% of the vote. Chad's Constitutional Council officially reported that 53% of registered voters had participated and that the president received nearly 65% of the ballots.

In December 2006, Déby negotiated and agreement with the FUC leader, Mahamat Nour Abdelkerim. Nour entered the government as minister of defense and two of his commanders were also given ministerial positions. Thousands of FUC combatants were to be integrated into the Chadian army, bringing considerable knowledge of the hills and caves of eastern Chad where rebels so often seek refuge.

In early 2008, new groups of rebels emerged to attack the capital N'Djamena, in an attempt to overthrow Déby. After coming within just miles of the presidential palace (and after being repulsed in part by shows of support for Déby by French troops), the rebellion seemed to falter, leaving about 1,000 injured and probably over 100 dead. While it ultimately failed to overthrow Déby, this surge of violence resulted in a worsening humanitarian crisis, as thousands of Chadians fled across the southern border into Cameroon. To further complicate matters, the Justice and Equality Movement of Sudanese rebels (who fight the Sudanese government and Illies across the border in Darfur) dispatched reinforcements from their sanctuary in eastern Chad to support Déby. This clarified the common interests between

Chad

Déby and the Sudanese rebels, and between the Sudanese government and the Chadian rebels.

After a brief lull in the fighting that followed the signing of a peace accord between the two neighboring countlies in early 2008, Chadian and Sudanese fighters began fighting again in May 2008. Diplomatic and economic relations between the two countries were cut off, and the border was militarized. That as many as 30,000 Chadians fled *into* the war-torn region of Darfur (Sudan) was a suggestion of the degree of social displacement occurring in the country. In November 2009, the International Red Cross and five other international aid organizations suspended work in the eastern region of Chad due to fears of abduction and issues of safety with their workers after a French employee was seized.

In May 2009, two months after the ICC issued an arrest warrant against the Sudanese president, Omar al-Bashir, for crimes against humanities in Darfur, the governments of Chad and Sudan agreed to a cessation of hostilities. A noteworthy shift occurred in February 2010, when President Deby met with Sudanese leader Omar al-Bashir in the Sudanese capital of Khartoum. It was their first meeting in six years and an attempt to begin to normalize ties; the leaders agreed to both support and monitor their shared border. In March, Chad agreed to let UN peacekeeping forces (known by the acronym MINURCAT) continue work for two additional months beyond their initial scheduled departure in mid-March. This was despite descriptions of the mission as a failure. In May 2010, at Chad's request, the UN Security Council unanimously voted to begin a full withdrawal of more than 4,000 peacekeepers with the final withdrawal scheduled to begin in October 2010.

The Endurance of Autocracy and State Weakness (2010s-present)

In 2011, Chad celebrated 50 years of Independence with parliamentary and presidential elections. The fracIpposition performed poorly and blamed the government's dominance of the media in the run-up to the parliamentary election in February. Nonetheless, some international observers held that the election was reasonably free and fair. President Déby's MPS took 113 of 188 seats, and 12 seats won by coalition partners brought the government to a total of 125. The remaining seats were distributed over more than two-dozen other parties. In response to the parliamentary deflading opposition candidates and parties boycotted the pIdential poll in which Déby took 84%I vote over token oppositioIMI, several people including an opposition MP were arrested in a coup attempt against President Déby. A few months later in October, Amnesty International, a London-based rights group, accused Déby's regime of illegally detaIning Ind killing critics.

Some of the big issues in Chadian politics in recent years have taken place or have origins outside of the country's borders. One is the issue of Chadian ex-President Hissene Habré, who had been sentenced to death *in absentia* for crimes against humanity during his time in office. In July of 2011, Senegal refused to repatriate the president, and in March 2012, the International Court for Justice took a role in the extradition case. Finally, in 2013, Senegal agreed to conduct a trial of Habré in a special purpose court known as the Extraordinary African Chambers. While the proceedings are forthcoming, this is seen as a potential precedent of African governments solving African problems of justice and impunity.

Chad has also been affected by the Arab Spring from its neighbors to the north, providing new challenges and risks for the temporarily stable country. Libya's revolution has threatened Chad's economic stability, as Col. Qaddafi was a supporter and benefactor of President Déby, a relationship not likely to be continued by Libya's new leaders. Tuareg nomads who had fought for the Libyan cause in 2011 are now returning south with some entering Chad. These fighters bring with them military and guerilla knowledge, potential weapons, and the possibility of partnership with the Muslims of the north, especially al-Qaeda in the Islamic Maghreb (AQIM).

The cross-border relations have also moved in the opposite direction, with Chadian troops playing a role in conflicts in both Mali and the Central African Republic. In Mali, Chadians assisted French troops who expelled Islamist militants from population centers. In the Central African Republic, troops from Chad moved in to attempt to stabilize the country following a coup that toppled that country's president. However, on April 16, 2014, all Chadian peacekeeping forces withdrew from the Central African Republic after allegations of aiding Muslim rebels and opening fire without provocation in Bangui on March 29, 2014. The instability around Chad's borders is clearly an ongoing dilemma for a country that is itself barely making steps towards its own domestic tranquility.

CONTEMPORARY THEMES

Chad is one of the poorest countries in the world and its social statistics are grim: Out of every 1,000 children born, 90 will die at birth and life expectancy is less than 50 years; furthermore, only 35.4% of the population over 15 years of age is literate. Misery has made the Sahel's thousands of unemployed easy targets for recruiters from extremist groups, further demonstrating the risks involved with the migration of the Tuaregs from Libya.

Cotton and livestock have traditionally been the country's principal moneymakers, but economic development has been irregular and inconsistent, characterized by alternations of growth and decline brought on by drought, civil war, and continuing political instability. Cotton is the main export crop and, until 2002, Chad's most lucrative source of income. Cotton fields cover 10% of Chad's cultivated land. Annual production varies between 150,000 and 200,000 tons, but the value of cotton exports has declined significantly. In 1999, cotton represented 43% of exports but dropped to 28% in 2002. In 2007, world cotton prices had reached their lowest level since the Great Depression of the 1930s. Livestock overtook cotton as the country's major source of income in 2002. There are 14 million head of livestock in Chad, including six million cattle, more than seven million sheep and goats, and over a million camels. Nearly 40% of the population is engaged in the livestock sector, which contributes about 20% of Chad's GDP. Cross-border smugglers, it is estimated, deprive the Chadian economy of close to two-thirds of its potential livestock taxes. Additionally, a rise in water temperatures in the nearby Gulf of Guinea has shifted the flow of rain clouds southwards and precipitation levels are low. Livestock are dying and long-term overgrazing and fast population growth have made the problem worse.

Economic development and poverty alleviation in Chad rest on oil production from southern oil fields at Doba. As of January 2009, reserves were estimated at 1.5 billion barrels, though Esso-Chad, the U.S.-Malaysian consortium, has announced another productive field near Timbré in southern Chad. Before that field comes online, peak production has been projected to double from present levels, eventually reaching 250,000 barrels per day. The crude oil from 315 wells is transported through a 650-mile pipeline to an offshore marine terminal near Kribi, Cameroon.

China's penetration of the Chadian oil industry illustrates the flexibility of ideology and subtlety of practice that guides its resource-acquisition policy. In contrast to neighboring Sudan, where Chinese state corporations have explored and developed oil fields, built a pipeline, and constructed refineries, in Chad, one of the few countries that maintained diplomatic relations with Taiwan, Beijing quietly bought shares of private companies that already possessed exploration and development

Chad

rights there. In 2003, for example, China National Petroleum Corp. (CNPC) and a subsidiary of China International Trust and Investment Corporation, Citic Resources Holdings, bought 50% of Swiss-based Cliveden Petroleum. Cliveden held a 50% share of an exploration concession covering 108 million acres in all of Chad's potential oil basins.

In August 2006, the Chadian government pragmatically decided to sever ties with Taiwan and reestablished diplomatic links with Beijing. Chinese Foreign Minister Li Zhaoxing was the first major leader to visit the country in January 2007, and before he left, he had cancelled much of Chad's debt to China and signed off on a "preferential loan" of some $26 million, plus a variety of other economic and development agreements.

Chad had the world's fastest growing economy in 2004, registering a one-time bump in GDP growth of 31%. Unfortunately, nearly all that growth occurred in the oil sector, and left poverty untouched. Moreover, by 2007 (after the uptick in investment), Chad had one of Africa's worst-performing economies (see "The Future" below). Chadians wonder where the benefits of oil production have gone when 80% of the population still has no access to drinking water, and when 34% of all children below the age of five are malnourished. One explanation is corruption: after oil revenues began to flow in 2004, Chad dropped precipitously on Transparency International's corruption perceptions index. Chad is currently experiencing an oil boom, but recent changes to rules regarding the spending of oil revenue have been extremely controversial. Chad is ranked as the world's most corrupt state in 2014.

Holding on to power secured from his father, General Mahamat Idriss Derby won 61 percent of the vote for the presidency In May 2024, but with major opposition leaders led by former Prime Minister Suces Masra claiming widespread vote rigging and outright suppression of political opponents who were prevented from running.

Similar results occurred in elections to parliament conducted in December 2024 as President Mahamat Idriss Deby's party, the Patriotic Salvation Movement, secured 124 of the 188 seats at the National Assembly while opposition parties continued their boycott. With the participation rate of only 51 percent of the electorate, opposition parties claimed this demonstrated voter doubts about the validity of the contest while the Deby's party portrayed the election as the last stage of the country's transition to democracy following the establishment of military rule in 2021. Also occurring were municipal and regional elections, the first in more than a decade, that reportedly pave the way for an era of decentralization "so long-awaited and desired by the Chadian people," this according to an official government statement. With the parliamentary election boycotted by more than 10 opposition parties, this included the main Transformers party, whose candidate, Succes Masra, came second in the presidential election, as opponents called the election a "charade" and expressed worries that it would be a repeat of the presidential vote, which election observers said was not credible. Chad also continues to confront many national security challenges, including attacks in the Lake Chad region by the Boko Haram armed group. Security forces also foiled an apparent attack on the presidency that the government referred to as a "destabilization attempt" with 19 fatalities.

FUTURE CONSIDERATIONS

The instability in Chad in many ways is a reflection of the instability in its neighbor to the east, Sudan. In 2010 and 2011, the conflict between the countries seems to have subsided, as seen in the back-and-forth meetings between the two presidents. Both presidents have notorious reputations (with Bashir currently an international criminal), but seem to have found common ground in restabilizing relations.

One could see the absence of Chadian unity in terms of a north/south division. Northerners are Arabized pastoralists with a long warrior tradition. Southerners are sedentary and Christianized, long subject to slaving raids by their northern neighbors. In reality, Chad's conflicts have as much to do with a vision of power and the nature of the state. Once lodged in N'Djaména, the group in power imposes a centralized view of the state and its authority, snuffing out resistance and denying individuality. In a situation where there are more than 200 different ethnic groups to be satisfied, a more reasonable course might involve greater decentralization and localized autonomy. But the central government has usually rejected federalism, seeing it as a loss of power and control over the meager resources available.

Stability in Chad would seem to be necessary for economic opportunity, but not sufficient. President Déby has maintained a fragile, Is intermittent, peace. Armed rebels have been offered amnesty and integration into the national armed forIposition political parties have been co-opted and their leaders given ministerial appointments. But as soon as one group reconciles with the government, a discontented faction hiIf, or another group seems to spring up. The Déby regime is still lacking in legitimacy and seemingly reliant upon tolerance of corruption to stay in power. One way that Déby has been able to stay in power so long is the state control of the press and rejection of dissenting views in the media. EveI the recent boom in oil prices has given only a modest booIo the economy, which was estimated to grow at just over 4% in 2010. Oil dependence also renders Chad's economy susceptible to the commodity's volatile price. The benefits of petroleum investment have had apparently little spillover into other industries, and Chad remains a country characterized by deep

Chad

and persistent poverty. Chad is thus a country that seems to have the advantage of certain natural resources, but the troubles of being trapped with a poor regime, poor governance, and poor neighbors.

Chad has been very instrumental in the fight against Boko Haram. Chadian forces have been able to defeat and pursue Boko Haram fighters into northeastern Nigerian towns of Damasak and Bago. This helped the Nigerian government's offensive in February 2015 to dislodge the militant group of places they had captured and occupied in the past. However, Chadian leadership has expressed frustration as a result of the lack of cooperation with the previous government of Goodluck Jonathan. With President Muhammadu Buhari in office in May 2015, and the move of the Boko Haram command center from Abuja to Maidugari, the epicenter of Boko Haram atrocities in the Borno state of northeastern Nigeria, we can expect more coordination between the two state in the fight and dismantling of Boko Haram.

The Republic of Congo

The hazards of the highway

Photo by G. Philippart de Foy
Courtesy APFT-ULB

BASIC FACTS

Area: 342,000 sq. km. (slightly smaller than Montana)
Population: 5,677,493 (June 2023 est.)
Capital City: Brazzaville
Government Type: Presidential Republic
Neighboring Countries: Gabon (west); Cameroon (northwest); Central African Republic (north); Democratic Republic of the Congo (east, south); Angola (southwest)
Official Language: French
Other principal Languages: Lingala and Munoukutuba (a Kikongo-based creole); both are lingua franca trade languages. Many local langIs and dialects (of which Kikongo has the most users).
Ethnic Groups: Kongo 48%, Sangha 20%, M'Bochi 12%, Teke 17%.
Principal Religions: Christian 50%, animist 48%, Islam 2%
Former Colonial Status: French Congo (1883–1910); French Equatorial Africa (1910–1960)
Independence Date: August 15, 1960
GDP (IMF 2023 est.): $2,584 (nominal), $5,155 (PPP)
Gini Index: 47.3 (World Bank 2013)
Currency: CFA, 1 USD = 594 Congolese francs (Apr. 2023)
Inflation Rate: 2.7% (2022 est.)
Chief Commercial Products: Oil, wood products and timber, potash, palm oil, cocoa, bananas, peanuts
Foreign Direct Investments (FDI) net inflows: 5,502,260,247
Literacy Rate: 80.6% (CIA 2021)
Life Expectancy: 62.51 years (CIA 2023 est.)
Head of State: Denis Sassou-Nguesso, President (since October 25, 1997)
Head of Government: Prime Minister Clement Mouamba, President (since 2016)

LAND AND PEOPLE

This fertile land lies immediately to the north of the great Congo River. Formerly a part of French Equatorial Africa, the country has the same general geographical features as Congo (Kinshasa) to the south. A low-lying, treeless plain extends 30 miles from the coast to the interior, succeeded by a mountainous region parallel to the coastline known as the Mayombe Escarpment. This is a region of sharply rising mountain ridges covered with jungle and dense growth. Further to the east extends the Niari River Valley, an important agricultural area, and to the north lies The Pool, a region of treeless hills and a succession of grassy plains, covers some 50,000 square miles. Part of Ihe Congo River Basin lies in the extreme northeast, a region If dense jungle and all but impassable plains. The climate is uniform and equatorial—hot and humid all year. NASA satellite data in 2014 has shown that there has been a "large-scale decline" in greenness in the Congo rain forest as the result of drought. This has a potential impact on the quantity of rainforest in Congo.

As in most of Sub-Saharan Africa, storytelling is the common way of recapitulating history in Congo, and stories are sung during common tasks and chores). A prominent form of music is the Congolese rumba.

Tribal patterns dominate the social life of the Republic of Congo. Although discrimination is legally prohibited, tens of thousands of indigenous Pygmy people, living largely in the northern forest regions, have the social status of modern-day slaves; many have Bantu masters to whom they are obligated from birth. The Congo's most important human rights organization, the *Observatoire congolais des droits de l'homme* (OCDH), has criticized the government for failing to issue the indigenous pygmies identity cards or register their births. (Symptomatically, the legislature passed a law in August 2006 affirming the right of pygmies to vote.) OCDH has also documInted significant numbers of indigenous pygmy women who have been victims of rape by Bantu men. According to the *Observatoire* spokesman, there were also cases of gang rapes, and "even of rapes perpetrated in police offices by the very people charged with protecting the population."

HISTORY TO PRESENT DAY

For early history, see *Historical Background and The Colonial Period: The French.*

French Colonialism and Post-Independence

Under the leadership of Félix Éboué, a black colonial administrator, French Equatorial Africa rallied to General Charles de Gaulle during World War II. A grateful de Gaulle made Éboué governor-general of FEA and honored the federation's capital by gathering colonial administrators for the Brazzaville Conference of 1944 to discuss postwar colonial reforms.

Following World War II, Congo was given a territorial assembly and representation in the French parliament, which

Congo

increased both political awareness and activity in the colony. With General de Gaulle's Fifth French Republic, Congo became an autonomous republic within the Franco-African Community in 1958 and opted for full independence in 1960.

The Abbé Fulbert Youlou, a Catholic priest instrumental in charting the course toward independence, was installed as president in 1960. His party, *Union Démocratique pour la Défense des Intérêts Africains* (UDDIA) drew its strength from southern peoples who had benefited most from colonial education and opportunity. The party advocated private ownership and close ties with France, but corruption, incompetence, massive labor unrest, and lack of French support led to a coup and Youlou's ouster in 1963. The three-day revolution was referred to as the "Trois Glorieuses"—mimicking the Parisian events of 1830.

Marxism under the MNR (1963–1989)

His successor, Alphonse Massamba-Débat, took inspiration from French Marxism, and created the National Revolutionary Movement (MNR) as the country's single party. Congo became a "people's republic" with a red flag and the *Internationale* as its anthem. Socialist-inspired economic policies ensued for the next 25 years.

Continuing north-south regional tension and administrative incapacity led the military to replace Massamba-Débat with Major Marien Ngouabi in 1968. Ngouabi maintained the socialist line, insisting that Marxism was a "universal science." He renamed the country the People's Republic of the Congo and replaced the MRN with the Congolese Labor Party (PCT) as the country's sole political party. With Ngouabi, a northerner, power shifted away from traditional power centers in the south. In highly politicized Brazzaville and other southern cities, opposition soon developed among both student and labor groups.

President Ngouabi was assassinated in March 1977; a military tribunal was hastily convened, which quickly accused and convicted Massambat-Débat of being behind the killing. He was executed and an 11-man military committee took control. Ngouabi's military successor, Col. Joachim Yhombi-Opango, lasted two years before he was at odds with the PCT.

In 1979, Yhombi-Opango handed over the presidency to the PCT, which selected Col. Denis Sassou-Nguesso as his successor. More politically attuned than his predecessors, Sassou-Nguesso maintained a delicate political balance among the leading political groups—the army, the trade unions, and Marxist intellectuals. Despite being the representative of the PCT's more militant wing, Sassou-Nguesso moderated the regime's Marxist rhetoric and established better relations with Western countries. With the fall of the Berlin Wall, Sassou-Nguesso began the task of dismantling Congolese Marxism.

The Republic of Congo and the Civil War (1990s)

The government dropped the party membership requirement for government Officials in 1990 and drafted a new constitution establishing a multiparty system. The country became "The Republic of Congo." In the March 1992 referendum, the new constitution was adopted, which provided for new multiparty elections. Ultimately, 14 political parties participated. The *Union Panafricaine pour la Démocratie Sociale* (UPADS), led by Pascal Lissouba (Massamba-Débat's prime minister), won 39 of the 125 assembly seats. In August Lissouba was elected president, defeating Sassou-Nguesso. Former president Sassou-Nguesso was granted amnesty for any acts committed during his years in office, but he refused to step aside completely.

The legislative elections of 1992 were inconclusive, and the coalition government that resulted lasted only until late 1992. New elections were held and were closely contested: President Lissouba's party won a razor-thin majority of 65 out of 125 seats in the National Assembly, and a period of shaky parliamentary government ensued.

Political opponents organized private militias to oppose the government and President Lissouba created his own personal militia, to avoid any reliance on the national army. Each of the militias had its own distinctive, colorful, and threatening name. Bernard Kolélas, the charismatic mayor of Brazzaville, had the "Ninjas." Sassou-Nguesso's were "Cobras," and President Lissouba's militia were the "Zulus." In 1997, conflict broke out in Brazzaville as the government moved to eliminate Sassou-Nguesso's Cobras militia.

President Denis Sassou-Nguesso

As the Cobras gained strength, Lissouba ordered more than $60 million in arms. Desperate for cash, Lissouba began discussions with an American oil company, and promptly lost the support of the French who refused to aid him against the forces of Sassou-Nguesso. Lissouba later charged that Sassou-Nguesso was supported by money coming from France's state oil giant Elf. Sassou-Nguesso also received interventionist support of Angolan forces. (Under Lissouba, Congo had become a launching pad for Cabindan rebels and a place through which Jonas Savimbi could sell the diamonds used to finance UNITA's war against the Angolan government.)

In the battle of the warlords Brazzaville was bombed and targeted by mortars, laid waste by internecine strife. Lissouba lost and fled into exile as Sassou-Nguesso's forces seized the capital. Elf returned to its damaged skyscraper office building and offered to contribute significantly to the rebuilding of Brazzaville, while Angolan forces established a seemingly permanent presence in the Congo.

Denis Sassou-Nguesso's bloody conquest of Brazzaville did not end Congo's civil conflict. The civil war continued in the south throughout most of 1999. Pointe-Noire, Congo's economic capital, was virtually cut off from the rest of the country. Water and electricity supplies were disrupted by rebel activity. Some 800,000 people in the south were dislocated, many fleeing to the forest to escape the depredations of the rebels, the government, and its allies. Supported by Angolan troops and helicopter gunships, as well as by remnants of the Hutu *Interahamwe* from Rwanda and a few Chadian and DR Congo fighters, government troops turned the tide of battle against the rebels by mid-year—not without compiling a horrific human rights record.

By the end of 1999, offers of amnesty and integration into government security forces in exchange for disarmament had secured cease-fire agreements with major militia commanders. Soon after, President Sassou-Nguesso managed a "national dialogue" that brought together representatives of the government, the internal and external opposition, plus other political groups and civic organizations.

Consolidation of Power under Denis Sassou-Nguesso (2000s)

President Omar Bongo of Gabon (who had married Sassou-Nguesso's daughter in 1990) mediated the process, and delegates focused on producing a draft constitution and preparing follow-up elections. Although billed as "all-inclusive," the national convention carefully excluded former president Pascal Lissouba and his last

Congo

prime minister, Bernard Kolélas. Having been sentenced to death (*in absentia*) by Congolese judicial authorities, the two men were, said the government, ineligible to take part in the deliberations.

The draft constitution that emerged—tailored to the style and personality of Denis Sassou-Nguesso—featured a strong presidential regime. The president of the republic, elected for a seven-year term—with one renewable mandate—would wield exclusive executive power extensively. He would, for example, appoint the prime minister and could not be impeached by parliament; he could also reject its legislation and rule by decree.

In January 2002 the new constitution was approved by referendum—84% of those voting, according to government figures. Despite the calls by opposition parties to boycott the vote, the government announced that 78% of all registered voters participated in the balloting. (Sassou-Nguesso needed massive support to legitimize his assumption of power through force of arms.)

With Lissouba and Kolélas excluded, and the principal remaining opposition candidate withdrawing at the last minute, the presidential election was held in March 2002. To no one's surprise, Denis Sassou-Nguesso was the victor—garnering 89.4% of the vote. None of the six other candidates won as much as 3%. Reports of low voter-turnout notwithstanding, the interior minister released hardly credible figures indicating 74.7% of the electorate had participated in the poll. Sassou-Nguesso used these estimates to tout his legitimacy.

With a resurgence of militia violence in the south—remnants of the Kolélas' Ninjas, now operating under the leadership of Rev. Frédéric Bitsangou, better known as Pasteur Ntoumi—legislative elections scheduled for April 2002 were postponed to May. When the National Assembly races were over, the president's PCT had won 53 seats and the *Forces démocratiques unies* (FDU: United Democratic Forces)—a coalition of parties supporting him—30, a clear majority in the 153-member house.

The elections brought neither stability nor security. Pasteur Ntoumi's Ninjas continued their depredations in the Pool region and even managed to attack the vital rail link between Brazzaville and Pointe-Noire and bring commercial traffic to a standstill. In conducting its campaign against the rebels, the Congolese army seemed oblivious to both professionalism and human rights.

In March 2003, the government and Ninja rebels signed an agreement to end the crisis in the Pool region. Pasteur Ntoumi agreed to end hostilities, disarm his fighters, and help the state to reestablish its authority in the area. In return, the government agreed to extend amnesty to the Ninjas and reintegrate some of their members into the national army.

That the government's commitment to the peace accord was hypocritical seemed obvious when it asked Pasteur Ntoumi for a list of 250 rebels to be integrated into the armed forces. The rebel leader rejected the proposal, calling the government's quota "a drop in the ocean." In reaction, he indicated he would only disarm his militiamen when the government opened up political space, forming a government of national unity in which his *Conseil national de la résistance* (CNR) could take part. The disarmament, demobilization and reintegration program (DDR)—administered by the UN Development Program and financed by the EU—made minimal progress. From 2001 to 2004, the government only demobilized some 9,000 ex-combatants.

In January 2006, the World Bank and IMF granted the government $17 million to disarm, demobilize and reintegrate 30,000 former combatants into the country's social fabric. Five years after signing a peace agreement thousands of Ninjas still await integration into the military or assistance returning to civilian life. The Pool area remains rife with weapons—between 37,000 and 40,000 according to one Swiss NGO. Incentives to surrender weapons have failed because the Ninjas have been required to turn them into officials in Brazzaville and fear reprisal if seen with their weapons. Left in the hands of the unemployed, the weapons pose a continuing security threat, and an easy resort to occasional banditry.

In the July 2009 presidential elections, the Constitutional Court had previously ruled out a leading contender, former prime minister Ange Edouard Poungui of the UPADS party (Lissouba's former party), on the grounds that he had not resided continuously in the country for the last two years. This left former finance minister Matthias Dzon of the ARD (*Alliance pour la République et la Démocratie*) as the leading opposition candidate. Various political parties boycotted the elections, and the result was another display of Sassou-Nguesso's control over Congo's fragile political system. Sassou-Nguesso claimed 78.6% of the vote, independent candidate Joseph Kignoumbi Kia Mboungou came in second with 7.46%, and Matthias Dzon gained only 2.3%. The election saw roughly 2,000 opposition supporters peacefully protesting on the streets of Brazzaville, with riot police reacting with tear gas. The official turnout of voters was reported as 66.42%. Although the head of the African Union observers, Dieudonne Kumbo Yaya, reported that his team was unaware of any fraud surrounding the election, this is a contested account. Various news correspondents reported witnessing accounts of fraud, ranging from money being handed out at polling stations to a lack of available voting cards. Sassou-Nguesso was ultimately able to extend his rule for another seven years, with considerable public discontent. Despite the lack of democracy Sassou-Nguesso's regime has experienced a period of relative stability.

A tragic accident in 2012 was when a fire broke out at a massive ammunition depot in Brazzaville. The explosion and resulting fires killed over 250 people and injured over 2,000 more. The explosion was so large it was seen and heard across the massive Congo River in Kinshasa, miles away. In October of 2012, defense minister Charles Zacharie Bowao was dismissed after an investigation found him to be accountable for the incident.

CONTEMPORARY THEMES

The object of armed struggle in Congo is the state's oil revenue, about 70% of state income and 94% of all its export earnings. (Timber exports produce the remaining export income.) From 65,000 bbl/d in 1980, oil production has risen to peaks of about 280,000 bbl/d. Congo is sub-Saharan Africa's sixth largest producer—after Nigeria, Angola, Egypt, Sudan, and Equatorial Guinea. Mostly conducted offshore, the oil sector was virtually untouched by the events of the civil war, compared to the severe damage that occurred in the rest of the economy.

At least 20,000 people were killed in the various phases of the war, and 800,000 people were displaced. Half of Congo's agricultural output was destroyed, particularly in the south where the richest agricultural land is located. Some 75% of the country's livestock was also destroyed. Congo's highly urbanized population, especially in Brazzaville, has felt the impact deeply. Since 1997, the percentage of the urban population below the poverty line has increased from 30% to 70% (2004). Half the population is unemployed, and life expectancy is only 58.52 years (2014).

Reduced conflict has allowed the government to reopen railroad service between Brazzaville and Pointe-Noire and dredge the port of Pointe-Noire, the government has invested $30 million in repairing the Congo-Ocean railroad linking Brazzaville and Pointe-Noire.

Reopening the Congo River, the railroad, and the port, all significantly benefit the timber industry. After oil, timber is Congo's most important source of income. There are two main areas of commercially

Congo

exploitable forests in Congo. In the south, forests cover more than 11 million acres, and by 1995, nearly 10 million acres were held as logging concessions. In the more isolated north, there are 22 million acres of commercially useful forests, but exploitation there has been much slower given transport difficulties.

During the war when river and rail traffic was curtailed, loggers in the north had to ship their timber by road via Cameroon to Douala, adding considerably to their costs. Normally, they would have floated logs downriver to the main river port of Brazzaville and then on to Pointe-Noire by train. In August 2006, President Sassou-Nguesso announced the continuing expansion of logging operations in Congo: from 1 million cubic meters in 2005, production increased to 1.5 million cubic meters in 2006.

The reality of Congo's diamond resources is totally uncertain, especially after the country was suspended in mid-2004 from participation in the Kimberley Process Certification Scheme, designed to keep illicit diamonds from the market. At best around 50,000 carats are produced annually, almost exclusively by individual miners. When the country's annual exportation figures of three million to five million carats could not be explained to a visiting Kimberley mission, Congo's participation was suspended, and the mission concluded that its entire production was illicit.

Given the terrible damage inflicted by years of civil war, investors are hesitant about placing money in the Congo. The country's biggest problem is finding the resources to repair infrastructure and productive capacity—estimated at nearly $2 billion. China has entered Congo's oil sector, long a French preserve, by granting loans through its Export-Import Bank that are paid back in oil. In 2003, for example, it advanced $238 million—85% of total estimated costs—to build a hydroelectric dam at Imboulou, some 133 miles north of Brazzaville, where the Congo and Kasai rivers meet.

Government deficits over the years created a huge total debt of $8.57 billion as of mid-2005—one of the world's highest per capita debt burdens. In 2007, major donors cancelled some 80% of Congo's foreign debt. In 2010, the Paris Club canceled $2.4 billion dollars of the Congo's debt. In 2013, Brazil stated that it would cancel or restructure its debt with Congo. The government did not help its image for financial restraint when the president hired 3,450 new civil servants in 2004, adding to an already-bloated 70,000 government employees. Nevertheless, following publication of audits of both SNPC and the government's oil revenues, the IMF expressed "guarded optimism" about Congo's economic and political situation and cautiously extended some $84 million in December 2004. The president then ousted finance minister Roger Andely in a January 2005 cabinet reshuffle; Andely had almost single-handedly been responsible for the transparency in oil accounts that led to IMF funding the month before. One year later, in January 2006, Prime Minister Isidore Myouba admitted the obvious: Congo did indeed conceal part of its oil revenues, sometimes using "unorthodox methods." They were justified, he argued, to protect Congo from "vulture creditors." In 2006, the IMF delayed relief to the country due to the allegations concerning corruption.

Whether or not additional funding will be forthcoming is questionable. The Publish What You Pay coalition says that $300 million of Congo's $1-billion oil revenues in 2004 simply evaporated, and independent auditors trying to make sense of the books were refused SNPC records. Global Witness, another close observer of the industry, has long argued that people close to President Sassou-Nguesso have profited from corrupt practices within the industry. In 2009, the French branch of Transparency International filed a complaint against Sassou-Nguesso and the presidents of Gabon and Equatorial Guinea, which accused the three of inappropriately acquiring real estate in France worth millions of dollars and embezzling public money for private use. In May 2009, a French judge announced that in relation to these corruption charges, an investigation would take place. However, the case was eventually halted in October 2009 due to the inability of the civil society groups to act as plaintiffs.

AIDS has appeared in Congo in the wake of civil disturbance and disruption. Nationally, government figures indicate 3.4% of the active population is HIV positive. Infection rates are higher in the southern provinces (with Pointe-Noire having an estimated rate of 5%) and among women. According to armed forces health officials, AIDS is the number one cause of death in the Congolese armed forces, a toll partially attributable to soldiers' frequenting of sex workers.

Unlike some of its neighbors, Congo has a relatively strong tradition of urbanization. One-sixth of the population has traditionally lived in the two principal cities, Brazzaville and Pointe-Noire. As a consequence, the country has one of the highest literacy rates in Black Africa, estimated at nearly 83%, though female literacy is generally lower—about 77%. Also related to this urban tradition is the relatively high percentage of Christians in the population—mostly Roman Catholic—and the early development of labor unions.

Major problems include widespread under- and unemployment with 75 percent of the workforce either self-employed or holding low-productivity jobs, a situation that has led to periodic unrest and tragic cases such as a stampede of people at the site of an army recruitment drive that resulted in 31 deaths in November 2023 With current 80-year-old President Neguseo seeking another term in office. In elections scheduled for 2026, opposition parties are gearing up to challenge his three-decades rule but with virtually no seats in the parliament and fears of potential massive vote rigging.

An attempted coup in May 2024 led by dissident Christian Malaga and evidently involving several Americans, including his son Marcel, was thwarted even as the coup plotters were able to breach the presidential palace.

Three opposition parties in the Republic of Congo have met for their first convention as a coalition to outline the group's goals ahead of the 2026 elections so they can unseat President Denis Nguesso, who has been in power since 1997. The Alliance for Democratic Alternation in

A marginalized minority, the indigenous Pygmy people of Congo's forest areas. This photo shows a group of Baka/Batwa children in an Ibamba village. ©Andrew Itoua/IRIN

Congo

202 is made up of the Democracy and Development party of former President Jacques Joachim Yhomby Opango, the Movement of Republicans, and the People's Party. The parties have grassroots support but no seats in parliament but have addressed the issue of political prisoners as a way to ease the political climate and promote social cohesion and national unity. Opposition figures have been found guilty of undermining internal state security after the 2016 elections when following the polling violence broke out after the opposition accused Nguesso, who had won 67 percent of the votes cast, of rigging the poll. The opposition coalition was launched with the aim of bringing change to a political landscape dominated by Nguesso. The 80-year-old president is set to run for a fifth term.

FUTURE CONSIDERATIONS

Oil output will rise over the next few years as new fields come online. The result has been several economic boom years, with growth around 7% in 2006, 2007, and again in 2009 (with one year's downturn in 2008 during the global economic crisis). French oil giant Total has already indicated its Moho-Bilondo field began production in 2008. Economically, Congo has potential and will benefit from high demand for natural resources in international markets. In February of 2013 Congo agreed to comply with the Extractive Industries Transparency Initiative (EITI) standards and disclose revenues from oil. The EITI provides countries with grants so that they can improve their governance and transparency concerning oil exploration and extraction. The EITI claims that the quality of reports from Congo has improved since 2013 when they first signed the agreement. While this is a step forward for transparency in Congo, it is too early to tell whether or not this will have a significant impact on the economy.

On the other hand, the political system remains disastrous. Increased oil revenues will not make the government any more democratic. Local human rights campaigners will continue to have risky careers. The invitation extended by Denis Sassou-Nguesso to former adversary Pascal Lissouba to return to Congo may have signaled a shift in the political winds towards some reconciliation, but Lissouba has not returned to Congo and has remained in exile in London. Electoral politics in Congo continues to be characterized by a lack of civil protections and the absence of democracy.

The Democratic Republic of the Congo

Kinois view the body of a policeman killed in faction fighting, August 2006. © Lionel Healing/AFP/Getty Images

BASIC FACTS

Area: 2,344,858 sq. km. (larger than Alaska, or roughly the size of Western Europe)
Population: 111,859,928 (June 2023 est.)
Capital City: Kinshasa
Government Type: Semi-Presidential Republic
Neighboring Countries: Congo (northwest); Central African Republic, South Sudan (north); Uganda, Rwanda, Burundi and Tanzania (east); Zambia and Angola (south)
Official Language: French
Other Principal Languages: Over 200 African languages are spoken. Most prominent are Kikongo, Lingala (a lingua franca trade language), Swahili, and Tshiluba (or Luba).
Ethnic Groups: Over 200 African ethnic groups of which the majority are Bantu; the four largest peoples—Mongo, Luba, Kongo and the Mangbetu-Azande make up about 45% of the population.
Principal Religions: Roman Catholicism 50%, Protestantism 20%, Kimbanguist 10%, Islam 10%, other sects and traditional beliefs 10%
Former Colonial Status: Personal possession of King Leopold II of Belgium (1885–1907); Belgian Colony (1907–1960)
Independence Date: June 30, 1960
GDP Per Capita (IMF 2023 est.): $695 (nominal), $1,447 (PPP)
Gini Index: 44.4 (World Bank 2013)
Currency: Congolese franc, $US1 = 2,041 francs (Apr. 2023)
Inflation Rate: 6.4% (2022 est.)
Chief Commercial Products: Diamonds, copper, coffee, cobalt, and crude oil
Foreign Direct Investments (FDI) net inflows: 343,601,083
Literacy Rate: 80% (CIA 2021)
Life Expectancy: 62.3 years (CIA 2023 est.)
Head of State: Félix Tshisekedi, President (since January 24, 2019)
Head of Government: Prime Minister Anatole Collinet Makosso (since May 12, 2021)

LAND AND PEOPLE

Note: This country has been known as Belgian Congo, Congo (Leopoldville), the Democratic Republic of the Congo, Zaïre, and most recently, Democratic Republic of the Congo.

The deep green region of the Congo has intrigued explorers, adventurers, and writers for centuries, becoming one of the popular stereotypes of Africa in the Western mind. Dark rain forests abounding in game adjoin huge mining developments and vast plantations, some of which have been broken down into smaller farms.

D.R. Congo

The very size of the Congo—as large as Western Europe—is one of its most distinctive features. Yet this huge nation has only a 25-mile-long coastline on the South Atlantic Ocean.

There are three distinctive features of this land mass: the immense river basin of the Congo and its tributaries, tropically hot and humid; the rich mining areas are located in the eastern sector and the upland plains in the northeast and southeast with tall grasses and mountains rising to almost 17,000 feet in the east near the Equator. The eastern lake region, which includes Lake Kivu and the western shores of lakes Tanganyika, Mweru, Albert and Edward, is unsurpassed in scenic beauty and abounds in wildlife.

Tributaries of the great Congo River flow from these lakes into the Lualaba River, which in turn becomes the Congo. From this point, the Congo surges in a wide, island-dotted course through the tropical forests, joined by its other tributaries. Three hundred miles inland from the Atlantic, at Malebo Pool (near bustling Kinshasa), the river widens into a lake, continuing on to the sea with a width of up to ten miles. The river is navigable for the most part and widely used in commerce, interrupted only by cataracts at Malebo Falls (formerly Stanley Falls) and below Kinshasa. Railway bypasses have been constructed at these cataracts to maintain the continuity of commerce.

Years of civil conflict have greatly affected the people of Congo, but the art industry has flourished in Kinshasa, and most particularly the music industry. Zairean/Congolese Soukous music, also known as Kwassa-Kwassa, originated in Kinshasa and became a popular musical sensation across Africa in the 1990s, leading many to consider Kinshasa Africa's music capital. Congolese music and dance remain popular on pan-African radio and on TV. Some foreign music has been adapted into the local rhythms to create new fusions of Congolese jazz, soukous, hip hop, and electronica. The Congotronics releases have become a worldwide sensation in recent years.

HISTORY TO PRESENT DAY

For early history, see *Historical Background* and *The Colonial Period: King Leopold and the Belgians*.

Independence and Early Problems (1957–1965)

Belgian rule in Africa was characterized by control through compulsion. Though little effort was made prior to independence to prepare the Congo for self-rule, local government reforms in 1957 presented an opportunity for political participation. Congolese *évolués*—the colony's miniscule educated elite—responded quickly. Elites from the Kongo ethnic group formed the *Alliance des Bakongo* (ABAKO) based in Léopoldville (now Kinshasa). Though ethnically based, ABAKO first articulated the demand for Congolese independence, and became a forceful voice of anticolonial protest, under the leadership of Joseph Kasavubu.

Once started, nationalist sentiments gathered enthusiastic followings. The most important multiethnic grouping dedicated to the Congo's national unity was the Congolese National Movement (MNC). With Patrice Lumumba at its head, the MNC became the most militant advocate of the colony's independence. When French Congo, across the river, was offered independence by President Charles de Gaulle in 1958, there was increased pressure on Belgium to grant independence to its colony. An impending threat of independence, coupled with tumbling world copper prices, led to a withdrawal of foreign capital from the country in the late 1950s, weakening the economy and creating widespread unemployment.

In January 1959, the Belgian administration's decision to cancel an ABAKO meeting in Léopoldville led to violent urban protests. Virtually the entire African population of the city took to the streets, and protest soon turned into looting. When finally suppressed, the Léopoldville riots officially resulted in 47 Congolese dead; in reality, many more were probably killed. Shocked by the extent and vigor of the protests, the administration advanced the timetable for independence.

In this turbulent atmosphere, Belgium summoned African leaders to Brussels in early 1960 and announced that independence would become effective on June 30. A multitude of new parties sprang up almost overnight. The intense political activity led Europeans to leave the Congo in droves. In parliamentary elections Lumumba's MNC won the greatest number of seats, but not enough to govern without coalition partners. After ten days of bargaining behind closed doors, Lumumba announced a 37-member cabinet, containing officials from no fewer than 16 parties. When independence was formally declared, Patrice Lumumba became prime minister and Joseph Kasavubu president of the renamed Democratic Republic of the Congo.

The country quickly deteriorated into lawlessness, rebellion, anarchy, revolt, and secession. Disintegration began when the *Force Publique*, Congo's army, mutinied on July 5, immediately followed by the intervention of Belgian paratroopers sent to protect the lives of Belgian citizens. Hundreds of whites were slaughtered and others beaten and tortured. The Congolese government was incapable of action, incapacitated by a lethal power struggle between Lumumba and Kasavubu, each of whom dismissed the other. Almost simultaneously Katanga, Congo's richest province, declared itself independent on July 11 under the leadership of Moïse Tshombe. On July 12, Tshombe and Kasavubu jointly appealed to the UN for assistance in restoring order.

The arrival of the UN peacekeeping force only increased the friction between President Kasavubu and Prime Minister Lumumba over the issue of Katanga's declaration of independence. Lumumba demanded that UN forces suppress the Katangese secession, by force if necessary, and Kasavubu categorically refused the idea. In September Lumumba turned to the Soviet Union for assistance in sending Congolese troops to Katanga, introducing cold-war politics into the Congo crisis. Amid further provincial secessions and increased violence, Army Chief of Staff Col. Joseph Mobutu announced on September 14 that the army would henceforth govern in association with a caretaker government headed by President Kasavubu.

President Kasavubu (center) and Premier Lumumba confer with Belgian army chief, 1960

D.R. Congo

The high way to travel — Photo by Maaike Göbel

Kasavubu decided to eliminate Lumumba once and for all. The army captured the charismatic leader in December, and Kasavubu turned him over to the self-proclaimed President of Katanga, Moïse Tshombe. Lumumba was killed shortly thereafter, with Belgian complicity and probably American and British foreknowledge.

Even though Kasavubu's sacrifice of Lumumba to the Katanga secessionists was intended to facilitate the breakaway province's return to a united Congo, the Katanga secession continued until early 1963 when Tshombe gave in to the central government. UN troops withdrew in midyear, and unrest and rebellion in the provinces continued as the central government was unable to assert its authority. From January to August 1964, rural insurgency engulfed five of Congo's 21 provinces, and in desperation President Kasavubu appointed Moïse Tshombe as premier. Ironically, the defeated secessionist used foreign mercenaries and Belgian paratroopers to put down secession and assert the central government's authority over a unified state. President Kasavubu, frightened and envious of Tshombe's growing popularity, fired him as premier, whereupon Colonel Joseph Désiré Mobutu took center stage and ousted the president in late 1965.

Africa's Quintessential "Big Man": Mobutu Sese Seko (1965–1997)

Conditions remained unstable in the eastern Congo even after Tshombe's exile and house arrest in Algeria. But General Mobutu maintained the loyalty of the army and skillfully played ethnic and political factions against each other to consolidate his control. Pressured by the U.S. and other foreign powers to hold elections, he created the Popular Movement for the Revolution (MPR: *Mouvement Populaire de la Révolution*) and was elected unopposed as president in 1970.

In 1971, Mobutu elaborated a campaign of cultural nationalism or "authenticity." He renamed the country Zaïre and himself Mobutu Sese Seko, donning a leopard skin cap as the symbol of his status and power as an African chief. Katanga became Shaba and the Congo River became the Zaïre River. Zaïriois, the citizens of the newly renamed country, were required to adopt African names.

The constitution was revised in 1974 to contain "Mobutuism," which embodied the president's thoughts and teachings. It became the required curriculum even in Zaïre's Catholic schools. Most plantations and farms owned by foreigners were nationalized, and all mineral ores had to be refined within Zaïre, even though there were insufficient facilities to perform the task.

Infrastructure deteriorated rapidly as the MPR state and its ideology of Mobutism proved inadequate to the tasks of national integration and governance. Increasingly the state was held together by little more than a web of client-patron relations sustained by state resources. The regime gave rise to the term "kleptocracy"—rule by thieves. Even in the midst of predation and decline, relative peace and stability prevailed until 1977 and 1978 when Katangan rebels based in Angola launched a series of invasions into Shaba (ex-Katanga). The rebels were driven out only with the aid of French, Belgian and Moroccan troops.

Elections in 1977 resulted in another victory for Mobutu and his party, but the legislature became meaningless as Mobutu increasingly ruled by decree. Despite dictatorship and kleptocracy, American aid continued to pour in on the theory that Zaïre was a bastion against communism. From 1965 to 1991, Zaïre received more than $1.5 billion in U.S. economic and military aid. While he was still favored by the U.S., Jonas Savimbi and UNITA, the Angolan anti-Marxist movement, received much of their assistance through Mobutu's Zaïre.

Realizing that his personal security and future were clouded, Mobutu summoned Israeli military personnel to train a presidential guard in 1982. They performed well, and the elite guard slowly became the only coherent and capable force in Zaïre. The remaining armed forces were expected to make their way by theft and corruption. Government workers were unpaid and were expected to survive the same way. Bribery and corruption became coping mechanisms for government workers. While workers scrambled to keep alive, President Mobutu became one of the richest men in the world. In 1992, according to the World Bank, 64.7% of Zaïre's budget was reserved for Mobutu's "discretionary spending." According to Transparency International, Mobutu embezzled $5 billion from his country.

With the collapse of the Eastern European socialist model, Zaïre was no longer seen as a necessary bastion against communism. Development programs were canceled, and the economy deteriorated even further. Pressure mounted to open up the political system. In April 1990, Mobutu agreed to end the ban on opposition parties and appointed a transitional government. Liberalization of the regime was, of course, illusory. May student protests at the University of Lumumbashi (ex-Elizabethville) were brutally suppressed. Anywhere from 50 to 150 students were killed, according to Amnesty International.

When soldiers threatened to rebel over unpaid wages, the government resorted

D.R. Congo

to printing more money—in higher denominations as inflation mounted—or gave them free reign to pillage and loot. In September 1991, they rioted and devastated Kinshasa. Some 2,000 French and Belgian troops had to be ferried in to evacuate 20,000 foreign nationals from the city. The president increasingly absented himself from his capital, seeking refuge in the sumptuous comfort of a fortress-palace at Gbadolite in northwest Zaïre. Conditions in the country continued to deteriorate.

Finally, after many promises and even more avoidance, Mobutu capitulated to the holding of a Sovereign National Conference in 1992. Over 2,000 representatives from various political parties and civil society attended. The conference took its "sovereign" power seriously and elected Étienne Tshisekedi, leader of the *Union pour la Démocratie et le Progrès Social* (UDPS) as prime minister.

By the end of the year, Mobutu had created a rival government with its own prime minister. Pro- and anti-Mobutu governments created a stalemate that was only broken when a compromise merged the two governments in 1994. A High Council of the Republic-Parliament of Transition (HCR-PT) was created with the resilient Mobutu as head of state. The HCR-PT repeatedly scheduled presidential and legislative elections over the next two years, but they never took place.

By now, Zaïre's economy was totally dysfunctional. So much of the state's resources had been diverted away into Mobutu's patronage network that capital investment was impossible. Several copper mines of Shaba, for example, had been flooded and idle for years. The Mobutu regime had become the mirror image of Leopold II's—personal, arbitrary, and venal.

In 1996 Mobutu traveled to Switzerland for extensive treatment of prostate cancer and died in exile in Morocco the following year. While in Switzerland, a Rwandan-backed rebel force captured much of eastern Zaïre as ethnic tensions in neighboring Rwanda suddenly engulfed Zaïre. Hutu militia forces (the *Interahamwe* driven from Rwanda in 1994) had attacked Rwanda from their Zaïre refugee camps. Despite repeated requests, the Mobutu government had done nothing to curb their violence, which quickly turned even more hostile when Hutu forces linked up with remnants of the Zaïrian armed forces (FAZ) to attack local Tutsi, the Banyamulenge, in eastern Zaïre. To prevent another genocide, Rwanda and its allies, particularly Uganda, invaded Zaïre.

Laurent Kabila (1997–2001)

Plucked from obscurity to provide a non-Tutsi face to the insurgency was the semiretired professional revolutionary Laurent Kabila. A Luba from Katanga, he had been long engaged in the anti-Mobutu struggle, but always in secondary roles. When Che Guevara arrived in eastern Zaïre, looking to spread Communist revolution beyond Cuba, he ran across Kabila and provided a contemptuous critique of his revolutionary potential. Despite being "the best of the Congolese leaders," Kabila was seen as "too addicted to drink and women," but he was available when the call to leadership came.

Once the insurgency began, there was little effective resistance. The Zaïrian army fled before the offensive; recognizing the imminent collapse of Mobutu's regime (and its opportunities for access to patronage), they had little loyalty except to themselves. The only thing that impeded Kabila's *Alliance des Forces Démocratiques pour la Libération du Congo-Zaïre* (AFDL) was the fact that there were no roads or bridges, just rutted, frequently flooded, and muddy areas that allowed trucks to pass irregularly. Because of these conditions, it took until May 1997 for the insurgent army to reach Kinshasa.

Laurent Kabila proclaimed himself president and took the oath of office on May 31, 1997. He promised democracy but said elections could not be held for two years because of the need to bring order to the country. To fit with its new aspirations, the country was once again renamed. Mobutu's Zaïre became the Democratic Republic of the Congo (DRC) once again. Laurent Kabila spent most of 1997–1998 consolidating his power.

By August 1998, it had become apparent that Kabila was little more than a mini-Mobutu. The security demands of Rwanda and Uganda were still unmet, Hutu rebels still posed threats from bases in the Congo, and enemies of the Museveni regime scampered back and forth across the border, doing damage to Ugandan citizens. Inside the Congo Banyamulenge Tutsi had little sense they would be incorporated into any national dialogue, and it became evident that Kabila was moving to place relatives and members of his own ethnic group in the most important positions of power. Nepotism was accompanied by corruption.

When Kabila sacked his Rwandan military advisors—the very people responsible for elevating him to presidential status—the crisis of confidence came to a head. A second rebellion arose in the east soon after the plane bearing the exiled advisors landed. A brilliant tactical flight to the west brought rebel forces close to the doors of Kinshasa and for a moment it looked as

D.R. Congo

Mobutu Sese Seko

though the regime was doomed. A fearful Kabila called upon his fellow authoritarians in Angola and Zimbabwe, whose presidents responded with interventionist forces. The western threat was ended and military action focused on the eastern front.

The Second Rebellion developed into Africa's first continental war. Besides Angola and Zimbabwe, Namibia, Chad, Sudan, and Libya came to the support of the Kabila government. Rwanda and Uganda supported local Congolese rebel factions. By mid-1999, the Democratic Republic of the Congo had been effectively partitioned, with the rebel coalition in control of the eastern third of the country and Laurent Kabila remaining in office by virtue of foreign arms.

Having enjoyed initial military success, the rebel forces opposing him soon fell to internal strife. The principal rebel group, the *Rassemblement Congolais pour la Démocratie* (RCD), split in two. Rwanda and Uganda, themselves divided on the best way to fight the war, supported different rebel factions. Yet a third rebel faction emerged under the leadership of Jean-Pierre Bemba, the leader of the *Mouvement pour la Libération Congolaise* (MLC). Backed by Uganda, Bemba took charge of the rebellion's northern front. Rwanda and Uganda themselves engaged in heated fighting around Kisangani on at least two occasions.

War and peace continued, intermittently bringing hope and despair to everyday Congolese. Peace prospects seemed hopeful in the summer of 1999 as warring states gathered in Zambia's capital, Lusaka. Conditions for ending the war were defined and a precise timetable was set, a sign of the terminal optimism of conference participants.

Within 24 hours of the signing, hostilities were to cease. To ensure compliance, an international force would collect weapons from civilians and supervise the withdrawal of all foreign troops. The agreement also envisioned tracking down and disarming armed groups, screening for mass killers and war criminals, and ultimately the handing over of suspected *génocidaires* to the International Criminal Tribunal for Rwanda (ICTR) in Arusha, Tanzania. (The "armed groups" were fundamentally the rebel oppositions destabilizing Rwanda, Uganda, and Burundi, along with Angola's principal *bête noire*: Jonas Savimbi's UNITA.)

Forty-five days after signing the Lusaka agreement, the DRC government, the RCD and MLC rebel groups, unarmed opposition groups and Congolese civil society were to begin open political negotiations amongst themselves—an Inter-Congolese Dialogue—leading to the creation of a new political dispensation for the Congo. President Kabila signed the Lusaka ceasefire to avoid losing the war. Rejection and delay provided time to rebuild his forces, but additional Chinese arms and North Korean training were of little avail.

In February 2000, the Security Council approved a worthless Congo peacekeeping force of 500, backed by about 1,000 soldiers. The 500 could hardly monitor a cease-fire only reluctantly and intermittently observed in a country the size of Western Europe. Unsurprisingly, the year 2000 was punctuated by regular violations of the cease-fire and dramatic successes of the rebel alliance.

In August 2000, Kabila announced his government would no longer observe the Lusaka accord because Congo was occupied by Uganda and Rwanda. In October, the Congolese army (FAC) and Illies attacked Rwandan and rebel forces on the southern Katangan Front. The attack was intended to open a corridor for Burundian Hutu rebels—members of the *Forces de la Défense de la Démocratie* (FDD)—to infiltrate Burundi. BurundiIalways considered the weakest link in the anti-Kabila alliance. If it could be destabilized, the government would have to withdraw its troops from the Congo.

The government coalItion was initially succeIsful, but its lines were overextended. Roads were in such miserable shape that the Zimbabwean heavy artillery could not be resupplied. When the Rwandan Patriotic Army) and its allies counterattacked, Kabila's troops retreated precipitously. The government's military failure was completed in early December when Rwandan troops and their RCD-Goma allies captured the strategic southeastern city of Pweto, a crucial gateway to the riches of Katanga province, Kabila's homeland. At least 200 of Pweto's defenders—Rwandan Hutu *Interahamwe*, Burundian Hutu rebels, and members of FAC—were killed. Those not killed, up to 10,000 including a full battalion of Zimbabwean soldiers, fled across the border into Zambia.

The rout of Kabila's forces prompted a debate within the Rwandan government. Some thought the victory should be exploited to destroy the Interahamwe in Katanga completely, and some even argued for tracking them down in Zambia. The diplomatically attuned successfully argued the backlash against such a move would simply be too costly. Indeed, Pweto was the high-water mark of Rwandan arms in the Congo; other events were soon to tip the balance toward more peaceful solutions.

Many in Kinshasa had the feeling the Kabila regime had entered its final stages by September 2000. In his regular search for plots, conspiracies, and opposition, President Kabila ultimately turned on his initial supporters. One of those was Anselme Masasu, a founding leader of the AFDL. Masasu had commanded the army of child soldiers (*kadogos*) from Eastern Congo that swept into Kinshasa in the wake of Kabila's victory. In October 2000, he was reported to have made subversive comments at a meeting of 1,200 *kadogos* and was subsequently arrested and tortured, along with many others of eastern origin. Some 47 were executed in the presence of president Kabila, who allegedly killed several himself. Anselme Masasu and eight of his companions were reportedly sent to Katanga where they were murdered on November 27. Masasu's murder resonated strongly among the *kadogos*, and its rumor was a factor in their massive desertion at the battle of Pweto. Others plotted more direct action to avenge the murder of their commander, with the assassination of Laurent Kabila.

Kabila was assassinated on January 16, 2001, 40 years to the day after the murder of Patrice Lumumba. According to the official version, he was shot by one of his own *kadogo* bodyguards, Rachidi Kasereka, who was, in turn, shot to death by Kabila's aide-de-camp, Col. Eddy Kapend. Col. Kapend and around 80 others were accused of plotting Kabila's death and were sent before a special military tribunal. Lawyers had little or no contact with them and little capacity to prepare their defenses. In January 2003, Kapend and 29 others were convicted of plotting and killing Kabila and sentenced to death.

The consequences of Laurent Kabila's death were significant for the Congo. His son, Joseph Kabila, elevated to the presidency by his father's inner circle and their Angolan and Zimbabwean backers, reached out for international understanding and support. With that in hand, he quickly reversed many of his father's decisions blocking implementation of the Lusaka agreement.

Joseph Kabila (2001–2019)

Joseph Kabila had long enjoyed the confidence of his father, alternating military assignments with more confidential

D.R. Congo

Former President Laurent Kabila

missions on his father's behalf. Quiet, direct and frank, Joseph is stylistically very different from his father. He rejected the "Marble Palace," built by Mobutu and favored by his father, and worked from the OAU's Kinshasa headquarters. Educated in Tanzania and Uganda, Kabila reportedly felt more comfortable speaking English than French. When elevated to the presidency he was serving as the army chief of staff. He was 29 years old—Africa's youngest president.

With the guidance of Sir Ketumile Masire, the OAU facilitator, participants in the Inter-Congolese Dialogue reached an agreement in the South African resort of Sun City in spring 2002. Nearly 400 delegates, representing the government, rebel factions, opposition parties, and civil society, met to thrash out plans to end conflict and begin Congo's reconstruction.

Follow-up meetings led to the withdrawal of Rwandan and most Ugandan and Zimbabwean troops by early November, and in December 2002, dialogue participants signed an agreement in Pretoria to share power in a transitional government. By March 2003, a transitional constitution was hammered out, and on April 2 delegates signed the last agreements to organize the transition—under Joseph Kabila and a power-sharing government—leading to the first democratic elections since independence. The agreement was fundamentally an accord among belligerents to maintain themselves at the center of the state in the post-war period. The spoils of office and impunity from crimes committed were powerful inducements to participate in transitional arrangements. The transition period was to be two years, but ultimately that was extended for another year.

Under the transitional agreements, President Kabila shared power with four vice presidents—one each from his government, the two main rebel groups, and the unarmed opposition. The vice presidents included Jean-Pierre Bemba, the leader of the MLC; Abdoulaye Yerodia Ndombasi, a longtime Kabila ally; Arthur Z'Ahidi Ngoma, a longtime opposition politician who represented the unarmed political opposition, and RCD-Goma's secretary-general, Azarias Ruberwa.

The transitional National Assembly and Senate agreed on the text of a new constitution that limited presidential powers, allowing a president to serve a maximum of two five-year terms. The minimum age for presidential candidates was lowered to 30 from 35, allowing Joseph Kabila (then 33) to run for office. Strikingly, the new constitution recognized as citizens all ethnic groups present at independence in 1960. That granted citizenship to the thousands of Rwandans, Hutu and Tutsi, whose presence had long been so contentious. In a national referendum held December 18, 2005, 84% of Congolese voters approved the new governing instrument.

Definitive adoption of the constitution permitted a vote on an electoral law and establishment of an electoral calendar that would end the transitional period. Presidential elections, which took place the end of July 2006, were the culmination of Congo's long and difficult transition. Despite a variety of problems, more than 70 individuals signed up to contest the presidency. Thirty-three made the electoral commission's final list of candidates. Besides Joseph Kabila, Vice Presidents Bemba, Ruberwa, and Z'Ahidi campaigned, along with several individuals associated with the former Mobuto regime, and Antoine Gizenga, once a colleague of Patrice Lumumba. (Rather than pay the nonrefundable $50,000 registration fee, Gizenga chose the alternative, offering 50,000 voters' signatures and photocopies of their identity cards, saying "I don't come with a financial guarantee, but a republican one.")

The election was Joseph Kabila's to win or lose. The People's Party for Reconstruction and Democracy (PPRD), founded by his supporters in 2002, was the only party to have established offices throughout the country, and it aggressively campaigned on the president's behalf. The president also benefited from absence of the other truly national party, Etienne Tshisekedi's UDPS, which opted to boycott the election. Kabila campaigned as an independent, above the political fray, but the state-controlled media skewed their coverage to benefit the president.

The best Kabila's opponents could hope for was a runoff election among the top two vote-getters, a not unlikely outcome given the large number of candidates. In

President Joseph Kabila

the first round, Kabila received 44.8% of all votes cast, not quite enough to avoid a runoff. The second-place finisher was Jean-Pierre Bemba with 20%. In the crucial third-place spot was the grand old man of Congolese politics, the octogenarian Antoine Gizenga; leading the *Parti Lumumbiste Unifié* (PALU), Gizenga gained the support of 13% of Congo's voters. The poll revealed a powerful regional divide in the country. President Kabila obtained a landslide victory in the East (including, improbably, 97% of the vote in the town of Bukavu); Jean-Pierra Bemba ran strongest in the West, and actually won a majority of votes in Kinshasa, where Kabila managed only a paltry 17%.

Fighting broke out between troops loyal to Kabila and those loyal to Bemba almost as soon as the results were announced on August 20. (Each had a personal guard during the transitional period. The president's praetorians numbered between 10,000 and 15,000, Bemba's crew was probably less than 500. Neither had been forced to disarm during the transition.) Bemba properties bore the brunt of a frontal attack with tanks and troops: two television stations belonging to Bemba and accused of broadcasting programs critical of Kabila, personal residences, and his personal helicopter. Heavy fighting left at least 23 civilians and soldiers dead. Under intense diplomatic pressure, Kabila and Bemba called upon their troops to withdraw and the fighting ceased.

Once the guns were silenced it was time for political deal making before the presidential runoff. Antoine Gizenga signed an agreement with President Kabila promising support in exchange for the post of prime minister. Gizenga's backing gave Kabila vital support in the west, and in Kinshasa, where he was weakest. The old oppositionist played his cards well. Kabila won the runoff, 58% to Bemba's 42%. True to his word, Kabila asked Gizenga

D.R. Congo

to become the new republic's first prime minister. In the National Assembly, Prime Minister Gizenga had an easy working majority. Parties supporting President Kabila dominate the legislature, taking some 220 out of 500 seats, while Gizenga's PALU won an additional 35. Jean-Pierre Bemba's MLC won 64 seats.

Bemba and the MLC came under pressure from the increasingly authoritarian Joseph Kabila. In March 2007, Bemba's personal guard refused a government ultimatum to disband and be integrated into the national army; Kabila's government assured Bemba would be protected by 12 policemen. When Bemba resisted, Kabila resorted to force, using army, police, presidential guards and even Angolan troops to bring down Bemba. The former vice president escaped with his life, finding asylum in the South African embassy, but the German ambassador estimated that somewhere between 200 and 500 had died in the violence.

The government issued a warrant to arrest Bemba, accusing him of treason "in using the armed forces for his own ends," and the DRC's chief prosecutor was quick to add that parliament would be asked to lift the immunity he held as a senator. The new leader of the opposition was thus hounded into exile. The MLC's party headquarters were destroyed, as were its television stations. Without a leader, the parliamentary opposition fell into disarray while party members reported police harassment and arrests. In June 2009, the International Criminal Court ordered Bemba to stand trial, charging him under suspicion of war crimes in relation to actions by his troops in the Central African Republic in 2002 and 2003. The trial of Bemba began in late 2010.

The year 2010 saw an echo of the conflict between Kabila and Bemba: further chilling repression of the opposition and unrest across the different regions of the country, even as some criminals were brought to justice. In June, a human rights advocate was found dead after being held briefly in police custody. Meanwhile, conflict raged again in North Kivu province in eastern DRC, as Ugandan rebels fought DRC troops. The army pushed back rebels, but a UN report accused the army of profiteering from the conflict. Still, better news came with the rather prompt trial and sentencing of army commander Kibibi Mutware and eight other officers for mass rape in early 2011. In November 2010, ex vice president Jean-Pierre Bemba was put on trial at the ICC for allowing his soldiers to rape and kill in Central African Republic between 2002 and 2003.

Additional good news for the Kabila government came with confirmation in July 2010 of a whopping $8 billion in debt

Étienne Tshisekedi, UDPS leader

relief by international financial institutions. This was soon followed with a further elimination of debt by the Paris Club, a consortium of creditor countries; that included an American agreement to eliminate $1.8 billion in DRC debt.

Since the risk to Kabila's 2011 reelection came from a united opposition, the government changed the electoral process to eliminate the second-round runoff. The elections on November 28, 2011 took place with a single round of voting, with the candidate receiving the most votes winning outright. President Kabila won the election with 49% of the vote, with Étienne Tshisekedi taking second place with 32%. The legitimacy of the election was disputed by opposing parties and the international community.

Since the 2011 elections, the great battle in DR Congo has shifted from Kinshasa politics back to the military front in the east. A number of rebel movements have emerged in the Great Lakes region along DR Congo's eastern border with Rwanda, Burundi, and Uganda. Of these groups, the most significant is the March 23 Movement, known for short as M23. This group is comprised primarily of members of the Tutsi ethnic group and is allegedly backed by the governments of Rwanda and Uganda (though both countries deny the charges). M23 went as far as to seize the catastrophe-weary provincial capital of Goma in late 2012. (Goma was the epicenter of the refugee crisis after the Rwandan genocide and has seen volcanic eruptions and outbreaks of various deadly communicable diseases.) Responding to the emergence of M23, a number of African countries signed an accord that pledged troops to stop the fighting, and the United Nations has prepared for an increasingly assertive presence that might even enable UN-backed troops to take an active war to the rebels. While the eastern Congo is not yet pacified, there are signs of dissension in the ranks of the rebels, with members of the rank-and-file deserting and even one of the former commanders, Bosco Ntaganda, turning himself in to the International Criminal Court after he split with M23.

The international response to M23 is establishing a precedent for more robust humanitarian intervention in situations where rebel groups are committing atrocities; of course, this has also had the effect of stabilizing the Kabila regime from what might have been an existential threat to its power of the sort previously experienced by Mobutu in the 1990s. UN forces joined Congolese troops in fending off M23 rebels, particularly condemning the Rwandan government for their involvement. The UN and the United States imposed sanctions on Rwanda for supporting M23 along the border with DR Congo, and the UN began using drones to patrol the border between the two countries. As Congolese and UN forces gained momentum, M23 rebels lost control of seized territories and cities. In November of 2013, M23 forces officially surrendered, bringing about renewed hopes that DR Congo and its eastern borders are beginning to stabilize. While Central Africa continues to rebuild from its long history of conflict, and UN peace forces continue to neutralize M23 forces and border conflicts, the DRC strives to resolve various conflicts – with Rwanda, the M23 rebels, and ongoing ethnic disputes within its own borders.

CONTEMPORARY THEMES

At the time of independence, DR Congo was one of the potentially richest nations in the world, with vast deposits of natural resources. The Congo contains 80% of the world's cobalt (essential in hi-tech and defense production), 10% of its copper, and one-third of its diamonds. There are also considerable reserves of gold, uranium, and manganese. Yet government corruption, mismanagement, and extravagance destroyed Congo's economy, and war only furthered the collapse. A statistical description of the Congo today is appalling. More than 70% of the population lives in absolute poverty and an even higher percentage is unemployed. The country's GDP has risen by around 7% in several recent years, suggesting some increasing investor confidence after 2003. Nonetheless, life expectancy is still estimated to be under 50 years.

Production in all key sectors declined dramatically under President Mobutu, and suffered worse during the 1997–2002 civil war. The mining sector imploded.

D.R. Congo

La Général des Carrières et des Mines (Gécamines), once the crown jewel of the Congo mining industry, reached near-terminal decline. State-owned Gécamines' production fell drastically from the late 1980s, when copper output was consistently 400,000 to 500,000 tons a year (t/y)—about 7% to 8% of global production. By 2005, its production was about 17,000 t/y. The World Bank has worked to restructure and revitalize the company, getting Paul Fortin, a Canadian, appointed as Gécamines' managing director. Copper production has improved since.

The difficulties of genuine reform in the mining sector are illustrated by one of the most delicate tasks—review of three mining contracts that account for 75% of Gecamines' mineral asset base. Approved in 2005 by the transitional government of Joseph Kabila, the contracts were signed without benefit of thorough analysis and evaluation. The World Bank's principal mining specialist described the assets transferred to the three companies involved as exceeding the "norms for rational and highest use of the mineral assets." The possibility of any contract revision is slight. The mining province of Katanga is Kabila's political stronghold, and he has installed his allies on the Gécamines board of directors. Any recommendation by Managing Director Fortin can be vetoed by the board.

Chinese companies have rapidly moved into Katanga's copper belt since President Joseph Kabila visited Beijing in March 2005. Beijing-based Colec is working to rehabilitate the Kamatanda mines and three copper and cobalt plants. Chinese businessmen in Katanga are also at the heart of a boom in ore-processing plants. Feza Mining, expected to produce 4,000 tons of copper alloy and 1,000 tons of cobalt annually, is joint Chinese–Congolese development. As a consequence of increased investment, sector analysts expect copper output to rise in the coming years.

Whether mining growth will relieve poverty and suffering in Katanga and in DRC is dubious. Global Witness succinctly described Congolese reality in its 2006 report, *Digging in Corruption*: "The mining sector in Katanga is characterized by widespread corruption and fraud at all levels. . . . Government officials are actively colluding with trading companies in circumventing control procedures and the payment of taxes. The profits are serving to line the pockets of a small but powerful elite—politicians and businessmen who are exploiting the local population and subverting natural riches for their private ends."

Apart from challenges in the mining sector and the economy more broadly, DRC still struggles with conflict in the region. To this day, the government accuses Rwanda of taking military action in Eastern DRC against the Hutu rebels. In January 2009, both governments started a joint venture against the rebels and the Tutsi rebel leader Laurent Nkunda was arrested in after attempting to cross over to Rwanda. In May 2009, in an attempt to bring peace to the North and South Kivu provinces, the government passed a law that gave amnesty to Congolese militias (but excluding foreign militias) operating in Eastern DRC. In April 2014, DR Congo further offered amnesty to some (though not all) members of the M23 movement.

Elected in 2019, President Felix Tshisekedi was reelected in January 2024 in a relatively peaceful electoral campaign and appointed Judith Suminwa as the first female prime minister of the sprawling country with promises to promote economic development with the governing party controlling 90 percent of the seats in the national assembly. Conflicts continue in the restive eastern region with its large reserves of gold, diamonds, and coltan, a mineral essential to production of mobile phones. Large swaths of territory have been seized in the region by Rwanda-backed militias as UN peacekeepers have been withdrawn.

The government of the DRC and Rwanda-backed M23 rebels have agreed to pause fighting while working toward a broader peace deal following negotiations in the Qatar capital of Doha conducted in April 2025. This follows a recent wave of violence, including a bloody assault and capture by M23 of the two large cities in eastern. The "cessation of hostilities" would apply "throughout the duration of the talks and until their conclusion" according to a joint statement. The peace push mediated by Qatar comes after the Gulf state successfully brokered an unexpected meeting in March 2025 between DRC President Felix Tshisekedi and Rwandan President Paul Kagame. This meeting paved the way for direct talks between DRC and M23 previously opposed by leaders in Kinshasa. The decades-long conflict has roots in the 1994 Rwandan genocide, with M23 made up primarily of ethnic Tutsi fighters who, after being integrated into the DRC army, later defected, citing discrimination and broken peace deals. Since 2021, the two sides have agreed to at least six truces that later collapsed. The latest bout of violence (since January 2025) resulted in thousands killed and raised fears of a wider regional war. On a related matter, the DRC suspended the party of ex-President Kabila over alleged links to M23.

The country also confronted a rising death toll from serious flooding prompted by heavy rains that cut access to more than half of the capital Kinshasa as authorities struggled to evacuate and support hundreds of families trapped in their homes. With major overflows from the Ndjili River, hundreds of buildings were submerged as many residents blamed the government for a poor respondence to the disaster, including lack of access to clean drinking from damaged water facilities. In 2022, at least 100 people were killed during similar flooding in Kinshasa.

FUTURE CONSIDERATIONS

The Democratic Republic of the Congo seemed to be emerging slowly from the horrific civil wars that ravaged the country between the mid-1990s and 2003, but its human rights record remains disastrous. In 2007 and 2008, Joseph Kabila's government signed pacts with a range of actors, including the government of Rwanda and a variety of armed groups in eastern D.R.C. These are intended to subdue the *interahamwe* militias of Rwandan origin, among other actors, and to provide buffer zones between lingering groups of rebels and the central government. In theory, this will facilitate respect of human rights on the part of the government. However,

Bridge repair in eastern D.R. Congo ©Paul Carlson Foundation

D.R. Congo

given the difficulty facing D.R. Congo in enforcing the rule of law across the vast territory—and especially along the eastern border—there is reason for skepticism.

Human rights abuses persist, as highlighted in a 2008 Human Rights Watch report that documented deaths of opposition leaders at the hands of government forces. This sense was only enhanced by the grisly death in June 2010 of the human rights activist Floribert Chebeya. However, there is a mix of reactions worldwide, as showcased by the recent statements of international actors. The head of the United Nations Mission in DR Congo (MONUC) remarked in August 2009 that previous joint UN-army operations, undertaken against Rwandan rebels, had been "largely positive," and in December 2009, a shortened five-month MONUC mandate was issued as part of a schedule to have a full withdrawal of UN troops by mid-2010. However, the UN High Commissioner for Human Rights made a September statement that the earlier North Kivu aggression (of October-November 2008) constituted war crimes, by both CNDP militia and the army itself. Human rights issues still plague the DRC, most recently with the M23 and other rebel groups in eastern D.R.C. committing systematic abuses, and with the ICC's conviction of warlord Thomas Lubango in 2012 for using child soldiers.

Economically, the country's problems remain enormous. There is little infrastructure to link the regions to Kinshasa, so the new constitution's creation of 25 semi-autonomous provinces (up from 11) was a concession to political reality. Each of the provinces has its own legislature, which will provide ample employment opportunities for the political class. Each will also be allowed to keep 40% of the revenues it earns, which is posited to generate local growth, but in the Congolese political economy may be likelier to provide opportunities for the localization of corruption.

The Republic of Equatorial Guinea

Selling yoghurt

Photo by Cayuela Serrano
Courtesy: APFT-ULB

BASIC FACTS

Area: 28,051 sq. km. = 10,830 sq. mi. (slightly larger than Vermont)
Population: 1,737,695 (June 2023 est.)
Capital City: Malabo
Government Type: Presidential Republic
Neighboring Countries: Cameroon (north); Gabon (east and south). The island portion of the country lies some twenty miles off the west coast of Cameroon.
Official Languages: Spanish and French
Other Principal Languages: Fang, Bubi, Ibo, and Pidgin English
Ethnic Groups: Bioko (primarily Bubi, some Fernandinos), Rio Muni (primarily Fang), Europeans less than 1,000, mostly Spanish
Principal Religions: Most people are nominally Roman Catholic; traditional tribal beliefs are intermingled with their Christian faith.
Former Colonial Status: Spanish Colony (island 1778–1968, mainland 1885–1968)
Independence Date: October 12, 1968
GDP per capita (IMF 2023 est.): $9,777 (nominal), $18,510 (PPP)
Gini index: N/A
Currency: CFA franc, $US 1 = 594 francs (Apr. 2023)
Inflation Rate: 4.0% (2022 est.)
Chief Commercial Products: Petroleum, timber, cocoa, agricultural food production
Foreign Direct Investments (FDI) net inflows: 1,933,000,000
Literacy Rate: 63.7% (CIA 2022)
Life Expectancy: 63.8 years (CIA 2023 est.)
Head of State: Brig. Gen. Teodoro Obiang Nguema Mbasogo, President (since August 3, 1979)
Head of Government: Prime Minister Manuela Roka Botey (since Feb. 1, 2023)

LAND AND PEOPLE

Equatorial Guinea is divided between the island of Bioko and the mainland known as Rio Muni. (Note: Between 1974 and the present, geographic place names have been changed from Spanish to African and then to other African designations and back to Spanish. The island, first known as Fernando Po, is now designated *Bioko* after an early king of the region. The mainland, formerly Rio Muni, became Mbini, but it is now again generally called Rio Muni.)

On the protected shoreline of hot and humid Rio Muni, a narrow white sandy beach quickly gives way to thick growth of interior rain forest filled with immense ebony, mahogany, and oak trees. Few roads penetrate into the interior, but the land is thick with streams (which include giant frogs up to a foot long and weighing eight pounds).

The scenic island of Bioko was the source of one of the best varieties of cocoa in the world until the 1970s. Production was on large plantations, using contract labor from Nigeria, but nearly all workers fled during the brutalities of the Macías Nguema regime. In its heyday, the island had an active port, and the international airport was the base from which relief supplies were flown into strife-torn Nigeria in the early 1970s. The recent oil boom in Equatorial Guinea has restored much activity on Bioko (and especially in the capital Malabo), though income inequality is atrocious.

The use of marijuana is widespread and traditional. Referred to as the "sacred weed of the people" and once used only in traditional ceremonies, marijuana has found its way into every level of Equatorial Guinean society. The drug provides, for the poor, escape from worsening poverty amid the riches of an oil boom.

HISTORY TO PRESENT DAY

For early history, see *Historical Background* and *The Colonial Period: The Spanish*.

The provinces known as Spanish Guinea were made internally self-governing in 1963, and their name was changed to Equatorial Guinea. Spain granted independence to Equatorial Guinea in 1968. In UN-supervised elections mainland Fang outnumbered the more educated Bubi of the island of Fernando Po, and their candidate, Francisco Macías Nguema, became the country's first president.

Macías Nguema quickly developed a paranoid style seen elsewhere in Africa. Prominent political figures were arrested

Equatorial Guinea

and executed on grounds they were plotting his overthrow. Family members were installed in key government posts, but they remained under close surveillance. The regime nationalized cocoa plantations and the economy spiraled downward. In 1972 Macías Nguema's handpicked National Assembly named him "President for Life." He assumed absolute personal power in 1973 and had the island of Fernando Po renamed in his honor. The president accumulated other titles as well: in addition to "President for Life," Macías Nguema was also "Grand Master of Education, Science and Culture."

As his paranoia increased, life became grimmer for the citizenry. Death squads formed by the "Macias Youth" roamed the countryside, raping, looting, and killing. Mass executions were held while loudspeakers blared a recording of "Those Were the Days, My Friend." Other regime opponents were buried up to their necks to be eaten alive by insects. Educated Guineans, mostly Bubi, were specially targeted for slaughter.

A militant atheist, Macías Nguema was especially venomous towards Christians. He ordered his picture to hang beside the altar of every church in the country and compelled priests and pastors to recite the slogan "All for Macias" at every service. The World Council of Churches branded him a "modern Caligula." One island visitor called the country "the concentration camp of Africa—a cottage-industry Dachau."

By 1979, when he was overthrown, Macías Nguema is believed to have murdered 50,000 Equatorial Guineans. Another 100,000, one-third of the country's population, had been driven into exile. Among the dead were two-thirds of the last elected national assembly and 10 of the 12 original cabinet ministers. Equatorial Guinea's small, educated class had been virtually eliminated through death or flight.

In the summer of 1979 Macías Nguema was overthrown by his nephew and deputy defense minister Lt. Col. Teodoro Obiang Nguema Mbasogo, who had been one of the principal architects of the Macías reign of terror; human rights groups had long accused him of personal involvement in a number of killings.

Obiang Nguema's governance of the country has been repressive and dictatorial. Until 1993, he operated through a single party, the Democratic Party of Equatorial Guinea (PDGE), and concentrated political power in his own hands and economic power in the hands of the Nguema clan. Though multiparty elections were introduced in 1993, nothing approaching democracy exists in Equatorial Guinea; President Obiang was elected to a seven-year term in 1996 in a contest dominated by fraud and intimidation. The government and 14 opposition groups signed a national pact in April 1997 agreeing to the basic conditions for future legislative elections. One month later, however, the government announced that a plot to overthrow the president had been uncovered. This set off another wave of political repression. Relations with Spain deteriorated when Spain granted asylum to Severo Moto, leader of the *Partido del Progreso de Guinea Ecuatorial* (PPGE) and alleged leader of the so-called coup. In pique, Obiang made French the official language of this former Spanish colony. In May 1997 Severo Moto, along with 11 others, was tried *in absentia* for treason, found guilty and sentenced to 101 years imprisonment and PPGE was banned in June.

A new separatist group emerged in January 1998, attacking three police posts and killing several people. It identified itself as the Movement for Self-determination for the Island of Bioko (MAIB) and demanded independence for the island's indigenous population of Bubi peoples, marginalized and excluded from the country's political and economic life by the mainland Fang. Mass arrests followed. Fifteen Bubi were condemned to death by a military court. The sentence was reduced in September (by "presidential grace") to life imprisonment after an outpouring of international protest.

March 1999 legislative elections could be called farcical were it not for the brutality of the Obiang Nguema regime. Opposition candidates were threatened, arbitrarily arrested, and prevented from campaigning. For the election itself, additional polling places were set up in schools, barracks, and state-owned enterprises, close to the governing party's adherents. Alliances between parties were prohibited. On election day armed soldiers or other security agents stood inside polling areas. Voters were often forced to cast their ballots publicly. Unsurprisingly, the PDGE won 75 of 80 parliamentary seats. Appeals to the National Electoral Commission would be unavailing. Its chairman was also the minister of the interior. The European Union and most other bodies who had been requested to send observers refused to sanction any of this by their presence.

The government strictly controls freedom of speech and press. Press laws authorize government censorship of all publications, and the Ministry of Information can require prepublication approval of article content. Self-censorship is the better part of valor. All electronic media are censured. The ruling party controls the country's main publications, radio, and television. It owns and operates Radio Malabo, the most widely heard station. Only in 1998 did the government allow the country's first private domestic radio station, Radio Ansonga, but that is owned by Minister of Waters and Forests, Fishing and Environment Teodoro ("Teodorino") Obiang Nguema, the president's eldest son. As a consequence of all this, NGO Freedom House placed Equatorial Guinea on its list of "the worst of the worst" in its 2005 report on the world's most repressive societies.

State and family are closely conjoined in Equatorial Guinea. The president's second son, Gabriel Mbegha Obiang Lima, became state secretary for oil, while his brother-in-law, Teodoro Biyogo Nsue, once Equatorial Guinea's ambassador to the UN, now manages family/country interests in the U.S., including a bank account of several hundred million dollars. The state security apparatus is dominated by his closest relatives, for this is a task that the president says cannot be entrusted in strangers: "I must be able to count on loyal people." (For his personal protection, Obiang relies on a contingent of Moroccan troops.)

It is the state security apparatus that is most responsible for Equatorial Guinea's appalling human rights record. Obiang's brother Armengol Ondo Nguema is director general of national security and one of the most feared men in the country. Another brother, Antonio Mba Nguema, is also part of the security service, as is his son-in-law, Julian Ondo Nkumu. The U.S. State Department's *Human Rights Practices Report* (2005) said the government's human rights record remained poor and it continued to commit or condone serious abuses, including torture and beating of prisoners and detainees, life-threatening prison conditions, arbitrary arrest, and incommunicado detention.

Because of Guinea's sleazy human rights record the U.S. kept President Obiang at arm's length until April 2006 when he met with Secretary of State Condoleezza Rice. The meeting came shortly before the visit of Chinese President Hu Jintao to Washington. China's national oil company had already signed an oil exploration

President Teodoro Obiang Nguema

Equatorial Guinea

agreement with Equatorial Guinea, and geopolitical considerations clearly weighed heavily in the decision. Secretary Rice's own State Department claimed President Obiang had made "small, haphazard steps toward the development of [a] participatory political system".

In the lead-up to presidential elections in late 2002, regime critics were subjected to the usual harassment, repression and torture; the country's four main opposition parties withdrew, saying the balloting was so rigged there was no way there could be a fair election. With well over 90% of the votes, Teodoro Obiang Nguema Mbasogo was reelected to another seven-year term as president. The constitution places no limits on the number of terms a president may serve.

In early 2004, rumors of an impending coup circulated in Malabo, but they were given substance in early March when 15 mercenaries were arrested in the country and another 64, allegedly on their way, were taken off a plane in Zimbabwe. The government hastily pointed fingers at its nemesis and scapegoat Severo Moto, head of the opposition Progress Party; the minister of information claimed the operation was funded by "enemies and multinational companies." The *Economist* magazine claimed to have documents linking Armengol Ondo Nguema, the president's brother and secret service chief, and the mercenary leader, Nick du Toit. Later investigations revealed some involvement of the son of former British prime minister Margaret Thatcher.

Dissent within the clan Nguema became very real over the years President Obiang has sought to assure the presidential succession by his eldest son, "Teodorino" Obiang Nguema, a young man whose flamboyant lifestyle has captivated the Western press, but whose trenchant criticisms of his uncles, the generals, has fostered bitter enmity in them and within the army. The younger Obiang has accused them of control and expropriation of both the economy and the apparatus of the state and deliberately absented himself from the country in protest. In a patriarchal political society, age remains important, and the generals detest the thought of taking orders from one junior to them.

Parliamentary elections in 2004 showed the regime was outwardly static. Seats had been increased in September 2003—to 100 from 80—to allow the "democratic opposition" to be represented in the legislature, but almost all the candidates of the two main opposition parties were rejected on technical grounds, and Obiang's PDGE took 98 of 100 seats, and 237 municipal councilors out of 244. The main opposition Convergence for Social Democracy (CPSD) got two seats in parliament and only seven on local municipal councils.

Criticized that the country's oil wealth had made little improvement in the lives of ordinary citizens, President Obiang launched a blistering attack on civil servants and his own cabinet as the parties responsible. In late June 2006, he was reported to have raged: "If it's necessary to change the government, the entire government will go. If it's necessary to replace every civil servant, they will all be replaced." Mincing no words, he went on to say that "corruption," "ignorance," "irregularities," and "badly taken decisions," had undermined the effectiveness of both cabinet and bureaucracy and produced the miserable conditions (or as the president phrased it, "difficult situation") in which the bulk of Equatorial Guinea's citizens lived.

Dutifully obedient to his president's wishes, Prime Minister Abia Biteo Borico submitted his cabinet's resignation in August, allowing the president to give the country "a new spirit and dynamism with a new governmental team." Ricardo Mangué Obama Nfubea (no relation to the U.S. president) was named prime minister. Mangué Obama Nfubea is ethnically a Fang, like Obiang. While the Fang—about 80% of the population—are the country's majority people, the prime minister's office has traditionally been reserved for a Bubi, the original inhabitants of Bioko Island. He served as prime minister for two years before falling out of favor with Obiang in 2008.

Further upheaval in Equatorial Guinea's politics followed in August 2008, when President Obiang dismissed his entire cabinet, replacing Mangué Obama Nfubea with Ignácio Milam Tang, also of the Fang ethnic group. The reshuffle was supposedly to root out corruption in the Mangué Obama Nfubea government, but also served to scramble any ambitious politicians who sought an independent power base.

In February 2009, gunfire erupted around the presidential palace. The government blamed 15 Nigerian rebels for the assault. While the attack failed, it showed the lingering divisiveness of politics in Equatorial Guinea and suggests that Obiang continues to face occasional challenges to his total grip on power. These challenges are outside the electoral arena; late 2009 saw Obiang re-elected with 95% of the vote from the November elections. Plácido Micó Abogo came in a distant second, with less than 4%. However, once again the elections were plagued with accusations of vote-rigging, manipulation, and intimidation, coming from both the opposition and groups such as Human Rights Watch.

The regime's strategy for dealing with opposition continues to be prompt elimination of threats: four regime opponents were captured in August 2010 and summarily executed as alleged plotters of the 2004 coup, just hours after being arrested and only one hour after sentencing in a military trial that allowed no appeal. Corruption and authoritarianism are thus central to life in Equatorial Guinea. Indeed, in May 2009, President Obiang was charged in France with using public funds for private purposes (in the same case as presidents Omar Bongo of Gabon and Sassou-Nguesso of the Republic of Congo), but the case was ultimately thrown out due to the leaders' positions as foreign heads of state.

Equatorial Guinea has continued to be a country where corruption and nepotism thrive. President Teodoro Obiang is now the world's longest ruling leader. He has been known to arrest political opponents and other populations (such as students) that may pose a political threat. In November 2011, a referendum of constitutional changes was passed, though it was widely acknowledged as further usurpation of power by the President. The President's son, Teodoro Nguema Obiang Mangue, has gotten into a number of international conflicts. The US hopes to seize $71 million of his assets and French police seized 11 sports cars belonging to Obiang Mangue in Paris in October 2011, because they were believed to have been acquired through corruption. President Obiang's response to this was to appoint his son to the Equatorial Guinea diplomatic mission to UNESCO, using the international organization to gain diplomatic immunity for his son and thus placing him above the law. He appointed this son (also known as Teodorin) to the vice presidency, even as France issued a warrant for his arrest.

Equatorial Guinea held elections—sort of—in May 2013. In a poll that international observers widely held to be neither free nor fair, the president's Democratic Party of Equatorial Guinea took all but one seat in each of the two houses of the legislature. In the Senate, the president's PDGE party 54 of 55 elected seats, and Obiang appointed 15 more Senators; in the Chamber of Deputies, the PDGE won 99 of 100 seats.

CONTEMPORARY THEMES

Equatorial Guinea's reversal of economic fortune began in the 1990s with the discovery of oil in the Gulf of Guinea. By 2005 oil production averaged 356,000 barrels per day (bbl/d). Equatorial Guinea has overtaken Gabon to become sub-Saharan Africa's third biggest oil producer (after Nigeria and Angola). Oil, with proven reserves of 1.77 billion barrels, accounts for 97% of the country's exports, and 80% of GDP, a gigantic share.

The oil economy means the people of Rio Muni no longer live in rural solitude.

Equatorial Guinea

Four-wheel-drive vehicles driving along the faded elegance of Spanish colonial boulevards suggest the ruling elite has begun to enjoy the economic fruits of political power. Symptomatically, as of April 2006, only Mercedes-Benz vehicles were permitted as taxis. By contrast, the dispossessed suffer daily water and power cutoffs and drinking water regularly polluted by drainage water, mainly because of broken pipes.

There are also reserves of 1.3 trillion cubic feet of gas. Marathon Oil Company has started site work to construct a liquefied natural gas (LNG) facility on Bioko Island; supply contracts have been signed with Nigeria, but those with Cameroon have been delayed because of disputed claims over areas of the Gulf of Guinea. As a consequence, Marathon's hope of supplying 3.4 million tons of LNG by late 2007 was delayed.

Gazprom, the Russian natural gas behemoth has entered the Guinean market. In September 2006 it concluded an agreement with the *Société nationale de gaz* (Sonagaz) for joint production of LNG.

With its oil bonanza, the country's economy has grown with enormous rapidity. In 2004, Equatorial Guinea was the fastest growing economy in the world; in 2005, the country's real gross domestic product (GDP) grew 15.4%. The average over roughly the last decade has been somewhere over 15%/year, though figures are far from transparent.

The average citizen, however, has yet to experience a higher standard of living from the oil revenues. The World Bank has been uncharacteristically blunt, saying that oil reve nue has had "no impact on Equatorial Guinea's dismal social indicators." Health-care spending, for example, has *declined* from 6% to just over 1% of the budget. Malabo, the capital, suffers from chronic water shortages.

How much money has come in, where it is deposited, and how it is being spent is unclear. President Obiang has told the IMF these statistics are state secrets. In January 2003 the *Los Angeles Times* lifted one small corner of the veil that conceals state patrimonialism. According to its investigations Equatorial Guinea kept an account with Riggs Bank in Washington, DC, where international oil companies directly deposited at least $300 million. The account was controlled exclusively by President Obiang. As he told a reporter for the *New Statesman*, "I am the one who arranges things in this country because in Africa there are a lot of problems of corruption . . . I'm 100 per cent sure of all the oil revenue because the one who signs is me."

The U.S. has attached great importance to developing Equatorial Guinea's oil sector to lessen its dependence on Middle Eastern suppliers. Washington's new enthusiasm for the country can be seen in the State Department's approval for Military Professional Resources Inc. (MPRI)—a private firm run by Pentagon retirees out of Alexandria, VA—to help the government develop a coast guard to protect its offshore oil fields. Those are being operated by American firms like ExxonMobil, ChevronTexaco, and Amerada Hess. In January 2007 the government signed a five-year deal with MPRI to train army units and the presidential guard.

Given increased American presence in the country, the U.S. reopened its embassy in Malabo in October 2003. Business was conducted by a chargé d'affairs rather than a full ambassador until November 2006, when the first American ambassador in eleven years arrived in Malabo.

China is poised to participate in Equatorial Guinea's oil bonanza. In February 2006, the China National Offshore Oil Company Africa Limited, a subsidiary of China's largest offshore oil producer (CNOOC), signed a product share contract with the country's national oil company giving it explorations rights over the next five years in an area of some 2,287 square kilometers.

In January 2007, Foreign Minister Li Zhaoxing made Equatorial Guinea the second stop on his seven-nation tour of Africa. The fruits of his discussions were announced in April: China Road and Bridge Corporation won a port construction deal valued at $425 million.

Oil revenues have allowed the Obiang regime to enrich and further entrench itself. As it had controlled jobs in the bureaucracy, awarding them to its faithful supporters, the clan Nguema controls access to the new, high-paying jobs of the oil industry. The best jobs are reserved for the PDGE faithful.

Developments in the petroleum sector have overshadowed the other important resource for the country's ruling clan: timber. Initially small scale, logging operations exploded around 1994 when huge Asian transnationals moved in. By the mid-1990s, there were more than 20 logging companies exploiting the rain forest on concessions reportedly owned by President Obiang. Forestry became the second most important economic sector after oil, but aggressive logging threatens the approximately 3.2 million acres of forestland in mainland Equatorial Guinea with over-harvesting.

The export of cocoa and coffee was once the backbone of the nation's economy, but under Macías Nguema the plantations were nationalized and destroyed. In the 1960s, nearly 98,000 acres were devoted to cocoa production, mostly on Bioko Island; by the 1980s, only 7,400 acres remained in production. Annual yields fell in cocoa and coffee collapsed. There were few incentives for farmers to continue cocoa cultivation until 2006, when the government was sloshing around in oil profits. In 2005, Equatorial Guinea exported about a million dollars' worth of cocoa. To provide additional incentives for the 2005–2006 agricultural campaign, the government pledged to subsidize the price offered farmers, nearly doubling what they would get on the open market. It also agreed to liquidate the debts farmers had built up with exporters during the 2004–2005 season.

Major political developments Include the death of prominent dissident Julio Obama Mefuman while imprisoned after being kidnapped from Sudan and reportedly subject to torture, Only one authorized opposition party exists in the country with the party of 80-year-old President Obiang controlling 90 percent of the seats in the national assembly.

On the international front, Russia has reportedly sent up to 200 troops to Equatorial Guinea to protect the presidency while saying that the Russians are training elite guards in the country's two main cities, the capital Malabo and Bata with reports of Russian troops deployed in the country first surfacing in August 2024. Many of the soldiers are reportedly from the Corps Africa, a paramilitary force previously known as Wagner before being renamed and officially coming under Russian military control.

With a population of only 1.7 million, the country is led by President Teodoro Obiang Nguema Mbasogo, the world's longest-serving president who has been in power since 1979 with his son, Teodoro Obiang Mangue, known for his lavish lifestyle, serving as the country's vice president while the subject of criminal charges and sanctions by other countries. Facing international criticism for its human rights record, including arbitrary killings and torture, Equatorial Guinea is pursuing military deals as well as gas and mineral exploration agreements with Russia and Belarus along with similar deals in the past with China. Domestically, the church pastor and former justice minister Rubén Maye Nsue Mangue, who was detained two years ago for referring to the president as a "demon . . . holding his people as prisoners," has been freed. Refusing to apologize to the head of state, he was accused of provoking public disorder with the justice ministry also barring him from preaching. Political opposition in the oil-rich state is barely tolerated along with major restrictions on the media, including the press.

Equatorial Guinea

FUTURE CONSIDERATIONS

The last few years have seen a handful of events that serve as useful shorthand for political life in Equatorial Guinea: an attack on the presidential palace in Equatorial Guinea in February 2009; the virtually uncontested victory of Obiang at the polls that year; and the summary executions of political opponents in 2011. The Nguema clan seems largely secure in power, though there is conflict and prospects for violence within the family. In short, there is no prospect for democracy here. The best the opposition can hope for from the new oil wealth is that the presence of hundreds of foreigners might restrain regime repression. Tensions within the clan, particularly focused on President Obiang Nguema's eldest son, could still explode in violence, as the abortive March 2004 coup suggests.

Known by some as "Africa's Kuwait," Equatorial Guinea has been, by some accounts, the fastest growing economy in the world in recent years. This does not, however, mean significant economic and social change for most citizens. Entirely an artifact of oil investment, the growth has failed to "trickle down" to the average person; the country's income inequality has been so staggering that it has become the subject of major exposés in the international press. The future remains bleak for those who are not directly benefiting from oil revenues, state patronage, or both. Given the sudden strategic importance of Equatorial Guinea (due to its location and its oil resources), there is a reasonable expectation that the country will receive considerably greater attention from the American government and international investors. Still, this is unlikely to mean greater democracy or improved living standards for most living in the country.

The Republic of Gabon

Gabonese school children chasing soap bubbles

Photo by Marian Zeldin

BASIC FACTS

Area: 267,667 sq. km. = 103,347 sq. mi. (slightly smaller than Colorado)
Population: 2,397,368 (July 2023 est.)
Capital City: Libreville
Government Type: Presidential Republic
Neighboring Countries: Equatorial Guinea (northwest); Cameroon (north); Congo (east, south)
Official Language: French
Other Principal Languages: Fang, Myene, Nzebi, Bapounou/Eschira, Bandjabi
Principal Religions: Christian 55%–75%, animist 10%, Islam less than 1%
Ethnic Groups: Predominantly Bantu tribes: Fang, Eshira, Bapounou, Bateke
Former Colonial Status: French Colony (1903–1960)
Independence Date: August 17, 1960
GDP per capita (IMF 2023 est.): $9,294 (nominal), $19,197 (PPP)
Gini Index: 38 (World Bank 2017)
Currency: Central Africa CFA franc, 1 USD = 594 CFA francs (Apr. 2023)
Inflation Rate: 2.9% (2022 est.)
Chief Commercial Products: Crude oil, timber, manganese, and uranium
Foreign Direct Investments (FDI) net inflows: 972,866,924
Literacy Rate: 85.5% (CIA 2021)
Life Expectancy: 69.7 years (CIA 2022 est.)
Head of State: Ali Bongo Ondimba (elected September 2009)
Head of Government: Prime Minister Alain Claude Bilie-Bynze (since Jan. 9, 2023)

LAND AND PEOPLE

Lying astride the Equator on the west coast of Africa, Gabon is a land of hot and humid rain forests where the coastal lowlands receive up to 150 inches of rain per year. A series of densely forested plateaus rise farther inland, spreading from the northeast to the southeast of the country with altitudes from 1,000 to 2,000 feet. The remainder of the land is covered by rounded mountains rising to heights of 5,200 feet. Gabon's exceptional biodiversity, preserved by their national forests that cover about 10% of the land, has led to its growing appeal as an ecotourism destination.

A common manifestation of culture in Gabon is through the use of masks that may be worn in ceremonies and for hunting, while some tribes center their art around the rituals for death. Because of the lack of systematic tourism and limited western influence, Gabonese art is seldom commercialized.

Gabon

HISTORY TO PRESENT DAY

For early history, see *Historical Background* and *The Colonial Period: The French*.

Under the constitution of France's Fifth Republic, Gabon achieved self-government in 1958 and full independence in 1960 under President Léon Mba. At independence there were two major political parties—Mba's Gabon Democratic Bloc (BDG) and the Social Democratic Union of Gabon, led by J. H. Aubame. Efforts by President Mba to eliminate his rival and institute a single-party state led to a rebellion of young military officers in February 1964. President Mba was deposed, but French troops intervened the next day and he was reinstated. Mba died in 1967 and was succeeded by Vice President Albert Bongo.

The Omar Bongo Regime (1967–2009)

After Bongo was reelected president, he announced that he was renouncing Roman Catholicism and adopting Islam, changing his name from Albert-Bernard to El-Hadj Omar. Bongo's single-party regime was authoritarian, quick to suppress the slightest sign of opposition, completely deaf to appeals for multiparty democracy, and utterly corrupt.

Declining oil prices in the 1980s brought on an economic downturn and increased political unrest. In 1990 budgetary belt-tightening—a consequence of austerities imposed by structural adjustment programs—set off street demonstrations by students and workers.

Shaken, Bongo at first rejected the notion of multiparty democracy, but quickly

Former President Omar Bongo

reversed his position. Opposition parties were legalized, but in parliamentary elections held in September and October the government demonstrated its reluctance to have its fate determined by voters. In what would become a recurring scenario, the election was manipulated and the opposition decried its fraudulence.

In December 1993, Bongo was reelected president by a modest 51% majority. His principal opponent was Father Paul Mba Abessole of the National Rally of Woodcutters (*Rassemblement National des Bûcherons*; RNB), but ten other candidates effectively diluted opposition voting. Complaints about electoral irregularities continued months afterward.

The same scenario was repeated in the presidential election of December 1998, when President Bongo was again opposed by Libreville's mayor, Paul Mba Abessole of the RNB, and Pierre Mamboundou of the High Resistance Council (*Haut conseil de la résistance*; HCR). The Ministry of the Interior announced final results: Bongo 66.55% and elected on the first ballot; Mamboundou, said the ministry, won 16.54% and Abessole collected 13.41%.

Observers noted the ministry had managed to add another 30,000 voters to the electoral lists a mere 48 hours before the election. Voters in precincts known to favor the opposition discovered that their polling place had been transferred to another site, usually at some distance. The regime even hired its own election observers—longtime friends of President Bongo in French legal circles—who dutifully reported that all was well.

International investigations revealed the nature and extent of Bongo's personal enrichment from Gabon's oil production. A U.S. Senate investigation named him as one of a "rogues' gallery" of foreign leaders who have funneled millions through American banks. In Switzerland an investigative judge developed testimony on the practice of offering "bonuses" to leaders of oil-producing states to secure exploration permits. Money—a minimum of $100 million—went into at least three accounts belonging to Bongo but held in another name. In October 2000, the Gabonese parliament offered protection to the president by amending the constitution to give former heads of state immunity from legal prosecution for any act committed in the performance of their official duties.

Legislative elections in December 2001 were yet another disaster. Opposition parties threatened to boycott when the electoral commission announced that the electoral rolls contained 778,000 eligible voters—nearly 75% of the country's population (in a country with large numbers of people under voting age). Cleanup reduced the number to a little less than 600,000, but 80% of those preferred not to go to the polls on election day.

Even though the courts invalidated 10% of the elections, (including one in which the winning candidate carried ballots from the polling place to the counting center) this scarcely affected the result. Bongo's ruling Gabonese Democratic Party (PDG) went into the election holding 90 of 120 seats and emerged with almost the same number. Some 24 parties put up candidates, but only eight could be considered oppositional. Even President Bongo's traditional rival, Paul Mba Abessole, broke with opposition calls to boycott the election.

Since becoming mayor of Libreville, Abessole had become an apostle of "convivial opposition," and the RNB participated in December's legislative elections with a clear eye to the future. Their reward

Oil storage at Port Gentil

Gabon

came in January 2002 when Bongo called for an "opening" of the government, and four members of the opposition were included in the new cabinet. Abessole was given the portfolio charged with human rights, but the Bongo clique retained control over all the more powerful ministries.

Control of state resources allowed President Bongo to fund and co-opt the opposition for years, and the regular migration from opposition to presidential supporter eroded public confidence in both the political system and individual politicians. Massive absenteeism continued to characterize elections and the turnout in the December 2002 local elections was so dismal that the opposition called for their annulment. One election official put it quite simply: "I don't know if the Gabonese have lost their sense of patriotism," he said, "but it's clear that they don't believe in elections any more."

Parliament amended the constitution in July 2003 to repeal a two-term limit for the head of state. Taking nothing for granted, parliament also amended the constitution to reduce the electoral process to a single round of voting: the candidate with the most votes on the first ballot, regardless of how few, will be declared the victor. The provisions guarantee lifetime tenure for President Bongo.

Already in power for 37 years, President Bongo ran again in the November 2005 presidential elections. None of his four opponents had much chance against the well-oiled electoral machinery of the PDG and President Bongo swept the field with 79% of the vote. Pierre Mamboundou, of the Union of Gabonese People (UPG), was expected to pose the greatest challenge, but received a paltry 13% of the vote, slightly down from his 16% showing in 1998. Zacharie Myboto, a former PDG heavyweight who had resigned from the party to run against the president, came in third with nearly 7%. The usual charges of electoral rigging were dismissed by Gabon's constitutional court, which declared Bongo officially reelected in January 2006.

The December 2006 legislative elections delivered a similar defeat to the opposition. The governing PDG won 82 of 120 seats in the National Assembly outright; 13 more deputies were elected from parties allied to it. The four "independents" were assumed to be favorable to the PDG. Pierre Mamboundou, runner up in the last presidential race, became the leader of the opposition when his UPG won eight parliamentary seats; the opposition Gabonese Union for Democracy and Development, led by the other defeated presidential candidate, Zacharie Myboto, won four seats. Given opposition thinness in the assembly, it posed little challenge to President Bongo.

Like Father, Like Son: Ali Bongo (2009–present)

Change of a sort finally came to Gabon on June 8, 2009, when Omar Bongo died in a Spanish Clinic at age 73. He had been Africa's longest-standing president, with an incredible 47 years in power. He left his country with no vice-president and a power vacuum. After a brief interim presidency of Senate speaker Rose Rogombe, elections were held on August 30, 2009. In September, the electoral commission announced that Ali Bongo Ondimba, Omar's son, had won with a plurality of 42% of the vote. André Mba Obame and Pierre Mamboundou, the two leading opposition candidates, each earned just over 25% of the vote. Unsurprisingly, the election was described as fixed by the opposition and critics, who focused on the dynastic element of the win. Riots occurred in Libreville and in Port Gentil, where opposition activists set fire to the French Consulate and broke into a prison, freeing hundreds of prisoners. Ali Bongo called for calm, and more importantly increased his security forces. In October, Gabon's Constitutional Court confirmed Bongo's victory.

December of 2011 witnessed another round of parliamentary elections in which the president's PDG party won 114 of the 120 seats available. Turnout was low at 34%, mainly due to a widespread boycott by the opposition and a general apathy in civil society. The trend seems to be that little of substance changes in Gabonese politics.

CONTEMPORARY THEMES

A Growing Economy

Gabon is among the richest of sub-Saharan Africa's tropical states due to several decades of oil, timber, and mineral extraction. It is the region's sixth largest oil producer, and crude oil exports are the backbone of the economy. Oil contributes 50% of GDP and represents 70% of total revenues. Sixty-five percent of government revenue comes from the oil sector, and budgets are seriously affected by price fluctuations in the world market. With a per capita income figure over $10,000, Gabon is a middle-income country, but there is also huge inequality and a lopsided income distribution. An estimated 21% of the population is unemployed, and one-third of Gabonese live below the international poverty line of less than one dollar a day. This poverty mostly lies in the inland area of the country where there are no roads with easy access and many areas that can only be reached by air.

Maize cropping in the rainforest
Photo by A. Binot
Courtesy of APFT–ULB

Oil is a nonrenewable resource and production in is slowing as Gabon's fields age and become exhausted. From a peak of 371,000 bbl/d in 1997, daily production declined to 242,000 bbl/d at present (2012–2013), and no major discoveries have been made in recent years. At the moment, much hope rests on ultra-deepwater drilling as a means to find new reserves.

Until the recent spike in oil revenues, Gabon's budgets usually ran in deficit, leading to a regular state of financial crisis. One critical aspect of the crisis is Gabon's huge accumulated debt—which soared to over $4 billion by 2008 and is still elevated at over $2 billion despite an oil price boom since that time. Debt servicing has exhausted as much as 50% of the budget in some years. Civil service salaries constitute another fifth of the budget, leaving little for investment and social services. The government is desperate to renegotiate its debt and to this end has sought assistance from the IMF, but Gabon is hardly a model of good governance and financial accountability. Lavish public spending regularly exceeds budgetary limits and needs to be significantly curtailed, yet one indicator suggested little belt-tightening: the prime minister appointed a cabinet of 50 members in early 2007.

As Gabon has seen its oil production (which is onshore) decline, it has eyed offshore possibilities. In February 2003, Gabon asserted sovereignty over the island of Mbanié in Equatorial Guinea's Bay of Corisco. The islet had been a point of contention since 1972 but took on strategic importance with the discovery of vast oil reserves in Equatorial Guinea's waters. In July 2004, the two governments announced an agreement to establish a Joint Oil Zone around the island, but its maritime boundaries were unresolved. In February 2006, UN Secretary-General Kofi

Gabon

Annan announced the two presidents had agreed to begin meetings on border demarcation; he expected the issue would be resolved "definitely before the end of the year." However, the issue is still simmering, and the UN continues to urge the two countries to resolve their dispute by establishing mutually agreed upon maritime boundaries.

Gabon's forestry sector is the country's second largest industry and, after the civil service, the country's second largest employer. Thick forests cover 76% of the country, and exports of timber have risen in recent years. In 1957, less than 10% of Gabon's forests were allocated as logging concessions; today more than half have been designated for logging. There is concern that, like oil, this resource may be rapidly exhausted. The government's new forestry code envisions a network of national parks, and President Bongo indicated the government planned to devote 10% of the national territory to the development of protected forest areas.

Having banned the cutting of its own old-growth trees in 1998, China became dependent on imported wood from places like Malaysia, Burma, Indonesia, and Gabon. China currently purchases some 65% of Gabon's annual 2.5 million cubic meters of mahogany exports. It also imports 1.5 million cubic meters of *Okoumé*, a softwood used in making plywood, that in turn is used to manufacture cheap bedroom furniture for export.

Chinese Investment and Concerns of Dependency

Gabon has become increasingly dependent on Chinese markets, and Chinese aid and cooperation loom large in Gabon's economic development. Omar Bongo traveled to China nine times, and over the decades met with Mao Zedong, Zhou Enlai, and Deng Xiaoping. When China's present leader, Hu Jintao, visited the African continent in February 2004, Gabon was his only sub-Saharan stop, after Algeria and Egypt—two other oil-producing states. In 2014, Gabon and China celebrated their 40th anniversary since the establishment of diplomatic ties.

As oil production faces prospects of declining volumes, the Bongo government pressed China and other investors to commit to development of its minerals sector. Gabon is the world's number two producer of manganese (after South Africa), and China is already the metal's principal importer. Huge reserves of iron, estimated at one billion tons, are located in the far north at Belinga, but the absence of adequate infrastructure to mine and move the ore has prevented development of the deposits. Given its voracious need for raw materials and its state corporations unhindered by the need to make a profit, China's seemingly uneconomic commitment to Belinga may be understood, however Gabon is still actively searching for investors. Development of Belinga will require construction of a hydroelectric dam on the Ivindo River to provide energy to operate mining equipment, two additional rail connections to the Transgabon Railroad, and construction of a deepwater port at Santa Clara to transport the ore.

China has already executed several high-profile projects in Gabon including hospitals in Franceville and Libreville and both the National Assembly and Senate buildings. One Chinese project became high profile when it fudged the boundaries of conservation and resource exploitation. China Petroleum & Chemical Corporation, more simply known as Sinopec, secured a concession to explore for oil in Gabon's Loango National Park, a small preserve of three climate zones—seashore, savanna, and forest—and photogenic wild-life—elephants, gorillas, and chimpanzees. (Tourist brochures referred to it as "Africa's Last Paradise.") Sinopec's environmental impact study was rejected by the Gabonese Environment and National Parks Ministry, which demanded the company cease its operations. This Sinopec refused to do, claiming authorization from the ministry of mines, and blissfully went about establishing the infrastructure of exploration.

Roads were cut into the forest, trees massively cleared away, and a village for 450 workers constructed. Dynamite facilitated destruction although its use is forbidden in a national park. Environmentalists were furious; the Gabonese government, which had lofted its eco-credentials by classifying one tenth of its territory a natural reserve, was embarrassed. Donors, including the EU, U.S., France, and the World Bank, which had set aside $10 million for Gabon's nature reserves, wrote letters of angry outrage. Ultimately the national parks council ordered Sinopec to halt its exploration activities. The company packed up men, machines, and dynamite sticks and departed paradise in October 2006.

In January 2014, another dispute against the Chinese oil company, Addax Petroleum Corp, was resolved as the company signed a 10-year contract for extraction in three Gabonese states with a price tag of 400 million dollars. The dispute started when Gabonese officials made complaints of the company including bad management practices, instances of corruption, avoiding taxes on oil exports, and lacking respect for the environment. Gabon continues to welcome Chinese corporations and investors in infrastructure and agriculture.

Politics and economy are very much family affairs in Gabon. Omar Bongo's eldest son Christian is a former deputy director-general of the National Timber Company (SNBG), which holds a monopoly on the commercialization of the two most valuable timber species—*Okoumé* and *Ozigo*. A deputy director-general of the *Union Gabonaise de Banques*, Christian Bongo was also president of the Transgabon Railroad's administrative council; the principal stockholders of the railroad are timber companies. He is now CEO of Gabon Airlines.

Social Development

Ali Bongo, before becoming President, was the chairman of the board of OPRAG (as well as defense minister), the country's port authority through which

The lagoon area near Port Gentil

Gabon

Gabon's principal natural resources—oil and timber—are shipped. This gave the current president a considerable position of leverage over the country's principal sources of wealth. It is not surprising that in Gabon the richest 20% of the population receives over 50% of the income, while 33% of all Gabonese live in poverty.

Situated on a strategically located peninsula, Libreville has experienced rapid growth. With a population of nearly 600,000, the city is dependent on imported food and is usually ranked among the most expensive cities in the world to live in. The poor of Libreville, seeking food and firewood in the surrounding area, contribute to enormous environmental pressures building up on the peninsula.

Over 89% of the population is literate. Two institutions of higher learning, Omar Bongo University (OBU) in Libreville and the Masuku University of Science and Technology at Franceville in the east, together enroll some 11,000 students in somewhat difficult circumstances. Built in the prosperous 1970s, OBU was designed to accommodate 3,000 students, but currently enrolls about 9,000.

Since 2011, the International Committee of the Red Cross (ICRC) has worked from Libreville in hopes of improving conditions for prisoners. On April 17, 2014, the ICRC signed an agreement with the Gabonese government to establish headquarters in Libreville. The organization hopes to continue their work in prisons while also promoting international humanitarian law between the armed forces and security forces, the authorities, universities, and the media.

Led by General Brice Nguema, a military coup was executed in August 2023 against his cousin President Ali Ondimba, shortly after reelection with his wife also subject to arrest on charges of money laundering. Former opposition leader Raymond Sima was appointed as prime minister while the former president was freed to leave the country.

The military leader of Gabon, Brice Oligui Nguema has won Gabon's presidential election by an apparent landslide winning 90 percent of the vote. Leader of the 2023 military coup, Nguema has been instrumental in ending 55 years of dynastic rule of the Bongo family in the eight-candidate race with the major opposition by Bilie-By-Nze winning a mere 3 percent. Promising to "restore dignity to the Gabonese people" by recovering "everything that has been stolen from the people," Nguema declared the country's foreign policy a success, citing increased international engagement and diplomatic achievements under his leadership including with the United States, France, Russia, and China. "Nguema inherits a country that spent five decades under Bongo rule," as the Bongo dynasty ruled Gabon through a web of patronage, distributing influential posts to allies and family members. Home to around 2.2 million people, Gabon holds substantial reserves of oil, gold, and manganese and is part of the Congo River Basin, a vital rainforest ecosystem. Yet, despite its natural riches, nearly 40 percent of young people remain unemployed, with the people focused on such immediate needs as restoring electricity, addressing food shortages, creating jobs, and ensuring the country's vast natural wealth (including oil, gold and manganese) benefits ordinary citizens. Once head of the Republican Guard under former President Ali Bongo, Nguema campaigned as a reformer wearing a baseball cap emblazoned with his slogan "We Build Together" and promising to clean up corruption, diversify the oil-heavy economy, and invest in agriculture, tourism, and industry as a third of the population still lives below the poverty line. Voter turnout in the election reached 70.4 percent, significantly higher than the 56.65 percent recorded in the disputed August 2023 vote, which saw Bongo declared the winner of a third term that resulted in a military coup. With the political establishment still deeply intertwined with the Bongo era, some in the country are wondering if this is a genuine break from the old system, or just a rebranding. With $3 billion in international debt, Gabon is under pressure to prove it can turn the page and build democratic legitimacy as the economy expanded by 2.9 percent in 2024, up from 2.4 percent the year before, buoyed by infrastructure development and higher output of oil, timber, and manganese.

FUTURE CONSIDERATIONS

Economically, Gabon still relies heavily on oil. These resources have made Gabon wealthier than most other African countries, and the recent surge of Chinese investment in Africa's energy sources will only contribute to this. However, oil revenues have not been widely distributed and there is a dramatic and depressing difference between the Gross Domestic Product (which counts the economic activity occurring in Gabonese territory) and the Gross National Income (which counts the income that Gabonese people themselves receive). Oil profits themselves also remain contingent on demand and the world price, and as reserves dwindle and fields dry up, it is essential that the Bongo government continue attempts to diversify and bring in foreign investment.

The Republic of Rwanda

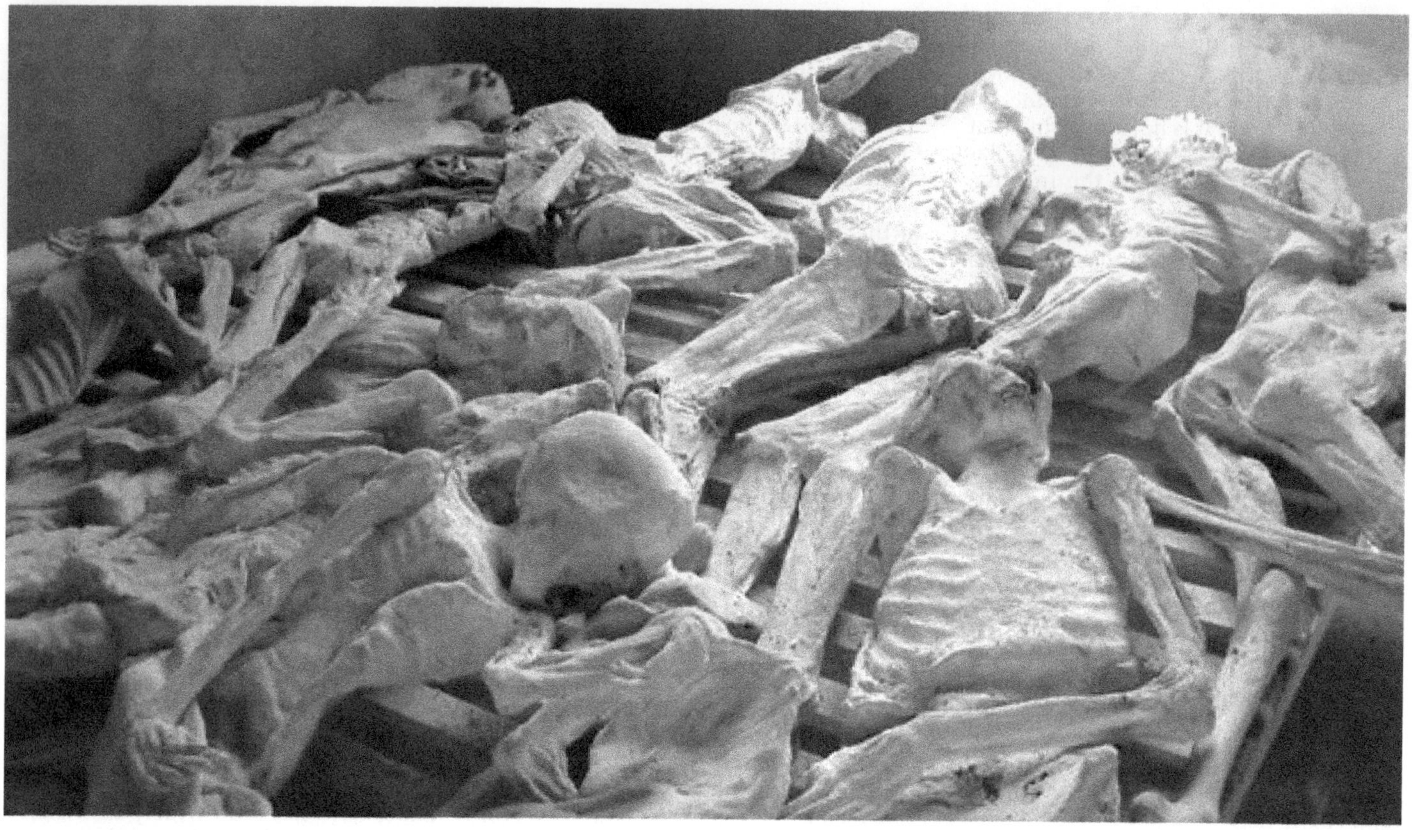

The Murambi Genocide Memorial

BASIC FACTS

Area: 26,336 sq. km. (slightly smaller than Maryland)
Population: 13,400,541 (June 2023 est.)
Capital City: Kigali
Government Type: Presidential Republic
Neighboring Countries: Democratic Republic of the Congo (west); Uganda (north); Tanzania (east); Burundi (south)
Official Languages: English, French, and Kinyarwanda
Other Principal Languages: KiSwahili
Ethnic Groups: Hutu 84%, Tutsi 15%, Twa (Pygmy) 1%. It is not possible to establish Rwanda's ethnic makeup accurately because the government has forbidden ethnic monitoring.
Principal Religions: Roman Catholic 50%, Protestant 40%, Muslim 2%, indigenous beliefs and other 8%
Former Colonial Status: Part of German East Africa (1899–1916); occupied by Belgian troops (1916); Belgian trust territory under the League of Nations and the United Nations (1923–1962).
Independence Date: July 1, 1962
GDP Per Capita (IMF 2023 est.): $970 (nominal), $3,090 (PPP)
Gini index: 43.7 (World Bank 2016)
Currency: Rwanda franc, 1 USD = 1117 Rwanda francs (Apr. 2023)
Inflation rate: 8.0% (2022 est.)
Chief Commercial Products: Coffee, tea, hides, and tin ore.
Personal Remittances: 280,069,130 (2020)
Foreign Direct Investments (FDI) net inflows: 291,726,096
Literacy rate: 75.9% (CIA 2021)
Life expectancy: 66.21 years (CIA 2023 est.)
Head of State: Paul Kagame, President (since April 22, 2000)
Head of Government: Prime Minister Edouard NGIRENTE (since August 30, 2017)

LAND AND PEOPLE

Rwanda is landlocked and lies in the eastern lake region of Africa and is composed for the most part of gently rolling hilly plateaus that once earned it the nickname the "African Switzerland." Sharp volcanic peaks rise in the west on the border of Lake Kivu. Another mountain range lies to the northwest, topped by Mt. Karisimbi (Rwanda's highest peak), at a height of 13,520 feet. Rwanda has a mild and temperate climate with two rainy seasons (February to April and November to January) – the temperature seldom rises above 80°F during the daytime and the nights are cool, with frost in the highlands and the mountains.

Centuries ago, the Virunga volcanoes, some of which are still active, dammed up a section of the Great Western Rift Valley, creating Lake Kivu. This lake drains into Lake Tanganyika to the south through the waters of the Ruzizi River. Volcanic activity thus diverted water that previously flowed northward to the Nile River, forcing it to flow westward to the Atlantic through the Congo River.

Music and dance are an important part of the lives of Rwandans, with the Intore Dance being the biggest exponent of this tradition. The Intore (or "the chosen ones," also called Rwandan Ballet) is a

Rwanda

musical tradition that celebrates heroism and victory. The traditional dance, once exclusive to the courts of the kings, can now be seen among the villages or at the National Museum of Butare.

HISTORY TO PRESENT DAY

For early history, see *Historical Background, The Colonial Period: The Germans* and *The Colonial Period: King Leopold and the Belgians.*

From Belgian Rule to Hutu Dominance (1960s)

In 1957, as the colonial period wound down in much of Africa, members of the majority Hutu ethnicity in Rwanda began to organize and articulate a political program to protest their maltreatment by the Tutsi ethnic group, which was a minority but dominated the political scene due to economic status and favoritism by the Belgian colonizers. The Hutus demanded a voice equal to their numbers and rose in revolt in 1959.

The 1959 revolution produced a civil war between Hutu and Tutsi and eventual consolidation of a Hutu-dominated state. The Tutsi king Mwami Kigeri V was forced into exile, along with thousands of other Tutsi, while hundreds of Tutsi were killed. With the success of the "Hutu Revolution," the colony of Rwanda abolished the monarchy and scheduled communal elections for 1960. Conducted under Belgian supervision, the elections resulted in a triumph for the *Parti du Mouvement de l'Émancipation du Peuple Hutu* (PARMEHUTU). Rwanda was declared a republic in January 1961 and became independent the next year under the leadership of Grégoire Kayibanda, Rwanda's first president. Ethnic clashes erupted again in 1963, driving more Tutsi into exile. Kayibanda gradually eliminated opposition parties; PARMEHUTU was the only party to present candidates for the elections of 1965 and the party returned to office in 1969.

Renewed strife between the Hutus and the Tutsi minority occurred in March 1973 following ethnic violence in neighboring Burundi. Kayibanda was criticized for being too lenient with the Tutsi, whose ethnic confreres were slaughtering thousands of Hutus in Burundi. At the same time regional tensions between northern and southern Hutus intensified. Suspecting Defense Minister Juvénal Habyarimana—the lone northerner in the cabinet—of disloyalty, Kayibanda ordered him arrested.

Juvénal Habyarimana and the MRND (1973–1994)

This resulted in a military coup by General Habyarimana on July 5, 1973, and a reordering of Rwandan politics. Power

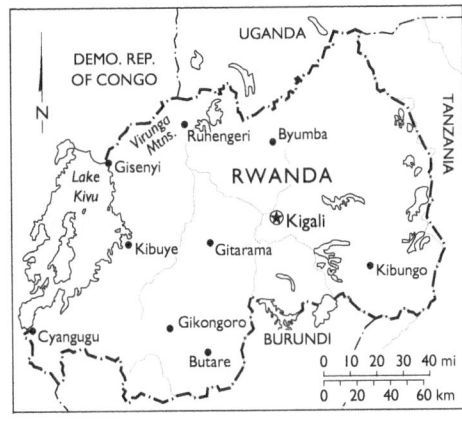

was shifted from civilians to military, and from Hutu of central Rwanda to those from the northern provinces. In 1975, President-General Habyarimana founded his own party, the *Mouvement Révolutionaire National pour le Développement* (MRND), assumed the party chairmanship, and so melded state and party hierarchies, that once were distinguishable from the other, down to the lowest level of administration. The regime increasingly discriminated against both Tutsi and Hutu not from the northwest. Within this privileged group there emerged an inner circle of friends and relatives of the president-general and his wife; the fruits of association with the presidential circle were great economic and political power, similar to other African countries. The *akazu*, or "little house," as this group was known, shared a Hutu supremacist ideology.

Habyarimana and the MRND held elections in 1978, 1983, and 1988, but were unopposed; by 1990, however, they faced increasing opposition from other sources. On October 1st of that year, the Rwanda Patriotic Front (RPF) attacked the country from its sanctuary in Uganda. The RPF was originally founded by the children of Tutsi refugees who had fled the country during the earlier Hutu revolution. President Habyarimana used the invasion as an excuse to arrest thousands of his opponents, both Tutsi and Hutu.

Under pressure from internal opponents, the international community, and the RPF invasion, Habyarimana finally agreed to a new constitution and multiparty elections in June 1991. The MRND was given a cosmetic change and was renamed the *Mouvement Républicain National pour la Démocratie et le Développement* (MRND). In April 1992, Habyarimana presided over the creation of a transitional government that included the opposition. For the first time the MRND became a minority party in the government, holding only 9 of 19 ministerial portfolios. Crucially, however, it maintained its control over local administration.

The new government also opened negotiations with the RPF. The result, known as the Arusha Accords, provided for the sharing of military and civilian power between the RPF, opposition parties, and the MRND. If implemented, this would have meant demobilization for many in Habyarimana's army and a significant loss of power, privilege, and profit for the Habyarimana inner circle.

To prevent such a loss, hardliners resorted to ethnic division and incitement to violence. They collectively stigmatized all Tutsi as accomplices of the RPF, and similarly launched public diatribes against Hutu opponents, especially those who did not hail from the northwest provinces. Hutu opposition parties were successively divided, each developing a wing that supported the government. Various Hutu parties mobilized radical youth wings, the most notorious of which was the MRND's *Interahamwe*. The parties then gave these youth wings military training and turned them into paramilitary groups. These groups created lists of persons to be eliminated, and local administrations (still controlled by the MRND) distributed arms to Hutu civilians. The gathered forces were organized for ethnic slaughter of Tutsis.

Fighting in Burundi following the assassination of its democratically elected Hutu president in late 1993 was the first major trigger, as Tutsis from Burundi poured into Rwanda by the tens of thousands. Clandestine and government radio stations in both nations fueled the flames of hatred. In Rwanda, the station RTLM (*Radio Télévision Libre des Milles Collines*) began broadcasting such messages as, "You [Tutsis] are cockroaches! We will kill you!"

Former President Bizimungu

Rwanda

President Paul Kagame

The Rwandan Genocide

The Rwandan genocide started on April 6, 1994, when a plane carrying President Habyarimana and the Hutu president of Burundi was shot down while attempting to land at Kigali airport. The enraged presidential guards embarked on barbaric slaughter of anyone considered the president's enemy—the Tutsi and any Hutu moderates. There is as yet no definitive forensic evidence from the crash telling who launched the rocket, but it is most probable that disgruntled Hutu military personnel were the perpetrators.

The genocide began with incredible speed, due to ample advance preparation and organization by elements of the Rwandan state in collaboration with Hutu militias. Within hours of the presidential plane crash, roadblocks sprang up around the capital Kigali to stop and kill Tutsi and suspected Hutu moderates. Members of Habyarimana's inner circle took control of the state and turned it into an instrument of genocide.

The genocide was horrifying in its dimensions. Conducted through the armed forces and the *Interahamwe* militia, the slaughter spread across the countryside, propelled by radio broadcasts and by killers who obligated other Hutu to kill or be killed. An unknown number of Rwandans participated in the killing. Trusted local institutions, from municipalities to churches, took part. Upwards of 900,000 people were killed over a 13-week period. Seventy-five percent of the country's Tutsi population was killed, most of them in the first five weeks. At the slaughter's peak, five people were killed every minute.

Western countries acted timidly and ineffectively, allowing the regime to consolidate its position in the early days after April 6 and continue the genocide thereafter. The magisterial Human Rights Watch report, *Leave None to Tell the Story,* is devastating in its condemnation of Western governments: "The Americans were interested in saving money, the Belgians were interested in saving face, and the French were interested in saving their ally, the genocidal government." "All of that took priority over saving lives." In 2008, the Rwandan government explicitly accused France of direct complicity in the genocide.

The genocide ended only with the successful military campaign of the Rwandan Patriotic Front (RPF) army, made up of diaspora Tutsi who had lived in Uganda and had been an important part of Yoweri Museveni's efforts to topple the government there. The RPF took the capital Kigali in July. Protected by a French "humanitarian" intervention, the Rwandan army and militias (trained and armed by the French) fled to Zaïre (now Democratic Republic of Congo), along with thousands of Hutu who now feared for their lives. Hutu militants took over the refugee camps and turned them into training grounds for yet another round of ethnic confrontation. The Tutsi search for security in this situation dominated every action of the RPF coalition government established by General Paul Kagame.

When President Mobutu of Zaire proved incapable or unwilling to control Hutu extremists in the eastern portion of that country, the RPF attacked and supported a successful rebellion against Mobutu. Laurent Kabila was installed in his place in 1997, and a year later, when Kabila himself had failed in his commitments to Rwandan security, a second intervention was undertaken, this time in support of Congolese Tutsi, called Banyamulenge, and other groups disenchanted with Kabila. Rwandan military activity in the Congo was not without criticism, including charges of rampant human rights abuses, smuggling, and corruption.

For the years from 1994 to 2000, the RPF government was nominally led by President Pasteur Bizimungu, a moderate Hutu who had been a critic of the Habyarimana regime, but Vice President Paul Kagame remained the central authority and retained the position of Minister of Defense. In April 2000, parliament elected Kagame as Rwanda's first Tutsi president. In his inaugural address, Kagame called upon diaspora Rwandans to return home to rebuild the country. He also justified the presence of Rwandan troops in the Congo as central to Rwanda's security concerns: Hutu *génocidaires* were sheltering in the Congo where they had been given arms and were allowed to carry out military training. Their only goal was to kill Rwandan citizens and destroy what had been reconstructed.

Following those guidelines, Rwandan military action focused on *Interahamwe* elements armed and employed by the Kabila government. Fighting resulted in a crushing defeat for the DRC government and its allies defending Pweto in early December 2000. Congo's then army chief of staff, Joseph Kabila, had to beat a humiliating retreat, abandoning his helicopter to escape the rout by ferryboat. Pweto marked a high-water mark for Rwandan arms and suggested the difficulty of its position before the international community. Hundreds of *Interahamwe* escaped across the border into Zambia, but the army held back from pursuing and destroying them, fearful of international reaction.

The Clinton administration, perhaps driven by the guilt of inaction during Rwanda's genocide in 1994, was lavish in praise and generous in support of the RPF government. Emergency military aid amounting to $75 million was dispatched soon after the RPF had installed itself in Kigali. After 2000, as the RPF established a stronger presence in the region, the Bush administration seemed more concerned about Rwandan militarism and its penetration into the Congo.

The government's priority was the arrest and trial of those Hutu strategists who conspired to create and implement the plan to destroy the Tutsi people. One example is Félicien Kabuga, described as "a mastermind behind the genocide." He was Rwanda's richest man, an owner of tea estates, transport companies and a variety of shops and factories. Part of the *akazu*—the Hutu elite that controlled wealth and power in Rwanda under president Habyarimana—Kabuga used his wealth to create *Radio Télévision Libre des Mille Collines* (RTLM), the most vile of the anti-Tutsi propaganda machines. He also used his wealth to import vast numbers of machetes to arm the *génocidaires.*

Kabuga remains at large, after failed attempts to capture him in Kenya, where his money apparently bought safety from prosecution for a time. Thousands of unrepentant Hutu extremists still shelter in the Congo; to Rwandans, they remain an omnipresent threat. In April 2005, the government signed cooperation agreements with police agencies in ten East Africa countries. Besides cooperation in eradicating illegal drugs and crime, the agreements will facilitate the transfer of criminals who flee to other countries to escape justice. The Rwandan government hopes the accords will help apprehend genocide perpetrators like Kabuga.

Rwanda

Ankole cattle grazing on the hills of Rwanda

The Aftermath: Attempts at Justice and Reconciliation

Some months after the genocide in 1994, the United Nations Security Council established the International Criminal Tribunal for Rwanda (ICTR), a special court intended to try the genocide masterminds. The court was headquartered created in Arusha, Tanzania and has operated since 1995. It has taken a methodical (some say slow) approach to justice. The total number of genocide leaders convicted has reached 46, with a dozen acquittals and 17 more cases in appeal as of 2013. The tribunal is intended to conclude its activities by the end of 2014, though there are still nine accused *génocidaires* still at large.

The relationship between Rwanda and Congo remains delicate. The Rwandan interventions in eastern Congo, with the formal objective of preventing another genocide, have killed thousands. Rwanda is known for supporting the Tutsi militia National Congress for the Defence of the People (CNDP) in Congo. Alleged support for these and other rebels resulted in the U.S., U.K., and the Netherlands suspending aid to Rwanda in 2012, though the Rwandan government denies that it is supporting rebellions in D.R. Congo.

In January of 2009, an agreement between the two countries led to the arrest of the general Laurent Nkunda, leader of the CNDP. The agreement establishes that Rwanda break up the CNDP and hand over Nkunda. Congo is meant to integrate the former CNDP's soldiers into the army and let Rwandan troops cross the border to fight against the Hutu militia, the Democratic Front for the Liberation of Rwanda (FDLR), composed of former génocidaires.

Domestically, President Kagame made some concrete steps toward national reconciliation. One symbolic and substantive example was the change of the previous mandatory national identity card, which bore the owner's ethnic identification, but does so no longer. The regime also established "solidarity camps" to reeducate both Hutu fighters returning from the Congo to seek reintegration into the Rwandan army and young Hutus who were arrested and imprisoned as child participants in the 1994 genocide. New national symbols—anthem, flag and coat-of-arms—were created in 2001. The new flag has a golden sun with 24 rays on a field of green, yellow, and blue. President Kagame said the colors stood for prosperity, wealth, peace, and happiness. Where the old national anthem lauded the supremacy of Rwanda's Hutu majority, the new one praises Rwanda's natural beauty and refers to its people simply as Rwandans. It was composed by a group of jailed Hutus awaiting trial on charges of genocide.

More than 120,000 prisoners were jailed for crimes arising from the 1994 genocide and kept in appalling conditions of incarceration. To break the judicial logjam, the government passed two pieces of legislation. One defined four categories of criminality, and the other created a system of grassroots justice—traditional village courts called *gacaca*. Under the new judicial legislation, only category one criminals—masterminds of the genocide—would be tried in the regular court system. All others would be brought before *gacaca* courts—ten villagers elected to hear and pass judgment.

Suspects would have to confront their own relatives and neighbors and those of their victims in a process that, it was hoped, would provide catharsis and social reconciliation. Those who had participated in the genocidal events of 1994 as children and have passed through a solidarity camp were expected to bear witness against those who had ordered and directed their murderous activities.

Truth-telling is at the heart of the child-participant's reeducation, and truth, perhaps more than justice, is the goal of the *gacaca* system. Rwanda's minister of justice described the system succinctly: "We've already seen in group trials that when people are brought together in a commune they do tell the truth. We take them to where the crime was committed, everyone comes, including witnesses, and they are charged there. The suspect fears to lie because everyone knows what happened."

The *gacaca* system has its flaws, but its roots are in traditional processes of reconciliation. The *gacaca* trials began in February 2005, but some were marred by a resurgence of violence. When a woman and her husband who were due to testify in one trial outside Kigali were hacked to death by unidentified people, most other witnesses refused to testify. Elsewhere genocide survivors have been murdered and others intimidated into fearful withdrawal of their witness; at least one *gacaca* judge has been murdered—by a relative—for not quashing an indictment.

In post-genocide Rwanda political life has been circumscribed. Given the experience of ethnic parties that fulminated group hatred, parties are prohibited from mentioning any ethnic affiliation. In local elections there is no party campaigning: candidates stand as individuals, not representatives of parties. On the other hand, women have, by design and by requirement, played a prominent role in Rwandan politics since 1994. As of 2008, Rwanda became the first and only country in the world with a national parliament that is majority female, 56.3% (by law Rwanda has a 30% quota). Few other countries come close to this gender parity, including, Sweden (47%), Cuba (43.2%—and the highest with no quota), Finland (41.5%), Netherlands (41.3%), and Argentina (40%). By comparison, the United States' legislature is 17% female.

Forming a political party in these circumstances is a risky business. Former president Pasteur Bizimungu, a Hutu who was the symbol of national reconciliation in the early post-genocide years, spent nearly one and a half years in jail after attempting to form his own political party—the Democratic Renewal Party (PDR). In his trial, which concluded in June 2004 and was widely seen as being at least partially motivated by politics, Bizimungu was sentenced to 15 years in

Rwanda

jail for embezzlement, inciting violence, and "associating with criminals." In April 2007, three years into his sentence, Bizimungu received a presidential pardon and was released from prison. By taking on such a high-profile individual, the government made abundantly clear its policies of reconciliation and unity would tolerate nothing that even hinted at "divisionism"—political language and appeal based on ethnic identity.

Hate speech is not tolerated. Rwandan police used all the high-tech capacity at their disposal to track down one hate monger who told genocide survivors, on live call-in radio, "we will kill you again." The punishment for incitement or genocide revisionism is ten to twenty years in jail. The president's attempt to mitigate ethnic identity has been criticized by human rights groups, who allege that outlawing ethnicity violates basic freedoms of expression. In 2007–08, around 1,300 cases involving genocide ideology were initiated in Rwandan courts. Some foreign critics, including journalists, are banned from the country.

Politics under Kagame in Contemporary Rwanda

The Rwandan parliament adopted a new constitution on April 23, 2003. The constitution created a semi-presidential regime, with a president elected by universal suffrage for a seven-year term (once renewable) and a bicameral parliament. Only 53 deputies of the 80-member National Assembly are elected by universal suffrage; the rest are designated in the name of their social category: 24 women, two youths, and one disabled person. The 26-member Senate is chosen indirectly. Local officials in each of Rwanda's 12 provinces select a senator and the president of the republic nominates eight; political parties appoint four, while colleges and universities elect the remaining two. Senators serve for a nonrenewable eight-year period.

One interesting (but potentially awkward) constitutional innovation attests to a desire to diffuse political power and emphasize unity in governance: the president, prime minister, and president of the National Assembly must all belong to a different political party. To prevent the dangerous hate mongering that facilitated genocide, political parties are strictly limited; they are not permitted to hold public meetings outside of electoral periods, and are strictly forbidden to make any reference, in any manner, to ethnic, religious, regional or clan differences. Several parties were forced to change their statutes and names: the Islamic *Parti démocrate islamique*, for example, became the "Ideal Democratic Party: *Parti démocrate idéal*, while the Christian *Parti démocrate chrétien* became the "Centrist" *Parti démocrate centriste*.

Eight political parties were registered to participate in the presidential and legislative elections that followed approval of the constitution. As the candidate of the RPF, Kagame won an overwhelming victory in August 2003 elections: 95% of the electorate supported him. His nearest opponent was Faustin Twagiramungu, a moderate Hutu. Twagiramungu had opposed President Habyarimana and helped revive the Republican Democratic Movement (MDR) of Grégoire Kayibanda, Rwanda's first president. He barely escaped assassination when the genocide began and became prime minister in the transitional government of July 1994. He received only 3.6% of the votes cast. In September of 2008, the parliamentary election guaranteed 42 of the 53 seats for the RPF coalition. The Social Democratic Party won 7 seats and the Liberal Party 4 seats. A coalition of about a dozen opposition parties called the United Democratic Forces remained in exile after the end of the genocide.

In April 2004, the tenth anniversary of the genocide, Kagame inaugurated a national genocide museum on one of Kigali's many hills; it stands atop five concrete tombs containing hundreds of coffins filled with the remains of an estimated 250,000 people killed in and around Kigali. On the occasion, Kagame said "We are prepared that what happened here should never happen again not only in Rwanda but anywhere in the world." Indeed, Rwanda was the first to send a peacekeeping contingent to Darfur as its genocide began to unfold.

The ceremonies of remembrance also displayed Rwanda's profound contempt for the shameful role of France in the decade-old events. In biting and undiplomatic language, Kagame detailed French activities in Rwanda, accusing the French government of arming and training government soldiers and militias and of being aware the extremists intended to commit genocide. France also provided an escape route to Zaïre for Hutu extremists as the RPF neared Kigale. It evacuated 394 regime officials by air—including President Habyarimana's widow—who were deeply implicated in planning the genocide. Unlike Belgium, France has yet to apologize for its actions in Rwanda.

In February 2005, French lawyers lodged six formal complaints with a military tribunal on behalf of genocide victims. The complaints allege complicity in the genocide on the part of French soldiers and have resulted in tense jurisdictional disputes in the judicial system. One courageous investigating judge, Bridgitte Raynaud, pursued her inquiry by traveling to Rwanda to conduct interviews, a move vigorously opposed by both the French Foreign and Defense ministries. Shortly after, she had compiled her preliminary report, the dossier was taken from her and handed over to another investigator. Military authorities appealed the validity of her investigation. Under pressure from her successor, Judge Florence Michon, the French government has announced the declassification of 105 military secret service documents relating to events in Rwanda.

President Kagame's outrage at France seemed to be triggered by an investigative report by a French judge looking into the downing of the Habyarimana plane in 1994. His conclusion, leaked to the Parisian daily *Le Monde* shortly before the tenth anniversary ceremonies, relied on regime dissidents and Kagame opponents who had long repeated the story that Kagame himself had given direct orders for the rocket attack on the plane. In December 2006, the judge recommended President Kagame be brought before the ICTR for "presumed participation" in the downing of Habyarimana's plane; arrest warrants on the same charges were also issued for eight of Kagame's close collaborators. Little judicial action is likely: in April 2007, the ICTR rejected a request from defendants before the court to prosecute Kagame for complicity in his predecessor's death.

President Kagame ended all diplomatic relations with France; French schools and cultural centers are shuttered, and Belgium looks after French interests. In August 2008, he charged that Paris had provided diplomatic, military, and logistical support to Hutus. In November 2009, France and Rwanda resumed diplomatic relations, although it is suspected that the tensions between the two nations will remain for some time. That same month, Rwanda was admitted to the Commonwealth, making it the second country (following Mozambique) to become a member without having a constitutional relationship to the United Kingdom or a British colonial history.

Despite the issues surrounding the relationship between France and Rwanda, recent events suggest some movement forward. In February 2010, President Nicolas Sarkozy of France paid an official visit to Rwanda. During this meeting—the first French presidential visit to Rwanda following the genocide—Sarkozy expressed regrets, saying "What happened here is unacceptable, but what happened here compels the international community, including France, to reflect on the mistakes that stopped it from preventing and halting this abominable crime." However, Sarkozy offered no official apology.

Meanwhile, in 2010, Kagame further consolidated his control of the political

Rwanda

system, giving rise to increasing objections to the non-democratic features of his rule. The election of 2010 saw Kagame win 93% of the vote, indicating that he faces no significant electoral challenge. Yet efforts to constitute a more viable opposition are emerging, albeit with resistance from the presidency. A new party known as the Rwanda National Congress was formed in late 2010 by prominent military officers. In February 2011, Kagame's government showed one response to opposition characteristic of authoritarian regimes by arresting an opposition leader on charges that many held to be trumped up. Bernard Ntaganda was sentenced to prison on charges of inciting ethnic conflict, but opponents of the ruling held that the motivation was to sideline a regime critic.

The last several years have been important for international court and genocide rulings in Rwanda. In June 2011, the former minister of family, Pauline Nyiramasuhuko, became the first female to receive a guilty verdict from the ICTR when it sentenced her to life imprisonment. In September of that year, Victoire Ingabire, previously a presidential candidate, was tried for denying genocide and affiliation with terrorists. (He was then sentenced in October 2012 to eight years in prison; his supporters claim the charges were trumped up and that the motivating factor behind his imprisonment was an attempt by the Paul Kagame regime to eliminate a political adversary.) The ICTR also overturned the convictions of two former ministers in February 2013, but sentenced another former minister, Augustin Ngirabatware, to 35 years in prison for his roles in organizing and inciting the genocide.

Alongside these events in the major international tribunals, Rwanda shut down its *gacaca* courts in June 2012. About 65% of the two million people tried in *gacaca* courts were found guilty. Human rights organizations criticized the courts for not meeting international legal standards.

CONTEMPORARY THEMES

Often described as the land of a thousand hills, Rwanda has an economy largely based on services and subsistence agriculture, 46% of the land is arable. It has engaged in a process of economic reconstruction following the genocide of 1994 which effectively cut Rwanda's GDP in half. Roads, bridges, and whole sectors of the economy were destroyed. Thanks to several years of relative stability, the GDP has grown annually, showing healthy growth rates averaging about 8–9% from 2005 to 2008. Growth is fueled by a booming construction industry (especially in Kigali) and increasing agricultural production. Given high population densities, questions of land use and allocation remain major issues.

Agriculture employs more than 90% of the population and contributes about one-third of GDP. Rwanda's most important exports are coffee and tea, which bring about 80% to 90% of export revenues. Tea production is strategically important to the country's economic development. Over the past 30 years it has grown consistently and now occupies 27,000 farmers and 30,000 workers. It is also the country's second most important export, representing 36% of total export earnings. In addition to coffee and tea, Rwanda also exports over 54 tons of flowers to European countries annually, making them the third largest export commodity.

The government's biggest economic problem, apart from security costs, remains the integration of more than two million refugees returning home. Housing, jobs, and land are of crucial importance. Some have been living as refugees since 1959. The fact that so many returnees did not speak French contributed to the decision to make English an official language. There are political and economic tensions between those who returned and those who stayed and survived the genocide. The victims have largely accepted integrating the former *génocidaires* into the society, and former FDLR soldiers are being promised new lives in Rwanda, after a process of indoctrination. But some survivors complain that returnees, with considerably more capital, are favored and privileged.

Rwanda needs to accommodate a population of over twelve million and steadily increasing demographic pressure. Population growth in 2014 was estimated to be 2.63% but by official estimates, a three percent annual population growth translates into a 93% increase in poverty. The population living below the poverty line is estimated at 45%. As a consequence, the government is drafting a law that may set a limit of three children per family. Rwanda is the most densely populated country in Africa.

As of the mid-2000s, Rwanda was a heavily indebted poor country (HIPC) with a total debt of $1.4 billion; its budget remained heavily dependent on foreign aid. At the July 2005 summit of the world's richest countries, known as the G-8, leaders pledged to cancel the debt of the world's most indebted countries, including Rwanda. The country became eligible for a 100% cancellation upon completion of certain requirements.

China has long been a significant investor in infrastructure projects, helping to build critical roads in a country without railways or navigable rivers. In May 2000, Chinese authorities agreed to fund a feasibility study for a rail link between Kigali and Northern Tanzania. China has also offered economic cooperation in agriculture (rice plantations and irrigation projects), energy (training in solar energy technology), and education. It has helped reestablish the Rwandan cement industry, while Chinese firms have rehabilitated the National Stadium and built the Kigali Conference Center. President Kagame has praised China for its policy of investment rather than aid, saying "The Chinese bring what Africa needs: investment and money for governments and companies."

About one-fifth of Rwandans live in urban settings, with an urbanization rate of 4.5% annually. On Rwanda's densely crowded hills. Houses are set within enclosures surrounded by cultivated fields. In addition to growing crops, most farmers also raise small livestock—goats, chickens, and rabbits. Only wealthy individuals have one or more cows. This pattern of family enclosures provides Rwandans with much valued privacy. Living close to their fields also allows farmers to better protect their crops from theft. Although most Rwandans are Christian, particularly among the Hutus, almost half retain traditional beliefs. Relations between the Rwandan government and the Catholic Church remain strained given the participation of clergy in genocide activities, and two priests have already been sentenced to death for participation in the genocide. Many Rwandans lost faith in their church, and though it is still a predominantly Catholic country, Rwanda's fastest growing religion is Islam.

HIV/AIDS affects an estimated 3% of the population (2012 est.). The virus was already working its way into Rwandan society by 1990, but the genocide contributed to its growth. The mass rape of Tutsi women was an integral part of the planned genocide for those who were not killed. According to the UN, more than two-thirds of the rape survivors were HIV-positive. One consequence of the 1994 genocide was that with so many men killed, female survivors in some cases prepared to share husbands in order to have a family. The practice of sharing men, known as *"kwinjira,"* is widespread in rural areas. Health officials say that it represents the greatest challenge to their efforts to combat the spread of AIDS. Kigale's street children, most of them AIDS orphans, were found to be sexually active at very early ages in a recent Johns Hopkins survey: 35% percent of children aged 6–10 were already sexually active, nearly half between 11 and 14 years, and over 81% at age 15 and above. The survey concluded that this is a "high risk population characterized by early sexual experimentation, multiple sex partners, unprotected sex, drug use and poor nutrition."

Rwanda

Malaria is another disease that strikes Rwanda. However, the country is an example of a successful policy against the disease through a strategy that combines the distribution of nets impregnated with long-lasting insecticides, indoor spraying, and medicines. In a short period of time, cases and deaths from malaria have dropped by two-thirds. This has contributed to recovery in life expectancy (which plummeted to under 27 years with the horrors of 1994) and its increase to an estimated 55 years as of 2013.

In April 2024, the country marked the 30th anniversary of the massacre of Tutsis as new mass graves in the country continue to be uncovered. Major foreign policy developments include a March 2024 decision by the United Kingdom to send African asylum seekers to Rwanda while the European Union has secured a deal with the country to acquire minerals for new forms of green energy.

Democratic Republic of the Congo (DRC) President Felix Tshisekedi and Rwandan President Paul Kagame held direct talks for the first time in March 2025 since Rwanda-backed M23 rebels seized two major cities in eastern DRC. In a joint statement issued with Qatar, whose emir mediated the talks in Doha, the countries called for an "immediate ceasefire" in eastern DRC with the two heads of State agreeing to continue the discussions to establish solid foundations for lasting peace. The DRC has accused Rwanda of sending weapons and troops to support the M23 rebels, which Rwanda has denied. The talks occurred after the M23 representatives pulled out of a planned meeting with the DRC government in Angola after the European Union imposed sanctions on some of the group's senior members, including leader Bertrand Bisimwa. The EU also sanctioned three Rwandan military commanders and other supporters of M23. The conflict in eastern DRC escalated in January 2025 when the rebels advanced and seized the strategic city of Goma, followed by Bukavu in February. M23 is one of about 100 armed groups that have been vying for a foothold in the mineral-rich eastern DRC near the border with Rwanda. The conflict has created one of the world's most significant humanitarian crises, with more than 7 million people displaced. The rebels are supported by about 4,000 Rwandan troops, according to United Nations experts.

FUTURE CONSIDERATIONS

Though Paul Kagame and the RPF will be remembered as the force that finally ended the Rwanda genocide and re-stabilized the country, they have also constituted a regime with a reputation for repression. Issues surrounding the freedom of other political parties and the press have begun to emerge, especially with relatively new opposition groups. In attempting to move past the genocide and its aftermath, President Kagame faces the balance between "progress and repression."

After the agreement with Congo, the Hutu militia FDLR was reduced to fragments hidden in the forest. The fear is that the FDLR—after losing their mineral revenues—will emerge from the jungle more desperate and dangerous. Also, other tensions might emerge from bringing the former Tutsi CNDP into Congo's army. With the question of security lingering, the legacy of the 1994 genocide remains present, as the country attempts

Rwandan peacekeepers, the first to be volunteered for service in Darfur, return home after a six-month stint in the genocidal region supporting the African Union mission. Logistical assistance for the homeward journey was provided by the U.S. Air Force.

Photo by Master Sgt. David D. Underwood, Jr., courtesy U.S. Air Force

Rwanda

to move through a painful reconciliation process. International tensions remain intact and have been mounting with the Democratic Republic of Congo since 2011, as the UN, the US, and other international actors have accused Rwanda of training rebels and thus promoting rebellion in the DRC. The UK redireected aid from the general budget towards poverty alleviation and education. And according to Human Rights Watch, the US government suspended military assistance to Rwanda under the Child Soldiers Protection Act.

April 2014 marked the twenty-year mark of the 1994 genocide. Rwanda over the past 20 years has achieved a remarkable peace and a surprising degree of social reconciliation, though there is a strong sense that the Kagame government has used a quite heavy hand to suppress tensions and to keep the lid on any dissent. While the country faces many of Africa's most significant problems—poverty, HIV/AIDS, unemployed youth, lingering ethnic tension, and apparent infringements on civil liberties—Rwanda also exhibits prospects for social development for the future. In 2010, the World Bank named the country its top reformer in the world for the ease of doing business, and sustained investments in service industries may yet see the country move ahead economically, albeit at the cost of authoritarian governance.

The Democratic Republic of São Tomé and Príncipe

São Tomé's volcanic shoreline

Photo by Fabien Violas

BASIC FACTS

Land: 1,001 sq. km. = 385 sq. mi. (About one-third the size of Rhode Island.)
Population: 220,372 (June 2023 est.)
Capital City: São Tomé
Government Type: Semi-Presidential Republic
Climate: Tropical; hot, humid; one rainy season (October to May)
Official Language: Portuguese
Other Principal Language: Crioulo
Ethnic Groups: Mestico, Angolares (descendants of Angolan slaves), Forros (descendants of freed slaves), *Serviçais* (contract laborers from Angola, Mozambique, and Cape Verde), Tongas (children of *Serviçais* born on the islands), and Europeans (primarily Portuguese)
Principal Religions: Roman Catholic, Evangelical Protestant, and Seventh-day Adventist
Independence Date: July 12, 1975 (from Portugal)
GDP Per Capita (IMF 2023 est.): $2,695 (nominal), $4,874 (PPP)
Gini index: 56.3 (2017)
Currency: São Tomé Dobras, $US 1 = 22.25 old dobra (June 2023)
Inflation Rate: 14.5% (2022 est.)
Chief Commercial Products: Cocoa, copra (for coconut oil), coffee, palm, and oil
Personal Remittances: 8,620,359 (2020)
Foreign Direct Investments (FDI) net inflows: 27,098,307
Literacy Rate: 94.8% (CIA 2021)
Life Expectancy: 67 years (CIA 2023 est.)
Head of State: President Carlos Manuel Vilanova (since October 2, 2022)
Head of Government: Prime Minister Patrice Trovoada (since Nov. 11, 2022)

LAND AND PEOPLE

São Tomé and Príncipe form an archipelago of two main islands and several associated islets lying just north of the Equator. São Tomé is 275 miles off the coast of Gabon; Príncipe is 125 miles off mainland Equatorial Guinea. Of volcanic origins, the islands have fertile central highlands from which numerous fast flowing streams carry soil to the ocean. Tropical rain forests cover 75% of the land area and shelter flora and fauna similar to that found on mainland Equatorial Guinea.

Wilder than Cape Verde and closer to Europe than the Caribbean, São Tomé and Príncipe represent a relatively unspoiled paradise for tourists. Clean beaches, the stunning Blue Lagoon, rain forest and mountains with the Obo Natural Park are all available to the intrepid. These would appear to be few: over the last decade the number of visitors to the islands has averaged around 6,000 a year. The climate is equatorial, with the driest and coolest months being from June to September. Roads are few, and any serious tourism requires four-wheel-drive vehicles. São Tomé, the capital, has a wealth of down-at-the-heels colonial architecture. The city's atmosphere is unrushed and unhurried. Blackouts are frequent, adding to the somnambulant mood. For many, the best cup of coffee in the world comes from local beans.

HISTORY TO PRESENT DAY

For early history, see *Historical Background* and *The Colonial Period: The Portuguese.*

Toward the end of Portuguese rule in Africa, a Committee for the Liberation of São Tomé and Príncipe was created in exile in 1960. It changed its name to the Movement for the Liberation of São Tomé and Príncipe (MLSTP) in 1972. Unlike its

São Tomé and Príncipe

counterpart in Guinea-Bissau, the MLSTP never mounted a guerrilla campaign against the Portuguese.

Following the overthrow of the Salazar dictatorship in 1974, African troops in São Tomé mutinied, and the new government agreed to hand over power to the MLSTP in 1975. Independence was granted on July 12, 1975. Most Portuguese had already departed, taking skills and capital with them. At independence, the Portuguese legacy was a 90% illiteracy rate, few skilled workers, and abandoned plantations.

The MLSTP became the nation's sole political party and ruled with little tolerance for opposition for 15 years. Its leader, Manuel Pinto da Costa, assumed the new nation's presidency, and Miguel Trovoada, another founder of the MLSTP, was elected prime minister.

To cope with the country's disastrous economic inheritance, President Pinto da Costa turned to Marxist-Leninist models of political and economic organization. The government nationalized most plantations, and no one was allowed to own more than 247 acres. The single ruling party largely absorbed the country's organizational life. Social control and surveillance were organized through a series of people's militias set up in workplaces and villages.

When cocoa prices collapsed in the mid-1980s, the economy was severely damaged. Popular dissatisfaction led to a process of liberalization, and multiparty democracy was introduced in 1990. Constitutional reforms included the direct election of the president, and Miguel Trovoada, whom Pinto da Costa had accused of complicity in a coup plot and had jailed from 1979 to 1981, returned from exile to battle his old comrade-in-arms for the presidency. Running as an independent, Trovoada won. He survived a coup attempt in 1995 and went on to win reelection to a second five-year term in 1996 against his old foe, Manuel Pinto da Costa. Despite this turn to more open elections, the country's political and economic crisis continued.

In November 1998 legislative elections the MLSTP, in alliance with the Social Democratic Party (PSD), won an absolute majority 31 of 55 seats in the National Assembly. President Trovoada's Independent Democratic Action (ADI: *Ação Democrática Independente*) became the official opposition. São Tomé's politics remained bitter, personal, and contentious.

The government continued to face serious social agitation in the late 1990s. Workers saw their own conditions deteriorating while rumors of a huge oil bonanza were rife. Civil servants, including doctors and teachers, regularly went on strike to protest their salaries and working conditions. In July 1999, president Trovoada admitted that salaries and pensions were

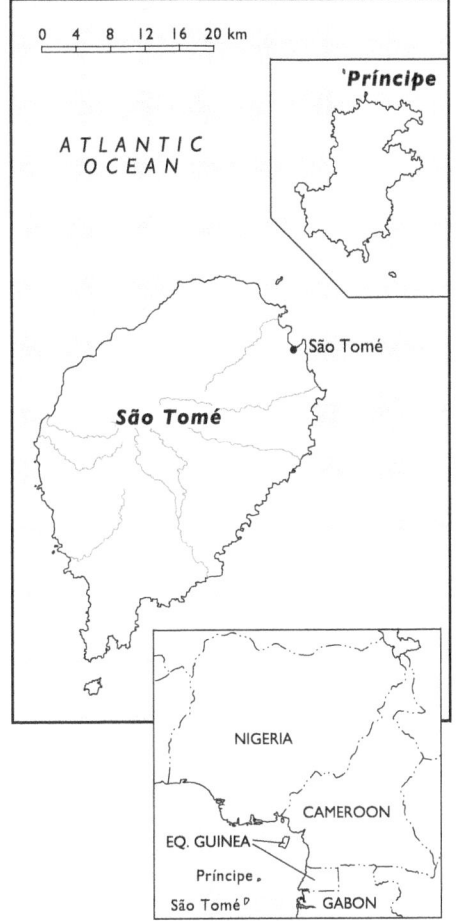

inadequate and sent a warning to the government: "São Tomé's oil cannot be a matter for political colleagues, friends and relatives. Its revenue should benefit citizens and the population as a whole." With remarkable candor Trovoada accused "a number of citizens and political leaders of eagerly getting themselves into positions to reap fabulous personal benefits."

The July 2001 election results came as a surprise to many. The best-known name—former President Manuel Pinto da Costa—went down to a humiliating defeat, unable to get enough votes to force a runoff election. Fradique de Menezes, a wealthy businessman, was elected president with 56.31% of the vote. Pinto da Costa received only 38.73%, with the remaining ballots distributed among three minor candidates.

Fradique de Menezes interjected an entrepreneurial dynamism into the campaign, while for most São Toméans, Pinto da Costa resurrected memories of authoritarian single-party rule and Marxist-Leninist economic policies under the MLSTP. Where da Costa spoke of a fair distribution of oil and gas revenues, de Menezes said he would encourage investment in agriculture, the mainstay of the country's economy.

In addition to wanting abandoned agricultural concerns to be rehabilitated, de Menezes argued that the bloated bureaucracy created by the MLSTP would have to be reduced and good managers for the public sector found. "We have made lots of mistakes in our 26 years of independence," he said. "We have destroyed what little we inherited from the colonial era. Does it make any sense that there should be only one hospital in the entire country?"

Stalemate between the new president and the MLSTP majority in parliament made cohabitation impossible. The National Assembly was dissolved and legislative elections held in March 2002. The political kaleidoscope shifted slightly, but politics continued pretty much as usual. The ADI went through an internal crisis, divided between supporters of ex-president Trovoada's son Patrice, and the party's secretary-general Carlos Neves. President de Menezes backed the formation of the Democratic Movement of Forces for Change (MDFM), which attracted a number of ADI dissidents and joined with the only other party to hold seats in the National Assembly—the *Partido da Convergência Democrática* (PCD). Wealthy and ambitious, Patrice Trovoada linked up five parties to create an opposition alliance, Ue-Kedadji (Light of Day).

Since party platforms were largely similar, voters could make few sharp distinctions; the election resulted in a virtual tie, the MLSTP winning 24 seats and the MDFM/PCD 23. Ue-Kedadji took the remaining eight seats. President de Menezes, who had hoped for a parliamentary majority, was forced to accept a coalition national unity government.

São Tomé has a semi-presidential political system that combines aspects of both presidential and parliamentary systems: the president who nominates the prime minister, who must be approved by the National Assembly. This generates some institutional conflicts, with both executive and legislature vying for primacy. Tensions between president and Assembly are regular, persistent, and potentially de-stabilizing. They spiked in early 2003 as President de Menezes dealt with the sensitive issues surrounding São Tomé's oil future and its relationship with the colossus to the north, Nigeria.

Finding three oil contracts signed by the Trovoada government grossly unfair, de Menezes rejected them and demand renegotiation. The president was also engaged in delicate negotiations with Nigeria over disputed boundaries, critical because of potentially vast oil resources located in the disputed territories. Since the negotiations were being handled almost exclusively by the president and his natural resources minister Rafael Branco, the institutional jealousy of the Assembly was roused. (Once the boundary dispute was settled, valuable exploration rights would be sold

São Tomé and Príncipe

off, a honey pot to which legislative factions did not want to be denied access.)

The legislature introduced legislation to amend the constitution and reduce the power of the presidency, including limiting the president's ability to negotiate international treaties. Terming the proposed reforms a "palace coup," President de Menezes vetoed the amendment package and dissolved the Assembly. Mediators managed to soothe ruffled feathers: the dissolution was withdrawn, and the Assembly agreed to a package of constitutional amendments to reduce the power of the presidency, but also reduce the possibility of hostile cohabitation between presidents and prime ministers.

Relations with Nigeria pit David against Goliath; the resources were utterly asymmetrical, with Nigeria having 800 times the population. To resolve the boundary dispute, President de Menezes deftly lined up a number of backers. Membership in the community of Lusophone (Portuguese-speaking) states gave access to the experience of East Timor, which renegotiated its oil contracts with Australia. More importantly, it brought the weight of countervailing influence from West Africa's other petroleum giant, Angola. Finally, de Menezes mobilized support in the United States, stressing São Tomé's democratic credentials, relative stability, and strategic location in an oil-producing area that could easily replace a hostile, dangerous, and unstable Middle East. The efforts by de Menezes worked as Americans pressured Nigeria to give up efforts to station a force of two hundred soldiers in São Tomé. Three questionable oil contracts were successfully renegotiated, and, once those impediments had been cleared away, the boundary settlement was finalized.

Despite successful conclusion of the boundary and contract issues, political tensions between the president and his critics persisted, fanning social discontent as the bulk of the population saw little improvement in the standard of living. On July 16, 2003, soldiers staged a *coup d'état*, seizing key sites and arresting government ministers. (President de Menezes himself was in Nigeria at the time.) The coup was mounted by local soldiers (who had grievances about living conditions, salary arrears, obsolete equipment, and government corruption) and members of a small, shadowy, and marginal political party, the *Frente Democrata Cristã* (FDC: Christian Democratic Front).

Universally condemned, the coup ended within a week. President de Menezes was reinstated but agreed to greater transparency in oil negotiations and greater respect for the separation of powers between the presidency and

Former President Fradique de Menezes
Photo by AFP/Andre Kosters

parliament. Parliament unanimously approved a general amnesty for the putschists, while Nigeria, South Africa and the United States agreed to take on the role of guarantors of the country's stability.

By March 2004, political tensions between president and parliament reached crisis proportions over the development of São Tomé's oil resources. Prime Minister Maria das Neves (MLSTP) demanded the resignations of her ministers of natural resources and foreign affairs, both of whom she accused of negotiating petroleum agreements without her knowledge. Both ministers were members of the president's Democratic Movement of Forces for Change (MDFM) party, and when the two other MDFM ministers resigned in solidarity, the prime minister's three-party coalition government was reduced to two parties and the slimmest of majorities in parliament.

After months of rivalry, Menezes dismissed das Neves in September 2004 when her name was raised in a corruption scandal. Damião Vaz d'Almeida, a former labor minister, was asked to form a government and managed to cobble together a coalition of MLSTP and ADI ministers. His tenure was brief. In June 2005, he resigned following controversial and disadvantageous oil exploration awards imposed by Nigeria as part of its Joint Development Zone agreement with São Tomé. As his replacement President Menezes appointed another MLSTP figure, Maria do Carmo Silveira, the former governor of the Central Bank. Testimony to the persistent tensions between president and government, Silveira was the sixth prime minister Menezes had appointed since his election in 2001.

Parliamentary elections in March 2006 provided no clear political mandate to São Tomé's contending factions and offered little prospect of future political stability for the country. The MDFM, which had previously been in opposition, took 23 of 55 legislative seats. Its main rival, the MLSTP, returned with slightly fewer seats—20. The big winner was Patrice Trovoada's Independent Democratic Action party (ADI), which increased its representation to 11 from its previous four. The remaining seat was won by the small *Novo Rumo* (New Direction) party.

To unseat President Menezes, the MLSTP unprecedentedly agreed not to run its own candidate in the July 2006 presidential elections; instead, it backed the ADI's Patrice Trovoada. The ploy was to no avail. Menezes won 58.85% of the votes cast, a decisive victory over Trovoada's 37.73%. In his concession speech, Trovoada wished his opponent "good luck," and continued by saying he would be "attentive to every measure taken by Fradique de Menezes as president of the republic, notably the way in which he exercises power."

For virtually the entire first term, President Menezes was confronted by hostile governments and parliaments. Constitutional amendments approved in early 2003, which took effect in September 2006 at the beginning of his second term of office, clarified the respective authority of both president and prime minister. In the new dispensation the president can appoint prime ministers, dissolve parliament and call elections.

The clarification of authority in a formal-legal sense has done little to sort out the political scene, however. Following Maria do Carmo Silveira, Tomé Vera Cruz took the prime ministerial post at the head of the winning coalition in April 2008. This lasted for a year, until Menezes appointed his rival Patrice Trovoada as prime minister. Trovoada's government lasted even less time, being defeated in a no confidence vote within months. Joaquim Rafael Branco of the MLSTP/PSD became the prime minister

The specifics of the situation changed again with legislative elections in August 2010. The ADI took a plurality of seats (26 of 55), MLSTP-PSD took 21, the PCD seven and the MDFM one. Trovoada was reinstated in the post of prime minister after the elections.

Presidential elections in 2011 resulted in the return of independence era leader Manuel Pinto da Costa. With Fradique de Menezes prohibited from running by term limits, the presidential field was open, and Pinto da Costa ran as an independent, having left his former party, the MLSTP. He advanced to a runoff against Evaristo de Carvalho of the ADI and emerged victorious with 53% of the vote. As had been

São Tomé and Príncipe

the case in several previous elections in São Tomé and Principe, the results were deemed free and fair by international observers. Patrice Trovoada served as prime minister for over a year but following a parliamentary no-confidence vote in his government in December 2012, Pinto da Costa replaced him with Gabriel Arcanjo Ferreira da Costa.

CONTEMPORARY THEMES

The country has been traditionally dependent on the export of cocoa. In 1975, Portuguese plantation farmers held 90% of all cultivated land on the islands. After independence, with a regime in the thrall of Stalinist economic thinking, the cocoa plantations were collectivized. Production collapsed and the plantations deteriorated. From exports of 11,400 tons of cocoa in 1900, production plummeted to 4,000 in 1996.

São Tomé's dependence on cocoa has been virtually total, and it suffers greatly from the fluctuation of cocoa prices on world markets. Any fall in prices is especially disastrous for small producers, many of whom are forced into debt. The islands have consequently faced vertiginous inflation and high unemployment.

The most important potential for São Tomé lies in its oil prospects. President de Menezes successfully renegotiated several onerous industry contracts, the worst of which goes back to 1997 when one of the minnows of the industry, Louisiana-based Environmental Remediation Holding Corporation (ERHC), secured a contract which gave it enormous control over the country's oil development. After a new contract with the company modifying overly generous provisions was initialed in 2003, São Tomé and Nigeria signed a settlement of their boundary dispute.

The settlement creates a Joint Development Zone (JDZ) out of the area of overlapping claims. The two states will jointly develop the JDZ and share the resources on a split of 60% for Nigeria and 40% for São Tomé. (Reserves in the JDZ could potentially amount to 14 billion barrels.) In February 2005, the two signed the first agreement for exploration in the JDZ with a consortium headed by ChevronTexaco and ExxonMobil. The signature bonus was nearly $125 million.

A second round of bidding for exploration rights in additional JDZ blocks in December 2005 proved highly controversial when many of the winners turned out to be obscure Nigerian firms with little experience and less capital, but with solid political connections in both Nigeria and São Tomé. The islands' attorney general found serious flaws with the whole process, much to his country's financial detriment. The entire bidding round was subject, he said, to "serious procedural deficiencies and political manipulation, including the award of interests to many unqualified firms or firms with inferior qualifications, technically and financially."

One of those companies was the already notorious Environmental Remediation Holding Corporation (ERHC). The firm, now called ERHC Energy and controlled by a Nigerian capitalist, had no experience with deepwater drilling and reportedly only one paid employee, its president. What it did have were preferential rights to equity in São Tomé's oil acreage and valuable fee waivers earned by providing technical and financial services in the 1990s. It exercised them in the December bidding round. According to Attorney General Adelino Pereira, ERHC's participation discouraged more qualified companies from bidding because of "reputational, financial and technical concerns." Because the company had no obligation to pay the requisite signature bonus, São Tomé lost approximately $60 million.

Actual oil production is many years off. While São Tomé awaits discovery and production from the JDZ, Nigeria is to provide it with 10,000 barrels of crude oil daily, thus providing an oil dividend income before actual production begins. The two nations set up a joint commission in 2009 to protect offshore crude oil fields.

Until oil investment and production revenues begin to flow, São Tomé will remain largely dependent on foreign aid. Foreign aid, mostly supplied by Taiwan, France, and Portugal, once accounted for about 80% of GDP and covered 95% of public investment. That represented one of the highest per capita aid rates in the world—$239.4 per person in 2003.

São Tomé's rain forest

The World Bank and IMF have agreed to help reduce the country's debt obligations through the Highly Indebted Poor Countries Initiative. In March 2007 São Tomé reached a completion point in the program; its debt reduction will amount to some $263.46 million.

São Tomé is central to the U.S. strategy for ensuring security of oil supplies from the Gulf of Guinea. In early 2004 it agreed to finance an $800,000 viability study for expanding São Tomé and Príncipe's international airport and building a deep-water port. The islands are an ideal location for monitoring satellite observations of the Gulf of Guinea.

Considered a model of parliamentary government and political stability, the island nation successfully thwarted a coup attempt in November 2022 allegedly led by Delfim Neves, the former leader of the national assembly, who lost his seat in the national elections won by the Independent Democratic Action (IDA) party that secured an absolute majority.

On the international front, the island nation signed a military accord that with Russia in April 2025 dealing with military training and delivery of old Soviet-era stockpiled explosives aimed at renewing the country's worn-out equipment. According to Prime Minister Patrice Trovoada, there was nothing special in the deal as he noted "many more commitments on the military side with the United States and NATO compared with Russia," dismissing the pushback from Portugal and others. An aid-dependent island country off the coast of West Africa, São Tomé and Príncipe is willing to work with all actors and does not demonize any one country.

FUTURE CONSIDERATIONS

São Tomé and Príncipe is one of the African continent's more democratic polities, though politics on the islands is tumultuous. President de Menezes went through a number of prime ministers and governments in his years in office. The political situation gives rise to frequent interpersonal and partisan tensions, but these do not appear to be going beyond what is to be expected in a democratic polity. Paradoxically, the trials and tribulations of the country's politics may be impressive: crises of particular governments in São Tomé and Príncipe have not become crises of the constitutional regime.

Somewhat more worryingly, concerns about a coup plot surfaced in February 2009, with the authorities turning back a small boat replete with armed men and detaining a number of people for questioning. In early 2010 the organizers of the attempted coup, including the leader Arlecio

São Tomé and Príncipe

Costa, were all pardoned and released from prison. The end of the de Menezes years seem unlikely to reshape fundamentally the personalist politics of the island nation, and the approach of the new Pinto da Costa presidency is an open question.

The question of political progress in the country is made all the more pressing with the prospects for economic change in the islands. With control of oil revenues at stake, political tensions in São Tomé are more important than ever. Foreign investment, combined with American naval interest in the oil-rich waters along this stretch of the Atlantic, make São Tomé and Príncipe a country to watch in the near future.

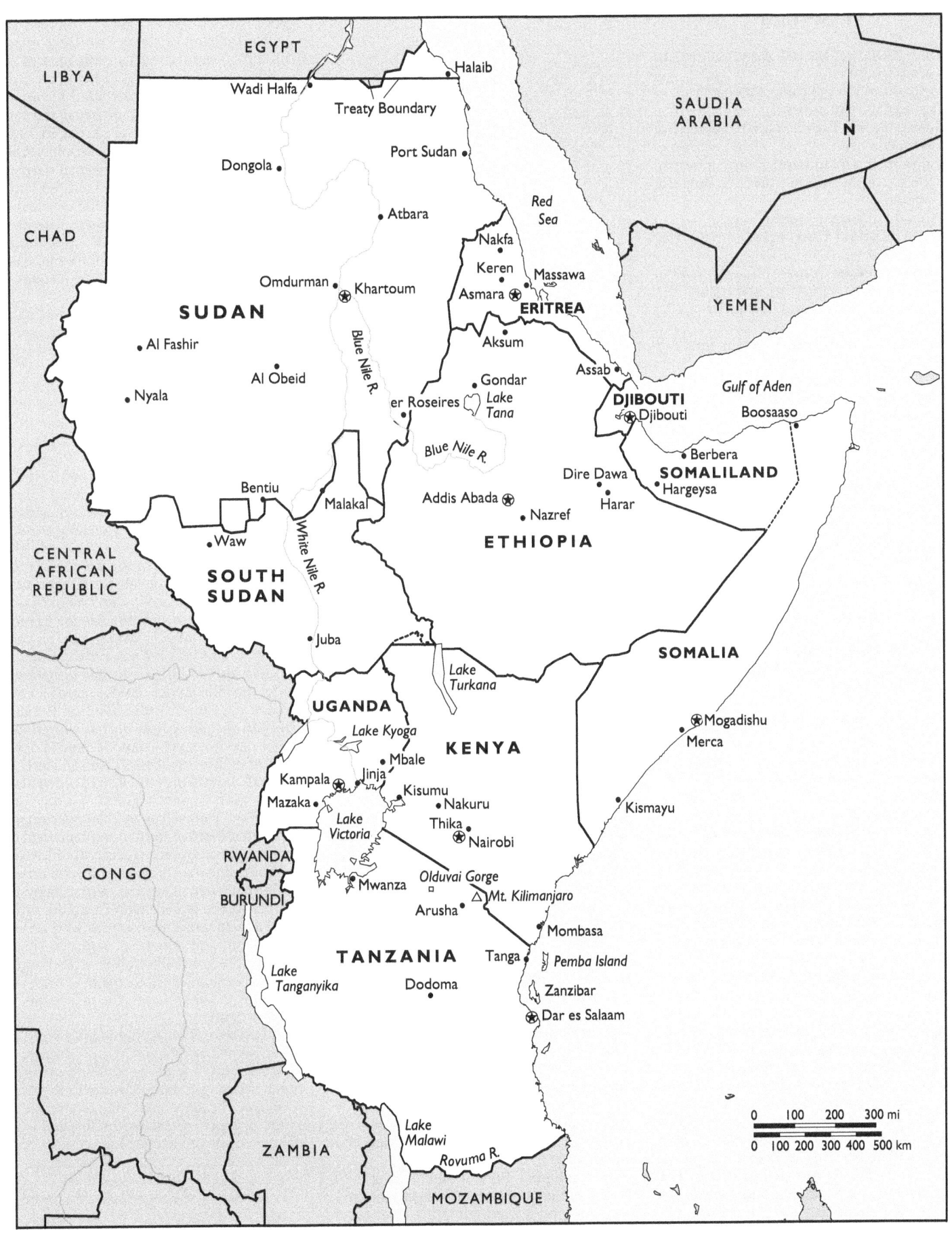

The Republic of Djibouti

BASIC FACTS

Area: 23,200 sq. km. (slightly larger than Massachusetts)
Population: 976,143 (June 2023 est.)
Capital City: Djibouti
Government Type: Semi-Presidential Republic
Neighboring Countries: Ethiopia (north, west, south); Eritrea (north); Somalia (south)
Official Language: Arabic, French
Other Principal Languages: Somali, Afar (Danakil)
Ethnic Groups: Somali 60%, Afar 35%, French, Arab, Ethiopian, and Italian 5%
Principal Religions: Muslim 94%, Christian 6%
Former Colonial Status: French Territory (1896–1977)
Independence Date: June 27, 1977
GDP Per Capita (IMF 2022 est.): $3,802 (nominal), $6,894 (PPP)
Gini index: 41.6
Currency: Djibouti franc, $US 1 = 177.7 francs (June 2022)
Inflation Rate: 3.8% (2022 est.)
Chief Commercial Products: Hides and skins, and coffee (in transit)
Foreign Direct Investments (FDI) net inflows: 152,998,239
Literacy Rate: 65% (CIA 2021)
Life Expectancy: 65.61 years (CIA 2023 est.)
Head of State: Ismail Omar Guelleh, President (since May 8, 1999)
Head of Government: Prime Minister Abdoulkader Kamil Mohamed (since April 1, 2013)

LAND AND PEOPLE

The Republic of Djibouti is a tiny, hot pocket of land strategically located at the entrance to the Red Sea. Its separate existence as a colony was derived from the deep, natural harbor at the city of Djibouti, through which Ethiopian exports and imports traveled overland since the beginning of the 20th century. The desert country of the interior is parched and bleak, an irregular landscape seen infrequently by other than the nomadic herdsmen who pass through.

The city of Djibouti is French in atmosphere; with large numbers of servicemen from France, Germany, and the United States. Over 20,000 Europeans live in the capital, and the city has seen some cultural challenges as a result: bars and restaurants serve the soldiers, but the police once tried to close many of these down as offensive to "good morals in a Muslim country." The cost of living is high as well (with a beer in town costing $6, or more than a day's wages.) The prices have helped keep U.S. servicemen largely confined to a camp that brings in its own supplies and contributes little to the economy.

A widespread practice is the use of *khat* (or *qat*), a stimulant common throughout the Horn of Africa. It is a social drug that is chewed and nor swallowed. Much of Djibouti's business activity grinds to a halt at midday; the midday heat has become a time to take breaks and chew the drug. Women are discouraged from chewing *khat*, and if they do it, it must be done in seclusion.

HISTORY TO THE PRESENT DAY

For early history, see *Historical Background* and *The Colonial Period: The French.*

Most of France's African colonies gained independence in 1960 (with Guinea as early as 1958), but the territory known as French Somaliland voted in 1958 to remain associated with France. French president Charles de Gaulle's August 1966 visit was marked by two days of public demonstrations by ethnic Somalis demanding independence. France conducted a second referendum in March 1967 in which 60% chose to remain associated with France, though the plebiscite engendered accusations of vote-rigging by the French authorities. In July of that year, the name French Somaliland formally changed to the French Territory of Afars and Issas to avoid any encouragement of expansionist ambitions in Somalia.

Hassan Gouled Aptidon, an Issa (a Somali clan), easily won the ensuing presidential elections and an interethnic government was formed with an Afar, Ahmed Dini, serving as prime minister. After a third referendum, the territory then became fully independent from France in 1977 and was renamed the Republic of Djibouti. The president declared a single-party state, and successive elections in 1981 and 1986 returned the unopposed president with majorities of over 90%. This affirmed Issa domination of Djibouti politics.

In November 1991, a devastating civil war erupted between the Issa-led government and a predominantly Afar rebel group, which termed itself the Front for the Restoration of Unity and Democracy (FRUD). Responding to criticisms of its monopoly of political power, Gouled Aptidon's government decided to permit multiparty politics and allowed the registration of four political parties in 1992. Only two, Gouled Aptidon's People's Rally for Progress (RPP)—the only legal party in Djibouti from 1981 to 1992—and the Party for Democratic Renewal (PRD) contested the National Assembly election. The PRD withdrew its candidates after claiming there were too many opportunities for electoral fraud. The RPP won all 65 Assembly seats with a turnout of only 50%.

In 1994, a moderate faction of the FRUD signed a peace agreement with the government, ending three years of civil war. In this accord the government agreed to recognize FRUD as a legitimate political party and named two FRUD leaders, Afars, to cabinet positions in 1995. In December 1997, elections the ruling RPP-FRUD coalition won all 65 legislative seats.

At the age of 83, the frail Gouled Aptidon announced that he would not stand for re-election in 1999, and in April a presidential election gave an overwhelming victory to his nephew Ismail Omar Guelleh, the *Chef de Cabinet* and longtime director of security services. Guelleh's campaign was slick and well-financed, with colored posters and distribution of thousands of green T-shirts and hats to Djibouti's unemployed. His opponent was the seasoned politician Moussa Ahmed Idriss, a leader in the campaign for independence who served in the French parliament from 1962 until 1967. The Iddriss campaign had substantially fewer resources, yet Idriss received about a quarter of the votes cast. It was an election in which both wings of FRUD participated rather than boycotted. Those who had reconciled themselves to the government supported Guelleh; those who remained in armed opposition urged support of Idriss.

The regime's severity to critics continued under President Guelleh, particularly in the press. The government owns the principal newspaper, *La Nation*, as well as the main radio and television stations. These support the government line, and charges of "distributing false information" can land an editor in jail and earn the newspaper a lengthy banning.

In February 2000, Ahmed Dini's wing of FRUD signed an agreement on "reform and civil harmony" with the Djibouti government, seeming to bring closure to the Afar rebellion. The agreement called for rehabilitation of zones devastated by the civil war, compensation of victims of the conflict, and "real devolution, granting a wide degree of autonomy to the regions concerned."

A section of the agreement on democratization suggested FRUD's sense of

Djibouti

exclusion from Djibouti politics. It referred to the need for "equitable representation" and an administration within which "the various national communities are equally represented." The reality of political power in Djibouti is that the Issa, the dominant Somali clan, control the ruling party and are disproportionately represented in bureaucratic and military ranks. Among the Issa, the president's subclan, the Mamassan, predominates.

Negotiations between the government and representatives of FRUD's armed faction on the specifics of the agreement began in April 2000, and they ultimately concluded with a peace accord signed in May 2001, and the demobilization of FRUD fighters went smoothly. Of 1,074 disbanded troops, some 300 were integrated into the government's forces and 700 returned to their villages. The peace agreement allowed the FRUD-Armé to be authorized as a political party when a multiparty system was approved in September 2002; as a legal party it is known as the *Alliance Républicaine pour le Développement* (ARD). Legislative elections scheduled for late 2002 were postponed to allow the numerous parties registered to organize and campaign effectively. They were ultimately held in January 2003.

In multiparty elections, two coalitions competed for seats in the country's 65-seat legislature. On the government side, the *Union pour la majorité présidentielle's* (UMP) list was dominated by nominees of President Guelleh's RPP (two-thirds) and FRUD-Legal (one-third). Two smaller parties were allocated two positions each on the list. The opposition rallied under the banner of the *Union pour l'alternance démocratique* (UAD: Union for Democratic Alternative) which was dominated by candidates of Ahmed Dini's ARD. With a winner-take-all district system, election results dramatically favored the governing coalition. UMP parties supporting President Guelleh won 62.2% of the votes, against 36.9% for the opposition, but took every legislative seat. Ahmed Dini of the UAD said the poll had been rigged and claimed his group had won at least 22 seats. Even the government was willing to admit the voter lists were hopelessly out of date. In an interview, the interior minister said they went back to the colonial period. "There are many dead people on the lists because our citizens do not normally report deaths," he said. "We have people who are 120 years old or more on the lists."

After the terrorist attacks of September 11, 2001, Djibouti became the hub of Western anti-terrorist activity. In addition to having France's largest military contingent, Djibouti has allowed U.S. and European forces (notably German, but also Spanish, British and Italian) to use its airport facilities. For Americans the main goal is to put American forces in position to strike cells of Al Qaeda in Yemen or East Africa. Indeed, it was CIA operatives in Djibouti who directed the launch of a Hellfire missile that struck a car carrying Qaed Salim Sinan al-Harethi, a close ally of Osama bin Laden, and the mastermind of the attack on the USS *Cole* in Yemen's port of Aden—an attack that killed 17 U.S. Navy sailors.

Djibouti's April 2005 presidential election was conducted without an opposition candidate. Longtime opponent Ahmed Dini Ahmed had died the previous September at age 72 and the only other candidate, Mohamed Daoud Chehem, withdrew in March citing difficulties in raising campaign funds. Opposition parties called a boycott and the police had to use tear gas to disperse hundreds of protesters who blocked the streets with burning tires, but President Guelleh was reelected to a second six-year term.

President Guelleh was thereafter preoccupied with events in neighboring countries, especially Somalia. The Ethiopian intervention to support Somalia's weak Transitional Federal Government was not helpful, he thought, and the use of American planes (from their Djibouti base) against Islamists fleeing Mogadishu in early 2007 was a cause for considerable embarrassment. In addition, Eritrean and Dijiboutian troops collided in June 2008 at the Ras Doumeira border area. Djibouti's government claimed Eritrea was responsible for the deaths of nine soldiers, but Eritrea denied launching the attack. In April 2009, the UN Security Council stated that Eritrea had not withdrawn its troops from a disputed border area of Djibouti; Eritrea responded by denying the claim and stating that they had no troops in Djibouti. In December, sanctions against Eritrea were approved by the UN, partly due to this border dispute.

Elections in 2011 largely repeated the results of the 2005 elections, and the Arab Spring protests of 2011 only briefly created tensions within the country (with two deaths in February). President Guelleh was reelected in a poll that saw another opposition boycott. On this occasion, Guelleh took nearly 81% of the vote, while Mohamed Warsama Ragueh took the remaining 19%. This third term for Guelleh was enabled by a constitutional amendment in 2010 that removed the two-term limit. Parliamentary elections in February 2013 resulted in 49 of 63 seats going to the Union for the Presidential Majority (UMP); opposition groups rejected the result and announced they would undertake rolling protests.

After years of serving as a base for anti-terror activities, Djibouti was targeted in 2014 by the militant Islamists al-Shabaab, effectively al-Qaeda's cell in the Horn of Africa. On May 24, the terror organization claimed responsibility for an attack on a Djibouti restaurant that killed three people (two of whom were the bombers) and wounded 15 more. In June 2014, western countries alerted their nationals that credible reports suggest al-Shabaab is planning more attacks in Djibouti, reportedly in retaliation for the presence of western military forces there.

CONTEMPORARY THEMES

The 1991–94 civil war expanded the army from 3,000 men to 18,000, devastated infrastructure and bankrupted the state. To pay for the war, public utilities were raided, and payments were delayed to creditors and state employees. When the government proposed reducing public salaries, which account for nearly 80% of the budget, a general strike was declared, and the government had to suspend planned reforms. Salary arrears to government workers continue to plague the government, and it remains dependent on the generosity of friends to make up budgetary shortfalls.

With less than 1% of its soil arable and with virtually no industry, Djibouti has had problems of food security following the increasing prices on imported food. Aside from livestock, its one traditional resource was salt, mined from a "lake" of salt deposits over 1,800 feet deep. From time immemorial, Afar nomads have brought their camels to Assal, loaded them with salt and led them to Ethiopia, where their cargo is exchanged for cereal and other goods. Large-scale exploitation of Assal's salt began in 1998 and trucking has replaced the traditional miner and his camel.

Today Djibouti's strategic location places it on one of the busiest sea-lanes of the world. Modernized to receive container cargoes, port facilities are the heart of the Djibouti economy. Border conflict between neighboring Ethiopia and Eritrea significantly increased activities at Djibouti port as

President Guelleh's campaign poster

Djibouti

Djibouti Nomad ©IRIN

Ethiopia diverted its trade from the Eritrean ports of Assab and Massawa. Eighty percent of all goods handled by the port are now destined for landlocked Ethiopia. As a consequence of significantly increased usage, the port has become so congested the government sought funding for a new and much larger facility at Doraleh, about five miles east of the current port.

The new facilities are being built in two phases—first an oil terminal and then a container area and free trade zone. The government hopes the project will make Djibouti a transshipment hub for the countries of the Common Market for Eastern and Southern Africa (COMESA). Most of the work is being done by companies based in the Persian Gulf state of Dubai. Dubai-based Horizon Terminals, Ltd. completed the new Doraleh oil terminal in February 2006. Another Dubai company, Dubai Ports World, announced plans to build a $300 million container terminal at Doraleh. The port officially opened in February 2009, it is the most modern and largest port terminal in East Africa. In addition to Doraleh, Dubai companies run the old port of Djibouti and the Djbouti airport. The commercial director of Djibouti port praised Dubai's contribution to his country's economic development: "Dubai has done in five years what France did not do during 115 years of colonization. And Dubai is doing it without showing any arrogance."

Strenuous efforts have also been made to improve rail and road connections between the port and Ethiopia to speed the transfer of imports. The 500-mile Djibouti to Addis Ababa railroad, constructed by France in 1897, suffers from dilapidated equipment more than 50 years old. The EU has granted a $40 million loan to upgrade the line. This includes enlarging its rails to accommodate modern trains, reinforcing viaducts and metal bridges, and replacing its communication system. With improvements the line will have the capacity to carry one million metric tons of freight annually.

Significant income is derived from the presence of foreign troops in Djibouti. France maintains a force of 2,800 strong there, making it France's largest foreign military base. The United States has made Djibouti a center for its war on terrorism, and 1,500 American soldiers are stationed there. The country also hosts an additional 800 German and 50 Spanish troops. The U.S. government has committed an additional $2 million to renovate state-run Radio Djibouti, along with $100,000 in annual rent, in exchange for a strategic transmission station the U.S. is building. The targeted audience is Yemen and the southern regions of Saudi Arabia.

As with other African leaders, President Guelleh is encouraging Chinese investment in his country. Chinese developers are being encouraged to build hotels and resorts in northern Djibouti to take advantage of unparalleled scuba diving opportunities. The government is currently in discussion with a Chinese national salt company to exploit local resources and hopes to interest other companies in its mining and thermal energy sectors.

Female Genital Cutting (FGC) has been common in Djibouti but is declining across Africa. A 2002 survey of 1,000 women by Djibouti's Health Ministry concluded that 98% of them had been circumcised; recent studies from as late as 2012 suggest FGC is still nearly universal in spite of international efforts to stop it; Article 333 of Djibouti's Penal Code outlaws the practice of FGC, but few people have ever been arrested. Infibulation, one of the most brutal forms of FGC, is the most prevalent in Djibouti. The inner labia and clitoris are first cut away, and then the remaining lips are sewn together, leaving only a small hole for urination and menstruation. The practice is a major contributor to Djibouti's relatively high maternal mortality rate: 69 deaths for each 10,000 live births.

A severe drought affecting much of Eastern Africa in later 2005 had a major impact on the traditional culture of Somali pastoralists. More than 150,000 were threatened as water holes dried up and pasturelands were degraded. Some affected populations abandoned their traditional pastures and moved entire villages to the outskirts of the capital as food security worsened.

Site of a United States military base, Djibouti has served as a transit point for Americans evacuated from Sudan beginning in 2023 during the flare up of conflict between contending factions in the war-torn country. Cases of migrant boats capsizing off the coast of Djibouti have also occurred most recently in April 2024, leaving 38 people dead including children.

Persistent issues include concerns over domestic human rights, continued drought with broad effects on local communities, and potential catastrophes afflicting migrant boats off the coast. With criticism of the government for employing surveillance and detention against opposition groups, monitoring of the situation is difficult as the ruling party remains dominated by President Guelleh and overall representation of major social groups remains limited. Suffering from an ongoing drought since 2020, large swaths of the population, including children, have been affected and are in need of humanitarian assistance. Migrant boats sinking off the coast largely consist of individuals seeking to reach Saudi Arabia via Yemen. A supporter of U.S. interests in the region, Djibouti troops have been deployed to neighboring Somalia to strengthen security and to combat Al-Shabaab. On the economic front, plans to diversify the economy have been pursued to reduce unemployment

A West Virginia Air National Guard crew lands its 1st C-5 in Djibouti

Photo by Sgt. Lee Harshman, courtesy U.S. Air Force

Djibouti

and become an emergent economy, though trade with Egypt actually declined in 2024.

FUTURE CONSIDERATIONS

President Guelleh has few resources with which to confront Djibouti's poverty, apart from its strategic location, and its economic future will continue to be dominated by services provided to the shipping industry and to Western governments seeking to maintain a presence in the volatile Horn of Africa. Still, unemployment and poverty look to be significant problems for the foreseeable future. The future of Djibouti—both economically and politically—will be inextricably linked to the presence of French and American troops in the region. Given the moderate version of Islam in the country, the government long avoided any severe consequences from the presence of these troops, but the 2014 terror attack shows that militant Islamists are now actively targeting the country for its cooperation.

Politically, Djibouti continues to be dominated by the single party, and there are few prospects for a robust opposition. The April 2010 approval of a constitutional amendment that allowed President Guelleh to run for a third term had a good deal of public support, and it seems likely the president would have won the 2011 presidential election in the absence of a boycott. While the country's residents cannot expect rich political contestation, there is little sign of broad civil upheaval emanating from the Arab Spring. The civil wars and conflict of previous decades seem to be contained, though terror in the Horn of Africa is increasingly a concern for the country.

The State of Eritrea

Downtown Asmara — Photo by Veronica Rentmeesters

BASIC FACTS

Area: 117,600 sq. km. (slightly larger than Pennsylvania)
Population: 6,274,796 (June 2023 est.)
Capital City: Asmara
Government Type: Presidential Republic
Neighboring Countries: Sudan (north and east); Ethiopia (south); Djibouti (southeast)
Official Languages: Tigrinya, Arabic, English
Other Principal Languages: Afar, Amharic, Arabic, Tigre and Kunama,
Ethnic Groups: Tigrinya 55%, Tigre 30%, Saho 4%, Kunama 2%, Rashaida 2%, Bilen 2%, other 5%
Principal Religions: Muslim, Coptic Christian, Roman Catholic, Protestant
Former Colonial Status: Italian colony (1890–1941); British trusteeship (1941–1952); absorbed by Ethiopia (1962–1991), defeat of Ethiopian forces (1991–1993), referendum in April 1993 resulted in total independence.
Independence Date: May 24, 1991
GDP Per Capita (IMF 2022 est.): $715 (nominal), $2,188 (PPP)
Gini index: N/A
Currency: Nakfa, $US 1 = 15 nakfa (June 2023)
Inflation Rate: 6.2% (2022 est.)
Chief Commercial Products: Livestock, sorghum, textiles, food, and small manufactures
Foreign Direct Investments (FDI) net inflows: 46,510,786
Literacy Rate: 76.6% (CIA 2018)
Life Expectancy: 67.19 years (CIA 2023 est.)
Head of State: President Isaias Afworki (since June 8, 1993)
Head of Government: President Isaias Afworki (since June 8, 1993)

LAND AND PEOPLE

Geological evidence indicates that Eritrea was a relatively flat plateau of green trees and grass prior to the arrival of modern mankind. At some unknown time, massive earthquakes caused the land to change into a terrain of sharp peaks accentuated by active volcanoes. Although the volcanoes are now dead, the peaks remain, often rising to more than 14,000 feet, with a craggy appearance caused by lava rock formations. Except for the coastal areas, the climate is moderate, with frost appearing above 11,000 feet. Variation in temperature from noon to midnight may be as much as 60 degrees Fahrenheit. Along the coast, the climate is hot and humid.

Eritrea has significant semiarid and desert regions where rainfall is irregular. Combined with the rugged terrain that dominates everywhere except the coast along the Red Sea, this makes the land somewhat inhospitable for agriculture. Rainfall depends upon prevailing wind direction. If the currents aloft are from southwest to northeast, moisture capable of generating rainfall arrives from central Africa's vast rain forest area. But if the prevailing pattern is from the northwest

Eritrea

to the southeast, the hot winds of the Sahara and sub-Sahara arrive and roast any crops that are planted.

Asmara, Eritrea's capital, is an Italian-style city, sometimes called a "second Milan." The Italian occupiers who built up Asmara in the 1930s left a legacy of experimentation in modern architectural styles. Among others, European Art Deco and Italian Futurism both found expression in colonial construction, and the city is known to architectural historians as one of the best concentrations of modernism in the world. To preserve this heritage, Asmara has established an historical district of one and a half square miles in the heart of the city; alterations to any significant buildings there are restricted.

Women are held in high esteem in Eritrea. During the war of liberation, at least a third of the 100,000-strong rebel force was composed of women. After the war, new laws made women fully equal to men with rights to own land, to choose their husbands and divorce them. Much remains to do to change the status of women at home more completely. The National Union of Eritrean Women estimates that a large majority of women—as high as 90% in recent years—are illiterate.

HISTORY TO PRESENT DAY

For details of early history, see *Historical Background* and *The Colonial Period: The Italians*.

The Italian conquest of Eritrea and later of Ethiopia effectively created a separate identity for each. After the Italians were expelled in 1941, the British assumed control over the territory. Under pressure from the British and Ethiopia, the UN adopted a plan for federating Eritrea and Ethiopia in 1950. This was intended to protect Eritrean autonomy, but almost immediately after the federation went into effect, Eritrean rights were violated by the Ethiopian imperial government. Political parties were banned in 1955, followed by the banning of trade unions in 1958. In 1959, the name "Eritrean Government" was changed to "Eritrean Administration," and Ethiopian law was imposed. Resistance to this administrative subordination was manifested by the creation of the Eritrean Liberation Front (ELF) in 1958.

Increasing pressure on Eritreans from Addis Ababa to renounce their autonomy was ultimately successful in November 1962. A compliant Eritrean Assembly voted unanimously for the abolition of Eritrea's federal status, reducing Eritrea to a simple province of the Ethiopian empire. The liberation struggle began in earnest at the same time.

In 1974, the Ethiopian monarchy collapsed, and power was seized by the military. Lt. Col. Mengistu Haile Mariam assumed power as head of state and chairman of the governing military council known as the Derg. The regime was totalitarian in style, financed by the Soviet Union and Eastern bloc, and assisted by Cuba in a massive militarization of the country. War against the Eritrean rebels continued through the late 1980s. When the Soviet Union, embroiled in Afghanistan, announced that it would not renew its defense and cooperation agreement with Ethiopia, army morale plummeted. The Eritrean People's Liberation Front (EPLF) joined with internal opposition to the Derg, advanced on Ethiopian positions, and ultimately drove Mengistu into exile in 1991.

The EPLF established a provisional government in Asmara in May 1991 with Isaias Afwerki as its head. Independence was overwhelmingly ratified in a UN-monitored referendum in April 1993. Freely contested elections led to a National Assembly that in turn appointed Afwerki as president of the Provisional Government of Eritrea (PGE). The EPLF renamed itself the People's Front for Democracy and Justice (PFDJ) in early 1994 and became the country's only political party.

The new government faced enormous challenges, including writing a constitution, creating a judiciary, reconstructing a school system, reintegrating refugees and demobilizing ex-guerrillas. Underlying all was the need to rehabilitate a badly damaged infrastructure and reform the collapsed institutions of a centrally planned economy. In March 1994, the National Assembly established a constitutional commission and members traveled throughout the country and to Eritrean communities abroad, holding meetings to explain constitutional

President Isaias Afwerki

options and solicit input. The new constitution that resulted from this broad consultative process was ratified by the constituent assembly on May 24, 1997.

At its peak fighting strength, the EPLF army grew to nearly 110,000 fighters—nearly 3% of the total population. Since a fragile peacetime economy could not support such numbers, the government began to demobilize 50% to 60% of the army in 1993. Those who had served longest and had the fewest civilian skills were given higher compensation, more intensive training and more psychological counseling. Special attention was given to women fighters who made up 30% of the EPLF's combat forces. By 1998, the army had shrunk to 47,000, but then the country went to war again with Ethiopia.

Hostilities with Ethiopia broke out in May 1998. At issue was a remote triangle of rocky, barren land (of 155 square miles) called the Badme Triangle. Unlocatable on most maps, the triangle became the focus of national pride on both sides of the border. Both Isaias Afwerki of Eritrea and Meles Zenawi of Ethiopia found themselves in a situation from which it was difficult to retreat as pride and personality on both sides generated entrenched positions. Negotiations had brought no resolution to the conflict by May 2000, and as soon as the last negotiators left, Ethiopia launched another massive attack. A surprise advance against a presumably impregnable pass brought crushing victory in 19 days, after which Ethiopia announced its war aims achieved.

A cease-fire was announced in June 2000 and actually lasted through the conclusion of December peace negotiations conducted in Algiers. The Algiers Agreement called for a pullback of troops and creation of a demilitarized zone manned by several thousand UN peacekeepers. A five-member Eritrea-Ethiopia Boundary Commission (EEBC) was established to demarcate the disputed border. Overall, the war had mobilized 200,000 fighters into the army, many of whom were young people rounded up in 1999 by the government and required to fight or face jail time. It cost the lives of 19,000 Eritreans, displaced tens of thousands, and set back development plans for decades.

The Boundary Commission rendered its decision in April 2002. The language of the 125-page decision was sufficiently obscure to allow both countries to claim victory: Badme was not explicitly mentioned in the text, for example. Both countries launched a propaganda campaign seeking to convince their citizens that the sacrifices of war had not been in vain.

Tensions between the two countries spiked as demarcation approached in spring 2003. In March, the EEBC affirmed

233

Eritrea

that Badme, the *casus belli* of recent conflict, was part of Eritrea. The Ethiopian prime minister rejected the decision, calling it "a blatant miscarriage of justice," as well as "illegal, unjust and irresponsible." Beating the drums and sounding the trumpets, he warned the decision could lead to "another round of war."

The Eritrean government continued to insist the border ruling be implemented. Finally, faced with international immobility, Eritrea acted. In October 2006, it moved troops and tanks into the demilitarized buffer zone. The UN-appointed demarcation panel began to visibly wash its hands of the whole affair by the end of November. It told both Eritrea and Ethiopia to resolve the six-year dispute or risk having the UN take the matter into its own hands. The threat did little to abate the enmity between Asmara and Addis Ababa. The United Nations' top peacekeeping official seemed to admit as much in early 2007 when described the peace process between the rivals as "failing." The 620-mile border remains undemarcated and a source of constant tension in the region. In February 2008, the UN began pulling troops out of the border area due to Eritrean government restrictions. This led to a shortage of fuel supplies and in July 2008 the UN mission withdrew officially. However, in August 2009, Ethiopia and Eritrea agreed to pay each other compensation for the war, which suggested a lessening of international tension.

As relations with Ethiopia deteriorated, the government mended fences with Sudan. It successfully mediated a settlement between Khartoum and the Eastern Front (EF), whose forces had been fighting a low-level insurgency for the past decade. The Asmara Peace Agreement was signed in October 2006. Its aims were similar to more familiar proposals for Southern and Darfur rebels: greater autonomy and control of natural resources. Under terms of the accord, the EF was to name an aide to President Bashir, get a junior minister's post and eight seats in parliament.

Eritrea's relations with Sudan were completely transformed, and with that transformation, the country began to be reevaluated as a major player in the conflict-filled region. From antagonism and support of hostile rebel movements, President Bashir praised the efforts of Eritrea to secure peace in Sudan. Even the EU, which had complained bitterly about a lack of transparency in Eritrea—and whose ambassador to the country had called it a dictatorship—changed its tune. In May 2007, Afwerki visited the EU Commission offices in Brussels to a warm reception, where the EU development commissioner singled out for praise Eritrea's efforts in Somalia, despite the country's questionable record there.

In Somalia, Eritrea reportedly funneled arms through the country's Islamic Courts Union rulers to rebel groups in Ethiopia, namely the Ogaden National Liberation Front (ONLF) and the Oromo Liberation Front (OLF). Eritrea also funded, armed, trained and advised insurgents, especially the al-Shabab militia, the most radical arm of the Islamic Courts Union. Eritrea reportedly continues to pass money to Islamist organizations in Somalia and in 2009 the UN imposed sanctions on Eritrea for supporting Islamic insurgents.

President Afwerki has yet to work out a redemptive relationship with his domestic opposition. Forming a new political party is still illegal, and the government has closed the private press and arrested dissidents, journalists, and prominent Eritreans whose only crime was to campaign for greater democracy. Dissidents have nonetheless organized a new political party—the Eritrean People's Liberation Front Democratic Party, or EPLFDP, to challenge the "autocratic and incorrigible" EPLF regime. As the first opposition party to emerge from within the EPLF, the new Democratic Party has more credibility than external opposition groups backed by Ethiopia and Sudan.

Relations with neighbors deteriorated further in 2008 and 2009 as troops from Eritrea and Djibouti clashed along the border between the two countries. Djibouti and the United States, among others, claimed Eritrea was the aggressor, though the government in Asmara denied any wrongdoing.

Conflict took on another troubling form in November 2008 when a group called the Red Sea Afar Democratic Organization (RSADO) attacked a military base, injuring and killing up to a hundred people. Asmara is now facing conflict within its territories as well as militarized territorial disputes along its western and southern boundaries.

Since 2009, the situation in Eritrea has remained dire and uncertain. In April 2009, the UN Security Council said Eritrea had not removed its troops from a disputed border with Djibouti; Eritrea denies having any troops there at all. In December the UN placed sanctions on Eritrea for supporting

Italian Art Deco architecture of Asmara

Eritrea

Islamist insurgents in Somalia. Human Rights Watch claimed that the Eritrean government has turned the country into a "giant prison," while the International Crisis Group warns that Eritrea may become a failed state. In December 2010, a WikiLeaks cable said that Eritreans were fleeing their country as the economy crashed and prisons overflowed. In 2010, rebel groups united to try to overthrow the government and met in Ethiopia to establish a parliament in exile with Ethiopia's support. In 2011, the UN accused Eritrea of a plot to attack an African Union summit in Ethiopia; the UN Security Council furthered its sanctions on Eritrea for continuing to support Islamist extremists in Somalia. In 2013, the major news out of Eritrea has been a brief mutiny by malcontents in the army that resulted in an occupation of the Information Ministry. While this event was soon neutralized by the government, the pattern of recent events suggests a combination of sclerosis in the regime alongside increasing manifestations of displeasure from opposition elements.

CONTEMPORARY THEMES

In the 1960s, when Eritrea was a province of Ethiopia, the economy was starved of investment and began to deteriorate. With the installation of the Mengistu regime in 1974, Ethiopia adopted a command economy and nationalized most private assets, further drying up investment. Recurrent drought, famine and nearly three decades of armed struggle intensified the destructive effects of centrally directed policies.

At its liberation in 1991, Eritrea inherited an economy neglected, isolated, and virtually destroyed by war. When independence was achieved in 1993, the government, turning its back on its own Marxist background, began an effort to rebuild infrastructure, liberalize the economy and aggressively seek foreign investment.

Those efforts were effectively ended by the 1998–99 war with neighboring Ethiopia. By spring 1999, Eritrea was bearing the costs of at least 40,000 refugees, driven out of Ethiopia. It had also gone on an expensive shopping spree for armaments. Eritrea purchased top-of-the-line fighter planes (MiG-29s), but these proved too sophisticated for inexperienced Eritrean pilots, and Eastern European pilots had to fly them. Because of the war, the achievements of years were lost in months; reconstruction costs were estimated at $800 million.

The economy has slowed or even reversed: GDP fell in 2003 and in 2006, while remaining flat in 2004 and 2005. All the while, population continued to grow at a rapid 4%; this meant a deteriorating standard of living. A catastrophic drop of nearly 10% occurred in 2008, and even the more recent recovery will mean Eritrea has had a lost decade or more. The country is not sharing in Africa's economic boom.

The consequences of war represent an enormous drag on the economy. Demobilization and reintegration efforts are costly; one in every 21 Eritreans serves in its armed forces—an estimated 202,000 out of a total population of 4.7 million—reportedly the highest proportion of a nation's population in military service in the world. Police periodically raid nightclubs or other hangouts of the young looking for draft dodgers, and they continue the practice of detaining and arresting the parents of individuals who have evaded national service duties.

Much of the cost of war was financed by the Eritrean diaspora. At the height of the war crisis in May 2000, when it was uncertain if Ethiopia would march on Asmara, 3,000 Eritreans living abroad bought land in the capital where they could ultimately build homes. These sales brought in a total of $29 million to the treasury. Throughout the war the government sold bonds and raised some $200 million in contributions from Eritreans who had emigrated abroad.

Port modernization is an important national issue. Work at Massawa has concluded and the port now has the capacity of docking big ships. Prior to 2005, large ships had to unload at Jeddah, Saudi Arabia, and their containers transshipped in smaller vessels to Eritrea. Plans for renovating the port of Assab have been put on hold since the war with Ethiopia, which shifted Ethiopia's trade through the port of Djibouti.

One potential bright spot has been the announcement by a Canadian mining company that it discovered high-grade gold at Bisha, less than 100 miles west of Asmara; exploratory drilling began in April 2005. The company noted the property has "excellent port facilities on the Red Sea."

Eritrea also continues to wrestle with social dilemmas such as HIV/AIDS, though the country has been much less hit by the pandemic than many countries in southern Africa. UNICEF estimates that about 1% of the population is affected. Life expectancy is estimated at about 60 years and the literacy rate at about 65% of adults.

Freedom of religious expression is limited in Eritrea. In 2002, all but four religions in the country—Islam, Eritrean Orthodox, Roman Catholic, and Evangelical Lutheran—were required to register with the government and cease all activities until their applications had been approved. Registration required a history of the group in the country, an explanation of its "uniqueness," and the benefits it offered over those already present. Reports indicate that those engaging in religious practices associated with unapproved churches are subjected to punishments by authorities.

Major issues include the involvement of military forces from Eritrea in the ongoing conflict in the Tigrsay region of nothern Ethiopia where Eritrean and Ethiopian forces fighting in concert against the Tirgray People's Liberation Front (TPLF) have been accused of war crimes especially mistreatment of women and arbitrary executions. While a peace deal was signed between Ethiopia and the TPLF in 2022, Eritrea is not an official party to the agreement though the government officially rejects the accusations of war crimes as a "fantasy."

Tensions continue to mount in March 2025 between Eritrea with its longtime foe Ethiopia over the latter's quest for direct maritime access to the Red Sea by the landlocked country. Seven years after restoring ties, Eritrea has begun a military mobilization deploying troops to joint border areas while Ethiopia has publicly ruled out conflict with Eritrea. Ethiopia has stressed using peaceful dialogue, but with Eritrea has struck a harsher tone, calling Ethiopia "misguided" over border tensions. Rising tensions include suspension of flights by Ethiopian Airlines to Eritrea and freezing bank accounts for no apparent reason. The Eritrean government has issued military mobilization directives to citizens below 60 years old, and called up reservists amounting to forced conscription in the authoritarian-led country while Ethiopia has also deployed troops and tanks on its northern border. Conflict in Ethiopia's northern region of Tigray has also signaled escalating hostilities between the neighboring countries as political disputes in Tigray, bordering Eritrea, have created political fragmentation with one of the factions reportedly allying with Eritrea. While Eritrean forces collaborated with Ethiopian troops during the Tigray war from 2020–2022, Eritrea was not invited to the negotiations between the federal government and rebel forces, which has driven a wedge between the two governments.

FUTURE CONSIDERATIONS

Pressures on the Afwerki regime are enormous and the response has typically been repression. The government takes a bashing for its less than sterling human rights record. The European Parliament has said President Afwerki rules the country "with an iron grip" and expressed concern over the country's "authoritarian trend." The U.S. State Department asserts that the regime has harassed, arrested, and detained members of minority religious

Eritrea

sects. The United States has reportedly even pondered placing Eritrea on the list of state sponsors of terrorism. Amnesty International calls torture, arbitrary detention, and political arrests "widespread." Despite the iron grip of the regime, it is possible domestic manifestations of discontent will become more prominent in the coming years, as evidenced by reporting on the activities of small rebel groups and even army mutinies.

The border demarcation with Ethiopia remains unsettled and volatile, with Ethiopia recently rejecting the latest attempt to secure a demarcation line. The years 2008–2009 saw the neighboring nation of Djibouti also drawn into the conflict, as Eritrean troops clashed with Djiboutian troops over the demarcation line between those two countries. The international community is concerned that full-scale war between could erupt once again now that the UN has voted to remove peacekeepers from the region, and since Eritrea is accused of violating a UN ultimatum to remove troops from disputed territory along the border with Djibouti. Such tensions dominate Eritrean political life, and the uncertainty these tensions generate makes much-needed economic investment untenable. With militarization, economic resources are also diverted from other productive ends. The Eritrean economy thus looks unlikely to advance until a range of regional conflicts is resolved.

The Federal Democratic Republic of Ethiopia

Earning a living on Lake Awasa

BASIC FACTS

Area: 1,104,300 sq. km. or 426373 sq. mi.
Population: 116,462,712 (June 2023 est.)
Capital City: Addis Ababa
Government Type: Federal Parliamentary republic
Neighboring Countries: Kenya (southwest); The Sudan (northwest); South Sudan (west); Somali Republic (east, southeast), Djibouti (east), Eritrea (northwest)
Official Language: Amharic
Other Principal Languages: Tigrinya, Oromo, Somali, Arabic
Ethnic Groups: Oromo (34.5 %), Amhara (26.9%), Somali (6%), Tigrayan (6.15%), Sidama (4%),
Principal Religions: Ethiopian Orthodox 43.5%, Islam 33.9%, Protestant 18.6%, Traditional 2.6%, Catholic 0.7%, Other 0.7%.
Former Colonial Status: Ethiopia has never been a colony in its history of almost 4,500 years. It was briefly occupied by the Italians under Mussolini (1936–1941).
National Holiday: National Revolution Day, September 12, 1974
GDP Per Capita (IMF 2023 est.): $1,475 (nominal), $3,724 (PPP)
Gini Index: 35 (2015)
Currency: Birr; $US 1 = 51.54 birr (Apr. 2022)
Inflation Rate: 26.84% (2021 est.)
Chief Commercial Products: Coffee, gold, leather products, oilseeds, beeswax, and honey
Foreign Direct Investments (FDI) net inflows: 1,200,000,000
Literacy Rate: 52% (CIA 2017)
Life Expectancy: 68.59 years (CIA 2023 est.)
Head of State: Sahle-Work Zewde, President (since October 25, 2018) Head of Government: Prime Minister Abiy Ahmed Ali (since April 2, 2018)

LAND AND PEOPLE

Ethiopia is a land with a rich and proud history that is even reflected in its geography. It is a land of sharp mountains rising to more than 15,000 feet. Their rough appearance is produced by volcanic rock formations. The Great Rift Valley depression enters the country in the southeast, and the majestic peaks on either side of the gorge march in parallel formation toward the Red Sea. Slightly above Addis Ababa, the mountains separate and those on the

left hand proceed north to the Red Sea at Asmara in Eritrea; the right-hand peaks extend toward the Somali Republic.

Some of Ethiopia's rugged terrain is surrounded by desert and arid land on all sides, encircled by mountains that form the Ethiopian highlands. The Blue Nile, originating from the waters of Lake Tana, flows through a gorge more than a mile deep and 20 miles across in places. The climate of the highland plateaus and mountains is temperate. Frost occurs regularly above 11,000 feet, where the daily range in temperature may span as much as 80° Fahrenheit from noon to midnight.

The Ethiopian Orthodox Church is one of the world's oldest, Christianity having become the state religion around the same time the Emperor Constantine converted to Christianity. Tradition has it that the first Christian to be baptized was an Ethiopian noble who was on his way home from a pilgrimage to Jerusalem when he met the Apostle Philip. Baptism scenes are a recurring motif in Ethiopian art. An extraordinary feature of the Ethiopian Church is its historic connection to the Old Testament and Jerusalem. Ethiopians celebrated the Sabbath on Saturday for over a millennium. Most Ethiopian churches are consecrated with a symbolic Ark of the Covenant, and tradition has it that the original Ark was brought to Ethiopia by Menelik I, son of the Queen of Sheba, following a visit to his father, King Solomon. The story of Solomon and the Queen is a popular motif in Ethiopian religious art. The original Ark is claimed by some to be in the Church of St. Mary of Zion in Aksum.

Ethiopia

Lalibela, in a mountainous region 400 miles north of Addis Ababa, was a "New Jerusalem" for Ethiopian Christians in the 13th century. Eleven medieval churches were carved out of solid rock there. They have been declared World Heritage sites by UNESCO and are principal tourist attractions for Ethiopian visitors.

HISTORY TO PRESENT DAY

For early history, see *Historical Background* and *The Colonial Period: The Italians*.

Emperor Haile Selassie (1930–1974)

History was made in Ethiopia on November 2, 1930, when Haile Selassie I was crowned as the emperor of Ethiopia. Originating from a family with roots that tradition holds trace all the way back to Solomon and the Queen of Sheba, Haile Selassie is held by many as playing a key role in the modernization of the country and thus is seen as a central figure in the history of Ethiopia and Africa at large. Within a year, he promulgated a constitution that provided for a two-chamber legislature, but in reality, he retained absolute power over the affairs of Ethiopia. A short time later, the Italians invaded and conquered the country, but faced stiff resistance for the duration of their five-year attempt at colonization. The impassioned entreaty made by Selassie to the League of Nations earned Ethiopia international acclaim, as Selassie was named Time's 1935 Man of the Year. With military support provided by the British, the Italians admitted defeat and the emperor was restored in 1941.

With Selassie's return came increased emphasis on the modernization of the country. The constitution was amended in 1955, providing for a Chamber of Deputies elected by universal suffrage to four-year terms, and a Senate selected by the emperor from among distinguished Ethiopians to serve for six years. Another important state institution was the Crown Council, a traditional institution, which included the crown prince and the archbishop of the Ethiopian Coptic Church, as well as other dignitaries drawn from the ruling class; it assisted in forming basic policy and was convened at the call of the monarch. Another important event connected with the rule of Haile Selassie was the annexation of Eritrea in 1962, but the Eritrean Liberation Front, formed in 1958, organized an armed resistance that would ultimately achieve independence in 1993 after more than three decades of struggle.

Over the course of the next two decades, Ethiopia remained a deeply conservative nation ruled by a select few wealthy landowners. The end of the monarchial system began in the 1970s with a series of natural and man-made disasters, causing the people to lose faith in the man who had ruled them for over forty years. Drought gripped the nation in 1972; rising prices and unemployment brought hordes of refugees to the cities from the parched countryside. The military, reacting to high prices, demanded higher salaries and started a limited military rebellion. Emperor Haile Selassie, aged and shaken, granted a partial increase. In the south, there were riots caused by an absence of land reform; peasants seized productive

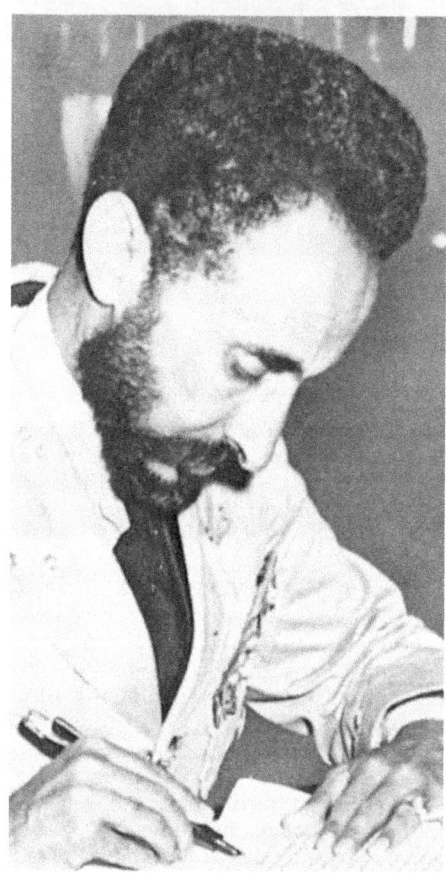

Former Emperor Haile Selassie

plantation land owned by absentee landlords. The wide-spread civil unrest led to the deposition of the aging Haile Selassie on September 12, 1974.

The Derg (1974–1991)

A provisional administrative council of soldiers, known as the Derg ("committee"), seized power and installed a socialist military dictatorship. Beginning what would become standard practice, the Derg summarily executed 50 members of the royal family, ministers, generals, and dignitaries of the imperial government. The emperor himself died of respiratory failure on August 22, 1975; whether he died of natural causes or was killed remains a subject of debate to this day.

Lt. Col. Mengistu Haile Mariam assumed leadership of the Derg in February 1977, after having his two predecessors killed. In only a few short months, Mengistu proceeded to turn Ethiopia into a totalitarian killing field. From 1977 through early 1978 thousands of suspected enemies of the Derg were tortured and killed in a purge known as the "Red Terror." The Derg officially adopted Communism, promulgated a Soviet-style constitution, and created the Workers Party of Ethiopia, complete with a hammer and sickle flag. Resistance to the Derg developed in all the major regions of the country, although much of which was equally inspired by Marxist-Leninist thinking and practice.

To deprive the rebels of popular support, the government resorted to "resettlement" and "villagization." Rejecting forced resettlement, peasants fled to Sudan and Somalia, creating huge refugee camps there. Many were shot in the back while fleeing, and thousands died in the squalor of the camps. The second program was designed to control rural peoples so they would be unable to support rebel movements. It also was intended to make the collectivization of agriculture easier. The government did not hesitate to use foreign aid, including food, to lure people into these programs.

Sensing Ethiopia's weakened condition, the Somali Republic unleashed a band of rebels (and later regular army troops) to seize the Ogaden Desert region, an area comprised largely of ethnic Somalians. By mid-1977, they had penetrated as far as Dire Dawa, one of the largest cities in the country. Mengistu's Soviet supporters sent massive quantities of arms and technical personnel to Ethiopia, placing the USSR in the embarrassing position of being patron and supporter of both sides of a war in which neither party had any interest in compromise. However, this conundrum for the USSR was brief; the Somalis ejected the Soviets from their nation and turned to the United States for support. Soviet arms in Ethiopia were then followed by a wave of Cuban troops—flown from Angola—to support the fledgling communist regime. By early 1978 the Somalis had been routed, but the Ogaden remains unstable even today.

The Liberation Fronts and the EPRDF

Incapable of dealing with drought and famine, the Derg's military dictatorship faced frequent regional insurrections against its repression, particularly in the northern regions of Tigray and Eritrea; these eventually brought down the regime. Officially created in February 1975, the Tigrayan Peoples Liberation Front (TPLF) announced its goal was "the establishment of an Independent Democratic Republic of

Ethiopia

Tigray." Allied with the Eritrean People's Liberation Front (EPLF), the TPLF waged incessant guerrilla warfare against the Derg. In 1989, the TPLF, representing a minority of only 7% of the Ethiopian population, merged with other ethnically based opposition groups to form the Ethiopian People's Revolutionary Democratic Front (EPRDF). By May 1991, as EPRDF forces advanced on Addis Ababa; Mengistu fled to Zimbabwe where he was granted asylum by President Mugabe. On May 27, EPRDF troops took control of the capital, and a transitional government was formed under the leadership of the TPLF chairman Meles Zenawi.

Meles Zenawi was born Legesse Zenawi, the third and youngest child of a member of the lower Tigrayan nobility. Like many other Tigrayan students, he saw himself as a victim of discrimination by the Amhara, who had dominated Ethiopian political life since the rule of Emperor Menelik. After two years as a premedical student, he dropped out of school to join the nationalist struggle in Tigray. It was at this point that he adopted his *nom de guerre* of Meles Zenawi, honoring Meles Tekle, a Tigrayan nationalist student killed in 1974. In 1985, Meles founded the Marxist-Leninist League of Tigray (MLLT) as a "vanguard party" within the TPLF. His intellectual model at the time was Envar Hoxha, the repressive ruler of Albania. Meles took over the leadership of the TPLF in 1989, linked with other opposition groups, and brought about the downfall of the Derg's military dictatorship.

One partner in the dictatorship's successful overthrow, the Eritrean People's Liberation Front, had already established—in May 1991—a separate regional government in the province; in April 1993, Eritreans voted for independence from Ethiopia.

In December 1994, the constituent assembly completed the new constitution of a Federal Democratic Republic of Ethiopia. It established a federal state and emphasized decentralized administration based on ten essentially ethnically defined regions; this was a revolutionary break with the highly centralized structures of the empire and its Marxist successor. Regions are granted broad powers for social and economic development, the right to raise and spend their own revenues. Most remarkably, they also have the right (in theory) to secede from the Ethiopian state. For the Tigrayan leadership at the core the EPRDF, the constitution was a means of redressing the grievances of Ethiopia's various "nationalities" against the Amhara.

In reality, political power in Ethiopia is relatively centralized around, the TPLF, and its allies within the EPRDF. Elections for Ethiopia's first popularly chosen parliament and regional legislatures were held respectively in May and June 1995. Numerous opposition parties boycotted the elections, resulting in a landslide victory for the EPRDF. As head of the dominant force within the EPRDF, Meles was thus appointed to a five-year term as prime minister.

The new system combined an appearance of pluralism with underlying centralization of power. With its ethnic and regional emphasis, Ethiopia spawned a plethora of new political parties, but most were created by or are satellites of the EPRDF, itself dominated by the TPLF. Meles Zenawi combines a variety of functions that emphasize his centrality: he is chairman of the TPLF, chairman of the EPRDF and prime minister. Despite the

Lt. Col. Mengistu Haile Mariam

constitution's commitment to regional and ethnic rights, the government continued to repress the opposition. People unwilling to join the EPRDF were castigated as "narrow nationalists," harassed, and imprisoned. In the Oromia and Somali regions especially, human rights groups have documented hundreds of "disappearances."

Centrifugal forces, reflecting Ethiopia's origins as a conquest state, tear at the heart of the new Ethiopia. Members of the Oromo Liberation Front have resorted to urban terror and earned a repressive response from the government. Afar separatists shuttle back and forth across the border with Djibouti, and Islamist Somali separatists continue to convulse the Ogaden. The model for each is the province of Eritrea, which gained its independence constitutionally.

War with Eritrea

Much to the surprise of the world community, minor hostilities occurred between Ethiopia and Eritrea in May 1998, escalating to major warfare in early June. At issue in the conflict was an obscure triangle of land called the Badme Triangle. At 155 square miles, rocky, and barren, the Badme triangle had little strategic value, but became the focus of national pride on both sides of the border. Both Prime Minister Meles and President Afwerki found themselves in a situation from which it was difficult to retreat. The internal pressures on Meles were particularly intense. Amhara imperialists had never accepted the loss of what they considered the Eritrean province, and the loss of the Red Sea ports rankled deeply, even among the Oromo majority. Galling too was the perception that the TPLF leadership had conceded too much by letting Eritrea secede and assume no share of the national debt.

As negotiators left in 2000, Ethiopia launched a massive attack. A surprise advance against a presumably impregnable pass brought crushing victory in 19 days, after which Ethiopia announced its war aims achieved. A cease-fire was announced in June 2000 and actually lasted through the conclusion of December peace negotiations conducted in Algiers. The Algiers Agreement called for a pullback of troops and creation of a demilitarized zone manned by several thousand UN peacekeepers. A five-member Eritrea-Ethiopia Boundary Commission (EEBC) was established to demarcate the disputed border. Overall, damages were calculated to be in the billions of dollars.

The EEBC held in March 2003 that Badme was part of Eritrea. Meles rejected the decision, calling it "a blatant miscarriage of justice," as well as "illegal, unjust and irresponsible." Beating the drums and sounding the trumpets, he warned the decision could lead to "another round of war." Ultimately, Eritrea moved troops and tanks into the demilitarized buffer zone in October of 2006; it claimed to be doing agricultural work, to which Meles caustically responded: "You don't need tanks to pick crops." By early 2007, the UN's top peacekeeping official admitted that the peace process was "failing." The 620-mile border remains unestablished and a source of constant tension in the region, even after the UN sent a peacekeeping force to monitor the disputed region.

EPRDF Control and Dissidence

Ethiopia held elections for a federal parliament and nine regional assemblies in May 2000. It was only the second time that

Ethiopia

nationwide elections had been held in the country. The opposition was given an unprecedented opportunity to air its grievances in a series of public debates. Largely attended, the debates were rebroadcast on state-run radio and television, but everywhere it was an uphill battle for the opposition.

Not a single opposition candidate managed to secure the 500 signatures necessary for nomination in the northern Tigray region. Elsewhere the EPRDF's satellite and creature parties dominated the electoral process. Prime Minister Meles' four-party coalition won overwhelmingly: 479 of the 547 parliamentary seats. When parliament convened in October, it reelected Meles to another five-year term.

The war and its resolution provoked dissent and impacted the leadership in both Ethiopia and Eritrea. In March 2001, 12 members of the TPLF central committee openly opposed Meles. These dissidents were narrowly defeated, removed from their party positions, and subjected to corruption charges that would keep them busy in the courts. Their supporters were also purged from their positions. Ethiopia's president, Negasso Gidada, spoke out in favor of the dissidents and described Meles as ruthless as the former dictator Mengistu Haile Mariam. He too soon found himself

Former Prime Minister Meles Zenawi

forced to resign, and parliament quickly elected Girma Wolde-Giorgis as a new president in October 2001.

The forced removal of these outspoken leaders marked a turn for the worst, as the EPRDF grew increasingly intolerant of dissent. A peaceful demonstration by Addis Ababa University students in April 2001 was violently broken up by the police. Two days of rioting ensued, resulting in the deaths of at least 31 people and injuries to hundreds of others. Thousands were interned without charges, and prominent human rights defenders were arrested as "instigators" of the riots. Antigovernment dissent by Oromo students at both high school and university levels was robustly repressed by the Oromiya state police, who regularly employ violence to disperse peaceful protesting of regional governmental policies. Oromiya, the largest and most populous Ethiopian state, is dominated by Oromos, Ethiopia's largest ethnic group. Federal and regional governments tend to view all forms of protest as instigated by the rebel Oromo Liberation Front (OLF), which has led a decade-long armed struggle for regional autonomy for Oromiya.

Parliamentary elections were held in May 2005 against this background of ethnic tension and political repression. The EPRDF faced two new electoral coalitions. One, the Coalition for Unity and Democracy (CUD) was made up of four parties and had at its core the All Amhara People's Organization. It called for liberalization of the economy and private ownership of land. It gave voice to the Amhara imperial vision of Ethiopia by opposing the constitution's emphasis on ethnic federalism. Instead, it called for more power for the central government and greater emphasis on being "Ethiopian" rather than being from a particular ethnic

Rock-carved Church of St. George, Lalibela

Photo by Judi Iranyi

Ethiopia

The Annunciation Photo by Judi Iranyi

group. The second coalition, the United Ethiopian Democratic Forces (UEDF), linked 14 parties (five inside Ethiopia and nine based abroad) with the Oromo National Congress as its dominant core. In contrast to CUD, the UEDF demanded greater regional autonomy.

When provisional election results were announced in late May it was clear the government would have a majority in parliament, but the opposition had cut deeply into its preponderance. The final returns, which were greatly delayed, gave the ruling EPRDF 296 seats, enough to form a government. The opposition took 174 seats, up from 12 in the previous legislature. CUD won a landslide victory in the capital, defeating the city's mayor and several ministers and taking all 23 seats representing the city.

The electoral results were bitterly, and lethally, contested at every stage. In June, CUD sought to prevent the release of provisional results, claiming massive vote rigging. Three days of violent protests against the alleged fraud resulted in many deaths in Addis Ababa. As the protests spread from the capital, thousands were arrested and Human Rights Watch reported that security forces killed "dozens of protesters and arbitrarily detained thousands of people across the country. One year later, the commission of inquiry examining the events reported that 193 civilians—nearly four times the number originally claimed by the government—and six members of the security forces were killed; 763 civilians and 71 member of the security forces were injured, many seriously.

CUD rejected the official election results announced in August and announced plans for massive antigovernment demonstrations for early October 2005. Their impact was blunted by large-scale arrests of opposition supporters beforehand, and when parliament met on October 10, the EPRDF majority once again elected Meles Zenawi prime minister. Its session was boycotted by 100 CUD deputies; those from the UEDF opposition faction rejected the boycott and took up their seats.

As tensions between CUD and EPRDF increased, it was clear that CUD chairman Hailu Shawel had the types of street demonstrations and popular actions that had toppled repressive regimes in Eastern Europe in mind. Amid a variety of protests, CUD called for strikes and boycotts of government-run breweries and state media. "The ruling party runs construction firms and printing companies, which will be targeted," the CUD spokesman added. He also asked drivers to honk their horns for three days and stay at home for five in mid-November.

Both sides reverted to form. Violent demonstrations rocked Addis Ababa for several days; thousands of opposition supporters were detained; at least 46 died. In mid-December, government prosecutors cast their nets broadly and heavily: 129 opposition leaders, reporters, and aid workers were charged with crimes ranging from treason to genocide. The trial of 111 defendants began in May 2006. It is the country's biggest court case since the genocide trial against the former Marxist dictator, Haile Meriam Mengistu, 14 years earlier. It remains ongoing.

Having dealt with the threat of domestic insurrection, the Meles government was soon faced with an even greater security threat to Ethiopia: the expansion of Islamist control in neighboring Somalia. From June to July 2006, the Islamic Courts Union (ICU) routed the warlords, imposed order on Mogadishu, and threatened the hopelessly weak Transitional Federal Government. To consolidate power, Islamist leaders fanned the flames of Somali nationalism against the traditional enemy—Ethiopia. After Ethiopia sent military forces to support the interim government, the ICU leader Sheikh Hassan Dahir Aweys ordered a "holy war" to drive the Ethiopians from Somalia.

By October, Meles bluntly said his country was "technically" at war with Somali Islamists. They were "spoiling for a fight," he told a Reuters reporter, "declaring jihad against Ethiopia almost every other week." ICU extremists also revived Pan-Somali irredentist claims to the territories of neighboring states (Djibouti, Ethiopia, and Kenya) occupied by Somalis. This combined with the Islamists' reliance on Eritrea and their military support of Ethiopian rebel groups (the Ogaden National Liberation Front and the Oromo Liberation Front) to draw the Addis Ababa government into war with the Mogadishu militants.

Ethiopia began military action against the Islamist regime in December 2006, with covert American support and intelligence. Ethiopian tanks, artillery batteries and military jets made quick work of the ill-equipped Islamist militia. The Ethiopian government announced it had detained 41 terrorism suspects from 17 countries who had been fighting for Somalia's Islamist movement. In June 2008, an agreement between the ICU and Somalia's transitional government included a provision for the removal of Ethiopian troops from the country. The Ethiopian withdrawal from Somalia was completed in early 2009. Ethiopia has since admitted to deploying reconnaissance missions in Somalia but denies deploying troops again.

Ethiopia's most recent general election was held on May 23, 2010, and results were announced in June. On this occasion, the EPRDF used a variety of methods to shore up support and weaken the opposition in advance of the election, and it restored its dominance to the point of becoming a virtual one-party state, winning far more seats than in the contested 2005 elections. At latest count, the EPRDF holds 499 of the 547 seats, and parties allied to the EPRDF won all but two of the remaining seats. Combined with a similarly dominant performance at the regional level, this gives the EPRDF a virtual monopoly on Ethiopian politics. While the electoral commission claimed that the 2010 election was free and fair, international observers (from the European Union) expressed concerns that the electoral process unduly favored the ruling party.

In 2011 and 2012, Ethiopia's conflicts with Eritrea and Somalia escalated. In March and April of 2011, Ethiopia accused Eritrea of planting bombs on the Ethiopian side of the border and openly declared its support for Eritrean rebels. In October 2011, American troops based in Ethiopia began flying drones over Somalia to fight against Islamist militants. In March 2012, Ethiopian soldiers attacked a region of southeast Eritrea that Ethiopia claimed served as a training ground for subversive groups. As of June 2012, Ethiopia openly had troops in Somalia, though these were moving out of the central region around the capital Mogadishu.

In December 2011, Amnesty International accused Ethiopia of drastically restricting freedom of expression, as the government increasingly restricted the media and the activity of non-governmental organizations. Two Swedish journalists

Ethiopia

who were captured and arrested by the Ethiopian government during a clash with ONLF rebels in July 2011 are found guilty of supporting terrorism and sentenced to 11 years in prison in December. The security situation further deteriorated in June 2012 when the ONLF raised an army post and claimed to kill more than 150 soldiers.

Amid these concerns about internal security and the war in Somalia, Ethiopia's political system was then shaken to its core in 2012 by the death of prime minister Meles Zenawi. Meles had ruled the country since 1995 but was still only 57 years old. His death removed the central pillar of the EPRDF regime: the prime minister had been applauded for his role in the liberation from the Derg and for stabilizing the country, as well as for his stewardship of the economy, but he also earned opprobrium for his hardline efforts to consolidate power and stifle dissent. In accordance with the constitution, deputy prime minister Hailemariam Desalegn of the EPRDF assumed the top post of prime minister, and he is likely to remain there (barring a vote of no confidence in his leadership) until the parliamentary term is completed in 2015.

On October 7, 2013, the Parliament of Ethiopia unanimously elected Mulatu Teshome Wirtu as its president, the third person to hold this office since the creation of the Democratic Republic in 1991. As a member of the Oromo Peoples' Democratic Organization (OPDO), one of the many satellite parties of the EPRDF, he stood out as a poster child for the modernization and growing international ties that the country has sought to develop in recent years. (Teshome received his Bachelor's and Doctorate degrees in Beijing, China.) Although still relatively new to his office, Teshome is no stranger to the EPRDF government, having held multiple positions over the last two decades, most notably serving as Deputy Minister of Economic Development and Cooperation in the 1990s and as Ambassador to China and Turkey. Although only holding a largely ceremonial position, many are interested to see what Teshome will do with his newly granted position, given the large amounts of investment and development of infrastructure that China has given to Ethiopia in recent years.

CONTEMPORARY THEMES

The EPRDF government has embarked on a program of economic reform that has far outpaced its commitment to democratization. This has included the privatization of state enterprises. While progress was slow, liberalization of the economy has been generally successful: the economy grew a striking 12.4% in 1996 before the war with Eritrea, and after several erratic years during the war (as Ethiopia experienced the effects of periodic drought), GDP growth improved considerably in the 2000s. After a 2003 decline of 3.9%, the GDP soared by 13.1% in 2004 and remained at or above 10% from 2005 (despite political instability) to 2008. Even facing the world financial crisis and global recession, the economy grew at a robust 8.7% in 2009, and Ethiopia is projected to be one of the world's top growing economies for 2010–2015.

Industrial development has been agriculture-driven. Small-scale agriculture involves 85% of the population, generates 80% of Ethiopian exports and contributed 47.7% to the GDP (2005). Only 10.9% of Ethiopia's total land surface is under intense agricultural cultivation. There has been much criticism of the government's agriculture-based industrial development policies. Seeking greater liberalization, critics have called for private land ownership, which, they believe, would help farmers secure bank loans and adopt modern agricultural techniques. Prime Minister Meles Zenawi has quashed any move in this direction: he has said land would remain state property.

Land tenure may be the central issue in Ethiopian development. Peasants have no security of land tenure and little incentive to produce above mere subsistence levels, but the regime itself has sold off large tracts to major investors. A report by the Oakland Institute in 2011 claimed that this was pushing small farmers off the land. And in January 2012, Ethiopia was accused of forcing thousands of people off land to be used for foreign investors. The consequence is the persistence of famine, whether under Imperial, Derg, or EPRDF governments. Under the emperor, peasants were deprived of their production by a feudal system; under the Derg and EPRDF, state ownership was substituted, continuing the disincentive to produce. (The government argues that if land were privatized before industrial growth has occurred, peasants would sell their holdings and move to the cities where they would be unable to find employment.)

Ethiopian economic development focuses on the necessity of increasing agricultural production. More than a million people died of starvation between 1984 and 1990. Since 1992, the government has established a series of grain storehouses to be better prepared when drought and famine occur. Without this advanced planning, the death toll from reoccurring drought and famine would be significantly greater. Though most Ethiopians usually produce enough food to support themselves, distributing and commercializing any excess faces difficulties. Most farmers live at least a half a day from a usable road.

AIDS is a greater threat than the periodic famines, which receive much greater international attention. Though prevalence rates are relatively low, populous Ethiopia has one the ten largest populations of people living with HIV/AIDS in the world. The disease is preventing further improvements in life expectancy in Ethiopia, which the World Bank has estimated at about 60 years.

Transportation inefficiencies, storage, and handling costs make product delivery in state-controlled agriculture slow and costly. It takes, for example, 20 to 30 days for a sack of grain to go from producer to consumer, instead of the two to three days it takes to cover the distance. As part of a food security program, the government has plans for major infrastructure developments of both transportation and dams. The World Bank is providing financing and at least 12 international construction firms, many of them Chinese, have bid on the projects that will focus on farm-to-market or feeder roads.

The government also has ambitious plans to develop irrigation agriculture. Since water management and increased electricity are essential for both agricultural and industrial development, the government plans to complete seven hydroelectric dams on the Blue Nile in the next five years. The dams would increase the present 340 megawatts electric-generating capacity of the country to 713 megawatts. Such proposals are viewed by Egypt with great concern, as Egypt is downstream, but utterly dependent on the flow of Nile waters from the Ethiopian highlands.

The birthplace of coffee, Ethiopia is Africa's leading coffee exporter. The crop accounts for the majority of the country's foreign exchange earnings. Nearly one million families are dependent on coffee for their income. Another 15 million households benefit indirectly from coffee sales. The international coffee market has proved volatile in recent years, with prices plummeting as a consequence of new entrants into the market around 2000 but recovering to very high international prices by 2008 and record highs by 2011. Starbucks and the government settled a trademark dispute in May 2007; Ethiopia will secure rights to three coffee names—Harar, Sidamo, and Yirgacheffe—through the U.S. Patent and Trademark Office. Oxfam International, the British NGO, estimated the agreement might worth as much as $100 million a year to Ethiopia.

A competing revenue source for farmers is *khat*, a shrub whose leaves have a psychotropic effect when chewed. Already a valuable traditional export to neighboring Djibouti and Somalia, the rewards of *khat*

Ethiopia

production are lucrative. Income from *khat* is often five times higher than coffee, and it can be harvested twice a year. Oxfam has warned that Ethiopia's coffee growing areas may increasingly be converted to fields of *khat* to meet the massive demand for the drug in East Africa and the Middle East.

Ethiopia is estimated to have 75 million head of livestock, the largest concentration in Africa. Its pastoralists face multiple afflictions. Regional diseases, like Rift Valley fever, can completely shut down a market when traditional buyers, like Saudi Arabia and the Gulf states, prohibit import of East African livestock. Persistent cycles of drought decimate herds, while those animals that survive bring less than optimal prices. Hides and skins remain important export items for Ethiopia, second only to coffee.

Despite drought, famine, and border warfare, about 200,000 tourists still come to Ethiopia every year, so attractive are its landscape and cultural treasures. The country has seven UNESCO World Heritage sites, and its paleontological remains are probably the most famous in the world. China has made Ethiopia one of eight African countries "approved" as a destination for Chinese tourists—little surprising since the country is one of its principal points of penetration into the continent.

The EPRDF government has made major efforts to attract Chinese investment since the late 1990s. More than 70 companies have been granted operating licenses. Manufacturers are producing goods ranging from pharmaceuticals to construction materials like iron and cement. Chinese businesses are involved in textiles, electricity, and mining, as well as major infrastructure projects from roads to hydroelectric dams and their associated irrigation projects. In March 2006, the Chinese company, Zhongyuan Petroleum Exploration Bureau, began its first oil exploration well in the Gambella basin of western Ethiopia. Zhongyuan employees working an oil field in the Ogaden region were attacked in May 2007 by unidentified gunmen; 74 people were killed, nine of them Chinese. The government blamed the ONLF.

Major foreign policy issues include a developing conflict with neighboring Somalia over an agreement between Ethiopia and the breakaway region of Somaliland granting landlocked Ethiopia access to the Red Sea in return for recognition of Somaliland as an independent state. Domestically, Ethiopian military forces are accused of arbitrary killings of civilians in the restive Amhara region where fighting with Fano militia is ongoing.

On the domestic front, the World Food Program (WFP) is suspending aid for 650,000 malnourished women and children in Ethiopia due to a lack of funding. The UN agency warned in April 2025 that 3.6 million people in Ethiopia overall are at risk of losing access to food aid in the coming weeks unless new financial support can urgently be sourced in light of cutbacks in aid funds, primarily from the United States. Included are two million mothers and children whose life-saving nutrition assistance in 2025 will fall short along with in-kind food assistance for up to one million refugees. The country faces continued conflict, instability, and drought while more than 10 million of Ethiopia's 130 million people face the threat of hunger. As the country slowly recovers from two years of a brutal civil war between federal forces and rebels in the northern region of Tigray, which ended in November 2022 and killed at least 600,000 people, tensions are again mounting with Eritrea over the quest for maritime access by landlocked Ethiopia. Continued violence and instability in the Amhara region of Ethiopia are also obstructing humanitarian operations with below-average rainfall in southeastern Ethiopia exacerbating conditions. Also concerning is an outbreak of a "rapidly spreading" cholera outbreak in the country's Gambella region in March that has worsened with the arrival of people fleeing violence in neighboring South Sudan, where the disease has spread. Several regions of the country are battling cholera outbreaks, with Amhara, the second-largest region, among the hardest hit with infection spread through food and water contaminated with the vibrio cholerae bacterium of fecal origin.

FUTURE CONSIDERATIONS

Some of Ethiopia's greatest contemporary challenges are in international relations. Conflict with Eritrea remains a concern, with the two countries seeming to be frequently at risk for further war, although the situation is monitored by UN peacekeeping forces. Such conflict, should it recur, would inevitably divert scarce economic resources to the military. On a positive note, in 2009, the two countries agreed in principle to pay each other compensation for the 1998–2000 border war. On the domestic front, future growth prospects are limited by weak infrastructure and other structural difficulties.

Domestically, the EPRDF regime has not found adequate ways to accommodate genuine dissent, other than coopting Iion elements into the dominant party. The legacy of the late Meles Zenawi is likely to persist under the government of his successor Hailemariam Desalegn: some effective management of economic and social development combined with a sphIin which the EPRDF dominates political life. The 2010 elections reconfirmed (or perhaps reestablished) the one-party nature of the regime, and this is likely to remain in place at beyond. the recent elections, Ethiopia's ethno-federal arrangement enables regions of the country to act with some autonomy from the central government, but the EPRDF's stranglehold on elected positions at the national, regional, and local levels means that top-down control remains intact. While the EPRDF is genuinely popular in many parts Ethiopia and deserves some of its popularity for its impressive development achievements in recent years, increased latituIthe opposition will be a prerequisite for Ethiopia to advance in a more democratic direction.

The Republic of Kenya

Modern Nairobi — Photo by Bev Klein

BASIC FACTS

Area: 582,750 sq. km. = 225,000 sq. mi. (larger than twice the size of Nevada)
Population: 57,052,004 (June 2023 est.)
Capital City: Nairobi
Government Type: Presidential Republic
Neighboring Countries: Tanzania (south, southwest); Uganda (west); South Sudan (northwest); Ethiopia (north); Somali Republic (northeast)
Official Languages: KiSwahili, English
Other Principal Languages: More than 60 languages are spoken. Prominently: Borana, Digo, Duruma, Embu, Gikuyu, Giryama, Gusii, Kalenjin, Kamba, Logooli, Luo, Luyia, Maasai, Meru, Pökoot, Saamia, Taita, Teso, and Turkana
Ethnic Groups: Kikuyu 22%, Luhya 14%, Luo 13%, Kalenjin 12%, Kamba 11%, Kisii 6%, Meru 6%, and other African 15%. Non-African (Asian, European, and Arab) 1%
Principal Religions: Protestantism 45%, Roman Catholicism 33%, indigenous beliefs 10%, Islam 10%, other 2%
Former Colonial Status: British Protectorate (1895–1963).
Independence Date: December 12, 1963
GDP Per Capita (IMF 2023 est.): $2,269 (nominal), $6,569 (PPP)
Gini Index: 47.7% (World Bank 2013)
Currency: Kenya shilling, 1 USD = 136.51 KES (Apr. 2023)
Inflation Rate: 7.2% (2022 est.)
Chief Commercial Products: Tea, flowers, coffee, and refined petroleum products
Foreign Direct Investments (FDI) net inflows: 944,327,305
Literacy Rate: 82.6% (CIA 2021)
Life Expectancy: 70 years (CIA 2023 est.)
Head of State: William Ruto, President (since Sept. 13, 2022)

LAND AND PEOPLE

Kenya lies on the East Coast of Africa, with coastline along the Indian Ocean and the interior stretching into the great lakes region of East Africa. North of the winding Tana River, there is an arid countryside that slowly rises to the southern mountains of Ethiopia. About 75% of the country is arid or semiarid. Nomadic pastoralists, like the Pokot, tend their cattle herds in the eastern regions and make frequent cross-border raids into Uganda. South of the Tana River, the coastline is hot and humid; this is the only part of Kenya that is truly tropical. This gives way immediately to thorn bush country of gently rising land extending about 175 miles from the coast.

The south-central portion of Kenya is a land of high plateaus stretching between the mountains. The capital Nairobi is over one mile above sea level and has a moderate climate year-round. Mount Kenya reaches a height of 17,040 feet 80 miles north of Nairobi. The Gregory Rift, extending in an almost straight line to the south from Lake Rudolf, is an immense trench almost 3,000 feet lower than the mountains that enclose it.

From the western side of these rift formations, the land slowly descends to the shores of Lake Victoria. The southeastern and south-central areas are temperate due to altitude, though the Equator divides these regions from northern Kenya. These are normally fertile lands; it is frequently possible in many sections to harvest two crops each year. Intermittent droughts, however, affect both productivity and hydroelectric potential. Given the limited availability of arable land, those droughts have also caused significant migration from the countryside To urban centers.

Kenya is the home of famous writers such as the renowned novelist Ngugi wa Thiong'o, as well as Jomo Kenyatta, a well-known anthropologist who became the country's first president. Ngugi was famous for the merits of his work as well as for his decision to stop writing in English and to write in his native Gikuyu instead. While Ngugi is presumed to be on short lists for the Nobel Prize in Literature, the country's first laureate came in 2004 when the Nobel Peace Prize was awarded to environmentalist and human rights campaigner Wangari Maathai. She became the first African woman to win the prize. Beginning in the late 1970s, she led the "Green Belt Movement," which mobilized poor women throughout the continent to replant millions of trees to slow deforestation and desertification. Long a political activist in Kenya, she challenged the regime of Daniel arap Moi when its policies and corrupt practices threatened Kenya's natural resources of parks and animals and forests. For her labors, she was frequently beaten and jailed.

HISTORY TO PRESENT DAY

For early history, see *Historical Background* and *The Colonial Period: The British*.

The Road to Independence: The Mau Mau, Jomo Kenyatta, and Oginga Odinga

The years leading up to independence saw Kenya become the first East African colony to include an African on its legislative council in 1944. At almost the same time, the Kenyan African Union (KAU) was created to campaign for better lands and independence for Africans. In 1947, the group chose as its leader Jomo

Kenya

Kenyatta, a prominent Kikuyu activist who had recently returned from a long residence in Europe. As noted in the chapter on colonial history, a Kikuyu-led secret society, the Mau Mau, launched a guerrilla campaign against white farmers in 1952. The revolt was based on the issue of land distribution and was specifically directed against European land ownership. When Kenya became a British crown colony, Africans were dispossessed from their lands, leaseholds were restricted to white settlers, and a "White-Highlands" policy herded the Kikuyu onto overcrowded reserves. The Mau Mau insurgency embattled Kenya for nearly five years. During the "emergency" declared by the colonial government, defense forces killed over 13,500 Africans, mostly Kikuyu; the Mau Mau killed 100 Europeans. In June 2013, The British government apologized for its treatment of thousands of Kenyans during the suppression of the Mau Mau insurgency and promised upwards of $33 million in compensation.Suspected of directing the Mau Mau, Jomo Kenyatta and nearly 100 other Africans were arrested immediately after the proclamation of the state of emergency. KAU was banned and its leaders charged with causing disorder or inciting other persons to cause disorder. In April 1953, Kenyatta was sentenced to a seven-year imprisonment for "managing the Mau Mau terrorist organization."

Following suppression of the Mau Mau insurgency in 1956, the British colonial government gradually steered the country toward African majority rule. African membership on the legislative council increased, and Africans assumed ministerial posts. In 1960, the British acceded to the principle of one man, one vote. The KAU, Ih had led Kenya's move toward independence, split along largely ethnic lines. Two leaders from the Luo tribe, Tom Mboya Iginga Odinga, formed the Kenya African National UnionINU), which sought Kenyatta's release. The KANU had strong representation from both the Kikuyu and LuIs. In opposition to KANU, other smaller tribes who feared Kikuyu and Luo domination formed the Kenya African Democratic Union (KADU). Ethnic division came to be an entrenched characteristic of Kenyan politics.

KANU elected Kenyatta (still detained even after having completed his sentence) its president *in absentia*. He was finally released in August 1961 and negotiated the arrangements that led to Kenya's independence in 1963. May 1963 elections resulted in an overwhelming victory for Kenyatta and KANU. As part of Kenyatta's ethnic Icing, he named Oginga Odinga vice president. A year later, following intense political lobbying and negotiation, KANU and KADU merged.

Odinga became increasingly disillusioned wIthe KANU government, which he felt had abandoned the socialist principles that had brought it to power. He advocated a ceiling on the amount of land that could be owned by any one individual (500 acres), but this troubled white farmers and KANU elites who had begun to accumulate property. The party closed ranks to divest itself of a troublesome critic. Fellow Luo and founder of KANU Tom Mboya pressed Odinga out; Odinga resigned the vice presidency, talking darkly of "international forces concerned with the ideological colonization of the country." The government's guiding star, he asserted, had become "personal gain." The ideological rift led to Odinga's expulsion from KANU and Imation of a left-wing opposition party, the Kenya Peoples' Union (KPU).

Elections in 1966 gave an overwhelming majority to KANU; Odinga's KPU won only a handful of seats. The KANU government nevertheless suppressed KPU. Tensions between the Kikuyu and Luo were exacerbated in 1969 when Tom Mboya, the most prominent Luo in the government (and still in his thirties), was assassinated on the verge of presidential and parliamentary elections. A Kikuyu man was convicted of the crime, but many Kenyans felt that Kenyatta was behind the assassination, having feared Mboya's power.

While touring the Luo heartland, Kenyatta encountered crowds of anti-government demonstrators. His bodyguards fired on agitated Luo demonstrators, killing several and wounding many more. The government blamed Odinga, placed him under house arrest, and banned the KPU.

With Odinga out of the picture, Kenyatta consolidated personal power. He was reelected unopposed. The 1969 general election also gave birth tIe single-chamber legislature in which KANU held overwhelming dominance. Kenya became a *de facto* single-party state. Kenyatta was reelected again in 1974 and died in office in 1978.

Daniel Arap Moi's Presidency (1978–2002): Consolidating Power

Kenyatta was succeeded by his vice president, Daniel arap Moi of the Kalenjin tribe. Moi won his own term of office in the 1979 elections and along with KANU officially made Kenya a single-party state in 1982. An attempted coup by members of the air force in August 1982 was quickly suppressed, but Luo involvement further marginalized Odinga and his Luo supporters. Odinga's son, Raila, was detained for alleged involvement in the plot. Moi disbanded the air force and closed the University in Nairobi, where student supporters of the coup were numerous.

KANU called early elections for September 1983, and Moi was reelected unopposed. He proceeded to govern an ethnically divided Kenya with increasing authoritarianism. Urban Kikuyus of Nairobi charged him with cronyism as he appointed fellow Kalenjin tribesmen to lucrative government positions. The secret ballot was abolished in favor of a "queuing" system where people have to publicly line up according to their political preferences. This led to intimidation and widespread election fraud. Voter participation plummeted; in some districts there was only a 20% turnout, down from the former 90%.

Maasai woman seated before a traditional plastered structure

Photo by Lance Fuchs

Kenya

Kenyan mother and children   Photo by Mary Ellen Grabski

Six opposition leaders, including an aging Oginga Odinga, formed the Forum for the Restoration of Democracy (FORD) to lobby for democratic chanID brought together Luo, Kikuyu and Luhya in common opposition to KANU's single-party monopoly. A massive demonstration in Nairobi in late 1991 (as the Cold War ended and many other countries in Africa made moves toward democracy) was met with tear gas and riot batons. The government dismissed the participants as agitators and anarchists.

Further protest came from international aid agencies—the International MIary Fund, the World Bank and several creditor nations—all of which cut off money-Itined for Kenya. This put tremendous pressure on the Moi regime, which made provisions for multiparty elections in 1992. Parliament repealed the one-party provision of the constitution and allowed several new parliamentary elections were scheduled for December 1992.

Moi successfully divided the opposition in the lead-up to the 1992 elections; divisions arose within the FORD, which had initially transcended traditional tribal rivalries. In August 1992, it split into two factions: FORD-Kenya, led by Oginga Odinga, and FORD-Asili, led by the Kikuyu Kenneth Matiba.

The election period was characterized by widespread ethnic tension and violence, deliberately manipulated by politicians. It was particularly virulent in the Rift Valley province. Hundreds were killed and thousands of potential voters were disenfranchised when forced to flee their homes. Young Kalenjin and Maasai were recruited into gangs to terrorize suspected opposition supporters—primarily members of the Kikuyu, Luhya, and Kamba ethnicities. These militants looted property, set homes ablaze, and killed several hundred. As people fled their lands, government supporters occupied them.

For added insurance, KANU legislators pushed through a constitutional amendment providing that a presidential candidate, to be elected, must win at least 25% of the vote in five of Kenya's seven districts. Since Moi and his Kalenjin tribesmen controlled a substantial minority of the vote through political patronage in several districts, this virtually assured that none of his three principal opponents stood a chance. Moi ended up a mere 36% of the vote, but earned another five-year term, beating out the two FORD candidates (Odinga and Matiba), and Mwai Kibaki of the Democratic Party. In the legislature, KANU elected 95 delegates in comparison to 88 for the opposition. Riots broke out on the opening day of parliament in 1993; Moi simply dissolved the legislature rather than face vocal opposition. The International Monetary Fund, infuriated by the printing of new currency to finance KANU's effort in the election, imposed more rigid conditions on future loans.

The regime's strongest critic, Oginga Odinga, died in 1994. His son, Raila, lost the struggle for leadership of FORD-Kenya, left the party and formed the National Democratic Party (NDP), which became a principal voice for the opposition.

The December 1997 elections reproduced the cycle of violence, conflict, and repression. Members of the thuggish KANU youth wing and security forces blocked meetings and rallies, while the government harassed and intimidated candidates and human rights workers. Once again opposition parties failed to unite behind a single candidate; their appeals were tribal rather than national. Moi was reelected by a mere 40% of the popular vote. KANU emerged with only 109 out of 222 seats, leaving the president needing coalition support in the parliament.

In 1998, the U.S. embassies in both Kenya and Tanzania were simultaneously bombed in al-Qaeda attacks, killing 224 people. This was followed several years later (on November 28, 2002) by a suicide bombing of an Israeli-owned hotel near the port city of Mombasa; simultaneously, an Israeli airliner escaped two missiles fired as it was taking off from Mombasa airport. In each case, Kenya's hotels and resorts subsequently experienced huge cancellations of reservations. In Mombasa, a leading imam, Sheikh Ali Shee, explicitly warned American and Israeli tourists to stay away.

The late 1990s were a period of economic uncertainty and public campaigns against Kenya's notorious corruption. In July, the International Monetary Fund (IMF) refused to lend any longer to Kenya, largely because corruption was so blatant it was constricting economic growth. Confirming the IMF's concern, the Commissioner-General of Kenya's Revenue Authority stunned the nation by disclosing that the country annually lost $1.68 billion through corruption. President Moi responded by creating the Kenya Anti-Corruption Authority (KACA). Corrupt bureaucrats were reportedly gripped by panic but remained calm enough to bring legal action against KACA. In December 2000, a three-judge constitutional court ruled the Authority illegal, setting off alarm bells within the donor community, which already knew the judiciary to be one of the most corrupt of Kenya's numerous corrupt institutions.

As part of a calculated set of responses to impress the IMF, Moi also appointed Richard Leakey, a well-known critic of Kenyan politics, to head its civil service. Leakey, part of the world-famous paleontology family, was a long-time friend of World Bank president James Wolfensohn, and his appointment achieved its desired goal. The IMF resumed lending to Kenya in July 2000, but with conditions that included enactment of anticorruption and economic crimes bills, and ethics legislation requiring public officials to declare their wealth and liabilities. Another condition—seen as humiliating by some Kenyans—required

Kenya

Former President Mwai Kibaki

weekly IMF inspections of the Central Bank of Kenya accounts. Leakey's tenure as head of Kenya's civil service lasted less than two years; he resigned in March 2001, and almost simultaneously the IMF stopped its lending to Kenya, citing "serious setbacks" to the fight against corruption.

Moi announced that he would step down at the end of his term in 2002 and made a number of changes to prepare KANU for the next set of elections. Speaking of the need for "new blood," he appointed the opposition leader Raila Odinga to his cabinet, forming Kenya's first coalition government in June 2001. Raila Odinga had previously been imprisoned without trial by Moi for six years following the attempted coup in 1982. In October, the president also appointed Jomo Kenyatta's son, Uhuru Kenyatta to parliament; this was rapidly followed by a cabinet post for Kenyatta.

KANU voted to absorb Odinga's smaller National Democratic Party (NDP) in March 2002, and Odinga was unanimously chosen as the new party's general-secretary. Four young politicians were chosen as vice presidents, the most prominent of which was Uhuru Kenyatta, clearly Moi's favorite. Moi was named chairman of KANU, with extraordinary powers that made him a virtual one-man party. Moi then pushed through the selection of Uhuru Kenyatta as his chosen successor in a move seen as an olive branch to Kenya's largest tribe, the Kikuyu, which had been largely marginalized for over two decades. Whatever electoral advantage might have come of this, however, was offset by the divisions the decision created in KANU.

Party barons and stalwarts defected in droves and marched into opposition. Led by Raila Odinga, they formed the "Rainbow Coalition" to incorporate all hues of opposition. Rainbow merged with the Liberal Democratic Party (LDP), while 13 other opposition parties, representing a variety of regions and all Kenya's major tribes, coalesced to form the National Alliance Party of Kenya (NAK). In short order NAK merged with LDP to form a super alliance known as the National Rainbow Coalition (NARC). They agreed to unite behind a single candidate to oppose KANU's Kenyatta: former presidential candidate Mwai Kibaki, who was also a Kikuyu.

At 71 years of age, Kibaki had already had a long political career. A founder of KANU, he had spent the last decade trying to drive it from the office. He had served as finance minister from 1969–1982, under

Kenya's Parliament opens in 2007

Das Parlament

Kenya

both Jomo Kenyatta and Daniel arap Moi, and then as Moi's vice president until he was removed in 1988. He had unsuccessfully run for president in 1992 and 1997.

Mwai Kibaki (2002–2012)

In December 2002, KANU faced united opposition and voters gave Mwai Kibaki a convincing victory: 62.2% of the vote to Kenyatta's 31.3%. The NARC was held together by a common hostility to Daniel arap Moi and his family and friends, many of whom had richly profited from his long tenure in office. Kibaki had made corruption and economic revitalization principal planks in his campaign. NARC won 125 of the 210 elected seats in parliament against KANU's 64.

The new government moved quickly to deal with corruption. President Kibaki appointed an anticorruption czar, John Githongo, a young journalist who had long campaigned against corruption as a newspaper columnist. A number of anticorruption commissions were organized, with quick results. By the end of 2003, half of Kenya's most senior judges—23 in all—had been suspended after an anticorruption commission had gathered evidence against them.

President Kibaki promised a draft constitution within 100 days of his election, but debate went on for over five years. At stake were interests that focused on efforts to curtail presidential powers and create the office of prime minister. Kibaki loyalists, including some fellow Kikuyus, wanted the presidency to retain its enormous powers. Supporters of Raila Odinga were furious that the president and his minions reneged on an alleged pre-campaign pact that promised the premiership to Odinga.

The issue of presidential and prime ministerial power in the new constitution split the NARC coalition, with Kibaki's National Alliance Party (NAP) and Odinga's Liberal Democratic Party (LDP) pulling in different directions. The cabinet was permanently divided; Kenyans took to the streets to protest delay with such vehemence that riot police had to intervene with tear gas and batons to control (and create) violence.

When the courts ruled the new constitution could not be simply adopted by parliament, but required a referendum, the two sides coalesced. Those supporting the government's 200-page draft constitution chose the banana as their symbol (to aid illiterate voters) and their opponents chose the orange. At least 24 people were killed in protests, MPs got in fistfights, and the cabinet was so badly divided it barely met. Orange campaigners argued the draft was designed to secure the political dominance of Kikuyu elites through a strong presidency. When Kenyans went to the polls in November 2005, they handed top banana Mwai Kibaki a humiliating defeat, with 57% of the voters rejecting the constitutional draft.

Corruption remained a major issue, with the British high commissioner to Kenya saying in 2004 that corruption accounted for about 8% of Kenya's total GDP. The anticorruption czar John Githongo had opened several dossiers dealing with fraudulent contracts signed by the Moi government and honored by Kibaki's. Representing an alliance of business and party interests, the contracts were typically signed with shell companies that provided nonexistent services to the government. Monies paid on the contracts were channeled back into party treasuries for campaigning. The president was duly briefed on his findings, but he took little action. Githongo's investigations named names. He received death threats and fled to England in February 2005.

Two especially outrageous corruption scandals were the Goldenberg and the Anglo Leasing affairs. The Goldenberg scandal, which took place in the early 1990s during the Moi presidency, involved fictitious gold and diamond exports; losses amounted to some $600 million. Top officials were implicated, including Moi and several of his ministers, but not prosecuted. The Anglo Leasing scandal involved a fabricated company that was awarded contracts to supply a system for producing passports that could not be forged. Millions of dollars were paid to the firm before the scam was detected in 2004. While not the first fictitious company, Anglo Leasing has now lent its name to describe this type of fraud. The Anglo Leasing investigations have covered contracts signed by both KANU and NARC governments. A recent study by the Kenya branch of Transparency International asserts that the country loses $1.2 billion annually to graft.

In October 2006, the Kenya Anti-Corruption Commission (KACC) recommended prosecution of four former cabinet ministers in connection with $300 million worth of faulty Anglo Leasing contracts. The four investigative reports were forwarded to Attorney General Amos Wako for prosecution, but he found them wanting, sent them back to the KACC, and effectively postponed any prosecution until after elections in 2007.

Kibaki ran for a second term in 2007. The NARC coalition reformulated as NARC-Kenya to support the president, and Kibaki was better positioned for the election than his potential rivals in mid-2007, being able to claim some economic success and plaudits for eliminating fees for primary school children. Kibaki also benefited from division within the opposition, but reelection was far from secure.

Potential opponents to Kibaki briefly coalesced in the Orange Democratic Movement, which included opposition leaders Uhuru Kenyatta (of KANU), Raila Odinga (formerly of the LDP), and another rival, Kalonzo Musyoka. By mid-2007, the Odinga and Musyoka factions had split the ODM into two pieces (the ODM under Odinga and the ODM-Kenya under Musyoka). Kenyatta split away from the ODM coalition and decided to

Nairobi slums, overrun with plastic bags

Photo by Mary Ellen Grabski

Kenya

back the incumbent Kibaki, as did former president and erstwhile Kibaki opponent Daniel arap Moi.

The split in the opposition seemed to advantage Kibaki and his coalition Party of National Unity (PNU) as the December elections approached, but the polling between the sitting president and Raila Odinga proved quite close, and through much of the fall of 2007 Odinga held a lead. After the elections, Kibaki claimed victory and was backed in his claim by the Electoral Commission, but there were widespread allegations of electoral improprieties that lit a fuse under Kenya's volatile political system.

Violent clashes broke out across the country in the wake of the election results. Thousands were displaced and over 1,000 killed in the ensuing months. The clash took on clear ethnic overtones, with Kibaki having drawn support from Kikuyu, while Odinga's support came from the Luo, as well as the Kalenjin and other smaller ethnic groups.

As the situation threatened to deteriorate into something approaching civil war, Kibaki and Odinga narrowly managed to pull it back from the brink with an unlikely power-sharing agreement: Kibaki would retain the presidency, but Odinga would be placed in the reinstated position of prime minister, a position abolished back in 1964 under founding father Jomo Kenyatta.

Kibaki and Odinga presided over a 40-member grand coalition cabinet that included Vice President Kalonzo Musyoka, and Uhuru Kenyatta and Musalia Mudavadi as new deputy prime ministers. The tenuous nature of the power-sharing agreement became clear in 2009 when Odinga accused Kibaki of sidelining the ODM. Odinga threatened to boycott future cabinet meetings, thereby generating a crisis of government. After inquiries into corruption in several ministries, Prime Minister Odinga dismissed two ministers, only to have his decision overturned by President Kibaki. Several of Odinga's allies in the Orange Democratic Movement then declared they would boycott cabinet meetings.

A New Constitution and New Generation: Uhuru Kenyatta and Raila Odinga

Despite this tension between president and prime minister, Kenya managed to hold a national referendum in 2010 that approved a new constitution. The 2010 charter was supported by both Kibaki and Odinga and approved by 67% of Kenyans. It is widely viewed as an improvement on the previous constitution that greatly centralized power. The new political dispensation created a Senate and 47 county governments to decentralize power, while also trimming presidential prerogatives. It eliminated the position of prime minister, effective as of the March 2013 general election. It further limited the size of landholdings (which brought opposition from major landholders such as former president Moi) and created a land board to adjudicate disputes.

The constitutional referendum reduced tensions between Kibaki and Odinga, partly due to a provision that prevented Kibaki from running again. Odinga thus became a front-runner for the presidency in 2013. Another potential candidate, George Saitoti, the Internal Security Minister (a powerful position in the Kenyan cabinet), died in a helicopter crash in the Ngong hills near Nairobi in June 2012.

In 2012, political news in Kenya came to be dominated by trials at the International Criminal Court (ICC) for six prominent Kenyans, including most notably Uhuru Kenyatta. The hearings and trial sought to establish the roles of political and media leaders in the election violence of 2007–2008. Of the six Kenyans summoned before the court, four progressed to a trial, including Kenyatta, the minister William Ruto (a Kalenjin minister known for his incendiary rhetoric and blatant appeals to tribalism), and radio announcer Joshua arap Sang.

During late 2011 and 2012, the Kenyan population was menaced by two deadly threats: drought and terrorism. The worst drought in decades hit the region in 2011, with the area in the north around Lake Turkana being especially hard hit. Neighboring Somalia suffered the drought, and tens of thousands of refugees fled across the border into Kenya, given the almost complete lack of government authority in Somalia. This swelled Kenya's refugee camp at Dadaab (near the Somali border) to a population of nearly half a million, making it the world's largest refugee camp.

At the same time, violence by Islamists from Somalia terrorized the Kenyan population, and open fighting has happened between the Kenyan government and Somali militants. In 2011, Somali raiders kidnapped several foreigners inside Kenya; the Kenyan government responded with raids into Somalia against the Islamist al-Shabaab militia. Kenya then initiated joint military efforts against al-Shabaab (which has been affiliated with al-Qaeda) along with the militaries of several other countries, including the United States, France, Ethiopia, and the Somali government. Al-Shabaab has retaliated with several grenade attacks on public locations (including pubs, bus stations, and churches) in Kenya's two largest cities of Nairobi and Mombasa. A deadly attack came in the eastern town of Garissa near the Somalia border on July 1, 2012, when 17 people were killed in grenade and gun attacks on two churches. Several attacks in Nairobi culminated in September 2013, when Somali militants from al-Shabaab took siege of a Nairobi shopping mall in retaliation for the presence of Kenyan troops as part of the African Union's Mission in Somalia. The four-day siege resulted in at least 67 deaths and almost 200 wounded.

A class in Nairobi

Kenya

Wangari Maathai, Nobel Peace Prize winner

Violent clashes took place across Kenya—on several pretexts—through 2012 and into 2013. First, in August 2012, battles over land resulted in over 100 deaths in the Tana River area along the southern coast. These were followed by rioting and burning of churches in the nearby city of Mombasa after a prominent Muslim cleric was assassinated in his car. Further fights in Garissa killed several soldiers, which led to retaliatory killings. And in June 2013, at least ten people were killed in a grenade attack perpetrated by unknown individuals in Banisa, near the borders with Somalia and Ethiopia. As a result, in March 2014, the Kenyan government began ordering Somali refugees from all across the country, and particularly the cities, to designated camps in an effort to minimize security threats and put an end to militant Islamist attacks. Similar government orders, however, were previously ruled unconstitutional by the Kenyan High Court in 2012.

In the midst of these paroxysms of violence around the country, it was remarkable that the election on March 4, 2013, took place as scheduled and with very little unrest. The election featured a sort of next-generation rematch between the two sons of Kenya's most prominent independence-era politicians. Uhuru Kenyatta and Raila Odinga fought a bitter campaign, though both pleaded with their supporters for peace and calm. Kenyatta allied himself with his former adversary, William Ruto, in order to supplement his renowned Kikuyu name with an explicit appeal to Ruto's Kalenjin ethnic group.

While Odinga led in much of the early polling (when his opponents were divided) and took the vast majority of the vote from the Luo ethnic group, Kenyatta consolidated his position as a leading contender and managed a narrow victory in the first round of voting by taking 50.5% of the vote. Odinga took 44%, with the remainder split among six other candidates. In both the National Assembly and the new Senate, Kenyatta's coalition took the largest number of seats, but failed to reach a majority. As a result, they cannot pass legislation without the support of other coalitions or independents. Odinga's coalition won the most governorships (23 out of 47) in newly established county governments.

The 2013 election took place against the backdrop of the International Criminal Court charges against Kenyatta and Ruto for incitement to violence and crimes against humanity after the 2007 elections. With Kenyatta's election, the situation has become especially thorny. While he has largely complied with requests from the ICC to appear and make statements, Kenyatta also appeared to leverage resentment against the ICC in the run-up to the election. (The court has increasingly come under fire in Africa for the fact that it has to date indicted only Africans of human rights crimes.) The prospect of a sitting president facing an international trial is difficult to imagine, not least due to Kenya's diplomatic and strategic value to the international community as an anchor in East Africa. Therefore, in October 2013, the African Union petitioned the ICC for immunity for sitting heads of state. A UN resolution petitioned the Security Council for a 12-month deferral of Kenyatta's case in the wake of terrorist attacks in Kenya and the need for international peace and security. While denied, Kenyatta's trial has nonetheless been postponed until October 2014 so more evidence can be gathered and submitted. It is still uncertain whether the power politics—within Kenya and internationally—will preclude a full trial for Kenyatta.

CONTEMPORARY THEMES

The Economy

Having meager mineral resources, the economy of Kenya has traditionally rested on agriculture and tourism. Prior to 1979 Kenya was relatively prosperous by African standards. A series of economic shocks—a spike in oil prices, drought, crop failure, and famine—increased borrowing and aid dependency. Government corruption siphoned off a large part of foreign aid, and the economy declined for years.

International donors insistently pressured President Moi to introduce economic liberalization, end corruption, and begin greater transparency in government. The IMF suspension of loans in 1997 sent the mismanaged economy into steep decline. Beginning in the mid-2000s, the consequences of changed policy began to set in, and Kenya reported GDP growth of about 6% in 2005 and 2006. Growth in 2007 (before the international economic crisis) hit 7%, the highest growth rate in three decades. It declined to the 2% range for the years 2008 and 2009 but rebounded to over 5% in 2010 and settled around 4.3% in 2012. Much of the recent improvement has been attributed to the revival of agriculture and the growth of related sectors like agribusiness.

Kenya remains in large part an agricultural country. It is the major source of income for the bulk of the population, employing over three-quarters of rural inhabitants. Despite its scale, agriculture contributes only about a quarter of GDP. An acute shortage of arable land, and uneven distribution of that which is arable, has meant that most farmers work plots of less than five acres.

Tea has been one focus of the government's attention, and the sector has been one of the economy's success stories. Kenya is now the world's second largest exporter of black tea. Liberalization of the market and favorable climatic conditions has produced bumper crops. The tea sector employs over two million people across the country, but the industry is threatened by the expansion of Chinese tea growing. Kenya's coffee industry has been similarly impacted by expanded coffee production

Kenya

in Asia. Small producers were long forced to be members of cooperatives that suffered chronic mismanagement and corruption. The result has been that farmers were often not paid for their produce.

Flower growing is a fast-growing part of Kenya's agricultural sector. Since the early 1990s, flower exports have increased around 20% per year. Kenya is now the EU's biggest source of fresh-cut flower imports—principally roses and carnations. Flower growing now surpasses coffee and probably tourism as a source of foreign exchange and is only second to tea as an income producer. Most flower farms are located in rural areas and thus have considerable impact on both the local population and environment. Cultivation is relatively labor intensive, requiring about 200 workers per 15 acres. The workers, mostly women, earn a little more than $1.50 per day, and the industry indirectly supports an estimated 500,000 people. There is increasing concern about the environmental and health impact of fertilizers and agricultural chemicals used by growers. Doctors report growing cases of bronchitis and breathing problems, severe headaches, loss of hair, and chest pains attributed to industrial chemicals.

With abundant wildlife, beautiful beaches, and a well-organized system of national parks, Kenya has long been a favorite tourist destination in Africa. Spending by tourists has been one of Kenya's most important foreign exchange earners, and constitutes over 10% of the economy. The industry directly employs a reported 300,000 people, while another 200,000 work in sectors that benefit from tourism. However, the US Embassy bombing in 1998, the Mombasa attacks of 2002, and recent attacks by Islamist militants have shaken the industry (as has competition from other African safari destinations). Some of the slack has been picked up by Chinese tourists. China granted Kenya "Preferred Destination Status" in 2004 and since then Chinese arrivals have more than doubled. China allocated Kenya Airways landing rights in several Chinese cities; direct flights between the two countries are expected to increase the number of Chinese visitors. Chinese President Hu Jintao visited Kenya in late April 2006, and at the conclusion of his tour several commercial agreements were signed. Potentially the most important was an oil-exploration deal that allowed China National Offshore Oil Corporation to explore off Kenya's Indian Ocean coast. The total area open to exploration is nearly 45,000 square miles; access to the area is reportedly free, with payment to be made only if reserves are discovered.

Kenya has also become a regional leader in information technology. The initial public offering of shares in Safaricom, a mobile phone service provider, generated a frenzy in Kenya in 2008, with reports of many citizens making their first ever equity investments by grabbing up single shares of the fashionable stock. Safaricom is a world leader in extending banking services to the poor in rural areas using transfers via mobile phone, an innovation that has the potential to alleviate poverty and spur economic growth. In the same vein, Kenya has become a world leader in mobile banking, with the M-PESA program enabling Kenyans to transfer cash value over their cell phones; because withdrawals can be made anywhere that phone cards are sold (including small kiosks and rural markets), millions of Kenyans who have never been bank clients have been able to access the financial system in new and socially beneficial ways. One big improvement has been in the ability of relatively well-off urban dwellers to send remittances to poorer family members in rural areas. While one must not expect technology to transform African economies overnight, Kenya does illustrate reasons for the enthusiasm. Broadband is also being extended across Kenya, making it a communications hub for much of East and Central Africa.

The country also seeks to be the transportation and trade hub for the east Africa region. Mombasa is already a leading port, but one of the most ambitious infrastructure projects in African history would make the city of Lamu an economic center of much greater scope and scale, with a port that would have five times the capacity of Mombasa. The project will link Kenya to the new nation of South Sudan and to Ethiopia, both of which are landlocked. Called the Lamu Port Southern Sudan Ethiopia Transport Corridor (LAPSSET), it is estimated to cost over $28 billion, or about a year and a half of the government's entire budget. The project envisions the port at Lamu (to be Africa's largest), major highways and railways into South Sudan and Ethiopia, and oil pipelines from South Sudan's oil fields to the port, possibly along with international airports and other investments that may bring the project into the $30 billion range.

Social Issues

Despite a seemingly robust economy, growth does not necessarily or immediately translate into improved life situations for ordinary Kenyans. Social statistics indicate that Kenyans on average are not significantly better off today than they were at independence, and a majority of Kenya's population still lives on less than two dollars a day, though such indicators as infant mortality have fallen impressively in the past decade.

Alongside the political system, the AIDS pandemic is one of Kenya's greatest dilemmas. The Kibaki government adopted a more public and activist stance than the Moi government, with the former president having described AIDS as the "greatest threat" to the country and urging all Kenyans to be tested for the HIV virus. Kibaki's government made AIDS education compulsory, even at primary school level; a shift in attitude and practice seems to have occurred as a result. The country's HIV/AIDS infection rates have declined, having previously been one of the world's highest. In part, the declining prevalence of HIV is attributable to the deaths of many living with HIV/AIDS, but it also suggests a slowing of the rates of transmission. There were about 2.5 million people living with the disease in 2000; it was about 1.6 million as of 2012. Prevalence is in the range of 6% of the adult population. (Government policy received little support from Luci Kibaki, Kenya's former first lady, who has told students that young people had "no business" using condoms.) Several Nairobi pharmaceutical companies are now producing high quality generic AIDS drugs, and the Health Ministry has acquired the drugs. Pregnant women, rape victims, and hospital inpatients have first priority. The country has also received considerable support from international sources and donors.

Largely peaceful national elections were conducted in 2022 with William

High above the plain Photo by Bev Klein

Kenya

Ruto securing just over 50 percent of the vote for the presidency. Major problems afflicting the country in 2024 primarily involve natural disasters—especially serious flooding of cities, towns, and the countryside from the effects of devastating cyclones striking the region with over 120,000 people displaced and 70 killed.

A devastating drought occurred in the northern regions in April 2025, the worst in 40 years. Forced to walk for several hours a day to the nearest borehole, where water levels are critically low, young women married off in their teens by desperate families, who live in stick-framed nomadic shelters pitched between black volcanic boulders on the arid plains of northern Kenya. Aid groups indicate climate change is making droughts more devastating and frequent and deepening inequality in insidious ways, such as a surge in the rate of child marriage, noticeably in communities in which there has been no rain for nine months and where livestock are dying from starvation and dehydration as the land becomes more sterile. Desperate families feel forced to offer up their daughters for marriage in exchange for a camel and a few goats, an arrangement that may provide the girl's family with sustenance for a few more months. This deepens existing gender inequalities and threatens women's incomes, health, and safety. Women and girls must walk great distances to collect water and fuel and are often the last to eat as many are forced into taking on insecure jobs or migrating, placing them at higher risk, especially of gender-based violence. Though women of all ages bear the burden of a worsening climate and a lack of money and food, younger girls are often the least protected and most at risk.

FUTURE CONSIDERATIONS

Kenya's peaceful election in 2013 suggests the country has come a long way from the deadly clashes between ethnic groups in 2007–2008. The election of Uhuru Kenyatta—and the eventual acceptance of the result by rival Raila Odinga—bodes well for political stability. The 2010 approval of a new constitution was hailed in Kenya as a major step forward towards increasing democratization, and the 2013 election was another step. Going forward, more identity groups in Kenya seem to have a slice of power, whether via a governorship, or a women's representative in the parliament. Despite this good news, the country will be anxiously awaiting news on the progress of Kenyatta's ICC trial, and it continues to face the destabilizing impacts of occasional clashes over land and religion. Neighboring Somalia appears to be stabilizing slowly, but there are still attempts by militants to wreak havoc in Kenya's remote northeast.

Economically, the country suffered some consequences from the shock to its stability in 2008 (and from the global financial crisis), but is relatively steady at present. Kenya's growth may well be able to hold at comfortably around 5%. That would be well above the population growth rate and would mean real improvements in the standard of living. Recent positive signs in the economy include the public offering by Safaricom and the expansion of broadband access through submarine cables under the Indian Ocean, a project that came to fruition in 2009; these both have the potential to make Kenya the information technology hub for East Africa. The sheer ambition of the port project at Lamu (along with other projects including the renovation of the international airport, a new technology park outside of Nairobi, and a rail system linking these) suggests a country that has confidence in its trajectory and prospects. If political stability can hold, domestic and international capital may increasingly be mobilized in the ways needed to promote development. Kenya looks like a risky—but promising—bet on the future.

Market day in Kenya

The Somali Democratic Republic

Life amid the ruins: soccer in Mogadishu   ©Jose Cendo, AFP/Getty Images

BASIC FACTS

Area: 637,657 sq. km. (slightly smaller than Texas)
Population: 12,693,796 (June 2023 est.)
Capital City: Mogadishu
Government Type: Federal parliamentary republic
Neighboring Countries: Djibouti (north-west); Ethiopia (west); Kenya (south-west).
Official Languages: Somali, Arabic
Other Principal Languages: Italian, English
Ethnic Groups: Darod (north-northeast); Hawiya (central area); Rahanwein (South); Ishaak (north central area); all of the foregoing are collectively referred to as Somali (85%); Bantu and other non-Somali 15% (including 30,000 Arabs)
Principal Religion: Sunni Muslim
Former Colonial Status: The north was a British protectorate (1897–1960); the South was an Italian colony (1892–1941); British administration (1941–1949); Italian trust territory (1949–1960).
Independence Date: July 1, 1960
GDP Per Capita (IMF 2023 est.): $544 (nominal), $1,374 (PPP)
Gini Index: N/A
Currency: Somali shilling, $US 1 = 569 (Apr. 2023)
Inflation Rate: 9.4% (2022 est.)
Chief Commercial Products: Livestock, bananas, hides, and fish
Foreign Direct Investments (FDI) net inflows: 105,500,000
Literacy Rate: 37.8% (CIA 2008)
Life Expectancy: 56.12 (CIA 2023 est.)
Head of State: President Hassan Sheikh Mohamud (since May 23, 2022)
Head of Government: Prime Minister Hamza Abdi Barre (since June 25, 2022)

LAND AND PEOPLE

The Somali Republic, the easternmost nation of Africa, covers an area often referred to as the Horn of Africa; it has a 1,700-mile coastline on the tropical waters of the Gulf of Aden and the Indian Ocean. Although the northern part of the country is hilly, reaching altitudes of 4,000 feet, the larger portion to the south is a flat, semi-arid land, which is uniformly hot. During the "dry season" there is almost no vegetation. However, acacia trees, with their roots reaching far into the land to obtain precious water, do survive.

Like men in Kenya and Ethiopia, Somalis and Somalilanders enjoy the stimulation that comes from chewing *khat,* a shrub whose leaves have a psychotropic effect when chewed. It works as an amphetamine-like stimulant, which causes extremely heightened feelings of excitement. The leaves are imported from Kenya and can cost the user up to five dollars a day, well beyond the average wage in the country. For importers, the profits of the *khat* trade are lucrative, and a number of the luxurious homes going up in Hargeysa (the capital of the self-declared autonomous republic of Somaliland), belong to *khat* traders.

Some of the great cultural achievements of Somalia can be found in its poetry. Oral verse is central to the Somali way of life. It is a means of mass communication, preserving history and shaping contemporary events, expressing personal and public sentiment and experience. Travelers invariably comment on the Somali love of harmonious sound, elaborate image, and alliterative arabesque. Distinguished poets were heard by huge audiences of national radio and showcased by the BBC's Africa Service; even under British rule, the metaphoric language stimulated the nationalist cause. The Somali poetic tradition remains today, not entirely muted by conflict or political repression. So embedded in Somali consciousness is poetry that it is part of the texture and discourse of clan reconciliation meetings, the bedrock of Somali politics. Among writers, the novelist Nuruddin Farah (most famous for his novel *Maps*) may be Somalia's greatest contribution to world literature.

HISTORY TO PRESENT DAY

For early history, see *Historical Background, The Colonial Period: The Italians; The British.*

Colonialism

Modern Somalia is the result of the merger of former British Somaliland and *Somalia Italiana* in 1960. Each came with a different colonial history and experience and those differences are at the heart of modern Somalia's present situation. British Somaliland became independent on June 26, 1960; five days later, on July 1, it joined Italian Somalia to form the Somali Republic. At independence, there was no common administrative language. English was spoken in the former British protectorate, Italian in the larger *Somalia Italiana*.

Somalia

Somali, though spoken by all, did not exist as a written language until the 1970s.

The British interest in Somaliland was strategic: control of the entrance to the Red Sea and cheap provisions for Aden, its garrison at the tip of the Arabian Peninsula. As a consequence, it adopted a strategy of indirect rule. Northern Somalis were left to follow their own customs; traditional procedures for resolving conflicts among nomadic clan groups remained in place. The British did not encourage modernization, partly because they feared the social disruption. Italy's treatment of Somalia was much different. Southern Somalis were forced to adopt Italian law, and Italy abolished nomad customs, especially traditional mechanisms for conflict resolution between clans. Resistance to Italy was intense and military confrontation continued to the late 1920s.

From British Somaliland emerged a well-educated elite, while Italy introduced mass education in the south, but at a relatively low level, creating a mass of very nationalistic semi-intellectuals. At unification there was little in common between the two partners save a vague sense of "Somali" identity. To preserve the union, which gave expression to that identity, northerners gave up much. The capital was located in the southern city of Mogadishu. Most of the technical positions in the new government were filled by better-trained northerners, but the bulk of political appointments went to southerners. Political parties proliferated, reflecting the fragmentary nature of Somali clan politics, and at one point Somalia had more parties per capita than any democratic state aside from Israel. (In the elections of 1969, more than 60 parties competed in a country of just a few million inhabitants.)

This multitude of parties expressed substantial differences in political style and orientation. With a dominant position in parliament, southern nationalists, pro-Arab and militantly pan-Somali, pushed the idea of a "greater Somalia"—a claim on Somali-inhabited areas of neighboring Kenya and Ethiopia. "Modernists," mostly northerners, stressed economic and social development and urged improved relations with other African states. Out of this welter of conflicting tendencies, the Somali Youth League gradually assumed a dominant position, successfully cutting across regional and clan loyalties. Under the leadership of Prime Minister Mohamed Ibrahim Egal (1967–69), a northerner educated in England, Somalia significantly improved its relations with Kenya and Ethiopia, but its fledgling constitutional democracy was brought to an end in October 1969, when army and police led by Maj. General Mohamed Siad Barre seized power in a bloodless coup. Prime Minister Egal was thrown in jail where he remained for 12 years.

The Reign of Siad Barre

Siad Barre was born in the Ogaden area of Ethiopia, an area once part of Italian East Africa but returned by the British to Ethiopia in 1948. Nicknamed "Afweyne" or "Mighty Mouth" by his fellow herdboys, Barre later traveled to Mogadishu for some formal education and ultimately became a member of the *Polizia Africana Italiana*. He rose within police ranks to become the first Somali commissioned as a full police officer, and by 1960, when Somalia became independent, Barre won accelerated promotion to the rank of brigadiergeneral of police. With the formation of the Somali National Army in April 1960, he transferred from police to army as one of its deputy commanders and he was promoted to commander in chief in 1965.

After the coup, Barre moved quickly to eliminate the institutions and personnel of Somalia's democracy. Siad detained important political figures like Prime Minster Egal, suspended the constitution, closed the National Assembly, banned all parties, and abolished the Supreme Court. The coup-makers designated themselves the Supreme Revolutionary Council (SRC) and assumed full executive and legislative power, concentrated in the hands of Barre himself: he became head of state and chairman of the SRC, its politburo, the cabinet, and the committees for defense, security, and judicial matters. His models were Nasser and Kim Il Sung, and like them, he cultivated a cult of personality. "Afweyne" would ultimately be touted as "The Father of Wisdom." The SRC renamed the country the Somali Democratic Republic.

The SRC introduced sweeping changes into Somali life, banning clan and kinship ties promising to root out all references to clanship. To replace traditional Somali private justice—blood vengeance or blood money payments between groups—the government introduced the death sentence for those convicted of homicide. On January 6, 2014, a soldier was executed by a firing squad after being found guilty of killing a child during a military operation in Mogadishu's main market. In the lawless state, homicide is still taken extremely seriously. In what is probably its most enduring achievement, the regime introduced a Latin script to make Somali a written language and aggressively pursued literacy in the new script.

In 1974, Barre signed a treaty of cooperation with the Soviet Union and gradually set in place the institutional functions of a Marxist dictatorship. The regime opted for "scientific socialism" and in a few years brought most sectors of the economy under state control. Banks, insurance companies, electrical power production, petroleum distribution, sugar estates and refineries, were all nationalized. One exception to this nationalization program was the large banana plantations, which represented significant foreign investment. State-run enterprises were created and given absolute monopolies as the foundation of an economy run on heavy government intervention. Private traders were prohibited from importing, storing, purchasing, or distributing food items.

An apparatus of state repression and militarization also emerged: The National Security Service (NNS), answerable to Siad Barre himself, began to create its own interrogation and detention centers, courts, and prisons. Barre also built a vast propaganda machine (obviously helped by literacy in the new script) that generated posters, poems, songs, and speeches to praise the "father of the revolution." Resources were lavished on an expansion of Somali military forces much to the consternation of neighboring countries, especially those with significant Somali minorities. For years Somalia had secretly assisted Somali, Oromo, Eritrean and other nationalities opposed to the central governments of Kenya and Ethiopia, but in June 1977, when the Ethiopian regime seemed both weakened by drought and politically vulnerable, the policy of clandestine support ended. The Somali army was instead authorized to intervene directly in Ethiopia to assist the Western Somali Liberation Front fighting for the return of the Ogaden to Greater Somalia.

Abdullahi Yusuf Ahmed, Former Transitional Federal President of Somalia

Somalia

The Somali eagle Photo by Ahmed in Burco

The Somali army entered the Ogaden in July and overran it.

Expansionist excess was severely punished, however. The Soviet Union, with alliances with both Ethiopia and Somalia, turned against Barre. War materiel was air-lifted to Ethiopia, and a Russian-directed Ethiopian army, with Cuban regiments in support, defeated Somali forces and sent their remnants scurrying back across the border. The army was humiliated and lost its legitimacy as the guardian of pan-Somali nationalism. The country was stunned, and soon overwhelmed by an influx of refugees fleeing the re-imposition of Ethiopian authority in the Ogaden. By 1979, there were officially 1.3 million refugees in the country, more than half of whom were located in the north. The regime's limited resources and even more limited capacity to deliver services increased tensions between the government and the northern clans.

Clan-based opposition grew, which Barre brutally repressed; he became increasingly dependent on his own clan and family, to whom he distributed the majority of government appointments (and attendant opportunities for corruption). Additionally, he used foreign aid dollars to line the pockets of regime officials. The regime also shifted its international alliances, signing on with the Americans after the debacle of the Ogaden war. It abandoned "scientific socialism" and granted U.S. forces access to Somali military facilities, many of which were upgraded. Somali officers were given training in U.S. military schools, and America came to the country's aid when invaded by Ethiopia in 1982.

Collapse of the State, Civil War, and Warlordism

Regime incapacity, economic mismanagement and human rights abuses moved Somalis from disillusionment to anger, and opposition increased to the points of civil war. A few senior officers who escaped a bungled coup attempt in 1978 fled to Ethiopia and created the first opposition movement: the Somali Salvation Democratic Front (SSDF). In 1981 a second opposition movement, the Somali National Movement (SNM) was created in London by disgruntled businessmen, religious leaders, intellectuals, and army officers, mostly from the northern Isaaq clan. SNM organized guerrilla operations out of Ethiopia against the regime, and by 1988 an all-out war developed.

As the civil war began, Siad Barre focused his wrath (and American-supported military might) on his northern opposition. The regime bombed Hargeysa, Somalia's second largest city and the former capital of British Somaliland and killed an estimated 50,000 people there through summary executions, aerial bombardments and ground attacks. Government planes even strafed streams of refugees fleeing the devastation.

The military assault was coupled with an attack on the economic base of Somaliland. The Barre regime destroyed market centers throughout the northwest, and mined transport routes, rendering them unusable. It poisoned wells upon which nomadic pastoralists depended. The closure of Berbera port from 1989 to 1991 shut off trade and the northern economy collapsed. Economic stress strained traditional kinship obligations of support. Social stress was intensified when a major drought hit the area in 1991–92 at the height of the civil war and famine killed between 300,000 and 500,000 and affected millions more.

Civil strife gradually expanded throughout Somalia, leading to the formation of other opposition movements. The United Somali Congress (USC) was formed in 1987 by largely Hawiye-clan exiles in Italy. The USC quickly divided into two rival factions based on different sub-clans. A faction led by General Aideed allied with the Somali National Movement, which provided arms. An Ogadeni-led Somali Patriotic Movement (SPM) was formed in 1989 when the highest ranking Ogadeni in the government, the minister of defense, was arrested. Siad Barre was increasingly isolated, defended only by his heavily armed presidential guard, drawn exclusively from his Marehan clan.

As 1990 drew to a close, rebel forces entered Mogadishu, and early the next year Barre and his loyalists fled the city. By then, little was left of Somalia as a country. Barre's regime represents the last stable Somali government. While Barre's original political campaign had included promises to dissipate clan warfare, when the future of his power became unclear, he poisoned relations between clans. The mistrust he created between clans has caused insuperable divisions which have made having a central government after his departure nearly impossible. Additionally, the army fractured into factions focused on rival clan leaders who became warlords' intent on control of territory and whatever resources remained that would sustain their power. The war in the south produced major population dislocations. A third of the population became internal refugees, and at least a quarter of a million migrated to Mogadishu. When fighting in the capital intensified, there was a similar outflow of people.

The humanitarian disaster brought about Operation Restore Hope, launched in 1992 under UN auspices. The operation started out to protect the delivery of humanitarian aid, but then refocused on creating a secure environment, which logically entailed demobilization of warlord factions. When General Aideed was identified as the chief troublemaker, the project changed its mission to focus on his capture. When the general's forces shot down an American helicopter (the infamous "Black Hawk Down" incident) and killed several American troops, the U.S. withdrew. The project yet again refocused, now seeking negotiation with General Aideed. TV images of a dead American soldier dragged triumphantly through the streets of Mogadishu shocked the American public and for several years

Somalia

left policymakers horrified at the prospect of committing American ground troops anywhere in the world.

The international humanitarian effort in Somalia was budgeted at 1.5 billion dollars a year. It was the most expensive humanitarian effort ever undertaken, and it was a failure. By early 2000, four warlords still contended over divided Mogadishu. General Aideed, who was killed in a gun battle with rivals in 1996, was replaced as faction leader by his son, a young man who somewhat ironically held American citizenship and once served in the U.S. Marine Corps. Various negotiations between southern faction leaders conducted in Egypt, Kenya, Ethiopia, and Libya achieved nothing.

Attempts at Governance

Djibouti's president Ismail Omar Guelleh convened the 13th Somali national reconciliation conference in May 2000. The conference in Arta, Djibouti brought together over 2,000 Somali clan elders, religious leaders, academics, businessmen (and for the first time a group of women) to thrash out new institutions for the new state. The conference elected a Transitional National Assembly was selected, which then proceeded to elect a transitional head of state. Abdulkassim Salat Hassan, a former interior minister of the Siad Barre regime, won out over some 20 rivals for the new office of transitional president. His term of office was set at three years, during which time the Transition National Government (TNG) he headed was to establish the procedures for creating permanent institutions for the renovated state.

Front and back of the Somali Shilling

Former Prime Minister Ali Mohamed Gedi

The leadership of Somaliland and Puntland rejected the results, complaining particularly about the predominance of individuals prominent in the Siad Barre regime, a government that did so much to destroy the north. The warlords in the northern regions suggested that the transitional president would have to negotiate with them to bring lasting peace to Somalia.

An overly optimistic international community awarded the Arta TNG Somalia's seats at the United Nations, the Organization of African Unity, and the Arab League. None of these designations improved the TNG's capacity to govern, or its acceptance by those it sought to govern. By the time its mandate ran out in 2003 it was little more than another Mogadishu faction.

Ethiopia did much to undermine the TNG. In early 2001, it gathered the major warlords in Addis Ababa in what was little more than a conference to undermine the Arta agreement. In March the attendees announced creation of a Somali Reconciliation and Restoration Council (SRRC). Given post-9/11 concerns about Somalia as a refuge for terrorists, the U.S. encouraged President Moi of Kenya to use his offices to reconcile the SRRC and the TNG. In May 2002, Kenya, Ethiopia, and Djibouti were designated by the principal regional organization—the Inter-Governmental Authority for Development (IGAD)—to persuade Somalia's faction leaders, clan leaders, and members of civil society to attend yet another peace conference.

A breakthrough occurred in August 2004, when the regional conference begun in 2002 selected a 275-person transitional federal parliament. By early October they had agreed on an interim president, Puntland's warlord chief Colonel Abdullahi-Yusuf Ahmed; in December, Yusuf appointed Ali Mohammed Gedi as prime minister. Gedi was a member of the Hawiye clan that dominates Mogadishu and much of southern Somalia. Gedi's cabinet, consisting of 79 individuals, reflected the delicacy of distributing employment possibilities among the various Somali clans spawning hope that the government might have success in its dealings.

Any hope for these transitional institutions dissipated once the parties returned to Somalia. The president, the prime minister and their supporters established themselves 56 miles north of Mogadishu in relatively peaceful Jowhar, a city over which they exercised no authority. In protest, the speaker of the transitional parliament, and about 100 MPs chose to return to Mogadishu, which remained a violent, divided city. For the Transitional Federal Government (TFG), the capital was

Somalia

Former Somaliland President Dahir Riyale Kahin

insecure and unwelcoming. Militia members, estimated to total 50,000, manned roadblocks (an important source of funding through extortion) and patrolled sections of the city to assert the power of their warlord patrons.

A new actor in Mogadishu's lawlessness was the Islamic Courts Union (ICU), which built upon the first Islamic Court set up in 1994 to provide law and order for the anarchic capital. Their effectiveness extended their dominion and brought them into competition with the city's warlords. Encouraged by American funding, the Mogadishu warlords created an Alliance for the Restoration of Peace and Counter-Terrorism (ARPCT) in February 2006. The coalition's founders charged that Islamic radicals were behind a wave of assassinations of intellectuals, military officials, and prominent civil society figures, all supporters of the Transitional Federal Government. A spokesman for the Courts denied all, but one month later, Issa Osman Issa blew himself up while assembling a bomb in a Mogadishu apartment. According to the police, Mr. Issa was a member of *Al-Ittihad Al-Islamiya*, a terrorist group with links to al-Qaeda; his bomb was to be used in an attack on Prime Minister Gedi.

Factional fighting in Mogadishu during the first half of 2006 was the worst in years. By early June, it was clear the victors were the militias of the Islamic Courts Union (ICU), who had driven the warlords out of the city. The ICU removed weapons from the streets and reopened the port and airport. By December, the ICU controlled most of southern Somalia, from the Kenyan border to autonomous Puntland. The TFG's diminished political space was no more than the area of Baidoa, where its military security was assured by Ethiopian troops.

At the heart of the ICU was *Al-Ittihad Al-Islamiya*, a terrorist group with links to al-Qaeda. Its operatives had worked with al-Qaeda since 1993 in various attacks on American interests, Iing the "Black Hawk Down" incident in Mogadishu and the bombing of the American embassy in Nairobi, Kenya. *Al-Ittihad Al-Islamiya's* chief, Sheikh Hassan Dahir Aweys, emerged as one of the most radical ICU leaders. The Sheikh featured prominently on both American and United Nations terrorist watch lists. In 2001, he was identified by the United Nations as an associate of Osama bin Laden, and member states were asked to freeze his assets.

Once in control, the Islamic Courts imposed strict *sharia* law: it banned live music, shuttered movie theaters, and closed video rental shops. Punishments for *sharia* violations became public ritual and spectacle: marijuana smokers were lashed and murderers executed. Religious obligations were enforced: all trade and public transportation were banned during prayer times. Indeed, prayer became mandatory. "Everybody must leave his business and go for prayer when the muezzin is heard," said a deputy security chief. "Anybody who does not obey will face painful punishment."

To consolidate power, Islamist leaders fanned the flames of Somali nationalism against the traditional enemy—Ethiopia. After Ethiopia sent military forces to support the TFG in its Baidoa redoubt, Sheikh Aweys ordered a "holy war" to drive the Ethiopians from Somalia. By October, Prime Minister Meles of Ethiopia bluntly said his country was "technically" at war with Somali Islamists. An ICU attack on Biadoa in December brought quick riposte. Ethiopian tanks, artillery batteries, and military jets, using the best American satellite intelligence, made quick work of the ill-equipped Islamist militia. The authority of the ICU simply dissolved; its leaders fled and abandoned Mogadishu.

In January 2007, combined military action, involving U.S., Ethiopian and Kenyan forces, pursued and tracked down the most wanted terrorists sheltered and employed by the ICU, though only with limited success. Some hint as to the richly fertile ground Somalia provided for international terrorism came in April 2007: the Ethiopian government announced it had detained 41 terrorism suspects from 17 countries who had been fighting for Somalia's Islamist movement.

Al-Shabaab

Into Somalia's political vacuum came a new armed Islamist group known as Al-Shabaab, part of which was an outgrowth of the ICU. The emergence of Al-Shabaab led to a row broke out in the transitional

Islamic Court Militia in Mogadishu ©Abdimalik Yusuf/IRIN

Somalia

government as President Abdullahi Yusuf Ahmed tried to force through a vote of no confidence in his own prime minister, who Yusuf felt was unwilling to confront the Islamists. Yet he failed to convince parliament and as a consequence, Yusuf stepped down on December 29, 2008, leaving the speaker of parliament in the presidential role till a new government could be elected.

On January 31, 2009, Sheikh Sharif Sheikh Ahmed was elected the new president of the Transitional Federal Government. The sheikh was a former member of the Islamic Courts Union, but his moderate Islamism proved unpersuasive to Al-Shabaab, which claimed it would only lay down arms after all foreign troops have left the country. In early January 2009, Ethiopian troops who had been present since 2006 left Somalia; Ethiopia argued they withdrew in victory, but Ethiopia's presence in Somalia seemed to have reunited radical Islamists under the banner of Al-Shabaab, and only a few thousand international troops from Kenya and Burundi remain in Somalia, barely protecting elements of the Transitional Federal Government. The UN has refused to send peace-keeping forces, noting there is no peace to keep. As a consequence, Al-Shabaab began to thrive. Within hours after Ethiopia left their strongholds in Somalia, Al-Shabaab took over important trade routes that were a source of funding for the weak transitional government.

In October of 2009, Al-Shabaab won control over the port city of Kismayo after defeating the rival Hizbul-Islam militia. The fighting killed at least 20 and pushed the Hizbul-Islam militia into smaller villages in the west. As Al-Shabaab grows in power, its influence around the continent has also increased. In early 2010 leaders declared they would begin sending fighters to support Islamist rebels in Yemen. They later declared a formal alliance with Al-Qaeda and claimed responsibility for the bombing of a restaurant in Kampala, Uganda in July 2010 that killed 74 people.

Fighting also broke out in the capital of Mogidishu in 2010 between government forces and Al-Shabaab fighters. Several thousand residents have been killed or wounded in 2010 and 2011, with Al Jazeera reporting in June 2011 that a large proportion of those wounded are children. Many thousands more have been forced to flee in addition to 1.5 million people already displaced by fighting. The TFG lost ground to the militants in Mogadishu, and another stalemate seems to have taken effect, with the TFG and Al-Shabaab each controlling different neighborhoods of the so-called capital.

The Transitional Federal Government continued to show signs of political dysfunction as well as military weakness in 2010 and 2011. Sharif Sheikh Ahmed dismissed then-Prime Minister Omar Abdirashid Ali Sharmarke in early 2010; the latter resisted, but ultimately resigned in late 2010, whereupon the president nominated the Somali-American Mohamed Abdullahi Mohamed. The TFG had originally claimed it would hold elections in 2011, but these seem doubtful as the government and the Transitional Federal Parliament (TFP) voted themselves extensions of their terms in early 2011. This was followed by an accord between Sharif Sheikh Ahmed and Parliament speaker Sharif Hassan Sheikh Aden. The agreement would postpone presidential elections by a year and remove Mohamed from the prime minister's role.

Outside of the corridors of the TFG, Somalia continued to be buffeted by a range of crises, including drought, famine, and continued conflict. In July 2011, the UN warned of prospects for famine in southern Somalia; soon thereafter, Somalis began fleeing the country into refugee camps in neighboring Kenya and Ethiopia. An unknown number of Somalis succumbed to hunger, with estimates ranging into the tens of thousands. Some of the most robust international responses came from Kenya, rather than wealthier countries.

While the drought brought terrible suffering, Somalia arguably took a turn for the better on the security front in 2011–2012. In what looked like an increasingly coordinated effort, international forces (from Ethiopia, Kenya, and the African Union, among others, with the U.S. military flying drones in support) attacked various al-Shabaab positions. The Islamist militia largely abandoned Mogadishu and successively lost control of a string of other important towns. The United Nations began to airlift aid into the capital for the first time in years; a suicide bomb attack in the city killed over 100 people in October 2011, but Kenyan forces in particular kept up pressure on al-Shabaab despite additional suicide bombings in Kenya. In 2012, al-Shabaab officially merged with al-Qaeda and became its Somali affiliate (though representatives of the two organizations had some spats over naming). International actors continued to step up pressure on the group, with the U.S. offering multi-million dollar bounties for information resulting in the capture or death of the group's leaders. (In response, al-Shabaab leaders announced a bounty of 10 camels for information on Obama's whereabouts, and 10 hens and 10 roosters for similar information on Hillary Clinton.) The most recent important successes of the international coalition have been the expulsion of al-Shabaab from several port towns, most notably the city of Kismayo, which fell to Kenyan forces in October 2012.

Despite some military success by international forces, al-Shabaab staged further attacks in neighboring countries in 2013–14. In September of 2013, four Somali al-Shabaab militants staged an assault on an upscale shopping mall in Nairobi, Kenya,

At the Burco, Somaliland market even satellite dishes are available

Photo by Ahmed in Burco

and killed 67 people. The event received major international attention; the terrorist group declared that the attacks come as retaliation for Kenya sending troops into Somalia in 2013 in efforts to help the UN-backed government tackle al-Shabaab. An attack on a restaurant in Djibouti—a small country that is home to several western military bases for the Horn of Africa—killed one person and wounded a dozen soldier.

Meanwhile, inside Somalia, al-Shabaab detonated a pair of car bombs that killed ten people at the Jazeera Hotel in Mogadishu on January 1, 2014. This attack used the now popular tactic of detonating one car bomb and then waiting for police and first responders to arrive and then detonating a second bomb. The militants have similarly targeted everything from hotels to schools with car bombs. The attacks on schools have taken from many the possibility for education and with the existing shortage of jobs, children as young as twelve have been joining al-Shabaab. An even more brazen attack came at the Somali Parliament in May 2014, where al-Shabaab detonated bombs and engaged in an hours-long gun battle, killing at least 10 security officers.

The United States has been increasingly active in its efforts to destabilize al-Shabaab leadership. In 2013, Navy Seals attempted but failed to capture al-Shabaab commander Abdukadir Mohamed Abdukadir. On January 27, 2014, the United States military carried out a successful air missile strike on al-Shabaab commander Sahal Iskudhuq.

As the security situation has remained in flux, reports have begun to trickle out of Mogadishu that the local informal economy (which is most of the economy, given that government efforts at official regulation and taxation are still nearly meaningless) was experiencing a surge in activity. There are indications that remittances are flowing into Somalia from the diaspora, and that residents are making small investments in their properties and small businesses. Meanwhile, public order has improved (albeit from abysmal levels) and there are even streetlights on some major thoroughfares—a big change for Mogadishu. International organizations even began to hazard guesses that the economy was growing at a modest clip, despite the lack of official statistics.

Amid these changes, Somali leaders set to the task of establishing formal branches of government and moving past the stage of the transitional (TFG) government. In August 2012, a new parliament was sworn in at Mogadishu airport. It reflected balance among Somalia's clans and set aside seats for women representatives (eventually to reach 30% of 275 seats in the lower house). The Federal Parliament is mandated to approve a new constitution and electoral system by 2016. This parliament in turn elected Somalia's current president, Hassan Sheikh Mohamud of the Peace and Development Party (PDP), in September. Soon after his election, Mohamud replaced prime minister Abdiweli Mohamed Ali with the independent Abdi Farah Shirdon.

Of course, this set of changes in the political sphere does not mean the war is over, as al-Shabaab continues to pose an existential threat to the regimg. Nonetheless, Somalia now has a nominal central government, some heightened international commitment, and arguably some prospects for a return to a modicum of stability, though these are far from guaranteed.

CONTEMPORARY THEMES

Somalia has been seen for some years as the epitome of the failed state. As such any estimates of its economic output are speculative; there are simply no agencies that can produce reliable knowledge about the country. That said, livestock was long among Somalia's most profitable sectors of the economy, but veterinary health facilities are weak and consequently, Somali herds are subject to periodic outbreaks of disease. In the south the most important commercial crop comes from banana plantations. The plantations, controlled by two major firms, one Italian and the other American (Dole), represent the only examples of agricultural production in the country that use modern techniques for irrigation and cultivation.

Piracy

Coastal waters off northern Somalia contain rich fishing grounds, but the absence of any governmental control of its waters has encouraged illegal plundering by a variety of fishing fleets. Using the newest and most destructive of techniques—drift nets and dynamiting to break up coral reefs where lobsters and other catch live—these mechanized fishermen destroy livelihoods of local fishermen, while also destroying of one of the world's most bio-diverse habitats. Traditionally, Somali fishermen used nets only between September and April, and only hooks in the hot season between May and August. Industrialized fishing operations do not follow such limitations, and have reaped significant profits at the expense of sustainability.

To stop illegal fishing, locals armed themselves and their boats and kept watch on the coast. When they captured a foreign fishing vessel, its occupants were forced to pay a cash fine for the illegal practice. What started out as self-protection by Somali fishermen was later distorted into full-scale piracy. The 2011 drought heightened incentives to engage in the lucrative practice of piracy as Somalia's two largest exports—livestock and bananas—are highly dependent on rainfall. Several pirate groups now operate along Somalia's 1,880-mile coastline, Africa's longest, and Somali waters are the world's most dangerous, according to the UN and NATO.

Despite allowing US vessels to patrol the Somali waters, the government has been unable to stop piracy. In 2008 and 2009, over a hundred attacks were recorded. In response to the increased piracy of one of the world's most important trade routes, the US, the EU, NATO, and several Asian countries sent part of their naval fleets to help control the problem, which could have severe economic consequences. As much as 30% of the world's oil passes through the Gulf of Aden, and the insecurity in delivering oil would contribute to higher and more volatile prices. Amongst merchant ships, fishing boats and other commercial ships, an oil tanker, the Sirius Star, was captured, and more than $25m demanded in ransom. Though few of the ships have had the same value as the Sirius Star, ransoms typically range between one and three million dollars, making piracy a very lucrative business. The owners of the Sirius Star eventually paid $3 million in ransom, before the tanker could continue with its $100 million worth of crude oil, after almost two months in captivity.

Many of the world's most powerful navies are involved in the protection of the Gulf of Aden. Since the October 2009 hijacking of a Chinese tanker, both the American and French navies have killed pirates and the EU has deployed its first ever joint naval force, called Operation Atlanta, in the region. Despite these efforts, hijackings rose in 2009, as did as the average ransom paid to pirates. In a country where the average income is around $250 a year, a low-level pirate can make up to $20,000 a year.

As the industry of piracy has grown, so has the sophistication of its perpetrators. For many pirates, spending weeks at sea with no success is common. As the foreign navies step up their presence in the area, it will be even more costly to embark on the sail (sometimes as much as 500 miles long) to intercept the commercial ships. The ships, weapons, gas and food the pirates need for their missions are huge expenses upfront, so a network of investors and suppliers has been created on Somalia's coast, who take percentages of the ransom money when a mission has been a success. In fact, the city of Eyl thrived for many years almost solely by being a safe-haven for pirates.

Somalia

However, 2013 saw Somali piracy drop to its lowest levels in eight years, with only 15 attacks, a forty percent drop from its peak in 2011. This extreme drop is being associated with international efforts to control the piracy off the coast of Somalia (perhaps along with improved prospects for other economic activities). Many ships have begun traveling with armed guards to discourage piracy activity. This coupled with the presence of international navies has been extremely successful. The re-securitization of the shipping lanes has encouraged the Gulf to reopen trade links. These are vital for Somalia to attract further foreign investment.

Terrorism

One of Somalia's main ongoing concerns has been terrorism, specifically by the militant Islamist group Al-Shabaab. The organization has able to recruit new members for financial reasons. And it is not surprising that as the profits from piracy have disappeared, some jobless Somalis have joined al-Shabaab and created a steady supply of militants.

In response, the United States military has authorized boots on the ground for the first time since 1994. The presence consists of a small group of military advisors, in Somalia. In efforts to counteract extremism in the Horn of Africa, these military advisors will help train regional armies. The United States is growing their military base in neighboring Djibouti (which al-Shabaab also attacked in March 2014, wounding several soldiers.

The international community was warned by the United Nations in February of 2014, that the previsouly-relaxed weapons ban on Somalia needs to be reinstated. The members of the lawless country's government have been actively diverting weapons to warlords and al-Shabaab militants. The embargo had been lightened to strengthen the national army in hopes of restoring some order to the country.

REPUBLIC OF SOMALILAND

In northwest Somalia lies the self-declared Republic of Somaliland, which declared independence from Somalia on May 18, 1991. The region (of 68,000 sq. miles, or about the size of the American state of Georgia) has some 3.5 million people and its own currency, the Somaliland shilling. It has not been recognized as a sovereign state by the international community (which remains intent on recreating a unitary state for Somalia) but has declared its capital at Hargeysa and its chief of state in Ahmed Mahamoud Silanyo.

In this region, British indirect rule did not destroy traditional Somali systems of conflict resolution, and Somali-style peace conferences, large-scale regional gatherings lasting anywhere from two to six months, managed to stabilize clan relationships. At a grand *shir*, or council, which concluded in February 1991, Isaaq clans representing 80% of the population of former British Somaliland reached an agreement with other clans. Independence was declared in the same year with the rallying cry "No More Mogadishu."

There have been at least three of these grand councils, called "national conferences," to work out the form and structure of the state. Two elected assemblies exist. One is essentially a small lower parliamentary house and the other is a council of elders, larger than the first and consisting of clan representatives. This council of elders cannot be dissolved by the president, and the council reflects the precarious nature of central power when facing the stronger ties within clans. When members of the council die, are recalled, or are incapacitated, they must come from the same clan or subclan. The system was ratified in a constitution approved by two-thirds of the representatives in February 1997. Submitted to a referendum, the constitution received overwhelming approval from Somalilanders in May 2001. In 1993, elders and citizens chose Muhammed Ibrahim Egal, the last prime minister of democratic Somalia, as president of the "Republic of Somaliland." He was re-elected to a five-year term as president in 1997, died in May 2002 and was immediately succeeded by Somaliland's vice president, Dahir Riyale Kahin who remained president until 2010.

Lacking international recognition, Somaliland has made remarkable progress on its own. Heavy weapons were surrendered voluntarily and often stored unguarded. State controls on the economy were virtually eliminated, and trade and commerce began to thrive. Even more remarkable has been the emergence of a stable and democratic political system operating under the rule of law. A constitution provides Somaliland's legal framework, and under its provisions for presidential succession the country made a smooth transition following the death of President Egal.

President Kahin presided over the next stage of Somaliland's political development—the preparation for presidential and parliamentary elections. Political parties were legalized and participated in municipal elections of December 2002. Of six parties participating, three emerged with sufficient support to be allowed to run candidates in the April 2003 presidential elections: the United People's Democratic Party (UDUB), the governing party founded by President Egal; Kulmiye or United Party, led by former planning minister Ahmed Mohamud Silanyo; and the Justice and Welfare Party (UCID), founded by Faisal Ali Warabe, a civil engineer who emphasized the notion of good governance in his campaign. In an important decision seen to limit the role of clan identity, the Supreme Court disallowed independent candidacies in the presidential elections. Each of the three candidates were forced to seek support among a broad range of clans and subclans.

The 2003 election was close. By a mere 80 votes, sitting President Dahir Riyale Kahin defeated his closest rival, Ahmed Mohamud Silanyo. Clan elders headed off a potentially volatile situation by convincing Silanyo to accept the results. That he did, and Somaliland avoided post-electoral violence. Somaliland's third experience with multiparty democratic elections came in September 2005, when voters elected members of parliament for the first time. The three parties put up 246 candidates for the legislature's 82 seats. International observers called the election generally free and fair and each of the parties will send a sizable delegation to parliament. UDUB won 33 seats, while Kulmiye and UCID took 28 and 21 respectively.

Perhaps as impressive as the lack of violence after the close election of 2003 was the alternation of power in 2010. In the 2010 presidential election, Ahmed Silanyo defeated President Dahir Kahin, taking just under 50% of the vote. Kahin took 33% and Warabe 17%. The relatively seamless transfer of power attested to the fact that Somaliland has far more of the attributes of a fully functioning state than Somalia itself. Apart from the symbols of nationhood (such as a flag, a currency, and national license plates), the de facto country's politics operates on a functioning constitutional basis. Perhaps most remarkably, in a deeply traditional society it has effectively moved from clan voting to individual voting in a multiparty democracy.

As of 2012, Somaliland and the government of Somalia began formal talks for the first time since Somaliland's unilateral declaration of independence in 1991. These meetings have been held in the United Kingdom and Dubai, and are sponsored by the U.K., Norway, and the European Union, with a view towards clarifying the relationship between the two entities and possibly reaching an accord or settlement.

The Somaliland government has an annual budget of around $18 million. Employing something like 26,000 people, it spends 70% of its revenues on salaries. Revenues are mostly derived from port duties at Berbera where activity has recently increased. UN agencies have used it for transporting food relief to

Somalia

Ethiopia, and the Ethiopian government has turned to it in a search for alternatives to the Eritrean port of Asab. Meanwhile, Ethiopian Airlines has begun twice-weekly flights to Hargeysa, Somaliland's capital. International flights from the Gulf states, East Africa, and Europe already land at Hargeysa and Berbera airports, generating about $1.5 million in revenues for the government. As of 2001, Somaliland businessmen began to pay income and profit taxes, which increased government revenues.

Wealth and profits are largely based on livestock trade, and remittances by overseas Somalis (estimated at $500 million a year), though the informal economy has diversified and is characterized by a range of services. Somaliland now has two universities and several vocational colleges whose construction was greatly aided by diaspora remittances. As *The Economist* magazine noted in July 2010, "the streets of Hargeysa, the dusty and tumbledown capital, hum with construction work and mobile phone chatter." Traders are working on export licenses for local products, and exploration has begun for oil and gemstones. A recently discovered reef of high-quality emeralds—several miles long—holds promise as an alternative source of income.

Despite the achievements of creating a working political system, police force and currency, there has been no official international acknowledgement of Somaliland's statehood; several countries have established contacts in Hargeysa, but none has offered diplomatic recognition. Somaliland's appeals for recognition faced their key setbacks with a series of murders targeting foreign aid workers in the mid-2000s. The series began in October 2003 with the shooting death of an Italian doctor, Annalena Tonelli, who was killed outside the hospital she had founded in Borama. This was followed by the murder of two British teachers the same month, unsettling aid workers and expatriates. When two German aid workers were ambushed and killed in March 2004, NGOs and international aid agencies decided to withdraw their personnel from Somaliland for security reasons. Eight men, all Islamic radicals, were sentenced to death for three of the murders in November 2005. Somali land has developed an impressive working state but there remains considerable room for improvement.

Mohamed Bihi Yonis, Somaliland's foreign minister. claims that Somaliland will soon gain international recognition. An important factor is that Somaliland follows old colonial borders, which gives the presumptive nation a sort of historical legitimacy with major international actors (some of which were themselves colonizers). Additionally, the recent discovery of oil in Somaliland has allowed the government to authorize several multinational companies' exploration licenses. Currently, the Somali government is working to lay claim to these contracts and the large financial payments. Advocates of an independent Somaliland hope that these large international investors could help lobby their home governments to recognize Somaliland. Currently, Turkey is mediating conversations between Somaliland and Somalia, and its Genel Energy company happens to be one of the largest investors in the oil exploration. Despite increased international interest, however, Western countries are arguing that African countries must be the first to recognize Somaliland. Yet African countries are hesitant to recognize Somaliland because of worries about precedent: as was the concern with the new nations of Eritrea and South Sudan, African leaders worry that independence could cause a ripple effect throughout the continent in support of other separatist bids.

Suffering from persistent drought, famine, and lack of internal security, the government of Somalia has attempted to create some measure of unity while confronting the continuing conflict involving the Al-Qaeda-linked terrorist group Al-Shabab, which retains considerable support in the countryside and is able to carry out attacks, including car bombings, in the capital of Mogadishu with more than 100 people killed in 2022 and an attack on a major hotel near the presidential palace in March 2024. Also persistent is the role of Somali pirates harassing international shipping off the coast with India naval units capturing a ship from a group of pirates in March 2024.

With al-Shabab forces seizing control of critical logistical hubs serving government forces just north of the capital city of Mogadishu in April 2025 which the government denied, the 16-year-long conflict continues unabated. A new African Union peacekeeping mission replaced a larger force at the start of the year, but funding for the operation is uncertain, with the United States opposed to a plan to transition to a United Nations financing model. Violence also rocked the domestic situation as an explosion was reported near the presidential palace minutes after a motorcade by President Hassan Sheikh Mohamud passed by with al-Shabab claiming responsibility.

FUTURE CONSIDERATIONS

Somalia's future depends on both internal and external consensus. The consensus is still fragile, although it is better than in recent years. The year 2012 witnessed the election of a functioning parliament and president that gave hope that normalized governance might follow. Yet the challenges should not be understated. Internal actors, be they clan elders, fundamentalist Islamist clerics, or the recalcitrant mini-states of Somaliland and Puntland, still struggle to settle on the amount of authority to be granted to the central government. Meanwhile, the anarchic state of affairs has led to external intervention, with the United States conducting air strikes and several African countries (especially Ethiopia, Kenya, and Uganda) having boots on the ground in an effort to stabilize the Horn of Africa.

Somalia has faced some of the worst human tragedies of modern times. For two decades and more, it was a failed state characterized by ongoing, open conflicts led by militants, armed clans, and pirates. In recent years, it is estimated that more than two million of the country's nine million people have been displaced or homeless. As much as 40% of the country's population may be reliant on foreign aid to survive. The 2011 drought led to thousands of deaths, and it is estimated that more than 50% of the population will be malnourished by 2015, if the crisis cannot be stopped.

While piracy has decreased, the militant group al-Shabaab remains a significant threat, both capitalizing on and furthering the disorder in Somalia (and beyond Somalia's borders). Even if international efforts led are able to end the reign of terror by al-Shabaab, there is no evidence suggesting Somalia would exit from its chaos. In fact, there is plenty of history to suggest that Somalia will struggle to consolidate anything like state authority and legitimacy.

On the political side, there is sporadic hope that the United Nations-backed government under Hassan Sheikh Mohamud will establish a viable rule of law (and eventually hold regular elections under a new constitutional order) at the expense of al-Shabaab and the violent clan groups that still threaten the cities and countryside. Successes in 2011 and 2012 began with the successes of rolling back al-Shabaab and have continued with the methodical introduction of more governing institutions. As yet, however, the new government has not proved it has the capacity to govern. The spurt of optimism in the past two years is warranted—given where Somalia was, it has come far—but governance has yet to be consolidated. Even if this progress continues and security can be established, Somalia has years to go before it frees itself from the status of failed state.

The Republic of South Sudan

South Sudanese celebrate their independence on July 9, 2011. ©IRIN

BASIC FACTS

Area: 644,329 sq. km. (slightly smaller than Texas)
Population: 12,118,379 (July 2023 est.)
Capital City: Juba
Government Type: Presidential Republic
Neighboring Countries: Democratic Republic of Congo (southwest); Central African Republic (northwest); Sudan (north); Ethiopia (east); Kenya (southeast); and Uganda (south).
Official Language: English
Other Principal Languages: Dinka, Nuer, Bari, Zande, Shilluk, Arabic
Ethnic Groups: Over 60, including Dinka (35.8%), Nuer (15.6%), Bari, Azande, Sudanese Arab, Shilluk, Luo, Murle, Mandari (2011 est.)
Principal Religions: indigenous beliefs 25%, Christian 5%
Former Colonial Status: Egyptian (1821–1885); British–Egyptian (1899–1956); part of Sudan (1956–2011)
Independence Date: July 9, 2011
GDP Per Capita (IMF 2023 est.): $467 (nominal), $516 (PPP)
Gini Index: 44.1 (2016 est.)
Currency: South Sudanese pound (SSP); $US 1 = 130.26 (Apr. 2022)
Inflation Rate: 16.0% (2022 est.)
Chief Commercial Products: Oil
Foreign Direct Investments (FDI) net inflows: 700,000,000
Literacy Rate: 34.5% (CIA 2019)
Life Expectancy: 59.71 years (2023)
Head of State: President Salva Kiir Mayardit (since July 9, 2011)
Head of Government: President Salva Kiir Mayardit (since July 9, 2011)

LAND AND PEOPLE

The climate in South Sudan is tropical, including swampy lowlands and is hot with seasonal rainfall that is heaviest in the south. South Sudan has terrain that gradually rises from plains in the north and center to southern highlands along the border with Uganda and Kenya; the White Nile, flowing north out of the uplands of Central Africa, is the major geographic feature of the country supporting agriculture and extensive wild animal populations. The Sudd (a name derived from floating vegetation that hinders navigation) is a vast swamp of more than 100,000 sq. km, fed by the waters of Lake Victoria and the White Nile. Comprising more than 15% of the total area of South Sudan, it dominates the center of the country and is one of the world's largest wetlands. The Nile emerges again from the Sudd to flow northward into Sudan.

South Sudan is divided between animists and Christian beliefs as well as by dozens of languages and ethnic groups. The two largest ethnic groups, the Dinka and Nuer, are segmentary societies with few traditions of overarching leadership and governance. Both are cattle raising people and were traditional rivals for pasturage and objects of mutual cattle raids. In the years up to 2011, South Sudan was governed by the Sudanese state in Khartoum; dominated by northerners, these governments traditionally exploited inter-ethnic rivalries between the leading groups, and intra-ethnic rivalries between segments within each group that vie with each other for scarce resources. Similarly, historical antagonisms between cattle pastoralists like the Nuer or Dinka and settled farming peoples create fissures that have worked against political unity in present-day South Sudan.

HISTORY TO PRESENT DAY

For early history, see *Historical Background* and *The Colonial Period: The British*.

Conflict and Separatism in Sudan

South Sudan is the world's newest country as of 2014. This country, which was formerly a part of Sudan, has been fraught with conflict for decades. That conflict has sometimes been between present-day Sudan (which is predominantly Muslim) and South Sudan (which is predominantly Christian), but conflict also persists between groups within South Sudan. Northern Sudan was conquered and unified by the Egyptian viceroy of the Ottoman sultan in 1821. Egyptian rulers claimed southern Sudan, but were unable to establish effective control over its fragmented animist populations. Access to southern Sudan was not possible until after 1839, and from that point both the Ottoman rulers and their Arab Sudanese subjects saw the south mainly as a source of manpower. Slavers from both groups aggressively raided southern peoples.

Sudan was governed by a joint British-Egyptian administration from 1889 to 1956, and during this colonial period, northern Arab Muslims were privileged by the administration, while black Africans of southern Sudan were persecuted.

Cultural differences between north and south (and between groups within the south) help explain Sudan's history of political instability and conflict. A civilian

South Sudan

President Salva Kiir

regime established at the independence of Sudan in 1956 lasted only until a military coup in 1958. After alternation between the military and civilian coalition governments, General Jaafar Nimeiry overthrew the regime in 1969, first backed by the Soviet Union and later (after he renounced Marxism) by the United States. In 1972, the Khartoum government reached a peace agreement with rebels in the south. Signed at Addis Ababa, the accord made the south a self-governing region, but offered only a brief respite to Sudan's endemic conflict. With American arms and support, General Nimeiry began an Islamization campaign in 1983, then suspended civil liberties and declared a state of emergency; his regime also curtailed rights and autonomy granted to southerners.

In response to the abrogation of southern autonomy, two army battalions mutinied in 1984 under the leadership of a southern Dinka, Colonel John Garang, whose Southern People's Liberation Army (SPLA) found a ready supply of arms from Marxist Ethiopia. By 1987, Soviet tanks and artillery supplied to the SPLA allowed it to fight positional battles and capture population centers. Subject to government bombardment and raids by its militias, massive numbers of southerners were displaced from their homes or fled to neighboring countries. The faction-ridden civilian government in Khartoum proved incapable of winning the war. When the negotiations with the SPLA rebels seemed on the verge of success, the Khartoum regime was overthrown by General Omar Hassan al-Bashir in 1989.

The new military regime stepped up the war against the south, motivated by the desire to spread militant Islam and to reap the wealth from huge southern oil reserves discovered in the 1970s. Emptying the oil producing regions of their black African animist populations became a deliberate government goal, even at the price of massive destruction and loss of life.

The overthrow of Ethiopia's Marxist regime in 1991 dried up the arms supply to the SPLA, and the organization broke into two factions. Under the leadership of Riek Machar, a Nuer faction broke off and proclaimed its goal of independence from Sudan. John Garang remained head of a largely Dinka SPLA and claimed his goal a unified, secular Sudan. The clash of three visions of Sudanese identity—an Arab-Muslim Sudan, a Sudan divided into two separate states, or a unified secular Sudan—continued for years.

By 1995, northern and southern opponents of Bashir's Khartoum regime joined forces. They formed the National Democratic Alliance (NDA), which mounted an offensive on three fronts in eastern Sudan by January 1997. The main spearhead came from Garang's SPLA, but also included elements from dissident northern groups.

In response, Khartoum rallied southern dissidents and signed a peace agreement with Riek Machar and other breakaway SPLA faction leaders in April 1997. Pro-Khartoum southerners were linked together under the name of the United Democratic Salvation Front (UDSF) headed by Machar; about 25 of their militias came together in the South Sudan Defense Force (SSDF) supported by Khartoum. However, in February and March 1999, Dinka and Nuer leaders held a series of reconciliation meetings that resulted in the Wunlit Covenant among major southern Sudanese elements. The meetings demonstrated the vitality of traditional conflict resolution procedures, as the groups reached agreement through consensus and traditional rituals, with the climax being the slaughter of a large white bull by spiritual leaders of the Dinka and Nuer communities. This symbolized peace and an end to the conflict between the southerners.

The growing unity of southern Sudanese actors posed a threat to Omar al-Bashir's regime in Khartoum. In late 1999 he dissolved Parliament and declared a state of emergency that allowed him to rule by decree. Bashir continued to terrorize civilians in southern Sudan. He called presidential and legislative elections for December 2000, but elections were not held in the south, allegedly for security reasons. In February 2001, John Garang's SPLA signed a memorandum of understanding with the Islamist northerner Hassan al-Turabi, in what appeared to be a marriage of convenience in opposition to Bashir, though Turabi and Garang were themselves arch foes. Bashir placed Turabi under house arrest until October 2003.

The Comprehensive Peace Agreement (2005)

In the meantime, the Bashir government began negotiating a peace settlement with its southern opponents. With Kenyan leadership, the IGAD (the Inter-Governmental Authority on Development consisting of Kenya, Eritrea, Ethiopia, Djibouti, Sudan, Somalia, and Uganda) brought the government of Sudan and the SPLA together at Machakos, Kenya and, to the surprise of many, produced a framework for peace in July 2002. Both sides made concessions. The government agreed to a referendum on self-determination for southern Sudan—to take place six and a half years later in 2010—and the SPLA accepted the application of *sharia* law in the North. The Machakos Protocol provided the framework and momentum for negotiation on several important issues: wealth-sharing, power-sharing, application of *sharia* in Khartoum, and defining the border between North and South.

A power-sharing agreement created a separate Government of Southern Sudan (GOSS), which received a "significant devolution of powers" from the national government. The agreement allowed Bashir to

South Sudan

remain president until national elections could be held, and Sudan obtained two vice presidents (appointed by the president). John Garang would be first vice president of the national government and president of the Government of Southern Sudan. Garang's SPLA gave rise to a political movement called the Sudan Peoples' Liberation Movement (SPLM). On the application of *sharia* law in Khartoum, it was agreed that non-Muslims would not be subject to its provisions in the capital. The rights of non-Muslims were to be protected by a special commission appointed by the president. Wealth-sharing agreements split oil revenues 50-50 between north and south, after deducting 2% to go to oil-producing communities. The parties agreed to a bicameral national legislature, in which the SPLM was allocated 28% of the seats, with an additional 6% going to other southern forces. The upper house, or Council of States, was to have two representatives from each of Sudan's states. The agreement called for a census to be held by the second year of the interim period and general elections by the end of the third year.

From these discussions emerged the Comprehensive Peace Agreement (CPA), which was officially signed in January 2005, ending 20 years of civil conflict between north and south that claimed the lives of as many as 1.5 million people. John Garang was accorded a tumultuous welcome when he arrived in Khartoum to be sworn in as national vice president in July; simultaneously he became the head of the autonomous GOSS for the next six years. Before the month was out, however, Garang died in a helicopter crash. This seemed suspicious to many in the SPLA, though the organization's leadership agreed with Khartoum's assertion that it was a genuine accident. Following a brief flare-up with riots in Khartoum after Garang's death, the SPLM moved quickly to fill the void, naming deputy chairman Salva Kiir as Garang's successor in the positions of national vice president and head of the Government of Southern Sudan. Kiir struggled to create an administration to implement the CPA, as Southern Sudan had limited educated and trained manpower, and Khartoum remained reluctant to fulfill its CPA obligations. Southern Sudan also faced the prospect of spoiler forces whose arms and ambitions had the power to destabilize the region.

For several years, conflict in Sudan was centered on Darfur, where the Bashir government led a genocidal war against minority groups. As 2007 progressed, north-south conflict returned as the SPLM briefly removed itself from government in protest over a perceived unwillingness by the government to enforce the 2005 peace accord. Arab militias later clashed with SPLM forces over the oil-producing province of Abyei, and this threatened to unravel the north-south accord. Bashir and Salva Kiir finally reached an agreement in August 2008 on managing Abyei, though the region returned to conflict in 2011.

In April 2010, Omar Al-Bashir won a presidential election in Sudan with 68% of the vote, to 22% for Yasir Arman of the SPLM; the SPLM took a comparable proportion of legislative seats. In a simultaneous election in South Sudan, Salva Kiir won reelection as president with an overwhelming 93% of the vote.

Referendum and Independence (2011)

After decades of conflict with the north, the semi-autonomous region of southern Sudan undertook a January 2011 referendum that resulted in an overwhelming vote for independence, with 99% of Southern Sudanese voting in favor. The referendum was a provision of the peace agreement in 2005.

In February 2011, clashes broke out in the south's most populous state of Jonglei between rebel leader George Athor and the South Sudan army. The GOSS accused Khartoum of backing the rebels and attempting to destabilize the south. In the same month, a further ominous sign emerged when a GOSS minister was assassinated in his office, though this incident was attributed to a personal dispute. Clashes also began in Abyei, which led the GOSS to suspend talks with the government of Sudan.

Fighting in the oil-rich province of Abyei reached new orders of magnitude in May 2011 as northern forces occupied a portion of the state, including the town of Abyei. This sent an estimated 100,000 people fleeing their homes, and the south responded with an attack on a Sudanese military unit, killing several dozen soldiers. Khartoum retaliated with more comprehensive movements of forces forward in Abyei, along with a more comprehensive bombing campaign in South Kordofan (which remained part of Sudan, yet is home to many southern sympathizers). This prompted US President Barack Obama to issue a statement calling for restraint on all sides. Simultaneously, Al Jazeera reported that Khartoum and the GOSS were seeking an accord on a plan to demilitarize Abyei, with the plan backed by a contingent of Ethiopian peacekeepers.

Independence came to South Sudan on July 9, 2011. After debating several options (including Southern Sudan, Kush, and Nile Republic), the government settled on the name South Sudan. Despite the trappings of sovereignty (including diplomatic recognition), South Sudan remained insecure. Conflict arose in border regions in 2011, and Salva Kiir and the GOSS (Government of Southern Sudan) rearmed to prevent re-invasion from the north in preparation for the 2011 plebiscite. According to Kiir, the GOSS needed to be ready with legitimate armed forces when the referendum came.

The main violent conflict between Sudan and South Sudan since independence first erupted over the disputed region of Abyei, though the regions of South Kordofan and other districts were soon subjected to fighting. According to peace agreements, Abyei will eventually be entitled to make its own determination about joining Sudan or South Sudan, but a

President Salva Kiir meets with Omar al-Bashir of Sudan in July 2012

South Sudan

referendum has been delayed by disagreements between north and south on stipulations for the vote. International arbitration courts in July 2009 ruled that a major oil field was to be located in the north, and that the Abyei was to be shrunken in size. This decision was tolerated by both sides, but the Khartoum government asserted control in much of Abyei as South Sudan's independence approached.

In 2012, South Sudan and Sudan clashed over control of oil fields at Heglig, located in the Sudanese province of South Kordofan. After several months, Sudan established clear control over the territory. The two countries then attempted to establish new agreements that would allow them to coexist. These agreements—brokered in part by the intervention of Ethiopia—included a demilitarized border and the removal of troops from Abyei. In recent months, Sudan and South Sudan have also reached accords on the continued flow of oil through pipelines from South Sudan to Port Sudan on the Sudanese coastline. This followed threats of boycotts by the two sides over disagreements stemming from the border conflict and the arrangements to share the revenues from the oil resources. Despite the agreements, tensions between the countries remain very high, and there is a likelihood of further skirmishes and economic turmoil in the coming years.

In July 2013, President Kiir dismissed Vice President Riek Machar and the rest of his cabinet, accusing them of instigating a coup. It is still uncertain as to whether Machar had actually planned a coup, but he was planning on running against Kiir in the next election. In December 2013, fighting broke out in Juba between government forces and rebel forces, led by Machar. A ceasefire was signed in January 2014; however, it was unsuccessful and the fighting continued. In May 2014, another ceasefire was signed by both sides. While Machar says that his forces are committed to upholding the agreement, he believes that Kiir's forces have already violated the ceasefire. Thousands of people were killed in the conflict and 1.5 million people were displaced from their homes. The UN has threatened to impose sanctions on both sides as they are guilty of the use of child soldiers and massacring civilians. The worst fighting took place in the oil-rich town of Bentiu in Unity State, where hundreds of unarmed civilians were murdered.

CONTEMPORARY THEMES

The civil war in South Sudan has had major repercussions on its already struggling economy. The country's economic future will largely depend on the outcome of the civil war and its substantial proven oil reserves. From the beginning of the conflict until the end of January 2014, oil production dropped 20%, which will have huge effects on world markets. If both sides do not reach uphold the peace agreement, it is possible that production will decrease even more and its economy will continue to struggle since the government derives about 98% of its budget revenues from oil. Not only has the civil war had major effects on oil production, but also its relationship with Sudan heavily influences its economy since the country seeks to build another pipeline. Beyond oil, South Sudan's economy depends upon agriculture and pastoral activity. South Sudan is one of the richest agricultural areas with its fertile soil and abundant water supply. Agricultural activity is mainly pastoral, with the main domestic livestock being cattle, along with smaller livestock such as sheep, goats, camels, and chickens.

The central economic question relates to the length of the conflict and its outcome. Despite its abundance of natural resources, South Sudan remains one of the most underdeveloped countries in the world. For example, only 15% of its citizens own a mobile phone. Before fighting broke out in late 2013, the country looked to undertake many development projects including railroad projects, tarmac key roads, redevelopment of the port at Lamu, and a hydroelectric dam. However, the government's focus is now entirely on restoring peace and the economy has felt significant negative effects from the conflict. Even before the conflict, South Sudan experienced widespread poverty and now, according to the UN, 3.7 million people are in need of food due the displacement of thousands of citizens and increased poverty.

Afflicted by both persistent drought and flooding along with an influx of people from neighboring Sudan, South Sudan is also dealing with Intercommunal conflicts especially in the oil-rich Abyei region claimed by both South Sudan and Sudan with upward of 400 people killed by marauding militias. Economic problems Include a cut-off of the oil pipeline running through Sudan and a widespread hunger crisis involving several million people brought on by fighting, climate change, and the huge influx of half million refugees from Sudan as Kenya Is conducting mediation talks to end ongoing conflicts.

With the potential return of civil war, ongoing violence against civilians, and the impact of recent cuts to healthcare services by the United States, the Vatican has urged South Sudan to honor the recently deceased Pope Francis by seeking peace. The arrest of the vice president, Riek Machar led the UN to warn of a rapidly escalating crisis and urged all parties to exercise restraint. The United Nations Mission in South Sudan (UNMISS) reports a significant increase in violence against civilians, including a rise in conflict-related sexual violence while US aid cuts have led to the closure of clinics, leaving cholera patients with limited access to medical care and resulting in deaths. South Sudan's opposition has said that the overnight arrest in March 2025 of First Vice President Riek Machar, longtime rival to President Salva Kiir, has invalidated their 2018 peace deal and risked plunging the country back into war involving a "polarized regional environment." This comes after weeks of escalating violence, which the Sudan People's Liberation Army In Opposition (SPLM/IO) describes a series of attacks by President Kiir's forces, in breach of the peace deal as the power-sharing agreement between Kiir and Machar over military power has been gradually unraveling, threatening a return of the civil war that killed around 400,000 people between 2013 and 2018. President Kiir, 73, has evidently been seeking to ensure his succession and sideline Machar for months through major changes in the

Conflict continues in Sudan *Das Parlament*

South Sudan

cabinet described by some as "clearly a power grab."

FUTURE CONSIDERATIONS

The independence of South Sudan has been one of the more stirring events in recent years in Africa. Yet instability and conflict remain, especially in Abyei and several other border regions including Jonglei and Unity state (and South Kordofan on the Sudanese side). Despite a relatively successful transfer of power and the avoidance of total war between the two states, the situation remains terribly precarious and subject to rapid escalation. Conflict comes both in the form of fighting and in the form of economic recriminations over the distribution of oil revenues.

While there continues to be tension between South Sudan and Sudan over oil, the major concern is the outcome of the civil war. Since the peace agreement was reached in May 2014, both sides appear to have stopped fighting. President Kiir cancelled the next elections to give the two sides more time to negotiate in order to effectively settle the conflict. There has been significant tension between the Dinka and Nuer ethnic groups since before the independence movement, so the future of South Sudan currently rests on whether these two groups can reconcile their differences and create an effective state to avoid future conflict and violence.

The Republic of the Sudan

Death in Darfur: A Janjaweed militiaman. AFP/Getty Images

BASIC FACTS

Area: 1,861,484 sq. km. = 718,723 sq. mi.
Population: 49,197,555 (June 2023 est.)
Capital City: Khartoum
Government Type: Presidential Republic
Neighboring Countries: Democratic Republic of Congo and Central African Republic (southwest); Chad (west); Libya (northwest); South Sudan (south)
Official Language: Arabic, English
Other Principal Languages: Nubian, Bedawi, Fur
Ethnic Groups: Sudanese Arab (approximately 70%), Fur, Beja, Nuba, Fullata
Principal Religions: Sunni Islam, small Christian minority (mostly in Khartoum)
Former Colonial Status: Egyptian (1821–1885); British–Egyptian (1899–1956)
Independence Date: January 1, 1956
GDP Per Capita (IMF 2023 est.): $975 (nominal), $4,471 (PPP)
Gini Index: 34.2 (2014 est.)
Currency: Sudanese pound (SDG), 1 USD = 598 SDG (Apr. 2023)
Inflation rate: 245.1% (2022 est.)
Chief Commercial Products: Oil, cotton, sesame, livestock/meat, and gum Arabic
Foreign Direct Investments (FDI) net inflows: 1,251,280,889
Literacy rate: 61% (CIA 2018)
Life expectancy: 67.45 years (CIA 2023 est.)
Head of State: President Umar Hassan Ahmad al-Bashir (since October 16, 1993)
Head of Government: Sovereign Council Chair Abd-al-Fatah al-Burhan (since April 11, 2019) was removed by military coup and replaced by a military council headed by Lt. Gen. Abd-al-Fatah al-Burhan

LAND AND PEOPLE

Sudan is the largest nation in Africa by area, covering almost one million square miles. The vast Sahara Desert lies in the northern sector and is succeeded by a semiarid plains country in the region near Khartoum, the capital city. This is followed by tropical plains with somewhat greater rainfall, but for the most part, the country is hot and dry. The Nile River, the longest in the world, is the main route of north-south communication and travel between the Mediterranean Sea and the lower part of the African continent. The river has two points of origin—the waters of Lake Victoria flow into the White Nile and pass through central Sudan. The Blue Nile originates to the east near Lake Tana in the mountains of Ethiopia. The two rivers join at Khartoum to form the main Nile, which proceeds through northern Sudan, interrupted periodically by rough cataracts. Were it not for the muddy waters of the Nile, much of Sudan would be empty. High mountains rise in the extreme east of Sudan, close to the Ethiopian border and along the Red Sea coast, and to the west on the Chad border.

UNESCO designated Gebel Barkel and four other Nubian locations as World Heritage sites in 2003. The sites contain tombs, temples, pyramids, living complexes, and palaces that testify to the importance of the ancient cultures of Napata, Meroë, and Kush. The 8th-century rulers of Kush conquered and ruled Egypt as the 25th dynasty. Non-recognition of Nubia's pharaonic heritage is one of the complaints this northern people lodges against Khartoum's Islamist regime.

HISTORY TO PRESENT DAY

For early history, see *Historical Background* and *The Colonial Period: The British.*

Origins of Internal Conflict

Sudan has been riven by internal conflict for most of its history. That conflict has usually been referred to as one between a Muslim North and a Christian South (in

Sudan

what became the country of South Sudan in 2011), but that conflict is neither exclusively regional nor exclusively religious given the country's enormous complexity. A central problem is defining the identity of the state. Northern Sudan was conquered and unified by the Egyptian viceroy of the Ottoman sultan in 1821. Egyptian rulers claimed southern Sudan but were unable to establish effective control over its fragmented animist populations. Access to the South was not possible until after 1839, and from that point both the Ottoman rulers and their Arab Sudanese subjects saw the South only as a source of manpower. Slavers from both groups aggressively raided southern peoples.

Only in the 1880s was a Sudanese identity articulated in opposition to the Egyptian conquerors. In 1881, the religious leader Muhammad Ahmad proclaimed himself the Mahdi or "expected one" and began to unify peoples in western and central Sudan. Drawing upon discontent with Ottoman-Egyptian exploitation, Muhammad Ahmad led a nationalist revolt that culminated in the capture of Khartoum in 1885. The self-proclaimed Mahdi died shortly afterwards, but his state survived until destroyed by an Anglo–Egyptian army under Lord Kitchner in 1889. Sudan was proclaimed a condominium in 1899 and governed by a joint British–Egyptian administration until 1956. Northern Arab Muslims were privileged by the condominium administration and in turn, looked down on the black African animists of the south. For black Africans of southern Sudan, the memory of slave raids brought an association between pale-skinned persons and enslavement.

Sudan's Muslim populations have been divided by their affiliations with rival religious brotherhoods. The followers of Muhammad Ahmad (the Mahdi) called themselves *ansars*, and this sect today is the largest of the Sudanese Muslim brotherhoods. During the period of Ottoman-Egyptian rule, Turkish-Egyptians developed close relations with another Muslin brotherhood, known as the Khatmiyya. The second most important brotherhood today, the Khatmiyya retains its original pro-Egyptian, anti-Mahdist identity.

Tomb of the Mahdi, Khartoum

Each of these two rival brotherhoods is associated with a separate political party. Mahdists are the core of the Umma Party, while the Khatmiyya forms the core of the Democratic Unionist Party (DUP). The leader of the Umma Party, Dr. Sadiq al-Mahdi, is a descendent of Muhammad Ahmad. Smaller than either the Ansar or Khatmiyya is the more militant Muslim Brotherhood led by Hassan al-Turabi. These sectarian groupings also have secular opponents (Muslims and non-Muslims) whose vision of Sudanese identity is not based on political Islam.

Cultural diversities help explain Sudan's history of instability and conflict. At independence in 1956, a civilian regime was incapacitated by internal division between its Muslim partners; it was overthrown by a military coup in 1958. The military in turn, reneging on its promises to restore civilian government, was driven from office and succeeded by another coalition government. Power sharing between Umma and Unionist parties could not overcome factionalism, economic stagnation, and ethnic dissidence in the south.

Jaafar Nimiery (1969–1985) and the North-South Conflict

Espousing pan-Arab-Nationalism and professing pro-Soviet sentiments, General Jaafar Nimeiry took advantage of dissatisfaction with this civilian regime and overthrew it in 1969. Soviet arms poured into Sudan, but only two years later disputes between Marxist and non-Marxist elements within the ruling military coalition resulted in an abortive communist coup. Anti-Marxist elements quickly restored Nimeiry, who did a political about-face and sought aid from the United States.

In 1972, the government reached a peace agreement with southern rebels. Signed at Addis Ababa, the accord made the south

Sudan States

Sudan

a self-governing region. Yet this offered only a brief respite to Sudan's endemic conflict. After Emperor Haile Selassie was overthrown in neighboring Ethiopia by a Marxist military coup in 1974, Sudan was seen as a bulwark against communism in the region. American arms poured into the country, and Sudan became another pawn on the chessboard of cold war politics.

Secure with American arms and support, General Nimeiry began an Islamization campaign in 1983. Traditional Islamic punishments drawn from Koranic *sharia* law were incorporated into the penal code. These included amputations for theft and public lashings for alcohol possession. When religious leaders like Sadiq al-Mahdi questioned the general's credentials for creating an Islamic state, they were thrown in jail. The Nimeiry regime suspended civil liberties and declared a state of emergency; it also curtailed rights and autonomy granted to southerners.

In response to the abrogation of southern autonomy, two army battalions mutinied in 1984 under the leadership of a southern Dinka Colonel John Garang. (The Dinka, an ethnic group predominantly from present-day South Sudan, have very different religious and cultural beliefs to the Arab-dominated Sudanese government at this time.) This began Sudan's long civil war. General Nimeiry himself fell in a bloodless coup a year later and was ultimately replaced by a civilian coalition again headed by Prime Minister Sadiq al-Mahdi; this civilian regime lasted from 1986 to 1989, but Garang's Southern People's Liberation Army (SPLA) found a ready supply of arms from Marxist Ethiopia and by 1987, Soviet tanks and artillery supplied to the SPLA allowed it to fight positional battles and capture population centers. Caught in the crossfire between government bombardment and SPLA raids, massive numbers of southerners were displaced or fled to neighboring countries. The faction-ridden civilian government in Khartoum proved incapable of winning the war, and at the very moment negotiations with the rebels seemed on the verge of success, the regime was overthrown by General Omar Hassan al-Bashir in 1989.

The Omar Hassan al-Bashir Regime (1989–present)

The new military regime under al-Bashir came to power with the backing of the militant National Islamic Front (NIF) party headed by Hassan al-Turabi. It quickly abolished the constitution, trade unions, and all political parties except the NIF. In addition, it eliminated press freedoms, imposed strict dress codes, and limited freedoms for women. The regime purged the army, police and civil administration to make way for more militant Islamists.

Support for the regime came from Iran, enabling the government to make massive purchases of arms from China and the former Soviet republics. These were used to step up the war against the south, which had become more strategically important following the discovery of huge southern oil reserves in the 1970s. Emptying the oil producing regions of their black African animist populations became a deliberate government goal, even at the price of massive destruction.

The overthrow of Ethiopia's Marxist regime in 1991 and questions about continued arms supply led to a factional breakup of the SPLA. One faction came under the leadership of Riek Machar (a Nuer) and proclaimed its goal of independence from Sudan. John Garang (a Dinka) continued to lead the SPLA and claimed his goal was a unified, secular Sudan. The clash of three visions of Sudanese identity—an Arab-Muslim Sudan, a Sudan divided into two separate states, or a unified secular Sudan—continued for years.

Dr. Sadiq al-Mahdi

By 1995, northern and southern opponents of the regime had joined forces in the National Democratic Alliance (NDA), and by January 1997 the NDA mounted an offensive on three fronts in eastern Sudan, led by Garang's SPLA, but also with elements from the Beja Congress and groups such as Sadiq al-Mahdi's Umma and Mohamed Osman al-Mirghani's Democratic Unionist Party (DUP). In April 1997, Khartoum signed a peace agreement with Riek Machar and rallied pro-government southerners from over two dozen militias, but in February and March 1999 Dinka and Nuer leaders reunified to oppose Khartoum.

Bashir faced growing unity among his southern enemies and a growing threat from within the governing National Congress Party (NCP), which was the new name for the former National Islamic Front. Bashir's response was twofold. First, he signed a peace agreement with Sadiq al-Mahdi, which drove a wedge in the NDA opposition. Second, he rallied a leading Muslim cleric to his side in preparation for his struggle with Hassan al-Turabi, the speaker of parliament and al-Mahdi's brother-in-law. As Turabi seemed on the verge of sidelining the president position in both party and state, Bashir's response amounted to an internal coup. In late 1999 Bashir acted decisively to curtail Turabi, dissolving Parliament and declaring a state of emergency that allowed Bashir to rule by decree. In May 2000, Turabi was suspended as NCP secretary-general and accused of plotting against the government. Formally expelled from the party in June, he announced the creation of a new political party, the Popular National Congress (PNC), better known now as simply the Popular Congress (PC).

With the principal spokesman for political Islam sidetracked, Bashir won the return of some of the northern political elite, including former president Numeiry and Sadiq al-Mahdi, who returned to lead his popular Umma Party. Ahmad al-Mirghani, a senior leader of the Democratic Unionist Party (DUP) and nominal president from 1986 to 1989, also returned after nearly 12 years of exile. At this time, Bashir also improved relations with formerly hostile neighbors, notably by allowing Ugandan army troops to pursue members of the rebel Lord's Resistence Army to their Sudanese hideouts.

Internally, however, Bashir continued to terrorize civilians living around the disputed Bentiu oil fields. Those fleeing the offensive reported that troops—backed by tanks, helicopter gunships and aerial bombardments—tortured, slaughtered and burned men, women and children in a drive to evict all non-Arabs from oil-producing areas.

Bashir called presidential and legislative elections for December 2000, but few participated. No elections could be held in the south for security reasons, and where they were held in the north, they were actively boycotted by the major opposition parties. Official reports indicated 63% of eligible voters went to the polls, a figure that produced hoots of derision from the opposition who claimed not more than 7% had participated. Bashir and the NCP won, overwhelmingly.

In February 2001, Hassan al-Turabi was arrested and jailed after his PNC had signed a memorandum of understanding with John Garang's SPLA. The linkage between Turabi and his arch foe Garang, was unexpected, unprecedented, and to many

Sudan

of his followers, inexplicable. Turabi remained under house arrest, a prisoner of the state that he had helped to create. He was freed in October 2003 while the Bashir government was negotiating a peace settlement with its southern opponents.

Sudan and its civil war rose high on Washington's list of priorities after the September 11 attacks. This was, after all, where Osama bin Laden had lived from 1991 until he was expelled in 1996. Even before those events, however, the House of Representatives had already passed the Sudan Peace Act in June 2001 by 422 to 2. The act would "punish those who trade in blood oil," said its sponsors, by imposing capital market sanctions on companies investing in Sudan. It would also provide $10 million to Sudanese opposition forces. To push the Sudanese peace process forward, President George W. Bush appointed former Senator John Danforth, an Episcopal minister, as Special Envoy for Peace in the Sudan.

The Comprehensive Peace Agreement

With Kenyan leadership, the IGAD (the Inter-Governmental Authority on Development consisting of Kenya and other neighboring countries) brought the Sudanese government and the SPLA together at Machakos, Kenya and produced a framework for peace in July 2002. Both sides made concessions. The government agreed to a referendum on self-determination for southern Sudan—to take place six and a half years later in 2010—and the SPLA accepted the application of *sharia* law in the North.

The Machakos Protocol provided the framework for negotiation on several important issues: wealth-sharing, power-sharing, application of *sharia* in the north, and defining the border between north and south. Wealth-sharing agreements came first, aided by experts from the World Bank and IMF. The agreement split oil revenues 50-50, after deducting 2% to go to oil-producing areas. A power-sharing agreement created a separate Government of Southern Sudan, which received a "significant devolution of powers" from the national government. The agreement allowed President Bashir to remain in office until national elections could be held, and Sudan obtained two vice presidents (appointed by the president). The first was John Garang, who also was appointed president of the Government of Southern Sudan. Garang's SPLA converted from a military force into a political movement called the Sudan Peoples' Liberation Movement (SPLM). *Sharia* law was applied in the capital city Khartoum, but it was agreed that non-Muslims would not be subject to its provisions and would have rights to be protected by a special commission appointed by the president.

The parties agreed to a bicameral national legislature. The majority of the National Assembly's seats were to be apportioned to the National Congress Party (52%), while the SPLM would be allocated 28%. Other northern political forces would receive 14%, with the remaining 6% going to additional southern forces. The upper house, or Council of States, was to have two representatives from each of Sudan's states. The agreement called for a census to be held by the second year of the interim period and general elections by the end of the third year.

From these discussions emerged the Comprehensive Peace Agreement (CPA), which was officially signed in January 2005, ending 20 years of civil conflict between north and south that claimed the lives of as many as 1.5 million people. Calling it a "new path" for Sudan, President Bashir signed a power-sharing constitution to implement the CPA in early July. Former prime minister and opposition leader Sadiq al-Mahdi condemned the new constitution, however, saying it was a mere bilateral deal between John Garang and Omar al-Bashir that would lead to a country ruled by two people.

John Garang was accorded a tumultuous welcome when he arrived in Khartoum in July to be sworn in as national vice president and head of the autonomous administration of southern Sudan for the next six years. Before the month was out, however, Garang died in a helicopter crash. The SPLM moved quickly to fill the void, naming deputy chairman Salva Kiir as Garang's successor. Kiir assumed Garang's offices as national vice president and head of the government of southern Sudan, but he struggled to create an administration to implement provisions of the CPA, as Southern Sudan had limited educated and trained manpower, and Khartoum remained reluctant to fulfill its CPA obligations. Southern Sudan also faced the prospect of spoiler forces whose arms and ambitions had the power to destabilize the region.

Even as the government made peace with southerners, however, resistance, rebellion, and insurgency emerged elsewhere. Some northern peoples, like the Beja and the Nubians, felt as marginalized as Garang's southerners and resentful at the exclusivity of the CPA. New groups also emerged in the western region of Darfur to press their demands during the Kenyan negotiations; the Bashir government's response to Darfur created a humanitarian disaster that culminated in genocide.

Darfur

The Sudan Liberation Army (SLA) in the region of Darfur took up arms against the government in February 2003, accusing it of ignoring the region and demanding a place at the negotiating table. Shortly afterwards a second armed group—the Justice and Equality Movement (JEM)—emerged to make the same claims. Both rebel groups recruited from the region's African (and largely Muslim) populations—notably Fur, Zaghawa, and Massaleit peoples—all of whom had historical conflicts with Arab pastoralists over water and grazing rights. In the 1980s, these traditional tensions had been intensified by the central government, which took to arming Arab militia groups to disrupt and destabilize black African communities that might be sympathetic to John Garang's SPLA.

With the emergence of the SLA and JEM, Khartoum armed Arab militias and gave them a free hand to target civilian populations suspected of supporting the rebellion. The most notorious of the militias were the *janjaweed*. Supplied with AK-47s and riding on horseback or camelback, the *janjaweed* attacked villages across Darfur, burning and looting entire settlements, raping, and pillaging. The *janjaweed* destroyed fields, orchards, and granaries, and branded those they raped on their hands to make them permanent outcasts. Attacks were frequently supported by government shelling, often from helicopter gunships, followed by the use of regular government troops.

More than 2.5 million people were displaced in Darfur. About two million lived in camps in Darfur and approximately 250,000 fled to Chad. Several hundred thousand died of disease, malnutrition, and violence. At the peak of the conflict, approximately four million people in Darfur, two-thirds of the population, were dependent on humanitarian aid for survival. In the midst of the fighting, humanitarian agencies were frequently prohibited from entering the area, or simply withdrew because it was too unsafe.

UN Secretary-General Annan identified the International Criminal Court (ICC) in The Hague as "the most logical place" to try suspects in the Darfur atrocities, and a special UN inquiry turned over a list of 51 names of potential suspects to the court in March 2005. The ICC handed down its first Sudanese war crimes indictments in February 2007. Charged were Ali Muhammad al Abd-al-Rahman ("Ali Kushayb"), the alleged *janjaweed* commander, and Ahmad Muhammad Harun, the former head of the government's Darfur task force. In a cruel twist, Bashir later appointed Harun as Sudan's minister of humanitarian affairs; as of July 2010, he was governor of the state of South Kordofan. According to the ICC, Ali Kushayb and Harun bore "criminal responsibility" for war crimes and crimes

Sudan

President Omar Hassan al-Bashir

against humanity, including torture, murder, and rape.

The Security Council voted to refer Darfur war crimes suspects to the ICC, but the Sudanese government made clear its refusal to permit any of its citizens to appear before the court. One major sticking point at the UN Security Council is that China, a permanent member, has the power to veto any action that would jeopardize its oil investments in Sudan. Additionally, both China and Russia are major arms suppliers to the Khartoum regime, a lucrative trade neither wishes to end.

Khartoum managed to dissemble and delay, postponing efforts by the international community to end atrocity and genocide in Darfur. Only by 2007 did the West move toward stronger words and deeds. On May 28, 2007, President George W. Bush announced heightened unilateral financial sanctions against 31 Sudanese firms, mostly in the oil business, and three individuals, including the aforementioned Ahmad Muhammad Harun.

China, which is the destination for some two-thirds of Sudan's oil production, objected to the international pressure. China itself increasingly became a focus of attention as the world increasingly concluded that the road to Khartoum lay through Beijing. In early May 2007—just a year before the Beijing Olympics—China announced that it had named a senior diplomat as its first ever special envoy to Africa, with Darfur his special focus.

As 2007 progressed, the crises in Sudan seemed to multiply with the return of north-south conflict and clashes with the neighboring nation of Chad. While Darfur continued to occupy the headlines, the conflict between north and south recurred as the SPLM briefly removed itself from government in protest over a perceived unwillingness by the government to enforce the 2005 peace accord. Arab militias later clashed with SPLM forces over the oil-producing region of Abyei, and this threatened to unravel the progress made on the north-south question. Bashir and the southern leader Salva Kiir finally reached an accord in August 2008 on managing Abyei, though the region returned to conflict in 2011.

In the meantime, Sudan briefly reached an accord with the Chadian government, under which both countries would stop harboring rebels that attack the other. Yet this accord, reached in early 2008, also proved fragile. Just weeks after raids by rebels into the Chadian capital of N'Djamena, rebels from Darfur conducted their own raids into the outskirts of Khartoum. The Chadian and Sudanese governments each accused the other of complicity with the respective rebel groups, and of destabilizing tactics; the two countries cut off diplomatic relations and seemed poised on the brink of outright war.

In August 2008, Bashir was indicted by the ICC for atrocities in Darfur, giving Sudan the dubious distinction of being the first country to have its head of state indicted for war crimes. Following the indictment, Hassan al-Turabi suggested that Bashir might turn himself into The Hague to face prosecution, which earned Turabi an arrest in January 2009. In March 2009, the International Criminal Court in The Hague issued an arrest warrant against Sudan's head of state, making him a fugitive from international justice. In practice, Bashir has still not been arrested despite making diplomatic visits to both Kenya and Chad.

The open warfare stage of the Darfur conflict has ceased. The Justice and Equality Movement (JEM)—the largest remaining rebel group in Darfur—signed a peace accord with the government in 2010, with a view towards some degree of autonomy for the region. President Bashir claimed that this showed the Darfur was over. However, the number of people displaced from Darfur in 2013 alone was estimated at 400,000. In 2013–14, conditions worsened in Darfur. Emergency aid workers and peacekeepers are still being attacked and killed. Less than 10% of people have access to clean water; the basic necessities are still not available and accessible to much of the population. The Darfur conflict has left an estimated 300,000 people dead and around two million displaced.

Amid the horrors of Darfur, conflict continued with in other regions of Sudan. Militarization and violence heightened in the central Sudanese state of South Kordofan (where alleged war criminal Harun is now governor). The Sudanese army increased its presence in the state in late 2008 (ostensibly in anticipation of an attack from Darfur's rebel groups), and clashes in 2009 over land rights resulted in several hundred dead. This threatened to add another locus to Sudan's crisis of internal strife.

The Secession of South Sudan (2011)

Sudan held a modestly competitive presidential election in April 2010. The result was a comprehensive victory for President Omar Al-Bashir of the National Congress, who took 68% of the vote, to 22% for Yasir Arman of the SPLM. The election was not wholly free and fair, though monitors reported mixed findings, which may imply perhaps a better-than-anticipated electoral process. The National Congress Party took a substantial majority of the seats (323 out of 450), and the SPLM took 99 seats, roughly proportional to the 22% garnered by its presidential candidate. In a simultaneous election in South Sudan, Salva Kiir won reelection as president with an overwhelming 93% of the vote.

The semi-autonomous region of southern Sudan held a January 2011 referendum in which 99% of Southern Sudanese voted in favor of independence, and flag of the new nation of South Sudan was hoisted in Juba on July 9, 2011. From 2009 to 2011, conflict arose in border regions between north and south, and this continued after South Sudan's independence. The Government of Southern Sudan (later the independent government of South Sudan) rearmed in anticipation of re-invasion from the north.

The most heated conflict between Sudan and South Sudan is over the disputed region of Abyei, which is rich in oil, though the regions of South Kordofan, Jonglei, and other districts are also subjected to tensions. According to peace agreements, the region will eventually be entitled to make its own determination about joining Sudan or South Sudan, but a referendum has been delayed by disagreements between north and south on stipulations for the vote. International arbitration courts in July 2009 ruled that a major oil field was to be located in the north, and that the disputed Abyei region was to be shrunken in size, and this decision was tolerated by both sides.

In February 2011, just months before independence, the Government of South Sudan, the GOSS, accused Khartoum of attempting to destabilize the south through backing for rebels led by George Athor. Further clashes in Abyei led the GOSS to suspend talks with the government of Sudan. In the midst of mutual recriminations, fighting in Abyei went to a new order of magnitude in May as

Sudan

Sudanese forces occupied a portion of the state, including the central town (also known as Abyei). This sent an estimated 100,000 people fleeing their homes, and the south responded with an attack on a Sudanese military unit, killing several dozen soldiers. Khartoum retaliated with more comprehensive movements of forces forward in Abyei. The Khartoum regime also conducted a more comprehensive bombing campaign in South Kordofan, which remained as part of Sudan yet is home to many southern sympathizers.

Khartoum and South Sudan engaged in open fighting over oil-rich parts of South Kordofan (Sudan) and Unity State (South Sudan) in 2012, with several hundred soldiers being killed between the two sides. Yet the two countries eventually reached two important yet precarious agreements in September 2012 and then in 2013. First, they agreed on a plan to demilitarize the border and the contested territory of Abyei, with the plan backed by a contingent of Ethiopian peacekeepers. Then, the two countries reached an agreement to keep landlocked South Sudan's oil flowing through a pipeline that passes through Sudan to the coast at Port Sudan. This came after both countries had made economic threats: South Sudan had threatened to shut off the flow of oil—from which Sudan takes a portion of the proceeds—while Sudan had threatened to refuse South Sudan the right to export its oil overseas. As of mid-2014, these agreements were holding, but the various tensions between the two countries continued to give rise to verbal threats and recriminations. The questions of oil revenues and exact border demarcation are still unresolved and create tensions between the two countries.

In the midst of this conflict, the Bashir regime seeks totalitarian control, though there are some cracks in the edifice. The government retains control over media, television, and radio, so there is a lack of freedom of information in the country. At the same time, internal party politics is more divisive. In late 2013, there was a significant split in the National Congress Party with many members breaking off to form a new party with the hope of reaching out to secularists and leftists and creating a democracy that encompassed all of its citizens. Soon after in response to this split, President Bashir reshuffling and revamped his cabinet by dropping many important figures including Vice President Ali Osman Taha.

CONTEMPORARY THEMES

Sudan's economic future depends in large part on its substantial proven oil reserves, which stood at approximately five billion barrels as of June 2010, but got cut down to 1.25 billion bbl with the independence of South Sudan; the division of oil-rich territories between north and south is a major source of conflict between the two. Sudan's crude oil exports began in August 1999 when a 1,000-mile pipeline from southern Sudan to the Red Sea was opened. They export 97,270 bbl per day. The pipeline was built by the Greater Nile Petroleum Operating Company (GNPOC), a consortium dominated by the state oil firms of China, Malaysia, and Sudan. China's assistance in the pipeline construction is being paid off in oil, and Khartoum is the biggest supplier of African crude to China's energy-hungry economy; Sudan recently accounted for approximately 10% of Chinese oil imports.

China's huge investment in Sudan's petroleum industry is at the heart of advocacy groups' divestment project. Individuals (like Warren Buffett and his Berkshire Hathaway company), mutual fund operators (like Fidelity), and state pension funds (like CalPERS) have been targeted by activists demanding they sell off the stocks of companies morally tainted by their association with and support of the government of Sudan. Buffett brushed the advocates aside, saying there was no evidence that PetroChina, listed on both the New York and Hong Kong stock exchanges, had any operations in Sudan. Its parent company, China National Petroleum Company (CNPC), he admitted, did work in Sudan, but as a subsidiary, PetroChina had no influence on CNPC's policies. (The argument was disingenuous, as the two share an intimate and symbiotic relationship. Managements of the two companies completely overlap; asset transfers, at subsidized rates, frequently take place between them, and CNPC is ultimately reliant on PetroChina for its financial health.)

High crude oil prices and increased production have meant impressive economic growth, at between 8% and 11% from 2005 to 2008. The last several years have seen more modest growth in the range of 3% to 6%. This has also meant a significant spike in net foreign investment—from $392.2 million in 2000, to $2.3 billion in 2005. One immediate consequence of all this money is inflation which continues to increase dramatically. Another consequence is a building boom which is transforming and modernizing once-sleepy Khartoum; bridges and office towers are rising, most notably in the glamorous al-Mogran project situated at the confluence of the Blue Nile and the White Nile. In the suddenly stylish city, the new petro-elite has access to the latest modern luxuries, including a spate of $165,000 BMWs.

The government cut fuel subsidies in September 2013 and the country responded with waves of demonstrations that left many dead. The subsidies hit the already struggling hard. The uprisings and protests did calm relatively quickly.

Oil and other industries (such as cotton ginning, textiles, and cement) provide work for 7% of the labor force and makes up 33.6% of the total GDP. Since the independence of South Sudan and the loss of a significant portion of oil revenues with it, the Sudanese government has increased its focus on mining especially gold mining. Sudan is experiencing somewhat of a gold rush with mines for many different minerals ramping up production and new reserves discovered in 2013. Many foreign companies have recently invested in the industry and obtained licenses to search for gold.

Before the oil boom, Sudan's economy was traditionally dependent on agriculture and pastoral activity. About 80% of the labor force makes its living through crop growing or animal grazing. Agriculture accounts for 27.4% of the total GDP. Principal food crops consist of millet, sorghum, rice, cassava, wheat, peanuts, beans, and bananas. Exports are primarily cotton, livestock, and gum Arabic. Sheep, goats, camels, and chickens are also reared. Sudan is an important supplier of sheep meat to the Arab world and is building new slaughterhouses in order to service this huge market.

At the Giad industrial complex, some 30 miles south of Khartoum, Sudan has a significant arms manufacturing capacity. Rocket-propelled grenades, machine guns and mortars are already produced there and the government is looking into the expansion of arms manufacture. It has signed an oil-for-manufactures agreement with the Russian republic of Tartarstan, bartering oil for various high-tech products, including military aircraft. Three Giad firms were placed on the list of companies subject to increased U.S. financial sanctions in May 2007. In 2012, an explosion destroyed an arms factory that was believed to be an Iranian-run plant providing arms to the Hamas Islamist organization in Palestinian territories. Many believed Israel was behind the explosion, though the cause remains undetermined.

The largest contemporary hydropower project in Africa, the Merowe Dam located in North Sudan was completed in 2008 and now supplies over 90% of the Sudanese population with electricity.

Apart from its history of conflict, Sudan remains a country with some of the longest-standing social problems still present in Africa. Slavery in Sudan still exists, and though numbers are declining this is still a salient issue. Over 45% of the population is below the poverty line. Sudan also is estimated to have the highest prevalence of female genital cutting (FGC) in the

Sudan

world. In many cases, FGC takes the most extreme form, known as infibulations, in which the labia are stitched together to cover the urethra and most of the vagina, leaving only a small opening for the passing urine and menstrual blood.

Other health indicators are also poor. Infant mortality and maternal death rates are very high, just above half of population has access to clean water, and nearly one-third of children are malnourished. The country is also under pressure from a substantial refugee population of over 300,000, mostly seeking asylum from Eritrea, and an increasing number of arrivals from South Sudan.

Major conflicts between the Sudanese Armed Forces (SAF) and the paramilitary Rapid Response Forces (RSF) and allied militias have led to cases of mass killings, torture, and rape—especially of non-Arab groups, such as the Masali Tribe, with entire villages burned to the ground concentrated in the West Darfur region. Street battles between the two contending forces have also broken out in the capital of Khartoum with a reported one half million refugees fleeing to nearby Chad.

At least 31 people, including children, were killed by the paramilitary Rapid Support Forces (RSF) in Khartoum's twin city of Omdurman in Darfur in April 2025, which the Sudan Doctors Network described as "the largest documented mass killing in the region." Victims were accused by the paramilitary group of affiliation with the Sudanese Armed Forces (SAF), but with the doctor's network calling the bloodshed a "war crime and a crime against humanity." Graphic video of civilians being killed circulated on social media as the Sudanese army has launched attacks to regain territory from the RSF in southwest Omdurman as well as western Omdurman, where the RSF also has a presence. Since April 2023, the RSF has been battling Sudanese army forces for control of the country in a brutal civil war, resulting in thousands of deaths and one of the world's worst humanitarian crises. Thus far, a reported 15 million people have been displaced and the death toll is estimated at 130,000.

FUTURE CONSIDERATIONS

For several years, Sudan was viewed mainly through the lens of the tragedy and the horror in Darfur. In the aftermath of the worst violence in Darfur, the arrest warrant from the International Criminal Court for the head of state Omar al-Bashir presents a test case for the reach of international justice. Despite the considerable evidence against him and his regime, Bashir was reelected in 2010. Yet the situation is ongoing: as of May 2014, 215,000 people were displaced from Darfur in this calendar year alone.

The role of China in Sudan is especially noteworthy, as it symbolizes the ideological tenets of Chinese involvement in Africa: "non-interference," or "respect of sovereignty" of other nations, which in practice mean a willingness to tolerate genocidal and dictatorial regimes. Amid massive suffering, Sudan's economy is growing largely for the reasons noted above: investment—especially from the Chinese—in the country's oil production.

The central question for the present and immediate future is the resolution of the ongoing conflict with South Sudan. Conflict subsided somewhat after the open small-scale war that took place in mid-2012 but heated up again in 2013. While both have reasons to prefer stability along the border, and have created a demilitarized zone as a result, Sudan and South Sudan still appear to be trapped in a security dilemma in which each state's security seems to come at the expense of security for the other. If conflict can be tempered and further conflict between the two states can be avoided, a major source of instability will dissipate. If Khartoum continues to press assert authority over several of the border regions, or if fights over the oil industry persist, then yet more violence is on the cards.

With refugees already spilling across the Sudan—South Sudan border, there is fear that major violence could increase along the border as well. Increasing violence in Southern Kordofan and Blue Nile states has already been noted in 2014. February 2014 was the month with the highest number of civilian casualties since conflict in those areas began in 2011.

President Omar Al-Bashir has repeatedly pledged to step down from his presidency in 2015, and this could be a huge crossroads in the future of Sudan. A clean transition of power from the man who has ruled since 1989 could show a new and improved truly democratic Sudan. On the other side, it could be an event that becomes the catalyst for another major civil conflict.

There are still many human rights and justice questions to answer in Sudan. Over 9,000 child soldiers are estimated to still be involved in fighting, and slavery is still present; an estimated 35,000 persons are enslaved in Sudan today. Human trafficking continues apace as well. Executions and torture are common forms of punishment for not only renegade warlords, but the Bashir government as well. Sudan is one of the worst countries in terms of women's rights violations, as is seen with the country's high rate of female genital cutting. With the exception of its economic growth and oil-led investment, Sudan remains emblematic of the problems that afflicted many African countries in previous decades, but which have fortunately been attenuated elsewhere: dictatorship, conflict, low levels of development outcomes, and lack of fundamental freedoms for many of the nation's citizens.

Darfur refugees, victimized by Janjaweed and government forces. ©IRIN

The United Republic of Tanzania

BASIC FACTS

Area: 947,300 sq. km. = 365,755 sq. mi. (includes the islands of Zanzibar and Pemba; twice the size of California).
Population: 65,642,682 (June 2022 est.)
Capital City: Dodoma
Government Type: Presidential Republic
Neighboring Countries: Mozambique (southeast); Malawi, Zambia (southwest); Congo (Kinshasa), Burundi, Rwanda (west); Uganda (northwest); Kenya (northeast)
Official Languages: Kiswahili (Swahili) and English
Other Principal Languages: Kiswahili (Swahili) is a mother tongue in Zanzibar and coastal Tanzania and a lingua franca of central and eastern Africa. Prominent local languages are Gogo, Ha, Haya, Makonde, Nyamwezi, Nyakyusa, and Sukuma.
Ethnic Groups: Mainland—Bantu 95% (more than 130 tribes); other 5% (including Asian, European, and Arab); Zanzibar—Arab, native African, mixed Arab and native African
Principal Religions: Mainland—Christian 30%, Islam 35%, indigenous beliefs 35%; Zanzibar—more than 99% Muslim
Former Colonial Status: German Colony (1885–1917); British Mandate under the League of Nations and Trusteeship under the United Nations (1919–1961)
Independence Date: April 26, 1964. Tanganyika became independent 9 December 1961 (from UK-administered UN trusteeship); Zanzibar became independent December 10, 1963 (from UK); Tanganyika united with Zanzibar April 26, 1964, to form the United Republic of Tanganyika and Zanzibar; renamed United Republic of Tanzania October 29, 1964.
GDP Per Capita (IMF 2023 est.): $1,348 (nominal), $3,600 (PPP)
Gini Index: 40.5 (2017)
Currency: Tanzania shilling, 1 USD = 2,354 Tanzania shillings (May 2023)
Inflation Rate: 4.4% (2022 est.)
Chief Commercial Products: Gold, coffee, manufactured goods, cotton, cashew nuts
Foreign Direct Investments (FDI) net inflows: 2,044,550,443
Literacy Rate: 81.8% (CIA 2021)
Life Expectancy: 70 years (CIA 2022 est.)
Head of State: Samia Suluhu Hassan, President (since March 14, 2021)
Head of Government: Samia Suluhu Hassan, President (since March 14, 2021)

LAND AND PEOPLE

Tanzania is a large, picturesque country lying just south of the Equator, extending between the great lakes of Central Africa and the Indian Ocean, with a 500-mile coastline. A fertile plain of up to 40 miles in width stretches along the coastline; the land slowly rises in the interior to a large central plateau averaging 4,000 feet in altitude. A mountain range of moderate height in the middle of Tanzania extends from north to south. At the north end of these peaks, Mount Kilimanjaro rises to the height of 19,340 feet—the tallest peak in Africa. Though only three degrees south of the Equator, Kilimanjaro was historically capped by snow and icy glaciers year around, though the famed snows are melting due to climate change. Farther to the northwest, the large freshwater Lake Victoria spreads across a semiarid plain.

A chain of towering mountains extends along the length of the entire western border, sharply descending to Lake Tanganyika, which is 2,534 feet deep. This long, narrow body of water was created centuries ago when an immense fault of land descended sharply, creating an earthquake and forming what is now called the Great Western Rift Valley. The large East African lakes contribute an area of 20,000 square miles of inland water to the area of Tanzania. Abundant rainfall supports dense vegetation in the coastal area, and the central plateau has an average of 25

Tanzania

inches of rainfall per year. In the higher elevations, cooler weather prevails and there is more abundant rainfall, produced by the rush of warm air up the high slopes of the mountains.

HISTORY TO PRESENT DAY

For early history, see *Historical Background, The Colonial Period: The Germans* and *The Colonial Period: The British*.

Independence, Union, and the Julius Nyerere Years (1960–1985)

As a result of pre-independence elections in 1960, the Tanganyika African National Union (TANU), led by its founder, Julius Nyerere, was installed in power. Nyerere was the son of a minor chief of the small Zanaki tribe and had been sent to a Catholic mission school as a boy. He later trained as a teacher at Makerere University College in Uganda and went on to Edinburgh University where he received a master's degree in 1949. When he returned home in 1953, he was one of only two Tanganyikans trained in foreign universities, and a year later he formed TANU to agitate against British rule. Under Nyerere's leadership, TANU effectively mobilized African sentiment and led the country to independence from Great Britain on December 9, 1961. Tanganyika was a de facto single-party state and Nyerere became the country's first president.

Meanwhile, the neighboring island nation of Zanzibar, independent in 1963, experienced a destabilizing revolution that would ultimately link it to Tanganyika. Before the 1964 revolution, Zanzibar—a collective noun that refers to both Zanzibar Island (or Unguja) and Pemba islands and their volcanic neighbors—was a highly stratified society. While 76% of the population was African, the Arabs (16%) monopolized political power and controlled the economy of the clove plantations a small Indian population dominated the trade. After World War II, the majority African population, who had experienced economic and social discrimination, began to challenge the existing racial structures of Tanganyika.

Political parties were first organized in the 1950s and reflected Zanzibar's racial divide. The Zanzibar Nationalist Party (ZNP) was largely Arab and Arabized Africans; the supporters of the Afro-Shirazi Party (ASP) were Africans, often descendants of a long mixture of Arab, Persian, and African heritage. In June 1963, Zanzibar gained internal self-government and July elections were held in which a ZNP-led coalition emerged victorious, with Sultan Jamsid ibn Abdullah becoming head of state and Prime Minister Hamadi, an Arab, becoming government leader. Zanzibar

Former President Julius Nyerere

was declared independent on December 10, 1963, but a month later on January 13, 1964, the Arab-dominated government was overthrown in a bloody revolution. Thousands of Arabs and Indians were massacred, the sultan deposed, and a republic declared, under the control of the 32-man Zanzibar Revolutionary Council led by Abeid Karume of the ASP.

The ASP monopolized political power as Zanzibar's sole legal party and used its control of state machinery to punish its enemies, usually ZNP supporters. All land was nationalized, political opponents thrown in jail and murdered, and a massive exodus of Arabs and Asians began amid continuing disorder. Karume appealed to neighboring Tanganyika for aid in maintaining law and order. Nyerere's government, fearing the consequences of continuing instability, dispatched Tanganyikan police forces, and in April 1964 Zanzibar and Tanganyika formed a union, later formally designated the United Republic of Tanzania.

In 1964, Nyerere proceeded to institutionalize the one-party system and TANU would become the sole means of organizing political expression in the country. The TANU followed Marxist-Leninist lines, and though Nyerere's socialism was more moderate than Karume's, the union strengthened left-radical pressures on TANU. The governing parties of each partner shared a similar outlook and had long cooperated with each other.

TANU soon faced instability on the mainland. Economic discontent had been fomented by trade unions and the army had mutinied in various parts of the country as soldiers protested low pay and the slow pace of Africanization of the lower officer grades. Nervous about a professional army, the government disbanded it and replaced it by a highly politicized Tanzanian People's Defense Force (TPDF). The emulation of "popular democracies" was intensified following Nyerere's visit to China in 1965.

President Jakaya Mrisho Kikwete

The Chinese told him that farmers were the most conservative members of society and must be uprooted from the land if socialism were to be built. Nyerere had used the KiSwahili term *ujamaa*, meaning "familyhood," to describe the ideal of communal cooperation he sought to develop, but this was given a more conventional socialist definition in TANU's Arusha Declaration of 1967. The government was asked to nationalize all means of production and to prepare development plans that did not rely on foreign assistance. Peasants were forcibly transferred to new Chinese-style planned villages without consultation and without compensation for the loss of their houses and farms. Unsurprisingly, production plummeted.

Nyerere's program damaged the productive economy, but it did emphasize public services, with heavy spending on education and health. Inspired by the Chinese experience, the government resettled peasant farmers in planned villages. This facilitated the distribution of services, but had disastrous effects on agricultural production, which plummeted. Government-owned industries and businesses were costly failures and a drain on national resources. As agricultural production diminished and the expenses of nationalized companies rose, national income fell, foreign debt increased, and Tanzania became increasingly dependent on the generosity of international donors.

In 1977, Tanzania adopted a new constitution, which explicitly subordinated all organs of state to the party. At the same time, TANU and the ASP merged to form a single party known as the Chama Cha Mapinduzi—the Revolutionary Party, or CCM for short. Within the union, Zanzibar maintained considerable autonomy—its own president, doubling as Tanzanian vice president, and chief minister, responsible for most affairs aside from defense and international relations. Under the constitution, Tanzania's lawmaking body, the

Tanzania

National Assembly, consists of 228 members, of whom 118 are elected from mainland constituencies and 50 from Zanzibar. Additional members are appointed by government and various "mass organizations," but given the leading role of the CCM and its monopoly of power, the legislature was relatively meaningless.

President Nyerere was confirmed in office by plebiscites held in 1965, 1970, 1975, and 1985. To reinvigorate a complacent party, an interesting variant on the one-party theme was introduced in the mid-1980s: CCM would approve two candidates for most constituencies, providing some illusion of democratic choice. Indeed, some government ministers were defeated in this manner.

Transition and Reforms: The Ali Hassan Mwinyi (1985–1995) and Benjamin Mkapa (1995–2005) Administrations

In 1985, Julius Nyerere retired from the presidency but retained the post of CCM chairman. His chosen successor was Ali Hassan Mwinyi, the former president of Zanzibar. During Mwinyi's two terms in office, the country was bankrupted and the regime lost its ideological support with the collapse of the Soviet Union. In 1986 the government finally launched a comprehensive economic reform and began to privatize some state companies and open the door to investment.

Surprisingly, the government introduced the notion of competitive democracy and the constitution was amended to make Tanzania a multiparty state in 1992. Benjamin Mkapa was elected president in Tanzania's first competitive election, held in 1995. The elections were chaotic, characterized by administrative ineptitude. The situation in the capital was so bad—election officials absent, ballots lost, polls opening late, if at all—that the election had to be reheld after being declared null and void. Opposition parties claimed that the disorganization was a CCM plot and withdrew, but when the dust settled (at least on the mainland) 30 years of single-party rule had given way to actual party competition. CCM continued to control parliament, winning 186 of 232 elective seats, and its candidate Mkapa beat three opponents, winning a total of 61.8% of ballots cast. In office, Mkapa continued his predecessor's efforts to liberalize the economy by liberalizing agricultural marketing, privatizing state-owned enterprises, and freeing exchange rates.

The 2000 elections went similarly to those in 1995. President Mkapa overwhelmed his opposition with nearly 75% of the vote, and CCM continued its dominance in parliament, holding 244 of 274 seats. Turmoil reigned in Zanzibar, however, where the CCM—always more authoritarian than its mainland counterpart—made life much tougher for its Civic United Front (CUF) opponents. Government security forces and the CCM militants harassed and intimidated CUF candidates and supporters on both Pemba and Unguja. On election day, ballots and registration lists conveniently failed to arrive on time in opposition strongholds. The situation on Pemba was such a disaster the Zanzibar Electoral Commission (ZEC) nullified the results and reran the elections. CUF boycotted the reruns, with the expected result: The ZEC announced that CCM's Amani Abeid Karume won the Zanzibar presidency with 67%, beating the CUF's Seif Shariff Hamad, who took 33%. The European Union, the OAU, and the United States all criticized the conduct of the election, but Amani Karume, the former minister of communication and transport and eldest son of Zanzibar's first president, Abeid Karume, seemed little inclined to make concessions to the opposition. CUF protests would continue to the elections of 2005.

Cloth market, Zanzibar

Photo by Beverly Ingram

The Jakaya Kikwete Administration (2005–present)

In preparation for presidential and parliamentary elections scheduled for October 2005, CCM's national congress chose Foreign Affairs Minister Jakaya Mrisho Kikwete as its standard bearer. Zanzibar's CCM branch acted with authoritarian dispatch to eliminate the candidacy of Dr. Mohammed Gharib Bilal against the incumbent, President Amani Abeid Karume.

The 2005 election results were a landslide victory for CCM and this raised questions about just how meaningful "multiparty" elections are in Tanzania. Presented a choice of candidates put up by ten political parties, Tanzanians chose the CCM's Jakaya Mrisho Kikwete overwhelmingly. He received 80.24% of all votes cast; his nearest rival was the CUF's Ibrahim Lipumba, who received 11.7% of the vote. The CCM also swept the parliamentary elections, winning 206 out of 232 elected seats. A distant second-place finisher was the CUF with 19 seats and three minor parties shared the seven remaining seats.

In Zanzibar, CCM pulled out all the traditional devices and ploys to limit its contentious CUF rival, leaving itself open to ongoing criticism for electoral manipulations. A month before elections, the head of the Zanzibar Electoral Commission reported that 700 people had registered to vote more than once and he expected that more names would be found. Indeed, a week before the election he announced the Commission had found 2,000 "bogus" names had been added to the electoral register. CUF claimed that its supporters had been victims of thuggish young men hired by the government to harass the opposition and public demonstrations and protests were suppressed with violence. CCM candidates carried 30 of the 49 legislative seats while CUF won the rest. In the presidential race, the CCM's Amani Abeid Karume won 53.2% of the vote; Seif Sharif Hamad, the CUF standard bearer, took 46.1%.

One explanation for CCM's domination of Tanzanian political space is the party's control of enormous financial resources that are lavishly spread about to assure electoral success. Indeed, vote buying is constitutionally permitted by a clause known as "takrim," which allows individuals, groups, or political parties to give gifts as a "show of African hospitality." No limits are placed on the amount, time, place, or purpose of such gifts. Former Prime Minister Joseph Warioba, probably Tanzania's foremost anticorruption figure, observed that in his country "democracy is on auction and only available to the highest bidder."

Elections in 2010 reconfirmed the CCM's dominance of Tanzania's political space on the mainland. Jakaya Kikwete won

Tanzania

reelection with 62.8% of the vote and Willibrod Slaa of the CHADEMA party took 27%. Slaa was a former Catholic priest who called the CCM "terrorists," and accused the government of fraud and rigging the vote during the counting and after the result. The CCM also won the parliamentary elections with ease, taking 259 of 350 total seats. CHADEMA won 48 and the CUF 36, with seven others going to smaller parties. In Zanzibar, CCM candidate Ali Mohamed Shein won as well, but by a narrow margin of 50% to 49% over the CUF candidate Seif Charif Hamad.

The Kikwete administration has largely followed the reformist tack of the Mkapa years, with a continued emphasis on public services. In light of reforms and pressing need, the country has received significant budgetary support from international donors, including the Millennium Challenge Corporation of the US government. (A brief glitch emerged in 2012, when it emerged that Tanzania had helped Iran evade oil sanctions by flagging tankers.) Political conditions are thus relatively stable in Tanzania, with presidential and legislative elections due again until 2015.

The dark cloud in terms of stability has been the recent emergence of strife between Christians and Muslims. In October 2012, groups of Muslims burned churches in the commercial capital of Dar es Salaam after reports that a Christian has desecrated a copy of the Koran; this resulted in over 100 arrests. Then in May 2013, a bomb attack in a church in the city of Arusha killed two and injured many more. These were not the first religiously-motivated attacks in Tanzania—in 1998, the U.S. Embassy was bombed by Islamist militants at the same time as the one in Nairobi, Kenya, killing a dozen people and wounding over 80 more. Yet the recent events raise the specter of religious conflict that has spread along the dividing lines between Muslim and Christian populations that cuts across the middle of Africa.

The next election will be in 2015. It is the fifth election since the introduction of the multi-party system in 1992. Current president Kikwete is ineligible to run for a third term. Members of the dominant CCM party that are possibilities for the position include: Edward Lowassa (Prime Minister, 2005–2008) and January Makamba (Deputy Minister of Communication, Science & Technology, and Member of Parliament).

CONTEMPORARY THEMES

Social issues: Education and Government Efficacy

One of President Nyerere's greatest achievements was improving education and literacy in Tanzania. Primary education was made universally accessible with a primary school in every village. When challenged with his policy failures by World Bank officials, the president is once reported to have responded "The British Empire left us a country with 85% illiterates, two engineers and twelve doctors. When I left office, we had 9% illiterates and thousands of engineers and doctors." However, investment in education later went into decline, and literacy fell to 63% by 1990. Concentrated effort (and international assistance) has begun to effect a change: literacy was up to 69.4% in 2006 and is estimated at between 75% and 80% among youth aged 15 to 24 (UNICEF 2009). Still, a quarter of Tanzanian adults still have no education, and women are likelier than men to miss out.

The government introduced free primary education in 2001 and school registrations shot up from four million to eight million children by 2007. In the initial period, many classrooms lacked teachers and were sorely dilapidated. Overcrowding was a serious problem in places like Dar es Salaam where classes averaged 145 children per classroom. A UNICEF report highlighted the key problems in Tanzania's educational system; these included a shortage of books and teachers who are poorly trained and unmotivated. The report also criticized teaching methods, and characterized the overall school environment as one of fear and boredom rather than interaction and real learning. Secondary education languished. While primary education was universalized, there was no concomitant expansion of public education at the secondary level, where fees have to be paid. As a consequence, Tanzania had the lowest rate of public secondary education in the world—just under 7%. The situation has begun to turn around. With the government helping communities across the country build secondary schools, more children are being encouraged to continue their schooling.

Retention of teaching staff remains a crucial problem because the government has done little to improve the living standards of teachers. Given the opportunity, they are likely to quit their jobs and try other options. One Oxfam researcher described it succinctly: "The majority of them feel that teaching is not a respected profession any more. The low status of teaching in society has to do with the deteriorating incomes and poor living conditions of teachers, which have cost them the respect of even the pupil."

The economic capital Dar es Salaam (Haven of Peace) has become a densely congested city of about three million. To "open up" the interior regions of the country and escape the congestion of the capital, centrally located Dodoma has been appointed the new official capital city (with the official move taking place in 1996), though some government offices remain in Dar es Salaam.

Corruption is at epidemic proportions in Tanzania ("In my country," said former Prime Minister Joseph Warioba, the chairman of President Mkapa's anticorruption commission, "you have to pay a bribe for everything.") The very public anticorruption campaign, which followed the Warioba Report, resulted in hundreds of state bureaucrats being fired and the dissolution of the President's cabinet in 2008, but there have been few prosecutions.

Government taxes and license fees are extensive. For example, there were recently 26 different taxes, levies and licenses imposed on the coffee industry, Tanzania's third biggest foreign exchange earner. A recent study found Tanzania's taxes to be the highest of five peer coffee-producing countries (Uganda, Ethiopia, Costa Rica, Guatemala, and Tanzania). The heavy hand of taxes and regulation has impacted small-scale coffee farmers, who account for 95% of the country's total output. They have the lowest yields in the region averaging an estimated 152 pounds an acre to Kenya's 625. Coffee production continues to decline, but in May 2007 Starbucks, the world's largest coffee retailer, signed an agreement with the Association of Kilimanjaro Specialty Coffee Growers that may lead to increased production.

The Economy: Agriculture, Tourism, and Mining

Most farmers are small-scale (with about four acres of land) and remain at virtually subsistence level. More than 90% of agricultural workers in Tanzania are women and many of them single mothers. They often work not only their own piece of land, but supplement their income by working on commercial farms, where they tend to be underpaid. Agricultural practice and inputs need improvement, but land legislation—rewritten in 1999—still makes it difficult for farmers to mortgage their land and find credit to develop their productivity. Local roads also need to be improved to provide access to markets, but even where there is access, liberalization has not raised the prices paid to farmers. Certainly, commodity prices have fallen generally, but in Tanzania, buyers have formed cartels that function to keep prices down even more. The Kikwete administration has initiated a nine-year development program to transform rural agriculture.

The island of Pemba, part of Zanzibar, produces 80% of the country's clove crop, but the Zanzibar government has been slow to liberalize the island's agricultural policy. For a long period, there has been only a single buyer for cloves—the

Tanzania

Zanzibar State Trading Corporation (ZSTC). The company has traditionally offered such low prices to producers that they have usually preferred to smuggle their crops to neighboring Kenya.

Tourism had replaced cloves as Zanzibar's principal source of foreign exchange, but has suffered with the rise of Islamist terrorism in the region. When Western nations warned their citizens of possible terrorist attacks in the islands in 2003, hotels almost immediately suffered 50% cancellation rates. During the 2003 Ramadan season, young Islamists beat up a number of Muslim women whom they considered inappropriately dressed. In March 2004, police had to use tear gas to disperse hundreds of demonstrators from the Islamic Awareness Society agitating for government adoption of Islamic *sharia* law. This concern has heightened in 2012 and 2013 with the emergence of occasional flare-ups between Muslim and Christian groups.

On the mainland, tourism is also an important economic sector, with the "big game" safaris playing a significant role. In 2010, one of the leading political issues became the government's plan to build a highway through the famed Serengeti National Park. President Kikwete and the government argued the project would be important for development, but conservationists objected to the plan on the ground that it would harm wildlife and disrupt important migration patterns. In June of 2011, the Tanzanian government announced that it would halt all plans to build a highway through the Serengeti Park but has not eliminated the possibility of building south of the reserve. The Tanzanian president is also making efforts to deter poaching of elephant tusks, which has become a very prominent issue all around the world.

In 2011, a ferry going from Zanzibar to Pemba capsized and over 200 passengers onboard died. Overloaded ferries were not an uncommon occurrence on Zanzibar, highlighting the lack of updated and adequate infrastructure on the island.

While tourism has become sensitive to international politics, mining has become the fastest growing sector of Tanzania's economy, led by rising gold sales. As the sector opened to private investment, mineral sales rose from $15 million in 1996 to more than $400 million in 2002. Sector growth has been continual: 15.4% in 2004 and 15.7% in 2005. It now contributes 3.5% of GDP. Gold accounts for the biggest portion of sector revenues and Tanzania was the third largest African gold producer (after South Africa and Ghana) in the mid-2000s. Despite industry growth, its impact on poverty reduction and job creation has been slim, and the entire mining sector has come under intense scrutiny. Pressure is building for the government to reexamine existing mining contracts to assure local communities a fair share of company profits.

Tanzania also possesses considerable deposits of gemstones—green tourmaline, sapphires, garnets, diamonds, rubies, and emeralds. Smuggling remains a problem, especially for Tanzanite, a precious blue stone found only in Tanzania southwest of Mount Kilimanjaro. In December 2002, the American Gem Trade Association named tanzanite an additional birthstone for the month of December. This was the first time a birthstone has been added to the existing list since 1912.

For any type of mining venture in Tanzania, infrastructure is a problem. Roads are inadequate and availability of water and electricity is often problematic. During the drought conditions of 2006 there were power shortages throughout the country and most hydroelectric stations had to produce well below capacity in the absence of sufficient water. Upon his arrival in Beijing for the Sino-African Summit of 2006, President Kikwete received an energy-assistance pledge from Chinese President Hu Jin Tao. Using coal mined in Tanzania's southern region, Chinese generators would help boost national electricity production.

International debt has been mitigated in recent years with debt relief from the G-8, the world's richest nations, which agreed to cancel Tanzania's multilateral debt. Tanzania was admitted to the World Bank's Heavily Indebted Poor Country (HIPC) program in 2001. As of 2005, debt totaled $6.2 billion, but 100% of the debt owed to multilateral institutions (such as the World Bank) was forgiven. The government is currently trying to reduce the budget deficit from 6.2% (last year) to 5%. Jakaya Kikwete recently announced his plan to launch Eurobonds (worth $700 million) in July 2014, but this will be delayed if the costs are too high.

Reflecting the decision of President Hassan to allow for greater tolerance of political opposition, government critics have called for major constitutional revisions—especially the creation of a truly independent electoral commission for management of all elections from the national to the local level. Like many neighboring countries, Tanzania has suffered from heavy flooding brought about by devastating cyclones with 155 people killed in April 2024.

While supporting greater political tolerance for the opposition in theory, the newly formed electoral commission barred the main opposition party, Chadema, from contesting presidential and parliamentary elections due in late 2025. Stating that the party failed to sign a mandatory code of conduct agreement by the required deadline for the polls, the commission's director of elections added that the disqualification announced in April 2025 extends to all by-elections until 2030. The announcement came days after Chadema leader Tundu Lissu was charged with treason, accused of inciting rebellion and attempting to stop the elections from going ahead with the charge carrying the possibility of a death sentence. A former presidential candidate and target for assassination in 2016, Lissu has long been a vocal critic of the governing Chama cha Mapinduzi (CCM) party and its leader, President Samia Suluhu Hassan, who is seeking a second term. Chadema had already warned it would boycott the polls unless meaningful electoral reforms were introduced. Human rights organizations and opposition groups have accused the government of clamping down on dissent, citing a pattern of unexplained abductions and killings of political activists that the government has denied. This follows police crack downs on planned protests against the government by Chadema in September 2024 in the Magomeni area of the capital Dar-es-Salaam. There, protesters were gathering for a rally against alleged killings and abductions of government critics and for defying a prohibition on the protests.

FUTURE CONSIDERATIONS

Tanzania has become a relatively stable polity in recent years, though it has not attained full democracy. Most indicators are respectable and improving, with elections being passable, if not flawless, and civil liberties being protected, albeit imperfectly. The country was singled out for praise from U.S. President Barack Obama for a variety

Mass production of sculpture for the tourist trade *Photo by Jude Barnes*

Tanzania

of achievements in advance of Obama's visit to Africa. Tanzania also received a visit from China's new president, Xi Jinping, in March 2013. There is little indication that the country will suffer from the broader inter-ethnic strife seen in its neighbor Kenya; rather, it is likely the country will continue on its relatively unspectacular trajectory. The biggest challenge that Tanzania faces is likely dealing with the political and religious tensions that persist on Zanzibar, where the opposition continues to be treated with force and violence. The question of greater autonomy for the island, indeed, whether it should become a separate state, will become more salient.

Economic growth picked up in the 2000s and averages around 7%. At this rate, Tanzania's economy will double in size every decade. Agriculture accounts for over 40% of GDP but occupies 80% of the work force. Tanzania is buffeted by extremes of drought and flooding. Prices for most of its main agricultural products—coffee, sisal, cotton, tobacco, cashew nuts, and tea—have tended to decline, though the country's terms of trade may have reversed in 2007 and 2008. In 2009 Tanzania joined Kenya, Uganda, Rwanda, and Burundi in the East African Community, an institution that allows the free movement of people and goods within the region. The country may remain one of the poorest on earth for some years to come, even as it moves in the right direction with relatively consistent and admirable economic growth.

The Republic of Uganda

Uganda's tropical rain forest   Photo by Pat Crowell

BASIC FACTS

Area: 241,038 sq. km. (slightly smaller than Oregon)
Population: 47,792,952 (June 2023 est.)
Capital City: Kampala
Government Type: Presidential Republic
Neighboring Countries: Rwanda (southwest); Tanzania (south); Congo-Kinshasa (west); South Sudan (north); Kenya (east).
Official Language: English and Swahili.
Other Principal Languages: Acholi, Chiga, Ganda, Karimojong, Lango, Masaaba, Nyankore, Nyoro, Kinyarwanda, Sogo, Teso.
Ethnic Groups: Numerous, including Baganda (16%), Banyankole (10%), Basoga (8%), Iteso (6%), Langi (6%), Acholi (5%), Bagisu (5%).
Principal Religions: Roman Catholic 42%, Protestant 42%, Muslim 12%, indigenous beliefs 3%, none 1%
Former Colonial Status: British Protectorate (1894–1962)
Independence Date: October 9, 1962
GDP (IMF 2023 est.): $1,105 (nominal), $3,224 (PPP)
Gini Index: 42.8 (World Bank 2016)
Currency: Uganda shilling, 1 USD = 3,737 shillings (May 2023)
Inflation Rate: 6.1% (2022 est.)
Chief Commercial Products: Coffee, fish and fish products, flowers, tobacco, electricity, cotton, and tea
Foreign Direct Investments (FDI) net inflows: 1,146,560,083

Literacy Rate: 79 (CIA 2021)
Life Expectancy: 69 (CIA 2023 est.)
Head of State: President Yoweri Kaguta Museveni (since seizing power on January 26, 1986)
Head of Government: President Yoweri Kaguta Museveni (since seizing power on January 26, 1986)

LAND AND PEOPLE

This fertile expanse of highland bestrides the Equator in central East Africa between the Eastern and Western Rift formations. Uganda, dotted with lakes, and with immense Lake Victoria in the south, lies at an altitude of between 3,000 and 6,000 feet. If this country were at a lower altitude, its climate would be hot, moist and oppressive, but it is quite pleasantly temperate with ample rainfall to support intense cultivation, interrupted by two short dry seasons. In the extreme northeast, the climate is dry and prone to drought.

Approximately 15% of the country is covered by fresh water. The Ruwenzori Mountains to the west divide Uganda from the Democratic Republic of the Congo, having altitudes of almost 17,000 feet. In the southwest, close to Rwanda, lies the Virunga range of active volcanoes. In the east are the Eastern Rift Mountains, where Mount Elgon rises to a height of 14,000 feet.

The Victoria Nile originates from the banks of Lake Victoria, heavily populated with hippopotamuses and crocodiles, and flows to Lake Kyoga, an irregularly shaped body of water with large swamps. From there the Nile flows north and west through the mountains to empty into Lake Albert. The Albert Nile flows northward, leaving Uganda at the South Sudanese border to continue more than 4,000 miles to the Mediterranean Sea.

Uganda is home to a range of ethnicities, among which the Baganda are the most politically prominent. The King of Buganda (kingdom of the Baganda ethnicity) is known as the Kabaka, and is a major force in national politics; the kingdom, which comprises a large area around the national capital Kampala, has some autonomy from the Ugandan state on customary matters. Illustrative of local culture and development challenges facing smaller ethnicities are the Karamojong, a pastoralist minority of 100,000 people in Uganda's northeast corner. The Karamojong are Nilotic, while the bulk of Ugandans are Bantus. Among several ethnic groups, the cow is central to economic and cultural life. Milk and blood (drawn during the dry season when the animal produces no milk) provide the principal sources of Karamojong protein. Wealth, power and status are all based on cattle ownership, but persistent drought has diminished their livestock and increased poverty, while the easy availability of arms has increased banditry and insecurity. Among the Karamojong, unemployment is high, literacy is low (recently estimated at a mere 6%, compared with a national average of over 70%), and diseases and child mortality are the highest in the country.

HISTORY TO PRESENT DAY

For early history, see *Historical Background* and *The Colonial Period: The British.*

Independence, Milton Obote (1963–1971, 1980–1985), and Idi Amin (1971–1979)
The United Kingdom of Uganda was granted internal autonomy on March

Uganda

1, 1962, becoming fully independent on October 9 of that year. The government initially consisted of a federation of the kingdoms of Buganda, Busoga, Butoro, and Bunyoro, which retained local autonomy, while the rest of the country was governed by the central government. Sir Edward Frederick Mutesa II, Kabaka of Buganda, became the first president and Sir William W. Nadiope, king of Bunyoro, was the first vice president. Prime Minister Milton Obote wielded considerable power within the central government. The cabinet was selected by a coalition of Obote's People's Congress Party (PCP) and the Buganda KabakaYekka Party; the formerly dominant Democratic Party was in the minority.

The post-independence era has been dominated by three figures. One is current president Yoweri Museveni, while the first two leaders Uganda to shambles, replete with starvation and widespread deaths. Milton Obote was the first (1963–1971, 1980–1985) and the second was the notorious military figure Idi Amin (1971–1979).

Obote took on the traditional kingdoms directly a few years into his rule. He first dismissed Kabaka Mutesa and seized the government in 1966, charging the Kabaka with making personal profits from the supply of arms in connection with a rebellion in neighboring Zaïre. The hereditary king barely escaped when the army stormed the presidential palace, and he lived in exiled poverty until his death in 1969. (His remains were ceremoniously returned to Uganda in 1971.) Obote then abolished the old constitution and the traditional kingdoms in 1967.

Having removed the threat from the kingdoms, Obote established the PCP as the sole party and steered Uganda sharply to a socialist economy. After Obote appointed more and more of his fellow tribesmen to public offices tensions mounted and political instability in the nation increased.

Milton Obote

Finally, the army revolted, uniting behind Idi Amin in January 1971.

General Amin, who had once been the Ugandan heavyweight boxing champion, was initially popular, but he quickly alienated major political constituencies with his scapegoating and terrorizing of the population. Some 70,000 Asians, mainly Indians and Pakistanis, were expelled in 1972 with little thought of their importance to the economy as merchants and traders. The expulsion won Amin immense support from those to whom he gave property and merchandise seized from Asian merchants.

As early admiration of Amin turned to fear, educated Ugandans began to leave the country. Brutality became the order of the day by 1974. Secret executions, massacres and torture were among his favorite methods, and he personally participated in some of these grisly acts. Military efforts to oust him failed, and perpetrators were executed on the spot. The economy collapsed by 1978, and the country seethed with unrest. Amin tried to distract attention from his failures by claiming that Tanzania had invaded Uganda; he "responded" by having his troops invade Tanzania. They captured about 710 square miles before withdrawing.

President Julius Nyerere of Tanzania used the Ugandan aggression as an excuse to get rid of Amin, and mounted a swift invasion of Tanzanian troops, augmented by Ugandan exiles. Though the Tanzanian army was undermanned, it was Amin's forces, demoralized by his behavior, who crumbled after fierce fighting had claimed the lives of many. The conquering Tanzanian army entered Kampala in April 1979 and was greeted as liberators. In the confusion, Amin escaped. Yusufu Lule was installed as president, but he was quickly replaced by Godfrey Binaisa, whose term of office was equally short-lived. Obote supporters plotted Binaisa's overthrow, and Obote returned to Uganda in May 1980.

December 1980 elections were stolen by Obote in outrageous fashion, and this drew his political rivals into rebellion, including Yoweri Museveni, who had contributed significantly to the military overthrow of Amin. Refusing to accept the fraudulent election results, he formed a guerrilla group and "went to the bush with only 26 guns and organized the National Resistance Army (NRA) to oppose the tyranny that Obote's regime had unleashed upon the population," as his website describes it. Five years of strife followed; an estimated one million fled and 300,000 lost their lives. Over time, the NRA built strength in the countryside, even serving as a sort of de facto government in some areas by establishing law

Idi Amin

and order and local administrations in territories it controlled.

The NRM and Yoweri Museveni (1986–present)

In January 1986, the NRA, shot its way into Kampala and seized control of the country, becoming the first guerrilla army to oust an incumbent African regime. Museveni became president as the head of the National Resistance Movement (NRM) and began the difficult task of rebuilding Uganda. This required an entire rethinking of the institutions and practices that had bedeviled and destroyed the country.

Chief among the objects of Museveni's criticism were the traditional political parties, which he castigated as "sectarian and divisive," responsible for the country's political and economic ills. Museveni banned political parties and organized political participation within the framework of the broad-based NRM. All Ugandans would belong to the NRM, and candidates would stand for office on personal merit rather than party platform; this became known as the nonparty movement system.

Since the regime had come to power by force of arms promising to restore democracy and individual liberties, one of its first projects was a constitutional commission that could develop the framework, which restored the rule of law. Once in existence, the commission toured the entire country and consulted broadly. The whole process demonstrated a remarkable shift from the tradition of top-down constitutions, but the transition from anarchy to constitutionalism was lengthy; the constitutional commission's draft was debated and ratified by a popularly elected constituent assembly only on July 12, 1995, and promulgated by President Museveni on October 8, nearly a decade after the NRA had seized power. The constitution that emerged from this process was equally lengthy. In its final

Uganda

form, the constitution weighed in with 287 articles and seven addenda, making the Uganda Constitution ten times longer than that of the United States.

The constitution outlawed traditional political party activities, including sponsoring candidates for election. Museveni claimed a country like Uganda, divided along ethnic and religious fault lines, could not afford the divisiveness of party competition; critics and opponents plausibly argued that this left the Ugandan state in a dominant position, with Museveni at its head. Parliament was constitutionally prohibited, however, from establishing a single-party state. After five years experience with the movement system, the constitution promised voters an opportunity to assess the system in a referendum.

President Museveni's personal rule was legitimized by May 1996 elections held in accordance with the new constitution. His election slogan was "No Change," and he campaigned on his record: He had ended Uganda's cycle of blood and dictatorship, boosted security through the army, and built economic success that saw the gross domestic product grow by 10% in 1994. He won handily, beating two opposition candidates. It was the first free and open presidential vote in 30 years. Parliamentary elections followed in July 1996 that included 214 directly elected members and a number of indirectly

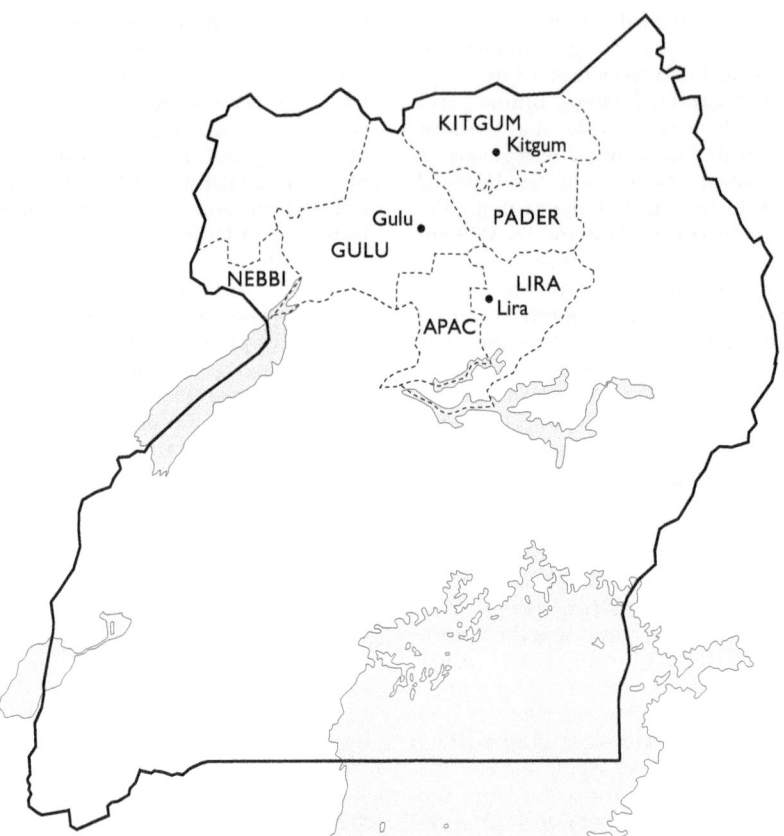

Northern Uganda, site of LRA activity

President Yoweri Museveni

elected seats for representatives of women (39), youth (5), workers (3), the disabled (5) and the army (10).

Museveni had inherited a wasteland in 1986, where piles of skulls remained at crossroads and the entire economic base had been destroyed: the economy was moribund and transportation and communication systems had been destroyed by war. The state was bankrupt; revenue from taxation was virtually nonexistent. To change course, the government made agreements with the IMF to liberalize the economy. Reforms included producer incentives and loans to rehabilitate infrastructure; the economy responded with eye-catching growth rates during reconstruction.

Rebels and Regional Conflicts

Although economic vibrancy returned to Uganda, not all its citizens shared in its changed conditions. In border areas to the west and north, the Uganda Peoples Defense Force (UPDF) faced ongoing resistance and rebellion from those marginalized economically and politically. In the north, resistance began with a mystic leader known as Alice Lakwena, who led the so-called Holy Spirit Movement in the late 1980s; Lakwena convinced her followers that her spiritual protection shielded them from bullets. This movement eventually gave rise to the Lord's Resistance Army (LRA), led by the mysterious Joseph Kony, Lakwena's cousin. Supported by Sudan's anti-Museveni regime, the LRA has waged war for years, often recruiting its soldiers by kidnapping children and sending them off to Sudanese camps for military training or sexual service. Those who flee or disobey are maimed or murdered as punishment. Kony's stated goal is to overthrow Museveni and rule Uganda in accordance with the Ten Commandments.

The rebels—Museveni calls them terrorists—have killed thousands, destroyed homes and property, and prevented the distribution of social services or development projects in an already poor region. More than 1.4 million people have been forced to leave their homes. At least 300,000 of them live in "protected villages" organized by the army to prevent the enemy from getting food and assistance from fellow Acholi tribesmen. Virtually the whole of northern Uganda became a humanitarian disaster area.

Sudan long offered support for LRA forces and other destabilizing elements as a tit-for-tat response. President Museveni shared with his colleagues in Eritrea and Ethiopia a common hostility to Sudan's Islamist regime and supported John Garang's SPLA rebel army in southern Sudan (which later became the independent nation of South Sudan) in its resistance to the government in Khartoum.

A successful guerrilla commander, Museveni has shown sympathy for more than Sudanese rebels. Uganda was the training ground for members of the Tutsi-led Rwandan Patriotic Front, which invaded and defeated the genocidal regime installed in Kigali in 1994. Museveni was also a central figure in organizing the forces that overthrew the Mobutu regime in Zaïre in 1997. Having once supported Laurent Kabila's rebels in this endeavor, Uganda then threw support to anti-Kabila rebels in the renamed Democratic Republic of Congo. For many, this raised

Uganda

fundamental questions about how a country as poor as Uganda could afford the increased defense expenditures necessary to conduct these operations. In part, the answer was that the war was self-financed through exploitation of Congo's rich resources. The war effort was early dominated by the question of resource extraction.

Congo's wealth tarnished the reputations of the Ugandan army and its officers, as corruption permeated the army operation. Timber prices in Uganda fell sharply because Ugandan troops in the Congo had flooded the market with cheap wood smuggled from the war zone. The tentacles of corruption spread throughout the region as ports in Kenya and Tanzania served as points of transshipment for timber, coffee and minerals headed for Asian markets. Corruption was also found much closer to President Museveni himself, especially in the person of his half-brother Major-General Salim Saleh.

Uganda's joint support with Rwanda of the anti-Kabila coalition in the Democratic Republic of Congo unraveled in 1999. In 2000, each country massed troops on its respective borders and seemed near war. Charges of supporting and training hostile forces were made by both parties, but diplomacy prevailed. Confidence-building measures—like exchanging military inspection teams—were created in 2002, but tensions remain.

The terrorist attacks on New York and Washington in September 2001 helped to transform Uganda's relations with Sudan. The UN placed the LRA on a list of terrorist organizations and, eager to be counted among the antiterrorists, Sudan gave permission for the Ugandan army to pursue Joseph Kony's forces into Sudanese territory.

Using heavy artillery, the Uganda People's Democratic Army (UPDA) launched operation "Iron Fist" against the LRA's Sudanese bases in March 2002. UN humanitarian organizations lamented that any hostage children had probably died under the bombs of the Ugandan army. The rebels responded by multiplying their attacks against Ugandan civilians in the north using even more violent and vicious tactics. The LRA took hostages, kidnapped children to replace fallen rebels, raped women, and castrated men and left them to bleed to death. One goal was to terrify local inhabitants and keep them from providing the army with intelligence on rebel locations and movements, while another was to delegitimize the Museveni regime by proving the army's incapacity to protect local inhabitants.

Despite army press releases, the UPDA could not defeat the LRA. The rebels moved across borders, finding sanctuary in Sudan or the Democratic Republic of Congo. In June 2005, President Museveni promised to forgive Kony if he surrendered, and got no response. In October, the International Criminal Court issued arrest warrants for Kony and five senior aides, but Kony remains at large, despite occasional meetings with emissaries at his jungle hideout.

Conditions in Northern Uganda, probably the least developed area of the country, spiraled downward. To resident Acholi people driven to refugee camps by LRA depredations and government policy, the army seemed more predator than protector. The rains failed for several years in a row, and the land became dry, dusty, and cropless. Schools were deserted and market stalls emptied and abandoned. Granaries were empty and underfed cattle, the pride of northern pastoralists, no longer provided the milk and blood of traditional sustenance. In some areas, people were living on one bowl of boiled leaves a day. UN officials called it the world's worst forgotten humanitarian crisis.

Those displaced by LRA violence became dependent on food handouts because it was simply too dangerous to live in villages and farm the land—even if the rains came. Insecurity also created the phenomenon of "night commuters"; every night as many as 20,000 children walk miles from their villages to the relative safety of cities where they spend the night in public buildings or on the streets.

The most sustained peace efforts in 20 years of conflict were initiated by Salva Kiir's government of Southern Sudan in 2006. The proposal was different from all other attempts to negotiate an end to the conflict. For the first time, negotiations would take place outside Uganda—in the Southern Sudanese capital of Juba—and would be structured and presided over by a third-party mediator, Riek Machar, Kiir's vice president.

For both the LRA and Uganda, the timing was crucial. Costs of the war to Uganda totaled a staggering $1.7 billion over its course, and donors (who fund 40% of the Ugandan budget) had become increasingly critical of defense expenses. The LRA also faced an increasingly hostile regional and international environment. The ICC had issued warrants for the group's top leadership, and the UN Security Council had called for coordinated military action against it. With the signing of the Comprehensive Peace Agreement (CPA) between Khartoum and Juba, it had also ostensibly lost its principal supplier of arms and money.

Joseph Kony declared a unilateral ceasefire on August 4, 2006. The offer was matched on August 19, when Salva Kiir and President Museveni jointly announced the UPDF would halt operations against the LRA, if the rebels agreed to assemble at two designated assembly points. These ad hoc initiatives were formally confirmed when a Cessation of Hostilities Agreement (CHA) was signed on August 26. Confidence-building measures were implemented between the two antagonists. Kony was permitted to visit his mother in Uganda for the first time in 20 years, for example, and he and President Museveni spoke several times by telephone. A renewed presidential offer of amnesty and efforts to suspend the ICC warrants seemed not to speed negotiations. The rebel delegation, which was being paid a per diem of $70, found reason to complain about the Sudanese mediator and seemed to be shopping for a more

Fighting corruption with billboards *Photo by Pat Crowell*

Uganda

favorable venue. Tired of delay, President al-Bashir of Sudan announced in early January that he was prepared to create a joint military force to eliminate the LRA: "We do not want them. If we cannot find a peaceful solution to the LRA conflict, then we must pursue a military solution."

Shortly afterward the LRA announced their disengagement from the peace process, citing security concerns and demanding the talks' relocation to a neutral country and mediator. Discussions resumed, at Juba, near the end of April 2008, and seemed to lead to the prospects for a peace settlement. Joseph Kony, however, failed to turn up to sign a peace agreement in late 2008. This prompted a new offensive from Ugandan and Congolese forces, along with those of Southern Sudanese leader Salva Kiir. This prompted Kony to seek a new ceasefire, but the LRA continues its activities. The conflict is unresolved, though the Ugandan government may now be gaining the upper hand, beginning with a claim to have killed LRA senior commander Bok Abudema in early 2010.

The year 2011–2012 saw a surge of global awareness and action against the LRA and Kony. In July 2011, the US deployed troops to assist Uganda in fighting the LRA. Uganda captured LRA commander Caesar Achellam in the Central African Republic and claimed this as a big win in the fight against the LRA. On the global stage, the biggest change in awareness came with the film KONY 2012, produced by Invisible Children, Inc. This 30-minute video became a YouTube sensation and incited a social networking campaign that sought to raise awareness about Kony and to have him stopped and arrested. In the first 25 days of being posted to YouTube, the video had over 86 million views and over 16.6 million views on Vimeo (another video-sharing website). The video went viral especially with youth and one poll estimates that half of America's young adults watched the video. The video and organization got a number of prominent celebrities and politicians to support and promote the campaign to "Stop Kony." The video propelled the United States Senate to pass a resolution and send troops to support the African Union in its efforts to arrest Kony. The video drew strongly mixed reactions around the world. Some argued that it was powerful, necessary, and highlighted what was most important in mobilizing support while others thought the video oversimplified the issue, stretched the truth, and didn't lead to sustained action. It remains an open question how much tangible action the film generated. Invisible Children produced a follow up video "Kony 2012: Part II—Beyond Famous" to address some of the critiques and concerns of the first video and to provide greater detail on the complex situation of the LRA.

Cross-border strife also continues in eastern Democratic Republic of the Congo, where several rebel movements are competing with Congolese forces for control of remote territories. As of June 2013, the United Nations is taking an increasingly assertive stance in fighting the rebel groups, and it accuses Uganda of supporting one of the largest—the M23 (or March 23) movement, which captured the provincial of Goma in late 2012. In response to the UN accusations, Uganda has removed its troops from under UN command in peacekeeping operations elsewhere in Africa.

Hesitant Moves toward Multipartyism

In the midst of fighting campaigns against rebels, the Ugandan government slowly changed the parameters of the "movement system." A referendum in 2000 asked if the movement system should be maintained or the country should adopt a multiparty system of democracy. The campaign became personalized and was widely interpreted as a referendum for or against Yoweri Museveni. Sensing the mood of a country relatively satisfied with Museveni's tenure, the opposition decided to boycott the vote. More than 90% of those who voted chose to retain the movement system.

There was little interest in Uganda's presidential election scheduled for March 2001, until Kizza Besigye entered the race. Dr. Besigye was no ordinary challenger. He was one of the original NRA fighters and Museveni's personal physician during the long bush war; he had also served as a minister in Museveni's NRM government but had become disillusioned. Besigye criticized regime corruption and nepotism, as well as Uganda's involvement in the Congo war. He accused the president of becoming increasingly autocratic and of turning the ruling movement into a party intolerant of competition. The president and his supporters experienced a sense of betrayal, and the campaign became violent and ramified regionally, as the Ugandan government accused Rwanda of contributing large sums to the Besigye campaign. Dr. Besigye's wife, a member of parliament, added to heightened suspicion between the two countries by accusing the Museveni government of aiding the *Interahamwe*, one of Rwanda's greatest bêtes noires.

President Museveni won the election by a huge margin, receiving 69.3% of the vote. Besigye ran second with 27.8% of the vote, but refused to accept the results, charging fraud and intimidation. The victory may have been sweet for President Museveni, but the campaign damaged his reputation.

Equally damaging was the April 2001 report of a panel of experts to the UN Security Council on "Illegal Exploitation of Natural Resources and Other Forms of Wealth in the Democratic Republic of the Congo." The report named names very near the president himself, specifically singling out Salim Saleh and his wife Jovia Akandwanaho, as being "at the core of the illegal exploitation of natural resources in areas controlled by Uganda." The report said Museveni had "put himself in the position of accomplice" by choosing not to act when information on corrupt practices was brought to his attention. The government denied the charges, but the accumulation of wealth by the president's family became a major factor in a growing opposition to Museveni. Parliamentary elections in June 2001 provided some hint of discontent. Becausee there are no parties, candidates were either for or against the government, and Museveni was faced with the defeat of 12 cabinet ministers, though only two were replaced by individuals who actually opposed the government.

With the approach of presidential elections in 2006, there were pressures to return Uganda to multipartyism. President Museveni seized the opportunity to polish his image by becoming a born-again democrat. In late February 2003, Ugandans learned their president, long the advocate of "no-party democracy," had decided to allow parties after all. By the end of March, the ruling NRM announced concurrence, and Uganda's constitutional court declared unconstitutional those parts of the Political Parties and Organisations Act, which forbade political parties from carrying out their activities. The decision liberated parties and transformed Uganda's political space. By early 2004, 50 political parties had applied for registration in preparation for the 2006 elections. The first to apply for the new designation was the NRM, rechristened the National Resistance Movement—Organisation (NRMO).

Against a background of increasing insecurity in the northern provinces and increasing political tension in the run-up to the 2006 general elections, Museveni sought repeal of constitutional provisions limiting a president to two five-year terms. The amendment needed only a two-thirds majority vote in parliament, which was obligingly offered by the NRM-dominated legislature in July 2005.

As a sop to democratic sensitivities, the government scheduled a referendum shortly afterwards to return Uganda to multiparty politics. Voters were presented with the simple question: "Do you agree to open up political space to allow those who wish to join different organizations/parties to do so to compete for political power?" Museveni traversed the country campaigning for a "Yes" vote, but six opposition parties denounced it as a

Uganda

democratic smokescreen and called for a boycott. They claimed Museveni had only accepted the referendum to distract people from the constitutional amendment designed, as they put it, to make him "president for life." Partly due to the boycott, less than 30% of eligible voters participated, but 92.5% of those agreed to return the country to multiparty competitive elections in 2006.

Donors became increasingly skeptical of the regime's democratic intentions. The United Kingdom cancelled millions in aid to Uganda, saying the country had not done enough to establish fair multiparty politics. Other European donors—Netherlands, Sweden, and Norway—also withheld or cut back their contributions. U.S. President George Bush reportedly urged Museveni to give up third-term plans, but the latter was not dissuaded.

Kizza Besigye returned to Uganda after four years of self-imposed exile to be the presidential candidate of the Forum for Democratic Change (FDC). In less than a month he was charged with treason, terrorism and rape, arrested, denied bail, and jailed. Antigovernment riots convulsed the capital, and donors cut off more funding. Uganda's attorney-general urged the electoral commission to deny Besigye's presidential candidacy, arguing his nomination would be "tainted." In early January 2006, however, Uganda's High Court released Besigye on bail and allowed him to campaign. Human Rights Watch described the campaign as "marred by intimidation of the opposition, military interference in the courts and bias in campaign funding and media coverage." EU observers criticized the "lack of a level playing field," but Uganda's Supreme Court threw out Dr. Besigye's petition to nullify election results based on allegations of massive malpractice.

Museveni won the 2006 elections with 59% of the vote and Kizza Besigye took 37%, on voter turnout of 65%. President Museveni's total vote was 10% lower than his 2001 performance; not unexpectedly, he did poorly in the northern regions and was soundly defeated in Kampala. In legislative elections the voters sent 80 MPs to defeat, including 17 who held ministerial portfolios. The NRM continued to dominate the legislature, with 190 seats in the 304-member body; the delegation from Besigye's FDC took a distant second place with 35 seats. The UPC won 13 seats and the DP nine; two smaller parties elected a single representative each and 37 members of the new parliament were elected as independents. First Lady Janet Museveni became an MP. Though losing the presidential race, candidate Besigye's woes were partially mitigated in March when a judge declared him innocent of the rape charge, calling the prosecution case "crude and amateurish."

Murchison Falls
Photo by Virginia Grady

The battle between Museveni and Besigye dominated Ugandan electoral politics again in the lead up to the 2011 elections, which ended with a similar result: Museveni won the election with 68% of the vote and Besigye took 26%. The challenger rejected the results and claimed fraud; international observers too found irregularities in the poll, but it was unclear if these affected the overall result. The NRM took 263 of 365 seats in the legislature, and the FDC 34, with the remainder going to smaller parties and a total of 43 independents. In both the presidential and legislative elections, the official results represented an increased vote for Museveni and the NRM relative to 2006.

In the meantime, Uganda suffered a resurgence in conflict and terror. Over the year, the ADF/NALU rebel groups in eastern DR Congo renewed their activity. While this primarily affected the DRC, it led Uganda to tighten border security. More frightening for Ugandans was the attack at a restaurant in Kampala during the World Cup final that killed 74 people and wounded many more. The Islamist group al-Shabab (from Somalia) claimed responsibility. This incident was followed by an attack on a bus from Kenya to Uganda in December that killed three people.

Political unrest ensued after the election as Besigye called upon Museveni opponents to demonstrate peacefully and engage in a "walk to work" protest the high cost of living and the regime's corruption. Against the backdrop of the Arab Spring in which many authoritarian regimes fell, the protests in Uganda quickly spread across Kampala, resulting in a handful of deaths and dozens of injuries. Besigye himself was arrested a total of four times and hospitalized after being attacked and pepper sprayed. While the protests seemed to subside by June 2011, Uganda still has not created a genuine multiparty system. In November 2013, Kampala mayor and prominent Democratic Party member Erias Lukwago was removed from office after the Kampala council found him guilty of "incompetence and abuse of office." The Democratic Party accused the NRM government of being behind this decision and it was not till the High Court of Kampala appealed the decision in March 2014 that Lukwago was able to return to office.

CONTEMPORARY THEMES

Social Issues

Uganda's HIV/AIDS program has come to be viewed as a model for states affected by the pandemic. A decade ago, estimates were that more than 18% of Ugandan adults were living with HIV/AIDS, which led to large number of AIDS orphans. The problem was recognized early, and the government made decisive early steps to manage the epidemic. Museveni appointed a bishop as one of the leaders of the Uganda AIDS Commission, but all the major sectarian communities participated. For its part, the Islamic Medical Association of Uganda worked with Imams to incorporate HIV/AIDS prevention information into their spiritual teachings. Openness of discussion and commitment to education also characterized the country's approach to AIDS. This was propelled by the public announcement and death from AIDS of Uganda's most famous popular singer, Philly Lutaaya in the late 1980s.

The Uganda AIDS program was reputed to be one of the most aggressive in Africa, featuring education and testing, counseling, and condoms. The most striking feature of Uganda's success is the drastic reduction in multiple partnering by Ugandan adults. Among women aged 15 and above, the number reporting multiple sexual partners fell from 18.4% in 1989 to 2.5% in 2000. Studies of the use of the drug nevirapine in Uganda showed the transmission of HIV from mother to child was reduced to about 13%. Overall, the HIV/AIDS prevalence rate in adults declined significantly, from estimates of 18.5% in the early 1990s to 4.1% in 2003, though it has since increased again to about 6.5% (2009). Over one million people are estimated to be living with HIV/AIDS and Uganda also has over a million AIDS orphans. The average life expectancy is just 53 years.

Uganda

While earning a reputation for progressive action on HIV/AIDS, Uganda has earned the opposite reputation for its treatment of homosexuals. Homosexuality is illegal. In late 2010, the Kampala newspaper "The Rolling Stone" made a very public exposé featuring names and pictures of homosexual men, under the headline "Hang Them." The activist David Kato was featured on the list and was beaten to death soon thereafter. In February 2014, President Museveni signed a bill making homosexuality punishable by life in prison. Similar to "the *Rolling Stone*" incident, the tabloid "Red Pepper" responded to this bill by publishing a list of Uganda's 200 most prominent gays. In response to this bill, the World Bank postponed a $90 million loan intended to improve Ugandan health services.

Economic Growth and Foreign Investment

Uganda was one of the poorest and most economically battered countries in the world in 1986, as social services had collapsed, and infrastructure had crumbled. Under Museveni, Uganda liberalized its economy and became the poster child of international lending agencies: Real GDP growth has been consistently high, averaging nearly 7% for the decade after 1995 and reaching over 10% in 2006, over 8% in 2007 and 2008, and even 7% in the midst of the world economic crisis in 2009. Economic growth is also reduced on a per capita basis by the effects of population growth, estimated at over 3% a year.

Uganda's economy is agriculture-based. The sector employs over 80% of the work force and contributes about a third of GDP. Coffee has traditionally been the country's biggest export earner. In the 1990s Uganda exported as much as four million bags of coffee, which accounted for 65% of its export income, but coffee declined around 2000 as plantations in Asia produced a glut on international markets and severely reduced prices. Coffee's decline was hastened by crop disease, aging trees, poor crop management, poor soil fertility, and poor post-harvest handling practices, and it was estimated that by the mid-2000s some 60% of coffee farmers had abandoned coffee production for crops with better returns.

Significant efforts have been made to diversify the economy, once almost totally reliant on coffee exports. Tea remains important, though struggling to regain its former status. By 1991, after years of horrific governing, Uganda produced only about a third of the tea it produced in 1972. Since then, strenuous efforts have been made to reclaim 42,000 acres that had returned to bush. Tea is now Uganda's third leading export, after coffee and fish. The government is seeking to further boost tea production, but marketing conditions are extremely difficult, and the high cost of Ugandan electricity and transportation are challenges; an erratic energy supply also discouraged investors from opening new areas for tea production. Together, coffee and tea accounted for about 22% of exports in 2010.

Fishing and fish processing have increasing importance among Uganda's exports (at about 8% in 2010), especially since the EU lifted its ban (because of sanitation and pesticide concerns) on imports in 2000. Yet the fishing industry still faces many challenges. Pesticide poisoning of lakes is related to a longer-range but potentially even more damaging problem: the water hyacinth. Probably brought in by Belgians as an ornamental plant, the hyacinth has no known natural predators and grows with amazing rapidity. The whole of Lake Victoria, the world's second largest freshwater lake, is threatened. Once colonized, the plant impedes fishing boats and kills off fish stocks.

Construction of a hydroelectric dam and 250-MW power station at Bujagali Falls, near the source of the Nile River is underway after delays. It was scheduled to begin in mid-2006, but the project was mired in corruption and controversy from its inception. Environmentalists argued against the dam, arguing the site supports the growing whitewater tourism industry and long term is a serious "hydrological risk," given the potential for serious drought due to global climate change. Supporters of the project argued that energy shortages constrained social and economic growth. The International Finance Corporation estimated that energy shortages and blackouts cut GDP growth by 1% in the 2005–2006 financial year. By increasing energy output, Bujagali would contribute to industrialization and economic growth. Finally, in April 2007 the World Bank approved a package of $360 million in loans and guarantees for the project.

One area of potential growth should be mentioned: oil. In early April 2003, the Canadian firm, Heritage Oil, announced that its explorations suggested Uganda had a potential oil reserve of "several billion barrels." Two wells were drilled, and oil was encountered. In early March 2007, the company it had a cumulative flow rate of 13,893 barrels of oil per day (bbl/d) from one of its wells in Western Uganda. In early 2010, Tullow Oil bought Heritage Oil's assets in Uganda. In February 2014, several oil companies (the British firm Tullow Oil, the French company Total SA, and the Chinese CNOOC Ltd.) signed a deal with the Ugandan government for the construction of an oil refinery and pipeline. Uganda can now expect nearly $10 billion in investment, $3 billion a year from oil by 2015 as well as the ability to begin exporting crude oil in 2017.

Having won election on six occasions since 1986 and ruled for 38 years, President Musevni has promoted his son, Muhoozi Kainerugaba, as army chief in an apparent move to groom him for ultimate rise to the presidency with elections scheduled for 2026. The Constitutional Court of Uganda has upheld a draconian Anti-Homosexuality Law that calls for life imprisonment and even execution for violators, the passage of which in 2023 led the World Bank to terminate loans to the country.

With the country scheduled to hold general elections in January 2026, the seventh since President Yoweri Musevni came to power in 1986, as in previous polls, political repression is on the rise and spilling over into neighboring countries. Opposition politician Kizza Besigye and his aide Obeid Lutale were abducted in Nairobi, Kenya in November 2024, appearing four days later in Kampala arraigned in a military court on security charges. Rendered to Uganda in clear violation of international laws prohibiting extraordinary rendition and due process, the two civilians faced military justice. Intended to silence dissenting voices, these actions have had the opposite effect, sparking a national debate on human rights and the proper role of the military. Widely seen as a potential successor to his aging father, General Muhoozi Kainerugaba heads a political pressure group, the Patriotic League of Uganda (PLU). This is in violation of prohibitions against serving military officers becoming involved in partisan politics. Since 2016, Uganda's Supreme Court has delayed ruling on a case, brought by Michael Kabaziguruka, a former member of parliament accused of treason, that challenged the trial of civilians before military courts arguing his trial in a military tribunal violated fair trial rights and that as a civilian, he was not subject to military law. In January 2025, the Supreme Court finally ruled that trying civilians in military courts is unconstitutional, ordering that all ongoing or pending criminal trials involving civilians must immediately stop and be transferred to ordinary courts. But President Museveni and his son have vowed to continue using military courts in civilian trials. The case of Besigye has now become a litmus test for Uganda's military justice system ahead of the 2026 elections while several supporters of the National Unity Platform (NUP), led by Robert Kyagulanyi, have been convicted by military courts for various offenses. Over 1,000 civilians have been prosecuted in Uganda's military courts since 2002 for such offenses as murder and armed robbery. Uganda has also deployed special forces in South Sudan as fears grow that its northern neighbor could descend into civil war. The building tension in South Sudan carries the fear for Uganda that a full-blown war could send refugees across the border and create

Uganda

further regional instability. Uganda has also sent troops across its eastern border into the Democratic Republic of the Congo in recent months, where rebel groups backed by Rwanda are fighting for control of eastern regions. On the domestic front, Uganda has officially declared the end of its latest outbreak of Ebola after cases emerged in the capital, Kampala in January 2025. Ebola infections are frequent in Uganda, which has many tropical forests that are natural reservoirs for the virus. The current strain has no approved vaccine.

FUTURE CONSIDERATIONS

Uganda's economic development has been impressive in recent years. Growth rates have been in the range of 8% or higher for many years, placing the country near the top of African charts for economic performance in the 2000s after decades of crisis and decline. The country is still dependent on international prices for agricultural products and on external aid, though foreign investment in the oil industry is changing the composition of the economy.

Uganda retains political stability, albeit precariously, which should facilitate investment in productive enterprise and in human capital over the long term. Diminishing civil strife and containing regional conflict are high-priority issues in Uganda. The conflict with the LRA remains unresolved and the bombings in Kampala in 2010 by the Somali Islamist militant group al-Shabab (an al-Qaeda-linked group) recalled the threat of regional terror. Uganda's progress may be overshadowed by violent conflict if there is further escalation on any of a number of fronts.

Finally, the political system remains problematic, albeit preferable to the chaos seen before 1985. The Museveni regime has changed its spots over the years with considerable success. In its latest incarnation, it is allowing a degree of multiparty competition yet harassing the main opposition, all while delivering successful economic performance and retaining donor support. The 2011 elections reflected the weakness of the opposition, and despite the plausible claims of fraud and disenfranchisement, Museveni and the NRM do indeed remain relatively popular among many Ugandans. However, the government's increasingly intolerant stance on the issue of homosexuality has led to international condemnation of the Museveni administration. Absent a major conflagration in the region that could come from an escalation of fighting in neighboring countries, Uganda looks likely to continue rather impressive economic growth with less-than-democratic governance. This may prove to be a relatively stable equilibrium for the country over the next several years.

INDIAN OCEAN ISLAND NATIONS

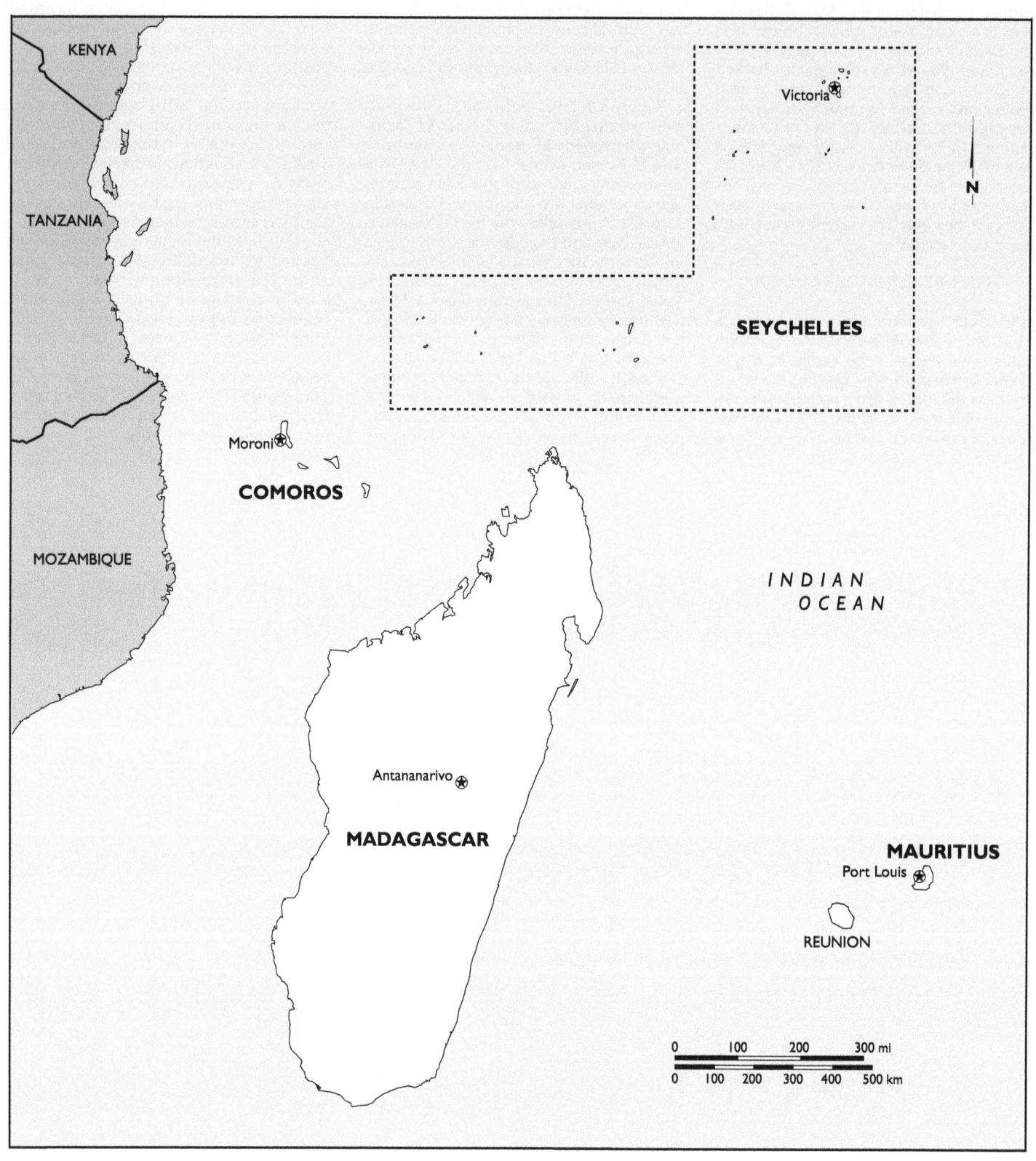

The Union of the Comoros

The Grande Mosque, Moroni ©IRIN

BASIC FACTS

Area: 2,235 sq. km.
Population: 888,378 (June 2023 est.)
Capital City: Moroni (on Grande Comore)
Government Type: Federal Presidential Republic
Official Languages: Arabic, French
Other Principal Languages: Comorian or Shikomoro (a blend of Swahili and Arabic).
Ethnic Groups: Antalote, Cafre, Makoa, Oimatsaha, Sakalava
Principal Religions: Sunni Muslim 98%, Roman Catholic 2%
Former Colonial Status: French Colony (to 1975)
Independence Date: July 6, 1975 (from France)
GDP Per Capita (IMF 2023, est.): $1,360 (nominal), $3,463 (PPP)
Gini index: 45.3 (2014)
Currency: Comorian franc, $US 1 = 446 francs (May 2023)
Inflation Rate: 5% (2022 est.)
Chief Commercial Products: Vanilla, ylang-ylang, cloves, perfume oil, copra, fishing, and forestry
Foreign Direct Investments (FDI) net inflows: 14,028,710
Literacy Rate: 62% (CIA 2021)
Life Expectancy: 67 (CIA 2023 est.)
Head of State: President Azali Assoumani (since May 26, 2016)
Head of Government: President Azali Assoumani (since May 26, 2016)

LAND AND PEOPLE

The Comoros group consists of three mountainous islands lying between Tanzania and the northern coast of Madagascar: Grand Comore (also known as Njazidja), Anjouan (Nzwani), and Mohéli (Mwali). Mayotte, a fourth island with a substantial Christian minority, opposed joining the other three and, although claimed by the Union, remains a dependency of France; in March 2009 referendum, Mayotte voted to be a French overseas department.

The people of the Comoros are a blend of Arab, African, and Indian Ocean heritage. They speak Comorian, which is closely related to the Swahili of East Africa but written in Arabic script. The language is enriched with borrowings from the many cultures that have made contact with the islands. Indian, Persian, Arabic, Portuguese, English, and French words have all been added to the basic African vocabulary. Given island isolation, there are four distinct dialects of Comorian spoken, each specific to one of the four islands.

The island of Grand Comore and its capital, Moroni, are dominated by the Karthala, one of the world's largest active volcanoes that erupted as recently as April

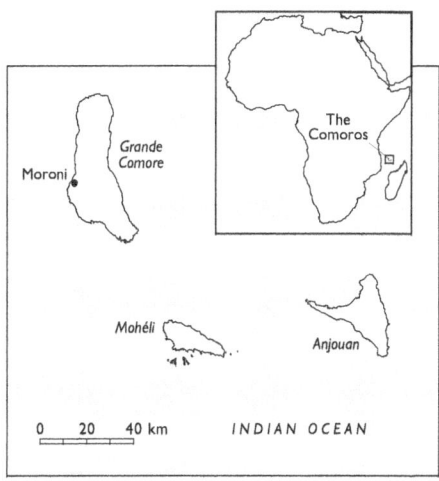

Comoros

Former President Ahmed Abdallah Mohamed Sambi

2005. Anjouan (also known as Nzwani) has been called the "pearl" of the Indian Ocean, a beautiful island with forested hillsides and rivers tumbling to the sea. It is essentially a triangle with approximately 31 miles on each side and a total area of 164 square miles. It is the most densely populated island in the Comoro archipelago, though most residents live in small communities found throughout the island. The major towns are Mutsamudu on the western side, the present capital, and Domoni on the eastern side, an ancient capital and seaport. Anjouan. Its volcanic peak, Mount Ntingi, 1,575 meters high, is covered with vegetation, including large ferns, tropical mahoganies, and wild orchids, in contrast with the three points of the triangle, which have been cultivated for centuries. Anjouan is the leading producer of essential oils including ylang-ylang, jasmine, cassis, basilic, palmarosa, and orange flower.

The dominant religion in the islands is Islam, and islanders are predominantly Sunni Muslims. Traditional Islam tended to incorporate local African belief and customs, like a belief in malevolent djinns and the importance of lavish weddings to secure social status. Surviving African traditions can also be detected in the property rights Comorian women enjoy. Islamic law tends to recognize only male ownership and inheritance of land, but in the Comoros, certain property, called *magnahouli*, is controlled by women and inherited through the female line, suggesting a surviving African matriarchal tradition.

Comorian marriages, especially among social elites, are prominent cultural events. Marriages are often prearranged between an older man and a younger woman and are celebrated by grand ceremonies. Before the marriage the groom is expected to provide a dowry for his bride, including expensive clothing, gold, and jewelry, which she is entitled to keep if they divorce. As proof of his status, the groom must also pay for a multi-day party to which the entire village and friends and relatives from around the country are invited; at the wedding, the groom is then allowed to wear a special sash signifying his status as a grand noble. Marriage tends to be matrilocal—the husband moves into the home of his wife—and sometimes polygynous. The practice reflects the survival of African matrilineal traditions and the practice of merchant traders who established families in more than one community.

In a deeply conservative Muslim society, women dress modestly, favoring colorful saris, but do not cover their faces. Against the fierce Comorian sun, women protect themselves with a yellowish facial cream, called *m'sidzanou*. Made of ground sandalwood and perfumed oils like ylang-ylang or jasmine, it is applied to the face as either a full mask or in a dappled pattern.

HISTORY TO PRESENT DAY

For early history, see *Historical Background* and *The Colonial Period: The French*.

After WWII, the islands became Overseas French Territories and were represented in the French National Assembly. Agreement was reached in 1973 to grant independence in 1978, but events moved more quickly. A referendum on December 22, 1974, saw over 99% of Comorians on the three islands of Grand Comore, Anjouan, and Mohéli vote for independence, while two-thirds of those on Mayotte (the only island that is majority Christian) voted to remain part of France. On July 6, 1975, the Comorian parliament declared unilateral independence. Deputies from Mayotte abstained from this vote, and Mayotte remains under French jurisdiction to this day.

The first president of the independent country, Ahmed Abdallah, lasted all of a month in his first term in the post before being overthrown in a military coup. The military in turn lost power to a revolutionary movement. The revolution was headed by the Communist-inspired Ali Soilih, but the firepower came from white mercenaries; this was the first incident in a theme of mercenary action that would play out multiple times over the subsequent years. Indeed, when Ahmed Abdallah reclaimed power from Soilih in 1978, it was with the support of the notorious French mercenary Bob Denard and his troops.

President Abdallah ruled for over a decade until 1989, surviving a string of coup attempts in large part because Bob Denard remained an important power player supporting and protecting the president behind the scenes. The French government seemed to support Denard's actions, at least tacitly, at this stage. (Denard, in the meantime, became a major businessman in Comoros.) Abdallah established a single-party state under the Comorian Union for Progress and was elected to the presidency unopposed in 1978 and again in 1984. His rule and his life came to an end only after he attempted to banish Denard from the islands. Abdallah was assassinated in a coup; while details are still murky, it came to be accepted that Denard played a major role.

Said Mohamed Johar seized the presidency and remained there from 1989 to 1995, when Denard attempted another coup by invading the island with about 30 men on inflatable boats. Johar was deposed, but on this occasion, the French government mounted a military operation and arrested Denard.

A string of acting and interim presidents followed the 1995 coup until the government of President Mohamed Taki Abdoulkarim, a deeply religious Sunni Muslim, was elected in 1996 following a mercenary-led coup that deposed President Djohar Said Mohamed. He went on to establish Islamic (*sharia*) law, announcing the death penalty, restrictions on the consumption of alcohol, and censuring women who wore mini skirts. In October 1996, Taki destabilized the Comoros by amending the constitution to strengthen the powers of the presidency and sharply erode the powers of individual islands. The islands of Anjouan and Mohéli grew increasingly frustrated: Taki's government directed little development money to these islands and unemployment rose to an incredible 90%. Islanders also thought themselves unfairly taxed in indirect ways. They had, for example, to make an expensive trip across the 50-mile straits to the capital to obtain any official documents. And always there was the nearby example of Mayotte.

Ex-President Azali Assoumani

Comoros

By remaining with France, the citizens of Mayotte enjoyed free education, health benefits and a minimum wage.

Rejected by France when reunion with the former colonial power was proposed, Anjouan and Mohéli declared unilateral independence in August 1997. A February 1998 referendum adopted a new independent constitution, but economic reality argued against independence. Anjouan and Mohéli have few exports, poor economies, and population problems; there was little basis for independent economies.

President Taki died suddenly of natural causes in November 1998 as the federation faced the prospect of secession, but the end result was that the three islands agreed to attend a reconciliation conference to be held in Madagascar in April 1999. In an effort to create a government of national unity, Tadjiddine Ben Said Massounde, the elderly president of the Comoros high court, was persuaded to accept an interim presidency and the opposition leader Abbas Djoussouf was appointed prime minister.

The Madagascar conference produced agreement on the tentative outlines of a new state that would give the islands greater autonomy. Each would have its local executive and parliament after a one-year transition. The central government would preside over defense, foreign affairs, the currency, and higher education and research. The federal presidency, elected by the National Assembly, would be rotated between the three islands every three years.

Riots broke out on Grand Comore when the details of the agreement were announced, and the government sent in heavily armed troops to restore order, whereupon the Comorian army staged the nation's 18th *coup d'état*. The army commander, Colonel Azali Assoumani, told his countrymen that the army had acted to insure "the survival of our nation and state," and that the army would remain in power for just a year. There was no return to civilian government in April 2000, however, and Anjouan continued its separatist push under Lt. Col. Said Abeid, who organized a series of farcical "elections" to legitimize Anjouan independence.

Colonels Azali and Abeid met in August 2000, and after a national reconciliation forum met in February 2001, a new constitution was approved by referendum in December 2001. According to the new charter, the islands would each elect their own president and be governed as "autonomous entities freely managing their own affairs." The Union of the Comoros would have a mandate limited to affairs of religion and nationality, currency, foreign, and defense policy. Elected every four years, the Union presidency would effectively rotate among the three islands, as each island would take turns holding a primary to nominate its top three candidates for the national election.

Elections in March and April 2002 began to implement the new dispensation, and Colonel Azali himself won the Union presidency, but voters on Grande Comore rejected their new constitution in a March referendum, forcing revision and delay of presidential elections there. After ratifying a revised constitution, Grande Comore chose former opposition MP Abdou Soule Elbak as its president. Tensions and mutual recriminations between the two presidents—island and federal—pushed Grande Comore near the brink of chaos.

Elbak called for equal control over Grande Comore's financial sector, pitting his government against the Union government and putting the business community in an administrative quandary. In early 2003 businesses received separate mailings from the two governments' finance ministries. Both presented themselves as the appropriate authority for the collection of fees, taxes, and licenses. Many businesses refused to become an arbiter between contending regimes and announced a freeze on tax payments until the conflict was resolved.

Diplomatic efforts by South Africa and the African Union produced an agreement on control of security forces and tax collection in August 2003. Island presidents would administer the police forces (the gendarmerie) stationed on their islands, while the Union president would control the country's army. A further reconciliation accord was signed in December 2003, defining the formula for sharing customs revenues. Twenty-eight percent would go to the Union; 32.5% to Grand Comore; 30.5% for Anjouan, and 9% for Moheli. This paved the way for legislative elections in early 2004.

Elections for local assemblies on each of the country's three islands in March 2004 were a huge victory for the supporters of island autonomy; they similarly won April elections to the federal assembly, taking 12 of 18 elected seats.

With a tenuous degree of institutional stability established, Azali focused on the Union's desperate economic situation, seeking to gain access to credit from international lenders, and especially France. Relations between Comoros and France remained chilly given Comoros' continued claims of control over the island of Mayotte, but a thaw occurred in January 2005 when French President Jacques Chirac received Azali Assoumani on an official state visit. It was increasingly in France's interest to restore aid and kick-start development plans, as well-off Mayotte was experiencing significantly increased illegal migration from the impoverished Comoros. In December 2005, France contributed 40% of the total $280 million pledged to assist development, conditional on the success of the Union's elections to the rotating presidency in 2006.

For the 2006 election, it was Anjouan's turn (per the agreement reached in 2001) to nominate the three candidates for the Union presidency. In the Anjouan primary election, Ahmed Abdallah Mohamed Sambi, a Sunni cleric and founding member of the Islamic National Front for Justice party, won 24% of the votes cast, while vice president of the federal National Assembly Mohamed Djanffari took second place with 13% of the votes and Abderemane Ibrahim Halidi, a former prime minister supported by President Azali, polled over 10%.

Ylang-Ylang flower

Photo by Powell Harrison

Comoros

Among these three, the Comorian population opted for the islands' leading Islamist, Ahmed Abdallah Sambi, to lead them for the next four years. Educated in Saudi Arabia and Iran, Sambi had long been known as "The Ayatollah." A familiar figure on the islands, Sambi had actively participated in public demonstrations against Israel, the war in Bosnia, and any reduction of taxes on alcohol. During his campaign, he repeatedly told audiences he intended to show "the true face" of Islam. His campaign was reportedly financed with Iranian money. At age 48, and a shrewd businessman, Sambi showed pragmatism, saying in an *Agence France Presse* interview he said he believed in an Islamic regime, but the Comorian economic situation did not permit it "for the moment."

Federalism in the Union continues to create tensions and potential for violence. In 2007, Anjouan selected Mohamed Bacar as the island's president. Bacar then held local elections in defiance of the central government, and these were almost certainly fraudulent. The center demanded Bacar re-run the elections or step down, and then blockaded the island. In 2008, the central government, backed by African Union troops, ultimately invaded the island, sending Bacar fleeing.

In 2009, Comorian voters voted nearly 94% in favor of a constitutional referendum that somewhat strengthened the central government and weakened island autonomy. The vote extending the union's presidential term to five years from four, eliminated certain autonomy provisions and established Governors instead of Presidents for each island; while Governors would still be elected, the elections would be simultaneous with national elections.

During 2010 and 2011, the Comoros managed what long seemed unlikely: it held a presidential election that looked likely to result in another peaceful transition of power from a sitting president to his successor. In this case, Sambi passed the reins to Ikililou Dhoinine. On the occasion of the 2010 election, the island of Mohéli (the least populous by far) had the right to nominate the three candidates. Dhoinine led after the first-round primary on Mohéli with 28% of the vote and took 61% in the national election, beating out Mohamed Said Fazul and Abdou Djabir.

Beginning April 20, 2012, and continuing through May of that year, Comoros experienced constant torrential rain causing flash floods and landslides. A state of emergency was declared as more than 50,000 people have been affected and over 9,000 people were displaced. The United Nations, African Union, Red Crescent, aid organizations, and countries have been providing aid relief efforts.

CONTEMPORARY THEMES

The Comoros islands are arguably caught in a poverty spiral. GDP has grown by under 2% for most of the past decade, which means a declining standard of living for a population that was growing even faster at about 2.4% annually. Endemic political instability is exacerbated by the government's regular revenue shortfall and foreign investors have shied away. Economic growth in 2011 was 2%, and the IMF estimates that Comoros' economy will grow by 2.5% in 2012 if the government continues to reform, citing "easing political tensions". This would mean that real GDP growth would (barely) exceed the rate of population growth. Meanwhile, Comoros has been receiving increasing amounts of aid from a number of Islamic countries, especially the United Arab Emirates and Kuwait.

External debt has remained a problem, but debt relief from multilateral lenders since 2009 should improve the economic outlook. The IMF, World Bank, and African Development Bank together are providing nearly $150 million in debt relief in response to economic reforms, which will dramatically reduce a debt total estimated at $280 million in debt (2007) that amounted to about 70% of the country's total GDP. Conditions involve greater control of budget deficits, including objectives for a ceiling on the public payroll and privatizations of government businesses.

The Comorian export economy is based on vanilla, cloves, and ylang-ylang, an essence popular in perfume making. Production of processed vanilla has been declining, a change attributed to aging vines, bad weather, and farmers discouraged by previous poor sales. Prices paid to vanilla farmers have also been volatile, dropping from $300/kg in 2003 to less than $50/kg in 2005. In 2006, the value of vanilla exports fell by half, driving even more producers out of the market. With world market prices and demand for cloves remaining high, Comorian clove farmers reported increases in volume and value in 2006, when the spice accounted for 66% of Comoros exports in 2006. The Comoros have long been the world's leading producer of ylang-ylang. Production is localized on Anjouan Island. Indeed, it was the island's feeling that it was not being given its fair share of ylang-ylang revenues that initially spurred its secession efforts.

The traditionally open and tolerant version of Comorian Islam is under intense pressure with the rise of Islamic fundamentalism, introduced mainly by young Comorians who have studied abroad. Lacking funds or blocked by immigration laws from studying in France, many seeking higher education were recruited by Islamic centers in Sudan and Saudi Arabia where Wahhabite fundamentalism prevailed. Comoros' chronic poverty and instability proved fertile recruiting grounds for the fundamentalists. One prominent recruit was Fazul Abdullah Mohammed, who became the leader of al Qaeda in East Africa until he was killed by government forces in Somalia on June 11, 2011. He was charged by the U.S. in the 1998 terror attacks on its embassies in Nairobi, Kenya, and Dar es Salaam Tanzania and a 2002 attack on a resort hotel in Kenya.

With the re-election of President Assoumani to a fourth term in January 2024, protests broke out among opposition groups in the capital city of Moroni that were met with tear gas fired by army troops as the former president, Ahmed Abdallah Sami (2006–2011), was convicted of "treason" for allegedly selling passports to the Bidoon people, an Arab and stateless minority. Economically, the island nation continues to suffer from grinding poverty with exports of commodities subject to wild price swings.

Located in waters serving as a major migration route for human trafficking, capsizing of overloaded boats are a frequent problem with thousands of people losing their lives, including women and children. In November 2024, traffickers deliberately capsized their boat between the Comoros island of Anjouan and the French island of Mayotte, with local fishermen rescuing five survivors out of 30 occupants. On the domestic political front, an overnight curfew was imposed after violent protests against President Azali Assoumani's re-election in January 2024 rocked the archipelago. Assoumani won a fourth five-year term with 62.97 percent of the vote after the country's electoral body declared him the winner against five opponents.

FUTURE CONSIDERATIONS

Political tensions between the Union and its member islands, arising from basic disagreement over the distribution of powers, are the central political dilemma in this small federation. The events came to a head in March 2008 when Comorian and African Union troops reinvaded Anjouan to quell a rebellion led by the separatist Mohamed Bacar. While the success of the mission to stop Bacar seemed to herald possible stability, the underlying conflict is not resolved. The status of the island of Mayotte is also the source of some tension. In a March 2009 referendum, the island voted to become a French overseas department by 2011. The Comorian government maintained that the result was "null and void," but the result has gone into effect and Mayotte is now considered a territory of France.

Comoros

Comoros has a troubled political history, with much instability and many coups (as highlighted by the role of the French mercenary Bob Denard). However, President Sambi's rule was comparatively stable and Ikililou Dhoinine's mandate is off to an uneventful start. There is some limited degree of political liberty on the islands now, but the simmering tension between the islands themselves is the dominant political story for the foreseeable future. Meanwhile, the economy is generally stagnant and dependent upon international prices for a handful of selected export commodities. Unless there is a considerable change in foreign investment, the future prospects for growth and development in Comoros are meager.

The Republic of Madagascar

BASIC FACTS

Area: 587,041 sq. km. = 226,658 sq. mi. (somewhat smaller than Texas)
Population: 28,812,195 (June 2023 est.)
Capital City: Antananarivo
Government Type: Semi-Presidential Republic
Neighboring Countries: 300 miles east of Mozambique
Official Language: French and Malagasy
Other Principal Languages: English
Ethnic Groups: Malayo-Indonesian (Merina and related Betsileo), Cotiers (mixed African, Malayo-Indonesian, and Arab ancestry—Betsimisaraka, Tsimihety, Antaisaka, Sakalava), French, Indian, Creole, Comorian
Principal Religions: Indigenous beliefs 52%, Christian 41%, Muslim 7%
Former Colonial Status: French Protectorate (1894–1960)
Independence Date: June 26, 1960.
GDP Per Capita (IMF 2023 est.): $536 (nominal), $1,916 (PPP)
Gini Index: 42.6 (World Bank 2012)
Currency: Malagasy Ariary, 1 USD = 4,415 Ariary (May 2023)
Inflation rate: 8.8% (2022 est.)
Chief commercial products: coffee, vanilla, sugarcane, cloves, cocoa, rice, cassava (tapioca), beans, bananas, peanuts; livestock products; meat processing, seafood, soap, breweries, tanneries, sugar, textiles, glassware, cement, automobile assembly plant, paper, petroleum, tourism
Foreign Direct Investments (FDI) net inflows: 350,695,431
Literacy Rate: 77.3% (CIA 2021)
Life Expectancy: 68.47 years (CIA 2023 est.)
Head of State: President Andry Rajoelina (since January 24, 2019)
Head of Government: Prime Minister Christian Ntsay (since June 6, 2018)

LAND AND PEOPLE

The Republic of Madagascar, the fourth-largest island in the world, is situated in the Indian Ocean off the southeastern part of Africa. The island split from the African continent 165 million years ago and has been isolated from the mainland by deep water for some 88 million years. As a consequence, 100 unique terrestrial mammal species are found on the island.

The west coast, facing the Mozambique Channel, is a low, tropically wet and dry region, particularly in the extreme south. A series of broad plateaus rise from the coast to increasing heights of 2,300 to 4,500 feet. More abundant rainfall occurs here, and the altitude tempers the otherwise hot climate. Almost daily rains fall during the summer and the weather from May to October is cooler when temperatures in the higher altitudes drop as low as the freezing point. Several mountain ranges rise above this tableland, including Mount Tsaratanana, which rises to 9,450 feet. The eastern shore is a hot, humid, rainy and narrow strip between the sea and the steep sides of the mountains.

Despite the diversity heritages of the people of the island, nearly all speak or understand the language called Malagasy, which—like the Malagasy people themselves—is a synthesis of Indonesian, Polynesian, African, Arab, and European influences. As in most preliterate cultures, traditional Malagasy oratory is replete with the unhurried telling of ancestral proverbs, metaphors, and riddles, often in a participatory dialogue of call and response. The last vowel in Malagasy names is not pronounced and its communication that is neither fast nor direct. For proponents of this oral tradition, the advent of cell phones and texting is a concern, with its emphasis on brevity, speed, and choppy communication that is not conducive to absorbing ancestral wisdom.

Although about 40% of the people are

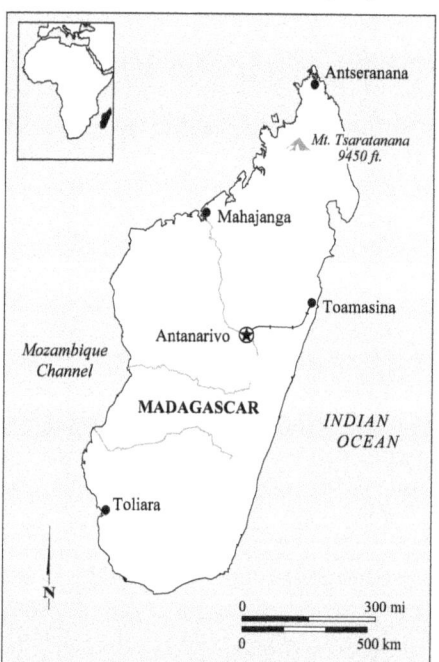

Christian, most have joined traditional beliefs with ancestor worship of Hindu origin—a religious combination of East and West. During the *Famadihana* ceremony, for example, the dead are exhumed and feted as guests just returned from an extended absence. They are entertained, danced with, regaled with stories of recent family events, turned to for advice, and then reburied with fine new shrouds and presents. This ceremony is said to placate the ancestors, who can bless or curse the activities of the living.

The capital of Antananarivo is located on the site of the old capital city of the Merina Kingdom in the high plateau region. Its population of nearly two million consists largely of Merina people. Of Indonesian origins, the Merina are physically distinct from the coastal peoples, having lighter features and straighter hair.

HISTORY TO PRESENT DAY

For early history, see *Historical Background* and *The Colonial Period: The French*.

Independence (1960) and Marxism under Didier Ratsiraka (1974–1991)

Philibert Tsiranana, a moderate, was the first president after independence in 1960, but when he was unable to deal effectively with a Maoist uprising in the South in 1971, all power was given to the military in 1972. Lt. Commander Didier Ratsiraka took over as President of the Supreme Council of the Revolution. Known as the Red Admiral, Ratsiraka was the instigator of the Malagasy socialist revolution of 1975 and even issued his own "little red book," in emulation of Chairman Mao of China. The Malagasy Republic was renamed the Democratic Republic of Madagascar and, backed by the military, Ratsiraka was re-elected to successive seven-year terms in 1982 and 1989. Violence marked the regime in the early 1990s, when Ratsiraka used the military to resist a pro-democracy movement. On August 10, 1991, the president ordered troops to fire on a crowd of protesters at the presidential palace. Fourteen people were killed and hundreds wounded, leading the International Monetary Fund to suspend its economic support to Madagascar.

The sixteen years of socialism under Ratsiraka from 1974 to 1991 were disastrous for Madagascar. Key sectors of the economy were nationalized: banks and insurance companies, export-import businesses, oil companies, and the principal firms in energy, mines, construction, and naval repairs all became state agencies. Expatriate businessmen left the country, usually without indemnification, and by 1985 only 10% of total investments were private.

During this time, factories operated at only 30% to 40% of their capacity and a massive state investment program built huge factories at enormous cost that were never able to function. Farmers soon lost confidence in the regime's cooperatives and returned to subsistence agriculture. With the deterioration of roads, provisioning cities with food became a problem and Madagascar, once a food exporting country, began to import foodstuffs, especially rice. By 1989, the annual average income fell below $210.

Madagascar

Former President Marc Ravalomana

Following large-scale protests in 1991 (as a wave of change swept across Africa with the end of the Cold War), the government instituted a High Authority for State Transition, presided over by Albert Zafy. The High Authority drafted and secured passage of a 1992 constitution that created a multiparty parliamentary democracy. In 1993, Zafy won the presidential election, but it soon became apparent that constitutional democracy did not guarantee governmental stability. In less than five years following its adoption, there would be six changes of government, three changes of prime ministers, and two motions of censure. Recognizing the weakness of executive authority confronted with a boisterously fragmented parliament, legislators revised the constitution to reinforce presidential powers. In 1996, after a long-running battle with parliament, President Zafy was impeached by the National Assembly and ultimately deposed by the High Constitutional Court.

The Return of Ratsiraka

Presidential elections in December 1997 resulted in the return of the Red Admiral, Didier Ratsiraka, to the presidential palace. A reformed Marxist, Ratsiraka spoke now of decentralization and economic liberalism and quickly called a referendum to decentralize governmental authority to six semiautonomous provinces in March 1998. These provinces were to be run by provincial councils elected by universal suffrage and, in turn, provincial councils would elect a provincial governor and exercise control over economic and social programs.

However, additional provisions in the referendum proposed significant increases in presidential authority. These included the power to nominate the prime minister (with no obligation to choose from the political majority in parliament), the power to dissolve parliament, and the power to nominate the most important magistrates of an "independent judiciary." Presidential impeachment also would become more difficult. Proponents said that the goal of these provisions was to end the permanent political instability created by the 1992 constitution.

The referendum presented voters with a single question, clearly framed by the advocates of a "yes" vote: "Do you accept the project to amend the constitution to give greater dimension to the development of all regions and to reinforce national unity?" The opposition called for a boycott of the election and only 34% of registered voters went to the polls, but the referendum passed by a razor-thin margin: 50.62%.

The new regional assemblies marked a shift of thinking on the part of the government. Previous regimes had emphasized national unity by concentrating authority at the center. Antananarivo, the capital, had traditionally been privileged politically and economically, to the detriment of distant regions. The new assemblies were to be granted limited taxing abilities to fund regional programs and money would still flow from the center as Antananarivo accounted for three-fifths of the state's tax collection.

With political skepticism growing, 60% to 70% of registered voters boycotted the December 2000 regional elections. When the final results were in, President Ratsiraka's AREMA (*L'Avant-Garde du Renouveau de Madagascar*) party and affiliated "independents" captured most of the 336 regional assembly seats. Only in the capital were President Ratsiraka's supporters beaten. Senate elections of February 2001 produced similar results with AREMA easily grabbing a majority of seats—49 out of 60. With AREMA dominating Madagascar's political space, President Ratsiraka seemed well positioned to call the shots in the presidential election.

Held in December 2001, the election pitted Ratsiraka—aged, ill, and tainted with corruption—against a self-made millionaire, Marc Ravalomanana, the youthful, dynamic, and popular mayor of Antananarivo. The election set capital against provinces, newly empowered by decentralization, with devastating consequences for the country. Official results—later annulled—gave Ravalomanana a clear lead, but not the absolute majority needed to win the election outright—46.49% of the vote to Ratsiraka's 40.64%. The incumbent president called for a second-round runoff, but Ravalomanana, accusing his opponent of fraud and vote rigging, claimed outright victory. He accused election officials of falsifying results and insisted that tally sheets drawn up by his own agents showed he won 52% of the vote, rather than the 46% claimed by the Interior Ministry. Ravalomanana supporters organized a general strike in January 2002 which closed the capital down. Daily protests continued for weeks, with no concession from Ratsiraka, and representatives of the Organization of African Unity (OAU) attempted mediation without success.

Marc Ravalomanana's Presidency and Crisis (2002–2009)

In February 2002, Ravalomanana declared himself president, staged an inauguration surrounded by judges and officers of the Ratsiraka regime, and appointed a prime minister. Ratsiraka loyalists withdrew to the coastal city of Toamasina and made it an alternative capital. After Ravalomanana announced his own cabinet, creating a second government, with every post in the country duplicated, including the governor of the central bank.

Ratsiraka decreed martial law in Antananarivo, but the army, deeply divided, remained neutral and his supporters resorted to direct action. The pro-Ratsiraka governor of Toamasina installed roadblocks on the main route to the capital, preventing movement of food or fuel to the capital. At least six bridges linking the inland capital to coastal ports were destroyed in an effort to strangle the city economically.

Amid increasing violence, Madagascar's Supreme Court annulled first-round election results in April and ordered a recount by the High Constitutional Court (HCC). After the recount, the HCC reported Ravalomanana had won an overall majority with 51% of the vote and 36% going to Ratsiraka. On May 6, Ravalomanana formally assumed the presidency and stepped up military action against Ratsiraka forces. Judicial success brought recognition by the United States at the end of June, quickly followed by France. The OAU, unsuccessful at diplomacy, saw its unity dissolve when Senegal endorsed President Ravalomanana on July 4. Three days later, on July 7, 2002, ex-President Ratsiraka flew to France and exile where

Oxen transport — Photo by Char Glacy

Madagascar

he remained until his return to Madagascar in 2011. Fearing the precedent of self-proclaimed presidents, it persisted in obtuseness, declaring that Ravalomanana's win had not been "legally constituted." Madagascar would not regain its seat until July 2003, when the African Union, the OAU's successor, finally recognized the Ravalomanana government.

President Ratsiraka had made a 180 degree turn to put in place a market economy during his term, but action to disengage the state through privatization of its large companies was slow, hesitant, and often indecisive. By the time he left office reluctantly in 2002, there had been some improvement: average annual income rose to $250—where it had been ten years before—and economic growth was around 6%. However, most benefits from economic liberalization went to a minority of urban dwellers employed in the textile industry, the country's largest export earner.

The political crisis following the December 2001 elections undermined the country's economic improvement for a time. Particularly hard hit were textile companies operating in economic development zones around Antananarivo who were unable to import fabric and thus had to close their factories and send their workers home. Overall, industrial output fell between 70% and 90%, and tourism virtually ceased, with revenues falling 95%. Commercial properties lost 50% to 60% of their tenants, and the World Bank estimated the dispute cost the country $12 million to $14 million a day. Economic growth for 2002 was a negative 12%.

The National Assembly elections were held in December of 2002, and though 40 parties vied for 160 seats, President Ravalomanana's *Tiako i Madagasikara* (TiM: I Love Madagascar party) won an overwhelming victory with an absolute majority of 102 seats. With National Solidarity, the wider coalition of parties supporting the president, pro-Ravalomanana forces controlled 132 legislative seats.

In response to the economic downturn, the Ravalomanana government liberalized the economy and opened it to foreign investment, including in real estate. With stability, Madagascar's economy achieved rather consistent growth above 5% for several years from 2003 until 2009, when the international crisis sent growth back into negative territory for a year. To mark a symbolic break with its socialist past, the government replaced the Malagasy franc with a precolonial currency, the ariary. The ariary was introduced in mid-2003 while the former Malagasy francs remained exchangeable until the end of 2009. With political and economic liberalization, international donors gave the first portion of $2.3 billion they had pledged to help reconstruct the country.

In the November 2003 local elections, the TiM was still generally successful, winning 29 out of 45 municipal government elections. It dominated the north and the capital region but appeared much weaker in other outlying areas as Madagascar's second city, the port of Toamasina, remained in AREMA control. The question of political amnesty for the events of 2002 was under consideration at this time, but given the center-periphery disconnect, some feared a general amnesty might lead to the return of political exiles that could destabilize the regime and the idea was rejected by the new government. For his role in the crisis and embezzlement of funds, former President Ratsiraka was sentenced, *in absentia*, to five years in prison, as was his daughter Sophie, found guilty of blowing up a bridge during the civil conflict.

Tropical cyclones hit the island in 2004, leaving thousands homeless and causing major damage to local infrastructure. Later that year the World Bank and International Monetary Fund write off nearly half of Madagascar's debt, which amounted to some $2 billion. With the economy in recovery, some degree of political stability returned with the December 2006 presidential elections. Despite a field of 14 candidates, President Ravalomanana thumped the opposition, winning a first ballot reelection with 55% of all votes cast. With nearly 12% of the vote, his nearest rival was the former speaker of parliament, Jean Lahiniriko, sacked by his TiM colleagues in the National Assembly after praising Iran's nuclear program. The third-place finisher was Roland Ratsiraka, the mayor of Madagascar's second city, Toamasina, and nephew of former-President Didier Ratsiraka, who received a little over 10% of the ballots in an election that saw some 65% of registered voters participating.

With popular backing, President Ravalomanana introduced a series of controversial constitutional reforms in early 2007. To facilitate local economic development, Madagascar's six autonomous regions would be phased out, replaced by the 22 regions of smaller size. To encourage greater foreign investment and closer ties with the anglophone world, Ravalomanana passed a reform to make English a national language. Most controversially, he proposed to increase presidential powers so that the president would have the authority to make laws directly if he declares a state of emergency. When submitted to the electorate in April, more than 75% approved the changes.

Political bitterness lingered within a restive army. From November 2006 to April 2007 security forces foiled at least three attempted assassinations of the president and at least 25 army officers were summoned for questioning. Another natural disaster occurred in 2008, when Cyclone Ivan hit the island and killed 93, leaving over 300,000 homeless.

Ravalomanana's downfall began in earnest in January 2009, when the government closed TV and radio stations run by the opposition. Protests turned violent, and dozens of Malagasys were killed, some by the authorities. In response, the mayor of the capital city Antananarivo, Andry Rajoelina, spearheaded a demonstrative opposition movement and called upon the president to resign. To heighten

Scenic coastline near Fort Dauphine

Photo by Ruth Evans

Madagascar

Former President Andry Rajoelina

President Hery Rajaonarimampianina

the stakes, the young, charismatic, and ambitious Rajoelina also declared himself the rightful leader of Madagascar.

Andry Rajoelina (2009–2013) and His Successor

Ravalomanana dismissed Rajoelina, but popular sentiment swung towards the mayor as more citizens were killed in clashes. Finally, in March, several top military officers declared allegiance to Rajoelina's shadow government, leading Ravalomanana to tender an ambiguous resignation and flee into exile in South Africa. Although international observers condemned the takeover and Ravalomanana periodically asserted his legitimate claim to power from abroad, Rajoelina began to consolidate power over the subsequent months. It soon became clear, however, that vital forces in Madagascar's political life remained opposed to Rajoelina. While Rajoelina had the backing of the military top command and the high court, a range of political movements continued to jockey for position in the government. Three of these groups coalesced around Madagascar's three former presidents: Ratsiraka, Zafy, and Ravalomanana.

Ravalomanana was tried *in absentia* for abuse of office in June and sentenced to four years of prison. Two months later, in August 2009, the new president (still just 35 years old) agreed to participate in an internationally mediated meeting with opposition leaders in Mozambique. The meeting was aimed to establish some degree of power-sharing in an attempt to calm political tensions. While Rajoelina agreed in principle, his appointments resulted in only a nominal inclusion of opposition groups in the power-sharing arrangement, with two ministers out of 31. According to the participant parties, this constituted a breach of the agreement.

In October, Rajoelina reached a new consensus with opposition forces on the appointment of a new prime minister, Eugene Mangalaza, who would assist in leading a unity government that would transition the country to the next election. By December, Rajoelina had also breached this precarious arrangement by dismissing Mangalaza in favor of a new prime minister, Cecile Manorohanta. However, this new appointment lasted all of one day before Rajoelina replaced her on December 20, 2009, with the military officer Albert Camille Vital. The shuffling and uncertainty was indicative of a president whose grip on power was insecure, especially as the appointment of Vital could be construed as a step by the president to ensure support within the military ranks.

Rajoelina hastily announced that parliamentary elections would be held on March 20, 2010, but these elections were later postponed multiple times. As his grip on power has looked increasingly shaky, Rajoelina also announced that a constitutional referendum would be held in August and a presidential election in November. In the meantime, international observers kept up their pressure, with the US and the EU both suspending new development aid flows in 2010.

In August 2010, a court sentenced former president Ravalomanana *in absentia* to life in prison for alleged killings of opposition supporters, thereby creating a deterrent to Ravalomanana's return. Then in November, Rajoelina's proposed referendum endorsed new constitutional provisions. One would allow the 36-year-old Rajoelina to run for president in 2011 by reducing the age requirement from 40 to 35 years, while another would allow him to remain as de facto leader until elections could be agreed upon. The referendum passed with 73% of the vote, according to official estimates, though international observers declared the process irregular.

Rajoelina sought to keep his political enemies closer by proposing a transitional unity government until the next elections, which were pushed back repeatedly until they were finally held in late 2013. In September 2011, eight political parties signed onto an interim government that intended to hold elections within a year. Opposition parties joined the new transition government in November of that year, despite reservations, and presidential and parliamentary elections initially were scheduled for November 2012. However, these were postponed to 2013 (first May, then June). In early 2013, Rajoelina reached a short-lived accord with Ravalomanana—brokered by the regional Southern African Development Community (SADC)—in which neither of them would contest the presidency, but the president then broke the agreement after Ravalomanana's wife Lalao announced her candidacy. After multiple delays, Rajoelina postponed elections once more to August 2013, and attempted to dismiss several members of the Transitional Senate that he has accused of sabotage.

Eventually, the special electoral court invalidated the candidacies of the principal contestants: Rajoelina, Ratsiraka, and Lalao Ravalomanana. The election then took the form of a proxy political battle between Rajoelina and Marc Ravalomanana. The former backed his ex-finance minister, Hery Rajaonarimampianina, while Ravalomanana backed one of his own former ministers Jean Louis Robinson. When neither secured a majority in the first round, the runoff election was held in December 2013, which Rajaonarimampianina won with 53% of the vote. There is as yet little indication of how much the new president will be able to establish legitimacy and become independent of the Rajoelina camp.

CONTEMPORARY THEMES

Madagascar faces continuing economic problems. Rural poverty has generated a migration to the cities, especially Antananarivo. The rate of change for urbanization between 2010 and 2015 is estimated to be near 5% per year, and about one-third of total population lived in urban areas in 2011. Now surrounded by shantytowns, the city is a microcosm of the island's problems: malnutrition, unhealthy living conditions, street children, traffic congestion, contaminated water, pollution, underemployment, and insecurity. Life expectancy is just 65.2 years.

Madagascar

One key to the government's development plans is improving the country's education system and infrastructure. Recognizing the importance of education for development, the government abolished school fees in 2002. Since then, there has been a campaign to build new classrooms, recruit teachers and distribute supplies as basic as pens, pencils, and paper. Similarly, road building was a necessity: Madagascar had 21,700 miles of useable roads, but these had dwindled to under 10,000 miles by 2001, making transport difficult, hazardous, expensive, and time-consuming. The EU offered assistance for road construction and maintenance and nearly $400 million has been spent on upgrading the system and 3,700 miles of new roads have been constructed.

Another major government priority is the agricultural sector, which dominates the labor force, employing some 85% of the working population. The sector is dominated by small-scale farms that produce both export and food crops. To improve production, various taxes and duties on fertilizers and machinery have been reduced Rice is Madagascar's main food crop, but production is not enough to satisfy internal consumption needs and the country must import additional quantities. In October 2003, thirty Vietnamese experts and technicians arrived to provide advice on increasing rice production. In 20 years, Vietnamese rice production increased 300% while in the same period Malagasy production rose by only 25%. Maize, bananas, sweet potatoes, groundnuts, pineapples, coconuts, and sugar are also grown for local consumption. Only about 6% of the land is arable. The economy's dependence on agriculture makes it subject to the caprice of nature as drought, locusts, and cyclones visit Madagascar nearly every year.

Vanilla used to be the number one export crop, but natural calamities, governmental inefficiencies in marketing, and high local taxes reduced production at the same time Mexico and Indonesia were increasing theirs. Madagascar produces nearly 60% to 65% of the world's vanilla supply. Some 70,000 vanilla farmers produce between 4,500 and 5,500 tons of green vanilla in a good year. After drying and processing, some 1,500 tons are available for export and can bring in $200 million or more to the economy.

Madagascar is rich in mineral resources, including a variety of precious and semi-precious gemstones such as garnets, emeralds, rubies and sapphires. In November 2007, President Ravalomanana opened a $3.3 billion nickel and cobalt mining project in Tamatave, the largest of its kind in the world. Development of large nickel deposits at Ambatovy, 80 miles east of the capital, is in progress. Estimates indicate the mine could become the third largest in production output in the world.

In December 2004, Exxon Mobil paid $25 million for exploration rights in 36,000 square kilometers of coastal water and the company sank its first exploration well in early 2007. In 2008, Madagascar produced its first barrels of crude oil in 60 years, leading the government to issue dozens of licenses to international oil companies for offshore oil exploration. China, too, has long maintained a presence in the country, first sending some medical teams since 1975 to treat millions of Malagasy, and more recently as investors in such projects as the construction of an international conference center, a cement factory, and investments in mineral resources.

The World Bank and IMF have recognized Madagascar's extreme poverty and qualified the country for debt relief of $1.9 billion under the Highly Indebted Poor Countries (HIPC) initiative. To reward good governance and sound economic policies, the world's richest countries also voted to cancel the debt owed by Madagascar to multilateral institutions (IMF, World Bank, African Development Bank) by HIPC countries at their July 2005 summit. Reduction of debt service payments has allowed the government to redirect debt service spending to poverty reduction programs.

While Andry Rajoelina was re-elected to a third term as president in November 2023, the contest was marred by low turnout and a boycott of the election by many of the smaller opposition parties with the winner securing 58 percent of the vote. Like many countries in the region, the island was hit by devastating cyclones in March 2024.

Concerned with the loss of native wildlife to international poachers, Madagascar has initiated repatriation agreements with partners, such as Thailand, to retrieve threatened species. These vulnerable to critically endangered species on the International Union for Conservation of Nature's (IUCN) Red List include ring-tailed lemurs, brown lemurs, radiated tortoises, and spider tortoises. In May 2024, Thai authorities seized a cargo of 1,109 endangered lemurs and tortoises originating from Madagascar in one of the country's largest wildlife trafficking busts to date, the result of an ongoing international investigation aimed at dismantling transnational criminal networks. Thai authorities tracked the convoluted route of an illegal wildlife shipment as it moved from Madagascar through Indonesia and Malaysia before entering Thailand, where the animals would have been sold into the multibillion-dollar global exotic pet market.

FUTURE CONSIDERATIONS

If the government stabilizes, reinvestment may take place—from domestic or foreign sources—and Madagascar needs substantial investment to accelerate economic advancement. Internationally, Madagascar was renowned for its unique ecosystems until recent years, but the news coming off the island in recent years has directed attention much more to the troubling questions of political turmoil and social uncertainty than to pristine beaches and exotic animals.

The Republic of Mauritius

Former President Anerood Jugnauth

BASIC FACTS

Area: 2,040 sq. km. (about the size of Rhode Island)
Dependencies: Rodrigues Island, the Agalega Islands and Cargados Carajos Shoals; Mauritius also claims sovereignty over the Chagos Archipelago, part of the British Indian Ocean Territory.
Population: 1,309,448 (June 2023 est.)
Capital City: Port Louis
Government Type: Parliamentary Republic
Neighboring Countries: Mauritius is located 550 miles east of Madagascar; Rodrigues is 350 miles northeast of Mauritius.
Official Language: English (official but spoken by less than 1% of the population)
Other Principal Languages: Creole (spoken by 80.5% of the population), Bojpoori (from Bihar, India) 12.1%, French, 3.4%, Hindi, Urdu, and Hakka
Ethnic Groups: Indo-Mauritian 68%, Creole 27%, Sino-Mauritian 3%, Franco-Mauritian 2%
Principal Religions: Hindu 52%, Christian 28.3% (Roman Catholic 26%, Protestant 2.3%), Muslim 16.6%, and other 3.1%
Former Colonial Status: French possession (1715–1810); British possession (1810–1968)
Independence Date: March 12, 1968
GDP Per Capita (IMF 2023 est.): $11,548 (nominal), $29,164 (PPP)
Gini index: 36.8 (World Bank 2017)
Currency: Mauritius Rupee, $US 1 = 45.32 rupees (May 2023)
Inflation Rate: 8.4% (2022 est.)
Chief Commercial Products: Clothing, textiles, sugar
Foreign Direct Investments (FDI) net inflows: 418,430,128
Literacy Rate: 92.2% (CIA 2021)
Life Expectancy: 75.13 years (CIA 2023 est.)

Head of State: President Pritivirajsing Roopun (since December 2, 2019)
Head of Government: Prime Minister Pracind Jugnauth (since January 23, 2017)

LAND AND PEOPLE

The landmass that is now the island of Mauritius is the result of volcanic activity that occurred thousands of years ago. The craggy, hardened lava, covered with fine ash and silt was in turn covered with a carpet of green vegetation that grows swiftly in the tropical sun. The island is a series of plateaus and interesting variations caused by small streams, waterfalls, crevices, and coastal indentations. The island of Rodrigues is a dependency of Mauritius. Mauritius has had minor disputes with Britain and France recently over claim to a few islands in the surrounding waters, but there has been no violence, and only court cases and diplomatic conversations.

The population of Mauritius is culturally diverse, reflecting the island's colonial history. Europeans brought in both Indians and Africans to work the sugar plantations. Today, about 63% of the population is Indian and overwhelmingly Hindu (52%). Thirty percent of the population is African-Creole, 5% Chinese, and 2% European. The various ethnic groups tend to have limited interaction with each other. The government has managed to increase literacy from 60% to 100% largely by making education free. University education remains elitist, restricted to a select few. Only 3% of Mauritians obtain university degrees. This impacts the government's efforts to attract high-tech companies.

HISTORY TO PRESENT DAY

For early history, see *Historical Background, The Colonial Period: The French*, and *The Colonial Period: The British*.

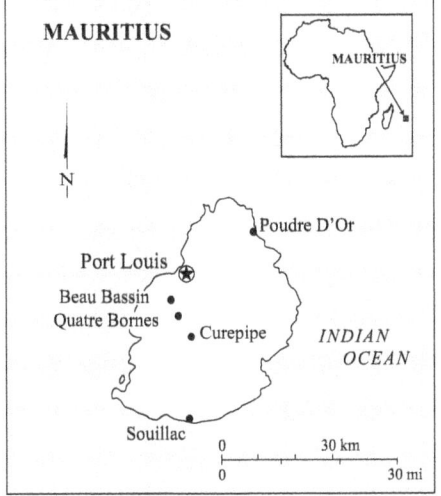

Following World War II, the worldwide surge of nationalism gradually entered Mauritius, particularly among those of Indian descent who had become a majority of the population. When Great Britain announced the withdrawal "east of the Suez" in 1966, Mauritius was intended to be a part of this plan. Ethnic diversity was the biggest problem—the Indian majority favored independence, but the Creoles were opposed.

To placate the Creoles, a complicated plan was devised to apportion the seats of the legislature among the ethnic groups, and elections were held. Hindu Indians were able to win a parliamentary majority; Creoles became the minority. Muslim Indians were unable to elect a single representative.

For about 41 years until 1982, Sir Seewoosagur Ramgoolam and his Labor Party dominated the political scene. The party was challenged in the June 1982 elections by a French Mauritian, Paul Bérenger. The vote was so split along party and ethnic lines that a coalition government emerged, headed by Anerood Jugnauth with Bérenger as finance minister. A second collapse in the government in mid-1983 led to a second election. To compete more effectively, Jugnauth organized the Mauritian Socialist Movement (MSM), which defeated Bérenger's Mauritian Militant Movement (MMM).

Jugnauth continued in power until late 1995 when he erred politically, proposing a constitutional amendment to incorporate vernacular languages (Hindi, Urdu, Tamil, Marathi, Telegu, Mandarin, and Arabic) into primary education. His principal associates in the coalition resigned, and the amendment failed. The Assembly had to be dissolved and new elections called. The language issue highlights the multiracial, multilingual, and multireligious nature of Mauritian society. Unlike many former British colonies, Mauritius retained the Westminster model, but without winner-take-all provisions. Each communal group constituting the Mauritian nation obtains representation in the National Assembly, but communal tensions can and do arise. In early 1998, Prime Minister Ramgoolam ordered a holiday to celebrate the Hindu festival, which drew the criticism of opposition leaders fearful of the economic consequences of too many sectarian holidays.

Class differences are sharp on Mauritius. Seventeen white Franco-Mauritian families own over half the island's cultivated land. They control not only agriculture but industry too. At the other end of the socioeconomic scale are the Creoles who often have no school certificates or vocational training. They frequently end up working as laborers, disaffected from a system in which they share so little.

Mauritius

Former Prime Minister Navin Ramgoolam

An opposition alliance won all 60 seats in the 20 island districts in 1995. Navin Ramgoolam, son of Sir Seewoosagur, became the new prime minister, but no basic changes in government economic development policies resulted.

Discontent with the state of the economy and dissatisfaction with the handling of communal tensions lay at the heart of the 2000 campaign. The MMM's Bérenger and the MSM's Jugnauth formed an electoral alliance. In a preelection pact the two agreed that if they won, Jugnauth would serve as prime minister for the first three years and Bérenger would rule for the next three, becoming the nation's first non-Hindu leader since independence. Despite 43 parties fielding candidates, the election was a straightforward fight between this alliance and Navin Ramgoolam's Labor Party-led coalition. When the final tallies were in, the MSM-MMM alliance won a smashing victory: 54 out of 62 seats in assembly.

The power-sharing agreement between Jugnauth and Bérenger was implemented in September 2003. President Offmann resigned and was replaced by Prime Minister Jugnauth, who left his position, making way for Paul Bérenger to become prime minister.

In the meantime, the government tried to make parliament more representative of minority interests. It announced a proposal in March 2002 to increase the size of the National Assembly, from 62 to 92 members. The additional 30 members would be proportionally chosen from parties that received more than 10% of the vote, but the constitutional amendment needed was never passed. Instead, Mauritius uses a two-tier election process. Sixty-two members are elected from 21 constituencies by popular vote. An additional eight members are chosen from a list of "best losers" to assure ethnic minority representation.

In the July 2005 parliamentary elections opposition leader Navin Ramgoolam successfully exploited a declining economy. Leading the Social Alliance, Ramgoolam criticized the Bérenger government for failing to prepare the island for the end of textile quotas and the elimination of EU sugar subsidies. The SA won 38 of 62 contested parliamentary seats and Ramgoolam was designated the island's new prime minister. Ramgoolam, 57, a doctor and lawyer who is the son of the first post-independence prime minister, returned to the job he held between 1995 and 2000.

Ramgoolam's job remained challenging, given the need to respond to problems of the domestic economy and the impact of globalization. This has put the Social Alliance on the defensive. Efforts to eliminate rice and flour subsidies and reform the pension system by extending the retirement age to 65 brought charges from the opposition that basic consumer items would now be unaffordable for many and that the budget was "pro-capitalist"—fighting words in a country that is socially oriented. A frustrated finance minister responded, bitingly, that the problem "is that there is no doctor or economist on the other side of the House." The opposition walked out, protesting the minister's "arrogance." It was the first time the opposition, the MMM and the MSM, had acted in accord in a long time.

The Mauritian Socialist Movement (MSM), headed by Pravind Jugnauth, the son of former-Prime Minister (and now President) Anerood Jugnauth was having internal problems even before the legislative elections of 2005. Pravind himself could not retain a seat in his own constituency and thus does not sit in the National Assembly, which complicates his ambition to someday become prime minister. The MSM took another body blow when Ashok Jugnauth, uncle of Pravind and brother of Anerood tendered his resignation from the party. When Paul Bérenger, erstwhile ally of Pravind Jugnauth, began to speak of Ashok as the next prime minister, what minimal unity the MMM-MSM coalition had enjoyed quickly dissolved.

In May 2010, Prime Minister Ramgoolam's Labour Party and the MSM allied with the Mauritian Social Democrat Party to defeat the MMM, taking 45 of 69 total seats. The coalition promised to deal with rising inflation and unemployment, and to support Mauritian exports, but strains emerged between the Labour Party and the MSM, leading to questions about whether the coalition can be effective.

In March 2012, President Jugnauth resigned from the ceremonial post due to "disagreements with members of the government," specifically the Prime Minister and a possible allegation against his son for fraud. Jugnauth views his resignation as a step in a return from a ceremonial position to active electoral politics, and the action heralds a new rivalry between Jugnauth and Ramgoolam. Vice President Monique Ohsan Bellepeau became acting president on March 31, 2012. The National Assembly elected Kailash Purryag as president on July 20, and he was sworn in on July 21, 2012, for a full term.

CONTEMPORARY THEMES

Mauritius has transformed its economy since independence when it was essentially dependent on the export of sugar to Great Britain. In the 1960s sugar accounted for nearly 80% of agricultural production and 86% of export earnings. Sugar is still king, but in the nearly 40 years since independence, Mauritius has diversified its economy to create supports in light manufacturing, particularly textiles, tourism and, more recently, information technology.

The sugar industry is facing difficult times. In 2005, the European Union agreed to end quotas and price subsidies given former colonial states and sugar prices were reduced by about a third over the period to 2009. The 18 sugar-producing countries affected, including Mauritius, lost significant export revenues as a consequence. To mitigate losses, the EU proposed a special fund to help such countries diversify and restructure their economies.

The government began a major reform of the sugar industry. It first consolidated small-scale holdings to increase productivity. It also invested in de-rocking to make sugar plantations amenable to mechanized harvesting. Last but not least, it promoted the planting of new cane fields, with sugar production estimated to expand from 50% to 81% of total land cultivated. Concentration and consolidation also occurred in sugar processing: seven of eleven sugar factories were slated for closure, while a voluntary retirement scheme was made available to support factory workers who lost their jobs.

To extract full value from the sugar cane, the government also commissioned more power plants to burn "bagasse," a residue from cane. After 2002, the industry began producing about 40% of the island's electricity using bagasse and import charcoal, and estimates are that 60% to 70% of Mauritian electricity may now be generated from renewable fuel. Similarly, molasses created during the sugar-refining process is being used to produce ethanol used in a blended fuel for vehicles. The Alcodis distillery has increased its ethanol production from a few million liters for

Mauritius

domestic consumption to 30 million liters for the export market.

Light manufacturing has also needed to adjust to more open trade. Dominated by textiles, the sector accounted for 21.4% of GDP in 2004. At one time there were more than 500 textile factories concentrated in Mauritius' Economic Processing Zone. They employed close to 90,000 workers, and they made Mauritius the world's second-largest exporter of woolen knits. Since the late 1990s, however, thousands of Mauritians have been cast out of the textile factories as they closed or downsized. With the ending of textile quotas beginning in 2005, low-cost production from Asia has begun to drive African production from the international marketplace. Textile firms have left for Asian nations, like China and India, where costs are lower. Job losses in textile manufacturing contribute significantly to the country's growing unemployment rate.

Tourism is the country's other large source of export revenues along with textiles and sugar, and it represents one of the greatest potential growth areas. Mauritius has always marketed itself as an upscale vacation site, but faced with declines in sugar and textiles, the government hopes to expand the industry—achieving two million arrivals a year by 2015. Some 860,000 visitors came in 2007.

Information and communication technology is slated to become a fourth pillar of the economy. The plan involves creating "cyber cities" that will provide a world-class telecommunications network via satellite and an expanding network of fiber-optic cables. To staff these investments, the government is investing heavily in education and overhauled the system, extending school hours and expanding the compulsory treatment of several subjects—including languages, mathematics, science, and information technology—in the curriculum. It has doubled the size of the computer engineering department at the University of Mauritius and set up a virtual learning center to give Mauritian students easy access to course materials used at MIT.

The government's diversification and development plans face practical difficulties. Budgetary deficits over the past few years have accumulated; public sector debt now amounts to two-thirds of GDP. The government now spends more on debt servicing than on education and health. The newly elected government plans to continue to spend on social projects but is also abolishing certain taxes imposed by the previous administration. As a result, financing spending will remain a problem. A fast growth rate could help reduce this deficit, but growth has been uneven since the global crisis of 2008 and 2009; it was around 5% prior, declined to about 2% in 2009, and recovered to an estimated 4% in 2010 and 2011. Meanwhile, unemployment has hovered at around 8%.

Another lingering issue that generates considerable bitterness is the legacy of Britain's 1968 removal of the Chagos archipelago from the administrative control of Mauritius. The archipelago includes the island of Diego Garcia, which was cleared of nearly 5,000 inhabitants in a harsh resettlement campaign and leased to the United States for use as a military and nuclear base. In return the British reportedly were able to obtain Trident submarines on favorable terms. The military base with its 12,000-foot runway is in a highly strategic location; originally intended to counter the Soviet threat, it has been used extensively by American and allied bombing missions in Iraq and Afghanistan.

A country heavily dependent on ecotourism, Mauritius has been struck by both natural and man-made disasters, including flash floods of major regions in January 2024 and a huge oil spill from a Japanese-owned supertanker off the coast in July 2020 with serious damage to coral reefs and local whale-spawning grounds with the island government allegedly withholding vital information on the spill from international NGOs and other interested parties.

Former Prime Minister Pravind Jugnauth was released on bail following an arrest on money laundering charges in February 2025. The country's anti-corruption agency seized suitcases of cash and luxury watches in raids, including those on Jugnauth's home. Coming 100 days after his landslide defeat in elections, his successor Navin Ramgoolam vowed to root out corruption through the Financial Crimes Commission (FCC). On the international front, the island nation is engaged in negotiations with the United Kingdom over an agreement to transfer the archipelago known officially as the British Indian Ocean Territory or Chagos Islands to Mauritius with annual payments by the British to secure the deal that is deemed necessary to guarantee the future of the joint military base, known as Diego Garcia. Resolving the legal dispute over the ownership of the islands, the deal finalized by the British Labour government has provoked reservations by the newly elected prime minister of Mauritius along with the United States Secretary of State, who cited the country's increasingly close ties with China.

FUTURE CONSIDERATIONS

Despite the relative wealth of Mauritius by African standards, the country continues to struggle with questions of economic reform, which often brings short-term pains with a promise of benefits only over the longer term. Rising inflation and unemployment have fueled discontent among the poor. Continued political stability in Mauritius will depend upon the government's ability to ease social suffering during the transitional period of its reform efforts without stripping itself of the revenues to continue development investment. Former president Anerood Jugnauth's rivalry with Prime Minister Navin Ramgoolam looks to be the next big story in the country.

Politically, Mauritius is one of Africa's great success stories, though the conditions on the island are unique and not easily replicated elsewhere. With a solid economy and some geographic separation from many of the continent's challenges, Mauritius has retained a solid democratic foundation for years. Stability in the island nation is a model for many other African countries, though Mauritius is not devoid of political intrigue.

A 2,000 rupee note with a traditional ox cart moving the island's important sugar crop

The Republic of the Seychelles

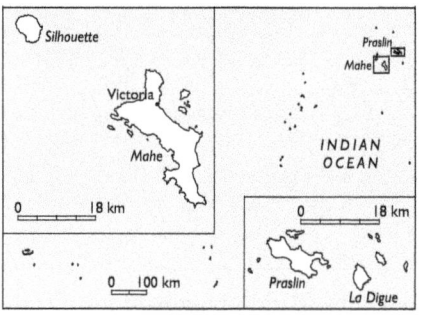

Presidential Palace — Photo by Powell Harrison

BASIC FACTS

Area: 455 sq. km., consisting of 115 islands (roughly 2.5 times the size of Washington, DC)
Population: 97,617 (June 2023 est.)
Capital City: Victoria (on Mahé)
Government Type: Presidential republic
Official Languages: Seychellois Creole (89%), English (5%), French (1%)
Ethnic Groups: Seychellois (mixture of Asians, Africans, and Europeans), Indian, Arab
Principal Religions: Roman Catholic 76%, Protestant 11%, Other Christian 2%, Hindu 2%, Muslim 2%, Other/None 6%
Former Colonial Status: French colony 1756–1814, United Kingdom colony until 1976
Independence Date: June 29, 1976
GDP Per Capita (IMF 2023 est.): $19,536 (nominal), $39,662 (PPP)
Gini Index: 32.1 (World Bank 2018)
Currency: Seychellois Rupee, 1 USD = 13.34 rupees (Apr. 2023)
Inflation Rate: 5.6% (2022 est.)
Chief Commercial Products: Processed fish (tuna), prawns, cinnamon bark, copra, tea, coconuts, and vanilla
Foreign Direct Investments (FDI) net inflows: 108,307,072
Literacy Rate: 96% (CIA 2018)
Life Expectency: 76 years (CIA 2023 est.)
Head of State: President Wavel Ramkalawan (since October 26, 2020)
Head of Government: President Wavel Ramkalawan (since October 26, 2020)

LAND AND PEOPLE

Located in the western Indian Ocean, 1,000 miles off the coast of East Africa, the Seychelles comprises 115 islands, spread over 154,000 square miles of the Indian Ocean. Lying just below the Equator, the islands have been dubbed a "Garden of Eden" because of the lushness and diversity of their scenery. The main archipelago consists of 42 granitic islands—thrown up by volcanic action to heights of a half mile above sea level—and 73 coral atolls, low, flat and only a few feet above the sea. Mahé, with its lush hills and luxurious beaches, is the largest and most populated of the islands, with almost 90% of the nation's total population. Praslin and La Digue are the other major islands. Others, like Denis Island, a coral atoll, Sainte Anne, Bird Island, and Cousine, the smallest of the granite islands, are privately owned nature reserves usually associated with an upscale resort. Fregate, only one square mile in size, was named after a bird and is now the home of tens of thousands of them.

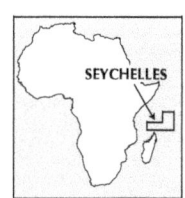

The population of the Seychelles is relatively homogenous, the result of frequent intermarriage between the island's original French settlers and Africans who settled after the islands were ceded to Britain in the early 1800s. Small Indian and Chinese minorities also exist. Most of the population is Roman Catholic, and almost everyone speaks Creole.

Upon assuming leadership in 1977, President René invited his fellow citizens to "create the new man, with his roots."

Seychelles

The "root" of this new Seychellois identity would be its "créolité"—its "creoleness." Since then government policy has affirmed and cultivated a common culture based on Creole roots. The language has become the first spoken and written language of everyone (English and French are the second and third languages), and the world's only Creole Institute can be found on Mahé. Each October Victoria hosts the world's largest Creole festival, featuring artists and writers from the diverse Creole world—Mauritius, Reunion, the French Caribbean islands, Guyana, etc.

In April 2002, the SPPF government celebrated 25 years of rule since the coup (or "liberation" as party stalwarts prefer to call it) that brought it to power. The government describes itself as "paternalistic"—a fusion of socialism and capitalism, and in many ways its achievements are striking. Gone are the days when 30 families—the *grands blancs*—controlled wealth and property on the islands. Free access to education and health, a right to housing, and guaranteed employment have created a costly social security system (although recently reformed) unequaled on the African continent. Seychellois have the highest per capita income of all the African states. The life expectancy at birth for the total population is 74.25 years, reflecting unprecedented access to healthcare not usually seen in other African states.

The islands boast two UNESCO World Heritage Sites. The first, Aldabra, is the world's largest raised atoll, and hosts the world's largest colony of giant tortoises (150,000 of them) along with the last remaining flightless birds in the Indian Ocean. The second is the Vallée de Mai on Praslin, the only place on earth where one finds the black parrot and the rare palm trees that bear the giant Coco de Mer or sea coconut, the world's largest and heaviest seed, perhaps better known for a voluptuous shape that reminds the erotically susceptible of portions of the female anatomy.

HISTORY TO PRESENT DAY

For early history, see *Historical Background* and *The Colonial Period: The French* and *The Colonial Period: The British*

The British colony of the Seychelles was granted self-government in 1975 and independence in 1976. James R. Mancham, the islands' first president, was overthrown in 1977 by a leftist *coup d'état* led by his prime minister, France Albert René. In 1979 René revised the constitution and created a one-party socialist state controlled by his Seychelles People's Progressive Front (SPPF).

René ruled at the head of the Leninist state until a multiparty political system was permitted in 1991 and Seychelles' first democratic multiparty elections were held in 1993. Then, René triumphed over former President James Mancham, and the SPPF retained control of the National Assembly.

In the March 1997 elections, President René was returned to power with 66.65% of the votes. James Mancham, leader of the opposition Democratic Party (DP), was the big loser, receiving only 14% of the vote, down from the 35% he had won in 1993. Reverend Wavel Ramkalawan, leader of the United Opposition (UO), drew 20% of presidential ballots, and his party replaced the DP as official opposition by winning 26% of the votes cast in legislative elections. Still, in Seychelles' mixed system of single member districts and proportional representation, that only earned the party three seats in the National Assembly. Once again, the SPPF swept the legislative elections, winning 30 seats. Mancham's DP saw its parliamentary representation drop from five seats to one.

Snap presidential elections were called in September 2001, well before the expiration of the president's term of office in 2003 and well before the country's increasingly difficult economic circumstances really began to hurt. With a bit of vote-buying, charged the opposition, René secured 54% of the vote, beating off a vigorous challenge from the Seychelles National Party's Wavel Ramkalawan, who won 45% of the votes.

Seychelles' opposition leader, Reverend Ramkalawan, has proved much less conciliatory than his predecessor and much more formidable. As such he became the object of a smear campaign by the SPPF-controlled press before the legislative election of 2002. (Despite its total dominance, the SPPF made few concessions to its opposition.)

Seychelles' radio and television service are government controlled and coverage of the political opposition is highly restricted. *Regar,* an independent weekly that supports the SNP, has been consistently targeted by President René and other government officials with costly defamation lawsuits. The courts, whose judges had all been appointed by René, inevitably found the paper guilty and fined it heavily. In December 2005, *Regar*'s offices were burned, damaging its printing press. The attack took place after the paper had exposed an alleged corrupt property deal implicating a senior member of the SPPF; as of mid-2007 no suspects had yet been charged. *Regar's* management suspended publication in October 2006 to protest its legal harassment. The decision to cease publication came after an unprecedented fine of 350,000 rupees—over $57,000—for publishing a photo of the Seychelles Tourism Board president fishing in restricted waters. The photo had already appeared in the *Seychelles Nation*, the government's daily newspaper.

President René called early parliamentary elections in December 2002, well before the normal expiration of the Assembly's mandate, and presumably before the impact of a declining economy would be felt by too many voters. Once again René and the government intimidated opposition SNP candidates and supporters: police were generally in attendance at all its meetings, but looked away when gangs of SPPF partisans menaced the opposition. The government also seemed to have given financing to James Mancham's Democratic Party, moribund since its disastrous defeat in 1998, to divide the opposition. Tacitly admitting the country's economic slowdown, the SPPF made "Things Can Only Get Better" its campaign slogan.

René's SPPF won handily, but saw its massive majority eroded, down from 30 to 24. Reverend Ramkalawan's SNP took the remaining 11 seats in the National Assembly. The Democratic Party failed to achieve the minimum 10% required to earn a seat by proportional representation.

President René retired from office in April 2004; he was succeeded by Vice President James Michel, but maintained his position as head of the SPPF. President Michel was elected president in his own right in July 2006, winning 54% of the votes to Reverend Ramkalawan's 46%.

When the government proposed legislation to ban political parties and religious groups from owning a radio station in late 2006, the opposition simply walked out. The boycott lasted five months. Fed up with stalemate, President Michel called a snap election for May 2007 hoping to secure an even larger SPPF majority. The voters—and some 85% participated—returned both parties to parliament with exactly the same representation as before: 23 members of the SPPF, 11 for the SNP.

Elections in 2011 further consolidated the power of the governing party, which changed its name from SPPF to Party Lepep (PL, or People's Party). President Michel of the PL was re-elected in May 2011 with results similar to the 2006 election: 55% to 41% for Ramkalawan of the SNP. Legislative elections in September and October were boycotted by the SNP and the New Democratic Party. The result was a sweep for the PL, which took 89% of the vote and all of the seats in the National Assembly.

CONTEMPORARY THEMES

Isolated in the vast Indian Ocean, the Seychelles promote themselves as an idyllic tourist location. Some 130,000 people visit the islands annually and account for 70% of their hard currency. The tourism

Seychelles

market is distinctly upscale, and until recently charter flights were not permitted, on the grounds that budget passengers would lower the tone of the island and not spend enough money. The number of visitors was at one time limited to 150,000 a year, with no more than 4,500 are permitted at any one time, though these caps have been lifted and tourism arrivals are eventually expected to reach 300,000. The government controls the quantity and quality of hotels and limits camping, such that accommodations are pricey. Still, Seychelles has experienced record visitation rates, with major increases in 2006 and 2007 before a decline in 2008 and 2009. With the rebound in 2010 and 2011, the government has contemplated again capping development in the tourism sector, given worries about sustainability. Seychelles hopes to take on a larger role in the worldwide tourism sector. In July 2012, Seychelles will be hosting the International Council of Tourism Partners general assembly meeting.

Seychelles has one of the highest living standards in Africa with a remarkable per capita income of over $10,000, but the economy is only recently coming out of major contractions due to the reliance on the tourism industry and crippling government interference. World Bank figures show GDP declined by over 10% during 2001–05. It was a rough period for the country: Seychelles' net international reserves were depleted and government debt grew alarmingly. The foreign currency shortage resulted in empty shelves in the shops, inflation, and a black market where a dollar cost ten rupees compared to the official rate of five. By mid-2001, the government was forcing foreign tourists to pay all their bills in foreign currency rather than local rupees. Because of its cash crunch, the government defaulted on its bonds, taking its place with other financial deadbeats like Liberia and Zimbabwe—all of whom are barred from borrowing from multilateral lenders. Its accumulated debt rose from $265 million in 2001 to $615 million in 2005.

The IMF blamed the crisis on excessive government involvement in the economy, including price controls, foreign exchange allocation, restrictive import licensing, and many government-owned monopolies in manufacturing and distribution. According to a recent EU study, government expenditures account for some 62% of GDP. The economy is dominated by the Seychelles Marketing Board (SMB), controlled by the government, the islands' largest employer. SMB possesses a variety of import and export monopolies and has a share of almost every enterprise. The IMF recommended liberalizing the economy: privatizing government monopolies, eliminating price controls, devaluing the rupee, permitting foreign investment, and dropping controls on foreign exchange.

The IMF declared the economy of Seychelles to have a market-based economy with full employment and a fiscal surplus in December 2013. Seychelles' GDP is poised to grow 3.3% this year, and have a remarkable unemployment rate of 2%. With a solid and liberalized fiscal system now in place, Seychelles is beginning to gather foreign investors and work to diversify its economy.

Seychelles' greatest natural resource, apart from its appeal to tourists, is fishing. Its exclusive economic zone gives it control of more than 386,000 square miles of Indian Ocean, abundant in rich fishing grounds. A fleet of patrol boats enforces the exclusion zone, and all fishing vessels must stop in Victoria port, register their catch, and pay the appropriate fees. Increasingly, however, high operating costs and the falling number of catches due to climate change have put Seychelles at a disadvantage

Fishing licenses and fees bring in some revenues (about $7 million annually), but the government decided that added value could be better achieved by processing the catch locally. In 1995, it joined with Heinz to build a new cannery on reclaimed land in Victoria harbor. President Michel announced in March 2006 that Lehman Brothers Merchant Banking had bought out the Heinz interest in the cannery (60%) and envisioned increasing annual production by 30%, from 85,000 tons a year to 110,000 tons over the following three years.

The beautiful coast of Seychelles is not without its risks, the most significant of which is piracy. As global anti-piracy efforts have increased in the Gulf of Aden to the north, Somali pirates have begun to move further South in and around Seychelles' waters. The Seychelles began to fight back in 2010 and 2011, first by passing legislation to facilitate prosecutions. Meanwhile, the United States has begun to supply the island nation with drone aircraft to fight pirates, and the government has finalized an Anti-Piracy agreement with the European Union that allows EU troops to be deployed on the islands. In 2010, the Seychelles successfully captured and convicted nine pirates in their first trial, and ultimately sent them to the Netherlands for further trial; more than 40 subsequent prosecutions were successful. The Seychelles also signed up to the International Criminal Court as part of these efforts to gain better control of their waters.

Concerned with preservation of its extensive natural habitat, the Seychelles created a zone of protection covering 30 percent of surrounding seas while the island nation has also dealt with heavy rains and an explosion at a weapons depot on the main island of Mahe in December 2023 that led to an official declaration of emergency.

Focusing on the country's self-proclaimed "Blue Economy" agenda, the restored wetland known as "Dan Sours" has been designated a new site for an agroforestry project while local public transport system is instituting a QR code payment system. Receiving a commitment of funding from the People's Republic of China, a 136-home social housing project is slated to begin construction in 2026.

FUTURE CONSIDERATIONS

After complying with many IMF suggestions, Seychelles' economy is poised to grow into the future. In 2012, Seychelles secured a 27-million-euro loan from the European Investment Bank to maintain a larger and cleaner water supply, a problem that has plagued the island nation that relies on rainwater catchment for potable water. Nonetheless, the Seychelles is currently experiencing significant "brain drain," and in 2013, it established the University of Seychelles, a partnership with the University of London, to keep qualified Seychellois within the country. With a now stable and relatively liberalized monetary and fiscal system, combined with incentives from the government, foreign investment and development is beginning to flood the tourism industry again. However, the government is looking to further diversify the economy away from the ever-volatile tourism industry by promoting small-scale manufacturing, farming, fishing, and the infamous offshore financial sector.

While the Seychelles has strict laws regarding sustainability, global climate change threatens its robust tourism and fishing industries in the near future. As Indian Ocean waters warm, large-scale deaths of coral reefs are being reported; this is a suspected cause of the approximately 20 percent decline in fisheries' catches over the last two years. Distant projected changes in global sea level will pose extreme difficulty for Seychellois (and their industries) living on low-lying coral atolls and beaches.

Political liberalization in the Seychelles has been ambiguous. The country has moved in the direction of somewhat increased political liberalism, as many middle-income economies do, but the state's leverage over the local media prevents the small island nation from being considered a full democracy. The boycott of the 2011 legislative elections by the opposition highlighted the dominance of the governing party. Still, political rights and some civil liberties are protected, which places the archipelago ahead many other countries on the African continent.

SOUTHERN AFRICA

Angola

BASIC FACTS

Area: 1,245,790 sq. km. = 481,000 sq. mi. (about four times the size of New Mexico)
Population: 35,981,281 (June 2023 est.)
Capital City: Luanda
Government Type: Presidential Republic
Neighboring Countries: Congo-Kinshasa (north); Namibia (south); Zambia (southeast)
Official Language: Portuguese
Other Principal Languages: Over forty African languages, including Tchokwe, Kikongo, Kwanyama, Mbundu, Nyaneka, and Umbundu
Ethnic Groups: Ovimbundu 37%, Kimbundu 25%, Bakongo 13%, Mestico (mixed European and African) 2%, European 1%, and other 22%
Principal Religions: Indigenous beliefs 47%, Roman Catholic 38%, Protestant 15% (1998 est.)
Former Colonial Status: Portuguese Colony until November 11, 1975; actual control passed in early 1975.
Independence Date: November 11, 1975
GDP Per Capita (IMF 2023 est.): $3,204 (nominal), $7,222 (PPP)
Gini index: 51.3 (World Bank 2018)
Currency: Angolan kwanza; $US 1 = 512.5 kwanza (Apr. 2023)
Inflation Rate: 23.9% (2022 est.)
Chief Commercial Products: crude oil 90%, diamonds, refined petroleum products, gas, coffee, sisal, fish and fish products, timber, cotton
Foreign Direct Investments (FDI) net inflows: 1,921,699,719
Literacy Rate: 71.1% (CIA 2015)
Life Expectancy: 62.51 years (CIA 2022 est.)
Head of State: President Joao Manuel Goncalves Lourenco (since September 26, 2017)
Head of Government: President Joao Manuel Goncalves Lourenco (since September 26, 2017)

The consequences of civil war: massive destruction of infrastructure
©IRIN

LAND AND PEOPLE

Most of Angola is a high, grassy plateau ranging from 3,000 to 4,000 feet above sea level, dotted by occasional trees and brush. The coastal belt, home to about 20% of the population, is from 15 to 60 miles wide, stretching from the tropical mouth of the Congo River, down to the palm-lined central beaches, and then on to the reddish sands of the Namib Desert in the extreme south. Mountains stretch eastward, splitting the country in half until the terrain gradually levels out, dipping northeast into the hot, steaming rain forest of Congo's river basin and southeast to isolated, semiarid land.

Angola's mountains are the source of numerous rivers, which fan out in all directions. The Kwanza (or Cuanza) River, Angola's largest, twists north for 600 miles in a half-circle and then drains into the Atlantic below cosmopolitan Luanda. The Cunene's cold waters gush southward down the mountains, slow as they pass through the plains, become sluggish in the silent desert, then turn westward and are caught by the huge Cunene Dam, which regulates its flow as it forms the 175-mile border with Namibia to the ocean. The Lucala river in the northeast meanders across sunny grasslands before reaching a wide, curved rock shelf where the placid waters suddenly plunge into a 350-foot gorge, sending up a heavy spray-mist that transforms the immediate area into a lush oasis, rich with dark mosses and tropical foliage—the Kalandula Falls (formerly Duque de Bragança Falls). Below the falls, the river moves across flat land and joins the waters of the larger Kwanza.

Until 1974, there were two cultures in Angola: Europeans (mostly Portuguese) businessmen and farmers, and the original inhabitants of the land. The latter lived a marginal existence in the cities and in the hinterland, working as laborers in the factories and fields of Angola. A small group of these lived as *assimilados*—they adopted European customs and the Portuguese language. Some now are the leadership of the Popular Movement for the Liberation of Angola (MPLA: *Movimento Popular de Libertação de Angola*), Angola's governing party.

HISTORY TO PRESENT DAY

For early history, see *Historical Background* and *The Colonial Period: The Portuguese*.

Portugal's abusive colonial policies in Africa generated increasing resistance and resentment in the 1950s. While assimilation had produced a small group of educated Angolans, mostly *mestiços* of mixed race, even these recognized for the poor treatment of the Africans. In the countryside, the settlement of white farmers and the use of forced labor embittered the rural peasantry. Anticolonial nationalist sentiment first coalesced in Luanda, the capital, with the formation of the Popular Movement for the Liberation of Angola (MPLA) in 1956, headed by Mbundu physician Agostinho Neto. The heart of the movement was a multiracial group of leftist urban intellectuals with its ethnic core

Angola

residing in the Mbundu people of Luanda and the surrounding area.

The MPLA, FNLA, and UNITA: Decolonization and Civil War

The MPLA's greatest rival in the early years was the National Front for the Liberation of Angola (FNLA). Led by Holden Roberto, the FNLA began as a spokesman for ethnic interests of Angola's northern Bakongo peoples, but by 1958 it expanded its goals to independence for all Angola. The FNLA created a national liberation army and sent young Angolans to North Africa to train with Algerian forces engaged in their own nationalist struggle. The Revolutionary Government of Angola in Exile (GRAE), headquartered in Leopoldville (now Kinshasa, Democratic Republic of the Congo), was also created and claimed sole representation of the interests of the Angolan people.

In 1964, Holden Roberto fell out with his foreign minister in the GRAE, Jonas Savimbi, and the latter created the National Union for the Total Independence of Angola (UNITA: *União Nacional para a Independência Total de Angola*). UNITA's membership was rooted in Angola's largest ethnic group, the Ovimbundu, peasant farmers who dominated the fertile central highlands. In 1965, Savimbi (who had earned a doctorate in political science from the University of Lausanne in Switzerland) and several of his followers went to China, where they received military training and became disciples of Maoism. Like its rivals, UNITA claimed to be the sole representative of the Angolan people.

Angola's march to independence centered on these three military-political groups: MPLA, FNLA, and UNITA, which shared a common enemy in Portugal, but maintained differing nationalist visions. Each was specifically rooted in a geographical and ethnic base and each drew on different sources of external support that intensified rivalries, both personal and ideological. At a time of intense ideological competition internationally, each of the groups ultimately became an extension of Cold War rivalries between East and West.

With its Marxist-Leninist orientation, the MPLA attracted the support of the international left. Its military cadres received training in Eastern Europe and Cuba. Recently independent African states with similar left-leaning inclinations provided sympathetic support and Soviet arms transited through Tanzania and Zambia to supply MPLA forces. The United States supported the pro-Western FNLA when it seemed the strongest of the groups, but it later shifted support to UNITA. The Soviet Union responded to U.S. support with increased arms deliveries to the MPLA, while Cuba sent military instructors and combat troops.

The nationalist struggles in the African colonies drained Portugal's resources and will. Some 11,000 Portuguese soldiers had been killed by 1974, and on April 25 of that year disgruntled military officers in Lisbon overthrew the Portuguese government and began the process leading to decolonization. Yet the transition to independence proved difficult in all colonies, including Angola. A transitional government involving all three nationalist groups was created, but Portuguese settlers resisted and rioted. Rivalries between the three nationalist groups intensified and external aid and intervention increased.

Organization of Africa Unity (OAU) negotiators brought together the MPLA's Agostinho Neto, the FNLA's Holden Roberto, and UNITA's Jonas Savimbi together in June 1975 to produce a draft constitution for independent Angola, but soon afterwards the transitional government collapsed and the FNLA and UNITA withdrew. Recognizing their individual military weakness against the MPLA army, the two groups united and began a civil war against MPLA.

South Africa supported the FNLA-UNITA alliance, having already worked with Portugal fighting nationalist guerrillas in Angola, and in August 1975, sent in an invasion force to protect hydroelectric facilities on the Cunene River. A larger South African-led force then invaded Angola in October, occupying six provincial capitals and coming within 62 miles of Luanda.

To combat this threat, the MPLA received a massive increase in Soviet military aid, while Cuba poured thousands of troops into the country. The military balance tipped in MPLA's favor, while the support of apartheid South Africa

Jonas Savimbi, former leader of UNITA

for the FNLA and UNITA tainted both groups. Portugal granted independence amid the chaos of civil war on November 11, 1975, marking the end of 400 years of Portuguese colonial rule.

The MPLA, in control of the capital, proclaimed the People's Republic of Angola. A rival "Democratic People's Republic of Angola" was proclaimed by the FNLA-UNITA alliance, but it was clear the MPLA, backed by 10,000 to 12,000 Cuban troops, had emerged on top. International recognition followed, and the MPLA moved to create a Marxist-Leninist single-party state. Agostinho Neto served as both MPLA secretary-general and president of Angola. With Cuban assistance the MPLA defeated the FNLA militarily, leaving only Jonas Savimbi's UNITA to dispute the government's legitimacy.

President Neto died following an operation on September 10, 1979, and was succeeded by his foreign minister, José Eduardo dos Santos. At this time, Angola faced continuing instability from internal and external elements. UNITA continued armed resistance to the MPLA government and South Africa also undertook incursions into Angola to root out guerrilla bases supporting the SWAPO (Southwest Africa People's Organization), the rebel group attempting to create an independent state in present-day Namibia; this resulted in clashes between Cuban and South African troops.

Negotiations and the Lusaka Peace Process

The linked external problems were resolved in a grand diplomatic solution of 1988. South Africa agreed to the independence of South West Africa (now Namibia), while Cuba and South Africa jointly agreed to withdraw their troops from Angola. The only irksome presence that remained was Jonas Savimbi and UNITA.

Between the MPLA and UNITA leadership lay the chasms of culture, history, and race. UNITA emerged as a factor in the liberation struggle from the perception that the MPLA was dominated by mixed-race intellectuals from the coastal cities. Historically the Luandan elite had looked down on countryside folk as inept and inferior. Savimbi sought to exploit and mobilize those differences, basing UNITA on the highland Ovimbundu people; it had always claimed to represent "real Africans," "sons of the soil," "living in the bush" against a better-educated, wealthy, cosmopolitan urban elite. (As almost living proof of the cultural division, dos Santos left Luanda to visit the rest of the country only once in a later seven-year span, during a brief campaign swing.) Savimbi's populist nationalism, with potential appeal to the dispossessed masses living in the

Angola

squalor of squatter shacks on the outskirts of Luanda, was deeply threatening to the status and perks of the urban elite.

Political negotiations between MPLA and UNITA resulted in a June 1991 ceasefire, but the lull in fighting was short-lived. Angola's single party constitution was amended to permit multiparty elections, and these were scheduled for September 1992. President dos Santos won a plurality of votes on the first ballot, but UNITA refused to accept the results, claiming widespread fraud. Within a few days, UNITA resumed the civil war. UNITA supporters were chased from Luanda, and the second round of elections was never held. Full-scale fighting continued until a peace accord was signed in Lusaka, Zambia in November 1994. The Lusaka Protocol called for demilitarization of UNITA and the creation of a national army integrating UNITA elements into the Angola Armed Forces, plus a government of national unity and the extension of state administration to areas formerly under UNITA control. Still, neither side was deeply committed to the peace accord, and the MPLA government continued to seek the total destruction of UNITA and the elimination of Jonas Savimbi.

The major Lusaka provisions were implemented by April 1998. UNITA had turned over almost all of the territory under its control to government administration, disarmed most of its soldiers and shut down its propaganda radio. For its part, the Angolan government recognized UNITA as an unarmed political party with the right to organize and campaign throughout the country. Savimbi was officially recognized as the main opposition leader with rights to hold regular consultations with President dos Santos, access to government media, and the right to visit Angolan embassies abroad. For his personal safety, Savimbi was permitted a bodyguard of 400 men, ultimately to be reduced to 150. UNITA's participation in a Government of National Reconciliation (GURN) was realized with the inclusion of 70 deputies in parliament and seven ministerial portfolios.

Again, however, the resolution proved ephemeral. In September 1997 the MPLA government suspended UNITA's ministers, vice-ministers, and parliamentarians, threatening GURN's existence. The government mounted an effort to destroy UNITA as a political party by inducing a number of UNITA figures participating in GURN to break with Savimbi and form a new party called UNITA-Renovado.

In the countryside, far from the probing eyes of reporters or UN monitoring teams, the Angola National Police (ANP) pursued another systematic approach to UNITA's destruction, violently targeting

President José Eduardo dos Santos

party leadership and grassroots structures. UNITA administrators, party officials and those simply accused of collaborating with UNITA were murdered. After UNITA closed its radio station, the government filled the airwaves with what Western diplomats referred to as "fabricated news reports of UNITA atrocities." The UN and the United States issued statements denouncing the use of "false information" and "provocative rhetoric." The government's intent was clear: to create an atmosphere of fear and justify a renewal of hostilities against its foe.

The Fall of Mobutu and Savimbi

As the long-standing Mobutu regime in neighboring Zaïre (now Democratic Republic of the Congo) finally crumbled in the 1990s, the MPLA saw another opportunity to destroy UNITA. It intervened militarily in Zaïre and Congo-Brazzaville to destroy Savimbi's support and supply bases across the border. Mobutu, who had long aided UNITA, was an obvious target; Angolan troops were sent to assist his opponent, Laurent Kabila. President Pascal Lissouba of Congo-Brazzaville had also aided UNITA, so when civil war erupted between Lissouba and ex-president Sassou-Nguesso, Angolan planes bombed the capital and helped dispatch Lissouba to exile. Angolan troops entered Congo-Brazzaville to ferret out UNITA bases from which Savimbi's forces had led attacks on the oil-rich enclave of Cabinda (see below).

The MPLA was willing to stir international conflict for domestic objectives, and made clear they would once again take up the fight against UNITA. At the MPLA party congress in December 1998 President dos Santos bluntly stated "the only way to achieve peace in Angola is through the political and military neutralization of UNITA and its president." By spring 1999, both the government and UNITA had restocked their weapons. With no peace to observe, the UN withdrew, its $2.2-billion mission having expired in utter failure.

Having spent half a billion dollars on new armament and possessed of overwhelming superiority in weaponry, the Angolan forced Savimbi and UNITA to take refuge in the countryside and resort to traditional guerilla tactics. By 2001 the government had eliminated UNITA's capacity to conduct conventional warfare, but had not destroyed the group. Savimbi's sphere of operations was limited to the province of Moxico, a vast under-populated region bordering Zambia. The government adopted a scorched earth policy in the province, removing any civilians that might have aided the rebels. The army eventually captured a number of Savimbi's leading officers and penetrated his security network. After more than 30 years of guerilla war, Savimbi was at last pursued, cornered, and killed on February 22, 2002.

Savimbi's death dramatically transformed Angola's political landscape. Within six weeks of his death, UNITA's military commander signed a cease-fire. Parliament voted a blanket amnesty covering "all civilians and soldiers, Angolan or foreign, who committed crimes against the security of the Angolan state." The civil war wound down, having devastated Angola for 27 years, and left more than 500,000 dead, 100,000 maimed, 100,000 orphaned, and 3.1 million—roughly a quarter of the population—displaced by the fighting. In the last year of the war alone, the government's scorched-earth policies forced 400,000 more people to flee their homes. GDP had fallen 48% over the previous 25 years. Infrastructure outside of Luanda, the capital, had been destroyed and the state's capacity to deliver services minimal. The state's vast oil wealth had contributed little to human development.

The MPLA after the War (2002–present)

As the threat from Savimbi was eliminated, the MPLA government found itself faced with growing demands for some negotiated settlement from civil society. Over the years, Angola's civil society had grown larger, stronger, and bold enough to condemn the government's war that had destroyed the country but not the enemy. Increasingly vociferous church groups and humanitarian organizations lead the way. Military destruction remained the preferred option for the government, however, which continued to buy arms wherever it could.

Dos Santos announced in August 2001 that he would not contest the next presidential election and would work on the reconstruction of Angola, but the promise was short-lived. At the party's fifth

Angola

Working to rebuild a bridge. ©IRIN

national congress in December 2003 dos Santos was unanimously reelected party president; there was no alternative candidate and voting was done publicly, by a show of hands.

In September 2008, Angola held its legislative elections. The MPLA had the majority of seats (82%), followed by UNITA (10%). This was also the country's first election with the new quota that establishes 30% of the candidates must be female. Although the opposition claimed fraud, the 2008 legislative election suggested some advances for democracy in the country, despite the disorganization of the process. Presidential balloting was tentatively scheduled for later in 2009, but dos Santos called for a new constitution before the elections can be held. In December 2009 he declared it would take another three years before Presidential elections could be held.

The MPLA still tolerates little dissent, though members of the *Partido de Apoio Democrático e Progresso de Angola* (PADEPA: Party for Democratic Support and Progress) have strongly and persistently tested the regime's boundaries. Several were arrested in September 2006 for allegedly instigating disobedience and rebellion by protesting the planned closure of Luanda's largest informal market, the Roque Santerio. (The beachfront property on which the market operates is much desired by politically well-connected developers.) In November 2006, police denied the group permits to demonstrate in front of the French Embassy to protest official corruption and to demand a return of public funds allegedly deposited by the fraudsters in French banks. One hundred and ten protesters were arrested for disturbing the peace as they approached the embassy, of which 27 identified themselves as members of PADEPA; tried and found guilty, they were sentenced to a month in prison, later converted to a $2000 fine.

It is unlikely most Angolans heard the news. While private media (print and broadcast) are permitted in Angola, they are tightly controlled. The government dominates broadcasting both on radio (with *Rádio Nacional de Angola*) and TV. Opposition parties are often denied broadcast time, and are infrequently mentioned in the government daily newspaper, the *Jornal de Angola*. The MPLA also cracks down on independent broadcasting, as was the case with the Catholic radio station Radio Ecclesia in February 2003, which the minister of information accused of practicing "antenna terrorism."

The MPLA has also refused to disband its civilian militias, armed by the government during the civil war, and seems to turn a blind eye when militia thugs intimidate UNITA organizers in the provinces. UNITA's leader, Isaïas Samakuva (chosen by a party congress in June 2003), has stated that the MPLA is "set on returning to the time of a one-party state." The MPLA retains the paramilitary Civil Defense Organization (*defesa civil*), which has been involved in several violent encounters. Police agents intimidate, rob, harass, and kill citizens, particularly those who may not agree with the government.

While remaining the principal opposition party, UNITA is weakened by internal division. In parliament, the MPLA, as it has done previously, has induced members to abandon UNITA and join the MPLA. Apart from assuring the MPLA a parliamentary supermajority, this floor-crossing by defecting UNITA members means the opposition loses considerable public election funding for having a smaller parliamentary delegation.

The MPLA passed a new constitution in January 2010 that was seen as strengthening the hand of dos Santos, though it nominally moved Angola from a presidential to a parliamentary form of government. The largest party in the National Assembly, the single-chamber parliament, now has the right to appoint its leader as president. With term limits for the presidency (of two five-year terms) going into effect only in 2012, dos Santos, who is already the continent's longest running current leader, could conceivably remain in the position until 2022. UNITA initially consulted with the MPLA on certain of the constitutional provisions, but its members of the assembly ultimately boycotted the final vote. At about the same time as the constitution was being passed, Angola hosted the African Nations Cup (of soccer) in January 2010, during which Cabinda separatists (see below) attacked the bus of the team from Togo.

In December of 2011, an anti-fraud law was passed that did little to ease tensions over the legitimacy of the current electoral system. Two months later in February 2012, opponents of the MPLA threatened a boycott of the upcoming presidential election and called for the replacement of the head of the National Electoral Commission, an MPLA party member. In an unpredictable turn of events, the Angolan courts (whose judges are appointed directly by President dos Santos) removed the Commission Head from her position. This was a blow to the MPLA, but also added some legitimacy to the government's claims of free and fair elections. Some civil society organizations have led small-scale protests against the government's authoritarianism, but none have manifested in larger movements.

In August 2012, dos Santos cemented his grip on power while buying a modicum of legitimacy through the holding of a reasonably free and fair election. The MPLA took 175 of 220 seats on 72% of the vote, with UNITA under leader Isaias Zamakuva winning 32 seats, and a new coalition known as CASA-CE (*Convergência Ampla de Salvação de Angola-Coligação Eleitoral*) taking 8 seats. In accordance with Angola's parliamentary

Angola

system, the MPLA duly selected its party leader (dos Santos) as president and head of government. UNITA claimed that the elections failed the test of transparency, but the poll received a relatively clean bill of health from international observers.

Cabinda

With an area of just a bit more than 2,800 square miles, the northern enclave of Cabinda is completely separated from Angola by a narrow stretch of land on either side of the Congo River. It exists as a consequence of colonial power politics. Leopold II, the dictatorial and entrepreneurial Belgian king, wanted access to the sea for the Congo Free State, his personal fief in the heart of Africa. The Portuguese government, possessed of little capacity to protest, was pressured into making the concession at the river mouth.

The enclave contains around 250,000 Cabindans, most of whom would probably prefer independence if given a chance. Cabinda produces nearly 70% of Angola's oil from its offshore wells. Like the people of the Niger Delta in Nigeria, Cabindans feel exploited, abused, and short-changed. Cabinda reportedly receives 10% of the taxes paid by the oil companies—Chevron is the dominant player on the Cabinda fields—but FLEC (*Frente de Libertação do Enclava de Cabinda*, or the Liberation Front for the Cabinda Enclave) has long argued this is insufficient.

In April 2001, the former president of Portugal, Mario Soares, commented on the continuing struggle for self-determination in Cabinda. The nearly 30-year liberation struggle was, said Soares, "no internal Angolan affair." "Anyone who supports self-determination," he added, "cannot deny the right of a population to discuss the issue, and when this reaches the pitch it has in Cabinda, it moves out of the realm of domestic politics." The speech was occasioned by kidnappings of Portuguese workers by various elements of the FLEC. Abducted to focus international attention on FLEC's demands for self-determination, some of the captured workers had been held for nearly a year when Soares spoke.

Cabindan separatism stems from several sources beyond the obvious economic incentives. Ethnically and linguistically, Cabindans are more closely akin to peoples of southwestern Congo. Historically, the enclave was administered separately by the Portuguese until 1956, and this provided a clear sense of distinctness from Angola. "In our souls, we don't feel we are Angolans, we are Cabindans," said one FLEC leader. There is also a sense of historical exclusion. Cabindan interests were not represented in discussions between mainstream nationalist groups and Portugal that resulted in independence.

Chinese Premier Wen Jiabao welcomed by President dos Santos, June 2006.

The feeling then and now was that the enclave was simply and arbitrarily annexed to Angola at independence. Even the recent Lusaka agreement was restricted to the MPLA government and UNITA and ignored FLEC demands.

For years, the dos Santos regime failed to eliminate the various FLEC factions, but with Jonas Savimbi's death in 2002 the Angolan army launched a massive offensive against FLEC forces. (One reason for Angola's military advance into the two Congos was to eliminate the support and refuge both UNITA *and* FLEC groups found there.) There were no official figures, but journalists and NGOs estimated the number of troops involved at anywhere from 10,000 to 35,000 soldiers, which could be as many as one soldier for every 10 Cabindans.

To deal with the separatists, the army adopted a scorched-earth policy, where destroyed villages, summary executions, rape, and torture featured prominently. It managed to capture the secessionists' forest strongholds and control the area through force and violence. In December 2004, Human Rights Watch reported that the army had "arbitrarily detained and tortured civilians with impunity."

Only a small fraction of Cabindans—about 10,000—have wage-paying jobs, and unemployment has been estimated as high as 90%. There is only one hospital for the entire province and the inhabitants of Angola's richest oil province have to queue up for gasoline. (Angola's only refinery is in Luanda, and gasoline, in insufficient quantities, is shipped by boat to Cabinda.) Most consumer goods have to be imported from Congo-Brazzaville at exorbitant prices.

Given the savagery of repression and its resultant insecurity, there were signs Cabindans might be willing to set aside their demands for independence temporarily in the mid-2000s. Father Jorge Kongo, an outspoken priest and human rights campaigner, noted that independence was no longer peoples' principal concern. Now, he said, they were more concerned with personal safety and survival. Yet, in February 2005 tens of thousands rallied in Cabinda city to support self-rule for the province.

With its usual dilatory pace and obscure tactics, the government forwarded discussion proposals "about a special status for Cabinda" to the Cabinda Forum for Dialogue (FCD) in February 2006. FCD, an umbrella group that includes representatives of FLEC and the Cabindan church among others, had been recognized as the representative body for the enclave's secessionist movements. Negotiations continued for several months, and in August 2006 the government announced that it had signed a peace agreement with General Antonio Bento Bembe, FLEC's secretary-general. The accord recognized Cabinda's unique history and provided "special designation" for the enclave, but not autonomy. The parliament voted amnesty for those who turned in their weapons, and some demobilized fighters will be trained and integrated, into the Angolan army or police. This status for Cabinda was upheld in the 2010 constitution.

However, this does not ensure FLEC has been mollified. When interviewed for his reaction to the 2006 agreement, FLEC president N'Zita Henrique Tiago (living in Parisian exile) said he was unaware of the agreement, and a FLEC spokesman

Angola

charged that Bembe had no power to speak for the group and was in reality on the government payroll. Symptomatically, General Geraldo Nunda, speaking in February 2007, expressed satisfaction at the completion of military matters in "northern" Cabinda. Elsewhere in the enclave, low-level violence reportedly continued. FLEC then claimed responsibility for attacking a convoy of Chinese mine workers in 2010, suggesting the conflict in the enclave remains ongoing.

CONTEMPORARY THEMES

Most Angolans have seen little benefit from the country's growing oil wealth, partly due to the long civil war and partly due to a concentration of wealth since the war's end. Some 60% to 70% of the population of Angola lives below the poverty line, and access to health services is abysmal, with only about eight physicians per 100,000 people. Infant mortality is extraordinarily high and life expectancy low. The devastation produced by more than 30 years of continuous conflict is catastrophic: bridges, streets and roads, communications systems, airstrips, hospitals, and schools all need reconstruction. Hundreds of thousands of people live in shantytowns of squalor and misery on the outskirts of the capital.

Luanda now has four million inhabitants, but only a small fraction have running water or modern toilets. Whole sections of the capital are nightmares of sanitation, with decades of accumulated refuse still backlogged for removal. In the absence of such potable tap water, millions of Luanda's poor pay up to 10,000 times more for drinking water—transported by expensive private delivery trucks—than the elite who are connected to water systems. These conditions have generated one of the continent's worst cholera epidemics in decades. Between February and June 2006, 43,000 Angolans were stricken by the disease; more than 1,600 died in this country that accumulated a budgetary surplus of $2 billion in 2005.

With the bulk of government resources devoted to defeating its armed opponents (military spending was 21.2% of GDP in 2000) or corruptly siphoned off to private coffers, Angola's health system collapsed. In an unusually frank report, Doctors without Borders (MSF: *Medecins Sans Frontières*) reported in 2000 that Angolan authorities displayed "a striking lack of interest in the health of their population." Between 1997 and 2001, the government allocated an average of only 3.3% of its expenditures to health care—less than half the average budgeted (7.2%) by members of the Southern African Development Community. In 2007, after five years of peace, the national budget still allocated less than 3.7% to health expenditures. Angola is thus a paradox: a country of great wealth and dramatic misery.

The war has also left a legacy of antipersonnel land mines—12 million to 15 million of them, more than one for every man, woman and child in the country. An estimated 70,000 to 200,000 people have lost limbs to them, and demining is a slow and laborious process.

While the distribution of wealth is problematic, economic performance has skyrocketed since 2002. Fueled by high oil prices and greater control of its diamond producing areas, Angola has turned in eye-popping growth statistics. From 2005 to 2007 GDP grew by between 18% and 20% per year, followed by growth of over 13% in 2008; this was probably the fastest growth in the world over that period, and approximately doubled the size of the economy in just four years. Angola is now roughly tied with Nigeria and Algeria as Africa's biggest oil producer. The government is using some of the oil revenues to build infrastructure, such as roads and sewage system. Angola became a member of the Organization of Petroleum Exporting Countries (OPEC) in 2007 and produced an average 2 million barrels per day (bbl/d) in 2008 and 2009. Oil income accounts for some 90% of the state's revenues and over 40% of GDP.

In addition to its oil resources, Angola is the world's fourth-largest diamond producer, accounting for 12% of world production and about 6% of the country's total export income. Diamond reserves are enormous: estimated at 40 million carats in alluvial diamonds and another 50 million carats in kimberlite form. The World Bank predicts that in the next two decades Angola could become the world's largest diamond producer.

These expectations are based on the government's increasing control of diamond-producing areas since the end of the civil war. The MPLA regime has also dealt somewhat brutally with a massive influx of foreigners who sought to take advantage of the country's diamond resources. To control illegal mining activities, the government conducted a series of raids from December 2003 through April 2004. Police and soldiers destroyed miners' huts, seized firearms, generators, sieves, scales and satellite phones. Amid stories of rampant torture and abuse, the government admitted it had expelled 11,000 people, largely Congolese, to end "exploitation of economic resources." After another round of expulsions of illegal Congolese miners by the Angolan government, the Congolese government expelled over 20,000 Angolans in October 2009.

Despite the abundance of natural-resource wealth, Angola long ran huge budgetary deficits, but with abundant oil, Angola has begun to pay down its debt and reduced its dependence on multilateral lenders. The dos Santos government has long claimed its long civil war was the principal cause of its huge external debt, though government profligacy and corruption contribute substantially as well. (The president's eldest daughter, Isabel, is widely reported to have extensive holdings in both oil and mining operations. Many of the Angolan generals own or have shares in the numerous security firms that are essential to business, especially the diamond business.) Regime elites have enriched themselves through their government connections; in recent years, Transparency International has consistently ranked Angola as among most corrupt countries in the world.

The books of the national oil company, Sonangol, are virtual state secrets. A Swiss judge elicited from the former president of Elf-Gabon the revelation that oil companies had paid hidden commissions—"bonuses" in "petrospeak"—of more than a billion dollars to secure Angolan exploration permits in 1998. Much of this revenue disappears off the books. An IMF report gave a five-year total (1997–2001) for money unaccounted for in state finances of $4.36 billion. Another IMF report indicated that more than $900 million had gone missing in 2003 alone. However, Angola denies allegations of wrongdoing and maintains that oil revenues are free of corruption.

With the IMF refusing to sanction loans for a time until some degree of transparency and accountability has been achieved, Angola turned to Chinese loans

Children receiving food aid at San'Antionia school, Benguela ©IRIN

Angola

to fund reconstruction and rehabilitation projects. The lines of credit or loans are large (two billion dollars in March 2004 alone), generous (interest-free), and repaid in oil, desperately needed by China's burgeoning economy. In an official visit in February 2005 by Chinese Vice Premier Zeng Peiyan, the two governments announced plans to develop a joint oil exploration project in Angola's offshore fields, an agreement for "the long-term supply of oil" to China, and development of a new refinery. In addition, Chinese companies are building a new finance ministry, a new justice ministry, and rehabilitating the Benguela railroad. The new Chinese-built Luanda General Hospital opened in March 2006, and in the same month, the first stone was laid in a project to build 5,000 apartments in Cabinda.

While oil and gas constitute 90 percent of Angolan exports, the country has withdrawn from OPEC (Organization of Petroleum Exporting Countries) citing excessive production quotas even as the majority of the population, especially among youth, live below the poverty line and demonstrate growing opposition to the ruling MPLA in favor of the opposition UNITA. Also afflicting the country is recurrent drought in the southern region with widespread hunger and limited access to water supplies as the water system infrastructure is limited to the well-off and politically connected segments of the population.

In an apparent effort to counter growing influence of the People's Republic of China (PRC) on the African continent, United States President Joe Biden visited Angola for three days in December 2024. Focus of the trip was the $800 million US-backed railway project in the Lobito Corridor, a strategic trade route that connects the resource-rich Democratic Republic of Congo (DRC) and Zambia to Angola, which hosts the port of Lobito, located on the Atlantic Ocean. Funded largely by the U.S. and the European Union, the Lobito Atlantic Railway project will see an existing rail network in the Lobito Corridor upgraded; this will allow for a faster export of cobalt and copper, among other minerals, mined from the DRC's Kolwezi mining town.

Angola announced in March 2025 that the country would serve as a mediator between the government of the Democratic Republic of the Congo and the Rwanda-backed M23 rebels. President Joao Lourenco saying the two countries would begin "direct peace negotiations" in the Angolan capital Luanda on March 18. Angola has previously acted as a mediator in the eastern DRC conflict that escalated in late January when the M23 took control of the strategic eastern Congo city of Goma and seized Bukavu, eastern Congo's second-biggest city. Rwanda denies backing the M23 armed group in the conflict, which is rooted in the spread of Rwanda's 1994 genocide into DRC, and the struggle for control of DRC's vast mineral resources.

FUTURE CONSIDERATIONS

With an oil boom attracting attention from the United States and China, there are reasons to believe that Angola will continue its recent run of rapid economic growth, despite a downturn in 2009. On the back of skyrocketing oil prices, Angola's economy grew at a clip far faster than even China through much of the mid- to late-2000s. But this is not to say Angolans can look forward to rapid improvements in their standards of living. The MPLA and UNITA have largely ended the traumatic period of arbitrary murder and pillage under the civil war, yet governance remains poor. Angola has shifted from being a conflict zone to a post-conflict zone, with elections that offered some hope for continued stability in the country, even if the country cannot be seen as fully democratic. In the current environment, the 2010 constitution has done little more than reconfirm the MPLA's centralization and dominance.

The economy and the political reality are quite contradictory at first glance but are characteristic of many poorly-governed "petrostates." State coffers are witnessing massive inflows, making improvements in public services and investment a real possibility. Still, this has translated into few gains for the majority of Angolans. While Angola may be one of Africa's largest oil exporters, it remains one of the continents poorest countries. Much government income is squandered in corruption, wasteful spending and inefficient services. Improving the capacity of the state to serve a broader population is a prerequisite for alleviating poverty. The government claims to be investing in agriculture, in an attempt to diversify the economy. The oil and diamond industries, in addition to being based on limited resources, bring substantial profits, but not massive increases in employment; this necessitates more broad-based government investment using the proceeds of natural resource wealth. The 2008 economic crisis

Angola

hit the Angolan economy by affecting the prices of both diamonds and oil. In January 2009 the government cancelled the World Diamond Summit, an indication that the industry is entering a crisis. The recession of 2008–2009 caused a halt in GDP growth for the year but GDP growth is expected to have returned to about 7% per year, according to the World Bank.

In sum, Angola offers some of the starkest contrasts in Africa: burgeoning investment and major prospects for international investors in a commodity boom, coupled with rampant poverty, corruption and poor governance, and a lack of state commitment to human capacity and welfare. Angola's most violent days may be behind it, but it is not clear that its best days are visible on the horizon until the MPLA develops stronger linkages to the majority of the population. The elections in 2012 marked the first time that dos Santos was actually up for a vote, as elections were cancelled due to violence in 1992 and due to constitutional changes in 2009. Dos Santos continues as president, and the MPLA dominates, but there is perhaps some incremental evidence that electoral politics will improve going forward. Of course, the political costs to the regime of holding the election were minimal since they were virtually certain of a victory that would reconfirm the dominance of the governing party. Whether the MPLA and dos Santos would allow democracy to flourish if they had an actual chance of losing is another matter.

The Republic of Botswana

BASIC FACTS

Area: 581,730 sq. km. (slightly smaller than Texas)
Population: 2,417,596 (June 2023 est.)
Capital City: Gaborone
Government Type: Parliamentary republic
Neighboring Countries: Namibia (west and north); Zambia (north); Zimbabwe (northeast); South Africa (south).
Official Languages: English (2.1%), Setswana (78.2%).
Other Principal Languages: Afrikaans, Herero, Kalanga, Kgalagadi, Kung and other Bushman languages, Mbukushu, Subia, Tswana, Yeye
Ethnic Groups: Tswana (or Setswana) 79%, Kalanga 11%, Basarwa 3%, other, including Kgalagadi and white 7%
Principal Religions: Christian 71.6%, Badimo 6%, other 1.4%, unspecified 0.4%, none 20.6%
Former Colonial Status: British Protectorate (1885–1966)
Independence Date: September 30, 1966
GDP Per Capita (IMF 2023 est.): $7,270 (nominal), $19,398 (PPP)
Gini Index: 53.3 (World Bank 2015)
Currency: Botswana 64pula, $US 1 = 13.19 pula (May 2023)
Unemployment Rate: 17.7%
Inflation Rate: 8.9% (2022 est.)
Chief Commercial Products: Diamonds, copper, nickel, coal and meat processing
Foreign Direct Investments (FDI) net inflows: 393,180,125
Literacy Rate: 88.5 (CIA 2015)
Life Expectancy: 66.04 years (CIA 2022 est.)
Head of State: President Mokgweetse Eric Masisi (since April 1, 2018)
Head of Government: President Mokgweetse Eric Masisi (since April 1, 2018)

LAND AND PEOPLE

Botswana is a large, landlocked country that lies in the transition zone between the dry deserts of South Africa and the forests of Angola. In the South, a vast area is covered by the shifting red sands of the Kalahari Desert, occasionally interrupted by limestone rock formations and clumps of grass and scrub brush at the few places where water is close to the land surface. Temperatures reach over 100°F in the summer (November–April) and as low as 20°F in winter (May–October). Rainfall can be 9 inches or less in the southern Kalahari Desert.

Moving north, the growth becomes increasingly thicker and there are frequent patches of trees. Annual rainfall slowly increases until it reaches a level required to support farmland where the food and cattle of the nation are produced in non-drought years. Vegetation becomes dense in the north, and the land turns into the marshland of the Okavango Delta, an inland swamp fed by the Okavango River flowing from the low mountains of Angola. There is no exit to the ocean for these waters. The country's elevation, averaging 3,300 feet, modifies its subtropical climate.

One of the highest concentrations of rock art in the world is located at Tsodilo. There are over 4,500 paintings in less than four square miles. The site, classified by UNESCO as a World Heritage site, is frequently referred to as the "Louvre of the Desert."

The government's resettlement plans for the San people, the indigenous population of the Kalahari have drawn international attention. Most of Botswana's population of 50,000 San have already been relocated into 63 resettlement villages, where the government says it can better provide water, health and education services. The resettlement villages, miles from the traditional hunting grounds of the San, have been likened to American Indian reservations.

HISTORY TO PRESENT DAY

For early history, see *Historical Background* and *The Colonial Period: The British*.

After gaining independence on September 30, 1966, the pre-independence government of Botswana continued in office. Elections since then have resulted in substantial majorities in the Legislative Assembly for the Botswana Democratic Party (BDP). There are three other small political parties, which actively compete in the free elections, but they have yet to dislodge the BDP from its dominant political position. The chiefs of the eight largest tribes are permanent members of a House of Chiefs, where they are joined by seven other sub-chiefs. The National Assembly consists of 57 directly elected representatives (four additional seats are nominated by the president), but it cannot act upon matters concerning internal tribal affairs without first submitting a draft to the House of Chiefs.

Elections held in 1969, 1974, and 1979 resulted in resounding victories for the BDP and its president Sir Seretse Khama, who had been reelected chief executive since independence. On each occasion, the BDP took between 68% and 80% of the vote, and selected Khama as head of state. Khama was to have served for another five years after the 1979 elections, but he died suddenly in June 1980. Vice President Quett K. J. Masire was installed to fill out his term and was reelected in September 1984. Khama's eldest son, Seretse Khama Ian Khama, was installed in May 1979 as Paramount Chief of the Bamangwato, the largest of the Twsana-speaking tribes; he also served as commander of the Botswana Defense Force until 1998.

For 18 years (1980–1998), President Masire maintained the multiparty traditions of democratic Botswana and exercised a conservative fiscal restraint on the use of the country's riches, producing 16 years of budget surpluses and large foreign reserves. After his initial election as president in 1984, he led his BDP to successive electoral victories in 1989 and 1994.

With a broadly diverse constituency—civil servants, trade unionists, businesspeople, cattle ranchers, and rural traditionalists—the BDP is subject to internal factionalism. As two-party factions vied for party control before the 1999 elections, President Masire decided to retire to avoid an open split in the party. He secured passage of legislation providing for the automatic succession of Botswana's vice president and in November 1997 announced his retirement, effective in six months. On April 1, 1998, he was succeeded by his vice president and finance minister, Festus Mogae.

Mogae quickly consolidated his own leadership of the BDP with a popular move. Almost simultaneous with Mogae's appointment to the presidency, Lieutenant-General Seretse Khama Ian Khama resigned as chief of the Botswana Defense Force. Having consulted with traditional Bamangwato leaders, he was given temporary release from his chieftaincy to pursue a career in politics. Moving swiftly to fill the vacant vice presidency, Mogae nominated general Khama. With the popular Khama on his side, Mogae effectively closed off internal opposition to his leadership of the BDP. An Oxford University graduate, Mogae was seen as a pragmatic,

Botswana

no-nonsense leader, capable of uniting and energizing a fractured and complacent BDP, as the young General Khama campaigned vigorously, often flying about the country in military helicopters to galvanize party and electorate.

The BDP's victory was abetted by a serious split in the opposition. In 1998, Botswana National Front (BNF) dissidents withdrew and formed the Botswana Congress Party (BCP). Separated, the two parties, along with the smaller Botswana Alliance Movement (BAM), contested the October 1999 parliamentary elections. Divided, the opposition was decimated. The BDP swept 33 of 40 elected seats, even winning four of eight urban seats traditionally occupied by the opposition.

Little changed in the October 2004 elections. The BDP, supported by its traditional rural base, took 44 of 57 directly elected seats in the National Assembly. Victory was again facilitated by opposition division: in most districts the opposition BNF and BCP parties put up rival candidates, allowing the governing BDP to win several districts with a plurality of votes. The BNF won 12 seats and the BCP one. Despite its dominance in the legislature, the BDP won only 52% of the vote nationwide.

Botswana's president is chosen by the National Assembly following legislative elections, and the BDP majority reelected President Mogae to his second five-year term. The October elections also confirmed the political strength of Vice-President Seretse Khama Ian Khama. Most of the BDP deputies were Khama loyalists, and several of the new cabinet members had served in the Botswana Defense Force, which Khama once commanded. Mogae indicated he would step down in 2008 to make way for Khama to succeed him, thus giving Khama 18 months as head of state before the next legislative elections in October 2009.

As promised, Mogae turned the reins over to Khama as president. Despite his lineage as the eldest son of Botswana's founding father, Khama has failed to quell differences within the BDP. In April 2007, four main opposition parties—Botswana Alliance Movement (BAM), Botswana National Front (BNF), Botswana Congress Party (BCP) and Botswana People's Party (BPP)—were in talks to form a united front to challenge the BDP and prevent the presidency from becoming "a dynasty."

Despite the fractious nature of the BDP, the party won a sweeping victory in the parliamentary elections in October 2009 and secured another five-year term for President Khama. The BDP tallied 53% of the vote, and won 45 of the 57 seats in the

The Okavango Delta Photo by Judi Iranyi

Botswana National Assembly. The BNF and the BCP each won about 20% of the vote and took six and four assembly seats, respectively.

With political and economic chaos in neighboring Zimbabwe, Botswana has had to confront an influx of refugees. Border communities are particularly affected and resentments are high. Xenophobia is rising with complaints about immigrants taking jobs from citizens and rising petty crime rates attributed to the refugees. Thousands of illegal immigrants are deported annually. Shortly after an outbreak of foot and mouth disease in the Zimbabwe border area, the government decided to build a

A young Botswanan woman
Photo by Joann Sandlin

13-foot electric fence along the entire 310-mile border to keep out diseased cattle. The solar-powered fence, capable of delivering a 220-volt shock (nasty but not fatal), will be patrolled 24 hours a day by security forces. In February 2010, Botswana recalled diplomats from Zimbabwe after a dispute over three Batswana game wardens who strayed in Zimbabwe and were detained. The officers were eventually fined and released, and normal diplomatic relations were resumed.

In January 2011, indigenous Basarwa bushmen went to court and won the right to drill boreholes for water on their ancestral land, which had been prevented because their lands are part of a wildlife conservation. In the meantime, the Kaza Conservation was finally enacted in 2012, having been initiated in 2003. Spanning Angola, Botswana, Namibia, Zambia, and Zimbabwe, this conservation park is nearly the size of Sweden and will be designed to protect threatened animals, thwart poachers, mitigate environmental problems, and increase revenue from tourism. The park has been created with the assistance of organizations such as the World Wildlife Fund and UNESCO.

Since 2011 and 2012, political discontent seems to be percolating in Botswana. In April 2011, civil servants went on a two-month strike over low pay. In party politics, talks took place in January 2012 among three political parties hoping to form a coalition against the BDP. These talks crumbled but signal more efforts to challenge the BDP in the near future.

Botswana

CONTEMPORARY THEMES

Health

Botswana has one of the highest HIV/AIDS infection rates in Africa and in the world. It was estimated by UNICEF in 2009 that about 25% of sexually active adults are infected (which is horrifically high, but also a major downward revision of estimates reaching 40% a few years prior). Life expectancy has dropped from over 64 years to 55 years, though this is an improvement on the years around 2002 when life expectancy was estimated to be around 49 years.

Botswana now has one of the most significant anti-HIV/AIDS campaigns in the world and one of the most advanced treatment programs in Africa. Yet, the grim figures emerge even after an extensive government education campaign. Billboards, posters and bumper stickers in cities and villages throughout the country warn of the dangers of unprotected sex, with messages like "Don't let casual sex kill Botswana's future" and "Be wise, condomise." The government provides free distribution of condoms in all public institutions.

Festus Mogae went to extraordinary lengths to publicize the public health crisis, and early indications are that Khama will do the same. A refreshing contrast with his South African counterpart Thabo Mbeki, Mogae mentioned HIV/AIDS in nearly every speech, and in March 2001 he chillingly warned his countrymen that Botswana faced extinction if it failed to slow the spread of the deadly virus within the next five years. He has tried to break the culture of silence and shame surrounding AIDS by personally revealing the results of his own HIV test (negative) and encouraging his ministers to do the same. As of January 1, 2004, HIV tests became automatic at government hospitals and clinics unless patients specifically decline them. Part of Botswana's effort is funded by the Bill and Melinda Gates Foundation, while the international drug company Merck has provides an unlimited supply of antiretroviral (ARV) medicines.

Economy

Since independence Botswana's economy has shown impressive growth, averaging 10% per year from 1976 through 1991, much of which was rooted in diamond mining. More recently it has shown signs of slowing down, with GDP growth under 5% in the years 2005 to present. The 2008-09 financial crisis made a significant impact on Botswana's economy. However, rapid and appropriate policy response by the government appears to have successfully mitigated the effects of that shock on the broader economy. Botswana's economy is still heavily based on diamonds: the country is the world's largest diamond producer, having 25% of the world diamond market in terms of value. Diamonds account for 70% of its export earnings, 30% of its gross domestic product and more than half of all government revenues. All of this is generated by Debswana, a company equally owned by the government and De Beers of South Africa. In the 2006 production year, Debswana set a new record—18.6 million carats. As of November 2009, Botswana has used an increase in diamond mining as a basis for a substantial economic recovery, a reversal of an earlier plan to cut diamond production because of a lack of demand.

Faced with significant unemployment—as high as 40%—Botswana has pressured its mining partner, De Beers, to help it enter the lucrative diamond-processing industry. Globally, rough diamond production worth $12 billion hugely increases in value—to around $65 billion—by the time it is sold in jewelry shops. Botswana had particularly strong leverage when it came time for De Beers to renew its diamond mining licenses: its high-quality stone account for about two-thirds of the De Beers output. As a consequence, De Beers agreed to transfer its diamond-mixing operations—mixing them into assortments to be purchased by those licensed to buy in bulk—from London to Gaborone by 2009.

An additional possibility of improving diamond revenues is to add value by cutting and polishing the gems locally. Internationally, the trade is dominated by low-wage India, which controls 95% of the market. Because of wage differentials De Beers was reluctant to pursue local diamond transformation, but after the Leviev Group, owned by the Israeli billionaire Lev Leviev showed interest in establishing a polishing plant in Botswana, De Beers reversed track. In May 2006, it signed an agreement with Botswana to set up facilities to cut, polish and market the stones. By the end of 2006, there were four diamond cutting factories in Botswana; eleven others have been licensed and are due to open in the subsequent years.

Despite the economic dominance of diamonds, the bulk of Botswana's workforce is employed in agriculture, though the primary sector contributes only 2.6% of GDP. The national cattle herd is almost three million head and represents an important source of food, income and employment, either directly or indirectly, through related industries (processing and canning meat products, hide tanning, shoes and other leather products).

The state-run Botswana Meat Commission (BMC) coordinates and processes meat production and has a statutory monopoly on the export of beef. European sales account for 90% of total exports. BMC efforts to revitalize the industry have been hindered by drought and periodic outbreaks of foot and mouth disease. The latest, in May 2006, was caused by infected cattle from Zimbabwe, where government and farmers are too poor to vaccinate cattle. Thousands of head of cattle had to be destroyed to control the disease; the country's two abattoirs were closed, jobs and revenues lost.

Dusk in the Kalahari *Das Parlament*

Botswana

Politics

The driving imperative of Botswana's government is diversification of the economy. Mining jobs account for only 3.6% of the country's workforce, and attempts to diversify into manufacturing have barely dented an unemployment rate estimated at 21%. Young, jobless voters have been the principal support of opposition parties, and the government has been unable to generate sufficient new jobs to absorb the 27,000 school leavers who enter the employment market each year. President Mogae singled out tourism, particularly safari tourism, as a potential area for investment. Botswana has developed a robust tourism industry based on high-end safaris with relatively limited ecological footprint in and around the Kalahari Desert and Okavango Delta. As of 2014, Botswana has banned commercial hunting to protect declining wildlife populations and to render tourism sustainable going forward. Safari tourism is a sustainable growth model, which the government hopes can replace the lucrative hunting industry.

The government welcomes diversification investment from any source, and China, which has already built hospitals, schools, and roads in the country, is a major potential investor. China has granted several African countries, including Botswana, "approved" status as a destination for its outbound tourists. There is, however, growing resentment from the grass roots about the country's increasing Chinese presence. "They do not contribute anything to Botswana," said one critic. "They do not even rent our houses. They would rather plant shacks on the site. It is even difficult for them to attract and keep local talent because they underpay us and subject us to insults and racist slurs."

Tensions with neighboring Namibia once ran high due to border disputes but have diminished. The border dispute over an island in the Okavango River was settled in Botswana's favor by the International Court of Justice in December 1999, and the two countries have agreed on a border demarcation. Unresolved are tensions created by Namibian desires to pump water from the Okavango River to its parched capital, Windhoek. This could upset the delicate ecosystem of the vast Okavango delta in northern Botswana, attracting millions of birds and animals, which are the country's principal tourist attraction. Namibia's plans would threaten the delta, which accounts for 75% of Botswana's earnings from tourism, contributes 6% to its gross national product, and employs thousands.

Major political developments include an arrest warrant issued in January 2023 against the former president Ian Khama (1998–2008) on charges of receiving stolen property and illegal possession of a firearm which Khama rejects by refusing to show up at court. Environmental problems include recurrent drought afflicting the crucial Okavanga Delta while the country deals with an apparent overpopulation of elephants, numbering 130,000, with offers to send 20,000 of the giant animals to Germany in protest of restrictions on importing elephant hunting trophies into the country.

At least 350 elephants died in 2020 apparently from a toxic brew of open water tainted by a species of cyanobacteria that released cyanotoxins. Approximately 20 watering holes in the country's Okavango Delta were contaminated across roughly 2,316 square miles. On the domestic political front, Duma Boko was sworn in as the new president after a landslide election victory defeated the Botswana Democratic Party (BDP), which had been in power for nearly 60 years. Heading the Umbrella for Democratic Change (UDC), the new president declared that after "our democracy has remained unbroken, unproven and untested, we tested this democracy . . . passed this test with flying colors." Boko's left-leaning UDC won 36 seats in parliament compared with just four for the conservative BDP, in a stunning reversal for the party that had governed diamond-rich Botswana since its independence from the United Kingdom in 1966. Former President Mokgweetsi Masisi, who conceded defeat two days after the vote as his party's colossal defeat became clear, was in the audience alongside leaders of other regional countries, including Namibia, Zambia, and Zimbabwe. The new president praised his predecessor's "statesmanship."

FUTURE CONSIDERATIONS

While Botswana is an African leader in many categories, including its historical record of democracy and economic growth, it is difficult to prognosticate about the medium-term in Botswana because the country's future depends on several factors. The first, of course, is the extent to which HIV/AIDS can be contained and reversed. Effective progress in combating HIV/AIDS in Africa has the potential to benefit Botswana more than any other country, given its relatively robust institutions and the stability that underpins the country's potential. Conversely, if the crisis continues unabated, then Festus Mogae's prediction of social collapse is a real possibility. The second factor is the future of international markets for diamonds and tourism.

Seemingly well-off, Botswana presents a paradox: despite rapid economic growth, its human development statistics have declined. Development has been uneven. Pockets of severe poverty persist in rural areas, the consequence of a contracting agricultural sector that was starved of investment and development while the mining sector was expanded. The 2008–09 financial crisis has contributed to uneven development. The crisis caused increased unemployment and reduced wages for the poorest population. Botswana's high Gini coefficient—the

Botswana

leading measure of inequality—places the country as the third most unequal in the world, with a wide gap between the wealthy and the poor.

Despite this large disparity between classes, Botswana has become a model for resource-rich countries of how to prudently manage natural resource wealth. Sound macroeconomic policies, good governance, and a high rate of public investment have transformed Botswana from one of the poorest countries in the world at the time of its independence into an upper middle-income country today.

Politically, Botswana remains stable and retains a good record of civil liberties, human rights, and political opportunities. This is despite the long predominance of a single party, the BDP. It plays an active role in the Southern African Development community (SADC) and has volunteered troops for humanitarian intervention in other nations. Seretse Khama Ian Khama's first years in the presidency as successor to Mogae have again illustrated the peaceful transitions that mark the country's record. If the spread of HIV/AIDS can be halted and reversed, Botswana will likely regain its mantle as sub-Saharan Africa's greatest success story.

The Kingdom of Lesotho

Catholic Church, National University of Roma, Lesotho　　Photo by Joe Joyner

BASIC FACTS

Area: 30,355 sq. km. (somewhat larger than Maryland)
Population: 2,210,646 (June 2023 est.)
Capital City: Maseru
Government Type: Parliamentary constitutional monarchy
Neighboring Countries: Lesotho is completely surrounded by South Africa.
Official Languages: Sesotho, English
Other Principal Languages: Zulu, Xhosa
Ethnic Groups: Sotho 99.7%, Europeans Asians, and others, 0.3%
Principal Religions: Christian 80%; indigenous beliefs 20%
Former Colonial Status: British Protectorate (1868–1966)
Independence Date: October 4, 1966
GDP Per Capita (IMF 2023 est.): $1,208 (nominal), $3,251 (PPP)
Gini index: 44.9 (World Bank 2017)
Currency: Basotho Maloti, $US 1 = 18.31 loti (Apr. 2023)
Inflation Rate: 6.1% (2022 est.)
Chief Commercial Products: Manufactures 65% (clothing, footwear, road vehicles), wool and mohair 7%, food and live animals 7%
Foreign Direct Investments (FDI) net inflows: 46,521,786
Literacy Rate: 81% (CIA 2021)
Life Expectancy: 59.87 years (CIA 2023 est.)
Head of State: King Letsie III (since February 7, 1996)
Head of Government: Prime Minister Nfsokoane Samuel Matekane (since Nov. 4, 2020)

LAND AND PEOPLE

Lying in between the peaks of the Drakensburg Mountains, Lesotho is completely surrounded by South Africa. One-fourth of the land is relatively low—from 5,000 to 6,000 feet above sea level. The warm sun raises the temperatures in this agricultural region during the summer. The rest of the nation is made up of scenic highlands from 6,000 to 9,000 feet, with some peaks rising as high as 11,000 feet above sea level.

The snow-capped Drakensburg Mountains form a natural boundary between Lesotho and KwaZulu-Natal Province of the Republic of South Africa; they also provide water for the neighboring country. Mountain snowmelt and gentle rainfall form small streams that unite to form the Orange and Tugela rivers, which flow into South Africa.

Bushmen tribes originally established a thinly populated society high in the mountains of Lesotho. Waves of Bantu migration from east and central Africa of the 17th century then reached the country and settled among the Bushmen. The two ethnic groups intermarried during succeeding generations, and their descendants are known as Basutos, or Basothos.

HISTORY TO PRESENT DAY

For early history, see *Historical Background* and *The Colonial Period: The British*.

An independence agreement was reached in 1966 whereby the colony called Basutoland, became independent from Britain on October 4, 1966, under Chief Leabua Jonathan. When friction developed between Leabua Jonathan and King Moshoeshoe (pronounced Mo-*shway*-shway), the hereditary monarch, Jonathan had the king placed under house arrest.

In the early 1970s, Chief Jonathan took steps to consolidate his power at the expense of democratic institutions. Elections held in early 1970 pitted Chief Jonathan's Basotho National Party (BNP) against the leftist Basotho Congress Party (BCP) led by Ntsu Mokhele. When Jonathan realized he was being defeated, he announced a state of emergency, arrested the opposition and took steps that led to the exile of the king. After agreeing to stay out of politics, the king returned the following year. In late 1973, Jonathan announced plans to make Lesotho a one-party state.

By the mid-1970s, security and stability were in peril. Mokhele and his followers in the BCP attempted a coup in early 1974, which failed. Fierce reprisals were taken against the leadership (some of whom escaped to South Africa and Botswana) and members of the BCP, as well as villages suspected of harboring BCP followers. Then, South Africa's apartheid regime raided Maseru and other parts of Lesotho in 1982–1983 in pursuit of ANC activists. Chief Jonathan denounced the raids and closed the borders. He further alienated South Africa—as well as the Catholic clergy—by visiting communist China, North Korea, Yugoslavia, Romania, and Bulgaria in mid-1983.

Elections were not held from 1970 into the 1980s. In July 1985, Chief Jonathan announced that balloting would take place in September, but when no opposition candidates registered to run by the August 14 deadline, he declared there was no need for an election. Jonathan continued instead to develop the institutions of a leftist single-party state. He formed a "Youth League of Chief Jonathan's Basotho National Party" and imported North Korean "advisers."

The trend towards leftism upset the conservative military, which finally ousted Chief Jonathan on January 20, 1986, and installed a Military Council headed by Major General Metsing Lekhanya. The military reopened the border with South Africa, and amnestied all imprisoned opposition leaders, including Ntsu Mokhele.

Lesotho

King Moshoeshoe, however, defied the military with a decree that all political activity would cease for two years. General Lekhanya ultimately sent the king into exile in the spring of 1990.

To legitimize itself, the military installed the eldest son of the king, Crown Prince Mohato Sereng Seeisa (King Letsie III) as monarch in late 1990. It also scheduled parliamentary elections for 1993, the first since the annulled election of 1970. The result gave the BCP all 65 seats in the National Assembly, and Ntsu Mokhele, now a centrist, became prime minister. Moshoeshoe II was restored to the throne in January 1995, but died under mysterious circumstances in an auto accident in early 1996 and was succeeded by the crown prince.

In July 1997, Mokhele split from the BCP after factions within the party sought to oust him from the party leadership. Mokhele took a majority of 40 members of parliament with him and created the Lesotho Congress for Democracy (LCD). The new formation then declared itself the government. King Letsie dissolved the squabbling parliament in February 1998 to prepare for May elections.

The new LCD party won 79 out of 80 parliamentary seats. As Ntsu Mokhele was sidelined from active politics by age and health, Pakalitha Mosisili was chosen to be prime minister. The opposition, stung by the magnitude of its defeat, mounted protests. The King's palace was blockaded by protesters, and electoral experts from Botswana, South Africa, and Zimbabwe, were called in to examine the election. The probe was completed in two weeks, but its publication was delayed, which only added fuel to the protesters' indignation. When finally released, the commission's report evinced "serious concerns" about the general election, but its overall conclusion, expressed in tortured prose and double negatives, was that "We cannot postulate that the result does not reflect the will of the Lesotho electorate."

Demonstrators closed government offices in the capital, Maseru, locked the gates of parliament, and shut down the Lesotho Bank. In the midst of the demonstrations junior army officers mutinied. They took senior officers prisoner and forced their resignation. Sensing a coup very much in the air, the government requested assistance from the Southern African Development Community (SADC).

South Africa and Botswana agreed to intervene to restore order. South Africa sent in an initial force of 600 soldiers on September 22, 1998, but was unprepared for stiff resistance from the Lesotho army. Botswana's forces, responsible for securing Maseru, were delayed, which had disastrous consequences for the city. Young Lesotho nationalists vented their rage

His Majesty King Letsie III

at South Africa by looting, burning, and destroying businesses owned by South Africans. The flames spread and much of the capital was reduced to ruins. Some 60 people died in the events.

Negotiations produced an Interim Political Authority (IPA) that would steer the country to new elections. The IPA consisted of two members from each of Lesotho's 12 political parties. It was supposed to conclude its work in 18 months, but eventually took four years to produce a plan to which all parties agreed: 80 Assembly seats would remain single-member districts while an additional 40 would be distributed by proportional representation.

The May 2002 election resulted in another sweeping victory for the LCD, which took 77 of the 120 seats for an absolute majority in parliament. The Lesotho People's Congress (LPC) secured 21 seats and other opposition parties took the rest. Observers were unanimous in declaring it free, fair, and transparent, undercutting the complaints of fraud issued by discontented losers.

Comfortable electoral majorities can lead to complacency, and aging leaders who do not retire when expected can prompt factionalism. Few were surprised when Lesotho's charismatic ex-foreign minister, Tom Thabane, took 17 other LCD members across the parliamentary aisle and joined the opposition to Prime Minister Mosisili in October 2006. Thabane's new party, the All Basotho Convention (ABC), was an open enticement for further LCD defections, something the government could not afford. His majority reduced to a dangerously thin two votes, Mosisili called upon the king to dissolve parliament.

Elections were scheduled for February 2007. Far better organized than its opponents, the LCD once again triumphed, taking 61 of the 80 contested constituencies. Its principal rival, the ABC took 17 seats. Of the 40 seats distributed proportionally, the LCD's alliance partner, the National Independence Party, won 21 and the ABC's ally, the Lesotho Worker Party, took 10. Prime Minister Mosisili thus began his new term with a governing alliance that held over two-thirds of the seats. Observers assessed the election as "credible, free and fair," but the opposition claimed collusion between the electoral commission and the LCD in the distribution of the proportional seats.

In 2009, the big news out of Lesotho was the government's report of an assassination attempt against the prime minister on April 22. Armed gunmen attacked Mosisili's home in Maseru, and three were killed by the authorities. Mosisili survived unscathed, but the unsettling event generated condemnation from South Africa's interim president and the Southern African Development Community (SADC). In April 2011, seven mercenaries were charged for this attempted assassination.

Because of the dispute over the 2007 election, in 2011 the government announced a new allocation system for seats in parliament for the May 2012 elections that included 80 members selected from district constituencies and 40 more by proportional representation of parties. In the meantime, the governing LCD split. Mosisili left the party to form the Democratic Congress (DC), and took a governing majority of parliamentarians with him. In the 2012 elections, Mosisili failed to win the required majority of the parliamentary seats. Former foreign minister Thomas Thabane of the All Basotho Convention party was sworn in as Prime Minister on June 8th, 2012. Thabane's ABC allied with the LCD, the Basotho National Party, and two other parties (but not Mosisili's DC) to form a coalition government. US Secretary of State Hillary Clinton congratulated Lesotho on the peaceful transition and commitment to democracy saying, "These successful elections demonstrate a commitment to multiparty democracy and represent a historic moment for the people of Lesotho as the country forms its first coalition government." Even Mosisili agreed, commenting that this peaceful transition demonstrates, "the growth of the country's democracy."

CONTEMPORARY THEMES

The people of Lesotho have a very high rate of literacy—roughly 90%—despite the fact that 80% live in rural areas. Sheep and cattle raising are among the main economic activities among the scenic peaks and plateaus, but all is not idyllic. Deeply impoverished, Lesotho has few employment opportunities, and Basotho men regularly migrate to South Africa to find work. Mobility and prolonged residence away from families have undoubtedly contributed to Lesotho's extremely high HIV/AIDS prevalence rate and consequent social and economic devastation.

Lesotho

United Nations estimates from 2009 are that almost 24% of Lesotho's economically productive population (between the ages of 15 and 49) is HIV positive. This is one of the highest rates in the world. Women are the most vulnerable, and at one time in the 2000s, 52% of all pregnant women in urban areas have tested positive for HIV. According to government figures 75% of all new infections are found among girls. Life expectancy has dropped to just 45 years from as high as 60 years for women in the early 1990s, according to the World Bank. AIDS deaths have left behind a growing legacy of orphaned and vulnerable children. Of the million people under the age of 18 in Lesotho, there are an estimated 200,000 orphans, of which about 130,000 are as a result of AIDS. Prime Minister Mosisili started a campaign for universal voluntary HIV/AIDS testing, but cultural taboos on talking about sex have complicated these efforts. The social stigma attached to HIV remains the greatest obstacle to dealing with the epidemic. In these conditions it's difficult to get the government's free antiretroviral drugs to the people who need them.

Lesotho celebrated 40 years of independence in October 2006 by unfurling a new national flag. It replaced one designed by the military government after the 1986 coup with its martial overtones: spears, club and shield on the same colors.

Approximately 85% of rural households depend on agriculture for their livelihoods, but harvests have been challenging. Only 11% of the country is suitable for cultivation, and the rest is comprised of rocky mountains and hills. Crop yields and livestock numbers have fallen since the 1970s due to drought, hailstorms, tornados, excessive rains, and other acts of nature. Disease, theft, and mismanagement have also diminished agricultural production. Cattle still do the bulk of plowing and stock theft has severely affected output. To confront these challenges, the government has attempted fixes ranging from purchasing a fleet of 50 tractors, to resettling farmers, to introducing alternative crops like seed potatoes, giant garlic and paprika. All the while, AIDS has only exacerbated the agricultural decline by weakening and killing those most capable of bringing in the harvest.

Lesotho is completely surrounded by South Africa, possessing no significant natural resources, and is economically dependent on its larger neighbor. As a result, large numbers of Basotho men traditionally leave to work in the mines of South Africa. At one time 70% of rural household income came from remittances sent by migrant workers. However, the decline of mining jobs in the late 1990s forced many Basotho men to return to Lesotho, where they faced extended unemployment; Lesotho's unemployment rate rose to a staggering 40% to 45%. Remittances once comprised about two-thirds of GDP (around 1990), but declined to about one-third in 1996 and are much less today.

The kingdom's principal revenues are now two sources: customs receipts from the Southern African Customs Union (SACU) and annual royalties from South Africa for water produced by the Lesotho Highlands Water Project (LHWP), known as Lesotho's "white gold." SACU receipts are in decline due to freer regional trade, but income from the LHWP amounts to about $30 million a year. The LHWP has become the largest single source of foreign exchange in the kingdom and provides 75% of the state's budget. With an elaborate series of dams, tunnels, and canals, the LHWP diverts the waters of the Orange River, in the mountains of Lesotho, to drier industrial areas of South Africa. Estimated to cost over $4 billion, the project was one of Africa's biggest civil engineering undertakings.

The LHWP, it should be noted, illustrates some of the ironies of development projects. The Mohale Dam inundated some of Lesotho's most fertile land, and the only region that produced a food surplus. In supporting the project, the World Bank argued that earnings from water sales to South Africa would far exceed the value of Mohale Valley crops. The second irony of the LHWP is that while it supplies South Africa with millions of cubic meters of water per year, Maseru and other lowland districts of Lesotho suffer serious water shortages. Feasibility studies for a Lesotho Lowlands Water Supply Scheme (LLWSS) to supply water to Maseru and the surrounding area have been conducted. The Millennium Challenge Corporation may help fund dams close to Maseru to support its small but developing industrial base, particularly its clothing manufactures.

As a consequence of the U.S. African Growth Opportunities Act (AGOA), East Asian textile firms rushed into Lesotho in the early 2000s to take advantage of cheap labor and reduced duties on African manufactured goods entering the U.S, investing more than $100 million and creating new jobs that made the industry Lesotho's largest employer with more than 50,000 workers. By 2003, the industry represented 10.5% of Lesotho's GDP and was the country's biggest foreign exchange earner, but beginning in January 2005 textile quotas were eliminated worldwide and factories began to close their doors. Over the December 2004 holiday period, six foreign-owned textile factories closed their doors, leaving 6,650 workers jobless; even worse, the owners—from China, Taiwan, Mauritius, and Malaysia—departed without informing or paying their employees. According to many factory workers, this treatment was indicative of horrific labor conditions in the industry.

Major political developments include the winning of 56 seats out of 120 in the parliament in the October 2022 elections by the recently established Revolution for Prosperity Party led by a millionaire businessman. Opposition politicians have also put forward a proposal for reclaiming large swaths of territory in South Africa, including the neighboring Free State, which has not been acted upon by the ruling government coalition. With one-third of the population living in poverty, the country is also plagued by outbreaks of gang violence.

Adding insult to injury, the country has also been hit by a major regional drought beginning in late 2024. Millions of people are going hungry across Southern Africa as the drought has destroyed crops and livestock. Lesotho along with Malawi, Namibia, Zambia, and Zimbabwe have all declared a state of national disaster while Angola and Mozambique have also been severely affected. Estimates are that 27 million lives have suffered, including 21 million children who are malnourished. Tens of millions of people in the region rely on small-scale agriculture, irrigated by rain, for their food and to make money to buy provisions. Aid agencies have warned of a potential disaster as the El Nino weather phenomenon led to below-average rainfall across the region with intensified effects from rising temperatures linked to climate change. The weather trends as well as the tariffs proposed by the United States in 2025 could have deleterious effects on the country's production and export of denim wear.

FUTURE CONSIDERATIONS

Lesotho is one of the world's lowest-income democracies. Unlike South Africa, the country has little industrial base to speak of, and relies on a variety of national survival techniques, including migrants'

Basotho Herdsmen ©IRIN

Lesotho

remittances and the exportation of its primary natural resource: water. A massive drought in 2007 meant some of the water resources literally dried up. This only serves to underline the precariousness of economic situations for the citizens of Lesotho. Poverty is endemic and unemployment is still estimated at a horrible 45%. Growth has been moderately positive but remains too slow to put a significant dent in these unemployment figures.

In the political arena, the country remains a democracy with fragmented institutions; the presence of about twenty registered political parties in a small country is indicative of the level of political activity. Prospects for future stability are called into question by internal struggles among and between leading political parties, as evidenced by the protests over the allocation of parliamentary seats following polling in 2007. The country's democracy seems relatively secure (despite the assassination attempt on the prime minister in April 2009), but not very efficacious.

The Republic of Malawi

Malawi's future   Photo by Sean Patrick

BASIC FACTS

Area: 118,484 sq. km. or 45,747 sq. mi.
Population: 21,279,597 (June 2023 est.)
Capital City: Lilongwe
Government Type: Presidential Repulic
Neighboring Countries: Mozambique (south, southwest, southeast); Zambia (northwest); Tanzania (northeast)
Official Languages: English and Chichewa
Other Principal Languages: Lomwe, Ngoni, NyakYusa-Ngonde, Nyanja, Sena, Tonga, Tumbuka, and Yao
Ethnic Groups: Chewa, Nyanja, Tumbuko, Yao, Lomwe, Sena, Tonga, Ngoni, Ngonde, Asian, and European
Principal Religions: Christian 82.7%, Islam 13%, Traditional 5%
Former Colonial Status: British Colony (1883–1964)
Independence Day: July 6, 1964
GDP Per Capita (IMF 2023 est.): $496 (nominal), $1,682 (PPP)

Gini Coefficient: 44.7 (World Bank 2016)
Currency: Malawian Kwacha, $USD 1 = 1022.7 kwacha (Apr. 2023)
Inflation Rate: 10.7% (2022 est.)
Chief Commercial Products: Tobacco, tea, cotton, coffee, and sugar
Foreign Direct Investments (FDI) net inflows: 715,693,148
Literacy Rate: 67.3 (CIA 2021)
Life Expectancy: 72.7 years (CIA 2023 est.)
Head of State: President Lazarus Chakwera (since June 28, 2020)
Head of Government: President Lazarus Chakwera (June 28, 2020)

LAND AND PEOPLE

Malawi, formerly known as Nyasaland, is a country of high mountains covered with lush, green foliage, interspersed with large, sparkling lakes and fertile plateaus. Situated on the western edge of the Rift Valley is Lake Malawi, which extends over three-fourths of the eastern boundary of Malawi.

The countryside of Malawi is dominated by sloping peaks. For the most part, these are 3,000 to 4,000 feet above sea level, but rise as high as 8,000 feet in the north. Immediately south of Lake Malawi are the Shire Highlands, a 3,000-foot high gently rolling plateau.

The altitude adds a bit of variation to an otherwise equatorial climate. From November to April, it is pleasantly warm with equatorial rains and sudden thunderstorms. Toward the end of March, the storms reach their peak, after which the rainfall rapidly diminishes. From May to September, wet mists float down from the highlands, invading the cool and dry reaches of the plateaus; there is almost no rainfall during these months.

Malawi is one of the most densely populated countries in Africa, with an average population of 117 per square kilometer. The shape of the country has tended to emphasize regional concentration of its various ethnic groups. This concentration has provided the basis of political support for the country's three main political parties. The United Democratic Front (UDF) draws its strength from the south; the Malawi Congress Party (MCP) is centrally based, and Alliance for Democracy (AFORD) is strongest in the north.

HISTORY TO PRESENT DAY

For early history, see *Historical Background* and *The Colonial Period: The British.*

Independence and the Rule of Hastings Banda (1964–94)

The history of modern politics in Malawi began in 1944 with the creation of the Nyasaland African Congress (NAC), a political body that provided a forum for the expression of African political aspirations, a desire long subordinated to the interests of European settlers. Under pressure from its settlers to create a larger economic space, in 1953 Britain combined its territories of Nyasaland with Northern Rhodesia (now Zambia) and Southern Rhodesia (now Zimbabwe) in what was called the Central African Federation. The move prompted bitter opposition from Africans, and the NAC gained popular support by mobilizing nationalist sentiment to oppose this new federation. One longtime opponent of British federation plans was Dr. Hastings Kamuzu Banda, an Edinburgh-trained medical practitioner. Though working in Ghana, Banda was active in the nationalist cause, and was finally persuaded to return to Nyasaland to lead the NAC in 1958.

As president of the NAC, Banda toured the colony and was able to effectively mobilize nationalist sentiment amongst the peoples of Malawi. Universal suffrage was demanded and disturbances ensued. Colonial authorities declared a state of emergency in 1959 and jailed the troublesome Dr. Banda. As pressures built, Banda was released in 1960, only to be invited a few months later to participate in discussions leading to a new constitution for Nyasaland. Under the new arrangements, Africans were granted a majority in the colony's Legislative Council. The country's first elections in 1961 gave Banda's Malawi Congress Party (MCP) 22 out of 28 seats, and Banda served as minister of natural resources and local government until becoming prime minister in 1963.

Malawi

In that year, the federation was dissolved and a year later, on July 6, 1964, Nyasaland became independent as Malawi.

Against the backdrop of democratic achievement at independence, Banda sought to cement his power and moved decisively toward dictatorship. A new constitution made Malawi a single-party state under the MCP in 1966, and Banda established himself as President-for-Life in 1970. He ruled with autocratic firmness for 30 years, ruthlessly suppressing any opposition. During the 1980s, elections involved only MCP candidates selected by Banda. Opposition figures died under very suspicious circumstances. Human rights violations, particularly those involving the MCP's Malawi Young Pioneers, which emerged as a paramilitary organization, became common. A cult of personality flourished around the dictator.

The economic legacy of the Banda regime was mixed to poor. Following some boom years in the 1960s and 1970s, the 1980s saw little in the way of growth or advancement. By the time of the end of the Cold War in 1991, Malawi was following the African pattern of an unstable and underperforming authoritarian regime.

A Partial Democratic Transition and the Muluzi Presidency (1994–2004)

Under external and internal pressures for political liberalization, the president-for-life grudgingly agreed to a referendum, which was held in 1993. He was stunned when 67% of parliament voted in favor of multiparty democracy. Illness overtook the president in late 1993, forcing him to go to Johannesburg for brain surgery. During his absence, political elites quickly formed a presidential council, adopted a new constitution, and abolished the life presidency. Malawi held multiparty elections in 1994 for the first time in three decades. Emerging victorious was the United Democratic Front (UDF), a new party whose political base lay in the densely populated south. The UDF's candidate for president, Bakili Muluzi, received 47% of the vote to Banda's 34%. Muluzi's UDF also won an 83-seat plurality in the National Assembly, where it joined with independents and disaffected opposition members to create a working majority. The elections demonstrated a marked regional division within the country. The UDF dominated the south, while Banda's Malawi Congress Party took the center and the Alliance for Democracy (AFORD) the north.

In 1995, the new government tried Banda and his supporters for the 1983 murders of opposition leaders. Well into his 90s, Banda was totally deaf, senile, and too ill to attend the sessions. A seven-member court controversially acquitted all defendants in December of that year. In early 1996, Banda addressed the nation on radio and apologized for any and all wrongs that might have occurred during his 30-year tenure. He died in November of 1996, and was remembered by many for his leadership of the nationalist struggle that gave Malawi independence; this was a surprising sentiment towards a leader who used an iron fist in the country for decades.

Former President Bingu wa Mutharika

For the presidential elections of May 1999, the MCP and AFORD formed an electoral coalition to oust President Muluzi. MCP leader Gwanda Chakuamba was designated the alliance's presidential candidate, and AFORD leader Chakufwa Chihana was chosen for the vice-presidential slot, much to the annoyance of the MCP deputy leader John Tembo. Once President Banda's right-hand man, Tembo was perhaps the MCP's longest-serving politician and had long been ambitious for the presidency.

President Muluzi was reelected with 52.4% of the vote to Gwanda Chakuamba's 45.2%, and the president's UDF won 93 seats in the National Assembly, just shy of a majority in the 192-seat house. The MCP won 66 seats and its AFORD ally picked up 29 seats. The opposition vigorously protested election irregularities and took their case to the courts but found no support there. Efforts to boycott parliament failed to find unanimity within the opposition, and rancorous division soon dominated Malawi's politics.

The MCP was soon split by a clash between Chakuamba and John Tembo, who was still smarting from being pushed aside as a vice-presidential candidate in the 1999 elections. The party suddenly had two leaders and two factions, with Tembo's faction opportunistically siding with the UDF in many parliamentary votes. The ruling UDF fared little better; President Muluzi's interest in seeking a third term (which would require a constitutional amendment) angered some party leaders who split off to oppose it.

The issue of a third term for Muluzi dominated political life for the next two years, dividing both the ruling party and opposition and rousing a storm of indignation in the country—led by the powerful religious lobby. Two attempts were made to amend the constitution to permit Muluzi to run for a third five-year term, but each failed. The president conceded defeat in March 2003, announcing he would not seek an additional term in office.

Punishment to those who had not supported third-term efforts was soon meted out. In early April, Muluzi discharged his entire cabinet, getting rid of anyone who had not supported the constitutional amendment and anyone who might have shown an interest in running for the presidency. Leaving nothing to chance, Muluzi also designated his potential successor—a 68-year-old economist, Bingu wa Mutharika. Dr. Mutharika had been deputy governor of the Reserve Bank of Malawi before being appointed economics minister in Muluzi's new "national unity" cabinet. To provide sectarian balance for his UDF ticket, President Muluzi chose fellow Muslim Cassim Chilumpha for the vice-presidential slot. Muluzi's authoritarian style and thwarted ambitions polarized Malawi, divided the UDF, and prompted a host of party defections. Two former UDF leaders—Muluzi's vice president Justin Malewezi and ex-Foreign Minister Brown Mpinganjira—both ran for the presidency.

Bingu wa Mutharika (2004–12), Joyce Banda (2012–14), and Peter Mutharika (2014–present)

The May 2004 elections showcased a deeply divided electorate and produced a minority victory for Mutharika as the UDF/AFORD nominee, though he won only 35% of the vote. His nearest rivals were John Tembo (MPC) with 27%, and Gwanda Chakuamba, who received 26% representing an opposition coalition of seven parties known as *Mgwirizano* (Unity). Observers stopped short of calling the election free or fair, and the opposition lodged a court challenge to the results. The new president also faced an opposition parliament with an opposition majority, as the UDF and AFORD combined to take only 55 seats of 193; the MCP alone had 57, Mgwirizano 25, and independents took 40.

Assumed to be little more than a Muluzi tool, Mutharika soon proved to be his own man as president. Where the previous administration had handled the country's

Malawi

monumental corruption problem with kid gloves, Mutharika declared "zero tolerance." At least five senior UDF figures faced criminal charges, and in February 2006 a former education minister was given a five-year prison term for corruption.

The president's relations with the UDF deteriorated completely. In February 2005, Mutharika resigned from the party, accusing Muluzi of frustrating his anti-corruption campaign and of plotting to assassinate him. He then launched his own Democratic Progressive Party (DPP), which drew support from independents and disgruntled members of the UDF. While this reconfigured the balance of power among political parties, Malawi's political scene remained bitter, personal, and dysfunctional. The parliamentary opposition attempted to impeach the president and tried to force those who defected to the DPP from their seats in the legislature.

For President Mutharika, working with a vice president chosen by former President Muluzi proved impossible. The president accused Vice President Cassim Chilumphaof insubordination, running a parallel government, and failing to perform his duties. After corruption charges against Chilumpha were dismissed by the courts, and an outright presidential firing of Chilumpha declared illegal, the vice president was arrested for treason in April 2006, charged with hiring South African assassins to murder President Mutharika. He went on trial, but later returned to parliament as an independent.

In 2009, the president was re-elected for second term. Mutharika had undoubtedly gained some popularity for his anti-corruption campaigns, but the elections were also imperfect. European Union observers (as well as reputable African observers such as John Kufuor of Ghana) noted in particular the pro-incumbent bias in the state-owned media. Opposition leader John Tembo of the MCP claimed the elections were fraudulent after receiving less than one-third of the reported vote, and former president Muluzi objected on the grounds that he should have been able to run again despite having served two terms. The Constitutional Court rejected his claim only days before the election.

In 2011, President Mutharika made a number of drastic political statements including calling on his party to beat up those who have insulted him and expelling British High Commissioner Fergus Cochrane-Dyet because he had called Mutharika "increasingly autocratic." Nineteen people died in a July anti-government protest. This caused Britain to stop all aid to the country due to economic mismanagement and failure to uphold human rights.

In April 2012, President Mutharika died of a heart attack and Vice President Joyce Banda of the People's Party became the new president. Joyce Banda is the country's first female president, having previously served as Minister of Foreign Affairs (2006–2009), vice president (2009–2012), and as Minister for Gender, Children's Affairs and Community Services as well as a Member of Parliament. She has been active and powerful within Malawi and across Africa in women's issues and humanitarian issues. Mutharika had tried to impeach Banda as vice-president because she did not support Peter Mutharika (his brother) as the next presidential candidate; it appeared that Banda herself intended to run for the position. Though the impeachment was never instituted, Mutharika did expel Banda from the DPP. Banda thus created a new political party—the People's Party—in 2011. The strained relationship between Banda and Peter Mutharika worsened upon Banda's assumption of the presidency. This culminated in Peter Mutharika (along with 11 others) being charged with treason by the Banda government in March 2013.

In one of her first actions as president in April 2012, Banda complied with IMF recommendations and devalued the currency by a third. This hit hard those low-income Malawians that rely on imported food and fuel, and led to some panic buying as citizens feared prices would skyrocket. The move was applauded, however, by some export farmers who hope this will make Malawian goods more competitive abroad.

Joyce Banda's term came to an end in 2014 when the regularly scheduled presidential election was held. The winner was Peter Mutharika, her bitter rival and younger brother of (and former adviser to) Bingu wa Mutharika. Despite the victory, Peter Mutharika's DPP won only a minority of the seats in the National Assembly. The DPP took 50 seats, the Malawi Congress Party 48, and Banda's People's Party took 26, while other parties and independence took 69 additional seats.

CONTEMPORARY THEMES

Malawi is among the lowest-income countries on earth. With little in the way of mineral resources, its economy is almost entirely agriculture-dependent; the sector supports nine out of ten Malawians, most of whom work as smallholders rather than on large plantations. Few smallholder farmers have access to productive land, a situation particularly difficult in the southern region where agriculture is dominated by large estates growing cash crops like tea and tobacco. Government policy under Mutharika sought to better support small-scale farmers, but he got no support from a hostile parliament. Tobacco, which alone accounts for about 70% of export revenue, demonstrates many of the problems of economic development in Malawi. World prices have declined, and farmers barely earn enough to repay loans taken

In Malawi the coffin maker is open 24 hours a day Photo by Ruth Evans

Malawi

Former President Joyce Banda
©IRIN

President Peter Mutharika

out for current crops. Economic weakness has furthered health problems: malnutrition is chronic and nearly half of all children have stunted growth.

Landlocked, Malawi faces high transport bills—estimated as high as a third or more of total import costs—though the situation may be improving. The shortest and cheapest route to the sea for Malawi was for some time the 48-mile rail link to Mozambique's port of Nacala. The track had fallen into disrepair during Mozambique's civil war (which ended in 1992) and Western donors helped rehabilitate it. More promising was the opening of a new Shire-Zambezi waterway that allowed Malawi to create an inland port with access to the Indian Ocean; unfortunately, tensions with Mozambique complicated the opening of the route in late 2010.

Malawi has one of the highest HIV/AIDS infection rates in the world. Statistics from UNICEF (2009) indicate nearly one million Malawians are HIV-positive, or about 11% of adults. The disease led to a decreased life expectancy in the 1990s and early 2000s, and it remains just under 54 years. The economic impact of Malawi's HIV/AIDS epidemic is significant. An estimated 5.8% of Malawi's farm labor force has died of AIDS.

The plight of the country's estimated one million AIDS orphans has been highlighted by the pop singer Madonna. Her charity Raising Malawi has built an orphanage which can house up to 4,000 children. More controversially, she was granted temporary custody of a Malawian baby boy whom she sought to adopt. She eventually was given the permission and is trying her case in the Malawi Supreme Court to obtain permission for another child.

In addition to the AIDS endemic, Malawi has also been struck by a number of societal issues, particularly the issue of marriage equality. In early 2010 two gay Malawian men, Tiwonge Chimbalanga and Steven Monjeza, were arrested for "carnal knowledge against the order of nature" and "gross indecency." Their cases drew widespread international condemnation and was called a significant step back for Malawi's human rights record by the US. In May 2010, the men were given a presidential pardon and released.

Concerned with Malawi's endemic corruption and fiscal management, the IMF stopped aid disbursements to the country in December 2000. (About a third of the country's annual budget was expected to disappear into the pockets of leading politicians and their clients.) The impact was critical: up to 80% of Malawi's development budget was funded by donors, and once the IMF had made its decision, most donors followed suit. Under Mutharika, the government put its financial house in better order. An IMF mission in late 2004 was "encouraged by recent signs that Malawi's economy is strengthening," and in August 2005 a new poverty reduction program was approved. It provides gradual reduction in domestic debt and debt servicing for the first time since the late 1990s.

The greatest challenge for the peop[e of Malawi is dealing with the multifaceted effects of global climate change on the agricultural sector, where episodic heatwaves, floods, drought, and outbreak of disease have reduced crop yields and resulted in major loss of topsoil and disruptions to electricity supply in rural areas. Particularly destructive was a prolonged dry spell from the impact of the El Nino in 2016–2017, which affected the major crops of maize, rice, cassava, and bananas. Fully one half of the population lives below the poverty line.

In June 2024, President Lazarus Chakwera confirmed the death of Vice President Saulos Klaus Chilima in the crash of a military aircraft. The country also continued to suffer from an ongoing drought afflicting the entire region and outbreaks of cholera while a persistent shortage of foreign currency dragged down living standards. The government increased support (especially for nurses) and cut back on travel by government officials and other public expenditures.

FUTURE CONSIDERATIONS

Despite several economic reforms made in recent years, Malawi remains one of the poorest countries on earth; per capita income is among the lowest in Africa, and the country comes near the bottom on the UN's Human Development Index. Economic growth was sluggish for years, though it was robust at rates of over 5% (and sometimes as high as 8% or 9%) from 2006 to up to the devaluation of 2012. Part of the volatility comes from the fact that Malawi's four major export crops—tobacco, tea, sugar and coffee—account for more than 90% of the country's export revenue.

The assumption of power by Joyce Banda has generated considerable political friction with Peter Mutharika, brother of the deceased president. While Mutharika may indeed have been guilty of attempting to prevent Banda's assuming the presidency, he appears as a *de facto* political prisoner. This exacerbates factional divisions in the country. The difficult relationship between opposition parties and the president mean trust is in short supply. Observers of Malawi can anticipate much of the opposition's energy will be spent fighting presidential initiatives, though opposition parties typically have minor impacts on African political outcomes.

While not the most repressive country on the continent, Malawi's democratic credentials remain quite suspect. Continued foreign aid may support the government budget to a large degree, and the economy to an extent, but Malawi does not look like a candidate to become one of Africa's model countries in economic or political terms in the coming decade.

The Republic of Mozambique

Electoral Remains ©IRIN

BASIC FACTS

Area: 799,380 sq. km.
Population: 32,513,805 (June 2023 est.)
Capital City: Maputo
Government Type: Presidential Republic
Neighboring Countries: Tanzania (north); Malawi, Zambia (northwest); Zimbabwe (west); South Africa, Swaziland (southwest); Madagascar lies 300 to 600 miles off the eastern coast.
Official Language: Portuguese
Other Principal Languages: Over 30, including Emakhuwa, Xichangana, Cisena, Elomwe, Echuwabo, Chopi, Chwabo, Lomwe, Makhuwa, Makonde, Marendje, Nyanja, Ronga, Sena, Shona, Tsonga, and Tswa
Ethnic Groups: Indigenous tribal groups 99.66% (Shangaan, Chokwe, Manyika, Sena, Makua, and others), Europeans 0.06% Euro-Africans 0.2%, Indians 0.08%
Principal Religions: Catholic 28%, Protestant 28%, Muslim 18%, other 7.2%, none 18.7%
Former Colonial Status: Portuguese colony (1498-1975)
Independence Date: June 25, 1975
GDP Per Capita (IMF 2023 est.): $587 (nominal), $1,556 (PPP)
Gini index: 54 (World Bank 2014)
Currency: Metical, $US 1 = 63.84 meticals (Apr. 2023)
Inflation rate: 8.5% (2022 est.)

Chief Commercial Products: Aluminum, prawns and other fish, cotton, cashew nuts, timber, sugar.
Foreign Direct Investments (FDI) net inflows: 4,998,799,334
Literacy Rate: 63.4% (CIA 2021)
Life Expectancy: 57.7 years (CIA 2023 est.)
Head of State: President Filipe Jacinto Nyusi (since January 15, 2015)
Head of Government: President Filipe Jacinto Nyusi (since Jan

LAND AND PEOPLE

The flat terrain of the coastline of Mozambique, filled with dense, tropical jungle in areas which are not cleared, gives way gradually to a series of plateaus and highlands, which gently rise toward high mountains in the part closest to the western borders. Towering green peaks are located in the Lake Nyasa area, where the temperature is moderated by the altitude. Most of the intense agricultural production takes place in the coastal lowlands and surrounding plateaus.

Among other artists, Mozambique is home to one of Africa's most internationally renowned writers, the novelist Mia Couto. Several of Couto's novels have been translated into languages beyond the original Portuguese, including *Under the Frangipani* (*A varanda do frangipani*). His novel *Sleepwalking Land* (*Terra sonâmbula*) was nominated as one of the top 12 African books of the 20th century by a panel of writers and critics.

HISTORY TO PRESENT DAY

For early history, see *Historical Background* and *The Colonial Period: The Portuguese*.

Struggle for Independence

Nationalist resistance to Portugal's colonialism was organized in 1962 by left-wing Mozambican exiles living in neighboring Tanzania. Under the leadership of Eduardo Mondlane, they formed the Mozambique

Mozambique

Liberation Front (FRELIMO: *Frente de Libertação de Moçambique*) and began a guerrilla war against the Portuguese in 1964. Mondlane was assassinated in 1969, but the war effort was continued and expanded by his successor, Samora Machel.

Portugal poured 70,000 troops into the colony to suppress the insurrection, but by the early 1970s it could do little more than defend the cities. Frelimo controlled most of the countryside and drained Portuguese manpower, resources, and will. Disgruntled army officers in Portugal overthrew the military regime in Lisbon in April 1974, and the new government granted Mozambique its independence a year later. FRELIMO created a single-party state organized on Marxist-Leninist principles with Machel as president.

The Portuguese colonial legacy was appalling, and the transfer of power was vindictive, with departing colonial officials burning government files and business records. After more than 400 years of Portuguese presence, more than 90% of Mozambique's population was illiterate. For the entire country there were only 80 doctors and 100 high school teachers. As the new government led by the Frelimo party imposed socialist organization and planning, including large-scale nationalization, a mass exodus of Portuguese colonists worsened. Over 100,000 left, taking with them the bulk of the country's administrative and managerial skills. What they could not take, they destroyed. Some famously drove tractors into the sea, while others ripped plumbing out of buildings or destroyed factories.

The Rise of FRELIMO, Samora Machel (1975–1986), and the Civil War

The decline of the colonizing power and rise of Frelimo hit especially hard in agriculture, the backbone of Mozambique's economy. Following Stalinist precedent, the Frelimo government collectivized agriculture, creating state farms and organizing agricultural cooperatives and communal villages. Some 4,000 commercial farms were abandoned, resulting in disastrous declines in export-crop production. Major portions of export earnings were devoted to the purchase of farm equipment, but there were too few skilled mechanics to maintain them and insufficient income to buy spare parts. Costly farm machinery lay idle and mechanized agriculture faltered.

Like its colonial predecessor, the Frelimo government based itself on the cities and among Lusophone urban elites, especially in the capital—renamed Maputo from its former name Lourenço Marques. The regime grew increasingly out of touch with the countryside. It appointed village "presidents" loyal to Frelimo and discarded traditional chiefs. Government-set prices for food crops were kept low to placate Frelimo's urban constituency, but they offered peasant farmers no incentive to produce. Not unexpectedly, farmers returned to subsistence production.

By 1983, even the most optimistic Marxists had to admit that Mozambican socialism had failed. Eighty percent of state resources had gone to state farms, but they represented only 10% of the country's agricultural sector. Given a shortage of trained manpower, basic record keeping, and production reports were virtually impossible. State farms and enterprises sent false reports to the government because they had no facts to report. When the government made it a crime to submit false reports, it got none at all.

Overt opposition to Frelimo's policies coalesced in 1976 with the aid of the white government of neighboring Rhodesia (which later became Zimbabwe). Fearful of Mozambican aid to Robert Mugabe's rebel forces fighting to dislodge it, the Rhodesian government organized Mozambican dissidents into an opposition army that called itself the Mozambican National Resistance (RENAMO: *Resistência Nacional Moçambicana*). When Mugabe's forces triumphed in Rhodesia, support of Renamo fell to the apartheid government of South Africa, equally terrified of black radicalism on its borders supporting its own black opposition, the African National Congress (ANC).

Rural, conservative, traditional, and speaking the indigenous languages of the illiterate populations of central and northern Mozambique, Renamo represented much that Frelimo was not. For 16 years, it engaged the Frelimo government in bloody civil war, destroying anything and everything that symbolized the Frelimo state, including roads and rail lines, utility lines, schools, clinics, stores, farms, and factories. The civil war brought the economy to a standstill and was a humanitarian catastrophe: it killed well over 100,000 and displaced more than a million people.

Faced with civil war and a collapsed economy, Frelimo's Fourth Party Congress in 1983 began to shift the state away from centralized planning and forced social organization. President Machel, who once thundered to his audience that "Our country will be the grave of capitalism and exploitation," began to solicit western investors.

By 1984, the government sought to cut off its Renamo opponent by severing the rebel group's ties with South Africa. A mutual agreement was reached at the border town of Nkomati: Mozambique would end sanctuary and support for ANC forces and in exchange South Africa would end its military support for Renamo. Despite the Nkomati Accord, the South African army continued to aid and supply Renamo forces, which in turn continued their depredations in Mozambique.

In October 1986, President Machel was killed when his plane, Russian built and piloted, crashed under mysterious circumstances shortly before landing in Maputo; suspicions of South African involvement remain. Frelimo's central committee met and elected foreign minister Joachim Chissano to the positions of party chairman and president.

At the Mozambique-Zimbabwe border Photo by David Johns

Mozambique

Joaquim Chissano (1986–2005), the Peace Accord, and the Cardoso Trial

President Chissano was regarded as a moderate and the man who had convinced Samora Machel to make overtures to western capital, and he expanded Machel's tentative opening to the West. The shift away from Marxism accelerated with the end of the Cold War. With Chissano as party leader, Frelimo's Fifth Congress ended the party's official Marxist-Leninist orientation in 1989. Chissano learned the language of Western democracy and economic liberalism. He facilitated transition to multiparty elections and acquiesced to economic reform policies proposed by the International Monetary Fund (IMF).

In October 1992, President Chissano and Renamo chief Afonso Dhlakama signed a peace accord. The two were separated by deep mutual suspicion, 16 years of devastating civil war, and diametrically opposed ideological visions. Frelimo has never accepted Renamo as a legitimate representative of those rejected and marginalized by its policies. Some in Frelimo still refer to Renamo as "bandits" to this day, but Mozambique has now seen several presidential and parliamentary elections that have been at least nominally multiparty proceedings.

The first electoral competition between the two antagonists came in 1994. Opposition to Chissano came from Dhlakama and ten other presidential candidates. The elections graphically showed the regional cleavage of Mozambique. Frelimo was popular in southern, more populated areas and swept the capital of Maputo. Chissano won slightly more than half the votes cast for president. Dhlakama ran strongly in the north—a thousand miles from Maputo—and central areas, winning 34% of presidential votes. Renamo ran ahead of its leader in parliamentary races, winning 112 of 250 seats in the Assembly of the Republic to Frelimo's 129.

Municipal elections in June 1998 were meant to implement Frelimo's decentralization policies. Instead, they displayed Frelimo's fundamental resistance to surrendering control over local authorities. Frelimo proposed to devolve authority to only 33 larger cities already organized and dominated by executive councils appointed by, and totally integrated into, the structure of the Frelimo state. Renamo encouraged the government to recognize the power of traditional rural authorities and demanded official recognition of their role in local communities. Frelimo rejected this, and Renamo declared an election boycott that resulted in 85% of registered voters absenting themselves from the polls. In 19 of the 33 constituencies allowed to elect municipal assemblies, Frelimo was the only party competing. In the northern

Mozambique Provinces

cities of Nampula and Beira, abstention rates were 92% and 90%.

Nationally, the Frelimo government liberalized the state-dominated economy and become the darling of donors and international lending agencies. Development money poured into Mozambique and economic growth rates accelerated for several years, though a downside was an expansion in underground and criminal activity.

In the December 1999 presidential election figures, President Chissano won a surprisingly close victory in his reelection bid, collecting 52.3% of the vote to Dhlakama's 47.7%. In elections for the 250-seat Assembly of the Republic, all minor parties received less than 5% of the vote and were completely shut out: Frelimo took 133 seats and Renamo 117. There were serious questions about the results and some diplomatic observers suspected Dhlakama actually won. On a split vote, Mozambique's Supreme Court ultimately rejected the request by Renamo and a coalition of smaller parties to invalidate the results.

Political tensions after the 1999 elections peaked in November 2000 when national protests went tragically awry in the northern community of Montepuez. Demonstrators converged on the police station and began to liberate arms and prisoners. Seven policemen were beaten to death after they had fired on the crowd; at least 18 demonstrators were shot to death. Nationally, over 40 people were killed in the demonstrations, most of them by police bullets. The next day security forces began a dragnet to arrest Renamo leaders and sympathizers throughout the northern region. Hundreds were arrested and most were jailed in deplorable conditions of overcrowding. In Montepuez, 84 prisoners died in a single night from asphyxia; their bodies were buried in a mass grave. Renamo accused the Frelimo regime of poisoning and killing the prisoners.

Mozambique then received an additional shock: Carlos Cardoso, the country's most respected investigative journalist, was assassinated gangland style. His exposés had revealed growing and pervasive corruption in the Frelimo state and his death highlighted the country's growing crime and criminality. Two years later, in November 2002, six individuals were tried for murder and complicity. The trial, broadcast live on radio and TV, was conducted in a high security prison in Maputo for safety reasons.

Testimony publicly confirmed the ramification of corruption through every level of the Frelimo state. At the heart of the conspiracy were two members of the rich, powerful, and politically well-connected Abdul Satar family. Cardoso was investigating how they defrauded a state-owned bank of $14 million, and the trial elicited allegations of international drug dealing, money laundering, and customs fraud, all of which was abetted by corruption in various state administrative structures.

One of the defendants—Aníbal António dos Santos Júnior ("Anibalzinho"), the man responsible for organizing the assassination and hiring the gunmen—was tried *in absentia*, having "escaped" a high security prison in September 2002 shortly before the trial began. It was a release that could have only been authorized at the highest level, and Attorney General Joaquim Madeira called it "a body blow to our judicial system." The minister of the interior (in whose jurisdiction the prison system falls) responded to a parliamentary inquiry with a question of his own: "In what part of the world do prisoners not escape from jails?"

Trial testimony brought the Cardoso murder very close to President Chissano himself. Three of the defendants testified that Nyimpine Chissano, the president's eldest son (and business partner of the Abdul Satars), had paid for the assassination. The lead investigator confirmed that one of the defendants had "confessed in a number of conversations" that Nyimpine Chissano son had ordered the assassination. When called before the court, Nyimpine denied everything, but the trial judge, courageously persisting in the face of threats on his life, opened a dossier for further investigation of "others" who might have been involved in the murder.

Mozambique

Former President Armando Guebuza

At the end of January 2003, all six were found guilty of Cardoso's murder and sentenced to jail for 23 to 28 years. Anibalzinho, captured in South Africa the day before the sentence was rendered, received the longest sentence. In addition to jail time, the defendants had to pay restitution to the Cardoso family of four billion *meticais*, about $175,000. The Mozambican press named the judge "personality of the year."

The case continued as soap opera: Anibalzinho escaped once again in May 2004, this time to Canada. Captured and retried, he was yet again found guilty on nine different charges in January 2006, and handed even stiffer punishment: 30 years in jail and payment of 14 billion meticais ($560,000) to his victim's children. Having granted extraordinary privileges to such a dangerous inmate—like having his meals brought in by relatives—Mozambican police claimed to have frustrated yet another escape attempt in March 2006. A young niece allegedly brought dinner and escape tools: a screwdriver secreted in a radio, small tubes of super glue hidden in a packet of soap, and a tin of shoe polish. (It would appear to take little to escape Mozambican confinement.) Less than 48 hours later, his privileges revoked, Anibalzinho fashioned a noose from his own trousers and tried to hang himself from the bars of his prison cell but was deterred by seemingly now more vigilant guards. Meanwhile, charges against Nyimpine Chissano for involvement in the Cardoso assassination remained in judicial limbo until he was found dead in his house in late 2007; while the cause of death was uncertain, it was claimed he had heart trouble.

The Armando Guebuza Presidency (2005–2015)

When President Joaquim Chissano announced that he would not run for a third term, he set off a political scramble between the socialist hardliners who thought Chissano had gone too far in economic liberalization and reformists who wanted to push further. In June 2002, Frelimo's central committee overwhelmingly elected Armando Guebuza, head of Frelimo's parliamentary group, the party's secretary-general and thus its candidate in the next presidential election.

Guebuza was a reformer who had a reputation for toughness and credibility with the left wing of Frelimo. A militant of the earliest Frelimo days, it was Guebuza who launched the "24/20" slogan at independence that gave Portuguese settlers 24 hours to leave with only 20 pounds of baggage. He was also associated with the forced removal program of 1983 where the urban unemployed were moved to sparsely populated northern rural areas. With the fall of the Soviet Union, Guebuza became a pro-Western, free-market liberal; in the process he became one of the country's richest men. He has extensive interests in a variety of sectors—banking, export-import, tourism, fishing, transport—and his business partners are frequently government colleagues or involved in state companies.

The revelations of the Cardoso trial badly damaged Frelimo's credibility and prestige. It also strengthened, in the words of one October 2006 governance-monitoring report, "the public's perception that organized criminal elements have connections with senior government officials." As one Frelimo legislator put it: "clearly the state has been highly infiltrated by organized crime." In urging officials to act promptly against corruption, he articulated the central dilemma facing Mozambique: "If the state does not control the bandits, the bandits will control it." In January 2007, the interior minister admitted that criminals had infiltrated the police and promised to reform police recruitment.

Despite the incumbent party's troubles, Renamo was not capable of capitalizing on crime and corruption in an electoral process still controlled by the Frelimo state. December 2004 presidential and parliamentary elections pitted Renamo's standard bearer Afonso Dhlakama against Frelimo's Armando Guebuza. Far better organized and financed, Frelimo won by a large margin. Guebuza took 64% of the vote and Dhlakama 32%. Frelimo captured nine of eleven provinces, winning 160 seats in the Assembly of the Republic, Mozambique's unicameral legislature; Renamo took the remaining 90 seats. Smaller parties were completely shut out.

Independent observers were not willing to call the election free and fair, and Renamo justifiably lodged complaints: in at least 100 polling stations in central and northern Mozambique (Renamo's traditional stronghold) official figures put the turnout at between (a suspiciously high) 92% and (an even more suspicious) 101%, almost all of which went to Frelimo candidates. The announcement of official results was delayed for more than two weeks, giving more than ample time to manipulate electoral computers.

Guebuza won reelection in October 2009 with a 75% majority, to which the opposition claimed fraud. Frelimo's exercise of power seems now to have given rise to an expectation of its semi-permanent dominance. In April 2007, one former interior minister told a training class at the national police academy that Frelimo should be "in practice a single party, though in a multiparty system." Other parties could continue to exist and stand in elections, he was reported saying, but "it was Frelimo

View of the Cahora Bassa Dam

AP/Wide World Photo

Mozambique

that should govern the country on its own and at all levels."

Dominance of the electoral process does not mean the Frelimo government is without challenges to its authority. In September 2010, riots erupted in several towns in Mozambique over rising prices (especially for bread and other food items). In Maputo, demonstrators blockaded streets with burning tires and began looting shops. Police intervened and shot at least six protestors dead, including two children. The incidents eventually subsided but represented another mark against the government.

After two decades of relative stability, the relationship between the Frelimo government and Renamo took a turn for the worse in 2013 and 2014 and raised prospects of a return to civil conflict. The tensions began when the government raided a remote base of Renamo leader Alfonso Dhlakama in October 2013. This prompted Renamo to declare that the 1992 peace accord was terminated, and the party boycotted municipal elections. Occasional skirmishes have flared between the two parties (which look increasingly like they may revert to armies). This has led to protests against the violence in some cities (including Maputo) and has also been accompanied by major exporters scaling back their operations due to the potential for disruptions to their supply.

CONTEMPORARY THEMES

Since the end of the civil war, Mozambique has become an important transit area for illicit drugs. Cocaine, for example, is shipped from Columbia to Brazil and then into Mozambique for redistribution to other parts of the world. Heroin is transported along a variety of routes, one of which passes from Pakistan to Dubai, then to Tanzania and into Mozambique, from whence it is distributed internationally. According to one observer of the Mozambique scene, the value of the illegal drug trade passing through the country represented more than all legal foreign trade combined.

Corruption at various levels of government facilitates the traffic. Customs officials are bribed to enable entry and removal of the drugs; immigration officers provide identity and residence papers to the traffickers; police are bribed to turn a blind eye to the trade, and judicial officers are put on the payroll in case the traffickers are ever (rarely) brought to trial. Attorney General Joaquim Madeira spoke openly about corruption and began to propose ways of dealing with it. His annual reports to parliament have detailed the processes by which the entire judicial system, including attorneys and judges has failed. The police too have been subject to his withering criticism. "It is not possible to combat crime with policemen who are allies of the underworld or who derive benefits from it," he told parliament in his 2001 report.

As the Cardoso case illustrated, criminal elements so corrupted the police and judicial systems they could at one time order the assassination of investigators and prosecutors with impunity. In his April 2007 report, Attorney General Madeira told how corruption investigators continued to be intimidated: their cars were photographed, their arrival and departure times checked. Madeira also reported that many suspects were refusing to cooperate with Mozambique's Central Office for the Fight against Corruption (GCCC), and told parliamentarians they lived in "a country where the criminals wear suits and ties and dresses, where they eat with us, laugh with us and work with us." Nearly 200 civil servants were dismissed in 2006 for corruption, but the greatest worry is that the magnitude of corrupt practices may have escaped the ability of parliament to control and monitor the state.

It did not help President Guebuza's pledge to take a tough stand against corruption when the head of Mozambique's anticorruption unit, Isabel Rupia, was dismissed from office without explanation in September 2005. A victim of an attempted assassination herself, Rupia was the country's most vigorous graft fighter. Some progress was made on the corruption front with the February 2010 conviction and sentencing of former minister Antonio Munguambe to 20 years in prison for embezzling $1.7 million in state funds. This is the biggest corruption conviction in Mozambique since 1975.

The international community has been determined to make Mozambique a showpiece of development, and foreign aid from the donor community has contributed as much as 60% of Mozambique's budget in recent years. Mozambique has garnered such support by creating one of the most open economic regimes in Africa and aggressively pursuing foreign investment. The consequence has been impressive economic growth figures, at over 8% in 2005 and 2006, and over 7% in 2007 and 2008 before slipping under 7% in 2009. Even with the global economic crisis, Mozambique has one of the most dynamic economies in southern Africa.

Mozambique's economy remains fundamentally agricultural in terms of the labor force, with farming employing 80% of the working population. Given the absence of transport and transportation links, most farmers produce only enough for their own subsistence needs. They toil with the most rudimentary of techniques: only a fraction of farmers use traction (animal or mechanical) or fertilizers or pesticides. The typical farmer has access only to rudimentary technology, such as a hoe for turning soil.

More than half of Mozambique's 23 million people continue to live in absolute poverty, the vast majority in rural areas distant from the economic success story of the capital Maputo. Industrial development has risen to over a third of GDP, while the agricultural sector has fallen to about one-quarter.

Until the advent of its aluminum plant, Mozambique's biggest export earner had been prawns, while cotton and cashews were once Mozambique's two largest cash crops and the nation's largest foreign currency earners. Production of both crops fell dramatically during the civil war, and both are subject to fluctuating demand and prices in the world market. Cotton, mostly grown in northern Mozambique, involves about 200,000 peasant families. Collapsing market prices have severely weakened production enthusiasm on the part of farmers, and the EU has granted economic assistance to help them shift to alternative crops. The country floated an international bond of nearly one billion dollars to enhance its fleet of tuna fishing boats, though some portion of the proceeds were reportedly used to outfit the navy to combat piracy.

Mozambique was once the world's largest producer of cashews, but the stock of trees was destroyed by war, ravaged by disease, and reduced in production as a consequence of aging. An estimated one million trees die or go out of production each year because of age, disease or neglect and on average only 300,000 have been planted annually to replace them. The cashew industry suffered greatly from trade liberalization that resulted in the closing of large, mechanized processing plants. The bulk of Mozambique's cashews are sold to India, and the government is seeking to convince Indian companies to take advantage of cheap labor and save transportation costs by opening their own processing plants in Mozambique. In recent years there has been a processing revival, based on smaller factories using intensive manual or semi-manual shelling methods. Currently some 18 factories are operating, employing nearly 6,000 workers. Mozambique's once thriving sugar industry was also revived in the 2000s due to rehabilitation efforts.

One huge megaproject has symbolized the country's economic vitality and potential, but also its economic limitations: the Mozal aluminum smelter located near Maputo. A joint venture between British, Japanese, and South African investors, Mozal represented an investment of $1.34 billion. The first aluminum was poured in

Mozambique

July 2000, and Mozambique's first aluminum exports were shipped in August of that year. Mozal completed an extension project in April 2003 that doubled its annual capacity.

One important energy project is the proposed Mphanda Nkuwa dam, which has been under consideration for over a decade. To be built by a Brazilian firm on the Zambezi River, some 43 miles downstream from the existing mega-dam at Cahora Bassa, Mphanda Nkuwa could generate over 1,500 MW. The project is estimated to cost $2.3 billion, and the government signed a Memorandum of Understanding with China's Eximbank for funding in April 2006. The Economist Intelligence Unit reported in 2009 that Mozambique had secured funding for the dam.

Cahora Bassa (or Cabora Bassa), built in 1974 by Portugal on the Zambezi River, supplies large amounts of electricity in the region and has potential for even greater, but has long faced financial challenges. Initially owned by Portugal (85%) and Mozambique (15%), the dam was to have been transferred to Mozambique relatively shortly after independence, when the Portuguese government's investment in the mammoth project had been paid off. That had to be postponed after Renamo blew up much of the transmission system's infrastructure. For years, the operating company was also burdened with unprofitable energy contracts (from its largest client, the South African energy giant Eskom) and deadbeat customers (the Zimbabwe Electricity Supply Authority). However, a contract with Eskom was eventually redrafted and power exporting increased in 2008. After years of delay, the transfer of Cahora Bassa to Mozambican control was finally completed by 2007. Ownership of the operating company, *Hidroeléctrica de Cahora Bassa* (HCB), has been restructured with Mozambique assuming full control of the company. Mozambique continues to seek investment to expand production through more turbines and the creation of sub-stations at Cahora Bassa.

The South African energy company Sasol has won the rights to commercialize Mozambique's natural gas riches. The Pande and Temane gas fields give Sasol proven reserves of 2.8 trillion cubic feet—enough gas for 30 years. The company will construct a pipeline to carry the gas to Maputo and South Africa. Ownership of the pipeline will be shared: 50% by Sasol, with the governments of South Africa and Mozambique each holding a 25% share. In the future, natural gas could easily vie with aluminum as Mozambique's most valuable export. It will also assist in alleviating Mozambique's need for additional electricity to power continued industrialization: a gas-fired power station in Inhambane province could produce 750 megawatts.

In northern Mozambique, Dublin-based Kenmare Resources has begun production of titanium from heavy mineral sands. Rich in titanium dioxide, the sands do not require smelting to be upgraded, and the project will reputedly become one of the world's lowest cost titanium producers. As with all major industrial projects in Mozambique, electricity is in short or nonexistent supply. Kenmare installed a 105-mile line to bring electricity generated by Cahora Bassa dam.

Elected in 2015, President Felipe Nyusi has had to deploy military forces to the gas-rich northern region of Cabo Delgado to deal with periodic incursions of ISIS-linked armed groups that have displaced more than 100,000 people. The region is a site for the construction of a liquified natural gas terminal developed by a French company with a similar project planned by the Exxon Corporation of the United States. Mozambique, like other countries in the region, has been hit with devastating cyclones with recovery aid provided by the World Bank.

In January 2025, Daniel Chapo was sworn in as president following a disputed election that sparked violent protests. The country's main opposition leader, Venancio Mondlane, returned home after two months in self-imposed exile and declared himself "the president-elect of the Mozambican people, . . . elected by the genuine will of the people" while claiming the government was perpetrating a "silent genocide" by abducting and executing members of the opposition to hide obvious irregularities in the October 2024 elections. Violent clashes broke out between state security forces and thousands of protesters who came to show support for the 50-year-old Pentecostal preacher. After the elections, the Mozambique Electoral Commission (CNE) was quick to declare the Frelimo Party, which has been at the helm of the country for 50 years, and its presidential candidate, Daniel Chapo, as the rightful winners with Chapo winning more than 70 percent of the votes. Mondlane, backed by the Podemos party, came in second and received just 20 percent. Several independent electoral missions concluded that the electoral process that led to Chapo declaring victory was neither free nor fair, citing irregularities during counting and alteration of results at both local and district levels. Mondlane and other opposition figures immediately denounced the election results, demanded a repeat of the polls, and encouraged supporters to rise up against Frelimo. The Frelimo government ordered a violent crackdown on all public expressions of dissent as more than 300 people, including several children, died in the violence. Tragic losses included Elvino Dias, a legal representative of Mondlane, and Paulo Guambe, an official from Podemos, who were both shot dead by unknown assailants in the capital, Maputo. It was after these killings that Mondlane made the decision to temporarily move abroad for his safety as the dispute over the elections has also wreaked economic chaos in Mozambique and the wider region, which also is suffering from a drought.

The port of Maputo

Mozambique

FUTURE CONSIDERATIONS

Progress has been slow for the average Mozambican in the search for economic progress. Current adult illiteracy rates of just over 50% still disguise regional and gender differences: about two-thirds of adults living in rural areas are illiterate, and probably over four out of five rural women are similarly disadvantaged. Low school enrollment remains a challenge to development plans. Development is highly unbalanced, with most centering in the southern regions, especially around Maputo.

That said, Mozambique has offered investment opportunities for some intrepid and well-financed capitalists. The Mozal aluminum smelter and hydroelectric power from the Cahora Bassa dam have been the motors of the industrial sector for several years, but Mozambique also appears to be a country where mining companies are prospecting for deposits ranging from coal to titanium to gold to natural gas. Mozambique's growth rate remained impressive and even topped 6% in the midst of the global economic crisis, though it turned downward in 2013–14 in the midst of the flare-up in conflict between the Frelimo government and Renamo.

Economic disequilibrium in the country, with poverty in the north, will continue to fuel political differences. Frelimo and Renamo seemed to have reached a pattern of peaceful (if wary) coexistence, but the events of the past year (2013–14) have raised more serious questions about the durability of the peace. The country will lack for full democracy for as long as Frelimo exerts dominance over the electoral system, and corruption remains a central issue, but the country has been advancing economically (from its low base) in recent years. If relative stability can be restored, economic recovery and investment opportunities mean Mozambique may be poised to move back in the right direction as a more favorable destination for international capital and a locus of greater opportunity for its residents.

The Republic of Namibia

Christus Kirche (Lutheran), Windhoek

Photo by Judi Iranyi

BASIC FACTS

Area: 824,292 sq. km. (about twice the size of California)
Population: 2,777,232 (June 2023 est.)
Capital City: Windhoek
Government Type: Presidential Republic
Neighboring Countries: Angola (north); South Africa (south, southeast); Botswana (east); Zambia (northeast)
Official Language: English
Other Principal Languages: Afrikaans common language of most of the population and about 60% of the white population, German; indigenous languages: Oshivambo, Herero, Damara, Nama and Kavanga
Ethnic Groups: Black 87.5%, white 6%, mixed 6.5% About 50% are the Ovambo people and 9% Kavangos; other ethnic groups are: Herero 7%, Damara 7%, Nama 5%, Caprivian 4%, Bushmen 3%, Baster 2%, Tswana 0.5%
Principal Religions: Christianity 80% to 90% (Lutheran 50% at least, other Christian denominations 30%), native religions 10% to 20%
Former Colonial Status: German colony until the Republic of South Africa asserted control of the territory (as South-West Africa), claiming a mandate under the League of Nations continued since the formation of the United Nations. The UN passed a resolution in 1966 declaring South-West Africa to be under direct UN control and designated the area Namibia in 1968.
Independence Date: March 21, 1990
GDP Per Capita (IMF 2023 est.): $5,100 (nominal), $11,440 (PPP)
Gini Index: 59.1 (World Bank 2015)
Currency: Namibian dollar, 1 USD = 18.31 Namibian dollars (Apr. 2023)
Inflation Rate: 5.5% (2022 est.)
Chief Commercial Products: Diamonds, copper, gold, zinc, lead, uranium; cattle, processed fish, and karakul skins
Foreign Direct Investments (FDI) net inflows: 493,302,263
Literacy Rate: 92.3 (CIA 2021)
Life Expectancy: 67.04 years (CIA 2023 est.)
Head of State: President Hage Geingob (since March 21, 2015)
Head of Government: President Hage Geingob (since March 21, 2015)

LAND AND PEOPLE

Just inland from the Atlantic Ocean, the narrow white beach of Namibia quickly disappears to reveal a 60-mile-wide stretch of red-colored Namib Desert that runs the entire length of the coastline. The barren Kalahari Desert stretches along the north and eastern borders of the territory, occasionally interrupted by formations of gray rock and thin scrub vegetation. The only rain in this region comes from torrential storms that occasionally gather—the desert quickly swallows the rapid downpour without leaving a trace of moisture. The entire country is hot and dry, with the exception of the thin Caprivi Strip, which stretches inland from the northeast corner of the country; this region gets more rainfall.

The central area of Namibia is a vast plateau suited to raising sheep and cattle. Here, there is somewhat more rain than the coast and deserts, which permits a thin forage to cover the soil. This region produces thousands of karakul sheep, the lambs of which are treasured for their shiny black, curly pelts used in fur coats.

HISTORY TO THE PRESENT DAY

For early history, see *Historical Background* and *The Colonial Period: British* and *The Germans*.

South African Control and the Struggle for Independence

Originally colonized by the Germans in the late 1800s, the discovery of diamonds in the territory in 1908, then led to an influx of Europeans to the area. South Africa seized the territory known as South-West Africa in 1915 and controlled it under League of Nations mandate. After the creation of the United Nations, all previously mandated dependent territories came under its supervision. In most cases, the mandates transformed into trusteeships, which required annual reports concerning the territory's development and progress towards eventual independence. South Africa applied for "permission" to make South-West Africa part of South Africa in 1946. The UN rejected the proposal but offered South Africa a trusteeship. South Africa rejected the offer and moved to incorporate the land within its national boundaries despite UN protests. By 1949, certain South African laws extended to South-West Africa, and its white representatives sat in the South African parliament. The UN condemned South Africa for its failure to live up to the terms of the

Namibia

UN Charter, but this meant nothing in the absence of force.

During the 1960s, nationalist sentiment coalesced in the South-West African People's Organization, or SWAPO, which sought majority rule and independence for the territory. While its political leaders headquartered in Dar es Salaam, Tanzania, SWAPO's fighters roamed the territory, recruiting volunteers, terrorizing farmers (black and white), sabotaging public utilities and ambushing army patrols. South Africa reacted quickly, rounding up and jailing hundreds of guerrillas, including the group's leader, Herman Toivo ja Toivo. The ruling white government sentenced Toivo to 20 years imprisonment on Robben Island, South Africa, after convicting him of "crimes against state security" in 1968. Backed by surrounding black-majority nations committed to the struggle against apartheid, SWAPO intensified its armed resistance.

By 1966, the UN decided to terminate the South African "mandate." It renamed the territory Namibia (derived from the name of the Namib Desert) and recognized SWAPO as the "representative" of the Namibian people. After considerable diplomatic pressure from the U.S., Canada, Britain, France, and West Germany, South Africa agreed to peace discussions that would include SWAPO representatives.

The first talks in early 1978 ended in failure, and while negotiations dragged on into the 1980s, the situation on the ground turned into a more generalized military conflict across the sub-region. Angola's Marxist regime's support of SWAPO and provision of refuge for its guerilla fighters further complicated the situation. South Africa, which was aiding UNITA rebels in their efforts to overthrow the Marxist regime in Luanda, invaded Angola in 1982–1984 to clean out SWAPO fighters. Clashes between South African forces and Cuban troops, present in the country since 1976, intensified the regional war. In 1983, South Africa declared a "linkage" policy: South African troops in Angola would not withdraw until Cuban troops withdrew first. Angola and Cuba responded firmly: Cuban troops would only depart after South African withdrew its forces.

Inside Namibia, SWAPO increasingly resorted to terrorist tactics, and government forces engaged in widespread atrocities in retaliation. SWAPO sought to punish defectors, accusing over 2,000 Namibians, some of whom had merely sought more democracy within the movement, of spying for South Africa. The organization sent many of these into crude prisons located in Angola, and simply "disappeared" others.

By 1988, the external actors saw the Namibian situation as counterproductive to their own interests. The involved nations reached a grand diplomatic solution in December 1988. South Africa agreed to the independence of Namibia, while Cuba and South Africa jointly agreed to withdraw their troops from Angola. Namibia would hold free elections for a national assembly that would draft a constitution leading to independence in April 1990.

Democracy In Namibia: The Sam Nujoma Years (1990-2004)

After a brief transition period, almost 98% of registered voters participated in elections for the constituent assembly. SWAPO took 57% of the vote, short of the two-thirds majority that would have given it free reign in writing a new constitution. The Democratic Turnhalle Alliance, a multiracial coalition of conservatives with white leadership, received 29% of the vote. In February 1990, the Constituent Assembly adopted a constitution, creating a multiparty system, limiting its executive president to two five-year terms, and enshrining a bill of rights. Distancing itself from its socialist background just as the Soviet Union collapsed, SWAPO voted to include provisions that granted private ownership of property and affirmed a mixed economy where foreign investment would be encouraged.

The Constituent Assembly converted itself into the National Assembly on February 16, 1990, and unanimously elected Sam Nujoma as Namibia's first president. The nation's first presidential election took place in December 1994, and Nujoma swept to triumphant victory, thrashing his DTA opponent Mishake Muyongo with nearly 70% of votes cast. SWAPO gained an overwhelming majority in parliament.

Nujoma's political dominance posed problems for SWAPO as it contemplated presidential elections in 1999. Despite the constitutional prohibition on more than two terms, Nujoma announced in April 1997, "I am still young and if the people of Namibia want me to continue making a contribution I will continue to do so." Dutiful and deferential to its leader, the 1997 SWAPO party congress recommended the amendment of the constitution to allow the president a third term.

SWAPO parliamentarians dutifully amended the constitution, but the move provoked a split in the party. Ben Ulenga, a former guerrilla, trade unionist and Namibian high commissioner (ambassador) in London, resigned from SWAPO and formed an opposition party—Congress of Democrats. He ran for president in the 1999 elections. Ulenga had impressive credentials as a candidate. His liberation struggle experience was impeccable—wounded in combat and 15 years detention on Robben Island in South Africa. His disillusionment with SWAPO began even before independence, when thousands of fighters disappeared without explanation in SWAPO detention camps. Nujoma's decision to seek a third term confirmed that disillusionment. Ulenga shocked the party with a scathing attack on Nujoma's rule, corruption, and the very idea of a third mandate for the president.

The Congress of Democrats was the first credible alternative to SWAPO to emerge, particularly in its traditional northern strongholds. Ulenga himself was also an Ovambo from the north, a center of SWAPO strength. The election was hard fought and included bullying tactics by SWAPO and its supporters. Ulenga accused his old party of corruption, arrogant leadership, and mismanagement of an economy struggling with a 35% jobless rate. Meanwhile, Mishake Muyongo, the longtime leader of the opposition DTA, damaged his party's reputation and undermined its challenge to SWAPO when he called for the secession of Caprivi.

The December 1999 election proved a smashing success for SWAPO; Nujoma obtained 76.8% of the vote, while Ulenga garnered only 10.5%. The DTA's Katuurike Kaura won 9.6%, and a fourth candidate trailed the field with a mere 3%. In the National Assembly elections, SWAPO increased its electoral support, winning 76% of the vote. Because the seats in the 72-member house are proportional to election results, SWAPO won 55 seats, the Congress of Democrats and the DTA each collected seven seats, and the United Democratic Front (UDF) got two, while the small Monitor Action Group settled for one.

President Hage Geingob

Namibia

The Namib Desert — Photo by Judi Iranyi

President Nujoma's authoritarian style did not change, affirmed by his single-handed commitment of Namibian armed forces in support of Laurent Kabila in the Congo. The actual number of troops committed, the number who died, or even the overall costs of the adventure remain shrouded in mystery. After his reelection, Nujoma also allowed Angolan troops to enter Namibian territory—without any reference to parliament—to search out and destroy bases and personnel of Jonas Savimbi's UNITA.

In late 1998, Nujoma faced secessionist agitation in the remote Caprivi Strip. The Strip, Namibia's panhandle, had long been a center of opposition. During the independence struggle South Africa stationed forces in Caprivi to fight SWAPO and received the collaboration of local peoples, which alienated them from SWAPO decision makers. As an opposition area, Caprivi regularly received less than its fair share in the distribution of development funds.

In his waning years as Namibia's absolute ruler, President Nujoma consciously followed some of the policy initiatives of Zimbabwe's Robert Mugabe, albeit in a much more constrained fashion and without the violence seen in Zimbabwe. Nujoma had his nation intervene in Congo and also raised awareness toward the land issue. In Namibia, whites—mainly Afrikaners and descendants of German settlers—make up only 6% of the population, but they own half the land. The government opted for a voluntary system of land acquisition (willing buyer, willing seller), but has been frustrated with the pace of change. According to government figures, Namibia spends over 20 million Namibian dollars ($2.5 million) every year to buy farms for redistribution. By 2004, however, only 124 farms had voluntarily changed hands, though redistribution to "landless peasants" may not fully describe the results. Government ministers, including Nujoma and his personally anointed nominee as SWAPO vice president, Hifikepunye Pohamba, purchased some of these.

After Nujoma

In November 2001, at age 72, President Nujoma announced that he would not be a candidate for office in 2004. Knowing that SWAPO would dominate national elections, Nujoma prioritized absolute control over the selection of his successor within the party. At SWAPO party meetings in 2002 and 2004, Nujoma successfully imposed his choices for party vice president, secretary-general, and deputy secretary-general on the membership. SWAPO appointed neither of the two principal figures earlier bruited as possible successors, Prime Minister Hage Geingob or Hidipo Hamutenya, then minister of trade and industry, to top party posts. Nujoma vigorously supported his lands minister, Hifikepunye Pohamba, as the party's next presidential nominee. He peremptorily fired Hidipo Hamutenya, his foreign minister, undercutting Hamutenya's support. In the end, most delegates (67%) dutifully voted for Pohamba, while a third voted for Hamutenya. The party in 2005 expelled the man who nominated Hamutenya (former Trade Minister Jesaya Nyamu), for promoting division, violence, and factionalism.

In the November 2004 elections, seven parties ran presidential candidates, but even the most successful of Pohamba's opponents, Ben Ulenga representing the Congress of Democrats (CoD), could garner only a feeble 7.3%, less than he had received in 1999. Pohamba swept the polls with 76.4% of the vote, a testimony to SWAPO's control of the election machinery. Outcry from protesters drew attention to possible corruption, and the High Court in Windhoek saw too many irregularities to approve the results. It ordered the Electoral Commission to recount the entire presidential election in ten days, but little changed. CoD, for example, earned precisely one additional vote. In parliamentary elections, SWAPO secured 75% of the vote, winning 55 out of 72 seats in the National Assembly. The CoD became the leading opposition party with a paltry five seats, with four going to the DTA and three to the United Democratic Front; five additional seats went to minor parties.

In his March 2005 inauguration address, President Pohamba pledged to address corruption "with a sledgehammer," and his first test on the issue came soon. By August, tales of government corruption unwound and swirled around the president. One of the biggest involved the disappearance of $5.2 billion siphoned off from the Social Security Commission (SSC)—whose income comes from monthly taxes levied on Namibian workers—and invested in Avid Investment Corporation; another $1.15 billion sunk into the Avid quicksand came from a SWAPO business arm, Kalahari Holdings. The principal facilitator of these transactions was Avid director Paulus Kapia, who was also deputy minister for works, transport, and communication; Kapia used his position as secretary of the SWAPO Youth League to secure the investments in Avid—and lucrative kickbacks for himself. The whole affair made headlines when Avid filed for bankruptcy and could not repay the SSC.

By the end of August, Pohamba had forced Kapia to resign from the cabinet, but the SWAPO politburo failed to expel him from the party; instead, it merely suspended his membership and asked that he resign from parliament. A protégé and spokesman for former president Nujoma, Kapia seemed to enjoy protection at the highest party level, illustrating Pohamba's greatest political problem: though his party enjoys unchallenged dominance in Namibia, the party presidency remained firmly in the grip of Sam Nujoma. It is a situation fraught with potential for tension and conflict. Not controlling the party, Pohamba found it difficult to initiate action against senior party officials who "are busy milking the system," as opposition leader Ben Ulenga remarked. Paulus Kapia finally resigned from parliament in November 2005, becoming the first government leader since independence in 1990 to be sacked for corruption.

Namibia

Rather than suggest clean government, most view this as indicative of tolerance of corruption within SWAPO. When Namibia's Ombudsman, Bience Gawanas, resigned to accept a position with the African Union, she noted that her office received daily complaints of unethical behavior and corruption, and lamented that the government lost millions of dollars to corruption that could have been used for national development.

In 2007, SWAPO reconfirmed Pohamba as the party's candidate for the 2009 general election, which he eventually won, continuing his and SWAPO's domination of Namibia's political scene. SWAPO received just under 75% of the vote in the election giving it control of 54 seats in the National Assembly. Its closest rival, Rally for Democracy and Progress (RDP), received just over 11% or eight seats. Nine opposition parties appealed the election claiming that it was irregular, but the high court dismissed their challenge in 2011. Namibia will hold elections again in 2014 and Pohamba will not be eligible for reelection, having served his constitutionally limited two five-year terms.

CONTEMPORARY THEMES

Economics and Political Issues

One of the most pressing economic and social issues in Namibia is land distribution. According to government statistics, about 75 million acres are owned by whites and only 5.4 million by black farmers. Absentee landlords own a further 7.1 million acres. (The state itself owns 5.6 million acres of land.) As a consequence of this arrangement, the World Bank indicates that income distribution in Namibia "is one of the most unequal in the world." Indeed, the UN's *Human Development Report* for 2006 ranked Namibia as the country with the most unequal distribution of wealth in the world. (The figures are somewhat misleading since they include none of the oil-producing sheikdoms.) A small minority—some 50,000 whites—have enjoyed most of the wealth of Namibia, while the majority have been living a much more meager existence, engaging in herding livestock to support themselves.

Namibia's modern market sector produces most of its wealth; the traditional subsistence agricultural sector supports most of its labor force. Much of the country's economy is dependent on natural resource exports. Namibia's main trading partner is South Africa. Diamonds are the principal export, and the Namibian economy depends greatly on Namdeb, its largest mining company. Namdeb, jointly owned by the Namibian government and De Beers of South Africa, accounts for 10% of the country's GDP and 30% of its exports; it is the biggest tax payer and, apart from the government, the country's largest employer.

The country has at least a 40% unemployment rate, and the government has cast about for any means of job creation in the diamond industry, where technology has increasingly replaced human labor. One possibility of adding value to diamonds is cutting and polishing. DeBeers opened a polishing factory in 1999 and young Namibians proved themselves the rivals of counterparts in traditional diamond-polishing centers like Tel Aviv, Antwerp, and Johannesburg. While quality was high, cost-effectiveness was not, largely because of high labor costs reflecting strong Namibian labor unions. Polishing a diamond in Asia cost between $10 and $15; in Namibia, the cost was almost double. Given the economic disadvantages, DeBeers' interest in Namibia waned. Nonetheless, the Leviev group, owned by the Israeli billionaire Lev Leviev, opened Africa's largest diamond-cutting factory in Namibia in 2004; the industry brings in profits and revenues from export, but even this factory employs only a few hundred Namibians.

Chinese demand for minerals has driven prices so high that interest in Namibian uranium has been revitalized.

Former President Hifikepunye Pohamba

The Rössing uranium mine, the country's largest, reached its highest production levels since independence in the mid-2000s, and has moved from survival mode to expansion. The uranium rush is on. Development of a second major mine, the Langer Heinrich, began in 2005 and the mine made its first product shipment in March 2007. Expansion has continued and will do so through 2011. With these mines, Namibia controls about 10% of the world's uranium production.

Energy to run its nascent industries is a major concern for Namibia. About half the country's daily power consumption of 500 MW is imported from South Africa, and the uncertainty of the electric supply from South Africa stimulated Namibia's development of its own energy sources in the Kudu gas field, located some 105 miles off the southern coast, with its proven reserves of 1.3 trillion cubic feet of natural gas. Long thought to be too expensive to be profitable, the project's finances were reassessed in light of rising prices and increased demand and it was given a go-ahead; the Russian gas giant Gazprom has become a major investor. Electricity production is now expected to begin in 2013. In July 2011, Namibia announced they had found an estimated 11 billion barrels of oil offshore.

One of the government's biggest proposals is for a hydroelectric project on the Kunene River, which is shared with Angola. After considering a site at the scenic Epupa Falls, the project was shifted for environmental reasons to the Baynes mountains, some 21 miles downstream. The site has a smaller inundation area, less evaporation, and should require less displacement than the original project. Completion of the project is not expected until about 2017. Additionally, construction on Africa's first solar-thermal power plant could begin in Namibia before the end of 2014.

Budgetary profligacy within the party-state—including patronage for a bloated civil service—means there usually is not much capital available for major infrastructure investments such as these. A principal cause is spending on the state bureaucracy. The Nujoma government began building a lavish new State House complex, completed in 2008, to accommodate the president and high state bureaucrats on a mountainside south of Windhoek. The massive complex was inspired by a presidential visit to North Korea and built by a North Korean company.

Social Issues

Namibia also faces major challenges with HIV/AIDS, which has spread more in southern Africa than in any other region of the world. The 2009 UNICEF estimates place HIV/AIDS prevalence at about 13%, or one of the highest rates in the world since prevalence rates were revised downward across the board in the late 1990s. Despite the presence of HIV/AIDS, life expectancy is back on the rise, and is now estimated at over 61 years, which is high by African standards. Improved treatment protocols and prevention have given hope that functioning polities like Namibia will be able to manage the pandemic more effectively going forward.

The SWAPO government has presided over democratization in Namibia and the country rates well in terms of many civil

Namibia

liberties, but one major exception is its targeting of Namibia's gay and lesbian community for special condemnation and harassment. The minister of home affairs has urged police to "eliminate gays and lesbians from the face of Namibia," and ex-President Nujoma once called gays and lesbians "unnatural," "ungodly," "un-African," and "idiots who should be condemned."

Elected in 2015, President Hage Geingob, age 82, died in February 2024 from a long illness. Nangolo Mbumba became acting president. Elections are scheduled for November 2024 with the ruling SWAPO party candidate, Ms. Nandi Ndaitwah, slated to run and become the first female president of the country. Citing the genocidal killing of the indigenous population by German settlers in 1904–1908, Namibia has criticized the decision by Germany in 2024 to join Israel in denying the charge of genocide against Palestinians in Gaza at the International Court of Justice (ICJ).

Sworn in as the first female president of Namibia in March 2025, Netumbbo Nandi-Ndaitwah extended the governing party's 35-year grip on power and represented one of the few women leaders on the African continent. Outgoing President Nangolo Mbumba, 83, handed power to Nandi-Ndaitwah at a ceremony that coincided with the 35th anniversary of Namibia's independence and was observed by leaders from neighboring states of South Africa and Tanzania. Popularly known as NNN and previously in the post of vice president, she is a veteran of the South West Africa People's Organization (SWAPO) that has led the sparsely populated and uranium-rich country since gaining independence from apartheid South Africa in 1990. Securing 58 percent of the vote, the often-chaotic elections were extended several times after logistical failures led to major delays. Outgoing leader Mbumba said the election of a woman "has been a long time coming."

On the economic front, Namibia continues to suffer from a drought afflicting the entire southern region. The country's farmers grow vegetables and other crops watered from one of the largest aquifers on earth serving as the lifeblood of the Kalahari Desert, which stretches across Namibia, as well as neighboring Botswana and South Africa. Desert villages such as Leonardville sit atop vast deposits of uranium as Rosatom, Russia's State Atomic Energy Corporation. It has spent years attempting to set up a mine in eastern Namibia after the country lifted a temporary ban on uranium mining in 2017. A Rosatom subsidiary, Headspring Investments, in 2011 proposed to use a controversial drilling method to extract the uranium, known as "in situ" mining, which involves injecting a solution that includes sulphuric acid down into the aquifer. While the prospect of financial reward has some locals supporting a potential mine in the area, Rosatom's proposal has also raised concerns among others in the country. Calle Schlettwein, the minister of agriculture, water and land reform, told Namibia's National Assembly in February that Headspring's activities could "endanger the groundwater" in Namibia, South

Herero women in their finery

Courtesy: CALTEX

Namibia

Africa, and Botswana, "destroying the economic basis for the entire region."

FUTURE CONSIDERATIONS

Namibia is one of Africa's few democracies, according to the independent monitoring organization Freedom House. Still, like his predecessor Nujoma, President Pohamba makes little distinction between state and party. SWAPO dominates political life, and the president has sanctioned the use of state power to silence party critics. In early May 2007, the government moved to control call-in programs on national radio. Central to the decision were claims that some callers regularly displayed a lack of respect for former president Nujoma; the liberation movement that legitimized itself in the independence struggle continues to demand deference, even in the presence of relative political liberties. SWAPO continued its political domination in 2009 and remains in power; Namibia will likely benefit from the emergence of a more robust and loyal opposition.

Economically, the country is better off than many African countries in the region, but troubles remain. Corruption continues to be pervasive inside government. SWAPO membership has long been a means of personal advancement. For many, becoming a politician has been a way to get rich quickly. During the April 2006 budget discussions in parliament, the Deputy Minister of Labor and Social Welfare made the point explicitly, arguing vehemently for "jobs for comrades." The omnipresent specter of HIV/AIDS across southern Africa gives further worry; apart from the human tragedy, this has severe economic consequences going forward.

South Africa

Johannesburg at night

BASIC FACTS

Area: 1,219,090 sq. km. (slightly less than twice the size of Texas)
Population: 58,048,332 (June 2023 est.)
Capital Cities: Pretoria/Tshwane (administrative); Cape Town (legislative); Bloemfontein (judicial).
Government Type: Presidential Republic
Neighboring Countries: Namibia (northwest); Botswana, Zimbabwe (north); Mozambique, Swaziland (northeast); Lesotho is enclosed by South Africa.
Official Languages: 11 official languages in the Constitution: Afrikaans, English, Ndebele, Pedi, Sotho, Swazi, Tsonga, Tswana, Venda, Xhosa, and Zulu.
Other Principal Languages: Fanagolo, a Zulu-based pidgin, widely used in towns and mining areas. Tamil and Urdu, especially in KwaZulu-Natal.
Ethnic Groups: Black African 79%, white 9.6%, colored 8.9%, Indian/Asian 2.5%.
Principal Religions: Christian 68% (about 60% of blacks, about 40% of Indians, and most whites and those of mixed race), Muslim 2%, Hindu 1.5% (60% of Indians), traditional and animistic 28.5%

Former Colonial Status: Member of the British Commonwealth as the Union of South Africa (1910–1961). Previously, British authority in a colonial sense was sporadic in the Orange Free State and Transvaal.
Independence Date: May 31, 1910 (from UK)
Freedom Day: April 27, 1994
GDP Per Capita (IMF 2023 est.): $6,485 (nominal), $16,091 (PPP)
Gini index: 63 (World Bank 2014)
Currency: Rand, $US 1 = 18.31 Rand (Apr. 2023)
Inflation rate: 5.7% (2022 est.)
Chief Commercial Products: Gold, other minerals and metals, food, chemicals.
Foreign Direct Investments (FDI) net inflows: 5,740,650,679
Literacy Rate: 95% (CIA 2019)
Life expectancy: 65.6 years (CIA 2023 est.)
Head of State: President Matamela Cyril Ramaphosa (since February 15, 2018)
Head of Government: President Matamela Cyril Ramaphosa (since February 15, 2018)

LAND AND PEOPLE

The Republic of South Africa occupies the southernmost part of the African continent, and touches both the South Atlantic in the west and the Indian Ocean in the east. This land of bright, sunny days and cool nights has a temperate climate year-round, with a mean annual

South Africa

temperature of slightly less than 60°F. The eastern coastal belt is humid, while western areas are drier. Some high mountain peaks are covered with snow during winter. Two-thirds of South Africa is desert, semi-desert, marginal cropland or urban. Altogether, only 12% is suited for intensive cultivation.

In the extreme southern Cape area, there is a period of rain between April and September, but December–May is warm and dry. The western coast is washed by the cool Benguela Current originating in Antarctica, which produces a climate that supports a large colony of penguins on the shoreline. Farther inland to the north, after the interruptions of the Cedarburg, Swartberg, and Louga Mountains, the land stretches forth in a vast, semiarid region known as the Karoo Desert. Here, periodic light rainfall supports some vegetation, which provides food for many species of wildlife. Occasional sharp projections of volcanic rock stand prominently in an otherwise flat land.

The eastern coast along the warm Indian Ocean supports almost every type of wild game known to southern Africa. In modern times, this climate has fostered the growth of high intensity agriculture similar to that found in southern California. Brilliant white sand beaches line the coast, adjacent to multicolored coral formations. The northwestern central territory is a land of high plains (veldt) stretching to the north from the scenic peaks of the Drakensburg Mountains. Receiving ample rainfall for the most part, its temperate climate supports rich farmland; the land also contains huge gold and diamond deposits.

The northeastern plains are lower than the high veldt to the south. Tourists from around the world travel to Kruger National Park. Here, all game live in protected areas, and visitors cannot get out of their cars except at designated campsites; traffic proceeds slowly along the road to enable their occupants to see and photograph the many species.

The people of South Africa are a rich and unique blend of peoples originating from several continents. A number of African peoples were the earliest inhabitants, and later exploration came from both the Atlantic Ocean and the Indian Ocean. Dutch and British settlers established footholds in the country and then fought over this most valuable of African colonies, with its temperate climate conducive to European agriculture (including world-class vineyards), its rich mineral deposits, and its concentrated populations. From the east came peoples from Asia that were the ancestors of many of today's Indian and Malay populations. The conflict between the races—and the eventual story of the end of institutionalized discrimination—is much the story of South Africa.

South Africa is one of the continent's leaders in artistic and scientific achievements. It has produced novelists such as Nobel Prize winners Nadine Gordimer and J.M. Coetzee, as well as prominent playwrights such as Athol Fugard and Zakes Mda. In addition to these, South Africa has developed a rich literature that has examined the country's social problems, including André Brink's *A Dry White Season*, and the works of black activist Steven Biko. Nobel Peace Prize winners include Nelson Mandela and FW de Klerk, as well as early ANC leader Albert Luthuli and Archbishop Desmond Tutu (see below). Among those in scientific fields, perhaps the best-known South African was the surgeon Dr. Christiaan Barnard, who completed the first successful heart transplant.

HISTORY TO THE PRESENT DAY

Before the arrival of Dutch East India Company employees in 1652, South Africa was thinly populated by Bushmen and very small bands of other peoples. Bartholomew Diaz had reached the southern Cape in 1486, six years before Columbus touched the West Indies. The rough, inhospitable appearance of the Cape region attracted only free Dutch burghers who were sent to grow grain and make wine to supply ships bound to and from Dutch East India possessions.

Settlement to the The Anglo–Boer War (1899–1902)

At the close of the 17th century French Huguenot refugee settlers, fleeing religious persecution under Louis XIV, joined the Dutch burghers in the Cape. The two peoples gradually melded into a single society and gradually expanded in a northeast direction; cattle-raising was their principal undertaking. Because of the need for farm labor, settlers brought slaves from West Africa and later from Asia. They added to modest numbers of indigenous Khoi or Khoikhoi people (known to Europeans by the now derogatory term *Hottentots*) working under conditions of virtual slavery. Most pioneers had multiple children. The children born of the union of settlers and slaves became the ancestors of today's Cape Colored population of South Africa.

After much competition between Dutch and English merchant capitalists, British interests ultimately came to dominate the Cape. In 1795, the Dutch asserted formal control, acting under the authority of the exiled Dutch Prince of Orange. All pretenses were abandoned in 1806 when Britain seized Cape Colony as a strategic base protecting its developing trade with India. The British abolished the

Trekkers' Monument, Pretoria

South Africa

In Kruger National Park

slave trade, which created labor shortages and set the interests of Dutch farmers at odds with the British colonial authorities. British authority heralded the arrival of substantial numbers of British colonists, increasing competition for land. The new settler farms and towns faced chronic shortages of labor since Britain abolished the slave trade in 1807. Increasingly, farmers enslaved native Africans to supply needed labor. When slavery in the region ultimately ended in 1834, about 35,000 people received emancipation.

Dutch farmers, known as Boers, chafed under British authority, and to escape it, many Boers trekked inland and northeastward into territories they called Orange Free State and Transvaal. This left the British in control of much of the coast, at Cape Colony in the west and Natal in the east. At the same time, numerous Bantu tribes from the north were occupying the area. Conflicts with the Bantu settlers were inevitable as white settlers became more numerous. The number of white settlers grew substantially during the period of the Great Trek, which pushed north and east of the Orange River in 1835–42.

The Dutch-descended Boers, having migrated to escape British authority, preferred to live in isolated communities where their independence could thrive. Inevitably, they would come in conflict with the British. Over a period of years at the end of the 19th century, the British tried various forms of government, the success of which directly related to their ability to leave the Boers alone; the British implemented trial self-government in the colonies of Natal, Transvaal and the Orange Free State. Discovery of immense sources of wealth in diamonds (1867) and gold (1886), however, brought in hordes of fortune-seekers. The Boers actively disliked the new people, calling them outlanders, but the processes of transformation had begun. The Boers could no longer maintain their lifestyle of isolation.

Towns sprang up virtually overnight because of the new mineral wealth. Johannesburg, laid out in 1886, soon had a population of more than 100,000, about half of whom were black. The Boer republics (Orange Free State and Transvaal) grew increasingly linked to the world economy through their supply of precious minerals. Cecil Rhodes consolidated the diamond industry under a single producer—De Beers Consolidated Mines—in 1889, and became prime minister of Cape Colony in 1890.

President Paul Kruger, the Boer leader of Transvaal, correctly concluded that Rhodes was financing an anti-Boer movement among the outlanders. The first tangible act was the aborted raid (1895) led by Rhodes' lieutenant, Leander Starr Jameson, allegedly in support of an outlander uprising. In the fallout, Rhodes lost his position as prime minister, and relations between the British and the Boers soured even more.

A minor dispute over voting rights of immigrants was the pretext for the Boer War of 1899–1902, but the area had become too valuable—following the discovery of gold in the Transvaal Highveld—to escape the ambit of British imperial control. The British fought ferociously for the land, even building concentration camps for Boer women and children, 25,000 of whom died of disease and neglect. (In separate camps, an estimated 14,000 Africans died.) Some 500,000 British troops were required to defeat over about 87,000 Boers, who knew the territory better and became effective guerrilla fighters. Although often thought of as a "white man's war," both sides employed Africans—at least 10,000 of them fought for the British. Eventually, though both sides wearied and weakened, the leaders of the Boer Republics sued for peace and signed the Treaty of Vereeniging on May 31, 1902, which recognized their military defeat: the Boers became British subjects. Left unresolved was the question of citizenship for Africans.

The Union of South Africa (1910) to the World Wars

Principally in response to the pleas of General Jan Christiaan (Boer commander-in-chief of the Republican forces in the Cape Colony during the final months of the war), the British established the Union of South Africa in 1910, granting self-government in Transvaal and Orange Free State. The constitution bound together the two former Boer republics with the British Cape Colony and Natal. The government established an administrative capital at Pretoria (in Transvaal), a legislative capital at Cape Town (in Cape Colony) and a judicial seat at Bloemfontein (in Orange Free State), an arrangement that still prevails.

At the same time, General Louis Botha and James Hertzog founded the South African Party. It was moderate, encompassing both English and Afrikaans speakers, stressing the equality of both, and pressing for independent status within the British Empire. Within a short time, however, Hertzog and the rural, conservative Boers split off to form the Nationalist Party (1914).

The Native Land Act (1913) limited the areas in which native Africans could own or occupy. Along with the Land Act of 1936, over 87% of the land ended up under the control of South Africa's white minority. The Native Land Act also restricted the movement of Asians. Controversy over these restrictions led to the creation of the Native National Congress—the precursor of the African National Congress—and a civil rights campaign among the Indian population, then led by the young lawyer, Mohandas K. (Mahatma) Gandhi. The Native Land Act of 1913 was the beginning of legal separation of the races—apartheid—which would be more fully enacted into law after World War II.

South Africa joined in World War I, fighting the Germans in their African possessions (German South West Africa and German East Africa, now Namibia and Tanzania, respectively). Hertzog appeared at the Paris Peace Conference at the close of the conflict to demand independence for South Africa, but Britain ignored him. Because no other logical power was in the

South Africa

region, South Africa received a League of Nations mandate to control the former German colony of South West Africa in 1919. This mandate continued without interruption until Namibia earned its independence in 1990. The British ultimately recognized the Union of South Africa as an independent nation within the British Commonwealth in 1931.

Until 1934, the government was controlled by either or both the South African Party (Smuts) and the National Party (Hertzog). When the two merged, adopting the name United South African Nationalist Party, conservative members of Hertzog's National Party withdrew and maintained the old party name under the leadership of Daniel F. Malan. Since the turn of the century, anti-black sentiments had been slowly crystallizing. Malan's National Party ultimately exploited these feelings.

South Africa declared war on the Axis Powers of World War II, but its participation was minimal because of its distant location from the fighting. Further, a sizable Boer contingent in parliament had no use for liberal English speakers. During the opening years of World War II, this group expressed little regret at a possible defeat of England by Germany.

The end of World War II was the end of the Hertzog-Smuts coalition, which had been in power since 1934. As 1948 elections approached, the National Party (NP), then led by Daniel F. Malan, campaigned on an openly racist platform, advocating that white South Africans insure their moral and financial future by enacting into law *apartheid*, the Dutch Boer word for "separate." The NP won a majority of seats in parliament (in alliance with the Afrikaner Party), taking 79 of 153 seats; this paved the way for the notorious institutions that would govern South Africa for the next four and a half decades.

Apartheid (from 1948)

Prime Minister Malan and the NP wasted no time in their efforts to deliver the promises made during the 1948 campaign. Several major acts created the basic structure of apartheid. Within a year, citizenship and other important rights for black Africans ended. Interracial marriage was banned, and black South Africans increasingly were restricted in where they could go and where they could work.

Perhaps the most fundamental law calculated to transform the country was the Group Areas Act of 1950, which placed race classification at the center of South African policy. Combined with earlier land acts, the Group Areas Act strictly limited the areas in which a person could live based on race. Provisions of the act forced an estimated 3.5 million black people to

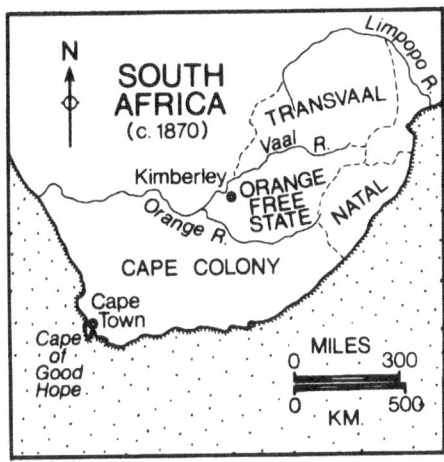

leave their native lands. The Group Areas Act essentially denied blacks any possibility of ownership based on their occupation of land. Thus, if a given tract was within a "white only" area, all that was necessary to oust a black person was proof that he was not white and therefore it was illegal for him to occupy that tract of land.

The Population Registration Act classified all South Africans by race at the time of his birth: black, white, Asiatic, Colored, or other. This determination controlled almost every aspect of a person's future—where he lived, worked, went to school, wages, voting (if any), property ownership, etc., and it became a foundation for the laws requiring that everyone have a passbook. In many cases, it was illegal for a person to be in a given area.

The Internal Security Act of 1982 granted virtual dictatorial powers to the government and abolished any semblance of civil rights that remained. It provided for the banning of organizations opposed to the state, made it illegal for individuals to belong to them, imposed involuntary censorship on the press, allowed detention without trial of persons suspected of terrorism, and imprisonment of anyone for ten days without any charges.

To enforce apartheid laws, the police developed an intensive system of espionage—informants and control calculated to strike fear into the hearts of all. The use of informants was widespread, enabling police to arrest would-be criminals before they attempted any crime. Prison facilities intentionally further exacerbated the ends of justice under apartheid. If the degree of proof of the guilt of an individual was dubious or flawed, he or she might well die in prison awaiting trial. "Slipped on the soap while taking a shower" . . . "fell downstairs" . . . and "died while trying to escape" were all heard with frequency in South Africa if, indeed, anything was heard at all.

Before the days of compulsory censorship, newspapers followed the principles of "voluntary" censorship. At the most fundamental level, this simply meant that newspapers avoided publishing anything embarrassing to the state. If a newspaper violated this imperative too seriously or too often (elusive quantities), paper supplies, bank credit and often telephone service evaporated. Worst of all, no official at whom a finger could be pointed ever did anything illegal. Things just happened.

The Publication Bill unashamedly demanded censored reporting of black activities in the press. It demanded that the media exercise "due care and responsibility concerning matters which can have the effect of stirring up feelings of hostility between different racial, ethnic, religious or cultural groups" in South Africa. True to the form of Boer religious conservatism, it professed to "avoid the spirit of permissiveness and moral decay sweeping the world and communications media in the country."

The African National Congress

The African National Congress initially formed in response to the Land Act of 1913. Passage of the act resulted in the expulsion of some people without adequate compensation from lands they and their ancestors had occupied for generations. The organization had little mass appeal prior to 1948 because of limited political awareness and limited economic strength. The group's leadership was generally conservative, hoping to deal with the white-dominated government in seeking redress for land seizures. After 1948, with the advent of apartheid, it became a militant force, openly sympathetic with communist thinking, and determined to

General Jan Christiaan Smuts

South Africa

oust the white minority from power and seize the economic wealth of the nation in the name of black power. In the immediate postwar period, communist rhetoric, and action terrified South Africa's government. It outlawed the South African Communist Party (SACP) in 1950 and the ANC, under the leadership of Nelson Mandela, responded with a campaign of civil disobedience.

Repression of the ANC and the SACP intensified, and at Sharpeville in 1960, the government killed nearly 70 black demonstrators and wounded another 180, many of whom purportedly the police shot in the back as they were running away. The ANC was promptly banned; in response, its military wing, Umkhonto we Sizwe (Spear of the Nation: MK), launched a sabotage campaign in 1961. The government issued warrants for the fugitive leadership of both the SACP and ANC in 1962.

After a year and a half as fugitive, Nelson Mandela was tried in 1964 (at what became known as the Rivonia trial) and found guilty. The sentence was life imprisonment without possibility of parole. The government sent Mandela to Robben Island Prison, noted for its harsh conditions. The leadership not arrested remained underground, taking refuge in neighboring and nearby nations such as Zambia (the location of its headquarters), Mozambique, Tanzania and Botswana. From these exile posts, men led by Oliver Tambo directed the affairs of the ANC.

During the 25 years after Mandela's trial, support for the ANC grew steadily on both the domestic and international fronts as apartheid became more rigid and even more reactionary and extremist. During the 1970s, the apartheid government forcibly resettled more than three million people in black "homelands," nominally giving these some independence, but, in reality, placing them under puppet governments and in impossible economic circumstances. Ironically, the ANC helped to found the Inkatha Freedom Party of the Zulus in 1974, feeling that the anti-apartheid movement ought to have some lawful presence in South Africa. The ANC successfully mobilized international public opinion against apartheid. In the United States, it enlisted the aid of the Congressional Black Caucus. Many governments worldwide embargoed trade and aggressively pursued other economic sanctions against South Africa.

Unrest in the Homelands and Soweto

During the 1960s and onward, there was a continual influx into black townships, which were located on the edge of every major and smaller city of South Africa; a reason for this was the starkly primitive conditions prevailing in rural areas and the influx of immigrants from surrounding African nations. South Africa tried to limit expansion of these urban slums by adopting an identity card (pass book) system intended to protect employed workers around the cities from competition by illegal immigrants. (The government did not repeal these "pass laws" until 1986.)

To take the population pressure off black townships, the government had established African Bantustans (or "homelands") with the Promotion of Bantu Self-Government Act in 1959. The act originally created eight (later ten) separate black tribal and geographical units. (The Bantu Administration and Development Department, known by its acronym, BAD, ran Bantustan affairs from Pretoria.) The Bantustan lands were overcrowded and overgrazed. Industry and employment were next to nonexistent; healthcare and education lacked resources. The Bantustans did not reduce the government's burden to provide decent housing and services to its black "citizens" and neutralize black political power, as was the white government's initial intention for giving them power. Technically, all township residents were required to vote in the homeland from which they or their ancestors had come, or in which the government assigned them to vote.

Meanwhile, the townships continued to grow, most notably Soweto, outside of the large city of Johannesburg. It had a great many four-room houses built by the government, and on the surface appeared reasonably presentable. In reality, only about 15% of them had inside running water and toilet facilities. The great majority of the homes had six to eight people crowded in very limited space with no heat.

The anti-apartheid disturbance in Soweto in mid-1976 was a major turning point and arose out of the 1953 language agreement. That agreement had

Port of Durban

established a 50–50 use of English and Afrikaans in secondary school instruction, but many schools ignored this in favor of English only. This was, however, unacceptable to Boer nationalists. Boer members of the parliament, led by the archconservative Dr. Andries Treurnicht, insisted on 50% Afrikaans in high school classrooms. Soweto teachers spread the word of the new policy enforcement, which alienated many black students who were learning English and viewed the apartheid NP as a largely Afrikaner party.

Protests against the NP and its pro-Afrikaans policy began on June 16 and within hours, a disturbance turned into a riot that lasted until the 24th; before the riot was over, 174 blacks and two whites died. There were 1,222 black casualties, contrasting sharply with six whites wounded. The government suppressed the riot with excessive force, and P. W. Botha retracted the demand that schools use Afrikaans as a language of instruction. The reaction of most students to the Soweto riot was to boycott schools as a way for the powerless to express their anger, and the slogan "liberation before education" became a watchword. However, it proved costly in later years: as a consequence of extended boycotts, a large number of potential black leaders were illiterate as black majority rule approached in 1994.

Attempted Reforms of Apartheid (excluding Blacks)

President Vorster adopted a "solution" to racial problems for the government in the form of a Bantu Homelands Citizenship Act (1970). The Act made every black South African, irrespective of actual residence, a citizen of one of ten homelands, each designated for specific ethnic groups. As such, the government classified blacks as "foreigners" and excluded from the South African body politic. Between 1960 and 1985, the government forcibly evicted 3.5 million blacks from their land under the homeland system.

The government granted each homeland internal self-government and when a homeland requested independence, it was to be granted. Transkei, in the southeast, with about 3 million inhabitants, was the first to opt for independence (1976). The next occurred the following year when the government granted self-rule to Bophuthatswana ("homeland of the Tswanas"), a nation in six separated areas with 2.1 million people. Most of its parts lay to the north, bordering Botswana. Venda, with almost half a million, became independent in 1979 and Ciskei in 1981. No nation in the world recognized these creations as "independent."

The "Black Homelands" solution addressed only a portion of South Africa's

South Africa

A spice market in Durban, where the Indian heritage is apparent.

Photo by Nancy Sprotte

social and economic impasse. More than 14 million black people lived in townships adjacent to the largest cities and industrial areas of South Africa; even the government classified them as "detribalized." However, to express themselves politically, they were required to vote in the homeland to which the government assigned to them (which had no role or vote in the white government of South Africa) whether or not they had ever been physically present. The system of identity cards intentionally served to determine who could live outside his or her "homeland."

President P. W. Botha, as early as 1980, saw the need for additional reform and embarked on a wide-ranging series of measures that would have revolutionized the system of apartheid. He proposed elimination of the Group Areas Act, the Slums Act and the Community Development Act; the names sounded innocent, but the laws were essential tools of apartheid. Conservatives in the National Party, led by the intractable Andries Treurnicht, resisted any reform whatsoever. They persuaded the president to embark on a "new" approach that ultimately led to violence and change in South Africa.

The plan was an attempt to placate both international opinion and internal resistance by blacks to white rule. It was supposed to be the answer to the exclusion of blacks from any participation in government. In the mid-1970s, the government concocted a new constitutional scheme.

To masquerade as democratic, the new constitution created a three-house National Assembly, with a large body restricted to white membership, and two smaller units to represent Coloureds and Indians, but no blacks. For blacks, control of the townships in which they were a majority was their only political representation. In this way, the government felt black leadership could contain increasing unrest in the townships and, at the same time, satisfy the hunger for self-rule. The leadership stood firm in the belief that they had given something of value to the blacks of South Africa. The ANC correctly saw it as no more than just another chapter in the book of apartheid.

The new National Assembly had a 185-seat white parliament, one for Coloureds (92 seats), and a third for Asians (46 seats). The smaller houses had no powers except with respect to matters of concern to the minority they represented. The larger white parliament could veto any act of the other two. This three-tiered system of parliament, coupled with black "home rule" proved to be white South Africa's most costly and serious mistake for it was instrumental in the downfall of white-controlled government.

The plan itself was unworkable, and it quickly gave way to a government by

South Africa

oligarchy: the Presidential Council of about 60 members proposed all laws and the parliament became a rubber stamp. Across the nation, blacks negatively reacted to this system, and protested by making South Africa ungovernable.

The ANC devised a two-pronged strategy. First, it used coercion and threats as a tool against non-Zulu black South Africans, trying to compel blacks within the townships to become members of the party or sympathizers with the cause. Second, the ANC leadership recognized that Inkatha, led by Chief Mangosuthu Buthelezi, was a potential rival that had to be eliminated or at least controlled in the struggle for power that was to come. The ANC programs (in both compelling sympathy and attacking Inkatha) resulted in terrible violence, but the police were virtually helpless to deal with it because of its sheer magnitude.

The ANC ordered a boycott of all township elections. Those who participated, and assumed office in township governments, received threats and ridicule. The ANC regarded those in township governments as traitors for cooperating with the despised, white-controlled government. They and their collaborators became targets of ANC and MK violence. The most grisly of deaths was from "necklacing"—having a tire filled with gasoline placed around one's neck and lit with a match. After violence rose, the ANC and its sympathizers began to use the turmoil as justification for disinvestment and sanction programs against South Africa by foreign businesses.

In the decade 1984–1994, over 20,000 blacks lost their lives fighting for the end of apartheid in South Africa. About half of them (11,000) died after 1990 when the government released Nelson Mandela from prison. The South African Defense Forces murdered about 1,500 of those killed. Ninety-four percent of the horrific township violence was murder of blacks by blacks. The commission that developed those figures also concluded that of the black-on-black homicides, those killed were about 85% ANC members or supporters, or lived in ANC-controlled areas.

Inkatha Freedom Party and Chief Buthelezi

In the early 1970s, the white government had come close to completely dismantling the ANC, having imprisoned the majority of the party's important leaders and demoralizing most followers. The system of spies and informants developed by the South African Defense Forces made it dangerous to belong to the underground organization or to be a communist comrade-in-arms. In order to try to maintain some form of legal pressure against apartheid, the ANC leadership recognized the need to have a Zulu-based organization to bring pressure on the white government.

The Zulus had a history of bad relations with the Xhosas, the second largest tribal group in South Africa, but the Xhosas were the core of the ANC. Thus, although they had no particular affinity for potential rivals, it was a matter of practicality for the ANC to encourage and assist the founding of the Inkatha Freedom Party (IFP) in 1974. Its leader was Chief Mangosuthu Gatsha Buthelezi, known for his ability to communicate with the white leadership, despite Inkatha's staunch opposition to apartheid. Buthelezi's attitudes largely reflected the lifestyles of most of the members of Inkatha, as well as most Zulu non-members.

Xhosas and Sothos tended to cluster with their families in shantytowns around large industrial and mining centers of South Africa, which led to children growing up in poverty and hardship. The Zulus, on the other hand, were the chief clientele of hostels—shelters for male workers with a minimum of comfort and convenience—where they lived for usually 27 out of 30 days. On days off, they went back home (where they had been sending their wages after expenses) to their wives and children. Living in this manner, their needs were minimal, their wages were comparatively high, and family tensions and quarrels were usually low level—since they didn't have time to escalate. Of equal importance, wives and children lacked the exposure to the crime, violence, and deprivations of the townships.

The NP leadership established an informal alliance with the IFP to help combat the ANC and rising violence. Members of the South African Defense Force armed and trained the Zulus. (As this became evident to the MK leadership, they redoubled efforts against Zulus.) Among Zulu customs, the carrying of traditional weapons was important as they were uniquely associated with the passage from boyhood to manhood. Though not carried at all times, their presence certainly marks the bearer as a Zulu. However, a South African judge in 1989 ruled that they were dangerous weapons and called for a law making them illegal to carry in public. The government agreed and told the Zulus they could not carry spears and axes as they had in the past. When resorting to violence, which Zulus considered to be for defensive purposes, they used modern weaponry.

Buthelezi and his followers were shocked at the decision. He and Goodwill Zwelithini, king of the Zulus, denounced the measure directly. Together with conservative white South Africans, the chief began to speak with regularity of a black state seceding from South Africa under his leadership. A system of strong federalism was favored, creating the equivalent of states' rights. This attracted favorable interest among many white conservatives, who wanted to establish a "white homeland" in the event of a black-dominated government in South Africa.

F. W. de Klerk and Nelson Mandela

With the townships in revolt and South Africa in a state of emergency, Nelson Mandela wrote to then President P. W. Botha in 1988, urgently stating the two should confer about matters vital to the future of the nation. Under a shroud of

Part of a large photomontage celebrating the development of freedom in South Africa

Photo by Cezar Ornatowski

South Africa

South African Vineyards Photo by Christine Farrington

secrecy, the conservative president Botha met with Mandela. Botha suffered a stroke in January 1989, but after a brief recuperation, he announced in March that he would resume his duties as president.

There was immediate opposition from the party leadership, which nominated Frederik W. de Klerk to run in the September elections. Three weeks before the elections, an angry and frustrated Botha made a television broadcast denouncing de Klerk, the ANC and anyone else he thought to be hostile and resigned his presidency. Despite Botha's objections, F. W. de Klerk (seen by most at the time as a conservative unlikely to concede to the ANC) became the NP leader and presumptive president. Soon thereafter, de Klerk defied expectations by beginning South Africa's transition from apartheid to democracy.

Nelson Mandela was born in Umtata (later within the homeland of Transkei) in 1918. When the apartheid government banned the ANC in 1962, Mandela went underground. The government apprehended Mandela and charged him under the anticommunist and antiterrorism laws, sentencing him to life imprisonment without hope of parole. While in prison, he kept abreast of current matters in South Africa, including the turn to violence and terrorism that characterized the period of 1984–1989.

When F. W. de Klerk became president in 1989, his government sought out more extensive contacts with Mandela. This ultimately led to his release from prison, along with Walter Sisulu and other prominent ANC activists. President de Klerk had correctly concluded that continued detention of Mandela would be counterproductive—and that his chances for meaningful negotiations had greater probability if he conducted them with the older generation of ANC leaders. These negotiations would start a reform program to dismantle apartheid.

The dismantling of the racist institution began with de Klerk's stunning and historic speech at the opening of parliament on February 2, 1990, in which he announced Mandela (now the leading symbol of anti-apartheid resistance) would be freed and the ANC unbanned. Among other changes, this allowed Black Africans the freedom to move about their own country. President de Klerk and the NP repealed the major apartheid laws in 1990 and 1991, after over 40 years.

The ANC next signed a peace accord that lifted the state of emergency. Almost immediately, the ANC made Mandela its deputy president, effectively making him the face and power head of the organization. He walked a tight wire astutely, keeping his base of followers mobilized, while negotiating with de Klerk, traveling abroad in search of desperately needed funding, and acknowledging that the rival IFP deserved some sort of recognition. A year later, in 1991, the international community lifted many of the sanctions against South Africa, as the apartheid government repealed most of its laws.

Mandela's conduct, which the more radical members of the ANC viewed as too concessionary, infuriated some supporters of black power who favored a confrontation and a seizure of the state by bloody revolution. Some of Mandela's early statements played to that audience, but shocked white South Africans: "We have waited too long for our freedom. We can no longer wait. Now is the time

South Africa

to intensify the struggle on all fronts. To relax our efforts now would be a mistake which generations to come will not be able to forgive." In the same speech, he insisted upon nationalization of South African industries, in particular, the immense Anglo-American Mining Company—a multinational consortium with worldwide interests as well as its diamond and gold mines in South Africa. In 1992, when he concluded that his advocacy of sanctions and disinvestment was the wrong policy, Mandela found that trying to turn away from these policies in order to attract investment to South Africa was far harder than he had imagined. His earlier position had generated suspicion and distrust regarding ANC's economic policy.

Many had expected Mandela to be a dedicated, violent revolutionary, gripped by the misjudgments of an uninformed old age. He instead showed an unwavering commitment to racial reconciliation, having understood the difference between a revolutionary movement and a political party charged with governing a country. Development of the country and improvement in the lives of its citizens would require, above all, the political stability that would give confidence and assurance to investors on whom that development largely depended.

The pressures on Mandela were tremendous, as he risked the disfavor of the militant wing of the ANC, conditioned by years of a struggle mentality and ideologically shaped by economic thinking that exalted the role of a highly centralized state. The tensions between Mandela's moderation, and the militants' more radical claims were constant. In the case of his wife, Winnie Madikizela-Mandela, they were even personal. After many months, they finally opted to part ways. Mandela thus separated himself from a figure romanticized by some of the most youthful and radical elements of the party as "Mother of the Nation."

Winnie Mandela

As an ANC activist, Winnie Mandela lived in internal exile for years. Violating her exile in 1986, she worked her way to Soweto, a black township outside of Johannesburg. A luxurious home, complete with swimming pool, had been built for her amid the two-room tarpaper and tin shanties of the town. There was a minor uproar of protest, so she did not immediately move in.

When she did move to Soweto, she formed a "soccer team" (known as Mandela United Football Club), a gang of young thugs that proceeded to terrorize Soweto and other nearby black townships. Trials of real and imagined offenders took place in her home, where she often "presided," allegedly issuing out sentences of beating and death. The most notable incident occurred in 1988 when the "team" kidnapped a 13-year-old Stompie Moeketsi from a Soweto Methodist Church shelter and took him to Winnie Mandela's house. They accused the boy of being a police informer and beat him severely, with Winnie Mandela herself reportedly taking part. Taken to a nearby field by the "team," he was murdered.

Acting through his lawyer from prison, Nelson Mandela ordered her to release three other kidnapped youths and to disband the "team," and the ANC ousted Winnie Mandela. During her trial, interruptions came from radical members of the ANC who threatened and actually kidnapped co-defendants and state witnesses, removing them from the country. After listening to her testimony, the judge (there was no jury trial in South Africa) called her a "calm, composed, deliberate and unblushing liar." The judge sentenced Winnie to six years in jail; an appeals court sustained the conviction in early June 1993 but vacated the prison sentence in a political decision.

Though Winnie Mandela's trial occurred after Nelson Mandela's release from prison, neither Mr. Mandela nor the ANC leadership rallied to Winnie's defense. An effort of radicals sought to rejoin Winnie to the ANC leadership by becoming president of the Women's Auxiliary. While her husband was trying to engage in meaningful negotiations with the white government, Winnie appealed to the militant sector of the ANC; they remembered her for her famous 1987 statement: "With our matchboxes and our necklaces, we shall liberate!"

Mandela divorced his wife in early 1996. One reason was that if Winnie were in any position of power, foreign investors would be hesitant to support the new South Africa. Mandela later remarried with Graça Machel, the widow of President Samora Machel of Mozambique.

By April 2003, a South African court found Winnie Madikizela-Mandela guilty of 43 charges of fraud and 25 of bank theft and sentence her to jail. "The state's evidence is overwhelming," said the judge as he found her guilty of obtaining bank loans worth more than $120,000 in the name of bogus employees of the ANC Women's League, of which she was president. The courts sentenced her to five years in jail, where she was to serve a minimum of eight months, with the rest of the time spent doing community service. Madikizela-Mandela resigned her parliamentary seat and positions in the ANC.

The End of Apartheid and the New Constitution (1990–1994)

In 1991, the various competing elements in South Africa began meeting informally and later in conferences of CODESA—Congress for a Democratic South Africa. Prior to negotiations, several apartheid

Soweto Township　　　　　　　　　　　　　　　　　　　　　　　　　Photo by Judi Iranyi

South Africa

laws had been repealed and political exiles (often common criminals) numbering 50,000 received amnesty and returned to South Africa. Periodic outbursts of violence, particularly between ANC and Inkatha supporters, interrupted the talks, and white extremists led by Eugene Terre'Blanche tried to stop the negotiations by attacking the conference center with armored vehicles.

Political sniping from the conservatives led de Klerk to have a national referendum on his policies, where his efforts were supported by 70% of whites, who thus for the first time voted to share power peacefully with the black majority. The "yes" vote in the referendum received an unexpected and tragic boost from the assassination of Chris Hani, a leader of the South African Communist Party and prominent member of MK. Mandela's appeals for calm in the wake of the Hani assassination were seen to bring the negotiating parties together, and the death itself seemed to present South Africans with a clear vision of the need for democratization over political violence.

The negotiations were delicate and oftentimes awkward. The ANC had to exercise caution because blacks distrusted the idea that whites would genuinely negotiate away their control of South Africa. Outside the conference room, Mandela was careful to level insults at de Klerk in a calculated attempt to reassure his own supporters that he was not giving in to white pressures. Behind the scenes, the parties worked towards consensus, led by the chief negotiators, Roelf Meyer of the NP and Cyril Ramaphosa of the ANC. The parties finally agreed that an interim government had to be elected to draw a permanent constitution and to govern, and it would have to provide minority (i.e. white) protection. The ANC senior leadership (but not its membership) quietly discarded black power.

Agreement on the interim constitution was signed on November 17, 1993, the result of months of painstaking negotiations. The substance of the document was a fundamental victory for the ANC. The constitution provided for elections and specified that the 400-member National Assembly would not represent any specific constituency. Lists prepared by each national party would contain possible representatives. The party's percentage of the total (national) vote would determine the number of seats for each party. A Senate of 90 people would consist of ten members selected by each of the nine provinces of South Africa. In effect, this placed virtually all decision-making power in the hands of the national parties. After the constitution's adoption, plans proceeded for elections on April 26, 1994.

Because of increased political violence and apprehension over the imminent elections, President de Klerk declared a state of emergency in KwaZulu-Natal on March 31, 1994, which infuriated Chief Buthelezi and made him even more adamant. Buthelezi demanded amendments to the constitution that would secure the position of King Goodwill Zwelithini and the historic Zulu kingdom. On April 5, 15,000 Zulus armed with spears and clubs marched through the town of Empangeni; the SADF forces considered them too dangerous to disarm.

The election commission said balloting in KwaZulu necessitated postponement. Mandela rejected this, and international mediators, including Henry Kissinger from the U.S., finally secured a breakthrough on April 19 after two days of talks. The Zulus would participate in the balloting, abandoning demands for amendment of the constitution. There was a guarantee to the continued status of the monarchy and the kingdom of KwaZulu-Natal. The real nature of the settlement was not apparent until almost a month after the elections. Zwelithini received the promise of more than a million acres of KwaZulu-Natal land. Buthelezi (jobless after the elections) would become home affairs minister in the new government lead by Mandela.

The 1994 Election: Freedom

Election officials made elaborate and painstaking preparations for the first popular balloting including all races in South Africa. The problem of illiteracy was immense—50%—so election officials placed pictures of the leaders of each party listed above that choice on the ballot. Overcoming fears of violence, and waiting in line for hours on end, more than 70% of those registered voted.

Besides the NP and the ANC, other parties and groups participated in the election. One was the Freedom Front (FF), formed in March 1994 and headed by former defense chief General Constand Viljoen, which appealed to many conservatives, though Viljoen himself had some views that suggested he favored integration. White conservatives formerly

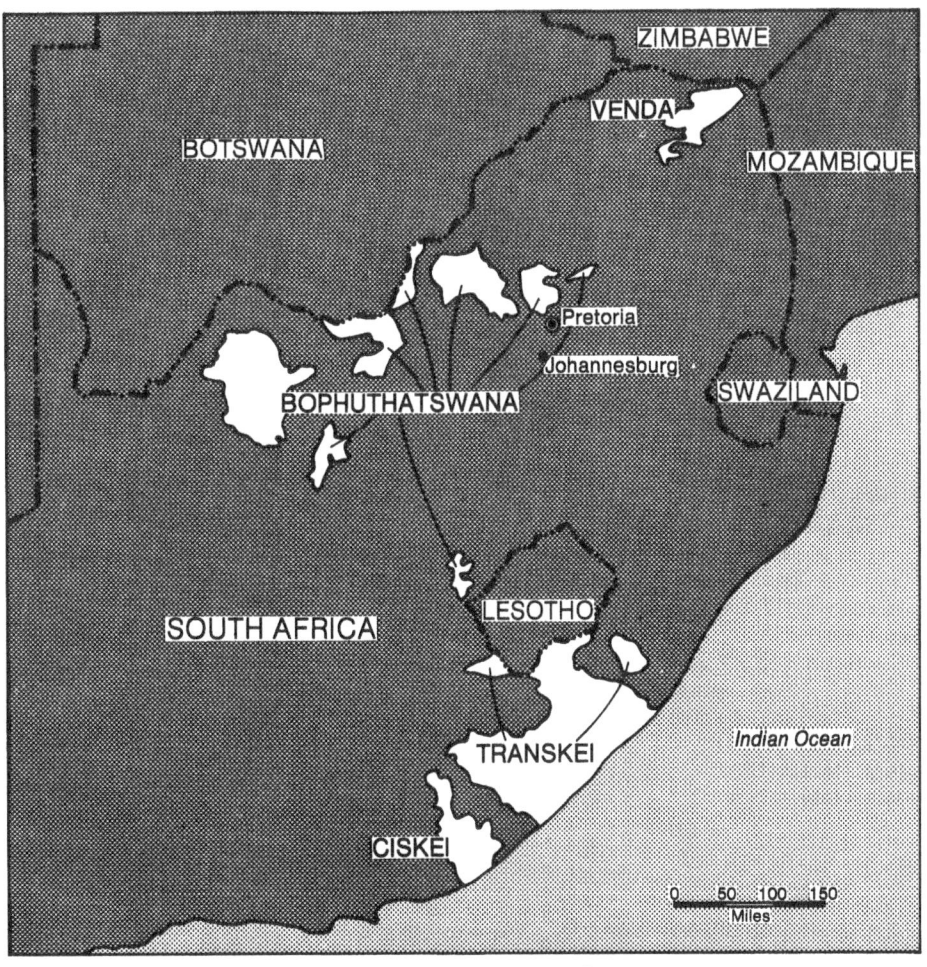

Black "homeland" republics

349

South Africa

Former President Thabo Mbeki

belonged to the Conservative Party (CP). Its principal objective was the creation of an all-white state by the interim constitution, a proposition few ever took seriously. It refused to register as a political party for the elections. The Democratic Party (DP) was the successor of two liberal parties popular among English speakers who opposed apartheid. Tony Leon served as leader of the party. The Pan Africanist Congress (PAC) and its militant wing, the Azanian People's Army, was a radical black party, which adopted a slogan "one settler [a white], one bullet."

As predicted, the ANC demonstrated nationwide appeal and dominated the election, securing a majority of Assembly seats. Nelson Mandela became the first black chief executive in this historic democratic election. The National Party and the Inkatha Freedom Party found their support more localized in Western Cape Province and KwaZulu-Natal. The National Party did well among Coloured and Asiatic Indian voters. The Freedom Front did well in areas dominated by rural whites.

Once in power the ANC demonstrated the balancing of ideology and practicality, required by the responsibility of governance. Its initial budget envisioned a million new housing units and a million new jobs over a five-year period, without the necessity of new taxes. The government adopted the Restitution of Land Rights Act, a very controversial measure, in late 1994 and established a Land Claims Commission and a Land Claims Court. The act directs "balancing the desirability of remedying past human rights violations against . . . the need to avoid major social disruption."

To the chagrin of those who preferred a state-controlled economy, the ANC encouraged foreign investment and announced plans for a significant privatization of state-owned companies. The two policies were interrelated, for privatization could assure the international business community that the state was moving towards a more liberal economy.

So great was President Mandela's moral authority, that he could successfully say "No" to the more outrageous demands from various sectors of the liberation struggle. When the leader of former guerrilla forces threatened to return to armed struggle over problems arising from the integration of these forces into the South African army, Mandela warned against a "suicidal plot."

Tensions ran high among South Africa's black population. During the election campaign, the ANC promised far more than could be realistically delivered to blacks. As the months wore on after the contest, their lives experienced minimal change. Symptoms of this malaise included a high crime rate, corruption, squatting on land, moving into nearby homes after ousting the occupants, and illegal strikes. President Mandela strongly condemned all of this in his February 1995 speech that opened parliament. He criticized what he termed "a culture of entitlement," and accused blacks who "misread freedom to mean license." He condemned those guilty of murdering police officers, taking hostages, rioting, looting, and other crimes.

Chief Mangosuthu Buthelezi

The Constitutional Commission completed its work on a new charter in May 1996. Some features of the document were praised for their symbolism, including the recognition of 11 official languages and an inclusive national anthem. At the institutional level, the Senate changed to a National Council of Provinces (now representing nine provinces, rather than the previous four) and others chosen provincially. The Bill of Rights extended a range of liberties and guarantees (more than that of the U.S.), but essentially continued the structure of government without change—maintaining a strong central authority, with the powers of provinces and smaller areas being strictly limited.

The 1999 Election and the Mbeki Years

The ANC party congress chose Thabo Mbeki as party president in December 1997. President Mandela increasingly relinquished governmental affairs to Mbeki in preparation for the 1999 presidential elections. Thabo Mbeki grew up groomed for leadership. Son of ANC leader Govan Mbeki, Thabo had earlier earned distinction for potential leadership from his father and his father's friend and colleague, Nelson Mandela. He left South Africa in 1962 for England where he studied economics at Sussex University. Like his father, Mbeki was a member of the Communist Party, and in 1970, he went to Russia for military training. On his return to South Africa in 1990, he resigned from the party. The ambiguities in Mbeki's background were numerous: steeped in Marxism, he also trained in Western economics, and nurtured in the idealism of a revolutionary movement and well versed in its Stalinist organizational style, he was seen as practical and pragmatic. The breadth of his intellectual background later became necessary to hold together his coalition partners and to get a handle on a legacy of problems created by apartheid.

Mbeki's accession to power marked a change in tone and language in the ANC's relationship with South Africa's white minority. Nelson Mandela signaled the shift in his valedictory speech to the 1997 ANC party conference. In a speech reportedly prepared by Mbeki, President Mandela departed from the soothing rhetoric of multiracialism that had eased the transition to majority rule. Whites had "demonstrated consistently" a desire to cling to the privileges they enjoyed under apartheid, he said. He accused some of being involved in a "counterrevolutionary conspiracy." The speech contained vintage Marxist rhetoric, stylistically out of character, highly controversial, an affront to those white South Africans who had long opposed apartheid.

South Africa

During his first term as president, Mbeki repeatedly returned to the subject of racism. "Racist" would become a potent political charge leveled against white critics of his policies. The term also had the added advantage of undermining black support of any such criticism. Thabo Mbeki's emphasis on race was one indication of how difficult the transition from liberation movement to political party would be for the ANC.

The ANC soon discovered being the party of power is quite different from being in opposition, and this affected its relationship with its traditional partners, the Congress of South African Trade Unions (COSATU) and the South African Communist Party (SACP). Membership in the three groups often overlaps, and leadership of the two partner organizations was frequently co-opted by the ANC leadership. After the 1999 election, for example, COSATU had to replace four of its principal officers elevated to parliament by virtue of membership on the ANC lists.

COSATU's new president, Willy Madisha, developed his career in the teachers' union and in the SACP. Its new general secretary, Zwelinzima Vavi, was a National Union of Mineworkers (NUM) organizer as well as a member of the SACP. Both COSATU and the SACP remained socialist in orientation. They were not part of the process that created a major piece of the government's economic legislation, GEAR (Growth, Employment and Redistribution), and both feared GEAR leaned too much towards a liberal capitalist economy. Both seem to prefer nationalization to privatization. The collision of the three partners seems inevitable, though "unity of the movement," at least in the short term, trumped the divisions among them.

Clifton Beaches near Cape Town   Photo by Rita Arendt

Big election issues for the ANC in 1999 were jobs and crime. Estimates put unemployment at 50%, making it one of the country's most urgent problems. An estimated 4.7 million people were unemployed and looking for work. GEAR had set a goal of 252,000 new jobs for 1997, but this did not adequately take into account the continuing recession in mining where the industry had to cut 50,000 mining jobs.

South Africa's second multiparty democratic election took place in early June 1999. Some 42 political parties participated. They ranged from God's People Party (dedicated to fighting Satan), to Keep it Straight and Simple (you work out the acronym). The ANC overwhelmed all, nearly winning a two-thirds majority with 266 seats. The National Party, burdened with the historical weight of apartheid and deprived of forceful leadership, fell to a fourth-place finish. Not even calling itself the New National Party (NNP) helped to slow its decline; it won only 28 seats.

The Democratic Party, a distant second-place finisher with a mere 38 seats, assumed the role of official opposition. White liberals congregated in the Democratic Party. The DP also benefited from defections from NNP, especially in the Western Cape Province. Its leader Tony Leon was articulate and fiery as an orator. As leader of the opposition, he provided some of the strongest criticism of the ANC. Chief Buthelezi's IFP won 34 seats.

In June 2000, the Democratic Party (DP), under Leon's leadership, merged with the New National Party (NNP) to form the Democratic Alliance (DA). In many ways, it was a merger of fish and fowl. The DP had inherited South Africa's white-minority liberal tradition. The NNP was, of course, the recently re-baptized National Party, which had created and enforced apartheid for 46 years. In many ways, the merger seemed to represent a voluntary death for the NNP. Loathed by black Africans as the party of apartheid, the NNP had little to offer, and it has won less than 7% of the votes cast. The question that remained was how long this awkward merger of DP and NNP would last.

According to the South African constitution, MPs lose their seats in parliament if their party dissolves. Therefore, the NNP and DP continued to exist in parliament until the 2004 national election. Such a situation was not to be, however, for leadership disputes in Western Cape Province at the end of 2001 shattered the alliance. . Grasping to keep the party and his own political career alive, NNP leader Marthinus van Schalkwyk withdrew from the DA, negotiated a new relationship with the ANC, and transformed the face of South African party politics.

The alliance was attractive for the ANC because the governments of Cape Town

King Goodwill Zwelethini

351

South Africa

Penguins, Boulders Beach, False Bay

and its province, which previously excluded the ANC, were now open to their politicians. At a national level, the ANC's political partners, COSATU and SACP, seemed left out of the loop regarding the new relationship, and some of their members expressed discomfort, adding to the strains within the triple alliance. Chief Buthelezi's IFP seemed to question its own relationship with the ANC, especially since an alliance between the ANC and the NNP could easily topple Inkatha's control of the KwaZulu-Natal provincial legislature. President Mbeki and the ANC quickly moved to use the new alliance to strengthen their domination of South African political space.

Sitting representatives passed legislation to permit "floor crossing"—allowing a representative to change parties without resigning from office and standing for reelection on a new party list. The opposition, with little more than a thin line of lawyers to defend themselves against the ANC juggernaut, challenged the legislation's legality and South Africa's Constitutional Court gave them partial victory. Municipalities permitted floor crossing, but at the provincial and national levels, the constitution required amendment before members could change parties. With more than a two-thirds majority in parliament, this posed no impediment for the ANC and its NNP partner.

Constitutional amendments to permit party changes at the national and provincial levels passed in February 2003. When the 15-day window in which lawmakers could change their political identities ended on April 4, the party changers reshaped the South African political landscape. Nine members of parliament crossed over to the ANC, giving the party 275 seats in the 400-seat body—a two-thirds majority of its own.

Thabo Mbeki's presidency inaugurated a new phase in South African politics. Nelson Mandela had used his moral authority to convince his fellow Africans to accept the new political system, and his moderation and restraint similarly convinced whites to support the new dispensation. A Truth and Reconciliation Commission sought to soothe the emotional pains on both sides of the racial divide. Acceptance and reconciliation seemingly gained; the new government moved to transform the legacy of injustice in contemporary South Africa. Four laws were passed early in 2000: the Promotion of Access to Information Bill,

Nelson Mandela

South Africa

Busy downtown Durban — Photo by Nancy Sprotte

the Promotion of Administrative Justice Bill, the Preferential Procurement Policy Framework and the Promotion of Equality and Prevention of Unfair Discrimination Bill.

Two of the bills give ordinary citizens the right to make the government—at all levels—accountable. The Promotion of Administrative Justice Bill forces the government to create mechanisms to explain its decisions, such as cutting welfare grants to affected members of the public. In theory, bureaucrats will think before acting, realizing they may have to justify any action they take. The Promotion of Access to Information Bill was a reaction to the secrecy with which the former white regime shrouded state affairs; it affirmed a right of access to "any information held by a public or private body," excluding defense, security, and foreign affairs information.

The two remaining bills sought to transform apartheid's legacy of racial injustice. The Preferential Procurement Policy Framework Bill gives preferences in government contracts to companies that have actively hired workers disadvantaged based on race, gender, or disability. The Promotion of Equality and Prevention of Unfair Discrimination Bill sought an end to traditional forms of discrimination. Its scope is vast. Discrimination is defined in the broadest possible terms and applied to 17 prohibited areas: race, gender, sex, pregnancy, marital status, ethnic or social origin, color, sexual orientation, age, disability, religion, conscience, belief, culture, language, and birth or any other recognized ground. Ambiguities of provisions in the four laws suggest that implementation of the laws will only take place over many years.

The Truth and Reconciliation Commission

Racial tensions still exist in South Africa, but given the bitterness of past experience, it is remarkable that any harmony at all is possible. One important institution that helped advance the reconciliation process was the Truth and Reconciliation Commission (TRC) established by act of parliament in 1995. Its purpose was to investigate crimes committed during the apartheid era, and as commission chairman, Mandela appointed Archbishop Desmond Tutu, the 1984 Nobel Peace Prize winner. Tutu had been the first black Anglican Dean of Johannesburg and had led the church in South Africa into an active struggle against apartheid.

The TRC heard 21,300 witnesses and compiled a dossier of human rights crimes committed by all sides during the apartheid era. A 3,500-page report submitted to President Mandela in October 1998 marked the conclusion of its investigative work. There was guilt aplenty in the report. The most serious culprit was the South African State itself. The commission's analysis of why this came about was simple and direct: racism was at the center of state action designed to protect the power and privilege of a racial minority. Consequently, white citizens adopted a dehumanizing attitude towards black citizens. They ceased to think of them as citizens and this "created a climate in which gross atrocities committed against them were seen as legitimate."

The commission also held the opponents of apartheid—the ANC and other liberation movements—morally and politically accountable for human rights violations. Thabo Mbeki, for example, had told the TRC that a number of ANC members—including 34 in Angola when the party was in exile—were executed by the movement's own security officials. At least one of those was wrongly executed by two ANC cadres who themselves were later put to death.

Important political figures did not escape the commission's condemnation. The commission found Winnie Madikizela-Mandela accountable for crimes committed by the Mandela United Football Club (MUFC). Killing, torture, assault and arson were all MUFC activities, the commission found that Madikizela-Mandela herself was aware of this criminal activity, but she chose not to address it.

The commission held Mangosuthu Buthelezi accountable as leader of the Inkatha Freedom Party for all the violence committed by its members. Between 1982 and 1994, IFP supporters caused the deaths of about 3,800 people in KwaZulu-Natal province alone, against 1,100 caused by the ANC. It was, the commission thought, a "systematic pattern" of murder and attacks by the IFP against its opponents, often in collusion with state security forces.

The commission was empowered to grant amnesty to those who asked for it and a separate panel existed to hold these hearings. Applicants were required to prove their crime had a political motive or was performed acting under direct orders. They were also required to offer full disclosure of their crimes and demonstrate

Winnie Madikizela-Mandela

South Africa

President Jacob Zuma

genuine contrition. The commission received 7,100 applications for amnesty and granted close to 1,000. It rejected the killers of Chris Hani—it was not a political crime according to the panel. It also rejected the amnesty application of five policemen involved in the death of the activist Steve Biko in 1977, and it refused a blanket amnesty to ANC leaders, arguing that the amnesty was for repenting individuals.

The legislation establishing the TRC entailed the idea that victims of state-sponsored violence deserve compensation from the state for their suffering. Since the conclusion of hearings, a third of the commission's panels have dealt with reparations to the victims. It received 20,000 requests for financial reparation. Of these, 17,000 claimants received initial payments totaling $3.7 million. However, a special government fund existed to give the bulk of financial reparations. President Mbeki announced the government would be making a one-time payment of 30,000 Rand ($3,800) to the 22,000 victims of apartheid designated by the TRC.

Mbeki's Government and the 2004 Elections

President Mbeki and his government came under increasing scrutiny as they confronted a number of issues and problems, many of their own making. Both the president's judgment and action on these raised questions about his capacity to lead. Part of the problem lies in the president's own style and personality. Mbeki demonstrated a governing style more restrained than that of Mandela. He was seen as cool, distant, and lacking a common touch. His rapport with the masses and charisma paled beside that of more popular and populist leaders. Indeed, it is widely reported that Nelson Mandela preferred Cyril Ramaphosa, the mineworkers' leader and principal negotiator of the transition from apartheid to majority rule, as his successor.

Thabo Mbeki's judgment and leadership also proved sorely lacking in several policy areas. The most tragic was the disastrous mismanagement of the HIV/AIDS pandemic (see "The Present: Contemporary Issues" below). In foreign policy, Zimbabwe loomed large. President Mbeki claimed the efficacy of "quiet diplomacy" before critics who demanded he condemn Zimbabwe's state-sanctioned violence against its opponents. The wisdom of that approach became ever more dubious as Zimbabwe collapsed economically under an increasingly dictatorial Robert Mugabe. The ANC and President Mbeki consistently refused to condemn comrade Mugabe and his thuggish antics. In this refusal, Mbeki abandoned moral leadership and jeopardized a visionary project for African development by alienating Western governments asked to finance the project. Disgusted with President Mbeki's moral flaccidity and lack of leadership on the Zimbabwe issue, South Africa's Nobel Prize-winning cleric Desmond Tutu unleashed a withering criticism: Mbeki, he said "would be booed in the street" if he were ever to ask ordinary Zimbabweans what they thought about his views on their country. "The people of Zimbabwe have no respect for Mbeki. They don't know why he is supporting Mugabe. They don't understand it."

Over the Mbeki years, certain internal democratic traditions of the ANC also eroded. In the early days, the national executive committee conducted lively debates on important issues, but its ultimate authority grew concentrated in an increasingly autocratic executive. Nothing better demonstrates presidential dominance in the South African political system than President Mbeki's decision to send an entire aircraft filled with weapons to rescue a beleaguered Jean-Bertrand Aristide in Haiti. The decision was single-handed, personal, and illustrative of the system's executive dominance.

Despite a lack of progress on Zimbabwe and obtuse obstructionism on the AIDS issue that shortened lives and increased suffering of South Africans, Thabo Mbeki was largely uncontested as the 2004 elections approached. Reelected ANC president in 2003, Mbeki led the party to a smashing victory—with nearly 70%—in the legislative polls of 2004, surpassing the 1999 results and gaining more than a two-thirds majority in parliament. The victory assured his election to a second four-year term as president of South Africa by the National Assembly.

The ANC entered the poll allied with the New National Party (NNP) of Marthinus van Schalkwyk, but it hardly needed support. It won 279 seats in the 400-seat assembly, while its coalition partner won a mere nine. The Democratic Alliance, shorn of all connection with the NNP, gathered support as the principal voice of opposition to the ANC; it won 50 seats in the legislature, 12 more than in 1999. Its electoral partner, Chief Buthelezi's IFP, dropped from 34 to 28 seats. The Freedom Front Plus party won support from the NNP's white Afrikaner support base, and Coloured NNP voters in Western Cape fled to the Independent Democrats (ID). The ID, led by Patricia de Lille, was barely a year old when she left the Pan African Congress during the Assembly floor crossings of early 2003. De Lille's was often the most vigorous voice of critical opposition in the assembly where she combined roles of gadfly and moral conscience to devastating effect. She becomes the first woman to lead a political party in parliament.

The ANC's electoral victory confirmed its dominance of South Africa's political space. It secured a majority in all but two provinces, Western Cape and KwaZulu-Natal. In each it became the dominant party, and having entered each province with a coalition partner, it emerged with a majority in the two provinces that had previously eluded it.

President Mbeki asserted his party's will over its coalition partners. In a display of personal confidence and power, he nominated premiers in all nine of South Africa's provinces. It provided an opportunity for a general housecleaning. ANC replaced incumbents in all but one of the premierships, opting to replace Mbhazima "Sam" Shilowa in Gauteng, who was seen as a rival to Mbeki. Four of the nine new ANC premiers would be women.

The Zuma Corruption Trial

Mbeki got an opportunity to deal with corruption at the national level in June 2005, when courts convicted Schabir Shaik of fraud and corruption; Shaik was the financial advisor to deputy president Jacob Zuma. The case, which riveted the entire country's attention, involved $200,000 in payments to Zuma to help secure business deals and negotiating a bribe for the deputy president with a French arms manufacturer. In his judgment, Justice Hilary Squires described as "overwhelming" the evidence of a "corrupt relationship" existing between Zuma and Shaik.

Shaik exhausted his appeals and entered prison in November 2006 to serve a 15-year term; the Court also required Shaik to surrender some $4.7 million in illegal gains to the state. Zuma reacted to the judgment by declaring his conscience

South Africa

Providing improved services: building a water-treatment facility ©IRIN

clear because "I have not committed any crime," but within two weeks President Mbeki bowed to the pressure of public opinion. The court's ruling, he announced before parliament, had "raised questions of conduct" and it would be in the best interests of the country to "release" Zuma from "his responsibilities as deputy president of the republic and member of the cabinet." Zuma remained deputy president of the ANC.

The delay of 12 days between the conviction of Schabir Shaik and Mbeki's firing of his deputy suggested Zuma did not go easily or willingly. He was widely seen as Mbeki's successor as both the ANC's and the Republic's next president, and he had powerful support within the tripartite alliance, especially among youth groups and labor's left wing. He also remained enormously popular in his native KwaZulu-Natal province. (His father was reportedly a Zulu chief and advisor to the Zulu king.)

The firing of Zuma earned Mbeki much praise from both home and abroad. Opposition leader Tony Leon offered praise for President Mbeki: "He faced a choice between two difficult paths. Each had its political costs. Yet in the end, he chose to uphold principle over politics. By so doing, he has led us to a great victory for our young democracy." *Business Day* offered a similar assessment: "South Africans must be grateful for what Mbeki did. When it can sometimes seem as if S[outh] A[frica] is becoming mired in corruption, its leader acted against the hardest possible target. If that didn't take courage, then the word has lost its meaning."

The *Mail and Guardian* moved the commentary from the personal to the political, calling the Zuma affair the country's "gravest post-apartheid political crisis." It was a crisis that highlighted developing divisions within the ANC, between those who supported President Mbeki's economic liberalism and those who thought Zuma, seen much more as a man of the people, might better return the party to its socialist ideals. Indeed, everything that followed the Zuma sacking seemed to reveal the down and dirty politics of succession, both to the presidency of the ANC (decided in 2007) and to the presidency of the republic (decided in 2009).

Byzantine, nasty, and complex, there would be enough intrigue to fill multiple spy novels as contending forces struggled for control of the ANC. Numerous hoax e-mails, the use of National Intelligence Agency personnel to spy on opponents, and the mysterious death of a mining magnate, accused of stealing millions, with close ties to the ANC, were the tips of the icebergs. When an accuser filed rape charges against Jacob Zuma in 2005, his supporters immediately saw it as a plot by Mbeki supporters (see below under "The Present: Contemporary Issues"), and his acquittal in June 2006 gave inspiration to his followers and stimulus to his campaign to become ANC president; at the same time, it raised concerns among other parties and opponents of Zuma that the future president was virtually above the law and living with impunity.

From Mbeki to Zuma

In November 2005, the courts indicted Zuma on two counts of corruption, but the case collapsed when the prosecution was unprepared. Over the next three and a half years, Zuma's lawyers delayed any attempt to secure evidence and move the case ahead. On September 12, 2008, the Courts ruled that the charges against Zuma were invalid because the prosecution had repeatedly followed incorrect procedure. Just over a week later, Mbeki resigned as president of South Africa after pressure from the ANC National Executive Committee, regarding his possible role interference in the trial. On January 12, 2009, the Supreme Court officially overturned the accusations against Mbeki, but his resignation stood.

The interim president was Kgalema Motlanthe, a close colleague of Zuma, who at the time of his appointment to the Presidency served as Deputy President of the ANC. On April 6, 2009, the National Prosecution Authority (NPA) announced that it dropped all charges of corruption, racketeering, tax evasion, money laundering and fraud against Zuma.

Despite a sentence to serve time through November 2021, Shaik walked out of prison in March 2009. The courts released Shaik on medical parole, a distinction for the terminally ill, expected to die within a rather short period. He only served 28 months of his 15-year sentence. Controversy surrounds his release, for Shaik has not commented to the media any specific explanation of any terminal illness, and most reports indicate that he appears healthy. *The New York Times* wrote an article indicating that Zuma played a role in the release of Shaik. A poll released at the Davos World Economic Forum in January 2007 showed that 63% of South Africans think their leaders are dishonest.

In April 2009, over 17 million South Africans voted in the national and provincial elections, electing Jacob Zuma the new President of South Africa. The ANC dominated the vote, though they narrowly lost the two-thirds majority they previously held, necessary to amend the constitution. The ANC took 264 of 400 seats in Parliament.

The opposition was led by the Democratic Alliance, led by Cape Town Mayor Helen Zille, which increased its contingent in Parliament to 67, after winning one-sixth of the vote. Following the

South Africa

resignation of Mbeki, defectors from the ANC formed a new party, Congress of the People (COPE), with the aim of creating a viable black-led competitor to end the ANC's quasi-monopolistic dominance of national politics. COPE was founded by former ANC luminaries, namely former ANC Chairman Mosiuoa "Terror" Lekota (who earned his nickname on the football pitch, not the battlefield) and former Premier of Gauteng province Mbhazima "Sam" Shilowa. COPE appointed Bishop Mvume Dandala as their candidate, a man with a squeaky-clean past compared to the controversial Zuma. Though analysts predicted COPE to make a significant impact on the election's playing field, the new party won 7.42% of the vote, taking 30 parliamentary seats. In 2011, The Democratic Alliance gained influence, nearly doubling its portion of the vote in local elections.

Meanwhile, the ANC showed increasing signs of further centralizing authority. In November 2011, the National Assembly passed an information bill that the ANC claimed was required to protect national security; critics argued the act threatens freedom of speech. More dramatically, South Africa was shocked in 2012 when police cracked down violently on striking mine workers in the town of Marikana, killing 34 and injuring nearly 80 more. Police claimed that the workers were threatening police lines with machetes and spears, but the violence was perpetrated by the police. This led to a major outcry that resulted in the government calling for an inquiry into the police action. The massacre led ANC youth leader Julius Malema to call for Zuma's resignation—though it should be noted that this happened concurrently with official investigations into Malema's probably fraudulent activities. The Marikana killings also served as an indicator that the long and important relationship between the ANC leadership and the broader movement of trade unions and workers may be badly frayed. If true, this could have major implications for the coming years and specifically for the prospects of another party winning national elections within the next generation.

The years from 2011 to the present have also seen an increased profile in international diplomacy: in January, South Africa acquired a seat on the UN Security Council for the 2011–2012 term, and in May, President Zuma became actively involved in mediating the Libyan conflict. South Africa also expanded its international presence in January 2013 when it sent additional troops to the Central African Republic as rebel movements descended upon the capital. However, thirteen of these troops were killed in clashes as the C.A.R. government fell, and the Zuma government announced in April 2013 that the South African troops would return home.

CONTEMPORARY THEMES

By regional standards, and even continental ones, the South African economy is huge. South Africa dwarfs its neighbors and represents as much as 40% of the entire economy of the continent. Nevertheless, the giant is sluggish. On February 5, 2009, Tito Bowen, governor of South Africa's central bank, predicted that the country would experience "a rough patch or the next three to four years." South Africa's moderate growth over the past several years has stagnated, and its openness to the global economy has made it vulnerable to the worldwide recession.

The Economy: Mining and Industry

Unemployment is a major issue in South Africa. In the early 2000s, independent estimates held that it was as high as 45% in many areas—much higher than official figures. For youths aged 16 to 25, a 2005 report estimated an employment rate of 52%. Three-fourths of South Africa's unemployed are black Africans, the principal constituency of the ANC. The government estimates that the economy must achieve a minimum of 6% growth to offset unemployment.

South Africa is rich in natural resources. It has, for example, the world's largest reserves of manganese (80%), chromium (68%), and platinum-group metals (56%). At least 40% of the world's total recoverable gold reserves are in South Africa. Yet even with gold fetching over $600/oz by mid-2006, the industry was facing difficulties, with rising costs and declining production. Labor costs keep rising (remaining gold reserves lie deeper and deeper, requiring greater amounts of labor) and worker militancy has cut production through strike action. In August 2005, some 100,000 members of the National Union of Mineworkers put aside their tools. The union demanded a 12% wage hike and rejected the offer of a 4.5%–5% wage increase coupled with bonuses tied to any rise in the domestic price of gold. It was the first industry-wide stoppage in 18 years and cost companies $12 million a day in lost revenue. After four days, the crippling strike ended when the miners accepted a revised offer of 6%–7% wage increases. As other producers in developing countries have come on line, South Africa's share of world gold production has dropped to about 10%, down from 80% in 1970. Overall, the once emblematic sector contributes 2% to the country's gross domestic product.

South Africa is the world's fourth largest diamond producer, after Botswana, Russia, and Canada, but like gold, this luxury industry experiences difficulty when global demand falters (as in 2009). De Beers, the foremost international

Township housing, Gugulethu — Photo by Judi Iranyi

South Africa

Goat herding in remote Northern Cape province ©IRIN

diamond concern, reported that five of its seven South African operations were loss-making in 2004, owing mainly to the strength of the rand. The company, once a virtual cartel, faces stiff competition from Russia. Alrosa, the state diamond company, which controls nearly the entire Russian production, plans to increase its output by 20%.

The government is shaping a new regulatory framework for the mining industry. In 2002, it enacted a law that formally transferred ownership of the country's resources to the state. Henceforth, companies exploiting those resources will have to pay royalties to the government. The initial percentages proposed by the government (around 3%) ran into stiff resistance. Most companies saw the proposed royalties as too high, especially since the government based the royalties on revenues rather than profits. The government and energy firms further negotiated the final wording of its Mining and Petroleum Royalty Bill. The planned royalty tax was to drop to 1% to encourage offshore oil and gas exploration.

South Africa lacks rich oil resources, but has considerable coal deposits, and coal is the primary fuel produced and consumed in South Africa. Estimates of recoverable coal reserves, the sixth largest in the world, are about 5% of world reserves. Coal is also the country's second most important foreign exchange earner, after gold, contributing 7% of export earnings. Production is concentrated in a few regions, with Mpumalanga Province accounting for 83% of total output. Nearly one-third of total coal production is exported—primarily to the European market. The bulk of domestically used coal generates electricity.

According to Interpol, South Africa is the fourth-largest cannabis producer in the world. An estimated 205,000 acres yield 387.2 million pounds of the drug. First introduced into the region some 500 years ago by Arab traders, cannabis (called "dagga" locally) is widely regarded as a traditional crop in many rural areas, particularly the Eastern Cape and KwaZulu-Natal. South African cannabis is some of the most potent in the world. Around a quarter of seizures worldwide involve the South African product. In some rural areas, farms produce up to three crops per year. While the producers are usually subsistence farmers for whom cannabis is a unique cash crop, the U.S. State Department reports that there are more than 100 drug syndicates operating in South Africa.

The recession of 2008 and 2009 took its toll on the stability of the South African rand. Because the value of the nation's currency depends so heavily on the prices of gold, platinum, diamonds, and other luxurious commodities traded, the rand loss nearly half of its value against the US dollar toward the end of 2008; it later recovered before drifting to its lows again by mid-2014. In reaction to the economic issues in 2008 and 2009, xenophobic violent attacks against refugees from Zimbabwe and other nations in sub-Saharan African made headlines worldwide. With already high levels of unemployment, many South African natives viewed the refugees as "leeches" who would only contribute to problem. Though as of June 2009 the violent xenophobic attacks have mostly ceased, anti-immigrant sentiment remains high. Meanwhile, worker strikes have been hitting South Africa recently. For example, Lonmin (a South African platinum producer) might go to court in a bid to stop a 16-week strike because of the levels of violence faced by workers who want to return to work is rising. Members of The Association of Mineworkers and

Cape Town harbor development with Table Mountain in the background
Photo by Rita Arendt

South Africa

One township declares its opposition to crime.   Photo by Char Glacy

Construction Union (AMCU) have been staging to strike, and they have been attacking workers trying to return to work. As many as four miners were killed in a recent altercation.

Black Economic Empowerment

The government has targeted the mining industry as a marquee sector in its drive for Black Economic Empowerment (BEE). Part of the government's plans to transform the economy by giving black Africans a significant share of major economic sectors, initial legislative drafts of BEE caused panic selling of mining shares in October 2002 when first released. Some shares dropped by 40% when it was learned the government was proposing that 51% of mining assets should be controlled by black South Africans within ten years. Negotiation reduced the amount transferred to black shareholders to 26% of equity by May 2014. As an incentive to the hard-pressed mining industry, empowerment requirements can drop to 16% if the company does enough to promote "benefaction"—increasing worker benefits.

BEE was a central goal of the Mbeki government. By 2014, the ANC would like to see that South Africa's black majority holds major (largely unspecified) stakes in the economy. Whites, about 12% of the population, still control the economy, the mines, banks, factories and farms. Whites own more than 70% of the land and dominate the banking, manufacturing, and tourism industries. According to government figures, white-run companies control 95% of the country's diamond production, 63% of platinum reserves and 51% of gold reserves.

As BEE deals unfolded, however, the Mbeki empowerment model came under increasing attack as enrichment of a few well-placed black businessmen, which has done little to improve the conditions of average South Africans. In October 2004, Kgalema Motlanthe, who then served as ANC Secretary-General, condemned the program as "narrow based", and saying "certain individuals . . . are the beneficiaries of repeated bouts of re-empowerment. We see the same names mentioned over and over again in one deal after another." Indeed, Cyril Ramaphosa and Mathews Phosa (a former premier of Mpumalanga province), both members of the ANC's national executive council, signed numerous empowerment deals, as has Tokyo Sexwale, the former Premier of Gauteng province. Ramaphosa's brother-in-law Patrice Motsepe became a very rich man after signing several major empowerment deals in the gold sector worth around $503.4 million. The opposition Democratic Alliance claims that Motsepe and Sexwale were involved in 60% of the $6.4 billion empowerment deals done in 2003. The benefits to BEE tycoons are startling against the backdrop of black South African poverty: when Standard Bank chose Saki Macozoma and Cyril Ramaphosa as empowerment partners, the deal netted each man around $30 million.

Much of the BEE criticism reflects internal ANC politics. (Rivals for future party leadership are more than happy to see criticism of the long-admired Cyril Ramaphosa, for example.) Left-wing opponents of the ANC's move to liberal economic policies still press for a rethink on the issue. The COSATU leader, Zwelinzima Vavi, has threatened to obstruct a pending $18.6 billion deal in the finance sector to bring in more black partners. The banks, he argues, should use their cash to build houses for poor blacks, fund small black businesses, and subsidize black farms. A similar line of criticism has also come from Desmond Tutu citing the fact that millions of South Africans live in "grueling, demeaning, dehumanizing poverty," while black empowerment "seems to benefit not the vast majority but an elite that tends to be recycled."

HIV/AIDS and Health

South Africa now has one of the highest rates of HIV infection and in terms of absolute numbers, the greatest number of HIV-positive people in the world. The statistics are appalling, with an estimated prevalence rate of 17.8%, and about 5.7 million HIV positive people. Patients with AIDS-related infections occupy nearly three-fourths of South African hospital beds. It has been estimated that as many as 700,000 children became AIDS orphans by 2010. In February 2005, the government released statistics showing annual deaths in the country had risen 57% from 1997 to 2003, with common AIDS-related diseases like tuberculosis and pneumonia fueling much of the increase. The mortality spike was greatest in the 15 to 49 age category.

Life expectancy has declined and is now estimated to be about 51.6 years (according to UNICEF in 2009), or the lowest levels since the 1960s. It is even lower in provinces like KwaZulu-Natal, which has one of the highest numbers of HIV/AIDS cases in the country. With more than 60% of new infections occurring in people 15 to 25 years old, the pandemic is expected to wipe out large segments of the very people who are needed to fight it—teachers, health professionals and government workers. With such a high percentage of the labor force HIV-positive, the economy is experiencing extreme difficulties. Additionally, the burden placed on non-positive family members to be caregivers is further affecting labor performance and the overall economy. The government was slow to recognize the problem and slower to respond, and some officials in the Mbeki administration were particularly negligent. Until subjected to a court order, the government refused to employ vaccines known to reduce the incidence of mother-to-child transmission of the HIV virus. In December 2001, the Pretoria High Court ordered the government to provide antiretrovirals (ARVs) to all HIV-positive pregnant women. Treatment Action Campaign (TAC), an AIDS lobby group, brought the case that has significantly ratcheted up techniques of public embarrassment for a foot-dragging regime. The Constitutional Court rejected the government's appeal in April, saying the government was violating the

South Africa

constitutional rights of women and their babies by not supplying Nevirapine, a drug long proven to reduce mother-to-child HIV transmission.

The embarrassments peaked in and around 2002 and 2003. At an international conference in July 2002, South Africa's health minister, Dr. Manto Tshabala-Msimang, said on record that the antiretrovirals were "poisons" killing "our people." She had also once suggested that those infected with HIV should eat beetroot and garlic. When parliament reopened in February 2003 and the government had not yet signed on to an AIDS treatment and prevention plan, advocacy groups descended on it in protest. TAC volunteers occupied government ministries and defied police to arrest them. By April 2003, TAC protesters had taken their cause international, demonstrating outside South Africa's diplomatic missions abroad to demand the government supply antiretroviral drugs to AIDS sufferers. Finance Minister Trevor Manuel announced in February 2004 that the government allocated an additional $305 million to fighting HIV/AIDS over the next three years, but it was not until two weeks before the April 2004 elections that the drugs began to appear. By the end of 2004, the World Health Organization estimated that 837,000 South Africans urgently needed antiretro-viral drugs, but only 78,000 received them through government programs. By November of that year, the government had already spent $6.3 million on the legal costs of defending the government's policy against activists in the courts.

Government delay on HIV/AIDS was directly attributable to President Mbeki himself. For starters, the president picked up notions—apparently from self-guided reading of the scientific dissidents on the internet—that there was no proven relationship between HIV and AIDS. His attitude only worsened the situation, for while his government delayed, people died and infections increased. He further criticized ARVs for both their costs and their toxicity. Mbeki's views also verged on paranoia and conspiracy theory. In October 2000, for example, he told a gathering of ANC officials that the CIA was part of a "conspiracy to promote the view that HIV causes AIDS."

According to South Africa's *Mail and Guardian* newspaper, Mbeki told the group the CIA was also working with big U.S. pharmaceutical manufacturers to undermine him. The reason for this, he explained, was the fear that his questioning of the HIV/AIDS link would lead to reduced profits in the sale of antiretroviral treatments. (In the midst of the debate speculation was rife that Mbeki

National Assembly Following the May 2014 Election

Party	Percentage of Vote	National Assembly Seats Won
African National Congress	62.15	249
Democratic Alliance	22.23	89
Congress of the People	6.35	25
Inkatha Freedom Party	2.40	10
Others	6.87	27
National Freedom Party		6
United Democratic Movement		4
Freedom Front Plus		4
Congress of the People		3
African Christian Democratic Party		3
African Independent Congress		3
Agang SA		2
Pan Africanist Congress		1
African People's Convention		1
Total		400

was financially invested in competitor treatments.)

President Mbeki reappointed his fellow AIDS obstructionist, Dr. Manto Tshabala-Msimang—"Dr. No" to AIDS activists—as health minister in April 2004. From that position she continued to urge people to follow a more healthful diet—lots of garlic and beetroot. Both Mbeki and Tshabala-Msimang came in for withering criticism from the UN special envoy to Africa on AIDS, the Canadian Stephen Lewis. In late 2005, Mr. Lewis published *Race Against Time* (Toronto: House of Anansi Press) a compilation of his lectures delivered as a private citizen. In the book, Mr. Lewis singled out the South African government and its president for what he called "bewildering policies and a lackadaisical approach to treatment of the nation's HIV-positive citizens."

The country's AIDS activists were further mortified when Jacob Zuma, who had headed the National AIDS Council when he was South Africa's deputy president, told the court at his rape trial in 2006 that he "took a shower" immediately after having sex with his HIV-positive accuser to "cut the risk of contracting HIV." TAC campaigners called the comments "ill-informed" and noted that there was no evidence that supported the idea that showers reduced the risk of HIV infection.

Proof of the disastrous consequences of misinformation came from the ANC's national health secretary, Dr. Saadiq Kariem, who admitted his concern that young people were misinterpreting Zuma's prevention claims. Following the trial, Kariem said, he had fielded calls from "ANC comrades enquiring whether a shower cap could help get rid of HIV." For her part, Tshabala-Msimang accused the press of misleading the public by publicizing Zuma's comments. In his final judgment, Justice Willem van der Merwe pointedly called Zuma's failure to use a condom with a woman whom he knew to be HIV-positive "inexcusable." For his part, the ANC president sought redemption through apology. Going on national radio after the courts acquitted him of rape, the 64-year-old Zuma apologized to the nation for having unprotected sex with an HIV-positive woman. "I should have been more cautious and more responsible," he told his interviewer. "I erred on this issue and on this, I apologize."

With Manto Tshabala-Msimang sidelined with serious health concerns (she would ultimately undergo a liver transplant before dying in late 2009), the government finally formulated a major policy shift and announced it in March 2007. The five-year (2007–2011) National Strategic Plan (NSP) marked a watershed in government thinking: ARVs are now a central tool in fighting HIV/AIDS, and the plan envisions a five-fold increase in the number of HIV-positive people receiving the drugs by 2011.

NSP's primary goal is to reduce new HIV infections by 50%. One means to that end is another key target of the plan: ensuring that 70% of all adults have an HIV test at least once in their lifetime. Ambitiously, the plan calls for 95% of pregnant women to take HIV tests by 2011, and HIV tests for 90% of their babies at six weeks. For those already afflicted, NSP aims to get antiretroviral medicines to 80% of the adults who need

South Africa

Cape Point, the tip of the Cape of Good Hope, where the Indian and Atlantic Oceans meet.
Photo by Connie Abell

them; only 24% of those in advanced stages of the illness were receiving ARVs by mid-2006 and 28% in 2007. Recent studies have shown that proper treatment of an HIV positive patient keeps the individual healthy and reduces the risk of transmitting the virus to a partner (even with unprotected sex) because treatment reduces an individual's viral load. Many advocates for increased funding for anti-retroviral treatment use the slogan, "treatment as prevention."

The plan could cost up to $6.2 billion, but delivery, not cost, may be a more difficult problem to overcome.

South Africa experiences a critical shortage of healthcare workers, especially in rural areas. A report by Doctors Without Borders concluded the country (and its neighbors) could not contain the disease without an increase in the number of doctors, nurses and medical assistants available. South African health officials are enlisting traditional healers, called *sangomas*, to detect signs of HIV and persuade their patients take tests and ARVs.

Crime

South Africa suffered a wave of crime in the 1990s and 2000s, and while there are reports that crime has diminished considerably in the period from 2003 to 2009, the wave has threatened to sink the state's capacity to protect its citizens and diminish its international reputation. (One study found that 60% of emigrants cited violent crime as a reason for leaving South Africa. North African states vying against South Africa to hold the soccer World Cup finals repeatedly stressed its insecurity.)

Car theft has long been one of the most common crimes in South Africa, and Johannesburg is notorious as one of the world's top cities for carjacking. Located in Gauteng province, Johannesburg's vehicles all bear license plates with the initials GP. Local cynics persist in saying it means "Gangster Paradise." As police worked to reduce one type of crime, however, criminals adapted and upgraded. Rather than individuals in cars, thieves began to target armored vehicles moving large cash shipments. In a typical attack, four cars would surround and stop the vehicle; some 20 hijackers would leap out with assault rifles, bringing traffic to a halt, while their associates ripped open the vehicle's roof. In the 2002–2003 reporting period, there were 374 such attacks. ATMs are another target of criminal violence. The efforts to battle crime in Johannesburg resulted in the placement of closed-circuit television cameras at nearly all traffic intersections in the huge metropolis. This reduced police response time and is reported to have reduced violent crime rates in the city.

South Africa's murder rate is one of the highest in the world. South Africans, black and white, rich and poor have been victims of crime, a fact made evident to South Africans when the former first lady Marike de Klerk was found murdered in her Cape Town apartment in December 2001. While murder rates seem to have declined, South Africa remains one of the few countries in which one is more likely to be murdered than die in an automobile accident. One particular murder that drew international attention was that of Reeva Steenkamp on February 14, 2013. Steenkamp was the girlfriend of Oscar Pistorius, an Olympic athlete known as the "Blade Runner" for his high-tech prosthetic legs known as blades. Pistorius acknowledged that he shot his girlfriend in his home but claimed that he mistook her for an intruder.

South Africa

Rape

Statistics have suggested that a woman born in South Africa has a greater chance of being raped than learning how to read. One in four girls faces the prospect of being raped before the age of 16. Some experts estimate that at least 60% of all rapes go unreported, and it is a crime where the police have made no progress.

Charlene Smith, an ANC activist and rape victim herself, highlighted cultural values that she argued created a culture of rape in South Africa, and surveys of public attitudes supported her analysis. In Johannesburg, which has the highest incidence of rape in South Africa, a survey conducted among 1,500 school children in Soweto township found that a quarter of all boys interviewed said that "jackrolling"—a South African term for recreational gang rape—was fun. Weaknesses in the criminal justice system contribute to a culture of impunity. Only about 7% of reported rapes result in convictions, leaving most rapists with little fear of punishment.

The rape trial of former deputy president Jacob Zuma brought the rape problem in South Africa under the klieg lights of publicity. Zuma allegedly raped a family friend—an HIV-positive woman in her 30s—at his Johannesburg home in November 2005. In responding to the allegations, Zuma claimed he had consensual sex, while the woman, a 31-year-old AIDS activist, claimed she had been violated by a father figure, a man she had known since she was five years old. Despite one of the world's most progressive constitutions that guarantees gender equality, operative law remains anachronistically biased against women. The country's Sexual Offenses Act, passed during the apartheid era, narrowly defines the crime and court procedure often requires the woman prove that she did not provoke the rape. In his defense Zuma was thus allowed to claim the woman wore a short skirt and sat "inappropriately," indicating she wanted to have sex with him. Following the norms of his traditional Zulu culture, he argued, to leave a woman in a state of arousal untouched would have been unacceptable and vilified.

Supporters of both accuser and defendant organized street demonstrations. Those supporting Zuma showed his political base in KwaZulu-Natal Province and among the most leftwing elements of the ANC tripartite alliance. Women's groups focused on the social and legal problems faced by the survivors of sexual violence. One of them, People Opposing Woman Abuse (Powa), estimated that one woman is raped in South Africa every 26 seconds, but only one in nine incidents is ever reported. Additionally, victims suffer further in a culture of silence and denial that surrounds the crime.

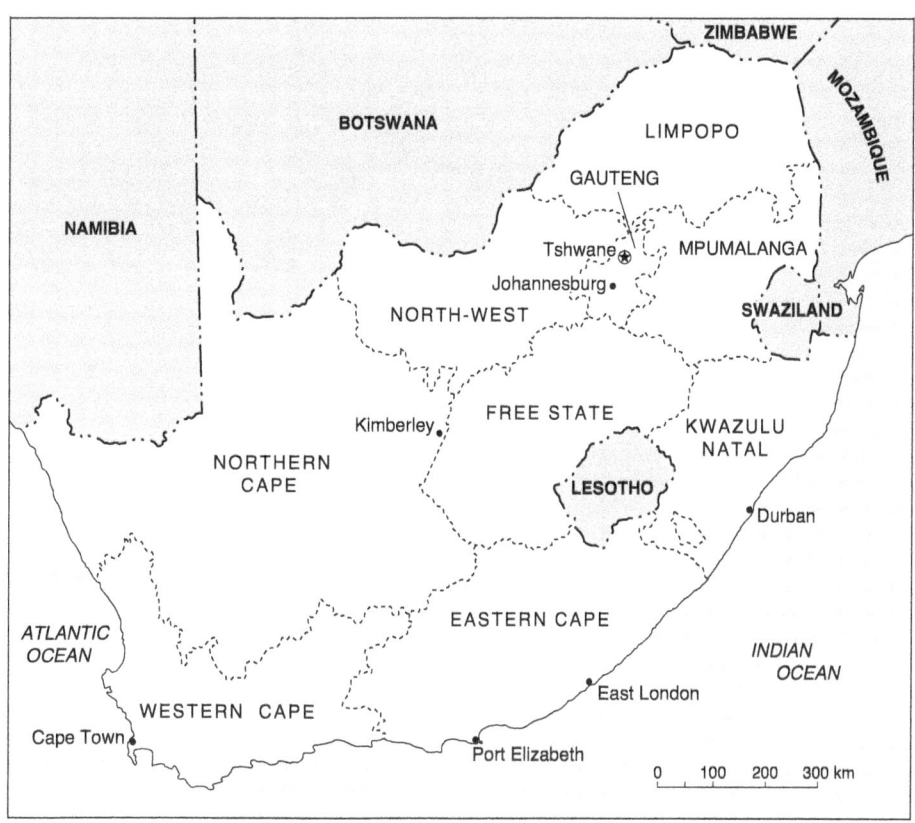

Provinces of South Africa

The case generated a tsunami of commentary. The president of the National Union Mineworkers seemed to express the values of an unreconstructed patriarchal culture when he justified Zuma's adultery. "We are not Christians," he told the union's national congress. "We don't listen to the Ten Commandments and we don't have to listen when Christians tell us adultery is wrong." (Zuma is a polygamist with three wives and at least 18 children.) Archbishop Desmond Tutu, South Africa's Nobel Prize–winning Christian cleric, thought the trial was "one of the worse moments" in the life of the country's democracy. "I've been saddened," he said, "by the reinforcement of the stereotype that when a woman accuses a man of rape, she is made out to be the guilty one, and her sexual history is brought up—whether true or not." That made it difficult for a woman to bring charges, he noted, because "she'll nearly always end up being the accused." Tutu reserved some of his sharpest words for the behavior of Zuma's supporters, who insulted the accuser and, shouting "burn the bitch," burnt her photograph outside the court. It was, he said, "abominable," and a sad day for the country's nascent democracy "when we can use our freedoms in such a way that it stomps all over the dignity of the accused." In early May 2006, Judge Willem van der Merwe ended the sordid trial by declaring the state had not proved the accused's guilt "beyond doubt." The accuser lived under heavy police protection during the trial due to threats against her life. She now lives anonymously in exile in a non-African country.

Education

Among the most important issues facing the ANC governments are the distribution of social services, particularly education. The crisis in education has been ongoing, a consequence of apartheid policies on curriculum and funding. Mbeki spoke often and with conviction of an African Renaissance, saying the new African century must produce doctors, engineers, and scientists. Yet the education system has been a shambles. Its desperate state is evident in the results of the 2000 matriculation exams—only 48.9% passed. The results were a shock and a call to arms.

Since then, the government has poured money into schooling and produced improved results. Matriculation (final school year) exams were successfully passed by 61.7% of those taking them in 2001 and 68.9% in 2002. The 2005 pass rate dropped slightly, to 68.3%, suggesting progress had reached a plateau. Indeed, in 2006 the pass

South Africa

Julius Malema, Leader of the Economic Freedom Fighters

rate fell even more, to 66.5%. Mitigating the seeming success of improved matric scores was the fact that the number of those passing the exam represented only 32% of those who entered the secondary school system two years before. South Africa's dropout rate is huge, sometimes reaching more than 50%.

The legacy of apartheid's inequalities and disparities is still apparent. A pattern of regional inequality in results reflects long-term inequality of resource distribution. The best-endowed provinces (Northern Cape, Western Cape, and Gauteng) performed best. The lowest pass rates occurred in the poor provinces with huge black and rural majorities. In 2006, the pass rate in Limpopo province, for example, dropped from 64.9% in 2005 to 55.7%, which prompted angry parents in the province to burn ANC T-shirts emblazoned with President Mbeki's face. Among the complaints: teachers working as municipal councilors, thus failing to fulfill their teaching responsibilities.

The causes of the crisis in education are manifold, though an obvious problem is the unequal disbursement of the basic material provisions, classrooms, and books, among schools across different areas of South Africa. KwaZulu-Natal, for example, faced a shortage of 14,000 classrooms in 2003, which would take nine years to eliminate. Beyond the physical, however, the whole delivery system—an educational bureaucracy, too many of whom are unqualified, unprepared and unmotivated—remains a challenge. A culture of learning has yet to be cultivated, and individual classrooms remain sites of threat and intimidation against both staff and students. Those who can afford it send their children to private schools.

Eastern Cape province demonstrates the deplorable conditions in which education must function in South Africa's poorest areas. In 2000, 17% of the schools had no toilets, 45% had no electricity, and 28% no water. In 2003, the provincial legislature's standing committee on education still complained about the shortage of classrooms, dilapidated mud structures, absence of toilets, electricity, telephones and water. Worse, it found a high degree of poor discipline among both teachers and students after visiting 157 provincial schools. "Drunkenness, absenteeism, truancy and use of drugs within the school premises could be cited as most striking examples," it said.

In his 2004 state-of-the-nation speech, President Mbeki promised that no children would learn outdoors by the next time he described the state of the nation. In early 2005, however, Minister of Education Naledi Pandor openly wondered in a parliamentary briefing why children continued to learn under trees when the provinces had the money to build classrooms. For the government the issue is crucial: education remains at the heart of its plans for social transformation. Parliament had apportioned more than twenty percent of the country's budget toward education, and the absence of constructed classrooms too openly displayed the government's inability to deliver services.

Despite ramped up construction and spending in the mid-2000s, the short-fall remained abysmal. In early May 2006, nearly 900 students were attending high school in Orlando, a suburb of Soweto Township, but there was only one qualified teacher to teach three basic science subjects; the library had no up-to-date books and the computer lab had no computers. According to the educational research unit at Witwatersrand University at about the same time, 43% of all South African schools had no electricity; 27% had no running water, and a staggering 80% had no library.

Of the many proposals for educational reform, perhaps the most controversial issue has been the question of language. The 2005 education reform plan made the teaching of English and Afrikaans optional, instead offering learners the choice of studying any two of the country's 11 official languages. According to official statistics, Zulu is the mother tongue of 23.8% of the population, followed by Xhosa, the mother tongue of 17.6%. Only about 8% of South Africans speak English as their first language. The proposal accords with the government's desire to develop the other nine official languages into media of instruction. Ultimately, the plan is to have universities teach in indigenous languages.

State Capture:

This is a type of systemic political corruption in which private interests significantly influence a state's decision-making processes to their own advantage. If there is any situation that has the potential to threaten South Africa's politics, government, and society it is state capture. In the middle of the growing concern of state capture in South Africa, is the Gupta Family who migrated from India in 1993 during the waning days of the apartheid regime in the country. The Gupta family, it is claimed have been so entrenched in the family of President Zuma to an extent that they have influence on the "hiring and firing" of individuals in the South Africa Cabinet. The President's son, Duduzane Zuma, was also a member of the Board of Directors of one of the Gupta's businesses. The Deputy President, Mr. Cyril Ramaphosa once called for an independent probe into claims of state capture and noted that it cannot be ignored since it has become an entrenched issue. Julius Malema, a former president of ANC's Youth League, and now the leader of the Economic Freedom Fighters also called for a criminal case into the Gupta family's business operations in South Africa. Although the Guptas left South Africa in April 2016, corruption seems to be problematic for the South Africa government despite its robust anti-corruption laws. Transparency International Corruption Index shows South Africa has not improved on reining in corruption. With

South Africa

the institutional, financial, and human resources that could be used to deal with the issue of corruption in South Africa, it is troubling to see that the country has not made progress in combating corruption.

Nelson Mandela's Death and Legacy

After battling health-related issues for years, Nelson Mandela passed away on December 5, 2013, at the age of 95 in his home in Houghton, Johannesburg. President Jacob Zuma announced the death publicly, and he declared that a national mourning period for 10 days, with all of South Africa's flags flying at half-mast. The news shook South Africa to its core, and large numbers of South Africans (both whites and blacks) broke down and wept in the streets upon hearing the news. Throughout the country, there were several impromptu memorial services to Mandela, but the official memorial service took place on December 10, 2013, at First National Bank stadium in Johannesburg. The program included tributes from several heads of state including President Barack Obama of the United States. (It should be acknowledged that Mandela had previously been considered a "terrorist" by the US government for many years, due to his role in MK, the armed wing of the ANC when it opposed the apartheid state.) Services also took place across the globe in cities such as Paris, New York City and Los Angeles. Mandela's state funeral was held on December 15 in his ancestral hometown of Qunu, Eastern Cape Province. Mandela will be remembered for many things, but his message of forgiveness and reconciliation resonates the most. As President Obama put it: "Mandela achieved more than could be expected of any man. We have lost one of the most influential, courageous, and profoundly good human beings that any of us will share time on this Earth. He no longer belongs to us—he belongs to the ages."

Elected president in 2018, Matamela Cyril Ramaphosa of the ANC has made support for the Palestinian cause in Gaza a centerpiece of the country's foreign policy by raising the charge of genocide against the state of Israel in the International Court of Justice (ICJ), which the main South African opposition party, Democratic Alliance, has opposed claiming neutrality on the issue. With general elections scheduled for May 29, 2024, the DA has focused more on domestic issues particularly the high murder rate of 80 people killed per day in the country, one of the highest in the world.

In the 2024 elections, the ruling African National Congress lost its parliamentary majority that it had held since 1994. The centrist Democratic Alliance (DA) came in second and the left-wing populist party, founded six months prior to the election and led by former president Jacob Zuma, finished in third place. In June 2024, the ANC, the DA, the Inkatha Freedom Party (IFP) and the Patriotic Alliance (PA), agreed to form a national unity government with Cyril Ramaphosa re-elected as president. In April 2025, President Ramaphosa ordered an inquiry to establish whether previous governments led by his party intentionally blocked investigations and prosecutions of apartheid-era cries, taking a step that survivors and families of those who were killed had demanded for decades. The landmark move addresses allegations of "improper influence in delaying or hindering" investigations leveled against post-apartheid governments led by the ANC after 25 survivors and relatives of victims of apartheid-era crimes launched a court case against his government in January, seeking damages. They alleged that successive South African governments since the late 1990s had failed to properly investigate unresolved killings, disappearances and other crimes during the time of forced racial segregation despite recommendations made by the post-apartheid Truth and Reconciliation Commission set up in 1996 by then-President Nelson Mandela under the chairmanship of fellow Nobel Peace Prize winner Desmond Tutu. One of the most prominent unresolved cases is that of the Cradock Four, a group of Black anti-apartheid activists who were abducted and murdered by security forces in 1985. Their bodies were burned and security officers were suspected of torturing them, but no one has been prosecuted for the killings and the circumstances of the deaths have never been fully revealed. These are among the thousands of crimes during apartheid where victims and families still haven't seen justice. Of equal concern is potential effects on HIV/AIDS prevention resulting from cutbacks to international programs proposed by United States President Donald Trump. Because the U.S. was responsible for funding nearly a fourth of what South Africa spends to combat HIV, some organizations have been forced to shut down certain programs while others have stopped operating entirely.

FUTURE CONSIDERATIONS

South Africa remains a country of contrasts. Rich in natural wealth, cosmopolitan and diverse, and culturally vibrant, it is also a country of horrific inequality. Violent crime continues (though there are indications it is on the decline), and there is continued evidence that highly educated people (blacks and whites) have left the country in large numbers. Economic and political tensions are on the rise after the Marikana mine incident in 2012.

The ANC remains South Africa's dominant political party, and the big political question is whether a viable opposition can emerge to challenge the dominance of the ANC. There are several possibilities, though none is a sure bet. First, there is the potential for a split within the party itself. Youth leader Julius Malema famously split with Zuma in recent years (while ending up accused of graft, fraud, and corruption). There is also the succession question as the ANC looks beyond Zuma (who was reelected party president in late 2012). It appears that Cyril Ramaphosa, a man who was a crucial negotiator in the transition from apartheid and was considered a possible successor to Mandela in the 1990s before he spent two decades becoming one of South Africa's most successful businessmen, is consolidating power as deputy leader of the party. If indeed Ramaphosa unites the ANC behind him, it will continue to be a daunting competitor for even the best-organized opposition.

That said, South Africa's opposition is showing some signs of strength, though it remains greatly outnumbered at present. The Democratic Alliance is now led by the dynamic Helen Zille, Premier of Western Cape province, and by the young Lindiwe Mazikubo as the party's leading face in parliament. The DA improved its showing in the 2011 elections at the municipal level, noting that it picked up support from blacks frustrated with the ANC, while consolidating its position as the single viable opposition party on the national level. It has long been expected that a plausible opposition will emerge from a splinter group within the ANC, but the DA is slowly improving the odds that it will be a force to be reckoned with going forward. The Congress of the People (COPE) continues to have a presence, and represents a possible pole of attraction for those former ANC members disaffected with the governing party. Finally, one of South Africa's heroes of the apartheid struggle, Dr. Mamphela Raphele, has declared with ample advance notice that she will start a new party known as Agang to contest the 2014 elections. Ramphele—an icon in her own right as well as the onetime partner of the legendary Steve Biko—has received public statements of support from another of South Africa's greatest figures: Archbishop Desmond Tutu.

Nelson Mandela's death will mark a turning point in looking ahead on South Africa's future. Mandela passed away during a tumultuous time in South Africa, given rising protests from miners and the impoverished masses, and increasingly

South Africa

public disillusionment with the ANC. Retired archbishop Desmond Tutu stated that he was "happy Nelson Mandela is dead—so he does not have to see what South Africa's current leaders are doing to the country." Recent allegations are that President Zuma spent huge sums of government money to upgrade his home as well as the homes of his family and village. This looks more like the corrupt rent-seeking of other African leaders from previous decades than the optimistic image of a forward-looking, modernized "rainbow nation" that Mandela cherished.

The future of South Africa will come down to how the ANC government handles several issues going forward: the HIV/AIDS epidemic, public service provision, political unrest, and the securing of an industrial and mining base that generates income and wealth for more than just a small fraction of the population. Failure in any one of these areas could turn Africa's greatest triumph of the 1990s into its greatest tragedy in the 21st century; conversely, stopping the epidemics and bringing a broader base of wealth and income opportunities could enable South Africa to remain the motor for much of the continent's development.

The Kingdom of Swaziland

King Mswati III

BASIC FACTS

Area: 17,364 sq. km. = 6,705 sq. mi. (slightly smaller than New Jersey)
Population: 1,130,043 (June 2023 est.)
Capital Cities: Mbabane (administrative); Lobamba (legislative).
Government Type: Monarchy
Neighboring Countries: Mozambique (northeast); South Africa (north, west, south).
Official Languages: siSwati, English
Other Principal Languages: Zulu, Afrikaans
Ethnic Groups: Swazi, a small number of other Bantu groups; European
Principal Religions: Zionist (mix of Christianity and indigenous practices) 40%, Roman Catholic 20%, Muslim 10%, Other 30%
Former Colonial Status: Under South African protection (1894–1906); British Protectorate (1906–1968)
Independence Date: September 6, 1968
GDP Per Capita (IMF 2023 est.): $4,146 (nominal), $11,492 (PPP)
Gini index: 54.6 (World Bank 2016)
Currency: Lilangeni (at par with the South African rand), $US 1 = 18.31 emalangeni (June 2023)
Inflation Rate: 4.8% (2022 est.)
Chief Commercial Products: Sugar, asbestos, wood and forest products, citrus, cotton, iron ore, coal, livestock, textiles
Foreign Direct Investments (FDI) net inflows: 26,584,894
Literacy Rate: 88.4% (CIA 2018)
Life Expectancy: 60.22 years (CIA 2023 est.)
Head of State: King Mswati III (since April 25, 1986)
Head of Government: Prime Minister Ambrose Manduulo Dlamini (since October 27, 2018)

LAND AND PEOPLE

High plateaus and forested mountains are found in western Swaziland, gradually descending from a maximum of 4,500 feet to a central region with an average altitude of 2,800 feet. These highlands give way to lowlands in the east, and the Lubombo Mountains rise at the easternmost border. The temperate climate is warm enough to permit large quantities of sugar cane to grow, but at the same time it is ideally suited for forest growth of excellent hardwoods.

Despite its small size, the country has an urban-rural divide that maps onto the tension between tradition and modernity. About 80% of Swazis live as peasant farmers on Swazi national land, or "king's land," distributed through local chiefs. Rural Swazis tend to be conservative and traditionalist, crediting past kings with resistance to foreigners and the formation of the Swazi nation. Urban dwellers are likelier to speak of political reforms, human rights, and democracy. The king, by custom the father of all his subjects and the embodiment of the nation, has stated that he would never recognize "anyone who comes to me saying he represents other Swazis."

HISTORY TO PRESENT DAY

For early history, see *Historical Background* and *The Colonial Period: The British*.

King Sobhuza ruled over present-day Swaziland from 1921 (under the British protectorate) up to and after the British granted independence on September 6, 1968, at formal ceremonies in Mbabane. Many foreign representatives were present at the transfer of power, along with King Sobhuza and his 112 wives. The first king reigned until his death in 1982.

King Sobhuza's Imbokodvo National Movement (INM) initially held all 24 seats of the National Assembly after the 1967 elections. Elections in 1972 saw Dr. Ambrose Zwane's Ngwane National Liberatory Congress (NNLC) Party claim three seats, leaving the INM with 21 of 24.

Within weeks after the 1972 election the king abolished the constitution and consolidated the power of the throne in Africa's last absolute monarchy. The king dismissed the Assembly, and announced he would appoint cabinet ministers and rule by decree. Political parties were banned in 1973. King Sobhuza later established a new bicameral parliament in 1979, consisting of a 50-member lower house and a 20-member upper house, but retained the right to dissolve parliament and choose 10 members of each house.

King Sobhuza died in August 1982, setting off a power struggle among the wives and 70 sons of the dead monarch. The struggles centered on Queen Regent Dzeliwe and Prince Sozisa Dlamini, the "Authorized Person" appointed by the deceased king to manage succession. The prince successfully deposed the queen regent, replacing her with Queen Ntombi, who in turn selected her son Makhosetive Dlamini to become crown prince, and thus the next king upon reaching the age of majority. The crown prince, the second-youngest son (and 67th child) of the late king, studied in Britain until 1986, when he reached the age of 18. He returned for his coronation on April 25, 1986, where he took the name Mswati III. He quickly moved to assert his power, reshuffling the cabinet, dismissing the *Liqoqo* (council of state), and replacing the prime minister.

Legislative elections have been held every five years since 1978, but the results have not been democratic. As a result of the ban on political parties, parliamentary candidates emerged through the *Tinkundla* system. Tinkundlas, or traditional assemblies, nominate candidates—generally conservative and loyal to the king—in all the chiefdoms of Swaziland. These hopefuls are pared down in primary elections, with the remaining candidates vying in secondaries for the 55 elected seats in the House of Assembly. The king appoints the remaining 10 Assembly members and chooses his cabinet (including a Prime Minister) from the Assembly. Current Prime Minister Sibusiso Dlamini, had held the post since 2008, and also did so from 1996 to 2003. Swaziland's senate has 30 members, none of whom is directly elected. Twenty members are now royal appointees and the remaining ten are selected by the Assembly.

The Swaziland Federation of Trade Unions (SFTU) became the most vocal opponents of Swaziland's absolute monarchy in the 1990s, despite being subjected to arrests and intimidation. The SFTU pressured authorities to create a commission

Swaziland

on a new constitution in 1994, after a series of strikes and firebombs of unknown origin, but royalists and traditionalists dominated the committee, but the king postponed indefinitely the consideration of the commission's findings.

The constitutional reform process dragged for several years before a traditional "Peoples Parliament" was summoned in September 2004 at the royal cattle kraal to discuss the constitutional drafts, where the king announced that parliament must review and pass a new law by mid-November. The calendar was strictly followed, but Mswati objected to certain provisions regarding the taxation of his family and the place of Christianity as an official religion. He finally signed the 164-page document in July 2005 after the changes he sought had been made (and a decade after the commission's creation). The new constitution affirmed the king's absolute authority over the legislature, security forces, and other institutions of government. The ban on political parties, in force for over 30 years, was retained. In one notable concession to democratic participation, the constitution allowed for the popular recall of members of parliament. It also made a break from tradition by declaring "Women have the right to equal treatment with men, including equal opportunities in political, economic and social activities."

Swazi absolutism underwent crises in the justice system beginning in November 2002, after a ruling from the high court (The Court of Appeal) that denied the king's power to issue laws by decree. The prime minister said the government would ignore the ruling. A second decision by the Court was also rejected, provoking a rule-of-law crisis: all six South African judges (on loan to Swaziland) on the Court of Appeal resigned in protest. The king later found himself the object of legal action again when the mother of a teenager he had chosen to be his tenth wife sued for the return of her daughter. The attorney general went to the judge hearing the case and threatened to have him fired if he did not drop the case. The judge refused, but soon resigned, presumably under pressure.

Between 2004 and 2007, Mswati made a habit of extravagant personal expenditures even as the country suffered drought and starvation. The king asked parliament for money to build palaces for his 11 wives in January 2004, at a cost of $15 million, almost as much as the country's health budget. (Two more wives have since been added to the royal family.) In April of that year, the king celebrated his 36th birthday with a party for over 10,000 guests gathered in the national football stadium and a purchase of ten new BMWs. In December, the king purchased a luxury limousine worth a half-million dollars; pictures of the vehicle were prohibited by royal decree. Ultimately, even Swaziland's parliament, filled with royal relatives, refused to approve purchase of a $48 million luxury plane for the king. One MP (Marwick Khumalo, the king's cousin) noted the kingdom could ill-afford such extravagance while 140,000 of the king's one million subjects were starving. Mswati's birthday expenses in 2007 were well over two million dollars while Swazi farmers were ruined by poor rains at the beginning of the year, followed by freak hailstorms, which destroyed the year's maize crop. This left nearly 300,000 Swazis (almost one-third of the population) living on food rations from international donors.

Opposition movements coalesced in 2008. The SFTU and other labor unions joined student organizations and other groups joined to form the Swaziland United Democratic Front (SUDF) in 2008. They have since called for a number of protests and rallies. While the regime broke up assemblies in September 2010 and April 2011 through arrests and detentions, the organization has persisted in rallying more Swazis to its cause. Members of the banned Peoples United Democratic Movement (PUDEMO) similarly stood up to the monarchy. Its members refused to participate in the 2008 legislative elections to protest the ban on party-affiliated candidates. The conflict between government and PUDEMO took on a more sinister tone in 2008 as a bomb attack occurred near a royal palace in September, the same month in which elections were held. (The King again appointed Sibususo Dlamini to the post of Prime Minister at this time, to which the SFTU and PUDEMO objected.) The authorities detained and held PUDEMO leader Mario Masuku for questioning regarding the incident. Masuku was released in September 2009 but continues to be a focus of police action, as in June 2010 when his house was searched for bomb making materials.

The years 2011 and 2012 saw volatility in the economy. In 2011, the economy reached a crisis point and the IMF declared Swaziland's budget crisis "critical." The government had run out of money and civil servants were given a 10% pay cut, which led to protests. For lack of funds, schools began shutting down and hospitals ran short of necessary medicines. Meanwhile, the budget deficit rose to double figures. The country was in turmoil and it was unclear if the King and his government would collapse. However, by June 2012, the *Economist* reported that Swaziland was expecting a budget surplus, that protests had died down, and that the government was almost back to "normal" provisions of services. Part of this change is credited to volatile receipts from a regional customs union, which collapsed in 2011 and rebounded in 2012; customs revenue is expected to fall again over time as trade between southern African countries gets freer.

In this turbulent economic time for Swaziland, Mswati continues his lavish personal spending (as well as the construction of a new international airport) but has not undertaken any of the reforms required for Swaziland to be eligible for international aid. South Africa offered Swaziland a 2.4-billion-rand loan in 2011 but has since withdrawn the offer because of concerns about management and the direction of the country. The African Development Bank has also frozen a promised loan to Swaziland of $100 million a year because of similar concerns.

Meanwhile, the political system remains oriented around the king and opposition is co-opted or marginalized. The main trade union (SFTU) disbanded and merged with others to form the Trade Union Congress of Swaziland (TUCOSWA) in 2012, but the government deregistered the TUCOSWA the following year. This has left the country without a legal trade union federation; trade unions and their federations have frequently been important advocates for political change in other African countries, so this action removed a potential basis for opposition. Electoral politics too is limited. Parliamentary elections in 2013 were held on a "no-party" basis, which complicated any cohesion of the opposition, and the king (and subordinate traditional chiefs) still retained the power to approve candidates. The elected prime minister was again Sibusiso Dlamini, who is a staunch ally of Mswati. Some

An Outdoor Laundry   Photo by Rita Arendt

Swaziland

opposition figures have been elected in the two largest cities (Manzini and Mbabane), most notably Jan Sithole of the Swaziland Democratic Party (SWADEPA), who was a former trade union leader. The question remains whether those in parliament constitute an opposition or have been effectively co-opted to support the monarchy. While there was some turnover among MPs, the king retains clear support in a mostly loyalist parliament.

CONTEMPORARY THEMES

Swaziland has the dubious distinction of what is likely the world's highest adult HIV/AIDS prevalence rate. There are some signs the epidemic may be leveling off, but this is likely due to the sheer number of those who have died from HIV/AIDS and thus are no longer counted in national health statistics. HIV prevalence was estimated at about 25% of the country's adult population in 2009. Campaigns to change male sexual behavior seem to have had some impact on behavior (with more men using condoms), but the consequences of the disease are devastating. By one estimate, over 60% of deaths in the country around 2002 resulted from HIV/AIDS. The number of AIDS orphans in the country may approach 100,000, or 10% of the Swazi population. Life expectancy reached a peak of 61 years in the early 1990s, then plummeted to just under 45 years by 2005; even if statistics have improved a bit since (49 is the life expectancy on 2012), this still means a year of life expectancy was lost with each passing year. King Mswati III has declared HIV/AIDS a "national disaster," but the government has not led effectively. One advisor described HIV/AIDS sufferers as "bad potatoes" and said they must be removed from society lest "all will go rotten." His solution was an isolation camp for victims of the disease.

Moving sugar cane from field to factory
©Mujahid Safodien/IRIN

Swaziland's economy has been anemic for years, with a GDP growth rate hovering around 2% each year since 2000. About 70% of the population lives on two dollars a day or less. The government has cast about for new growth industries with limited success, once attempting an ambitious program to develop transportation and tourism, featuring a new international airport, international conference center and luxury hotels, new highways, an industrial park and an amusement park.

A major contributing factor to the country's economic malaise is a continuing drop in agricultural productivity, compounded by drought. Seventy percent of Swazis earn their living from agriculture, but the sector weakened in the years after 1999. One relative bright spot until recently was Swaziland's principal export, sugar. The country is one of the world's lowest cost producers, and the sugar industry has been its biggest employer, accounting for nearly 20% of the labor force, and earns over 10% of the country's foreign exchange. However, prevailing weather conditions reduced production in drought years. The industry was also hurt by an EU decision to slash dramatically the above-market subsidy price it paid for Swazi sugar beginning in 2007. Earnings plummeted, even as production increased modestly in 2010 and 2011.

The government has also contemplated resuscitation of local cotton production as a cash crop, which had declined from the 1990s into the mid-2000s, and conversion of cotton into textiles. Here again, early hopes fell flat. Taiwanese interests built factories to take advantage of special benefits for Swazi manufactures offered by AGOA (America's African Growth and Opportunities Act). This briefly added 28,000 new jobs, but eliminations of quota restrictions on clothing worldwide led manufacturers to move operations to China and India. Over half the country's 31 textile companies shut their doors by the end of 2005.

One clear growth industry has been marijuana, or "dagga" as it is known locally, which grows well in Swaziland's mountainous northern region. "Swazi Gold" is internationally known for its potency and has been a major money earner for Swazi farmers: when a ten-kilogram bag of maize sold for $11, a ten-kilogram bag of dagga sold for $405. International crime syndicates provide what might be called "agricultural extension services" to fund and organize large-scale production.

The Swazi economy is highly dependent on neighboring South Africa, which surrounds the country on three sides. The currency is pegged to the South African rand; all its oil is imported from South Africa, as is nearly all electricity and 85% of its consumer goods. Trade is well over 100% of GDP, as is the case in many small countries.

Dependency on the South African economy has also hurt government revenues. An incredible 75% of government revenue in 2009 came from customs receipts from the Southern African Customs Union (SACU), with the remainder coming from income tax, sales tax, and a few other tolls and duties. Yet SACU revenues have declined precipitously (then vacillated dramatically in 2011 and 2012) as South Africa has pushed for freer trade among the countries of the region. The result has been escalating government borrowing, even as the government has declared it may need to fire and cut the pay of civil servants; the pinch has meant worsening relations with both international creditors such as the International Monetary Fund and with Swazis domestically who are bracing for dramatic budget cuts. The response for the longer term has been the creation of a central tax-collection agency in 2010 (the Swaziland Revenue Authority), which is paving the way for the introduction of a value-added tax.

Renamed Eswatini in April 2018, meaning "land of the Swazis" in the indigenous language, the country remains the last absolute monarchy in Africa with political parties officially banned and members of the national parliament playing only an advisory role to the king. Major domestic issues include protecting wildlife and plant life biodiversity in the country's indigenous forests from illegal poachers.

In the heart of the Jilobi Forest, a biodiversity hotspot in Eswatini's eastern region of Lubombo, three chiefdoms inhabiting the territory had longstanding disputes, and tensions used to run high. But recently, an urge to preserve their shared land has caused them to retire their rivalry. "There were disputes over boundary lines and resources management that strained relations and hindered peaceful coexistence," said Muzi Maziya, from the Lukhetseni constituency, one of the chiefdoms in the remote area of the country. "Most of the disputes resulted in illegal activities like wood-cutting and livestock theft by outsiders and people from the communities who took advantage of the polarization." The rivalries, which date back to the 1980s among the chiefdoms of Maphungwane, Tikhuba, and Lukhetseni, posed a major threat to the diversity of the Jilobi Forest because members of one community would steal cattle that belonged to a neighboring chiefdom in a bid to discourage farmers from grazing on land under dispute. This resulted in the poaching of wild animals, such as warthogs and Samango monkeys, and illegal harvesting of plants for medicines and food. The forest holds cultural significance for the

Swaziland

Maziya clan of Maphungwane and for the Dlaminis of Lukhetseni, with a common belief that the souls of their ancestors roam the forests. Hence, they believe the land should be preserved and never disturbed. But unsustainable land practices, medicinal plant harvesting without consent, and poaching have threatened this natural asset. People regularly employ sustainable farming practices that include protecting the area from pests and diseases and avoiding protected areas that are home to endangered species (like the endemic cycad and Samango monkey and the ironwood tree used for house construction and furniture making). Recent surveys show the rich biodiversity and unique butterflies found in the Jilobi Forest that are at stake from the rapid harvesting of the forest.

FUTURE CONSIDERATIONS

Swaziland's future looks worse than many of its neighbors. At a time when many African economies are surging after the global financial crisis, Swaziland has stagnated. GDP growth has been minimal, and as successive industries have come under economic pressure from international competition, the prospects are weak for more Swazis to move out of poverty.

Politically, the situation seems little better. Even for a deeply traditional society, the Swazi absolute monarchy seems antiquated with its ostentatious and polygamous monarch. A former advisor to the King has described him as "unbalanced," "not intellectually well-developed," and influenced by witchcraft. King Mswati has a royalist following (including most of the parliament) but is deeply unpopular with the other main political organizations in the country, such as the banned party PUDEMO and the now unofficial trade union (TUCOSWA). Declining economic conditions are likely only to exacerbate further the political tensions in the country. In the end, the future outlook for Swaziland is a rather depressing status quo.

The Republic of Zambia

Victoria Falls Photo by Joe Joyner

BASIC FACTS

Area: 752,618 sq. km. (slightly larger than Texas)
Population: 20,216,029 (June 2023 est.)
Capital City: Lusaka
Government Type: Presidential Republic
Neighboring Countries: Angola (west); Congo-Kinshasa (northwest); Tanzania (northeast); Malawi (east); Mozambique (southeast); Zimbabwe, Botswana, and Namibia (south)
Official Language: English
Other Principal Languages: Over 30, including Bemba, Chichewa, Lamba, Lozi, Luvale, Nsenga, and Tonga.
Ethnic Groups: African 99%, European 1%
Principal Religions: Christian 50%–75%, Muslim and Hindu 24%–49%, indigenous beliefs 1%
Former Colonial Status: British South Africa Company administration (1895–1923); British Colony (1924–1964)
Independence Date: October 24, 1964
GDP per capita (IMF 2023 est.): $1,423 (nominal), $4,041 (PPP)
Gini Index: 57 (World Bank 2015)
Currency: Zambian kwacha, 1 USD = 18.08 kwacha (May 2023)
Inflation Rate: 15.7% (2022 est.)
Chief Commercial Products: Copper, cobalt, zinc, lead, and tobacco
Foreign Direct Investments (FDI) net inflows: 1,507,800,000
Literacy Rate: 86.7% (CIA 2018)
Life Expectancy: 66.6 years (CIA 2023 est.)
Head of State: President Hakainde Hichilema (since August 24, 2021)
Head of Government: President Hakainde Hichilema (since August 24, 2021)

LAND AND PEOPLE

The Republic of Zambia is located in south-central Africa, stretching 750 miles west from the mountains of the great Western Rift. This is a high plateau country with an average elevation of 3,500 feet above sea level, which renders its equatorial climate more temperate. Topical high heat and humidity are found mainly in low river valleys.

The rolling countryside alternates between the plains grasslands and forests of widely spaced trees. Abundant wildlife is supported by the vegetation, which grows rapidly during the rainy season. The country is drained by two major river systems: the tributaries flowing north to the Congo River, and the Zambezi River, which flows southeast through Mozambique to the Indian Ocean. One of the incomparable sights in the world is found at Victoria Falls, near Livingstone in the south. Swampy Lake Banguelu spreads across in the north-central part of the country, while the deep blue waters of Lake Mweru and Lake Tanganyika are found in the North.

Zambians in rural areas tend to be conservative and closely knit within their communities. At the same time, Zambia is one of sub-Saharan Africa's most urbanized countries. Nearly one-half the population is concentrated in a few urban zones (especially in the so-called Copperbelt), and rural areas are underpopulated. While agriculture supports half the population, with corn being the principal food crop and money earner, it is copper that dominates the Zambian economy.

Most Zambians are Christian, particularly in the more densely populated south and west, but many in rural areas retain traditional beliefs. While the country has never witnessed a major civil war, racial, religious and tribal frictions have been frequent since independence.

HISTORY TO PRESENT DAY

For early history, see *Historical Background* and *The Colonial Period: The British.*

Independence and Kenneth Kaunda (1964–1991)

Northern Rhodesia became fully independent from Great Britain in 1964, taking the name Zambia from the Zambezi River. A republican form of government was established with a single legislative house and a directly elected president. The legislature was initially composed of 75 members, but later increased in size and until 1969, ten seats were reserved for the white minority. Initially there were two major parties—the United National Independence Party (UNIP) led by Kenneth Kaunda, and the African National Congress (ANC) led by Harry Nkumbula (who died in 1984 in neighboring Zimbabwe).

Kenneth Kaunda was elected first president in 1964, and after winning a large majority in 1968, he embarked on moves to consolidate power. Kaunda abolished the opposition ANC in the name of "national unity," and crafted his own philosophy of "humanistic socialism." He led a massive nationalization of major enterprises beginning in late 1970 and created state-owned businesses and state-run marketing facilities. Because of poor planning and lack of technical skills, the economy suffered, particularly in agriculture.

In the early 1970s, Kaunda heightened political repression and silenced organized political opposition. Zambia was officially made a one-party state under the UNIP. The Assembly was dissolved in 1973 and new elections were set; under the new system, a candidate had to have the approval of the UNIP Central Committee before he could run in the general election; several winners of primary elections were eliminated in this way. Twenty other candidates were announced in their stead as "official candidates" of the party, insuring their election.

Elections were held in 1973, 1978, 1983, and 1988, each with the same result: UNIP was the single party represented in the National Assembly and Kenneth Kaunda was reelected president unopposed. By the time of Kaunda's sixth term in 1988, however, voter turnout was quite low, indicating increasing dissatisfaction with the regime.

Zambia had several economic boom years in the early post-independence period, largely due to high world prices for its main export: copper. However, state

Zambia

mismanagement, weak investment, and declining (and volatile) copper prices through the 1970s brought about economic crises in the early 1980s. To receive desperately needed funds from the International Monetary Fund and the World Bank, Zambia instituted economic austerity programs that cut government spending. It also effectively devalued the currency (the kwacha) by allowing the market to set its exchange value. These reforms failed to improve economic conditions in the short-term and proved unpopular, and Zambia broke with the IMF in May 1987, decreeing that only 10% of its export earnings would be used to repay and service external debt. External assistance was frozen just as the country was again gripped by drought. Inflation reached 400% by the 1990s.

Zambia has long been copper dependent. The metal traditionally produced 80% of national export revenues, and one mining company, Zambia Consolidated Copper Mines (ZCCM) once contributed 25% of GDP. But socialist planning and administration during the Kaunda years stunted development with two decades of under-funding and a shortage of capital investment; copper production fell from a peak of 720,000 tons in 1969 to about 320,000 in 1996.

The economy deteriorated by 1990 as copper revenues sank. State enterprises, already bureaucratically inefficient, became heavily indebted and deficit budgeting worsened the debt and spurred inflation; goods and services were in short supply. Business confidence evaporated and consumer frustration mounted. Ultimately, increased food prices provoked riots and an attempted coup.

Transition and the Frederick Chiluba Presidency (1991–2002)

Confronted with growing calls for political change, and President Kaunda

announced the first multiparty elections in 23 years for October 31, 1991. Kaunda's opponent was Frederick Chiluba, a labor leader and head of the Movement for Multiparty Democracy (MMD). Chiluba accused Kaunda of being out of touch and failing to control the inflation rate, and stressed the need to improve economic management and eliminate corruption. After 27 years in power, Kaunda and UNIP were soundly defeated by Chiluba and MMD, which gained 125 of the 150 legislative seats.

During his first term President Chiluba reversed socialist policy and introduced far-reaching market reforms, with mixed success. The government privatized more than 300 unprofitable state-owned industries, and about 82% of these were sold to Zambians, but many of these went to well-connected members of the governing party. The state mining conglomerate, ZCCM, was broken up and its constituent parts sold off after delays that only diminished the sale value. New management and capitalization failed to halt production declines and the mines were shut down by the new owners for almost a year while the government sought a new buyer. Chiluba also ended the government monopoly on foodstuffs. This resulted in higher food prices, but the country's high external debt was lowered by $2 billion. Despite the new market discipline and the change in government, the old problems of inflation, currency devaluation, and corruption persisted.

As the November 1996 elections drew near, Kenneth Kaunda prepared for a comeback and Chiluba prepared to sideline him. The MMD pushed through two constitutional amendments specifically designed to eliminate Kaunda. The first required that both parents of a candidate be Zambian. (Kaunda's parents were both from Malawi.) The second removed the requirement that a candidate win more than half the ballots to be declared president, making it possible to be elected president with a plurality of votes. Furious but helpless, Kaunda's followers boycotted the election. With only 40% of registered voters turning out, Chiluba and his MMD were reelected in 1996, gaining 131 seats in the legislature. Kaunda threatened continued civil disobedience and strikes but was muted by a threat of criminal prosecution. Again, the economy showed few signs of change: it zig-zagged its way from good year to bad through Chiluba's second term.

Elected as a reformer committed to term limits, Chiluba spent most of 2000 and 2001 seeking ways to secure himself a third term. Chiluba coyly refrained from expressing any public desire for a third term, but his minions busily pursued his ambition. The aspiration divided cabinet, party, and country. Those who opposed a third term were summarily dismissed, as were any MMD members who announced their own candidacy for the 2001 elections (as was the case with cabinet member Ben Mwila). Political frustration spilled into the streets, as violent protests erupted and police intervened with tear gas. Finally, the president announced in May 2001 that he would not seek a third term.

Thwarted from a third term, Chiluba handpicked his successor, plucking former vice president Levy Mwanawasa out of political retirement to be the MMD candidate. Mwanawasa switched parties to join the MMD only a day before his appointment, angering MMD heavyweights who sought the job for themselves. One of Zambia's leading lawyers, Mwanawasa had once served as solicitor general under Kenneth Kaunda and had been the first MMD vice president in 1991. He resigned from the office in 1994, criticizing the MMD's tolerance of corruption and drug trafficking. This earned him a reputation as a man of integrity, but the way candidate Mwanawasa had been chosen raised concerns he would be Chiluba's puppet.

Levy Mwanawasa (2002–2008)

The December 2001 presidential and parliamentary elections were overtly rigged by the Chiluba government; the EU's chief official observer described the results as both untrue and unreliable. The Electoral Commission of Zambia (ECZ) nevertheless declared the MMD's Levy Mwanawasa the victor, saying he had won a plurality of 29% of the ballots against 27% for Anderson Mazoka, a businessman and political newcomer who had only recently founded the United Party for National Development (UPND). Nine other candidates split the remaining votes.

Former President Levy Mwanawasa

Zambia

In parliamentary elections the MMD won 66 seats in the 158-member National Assembly. UNIP won 11 seats, while the Forum for Democracy and Development (FDD) took nine and the Heritage Party four, with the remaining seats attributed to other minor parties.

The opposition quickly launched a series of legal challenges to the elections with Zambia's Supreme Court. The court annulled results in four district elections and stripped the MMD of its deputies. Mwanawasa said he would resign as president if the court invalidated the election results, but that proved unnecessary when the court finally rejected the opposition challenge in February 2005, saying that voting was flawed, but that the errors did not affect the final result.

Mwanawasa gained popularity as president for a vigorous anticorruption campaign that even netted his former benefactor: ex-President Chiluba. The task force identified office buildings and houses that Chiluba and other officials owned in Britain, Belgium and other countries and announced it planned to seize those believed to have been purchased with state funds. Because public monies had been used to acquire assets in Britain, Zambia's attorney general lodged a civil suit against Chiluba and four of his associates in a London High Court. In May 2007, the judge found Chiluba and company had conspired to misappropriate around $46 million from Zambia's coffers to purchase property and luxury items ranging from motorcycles to jewelry. The judge caustically noted that Chiluba, who earned about $105,000 in salary over ten years, managed to pay an exclusive men's shop in Geneva $1.2 million. Of that, $500,000 was spent on clothes for Chiluba. Much to the consternation of the former president, the Zambian government had seized a full warehouse of wardrobe items: 349 shirts, many of them with the presidential monogram; 206 jackets and suits; and 72 pairs of shoes, many handmade in Switzerland with special high heels to help raise his stature, physically at least. None of the defendants appeared in court, refusing to recognize its jurisdiction.

The Chiluba trial deeply divided the MMD and weakened Mwanawasa's support, particularly in the north. Chiluba backed the formation of a new party (the Party for Unity, Democracy and Development, or PUDD), which further eroded Mwanawasa's base; ultimately, erstwhile allies drummed up impeachment proceedings, which the president survived. To balance his loss of support in the north, the president reshuffled his cabinet (and even fired two vice presidents), bringing in politicians from traditional opposition areas in the south. He expanded the cabinet and broadened ethnic and regional representation in the government; this threw the opposition into disarray as members crossed the aisle to join the government benches.

Mwanawasa then faced paralyzing strikes by government workers, which proved damaging as the government was under enormous international pressure to get its financial house in order. The IMF withheld $100 million in aid when the government could not stanch budgetary hemorrhaging. Western donors followed suit, leaving the government with nothing to offer its angry workers but future installment payments. Budget deficits prevented Zambia from moving forward in the Highly Indebted Poor Countries initiative (HIPC), a program designed to reduce its crippling debt service costs. The impact on social services was devastating: in 2004, for example, it spent $156 million more on debt repayment than it did on education.

The Mwanawasa government presented an austerity budget in February 2004, promising to increase revenues by increasing taxes and to cut costs by freezing the salaries of public employees. The move set off immediate protests, but the political gamble paid off: by early 2005 Zambia was included in HIPC, and in April the World Bank approved a $3.8 billion debt relief package. A few months later, the world's richest countries, collectively called the G-8, agreed to cancel the multilateral debt of 19 of the world's poorest countries, Zambia included. About 95% of the country's $7 billion external debt disappeared by the end of 2006.

Civil society NGOs and opposition groups called for a new constitution. In response, President Mwanawasa appointed a Constitutional Review Committee in 2002, and it reported out in August 2005 with its principal recommendations: presidential election by majority (50% + 1 vote rather than plurality), the vice president elected as the running mate of the presidential candidate, and elimination of the controversial Chiluba-instigated amendment requiring both parents of a presidential candidate be of Zambian birth. Government, opposition, and civil society remained at an impasse as to what the new text should say, how it should be adopted, and when it should be implemented. The Oasis Forum, an umbrella group composed largely of lawyers and church bodies, demanded a constituent assembly be summoned to approve a new text before the 2006 general elections, but Mwanawasa held firm that the 2006 elections would be held under the pre-existing constitution, and set the elections for late September, giving his opponents a relatively short time to campaign.

Mwanawasa entered the 2006 election season with a solid record of economic accomplishment: GDP growth had been stable and positive, and was a solid 5% in 2006; inflation had dropped to 8% from 30% in 2001, and international lenders had agreed to write off a large chunk of Zambia's foreign debt to reward "good economic management." With surging commodity prices, export earnings had grown and once-closed copper mines had been reopened. Yet the record was more appreciated abroad than at home. The practical benefits had yet to seep down to the average Zambian, and the president's opponents seized on the disconnect between statistics and life reality.

The most formidable rival was the fiery populist, Michael Sata, leading the Patriotic Front (PF). Sata promised to slash the high tax rates paid by government workers and blamed outsiders (especially Chinese and Indian businessmen) for keeping wages low. Sata even vowed to recognize the independence of Taiwan if elected, which was a provocation to Chinese state-backed investors. The other candidate with a chance was Hakainde Hichilema, a successful businessman chosen to lead the United Democratic Alliance (UDA). The UDA brought together the three largest parliamentary opposition parties—the Forum for Democracy and Development (FDD), the United National Independence Party (UNIP), and United Party for National Development (UPND). Its intended candidate was UPND's Anderson Mazoka, who had barely lost the controversial 2001 election to Mwanawasa, but Mazoka died of kidney failure in May 2006.

In the end, President Mwanawasa received 43% of the vote, beating Sata (with 29%) and Hichilema, who tallied a respectable 25% with the strong support of ex-President Kaunda's UNIP. Simultaneous parliamentary elections gave the MMD a solid bloc of 74 seats in a 150-seat legislature. In a move that would prove to be of greater consequence than expected, Rupiah Banda was appointed as the vice president.

Mwanawasa suffered a stroke in June 2008 (his second) and never fully recovered, and he died in August 2008. In his final years, Mwanawasa gained considerable international respect for his willingness as the chairman of the Southern African Development Community (SADC) to take a firm stand against the dictatorial Robert Mugabe in Zimbabwe. While controversial in Africa, this was appreciated overseas, especially given the comparatively feeble statements of South African president Thabo Mbeki on the matter. Mwanawasa was succeeded by Vice President Rupiah Banda, who took the presidency on an interim basis until an election was held.

Zambia

Mwanawasa's death was mourned even by his rival Michael Sata.

The Rupiah Banda Interregnum and Michael Sata (2011–present)

Mwanawasa's death necessitated (by law) another presidential election in October 2008. In that poll, Rupiah Banda of the MMD earned over 41% of the valid votes, while Michael Sata of the Patriotic Front came in close behind with 39% and Hakainde Hichilema took most of the remainder with 20%. Sata rejected the results and Banda's presidency, calling the election fraudulent. In November, violent protests and post-election riots broke out in Lusaka and Kitwe. The conflict eventually subsided, but tensions remained ahead of the election slated for 2011.

In late 2010, another issue reemerged that has surfaced from time to time: that status of the Western Province, formerly known as Barotseland. The region was incorporated into Zambia's unitary state along with Northern Rhodesia upon independence in 1964 in the Barotseland Agreement, and some in the region have periodically clamored for greater autonomy; in 2010, traditional leaders in the Barotseland Royal Establishment (BRE) sought more explicit constitutional recognition for the region in a revised constitution. Clashes between youth demonstrators and police in the provincial capital Mongu in October 2010 and January 2011 brought the issue back to the fore, as at least two young demonstrators were killed and many arrested. The issue has become electoral, with the MMD government seeking to control agitation while opposition candidate Michael Sata has attempted to draw support in Western Province by empathizing with the protests.

After losing three presidential elections (2001, 2006, 2008) and spending ten years in opposition, Michael Sata won the presidency in September 2011. He won 43% of the vote (most notably taking much of the urban vote) while the incumbent Rupiah Banda, took 36%. Sata has shown anti-Chinese sentiments, which leaves some of the investment community in Zambia nervous. Most recently, after some contradictory statements, Sata has supported foreign investors on the condition that they provide better labor conditions for Zambian workers and increase the role of Zambians in management. Generally, Sata has adopted an overtly populist stance with a centralizing streak, which has been manifested in a tightening of restrictions on foreign currency flows. The economy continues to grow apace, but the contradictions in the government's economic policy have led to questions among western observers about the sustainability of the Zambian model.

CONTEMPORARY THEMES

Social Issues

Zambia suffers from the pandemics of southern Africa: HIV/AIDS and tuberculosis. The government was slow to respond after 1984 when the first AIDS case appeared in Zambia, and through the 1990s continued to provide a subpar (if any) response to the disease, but the 2000s saw the government become proactive in confronting the epidemic. An estimated 13.5% of all adults aged 18–49 are HIV-positive, or a total of about one million of the country's 14 million people. Some areas of the country have a prevalence rate of 25% and in 2009 there were 76,000 new infections among adults; this means an estimated 200 adults per day were infected. As a consequence of the epidemic, life expectancy has dropped to only about 46 years (World Bank 2009 estimate), a figure among the lowest in the world. UNICEF estimates there are 75,000 street children in the country, many of them AIDS orphans. Many wind up on the streets of Zambia's cities, especially the capital, Lusaka. In 2004, manufacturing of cheap generic antiretroviral (ARV) drugs began with Cuban assistance, and these are now distributed free of change. While this greatly improved access, the AIDS prevalence rate has dropped down to 14.3% as of 2014, though some patients have wrongly gone off the drug once feeling better (ARVs are needed for a lifetime).

Foreign Investment

Economically, Zambia has benefited from the burgeoning economies in China and India, which have driven up prices for copper and other commodities. The boom has brought higher profits, tax revenues, and foreign investment in Zambian mines. Projects previously thought too expensive are now deemed feasible. India's Vedanta Resources purchased 51% of Konkola Copper Mines (KCM) shares for a rock-bottom price of $25 million in August 2003; it later invested $400 million into the massive Konkola Deep project, which had been studied and restudied for two decades, which is expected to extend the mine's life another 22 years. The government, which owns 20% of Konkola, hopes national copper production will triple from previous levels to over a million tons by 2015. There are some modest signs of industrial diversification as well, though the emphasis is still mining; Zambia now produces 20% of the world's emeralds, and is also endowed with rich deposits of amethysts, aquamarines, and red garnets. The Zambian government has increased its efforts in countering drug and human trafficking and the black-market trade of illegal goods, such as ivory.

Landlocked Zambia requires transportation improvements, since extracted minerals are expensive compared to, say, Chilean copper (which is mined near deepwater ports). Konkola, for example, ships all its output by rail to Durban, South Africa or Dar es Salaam, Tanzania. Both ports are more than 1,200 miles away and the journey takes several days. Poor roads mean that truck transport is prohibitively expensive. The Southern Africa Development Community (SADC) is planning a $200-million railroad line connecting Zambia's copper mines to the Benguela railroad line in Angola. The 400-mile connector is expected to reduce transportation costs.

China has had a long interest in Zambia and has recently become a major economic player responsible for investment and assistance in a variety of areas, from telecommunications, medicine, education, and tourism (designating Zambia "Approved Destination Status" for Chinese tourists) to infrastructure improvements. In 2010, President Hu of China met with President Banda in Beijing, and the two signed accords that year to establish a "joint economic zone" for Chinese investment in Zambia, along with concessionary loans from China to Zambia for such projects as a major hydroelectric dam on the Kafue River. The major caveat to the close economic linkage is the conflicting relationship that has emerged between many Chinese employers and Zambian nationals. Tensions between these two groups have created a major issue for Chinese-Zambian economic relationship in recent years as poor working conditions inside Chinese-owned mines have led to violence between Zambian miners and Chinese managers. In response to these subpar safety conditions, the Zambian government took control of the Chinese-operated Collum Coal mine in February 2013 and declared it would operate the mine until new investors are found.

Along with a major outbreak of cholera that reportedly killed 400 people, Zambia, like many surrounding nations in southern Africa, is experiencing serious drought brought about by the El Nino weather pattern, which has severely affected food production, especially of the primary maize crop, along with domestic electricity production from hydro power. Estimates are that one million hectares (2.5 million acres) of cropland have suffered severe degradation.

Along with neighboring Zimbabwe, Zambia has experienced a major drought that has destroyed harvests and sent the Zambezi River's water flows to a historic low. For decades, the Kariba Dam on the River had provided the bulk of electricity consumed in Zambia and Zimbabwe.

Zambia

Beginning in September 2024, Zambian officials ordered that, owing to desperately low water levels, only one out of six turbines on its side of the lake could continue to operate, leaving entire cities deprived of electricity, sometimes for days on end. Sporadic access to power has become the norm since. In 2022, as record low rainfall has led to a glaring imbalance between the water intake level at Lake Kariba, the world's biggest dam reservoir, and water consumption by Zimbabweans and Zambians, which has hit hard urban households (75 percent of which normally have access to electricity). Rural areas are also suffering from the dramatic reduction in precipitation as Zambia experiences its driest agricultural season in more than four decades. The worst-affected provinces usually produce half of the annual maize output and are home to more than three-quarters of Zambia's livestock population, which is reeling from scorched pastures and water scarcity as crop failure and livestock losses are fueling food inflation. UNICEF has reported that more than 50,000 Zambian children under the age of five are at risk of falling into severe wasting, the deadliest form of malnutrition. Zambia has also been battling a cholera outbreak with more than 20,000 reported cases, as access to water has become increasingly scarce. This is a water, energy, and food emergency, all at once blamed on climate change. With prioritization of urban areas over rural ones in development. Zambia's Gini coefficient, a measure of income inequality, is among the world's highest as workers in cities are much more likely to earn regular wages, while the poorest layers of the population depend on agricultural self-employment and the vagaries of the climate. The massive gap between rich and poor appears not accidental as tax reforms in recent decades have benefited wealthy urban elites and large rural landowners, but subsistence farmers and agricultural laborers are left out.

FUTURE CONSIDERATIONS

After independence, Zambia went from one of Africa's wealthiest states to one of its poorest, but it appears to have turned a corner once again in the last decade with the introduction of foreign investments in the countries lucrative mining industry. The country's outlook continues to depend in large part on commodity prices, with high prices benefiting this mining-intensive economy. Of course, this makes the economy especially vulnerable to global economic downturn. Economic growth from 2007 to 2012 was estimated at about 6% (or roughly the continental average) per year, and at times peaked at over 7%. Economic reform seems to have put the country on a better trajectory than before, and *The Economist* magazine anticipates this could be one of the 10 fastest growing economies in the world over the coming years, assuming global demand for copper and other commodities remains high.

Politically, Zambia has some free political contestation and some reasonable degree of civil liberties. Though democracy is incomplete, the 2006 elections were widely viewed as an improvement upon prior presidential elections. The passing of Levy Mwanawasa triggered the more discordant election of 2008 between Rupiah Banda and Michael Sata. While the post-election strife seems to have passed, there is little doubt that the response to the 2008 election was something of a setback for Zambia. The electoral turnover to Michael Sata in 2011 has generated some optimism that Zambia can handle the vicissitudes of democratic alternation. However, recent developments have led to questions about Sata's tolerance for political dissenters. One more conspicuous case was the arrest in 2014 of political opponent Frank Bwalya on defamation charges for comparing the president to a potato. For the time being though, this suggests a modicum of stability in an era when commodity prices and investment may make a lasting contribution to human and social development. Observers will also be keeping a watchful eye on the recent minor unrest in the Western Province over the so-called Barotseland Agreement; while limited at present, any further secessionist agitation would raise eyebrows.

Modern Lusaka ©IRIN

The Republic of Zimbabwe

Bridge at Victoria Falls connecting Zimbabwe and Zambia

BASIC FACTS

Area: 390,757 sq. km. (slightly larger than Montana)
Population: 15,418,674 (June 2023 est.)
Capital City: Harare
Government Type: Semi-Presidential Republic
Neighboring Countries: Zambia (northwest); Namibia (west); Botswana (southwest); South Africa (south); Mozambique (east)
Official Language: English
Other Principal Languages: Shona, Sindebele (Ndebele)
Ethnic Groups: Shona 82%, Ndebele 14%, other African 2%, mixed and Asian 1%, white less than 1%
Principal Religions: Syncretic (part Christian, part indigenous beliefs) 50%, Christian 25%, indigenous beliefs 24%, Muslim and other 1%
Former Colonial Status: Administered by the British South Africa Company (1889–1923); Autonomous state within the British Commonwealth (1923–1965); unilateral independence as Rhodesia (1965–1980), recognized independence (1980).
Independence Date: April 18, 1980
GDP Per Capita (IMF 2023 est.): $1,851 (nominal), $2,627 (PPP)
Gini index: 50.3 (World Bank 2019)
Chief Commercial Products: Tobacco, gold, ferroalloys, diamonds, and cotton, platinum, textiles
Inflation Rate: 86.7% (2022 est.)
Currency: Has adopted several currencies, including the US dollar, Botswana pula, pound sterling, and South Africa rand. Also, 1 USD = 361.9 ZWL.
Foreign Direct Investments (FDI) net inflows: 544,800,000
Literacy Rate: 89.7% (CIA 2021)
Life Expectancy: 63.74 years (CIA 2023 est.)
Head of State: President Emmerson Dambudzo Mnangagwa (since November 24, 2017)
Head of State: President Emmerson Dambudzo Mnangagwa (since November 24, 2017)

LAND AND PEOPLE

Zimbabwe is hot and humid in the southern river basin areas. Cluttered forests of hardwood and scrub vegetation predominate in these lowlands. Central Zimbabwe is a series of fertile plateaus, whose higher altitudes moderate the tropical climate. During the winter, occasional frosts may occur. Most of the land not forested is under cultivation.

Victoria Falls, located on the Zambezi River is one of the greatest sights of Africa—they are more than twice as high as Niagara Falls and have a width of about one mile. The waters of Lake Kariba stretch downstream (northeast) from the falls to the 420-foot-high Kariba Dam that provides electric power to both Zimbabwe and Zambia.

Social commentary in Zimbabwe has long been the subject of the country's foremost artists, including musicians such as Thomas Mapfumo. Born in colonial Rhodesia in 1945, Mapfumo recognized early on how colonists exploited Africans and he sympathized with those fighting against white rule. His songs in his native Shona came to be known as *chimurenga* music, or music of the struggle. After the liberation, however, Mapfumo became increasingly disenchanted with Zimbabwe under Robert Mugabe, and his later music came to criticize the regime's corruption and violence on behalf of the unfortunate. The album *Chimurenga Explosion* in 2000 had at least one of its cuts, "Disaster," denied airtime, and other songs have similarly been banned from the airwaves. Mapfumo has moved his family to the United States and vows not to return to Zimbabwe while President Mugabe remains in office. Another popular musician—Hoseah Chipanga—also took up the role of regime critic at the 2006 pre-Independence Day ball, attended by regime elites and diplomats. Oliver Mtukudzi, a

Zimbabwe

former bandmate of Mapfumo, is another of Zimbabwe's most internationally renowned musicians. Among Zimbabwe's top literary talents are the women authors Yvonne Vera and Tsitsi Dangarembga, the latter of whom wrote the much-acclaimed novel *Nervous Conditions*.

HISTORY TO PRESENT DAY

For early history, see *Historical Background* and *The Colonial Period: The British*.

By 1923, white settlers in present-day Zimbabwe gained self-rule from the British South Africa Company for their colony. The settlers generally referred to the colony as Rhodesia, named after adventurer and industrialist Cecil Rhodes, but the British called the area Southern Rhodesia to distinguish it from the colony north of the Zambezi River known as Northern Rhodesia. In 1923, white electors rejected the possibility of joining South Africa, opting instead to have Rhodesia become an autonomous member of the British Commonwealth. British settlers chose a parliament; with very few exceptions, Africans could not pass the educational tests required to gain voting rights. Whites further solidified their control in 1931 with the passage of the Land Apportionment Act, which gave about 150,000 settlers exclusive rights to roughly one-half of the choicest land; the 3,000,000 native Africans were left with the remaining poorer land.

In 1953, Southern Rhodesia joined with Northern Rhodesia and Nyasaland to form the Central African Federation. The federation was dissolved in 1963, and Northern Rhodesia and Nyasaland earned independence as Zambia and Malawi respectively. Fearing a similar development, white Southern Rhodesians rejected the governing United Federal Party and replaced it with the more conservative Rhodesian Front (RF). By 1964, Ian Douglas Smith led the RF, and the party swept the 1965 elections. After several attempts to persuade Britain to grant independence, the Smith government announced the Unilateral Declaration of Independence (UDI) on November 11, 1965.

Unilateral Declaration of Independence (1965)

African nationalist organizations began to flourish after 1953, a development greeted with hostility by colonial officials. The first commanding nationalist figure was Joshua Nkomo. In 1961, Nkomo (an Ndebele) joined with Robert Mugabe (a Shona), and Reverend Ndabiningi Sithole (an Ndau) to form the Zimbabwe People's Union (ZAPU). By 1963, however, Sithole, Mugabe and other Shona intellectuals, disappointed with his leadership, split from Nkomo and formed the Zimbabwe African National Union (ZANU). The split shattered what had been a multi-ethnic and multiregional anti-colonial movement. It shaped political rivalries well into the post-independence period. Two movements claiming nationalist goals each became ethnic and regional movements that were already divided by the advent of UDI in 1965.

United Nations resolutions condemned white rule in Rhodesia, and one forbade any member nation to trade with Rhodesia. Since Rhodesia was one of the very few sources outside the U.S.S.R. of chrome ore vital to the manufacture of hard steel, the U.S. Congress allowed the resumption of Rhodesian chrome purchases in 1971, infuriating many African nations. Faced with international sanctions, Rhodesia turned to the development of import-substitution industries, ironically providing the basis for one of Zimbabwe's greatest economic strengths: a richly diversified economy.

ZANU and ZAPU took refuge in neighboring Zambia and began launching minor guerrilla attacks against the regime by 1965. In an attempt to find and deal with more moderate nationalist elements than ZANU and ZAPU, Ian Smith allowed the creation of a third nationalist movement, the United African National Council (UANC) led by Abel Muzorewa, a bishop of the American United Methodist Church. Smith opened talks with Muzorewa and two other black leaders, Chief Jeremiah Chirau and Reverend Sithole, who had lost out in a ZANU leadership struggle with Robert Mugabe. Smith excluded both ZAPU and ZANU from the talks.

All-out guerrilla war began in 1972 against isolated white farmers in the northeast of the country. With the collapse of Portuguese colonial authority in 1974, ZANU guerrilla forces found a permanent base of operations in Mozambique under Robert Mugabe. Joshua Nkomo and his ZAPU supporters raised their own guerrilla army, largely Ndebele speakers from the southwest, and opened a second front in the guerrilla war, operating out of Zambia. Both Mozambique and Zambia suffered terribly as targets of Rhodesian retaliation and by 1976 both countries pressured the two guerrilla movements to fight the Smith regime jointly. This resulted in the creation of the Patriotic Front of Zimbabwe.

As more whites began to flee the country in 1978, Smith signed an "internal settlement" with Muzorewa, Sithole and Chirau providing for qualified majority rule and elections with universal suffrage. Mugabe and Nkomo scoffed at this settlement and branded the other black leaders "Uncle Toms." Patriotic Front leaders rejected an offer of total amnesty. In the parliamentary elections of 1979, Muzorewa's UANC won 51 of the 72 seats allotted to African candidates, beating the ZANU splinter group led by Reverend Sithole, which won only 12 seats. Muzorewa became Rhodesia's first black prime minister, but whites retained key positions within the government and the army.

The guerrilla war continued and the U.N. lifted none of their sanctions. Britain intervened to end the crisis by creating a government that included all nationalist elements. The Lancaster House Conference began in London in September 1979 with Muzorewa, Nkomo and Mugabe. After endless weeks of fruitless discussions against a background of continuous fighting back home—an average of 100 lives were lost each day—the white minority finally consented to hold multiracial elections, supervised by the British, in 1980. These, it was agreed, would lead to independence for Zimbabwe.

Independence and Early Post-Independence

The Lancaster House constitution that established Zimbabwe's independence operated from 1980 to 1990, guaranteeing whites representation in parliament and protecting white economic interests. The constitution established a bicameral legislature, with reserved seats for whites in both houses. Also, the new government prohibited compulsory land acquisition, as well as the establishment of a one-party state, before 1990. The three leaders accepted the draft constitution, and a total of nine political parties prepared for the upcoming elections. Both elements of the Patriotic Front, Nkomo's PF-ZAPU and Mugabe's ZANU-PF, ran separate candidates, as did the Muzorewa and Sithole organizations.

The 1980 election was a stunning triumph for Mugabe. ZANU-PF won 57 of 80 black seats in the House of Assembly. Nkomo's ZAPU was successful in 20 contests, mostly in Matabeleland, while Bishop Muzorewa won only three seats. The white minority was badly frightened at the prospect of having the Marxist Mugabe as prime minister, but he promised them equal treatment as with all other Zimbabweans. With representatives of 100 nations on hand, Zimbabwe achieved independence on April 18, 1980.

President Mugabe's politics was initially conciliatory and successful. Mugabe appointed his political rival Nkomo to a high-ranking cabinet position and included two prominent white Zimbabweans as well.

The tasks of the new government were enormous. It had to integrate three different armies—the guerrilla forces of ZAPU

Zimbabwe

and ZANU, and the Rhodesian Defense Forces. It had to reestablish social services and education in the rural areas, and resettle a million refugees, displaced by nearly 15 years of civil conflict. Mugabe adopted a cautious approach to socializing the economy. The government raised prices for cash crops to placate farmers, and Mugabe assured white farmers that the government would not confiscate their property, despite popular pressures for land reform. These policies produced surpluses that allowed Zimbabwe to weather the drought-caused crop failures of 1982–1984 better than most of her neighbors.

Fissures within the Patriotic Front soon developed. Authorities allegedly found a cache of arms on Nkomo's farm and accused him, along with his closest aides, of trying to overthrow the ZANU-PF government. Mugabe expelled Nkomo and his aides from the cabinet in 1981. Nkomo's followers began a loosely organized campaign of dissidence. Centered in Matabeleland, the dissidence involved attacks on both white farmers and government targets. The government responded with the full force of emergency powers first granted the Smith regime and renewed annually ever since.

The government began an increasingly horrific crackdown in Matabeleland after 1981. The repression began with sweeping raids, strict curfews, and even withholding of food shipments in order to starve the area into submission. In 1983, the Mugabe sent the notorious Fifth Brigade, trained by North Korea, to suppress dissidence. The brigade, known as *Gukurahundi*, or "storm that destroys everything" accomplished its goal with ghastly violence. According to the Catholic Commission for Justice and Peace, the Fifth Brigade was responsible for the deaths of an estimated 20,000 people between 1983 and 1987. The Matabeleland campaign demonstrated the regime's willingness to use violence and terror against its own people to consolidate its power.

In the 1985 general election, held at the height of the Matabeleland massacres, ZANU garnered 76% of the vote and increased its parliamentary majority by eight seats. Two years later, parliament eliminated seats reserved for whites. In November, amendments to the constitution created the post of executive president with enhanced powers, combining the roles of head of state and head of government. Mugabe then won a new election to the presidency for a term of six years.

ZANU-PF and the One-Party State

In the same month, the two main political parties agreed to unify. Nkomo's ZAPU was absorbed into the ruling party, ZANU-PF. It marked the triumph of the Shona branch of Zimbabwean nationalism and the creation of a de facto one-party state. Nkomo later was named second vice president. ZANU-PF asserted it would "seek to establish a socialist society, on the guidance of Marxist-Leninist principles, and to establish a one-party state."

Despite state repression of political opposition, four opposition parties contested the March 1990 general election, the largest of which was the Zimbabwe Unity Movement (ZUM) led by Edgar Tekere. Mugabe won 78% of the vote, but pre-election violence and intimidation cast increasing doubt on any semblance of democracy.

President Mugabe proposed to institutionalize the one-party state later that year, but this led to strains within the party as churches, trade unions, and students all strongly opposed the proposal. Ultimately, a majority of the Politburo rejected the Mugabe plan. With the collapse of the Soviet Union and the decline of communism worldwide, enthusiasm for Marxist-Leninist doctrine declined in Zimbabwe. In June 1991, ZANU-PF's central committee dropped references to "Marxism-Leninism" and "scientific socialism" from the party's constitution.

Economic issues dominated Zimbabwean politics in the 1990s. With the expiration of the Lancaster House prohibition on forced land purchases, President Mugabe announced that the government would amend the constitution to speed up land redistribution. The Land Acquisition Act of 1992 allowed for the compulsory purchase of 13,585,000 acres of predominantly white-owned land. The commercial farming community fiercely opposed the plan and was able to delay its implementation. A regional drought in 1992 brought great suffering, and the Mugabe government, blamed for inadequate planning for the anticipated crop failure, became increasingly unpopular.

As ZANU-PF's support waned, it moved to accelerate land redistribution. The government published a list of farms it would be purchasing on a compulsory basis in May of 1993. The list included seventy farms, some of them the most productive in the country, amounting to nearly half a million acres. A year later, news broke that a government minister was leasing the first farm seized under the Land Acquisition Act; this was an early indication the government was more concerned with self-enrichment than the needs of small farmers who were supposed to be the beneficiaries of redistribution.

Diamond mining, Zimbabwe *Das Parlament*

Zimbabwe

Elections in the mid-1990s confirmed the one-party state: ZANU-PF won its fourth successive electoral victory in 1995 parliamentary elections, taking 118 of 120 seats, and Mugabe won reelection to another six-year term in March 1996, though less than one-third of the electorate voted, suggesting diminishing legitimacy.

Despite electoral victories, Mugabe's regime showed some cracks. Several legislators, emboldened by the example of President Mandela's leadership in neighboring South Africa, reacted vigorously to a series of corruption scandals. The media broke stories of high ZANU-PF officials looting of the veterans' compensation fund, leading 100 ZANU-PF legislators called for an official audit of the fund. Legislators also rejected a contract for a new terminal at the Harare International Airport when government planners awarded it to an inexperienced Cypriot company with close ties to President Mugabe's nephew.

Public demonstrations against the regime increased. Civil servants, railway workers, doctors, and nurses, among others, protested wages and work conditions. Veterans of the liberation struggle, mostly poorly educated peasant farmers living in poverty, demanded payment and pensions for service. Food riots in January 1998 forced the government to send in the army when the police could no longer control the situation. The regime seemed to be unraveling.

A Regime of Personal Rule

By 1998, Robert Mugabe's control over party and state in Zimbabwe had little credible or effective opposition. Every constitutional amendment and each election since independence had concentrated authority in his hands, and there were few checks to assure accountability. Robert Mugabe's Zimbabwe became a regime of personal rule.

Mugabe's economic mismanagement resulted in an economic meltdown by the late 1990s. The value of the Zimbabwe dollar plummeted as inflation soared and basic commodities became unaffordable to most Zimbabweans. In response, unions organized massive "stay-aways" from work. The government acquiesced to some popular demands, rescinding fuel price increases and introducing price controls on basic commodities. With government control over the economy accentuated and the regime looking increasingly like a pariah, the International Monetary Fund withdrew loan support.

Intensifying the domestic political crisis was President Mugabe's decision to intervene on behalf of fellow authoritarian president Laurent Kabila when a rebellion convulsed the Democratic Republic of Congo (DRC) in August 1998. The Zimbabwean government went on an arms-buying spree, purchasing fighter aircraft from China and Swiss-designed cluster bombs. It spent over $1 million daily to keep about 11,000 troops in the Congo, and used the state-owned oil company to divert fuel to the war effort, despite acute shortages and massive lines at the gas pumps in Zimbabwe. To pay the costs of war, Zimbabwe signed deals that treated the DRC as a neo-colony; one concession from the Kabila government would allow Zimbabwe to log some 84 million acres (15% of the Congo's territory) of rain forest. The concession went to the ZANU-PF business empire controlled by Emmerson Mnangagwa, the speaker of parliament and Mugabe's financial right-hand man. While the ventures failed miserably by mid-2003, they may have had the desired effect: by most accounts, Mugabe's Congo escapade was designed mainly to secure the loyalty of the army and provide enrichment opportunities for cronies. Polls indicated that 70% of Zimbabweans opposed the presence in the Congo.

Faced with mounting criticism, the dictatorship became increasingly maniacal as Mugabe attacked and threatened his critics. The few independent newspapers remaining in Zimbabwe were subjected to criticism and intimidation. Mugabe punished labor unions with a six-month ban on strikes in response to their demands for political reforms and their public anger over economic hardship. In his rhetoric, Mugabe sought scapegoats for each of Zimbabwe's crises. When fuel shortages occurred, for instance, he accused white industrialists and farmers of hoarding it. He also railed against foreign leaders for trying to destabilize Zimbabwe, especially singling out British Prime Minister Tony Blair (1997–2007), the head of government in what was once Rhodesia's colonial power. Mugabe increasingly claimed that domestic opponents were the stooges of neo-imperial powers.

After 1999, Zimbabwe continued its downward spiral into economic crisis and political violence. Corruption and cronyism ran rampant. As investment and commercial farming declined, foreign exchange nearly disappeared. Inflation soared (eventually becoming hyperinflation), as did the unemployment rate and poverty rate. Interest rates rose and the Zimbabwe dollar declined further.

The Movement for Democratic Change (MDC)

Economic collapse gave rise to a new and important opposition party. In September 1999, the Zimbabwe Confederation of Trade Unions (ZCTU) launched the Movement for Democratic Change (MDC) under the leadership of

President Robert Mugabe

its secretary-general Morgan Tsvangirai. In the months to come, the MDC became the kind of opposition the Mugabe regime had never seen before, mobilizing opposition and building upon preexisting grassroots organizations.

Simultaneously, deteriorating conditions led to a push to amend Zimbabwe's constitution. President Mugabe appointed an official Constitutional Commission to recommend changes. It held hearings and learned that Zimbabweans overwhelmingly wanted to limit Mugabe's power, but the process was dominated by Mugabe loyalists and ended in farce. A draft revision actually strengthened and consolidated the president's powers and allowed confiscation of white-owned farms without compensation. The draft went through the final meeting of the 400-member constitutional commission without a vote. Despite delegates screaming their opposition, Constitutional Commission chairman, Judge Godfrey Chidyausiku, declared "the draft is adopted by acclamation."

The MDC grew in organization and strength, however, and worked with commercial farmers to organize a successful "No" campaign in the February 2002 referendum on the new constitutional amendments. The government, which had never lost an election in 20 years, used its power over state print and broadcast media to reject all opposition advertising and virtually all statements critical of the draft constitution. Despite intimidation, the opposition handed President Mugabe his first defeat since independence, despite the government's populist promise of white lands for black Zimbabweans. Fifty-five percent of voters rejected the proposed amendments.

Land Invasions and the End of Commercial Farms

Mugabe orchestrated a campaign of violence after the referendum's defeat, directing his ire at commercial farmers (who

Zimbabwe

were usually white) and some of their black employees who had been active in the campaign against the referendum. Many white farmers were humiliated and killed, while black farm workers had their homes and property destroyed, and most were forced to participate in subsequent farm invasions. The government claimed the country was witnessing "spontaneous" invasions of white-owned farms by "war veterans" disillusioned by the rejection of the constitutional amendment that would have allowed land confiscation and redistribution. In reality, many of the self-styled "war veterans" were born after the liberation war was over, or were otherwise far too young to have ever served. They were in fact from young, urban unemployed, carefully organized and dispersed throughout the country by ZANU-PF with logistical precision.

The farm invasions began within a week of Mugabe's referendum defeat and ultimately involved 50,000 pro-Mugabe squatters invading about 1,400 farms. A lead coordinator of the land seizures was General Perence Shiri, the head of Zimbabwe's air force who had also commanded the Fifth Brigade massacres in Matabeleland in the 1980s—the most notorious example of Zimbabwe's state employing coercion against its own citizens. General Shiri's name also appeared on a list of 28 senior government and military figures given farms seized from whites.

In June 2000, parliamentary elections took place against the backdrop of farm invasions. Mugabe and the ZANU-PF resorted to further terror to silence rural supporters of the MDC. Government-sponsored violence resulted in the deaths of some 30 people, and thousands were beaten, raped and intimidated. Still, MDC voters went to the polls and made the best showing by any opposition party in Zimbabwe's history: the MDC won a remarkable 57 out of 120 seats, while ZANU-PF won 62, and the remaining seat went to Rev. Sithole's ZANU-Ndonga. Several ZANU-PF bigwigs were defeated, including parliamentary speaker Emmerson Mnangagwa, though Zimbabwe's constitution allows the president to appoint an additional 30 members to parliament; using this option Mugabe returned Mnangagwa to the House of Assembly, where he won election as speaker.

The MDC challenged nearly 40 of the election results in court. Justices annulled election results compromised by violence and intimidation, putting elements of the judiciary at odds with Mugabe. Outright assault on justices started when courts ordered black squatters to end their illegal occupations of white-owned farms. War veterans (and fake war veterans), who had become the regime's paramilitary,

Robert Mugabe and the Zimbabwean military *Das Parlament*

invaded judicial premises and threatened judges. The police did little, and the regime informed the justices that it was unable to protect them or their families. Under coercion, the chief justice of Zimbabwe's Supreme Court retired early. To fill the vacancy, Mugabe appointed Judge Godfrey Chidyausiku, the former chair of the notorious constitutional commission that had proposed constitutional amendments to increase Mugabe's authority.

Mugabe and the Media

The regime intimidated the independent media as well as commercial farmers, opposition supporters, and judges. The *Daily News*—the only remaining independent newspaper and an outspoken critic of the Mugabe regime—faced much harassment and intimidation. War veterans assaulted *Daily News* journalists, fired steel bolts into its offices, and set up roadblocks outside Harare to confiscate copies of the newspaper and prevent its distribution to outlying areas where two-thirds of the population lives. A massive explosion rocked the paper's printing works, destroying five of the *Daily News's* six presses. Investigators later determined five Soviet made anti-tank land mines, favored for their ability to toss a ten-ton tank into the air, caused the destruction, and that munitions experts had set them off after placing them for maximum effect.

The Media Institute of Southern Africa (MISA) consistently ranks Zimbabwe as the worst offender of media freedom in the sub-region, given the raft of anti-media laws enforced by the regime. Equally inimical to press freedom is the strategy of the country's Central Intelligence Organization (CIO) to own papers through shell companies or silent shareholders. In May 2006, the Paris-based international media watchdog, Reporters Without Borders, classified Robert Mugabe as a "predator" of press freedom, along with Cuba's Fidel Castro and China's Hu Jintao.

Radio is far cheaper than newspapers and more effective in reaching a rural audience. It has thus been a major concern of the regime since Zimbabwe's Supreme Court declared the state's broadcasting monopoly unconstitutional in September 2000. Since independence in 1980, there has been no private broadcasting station in the country. Shortly after the court's decision, Capital Radio, financed by foreign charities, started operations broadcasting music, but its life was brief. Within days, armed police swept into the station's office, seized its equipment, and accused it of being a "pirate" station.

ZANU-PF majorities in parliament rushed a restrictive broadcasting act through parliament in April 2001 with little debate. The bill required broadcasters to have a license, but licenses would be severely limited, and radio stations could not operate if financed by foreign interests. The law held that the government retained the power to shut down broadcasters if they did anything that was "prejudicial to the defense, public safety, public order, public morality or public health of Zimbabwe." Zimbabwe's information minister, Jonathan Moyo, made the government's position clear: "If there is a court which allows [independent

Zimbabwe

broadcasting] in Zimbabwe, we [the government] will not allow it. It compromises our national security."

In the spring of 2001, Chenjerai Hunzvi (nicknamed "Hitler" Hunzvi) and his "war vets" brought their chaos to the cities, attacking businesses and charitable institutions in an orgy of theft, kidnapping, and extortion. The regime tolerated and tacitly encouraged Hunzvi's "war vets," since they were attacking the base of the opposition MDC's support. It only halted the attacks when Hunzvi's forces threatened to invade embassies. Hunzvi ultimately died in early June 2001, reportedly of malaria of the brain.

To ensure victory in the presidential election of March 2002, Mugabe continued to mobilize police, army, and youth militia to intimidate and terrorize the population. According to official figures, Zimbabweans cast nearly three million ballots in the election, with Mugabe winning 56% of the vote and Morgan Tsvangirai winning only 42%, with three minor candidates taking the remainder. ZANU-PF spokesmen claimed Mugabe won because people supported his seizure of white-owned land and saw the MDC and Tsvangirai as the stooges of white colonialists.

In reality, Mugabe won the election through massive fraud, manipulation, and terror. Suspected MDC supporters were brutally beaten, bullied and robbed of their voter registration cards to prevent them from voting, often while police looked on. The government implemented the Public Order and Security Act to prohibit MDC rallies and to ban loudspeakers at the few permitted meetings. Further fraud occurred when officials reduced voter rolls in pro-MDC urban areas and augmented them in rural ZANU-PF strongholds. In the cities, state officials halved the usual number of polling places deliberately lengthened the wait for voters at the locations that did open, forcing to stand in the hot sun for hours, or go home without voting. Lines grew so long that the courts had to order an additional day of voting in the urban centers. In areas suspected of being sympathetic to the MDC, ZANU-PF set up militia camps near polling stations to better threaten potential voters. The government rejected the use of see-through ballot boxes and prevented election monitors from getting near polling stations. Widespread disparities in voting reports further delegitimized the election. In its petition to the courts to invalidate the election, the MDC showed there were nearly 186,000 "missing" votes and perhaps as many as 246,000 "additional" votes. Consensus opinion from civil society groups charged with assessing the electoral process agreed the vote was unfree and unfair.

The Politics of Survival

Zimbabwe under Robert Mugabe provides a model in political survival for authoritarian regimes. The first step is to take down opposition leadership. Mugabe put Morgan Tsvangirai and two other pro-democracy leaders, Welshman Ncube and Renson Gasela, on trial for treason on the charge of plotting to assassinate the president. The evidence was murky: a four-hour fuzzy, often inaudible, secretly video-taped meeting between Tsvangirai and Ari ben Menashe, an international fraudster who admits to receiving $100,000 from the Mugabe regime as a "retainer fee." The judge was Paddington Garwe, a Mugabe appointee installed after Mugabe had purged the higher courts of judges who ruled against farm seizures; Judge Garwe took over one of those farms. The possible sentence was the death penalty. Despite this, Judge Garwe cleared Tsvangirai of the treason charges in October 2004, saying the state had failed to prove its case against him. Yet the state appealed Judge Garwe's decision, and in May 2005, it reinstated a second treason charge over Tsvangirai's call for mass protests in June 2003. Finally, the courts dropped the charges in August 2005.

A number of parliamentary by-elections were held after 2000, to replace members who had died, or in one case, an opposition MP who fled the country in fear for his life. ZANU-PF sought to use these by-elections to reduce the MDC's representation below 50, in order to regain the two-thirds majority necessary to make constitutional changes on its own. After violent campaigns, the ZANU-PF won the first seven such races, and the MDC's parliamentary delegation was indeed reduced to 50.

Mugabe also aimed to render MDC local politicians powerless. Zimbabwe's two largest cities, Harare and Bulawayo, both had MDC mayors, but Mugabe appointed new governors to run them and required the mayors to report to the governors, effectively reducing the MDC's authority and political activity. To avoid future opposition victories in mayoral elections, the government announced it would gerrymander the cities' boundaries, folding districts of urban Harare or Bulawayo into rural areas, traditional ZANU-PF strongholds. The MDC continues to control many elected local government positions, but these politicians have little in the way of autonomy or resources.

Torture and arbitrary imprisonment became routine for regime opponents, and the Mugabe government continued its assault on the last two institutions still showing signs of independence: the press and the judiciary. The regim intimidated, abused, jailed or deported reporters both

Morgan Tsvangirai

domestic and foreign. The government tried to destroy the *Daily News* financially (prohibiting all government advertising on its pages) as well as physically (with the explosion at its presses). In the judiciary, some men of principle still, but infrequently, deliver independent rulings. Judge Benjamin Paradza, a black judge on Zimbabwe's High Court and former fighter in Mugabe's guerilla army, was such an independent voice, having overturned state eviction notices against white farmers whose land the government was trying to seize. The government had warned Paradza, when appointed to the bench, "not to embarrass the government with his court rulings." In mid-February 2003, Mugabe's police arrested Paradza (over constitutional prohibitions against the arrest of sitting jurists). The courts convicted Judge Paradza, widely regarded as the last independent judge in Zimbabwe, of alleged corruption in January 2006. He fled the country before sentencing, ultimately landing in New Zealand. In absentia, the courts sentenced him to three years in prison.

The regime also used food as a weapon. Zimbabwe was once known as the breadbasket of Africa for its rich and abundant agricultural production, but political misrule, economic mismanagement, corruption, and drought combined to create catastrophic food shortages in early 2003. More than half Zimbabwe's 12 million people were at risk of starvation. The government used its monopoly on grain imports to channel food to friends and supporters and interfered with international food aid intended for distribution to others. Rural villagers were threatened, cajoled, and denied food if there was any possibility they might support the MDC. Shopping centers controlled by

Zimbabwe

ZANU-PF often turned MDC supporters from bread lines. (Some MDC supporters put principle aside and bought ZANU-PF cards in order to eat.) Didymus Mutasa, ZANU-PF's organizing secretary, spoke ominously at an August 2002 rally saying: "We would be better off with only six million people, with our own people who support the liberation struggle. We don't want all these extra people."

Implausibly, the government announced a bumper harvest of maize in 2004 and told the international donor community it would not need emergency food, but it refused to let United Nations staff assess the state of the country's crops and food stocks. The global community dismissed the food production figures and the Catholic archbishop of Bulawayo, Pius Ncube, became a leading domestic critic. He claimed the government was "not telling the truth," noting that much land was lying fallow, and condemned the "evil and systematic denial of food to hungry people." By 2005, five million Zimbabweans were in urgent need of food aid.

As the March 2005 parliamentary elections approached, the MDC leadership and supporters (focused on survival) grew disorganized and dispirited, but politics within the ZANU-PF heated up as party elites jockeyed to secure the vice-presidential spot, seen as identifying the next-in-line to succeed Zimbabwe's aging dictator. The initial front-runner was Emmerson Mnangagwa, the speaker of parliament and Mugabe's link to ZANU-PF's economic empire, who seemed to have sewed up the support of provincial leaders in the race for party vice president. His enemies in the Politburo convoked an emergency meeting, and a faction led by the influential former defense chief, General Solomon Mujuru, bulldozed through a resolution calling for a woman to fill the vice presidency position. General Mujuru's intended candidate was his wife, Water Resources and Infrastructural Development Minister Joyce Mujuru, who ultimately became Vice-President in December 2004. Information Minister Jonathan Moyo, who had tried to rally provincial leaders to Mnangagwa, was reprimanded for opposing Mujuru, dropped from his party position, and denied the party's nomination in the March 2005 elections. He successfully ran as an independent, suggesting ZANU continued in disarray.

The March 2005 parliamentary election conformed to the usual Zimbabwean standards: ZANU-PF victory achieved through fraud, intimidation, ballot stuffing, and prevention of participation for many of the living coupled with active participation of the dead. Official results gave ZANU-PF 78 of 120 contested seats; MDC managed 41 seats, and former Mugabe information minister Jonathan Moyo took the lone independent seat in parliament.

May 2005 also saw the regime launch yet another assault on its citizens. Called Operation *Murambatsvina*, a Shona word meaning, "clean out the garbage," the government initiative was designed to rid Harare's shantytowns of illegal structures and informal businesses. *Murambatsvina* bulldozers leveled the cardboard shacks and solid cinder block homes of Harare's marginalized poor. Direct police action killed at least six people and many of the more vulnerable—children, AIDS victims, and the elderly—succumbed to exposure in Zimbabwe's midwinter cold. Hundreds of thousands of people were displaced as *Murambatsvina* was extended to other cities that were strongholds of opposition supporters. Of those affected by *Murambatsvina*, Police Commissioner Augustine Chihuri claimed they were a "crawling mass of maggots bent on destroying the economy." Many analysts saw the operation as a means of forcing potential opposition supporters out of the cities into rural areas where the government's control of the food supply would make them more acquiescent.

With the 30 seats President Mugabe appointed to the House of Assembly, ZANU-PF had a two-thirds majority in parliament and the party could change the constitution at will. It did so in late August 2005, amending the constitution for the 17th time since independence. With its 22 clauses, the Constitutional Amendment Bill stripped landowners of the right to appeal against government expropriation of their lands and allowed the government to deny passports to its enemies if deemed in the national interest.

The amendment bill also created a 66-seat Senate, which seemed to have no other purpose than to provide comfortable sinecures for aging ZANU-PF politicians. The body has 50 elected members and six appointed by President Mugabe; traditional chiefs would fill the remaining ten seats. The government quickly called elections for November 2005 (allowing senatorial salaries to begin as soon as possible), but voters were mostly indifferent. A record low turnout of less than 20% sent 43 ZANU-PF faithful to the new body, and only seven from the MDC.

The MDC was split over whether to boycott the senate election and these divisions further eroded its effectiveness as an opposition party. Party leader Tsvangirai called for a boycott, arguing the regime had never and would never permit a free and fair election. Others, largely Ndebele from the Southern provinces—savagely repressed by the Mugabe regime in the 1980s—refused to have ZANU-PF senators represent them and urged participation. In February 2006, the pro-senate faction elected as its leader Arthur Mutambara, a former student leader who had gone on to be a NASA research fellow. Mutambara said he returned to Zimbabwe after 15 years of exile in South Africa to provide new blood and leadership to the opposition, and he created a faction known as MDC-M (for MDC-Mutambara). As the rancorous division unfolded, ZANU-PF politicians gloated and rumors surfaced of the country's security services dispersing millions of Zimbabwean dollars to destabilize the opposition.

Mugabe launched further crackdowns in 2007. Physical assaults against MDC leaders and offices landed Morgan Tsvangirai and others in hospitals. Tsvangirai's bashed and bandaged head became an iconic image of Mugabe's repression. Mugabe also attacked on the last defenders of basic freedoms in the country: lawyers and churches. The regime arrested and charged two of Tsvangirai's defense attorneys with "defeating the course of justice." When colleagues protested the arrests, the police beat them up as well. Zimbabwe's Catholic bishops worded strong letters about how "the state responds with ever harsher oppression through arrests, detentions, banning orders, beatings and torture." Even more remarkably, they supported Morgan Tsvangirai's refusal to participate in the 2008 elections if they were conducted under the present constitution. "In order to avoid further bloodshed and avert a mass uprising," they wrote, "the nation needs a new people-driven constitution that will guide a democratic leadership chosen in free and fair elections." For Mugabe, the bishops were on a "dangerous path," and warned the Church: "Once [the bishops] turn political, we regard them as no longer spiritual and our relations with them would be conducted as if we were dealing with political entities."

Politicians in both the ruling ZANU-PF and the opposition MDC attempted to counter Mugabe as the country moved towards the elections for president and parliament in 2008. From within the ZANU-PF, Mugabe faced a potential battle for the party nomination from one of his former ministers, Simba Makoni. Mugabe supporters within ZANU-PF managed to exclude Makoni from the vote by citing obscure qualification rules; this led Makoni to declare as an independent candidate. Makoni was then menaced with violence by Mugabe backers (including the "war veterans" that had occupied farms across the country), who trotted out the usual accusations that Makoni was a pawn of the West and a stooge who was hoping to split the ZANU-PF vote to give the presidency to Tsvangirai.

Zimbabwe

Tsvangirai won the most votes in the first round of the presidential election on March 29, 2008, but the Zimbabwe Electoral Commission tallied this share at 47.9%, under the 50% needed to win the presidency outright. Mugabe was purported to win 43% of the vote, and Makoni over 8%. This result would ensure the necessity of a second-round runoff between Tsvangirai and Mugabe. The MDC cried foul, with Tsvangirai saying the presidency was being taken from him in a "scandalous daylight robbery."

In the parliamentary elections that same day, incredibly, the ZANU-PF lost its majority in the House of Assembly for the first time ever, taking only 99 of 210 seats. Tsvangirai's wing of the MDC (known as MDC-T) took 100 of the 210 seats and Arthur Mutambara's wing (the MDC-M) took 10 seats, with Jonathan Moyo retaining his sole independent seat. The two MDC factions ultimately agreed to cooperate, and this gave the combined MDC a clear parliamentary majority. In the Senate, meanwhile, ZANU-PF took 30 of the 60 elected seats (with MDC-T and MDC-M winning 24 and 6, respectively), and Mugabe's appointment powers over remaining seats gave it a majority there.

Tsvangirai insisted he was the outright winner of the presidential election but did not (for some time) rule out competing in the runoff. Third-place finisher Simba Makoni threw his support behind Tsvangirai, and it seemed clear the MDC candidate would receive the majority vote, if there were a free and fair election. This led the ZANU-PF and its allies to ramp up repression. Tsvangirai faced death threats and attacks on his office and person, in addition to legal impediments, such as accusations of treason. Similarly, MDC Secretary-General Tendai Biti was accused of treason in June 2008 upon his return to Zimbabwe from South Africa and was threatened with the death penalty for (among other trumped-up charges) alleging that Tsvangirai had won the presidency outright in the first round.

Just before the runoff scheduled for June 27, 2008, Tsvangirai pulled out of the runoff, claiming that Mugabe and his supporters had made a credible election impossible, that the election was rigged, and that preventing his victory in the first round of voting allowed the ZANU-PF time to manipulate the results. Mugabe won the sham election uncontested; most international observers did not recognize the result as legitimate. Tsvangirai too denounced the result, occasionally from his refuge in the Dutch Embassy, where he fled on at least two occasions in fear for his life. African countries attempted to reconcile the two parties and craft a government of national unity.

Artists at Shona Sculpture Park near Harare with sculpture of an AIDS victim
Photo by David Johns

"Power Sharing": the Inclusive Government and New Constitution

After years of recrimination and violence toward Mugabe's opponents from military and paramilitary personnel, power-sharing negotiations surprisingly culminated in an accord between the MDC and the ZANU-PF on August 16, 2008, known as the Global Political Agreement (GPA). According to the GPA, Morgan Tsvangirai agreed to serve as a Prime Minister alongside President Mugabe; he was sworn in as Prime Minister on February 11, 2009. Tsvangirai attempted to leverage his position to build a power base within Zimbabwe's political system, but Mugabe almost certainly had no interest in ceding real power as part of the "Inclusive Government." Rather, he hopes the Prime Minister's spot will contain his opponent and allow a shifting of blame if Zimbabwe spirals further. The suspicion between Mugabe and Tsvangirai worsened with a highway accident that injured Tsvangirai and claimed the life of his wife in early 2009. While Tsvangirai openly suggested there was no foul play, the MDC conducted its own investigation into the incident. At the end of 2011, President Magube declared his plan to run again in the upcoming election and called the current power sharing government a "monster."

From 2009 to 2011, Morgan Tsvangirai's stand on the ZANU-PF has vacillated between tame collaboration and outraged criticism. In June 2009, the government started reviewing its constitution, and Tsvangirai went on a tour of various European nations and the US to gain donor support. However, when US and EU delegates arrived in September 2009, they both retained their imposed sanctions; a month later, Mugabe called for a new start to relationships with the West. In January 2010, Tsvangirai again called for the easing of sanctions, arguing that the Inclusive Government had improved governance. In later 2010, however, Tsvangirai asserted that ZANU-PF was ignoring and sidelining the MDC, and that the Inclusive Government had once again become dominated by Mugabe's party. A joint press conference with Mugabe and Tsvangirai seemed to paper over the differences in December 2010, but March 2011 brought renewed criticism from the Prime Minister. In February 2012, the EU lifted sanctions against some Zimbabweans but kept restrictions against President Mugabe. The UN commissioner for human rights, Navi Pillay, later asked the West to lift sanctions from more prominent Zimbabweans because she argued that such sanctions were hurting the country's vulnerable citizens.

Zimbabwe

A largely symbolic shift in Zimbabwe's politics occurred when the country overwhelmingly approved a new constitution in a referendum in March 2013. Supported by about 95% of voters, the new constitution sets two-term limits (of five years each) for the presidency, removes the presidential veto power, and devolves power to 10 provinces, among other provisions. Since the two-term limit does not apply retroactively, Robert Mugabe is eligible to run for the presidency once again, and he has shown every intention of guaranteeing himself a victory. He has tried to schedule elections hastily for July 31, 2013, though the regional body known as SADC (the Southern African Development Community, which is offering financial support for the balloting) may be able to secure a postponement that would allow opponents to organize and contest the election. Morgan Tsvangirai has demanded several additional weeks (into August 2013) to prepare for the polling. In July 2013, Mugabe won a seventh term in office and his ZANU-PF party won three quarters of the seats in parliament; the Movement for Democratic Change deemed these results unfair and boycotted the opening of parliament two months later. In August 2013, southern African leaders asked the West to lift sanctions on Zimbabwe but the United States refused to do so until more significant political reforms occur in the country.

CONTEMPORARY THEMES

Zimbabwe's contemporary crisis is political in origin but has a wide range of consequences beyond the political sphere. The economy essentially collapsed from 2000 to 2008, with the GDP of Zimbabwe dropping over 54%, the worst performance of any African economy. In 2009, the GDP real growth rate was estimated at about 6%, a dramatic improvement reflecting recovery, but far short of what is needed to return the economy to pre-crisis levels. In 2010 and 2011, it appears the economy is recovering further, with industrial and agricultural production picking up from their low bases. In November 2011, the Kimberley Process (which regulates aspects of the global diamond trade) lifted a ban on exported diamonds from two of Zimbabwe's fields. In 2012, Zimplats (platinum producer) transferred a majority stake to Zimbabwean shareholders.

Zimbabwe's hyperinflation was likely the second worst in history (after Hungary immediately after World War II), with prices doubling about every 24 hours at its peak, and the current consequence is that the country no longer has its own currency. Most stores quit taking Zimbabwean dollars over the end of 2008, and the country ceased issuing the Zimbabwean dollar in 2009. Business first "dollarized" (accepting the American dollar, that is), and business is now conducted in a mix of US Dollars, South African Rand, Euros, British Pounds, and currencies of other neighboring African countries. An estimated 95% of the population lacks employment in the formal sector, and about 80% of the population lives on less than a dollar a day. Although the financial situation has stabilized to a degree, Zimbabwe still faces constraints on lending and investment because of investor concerns that proceeds will be misdirected toward Mugabe and regime elites. Many argue that the dire need for investment was the real motivation behind Mugabe's decision to accept the unity government. Still, as of 2014, Zimbabwe has made only a "token payment" on its arrears of international debt; the country has been in default on its payments to the International Monetary Fund since 1999. Both the United States and the European Union have sanctions on Mugabe and members of his inner circle, though the EU has lifted some of its sanctions, allowing Zimbabwean businesses to work with other European companies.

Traditionally, Zimbabwe earned its principal revenues from agricultural exports, but this sector suffered terribly in the crisis. Tobacco was the principal commercial export, but violence orchestrated by ZANU-PF disrupted the agricultural sector, especially food and tobacco. The government's confiscation of commercial farms for distribution to the landless has destroyed the most vibrant component of a desperate economy. The big farms not only kept Zimbabwe fed but produced 30% of its total exports. Tobacco was the single biggest earner of foreign exchange—about 35%—and traditionally contributed at least 15% of Zimbabwe's GDP, but exports of the crop fell by more than half in the few years after 2001.

The effects of the regime's disastrous economic policies were apparent in declining exports and loss of foreign exchange from the country's massively rich mineral deposits, which include gold, ferroalloys, nickel, copper, and chromium. Gold was traditionally Zimbabwe's second most important source of export earnings, but production there too declined over the decade of crisis. Zimbabwe first mined platinum in 1994 and became the world's second largest producer of platinum after South Africa; platinum emerged as one of the country's major foreign exchange earners. Even here, however, bad economic policy wrought havoc: in March 2006, the minister of mines announced that 51% of all foreign mining shares would be transferred to the government, half of them without compensation. The government extended this confiscation of assets without compensation to all foreign-owned business in mid-2007, further complicating investment. Given the state of the country's finances, little capital was available to expand production. In recent years, the Zimbabwean government has become increasingly strident about ownership of the nation's mines, and it moved in April 2014 to cut some companies from its mining fields.

Zimbabwe's economic implosion can be traced to Mugabe's violent land reform program, which failed miserably for several reasons. First, the program was rife with corruption: top government officials and well-connected ZANU-PF elites grabbed much of the best and richest farmland at the expense of the landless poor. Second, production declined as those resettled (estimated at over 300,000 families), had inadequate experience, equipment, and resources (to buy fertilizer, for example). Only a small percentage of the land listed has been cultivated, and that in rudimentary circumstances. Formerly productive lands have languished, leaving the country without food or the cash crops needed to purchase imports. Third, farm employment also declined, with several hundred thousand jobs disappearing, mostly for black farm workers.

Regardless of Mugabe's populist and racial appeals, black Zimbabweans are the majority of those who have suffered the agonies of hyperinflation, economic collapse, and dictatorial rule. For the remaining white Zimbabweans, especially commercial farmers, the future is still unsettled. From a peak more than 5,000 white-owned farms in 1980, the Commercial Farmers Union claims less than 200 are left as of 2010, and that number continues to decline as the remaining farmers depart, age, or die. After years of violence, the regime now sends conflicted messages. At his 85th Birthday in February 2009, Mugabe issued a thinly veiled threat to the few remaining white farmers to quickly vacate their farms; conversely, in 2010, the government considered compensating farmers for the land taken from them in invasions, likely in an attempt to reestablish a cash crop economy.

The government accumulated a growing external debt, much of which came from the regime's system of patronage and pre-electoral payoffs. Party faithful win lucrative appointments in state corporations, which almost inevitably lose money, and unbudgeted spending sprees usually precede tough elections. To avoid action by disgruntled civil servants, the government granted huge salary increases—between 200% and 300%—in April 2006. In 2009, the government's wage bill was well

Zimbabwe

over 50% of GDP. This necessitated further borrowing or printing more money. Only recently has inflation started to decrease, with a rate in June 2009 stated to be as low as 3%. By 2013 however, the inflation rate had increased to 8.5% and appeared to be increasing again as the Zimbabwean economy faltered.

Foreign capital flowed out of Zimbabwe during the crisis and inflation destroyed domestic savings as a possible source of investment. Without investment, job creation came to a near standstill and old jobs disappeared as the economy shrank. In these circumstances, the Mugabe regime adopted a "Look East" policy, turning to Asia (and particularly China) for investment. Chinese investment is famously indifferent to political or human rights concerns, and China is now Zimbabwe's biggest foreign investor and a major destination for exports; the country even granted Zimbabwe "Approved Destination" status for Chinese tourists, though Chinese tourists have been scarce.

Alongside Zimbabwe's many other tragedies, AIDS takes a horrific toll. UNICEF estimated that 1.2 million Zimbabweans were living with HIV/AIDS in 2009, or about 14.3% of the active adult population. This is one of the highest infection rates in the world, though it still represents a major decline from much higher estimates of HIV/AIDS prevalence a decade earlier. Unfortunately, the decline in AIDS rates may be due in large part to many AIDS deaths; at one point, an estimated 3,000 Zimbabweans a week were dying of HIV/AIDS, and the World Bank projected life expectancy fell by over 20 years (from 61.3 to only 41.1 years) in just the 15 years between 1989 and 2004. From this place among the worst indicators in the world, the estimate has recovered slightly, to over 55 years in the 2014 estimate. Left behind are AIDS orphans—estimated at more than one million since the 1980s—deprived of traditional family support and often abandoned to life on the streets of the larger cities. In the rural areas, the surviving elderly people have to care for the country's AIDS orphans. UNICEF estimates that nearly one in five Zimbabwean children was an orphan by 2010, 80% of them because of AIDSZimbabwe has also suffered other humanitarian crises in the last few years. A recent cholera outbreak infected over 60,000 people and killed almost 5,000; cholera is a curable disease, but most Zimbabweans cannot afford the (relatively inexpensive) treatment. Economic and political refugees fleeing the crisis have poured into neighboring South Africa (sometimes braving crocodile-infested waters to do so), over the mountains into Mozambique, and elsewhere. In late 2008, many of these refugees suffered at the hands of a wave of xenophobia throughout South Africa, though that appeared to have mostly ceased in 2009.

Like much of southern Africa, Zimbabwe is suffering from severe drought brought about by climate change with the primary corn crop affected turning the once grain-exporting nation into a food importer with assistance provided by major international food organizations and aid groups. With 60 percent of the population living in rural areas, the government has requested $2 billion in international aid as a formal state of disaster was declared in April 2024.

Outbreaks of protests in March 2025 reflected continued opposition to Zimbabwean President Emmerson Mnangagwa who came to power in 2017 after the army overthrew former President Robert Mugabe. Decrying what protestors insist is a corrupt political elite and a struggling economy, the protests were met by arrests, indicating a complete intolerance for any form of dissent. An internal split has roiled the ruling ZANU-PF party, which has been in power since independence in 1980. It pits supporters of Mnangagwa, who want him to rule until 2030, this despite a two-term constitutional limit that would see his term end in 2028, and those opposed. Blessed "Bombshell" Geza, a veteran of Zimbabwe's war of liberation from Great Britain, called for the mass demonstrations after being expelled from ZANU-PF in March after calling on the president to go and is now wanted by the police for charges including undermining the president's authority. He has accused the government of corruption and jailing dissenting voices without trial, and argued that Mnangagwa, who promised jobs and democracy, is surrounded by "criminals." For many Zimbabweans, the recent protests offered a moment of hope as they continue their push for economic and democratic reforms. Polls have been marred by violence, repression, and torture of opposition members, and election rigging. Under Mnangagwa, opposition party leaders have been jailed for gathering together while the country has faced an economic crisis for three decades with high food prices, loss of currency value, and low wages.

While residents of poor areas have lived without running water for more than 20 years and must buy drinking and bathing water from mobile storage tank providers, wealthy residents in Harare's leafy suburbs have cushioned themselves from the water shortages by drilling private boreholes. Across the country, most people have lost a stable income as the economic crisis is forcing businesses to close with people largely work in the informal economy as vendors, "pirate taxi" drivers (operating private cars without a business registration), waiters in back yard food courts, and as security guards. A common belief is that Mnangagwa is running the country like a family business, benefitting his family and friends, with individuals close to top government officials repeatedly winning government contracts and benefiting from taxpayers' money. Mnangagwa has appointed his son, David, as deputy finance minister and his nephew Tongai as the deputy tourism minister. People surrounding the president buy helicopters and private jets in a country where the majority are unemployed, roads are potholed, and hospitals don't have cancer radiotherapy machines. Dilapidated infrastructure is a constant issue; roads built in the 1990s have not been maintained, bus terminals are run down, and sewers are frequently blocked, posing a health hazard. At the same time, the government has offered to pay white landowners $3.5 billion in a compensation deal to get seized and back while also currying favor with the United States by ending tariffs while the country confronts a severe regional drought.

FUTURE CONSIDERATIONS

From one of the most promising countries in Africa, called the "breadbasket" of the continent in the 1980s, Zimbabwe has become one of the continent's basket cases. Political violence and the destruction of the productive (real) economy ruined the country in the decade up to 2009. Zimbabwe's immediate future is bleak, regardless of considerable foreign humanitarian aid at the end of the most brutal phase of the conflict.

Given the depth of the catastrophe of the mid-2000s, Zimbabwe bottomed-out by 2009, and the years since 2010 have

The sophisticated architecture of ancient Zimbabwe Photo by David Johns

Zimbabwe

actually seen some modest economic rebound. The adoption of international currencies has given an anchor to the economy, and the fact that aggression against commercial farmers was so complete means that any further damage that can be done pales in comparison. Zimbabwe actually had decent harvests in over the two years up to 2011, which has mitigated concerns about food security in the short-term. Despite recent fluctuations in crop production, investors such Econet Wireless have augmented crop production with its EcoFarmer initiative in 2014 which provides better agricultural technology and insurance for Zimbabwean farmers.

Meaningful political change in Zimbabwe is unlikely until Robert Mugabe is out of power and the ZANU-PF fundamentally alters course from his despotic rule. The advent of the Inclusive Government was just the start of possible positive change, but it has seen only modest results. The government still has not established a secure rule of law nor property rights, and it is not yet clear whether the new constitution will have any real impact on the conduct of Zimbabwean politics. The influence of Tsvangirai offered some glimpse of hope (at least relative to the atrocities of recent years), but human rights conditions remain precarious even today and tensions within the unity government fester. Though the regime claims to want to hold elections, stabilize the economy, and bring displaced people home, it is unlikely any substantial progress will be made until the MDC or other opposition movements gain greater leverage. Since such a genuine shift in power is anathema to top actors in the ZANU-PF, and since the Mugabe machine has various levers it can pull at election time, Zimbabwe's problems are unlikely to find satisfactory resolution in the short term. Some members of the international community appear to have concluded that economic aid will not make significant change until Mugabe passes from the scene. Yet the death of one authoritarian leader seldom leads to a peaceful and positive transition. Although Tsvangirai and his MDC once appeared capable of providing a viable opposition for Zimbabwe, recent internal conflicts have made that unlikely; in 2014, the MDC suspended Tsvangirai for "fascist tendencies". Zimbabwe is in dire straits at the present moment, and most hopes center on the death of Robert Mugabe eventually facilitating slow change that will only occur over time.

Web Sites and Selected Bibliography of Key English Language Sources

Web Sites and Selected Bibliography of Key English Language Sources

General Web Sites

Africa South of the Sahara: Selected Internet resources http://www-sul.stanford.edu/depts/ssrg/africa/guide.html. Prepared by Karen Fung for the Information and Communication Technology Group (ICTG), African Studies Association, USA. A comprehensive introduction.

African Studies Internet Resources. Prepared by Joseph Caruso, Columbia University. http://www.columbia.edu/cu/lweb/indiv/africa/cuvl/

An A–Z of African Studies on the Internet. Prepared by Peter Limb, Michigan State University. http://www.lib.msu.edu/limb/a-z/az.html

International Governmental Agency Sources:

UN Conference of Trade and Development http://www.unctad.org/. Statistical data on Least Developed Countries and discussion of poverty strategies.

UN Development Programme. *Human Development Reports*. http://hdr.undp.org. Provides important material on country achievement on life expectancy, educational attainment and adjusted real income.

UN Economic Commission for Africa. http://www.uneca.org/. ECA is the regional arm of the United Nations, mandated to support the economic and social development of its 53 member states. Its annual economic reports are useful.

Integrated Regional Information Networks (IRIN), part of the UN Office for the Coordination of Humanitarian Affairs (OCHA): http://www.irinnews.org/. Current news on humanitarian issues. Its focus reports and specials often contain useful political insights.

The International Monetary Fund (IMF). http://imf.org/external/country/index.htm. Useful material on country projects and debt alleviation.

World Bank in Africa. http://www.worldbank.org/afr/. Useful statistical material and poverty alleviation projects.

U.S. Government Sources:

Central Intelligence Agency (CIA) *The World Factbook* http://www.cia.gov/cia/publications/factbook/index.html. Basic material on land, people, government and economy for each country.

Department of Energy. Energy Information Agency. http://www.eia.doe.gov/. Country analyses provide useful material on energy resources of producing states.

State Department:

Bureau of African Affairs: http://www.state.gov/p/af/. Particularly useful are its *Background Notes* for individual countries.

Bureau of Democracy, Human Rights, and Labor: Annual *Human Rights Reports* for each country: http://www.state.gov/g/drl/hr/.

Annual *International Religious Freedom Reports*: http://www.state.gov/g/drl/rls/irf/.

Bureau for International Narcotics and Law Enforcement Affairs Annual *International Narcotics Control Strategy Report*: http://www.state.gov/g/inl/rls/nrcrpt/.

Counterterrorism Office. Issues the annual *Patterns of Global Terrorism* report: http://www.state.gov/s/ct/

Non-governmental Organizations (NGOs)

Amnesty International http://amnesty.org/. The human rights situation country by country.

Freedom House. www.freedomhouse.org.

Global Witness. http://globalwitness.org/. The group is dedicated to breaking the links between natural resources, conflict, and corruption. Its reports on trafficking conflict diamonds and illegal timber cutting provide in-depth studies of those linkages.

Human Rights Watch. http://hrw.org/. Excellent reports on a range of human rights issues.

Institute for Security Studies. http://www.iss.co.za/. A South African research institute. Excellent studies, mostly on Southern African issues.

International Crisis Group (ICG). http://www.crisisweb.org/. An independent, nonprofit, multinational think tank. Its reports on Central, Southern, and West Africa, as well as the Horn of Africa are packed with information and insight.

Transparency International. http://www.transparency.org. A German NGO. Its annual *Global Corruption Report* is in English.

News Agencies

www.economist.com. *The Economist* magazine is the sole major newsweekly with regular coverage of African affairs.

http://news.bbc.co.uk. BBC news has more comprehensive coverage of Africa than major U.S.-based papers such as the *New York Times*, *Washington Post* or *Los Angeles Times*. North African news is often covered under its "Middle East" rubric.

http://allafrica.com/. Republishes current news stories and topical features from some 100 African newspapers and agencies. For detailed African news, the best site.

Books: General

Adams, William and Andrew Goudie, eds. *Physical Geography of Africa*. New York: Oxford University Press, 1999.

Ali, Taisier M. and Robert O. Matthews, eds. *Civil Wars in Africa: Roots and Resolution*. Montreal: McGill-Queen's University Press, 1999.

Anshan, L. *A History of Chinese Overseas in Africa*. Beijing: Chinese Overseas Publishing, 2000.

Appiah, Kwame Anthony. *In My Father's House: Africa in the Philosophy of Culture*. Oxford: Oxford University Press, 1992.

Ayittey, George B. N. *Africa Unchained: The Blueprint for Africa's Future*. New York: Palgrave, 2005.

Bates, Robert. *Markets and States in Tropical Africa: The Political Basis of Agricultural Policies*. Berkeley: University of California Press.

Bates, Robert. *When Things Fell Apart: State Failure in Late-Century Africa*. Cambridge: Cambridge University Press, 2008.

Bayart, Jean-Francois, Stephen Ellis, and Béatrice Hibou. *The Criminalization of the State in Africa*. Oxford: James Currey, 1999.

Bayart, Jean-Francois. *The State in Africa: The Politics of the Belly*. New York: Longman, 1993.

Berkeley, Bill. *The Graves are Not Yet Full: Race, Tribe, and Power in the Heart of Africa*. New York: Basic Books, 2001.

Boardman, Henry G. *Africa's Silk Road: China and India's New Economic Frontier*. Washington: World Bank Publications, 2007.

Bøås, Morten, and Kevin C. Dunn. *African Guerillas: Raging Against the Machine*. Boulder, CO: Lynne Rienner, 2007.

Boone, Catherine. *Political Topographies of the African State: Territorial Authority and Institutional Choice*. Cambridge: Cambridge University Press, 2003.

Bratton, Michael and Nicolas van de Walle. *Democratic Experiments in Africa: Regime Transitiosn in Comparative Perspective*. Cambridge: Cambridge University Press, 1997.

Chabal, Patrick and Jean-Pascal Daloz. *Africa Works: Disorder as Political Instrument*. Oxford: James Currey, 1999.

Chabal, Patrick, et al. *The History of Postcolonial Lusophone Africa*. Bloomington: Indiana University Press, 2002.

Bibliography

Chazan, Naomi, Lewis, Peter, Mortimer, Robert A., Rothchild, Donald and Stedman, Stephen John. *Politics and Society in Contemporary Africa*. Boulder, CO: Lynne Rienner, 1999.

Collier, Paul. *The Bottom Billion: Why the Poorest Countries are Failing and What Can Be Done About It*. Oxford: Oxford University Press, 2007.

Cowen, Michael and Liisa Laakso, eds. *Multi-Party Elections in Africa*. New York: Palgrave, 2002.

Davidson, Basil. *Africa in History [Revised and Expanded Edition]*. New York: Touchstone, 1995.

Dickovick, J. Tyler. *Decentralization and Recentralization in the Developing World: Case Studies from Africa and Latin America*. University Park: Penn State University Press, 2011.

Dowden, Richard. *Africa: Altered States, Ordinary Miracles*. New York: Public Affairs, 2010.

Easterly, William R. *The White Man's Burden: Why the West's Efforts to Aid the Rest Have done So Much Ill and So Little Good*. New York: Penguin, 2006.

Ellis, Stephen and Gerrie Ter Haar. *Religious Thought and Political Practice in Africa*. London: Hurst, 2004.

Englebert, Pierre. *State Legitimacy and Development in Africa*. Boulder, CO: Lynne Rienner, 2002.

Englebert, Pierre. *Africa: Unity, Sovereignty, and Sorrow*. Boulder, CO: Lynne Rienner, 2009.

Fietzek, Gerti. *Under Siege: Four African Cities—Freetown, Johannesburg, Kinshasa, Lagos*. Ostfildern-Ruit, Germany: Hatje Cantz, Verlag, 2002. (Distributed in USA by Art Publishers).

French, Howard W. *A Continent for the Taking: The Tragedy and Hope of Africa*. New York: Alfred A. Knopf, 2004.

Freund, Bill. *The Making of Contemporary Africa: The Development of African Society Since 1800*. Boulder, CO: Lynne Rienner, 1998.

Gikandi, Simon, ed. *Encyclopedia of African Literature*. London: Routledge, 2003.

Good, Kenneth. *The Liberal Model and Africa: Elites Against Democracy*. New York: Palgrave, 2002.

Guest, Robert. *The Shackled Continent: Power, Corruption and African Lives*. Washington, DC: Smithsonian Institution Press, 2004.

Gyimah-Boadi, E., ed. *Democratic Reform in Africa: The Quality of Progress*. Boulder, CO: Lynne Rienner, 2004.

Harbeson, John W. and Rothchild, Donald, eds. *Africa in World Politics: Reforming Political Order*. Boulder, CO: Westview Press, 2008.

Herbst, Jeffrey. *States and Power in Africa: Comparative Lessons in Authority and Control*. Princeton, NJ: Princeton University Press, 2000.

Hunter, Susan. *Black Death. AIDS in Africa*. NY: Palgrave, 2003.

Hyden, Goran. *African Politics in Comparative Perspective*. Cambridge: Cambridge University Press, 2006.

Joseph, Richard, ed. *State, Conflict, and Democracy in Africa*. Boulder, CO: Lynne Rienner, 1999.

Joseph, Richard and Gillies, Alexandra, eds. *Smart Aid for African Development*. Boulder, CO: Lynne Rienner, 2009.

Kalipeni, Ezekiel, Susan Craddock, Joseph R. Oppong, and Jayati Ghosh, eds. *HIV and AIDS in Africa: Beyond Epidemiology*. London, Blackwell Publishers, 2004.

Karl, Terry Lynn. *The Paradox Of Plenty: Oil Booms and Petro-States*. Berkeley: University of California Press, 1997. [Though the work focuses on Venezuela, it is abundantly relevant to Africa's petro-states.]

Keppel, Gilles. *Jihad: The Trail of Political Islam*. Cambridge, MA: Belknap Press of Harvard University Press, 2002.

Kevane, Michael. *Woman and Development in Africa: How Gender Works*. Boulder, CO: Lynne Rienner, 2004.

Larémont, Ricardo René, ed. *Borders, Nationalism, and the African State*. Boulder, CO: Lynne Rienner, 2005.

Larémont, Ricardo René, ed. *The Causes of War and the Consequences of Peacekeeping in Africa*. Portsmouth, NH: Heinemann, 2002.

Le Vine, Victor T. *Politics in Francophone Africa*. Boulder, CO: Lynne Rienner, 2004.

Lewis, Peter, ed. *Africa: Dilemmas of Development and Change*. Boulder, CO: Westview Press, 1998.

Lindsay, Lisa A. and Stephan F. Miescher, eds. *Men and Masculinities in Modern Africa*. Portsmouth, NH: Heinemann, 2003.

Lindberg, Staffan. *Democracy and Elections in Africa*. Baltimore: Johns Hopkins University Press, 2006.

Mamdani, Mahmood. *Citizen and Subject: Contemporary Africa and the Legacy of Late Colonialism*. Princeton, NJ: Princeton University Press, 1996.

Meredith, Martin. *The Fate of Africa: From the Hopes of Freedom to the Heart of Despair. A History of 50 Years of Independence*. New York: Public Affairs, 2005.

Miers, Suzanne and Martin A. Klein. *Slavery and Colonial Rule in Africa*. Portland, OR: Frank Cass Publishers, 1999.

Miles, William F.S. *Political Islam in West Africa: State-Society Relations Transformed*. Boulder, CO: Lynne Rienner, 2007.

Morris, James. *Butabu: Adobe Architecture of West Africa*. NY: Princeton Architectural Press, 2004.

Moss, Todd J. *African Development: Making Sense of the Issues and Actors*. Boulder, CO: Lynne Rienner, 2007.

Moyo, Dambisa. *Dead Aid: Why Aid is Not Working and How there is a Better Way for Africa*. New York: Farrar, Straus, and Giroux, 2009.

O'Connor. David and Andrew Reid, eds. *Ancient Egypt in Africa*. London: University College London Press, 2003.

Olivier de Sardan, Jean Pierre. *Anthropology and Development: Understanding Contemporary Social Change*. London: Zed Books, 2005.

Patterson, Amy. *The Politics of AIDS in Africa*. Boulder, CO: Lynne Rienner, 2006.

Posner, Daniel. *Institutions and Ethnic Politics in Africa*. Cambridge: Cambridge University Press, 2005.

Renner, Michael. *The Anatomy of Resource Wars*. Washington, D.C.: Worldwatch Institute, 2002.

Reno, William. *Warlord Politics and African States*. Boulder, CO: Lynne Rienner, 1999.

Rosander, Eva Evers, and David Westerlund, eds. *African Islam and Islam in Africa: Encounters between Sufis and Islamists*. Athens, OH: Ohio University Press, 1997.

Rotberg, Robert I., ed. *State Failure and State Weakness in a Time of Terror*. Washington, DC: Brookings Institution Press, 2003.

Rothchild, Donald. *Managing Ethnic Conflict in Africa: Pressures and Incentives for Cooperation*. Washington, DC: Brookings Institution, 1997.

Schatzberg, Michael G. *Political Legitimacy in Middle Africa: Father, Family, Food*. Bloomington: Indiana University Press, 2001.

Segal, Ronald. *Islam's Black Slaves: The Other Black Diaspora*. New York: Farrar, Straus and Giroux, 2001.

Singer, P. W. (Peter Warren) *Corporate Warriors: The Rise of the Privatized Military Industry*. Ithaca: Cornell University Press, 2003.

Van de Walle, Nicolas. *African Economies and the Politics of Permanent Crisis, 1979–1999*. Cambridge: Cambridge University Press, 2001.

Villalón, Leonardo and Peter VonDoepp. *The Fate of Africa's Democratic Experiments: Elites and Institutions*. Bloomington, IN: University of Indiana Press, 2005.

Visonà, Monica Blackmun, et al. *A History of Art in Africa*. New York: Harry Abrams, Inc., 2001.

Vogel, Joseph O., ed. *The Encyclopedia of Pre-colonial Africa: Archaeology, History, Languages, Cultures, and Environment*. Walnut Creek, CA: Alta Mira Press, 1997.

Bibliography

Widner, Jennifer, ed. *Economic Change and Political Liberalization in Sub-Saharan Africa*. Baltimore: Johns Hopkins University Press, 1994.

World Bank. *Breaking the Conflict Trap: Civil War and Development Policy*. New York: Oxford University Press, 2003.

World Bank. *World Development Report 1997: The State in a Changing World*. New York: Oxford University Press, 1997.

World Bank. *World Development Report 2003: Sustainable Development in a Dynamic World: Transforming Institutions, Growth, and Quality of Life*. New York: Oxford University Press, 2002.

World Bank. *World Development Report 2005: Investment Climate, Growth, and Poverty*. New York: Oxford University Press, 2004.

Wunsch, James and Dele Olowu, eds. *The Failure of the Centralized State: Institutions and Self-Governance in Africa*. San Francisco: Institute for Contemporary Studies, 1995.

Young, Crawford. *The African Colonial State in Comparative Perspective*. New Haven, CT: Yale University Press, 1994.

Young, Crawford. *The Politics of Cultural Pluralism*. Madison, WI: University of Wisconsin Press, 1976.

Zartman, I. William, ed. *Collapsed States: The Disintegration and Restoration of Legitimate Authority*. Boulder, CO: Lynne Rienner, 1995.

Zeleza, Paul Tiyambe, ed. *Encyclopedia of Twentieth-Century African History*. London and New York: Routledge, 2002.

Zell, Hans. *The African Studies Companion: A Guide to Information Sources*. Third Edition. Locharron, Scotland, Hans Zell Publishing Consultants: 2003.

West Africa

Achebe, Chinua. *Home and Exile*. Oxford: Oxford University Press, 2000.

Amadi, L.O. *Dictionary of Nigerian History: from Aba to Zazzau*. Bethesda, MD: International Scholars Publications, 1998.

Beah, Ishmael. *A Long Way Home: Memoirs of a Boy Soldier*. New York: Farrar, Straus and Giroux, 2007.

Clapham, Christopher S. *African Guerrillas*. Bloomington, IN: Indiana University Press, 1998.

Clark, Andrew Francis and Lucie Colvin Phillips. *Historical Dictionary of Senegal*. Lanham, MD: Scarecrow Press, 1994.

Daniels, Morna. *Côte d'Ivoire*. Santa Barbara, CA: ABC-CLIO, 1996.

Decalo, Samuel. *Historical Dictionary of Benin*. Lanham, MD: Scarecrow Press, 1995.

Decalo, Samuel. *Historical Dictionary of Niger*. Lanham, MD: Scarecrow Press, 1996.

Decalo, Samuel. *Historical Dictionary of Togo*. Lanham, MD: Scarecrow Press, 3rd ed. 1996.

Dunn, D. Elwood. *Historical Dictionary of Liberia*. Lanham, MD: Scarecrow Press, 2001.

Eades, J.S. and Christopher Allen. *Benin*. Santa Barbara, CA: ABC-CLIO, 1997.

Falola, Toyin. *The History of Nigeria*. Westport, CT: Greenwood Publishing Group, 1999.

Farah, Douglas. *Blood from stones: the secret financial network of terror*. New York: Broadway Books, 2004

Ferme, Mariane C. *The Underneath of Things: Violence, History and the Everyday in Sierra Leone*. Berkeley: University of California Press, 2001.

Forrest, Joshua B. *Lineages of State Fragility: Rural Civil Society in Guinea-Bissau*. Athens, OH: Ohio University Press, 2003.

Gifford, Paul. *Ghana's New Christianity: Pentecostalism in a Globalising African Economy*. Bloomington: Indiana University Press, 2004.

Hirsch, John L. *Sierra Leone: Diamonds and the Struggle for Democracy*. Boulder, CO: Lynne Rienner, 2001.

Huband, Mark. *The Liberian Civil War*. Portland, OR: International Specialized Book Services, 1998.

Hughes, Arnold. *Historical Dictionary of The Gambia*. 3rd ed. Lanham, MD: Scarecrow Press, 1999.

Human Rights Watch. *Chop Fine: The Human Rights Impact of Local Government Corruption in Rivers State*. Nigeria. New York: Human Rights Watch, 2007.

Human Rights Watch. *How to Fight, How to Kill*. New York: Human Rights Watch, 2004.

Human Rights Watch. *The Price of Oil: Corporate Responsibility and Human Rights Violations in Nigeria's Oil Producing Communities*. New York: Human Rights Watch, 1999.

Human Rights Watch. *Revenge in the Name of Religion: The Cycle of Violence in Plateau and Kano States*. New York: Human Rights Watch, 2005.

Human Rights Watch. *Rivers and Blood: Guns, Oil and Power in Nigeria's Rivers State*. New York: Human Rights Watch, 2005.

International Crisis Group. *Guinea: Change or Chaos*. Brussels: ICG, February 2007. Available online at http://www.crisisweb.org/

International Crisis Group. *Nigeria's Faltering Federal Experiment*. Brussels: ICG, October 2006. Available online at www.crisisweb.org/

Kourouma, Ahmadou. *Waiting for the Vote of the Wild Animals*. Translated by Carrol F. Coates. Charlottesville: University Press of Virginia, 2001.

Lobban, Richard. *Cape Verde: Crioulo Colony to Independent Nation*. Boulder CO: Westview Press, 1995.

Lobban, Richard. *Historical Dictionary of Cape Verde*. Lanham MD: Scarecrow Press, 3rd ed. 1995.

Maier, Karl. *This House Has Fallen: A Journey Through Nigeria's Heart of Darkness*. New York: Public Affairs, 2000.

Mbacké, Khadim. *Sufism and Religious Brotherhoods in Senegal*. Interpretive translation by Eric Ross; edited by John Hunwick. Princeton, NJ: Markus Wiener Publishers, 2005.

McFarland, Daniel M. *Historical Dictionary of Burkina Faso*. Lanham, MD: Scarecrow Press, 1998.

Mundt, Robert J. *Historical Dictionary of Côte d'Ivoire (the Ivory Coast)*. Lanham, MD: Scarecrow Press, 1995.

Obi, Cyril I. *The Changing Forms of Identity. Politics in Nigeria under Economic Adjustment: The Case of Oil Minorities Movement of the Niger Delta*. Report No. 119. Uppsala: Nordic African Institute, 2001.

Okonta, Ike and Douglas Oronto. *Where Vultures Feast: Shell, Human Rights, and Oil in the Niger Delta*. San Francisco: Sierra Club Books, 2001.

Paden, John N. *Muslim Civic Cultures and Conflict Resolution. The Challenge of Democratic Federalism in Nigeria*. Washington: Brookings, 2005.

Pham, John-Peter. *Child Soldiers, Adult Interests: The Global Dimensions of the Sierra Leonean Tragedy*. New York: Nova Science, 2005.

Richards, Paul. *Fighting for the Rainforest: War, Youth and Resources in Sierra Leone*. Portsmouth, NH: Heinemann, 1996.

Rotberg, Robert I., ed. *Crafting the New Nigeria: Confronting the Challenges*. Boulder, CO: Lynne Rienner, 2004.

Rovine, Victoria L. *Bogolan: Shaping Culture through Cloth in Contemporary Mali*. Washington: Smithsonian Books, 2001.

Söderling, Ludwig and J. Clark Leith. *Ghana-Long Term Growth, Atrophy and Stunted Recovery: Research Report No. 125*. Uppsala, Sweden: The Nordic Africa Institute, 2003.

Suberu, Rotimi T. *Federalism and Ethnic Conflict in Nigeria*. Washington, DC: United States Institute of Peace Press, 2001.

Central Africa

Adelman, Howard and Govind C. Rao, eds. *War and Peace in Zaire/Congo: Analyzing and Evaluating Intervention: 1996–1997*. Trenton, NJ: Africa World Press, 2004.

Ballentine, Karen and Michael Nest, eds. *The Democratic Republic of Congo: Economic Dimensions of War and Peace*. Boulder, CO: Lynne Rienner, 2005

Bibliography

Azevedo, Mario. *Chad: A Nation in Search of Its Future.* Boulder, CO: Westview Press, 1997.

Bocquené, Henri. *Memoirs of a Mbororo: The Life of Ndudi Umaru: Fulani Nomad of Cameroon.* New York: Berghahn Books, 2002.

Burr, J. Millard and Robert O. Collins. *Africa's Thirty Years' War: Chad, Libya, and the Sudan, 1963–1993.* Boulder, CO: Westview Press, 1999.

Dallaire, Romeo. *Shake Hands with the Devil: The Failure of Humanity in Rwanda.* New York: Random House, 2003.

Decalo, Samuel. *Historical Dictionary of Chad.* Lanham, MD: Scarecrow Press, 1997.

DeLancey, Mark W. *Historical Dictionary of the Republic of Cameroon.* Lanham, MD: Scarecrow Press, 3rd. ed. 2000.

De Witte, Ludo. *The Assassination of Lumumba.* Trans. Ann Wright and Renée Fenby. New York: Verso Books, 2003.

Doom, Ruddy and Jan Gorus, eds. *Politics of Identity and Economics of Conflict in the Great Lakes Region.* Brussels: VUB University Press, 2000.

Dunn, Kevin. *Imagining the Congo: The International Relations of Identity.* NY: Palgrave, 2003.

Eggers, Ellen K. *Historical Dictionary of Burundi.* Lanham, MD: Scarecrow Press, 1997.

Gondola, Ch. Didier. *The History of Congo.* Westport, CT: Greenwood Press, 2002.

Fegley, Randall. *Equatorial Guinea.* Santa Barbara, CA: ABC-CLIO, 1992.

Global Witness. *Digging in Corruption: Fraud, abuse and exploitation in Katanga's copper and cobalt Mines.* Washington, DC: Global Witness Publishing, 2006. Available on line.

Gourevitch, Philip. *We Wish to Inform You That Tomorrow We Will Be Killed With Our Families: Stories from Rwanda.* New York: Farrar, Straus, Giroux, 1998.

Gross, Jean-Germain, ed. *Cameroon. Politics and Society in Critical Perspectives.* Lanham, MD: University Press of America, 2003.

Hatzfeld, Jean. *Into the Quick of Life.* London: Serpent's Tail, 2005.

Hatzfeld, Jean. *Machete Season.* New York: Farrar, Strauss, Giroux, 2005.

Hochschild, Adam. *King Leopold's Ghost.* New York: Houghton Mifflin Co., 1999.

Human Rights Watch. *Closing Doors? The Narrowing of Democratic Space in Burundi.* New York: Human Rights Watch, 2010.

Human Rights Watch. *The Curse of Gold.* New York: Human Rights Watch, 2005.

Human Rights Watch. *Leave None to Tell the Story: Genocide in Rwanda.* New York: Human Rights Watch, 1999 [Reissued April 2004 with update].

Human Rights Watch. *Some Transparency, No Accountability: The Use of Oil Revenue in Angola and Its Impact on Human Rights.* New York: Human Rights Watch, 2004.

Human Rights Watch. *Sudan, Oil, and Human Rights.* New York: Human Rights Watch, 2003.

Human Rights Watch. *"They Came Here to Kill Us:" Militia Attacks and Ethnic Targeting of Civilians in Eastern Chad.* New York: Human Rights Watch, 2007.

International Crisis Group. *Burundi: Democracy and Peace at Risk.* Brussels: ICG, November 2006.

Jefremovas, Villia. *Brickyards to Graveyards: From Production to Genocide in Rwanda.* New York: State University of New York Press, 2002.

Kalck, Pierre and Thomas O'Toole. *Historical Dictionary of the Central African Republic.* Lanham, MD: Scarecrow Press, 2nd ed. 1992.

Khadiagala, Gilbert M. *Security Dynamics in Africa's Great Lakes Region.* Boulder, CO: Lynne Rienner, 2006.

Lemarchand, René. *Burundi: Ethnocide as Discourse and Practice.* New York: Cambridge University Press, 1994.

Liniger-Goumaz, Max. *Historical Dictionary of Equatorial Guinea.* Lanham, MD: Scarecrow Press, 1998.

Liniger-Goumaz, Max. *Small Is Not Always Beautiful: The Story of Equatorial Guinea.* London: Hurst, 1988.

MacGaffey, Wyatt. *Kongo Political Culture: The Conceptual Challenge of the Particular.* Bloomington: Indiana University Press, 2000.

Mamdani, Mahmood. *When Victims Become Killers: Colonialism, Nativism and the Genocide in Rwanda.* Princeton: Princeton University Press, 2001.

Melvern, Linda. *Conspiracy to Murder: The Rwanda Genocide and the International Community.* London: Verso Books, 2004.

Nzongola-Ntalaja, Georges. *The Congo. From Leopold to Kabila: A People's History.* New York: Palgrave, 2002.

Peterson, Dale. *Eating Apes.* California Studies in Food and Culture, 6. Berkeley: University of California Press, 2003.

Peterson, Scott. *Me against My Brother: at War in Somalia, Sudan and Rwanda.* New York: Routledge, 2000.

Petterson, Donald. *Inside Sudan: Political Islam, Conflict, and Catastrophe.* Rev. ed. Boulder, CO: Westview Press, 2003.

Popenoe, Rebecca. *Feeding Desire: Fatness, Beauty, and Sexuality among a Saharan People.* New York: Routledge, 2004.

Pottier, Johan, et al. eds. *Re-Imagining Rwanda: Conflict, Survival and Disinformation in the Late Twentieth Century.* Cambridge: Cambridge University Press, 2002.

Review of African Political Economy, 29:93/94 (September/December 2002). Special issue devoted to "State Failure in the Congo: Perceptions & Realities."

Roberts, Adam. *The Wonga Coup: Guns, Thugs and a Ruthless Determination to Create Mayhem in an Oil-Rich Corner of Africa.* New York: Public Affairs, 2006.

Scroggins, Deborah. *Emma's War.* New York: Pantheon, 2002.

Trefon, Theodore, ed. *Reinventing Order in the Congo: How People Respond to State Failure in Kinshasa.* London: Zed Books, 2004.

Walker, John Frederick. *A Certain Curve of Horn: The Hundred-Year Quest for The Giant Sable Antelope of Angola.* New York: Atlantic Monthly Press, 2002.

Wallis, Andrew. *Silent Accomplice: The Untold Story of France's Role in the Rwandan Genocide.* London: I.B. Tauris, 2006.

Warburg, Gabriel. *Islam, Sectarianism, and Politics in Sudan Since the Mahdiyya.* Madison: University of Wisconsin Press, 2003.

Wrong, Michela. *In the Footsteps of Mr. Kurtz: Living on the Brink of Disaster in the Congo.* New York: HarperCollins, 2001.

Zamponi, Lynda F. *Niger.* Santa Barbara: ABC-CLIO, 1994.

Southern Africa

Allen, John. *Rabble-Rouser for Peace: The Authorized Biography of Desmond Tutu.* New York: Free Press, 2006.

Ashforth, Adam Philip. *Witchcraft, Violence and Democracy in South Africa.* Chicago: Chicago University Press, 2004.

Barber, James. *Mandela's World: The International Dimension of South Africa's Political Revolution 1990–99.* Athens, OH: Ohio University Press, 2004.

Bauer, Gretchen and Scott D. Taylor. *Politics in Southern Africa: State and Society in Transition.* Boulder, CO: Lynne Rienner, 2004.

Beck, Roger B. *The History of South Africa.* Westport, CT: Greenwood Publishing Group, 2000.

Blair, David. *Degrees in Violence: Robert Mugabe and the Struggle for Power in Zimbabwe.* London and New York: Continuum Books, 2002.

Bond, Patrick. *Elite Transition: From Apartheid to Neoliberalism in South Africa.* 2nd edition. Scottsville, SA: University of KwaZulu-Natal Press, 2006.

Booth, Alan R. *Historical Dictionary of Swaziland.* Lanham, MD: Scarecrow Press, 2000.

Boraine, Alex. *A Country Unmasked: Inside South Africa's Truth and Reconciliation Commission.* New York: Oxford University Press, 2000.

Bowen, Merle L. *The State Against the Peasantry: Rural Struggles in Colonial and*

Bibliography

Postcolonial Mozambique. Charlottesville: University Press of Virginia, 2000.

Campbell, Catherine. *Letting Them Die: Why HIV/AIDS Prevention Programmes Fail*. Oxford: James Currey, 2003.

Chan, Stephen. *Citizen of Africa: Conversations with Morgan Tsvangirai*. Cape Town: Fingerprint Co-operative, 2005.

Cilliers, Jakkie and Christian Dietrich, eds. *Angola's War Economy: The Role of Diamonds*. Pretoria, SA: Institute for Security Studies, 2000.

Crais, Clifton. *The Politics of Evil: Magic, State Power and Political Imagination in South Africa*. Cambridge: Cambridge University Press, 2002.

Crosby, Cynthia A. *Historical Dictionary of Malawi*. Lanham, MD: Scarecrow Press, 1993.

Eades, Lindsay Michie. *The End of Apartheid in South Africa*. Westport, CT: Greenwood Publishing Group, 1999.

Englund, Harri, ed. *A Democracy of Chameleons: Politics and Culture in the New Malawi*. Uppsala: The Nordic African Institute, 2002.

Forester, Peter G. and Bongani J. Nsibande, eds. *Swaziland: Contemporary Social and Economic Issues*. Aldershot: Ashgate Publishing, 2000.

Galli, Rosemary. *People's Spaces and State Spaces: Land and Governance in Mozambique*. Lanham, MD: Rowman & Littlefield Publishers, 2003.

Gillis, D. Hugh. *The Kingdom of Swaziland: Studies in Political History*. Westport, CT: Greenwood Publishing Group, 1999.

Giliomee, Hermann. *The Afrikaners: Biography of a People*. Charlottesville: University of Virginia, 2003.

Graybill, Lyn S. *Truth and Reconciliation in South Africa: Miracle or Model?* Boulder, CO: Lynne Rienner, 2002.

Grotpeter, John J. *Historical Dictionary of Zambia*. Lanham, MD: Scarecrow Press, 1998.

Gukurahundi in Zimbabwe: A Report on the Disturbances in Matabeleland and the Midlands 1980–1988. Johannesburg: Jacana Media, 2007.

Gumede, William Mervin. *Thabo Mbeki and the Battle for the Soul of the ANC*. Capetown, SA: Zebra Press, 2005.

Hall, Margaret and Tom Young. *Confronting Leviathan: Mozambique since Independence*. Athens, OH: Ohio University Press, 1997.

Hammer, Amanda and Brian Raftopoulos and Stig Jensen, eds. *Zimbabwe's Unfinished Business: Rethinking Land, State and Nation in the Context of Crisis*. Harare: Weaver Press, 2003.

Hansen, Karen Tranberg. *Salaula: The World of Secondhand Clothing and Zambia*. Chicago: University of Chicago Press, 2000.

Harrison, Graham. *The Politics of Rural Democratization in Mozambique: grassroots governance in Mecúfi*. Lewiston, NY: Edwin Mellen, 2000.

Hassan, Fareed M.A. *Lesotho: Development in a Challenging Environment: a Joint World Bank-African Development Bank Evaluation*. Abidjan: African Development Bank; Washington, DC: World Bank, 2002.

Henning, Melber, ed. *Reexamining Liberation in Namibia: Political Culture since Independence in Namibia*. Uppsala: Nordic African Institute, 2003.

Hodges, Tony. *Angola: Anatomy of an Oil State*. 2nd edition. Oxford: James Currey, 2004.

Human Rights Watch. *Deadly Delay: South Africa's Efforts to Prevent HIV in Survivors of Sexual Violence*. New York: Human Rights Watch, 2004.

Human Rights Watch. *Not Eligible: The Politicization of Food in Zimbabwe*. New York: Human Rights Watch, 2003.

Huddlestone, Sarah. *Face of Courage: Morgan Tsvangirai*. Cape Town, South Africa: Double Storey Books, 2005.

Hyam, Ronald amd Peter Henshaw. *The Lion and the Springbok: Britain and South Africa since the Boer War*. Cambridge: Cambridge University Press, 2003.

International Crisis Group. *Zimbabwe: An End to the Stalemate?* Pretoria/Brussels: ICG, March 2007. Available online at http://www.crisisweb.org/

International Crisis Group. *Swaziland: The Clock Is Ticking*. Pretoria/Brussels: ICG, July 2005. Available online at http://www.crisisweb.org/

Jackson, Ashley. *Botswana 1939–1945: an African Country at War*. New York: Oxford University Press, 1999.

Jacobs, Sean and Richard Calland, eds. *Thabo Mbeki's World. The Politics and Ideology of the South African President*. NY: Palgrave, 2003.

Johnston, Deborah. *Lesotho*. Santa Barbara, CA: ABC-CLIO, rev. ed., 1997.

Lodge, Tom. *Politics in South Africa: From Mandela to Mbeki*. Bloomington: Indiana University Press, 2003.

Mandela, Nelson. *Long Walk to Freedom: The Autobiography of Nelson Mandela*. New York: Back Bay Books, 1995.

Melber, Henning, ed. *Reexamining Liberation in Namibia: Political Culture since Independence*. Uppsala: Nordiska Afrikainstitutet, 2003.

Meredith, Martin. *Our Votes, Our Guns: Robert Mugabe and the Tragedy of Zimbabwe*. New York: Public Affairs, 2002.

Newitt, Malyn. *A History of Mozambique*. Bloomington, IN: Indiana University Press, 1995.

Pitcher, M. Anne. *Transforming Mozambique: The Politics of Privatization, 1975–2000*. Cambridge: Cambridge University Press, 2002.

Raftopoulos, Brian and Tyrone Savage, eds. *Zimbabwe: Injustice and Political Reconciliation*. Capetown, SA: Weaver Press, 2005.

Ross, Robert. *A Concise History of South Africa*. New York: Cambridge University Press, 1999.

Saunders, Christopher C. and Nicholas Southey. *Historical Dictionary of South Africa*. Lanham, MD: Scarecrow Press, 1999.

Schoeman, Stanley and Elna Schoeman. *Namibia*. Santa Barbara, CA: ABC-CLIO, rev. ed. 1997.

Sheldon, Kathleen E. *Pounders of Grain: A History of Women, Work and Politics in Mozambique*. Portsmouth, NH: Heinemann, 2002.

Tekere, Edgar. *A Lifetime of Struggle*. Harare: Sapes Books, 2006.

Temkin, Ben. *Buthelezi. A Biography*. Portland, OR: Frank Cass Publishers, 2003.

Terreblanche, Sampie (Solomon Johannes), *A History of Inequality in South Africa, 1652–2002*, Scottsville, SA: University of KwaZulu-Natal Press, 2003.

Tomlinson, Richard. et al. eds. *Emerging Johannesburg: Perspectives on the Post-Apartheid City*. London: Routledge, 2003.

Walker, Liz, et al. *Waiting to Happen: HIV/AIDS in South Africa—The Bigger Picture*. Boulder, CO: Lynne Rienner, 2004.

Woods, Anthony. *The Creation of Modern Malawi*. Boulder, CO: Westview Press, 1998.

Indian Ocean Island Nations

Allen, Philip M. *Madagascar: Conflicts of Authority in the Great Island*. Boulder, CO: Westview Press, 1995.

Bennett, George and Pramila Ramgulan Bennett. *Seychelles*. Santa Barbara, CA: ABC-CLIO, 1993.

Bradt, Hilary. *Madagascar*. Santa Barbara, CA: ABC-CLIO, 1994.

Metz, Helen Chapin, ed. *Indian Ocean: Five Island Countries*. Washington, DC: U.S. GPO, 3rd ed. 1995.

Dick-Read, Robert. *The Phantom Voyagers: Evidence of Indonesian Settlement in Africa in Ancient Times*. Winchester: Thurlton Publishing, 2005.

Ottenheimer, Martin and Harriet Ottenheimer. *Historical Dictionary of the Comoro Islands*. Lanham, MD: Scarecrow Press, 1994.

Scarr, Deryck. *Seychelles since 1770: History of a Slave and Post-Slave Society*. Lawrenceville, NJ: Africa World Press, 1999.

Storey, William K. *Science and Power in Colonial Mauritius*. Rochester, NY: University of Rochester Press, 1997.

Bibliography

Eastern Africa

Aboubaker Alwan, Daoud. *Historical Dictionary of Djibouti*. Lanham, MD: Scarecrow Press, 2000.

Ali, Ayaan Hirsi. *Infidel*. New York: Free Press, 2007.

Amnesty International. *Sudan: The Human Price of Oil*. London: Amnesty International, 2000.

Baltimore, The Walters Art Museum. *Ethiopian Art: The Walters Museum*. Lingfield, UK: Third Millennium Publishing, 2001.

Burr, Millard and Robert Collins. *Revolutionary Sudan: Hasan al-Turabi and the Islamist state, 1989–2000*. Leiden; Boston, MA: Brill, 2003.

Coalition for International Justice. *Soil and Oil: Dirty Business in Sudan*. Washington: CIJ, February 2006. Available online at www.cij.org

Crummey, Donald. *Land and Society in the Christian Kingdom of Ethiopia: from the Thirteenth to the Twentieth Century*. Champaign, IL: University of Illinois Press, 1999.

Darch, Colin. *Tanzania*. Santa Barbara, CA: ABC-CLIO, rev. ed. 1996.

Deng, Francis Mading. *War of Visions: Conflict of Identities in the Sudan*. Washington, DC: Brookings Institution Press, 1995.

De Waal, Alexander. *Islamism and its Enemies in the Horn of Africa*. London: Hurst & Co., 2004.

Elkins, Caroline. *Imperial Reckoning: The Untold Story of Britain's Gulag in Kenya*. New York: Henry Holt, 2005.

Fegley, Randall. *Eritrea*. Santa Barbara, CA: ABC-CLIO, 1995.

Forster, Peter G. and Sam Maghimbi, eds. *Agrarian Economy, State, and Society in Contemporary Tanzania*. Brookfield, VT: Ashgate Publishing Company, 1999.

Fozzard, Adrian. *Djibouti*. Boulder, CO: Westview Press, 1999.

Gregory, Robert G. *South Asians in East Africa: An Economic and Social History, 1890–1980*. Boulder, CO: Westview Press, 1993.

Heldman, Marilyn with Stuart C. Munro-Hay. *African Zion: The Sacred Art of Ethiopia*. New Haven: Yale University Press, 1993.

Henze, Paul B. *Layers of Time: A History of Ethiopia*. New York: Saint Martin's Press, 1999.

Henze, Paul. *Eritrea's War*. Summerset, NJ: Transaction, 2002.

Human Rights Watch. *Entrenching Impunity: Government Responsibility for International Crimes in Darfur*. New York: Human Rights Watch, 2005.

Human Rights Watch. *"If We Return, We Will Be Killed": Consolidation of Ethnic Cleansing in Darfur, Sudan*. New York: Human Rights Watch, 2004.

International Crisis Group. *Darfur Rising: Sudan's New Crisis*. (Africa Report No. 76). Brussels: International Crisis Group, 25 March 2004. (http://www.crisisweb.org/)

Iyob, Ruth and Khadiagala, Gilbert M. *Sudan: The Elusive Quest for Peace*. Boulder, CO: Lynne Rienner, 2006.

Johnson, Douglas H. *The Root Causes of Sudan's Civil Wars*. Bloomington: Indiana University Press, 2003.

Khalid, Mansour. *War and Peace in Sudan: A Tale of Two Countries*. New York: Kegan Paul, 2003.

Killion, Tom. *Historical Dictionary of Eritrea*. Lanham, MD: Scarecrow Press, 1998.

Levine, Donald N. *Greater Ethiopia: The Evolution of a Multiethnic Society*. Chicago: University of Chicago Press, 2000.

Little, Peter D. *Somalia: Economy Without State*. Oxford: International African Institute in association with James Currey, 2003.

Maathai, Wangari. *Unbowed*. New York: Knopf, 2006

Maloba, Wunyabara O. *Mau Mau and Kenya: An Analysis of a Peasant Revolt*. Bloomington, IN: Indiana University Press, 1998.

Marcus, Harold G. *A History of Ethiopia*. Berkeley, CA: University of California Press, 1994.

Maxon, Robert M. *Historical Dictionary of Kenya*. 2nd ed. Lanham, MD: Scarecrow Press, 2000.

Menkhaus, Kenneth John. *Somalia: State Collapse and the Threat of Terrorism*. New York: Oxford, 2004

Mosely Lesch, Ann. *The Sudan: Contested National Identities*. Bloomington, IN: Indiana University Press, 1998.

Mukhtar, Mohamed Haji and Margaret Castagno. *Historical Dictionary of Somalia*. Revised edition. Lanham, MD: Rowman & Littlefield, 2003.

Munro-Hay, Stuart and Richard Pankhurst. *Ethiopia*. Santa Barbara, CA: ABC-CLIO, 1995.

Negash, Tekeste. *Eritrea and Ethiopia: The Federal Experience*. New Brunswick, NJ: Transaction Publishers, 1997.

Neyko, Balam. *Uganda*. Santa Barbara, CA: ABC-CLIO, rev. ed. 1996.

Oded, Arye. *Islam and Politics in Kenya*. Boulder, CO: Lynne Rienner, 2000.

Ofcansky, Thomas P. and Robert M. Maxon. *Historical Dictionary of Kenya*. Lanham, MD: Scarecrow Press, 1999.

Ofcansky, Thomas P. and Rodger Yeager. *Historical Dictionary of Tanzania*. 2nd ed. Lanham, MD: Scarecrow Press, 1997.

Pankhurst, Barbara. *The Ethiopians*. Malden, MA: Blackwell Publishers, 1998.

Pausewang, Siegfried, et al. *Ethiopia Since the Derg. A Decade of Democratic Pretension and Performance*. New York: Palgrave, 2003.

Peterson, Scott. *Me against My Brother: At War in Somalia, Sudan and Rwanda*. New York: Routledge, 2000.

Prouty, Chris and Eugene Rosenfeld. *Historical Dictionary of Ethiopia and Eritrea*. Lanham, MD: Scarecrow Press, 2nd ed. 1994.

Prunier, Gerard. *Darfur: Ambiguous Genocide*. Ithaca, NY: Cornell University Press, 2005.

Reeves, Eric. *A Long Day's Dying: Critical Moments in the Darfur Genocide*. Toronto: Key Publishing House, 2007.

Rotberg, Robert I., ed. *Battling terrorism in the Horn of Africa*. Washington: Brookings Institution, 2005.

Schraeder, Peter J. *Djibouti*. Santa Barbara, CA: ABC-CLIO, 1991.

Sudan Divestment Task Force. *PetroChina, CNPC, and Sudan: Perpetuating Genocide*. Available online: http://www.sudandivestment.org/docs/petrochina_cnpc_sudan.pdf

Tripp, Aili Mari. *Museveni's Uganda: Paradoxes of Power in a Hybrid Regime*. Boulder, CO: Lynne Rienner, 2010.

Woodward, Peter. *The Horn of Africa. Politics and International Relations*. Rev. ed. New York: Palgrave, 2003.

Wrong, Michela. *I Didn't Do It for You: How the World Betrayed a Small African Nation*. New York: HarperCollins, 2005.

North Africa

Abdo, Geneive. *No God but God: Egypt and the Triumph of Islam*. New York: Oxford University Press, 2000.

Adamson, Kay. *Algeria: A Study in Competing Ideologies*. Herndon, VA: Cassell Academic, 1998.

Ahmida, Ali Abdullatif. *The Making of Modern Libya: State Formation, Colonialization, and Resistance, 1830–1932*. Albany, NY: State University of New York, 1994.

Arnold, Guy. *The Maverick State: Gaddafi and the New World Order*. Herndon, VA: Cassell Academic, 1996.

Beattie, Kirk J. *Egyptian Politics During Sadat's Presidency*. New York: Saint Martin's Press, 2000.

Borowiec, Andrew. *Tunisia: a Democratic Apprenticeship*. Westport, CT: Greenwood Publishing Group, 1998.

Bouqia, Rahma and Susan Gilson Miller, eds. *In the Shadow of the Sultan: Culture, Power and Politics in Morocco*. Cambridge: Harvard University Press, 1999.

Burr, J. Millard and Robert O. Collins. *Africa's Thirty Years' War: Chad, Libya, and the Sudan, 1963–1993*. Boulder, CO: Wesview Press, 1999.

Ciment, James. *Algeria: The Fundamentalist Challenge*. New York: Facts on File, 1997.

Bibliography

Daly, Martin W., ed. *Modern Egypt from 1517 to the End of the Twentieth Century.* New York: Cambridge University Press, 1999.

El-Kikhia, Mansour O. *Libya's Qaddafi: The Politics of Contradiction.* Gainesville, FL: University Press of Florida, 1997.

Findlay, Anne M., et al., *Morocco.* Santa Barbara, CA: ABC-CLIO, 1995.

Gould, St. John. *Morocco.* NY: Routledge, 2002.

Howe, Marvine. *Morocco: The Islamist Awakening and Other Challenges.* New York: Oxford University Press, 2005.

Human Rights Watch. *Egypt: In a Time of Torture.* New York: Human Rights Watch, 2004.

Jensen, Erik. *Western Sahara: Anatomy of a Stalemate.* Boulder, CO: Lynne Rienner, 2004.

King, Stephen J. *Liberalization against Democracy: The Local Politics of Economic Reform in Tunisia.* Bloomington: Indiana University Press, 2003.

Lawless, Richard I. *Algeria.* Santa Barbara, CA: ABC-CLIO, 1995.

Long, David E. and Bernard Reich. *The Government and Politics of the Middle East and North Africa.* 4th ed. Boulder, CO: Westview, 2002.

Murphy, Emma C. *Economic and Political Change in Tunisia: From Bourguiba to Ben Ali.* New York: Saint Martin's Press, 1999.

Naylor, Phillip Chiviges and Alf Andrew Heggoy. *Historical Dictionary of Algeria.* Lanham, MD: Scarecrow Press, 2nd ed. 1994.

Niblock, Tim. *"Pariah States" & Sanctions in the Middle East: Iraq, Libya, Sudan.* Boulder, CO: Lynne Rienner, 2001.

O'Conner, David and Andrew Reid, eds. *Ancient Egypt in Africa.* London: University College of London Press, 2003.

Park, Thomas K. *Historical Dictionary of Morocco.* Lanham, MD: Scarecrow Press, 1996.

Pazzanita, Anthony G. *Historical Dictionary of Mauritania.* Lanham, MD: Scarecrow Press, 1996.

Pennell, C. R. *Morocco Since 1830: A History.* Millwood, NY: Labyrinth, 2000.

Perkins, Kenneth J. *A History of Modern Tunisia.* Cambridge: Cambridge University Press, 2004.

Quandt, William B. *Between Ballots and Bullets: Algeria's Transition from Authoritarianism.* Washington, DC: Brookings Institution Press, 1998.

Rubin, Barry. *Islamic Fundamentalism in Egyptian Politics.* New York: Palgrave, 2002.

St. John, Ronald Bruce. *Historical Dictionary of Libya.* Lanham, MD: Scarecrow Press, 3rd ed. 1998.

Stora, Benjamin. *Algeria, 1830–2000: A Short History.* Ithaca, NY: Cornell University Press, 2001.

Sullivan, Denis J. *Islam in Contemporary Egypt: Civil Society vs. the State.* Boulder, CO: Lynne Rienner, 1999.

Takeyh, Ray. *The Origins of the Eisenhower Doctrine: The U.S., Britain and Nasser's Egypt, 1953–57.* New York: Saint Martin's Press, 2000.

Vandewalle, Dirk. *Libya since Independence: Oil and State-Building.* Ithaca, NY: Cornell University Press, 1998.

White, Gregory. *A Comparative Political Economy of Tunisia and Morocco: On the outside of Europe looking in.* Albany, NY: State University of New York Press, 2001.

Willis, Michael. *The Islamist Challenge in Algeria: A Political History.* New York: New York University Press, 1997.

About the Author

Lawrence R. Sullivan, professor emeritus Adelphi University, Garden City New York, provided additional contributions on recent developments for each of the 54 African nations.